HORROR

THE AURUM FILM ENCYCLOPEDIA

HORROR

EDITED BY
PHIL HARDY

WITH CONTRIBUTIONS BY
TOM MILNE, KIM NEWMAN, PAUL WILLEMEN
JULIAN PETLEY, TIM PULLEINE

ILLUSTRATIONS BY THE KOBAL COLLECTION

AURUM PRESS

This book is dedicated to David Pirie, who first charted the territory.

Acknowledgements

As the title page shows, this book is the result of the close collaboration of a large number of writers. It is they first and foremost who are its creators; certainly without them there would be no *Encyclopedia of Horror*. By the same token there would not have been a book without the assistance of a number of people who took on the unglamorous and highly complex task of organizing its production with a degree of commitment that went well beyond the call of duty. These include Anne Yelland, who oversaw the production of the first edition in a wholly sympathetic fashion. Luckily for the book Geoff Barlow and Theresa Wright found a similar enthusiasm for this edition. Sheila Murphy believed, which is not always an easy thing for a publisher when their author is as demanding as Stephen King but their sales don't quite match. Once again thank you Robert Updegraff, who made (almost) painless the process of illuminating the manuscript – we'll have that bottle next time round. Thanks are also due to Dave Kent of the Kobal Collection, who found stills and still more stills.

Sometimes when a book finally enters the real world it finds readers who want to make it better. This has been such a book. Many of the corrections to the existing text are the result of readers' letters. Sadly I must admit that there could have been even more but a persistently wayward file of letters from readers refuses to come out of hiding. Accordingly, the list that follows of readers who have sent in corrections is shorter than it could be. Among those who have made suggestions and corrections and offered advice are: *Variety*'s Fred Lombardi, Dobal Raoul, Bill Warren, J. Chapman, Earl Bobert and Stephan Zahner. Thanks too to those who sadly wrote in vain. But remember there will be another edition soon, so please read carefully and put pen to paper rather than just tut-tutting. Many thanks everyone.

Lastly, I thank *Variety* for kindly allowing me to republish material originally published by them.

First published 1985 by Aurum Press Limited, 25 Bedford Avenue, London WC1B 3AT
Revised updated edition 1993

A catalogue record for this book is available from the British Library

ISBN 1 85410 263 X

10 9 8 7 6 5 4 3 2 1
1997 1996 1995 1994 1993

Design by Robert Updegraff
Printed in Great Britain by The Bath Press

Photographs from the Kobal Collection courtesy of: A Erre Cinematografica; A Turman Foster; A Vortex; ABP; AFC; AIP; Academy; Academy Pictures; Achilles; Alameda Films; Alfa Films; Alive; Allied Artists; Alta Vista; Ama Film; Amblin Entertainment; American Cinema; Amicus; Amusement Securities; Anabel Films; Ancla Century; Anglo Amalgamated; Aquila Film Enterprises; Argyle Enterprises; Argyle Productions; Armitage; Arrivision; Art Cinema; Artemis; Artistes Associés; Ashley Productions; Associates and Aldrich; Aston Film; Atlantica Cinematografica; Australian International Film Corporation; Avco Embassy; BEF Film Distributors; BHP; BLT Productions; Barrandov; Benmar Production; Bernie Brillstein Production; Bing Crosby Productions; Birthday Film Company; Black Rhino; Blood Relations Company; Borough Park Productions; Braddock Associates; Brandywine-Ronald Shusett Productions; British Lion; Bungei; CC Champion; CCC; CEC; CFC; CIC; Cadre Films; Cal-Am Productions; Camp Hill Productions; Canadian Film Development Corporation; Cannon; Capitolina Produzioni Cinematografiche; Caralan; Carl Theodor Dreyer Filmproduktion; Carlin Company; Carlo Ponti-Jean Pierre Rassam Production; Carlos; Carmel; Carolco; Chadwick; Champs Elysées-Lux; Cheviot; Chips Productions; Chromage; Cine Allianz Tonfilm; Cinegai; Cinema 77; Cinemarque; Cinevideo; Cinevog; Cirio H Santiago Productions; Columbia; Comacico; Compton; Consorzio Italiano Films; Contemporary Film-Makers; Corona Filmproduktion; Cosmopolitan; Crossbow Productions; Crown International; Curtwell; Daiei; Dan Curtis Productions; Dania Film; David F Friedman; David Lynch; De Laurentiis; Debra Hill Productions; Decla Bioscop; Decla Film; Delphi; Delphi Productions; Deutsche Bioscop; Dialchi Film; Diana Films; Dieter Geissler; Discobolo Cinematografica; EMI; Ealing Studios; Edison; Elliott Kastner-Jay Kanter-Alan Ladd Jnr Productions; Embassy Productions; Emmeci Cinematografica; Emmepi Cinematografica; Empress Productions; Essay Films; Estudios America; Euro International Films; Euroamerica; Eva Films; Evans Productions; Excalibur Films; Explorer Film; Falcon International; Famous Players; Famous Players-Lasky; Fanfare; Fantale Films; Faro Film; Fenady Associates; Fenix Films; Film Futures; Film House; Filmar Compagnia Cinematografica; Filmedis-Filmel; Filmgroup; Filmica Vergara; Films de la Beotie; Filmways; Filmways Australasia; Flaminia Produxioni; Fox; Francinor; Frank Yablans Presentations; Freedom Arts Pictures; Fries; Fulvia Film; Galatea Films; Gaumont; Gaumont-British; Geffen; Georgetown Productions; Getty Pictures Corporation; Glendale; Global; Goldstar; Goldwyn; Gramercy; Greenbaum Film; Grenade Films; Grenadie Films; Grenadier Films; Gruskoff; Guardian Trust Company; H R Sokal Film; HBO; Halperin; Hammer; Harbor-Herman Cohen Productions; Harristown Funding; Hawk Films; Helios Film; Hemdale; Henkel; Heritage; Herschell G Lewis Productions; Hesperia; HiFi Stereo 70; Hit Pictures; Hollywood Pictures; Hooper Production; Host-Rohar Productions; Hoya Productions; Humongous Productions; Iberia Filmes; Iduna Film; Image Ten; Intercontinental Industries; International Cinematografica; International Film Investors; Inernational Productions; Interplanetary; Interscope; Intersound; Invincible; Janus Films; Jerry Gross Productions; Jolly Films; Joseph E Levine; Joseph M Schenck Enterprises; Jouer; Judica Productions; Junior Filmi; KL Productions; Karr International; Katsu Productions; Keith Barish; Kenneth Shipman Productions; Kindai Eiga Kyokai; Kingsmere Properties; La Loggia Productions; Largo Entertainment; Laser Film; Laurel; Layton; Leander Films; Leo Lax Film; Libbert; Lightning; Lipow Film; Lippert; Lorimar; Luis Films; Lycanthrope Films; MCA Theatricals; MGM; MI; Magnum; Mainline; Majestic; Maljack; Manitou Productions; Manuel Salvador; Mardi Gras; Marianne Productions; Mars Production Group; Masada Productions; Maya Films; Medusa; Melvin Simon Productions; Meridian; Merlin; Metromedia Producers Company; Metropolis; Michael Findlay; Michael Powell Theatre; Millco; Miramax; Monarch Releasing Corporation; Monarchia Films; Morgana Films; Mutual; Navaron Films; Neptun Film; Neutral Film; New Line Productions; New World; The Night Company; Ninjin Club; Nordisk; Nucleo Film; OCL Industries; Oak Industries; Oliane Productions; Orbita; Orion; Orion Pictures; PRC; Pagu; Palace Pictures; Palomar Pictures; Pan Arts; Pan Film; Panda Film; Panitalia; Paragon; Paramount; Paris Films; Pathé; Pea Films; Pelleport Investors; Penta Films; Peri Productions; Pete Walker-Heritage-Ltd; Peter Rogers Productions; Pethurst; Picnic Productions; Plata Films; Poseidon Films; Prana Film; Premiere; Present Day; Pressman Williams; Pressman-Williams Enterprises; Prisma Film; Proa Films; Producers Associates; Production de Peliculas; Productions Georges de Beauregard; Productions Simone Allouche; Produzioni Intersound; Profilmes; Pyramid Entertainment; QM Productions; Queen of Evil; REP; RKF; RKO; Rapid Film; Red Bank Films; Regal; Renaissance Pictures; Rialto Film; Richard Oswald Film; Richard Shepard Company; Riviera International; Roffman-Taylor; Ronald J Kahn; Roto Film; Roxy; Russo Productions; Ryntare Productions; SIM Entertainment; SIS Productions; Sabre; Sandy Howard Productions; Santa Clara; Saticoy; Scimitar; Secret Film Company; Seda Spettacoli; Serena Film; Sergio Kogan; Seven Arts; Shochiku; Showking; Sigma Cinematographia; Silver Screen; Sir Nigel; Société Cinematographique Lyre; Société d'Expansion du Spectacle; Sofidoc; Solofilm; Soma Film Produktion; South Australian Film Corporation; Spa Cinematografica; Star Films; Stardust; Steckler Production; Steve Krantz Productions; Studio Films; Studio One; Sueva Films; Svensk Filmindustri; TMS; TV13; Taft Entertainment Company; Taurean Films; Tecisa; Tefi; Tekli; Tigon; Tigon British; Titan; Toei; Toho; Tokyo Eiga; Top Film; Tor Productions; Towers; Translor Films; Translux; Tri-Star; Triad; Tritone Cinematografica; Troma; Twentieth Century Fox; Tyburn; Tyburn Film Productions; Ulysée Film; Unicapital; Unicorn; United Artists; Universal; Vanguard Film; Variety Film; Venture Films; Vestron; Victorian Film Commission; Vitascope; Vulcan; Vulsinia Film; Walt Disney; Warner Brothers; Warren-Chaney; Werner Herzog; Wescom Productions; William Castle Productions; Winkast; Wolfgang Hartwig; World Arts Media; World Film Services; X Films; Zenith International; Zev Braun Productions

The Kobal Collection would like to thank the following organisations and individuals for their help in supplying additional photographs for this book:
Michelle Snapes and the staff of the National Film Archive, London (16, 18(B), 35, 58, 95, 99, 101, 110, 128, 171, 177, 178(R), 181, 182, 191, 196, 203, 209, 222, 281, 294, 341); David Del Valle; The Euro-Collection; Phototeque; Al McKenzie; Terry Ellacott: Stills; Stiftung Deutsche Kinemathek; Memory Shop; Movie Memories; Cheryl Thomas.

Contents

The index gives the year under which all film titles (including alternative titles) having entries are to be found.

Notes on the entries

The entries are arranged chronologically throughout the volume and alphabetically within each year. The definite and indefinite articles in all titles have been disregarded in establishing alphabetical order. Unless otherwise indicated, all films are in colour, and were made in the United States of America. The index gives the year under which all titles having their own entries are to be found. The titles of all such films are printed in bold throughout the book (except for all subsequent references to a title in the same entry), with their date for ease of cross-referencing. All other films mentioned are printed in italics.

The running time of a film can vary considerably because different versions are often released in different territories. Accordingly, where such versions are known to be in circulation, the different lengths are listed in brackets after the original running time. All such lengths relate to theatrical screenings; on television, because of the medium's faster projection speed, a film will generally run (excluding commercial breaks) approximately four minutes per hundred shorter. The running time of silent films varies a great deal. The most accurate description would be to give the footage, rather than a running time; however, for the sake of consistency, length has been converted into time, calculated on an average projection speed of 20 frames per second. In fact, projection speed usually varied between 18 and 22 frames per second, although occasionally it exceeded these conventional boundaries.

For the purposes of this book, the date of a film has been generally taken as the year of its making, rather than its release, except in a few unusual circumstances in which case the different dates are mentioned in the text. In the case of some films, even this is open to debate, and many of the sources are inconsistent if not actively in dispute. In these cases, I have opted for the date most often ascribed. Where the date is in doubt, you are advised to consult the index to find the year under which the title has been entered. Similarly, often films are given different titles for different markets. Accordingly, if a film seems to be missing, you are advised to consult the index to find out which title has been used here. It is particularly important to do this with foreign films, all of which have been entered under their original, rather than English language, titles.

Although the credits have been exhaustively researched, inevitably some are missing, especially in the early period. Indeed, in some cases, a film has been 'lost': inclusion of a title, particularly a silent film, does not imply that a print is available. Moreover, some of the prints that have survived are known to be incomplete. In the case of 'lost' films, information has been based on contemporary reviews and publicity sources; consequently, such information must be treated with the greatest caution. Most silent films were tinted in the sense that night sequences would be tinted blue and scenes with fire tinted red. However, the vast majority of surviving prints are in black and white only, and without checking this against the original prints, most of which have been long since destroyed, any information as to the nature of a film's tinting would be, at best, guesswork. Accordingly, silent films have been designated as black and white, except in those cases where we positively know the films were extensively tinted.

Producer credits for films from countries where the film industry has been nationalized are meaningless, and have been omitted in nearly all cases. In such circumstances, the production functions of people conventionally called 'producers' correspond more closely to those of the studio general manager or production manager in Hollywood. Where a name has been given for that function, this is to be understood as a creative production/management function. The contributions of those in a supervisory function have, where known, been signalled in the text.

In the Far East, not only in Japan, but also in Hong Kong, Taiwan, the Philippines, India, Korea, Malaysia, Singapore and Thailand, undoubtedly more horror films have been made than are mentioned in this volume. Any information about such films – indeed about any films which are missing from this book – will be gratefully received.

Abbreviations and Explanation of Terms

aka	also known as
b/w	black and white
sepia	Sepiatone
scope	all wide-screen anamorphic systems such as Cinemascope and Warnerscope, except:
pv	panavision
vv	Vistavision

Countries

ARG	Argentina
AUST	Australia
BEL	Belgium
CAN	Canada
CZECH	Czechoslovakia
DEN	Denmark
EG	East Germany
FIN	Finland
FR	France
G	Germany (before 1939 and after 1990)
GB	Great Britain
GR	Greece
HUN	Hungary
ICE	Iceland
IT	Italy
JAP	Japan
MEX	Mexico
NETH	Netherlands
PHIL	Philippines
POL	Poland
ROK	Republic of Korea
ROM	Romania
SP	Spain
SW	Sweden
SWITZ	Switzerland
THAI	Thailand
US	United States of America
USSR	Union of Soviet Socialist Republics
WG	West Germany

Studios

AA	Allied Artists
COL	Columbia
FOX	Fox and (after 1935) 20th Century Fox
MGM	Metro Goldwyn Mayer
MON	Monogram
PAR	Paramount
REP	Republic
RKO	RKO Radio
U	Universal
UA	United Artists
WB	Warner Brothers

Credits

d	director
p	producer
s	screenwriter
c	cinematographer
se	special effects
lp	leading players
co-	in collaboration with

Preface to the First Edition

At the time of writing, the horror film stands in an odd position. A declining force at the box office, though not in the video market, in recent years the genre has probably received more attention from critics and censors alike than at any moment in its history. Interestingly, this renewed critical interest in the horror film comes just as, in America at least, science fiction – previously a genre, like horror, in which fear and terror were central – has acquired a far more escapist inflection, more in keeping with the needs of a Reaganite America and, in so doing, has supplanted horror at the box office. Certainly the contemporary horror film has never seemed blacker. On the one hand, there has been an endless stream of women-in-peril movies with their conservative, not to say reactionary, views of women and sexuality; another strand has been the more complex (and more interesting) cannibal/zombie movies in which such sacred cows as Mom's Apple Pie and the family have been challenged and questioned in a variety of ways. What both these strands of film-making have in common is a commitment to bloody and prolonged violence. The debate about 'video nasties' in the UK, and to a lesser extent the USA, though rife with the kind of misinformation that comes from most of the would-be censors not having seen the films in question, nonetheless is an indication of how far the modern horror film has developed from the once-shocking films of the sixties. That it is about *video* nasties is also significant, confirming the changes in distribution that have accompanied the phenomenal growth of the exploitation film in recent years. One result of this has been further confusion as to what constitutes a film. Where once a film was a film was a film, now in addition there is the telefilm, a film made for TV but not generally theatrically released, and the videofilm, a video made for direct video distribution. (For reasons of space, only a limited number of these, often very amateur, productions are included in this volume.) Seen in isolation from a sense of history of the genre these debates are both more shocking and naïve than they need be, seen in the context of that history they are far more revealing.

The aim of this book is to document that history and serve as a critical guide to the glorious (and many not so glorious) movies that comprise the horror genre. What distinguishes this volume from others is its scope, which is truly encyclopedic, and its structure. The heart of the book is some 1,300 entries, arranged chronologically and alphabetically within each year, which are devoted to individual films. These entries range from a hundred words to a thousand in a direct reflection of the film's interest and/or historical importance in the development of the genre. Each entry comprises fully researched credits (director, producer, studio, writer, cinematographer and where possible a minimum of six leading players), a brief synopsis of the plot and, most importantly, informed critical comment on the film. Where relevant, cross reference is made to other movies. Thus it is possible to follow the careers of important stars, directors and producers and key themes of the genre through the book. In addition to the entries, this volume also contains numerous appendices, including critics' top tens, a ranking of horror films by their rental earnings and a list of Oscars won by horror films. Taken together, the appendices represent the most comprehensive statistical overview of the genre ever published.

Even more significant than the fact that more films are covered in this encyclopedia than in any other book devoted to the horror film published hitherto, is the wide range of films included. In contrast to previous books which have concentrated almost exclusively on British and American films, I have attempted to disturb this parochial and limited notion of the genre by covering in depth the silent cinema and the horror cinema of countries such as Japan, Italy, Mexico and Spain. As a mark of this international perspective, for this volume we have continued with the procedure, adopted in *Science Fiction*, of listing films by their original title in their country of production. For reasons of space and scholarship the encyclopedia is only intended as a guide to the more rarified areas of horror thrown up by the, previously little researched, *popular* cinema of such countries as Mexico, Spain and Japan. Hopefully other scholars and researchers will follow the trails laid down by this volume and uncover more of the strange wonders of such national cinemas.

Precisely because this is an encyclopedia rather than a personal view of the horror film, I have been concerned with broad rather than narrow notions of the genre. Such a perspective necessarily means that there is considerable overlap between this volume and *Science Fiction*. In the introduction to that volume I dealt at some length with the difference between science fiction and horror as genres. That said, film-makers make films, and it is only critics who worry about genres. Accordingly, even though Baron Frankenstein and Dr Jekyll are figures of science fiction (by virtue of the scientific basis of the horrors they unleash), they can (and indeed have more often than not) be claimed for the horror genre by virtue of theme and look. For this reason, in the main, I have opted for having an entry (almost always written from different perspectives) in both volumes where the film seemed to warrant it. At the same time, mindful of space and of the fact that so many movies of recent years could claim a place in either volume, where it seemed appropriate having put a film in *Science Fiction* I have not repeated it here simply because it has some horror inflections. Thus, the films of David Cronenberg are in *Science Fiction* but not this volume. Just as *Science Fiction* and *Horror* are closely connected genres, so the volumes devoted to them in *The Film Encyclopedia* series are complementary. Of course, both genres could have been combined under the notion of fantasy films, but to do so would be to so limit coverage of both science fiction and horror films as to make the book a backward, rather than progressive, step. Accordingly, readers are advised, where possible, to use the two volumes together. With this in mind, where a film has an entry in both volumes and further information and/or corrections to existing information have come to light, the facts in an entry in *Horror*, take precedence over those in an entry in *Science Fiction* on the few occasions they are in conflict. Needless, to say, I am indebted to the readers, too numerous to mention individually, who have written in with comments and corrections to both *The Western* and *Science Fiction*. I only hope that readers of this volume will be as generous with their time and send in further information thereby helping us slowly to excise the mistakes that inevitably creep into such a mammoth undertaking as this.

In the course of preparing this volume, I have relied heavily on Walt Lee's invaluable work, *A Reference Guide to Fantastic Films*, David Pirie's *Heritage of Horror*, which remains the classic account of the English horror film, and Don Willis' three-volume *Reference Guide to Science Fiction, Horror and Fantasy Films*. I have also made use of the reviews in *Variety* and, for more recent films, *The Monthly Film Bulletin*. With these to lean on I have sought to construct what, I hope, is the most comprehensive guide in book form to the horror film so far produced.

Keep your eyes about you and beware the full moon!

Phil Hardy
London 1985

Preface to the Second Edition

Bravely (I think, anyway), I have not altered the original 1985 introduction to this book ('The Horror Film in Perspective'), or doctored the original preface – the latter opened with a statement to the effect that horror was 'a declining force at the box office'. Nor have I excised the niceties of some of the neat distinctions I previously made between science fiction and horror – 'Thus, the films of David Cronenberg are in *Science Fiction* but not in this volume'. I have, nonetheless, responded to critical reviews and letters that have pointed out that some omissions, however arguable, were simply unhelpful. Hence, in the body of the text, as well as correcting as many of the errors as possible, I have rent the fabric to include entries on **Let's Scare Jessica to Death** (1971); **Blood Waters of Dr Z** (1972); **Curse of Bigfoot** (1972); **Don't Look Now** (1973); **King Kong** (1976); and **Dawn of the Dead** (1979). I'm not suggesting that all these films are of equal value, merely that each in its own way highlights issues and themes that are central to the genre. Sadly, book production being what it is, to include these films two minor outings and a couple of illustrations have had to be deleted. The films lost are *Don't Look in the Basement* (1973) and *Kiss of the Tarantula* (1976). But at least they are in the first edition. Similarly, though there are other titles that should be included in a perfect world, I have resisted the impulse, aided by timely and pressing advice from my publishers. The unhappy truth is that too many changes to the existing text would have made the production of a new edition impossible.

I raise these issues immediately not out of embarrassment, but because they are valid and because they highlight the essential fact that this is a new book, with vast amounts of new material, and yet is still the same old horror encyclopedia that people have come to love over the years. I have no qualms about this last statement. Of all the books I have been responsible for, I have had more letters about *Horror* than about any other. Accordingly, I know its re-appearance will be welcomed in many quarters.

As is usually the case in books like this, as editor I must take full responsibility for errors of omission and commission. However, I cannot claim the credit for the scholarship, research and insight that the entries contain. This is due to the major contributors, Paul Willemen, Tom Milne and Kim Newman. In particular I would like to thank Kim Newman, who was responsible for the major revision that this edition represents. He also spelt most of the characters' names correctly.

This edition comes at a time when the debate about violence in the cinema has resurfaced and there have been calls for (self) censorship from various quarters. Horror movies, it must be said bluntly, are violent, and more often than not the violence is directed at women. Some films deal with or are about that violence; most merely present it, often graphically and with exploitative intent. Consider **Singapore Sling** (1991), which features one of the nastiest sequences in recent cinema: a character straps a steak knife to his groin and sodomizes a woman to death. The film is of some interest as a sort of classical Greek tragedy – it is a Greek production – revisited and crossed with a forties *film noir* (complete with voice-over), but the scene described above has no redeeming social or artistic feature. It does, however, represent a recurrent male fantasy which needs to be dealt with rather than suppressed. If horror as a genre has any important social characteristic, it lies in its direct conduit to the unconscious, in its ability to catch the pathology of the times. To those who might object to the subject matter, let alone the approaches taken to it, of some of the films under discussion here, I would point out that the films are written about critically rather than simply celebrated and that whether we like it or not the concerns at the centre of these films are real. Just how real they are can be seen in the way that in the nineties the horror film has found a home in mainstream US cinema: witness the fright machine of **Cape Fear** (1991), the big-budget Dracula, **Bram Stoker's Dracula** (1992), the Oscar-laden **Silence of the Lambs** (1991) and the designer sexuality meets violence of **Basic Instinct** (1992). These films are testaments to the drive of the horror narrative in which plot and character are secondary to obsession and fantasy. Even more ironic, at a time when family values are being vacuously celebrated, are the host of horror films (including, at random, **The People Under the Stairs** (1991), **The Stepfather** (1986), **Blue Velvet** (1986), **The 'burbs** (1988) and **Society** (1989), which from a variety of angles confirm the central thesis of Philip Larkin's oft-quoted poem, 'This Be The Verse':

> They fuck you up, your mum and dad.
> They may not mean to, but they do.
> They fill you with the faults they had
> And add some extra, just for you.

Phil Hardy
London 1993

The Horror Film in Perspective

A central element of both horror and science fiction films is a concern with fear and terror. However, whereas in general science fiction is also critical of the social (and scientific) forces which fuel that terror, horror films lack that critical element. If science fiction's futures (and pasts) are created out of reactions to a given present, the horror film has no such social grounding. Quite simply, horror (be it film or literature) deals with fantasies and ideologies rather than social realities. Thus, shifts and developments within the horror genre can be traced less to changes in material conditions than to changes in the value systems through which a society is seen and reflected. The assorted vampires that so sensuously stalked the world's cinema screens in the sixties, for example, were just one aspect of the sexual revolution of the period. Similarly the families of cannibals and zombies who slashed and dismembered their way through the seventies are the meeting point of a sudden increase in the heights of cinematic realism possible (courtesy of new sophisticated technology and special effects) and a bizarre distortion of the sudden escalation within Western culture of an intense physical concern for the well-being of our bodies.

Of course, all cultural artefacts, though especially those of popular culture, reflect the times that produce them. What is particularly fascinating about horror as a genre, however, is just how direct a conduit it is to the unconscious: the particular fantasies of particular times can be identified quite precisely. The major fantasies brought into play in the sixties, for example, are oedipal, while those of the seventies are generally the infantile complexes associated with the (pre-oedipal) oral stage of child development. From another perspective, the major themes of the sixties are incest and necrophilia while those of the seventies are cannibalism. Such a reductionist approach, while it does not 'explain' away the films, helps make clear why it is that the horror film has been so often attacked: it speaks of the unspeakable.

'Depressing, degrading – for all lovers of the cinema only two words describe this film'; '[this film] deserves a new certificate "SO", For Sadists Only'; '[this is] amongst the half-dozen most repulsive films I have ever encountered'. These comments were made not about any of the infamous 'video nasties', like **I Spit on Your Grave** (1978) or **The Driller Killer** (1979), which have caused such a furore in the United Kingdom and United States in recent years, but about **The Curse of Frankenstein** (1957), Hammer and Terence Fisher's epoch-making entry into horror. This 'moral panic', which had earlier in the decade surfaced in connection with horror comics like *Tales From the Crypt* and *The Vault of Horror*, and can be found in most of the reviews of the first wave of British horror films of the fifties, has direct links with the present concern over 'video nasties'. Then, as now, it was the 'sadistic' content of the films that was highlighted by their critics. Similarly, little distinction was made between critically worthwhile films, such as **Les Yeux sans Visage** (1959) or **Peeping Tom** (1960) and the many lacklustre imitations Hammer spawned. I have no interest in defending *all* horror films – indeed such a concern would be inappropriate in an encyclopedia whose thrust is both critical and historical – but the uninformed way in which they have been attacked, and the uncritical way in which they have been generally received, needs some comment.

Horror films have been treated with disdain and contempt by most reviewers. By their major audience – adolescents, who see the films at drive-ins, in triple-bills or late at night on television – they are generally treated with embarrassment, guffaws, giggling and sniggering. Their makers, on the other hand, turn seemingly unendingly to parody in attempts to defuse the fantasies they have set in motion. In all these responses there is a refusal to take the films and the fantasies they exploit seriously. In itself, this isn't surprising; after all, the price of civilization and culture is a degree of repression. What is surprising, though, is the vehemence with which the dreams and nightmares that horror films represent have been rejected by avid audiences and censors alike. In the individual entries to this book, the films and the fantasies that underpin them are examined in detail. Here I want to examine horror as a genre and suggest through a historical sketch why the horror film, rather than any other film genre, has become such an important avenue to the unconscious.

Origins of the genre

As a genre horror has its origins in the gothic novels of the late 18th and early 19th century, in particular those of Mrs Radcliffe, M. G. Lewis and Charles Maturin, all of whom were British. These novels all exhibited a vulgarized romanticism in which the creation of sensations and a morbid fascination with death, pain and solitude were recurring features. This is most notable in the case of Lewis, who long after the *succès de scandale* of *The Monk*, mounted several truly sensational plays which made extensive use of stagecraft, lighting and stage machinery to achieve their effects. Accounts of the audience response read like descriptions of the audience at a horror film: 'Never did Covent Garden present such a picture of agitation and dismay. Ladies bathed in tears – others fainting – and some shrieking with terror – while such of the audience who were able to avoid such demonstrations as these sat aghast with pale horror painted on their countenances'. Similarly, Mary Shelley professed herself 'much amused' by an adaptation of her novel, *Frankenstein*, reporting that 'it appeared to excite a breathless eagerness in the audience'. This theatrical backdrop is of special significance to the Anglo-American tradition of horror. It announced the kind of sensationalism that film-makers would seek first to duplicate, and then to further intensify with apparatus and techniques newly available to them. Equally important, it was these theatrical versions of *Frankenstein* and *Dracula*, *not the novels themselves*, that were the models for the classic Universal interpretations of Mary Shelley and Bram Stoker's supreme gothic achievements. Indeed, there is a long theatrical tradition on Broadway of horror plays (and spoof horror plays, many of which were translated to the screen in the twenties), of which the latest example was Frank Langella's enormously successful *Dracula*, which like the Bela Lugosi version was also filmed (by John Badham in 1979).

In Europe too, the theatre was a major influence on the development of the cinema but its effects were felt far more widely. The European gothic tradition, like its British counterpart, can be described in Morton Kaplan's words as 'a class of melodrama characterized by the subordination of events to the production of terror', but its terrors for the most part were of a much more philosophical nature. The German *Schauerromane* – a strand of gothic literature – in particular, call into question the very world we live in as they simultaneously titillate their readers with sadistic and erotic fantasies. In the *Schauerromane* also, the uncanny (*unheimlich*) has a much more prominent role than elsewhere. Where Conan Doyle's Sherlock Holmes can be seen as a 20th-century culmination of the Anglo-American need for explanations of those acts which seem unexplainable – Joseph Wood Krutch has remarked that Edgar Allan Poe 'invented the detective story in order that he might not go mad' – the German silent cinema, and especially its horror films, dwelled on the unexplainable.

A brief comparison of the opening of James Whale's **Frankenstein** (1931) and Robert Wiene's **Das Cabinet des Dr Caligari** (1919) is instructive here. Whale's film begins *in medias res*. The first image is of hands, seen in close-up, which initiates a long tracking shot through what we quickly surmise is a graveyard in which a funeral service is being conducted. There is no establishing shot: Whale opens on a shock effect – the hands on the rope in close-up which also introduces an image that recurs throughout the film – and concludes the tracking shot with an image of a churchyard statue that momentarily seems to be a supernatural spirit. Whale's aim here is not to provide us with a *context* for what will follow, but to introduce the shocks and terrors that lie ahead. Wiene's film opens very differently: two men sit in a stylized garden on a bench in front of a high, forbidding wall. The figures, eyes staring blankly from pale faces, seem as lifeless as the garden. The old man leans towards his disinterested young companion and starts to speak: 'Everywhere there are spirits....They are around us....They have driven me from hearth and home, from my wife and children.' As he speaks, we see that the wall behind them is strangely patterned by the shadows of a tree moving in the slight wind. In cold, plain prose the sequence might seem bland, but on screen, as S. S. Prawer has pointed out, 'the *mise-en-scène* of the opening sequence slides us from a "normal" world to the distorted one presented in the stylized settings that are yet to come'. In the recently discovered complete print of the film, this is all the more evident, for not only is the prologue tinted but the intertitle on which the old man's words are written is decorated in the expressionist manner of the rest of the film. Both film-makers start by taking us out of our familiar, everyday world, but in radically different ways, one shocks us, the other prepares us for a literally distorted world in which fantasies reign. Of the two films, *Caligari* is the better because it is both more truthful (the debate about the framing devices of the film notwithstanding) and more fearful. That said, Whale's film is the more robust. Its cocktail of influences resulted in a world far less fragile, if less imaginative, and a world that could be returned to time and time again, as Universal did throughout the thirties and forties. Where *Caligari* represents a style and a vision, *Frankenstein* represents a formula and the beginnings of a genre.

Before the coming of sound, European horror films were more interesting than their American counterparts simply because they were more serious (though this was not always to

The climax of the marvellous opening sequence of James Whale's seminal Frankenstein *(1931).*

their advantage as the sterile academicism of a film like **La Chute de la Maison Usher**, 1928, demonstrates). Films like **Nosferatu, Der Muede Tod** (both 1921) and **Der Student von Prag** (1926) addressed their material with a far deeper concern than is evident in American films like **The Phantom of the Opera** (1925) and **The Cat and the Canary** (1927), in which both shocks and comic turns are used to distance viewers from the terrors on display. *Caligari* is further strengthened by its use of hypnotism, and intensified by the image of the thick-spectacled Werner Krauss staring into the camera as if he were hypnotizing the audience as well as Conrad Veidt's somnambulist. What makes the film so powerful is that this theme of 'the look' – the camera looking at the world (voyeurism) and into the unconscious (and so becoming the vehicle of fantasies) – is articulated, in the manner of Fritz Lang and Carl Dreyer, in the very look of the film itself, in its style, as well as its content. It is this duality that is missing from American silent and early sound films. Accordingly, though films like *Caligari* were stylistically influential in America as supreme examples of expressionism, the films made under their influence (including *Frankenstein*), with few exceptions, have at their best an innocence and pragmatism, and at their worst a hollowness, that reveal how little of the spirit of films like *Caligari* crossed the Atlantic.

The sound era

With the coming of sound, the internationalization of the film market and the swift control of that market by the USA, the aesthetics of Hollywood became dominant the world over. Even in Europe, expressionism became little more than a minor stylistic influence, rather than the way of looking it had been. Thus, until the fifties when significant changes in the modes of production and distribution took place, there were no movies as delirious and all-encompassing as *Caligari*. Though stylistically worlds apart, the films of Terence Fisher in England, Mario Bava in Italy and Roger Corman in the USA, echo some of this delirium. Alfred Hitchcock, for whom a formative influence had been Fritz Lang's **Der Muede Tod** (1921), laid the foundations for the next significant development of the horror film with **Psycho** (1960). Until then, for the most part, the formula of Universal's monster films held sway to ever-diminishing returns as the horror film toyed with the themes of Mary Shelley and Bram Stoker, rather than interrogating and breathing new life into them.

If one looks at stills from James Whale's **Frankenstein** and Tod Browning's much over-praised **Dracula** (both 1931) the illustrations retain their power; but the films themselves are far less powerful. It is not so much that the films are stilted (though in the case of the Browning-Lugosi collaboration the film is very flat), or even merely old, but that the strategies that the writers and directors adopt undercut the mythical dimension of their material. In doing so, they made it possible for those who followed in their footsteps, to cut down the characters of Frankenstein, Dracula and the Wolf Man in film after film until they were simply foils to be set against Abbott and Costello, Old Mother Riley and the Bowery Boys. Only rarely do American films of this period address themselves to notions of sexuality (**Dr Jekyll and Mr Hyde**, 1932), perverse obsessions (**Mad Love**, 1935) and sadism (**The Most Dangerous Game**, 1932) – only rarely do they attempt to speak the unspeakable. Oddly enough, the one film to enter the mythic, **King Kong** (1933), did so so wholeheartedly that it is seemingly open to an infinite number of interpretations. It has often been seen as a *macho* fantasy of domination – and a leaf through the illustrations of this book reveals just how prevalent the image of man the gorilla is. A more complex reading sees Kong, who is after all found by a movie crew, as a giant man who for all his size is humbled by forces that he cannot comprehend, just as the film's audiences were humbled by a force they could could not comprehend, the Depression.

'To show that, unconsciously, we all live in fear – that is genuine horror. Many people today are constantly prey to a kind of fear they don't wish to analyse. When the audience, sitting in a darkened room, recognizes its own insecurity in that of the characters in the film, then you can show unbelievable situations in the certain knowledge that the audience will follow you.' The speaker here is Jacques Tourneur, director of **Cat People** (1942), **I Walked with a Zombie** and **The Leopard Man** (both 1943) and he articulates an aesthetic of disquiet which is far removed from that of *Frankenstein* and the like. His films hark back to the notions of evil and sexuality common in German silent films, but treat them from a psychological, rather than a mythic, perspective. In this, he pre-dated Hollywood's general discovery of Freud. Similarly, in place of the gothic decorations of the Universal films, Tourneur opted for a camera style in which virtually all his scenes have visible light sources, all the shadows have *real* origins, whether just out of the frame or in the minds of the characters. These, and his other films for producer Val Lewton, were immediately praised for their 'suggestiveness', as opposed to the obvious horrors of the Universal monster films. Later, and more evasively, this quality was even more fulsomely praised for its direct contrast to the graphic technicolor realism of today's 'splatter movies'. These were seminal films, but they had little immediate influence. By the end of the forties, horror was virtually a dead genre and in the early fifties, science fiction replaced horror as fears of Armageddon supplanted the far less palpable fears the horror film traded in.

The rebirth of horror

By the mid-fifties in the USA, the monsters of the science fiction creature-features, began to mutate and revert back to the trappings of their horror ancestors and science fiction-horror hybrids like **I Was a Teenage Werewolf** (1957) proliferated. But it was outside of the USA, in Italy and the UK in the hands of Riccardo Freda, Mario Bava and Terence Fisher that horror was, literally, reborn as a genre. Freda's **I Vampiri** (1956), a modern version of the Erzsebeth Bathory legend, initiated a macabre stream of hallucinatory nightmares which dealt explicitly with a variety of (male) sexual fears and were publicized as such. The blurb on the poster for Bava's **L'Orribile Segreto del Dr Hichcock** (1962) when it was released in the USA as *The Terror of Dr Hichcock*, for example, ran 'His secret was a coffin named Desire!' and 'The candle of his lust burnt brightest in the shadow of the grave!'. Fisher's **The Curse of Frankenstein** (1957) and **Dracula** (1958), although more traditional in terms of subject matter, were equally revolutionary films. In the first, Fisher refocused attention on the Baron as a Byronic man of science and over-reacher whose surgical skills cut through previous nostalgic brass and mahogany visions of the Victorian past. In the second, he presented Dracula as a feudal relic transformed into a sort of 19th-century James Bond through the blood of his adoring victims. Common to both directors (but put to radically different effects by them) was colour, and a consequent degree of realism in their images, in the amount of blood on display, for example. More significantly, their work represented not merely an increase in shock effects – though the resurrection sequence in Mario Bava's **La Maschera del Demonio** (1960) is spectacular compared to earlier similar efforts – but a newfound intensity and consistency of viewpoint. Their characters are caught in a mutable middle-ground between dark fantasies and 'reality'; as the characters are warned in Bava's **Ercole al Centro della Terra** (1961), 'Do not believe in what you think you see'. In this, Bava and Freda were greatly helped by the presence of Barbara Steele (with Christopher Lee, Vincent Price and Peter Cushing, one of the stars of the modern horror film) whose face had an uncanny ability to suggest both pleasure and pain simultaneously.

Bava's prowling camera had its counterpart in America in the films of Roger Corman. He brought to his series of Edgar Allan Poe adaptations that commenced with **House of Usher**

Nobuko Otowa (right) and Jitsuko Yoshimura as the peasants who live by killing soldiers and selling their armour in Shindo's impressive Onibaba *(1964).*

in 1960, a baroque lyricism and, at the same time, made explicit the dark themes of Poe. Thus *House of Usher* is only intelligible once the fact that Roderick Usher's guilt stems from his incestuous desires for his sister is accepted. In re-interpreting Poe, whose gothic fantasies are peculiarly American, Corman opened the way for a particularly American inflection to the horror film. But it was Alfred Hitchcock, the British poet of repression who had learnt his craft from the German masters, who made the first truly *American* horror film, **Psycho** (1960). The film's enormous success had immediate effects: in America William Castle launched a series of *Psycho*-derived movies and in Britain Hammer did the same. The significance of *Psycho* goes far deeper, however. In its shower sequence, it introduced a specific application of special effects that the horror movie would later make its own; it introduced the knife and the 'slasher' to horror; it introduced the theme of the woman-in-peril; it was set in a contemporary believable world, instead of in a shrouded past; it made explicit the conservative view of sexual activity outside marriage (and at lunchtime!) as being punishable by death; and it was set in the mid-West, the location of most subsequent American horror films, and so on. Although it 'introduced' numerous themes, *Psycho* is not important in strict chronological terms. Its influence on the development of the American horror film lies in the particular blend of these themes and elements that the film yoked together. Quite literally, *Psycho* forms the bridge to the 'splatter movies' of the seventies. Robert Bloch's script was based on the case of the infamous Ed Gein, the Wisconsin necrophile who graduated from robbing graves and mummifying the bodies to pursuing live victims. The Gein case also provided the source material for **Deranged** and **The Texas Chainsaw Massacre** (both 1974), the film that made

'splatter movies' headline news. Similarly, Hitchcock's manipulation of the perspective he offers audiences, making explicit the voyeurism implicit in looking at the cinema image, has been borrowed and aped by numerous subsequent directors (Brian de Palma being just the most obvious example) until it has become almost a stylistic *sine qua non* of the modern horror film.

The impact of films like **The Curse of Frankenstein** (1957) and **Psycho** (1960), though they elaborated specifically national themes, was worldwide in that their success led to a renaissance of the genre. However, the resulting flood of films were not all inflected by the themes and styles of Bava, Corman, Fisher, Freda and Hitchcock. In Mexico, for instance, horror movies either used traditional national characters like the Mourning Mother and the Aztec Mummy (often pitting them against that Mexican speciality, the masked wrestler) or, in direct contrast to 'international trends', returned to the styles and notions of horror of the thirties. Thus, **El Vampiro** and **El Ataud del Vampiro** (both 1957) are oldfashioned in form. And, though subsequent films would be seasoned with soft-porn sequences, in their commitment to a linear narrative and the simple pleasure of directly staged action, they remain oldfashioned in feel. Surprisingly, even the mix of surgery and sadism inaugurated by Jesús Franco's gruesome **Gritos en la Noche** (1962), which was particularly influential throughout Latin America, had little impact in Mexico. Similarly, in Japan, although attempts were made to follow international trends and Dracula and other figures of European culture were inserted into traditional stories in the main, national themes and motifs held sway.

The net effect of the revolution in the horror film that occurred in the late fifties and early sixties was the emergence of a genre capable of dealing with far more complex and dense themes (some echoing back to those of the silent period) than those of the thirties. This is not to say that the majority of the films were necessarily any better, as a comparison of **La Residencia** and **Taste the Blood of Dracula** (two films picked at random from 1969) makes clear. In *La Residencia*, Narcisco Serrador takes a completely exploitative attitude to his material, and draws on **Psycho** (1960) and **Gritos en la Noche** (1962) to little effect. Peter Sasdy's *Taste the Blood of Dracula* explores in a genuinely interesting way the theme of Victorian family first outlined by Fisher in **Dracula** (1958). That said, however, unlike many later (s)exploitation films, *La Residencia* is merely objectionable. Although in its articulation of male violence against women for profit, it in no way engages with or interrogates the fantasies it rests on, neither is it pathological as are the films of José Mojica Marins (**Esta Noite Encarnarei no Teu Cadaver**, 1966, and **O Estranho Mundo de Zé do Caixao**, 1968, for example) nor is it wholly constructed around the theme of violence.

The seventies

By the seventies, when special effects made even the cheapest of Z-grade films truly shocking, and the theme of violence against women – stalked by knife-wielding 'slasher-killers' or chased by cannibals – became omnipresent, the problems posed by exploitation pictures could not so easily be dismissed. To ban them, as so many people have proposed, is merely to attempt to repress the very fears the films articulate in however garbled a manner. To champion them unthinkingly in the name of 'liberalism', on the other hand, is to forget the power of the fantasies they represent. More importantly, these films need to be understood. The themes and subject matter of 'splatter movies' are not as different from mainstream film-making as one might think. Consider blockbusters like **The Exorcist** (1973) and **The Omen** (1976), with their tales of possession and the coming of the Antichrist *and* their reaffirmation of family life, even at the cost of the possible annihilation of the world. At the time of their release, both films were, bizarrely enough, treated with a degree of theological seriousness – as if such crude 'shockers' could enter into arcane theological debate – that was the inverse of the contempt with which the exploitation movies were dismissed. Or consider the series of 'Superman' movies, in which the world was set to rights quite literally by someone whose body could not be cut into pieces, be it by chainsaws or scalpels. Significantly, in *Superman III* (1983) even the Man of Steel is revealed to have baser instincts. Quite clearly, in general in the seventies, and in the USA in particular, a sense of imminent doom hung in the air (the fallout from the Vietnam war and Watergate?), and was held at bay only by the likes of Superman. Certainly, in contrast to earlier decades in which, although the children of the night were forever threatening to extinguish the light of reason, they were held at bay by the efforts of the likes of Van Helsing, in the seventies the assumption of so many horror films has been that mankind is doomed and that the day of zombies and cannibals, let alone the Antichrist, has come. At the very least, the number of sequels to films like **Halloween** (1978) and **Friday the 13th** (1980) suggest that getting rid of the likes of the 'Boogeyman' is as time-consuming as ridding the world of Dracula.

From this perspective, the strand of recent American horror movies best represented by **The Texas Chainsaw Massacre** (1974) and **The Hills Have Eyes** (1977), is particularly interesting. Unlike *Halloween* and its clones, they are not mere 'shock machines' in the tradition of Dario Argento. Nor, like so many contemporary American horror films, are they Hitchcock imitations. As several critics have pointed out, at the centre of these films is a crude parody of the brave frontiersmen of the past, the men who opened up the West (though on the evidence of Michael Lesy's book, *Wisconsin Death Trip*, dementia played a far more prominent role in frontier life than has been hitherto acknowledged). Thus, in *The Texas Chainsaw Massacre*, the once proud figure of Leatherstocking, hero of James Fenimore Cooper's pioneering novels, has been transformed into Leatherface, the wielder of the chainsaw (and, significantly, the chainsaw is presented as a weapon of mutilation rather than a symbol of procreation). Similarly, *The Hills Have Eyes*, though its stated factual basis is in Scotland and its mythical basis lies in the Grimm fairytale notion of a stolen baby, replays the idea of a family – and that they are a family is significant – of pioneers preying on those who have followed them. Films like **The Driller Killer** (1979) and **Ms 45** (1980), in a similar way, examine the urban nightmare in which women are commodities for sale in a far more thorough-going fashion than more socially committed films like Richard Brooks' *Looking for Mr Goodbar* (1977) and Tony Garnett's *Handgun* (1982). Of course, only a relatively small number of cannibal and women-in-peril movies situate themselves in this broad cultural context. Nonetheless, even at their most exploitative such films have a degree of honesty about them, especially at a time when 'gore' is a fact of life in the West, that urges caution against a wholesale dismissal of the modern 'exploitation' horror film. At the same time, the size of the market for such exploitation films and minimal control producers and distributors demand over writers and directors has made the area a fertile one for the likes of Wes Craven at precisely the time when , for the most part, socially conscious cinema in America is all but dead.

Ironically, the present debate about modern (exploitation) horror films has been conducted against the backdrop of a marked decline in the actual number of horror films made in recent years. Their place has been taken by science fiction movies which, since the mid-seventies, have spoken of a far more optimistic future. Less convincing, especially in the light of their newfound optimism, but far more appealing to a Reaganite America, the science fiction film has (temporarily) displaced the horror film. Its eclipse notwithstanding, horror remains the most probing and problematic of film genres and the one most in need of examination. Hopefully by providing a much-needed historical dimension, this work will contribute to such a re-evaluation and exploration.

1896-1919

Previous pages: *The aesthetics of paranoia:* Das Cabinet des Dr Caligari *(1919).*

Tales of Terror

Horror had little role to play in the earliest days of the cinema. In the flickerings that resulted from the combination of the trickeries of science and magic, the emotions engendered by horror had little place. Thus, although George Méliès' **Le Manoir du Diable** (1896), with its image of the Devil as a vampire bat, is undoubtedly the first horror film, in atmosphere and feeling the film is far closer to the tradition of comic fantasies in which smiling amazement, rather than terror, was the expected reaction.

It was only as films grew longer and audiences more sophisticated that the horror film took its rightful place in the cinematic spectrum. In retrospect, the speed with which the subsequently identified 'traditional' themes and sources of the horror film then emerged is quite surprising. By 1920, Frankenstein had made his screen debut (in 1910), as had Robert Louis Stevenson's classic double figure, Dr Jekyll and Mr Hyde (in **Ein Seltsamer Fall**, 1914); the werewolf had put in an appearance (in 1913, in **The Werewolf** which significantly also introduced a specifically American inflection to horror with its use of Red Indian mythology); Conan Doyle's own monstrous hound had begun stalking the moors (in **Der Hund von Baskerville**, 1914) and the first of the cinema's ape-men was set loose (in **Balaoo**, 1913). Also, Edgar Allan Poe was speedily identified as a key source (with the French **Le Système du Docteur Goudron et du Professeur Plume**, 1912, the American **The Avenging Conscience**, 1914, and the German **Die Pest in Florenz**, 1919). But what is most marked about the period, especially considering the small number of films made, is the variety of approaches to horror they represent, ranging from the mysticism of **Der Schatten des Meeres** (1912) to the athleticism of **L'Atketa Fantasma** (1919), which introduced the contemporary masked-wrestler figure whose descendants would include the likes of the Mexican Santo and the Blue Demon, among others.

Soon, however, this stylistic pluralism would be shattered. In Europe, the imaginative possibilities of film remained uppermost in the minds of film-makers, though the dominant influence of German expressionism was as inhibiting for some as it was exhilarating for others; in America, fast-paced action held sway. The two films that represent this trend best are Robert Weine's classic **Das Cabinet des Dr Caligari** (1919) and the action serial **The Crimson Stain Mystery** (1916). The one, in its rigorous undercutting of the contemporary melodramatic realism, paved the way for the magnificent work of Fritz Lang and others in the twenties, while the other confirmed that action would be the mainstay of the American cinema in the following decade – except, ironically, for the horror film which, for the most part, would retreat to an even cruder theatricalism than that of Weine.

1896

Le Manoir du Diable *aka* **The Haunted Castle** *aka* **The Manor of the Devil** *aka* **The Devil's Manor**

(STAR; FR) b/w 2min

This is strictly speaking the first vampire movie. On a set representing a hall in a medieval castle, a large bat flies in, circles round and is transformed into Mephistopheles. Conjuring up a cauldron, Mephistopheles produces from it a pretty girl, followed by a stream of phantoms, skeletons and witches until one brandishes a crucifix and the demon vanishes in a puff of smoke. The Devil also appears as a bat, rather more vampirically erotic in intent if not in deed, in *Le Diable au Couvent* (1899). But although the work of Méliès teems with demons, monsters, apparitions and bizarre mutilations, on very rare occasions gruesome in effect – like the giant of the snows when it crushes a hapless explorer in *A la Conquête du Pôle* (1912) – he was too steeped in the pantomime tradition of amusing fantasy to figure in the history of horror.

d/p/s Georges Méliès *lp* Georges Méliès

1909

Den Graa Dame *aka* **The Grey Lady** *aka* **The Grey Dame**

(NORDISK; DEN) b/w 14(10)min

This picture is the sixth in the Sherlock Holmes series Nordisk had started in 1908, starring and directed by Larsen. A legend holds that anyone seeing the ghost of a woman in grey – instead of a hound – will die soon afterwards. Holmes is called in to solve the problem and discovers that the culprit is a rich patriarch's nephew who dresses up as the grey lady's ghost in order to scare and kill people and earn himself a fortune in the process. By all accounts this was a fast-paced adventure story, full of secret rooms and passageways and the spectral appearances were the highlight of the movie. Larsen left the series after this episode and was replaced first by Otto Lagoni, then by Alwin Neuss and finally by Holger Rasmussen.

The next major Holmes movie was part of the German series which began with **Der Hund von Baskerville** in 1914, in which Neuss continued in the role he had played briefly in Denmark.

d/s Viggo Larsen *p* Ole Olsen *c* Axel Sorensen *lp* Viggo Larsen, Forest Holger-Madsen, Gustav Lund, Elith Pio

Sherlock Holmes in danger in Den Graa Dame.

Charles Ogle as the screen's first Frankenstein.

1910

Frankenstein (EDISON) b/w 16min
The first attempt to capture Mary Shelley's *Frankenstein or The Modern Prometheus* on film (though there had been many stage adaptations), this is an extraordinary effort for its time. Written and directed by Dawley, the film successfully reinterprets, rather than condenses, the original material. Billed as a 'liberal adaptation of Mrs Shelley's tale', the film – its makers claimed – also 'tried to eliminate all the actually repulsive situations and to concentrate upon the mystic and psychological problems that are to be found in this weird tale'.

Frankenstein (Phillips), a young medical student, tries to create chemically a perfect human being. Unfortunately, the result of his experiments is a misshapen monster (Ogle), who flees into the night. Frankenstein, sickened, is nursed back to health by his sweetheart, but on the eve of his wedding is visited by the monster. During the ensuing struggle, the monster sees himself reflected in a mirror and, horrified, takes off into the night, but later breaks into the bride's room. Her shrieks bring Frankenstein running, there is another struggle and, overcome 'by love', the creature fades away.

The curiously mystic finale sits oddly with the beautifully built-up dark mood which, after James Whale's classic **Frankenstein** (1931), was at the centre of, if not central to, all subsequent versions of the tale.

d/s J. Searle Dawley *p* Thomas A. Edison *lp* Charles Ogle, Augustus Phillips, Mary Fuller

1912

Conscience *aka* **The Chamber of Horrors**
(VITAGRAPH) b/w 10min
More a cautionary moral tale than anything else, *Conscience* makes use of a setting that was to become a horror movie favourite: the chamber of horrors. Persuaded to elope by her lover Eric, Eleanor Donelly defies her police officer brother to go to New York, where the young couple are married. Soon deserted by Eric and desperate for food for her baby, Eleanor tries to steal a bottle of milk. Fleeing in terror from a policeman, she takes refuge in a chamber of horrors. Coincidentally, fallen among disreputable companions, Eric has meanwhile accepted a wager daring him to spend a night in the same chamber of horrors. In the morning, seeing Eleanor in the shadows as she wakes and rises, Eric dies of fright while Eleanor goes mad.

d Maurice Costello *p* Albert E. Smith *lp* Rose Tapley, Maurice Costello

Der Schatten des Meeres *aka* **The Sea's Shadow** *aka* **Im Schatten des Meeres** *aka* **In the Shadow of the Sea**
(MESSTERS PROJEKTION; G) b/w 40min
On a dark night, the shadowy figure of Death emerges from the sea and enters a fisherman's hut to persuade an unhappy woman (Porten) to follow him into a watery grave. This poetic exploration of suicide, based on a Swedish legend, provides Messter with an opportunity to combine heavy melodrama with elements of Nordic mysticism and to compete with the strong Scandinavian film industry of the period. The result deserves respect for its success in conveying the rhythms of oral storytelling and for the lyrical passages of the film's second act.

Stark, Porten's husband at the time and frequent co-star, usually made uninspired, naturalistic dramas which suggests that the introduction of the darkly romantic elements can be attributed to Messter and Froehlich. Messter was a prominent German film pioneer, inventor and entrepreneur. He directed most of his company's films until 1910 and controlled his own equipment, production and distribution companies until they were taken over by UFA in 1917. His Berlin-based empire experimented with animation (1897) and sound films (1903) and introduced the star system into Germany. Under Messter's supervision, Porten, the daughter of opera singer and film director Franz Porten, became the first German screen star. She later founded her own production company with Froehlich.

d Curt A. Stark *p* Oscar Messter *c* Carl Froehlich
lp Henny Porten, Curt A. Stark, Fran Retzlag, Lizzy Krueger

Le Système du Docteur Goudron et du Professeur Plume *aka* **The Lunatics**
(ECLAIR; FR) b/w 15min
Tourneur's third film after a varied career as interior decorator, illustrator, stage and film actor, and as assistant to Emile Chautard at Eclair. Reputedly the best of several films transposed from the Théâtre du Grand Guignol repertory of one-acters, it was adapted by de Lorde (one of the Grand Guignol's regular writers) from his own dramatization of Edgar Allan Poe's short story (*The System of Dr Tarr and Professor Feather*) about a visitor making a tour of inspection of a lunatic asylum who finds to his discomfiture that it has been taken over by the inmates after a mutiny. As with all Grand Guignol productions, subtlety is beside the point (the visitor is even provided with a pretty wife to double the threat), but Tourneur manages to inject some in the film's most notorious scene, where the supposed director of the asylum is describing for the benefit of the visitors his new cure for insanity: first cutting out an eye, then slitting the throat. Interrupted by noises off-screen, he rushes into the next room and reappears with bloody hands while blood slowly oozes under the door from the next room and begins to arouse feral instincts in the inmates surrounding the visitors.

Tourneur filmed another de Lorde playlet (*Figures de Cire*, 1912) before his departure for America. The Poe story was remade in Mexico, erratically but often brilliantly, as **La Mansión de la Locura** (1972). In 1920, a famous season of Grand Guignol plays in London, starring Sybil and Russell Thorndike, sparked off a miniseries of one-reelers under the general title *Grand Guignol*.

d Maurice Tourneur *s* André de Lorde *lp* Henri Gouget, Henri Roussell, Renée Sylvaire

1913

Balaoo *aka* **Balaoo the Demon Baboon** *aka* **Balaoo ou des Pas au Plafond** (ECLAIR; FR) b/w 24min
This curious little tale of an ancestor of King Kong's who also died for love, is based on the serial by Gaston Leroux (author of *The Phantom of the Opera*) and directed by Jasset, Louis Feuillade's chief rival for the title of serial king until his death in 1913. While experimenting along Darwinian lines, Dr Coriolis succeeds in transforming an ape into a gentle, semi-human creature called Balaoo (Bataille) who worships the doctor's pretty niece Madeleine. Balaoo is still mischievous by nature, however, and delights in tormenting people, taking to the trees when punished and eventually running away to sow widespread terror. Befriended by a poacher who saves his life, Balaoo becomes his willing slave, even committing murder to rid the poacher of an enemy in a crime which goes undetected since the only clue is a puzzling set of footprints on the ceiling (Jasset shot the scene is a set built upsidedown). But after kidnapping Madeleine on the amorous poacher's orders, Balaoo rebels, knowing that she is lost to him for ever. Though mortally wounded, he sets a deadly trap for the poacher and manages to alert the doctor to his niece's peril. Two American remakes, *The Wizard* (1927) and *Dr Renault's Secret* (1942), played down to the tender romantic aspects to concentrate on science fiction comedy-horrors.

d/s Victorin Jasset *lp* Lucien Bataille, Camille Bardou, Henry Gouget

The Werewolf (BISON) b/w 18min
Seemingly the first werewolf, although there had been a were-snake in the lost *The Vampire* (1913) – in which a vampiric native woman in India turns into a snake to kill the explorer who shot her. Here, attaching the theme to American Indian mythology, the plot concerns a Navajo witch-woman who thinks she has been deserted by her husband (actually he has been killed) and who raises her daughter to hate all white men. The daughter becomes a werewolf seeking revenge.

The Wolf Man (1924), sometimes listed as a horror film (it was directed by Edmund Mortimer and starred John Gilbert), is about a man who becomes a vicious brute when drunk.

d Henry McRae

1914

The Avenging Conscience (MUTUAL) b/w 80min
Over-elaborate and at times unduly naïve, this adaptation of Poe's *The Tell-Tale Heart* (with injections from the poem 'Annabel Lee') nevertheless stakes a fair claim as the horror cinema's first masterpiece. Walthall plays a young man frustrated in love (for Sweet) by opposition from his tyrannical uncle (Aiken). Brooding over thoughts of murder, he is assailed by visions: Moses and the Ten Commandments, Christ on the Cross, but also a grisly little tableau in which a spider traps a fly in its web, and is then devoured in its turn by ants. Concluding that life 'is a long system of murder', he duly kills his uncle and walls up the body.

Using a veritable barrage of double exposures and framing devices that re-shape the screen space and supporting his narrative with a mosaic of Poe allusions, Griffith gives at least the semblance of psychological depth to his portrait of a murderer. The editing, extremely effective as conscience takes hold – with the ticking of a clock, the rhythmic tapping of a policeman's shoe, the repeated cry of a bird, all echoing the tell-tale beating of the dead man's heart – builds to a superb crescendo as the murderer is assaulted by the nightmarish creatures of conscience.

Disappointingly, but typically of Griffith and the period, it is all revealed at the end to have been a dream occasioned by the reading of Poe.

d/p/s D. W. Griffith *c* G. W. Bitzer *lp* Henry B. Walthall, Blanche Sweet, Spottiswoode Aitken, Ralph Lewis, Mae Marsh

Lyda Salmonova (right) in Der Golem, *the first of the many versions of the legend of the clay statue (seen behind Salmonova) brought to malevolent life through unrequited love.*

The Basilisk (HEPWORTH; GB) b/w 28min
This mild British attempt at horror is notable chiefly for anticipating at its climax Universal's use of green – 'the colour of fear' – as a tint for some of the original prints of **Frankenstein** (1931). Felton is a mesmerist with occult powers who endeavours to draw a beautiful woman (Taylor) into his clutches. Meeting with resistance and bent on destruction, he compels her to stab her fiancé (Powers) to death, a fate from which both are saved when a snake conveniently kills the villain.

d/p/s/c Cecil M. Hepworth *lp* William Felton, Alma Taylor, Tom Powers, Chrissie White, Cyril Morton

Der Golem *aka* **The Golem** *aka* **The Monster of Fate** (DEUTSCHE BIOSCOP; G) b/w 60min
Two years before Gustav Meyrink's famous novel introduced the golem to the world, Wegener had heard the legend while on location in Prague in 1913. He became so fascinated with the story of the clay statue manufactured by Rabbi Loew in the 1580s to save the Jews of Prague from a pogrom threatened by Rudolf II of Habsburg, that he played the creature three times on the screen and directed two of the films himself.

This version is set in the 20th century. The monumental hulk (golem means shapeless mass) is uncovered by workmen in the ruins of a synagogue and sold to an antiquarian who

Left: *Christ as* The Avenging Conscience *in D. W. Griffith's spirited adaptation of Edgar Allan Poe's tale,* The Tell-Tale Heart.

brings it to life. Used as a servant, the creature eventually rebels, partly because its love for Salmonova (Wegener's wife) remains unanswered. After going on a murderous rampage, it is destroyed in a fall. The appearance of the creature, designed by the sculptor Belling, remained largely unchanged throughout Wegener's subsequent essays in the role including the comedy *Der Golem und die Taenzerin* (1917), where he pretends to be the golem in order to frighten a beautiful dancer he wishes to seduce. In 1920 he directed himself in the classic version of the legend, set in the appropriate period. The Danish director Urban Gad, the husband and director of Asta Nielsen, is often credited with a golem film, but the existence of such a film is more than doubtful.

d/co-s Henrik (Heinrich) Galeen *co-s* Paul Wegener *c* Guido Seeber *lp* Paul Wegener, Lyda Salmonova, Carl Ebert, Jacob Tiedtke, Rudolf Bluemner

Der Hund von Baskerville *aka* **The Hound of the Baskervilles**
(VITASCOPE; G) b/w 2 parts (65,55min)
The first two feature-length instalments of a series based on Conan Doyle's most often filmed novel. Part 1 is the first faithful adaptation of the story, although the Watson character is left out of the proceedings. A contemporary source describes the hound as 'a monstrous Great Dane with flaming eyes and fire emerging from its mouth'. Holmes is played by Neuss, who took over the role from Viggo Larsen shortly after the release of **Den Graa Dame** (1909) in an earlier series for Nordisk Films. Fichtner is Lord Henry, Weisse his fiancée Laura Lyons, Kuehne plays the villain, Stapleton, and Van Horn the mysterious butler. Part 2, *Des Einsame Haus*, was made by the same cast and crew except for the replacement of Freund by Brandes as cinematographer. It tells of Stapleton's escape from prison and his return, in disguise again, to Baskerville Castle. He builds a submersible house in a nearby lake where he imprisons Sir Henry and Laura. Holmes rescues them as the house slowly sinks into the lake, trapping the villain. Both parts were released in 1921 in a slightly shortened version, possibly as competition for a rival's success with parts 5 and 6 of the series, *Dr Macdonald's Sanatorium* (1921) and *Das Haus Ohne Fenster* (shot in 1920).

Meinert later became production supervisor for Decla Film and played an important part in the production of **Das Cabinet des Dr Caligari** (1919).

d Rudolph Meinert *p* Josef Greenbaum *s* Richard Oswald *c* Karl Freund, Werner Brandes *lp* Alwin Neuss, Friedrich Kuehne, Erwin Fichtner, Hanni Weisse, Andreas Van Horn

Right: *Hanni Weisse and Alwin Neuss in the first German adaptation of* The Strange Case of Dr Jekyll and Mr Hyde, Ein Seltsamer Fall.

Ein Seltsamer Fall (VITASCOPE; G) b/w 50min
The first German film adaptation of Stevenson's classic tale *The Strange Case of Dr Jekyll and Mr Hyde*, this was released while Germany was at war with Great Britain. The motif of the double or of a character split into two antagonistic personalities was a familiar one in German literature long before Stevenson. Albert Basserman, in his first major screen appearance, had scored a triumph with such a character in Mack's previous 'double' film, *Der Andere* (1913), where he played a lawyer sometimes overcome by his unconscious desires. Murnau later returned to the theme with **Der Januskopf** (1920).

d Max Mack *s* Richard Oswald *lp* Alwin Neuss, Hanni Weisse, Lotte Neumann

1915

Der Hund von Baskerville *aka* **The Hound of the Baskervilles**
(GREENBAUM FILM; G) b/w 2 parts(50, 50min)
When Greenbaum left Vitascope to form his own company, he took with him most of the cast and the scenarist responsible for the first two episodes of that company's series **Der Hund von Baskerville** (1914). He immediately made and released two more instalments while Vitascope, now renamed PAGU, countered this act of piracy (in fact, neither company had cleared the rights with Conan Doyle) by releasing its own episode 3 entitled **Der Hund von Baskerville: Das Dunkle Schloss.**

The two Greenbaum films, written and directed by Oswald, were designed by Hermann Warm, better known as the designer of **Das Cabinet des Dr Caligari** (1919). The Greenbaum part 3 was called *Das Unheimliche Zimmer*. Stapleton (Kuehne), having escaped from the sinking house at the end of part 2, returns to do more mischief to Sir Henry (Fichtner) and his fiancée, played by Irrah since Weisse had stayed behind at Vitascope where she continued to play Laura Lyons in their rival part 3. To complicate matters further, Greenbaum-Oswald's part 4, entitled *Die Sage von Hund* was submitted to the German censor before their part 3. Part 4 tells of Sir Henry's evil ancestor who killed his wife and her faithful dog, causing the dog to haunt the area. The censor's certificate describes it as 'a costume drama with Knights'. The role of the woman is taken on by Borke, while the rest of the cast simply re-enact their respective roles in a period setting. However, both Greenbaum's 'pirate' films were banned for the duration of the war after the more powerful Vitascope-PAGU had lodged complaints against Greenbaum.

d/s Richard Oswald *p* Josef Greenbaum *lp* Alwin Neuss, Friedrich Kuehne, Erwin Fichtner, Andreas Van Horn, Tatjana Irrah, Hilde Borke

Sherlock Holmes (Alwin Neuss) in danger in Rudolph Meinert's stylish Der Hund von Baskerville.

1915

Der Hund von Baskerville: Das Dunkle Schloss *aka* **The Hound of the Baskervilles: The Dark Castle**
(PAGU; G) b/w 50min
In competition with Josef Greenbaum and Richard Oswald, PAGU continued the series which they had started (when the company was called Vitascope) with **Der Hund von Baskerville** in 1914 before Greenbaum, the producer, left them taking most of the artists involved with him. PAGU's part 3, *Der Hund von Baskerville: Das Dunkle Schloss*, starred Burg as Holmes while Kuehne again played the villain (as he continued to do for Greenbaum) and Weisse remained Laura Lyons. After complaints from the powerful PAGU Greenbaum's films were banned, but after the war Greenbaum again hired some of the people associated with the series and released 'his' parts 5 and 6 entitled *Dr Macdonald's Sanatorium* (1921) and *Das Haus Ohne Fenster* (1920). To counter this new move, PAGU re-released a shortened version of their own original two episodes made in 1914, as one single feature.

d Willy Zehn *lp* Eugen Burg, Friedrich Zelnik, Friedrich Kuehne, Hanni Weisse

1916

The Crimson Stain Mystery
(ERBOGRAPH) b/w 16chaps
This mad-doctor serial has Dr Burton Montrose (McGrane) discover an enzyme which he believes will give the human brain super-intellectual powers. The plot, which emphasizes the horror rather than the science elements, has his experiments go disastrously wrong: in developing superior brains, the human guinea-pigs also become hideous, murderous mutants who form a gang preying on the wealthy. When the police prove helpless, a crusading newspaper publisher puts his detective son (Costello) to work. He starts out with only one clue, a telltale crimson stain said to be visible in the eye of the leader of the gang. But, aided by the doctor's daughter (Grandin) whom he falls in love with en route, spurred on by his father's murder and hindered by a vampiric temptress from the gang (Olonova), Costello finally discovers that the Crimson Stain is none other than the doctor, an unhappy victim of his own experiments.

d T. Hayes Hunter *s* Albert Payson Terhune *c* Ludwig G. B. Erb *lp* Maurice Costello, Ethel Grandin, Olga Olonova, Eugene Strong, Thomas J. McGrane

Life Without Soul (OCEAN) b/w 70min
The first feature-length version of Mary Wollstonecraft Shelley's novel, *Frankenstein or The Modern Prometheus*, brought the story up-to-date (1915) and added a great deal of spectacle, which required location shooting in Florida, Georgia, Arizona, New York and the Atlantic Ocean. Frankenstein became Dr William Frawley and the monster 'the Creation'. Standing, the English-born actor who played the artificially created man, used little special makeup, but was highly acclaimed for his performance. 'His embodiment of the man without a soul adequately conveys the author's intent. He is awe-inspiring but never grotesque, and indicates the gradual unfolding of the creature's senses and understanding with convincing skill. At times he actually awakens sympathy for the monster's condition, cut off as he is from all human companionship' was the opinion of Edward Weitzel in *Moving Picture World*. Thus Standing would seem to have foretold Boris Karloff's classic interpretation of 1931. Despite much exciting advertising – 'A photoplay embracing a theme never before attempted in cinematography, and stupendous in its execution!' – the film failed to get a decent release, and was re-edited and re-released by the Raver Film Corporation in May 1916. They added 'scientific films showing the reproduction of life in the fish world' and a tinting and toning colour scheme throughout.

d Joseph W. Smiley *p* John l. Dudley *s* Jesse J. Goldburg *lp* Percy Darrell Standing, William A. Cohill, Jack Hopkins, Lucy Cotton, Pauline Curley, David McCauley

1917

Das Bildnis des Dorian Gray *aka* **The Picture of Dorian Gray**
(RICHARD OSWALD FILM; G) b/w 80min
Having adapted Conan Doyle's *The Hound of the Baskervilles* (**Der Hund von Baskerville**, 1914) and Stevenson's *The Strange Case of Dr Jekyll and Mr Hyde* (**Ein Seltsamer Fall**, 1914), Oswald turned to Oscar Wilde for this variation on the familiar 'double' motif in which 'the soul' is represented by a painting rather than by another character. It was the first of a series of fantasy thrillers Oswald directed with Aldor in the lead. The set designs were furnished by Manfred Noa, a talented art director who had worked with Oswald before on *Hoffmanns Erzaehlungen* (1916).

An obscure American director, Fred Durrant, made the first film adaptation of Wilde's novel on record in 1913. The best known and best made version remains Albert Lewin's **The Picture of Dorian Gray** (1945). Massimo Dallamano made a botched version, **Il Dio Chiamato Dorian** (1970).

d/p/s Richard Oswald *c* Max Fassbender *lp* Bernd Aldor, Lupu Pick, Ernst Pittaschau, Andreas Van Horn, Lea Lara, Ernst Ludwig

Hilde Warren und der Tod *aka* **Hilde Warren and Death**
(MAY FILMS; G) b/w 80min
This early version of **Rosemary's Baby** (1968) was scripted by Lang for May, a director best known for his adventure serials. May's wife played the part of Hilde, a famous actress made pregnant by a condemned murderer. She becomes prey to visions of Death: an emaciated, spectral figure played by Lang himself. When it becomes clear that the child is in the father's image, she overcomes her maternal feelings and kills her evil offspring. Finally, when Death again appears to her in prison, she acquiesces to his embrace.

Many of Lang's scripts of the period presented explicit but highly stylized fantasies linking sex and death, such as **Die Pest**

A poster for Das Bildnis des Dorian Gray.

Hilde Wolter (centre) as the demonic Alraune *in the first of the many versions of Hanns Heinz Ewers' novel of the same name.*

in Florenz, **Totentanz** and **Lilith und Ly** (all 1919). It is interesting to note that in **Der Muede Tod** (1921), his best known Death movie, Lang put a very different slant on the story by making Death the central and even sympathetic character: a weary figure tired of killing but condemned to repeat his implacable task for all eternity.

d/p Joe May *s* Fritz Lang *c* Curt Courant *lp* Mia May, Hans Mierendorff, Bruno Kastner, Ernst Matray, Fritz Lang, Georg John

1918

Alraune (NEUTRAL FILM; G) b/w 88min
In contrast to the Victorian gothic novels which invariably suggested some logical explanation, however implausible, for the events described, the German *schauerromane*, produced under the influence of high romanticism, unapologetically cultivated the uncanny and the irrational, in the tradition of E. T. A. Hoffmann and Edgar Allan Poe. One of the movement's most accomplished practitioners was Hanns Heinz Ewers, the author of *Das Grauen* (1907), *Vampir* (1920) and the smash hit of *trivial literatur*, *Alraune* (1913).

The novel was filmed many times between 1918 and 1952. This version by a minor figure, Illes, and one by Kertesz, both released in 1918, constitute the first and by all accounts the least successful adaptations. The plot concerns a mad doctor, Ten Brinken, who artificially inseminates a prostitute with the semen of a hanged man. The result is the beautiful but demonic Alraune (Wolter) who eventually turns against the mad doctor in a reversal familiar from the Frankenstein stories as well as from the legends of alchemy and **Der Golem** (1914, 1920). Ewers' novel, however, concentrates more on the evocation of a broodily perverse sexual atmosphere, best rendered in Galeen's **Alraune** (1928).

d/c Eugen Illes *lp* Hilde Wolter, Gustav Adolf Semler, Friedrich Kuehne, Max Auzinger, Ernst Rennspies

Alraune (AUSTRIA, HUN) b/w 80min
This version of Hanns Heinz Ewers' popular novel was directed by Kertesz, a Hungarian who became famous in Hollywood under the name Michael Curtiz, making pictures with Errol Flynn as well as **Doctor X** (1932), **Mystery of the Wax Museum** (1933) and *The Walking Dead* (1936). Instead of using the artificial insemination of a prostitute with a hanged man's semen, the mad doctor here fathers a child by making the unfortunate woman copulate with the mandrake root itself. No copies appear to have survived from either of the two Alraune films made in 1918. Many sources list another version made in 1919 entitled *Alraune und der Golem*, but it is extremely doubtful that such a film was ever made and only a pre-production publicity poster remains. Similarly, a film called *Alraune and the Gypsy* (1913), although definitely shown, bears no relation to Ewers' story and merely features a woman who disturbs the conventional moral codes. The classic adaptations of the story were made in 1928, 1930 and 1952.

d Mihaly Kertesz (Michael Curtiz), Fritz Odon *s* Richard Falk *lp* Guyla Gal, Rozsi Szollosi, Jeno Torzs, Margit Lux, Kalman Kormendy

1919

L'Atketa Fantasma (A. DE GIGLIO; IT) b/w 85min
At a time when Maciste, played by the wrestler Bartolomeo Pagano, was king of the Italian superheroes, this Turin-based production launched a masked wrestler who anticipated not only the Mexican adventures of Santo and his colleagues, but Superman as well. The plot concerns a timid man, Audreses (Guaita-Ausonia) whose girlfriend Jenny (Zara) becomes involved in a series of outlandish adventures triggered by her possession of an antique jewel. A masked, bare-chested wrestler rescues her a number of times before he is revealed to be none other than the heroic side of her timid suitor.

d Raimodo Scotti *p* A. de Giglio *s* Reneę de Liot *lp* Elsa Zara, Mario Guaita-Ausonia, Gaetano Rossi, Dino Bonaiuti

Das Cabinet des Dr Caligari *aka* **The Cabinet of Dr Caligari** (DECLA FILM; G) b/w 82min
In a little village on the Dutch border, a fairground magician Caligari (Krauss) exhibits a somnambulist called Cesare (Veidt) who, at night, dressed in a black bodystocking and with ghostly white face, slithers through the town murdering on the phoney doctor's orders. A student, Francis (Feher) keeps an eye on Caligari after his friend has been found dead. Cesare is dispatched to kill Francis's fiancée, Joan (Dagover), but is struck by her beauty and abducts her instead, fleeing over the rooftops with her in his arms until he falls dead, exhausted. Caligari is then discovered to be the evil director of a local asylum who, confronted with the body of Cesare, goes mad. The whole story is told from Francis's point-of-view.

Such was the plot written by Mayer on the basis of an idea from the Czech poet Hans Janowitz. Decla's production supervisor, Rudolph Meinert, gave the script to the set designer Hermann Warm. In collaboration with Walter Reimann and Walter Roehrig, fellow members of the expressionist *Der Sturm* group in Berlin, with whom he had regularly worked, he proposed a completely unprecedented style for the sets, costumes and makeup. Meinert recognized the commercial potential of using an 'insane' style which was guaranteed to create a sensation and it was agreed to make the whole piece as insane as possible, in spite of the reservations expressed by Pommer and the other studio bosses. In order to signal the body of the film as 'insane', a prologue and epilogue were added, partly at the suggestion of Fritz Lang who had been approached to direct the movie but was unavailable at the time. A routine cameraman and director were assigned to the project: the director was supposed to take care of the actors while the cameraman simply photographed the light patterns already painted on the sets and backdrops. Unfortunately, the team was so carried away with aesthetic experimentation that they failed to reflect on the political implications of their agreement to put a frame around the central story to show that the student was an inmate in an asylum and that his paranoid fantasies were thus responsible for the film's insane style. The First World War had just ended and, while the general disillusion resulting from such carnage in the cause of international trade/competition had left its imprint on Mayer's script, the added frame reversed the political meaning of the movie. Instead of suggesting that 'the authorities' were insane criminals who ordered wholesale murder to be committed by blindly obedient soldiers, the film as it stands creates the impression that only strongly authoritarian institutions ruled by benign dictators can contain the insane fantasies of intellectuals. But these overtones became clear later in the light of the rise of Fascism, prompting Siegfried Kracauer to entitle his classic history of the German cinema *From Caligari to Hitler*. At the time of the film's release, its formal aspects had a far greater impact than its political implications.

In many ways a very theatrical movie, it nevertheless showed cinema's potential for creating a subjective and discursive world, a world drastically different from the melodramatic realism prevalent at the time. No longer was it the uncanny ability of film to make the weirdest happenings seem 'real' which provided the thrill, but the exact opposite: the cinema's potential for transcending the limitations of photographic realism. There had been such moments in previous films, but it was the overall impact of *Das Cabinet des Dr Caligari* which liberated both film-makers and audiences from the suffocating naturalist conventions that dominated the novels and plays of the late 19th century and their film adaptations. This liberating effect could be seen in the succeeding years, not so much in the awkward *Caligari* imitations attempted by the likes of Hanns Kobe (*Verlogene Moral*, 1921) or even by Wiene himself *Raskolnikow*, 1923), but in Paul Wegener's **Der Golem: Wie Er in die Welt Kam** (1920) and in Fritz Lang's boldly experimental approach to cinematic narration **Der Muede Tod** (1921). The American movie **The Cabinet of Dr Caligari** (1962), although scripted by Robert Bloch, is merely an inept thriller seeking to trade on the German classic's reputation.

The original silent release print was elaborately tinted in green, brown and cold blue.

d Robert Wiene *p* Erich Pommer *s* Carl Mayer, Hans Janowitz *c* Willy Hameister *lp* Werner Krauss, Conrad Veidt, Lil Dagover, Friedrich Feher, Hans von Twardowski, Rudolf Klein-Rogge, Rudolf Lettinger

Lilith und Ly *aka* **Lilith and Ly**

(FIAT FILMS; AUSTRIA) b/w

No copy of this film appears to have survived. As in **Hilde Warren und der Tod** (1917) and **Die Pest in Florenz** (1919), Lang puts Death on the screen, but here in a slightly different form, combining the legend of the golem with vampire themes in a setting that recalls the more classic representations of vampires: instead of casting no reflection in mirrors, Lang's vampire lives only as an image in a sort of TV screen invented by his central character, Frank Landow. Having discovered the secret of creating life, by means of a special ruby, he animates a statue of Lilith and falls in love with her. She is revealed to be a vampire and Landow is forced to watch her on his screen becoming stronger as his own life drains away. In addition, he sees his new love, Ly, also being taken over and fading away until he manages to free himself by smashing the images he had created in the first place: the statue and the screen. Casting the blood red ruby in a stream, Landow removes the menacing incarnation of female desire, Lilith, and achieves, or perhaps one should say 'contents himself with', domestic happiness by the side of Ly who has been drained of desire, at least symbolically.

Lang's script for **Totentanz** (1919) can be seen as a companion piece to this picture, presenting the other side of the asymmetric relationship between male and female desire.

d Drich Kober *s* Fritz Lang *c* Willy Hameister *lp* Elga Beck, Hans Marschall, Ernst Escherich, Franz Kammauf

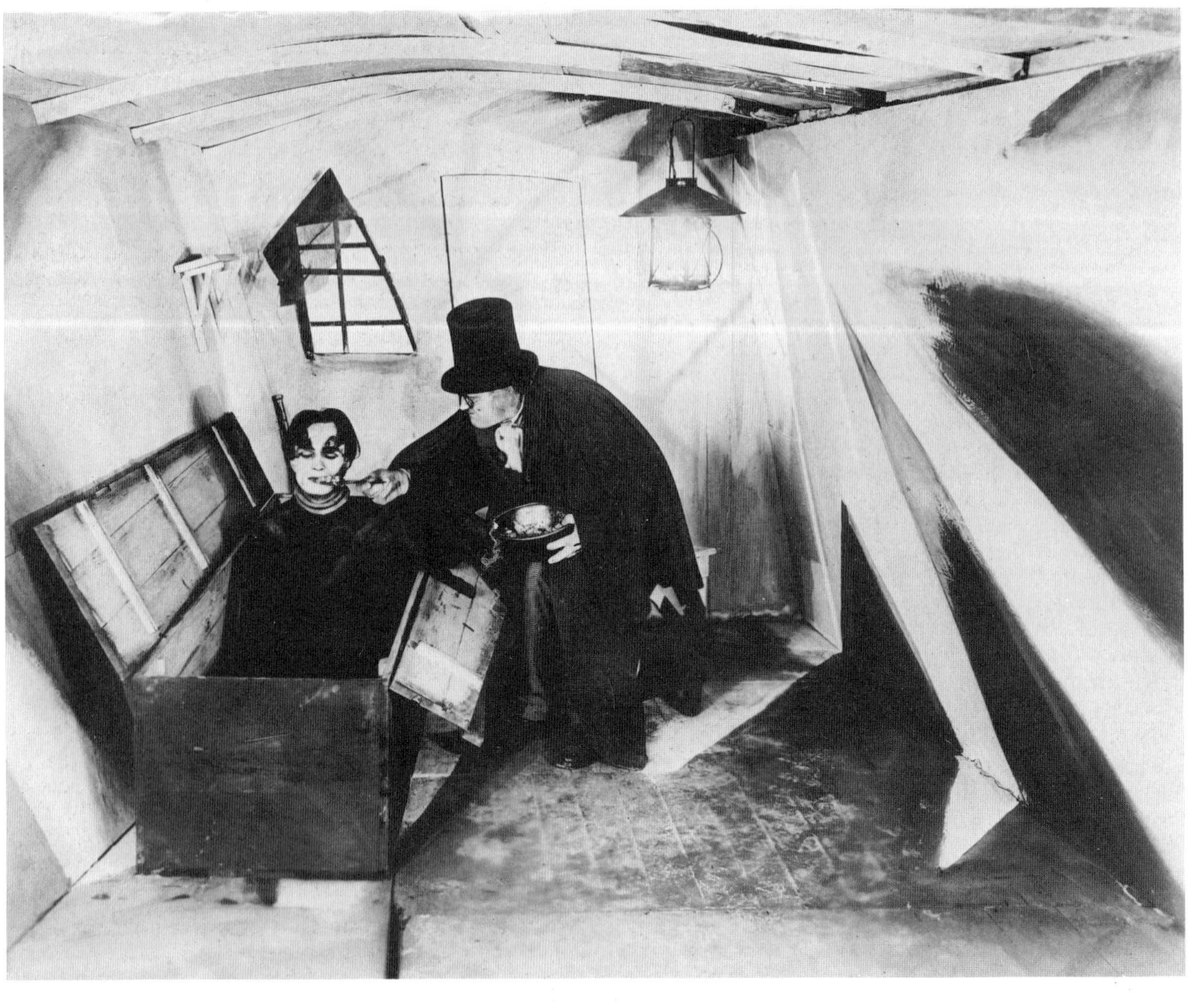

Master and slave, Werner Krauss (right) and Conrad Veidt, in Robert Weine's expressionist classic, Das Cabinet des Dr Caligari.

Sascha Gura (left) as the femme fatale *in Fritz Lang's* Totentanz, *one of his many tales of 'Hate, Murder and Revenge'.*

Die Pest in Florenz *aka* **The Plague in Florence**
(DECLA FILM; G) b/w 96min
After **Hilde Warren und der Tod** (1917), Lang again put Death on the screen with this story adapted from Poe's *The Masque of the Red Death*. The difference here is that Lang makes the figure which causes evil, corruption and debauchery a woman (Kierska), the first of the many *femmes fatales* that populate Lang's movies. Her sensual presence seduces the city's ruler Cesare (Mannstaedt) and his son (Wikman). When Cesare, in a jealous rage, orders Kierska to be tortured, his son is driven to patricide and takes over the city, turning its churches into sites of sexual frenzy. A Franciscan monk (Becker) tries to intervene, but he too falls under the woman's spell and kills his rival in order to possess her. Eventually Death (Brandt) comes to stalk the city and everyone, rich and poor, succumbs to the horrors of the plague.

In this picture Death and the woman are two different figures but in **Lilith und Ly** (1919), Lang combined them into the single figure of the vampiric woman who seduces and kills in the same gesture.

The art direction for this lavishly produced film (for which thousands of extras were employed) was by four different artists. Architect Franz Jaffe designed the set of Florence, Hermann Warm was responsible for the interiors and Walter Reimann and Walter Roehrig furnished the murals and backgrounds. With the exception of Jaffe, the same team wrote and designed the best-known work of the silent cinema, **Das Cabinet des Dr Caligari** (1919). Lang later incorporated elements of *Die Pest in Florenz* into his first fantastic masterpiece **Der Meude Tod** (1921), while Rippert, who had established himself with the successful serial *Homunculus* (1916), went on to direct another Lang script, **Totentanz** (1919).

d Otto Rippert *p* Erich Pommer *s* Fritz Lang *c* Willy Hameister, Emil Schuenemann *lp* Otto Mannstaedt, Anders Wikman, Theodor Becker, Marga Kierska, Julietta Brandt, Karl Bernhard, Franz Knaak, Erner Huebsch, Hans Walter

Totentanz *aka* **Dance of Death**
(HELIOS FILM; G) b/w 84min
Lang's third sex-and-death fantasy was filmed by Rippert who also directed his **Die Pest in Florenz** (1919). No copy appears to have survived but a contemporary source gives an idea of the story. A cripple (Krauss) uses a beautiful dancer (Gura) to lure people to their doom. As the plot synopsis says: 'her body attracts men as light attracts insects, though they know that they will suffer death as a consequence'. When she falls in love, Krauss promises to set her free if her lover manages to escape from the labyrinthine catacombs underneath his house. But the lover, who is also revealed to be a murderer, dies. In the end, Krauss is killed and Gura dances herself to death next to the coffin containing the corpse of her lover. While in **Lilith und Ly** (1919) the *femme fatale* figure threatened to destroy the hero, in this movie the heroine becomes the victim of warped and violent men: a misanthropic tyrant on crutches and a potent but homicidal lover. The art direction was by Hermann Warm, better known for his work on **Das Cabinet des Dr Caligari** (1919).

The film is not to be confused with the Urban Gad-Asta Nielsen drama, *Der Totentanz* (1912), about a woman who comes under the Svengali-like influence of a demonic composer.

d Otto Rippert *p* Erwin Rosner *s* Fritz Lang *c* Willy Hameister *lp* Sascha Gura, Werner Krauss, Joseph Roemer, Richard Kirsch

Unheimliche Geschichten *aka* **Tales of the Uncanny** *aka* **Five Sinister Stories** *aka* **Tales of Horror**
(RICHARD OSWALD FILM; G) b/w 112min
Having adapted E. T. A. Hoffmann's stories as interpreted by Offenbach in his *Hoffmanns Erzaehlungen* (1916), Oswald turned to a variety of authors for his second omnibus movie. He used a combination of Poe's *Black Cat* and *The System of Dr Tarr and Professor Feather* for one episode and Stevenson's *Suicide Club*, Anselma Heine's *Die Erscheinung*, the scenarist Liebmann's story *Die Hand*, and his own *Der Spuk* for the other four. He later remade the Poe stories as a comedy in his sound film **Unheimliche Geschichten** (1932). Oswald was capable of making an occasional interesting film but he became best known for so-called sex education movies and anodyne costume dramas. He also made an inferior version of **Alraune** (1930) and a seemingly endless adaptation of Conan Doyle's *The Hound of the Baskervilles* (**Der Hund von Baskerville,** 1914).

The definitive version of Poe's *The System of Dr Tarr and Professor Feather* was eventually provided by the Mexican director Moctezuma, **La Mansión de la Locura** (1972).

d/p/co-s Richard Oswald *co-s* Robert Liebmann *c* Carl Hoffmann *lp* Conrad Veidt, Anita Berber, Reinhold Schuenzel, Georg John, Hugo Doeblin, Paul Morgan

Wahnsinn *aka* **Madness**
(VEIDT FILM; G) b/w 70min
Shortly after his masterly performance as the somnambulist in **Das Cabinet des Dr Caligari** (1919), Veidt made his début as a director with this story about a banker who suffers a mental breakdown. A gypsy foretells that he will come across a trunk which will signify either happiness or death for him. In the end, he gets locked into the trunk and dies of suffocation. Veidt, who played the lead as well as directing, uses all manner of 'expressionist' lighting effects to convey his character's delusions. Contemporary critics pointed to similarities with Paul Leni's *Prinz Kuckuck* (1919) and expressed a wish to see the actor in a part that didn't require him to play a madman. His best performance as a man obsessed, however, came in 1926 with **Der Student von Prag**. Schuenzel, soon to become a director as well, here plays the part of the banker's thieving assistant, while the *femme fatale* is Hegesa. The story was adapted from a novella by Kurt Muenzer.

d/p Conrad Veidt *s* Margarete Lindau-Schulz, Hermann Fellner *c* Carl Hoffmann *lp* Conrad Veidt, Reinhold Schuenzel, Gussy Hole, Grit Hegesa

The 1920s

The Twenties

European Nightmares and American Daydreams

The twenties saw a marked contrast between European and American approaches to horror. For the most part, in America, the horror film was seen as merely offering film-makers the opportunity to raise goose bumps and gasps from audiences; in Europe, the genre's grander and darker possibilities were grasped. Thus for instance, in comparison to both earlier and later American versions of the Frankenstein story (in 1910, 1915 and 1931) which exploited the spectacular possibilities of the novel in a theatrical way, F. W. Murnau and Heinrich Galeen in their classic **Nosferatu** (1921) – which introduced the vampire to the cinema – interrogated Bram Stoker's novel to bring out its sexual current all the more clearly. In a similar fashion, Paul Wegener brought to life the legend of the golem (**Der Golem**, 1920), making use of lighting and design to produce a sense of claustrophobic atmosphere in advance of anything being attempted in America, and in **Körkarlen** (1920), Victor Sjöström – mining similar territory to D. W. Griffith – showed himself in advance of Griffith in his handling of a complex narrative. In place of the willingness of European directors to experiment and probe at the disturbing world of dreams, seen at its most exhilarating in a film like **Häxan** (1922) and at its worst in a piece of studied surrealism like Jean Epstein's **La Chute de la Maison Usher** (1928), in America, directors, for the most part, produced efficient (and self-censored) shock machines.

Griffith's **One Exciting Night** (1922) sparked of a trend for haunted-house spoofs that climaxed in **The Cat and the Canary** (1927) in which the real fears that horror deals in are distanced by laughter and a sense of artifice. Equally noticeable was the theatricality of American acting in the first half of the decade. Thus John Barrymore's performance in **Dr Jekyll and Mr Hyde** (1920) – in which he achieved the transformation scenes without the use of either makeup or camera trickery – though it was acclaimed at the time as the greatest acting the screen had ever seen, in retrospect palls beside performances by, for example, Conrad Veidt and Lon Chaney. Chaney's first films (**The Hunchback of Notre Dame**, 1923 and **The Phantom of the Opera**, 1925) were marred by their double-faced attitude to the monstrosity of the characters he played, but from the time of **The Unholy Three** (1925) and his association with Tod Browning, his films achieved a disturbing masochism and perverse sexuality that was all the more chilling because of the naturalistic way Chaney played the parts. Oddly enough, however, it was two European émigrés, Benjamin Christensen (with the magnificent **Seven Footprints to Satan**, 1929) and Paul Leni (with *The Cat and the Canary* and **The Man Who Laughs**, 1928) who showed themselves to be the masters of the slight horrors that the American cinema specialized in. Their going to Hollywood anticipated the stream of émigrés of the thirties. But, by then, following the advent of sound, Hollywood notions of film-making and American films were dominant the world over and it was American attitudes to horror that the rest of the world imitated.

1920

Dr Jekyll and Mr Hyde

(FAMOUS PLAYERS-LASKY) b/w 63min

Highly praised at the time for Barrymore's performance, and undoubtedly the best of the seven American silent versions of Stevenson's story, this is now very dated. Barrymore's much vaunted first transformation on screen without makeup – really just one shot in which, after bending over doubled in agony, he raises a face twisted in an evil grimace, supported by a dissolve which shows his hand turning into a claw – is impressive ham, but ham nonetheless. Even as Jekyll he is too much given to theatrical posing, and despite excellent camerawork from Struss, the film really comes alive only in isolated moments. One such moment comes when Jekyll, waking from nightmarish sleep, realizes that the transformation is now taking place even without the potion. A monstrous spider scuttles across the floor, climbs up on the bed, and settles smotheringly on top of him. This naïve yet extraordinarily effective piece of symbolism is somehow made all the more powerful by the fact that the spider has distinctly human features. In fact it has the face of Hyde, though this is not usually apparent because of poor quality prints of the film.

Thematically, however, the film is a disappointment partly because it adheres to the Victorian attitudes of the Richard Mansfield stage adaptation of 1897 on which it is based, rendering them even more innocuous by turning Jekyll's prospective father-in-law (Hurst) into a version of Lord Henry from Oscar Wilde's *The Picture of Dorian Gray*. It is Hurst's cynical *carpe diem* philosophy which leads the idealistic Jekyll to experiment in the hope of separating the good and the evil in human nature; and it is also Hurst, trying to bring the 'prig' Jekyll down off his high horse, who deliberately introduces him to temptation (Naldi). Thus cast as a double-dyed villain (who gets his rightful comeuppance at Hyde's hands), Hurst simply obscures the issue of moral responsibility for Jekyll's tragedy.

d John S. Robertson *p* Adolph Zukor *s* Clara S. Beranger *c* Karl Struss, Roy Overbaugh *lp* John Barrymore, Martha Mansfield, Brandon Hurst, Charles Lane, J. Malcolm Dunn, Nita Naldi

Previous pages: Häxan *(1922), Benjamin Christensen's surrealist mélange of fact and fiction.*

Der Januskopf, *yet another (unauthorised) version of Stevenson's* Dr Jekyll and Mr Hyde.

Director Paul Wegener as Der Golem *in the classic version of the legend.*

Dr Jekyll and Mr Hyde

(LOUIS B. MAYER PRODUCTIONS) b/w 40min

Together with the Robertson-Barrymore version and the short comedy starring Hank Mann, Mayer's was the third adaptation of the Stevenson novel that year. To avoid copyright problems, Mayer updated the setting, locating it in contemporary New York and changing the plot structure quite dramatically. In this film, Jekyll dreams the tribulations that might ensue from his experiments and, having woken up, he abandons his attempts to develop a potion that might separate the good from the evil in an individual's personality. Apparently, the film was so cheaply and quickly made that the director withdrew his name from the credits. Lewis' acting of the Hyde character bears a marked similarity to the roles he played in a number of serials. He was the villain in *The Iron Claw* (1916) and in *The Hidden Hand* (1917), as well as incarnating the Clutching Hand in Pearl White's *The Exploits of Elaine* (1914). Mayer, who had made his first fortune distributing Griffith's *Birth of a Nation* (1915) on the East coast, went to Hollywood in 1917 and set up as a producer, with his own company, in 1920. With the foundation of MGM in 1924, he became one of the most powerful studio bosses in film history.

p Louis B. Mayer *lp* Sheldon Lewis, Alexander Shannon, Dora Mills Adams, Gladys Field, Harold Forshay, Leslie Austin

Der Golem: Wie Er in die Welt Kam *aka* The Golem: How He Came into the World

(PAGU; G) b/w 85min

This is the classic film version of the legend, achieved by a brilliantly productive collaboration between Germany's foremost cinematographer, Freund, an inspired special effects man, Boese, the celebrated architect Hanns Poelzig and director Wegener's theatrical flair. Dissatisfied with the compromises he had to make on his previous attempt to film the story (**Der Golem**, 1914) Wegener decided to recount the legend exactly as he had heard it told in Prague in 1913 when he was on location there shooting the first version of *Der Student von Prag* (1913), before Gustav Meyrink's famous novel about the golem had been published.

Rabbi Loew (Steinrueck) creates the clay giant in order to save the Jews from Rudolf II's tyranny, but his libidinous assistant, Famulus (Deutsch) gains control of it and orders it to kidnap the lovely Miriam (Salmonova). Eventually, the creature rebels against the menial and criminal tasks it is required to perform and goes on the rampage. In the end, a little girl offers the hulk an apple and when he bends over to accept it, the child snatches the sacred, life-giving star of David from his chest, turning him into a lifeless lump of clay again.

The picture marked a decisive step forward in German, as well as world, cinema, blending all the resources of acting, set design, photography and direction into a wonderfully orchestrated piece of film which did not rely on ostentatious expense to achieve its effects. Poelzig's set of old Prague creates a sense of claustrophobia and instability with its oblique and jagged lines, while Freund's virtuoso lighting weaves its own magic spells with dancing lights, deep shadows and ghostly superimpositions. The style was later refined in a number of German fantasy films (such as **Nosferatu – Eine Symphonie des Grauens**, 1921 and **Schatten**, 1923) and subsequent golem movies (for example, **Golem**, 1936; *Cisaruv Pekar*, 1951; **It**, 1967) tried to recapture the uncanny atmosphere of Wegener's version, unsuccessfully. An Austrian company revived the creature in broad rural comedy, *Der Dorfsgolem* (1921), using the hulk as a cheap source of labour.

co-d/co-s Paul Wegener *co-d/se* Carl Boese *co-s* Henrik (Heinrich) Galeen *c* Karl Freund *lp* Paul Wegener, Albert Steinrueck, Ernst Deutsch, Lyda Salmonova, Otto Gebuehr, Hanns Sturm, Loni Nest, Greta Schroder, Max Kronert

Der Hund von Baskerville *aka* The Hound of the Baskervilles

(GREENBAUM FILM; G) b/w 2 parts (73,84min)

Released as parts 5 and 6 of the series initiated in 1914 at Vitascope, this is in fact the sixth Baskerville film but Greenbaum apparently refused to acknowledge the existence of PAGU's part 3 made in 1915. He insisted that when he left Vitascope-PAGU in 1915 to form his own company, he had every right to take 'his' successful production personnel and ideas with him. Needless to say, PAGU disagreed and arranged for Greenbaum's parts 3 and 4 to be banned throughout the war period. However, in the confusion that followed the defeat of Germany, Greenbaum again took the opportunity to continue a series he regarded as his property. By now, the story was no longer related to Conan Doyle's novel except through the names of the characters. Episode 5, *Dr Macdonald's Sanatorium*, was written by Liebmann, a prolific author of fantasy stories, and based on a tale provided by Irene Daland. The only known member of the cast is Kaiser-Titz who played Holmes. The German censor passed the episode for public release in June 1921, although part 6, *Das Haus Ohne Fenster* was passed much earlier in September 1920, thereby further confusing to the complicated production history of this series.

d Willy Zehn *p* Julius Greenbaum *s* Robert Liebmann *lp* Willy Kayser-Titz, Lu Juergens, Erwin Fichtner, Ludwig Rex

Der Januskopf *aka* Schrecken *aka* Love's Mockery *aka* The Janus Head *aka* Janus Faced *aka* The Head of Janus

(DECLA BIOSCOP/LIPOW FILM; G) b/w 107min

As was the case with Murnau's **Nosferatu** (1921), this adaptation of Stevenson's *Dr Jekyll and Mr Hyde* was made without clearing the rights with Stevenson's estate. Janowitz, the Czech poet responsible for the original *Caligari* story, left the names of Stevenson's original characters in the script, but these were changed in order to camouflage the story's source. The trick apparently worked since, although the credits drew their attention to the use of 'an English original', none of the contemporary German critics recognized Stevenson's work. In part, this was because the theme of the double was already familiar at the time in Germany. Characters split into good and evil polarities, the bad side actually doing what the good side secretly wished to do but didn't allow himself to indulge in, had been used in many films derived from stories by such writers as Chamisso, Poe, Wilde, Ewers, Hoffmann and Dostoevsky. In addition, the early popular versions of psychoanalysis tended to reinforce these myths and had informed films since before the First World War (*Der Andere*, 1913, for example). So, for a German audience, in spite of the previous film version of the Stevenson story (**Ein Seltsamer Fall**, 1914), this would have been perceived as just one more variation on a very familiar theme.

The story tells of a rich Dr Warren who periodically turns himself into the evil Mr O'Connor, both parts played by the superb Veidt. The film appears to have been lost which is particularly sad in view of the appearance of the then little-known Hungarian, Lugosi, in the role of Dr Warren's butler.

d Friedrich Wilhelm Murnau *s* Hans Janowitz *c* Karl Freund, Carl Hoffmann *lp* Conrad Veidt, Margarete Schlegel, Willy Kayser-Heyl, Margarete Kupfer, Gustav Botz, Bela Lugosi, Jaro Fuerth, Manus Stifter, Marga Reuter

Körkarlen *aka* **The Phantom Carriage** *aka* **The Phantom Chariot** *aka* **Thy Soul Shall Bear Witness** *aka* **The Stroke of Midnight** *aka* **Clay**
(SVENSK BIO; SW) b/w 110(80)min
Although in many respects this film resembles a D. W. Griffith-type melodrama warning of the evils of the demon drink, Sjöström transcends the limitations of his format both through the complex narrative structure, which embeds flashbacks within flashbacks, and by putting the emphasis on the orchestration of the images themselves, demonstrating that cinema is as much a matter of visual style as of storytelling technique. In this way, Sjöström and fellow Scandinavian director Stiller pointed the way for cinema's liberation from the literary, a lesson quickly learned in France and Germany. Sjöström's leitmotiv, a ghostly carriage driven by Death rolling through foggy nights and along the seashore, is so powerful that it goes far beyond the symbolic meaning it is supposed to convey to become a celebration of cinema itself. These images infuse the whole movie with a macabre poetry that far outweighs the banality of the story, which was adapted from Selma Lagerlöf's novel.

The film tells of a drunk (Sjöström) who scoffs at the legend that anybody who dies on the stroke of midnight on New Year's Eve will be condemned to drive the coach of death for the next year. In the end, realizing the misery his drinking has caused his family, he repents. But the image of the chariot haunts the memory long after we have dismissed the 'human drama' as sentimental nonsense.

Körkarlen was released on 1 January 1921 and re-edited to make the complex flashback structure a little easier to understand for American audiences not used to such intricate narrative construction. Although not its director's best work, the film proved a success and was remade later in France by Julien Duvivier (*La Charette Fantôme*, 1939) and again in Sweden by Arne Mattson as *Körkarlen* (1958)

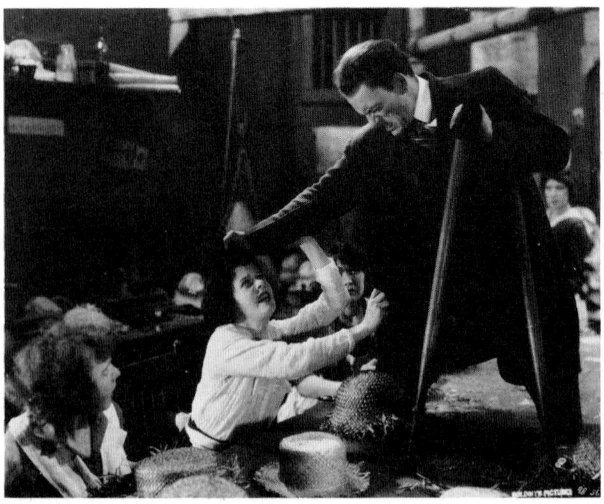

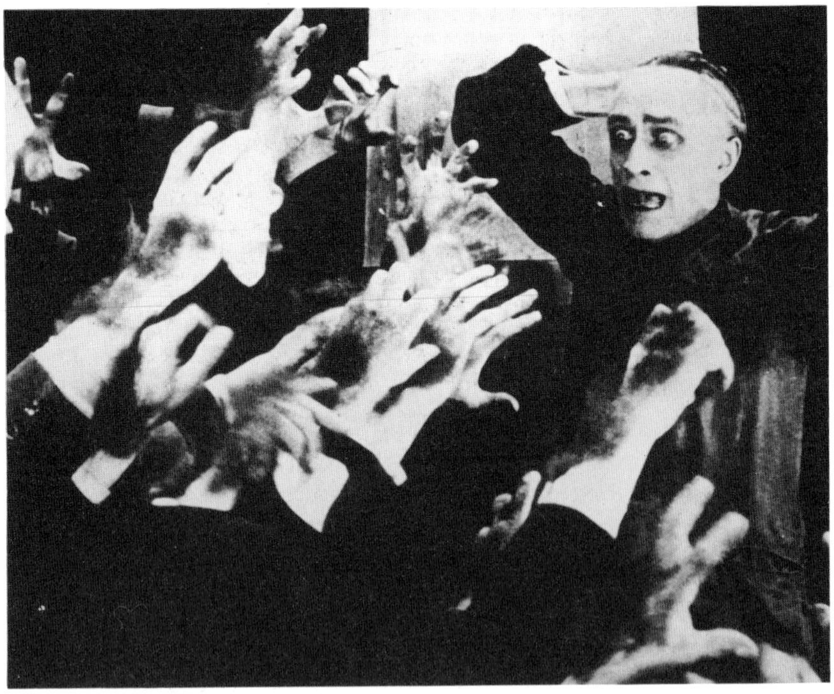

Conrad Veidt as Dr Warren/Mr O'Connor in Der Januskopf *an 'unofficial' version of Robert Louis Stevenson's classic tale.*

d/s Victor Sjöström *p* Charles Magnusson *c* Julius Jaenzon *lp* Victor Sjöström, Hilda Borgstrom, Astrid Holm, Tore Svennberg, Concordia Selander, Lisa Lundholm, Olaf Aas, Nils Arehn, Tor Weijden

Il Mostro di Frankenstein *aka* **Frankenstein's Monster** *aka* **The Monster of Frankenstein**
(ALBERTINI FILM; IT) b/w
Although no print of this movie appears to have survived, it is worth mentioning if only because it was the last Italian horror movie for nearly 50 years, until Riccardo Freda and Mario Bava made **I Vampiri** (1956). This was partly due, no doubt, to the strict censorship which removed 'sensational' shots from fantasy pictures. In painter Domenico Gaido's *La Maschera dello Scheletro* (1919), for example, all scenes with the gruesome masked skeleton were cut out leaving contemporary critics wondering about the title as well as the terrifying image on the poster. Producer Albertini took the part of the Baron while Guarracino played the creature. At the time, the athletic Albertini was the major box-office rival of wrestler Bartolomeo Pagano who had the role of Maciste in Italian fantasy movies.

d Eugenio Testa *p* Luciano Albertini *s* Giovanni Drivetti *c* Alvaro de Simone *lp* Luciano Albertini, Umberto Guarracino

Nachtgestalten *aka* **Eleagable Kuperus**
(RICHARD OSWALD FILM; G) b/w 106min
Karl Hans Strobl was Austria's foremost author of *schauerromane* (horror stories in the tradition of Edgar Allan Poe and Hanns Heinz Ewers). His ghost story *Eleagable Kuperus* was published in 1910 and Oswald's adaptation, according to contemporary sources, contained excellent performances by Wegener and Veidt in a generally distinguished cast. A notable appearance which also gives a clue about the plot, was that of Charell, who later achieved fame as the director of the extremely successful comedy *Der Kongress Tantz* (1931), in the role of a gorilla.

d/p/s Richard Oswald *c* Carl Hoffmann *lp* Paul Wegener, Conrad Veidt, Erna Morena, Anita Berber, Reinhold Schuenzel, Erik Charell, Theodor Loos

The Penalty (GOLDWYN) b/w 70min
Along with *The Miracle Man* (1919), in which he was a fake cripple 'cursed' by a blind faith healer, this was the first indication of Chaney's curious, almost masochistic, pre-

Lon Chaney as the double amputee turned master criminal in The Penalty.

Right: *Lil Dagover and Bernhard Goetzke as the stranger who abducts her in Fritz Lang's essay in fatalism,* Der Muede Tod.

occupation with deformity, possibly a consequence of his upbringing by deaf-mute parents, and which lay behind his reputation as the man of a thousand faces. Here he plays Blizzard, a ruthless criminal warped since childhood by an operation in which both his legs, crushed in an accident, were amputated below the knee by a careless surgeon who might have saved them. Sworn to vengeance against society in general and the surgeon in particular, he grows up to be king of the San Francisco underworld with a sinister gang of thugs, molls and dope fiends at his command. Rattling along like a serial with movable fireplaces and trapdoors that open on to secret lairs as he lures his enemies into his clutches, the film works up to a melodramatically moral climax in which, suffering from a blood clot on the brain and operated on successfully, Chaney realizes that there is good in the world. Literally playing the part on his knees, Chaney scurries about and even climbs rope ladders with chillingly arachnoid speed. The agony that twists Chaney's face into a remarkable semblance of Blizzard's warped mentality lends the film a distinctly macabre tone.

d Wallace Worsley *p* Sam Goldwyn *s* Charles Kenyon *lp* Lon Chaney, Claire Adams, Kenneth Harlan, Charles Clary, Ethel Grey Terry

1921

Der Muede Tod *aka* **Between Two Worlds** *aka* **The Weary Death** *aka* **The Three Lights** *aka* **The Light Within**

(DECLA BIOSCOP; G) b/w 110min

Surrealist film-maker Luis Buñuel has said that it was Lang's *Der Muede Tod* which first made him realize the potential of cinema. Similarly, Hitchcock is said to have been so impressed by the film that it finally made him decide to become a film-maker as well. Even the American megastar Douglas Fairbanks pillaged the film, no doubt wanting the best that money could buy, for his *Thief of Baghdad* (1924).

Subtitled 'A German Folksong', Lang's picture was badly received on its release and criticized for not being sufficiently 'German'. But, abroad, it soon acquired a reputation to equal that of **Das Cabinet des Dr Caligari** (1919). Set in the early 19th century, the film begins in an inn in a small village where, one windy night, a young couple (Dagover and Janssen) stop to rest. A few tables away sits the stony stranger (Goetzke) who bought land by the cemetery and built a huge wall without windows or doors around it. When the stranger abducts the young bridegroom, Dagover desperately looks for a way through the wall until, in a dream, a gothic archway opens up revealing a steep, narrow stairway chiseled in light, leading up to a forest of candles, each representing a life. Death recounts three tragic tales to her, set in Baghdad, renaissance Venice and fairytale China. Every time, Dagover sees herself and her lover acting out the story, as in a nightmare, unable to alter its course and driving her lover deeper and deeper into Death's realm. Still not resigned, she seeks someone to take her lover's place voluntarily, while Death, weary with wisdom, patiently awaits the inevitable outcome. In the end, she realizes that the only way of joining her lover is to commit suicide.

Although there are some brilliantly achieved effects in all three stories, it is the framing narrative – Death and his eerie realm and the village setting with its alchemist's apothecary where, as Lotte Eisner writes 'skeletons and stuffed animals jut out from the darkness like phosphorescent phantoms' – which stays in the mind. Although the script by von Harbou (Lang's wife) is weak and overly sentimental, the visuals are firmly under Lang's control. The art direction is by Robert Herlth, Hermann Warm and Walter Roehrig; Warm and Roehrig had worked with Lang before and were responsible for the design of *Das Cabinet des Dr Caligari*. *Der Muede Tod* was only briefly released in the US in 1923 under the title *Between Two Worlds*.

d/co-s Fritz Lang *p* Erich Pommer *co-s* Thea von Harbou *c* Fritz Arno Wagner, Erich Nitzschmann, Hermann Saalfrank *lp* Bernhard Goetzke, Lil Dagover, Walter Janssen, Rudolph Klein-Rogge, George John, Eduard von Winterstein, Max Adalbert, Wilhelm Diegelmann, Karl Platen, Hans Sternberg

Below: *Max Schreck as* Nosferatu.

Nosferatu – Eine Symphonie des Grauens *aka* **Nosferatu – A Symphony of Horror** *aka* **Nosferatu the Vampire** *aka* **Terror of Dracula** *aka* **Dracula** *aka* **Nosferatu – A Symphonie of Terror** *aka* **The Twelfth Hour** *aka* **Die Zwoelfte Stunde** *aka* **Eine Nacht des Grauens**

(PRANA FILM; G) b/w 95min

This unparalleled masterpiece, scripted by Hanns Heinz Ewers' disciple, Galeen, designed by a spiritualist, Albin Grau, photographed by a virtuoso cinematographer and directed by one of the three undisputed masters of the German cinema (with Lang and Lubitsch), offers a fairly straightforward adaptation of Bram Stoker's classic novel. However, Stoker's estate was displeased with the unauthorized use of the novel and sued the German producers. An English court ordered all copies of the film to be destroyed and the negative to be burnt. Fortunately, this order was unenforceable in Germany, but it prompted the producers to divest themselves of the hot property and they sold all their film material, including Murnau's out-takes, to Deutsche Film Produktion, who hired a Dr Roger to 'amend' Murnau's film and a longer, sonorized version entitled *Die Zwoelfte Stunde*, was released. This version was then further butchered for its American release in 1929. Since then, scholars in various countries have been trying to piece Murnau's masterpiece back together again. But what has survived amply justifies the film's reputation as one of the finest cinematic achievements to date.

Murnau's inspired editing, framing, lighting, distorting relations of space and time and his direction of the weirdly jerky figure of Count Orlok (allegedly played by Schreck), the way he imbues both location and studio shots with an eerily disturbing atmosphere, all combine to make the film the perfect illustration of Jean Cocteau's dictum that cinema is the registration of Death at work. Released in 1922, it ran into widespread incomprehension and even critical hostility, although it proved a success in Europe until it had to be withdrawn because of legal action, and was acclaimed by the surrealist poets and artists who laid the foundations of its reputation. What appealed to them most was the depiction of the relationship between Nina (Schroeder) and the vampire. Although the film's plot is close to Stoker's, with the significant exception of Nosferatu's sea journey, its emotional and intellectual emphases are drastically different. Jonathan (von Wangenheim) is the vampire's 'decent' mirror image as shown particularly clearly at the beginning when the two protagonists approach each other, each framed by an archway; van Helsing (Gottowt) is reduced to an ineffectual old man and the film's centre is Nina, who does not have to be rescued from the vampire (as in the novel and in Terence Fisher's **Dracula**, 1958) but abandons herself to him with a chilling ecstasy in order to destroy the repressed evil he represents. It is the fusion of Nina and Nosferatu, her change from a virginal, idealized bride to someone who 'knows' the dark side of sexuality, which constitutes the climax of the movie: the sun rises and she, now irrevocably 'soiled' and no longer available for romantic idealization, dies. This fantasy logic which dictates that she must die generates the horror embodied by the film, the tragic necessity that ideal love objects must be lost if we ('society' in the film) are to live. Failure to resolve this contradiction, as shown by the figure of Jonathan, means madness, being overwhelmed by the forces of darkness. The rich complexity of Murnau's film, including its intricate, stunning visual textures and narrative patternings, makes it a valid model of cinema rarely equalled today.

In 1979, Werner Herzog attempted to duplicate Murnau's achievement, but in spite of Klaus Kinski's performance and the shot-by-shot repetition of some of Murnau's sequences, Herzog's version fails to match the original's symphonic mastery of light and rhythm and testifies to a radical incomprehension of Murnau's insights into the fantasy at stake in his masterpiece.

d Friedrich Wilhelm Murnau *s* Henrik (Heinrich) Galeen *c* Fritz Arno Wagner *lp* Alexander Granach, Max Schreck, Gustav von Wangenheim, Greta Schroeder, John Gottowt, Ruth Landshoff, G. H. Schnell, Gustav Botz

1922

The Ghost Breaker

(FAMOUS PLAYERS-LASKY) b/w 57min

A half-hearted comedy chiller based on a 1909 play by Paul Dickey and Charles W. Goddard, this was previously filmed even more half-heartedly under the same title in 1914. It was later remade more wittily as **The Ghost Breakers** (1940), and again as **Scared Stiff** (1952). A tediously protracted prologue has Reid's personable young hero reluctantly involved in a Kentucky family feud, from which he escapes (accompanied by the inevitable black servant, played by Hiers) into an encounter with a beautiful heiress (Lee) who persuades him to help rid her father's castle in Spain of its ghosts. The usual scary hauntings turn out to have been engineered by the villainous Duke d'Alba (Carewe) a neighbour determined to find the supposed hidden treasure that will enable him to marry the heiress. Reid and Lee find a greater treasure in their love.

d Alfred Green *p* Jesse L. Lasky *s* Walter de Leon *c* William Marshall *lp* Wallace Reid, Lila Lee, Walter Hiers, Arthur Carewe, J. Farrell McDonald, Snitz Edwards

Häxan *aka* Witchcraft Through the Ages

(SVENSK FILMINDUSTRI; SW) b/w 94(76)min

A powerful piece of fiction combining documentary footage, animated sequences and dramatic fiction, *Häxan* has been described by surrealist film historian Ado Kyrou as an indictment of 'the criminal church, its inquisition and its instruments of torture'. He added, 'this document should be shown in every school in the world'. Based on the records of witchcraft trials of the 15th and 16th centuries, the film presents, in a highly colourful fashion, some of the traditional motifs associated with sorcery – confessions extracted under torture, a witches' sabbath and black mass – and contemporary scenes of possession. Many sequences are genuinely grotesque, with echoes of Bosch or Goya, but there is also a humorous dimension to the movie, with the director casting himself as the devil who seduces a woman while her husband is asleep next to them in bed and as the psychiatrist who is supposed to give a reasonable explanation for the strange happenings. Circulated in a number of different versions, including a sound copy narrated by William Burroughs (1966), the original print with its wonderfully tinted sequences has now been restored.

Danish director Christensen had started out as an opera singer before turning to acting and scriptwriting. Before making *Häxan*, he had been responsible for a number of thrillers in Denmark and, like many of the foremost

The devil manifest in Häxan.

Lon Chaney, the man of a thousand disguises, here bowed under a 72-pound rubber hump as The Hunchback of Notre Dame.

Scandinavian film-makers, had a career in Germany before moving to Hollywood in 1926 where he directed some remarkable fantasy comedies, including *The Haunted House* (1928) and **Seven Footprints to Satan** (1929).

d/s Benjamin Christensen *p* Ernest Mattison *c* Johan Ankerstjerne *lp* Maren Pedersen, Oscar Stribolt, Clara Pontoppidan, Benjamin Christensen, Tora Teje, Elith Pio, Karen Winther, Emmy Schoenfeld, Johs Andersen

One Exciting Night
(D. W. GRIFFITH INC) b/w 128min
Though this is not one of Griffith's better films, it is worthy of note because it sparked off the vogue for haunted-house spoofs which more or less smothered any real flowering of horror movies during the silent cinema's years of maturity in America. Borrowing much of his thinly disguised plot from *The Bat* (a current Broadway hit – filmed in 1926 – which he had considered buying but instead pastiched to save money), Griffith hedged his bets by hiring the leading man (Hull) from the stage version of *The Cat and the Canary* as his hero. A prologue set in Africa established Dempster as a somewhat mysterious orphan. Sixteen years later, sought in marriage by a wealthy older man (Wallace) whom she dislikes but who has a hold over her adoptive mother, she meets and falls in love with a young man (Hull) at a country house party. But bootleggers are trying to get away with their hidden loot, mysterious figures lurk, strange noises are heard and the chief bootlegger is killed. Hull is suspected, Dempster is menaced, and, to add to the alarms, a storm breaks out. In the end, revealed to be an heiress with Wallace unmasked as the killer, Dempster and Hull are free to marry.

Already labouring over the comedy element, Griffith is not helped by a truly horrendous blackface performance by Strong as the cowardly negro servant, while his excitements are perversely hampered by some genuine hurricane footage he had happened to shoot earlier and which stresses the artificiality of the studio storm and the shaky sets (in particular a pasteboard tree threatening to crush a helpless Dempster). Disastrously pedestrian, *One Exciting Night* has none of the touches of brilliant visual fantasy which Griffith brought to *The Sorrows of Satan* (1927), notably in the extraordinary, Busby Berkeley-ish 'War in Heaven' prologue (Lucifer being cast down by the angels). This was admittedly conceived and staged by the designer Norman Bel Geddes, but the climactic moment when Satan materializes to claim the hero – seen only as the shadow of gigantic bat-wings dwarfing the terrified victim and apparently sprouting from his shoulders – is pure Griffith.

d/p D. W. Griffith *s* Irene Sinclair (D. W. Griffith) *c* Hendrik Sartov, Irving B. Ruby *lp* Carol Dempster, Henry Hull, Morgan Wallace, Porter Strong, Margaret Dale

1923

Au Secours! (ABEL GANCE; FR) b/w 18min
When the great comedian Linder returned from his second visit to America, having completed *Seven Years Bad Luck* (1923) there, Gance was deep in preparation for his *Napoléon* (1927) and having trouble with his backers. Linder bet Gance he could not make a film with him in three days. Gance accepted, although he appears to have taken a week to shoot *Au Secours!*, a delightful Grand Guignol spoof in which Max (Linder) accepts a bet that he will not be able to stay among the ghosts at the Manoir de la Marjolaine until midnight without calling for help. Once Max, armed only with his wit, enters the gloomy portals, the beautifully staged and timed gags come thick and fast. Knocking the head off a dummy tiger, he is startled to see the body walk away and return carrying its head; a ghastly presence weightily forces the door against him, and in walks a diminutive duckling; a gigantic skeleton suddenly straddles him, one leg on either side. Abruptly the tone changes as he sees his sweetheart seemingly menaced by a brutish rapist (a brilliantly shot sequence with the nightmarish figure looming through the curtains behind gauze hangings). Panic-stricken, he calls for help, and the grinning monster reveals himself to be just another illusion staged to win the bet. An engaging satire, the film is also a reminder that Linder had started his career as a serious dramatic actor. Since Linder was under American contract at the time, the film could not be released and was not seen until it was shown on French television in 1958.

d/p/co-s Abel Gance *co-s* Max Linder *c* Georges Specht *lp* Max Linder, Gina Palerme, Jean Toulout

The Hunchback of Notre Dame
(U) b/w 133min
The problem with Victor Hugo's novel, more obvious in the watered-down version that made it to the screen, is that it is basically a historical romance. Anyone coming to the film with expectations of a horror movie is therefore in for long stretches of tedium, compounded by the fact that Quasimodo, for all his monstrous ugliness, is unquestionably a good guy and so lacks any real menace.

The problem is all too apparent in this version, for which Chaney and the film were given full star treatment by Universal – a year to prepare the enormous sets, a four-month shooting schedule and a cast of 3500 supporting players and extras. Equal care went into bowdlerizing the script, which focuses either on spectacle or on Quasimodo, the horribly deformed hunchback bellringer of the cathedral of Notre Dame in Paris, and his lovesick hopes for the beautiful gypsy Esmeralda (Miller), who once did him a kindness and whom he protects, but who loves another. The harmless grotesquerie of the King of the Beggars (Torrence) and his Court of Miracles is retained, but in all other respects the social, religious and sexual aberrations that are central to Hugo's novel are missing. Surprisingly ineptly mounted, despite its lavish budget, and wretchedly directed by Worsley with constant flurries of extras milling around, the film survives solely through Chaney's remarkable performance. In spite of his being dubbed the man of a thousand faces, what sticks in the memory is not his (fairly conventional) facial makeup but the way he uses his body. Bowed under the 72-pound weight of a rubber hump that made it difficult for him to stand up straight, Chaney adopts a weird apelike crouch, as though his legs were too rickety to support him, but which allows him to scuttle round in a manner frighteningly part-simian and part-arachnoid.

There were a number of earlier silent versions of Hugo's novel, none of them very horrific – including *The Darling of Paris* (1916), which even had Quasimodo winning Esmeralda – and two sound remakes: **The Hunchback of Notre Dame** (1939) and **Notre Dame de Paris** (1956).

d Wallace Worsley *p* Carl Laemmle *s* Edward T. Lowe *c* Robert Newhard, Tony Korman *lp* Lon Chaney, Ernest Torrence, Patsy Ruth Miller, Norman Kerry, Kate Lester, Brandon Hurst

The Last Moment
(J. PARKER READ JNR PRODUCTIONS) b/w 60min
A typical twenties comedy-chiller. Hercules Napoleon Cameron (Hull), a dreamer who finds his adventures in books, is scouring the waterfront for a friend's missing father when – along with his girlfriend Kenyon – he is shanghaied aboard a ship bound for the South Seas and commanded by a brutal captain (Wolheim) who maintains his reign of terror with the aid of a vicious apelike monster (Peterson) kept in a cage. During a storm the monster escapes, killing the captain and crew. Fearing their last moments have come, Hull is emboldened by Kenyon's despairing declaration of love to fend the monster off until they can jump overboard. It follows as they swim for shore, but Hull manages to clobber it with a particularly large abalone.

d/p J. Parker Read Jnr *s* J. Clarkson Miller *c* J. O. Taylor *lp* Henry Hull, Doris Kenyon, Louis Wolheim, Louis Calhern, Jerry Peterson

Schatten *aka* **Warning Shadows** *aka* **Die Nacht der Erkenntnis**
(PAN FILM; G) b/w 97(62)min
Although a relatively banal story concocted by a practising spiritualist, Albin Grau – who had collaborated on **Nosferatu** (1921) – Robison's film about a man's obsessive jealousy pioneered many of the images and techniques of the psychotic horror thriller. It uses the play of shadows, tricks of the light and mirrors to create a hallucinatory world determined by the central character's delusions and unconscious desires, and is breathlessly photographed by the great Wagner, cinematographer of *Nosferatu* and **Der Meude Tod** (both 1921). The backlit figure of a mysterious person roaming around a house at night, the suggestion of sadistic sexual scenarios, the closeups of grotesquely distorted faces, the vast rooms in which a bright pool of light only emphasizes the menacing darkness all around, all became part of the basic conventions of the genre as practised most expertly by Alfred Hitchcock (**Psycho**, 1960) and Mario Bava (*La Ragazza che Sapeva Troppo*, 1962, and, especially, **Sei Donne per l'Assassino**, 1964).

A sequence from Maurice Tourneur's stylish, if frothy, While Paris Sleeps.

Left: Ruth Weyher as the flirtatious damsel in distress in the superior Schatten.

Robison was an American *émigré* who got a degree in medicine in Munich before becoming an actor and, in 1914, a scenarist and director in Germany. He specialized in macabre fantasy stories such as *Die Nacht des Grauens* (1916), *Zwischen Abend und Morgen* (1923) and **Der Student von Prag** (1935). *Schatten*, originally shown without any intertitles, was re-released in various versions with titles added and scenes altered. The basic plot concerns an apparently flirtatious wife (Weyher), her jealous husband (Kortner), and indiscreet lover and some friends as well as a servant. A travelling magician (Granach) arranges, through hypnosis, for them to experience the scenarios they fear/desire by showing what would happen if they acted in accordance with their wishes. The entire action takes place within one evening, in one house.

d/co-s Arthur Robison *co-s* Rudolf Schneider *c* Fritz Arno Wagner *lp* Fritz Kortner, Ruth Weyher, Gustav vonWangenheim, Alexander Granach, Fritz Rasp, Ferdinand von Alten, Karl Platen, Lilli Herder, Eugen Rex, Max Guelstoff

While Paris Sleeps (PAR) b/w 54min
An interesting precursor to **Mystery of the Wax Museum** (1933), even if – as might be expected from a film based on a novel pseudonymously published by Pan (Leslie Beresford) in 1919 called *The Glory of Love* – it lays lyrical stress on the splendours and miseries of young love with a little judicious borrowing from *La Dame aux Camélias*. Chaney plays Henri Santodos, a sculptor in the Latin Quarter who is passionately in love with his model (Manning), but she meets and falls in love with a young American tourist (Gilbert). Pressed by the young man's father not to ruin the boy's life, Manning agrees to give him up provided they can share on evening of happiness together at the Mardi Gras festival. Insane with jealousy

Right: *Richard Talmadge (centre) as the young innocent in* On Time, *one of the many American attempts of the period to mix comedy and horror.*

however, Chaney, with the help of the mad curator of a wax museum, decides to get rid of his rival. Gilbert is kidnapped and tortured but rescued before he can be added to the waxworks' collection. The film's release was delayed for three years by Paramount, who thought it too macabre. When it did eventually appear, however, no one raised an eyebrow.

An exquisite visual stylist who worked in America from 1914 until 1926 (when he was fired from *The Mysterious Island*), Tourneur was probably at his best with the light fantasy of *The Blue Bird* (1918), or the picturesque adventure of *The Last of the Mohicans* (1920). He did dabble in the macabre, however, as his **Le Système du Docteur Goudron et du Professeur Plume** (1912) and *La Main du Diable* (1942) witness.

d/p Maurice Tourneur *c* René Guissart *lp* Lon Chaney, Mildred Manning, John Gilbert, J. Farrell MacDonald, Hardee Kirkland

1924

On Time (CARLOS) b/w 67min

Like **While London Sleeps** (1926), an example of the Broadway-influenced popularity of horror as a seasoning. Talmadge, stunt double for Douglas Fairbanks and Harold Lloyd, among others, plays a Fairbanksian role as a young man disheartened by his failure to make a fortune in six months as he had promised his sweetheart (Dove). When she gives him a Chinese idol for luck, he is promptly offered a job by a mysterious Chinaman which will bring him $10,000 if he follows instructions for one full day. He immediately finds himself whisked into a series of wild adventures, including a mad doctor's attempt to transplant a gorilla's brain into his head. These turn out to be a movie agent's test, and he is rewarded with $10,000, a Hollywood contract, and his sweetheart's hand. Flatly staged by Lehrman, who had directed Chaplin's first Sennett comedies, it has none of the flair and visual excitement which Benjamin Christensen brought to the rather similar **Seven Footprints to Satan** (1929). Fittingly, Talmadge later became a stunt director.

d Henry Lehrman *p* Richard Talmadge *s* Garrett Fort *c* William Marshall *lp* Richard Talmadge, Billie Dove, Charles Clary, Stuart Holmes, Tom Wilson, Fred Kirby

Conrad Veidt in the Ivan the Terrible episode of Paul Leni's Das Wachsfigurenkabinett, *an expressionist masterpiece.*

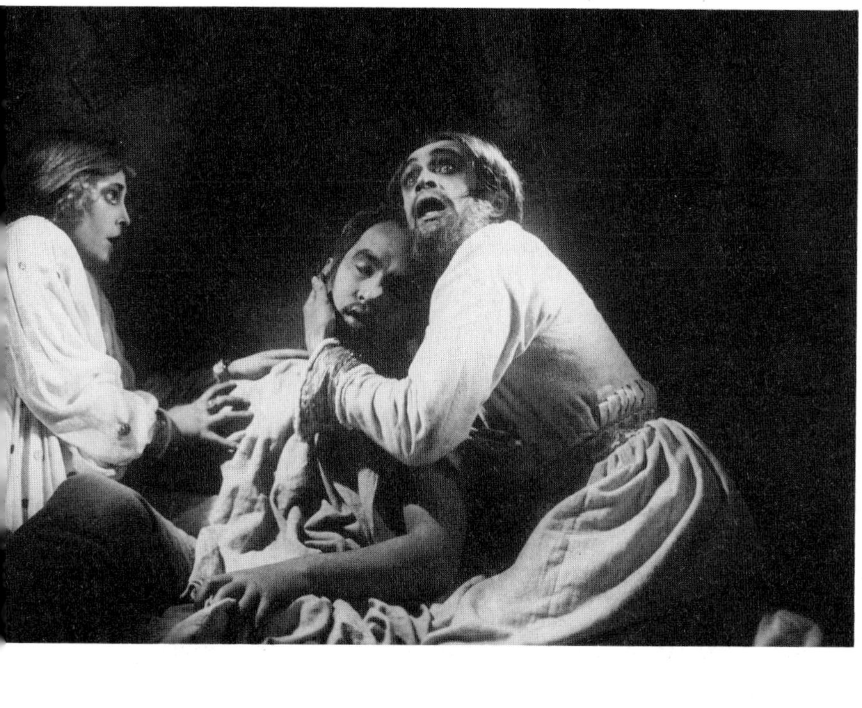

Orlacs Haende *aka* **The Hands of Orlac**
(PAN FILM; AUSTRIA) b/w 92min

Maurice Renard's novel *Les Mains d'Orlac*, published in 1920, is generally acknowledged to be his weakest work although its story of a piano player who loses his hands in an accident does lend itself to visualization. Orlac (Veidt) is given a hand transplant allowing him to play again, but it emerges that the new pair belonged to a murderer and Veidt finds that they have a will of their own. Wiene, best known as the director of **Das Cabinet des Dr Caligari** (1919), here adopts an inappropriately realistic style all too rarely interrupted by more stylized moments. The film's strength lies in Veidt's sensitive portrayal of a man alienated from his own hands, fearing that they may obey another will, possibly even acting out his own unconscious desires against his conscious efforts to contain and repress them. Kortner also shines as the diabolical blackmailer, Nero, who intensifies Veidt's distress. The misogynist aspects of the story, here revolving around the role of Veidt's maid (Cartellieri) are standard for a horror movie of this early period and betray some of the culturally determined fantasies that underpin such scenarios.

Renard's story was remade in Hollywood by the German *émigré* cinematographer turned director Karl Freund as **Mad Love** (1935). In 1960, E. T. Greville returned to the story with a Anglo-French co-production entitled **The Hands of Orlac,** starring Mel Ferrer and Christopher Lee.

d Robert Wiene *s* Ludwig Nerz *c* Hans Androschin, Guenther Krampf *lp* Conrad Veidt, Fritz Kortner, CarmenCartellieri, Alexandra Sorina, Fritz Strassny, Paul Askonas

Das Wachsfigurenkabinett *aka* **Waxworks** *aka* **Three Wax Men**
(NEPTUN FILM; G) b/w 93(84)min

Leni's remarkable omnibus movie connects its three episodes with a framing narrative in which a writer, played by the future Hollywood director Dieterle, furnishes the operator of a fairground waxworks (Gottowt) and his daughter (Belajeff) with stories for three of their wax statues. The first and somewhat botched episode features Jannings overacting in an oriental fairytale, in which he plays the part of Harun al-Rashid in sets and costumes that are all swirling lines. The Ivan the Terrible episode features Veidt and is an object lesson in 'expressionist' stylization, although by this time expressionism as an art movement was long dead. The sets required Veidt to distort his body into angular shapes as he passes through low doors or hides in a nightmarish torture chamber witnessing the death of his victims. Veidt's virtuoso performance no doubt inspired Eisenstein's direction of Tsherkassof in his *Ivan Groszny* (1944-6). The last episode is presented as a dream in which the narrator and his girlfriend are stalked by Jack the Ripper (Krauss). This brief story combines feverishly beautiful décors with an unleashing of the silent cinema's full stylistic potential, with disturbing superimpositions, hallucinatory framings and a restlessly mobile camera weaving through the shadows.

After this astonishing demonstration of versatility and stylistic ingenuity, Leni went to Hollywood. A few years later, Veidt followed and they worked together again in California on **The Man Who Laughs** (1928), although Leni's best-known American movie remains **The Cat and the Canary** (1927). Scenarist Galeen subsequently returned to directing. His best works as a director are **Der Student von Prag** (1926) and **Alraune** (1928).

d Paul Leni *s* Henrik (Heinrich) Galeen *c* Helmar Lerski *lp* Wilhelm (William) Dieterle, Emil Jannings, Conrad Veidt, Werner Krauss, Olga von Belajeff, John Gottowt, Georg John

1925

The Monster (MGM) b/w 71min

Based on a Broadway play by Crane Wilbur (later the screenwriter of **House of Wax**, 1953), whose tiresome spoof horrors dogged the last years of the silent movie in America, this is a film of considerable charm about a rustic youth (Arthur) whose correspondence course skills as a detective land him in an old dark sanatorium where the sinister Dr Ziska (Chaney) is collecting bodies in pursuance of his mad dream of discovering the secret of life by transferring a female soul to a male body. West was an extraordinarily talented film-maker whose career mysteriously collapsed in the early thirties even before his involvement in the Thelma Todd scandal. He evolved a striking native brand of expressionism in his three sound features, *Alibi* (1929), **The Bat Whispers** (1930) and *Corsair* (1931). Here the ambience is closer to Louis Feuillade, with a superbly minatory opening sequence: a dark, nocturnal forest in which a hooded figure with a scarred, skeletal face from its perch in a tree lowers a vast mirror camouflaged with foliage on to the roadway; a speeding car crashes as it swerves to avoid the mirror image rushing to meet it; alarming subterranean upheavals as the earth opens and another sinister figure emerges from a concealed pit to make away with the body. There are several other bravura passages in the Feuillade vein, notably one (brilliantly shot and lit by Mohr) in which the hero escapes from the sanatorium by tightrope-walking the telegraph wires while a villain shins up to cut them.

Unusually for this sort of film, West adds to the pleasure by taking the time to establish not only his small-town atmosphere but his characters (a wonderfully bizarre collection, with Chaney belying the suave effect of a Noël Coward dressing-gown and cigarette holder only by his alarmingly fixed manic grin). Equally to the point, West manages the usual flurry of haunted-house tricks with flair and discretion. Some, like the moment when the sofa on which the heroine is lying begins to descend through the floor and two live arms snake out of the murky depths to encircle her waist, lend the film a touch of Cocteau magic. Others, in particular the scene in which Chaney exultingly prepares to embark on his great experiment, suggest (in setting, laboratory paraphernalia, and acting style) that James Whale might have remembered *The Monster* while filming **Frankenstein** (1931).

d/p Roland West *s* Willard Mack, Albert G. Kenyon *c* Hal Mohr *lp* Lon Chaney, Gertrude Olmstead, Hallam Cooley, Charles A. Sellon, Walter James, Knute Erickson

Harry Earles as the malevolent midget in the disturbing The Unholy Three.

The Phantom of the Opera (U) col seq 94min

Chaney's second major vehicle, this is a distinct improvement on **The Hunchback of Notre Dame** (1923). A simplification of Gaston Leroux's superb novel (omitting, in particular, the Persian prologue which not only explains how Erick the Phantom acquired his hideously scarred face and twisted personality, but why a vaguely Middle Eastern detective is lurking in the film), it takes some time to get going. For a while, the new managers of the Paris Opera, warned to beware of the Phantom who reserves box no. 5 for his exclusive use and is sometimes seen there darkly cloaked and refusing to speak, find themselves embroiled in the standard haunted-house routine as creaky threats, warnings, apparitions and disturbances sow alarm backstage as the Phantom remorselessly pursues his goal of having pretty Christine (Philbin), his silver-voiced young protégée from the chorus, replace the reigning diva. But once resistance crumbles after a chandelier crashes down on the crowded auditorium during a performance and the Phantom, having hitherto been merely 'a voice like an angel' tutoring Christine from a secret hiding-place behind the walls of her dressing-room, summons the breathlessly expectant girl to his presence through a mirror on the wall, the film lifts itself on to another plane.

As though mirrors had the same magical properties as in Jean Cocteau's *Orphée* (1950), the strange, dreamlike journey

Left: *Lon Chaney and Mary Philbin, the object of his desire, in Rupert Julian's scrappy* The Phantom of the Opera.

through the catacombs begins as the Phantom escorts her on horseback and by gondola, white veil trailing, to his underworld realm. The sets here, dominated by the organ that lends an air of a funeral parlour, are macabrely apposite as the Phantom declares his love and hope of redemption through the horrified girl who finds the fairytale bower made ready for her adjoining a crypt housing the coffin in which the Phantom sleeps with two candles burning at his head. The unmasking of the Phantom is a superb double shock as Christine advances behind him while he sits at the organ and suddenly snatches away his mask, still romantically hoping – both are facing camera – the face of an angel will be revealed instead of the livid, skull-like ruin we see. The scene is one of Chaney's best, matched only by the marvellous masked ball where, having allowed Christine to go free after swearing never to see her lover again, the Phantom makes his majestic entry down the grand staircase of the Opera costumed as the Red Death, then steals away to perch demoniacally among the statuary on the roof, his cloak billowing wildly in the wind as he eavesdrops on the lovers secretly planning their escape.

If the rest of the film is as scrappy as the beginning – though charged with a vivid, serial-style excitement as the Phantom's revenge is foiled – it is no doubt due to persistent director troubles. Chaney himself had to direct some scenes and Julian was eventually replaced by Edward Sedgwick.

d Rupert Julian *p* Carl Laemmle *s* Raymond Schrock, Elliot J. Clawson *c* Virgil Miller *lp* Lon Chaney, Mary Philbin, Norman Kerry, Arthur Edmund Carewe, Snitz Edwards, Gibson Gowland

The Unholy Three (MGM) b/w 77min

Browning had been a carnival barker, clown and blackface minstrel before joining D. W. Griffith in 1913 as actor and assistant director, making his début as a director on two-reelers in 1915. He and Chaney made ten films together, and although they had met twice previously (*The Wicked Darling*, 1919 and *Outside the Law*, 1921), *The Unholy Three* is the first in the remarkable series of collaborations which was a true marriage of kindred spirits in which Chaney gave body to the macabre figments of Browning's carnival background.

Based on a novel by Tod Robbins, who also provided the source material for **Freaks** (1932), it is curiously muted compared to the gruesome fancies of that film. Nevertheless, its story of a weird family circle formed by three carnival refugees – Chaney's ventriloquist in drag as granny, McLaglen's strong man in moronic attendance as the son-in-law, and Earles' malevolent midget posing as baby – provides many a *frisson*. 'The unholy three' run a pet shop as cover for their ingenious criminal activities (the ventriloquist provides voices for parrots; the wealthy people who buy them subsequently call to complain; granny pays a visit to consult, bringing baby in a pram to case the joint). Slightly tongue-in-cheek – baby sports a huge cigar as he checks his bonnet and bootees and a murderous ape is casually thrown in for the finale – the film also displays considerable subtlety in depicting the tangle of loyalties and passions which tear the trio apart. Crucial here is the character of the midget (a marvellous performance by Earles), first seen throwing a tantrum during his carnival act, where his flurry of insults hurled at the mocking audience climaxes in his kicking a child's teeth in. Soon revealed as a mini-Hitler whom the strong man serves as an adoring slave, delightedly adding murder to the accomplishments of the unholy three, he merely sneers when an innocent (Moore) is found guilty of the murder. Chaney, in love with the pretty pickpocket (Busch) who serves as a fourth member of the gang finally does the decent thing. But the midget, stirred not only by the sense that his authority is being flouted but by a perverse sexual jealousy when the strong man also reveals an amorous interest in Busch, sets a self-destruct mechanism in motion by letting the ape loose. Not quite as controlled as **The Unknown** (1927), perhaps, *The Unholy Three* is a remarkable film just the same.

d/p Tod Browning *s* Waldemar Young *c* David Kesson *lp* Lon Chaney, Mae Busch, Harry Earles, Victor McLaglen, Matt Moore

Lionel Barrymore (right) in The Bells, *the best version of Henry Irving's famous story.*

1926

The Bells (CHADWICK) b/w 70min

This is by far the best version of Henry Irving's famous story about the troubled workings of conscience which had been filmed previously both in America (1913, 1914, 1918) and in Britain (1914, with Irving's son, H. B. Irving, in the lead). Barrymore plays the Alsatian innkeeper harried by debts who murders a wealthy traveller, only to be tormented into expiation of his crime years later when, now the universally respected burgomaster, his guilty conscience is awoken by chance circumstance.

Barrymore won all the praise at the time, but the performance that really catches the eye is Karloff's as a fairground mesmerist. Played with a quiet, inscrutable menace that is extremely effective by contrast with Barrymore's histrionics, the character appears to have been brought into the play with **Das Cabinet des Dr Caligari** (1919) in mind. Certainly Karloff's presence in top hat, cape and thick glasses is an inescapable reminder of Caligari as he blandly invites Barrymore (before he has even committed his crime) to become a subject in his demonstration of hypnotism, which can 'make criminals confess and the good tell of good deeds'. The ending, with Barrymore driven to paroxysms of terror in the belief that the sleigh bells he heard on the night of the murder have returned to haunt him, is considerably enhanced by Karloff's reappearance in Barrymore's nightmare in which he is hypnotized at this trial into revealing the whereabout of the body and putting the rope around his own neck. In this version, curiously, the guilty man dies with his conscience unassuaged by confession.

The play (adapted by Leopold Lewis from the French of Emile Erckmann and Alexandre Chatrian, *Le Juif Polonais*) was filmed again three times, very dully: in Britain as *The Bells* (1931), in Australia as *The Burgomaster* (1935), and in France as *Le Juif Polonais* (1937).

d/s James Young *p* I. E. Chadwick *c* William O'Connell *lp* Lionel Barrymore, Fred Warren, Boris Karloff, Gustav von Seyffertitz, Edward Phillips, Lola Todd

1926

Kyoren no Onna Shisho *aka* Passion of a Woman Teacher

(NIKKATSU SHINGEKIBU; JAP) b/w 85min

Mizoguchi, one of the undisputed masters of world cinema, had made more than 30 features in less than four years by the time he turned to this 19th-century story associated with the bard Encho Sanyutei. It tells of the unrequited love of a samisen player's daughter (Sakai) for a blind masseur. Her lover (Nakano) prefers one of her students (Okada). This makes her commit suicide and she becomes a vengeful ghost driving the insensitive lovers to a gruesome death.

Since the earliest surviving print we have of a Mizoguchi film is of *Taki no Shiraito* (1933), his 50th movie, little is known about the 49 he directed between 1922 and 1932, but his approach to ghosts in the lyrical classic *Ugetsu Monogatari* (1953) makes it unlikely that his treatment of the story was as horrific as Nakagawa's version, **Kaidan Kasanegafuchi** (1957).

d Kenji Mizoguchi *s* Kawaguchi Matsutaro *c* Tatsuyuki Yokota *lp* Yoneko Sakai, Eiji Nakano, Yoshiko Okada

The Magician (MGM) b/w 77min

Along with the Tod Browning-Lon Chaney collaborations, this is one of the few serious American horror movies in a time of spoofs. Based on a novel by Somerset Maugham inspired by the life and reputation of Aleister Crowley, its view of occult evil is distinctly oldfashioned by comparison with, say, Edgar G. Ulmer's **The Black Cat** (1934), yet absolutely in keeping with darkly Germanic tone Ingram brought to the film, not least by casting Wegener – director and star of **Der Golem: Wie Er in die Welt Kam** (1920) – as Oliver Haddo, the mad sorcerer obsessed by a dream of creating artificial life. Animation of his homunculus requires the heart-blood of a virgin, and at the inevitable fairground (echoing **Das Cabinet des Dr Caligari**, 1919) he happens on Terry, and duly abducts her on the eve of her wedding.

In one sense the film is merely a series of stagy tableaux as the heroine is strapped to the operating table, the magician prepares himself, the hero (Petrovitch) arrives for a fight to the death, an angry mob goes on the warpath, and both the laboratory and castle go up in the traditional holocaust. But Ingram was a supreme visual stylist, and the film is also a series of electrifying images. Not the least astonishing is the stunningly lit sequence where Wegener hypnotizes Terry and – with the fiery furnace roaring beneath the laboratory floor implying that she is already in hell – she finds herself in a hallucinatory bacchanal in which she is wooed, with a heady eroticism perhaps explained by the fact that the film was shot far from Hollywood at the Victorine Studios in Nice, by a statue of Pan come to life (and played virtually nude by Stowitts, an American dancer from the *Folies Bergère*). It seems almost certain that the laboratory sets and gestures must have been a formative influence on James Whale's conception of **Frankenstein** (1931).

The assistant designer here was Michael Powell.

d/p/s Rex Ingram *c* John Seitz *lp* Alice Terry, Paul Wegener, Ivan Petrovitch, Firmin Géier, Gladys Hamer, Stowitts

Alice Terry as the virginal maid wooed, literally, by Pan (Stowitts) in the delirious The Magician.

Der Student von Prag *aka* The Student of Prague *aka* The Man Who Cheated Life

(H. R. SOKAL FILM; G) b/w 140min

Together with **Alraune** (1928), this is Galeen's best work. Galeen, who began his career as a journalist and secretary to the popular novelist Ewers, is linked with nearly all the best fantasy films in Germany (including the superb **Nosferatu**, 1921), either as a director or as a scenarist.

The story of Balduin (Veidt), a poor student in the Prague of the 1820s who sells his mirror image to a mysterious stranger, Scapinelli (Krauss), was derived from Poe's *William Wilson* and had been transformed into a script by Ewers and Paul Wegener in 1913 for a film directed by Stellan Rye. But whereas that version was hampered by limited technical facilities, Galeen's film was able to benefit from an extraordinarily rich and inventive 13 intervening years of German cinema. Together with art director Hermann Warm (of **Das Cabinet des Dr Caligari** (1919) fame) and cinematographer Krampf, Galeen created a festival of light and shadow in windswept landscapes and stiflingly claustrophobic rooms, giving the whole film an atmosphere of hallucination. Krauss's grand but menacing gestures, which provoke marvellous shadows that dominate the key scenes of the picture, contrast well with Veidt's enthralling, interiorized style of acting as the man without a shadow and a reflection. He left Germany soon afterwards to pursue a career in Hollywood but later returned. Kober, the director of Lang's **Lilith und Ly** (1919) is here demoted to the post of assistant director and actor.

A third version of this story was made by American émigré Arthur Robison in 1935.

d/co-s Henrik Galeen *co-s* Hanns Heinz Ewers *c* Guenther Krampf, Erich Nitzschmann *lp* Conrad Veidt, Werner Krauss, Agnes Estherhazy, Fritz Alberti, Erick Kober, Ferdinand von Alten, Elizza La Porta, Sylvia Torf, Max Maximilian, Marian Alma

Left: *Werner Krauss lays temptation before Conrad Veidt in* Der Student von Prag.

Unknown Treasures (STERLING) b/w 63min
This stock thriller involves much creeping around an old dark house where a young man (Agnew) hopes to find stolen securities belonging to the banker uncle of the girl he loves (Hulette) but to whom he is too poor and too proud to propose. As an encouragement, the uncle obligingly has some securities hidden in the house. But instead of finding them, Agnew finds the strangled corpse of his cousin (Miljan), also in love and also searching. Agnew eventually solves the mystery, and the villainous caretaker who stole the bonds (von Seyffertitz) is killed by the ape he trained to kill on command but which rebels.
d Archie Mayo *s* Charles A. Logue *c* Harry Davis
lp Gladys Hulette, Robert Agnew, John Miljan, Gustav von Seyffertitz, Jed Prouty

While London Sleeps (WB) b/w 66(52)min
A curiosity illustrating the popularity at the time not so much of horror films as of comedies or adventures with a judicious dash of seasoning. Even Rin-Tin-Tin followed an unlikely suit. Here the wonder dog is owned by a notorious Limehouse criminal known as the London Letter who maltreats him while using him as a lookout. When Inspector Burke of Scotland Yard (Jennings) is on his trail, the London Letter commands his pet killer, a semi-human apelike monster (Kotsonaros) to kidnap Jennings' daughter (Costello). But, devoted to the girl who had rescued him from his master's abuse, Rinty attacks and kills the monster in a savage fight, while Burke and his men deal with the London Letter. The British release version was heavily cut and cleaned up to turn it into a standard Rin-Tin-Tin adventure.

d H. P. Bretherton *s* Walter Morosco *c* Frank Kesson
lp Helene Costello, Walter Merrill, John Patrick, Otto Matiesen, George Kotsonaros, DeWitt Jennings

1927

A surprisingly modern-looking representative of evil from the best version of the most famous of all haunted-house spoofs, Paul Leni's The Cat and the Canary.

The Cat and the Canary (U) b/w 86min
This is the most famous of all the haunted-house spoofs, with its collection of greedy relatives assembled for the reading of a will, mutual hatreds circulating around attempts to eliminate the pretty heiress by proving her a victim of hereditary insanity, and complications caused by the supposed escape of a homicidal maniac who imagines himself to be a cat tearing canaries to pieces.

The opening, as a hand lovingly brushes away the cobwebs to reveal the credits, is magnificent. In an old dark house with spiky battlements perched gothically on a hilltop, old Cyrus West cringes in an armchair, menaced by shadows that become huge medicine bottles with monstrous cats (his relatives) snarling, spitting and weaving between them. Continuing the brisk, brilliantly skilful series of dissolves and superimpositions, Leni then whisks through the details of will and codicils until a hairy, claw-like hand grasps the envelope and – 'for 20 years it was said his tormented ghost wandered' – the camera begins to track along a corridor hung with white, billowing dust-sheets, following the faint beam of a torch through deserted rooms until a gloved hand gropes for a secret panel, opens it, and furtively inserts a sealed envelope into the safe.

After this, given the need to assure the audience that nothing really unpleasant will happen and that it is safe to laugh (even the one murder takes place off-screen), there is little that Leni can do but mark time, continuing to build an atmosphere that is simultaneously exposed as false by the cringing comic cowardice of the characters. Drawing on his expressionist resources, Leni nevertheless works wonders for a while: characters lurching out of the darkness until their backs ominously blot out the entire screen; disembodied hands hovering timidly, curling round doorways, slowly reaching for the heroine's throat; an uncanny resurrection of Caligari as the mysterious, mincing stranger with pebble glasses and limp hands advances to announce 'I am the doctor'; and, most arresting of all, the extraordinary double exposure showing the mechanism of a clock that hasn't struck since old Cyrus died, laboriously gathering its forces to start up again as the lights dim and the assembled company await the stroke of midnight.

Based on a play by John Willard first performed in 1922, *The Cat and the Canary* was remade three times: twice under the same title (1939, 1978) and once as **The Cat Creeps** (1930).

d Paul Leni *p* Carl Laemmle *s* Robert F. Hill, Alfred A. Cohn *c* Gilbert Warrenton *lp* Laura LaPlante, Creighton Hale, Lucien Littlefield, Flora Finch, Arthur Edmund Carewe, Tully Marshall

The Gorilla (FIRST NATIONAL) b/w 79min
An adaptation of Ralph Spence's successful Broadway play, this is the standard old-dark-house spoof, involving a series of murders generally supposed to have been committed by a gorilla. Falling under suspicion when her father becomes the latest victim, Day, her sweetheart Glass (the old man's secretary, also under suspicion), and a friend (Pidgeon) receive a message warning them to leave the house before midnight. The sudden unannounced arrival of two bizarre individuals (Murray and Kelsey), who turn out to be detectives, does nothing to lessen the nocturnal alarms of strange noises and mysterious disappearances that culminate in the capture of a sailor who confesses to having impersonated the marauding gorilla. But Glass, finally revealing that he too is a detective, unmasks Pidgeon as the real gorilla-suited killer. Santell's often imaginative use of the settings is rather hampered by the crude slapstick antics of the two detectives (Murray was a Mack Sennett alumnus) which only occasionally pay dividends.

The film was remade twice, in 1930 and 1939, both times under the same title.

d/p Alfred Santell *s* Al Cohn, Henry McCarty *c* Arthur Edeson *lp* Charlie Murray, Fred Kelsey, Alice Day, Gaston Glass, Walter Pidgeon, Tully Marshall

London After Midnight *aka* **The Hypnotist**
(MGM) b/w 63min
Chaney's brief appearance here with debauchedly drooping eyelids, needle-sharp teeth, water-melon grin and wearing

Left: *A poster for* The Unknown, *yet another of Lon Chaney's essays in morbid self-mutilation.*

cloak and stovepipe hat constitute Hollywood's first real (though fake) vampire. Based on a story by Browning himself, the film's opening shot is of a murder. Five years later, still investigating what he believes to have been murder and not suicide, Detective-Inspector Burke of Scotland Yard (Chaney) sets in motion a cunning plot to expose the murderer by first suggesting that the killing was the work of vampires and demonstrating that the dead man's coffin is empty. Strange nocturnal apparitions (the inspector and female assistants posing as vampires) then enable him to narrow his suspects down to two: the dead man's best friend (Walthall) and his nephew (Nagel). An accomplished hypnotist, the inspector puts each suspect in turn into a trance on the scene of the crime. Re-creating the circumstances of the murder, he draws a blank with Nagel (who loves the heroine, Day), but exposes Walthall as the killer.

Browning himself remade the film as **Mark of the Vampire** (1935), although the secnario was rearranged and the Chaney role split into three.

d/p Tod Browning *s* Waldemar Young *c* Merrit B. Gerstad
lp Lon Chaney, Marceline Day, Henry B. Walthall, Percy Williams, Conrad Nagel, Polly Moran, Edna Tichenor

The Show (MGM) b/w 70min

Something of a forerunner to **Freaks** (1932), *The Show* is based on a novel by Charles Tenney Jackson (who also wrote *The Day of Souls*). Set in a Budapest carnival, with an opening sequence which offers a quick tour of 'The Palace of Illusions' – a sideshow presenting such freaks and marvels as the Human Spider, the Living Half-Lady and a pair of mermaids – and made just before **The Unknown** (1927), the film dramatizes a similarly tormented sexual triangle involving a conceitedly handsome roughneck (Gilbert), the girl who adores him (Adorée), and the malevolent Greek (Barrymore) who loves her. All three are involved in a sideshow illusion presenting the death of John the Baptist, and the effective climax has the fiendish Barrymore failing to substitute a papier-mâché axe for the real one during the act and cutting off Gilbert's head (a neat shock effect that turns out to have happened only in Barrymore's imagination). For further excitement, a rampaging poisonous lizard (actually a gila monster) is thrown into the action, and there is a sentimental subplot concerning Adorée's blind and dying father, designed with the intention of teaching Gilbert the true meaning of love and humility – and succeeding.

Lacking any real conviction, *The Show* unfortunately fails to match the psychological subtlety and stark tension that make *The Unknown* so distinguished.

d Tod Browning *s* Waldemar Young *c* John Arnold
lp John Gilbert, Renée Adorée, Lionel Barrymore, Edward Connelly, Gertrude Short, Andy MacLennan, Edna Tichenor

The Unknown (MGM) b/w 61min

Browning and Chaney followed **The Unholy Three** (1925) with two melodramas offering colourfully grotesque characterizations: *The Blackbird* (1926), in which Chaney played a tough Cockney crook doubling in disguise as the crippled Bishop of Limehouse, and *The Road to Mandalay* (1926), where he was Singapore Joe, a one-eyed, hideously pock-marked brothel-keeper who dies to defend his daughter's virtue. After this they made *The Unknown*, the peak of their collaboration and one of the most resplendently morbid films ever made.

Based on a story by Browning himself, *The Unknown* features Chaney as Alonzo the Armless Wonder, a circus artiste who uses his feet to perform a knife-throwing act. Actually not armless at all but a strangler wanted by the police and concealing the tell-tale evidence of a hand with two thumbs by his masquerade, he falls for a pretty equestrienne (Crawford) who is being courted by the strong man (Kerry). But Crawford suffers from a neurotic condition, brought about by all the lecherous pawing she has undergone, which means that she cannot bear to be touched by men. Mistaking her gratitude for love when he intervenes to rescue her from Kerry's eager attentions, Chaney is reminded by his hunchback assistant (George), a sort of mocking *alter ego*, that marriage will inevitably mean discovery of his arms and probably exposure and loss of his love (all the more so in that he has been obliged to kill the carnival owner – unaware that he was Crawford's father – who had discovered his identity). So, in a bizarre solution that smacks of self-emasculation, Chaney decides to have his arms

John Gilbert with 'spider woman' Edna Tichenor in The Show.

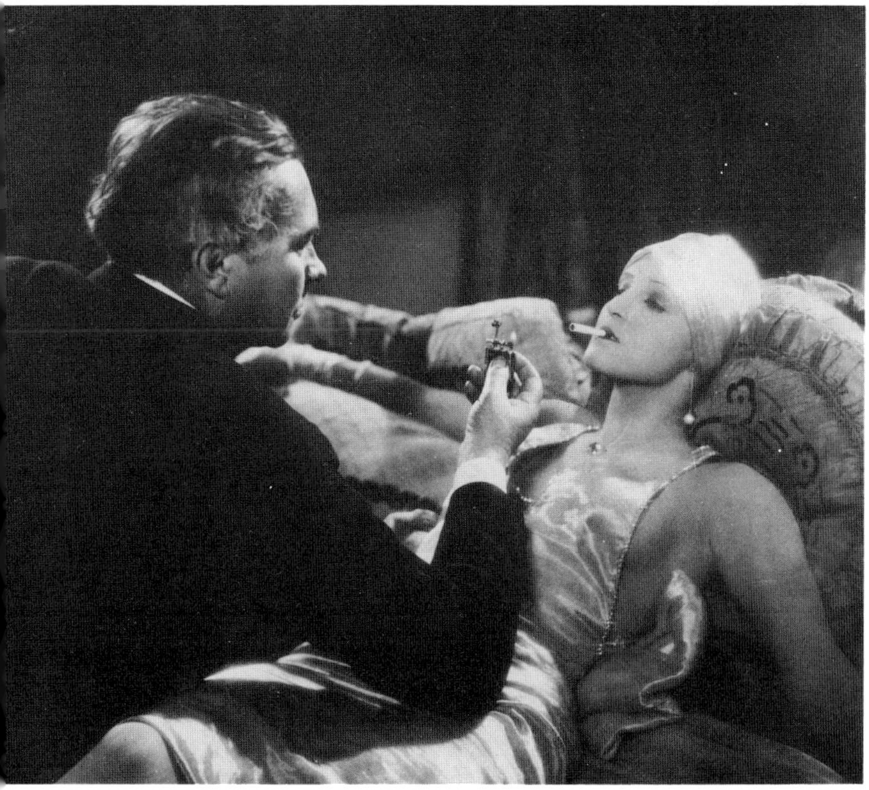

Brigitte Helm and her 'father' (Paul Wegener) in the best version of Hanns Heinz Ewers' novel Alraune.

amputated, blackmailing a reluctant doctor into performing the operation, only to discover after it is too late that his love has overcome her psychological block and fallen for Kerry.

The tormented tale is worthy of the Theatre of the Absurd, but staged with an intensity and emotional directness that lift it into areas of *amour fou* and wholly justify the Grand Guignol ending in which Chaney plans a splendidly theatrical punishment for the strong man by speeding up the treadmills on which two huge carthorses pit their strength against Kerry as part of his act. But half-changing his mind, Chaney slips and is trampled to death before achieving a vengeance designed, with poetic justice, to pull his rival's arms from his body.

One of the truly great silent movies, *The Unknown* is unusual (like several other Browning movies, notably **Dracula**, 1931 and **Freaks**, 1932) in the depth and darkness of its undertones of sexual phobia.

d Tod Browning *s* Waldemar Young *c* Merritt B. Gerstad *lp* Lon Chaney, Joan Crawford, Norman Kerry, Nick de Ruiz, John George, Frank Lanning

1928

Alraune *aka* Unholy Love

(AMA FILM; G) b/w 140min

Finished late in 1927, this is the best film version of Ewers' bestselling novel, filmed twice before (1918) and twice later (in 1930 and 1952). Wegener is Ten Brinken, the mad doctor who artificially inseminates a prostitute with a hanged man's semen. According to the legend, this emission causes the mandrake root to grow beneath the gallows, and throughout the film, there is a compelling bond between the result of the experiment, Alraune (Helm), and her root, her little piece of man vulnerable only to destruction by fire. She also lives in constant incestuous tension with her 'father' who is simultaneously fascinated, appalled and seduced by the eerily sensuous creature he has created. The film does not make clear whether the 'evil' Alraune merely fashions herself in the mirror of Ten Brinken's obsessions and expectations, or whether it is the otherness of Alraune's desires that fascinate and seduce the older man who wants to 'know' her in all senses of the word but finds that he cannot. The whole texture of the picture is suffused with a sense of enchantingly perverse sexuality and although it never quite matches the shadowy magnificence of Galeen and Ewers' previous collaboration (**Der Student von Prag**, 1926), *Alraune* remains one of the silent cinema's most sensuous works.

Helm repeated her role two years later under Richard Oswald's direction, but that film was ruined by the director's attempt to treat this sinisterly romantic *schauerromane* as if it were a realistic novel. Gert, soon to become a major figure as a result of G. W. Pabst's *Tagebuch einer Verlorenen* (1929) and *Der Dreigroschenoper* (1930), makes a brief appearance.

d/co-s Henrik Galeen *p* Helmut Schreiber *co-s* Hanns Heinz Ewers *c* Franz Planer *lp* Brigitte Helm, Paul Wegener, Ivan Petrovich, Georg John, Valeska Gert, John Loder, Hans Trautner, Louis Ralph, Mia Pankau

The Black Pearl (TREM-CARR) b/w 58min

Stock old-dark-house thrills, notable only (for the period) in that they are played straight. Based on a novel by Mrs Wilson Woodrow, the film's starting point is the old chestnut of a gem stolen from the eye of a sacred Indian idol that brings a curse upon the head of its possessor, old Silas Lathrop (Curran). Subjected to a hail of sinister death threats pinned to daggers, the old man decides to gather his family for a reading of his will. He is predictably killed, along with several members of the family, before the mystery is cleared up by a detective masquerading as the butler (Stockdale) with the aid of resourceful heroine Lee – something of a specialist in this sort of thing since she also appeared in **The Ghost Breaker** (1922), **The Gorilla** (1930) and **The Unholy Three** (1930).

d Scott Pembroke *s* Arthur Hoerl *c* Hap Depew *lp* Lila Lee, Ray Hallor, Carlton Stockdale, Thomas Curran, Adele Watson

La Chute de la Maison Usher *aka* The Fall of the House of Usher

(JEAN EPSTEIN FILMS) b/w 55min

This is one of the showpieces of the French avant-garde – but at the opposite end of the spectrum from a film like *Un Chien Andalou* (1929), which might almost be taken as a riposte from Luis Buñuel, who had been assistant director on Epstein's film, but spoken disparagingly of his conception and quit. This version is, in fact, a travesty of Poe and sidesteps the troubled brother-sister relationship by making Roderick and Madeline man and wife. So when the friend (Lamy) arrives to see Roderick Usher (Debucourt), he finds him – in a theme appropriated from 'The Oval Portrait' – feverishly painting a portrait of his ailing wife (Gance) aware that life is draining from her as his work progresses but driven on by the demands of family tradition. She duly dies, is buried, and returns from the grave – though not to destroy him but to save him from the conflagration started by lightning that is destroying the House of Usher: a piously catholicized theme that is supported by metaphorical intimations of regeneration (a shot of copulating toads interpolated during the funeral sequence, for example).

Though often dazzling visually with its bravura display of superimpositions, slow motion and sensuously tracking/panning camera movements (not to mention exteriors shot with exquisitely autumnal melancholy), the film is basically an empty exercise in style. Roger Corman's **House of Usher** (1960) captured the troubled undertones of Poe much more honestly.

d/p/s Jean Epstein *c* Georges Lucas, Jean Lucas *lp* Margaret Gance, Jean Debucourt, Charles Lamy, Abel Gance

The Leopard Lady (DE MILLE) b/w 75min

Featuring the murderous ape which seemed ubiquitous during the twenties, this close relative to **Murders in the Rue Morgue** (1932) was based, almost inevitably, on a play (by Edward Childs Carpenter). An animal trainer known as the Leopard

Lady, Logan joins a circus to investigate a series of thefts and murders on behalf of the police. She discovers the culprit to a Cossack (Hale) who has trained his ape to kill for him, but hesitates to turn him in because he once saved her life. Her doubts vanish when her fiancé (Armstrong) nearly becomes the ape's next victim.

d Rupert Julian *p* Bertram Millhauser *s* Beulah Marie Dix *c* John J. Mescall *lp* Jacqueline Logan, Alan Hale, Robert Armstrong, Hedwig Reicher, Dick Alexander

The Man Who Laughs (U) b/w 113min
Leni's best American film, this is a superb piece of UFA-influenced gothic. Like **The Hunchback of Notre Dame** (1923), also adapted from a Victor Hugo novel, it is a historical romance, shot through with an eloquently macabre chill. In the superb prologue, Veidt is the Scottish nobleman sentenced to death by King James II for political defection, who as an added refinement of cruelty while he is executed in the barbarous iron maiden of Nuremberg, is subjected to the torture of having his young son Gwynplaine's face carved into a hideous fixed grin. Escaping from the palace into the snowy night (a marvellous nightmare of pursuit in which his path is strewn with dark shadows, demonic stone faces and corpses dangling from gibbets), the boy befriends a blind girl and together they find shelter with a mountebank (Gravina). Reaching manhood, Gwynplaine (Veidt again) is loved by the blind girl (Philbin), who cannot see his hideous face which he hides from the audience too under the painted grin of a clown at Southwark fair. His happiness is shortlived, however, and he's recognized by the late King's monstrous jester (Hurst), whisked back to court, and restored to his rightful title and estates by the vicious Queen Anne merely so that he can serve in a cruel plot designed to humble her lascivious sister (Baclanova).

The second half of the film is heavy-handed, especially in its pursuit of a happy ending for Veidt and Philbin, but with its resplendent sets, expressive camera angles and exquisite low-key lighting, *The Man Who Laughs* is invariably a pleasure on the eye. At its best, Leni's direction is reminiscent of Stroheim and the film's highlights include the long, low-angled tracking shot that turns King James and his jester into demoniacally prancing grotesques as they hurry to witness the torture and punishment they have conceived; the Hogarthian images that introduce the scenes at Southwark fair; and the perverse eroticism of the scene in which the Queen's sister (a fine performance by Baclanova, the treacherous Cleopatra of **Freaks**, 1932), sardonically characterized by the black monkey which accompanies her everywhere, lures Veidt to her bedroom purely to torment him.

Conrad Veidt and Olga Baclanova in the erratic The Man Who Laughs.

d Paul Leni *p* Carl Laemmle *s* J. Grubb Alexander *c* Gilbert Warrenton *lp* Conrad Veidt, Mary Philbin, Olga Baclanova, Josephine Crowell, George Siegmann, Brandon Hurst, Cesare Gravina

The Terror (WB) b/w 85min
The second all-talking feature ever made (it followed Bryan Foy's *The Lights of New York*, 1928), even *The Terror*'s credit titles were spoken (by Nagel) instead of written. Based on the Edgar Wallace play which had been a huge hit in London the previous year, and which owed something of a debt to both **The Phantom of the Opera** (1925) and the 1922 John Willard play which furnished **The Cat and the Canary** (1927), it features a homicidal maniac escaped from an asylum who lurks in the catacombs below an old English country mansion now used as an inn, terrorizing the guests by his habit of playing the organ underground and wandering about at night in a cloak complete with hangman's hood. During one storm-bound night of murder and mysterious prowlings in which a medium (Fazenda) holds a seance and a bumbling fuddy-duddy (Horton) proves to be a man from Scotland Yard, the soundtrack had a thorough workout recording not only the howling wind, beating rain and wailing organ but the croak of a sinister toad and the endless screams McAvoy was induced to utter.

In one way, at least, the film was an object lesson in the problems that sound was to bring, since audiences were regaled with an 'English' atmosphere which involved Scotland Yard men snarling in Brooklyn accents, a heroine shrilling 'Daddy, can you hear the organ?', and the inescapable impeccably dressed butler opening the door to greet guests with the solemn enunciation, 'I am the butler'. To compensate for the need to have the characters huddle close to the microphone in tight groups for the dialogue scenes, del Ruth moved his camera energetically wherever possible, suspending it overhead for the seance round a table and hurling it on rollers up to McAvoy's face as she screamed. But the overall effect was still stiff, stagy and more than a little ludicrous.

d Roy del Ruth *s* Harvey Gates *c* Barney McGill *lp* May McAvoy, Louise Fazenda, Edward Everett Horton, Alec B. Francis, Conrad Nagel, Matthew Betz

May McAvoy about to let forth one of the endless screams that formed the subject of The Terror, *as befits a film whose lasting claim to fame is that it was the second all-talking feature film ever made.*

West of Zanzibar (MGM) b/w 68min
Not perhaps the most convincing of Browning's films, this is nevertheless given a frightening ferocity by Chaney's performance as the malevolent Dead Legs, a Limehouse

magician who loses the use of his legs when pushed off a balcony by an ivory trader (Barrymore) about to run off with his wife. Soon afterwards the wife dies, leaving a daughter whom Chaney believes to be Barrymore's bastard. Blindly obsessed by a thirst for revenge, he takes the child to Africa and secures his position as a trader by becoming the terror of the natives as a sort of voodoo witch-doctor (playing on their superstition through his magic and even having an assistant pose as a monster).

Despite the highly artificial evocation of Africa, Browning builds an atmospheric dark, cramped tension centred around the image of the paralysed Chaney dragging himself serpentlike across the floor. Contrivance creeps in when Barrymore turns up again to find the now grown-up daughter (Nolan) a prostitute in the brothel where she has been lodged. Chaney is finally persuaded that Nolan is indeed his daughter just as an even better revenge presents itself (if Barrymore is killed, according to native belief the daughter must also die), and has to make a last-minute sacrifice of his own life. Arbitrary melodrama, perhaps, but neatly prepared for by the illusion which opens the film – a stage act in which a skeleton in a coffin transformed into a beautiful woman – and which Chaney uses again at the end, after recovering his illusions, in order to save his daughter.

The remake, *Kongo* (1932), lost the intensity Browning brings to this film but featured a striking performance by Walter Huston in the Chaney role.

d Tod Browning *p* Irving Thalberg *s* Elliott Clawson, Waldemar Young *c* Percy Hilburn *lp* Lon Chaney, Lionel Barrymore, Mary Nolan, Warner Baxter, Kalla Pasha

1929

Black Waters

(BRITISH AND DOMINION/WORLD WIDE) b/w 90(81)min

Strictly speaking, the first British sound film (though made in America, where the equipment was situated), beating Hitchcock's *Blackmail* (1929) to that honour. Adapted from John Willard's play *Fog*, it follows much the same formula as his **The Cat and the Canary** (1927). A group of characters arrive for assorted reasons at a deserted wharf in San Francisco. It is midnight, a strange drumming noise can be heard from a ghostly-looking yacht moored there, and an old watchman urges them not to go aboard, muttering dire warnings about voodoo and cannibals. On board they encounter a sinister black giant (Johnson), find a reporter (Ames) being held prisoner, and realize that the hawser has been cut. As they drift in the night, members of the party disappear one by one, dispatched by the giant's blowpipe or worse, until only the young lovers (Loder and Brian) and a reverend gentleman (Kirkwood) are left. The latter is revealed as a madman who believes he has reason to kill each of his guests and who is killed Johnson whom he brutalizes, but leaves a bomb set to explode in five minutes, which Loder manages to find and throw overboard. Excellent camerawork helps the plot which luridly anticipates Agatha Christie's *Ten Little Indians*, but the very talkative script is not made any more bearable by comic relief from Hamilton as a stuttering valet.

d Marshall Neilan *p* Herbert Wilcox *s* John Willard *c* David Kesson *lp* James Kirkwood, Mary Brian, John Loder, Robert Ames, Frank Reicher, Noble Johnson, Lloyd Hamilton

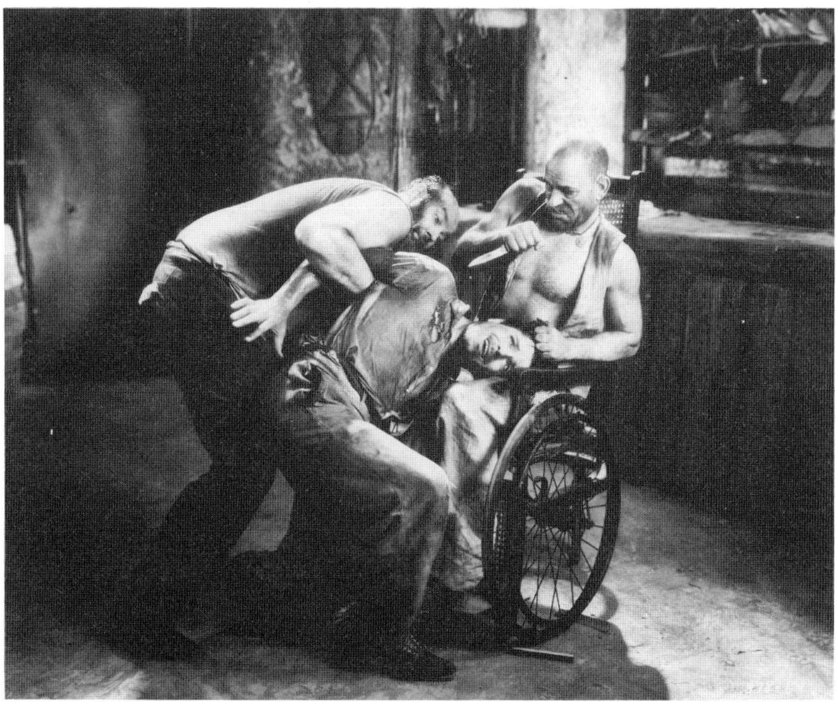

Lon Chaney (right) as Dead Legs in the melodramatic West of Zanzibar.

Der Hund von Baskerville *aka* The Hound of the Baskervilles

(SUEDFILM/ERDA FILM; G) b/w 115min

The last silent film of both Oswald and Sherlock Holmes, this was a commercial disaster. The reasons were threefold: the miscasting of Blackwell in the central role, Oswald's pedestrian direction and, most importantly of all, because sound cinema was rapidly displacing the silent movies. Having adapted the novel once before (1914-15), this time Oswald stayed closer to Conan Doyle's plot and used brooding, shadowy images to depict the moors. The script is by realist Viennese film-maker and scenarist Klaren, one of Juttke's regular collaborators, who later became famous as the director of *Wozzeck* (1947) in East Germany. American actor and entrepreneur Blackwell plays Holmes as a macho adventurer, the style he had adopted for Bulldog Drummond a few years earlier, and Seroff's Watson is a younger sidekick than the image provided later by Nigel Bruce.

The international cast, which includes a Russian (Murski) as Sir Hugo and an Italian (Pavenelli) in the role of Sir Henry, is dominated by Rasp's portrayal of the villain. Indeed, he was so well known for his marvellous villains that a contemporary audience would have had little difficulty in guessing who was behind the nefarious doings on the moors.

The next German Holmes movie, *Sherlock Holmes und das Halsband des Todes* (1962), again imported an Anglo-Saxon actor, this time Christopher Lee, to play the detective, and was also directed by an Englishman, Terence Fisher.

d Richard Oswald *s* Georg C. Klaren, Herbert Juttke *c* Frederik Fuglsang *lp* Carlyle Blackwell, George Seroff, Fritz Rasp, Alexander Murski, Livio Pavanelli, Betty Bird, Alma Taylor

The Last Performance (U) b/w 69min

This film features a superb performance from Veidt as Erik the Great, a sinister stage magician who exerts hypnotic control over his assistant Buffo (Fenton). Arriving in New York from Budapest and making the big time, Veidt falls for the pretty assistant Julie (Philbin) who joins the act, and though she is 20 years his junior, arranges a reception at which he means to announce their engagement. But the jealous Fenton arranges for him to discover that Philbin loves Mackaye, a starving young man caught rifling Veidt's apartment and brought into the act at her suggestion. Consumed with rage, Veidt plans to kill Mackaye during the act while performing a sword trick. But Fenton is the one stabbed to death, Mackaye is arrested for his murder, and Veidt confesses before theatrically stabbing himself.

Although he did make the extravagantly stylish *Broadway* (1929), Fejos was clearly more at home with the simpler and humbler emotions of *Lonesome* (1929), a charming 'big city' tale in much the same vein as F. W. Murnau's *Sunrise* (1927) and *City Girl* (1930). Although *The Last Performance* was

Left: *Conrad Veidt who gives a superb performance as the obsessed magician in Paul Fejos'* The Last Performance.

filmed on the sets used for **The Phantom of the Opera** (1925) and is strikingly shot by Mohr – using the ultra-mobile crane he and Fejos had designed for *Broadway* – the plot is not sufficiently extravagant to suspend disbelief and tends to lumber unconvincingly. Clearly influenced by the UFA style in general and by Karl Freund's camerawork for E. A. Dupont's *Variety* (1925) in particular, Mohr paid tribute by having his camera fly on a trapeze in an early shot. He also improvised the cinema's first zoom effect by sending the camera rushing down on steel cables to the magician's cabinet just as it is opened for the shock discovery of Buffo's body transfixed by swords.

d Paul Fejos *p* Carl Laemmle Jnr *s* James Ashmore Creelman *c* Hal Mohr *lp* Conrad Veidt, Mary Philbin, Leslie Fenton, Fred Mackaye, Gustav Partos, William H. Turner

The Last Warning (U) b/w 88min

This is Leni's last film; he died of blood poisoning in September 1929. A companion piece to **The Cat and the Canary** (1927), its spoof horrors are set this time in a theatre – actually the replica of the Paris Opera built for **The Phantom of the Opera** (1925) and pressed into service again – which has been dark for five years since the leading man was murdered during a performance and his body disappeared. The playwright (Love) decides to try again with the same play and most of the original cast but rehearsals are disturbed by strange noises, falling scenery and treacherous trapdoors. The plot gets sillier and sillier as a mysterious phantom prowls (only supposedly a ghost), issues an unheeded last warning that the theatre must not reopen, and presides over an opening night when the stage goes dark and the new leading man disappears at precisely the same point in the play. It is all hollow stuff, neither very amusing nor very scary, although Leni and Mohr play stylish games, keeping the screen filled with dark corners and menacing shadows, and swinging the camera on ropes as the phantom leaps from balcony to balcony in the climactic scene. Best of all is the opening sequence, a brilliant impressionistic montage of Broadway nightlife with the façade of the theatre becoming a demoniacally grinning mask. The film was remade as **House of Fear** (1939).

d Paul Leni *p* Carl Laemmle Jnr *s* Alfred A. Cohn, Robert F. Hill, J. G. Hawks *c* Hal Mohr *lp* Laura LaPlante, Montagu Love, Roy d'Arcy, Margaret Livingston, John Boles, Mack Swain, Slim Summerville

The surreal splendours of Seven Footprints to Satan.

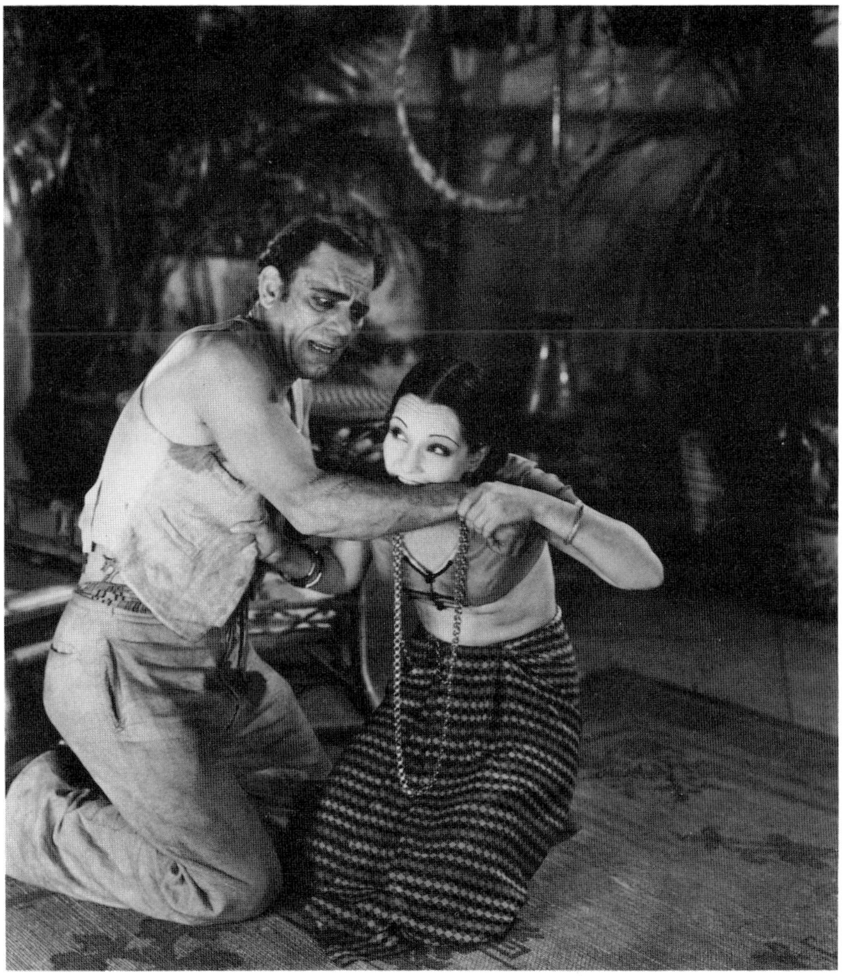

Lupe Velez as the spirited daughter in Tod Browning's lacklustre Where East Is East.

Seven Footprints to Satan
(FIRST NATIONAL) b/w 60min

Between 1926 and 1929, Christensen, the Danish film-maker best known for his remarkable **Häxan** (1922) and his performance as the ageing homosexual artist in Carl Dreyer's *Mikael* (1924), made seven films in Hollywood, most of which appear to have been lost. His first two Danish films, both serial-style thrillers – *Det Hemmelighedsfulde X* (1913) and *Haevens Nat* (1915) – demonstrate a technical skill and sophistication in advance of D. W. Griffith, and a visual flair that echoes the best of Louis Feuillade. Even in those days Christensen was 'painting with light' in the way that Josef von Sternberg was to do later.

Seven Footprints to Satan is dazzling in its virtuosity right from the startling opening in which an elderly professor (Mong) arrives to find the dashing young hero (Hale) in the dark doing some target practice at a row of guttering candles. Yearning for adventure, Hale soon gets his wish as he and his sweetheart (Todd) are whisked off in a car without windows when a fabulous diamond disappears during a reception at her home and the pair set out to notify the police. Deposited instead at a castle belonging to a mysterious stranger known as Satan and given tantalizing clues as to the whereabouts of the jewel, they are subjected to the usual horror-comedy barrage of terrors which turn out (in the debunking prevalent at the time) to be merely an amiable ruse to give Hale his fill of adventure. But in Christensen's hands the parade of madmen, witches, dwarfs and gorillas waving guns and manipulating secret panels becomes a startling symphony of light and shadow, sometimes chillingly bizarre, sometimes strikingly beautiful, always invested with a darkly mocking wit. A semi-naked girl appears in a doorway, for instance; we see gorilla feet clad in evening-dress trousers following her; gorilla paws clutch at her as other unseen hands lash her to a pillar; a hand starts creeping through a fanlight. The denouement, though disappointingly rationalized (and a complete betrayal of Abraham Merritt's excellent source novel), is again superbly realized as the hero, aided by a weird dog-man and contriving to release his sweetheart from a coffin, finds himself in a vast amphitheatre where seven steps, each one illuminated with a vast numbered footprint, lead to Satan's throne.

Christensen made two other films in much the same vein, *The Haunted House* (1928) and *The House of Horror* (1929). He returned to Denmark with the coming of sound and made more films there, none of them of horror interest.

d Benjamin Christensen *p* Wid Gunning *s* Richard Bee *c* Sol Polito *lp* Thelma Todd, Creighton Hale, Sheldon Lewis, William V. Mong, Sojin, Nora Cecil

Stark Mad (WB) b/w 74min

Standard horrors, set for a change in the jungles of Central America, with Fazenda on hand for light relief. Gillingwater organizes an expedition to hunt for his missing son but finds only the latter's guide (Beranger), who has been driven mad by his experiences. Camping out in a ruined Mayan temple where a huge ape is mysteriously chained, the party find messages warning them to leave at once. The missing son's fiancée (Logan) disappears, a member of the party is carried off by a terrible taloned monster and another is killed by an arrow. Regaining his senses after killing a sinister intruder, Beranger reveals that the dead man was a demented hermit who lived in the temple with his pets and had done away with Gillingwater's son months earlier.

d Lloyd Bacon *s* Robert Lord *c* Barney McGill *lp* H. B. Warner, Louise Fazenda, Irene Rich, Jacqueline Logan, Henry B. Walthall, Claude Gillingwater, André Beranger

Where East Is East (MGM) b/w 75min

Despite another striking performance by Chaney, this is a curiously lacklustre (and even sentimental) film. As Tiger Haynes, a wild-animal trapper, Chaney is hideous to behold because of the many maulings that have scarred him but he has a heart of gold. The apple of his eye is his daughter (Velez), whom he gives with his reluctant blessing to the son of an American circus owner (Hughes). But when his wife (Taylor) tries to seduce the young man, the enraged Chaney lets loose a gorilla (made savage by her own earlier mistreatment) on her. Trying to oblige when Velez pleads for her mother's life, Chaney is badly mauled, but survives long enough to see the young couple married. The film is not improved for modern tastes by its macho ethos (the young suitor is approved only after he bravely dominates an escaped tiger) and racial stereotyping (the treacherous mother is Eurasian).

d/p Tod Browning *s* Richard Schayer *c* Henry Sharp *lp* Lon Chaney, Lupe Velez, Estelle Taylor, Lloyd Hughes, Louis Stern

Right: *Louise Fazenda in danger in* Stark Mad.

The 1930s

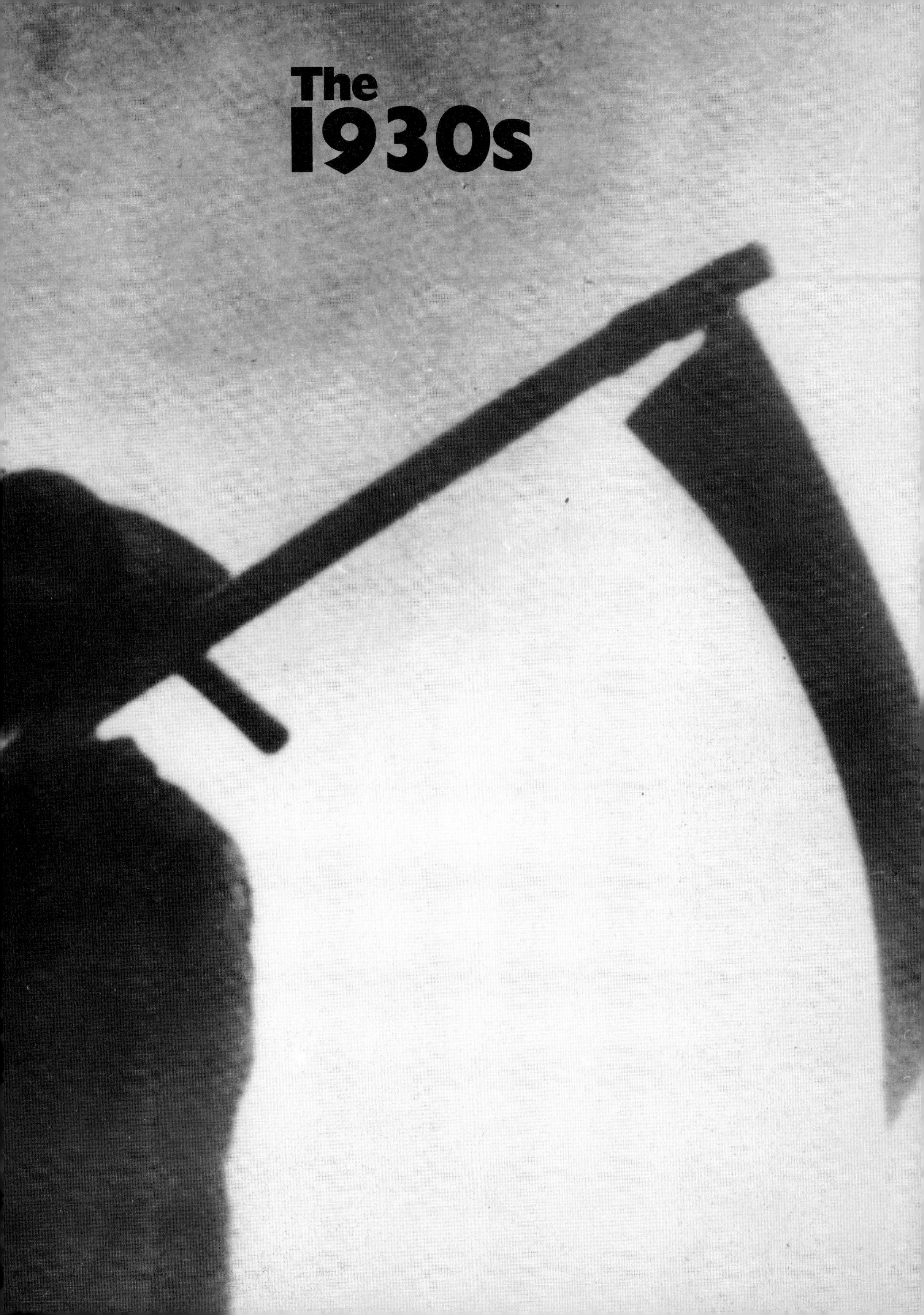

The Sons and Daughters of Universal

Before the thirties, one can only talk of a horror genre loosely; after the phenomenal success of **Dracula** and **Frankenstein** (both 1931) its codification swiftly followed as Universal set about making itself the home of horror. The company subsequently unleashed mummies (starting with **The Mummy**, 1932) and werewolves (starting with **The Werewolf of London**, 1935) to join Dracula and Frankenstein's monster and terrify willing audiences, and made of Bela Lugosi and Boris Karloff if not the first horror stars then the first actors for whom horror would be both the backbone and the limiting factor of their careers. In retrospect, few of the decade's great horror movies were actually made by Universal (**Dr Jekyll and Mr Hyde**, Tod Browning's **Freaks** – which was far superior to his *Dracula* – and **The Most Dangerous Game**, all 1932; and **King Kong**, 1933, the ultimate monster movie) and those that were (Edgar Ulmer's delirious **The Black Cat**, 1934, and the beguiling **Dracula's Daughter**, 1936) ran counter to the grain of the Universal notion of horror which was far more innocent and naïve (the original *Frankenstein*), witty (James Whale's blackly comic sequel, **The Bride of Frankenstein**, 1935), and finally exploitative (**Son of Frankenstein**, 1939), as the decade wore on. With different inflections, this cyclical attitude would be repeated by later studios, producers and actors when they tied their stars to horror.

Outside the United States, the horror tradition all but died. Thus, Carl Dreyer's intense and powerful **Vampyr** (1931) could only find a small audience. But at least it was made; elsewhere in Europe film-makers' attentions were on much more immediate events. Only in Mexico did a native horror tradition flourish with films like **La Llorona** (1933), which made use of a specifically Mexican legend, and the guilt-ridden **El Fantasma del Convento** (1934) which echoed the gothic horrors of M. G. Lewis' *The Monk*.

By the end of the decade, as Universal had learnt even earlier, the horror genre deteriorated into a series of pastiches and remakes which operated as little more than vehicles for their stars. Thus, **The Cat and the Canary** (1939) was the film that made Bob Hope a star, **The Face at the Window** (1939) a vehicle for the stylish barnstorming of Todd Slaughter and **The Gorilla** (1939), in which Bela Lugosi met the Ritz Brothers and a gorilla suit, a tiresome would-be horror comedy. The price of horror's success in the thirties, it seemed, was its ghettoization, with the concomitant assumption that horror films were no longer serious, and a dilution of the fears it represented.

1930

Alraune *aka* **Daughter of Evil**
(UFA; G) b/w 103min
Barely two years after Galeen's masterful silent adaptation of Hanns Heinz Ewers' popular novel, Helm repeated her role as Alraune, the offspring of a prostitute artificially inseminated by scientist Ten Brinken (Bassermann) with the semen scooped from the ground beneath a hanged man. The classic nature-nurture fantasy (made at a time of intense debate on racial and genetic purity), was ruined by Oswald's pedestrian direction which played the story for realism and inserted lots of dialogue. Ostensibly this was to achieve better character development, but the suspicion remains that it was merely in order to exploit the novelty of sound cinema, even at the cost of destroying the sense of brooding, perverse sensuality that had energized Helm's performance in Galeen's film.

The 1952 version of the story, *Alraune*, the last to date, tried to reintroduce a sexually charged atmosphere through Hildegarde Neff's performance, but it failed in all other respects.

d Richard Oswald *p* Erich Pommer *s* Charlie Roellinghoff, Richard Weisbach *c* Guenther Krampf *lp* Brigitte Helm, Albert Bassermann, Agnes Straub, Kaethe Haack, Bernhard Goetzke, Harald Paulsen

The Bat Whispers (ART CINEMA) scope b/w 88min
Along with *The Cat and the Canary*, *The Bat* was probably the most famous of all the Broadway spoof horrors. First staged in 1920, adapted by Avery Hopwood and Mary Roberts Rinehart from the latter's 1908 novel *The Circular Staircase* (which was filmed under that title in 1915), the play was about a master

Previous pages: Vampyr *(1931): Carl Dreyer's symphony in grey.*

Below: *Brigitte Helm as* Alraune *in her second, and less successful, attempt at the role.*

A sequence from The Bat Whispers, *the best of the many spoof horror films that had their origins on the Broadway stage.*

criminal known as the Bat who announces a jewel theft in advance but is foiled by a rival crook who gets in first. The trail leads to a house leased by a wealthy spinster where, with the plot complicated by another exploit of the Bat's involving the death of a banker and disappearance of a young cashier who loves the spinster's niece, the household is soon subjected to terrifying nocturnal disturbances as the Bat tries to locate his loot. Though a detective is present and the cashier is posing as a gardener in the hope of finding out what happened, it is the cool spinster who clears up the mystery, revealing the identity of the Bat (who had killed and is posing as the detective).

West's first film version, *The Bat* (1926, seemingly a lost film like **London After Midnight**, 1927), fóllowed the play fairly closely, emphasizing the mystery element stressed in *The Circular Staircase* and Miss Cornelia Van Gorder's sterling role in solving it. *The Bat Whispers* is very different in that it displaces Miss Cornelia (Hampton) to bring the Bat (Morris) right to the very heart of the film, starting with an extraordinary, vertiginous camera movement swooping down as though in flight – on the stroke of midnight from the clock tower – and through an open window, as the Bat, now seen to be hanging upsidedown from the frame, swings in to enfold his victim in strangling darkness. For the film, technician Charles Cline built a lightweight camera dolly even more mobile than the one designed by Paul Fejos and Hal Mohr and used on *Broadway* and **The Last Performance** (both 1929). With it West was able to create remarkable effects (some of them accomplished with miniature sets) like the camera's sudden dash with the unseen Bat across acres of lawn, zooming straight to an upper window and – with the darkness following a flash of lightning masking the cut – inside the house and along dark corridors to a half-open doorway from which voices can be heard in faint conversation. If the material is the routine mixture of screams and laughs, West's direction is often truly startling, with scenes executed in shadowplay, the camera performing stunning arabesques, and one hallucinatory moment when, locked into a candlelit room with the heroine (Merkel), the Bat can just be seen silhouetted against the wall and spreading his wings before he literally seems to melt into the darkness.

Prints were originally available in either standard 35mm (shot by June) or a special 65mm format (shot by Planck). For a few months in 1930 several widescreen formats were in use: Fox Grandeur (*Happy Days*, *The Big Trail*), Warner Brothers' Vitascope (*Kismet*), MGM's Realife (*Billy the Kid*), RKO's Natural Vision (*Danger Lights*), but cinema managers found the equipment expensive to install and cinemagoers baulked at the raised prices.

There was an atrocious remake, **The Bat** (1958).

d/p/s Roland West *c* Ray June, Robert Planck *lp* Chester Morris, Una Merkel, Maud Eburne, William Bakewell, Grayce Hampton, Gustav von Seyffertitz

The Cat Creeps (U) b/w 71min

This is the first sound remake of **The Cat and the Canary** (1927), and sticks closely to the original plotline with Twelvetrees doing the screaming, Hersholt as the sinister doctor, and Hamilton as the Cat. Horribly hampered by the laborious dialogue scenes, the film's saving grace is Mohr's effective camerawork which makes good use of the camera crane he had developed on *Broadway* and **The Last Performance** (both 1929).

d Rupert Julian *p* Carl Laemmle Jnr *s* Gladys Lehman, William Hurlbut *c* Jerry Ash, Hal Mohr *lp* Helen Twelvetrees, Raymond Haskell, Neil Hamilton, Jean Hersholt, Montague Love

The Gorilla (FIRST NATIONAL) b/w 65min

Ralph Spence's Broadway horror spoof was trotted out again for the coming of sound, retaining its plot virtually unchanged from **The Gorilla** (1927) but with Pidgeon now promoted to the hero's role. Amid the statutory flurry of sliding panels and opening trapdoors, verbal wisecracks take over from the earlier slapstick antics of the two detectives (Frisco and Gribbon). But there is a pleasing new sight gag which starts with Frisco being persuaded by his partner to don a gorilla suit to facilitate the hunt, helpfully tying a white ribbon round his neck for purposes of identification. Later, watching interestedly from the safety of a tree as his partner is chased up and shaken out of another tree, Frisco suddenly realizes that the (supposedly) real gorilla is now perched beside him, coyly removing the white ribbon and placing it round its own neck like some alarming love token. Otherwise the film is pretty stiff.

d Bryan Foy *s* B. Harrison Orkow, Herman Ruby *c* Sid Hickox *lp* Joe Frisco, Harry Gribbon, Lila Lee, Walter Pidgeon, Purnell Prat

The Unholy Three (MGM) b/w 75min

Virtually a carbon copy of the silent **The Unholy Three** (1925), with Chaney and Earles repeating their roles as ventriloquist and midget, and Linow replacing Victor

Right: *Helen Twelvetrees menaced ever so decorously in* The Cat Creeps, *the first sound remake of* The Cat and the Canary *(1927).*

McLaglen as the strong man. Sound makes two notable differences. This was Chaney's first and only sound film, made while he was still recovering from an operation for cancer of the throat and released less than a month before he died. It proves conclusively that he could have made the transition to sound with ease – did, in fact – since his delivery of lines, not to mention his vocal mimicry as the old woman, is superb. Although Conway's direction lacks the controlled intensity of Browning's, sound does heighten the climactic scene in which Chaney, trying to remain incognito while using ventriloquism to clear the innocent man being tried for murder, is betrayed by a vocal lapse which reveals his identity instead of lamely ending up by confessing as in the earlier version. Earles' performance, on the other hand, suffers from the addition of sound because of his problems with the language. On several occasions his sadistic glee – when mimicking his murder victim's cries for mercy, for instance, or mocking Lee's despair when her lover is arrested by dandling the ventriloquist's dummy on his knee and chanting 'I *wish* I had someone to *love* me' – almost fails to come across because of the difficulty in catching what he is actually saying. Significantly, one of Earles' best moments comes when he lapses into his native German to croon lovingly over the jewels which occasioned the murder. It is indicative of the suspicion surrounding early talkies that Chaney felt it necessary to issue a signed affidavit assuring the public that the voices he used in the film were his own and not dubbed.

d Jack Conway *s* J. C. Nugent, Elliot Nugent *c* Percy Hilburn *lp* Lon Chaney, Lila Lee, Henry Earles, Elliot Nugent, Ivan Linow

1931

Doctor X (FIRST NATIONAL) 77min
This is a film that sadly belies its reputation. The main problem is that Tracy's wisecracking reporter hero – supposedly, the comic relief – is unkindly shown up by the smoothly sardonic edge with which Atwill delivers his lines. Also, in trying to rival Universal's **Frankenstein** (1931) with a ghoulish yarn about a moon murderer who kills by scalpel and cannibalizes his victims, First National lamely turn the film into a whodunit where it is all too obvious who did it (Foster's one-armed doctor who adds an arm of synthetic flesh which also furnishes him with a scary face). Curtiz manages some fine expressionistic touches, and the sets (gothic mansion, of course) are splendid but with most of the grisly effects turning risible, the good moments (Wray discovering that she is partnering the real killer in a re-enactment of his crimes, for example) seem few and far between. A few first-run prints were issued in the early two-colour Technicolor process.

d Michael Curtiz *s* Robert Tasker, Earl Baldwin *c* Richard Tower, Ray Rennahan *lp* Lionel Atwill, Fay Wray, Lee Tracy, Preston Foster, Arthur Edmund Carewe, Mae Busch

Dr Jekyll and Mr Hyde (PAR) b/w 98(90,81)min
Unlike the John Barrymore **Dr Jekyll and Mr Hyde** (1920), Mamoulian's version stoutly defends the healthy normality of sex. Taken by his leeringly lecherous future father-in-law to the depravity of Soho (where the lower orders are doing a bit of mild drinking while Nita Naldi does a Spanish-style dance), Barrymore's Jekyll shrinks in disgust as Naldi offers to kiss him. The equivalent scene in Mamoulian's version has Jekyll (March) responding cheerfully but circumspectly to flirtatious provocation from the sluttish Ivy (Hopkins): obviously sexually attracted and not ashamed of it, he disengages himself simply because he is already in love (with Hobart).

Contrary to his usual impressionistic practice, Mamoulian opens the film with a lengthy subjective sequence, uninterruptedly adopting Jekyll's point-of-view as he carols his joy at his coming marriage by pounding out Bach at the organ, is reminded by his manservant that he has a lecture to deliver, and makes his way to the university amphitheatre. So little thought of at the time that it was excised from some prints, this subjective sequence fills several functions. Firstly, it obviously establishes Jekyll's nature as one of introspection, a moody self-absorption to which his future father-in-law's indignant insistence that the date of the wedding cannot be brought forward (and the dialogue makes it amply clear that Jekyll's sexual need is paramount in motivating the request) soon adds the dimensions of mania. Secondly, the ostentatious flourish with which the sequence ends – the camera panning full circle round the amphitheatre and cutting to the first objective view of Jekyll as he utters the first word of his lecture on the possibility of separating good from evil in the human mind – indicates the arrogance of the man who sees himself as the centre of the universe and is about to usurp God's role as

Left: *Henry Earles, Lon Chaney and Ivan Linow in the remake of* The Unholy Three.

Bela Lugosi as Dracula, *the classic suitor, with Helen Chandler as the damsel in distress.*

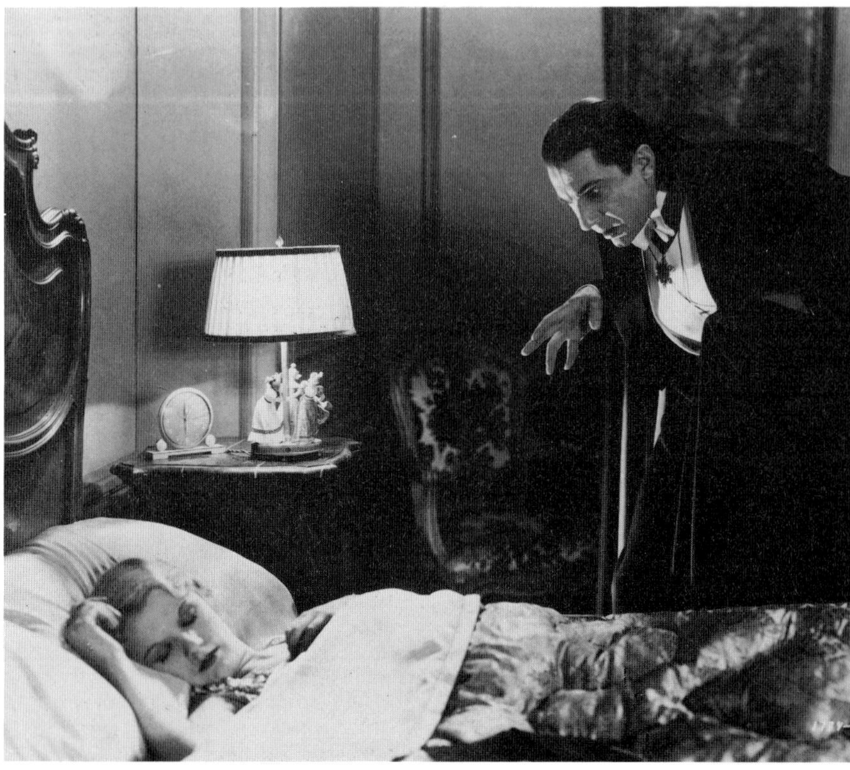

Above: *Boris Karloff as the saddest of all man-made monsters in the classic* Frankenstein.

creator. Thirdly, and perhaps most importantly, it establishes Jekyll as a basis not only for the series of diagonal wipes which associate Hopkins and Hobart within the frame, but for the system of cuts and dissolves which link Hyde's ecstasies and Jekyll's shame to the same root cause.

The film, in other words, openly traces the cause of Jekyll's troubles to the frustration by social convention of his perfectly natural sexual desires. And one of its most remarkable features is the consistency with which Jekyll and Hyde are viewed as two halves of a schizophrenic personality. Far from representing a liberation of Jekyll's sexuality, Hyde is the product of its ruthless suppression: where Jekyll's initial encounter with Hopkins was suffused with a heady eroticism, Hyde's dealings with her are pointedly asexual, dominated instead by a cold, murderous sadism. Still by far the best film of the story, with superb performances from March and Hopkins, it also has the incomparable Struss behind the camera, producing a marvellous chiaroscuro vision of Stevenson's London as a fog-laden, gaslit warren of glistening streets, towering stairways and shabby dens, haunted by the shadow of Mr Hyde, alternately bestially small or towering like a giant, as he prowls with black cloak swirling like a matador's cape.

d/p Rouben Mamoulian *s* Samuel Hoffenstein, Percy Heath *c* Karl Struss *lp* Fredric March, Miriam Hopkins, Rose Hobart, Holmes Herbert, Halliwell Hobbes, Edgar Norton

Dracula (U) b/w 85min

For a film by a major director which became Universal's biggest box-office hit of the year and which provided the impetus for a whole generation of horror movies, *Dracula* really isn't terribly good. One reason for this may be that Browning, who very often dreamed up his own scenarios, here did not even go back to the book: the script is based on the Hamilton Deane play, as Americanized by John L. Balderston, in which Lugosi had appeared on Broadway in 1927. Universal originally bought the rights as a vehicle for Lon Chaney. When Chaney died it was inherited by Lugosi, and it may well be that this change, with Lugosi so familiar with the play after a two-year run, inhibited Browning from rethinking the material. At all events, the first 20 minutes – predominantly silent, with the arrival of Renfield and the drive to Castle Dracula with a bat leading the way – are astonishingly fluid and brilliantly shot by Freund despite the painted backdrops. There are innumerable imaginative touches to treasure here: the sinister emphasis of Lugosi's first line ('I ... am Dracula. I bid you welcome') and the sonorous poetry of his invocation to the children of the night; the moment when Dracula leads the way up his castle stairway behind a vast cobweb through which Renfield has to fight his way as he follows; and the vampire women, driven off by Dracula, reluctantly backing away from the camera while it continues hungrily tracking in to Renfield's fallen body.

Thereafter the pace falters, and with the London scenes growing in verbosity and staginess, the hammy limitations of Lugosi's performance are cruelly exposed. But the brilliant moments continue (Renfield's frenzy in his cell, for instance), and Freund's camerawork rarely falters.

d Tod Browning *p* Carl Laemmle Jnr *s* Garrett Fort, Dudley Murphy *c* Karl Freund *lp* Bela Lugosi, Edward Van Sloan, Dwight Frye, Helen Chandler, David Manners

Frankenstein (U) b/w 71(67)min

Mary Shelley's novel had been filmed three times in the silent era: in 1910 by the Edison company; in 1915 as **Life Without Soul**; and in Italy in 1920 as **Il Mostro di Frankenstein**. Intriguingly, the cast originally lined up for the first sound version featured Bela Lugosi, Leslie Howard and Bette Davis. At that point the director was to be Robert Florey, who had selected the novel from several subjects suggested by Universal's story editor Richard Schayer as possible follow-ups to **Dracula** (1931). The idea was for Lugosi to play the scientist but Universal objected, so Howard became Henry Frankenstein (with Davis as his fiancée), and tests were shot by Paul Ivano on the *Dracula* sets with Lugosi as the monster. The studio were unhappy with the makeup Lugosi had devised for himself and Lugosi was unhappy because the monster was a non-speaking role; and the project, complete with Florey's storyline (he contributed, most notably, the twist whereby the monster is given a madman's brain and the ending in the windmill) was inherited by Universal's up-and-coming director James Whale. Whale promptly substituted Colin Clive for Howard, brought in the little-known Karloff (whom he had seen in the Los Angeles stage production of *The Criminal Code* and in the gangster movie *Graft*, 1931), and gave the task of creating a suitable makeup for the monster to Jack Pierce. Davis had by then vanished from the cast and was replaced by Clarke, since the Laemmles felt that her star potential might be marred by an appearance in a horror movie. The rest, as they say, is history, although it is still sometimes reported that the scene in which the monster is shown throwing the little girl into the lake was cut from release prints because preview audiences found it too harrowing. Actually it was removed at Karloff's insistence, because he felt that the scene as shot betrayed the character he had created: where Karloff had wanted to *place* the child in the water, Whale made him throw her in. Censorship was responsible for the removal of the scene in which the monster is seen killing the hunchback Fritz by impaling him on a hook. Most prints are also shorn of Clive's exulting line when he cries, after the famous 'It's alive! It's alive!' as the monster gives its first sign of life, 'In the name of God, now I know what it feels like to *be* God'. Originally left intact, this line was censored out (leaving a jump cut) when the film was re-released.

Although one of the most celebrated and influential movies ever made – it even sparked off a horror revival when shown on American TV in 1957 – it does not by any means represent Whale's best work. Whale's delight in the eccentricities of human behaviour, in outcast monsters and other grotesques whom he encourages to take the plot by the scruff of the neck and make free of it to create self-contained little farces of their own, is much better served by the quirkish humours of **The Old Dark House** (1932), *The Invisible Man* (1933), and above all, **The Bride of Frankenstein** (1935). The stark, solid, impressively stylish film, obviously influenced by the sculptural/architectural massiveness of Paul Wegener's **Der Golem: Wie Er in die Welt Kam** (1920), stalks through its plot – Baron Frankenstein (Clive) and his feverish dreams of creating life; his success when his graverobbing hunchback assistant (Frye) steals a murderer's brain to go with the patchwork quilt of human fragments; his despair when the man he creates becomes a monster – with immense solemnity. With Karloff giving one of the great performances of all time as the monster whose mutation from candour to chill savagery is mirrored only through his limpid eyes, the film's great imaginative coup is to show the monster 'growing up' in all too human terms. First he is the innocent baby, reaching up to grasp the sunlight that filters through the skylight. Then the joyous child, playing at throwing flowers into the lake with a little girl whom he fondly imagines to be another flower to float. And finally, as he finds himself progressively misjudged by the society that created him, the savage killer as whom he has been typecast. Illuminated by Karloff's performance, the film has a weird, fairytale beauty not matched until Jean Cocteau made *La Belle et la Bête* (1946). But its importance lies in the fact that its monster is put forward at least ambivalently as hero, inducing a note of discreet but profound eroticism to the genre as well as an indication that it was perfectly capable of challenging – even undermining – social conventions.

d James Whale *p* Carl Laemmle Jnr *s* Garrett Fort, Robert Florey, Francis Edward Faragoh *c* Arthur Edeson *lp* Boris Karloff, Colin Clive, Mae Clarke, Frederick Kerr, Dwight Frye, John Boles, Edward Van Sloan

The Hound of the Baskervilles

(GAUMONT-BRITISH; GB) b/w 75min

Rendel as Holmes and Lloyd as Watson, here save Stuart's Sir Henry from the Baskerville doom on a Dartmoor that looks rather like Hampstead Heath. This second British version of Conan Doyle's story is just as pedestrian as the first, which was filmed in 1921 with Eille Norwood as Holmes. The temperature is not noticeably raised in either version by a hound which glows with phosphorescent paint. Other early film versions of the story were made in France (1914) and Germany (1914, 1915 and 1929).

d/co-s V. Gareth Gundry *p* Michael Balcon *co-s* Edgar Wallace *c* Bernard Knowles *lp* John Stuart, Reginald Bach, Robert Rendel, Frederick Lloyd, Heather Angel

The shadowy world of Carl Dreyer's Vampyr, *one of the undisputed masterpieces of the genre.*

Vampyr *aka* Vampire *aka* The Strange Adventure of David Gray *aka* Castle of Doom

(CARL THEODOR DREYER FILMPRODUKTION; G)
b/w 82(70)min

In this uniquely beautiful and disturbing film Dreyer wanted 'to create a daydream on the screen and to show that the horrific is not to be found around us but in our own unconscious mind'. Loosely based on Sheridan LeFanu's *Carmilla*, the script also borrows from other stories contained in his collection *In a Glass Darkly*. In fact, Dreyer himself took full responsibility for the script. The movie suggests rather than tells the story of a young man, David Gray (Allan Grey in the German version), who becomes involved with two sisters: Leone (Schmitz), who appears to be dying from a mysterious illness, and Gisele (Mandel) who appears to be held captive. Both are under the influence of an old person, probably female, referred to as Marguerite Chopin (Gérard) and of a doctor (Hieronimko). There is also a one-legged man whose shadow has been detached from him. When Gray and a servant stake Chopin, whom they assume to be a vampire after Gray has read a book on the subject left him by the sisters' dead father, Leone's face relaxes but it seems she dies anyway. Gray and Gisele cross a river in dense fog and reach the shore to which, at the beginning of the movie, a shadowy figure carrying a scythe had gone to the accompaniment of a faintly tolling bell. Like the celebrated sequence in which Gray imagines he is dead, sealed in a coffin but able to see as he is carried to his grave, the entire film is riddled with disjunctive editing, impossible point-of-view shots and seemingly incoherent events (the one-legged man and his shadow, for example), which make it impossible for the viewer to settle on any particular 'view' with any certainty. The sparse, cryptic, softly spoken lines – acted on location in German, French and English – together with the repeated use of a voice off and an eerie soundtrack (composed especially by Wolfgang Zeller) and the spatial dislocations provoked by the editing style combine to make an abstract movie proceed with the movement of dream logic. Many

Left: *John Stuart under threat from* The Hound of the Baskervilles, *a thoroughly pedestrian version of Conan Doyle's story.*

images remain engraved in the mind: the witches' sabbath in a cavernous space, signified by means of shadows on a huge wall decorated with large carriage wheels; the face of Schmitz as her lips pull back to reveal her teeth as she stares with a demonic craving at her sister; the face of Gerard as she looks into the dead hero's coffin, and so on.

The look of the film is as unique as its narrative structure. Instead of heavily contrasted chiaroscuro, the images are hazy, dissolving into shades of grey. Mate and Dreyer hit on the visual style by accident: some rushes were produced with the fault because of a false light in the lens, and they decided to reproduce the effect throughout. The contribution of the celebrated designer Hermann Warm was minimal, although some of the compositions are reminiscent of the way Murnau used light in **Nosferatu** (1921), also designed by Warm. The picture was financed privately by the Dutch aristocrat Nicolas de Gunzburg who, under the alias of Julian West, also played the part of Gray. With the exception of Schmitz, the cast was non-professional, although Mandel had experience as a (nude) photographer's model. The whole film was shot on location in the summer of 1931.

The director's previous film, *La Passion de Jeanne d'Arc* (1927) had been a flop, as was *Vampyr* when it was first released in Germany in 1932, possibly because audiences were not prepared for such a disconcerting work in a year that saw scores of frantic operettas and Universal's rather different approach to the genre. Dreyer did not make another movie for 12 years, when he returned to the theme of the cruel terror exercised by unconscious forces when they are given legitimacy by institutionalized religions with *Vredens Dag* (1943).

d/p/co-s Carl Theodor Dreyer *co-s* Christen Jul *c* Rudolf Mate *lp* Julian West (Nicolas de Gunzburg), Henriette Gérard, Sibylle Schmitz, Rena Mandel, Jan Hieronimko, Albert Bras

1932

Freaks *aka* Forbidden Love *aka* Nature's Mistress *aka* The Monster Show

(MGM) b/w 90(61)min

This is a nightmarish collision between normality and abnormality. Baclanova, a trapeze artist, marries a dwarf (Earles) for his money, planning to poison him with the aid of her strongman lover (Victor). As a result she is subjected to hideous mutilation by the vengeful circus freaks, who turn her into a chicken-woman.

Tod Browning's nightmarish Freaks.

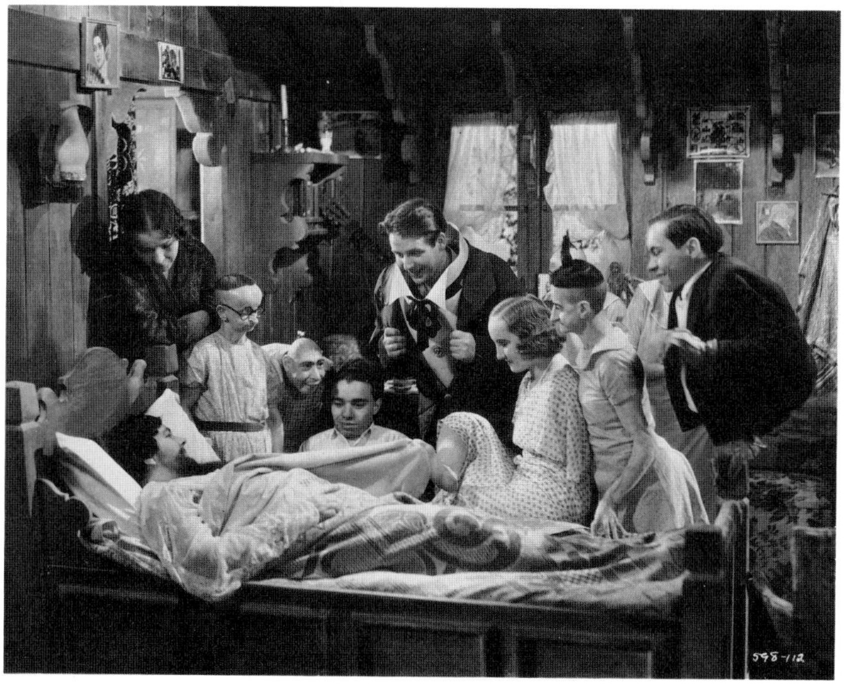

Because of its use of real freaks and its unfortunate early history – banned in Britain, shelved by MGM after disastrous premières and then snapped up for exploitation by Dwain Esper (of **Maniac**, 1934, fame) – *Freaks* acquired an unsavoury reputation which lingers on even though denied by the film itself. If the last scenes are horrific enough to satisfy the most ghoulish tastes, the revelation of the film is its warmth and humanity. Browning manages to evoke the closed world of freaks, the intensely human emotions contained within inhuman exteriors, in such a way that fascinated revulsion turns into tender comprehension. His first introduction to the freaks comes as a local squire walks through a forest, his gamekeeper babbles wildly about having seen grotesque creatures in the wood, and the camera focuses on a clearing in which *things* crawl, dance and hop obscenely. The squire angrily protests, and Madame Petralini (Dione), the motherly body in charge of the freaks, explains that they are merely playing in the sun on a day off from the circus. An instinctive huddling of the terrified freaks against Dione, a gesture from a pin-headed woman who lovingly touches her face, and the scene suddenly turns from a *Walpurgisnacht* revel into a charming idyll. The brilliance of the film lies in the care with which its sideshow context is evoked – on the one hand, the 'normal' circus folk, with their cruel, unthinking mockery of the freaks; on the other, the freaks themselves, joyous, eager to accept anybody who will meet them halfway. Frozo the clown (Ford) and his girl Venus (Hyams), who take the freaks as they are, link these worlds in two wholly charming scenes: teasing one of the pin-headed women about her new dress, and joking with the bearded lady about the birth of her baby. These scenes, and more particularly the sequence of the wedding banquet, provide an emotional basis for the horror of the climax. The wedding banquet is a brilliant piece of *mise-en-scène*, with the freaks assembled around a long table in joyous celebration of the marriage between Baclanova and Earles, culminating in the wild progress of a dwarf down in the centre of the table, clutching a loving-cup of wine and accompanied by a mounting chant of 'We accept her, we accept her, one of us'. The intensity, the laughter, the strange ritual of the chant, make Baclanova's revulsion perfectly natural. But she is still unable to consider the freaks as other than unfeeling monsters, and inflicts the final insult on her tiny husband by carrying him piggyback round the room. After this, and the subsequent slow poisoning of Earles, there is no doubt whose side the audience is on.

The macabre finale, lit in chiaroscuro, is even better. As Baclanova and Victor go about their business of poisoning Earles, eyes watch constantly, peering in at windows and from beneath caravans. The freaks gather their forces. A storm breaks, the rain comes pouring down, knives appear and there is nothing on the soundtrack but the storm, the caravans rolling, a melancholy tune played by a dwarf on a pipe; the steaming rain, the thick mud full of crawling shapes in the darkness, and Baclanova and Victor running screaming in terror.

d/p Tod Browning *s* Willis Goldbeck, Leon Gordon, Edgar Allan Woolf, Al Boasberg *c* Merritt B. Gerstad *lp* Wallace Ford, Olga Baclanova, Harry Earles, Daisy Earles, Henry Victor, Leila Hyams, Rose Dione

Island of Lost Souls (PAR) b/w 72min

Although H. G. Wells disapproved of it, this is a remarkably fine adaptation of his novel *The Island of Doctor Moreau*. Struss's cinematography is magnificent and the film boasts a superb performance by Laughton as the fiendish, whip-cracking scientist whose experiments in surgical grafting between humans and animals have produced a pathetic series of bestial mutants, kept under hypnotic control by regular assemblies devoted to a liturgical chanting of the master's 'law' (with Lugosi as his beast-man foreman, 'sayer of the law').

Although less suave than Count Zaroff of **The Most Dangerous Game** (1932) – in spite of his Mephistophelean

Charles Laughton as the decadent Doctor Moreau in Island of Lost Souls.

goatee, Laughton's Moreau looks sweaty and rumpled compared to the impeccable Zaroff – Moreau is his blood brother in the mind. Moreau's equivalent to Zaroff's cool intellectual sadism, again suffusing the film with a perverted eroticism, is his plot to have Arlen mate with Burke – the beautiful woman he has created from a panther but who is already reverting – just to see what the results of cross-breeding will be. Interestingly, though, *Island of Lost Souls* anticipates **King Kong** (1933) in its embodiment of the underground spirit of revolt, a spirit extremely timely in its appeal to victims of the Depression years, who not only resented their material deprivations but were all too willing to blame a system which appeared to thrive on an arbitrary suspension of the individual's inalienable right to the pursuit of happiness. The delirious final revolt here, with the master dragged away to the 'house of pain' in which he created his subservient brutes, echoes the wilder excesses of the French Revolution.

Presumably because of its vivisectionist aspects, the film was banned in Britain until 1958. Lost somewhere among the beast-men are Randolph Scott and Alan Ladd. First filmed in France in 1913 in a thinly disguised version as *L'Ile d'Epouvante*, the Wells novel was remade as **Terror Is a Man** (1959), and as **The Island of Dr Moreau** (1977).

d Erle C. Kenton *s* Waldemar Young, Philip Wylie *c* Karl Struss *lp* Charles Laughton, Richard Arlen, Leila Hyams, Kathleen Burke, Bela Lugosi

The Mask of Fu Manchu

(COSMOPOLITAN/MGM) b/w 72(67)min

After completing **The Old Dark House** (1932), Karloff was loaned to MGM to take over a role that had been played by Warner Oland in *The Mysterious Dr Fu Manchu* (1929), *The Return of Dr Fu Manchu* (1931) and – playing second fiddle to Anna May Wong – *Daughter of the Dragon* (1931). As the MGM advertising campaign claimed, this was 'a new Fu Manchu', still the deadly master criminal of Sax Rohmer's novels but tailored to suit Karloff's image, with the character's nobler aspects toned down and replaced by pure sadism. Gloriously creaky claptrap, the plot (something to do with the sword and mask of Genghis Khan being the key to world domination) is shoved aside to make way for a non-stop welter of fiendish tortures as the dastardly Yellow Peril plays cat-and-mouse with both Scotland Yard's Nayland Smith (Stone) and the brave British archaeologists who secured the relics from Genghis's tomb. Karloff presides with impeccably urbane wit over the ingenious tortures, earning grateful plaudits by suspending Stone (alias Andy Hardy's perennially pompous papa) over a pit of drooling crocodiles, but is very nearly upstaged by Loy as his sadistic-nymphomaniac daughter, who gleefully has the stalwart hero (Starrett) tied up and whipped as a prelude to injecting him with a serum that will reduce him to a helpless love object. Imaginatively designed and superbly shot, it is all great fun: even the imperialist xenophobia – all orientals are villainous heathens – can hardly be taken seriously.

d Charles Brabin, Charles Victor *p* Irving Thalberg *s* Irene Kuhn, Edgar Allan Woolf, John Willard *c* Gaetano Gaudio *lp* Boris Karloff, Lewis Stone, Karen Morley, Jean Hersholt, Myrna Loy, Charles Starrett

The Monster Walks *aka* The Monster Walked

(MAYFAIR) b/w 65(57) min

This lavish imitation of **The Cat and the Canary** (1927) opens tolerably stylishly with the arrival during a howling storm of the heroine (Reynolds) at the family mansion where her father's body is laid out in a candlelit room. All too soon a sinister housekeeper is prowling, a partially paralysed wicked uncle (Lewis) is plotting the demise of the heiress, and a maddened ape gibbers in the basement. Ordered to murder Reynolds and lay the blame on the ape, the housekeeper's half-witted son (Auer) instead kills his mother by mistake, but gets his comeuppance from the ape while trying to goad it with a whip into attacking Reynolds whom he has tied to a post. The limp thrills are marginally brightened, no thanks to the script, by a characteristic performance from Best in his début as the inevitable cowardly black servant.

Ellis went on to script a number of Charlie Chaplin films. Strayer's second horror film, **The Vampire Bat** (1933), was rather better.

d Frank Strayer *p* Cliff Broughton *s* Robert Ellis *c* Jules Cronjager *lp* Rex Lease, Vera Reynolds, Mischa Auer, Sheldon Lewis, Martha Mattox, Sleep 'n' Eat (Willie Best)

The Most Dangerous Game *aka* The Hounds of Zaroff

(RKO) b/w 78(63)min

This is one of the most authentically sadean films ever made. Count Zaroff (Banks) is a connoisseur of arcane pleasures, and the owner of a remote island in the Malay archipelago to which he ensures that passing ships are attracted and then wrecked on the reeds. Only those strong enough to swim ashore *and* to avoid the sharks will do, since Zaroff is a sportsman and believes in playing the game. 'First the hunt, then the revels', he purrs, delighted to discover that his latest victims include not only a beauty (Wray) but a big-game hunter (McCrea), almost his match in celebrity, as he suavely intimates the rules governing the sport he has devised to revive his jaded palate: a hunt for human prey, with the latter given a knife, a few hours start, a guarantee of freedom if he survives the night, and the knowledge that no one has yet survived (even though, to even

Myrna Loy and Boris Karloff, with Charles Starrett as the innocent hero, in the surprisingly sadistic The Mask of Fu Manchu.

Joel McCrea and Fay Wray in flight in the superior The Most Dangerous Game.

the odds and render the game more piquant, Zaroff uses only a bow and arrow).

What surprises about this long exposition in which Zaroff expounds his sadean reasoning, trying to win McCrea over as a fellow-aesthete but foundering on the latter's stolid insistence that he is a hunter and not a murderer, is that far from even fringing boredom, it retains the excitement of a duel. And a duel it is, with the presence of Wray – the character does not appear in Richard Connell's original story – lending a darkly erotic meaning to Zaroff's 'revels'. The theme is hinted at almost from the beginning, when the castaways enter Zaroff's mansion by a door with an ornate knocker in the form of a satyr bearing a swooning maiden in his arms. Greeting them from his ornate stairway in impeccable evening-dress, Zaroff is backed by an identical motif, this time a wall tapestry of a centaur and his captive. The old-world elegance (a silver candelabra is used to light the way) and its decadence (the sinister trophy room with its macabre exhibits, reserved as a *divertissement* for evenings of especial ennui) are not only kept in perfect counterpoint through this part of the film, they continue – but reversed, as it were – during the climactic hunt. Remarkably excitingly staged, the hunt sequence shows McCrea the hunter, defending not only himself but his mate as represented by Wray, justifiably resorting to such dirty tricks as angled, sharpened stakes planted to get rid of Zaroff's hounds and henchman, but in fact becoming the killer he refused to be. Sticking with honour and rectitude to the rules, having as he thought delivered the *coup de grâce* and found that it did not take, Banks concedes defeat: 'Yes ... yes, I insist, you have beaten me'. But McCrea still kills him, literally stabbing him in the back. Justifiably, but ...

It takes only a very short stretch of the imagination to see the fiendishly megalomaniac Zaroff as a prototype fuehrer who even lists the members of inferior races who have fallen to his strength, but it seems more likely that, as with **White Zombie** (1932), the film's reference point is American isolationist fears during the Depression, with Zaroff, like Lugosi's Murder Legendre, symbolizing decadent Europe. Connell's story inspired a number of remakes, mutations and travesties, not always horror films: **A Game of Death** (1945), *Johnny Allegro* (1949), *Kill or Be Killed* (1950), **The Black Castle** (1952), **The Black Forest** (1954), *Run for the Sun* (1956) and **Bloodlust** (1961).

co-d Ernest B. Schoedsack *co-d/co-p* Irving Pichel *co-p* Merian C. Cooper *s* James A. Creelman *c* Henry Gerrard *lp* Joel McCrea, Fay Wray, Leslie Banks, Robert Armstrong, Noble Johnson

The Mummy (U) b/w 78(63)min

The reputation of this film as a classic is based on one superb sequence in which a young archaeologist (Fletcher), unable to resist peeking into the newly unearthed mummy case he has been warned not to open, reads aloud from a parchment without realizing he is intoning an incantation for raising the dead. A single baleful eye flickers open, the hands stir, one of them seizes the fateful parchment, and a wisp of grave-soiled bandage (all we are shown of the perambulating mummy) slowly disappears through the doorway, leaving the terrified young man gibbering with insane laughter.

Freund, the great German cinematographer particularly noted for his work with F. W. Murnau and here moving behind the camera for the first time after photographing **Dracula** (1931) and **Murders in the Rue Morgue** (1932), directs with a measured Teutonic gravity. The style might have been highly effective in suggesting the timeless obsession of the mummy's quest as, now in the guise of a tolerably mummified Egyptian archaeologist (still played by Karloff), he stalks Cairo for the English girl (Johann) he believes to be a reincarnation of the princess for whom he died. But the mesmerizing quality of the quest is disrupted by a quaintly absurd flashback (seen inset in a magic pool uncomfortably reminiscent of a television set), and the carefully calculated mood constantly undercut by a trite script which includes such absurd lines of dialogue as 'Let us go and sit under the Egyptian stars', obviously designed to foster the illusion of local colour. The result is dull and ponderous, distinguished chiefly by the exemplary discretion of Karloff's performance.

d Karl Freund *p* Stanley Bergerman *s* John L. Balderston *c* Charles Stumar *lp* Boris Karloff, Zita Johann, David Manners, Arthur Byron, Edward Van Sloan, Bramwell Fletcher

Murders in the Rue Morgue (U) b/w 75(61)min

Stemming less from Poe than from **Das Cabinet des Dr Caligari** (1919), Lugosi's Dr Mirakle (one of his most engaging performances) starts with the great advantage that his adventure is stunningly shot by Freund. A fairground hypnotist who haunts the Boulevard de Crime – in a Paris of lean-to houses and distorted perspectives that looks as if it were an expressionist Prague waiting for the reappearance of the golem – Mirakle is a sort of perverted Darwinist whose life's work is the crossbreeding of apes and humans. For this he needs subjects, and like Caligari with his Cesare, he has a trained gorilla (Gemora) to carry girls off across the rooftops on his behalf. Aided by Janos, the Black One (Johnson), a more

Right: *Boris Karloff brought to life in Karl Freund's pedestrian* The Mummy.

Left: *Bela Lugosi and ape in the imaginative* Murders in the Rue Morgue.

literal Cesare figure, he can then carry out his experiments in the privacy of his laboratory. Many contemporary reviewers complained about the sadistic nature of the experiments, and, although the film is mild by today's standards, many of its scenes – notably one in which Francis is bled to death on the rack and then brutally dumped in the river – still carry a minatory charge. A darkly erotic undertone flows through the film, with no one deceived by the notion that gorilla blood is what the girls are getting (or maybe it is partly sexual frustration that makes Erik the gorilla strangle his master in the end).

Perhaps too derivative to be considered one of the great Universal horrors (directing it was Florey's compensation for missing out on **Frankenstein**, 1931), *Murders in the Rue Morgue* is nevertheless hugely enjoyable and, taken together with **The Beast with Five Fingers** (1946), good enough to make one regret that Florey's imagination was let loose so rarely. Poe's story was first filmed in 1910 as *Sherlock Holmes in the Great Murder Mystery* and was remade as **Phantom of the Rue Morgue** (1954) and **Murders in the Rue Morgue** (1971).

d Robert Florey *p* Carl Laemmle Jnr *s* Tom Reed, Dale van Every, John Huston *c* Karl Freund *lp* Bela Lugosi, Sidney Fox, Leon Waycoff (Ames), Arlene Francis, Noble Johnson, Charles Gemora

The Old Dark House (U) b/w 74min

In a retrospective comment about his novel *Benighted*, which he describes rather grandly as a philosophical thriller, J. B. Priestley explained that 'The intelligent modern novelist cannot help being concerned with ideas and states of mind. We live in a self-conscious, introspective Hamlet-ish age, and it is natural that fiction should reflect this spirit. It is not so much our hero's outward fortunes that engage us as the drama of his succeeding states of mind, the vague and changing pageant of his ideas'. Rather tartly, after observing that the novel was a failure in Britain, Priestley notes that 'My American publishers, presumably determined to make money out of one of my books or perish in the attempt, promptly abandoned my title, which has of course a double meaning and tells you almost everything about the novel, and with the title any pretensions the book might have to be a psychological or philosophical novel. They called it *The Old Dark House* and brought it out as a thriller. So disguised, it had a very good sale indeed ...'

Whale fortunately ignores these pretensions, which are hardly supported by the novel itself, and which furthermore reflect an attitude to horror movies (and novels) that remains unchanged to this day. Instead, he follows Priestley's American publishers by using the plot as a springboard for a classic display of old-dark-house horrors as five travellers stranded by a storm – a married couple (Massey and Stuart), their cynical friend (Douglas), a bluff Yorkshire magnate (Laughton) and his chorus girl (Bond) – are obliged to take refuge in a ramshackle mansion somewhere in the wilds of Wales. Allowed free rein for the first time in his career, Whale's black humour revels delightedly in a crescendo of bizarrerie as the host household proceeds to disgorge a strange menagerie in which Karloff's mute, black-bearded and lecherously drunken butler, Thesiger's alarmingly effeminate lord of the manor, his birdlike sister and his bedridden centenarian father, are all effortlessly topped by the ineffable *frisson* with which the diminutive homicidal pyromaniac kept locked in the room at the top of the stairs finally makes his appearance near the end. As much as anything, the delight of the film is the subtlety with which Whale shades comedy of manners into tragedy of horrors, with conventional values (decency and decorum still hold sway among the visitors) being tested and found wanting in a situation where abnormality holds sway. Funny it may be, but there is a nightmarish edge to the mockery of social niceties with which Thesiger, playing the perfect host with waspish effeminacy, politely presses his uninvited dinner-guests to 'Have a po-ta-to?' while his sister proffers the soggy object on a fork, or qualifies his offer of a drink with a defensive and supremely decadent leer: 'It's only gin, you know, gin. I *like* gin!'

d James Whale *p* Carl Laemmle Jnr *s* Ben Levy, R. C. Sherriff *c* Arthur Edeson *lp* Boris Karloff, Charles Laughton, Raymond Massey, Melvyn Douglas, Gloria Stuart, Ernest Thesiger, Brember Wills, Lillian Bond, Eva Moore

Unheimliche Geschichten *aka* Tales of the Uncanny *aka* The Living Dead *aka* Extraordinary Tales *aka* Asylum of Horror

(ROTO FILM; G) b/w 89min

Finished late in 1931, this film extends three of the stories Oswald had used in his 1919 movie of the same title – Poe's *The System of Dr Tarr and Professor Feather* and *The Black Cat* and Stevenson's *The Suicide Club* – into a full-length comedy. The mixture, played as a crazy comedy, pokes fun at all the classic motifs of the genre but seems to single out Paul Leni's **Das Wachsfigurenkabinett** (1924) as a special target for parody. The picture features Wegener, who had played the title role in **Der Golem** (1914 and 1920) and the father of **Alraune** (1928). Here he is a mad scientist who kills his wife and is locked away in an asylum which he then takes over and uses as a suicide club. The actor, soon to become one of the Nazis' most

A classic example of a horror sequence: The Old Dark House.

Unheimliche Geschichten*: one of the rare examples in the German cinema of a successful black comedy.*

prestigious collaborators in the world of the theatre and cinema, seems to relish the opportunity to send up both himself and all the gothic paraphernalia of the genre.

The film is one of the rare examples in the German cinema of well-done black comedy.

d Richard Oswald *p* Gabriel Pascal *s* Heinz Goldberg, Eugen Szatmari *c* Heinrich Gaertner *lp* Paul Wegener, Harald Paulsen, Bert Reisfeld, Roma Bahn, Mary Parker, John Gottowt, Paul Henckels, Ilse Feurstenberg, Viktor de Kowa

White Zombie

(AMUSEMENT SECURITIES/UA) b/w 73min

This is one of the underground classics of horror. Made on a shoestring and atrociously acted, the film nonetheless emerges as a strangely poetic fairytale about a beastly zombie master and the beauty he lures to his lair and functions in a dislocated, dreamlike manner reminiscent of Carl Dreyer's **Vampyr** (1931). As pretty Madeline (Bellamy) arrives in Haiti to marry her fiancé (Harron), her experience is almost as disorienting as David Gray's at the start of *Vampyr*: a twilight coachride past a furtive burial ceremony at a crossroads, then a troubling encounter by the wayside with Murder Legendre (Lugosi), a sonorously satanic zombie master who supplies labour for the local mills and who inexplicably steals her scarf. Unknown to her, a fellow traveller (Frazer) has enlisted Legendre's evil powers in the hope of bending her beauty to his lecherous will, and both men eventually become locked in a deathly struggle for possession of her temporarily spiritless body, kept captive in Legendre's castle, a quaint Gustave Doré eyrie perched on a clifftop. Echoes of Dreyer surface even more tangibly during a visit to the mill where Legendre's zombie slaves ceaselessly labour to turn a huge wooden wheel, its creaks and groans carrying precisely the same ominous charge as the rumbling machinery of the flour mill in *Vampyr*. The most striking resemblance to Dreyer's film is, in fact, in the orchestration of sound: haunting snatches of music (including a spiritual) and long passages of silence, with dialogue serving less as communication than as incantation (and providing Lugosi with a line as memorable as his 'Children of the Night' speech in **Dracula** (1931), when Harron asks who the zombies are and is told, 'For you, my friend, they are the angels of death').

The film has been rather laboriously interpreted as a parable about American isolationist fears during the Depression, with Lugosi as an archetypal symbol of decadent Europe determined to enslave the unwary. But it really needs no such excuses, since its network of strange and perversely erotic images – the voodoo doll wrapped in Madeline's scarf and thrust into a candle flame as a vulture screeches; Madeline arriving for her wedding in a long white gown that uncannily resembles a shroud; the single poisoned rose offered like some bizarre love token in a bridal bouquet – weave a potent spell that is hardly broken by occasional miscalculations where Halperin tries to inject some conventional horror motifs (notably long-held closeups of Lugosi's supposedly mesmeric eyes).

This was in effect the first zombie film: the term came into common use only with the publication of William B. Seabrook's *The Magic Island* in 1929. Halperin's other horror films, **Supernatural** (1933) and **Revolt of the Zombies** (1936) are disappointingly conventional.

d Victor Halperin *p* Edward Halperin *s* Garnett Weston *c* Arthur Martinelli *lp* Bela Lugosi, Madge Bellamy, John Harron, Robert Frazer, Joseph Cawthorn, Clarence Muse

Right: *Bela Lugosi as Murder Legendre in the impressive* White Zombie.

1933

The Ghoul

(GAUMONT-BRITISH; GB) b/w 85(73)min

Karloff's first British film, an obvious attempt to cash in on the success of **The Mummy** (1932), has him play an Egyptologist who believes that if he can present a jewel called the eternal light to the god Anubis on the first full moon after his death, he will be granted eternal life. He dies but the jewel, taken with him to the tomb bandaged to his wrist, is stolen by his club-footed servant (Thesiger); and he returns from the dead (hollow-eyed but possibly having suffered only a form of catalepsy, as the script suggests to cover the illogicality) to seek both the talisman and revenge.

These first scenes have something of the Universal mood and manner, but the second half, saddled with some inappropriate comedy, rapidly degenerates into wild haunted-house antics as the dead man's heirs are assembled by a conniving lawyer (Hardwicke), various crooked elements join in the hunt for the jewel, and Karloff prowls round committing the odd murder

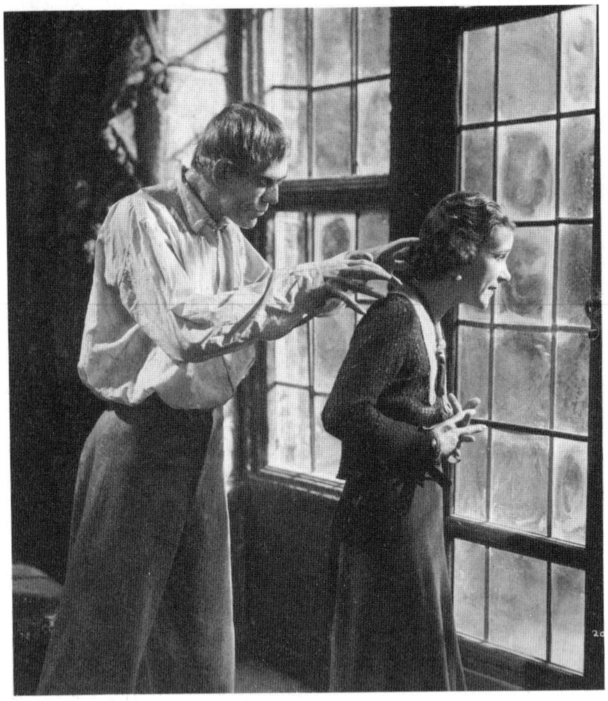

Left: *Boris Karloff menaces Kathleen Harrison in* The Ghoul.

before being destroyed by fire. The excellent cast also features Richardson, in his first screen appearance, as a phoney vicar.

The Frank King-Leonard Hines novel on which the script is based was remade farcically as **What a Carve-Up!** (1961).

d T. Hayes Hunter *s* Roland Pertwee, John Hastings Turner, Rupert Downing *c* Guenther Krampf *lp* Boris Karloff, Cedric Hardwicke, Ernest Thesiger, Dorothy Hyson, Anthony Bushell, Ralph Richardson, Kathleen Harrison

King Kong (RKO) b/w 100min

As a film, *King Kong* is barely average: crudely acted, little more than competently directed, and with (famed) special effects which vary wildly from the magnificent (Kong's first eruption from the jungle to stand framed in the vast stockade gateway) to the mediocre (Kong's destruction of the toy subway train, his stilted climb up the Empire State building). It can't even boast originality – there had been a screen history of prehistoric monsters just as huge and twice as ferocious. None, it is true, of whom it could be said ''Twas Beauty killed the Beast'. Yet what was Kong *really* going to do with his miniature Wray other than tear her limb from limb or eat her?

This is where the mythical dimension makes its appearance, and turns a recognizably humanoid, yet possibly Olympian ape – first cousin to the gods of ancient Greece and Rome – into the stuff of dreams and aspirations. As such, of course, he embodies a macho ideal on to whom erotic fantasies of sexual conquest can be projected, but equally importantly he's the symbol of subversive power, born of the Depression but still answering the eternal urge to rebellion. Was it merely a happy accident that made him a captive of a film crew, a spirit of non-conformism destined to be brought to heel and tamed by the dream palace, the super-tranquillizer whose palliatives everybody bought but perhaps, secretly, resented? The real – the mythical – tragedy of Kong isn't that he didn't get to make love to Wray, but that if even he fails to non-conform, then there is indeed cause for despair.

Derivatives (*Son of Kong*, 1933; *Mighty Joe Young*, 1949) and the latterday remake (*King Kong*, 1976) fail (and fall out of the scope of this work) precisely because they allow reality to destroy the myth.

d/p Merian C. Cooper, Ernest B. Schoedsack *s* James Creelman, Ruth Rose, Edgar Wallace *c* Edward Lindon *se* Willis O'Brien *lp* Fay Wray, Robert Armstrong, Bruce Cabot, Frank Reicher, Sam Hardy, Noble Johnson

La Llorona *aka* **The Ghost** *aka* **The Crying Woman**

(ECO FILMS; MEX) b/w 73min

It seems appropriate that the first major Mexican fantasy horror story should feature the peculiarly Hispanic character, la Llorona – the wailing maternal ghost mourning her dead child. The character figures in a great many Mexican movies, including *La Herencia de la Llorona* (1946), *El Grito de la Muerte* (1958), *La Llorona* (1959) and **La Maldición de la Llorona** (1961).

This ghost melodrama, co-scripted by de Fuentes, the first master of the Mexican cinema, is structured somewhat like D. W. Griffith's *Intolerance* (1916), partly to achieve the same effect of repetition throughout different historical epochs. Within the narrative framework, two other stories are recounted: the first from a book read by the father-in-law (Martinez) of the central character, Dr Cortes (Pereda); the second a story found in a book belonging to the person who murdered the father-in-law. Each tells the tale of a woman who commits suicide over the loss of a four-year-old child. The first, set in the distant past, has an abandoned woman, Ana (Lamar), kill herself and her bastard son as her faithful suitor (Pereda) and her fickle lover, Rodrigo Cortes (Marti) fight a duel which is interrupted by the sight of Ana's wailing ghost rising to the sky. The second story has *La Malinche* (Zea) curse the Cortes family for taking away her four-year-old child. She goes insane, commits suicide and rises to the heavens as a wailing ghost. The framing story starts with a birthday celebration, interrupted by a murder and a kidnap attempt, a chase and the shooting of the villain as he is about to knife the family's four-year-old son. The culprit is the boy's grandmother, wearing an enormous pseudo-Aztec ring, thereby closing the circle by referring back to Ana Xicotencatl and pre-Christian superstitions, which are seen to persist within the 'modern' Mexico exemplified by the surgeon and his wife (Zuri).

The movie is full of artistry and Cuban director Peon achieves spectacular spectral figures with slow camera movements and superimpositions. De Fuentes went on to make the best-known Mexican fantasy film of the period, **El Fantasma del Convento** (1934). Also worth noting is the contribution of Noriega Hope, one of Mexico's best-known silent film-makers.

d Ramón Peon *p* Juan Duque de Estrada *s* Guz Aguila, Carlos Noriega Hope, Fernando de Fuentes *c* Guillermo Baqueriza *lp* Ramón Pereda, Virginia Zuri, Carlos Orellana, Adriana Lamar, Alberto Marti, Paco Martinez, Maria Luisa Zea, Conchita Gentil Arcos, Esperanza del Real

King Kong *at bay.*

Allen Vincent and Glenda Farrell seek information in Mystery of the Wax Museum.

Murders in the Zoo (PAR) b/w 66(55)min

An unjustly neglected film which opens with Atwill leaving a man to die among the snakes in an Indian jungle after sewing his lips together according to 'symbolic Oriental custom'. An insanely jealous husband – small wonder, since his wife is played by Burke, the sultry panther-woman from **Island of Lost Souls** (1932) – he is later asked by Burke if her lover sent her any message before (as she thinks) leaving. 'He didn't say anything', Atwill replies with the sardonic aplomb of which he was a master. A wealthy sportsman-zoologist, he uses his curatorship of the zoo as a means of dispatching his wife's amorous fancies (including feeding one of them to the lions). The bulk of the film is concerned with his grisly and successful plot – while his daughter (Patrick) is romanced by the zoo's toxicologist (Scott) – to have Burke disappear into the crocodile pool while her latest lover is subjected to the bite of a black mamba.

Beautifully shot by Haller in Paramount's caressing low-key style, literately written (Wylie also co-scripted *Island of Lost Souls*) and very well acted, it has something of the same intense intellectual sadism as **The Most Dangerous Game** (1932). Even the comedy supplied by Ruggles, oddly getting top billing as the zoo's nervously befuddled press agent, is less intrusive than usual.

d Edward Sutherland *s* Philip Wylie, Seton I. Miller *c* Ernest Haller *lp* Charlie Ruggles, Lionel Atwill, Gail Patrick, Randolph Scott, John Lodge, Kathleen Burke

Mystery of the Wax Museum (WB) 78min

Although not the first horror film to be shot in the two-colour Technicolor process – that was **Doctor X** (1932), also directed by Curtiz – this was the first to be generally released in colour after its first run. Weighed down with the same laborious comedy elements and the same tendency to angle towards the whodunit, it is as much of a disappointment, for all its reputation, as *Doctor X*. Its reputation was no doubt largely the product of novelty: not just Technicolor but the fact that, unlike the other major horror movies of the early thirties, it was set in a recognizably contemporary, bustling New York (even if moving from Broadway into the wax museum was to move back into the timeless, placeless world of horror movies).

Atwill is splendid throughout as the sculptor forced to wear a waxen mask when his face is hideously scarred by fire, and who finds a substitute for sculpture in killing people, encasing them in wax, and turning them into exhibits. But the film really only comes alive in the climactic sequence of the fire, with the waxen figures twisting and writhing as though alive while the terrified Wray, first striking at Atwill's face and then clawing at it as she realizes it is a mask, reveals for the first time the monstrous, shrivelled thing beneath. A remake, **House of Wax** (1953), shifted the locale to Baltimore.

d Michael Curtiz *s* Don Mullaly, Carl Erickson *c* Ray Rennahan *lp* Lionel Atwill, Fay Wray, Glenda Farrell, Frank McHugh, Allen Vincent, Holmes Herbert

Night of Terror (COL) b/w 65min

A routine horror story with comedy elements, this has the wealthy uncle of a young scientist murdered, supposedly by a maniac at large. While the scientist (Maxwell) is buried underground to prove his claim that he has discovered a formula enabling humans to live without oxygen, further murders occur. It eventually transpires that the burial is a fake, enabling Maxwell to remove anyone who stands between him and his uncle's estate. Lugosi is stirred into the plot as a turbanned Hindu uttering trancelike statements, and Meeker plays the inventor of a method for raising the dead. The comedy elements, apart from the customary terrified black and a dim detective, include a gag ending where the killer returns from the dead and threatens to haunt the audience if they reveal the plot.

d Benjamin Stoloff *s* Beatrice Van, William Jacobs, Lester Nielson *c* Joseph A. Valentine *lp* Bela Lugosi, George Meeker, Tully Marshall, Bryant Washburn, Edwin Maxwell

Supernatural (PAR) b/w 64min

With a bigger budget than usual on the strength of his success with **White Zombie** (1932), Halperin here loses his flair under a bland glossy veneer. Apart from a fine opening montage and occasional eerie moments, this is a largely risible, erratically acted, creaky contrivance involving a fake spiritualist (Dinehart) given to Borgia-like antics with a poisoned ring to get rid of anyone who gets in his way. After betraying his associate (Osborne) to the police – a three-time murderess, she goes to the electric chair still thirsting for vengeance – Dinehart turns his mercenary attentions to a wealthy heiress (Lombard), claiming to have contacted the spirit of her recently dead brother. But Lombard's doctor (Warner), dabbling with theories that spirit transmigration is possible, happens to have obtained permission to experiment with Osborne's body; and in his laboratory, seized by the spirit of the dead murderess, Lombard attacks and kills the evil spiritualist. Her own personality then returns to ensure a happy ending with fiancé Scott.

d/co-p Victor Halperin *co-p* Edward Halperin *s* Harvey Thew, Brian Marlowe *c* Arthur Martinelli *lp* Carole Lombard, Randolph Scott, Vivienne Osborne, Alan Dinehart, H. B. Warner

Right: *Carole Lombard as voyeur in* Supernatural.

The Vampire Bat (MAJESTIC) b/w 67(60)min

One of the best of the independent films churned out to meet the new vogue for horror (most of which were more darkish thrillers than pure horror). The plot features a Central European village terrorized by a series of murders in which the bodies are found drained of blood. Although the police chief (Douglas) insists that the killer is human, the village has become infested with bats and superstitious fears run to vampires. The culprit is a mad doctor (Atwill) who has succeeded in creating life – a sponge-like substance which needs fresh blood so that it can thrive and grow. When the murders continue after the village idiot (Frye) has been staked as a vampire, largely because of his fondness for bats, Atwill over-reaches himself by menacing one of his assistants (Wray) who has stumbled on the truth. Seeing her danger, another assistant (Frazer), bound by hypnotism to obey orders, comes to his senses and kills both Atwill and himself, wrecking the laboratory in the process. The resemblance to **Frankenstein** (1931) – the presence of Frye, the torchlit pursuit by the incensed villagers – is hardly surprising since much of the film was shot at Universal on the village sets from *Frankenstein*, while the interiors are from **The Old Dark House** (1932). Even the dialogue comes close to pastiche, as when Atwill cries 'Think of it, I have lifted the veil! I have created life, wrested the secret of life from life'. But, backed by clever camerawork, the admirable quartet of Atwill, Wray, Frye and Douglas keep the film afloat.

d Frank Strayer *p* Phil Goldstone *s* Edward T. Lowe *c* Ira Morgan *lp* Lionel Atwill, Fay Wray, Melvyn Douglas, Dwight Frye, George E. Stone, Maude Eburne

1934

The Black Cat *aka* House of Doom *aka* The Vanishing Body (U) b/w 66min

This was the first and best of Universal's three co-starring vehicles for Karloff and Lugosi; it was followed by **The Raven** (1935) and a science fiction piece, *The Invisible Ray* (1936). A honeymoon couple stranded in Austria (Manners and Wells) are befriended by psychiatrist Dr Vitus Werdegast (Lugosi) and shelter in the opulent mansion built by the old friend he is visiting, architect Hjalmar Poelzig (Karloff), over the ruins of the fort of Marmaros where, during the First World War, thousands of men were betrayed into death by Karloff. Imprisoned as a result of his betrayal at the hands of Karloff, Lugosi has returned after 15 years in a Russian prison, seeking his wife, daughter and revenge, only to find that Karloff had married first his wife – now dead and displayed in a glass case that preserves her beauty – then his daughter. Realizing that Karloff, having killed his daughter, means to sacrifice Wells in a black mass, Lugosi accepts a wry challenge to play chess for her life. He loses the game but overpowers Karloff and proceeds to flay him alive. Attacked by mistake by Manners, Lugosi allows the young couple to escape, then blows the house, himself and Karloff to pieces.

Although the plot has nothing to do with Poe's story, and very little to do with cats except for a brief scene illustrating Lugosi's aelurophobia, *The Black Cat* is quintessential Poe in that it weaves an almost abstract web of anguish out of its all-pervasive sense of evil. Rejecting the straightforward Poe adaptation originally planned, Ulmer devised a new plotline – essentially a mortal duel conducted by two men beyond mortal concerns, one because he has reached the limits of suffering, the other because he has passed the limits of cruelty – inspired by the life and legend of Aleister Crowley, then very much in the news with the publication of Nina Hamnett's autobiography *Laughing Torso* in 1933 and Crowley's libel suit against her. One of the more notorious Crowley stories, explaining the unusual *frisson* attached to Lugosi's 'morbid fear of cats', concerned a black cat whose blood was drunk at a black mass; and Karloff's mansion, a Bauhaus glitter of steel, glass and marble, rising out of what had been the graveyard of thousands and poised precariously over a foundation relic of dynamite, is a brilliantly imaginative transposition of Crowley's Abbey of Thelema. 'I can still sense death in the air', Lugosi murmurs as he is shown through the mausoleum, down secret passages and spiral staircases, past glass cases containing embalmed bodies and walls designed as huge illuminated charts dating from the war years; and his apprehension is echoed by Mescall's stealthily prowling camera, which seems to be in the throes of a somnambulistic nightmare of terror.

By contemporary horror film standards almost nothing happens, yet the sense of evil grows almost tangible under the oppressive pall cast by sadism, satanism and necrophilia. Our first introduction to Karloff, superbly shot by Mescall through a gauze mosquito-net and with an hallucinating sense of slow motion as he rises from bed to greet his unexpected guests, already has the unmistakable suggestion – the stiff movements, the skintight black pyjamas, the sepulchral aspect of the four-poster – of walking death. Later Karloff, in a superb speech implying that both of them died morally in the incidents 15 years before and bringing all the *angst* of the First World War into play, defines the name of the game as a sort of euthanasian suicide pact: 'Are we not both the living dead? And now you come to me playing at being an avenging angel, childishly thirsting for my blood. We shall play a little game, Vitus. A game of death, if you like.' Strange, hypnotic, tormented and eliciting the best performances of their careers from Karloff and Lugosi, *The Black Cat* is one of the masterpieces of the genre.

Left: The Vampire Bat, *one of the earliest imitations of* Frankenstein *(1931)*.

The Ghost Walks, *a late addition to the cycle of Broadway-derived horror spoofs.*

David Manners, Jacqueline Wells and The Black Cat *in Edgar Ulmer's masterpiece.*

d/co-s Edgar G. Ulmer *p* E. M. Asher *co-s* Peter Ruic *c* John J. Mescall *lp* Boris Karloff, Bela Lugosi, David Manners, Jacqueline Wells (Julie Bishop), Lucille Lund

Dos Monjes *aka* **Two Monks**
(PROA FILMS; MEX) b/w 85min
Five months after his collaboration with de Fuentes on **El Fantasma del Convento** (1934), Bustillo Oro finished this effective follow-up, which was much praised by the surrealist poet André Breton. Two eternal triangle stories are told from within the neutral-neutered setting of a monastery. Xavier (Villatoro) recounts how his best friend, Juan (Urruchua) tried to steal his girl, Ana (Haller), and accidentally shot her. Then Juan narrates the same story from his point of view: he and Ana had been lovers but were separated until they met again in Xavier's house; although still in love with each other, they decided not to upset their friend and to separate again, but Xavier chances upon them and jumps to the wrong conclusion, grabs his pistol and accidentally shoots Ana. After the tragedy, both narrators became monks and the stories are recounted in the monastery's confessional. The film ends with the demented Xavier playing the organ and dying prey to hallucinations.

In each story, the sets mirror the subjectivity of the narrator with designs reminiscent of **Das Cabinet des Dr Caligari** (1919) or, the picture's more obvious antecedent, **Schatten** (1923). The director's interest in German expressionism – a preoccupation dating back to his early career as a theatre director in the artistically turbulent twenties in Mexico – dominates the film: in Xavier's story he is dressed in white and Juan in black, while in Juan's story this is reversed; décor and lighting are often non-realist and scenes are composed in tableaux, to take just a few examples. In spite of the conventionality of the melodrama, the slow pace and stilted dialogue, the film remains of interest, not least for its experimental approach to narrative. Not simply a precursor of Akutagawa and Kurosawa's *Rashomon* (1950), the movie's refusal to provide a stable position from which the 'truth' can be established finally propels the narrative on to a new level characterized by madness and music instead of sanity and speech when the image track, almost static up to that point, erupts into a frantic rhythm, edited by the director himself.

Bustillo Oro's subsequent work, such as the expressionist thriller *El Misterio del Rostro Palido* (1935), the epic *Nostradamus* (1936) and **El Hombre Sin Rostro** (1950), did not fulfil the promise shown here in his first sound film.

d/co-s Juan Bustillo Oro *p* San Vicente Brothers *co-s* José Manuel Cordero *c* Agustin Jimenez *lp* Magda Haller, Victor Urruchua, Carlos Villatoro, Emma Roldan, Manuel Noriega, Sofia Haller

El Fantasma del Convento *aka* **The Phantom of the Convent**
(PRODUCCIONES FESA; MEX) b/w 85min
De Fuentes, the first master of the Mexican cinema, shot this oppressive movie on location in the Teotzotlan monastery. The macabre and lyrical story can be read in two ways. Cristina (Roel), the wife of Eduardo (Villatoro), tries to seduce their friend, Alfonso (del Campo). One night, they lose their way and are guided by a mysterious stranger to an eerie monastery. Over a meal, the old Father Superior (Martinez) tells them the story of a monk who seduced a friend's wife: when he died, the monk could not find peace in death and returned to his cursed cell. Alfonso, about to give in to Cristina's advances, finds the fateful cell and enters it. The sinful monk's mummified corpse gestures towards a book dripping with blood and when the cadaver of Eduardo appears to him as well, Alfonso sinks into a delirium. When he wakes, the trio find out that the monastery has been a ruin for many years and the crypt with the mummified monk has become a tourist attraction. During a final meal in the spectral setting, Cristina accuses Alfonso of cowardice.

While the story can be understood as accusing women of being vessels of the devil, the visual aspects of the fantasy contrast the dessicated bodies of the monks and the monastery's ascetic blankness to the vibrant sensuality of the dark-haired Roel whose sexuality neither marriage, religion nor superstition can repress. Desire and repression are shown as two sides of the same coin. Repression is signified through the story's literary content and the Father Superior's tale which is spoken rather than shown, while desire disturbs and positively animates the movie's imagery. The entire picture, with its ghostly, self-flagellating monks, empty coffins and shadowy bats, bathes in an uncanny atmosphere, with the cell scene as the undoubted highpoint of the film. Although excellently shot, however, the story is rather slow-paced.

Co-scenarist Bustillo Oro went on to direct another classic monk story, **Dos Monjes** (1934).

d/co-s Fernando de Fuentes *p/co-s* Jorge Pezet *co-s* Juan Bustillo Oro *c* Ross Fisher *lp* Marta Roel, Carlos Villatoro, Enrique del Campo, Paco Martinez, José Rocha, Victorio Blanco

The Ghost Walks (INVINCIBLE) b/w 66(62)min
The usual homespun collection of storm effects, sliding panels, bumps in the night and mysterious prowlings as a Broadway producer (Carle) and playwright (Miljan) take refuge in an old, dark house after finding the road they are driving along (to the playwright's home) blocked by a fallen tree. Twist number one reveals that it was all a put-up job by the playwright, and that the terrors are from the new play he hopes to persuade (with the help of actor friends) the producer to stage. Twist number two (a bit much, this one) introduces a real escaped lunatic (Charters), panicking the actors and playwright but greeted with derision by the now determinedly sceptical producer. The standard mixture of comedy and terrors, *The Ghost Walks* is more competently staged than scripted.

d Frank Strayer *p* Maury M. Cohen *s* Charles S. Belden *c* M. A. Anderson *lp* John Miljan, June Collyer, Richard Carle, Spencer Charters, Johnny Arthur

1934

House of Mystery (MON) b/w 63min

Like **The Black Pearl** (1928), this belated addition to the horror spoof cycle of the late twenties (based on a play by Adam Hull Shirk), resorts to the hoary device of the curse of the violated Indian temple. Haunted by a ghostly creature long years after he killed a sacred Hindu temple ape to abscond with jewels and a pretty dancer, a crippled recluse (Clement) decides to heed the high priest's warning that wealth amassed from the jewels will bring only misfortune. Accordingly, he assembles the investment cartel claimants to his fortune for the usual old-dark-house mystery which include one murder during a seance, another when a gambler (Hayes) masquerades as the ghostly ape in the hope of stealing the jewels, and the final revelation that the whole thing was a plot by the old man to try to cheat fate. Ponderously directed by Nigh, who was also responsible for a totally unrecognizable remake called **The Ape** (1940), the film is not aided by distinctly unfunny comic relief from Lowry, a radio star making his only film appearance as a brash insurance salesman.

d William Nigh *p* Paul Malvern *s* Albert de Mond *c* Archie Stout *lp* Ed Lowry, Verna Hillie, John Sheehan, Clay Clement, Brandon Hurst, George (Gabby) Hayes

Maniac (ROADSHOW ATTRACTIONS) b/w 67min

This fascinating exploitation picture was made by Esper and Stadie, the Hollywood husband-and-wife team whose films – other titles include *Marihuana, Weed with Roots in Hell* (1936), *Narcotic* (1937) and *How to Undress in Front of Your Husband* (1937) – were shown at burlesque theatres and roadhouses rather than at regular theatres. Partly based on Edgar Allan Poe's *The Black Cat* and using clips from **Häxan** (1922) in superimposition to suggest madness, it has a truly awesome camp/movie-buff plot. Carpenter plays a mad doctor, a sibling Frankenstein who blackmails Woods, formerly a vaudeville impersonator (a useful accomplishment in pursuing nefarious projects), into helping him acquire the corpses he needs to pursue his dream of bringing the dead back to life. He succeeds, but is accidentally killed by Woods, who impersonates him in time to deal with a woman arriving for a consultation because her husband (Edwards) thinks he is the killer ape from Poe's *Murders in the Rue Morgue*. Taking a random stab at administering an injection, Woods sends the maddened husband screaming off to pursue and rape a young woman. Undeterred, he then decides to bring the dead Carpenter back to life to forestall possible charges of murder. Infuriated when interrupted by a black cat as he prepares to operate, he gouges out one of its eyes and hides Carpenter's body by walling it up in the cellar, only to be betrayed to the police (after other wild adventures) by the squeals of the cat bricked in with the body. Aside from the fact that it features little or no blood, the film is very much a precursor of what was to come, exploiting some mild nudity and offering several gleeful examples of 'bad taste', notably when Woods eats the eye he has plucked from the black cat with ghoulish relish. A curiosity more than anything else, it is abominably acted and distinctly poor in all technical departments.

d/p Dwain Esper *s* Hildegarde Stadie *c* William Thompson *lp* Bill Woods, Horace Carpenter, Ted Edwards, Phyllis Diller, Thea Ramsey, Jennie Dark

1935

The Black Room (COL) b/w 75(67)min

A heavily stylized period piece, more gothic melodrama than pure horror movie, *The Black Room* features Karloff as twin Czech brothers plagued by a curse which foretells that, just as the family began with an elder twin killing the younger, so it will end. Separated from his brother for fear of fulfilling the curse, Anton only returns when Gregor reports that he has walled up the black room where the 'murder' is to take place. In fact, Gregor uses the black room to dispose of village wenches once they have served his debaucheries. Since suspicion is now rife among the villagers, Gregor kills the well-liked Anton, announces his renunciation of the estate and departure and assumes the identity of his brother (mimicking his paralysed arm). After further villainies involving his attempts to secure an unwilling bride (Marsh), he is attacked by Anton's faithful mastiff and falls on to a dagger still clutched by the remains of his dead brother in the black room, who thus fulfils the curse. One superb sequence has Marsh's father (Hall) discover the masquerade when he sees in a mirror that Gregor is using his supposedly paralysed arm. His own murder follows immediately, off-screen to maintain the elliptical mood.

Elsewhere Neill's direction is solid, if a little heavy-handed, and the strikingly handsome sets tend to be occupied by too many 'rhubarbing' villagers. But Karloff's performance is outstanding throughout, particularly in the subtle mime sequence in which the bad twin carefully rehearses his transformation into the brother he has killed.

d Roy William Neill *p* Robert North *s* Henry Myers, Arthur Strawn *c* Al Siegler *lp* Boris Karloff, Marian Marsh, Robert Allen, Katherine de Mille, Thurston Hall

The Bride of Frankenstein (U) b/w 80min

By late 1933, the sequel for which Universal had been agitating ever since the returns started coming in on **Frankenstein** (1931) had been definitely slated as a vehicle for Karloff and Lugosi to follow **The Black Cat** (1934), with Lugosi in a mad-doctor role that eventually became Thesiger's Dr Praetorius; the title had been changed from *The Return of Frankenstein* to *Frankenstein Lives Again*; and R. C. Sherriff had turned down an invitation to work on the script ('It was dreadful stuff. I should have spent the summer writing pulp, and been ashamed of every page I wrote') after completing *One More River* (1934). Whale himself, unable to prevaricate any longer, had resigned himself to the inevitable in the hope that he could wring a little more mileage out of the characters by going back to Mary Shelley's storyline and her conception of Frankenstein's creature as more sinned against than sinning. Although the horrendous Dr Praetorius emerges as the real villain of the piece and Karloff's monster is shown in a more sympathetic light than in *Frankenstein*, this point was originally made clearer by scenes (cut from the release prints) in which Dr

Below: *Boris Karloff as the inhabitant of* The Black Room.

Elsa Lanchester, weirdly compelling as The Bride of Frankenstein.

Praetorius' demented bodysnatching assistant Karl (Frye) was shown committing a series of gruesome murders for which the monster was blamed and ruthlessly hunted down. Another bizarre sequence involving Frye was also deleted, perhaps because it was felt that Praetorius was already quite perverse enough: introducing Frankenstein to his assistant, Praetorius cheerfully explained that he keeps his hold on Karl because of the latter's terror after an incident in which Karl unwittingly bodysnatched a cataleptic woman whom he, Praetorius, dissected alive before being alerted to the situation by the poor lady's screams.

Matching the black humour with which Whale kept his boredom at bay, and excelling even his makeup job for the monster, Jack Pierce created a weirdly compelling figure out of the bride simply by including grisly reminders of her origins in the shroudlike floor-length robe (designed to conceal the huge shoe-lifts Lanchester wore), the mummy-wrapped hands and arms, and the hair frizzed out in electric shock and shot through with lightning streaks of silver. Since the monster had been burned alive in the windmill at the end of *Frankenstein*, Pierce also took the trouble to resuscitate him with his hair singed off, and one side of his face and a hand burned by the fire: a meticulous piece of craftmanship that was rather undercut by the fact that Universal, concurrently re-releasing *Frankenstein* and touchingly worried is case audiences wondered how the monster came to be alive, excized the final scene in the burning windmill from the new prints.

As it finally and superbly emerged, preceded by a prologue in which Byron and the Shelleys discuss the story – a drawing-room charade which points to the comedy of manners to come – *The Bride of Frankenstein* is closer in mood the **The Old Dark House** (1932) than to *Frankenstein*. One of its best sequences, managing the lightning shifts in tone with amazing skill, is the one where the monster, driven by vengeful hunters from his refuge and from the only person who never shrank from him in horror – the blind hermit who teaches him to speak, smoke, love music and savour the meaning of the word friendship – takes shelter in a dank and dusty crypt. Seeing the body of a beautiful young girl lying in a coffin, he advances and queries 'Friend?' with heartrending hopefulness. A moment later he has to hide as Dr Praetorius, arriving on a graverobbing expedition, settles down to picnic on the coffin and to react with impeccable *savoir faire* as the monster emerges threateningly from the shadows. 'Oh, I thought I was alone,' he says, 'Good evening! Have a cigar? It's my only weakness'. It is this encounter which provides the main impetus for the plot, since Praetorius, having promised to make the monster a mate, does so only with the enforced aid of Frankenstein. Characteristically, however, it is a social lapse that fuels the climax – catching her first sight of her intended, the bride reacts with an appalled hiss – in which the disillusioned monster goes on another rampage and causes a conflagration in which he, Praetorius and the bride all perish.

d James Whale *p* Carl Laemmle Jnr *c* John Balderston, William Hurlbut *c* John J. Mescall *lp* Boris Karloff, Colin Clive, Elsa Lanchester, Ernest Thesiger, Valerie Hobson, Dwight Frye

Condemned to Live (INVINCIBLE) b/w 65min

Like Strayer's **The Vampire Bat** (1933), this is one of the better independents of the period, unusual in attempting to deal seriously and sympathetically with vampirism. Although he doesn't realize it, a kindly professor (Morgan) is the vampiric werewolf terrorizing a Central European village, watchfully shadowed by his devoted hunchback servant (Auer) and spirited away before his guilt can be discovered. Morgan's friend, Dr Bizet (Cordoba), discovers that the professor's mother was bitten by a giant bat in Africa just before giving birth and that a local doctor had suspected vampiric tendencies in the child, and Cordoba is just in time to prevent the professor from attacking his fiancée (Doyle). Also trying to intervene and mistaken for the killer, the hunchback flees with a mob of enraged villagers in pursuit and, aware of the truth, the despairing professor saves the hunchback by confessing his guilt, then leaps to his death, followed by the heartbroken hunchback.

The prenatal influence (rather clumsily established in a prologue) is not particularly convincing in itself, but is more persuasively allied to a discreet sexual motif probably suggested by **Dr Jekyll and Mr Hyde** (1932). A staid middle-aged man, the professor is engaged to a much younger woman who has only agreed to the marriage to please her dying father, and who moreover loves a young man her own age (Gleason). Realizing this, Cordoba promptly advises his friend to abandon the marriage: the implication is inescapable that the professor's vampiric tendencies are connected to his belatedly aroused sexual instincts. Too poverty-stricken to afford special effects (though looking quite presentable since it employed Universal sets, notably from **The Bride of Frankenstein**, 1935), the film sensibly settles for excellent camerawork, dialogue and performances (Morgan in particular).

d Frank Strayer *p* Maury M. Cohen *s* Karen DeWolf *c* M. A. Anderson *lp* Ralph Morgan, Maxine Doyle, Mischa Auer, Russell Gleason, Pedro de Cordoba

The Crime of Dr Crespi (REP) b/w 63min

Stroheim's first horror movie, following his schizophrenic ventriloquist in *The Great Gabbo* (1930), this is a full-blooded entry in the mad-doctor stakes. Although publicized as a Republic production and referred to by its star as 'The Crime of Republic', it was actually shot in New York by the failing Liberty Pictures, taken over when Herbert J. Yates established Republic. Nominally based on Edgar Allan Poe's story *The Premature Burial*, it features Stroheim as a distinguished surgeon who harbours a mad thirst for revenge against the man

Left: *A poster for* The Crime of Dr Crespi.

(Bohn) who married the woman he loves (Russell). His chance comes when he is required to operate on Bohn, who seemingly dies during surgery. Actually, Stroheim has administered a drug to induce a cataleptic trance, and revels in his revenge as his victim is buried alive, only to be dug up by two suspicious colleagues (Frye and Guilfoyle) and then wander the hospital as a ghostly, terror-maddened figure eventually driving Stroheim to suicide. Cheap, lurid and hesitantly directed, it nevertheless can boast moody camerawork and excellent supporting performances to counterbalance Stroheim's over-the-top portrayal of lecherous sadism. Nice details abound (Stroheim's desk, for example, is graced by the skeleton of a dwarf), and there is one superbly ghoulish sequence in which Stroheim pays a nocturnal visit to the morgue to taunt Bohn with the horrible fate that awaits him. Poe's story was filmed again in 1961.

d/p John H. Auer *s* Lewis Graham, Edwin Olmstead *c* Larry Williams *lp* Erich von Stroheim, Dwight Frye, Paul Guilfoyle, John Bohn, Harriett Russell, Edward Van Sloan

The Great Impersonation (U) b/w 67min

The second of the three film versions of the E. Phillips Oppenheim espionage thriller set largely in an old dark house where a tremulous wife (Hobson) wonders if her husband is really his double, a dastardly German spy (Lowe in a dual role), this is also the best. Although the film is uncomfortably complacent in its attitudes (to both the aristocratic hero and the Hunnish spy), sets from **Frankenstein** (1931) and **The Old Dark House** (1932) are put to good use, and there is some conventional creepy fun to be had from Dale as the inevitable sinister housekeeper and Frye as a maniac who haunts the Black Bog with blood-curdling screams. The other two versions, filmed under the same title in 1921 and 1942, were much more staid.

d Alan Crosland *p* Carl Laemmle Jnr *s* Frank Wead, Eva Greene *c* Milton Krasner *lp* Edmund Lowe, Valerie Hobson, Frank Reicher, Brandon Hurst, Spring Byington, Dwight Frye, Esther Dale

Mad Love *aka* **The Hands of Orlac**

(MGM) b/w 86(67)min

This is by far the best of the many versions and variants of Maurice Renard's novel *Les Mains d'Orlac*, although Freund, a master behind the camera, is no more at ease directing than he was with **The Mummy** (1932). The film, however, boasts an astounding performance from Lorre in his first American role as the macabre Dr Gogol, so madly infatuated with the wife (Drake) of a celebrated concert pianist (Clive), that when the latter's hands are mutilated in a train wreak, he conceives a diabolical plan to graft the hands of a knife-thrower guillotined for murder (Brophy). That there is something twisted behind the shaven head and dead face is indicated by an opening sequence in which, enraptured, Lorre watches a Grand Guignol stage performance in which Drake plays a faithless wife put to the torture, and later turns her into a waxwork image to be worshipped, serenaded on the piano, and read poetry to in the privacy of his own weird home.

The sense here of a mind fascinated by sadism yet capable of tenderness is accentuated by the paradoxical contrast between motives in the sequence where Lorre performs the grafting operation on Clive: on the one hand, Lorre's fiendish purpose, on the other the professional skill and concern he displays. But increasingly deranged by his mad love, Lorre proceeds to what must be one of the most macabre impersonations in all cinema when, in the hope of driving Clive (already unhinged by the knife-throwing propensity of his hands) completely mad, he appears muffled up to the eyes (even they are behind dark glasses) and then does a terrifying striptease to reveal the metal gauntlets (replacing his amputated hands) and steel neck-brace

Peter Lorre makes love to Frances Drake in the sublime Mad Love.

Above: *Bela Lugosi and Carol Borland in the imaginative* Mark of the Vampire.

(holding on his guillotined head) that identify him as the executed murderer. If the ending is by contrast both conventional and perfunctory (about to strangle Drake, Lorre is nailed by Clive's new knife-throwing skills), it is just one of the several flaws – along with the uncertainties in pacing and clumsy comic relief from Healy's reporter – that demonstrate that Freund did not really have the instincts of a director. *Mad Love* is a remarkable film all the same.

d Karl Freund *p* John W. Considine Jnr *s* P. J. Wolfson, Guy Endore, John L. Balderston *c* Chester Lyons, Gregg Toland *lp* Peter Lorre, Frances Drake, Colin Clive, Ted Healy, Edward Brophy, Isabel Jewell

Mark of the Vampire (MGM) b/w 60min
This remake of **London After Midnight** (1927) features Atwill as the police inspector and Barrymore as the hypnotist who solve a murder by convincing the assembled suspects that vampires (actually a troupe of actors led by Lugosi) are at work. The original was made at the height of the vogue for horror spoofs. Here, despite the obligatory light relief involving panicky servants which marred so many films of the period, and despite the last shot of the chief vampire revealed in all his actor-managerial vainglory, comic disbelief is never allowed to gain a foothold.

The film begins *in medias res*, with a stunningly shot sequence in which the camera pans down a church from the cross on its steeple, prowls through a sinister gypsy encampment, picks up an old crone wandering through the pale shadows of a graveyard as a carriage rattles by, an owl hoots, and, already unnerved, she flees in panic from the harmless yet diabolically twisted gravedigger's fork that appears to be clutching her arm in a mortal embrace. From this point on, remarkably well acted in a muted mood, the film goes from strength to strength as Wong Howe's photography caressingly illuminates the horrendously beautiful images of a moon-faced vampire (Borland) strolling through the pallid night with features as blank as snow, or the dead man who is actually an actor (Herbert) sitting at a cobweb-shrouded organ funereally entertaining an audience of vampires, while assorted bats, rats and unidentifiable crawling creatures lend their Murnau-esque presence. Even after the revelation that we are watching a mundane detective story rather than supernatural horrors, the atmosphere continues strange and haunting as the hypnotized killer (Hersholt) relives his crime. So cleverly delayed is this revelation, in fact, that one is left still busily working out its implications while the killer is arrested and the chief vampire removes his makeup and still wondering how actors could have managed the scene where Borland wanders the night accompanied by a fluttering bat, or indeed the one in which she is airborne on her wings. No doubt at least partly because it was apparently extensively cut before release, *Mark of the Vampire* satisfies in very much the same way as *La Nuit du Carrefour* (1932), which remains a nocturnal mystery even after Pierre Renoir's Inspector Maigret has proudly announced his solution.

d Tod Browning *p* E. J. Mannix *s* Guy Endore, Bernard Schubert *c* James Wong Howe *lp* Bela Lugosi, Lionel Barrymore, Elizabeth Allan, Jean Hersholt, Lionel Atwill, Carol Borland, Donald Meek

Ouanga *aka* **Drums of the Jungle** *aka* **Crime of Voodoo** (TERWILLIGER) b/w 63min
Terwilliger, once a screenwriter for D. W. Griffith, tried to film this voodoo tale in Haiti with authentic participants, but was forced to retreat to Jamaica by unrest and the delivery of an ouanga (token of a voodoo curse) as soon as his purpose was made known. Washington, the black girl who attempted to pass for white in *Imitation of Life* (1933), plays a voodoo priestess whose power (supplemented by hypnotism and human sacrifice) is insufficient to bend the will of the white man she loves (Leonard). In revenge she has zombie helpers kidnap Leonard's fiancée (Paxton) and take her to the hills for a voodoo sacrifice which Leonard manages to circumvent. An all-black remake, *Pocomania* (1939), also filmed in Jamaica, was directed by Arthur Leonard with a reworked script (also by Terwilliger) in which the priestess aims her malice at her half-sister so as to gain control of her estate. Both versions are pretty rough and ready, but the remake is further burdened with a lengthy travelogue opening.

d/p/s George Terwilliger *c* Carl Berger *lp* Fredi Washington, Sheldon Leonard, Philip Brandon, Marie Paxton, Winifred Harris

The Raven (U) b/w 62min
The second of Universal's trio of co-starring vehicles for Karloff and Lugosi, *The Raven* is less polished than **The Black Cat** (1934). Lugosi is the brilliant surgeon who goes berserk when frustrated in his passion for a beautiful young dancer (Ware) on whom he is persuaded to operate when she is scarred in a crash. What makes the film out of the ordinary is Lugosi's fanatical devotion to Poe, strikingly introduced when his first appearance is heralded by the shadow of a raven on the wall while his off-screen voice sonorously intones Poe's poem. A museum representative has come to inquire about the possibility of acquiring his Poe collection, remarking – as Lugosi gloatingly boasts that he has built several of the torture chambers imagined by Poe – 'What a curious hobby'. 'It's more than a hobby,' Lugosi retorts, his ominous tone underscored by a lingering closeup of his supposedly hypnotic eyes (the shot that became such a cliché in early Lugosi films). The film achieves an enjoyable delirium as Lugosi (who also has fits of

organ-playing) brings Poe's murderous pendulum, perambulating room and torture chamber with shrinking walls into play in pursuit of the heroine, gleefully chuckling at his seeming moment of triumph, 'What torture, what delicious torture ... Poe, you are avenged!'

If Lugosi's melodramatic delivery at times tends to bring the film perilously close to parody, the balance is restored by Karloff's soberly malevolent performance as the shaggy-bearded killer who comes to plead with Lugosi to transform his appearance by plastic surgery ('Maybe if a man looks ugly he does ugly things'), and whom Lugosi tricks into doing his bidding ('Torture and murder, things like that' he airily explains) by making him even uglier. A superb scene has Lugosi confront Karloff with his even more hideous post-surgical appearance in an octagonal room whose walls are mirrors which Karloff smashes, snarling with the same anguished rage as his Frankenstein monster. Often criticized as self-parodic, with Lugosi's 'Poe, you are avenged!' coming in for particular mockery as pure self-indulgence, *The Raven* is in fact about a peculiarly twisted concept of revenge. Remarkably well scripted, it very nearly brings off its notion that, in pursuing the heroine so monomaniacally, Lugosi's Dr Vollin is trying to demonstrate that while Poe's potential for greatness was destroyed by the lost Elenore ('When a man is denied his great love, he goes mad'), he himself will achieve that greatness.

d Louis Friedlander (Lew Landers) *p* David Diamond *s* David Boehm, Jim Tully *c* Charles Stumar *lp* Bela Lugosi, Boris Karloff, Irene Ware, Lester Matthews, Samuel S. Hinds

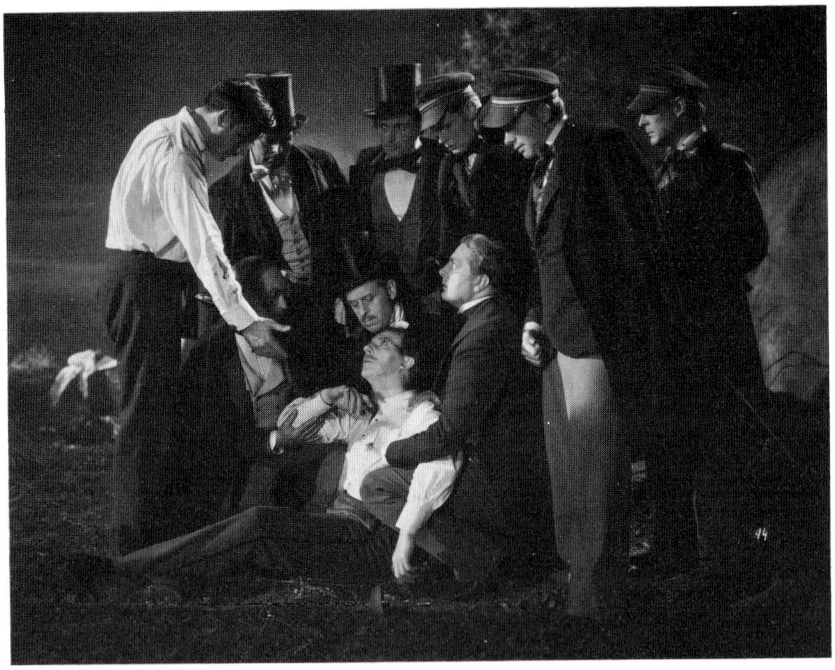

The duel scene from the third version of Der Student von Prag, *directed by Arthur Robison.*

Der Student von Prag *aka* The Student of Prague

(CINE ALLIANZ TONFILM; G) b/w 86min

The third, last and somewhat anachronistic, version of Hanns Heinz Ewers' adaptation of E. T. A. Hoffmann's story *Sylvesternacht*. It tells of Balduin (Wohlbrueck) who sells his mirror image to the mysterious Scapinelli (Loos) and finds himself persecuted by his double who acts out his unconscious desires. Henrik Galeen's 1926 version of the story achieved its uncanny intensity through Veidt's acting and the use of sombrely romantic imagery. Robison, who died during shooting, here tried to match the atmosphere he had created in his best work, **Schatten** (1923), but failed, partly because the script develops too slowly and is too wordy, undermining the necessary dreamlike qualities. In addition, the enterprise was so out of step with the times that even on its release it was seen as a throwback to the twenties. A year later, in context of the Nazi arianization campaign, it was banned, largely because Robison was an American émigré.

Wohlbrueck, a fine actor, left Germany soon afterwards and enjoyed a remarkable career under the name Walbrook, starring in *Gaslight* (1939), a number of Michael Powell movies and Max Ophuls' *La Ronde* (1950). Here, however, the limelight is stolen by his female co-star, Wieck, best known today for her role as the cool sensuous teacher in *Maedchen in Uniform* (1931).

d/co-s Arthur Robison *p* Fritz Klotzsch *co-s* Hans Kyser *c* Bruno Mondi *lp* Anton Wohlbrueck, Dorothea Wieck, Theodor Loos, Erich Fiedler, Edna Greiff, Volker von Collande, Karl Hellmer, Fritz Genschow, Elsa Wagner

Left: *Bela Lugosi with friend in* The Raven.

The Werewolf of London (U) b/w 75min

Universal's first attempt at lycanthropy since 1913 offers two werewolves for the price of one. Though clumsily directed by Walker (his only horror movie), it is lifted out of the rut by Oland's superbly sinister performance as the oriental werewolf who bites Hull, a botanist exploring Tibet in search of a rare flower which blooms only at midnight. With London subsequently terrorized by a series of brutal murders, a mortal struggle develops between the two werewolves for possession of the specimen of *Marifasa lupina* – the only known antidote to lycanthropy – which Hull brought back from Tibet and is now nursing in his laboratory. Oland is killed by Hull, who is shot by the police as he attacks his beloved wife (Hobson). Hull manages the terrors of approaching transformation quite well, but is both dull and unsympathetic as the botanist while as the werewolf, despite an intelligent makeup job by Jack Pierce which leaves his face almost as naked as Boris Karloff's in **Frankenstein** (1931), he looks more eccentric than frightening.

When Universal returned to the werewolf theme in 1941 with **The Wolf Man**, they fleshed out the legend with gypsy curses and silver bullets. If the wolf-man has remained the dullest of Universal's monsters, it was largely an accident of birth. Guy Endore's superb novel, *The Werewolf of Paris*, was published in 1933. Endore was snapped up as a screenwriter by MGM and Universal rushed to get its own werewolf on to the screen. Endore made his début as co-scriptwriter of **Mark of**

Right: *Gloria Holden in the marvellous* Dracula's Daughter.

the Vampire (1935). It was left to Hammer Films to concoct a much more persuasive werewolf myth for **The Curse of the Werewolf** (1960) by reverting to Endore's view of the process whereby the admixture of degenerate cruelty and spiritual aspiration in mankind's history combines to produce a creature (a baby born on Christmas Eve, so the legend goes, will be born a werewolf) in whom the forces of good and evil are locked in battle. In all other respects, however, the Hammer film is a travesty of Endore's novel. It does not reach back to the Middle Ages to show the start of the evolution when, because of a feud between two baronial families, a man is kept incarcerated and fed only on raw meat until, when he finally escapes, he has become part animal. It does not trace the complex interaction between this brutish instinct (or its descendants over the years) and the charitable impulses it encounters, until out of the original man-wolf is born a wolf-man. Nor, most unforgivably, does it show how one such lycanthrope grows up to be a medical student during the terrible year of 1870 in Paris when, with the besieging Prussians shelling the city, the Commune indulging in wholesale slaughter of political enemies, and Versailles exacting revenge with equal indiscrimination, the starving, disease-ridden populace divided its time between eating rats, denouncing friends, and committing unspeakable crimes. Bringing out all the overtones of diabolism, cannibalism and sexual perversion inherent in the werewolf myth, Endore also asks the very pertinent question: what price one certified lycanthrope in a society where lycanthropic behaviour is the norm?

d Stuart Walker *p* Stanley Bergerman *s* Robert Harris *c* Charles Stumar *lp* Henry Hull, Warner Oland, Valerie Hobson, Spring Byington, Lester Matthews, Zeffie Tilbury

1936

El Baúl Macabro *aka* The Macabre Trunk

(PRODUCCION PEZET; MEX) b/w 77min

Pereda, the surgeon-hero of **La Llorona** (1933), repeated his medical role in this awkward variation on **Frankenstein** (1931), which anticipates Jesús Franco's **Gritos en la Noche** (1962). Dr del Vialle is the mad scientist who kills young women and uses their blood to keep his wife (Fernandez) alive. The picture's most interesting and, for the period, daring images are those showing Fernandez's lovely body lying on the surgeon's table, naked except for a sheet which covers her to the shoulders.

The Werewolf of London, *Universal's first essay in lycanthropy of the sound era.*

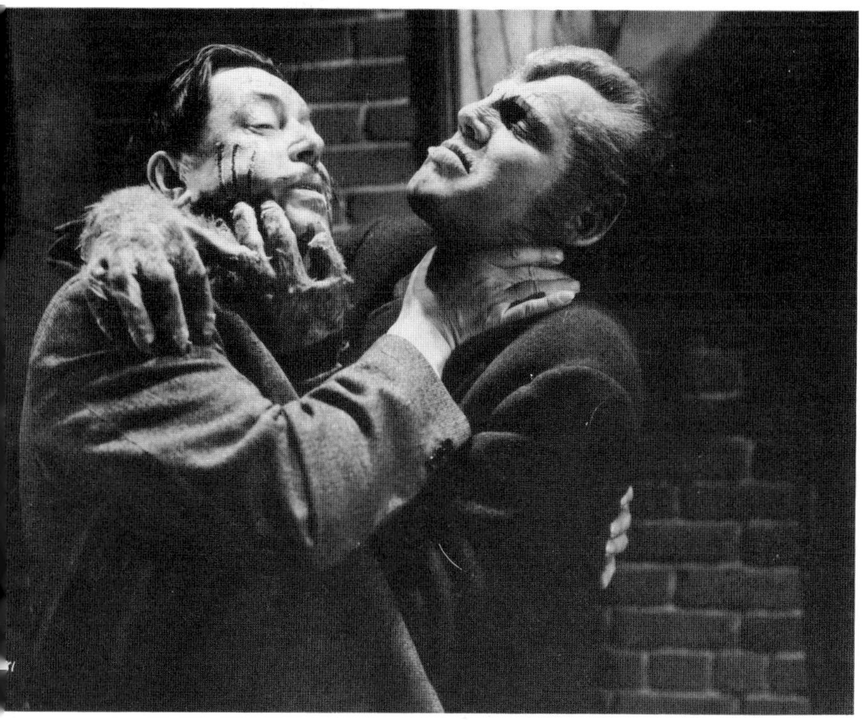

The scenarist Dada, who had just finished his only directorial effort (*Tres la Reja*, 1936), is best remembered for littering the Mexican cinema with banal songs in even more banal melodramas and Zacarias also contributed musical dramas, often starring Pereda, to Mexico's early sound cinema. Although he achieved some notoriety by introducing Maria Felix to the screen in *El Peñon de las Animas* (1942), Zacarias remained an undistinguished professional. Cardona became one of the more prolific directors of fantasy films, including **La Mujer Sin Cabeza** (1943), *El Museo del Crimen* (1944) and a new version of *La Llorona* (1959).

d/co-s Miguel Zacarias *p* Jorge Pezet *co-s* M. Dada, Alejandro Galindo *c* Alex Phillips *lp* Esther Fernandez, Ramón Pereda, René Cardona, Carlos Lopez (Chaflan), Manuel Noriega, Enrique Gonce, Ruperto Batiz, Juanita Castro

Dracula's Daughter (U) b/w 72min

Curiously neglected, perhaps because it had no stars, this first sequel to **Dracula** (1931) – based on Bram Stoker's story *Dracula's Guest* – is in many ways the better film, though obviously made on an extremely low budget. Picking up exactly where *Dracula* left off, it has the police arrive at Carfax Abbey, find Van Helsing (Sloan again) with the bodies of Dracula and Renfield, and arrest him for murder. A strange woman in black (Holden) appears and, after hypnotizing the police guarding it, removes Dracula's body. In a lonely forest, holding a crucifix and intoning an exorcism, she consigns her father's body to the flames. As Dracula's daughter condemned to the nocturnal agitations of a vampire, she yearns to be free, and confides her problem to Dr Garth (Kruger), a sympathetic psychologist who advises her that she must confront her problem if she wishes to be free of it.

After this slow, moody, beautifully shot – by Robinson – and acted – in an extraordinarily effective low-key tone – first impressive part, the film begins to stutter a little. It never, however, falls apart completely and stills boasts at least one remarkable scene in which, determined to test her resolve to resist, Holden has her slavishly devoted retainer (Pichel) bring her a model to pose for her. The erotic undertones as she asks the girl (Grey) to lower her shoulder straps for a head-and-shoulders portrait – and almost loses control, whereupon the camera cuts to a grinning mask on the wall – are far more subtly expressive than the explicit lesbian nudges offered in **Et Mourir de Plaisir** (1960) and the films that followed in its wake. Even the flurry of action towards the end – acknowledging the impossibility of cure but in love with Kruger, she tries to force him to go to Transylvania with her by kidnapping his fiancée Churchill – contrives to maintain the mood of bleak and hopeless desperation that only ends when she finally sacrifices herself to save the man she loves from death at hands of the jealous Pichel.

d Lambert Hillyer *p* E. M. Asher *s* Garrett Fort *c* George Robinson *lp* Otto Kruger, Gloria Holden, Marguerite Churchill, Edward Van Sloan, Irving Pichel, Nan Grey

A Face in the Fog (VICTORY) b/w 66 min
This low-budget chiller which looks suspiciously like a remake of **The Last Warning** (1929), on which Hill served as associate director, is credited as being adapted from a short story by Peter B. Kyne. A mad hunchback known as the Fiend is haunting the theatre, terrorizing the cast of the play being performed there (engagingly titled 'Satan's Bride'). With several deaths already from some mysteriously untraceable cause, a drama critic (Collyer) is saved from the Fiend's attention by a reporter (Hughes) who has indiscreetly intimated in print that she knows who the killer is. She doesn't but after one arrest (proven false by another murder) and a brush with a suspect hunchback, Hughes inadvertently establishes that the Fiend is a vengeful playwright (Gray) whose brother had died in a theatre fire during a show staged by the same producers ten years before. His murders had been committed with bullets of frozen poison. This usual ramshackle Katzman production includes the usual comic relief (a blundering photographer played by St John) but – oddly – no fog.

d Robert Hill *p* Sam Katzman *s* Al Martin *c* Bill Hyer *lp* June Collyer, Lloyd Hughes, Lawrence Gray, Jack Mulhall, Al St John

Faehrmann Maria *aka* **Ferryboat Woman Maria** *aka* **Death and the Maiden**
(PALLAS FILM; G) b/w 97(85)min
This is an enchanting ghost story based on a Nordic legend also alluded to in Carl Dreyer's **Vampyr** (1931) and featuring the same female star, the inexpressive Schmitz with the perversely lustful smile. Using sinister forestscapes in the night with spectral, white-faced riders in black capes pursuing a man claimed by Death and hailing a ferryboat from the other side of the river, Wisbar's movie often recalls the atmospheres evoked in F. W. Murnau's **Nosferatu** (1921). In the end, Maria (Schmitz), who operates the ferryboat, falls in love with the horsemen's prey and entices Death into a swamp where he slowly sinks into the mire. Shortly after finishing this picture, his greatest achievement, Wisbar emigrated to the United States where he remade the story as **Strangler of the Swamp** (1946).

d/co-s Frank Wisbar *co-s* Hans Jeurgen Nierentz *c* Franz Weihmayr *lp* Sybille Schmitz, Peter Voss, Aribert Mog, Carl de Vogt, Karl Platen, Eduard Wenck

Golem *aka* **Le Golem** *aka* **The Golem** *aka* **The Legend of Prague** *aka* **The Man of Stone**
(BARRANDOV/METROPOLIS; CZECH, FR) b/w 100(83)min
One of the most striking features of Paul Wegener's performance as the monster of clay in **Der Golem** (1920) is that – as with Boris Karloff in **Frankenstein** (1931) – his massively impassive face is belied by extraordinarily expressive eyes. In contrast, Duvivier's golem (Hart) looks like a well-fed wrestler in a rubber suit with a permanent scowl on his deep-tanned face, and expresses precisely nothing beyond his tackily conventional monsterhood. Moreover, although Duvivier's version of the Jewish folk tale makes perfunctory gestures towards re-creating the bizarre huddle of twisted roofs and canted walls designed by Hans Poelzig for the ghetto scenes in *Der Golem*, he is really more concerned with the vastly opulent palace sets which look as though they might have been intended for a version of *Quo Vadis?* (an impression fuelled by the lions waiting, as a change from their usual Christian dead, for Jewish martyrs), and in which much play is made of a 'sophisticated' subplot providing the excuse for some highly inappropriate romantic comedy. To the film's credit is some stylish camerawork. Genuine inspiration, however, is apparent only in Baur's superb performance as the mad Emperor Rudolph II, a man driven by the terrors of a solitude in which he fears constantly for his life to commit unspeakable cruelties that clearly amaze his childlike soul (and to combat which the golem is brought back to life in the ghetto). There is also one brilliant sequence in which, goaded by his uncontrollable terror, Baur sets off alone on a nocturnal odyssey through shadowy corridors and echoing halls, intent on destroying the golem but instead coming face to face with his nightmare, shyly confiding his terrible loneliness to someone who will at last listen: 'You should understand that; like me you're half-man and half-spectre. Just make a small sign and I'll know you're my friend.'

d/co-s Julien Duvivier *p* Charles Philippe *co-s* André-Paul Antoine *c* Václav Vich, Jan Stallich *lp* Harry Baur, Germaine Dussey, Roger Karl, Ferdinand Hart, Jany Holt, Charles Dorat

Mummy's Boys (RKO) b/w 68min
This is a dire attempt to parody **The Mummy** (1932), with Wheeler and Woolsey on an expedition to return stolen treasures to the Pharaoh Maritime's tomb, since a curse has destroyed the archaeologists who removed them. Even the perambulating mummy turns out to be a fake, and a banal murderer is responsible.

d Fred Guiol *p* Samuel J. Briskin *s* Jack Townley, Philip G. Epstein, Charles Roberts *c* Jack McKenzie *lp* Bert Wheeler, Robert Woolsey, Barbara Pepper, Moroni Olsen

Harry Baur (centre) as the megalomaniac Emperor Rudolph II in Julien Duvivier's version of the Golem *legend.*

Victor Halperin's *disappointing* Revolt of the Zombies.

Revolt of the Zombies
(HALPERIN/ACADEMY) b/w 65min
Halperin's return to the theme of the living dead is a dreary disappointment after **White Zombie** (1932), despite an intriguing opening in which, to demonstrate their invulnerability to bullets and worth as soldiers, a Cambodian high priest brings a company of zombies to the Franco-Austrian front during the First World War. Concluding that zombies are a menace to civilization, the powers agree to send a postwar expedition to Cambodia to find and destroy the formula which creates them. The film promptly degenerates into a silly triangular affair, which though it echoes *White Zombie*, is even more atrociously acted and lacks that film's saving graces. Jagger falls for Stone who loves Noland, finds the formula and uses it to impose his will until the power of love makes him realize what he has done, whereupon he leaps to his death, thereby freeing his slaves.

d/co-s Victor Halperin *p* Edward Halperin *co-s* Howard Higgin, Rollo Lloyd *c* J. Arthur Feindel *lp* Dorothy Stone, Dean Jagger, Roy d'Arcy, Robert Noland, George Cleveland

1937

Super-Sleuth (RKO) b/w 75(70)min
This is basically a fast-moving whodunit parody with Oakie – admirably abetted by wisecracking Sothern – in his element as a bumptious movie star who lets his role as the screen's greatest detective spill over into real life when he arrogantly takes the police department to task for incompetence. With the police chief (Kennedy) soothed by a tactful invitation to act in a movie, much of the action – including the crucial murder – takes place (as fascinatingly as always) inside the studio. But the film also wanders engagingly into horror territory by way of a mad criminologist (a marvellously sinister Ciannelli) deferred to by Oakie as his chief adviser on methods of detection, but who also happens to be the poison pen letter-writer, the killer, anything but a fan of detective movies, and the possessor of a fiendish chamber of horrors into which Oakie is lured. Trivial but entertaining.

d Ben Stoloff *p* Edward Small *s* Gertrude Purcell, Ernest Pagano *c* Joseph H. August *lp* Jack Oakie, Ann Sothern, Edgar Kennedy, Eduardo Ciannelli, Willie Best, Paul Guilfoyle

1939

The Cat and the Canary (PAR) b/w 75min
The film that made Hope a star, this is a suitably revised adaptation of John Willard's classic horror comedy, first filmed under the same title by Paul Leni in 1927. The plot is retained surprisingly intact but decorated with a flurry of characteristic wisecracks for Hope ('Don't these big empty houses scare you?' 'Not me, I used to be in vaudeville'), here caught on a halfway mark between juvenile lead and his later cowardly persona. Obviously modelled on Leni's film, with the credits superimposed over forlornly flapping shutters, the opening is highly effective as the camera discovers the mist-shrouded house quietly rotting in the middle of a Louisiana swamp and peers through a cobwebby window at the sinister housekeeper (Sondergaard) and the black cat that shadows her. Though quite stylishly staged in elegant sets, with wonderfully sepulchral performances from Sondergaard and Zucco (as the lawyer who disappears in the clutch of a hairy paw), the wisecracks tend to keep the thrills at bay until the climax. In this long, cleverly sustained, sequence Goddard's intrepid heiress is shadowed through dank underground passages by the Cat, the supposed escaped maniac who finally exposes his own game rather lamely, before being summarily dispatched by Sondergaard. Whereupon in an outrageous cheat, since a physically dissimilar actor was used throughout his masquerade, he proves to be Montgomery. The success of the film led to a repeat performance from Hope and Goddard in **The Ghost Breakers** (1940).

d Elliot Nugent *p* Arthur Hornblow Jnr *s* Walter de Leon, Lynn Starling *c* Charles Lang *lp* Bob Hope, Paulette Goddard, John Beal, Douglass Montgomery, Gale Sondergaard, George Zucco

Dark Eyes of London *aka* **The Human Monster**
(ARGYLE PRODUCTIONS/PATHE; GB) b/w 76min
This was the first British film to receive the censors' new 'H' certificate introduced in January 1937. Based on Edgar Wallace's 1924 novel, the film gave Lugosi his last real acting opportunity in a dual role as Dr Orloff, head of a Greenwich insurance company, and as Mr Dearborn, director of a home for the blind where newly insured victims are drowned in a tank and their bodies dumped in the Thames by Lugosi's monstrous blind henchman Jake (Walter). Williams is the rather too boyishly Oxbridge man from Scotland Yard and Gynt the conventionally intrepid heroine determined to find

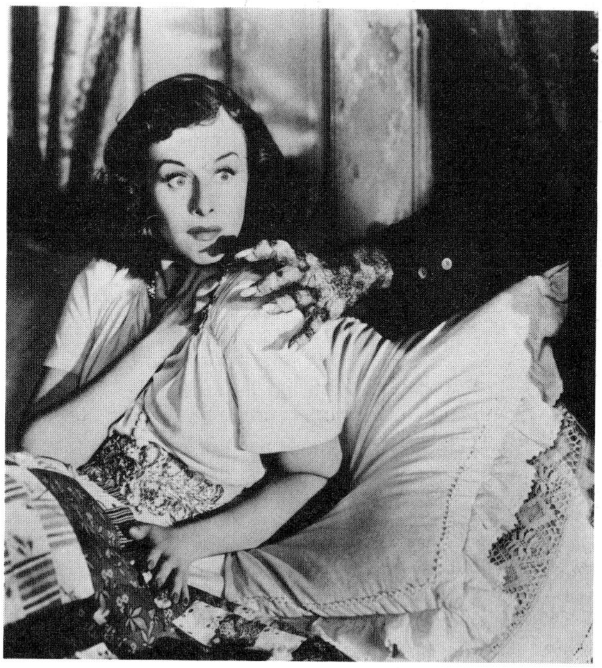

Right: *Paulette Goddard menaced in* The Cat and the Canary, *the film that made Bob Hope a star.*

Left: *Bela Lugosi (centre) in the inept Ritz Brothers vehicle,* The Gorilla.

out what happened to her father. The atmosphere is beautifully sustained from the opening shot of a corpse floating in the river to the final one of Lugosi as he sinks into the mudflats, evoking a sort of D. W. Griffith Limehouse crossed with Brecht's *Threepenny Opera* as Braille messages are typed by a zombie-like secretary and carried through the streets by blind messengers, while at headquarters the blind inmates work to the accompaniment of non-stop organ music occasionally interrupted by strange and frightening screams. Lugosi has one nicely diabolic moment when he realizes that his blind-mute messenger Lew (Owen) is the man who can hear too much, and uses an electrical apparatus to make him deaf as well. Owen eventually goes into the tank like the insurance victims, leaving Walter – his only friend, in a bizarre relationship reminiscent of that between the monster and Ygor in **Son of Frankenstein** (1939) – to go berserk, strangle Lugosi, and hurl his body from the roof.

d/co-s Walter Summers *p/co-s* John Argyle *co-s* Patrick Kirwan *c* Bryan Langley *lp* Bela Lugosi, Hugh Williams, Greta Gynt, Wilfred Walter, Arthur Owen

The Face at the Window (PENNANT; GB) b/w 65min
Slaughter, the last of the great barnstormers who toured the provinces until his death, made a number of films with alluringly horrific titles like *Sweeney Todd the Demon Barber of Fleet Street* (1935), *Maria Marten: or the Murder in the Red Barn* (1935), *The Crimes of Stephen Hawke* (1936), *Crimes at the Dark House* (1940), *The Curse of the Wraydons* (1946) and *The Greed of William Hart* (1948). Though saturated with evil deeds, they are not strictly horror movies, since Slaughter's stock-in-trade was the Victorian melodrama or the like (*Crimes at the Dark House*, for example, is an adaptation of Wilkie Collins' *The Woman in White*) with largely theoretical horrors used for melodramatic relish. The exception, perhaps simply because it happens to be the most cinematically effective of his films, is *The Face at the Window*, based on a play by F. Brooke Warren which had been adapted less well three times before (in Australia in 1919 and in Britain in 1920 and 1932).

Although principally the story of a fiendish killer, the Wolf (Slaughter), who terrorizes the Paris of the 1880s, stabbing his victims while their attention is focused on a bestial face at the window (his maniac half-brother), the film also boasts a scientist who revives corpses by electricity, and who proposes to do just that in order to have one of the Wolf's victims reveal the killer's identity. The movie is, and Slaughter's knowing performance readily acknowledges, preposterous rubbish but there are two points to be made. One is that Slaughter is extraordinary: a prancing pantomime demon, totally stylized in word and gesture, who nevertheless manages to transmit an authentic shudder of sadism along with the amusement simply by taking his audience into his confidence, assured that they will share his pleasure as he gleefully contemplates his crimes (the only comparable expression of sheer delight in evil that comes to mind is Jean-Louis Barrault's performance as the Mr Hyde of Jean Renoir's **Le Testament du Docteur Cordelier**, 1959). The other is that King, by directing the film as a series of virtually static theatrical tableaux, has (no doubt accidentally) created a sort of blank filmic space with in which Slaughter's intricate movements create the *mise-en-scène*.

d/co-p George King *co-p* Randall Faye *s* A. R. Rawlinson *c* Hone Glendenning *lp* Tod Slaughter, Marjorie Taylor, John Warwick, Leonard Henry, Aubrey Mallalieu

The Gorilla (FOX) b/w 67min
This abysmal remake of the Ralph Spence play first filmed in 1927, features three detectives instead of two prowling the old dark house on the trail of the killer gorilla. Dwan directs confidently enough around Atwill and Lugosi as the amusingly sinister though predictably red-herring menaces, but can do little with the appalling mugging of the Ritz Brothers, who are given insufficient comic material to work with and make up for it by cringing in endless variations on terror.

d Allan Dwan *p* Darryl F. Zanuck *s* Rian James, Sid Silvers *c* Edward Cronjager *lp* The Ritz Brothers, Patsy Kelly, Anita Louise, Lionel Atwill, Bela Lugosi, Joseph Calleia

Right: *Basil Rathbone as Holmes, with hound, in* The Hound of the Baskervilles.

La Herencia Macabra *aka* **The Macabre Legacy** (PRODUCTORA DE PELICULAS; MEX) b/w 83min
A mad doctor film on a par with Michael Curtiz's work (**Doctor X**, 1932; **Mystery of the Wax Museum**, 1933). The plastic surgeon Dr Duarte (Arenas) injects his wife's lover (Armengod) with a disfiguring virus. When she (Frank) tries to steal the antidote, he performs an operation on her and lets it be known that she died, but buries a wax effigy instead of her body and keeps her in a secret room. The crazed surgeon eventually dies of a heart attack when he sees a cat attacking his wife. Bohr who also edited the picture and wrote the score, creates some memorable images, a testament to his genuine sense of cinema. One outstanding sequence has the doctor fall asleep during a dinner; his premonition of his wife's adultery generates images in which her feet are seen to mingle with those of his assistants.

The film was not released until 1944 and there is some confusion as to its title: a picture with the same credits, entitled *La Traicionera* is mentioned in a yearbook for 1945, but the still accompanying it is from Bohr's movie. The credits are also noteworthy for mentioning a 'bacteriological consultant'.

Bela Lugosi (right) in the intriguing Dark Eyes of London.

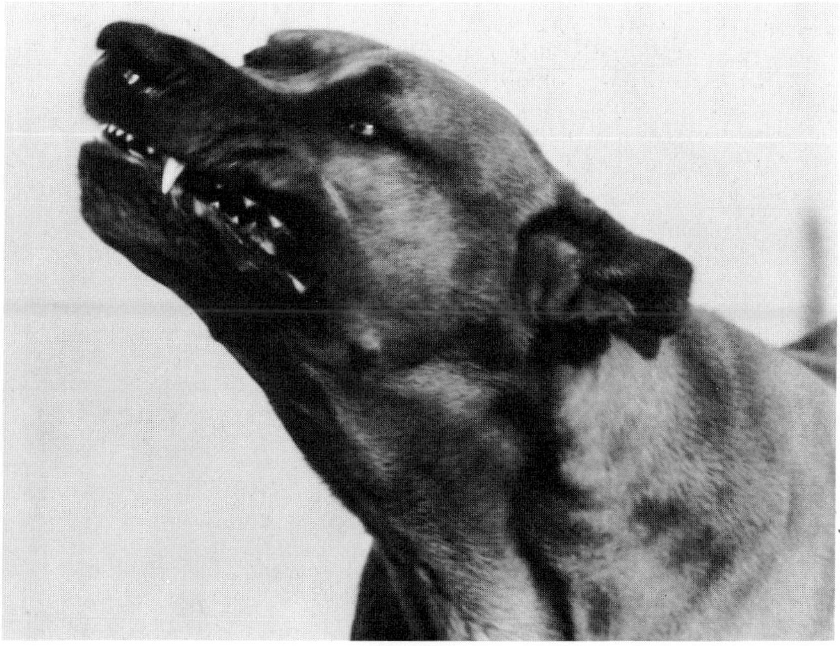

d/co-s José Bohr *p* Enrique M. Hernandez *co-s* Xavier Davila *c* Jack Draper *lp* Miguel Arenas, Consuela Frank, Ramón Armengod, Luis Aldas, Aurora Walker, Agustin Insunza, José Rubio, Manolo Fabregas, Maria Virginia

The Hound of the Baskervilles (FOX) b/w 80min
This is the first of the 14 films in which Rathbone and Bruce played Holmes and Watson, and is notable as the only one of the series to mention Holmes's habit: 'The needle, Watson!' he mutters aside, retiring wearily to bed as the end title comes up. The other curious fact of the film is that, perhaps because its studio version of Dartmoor is so cramped, it makes little effort to play up the horror of the hound, aside from having it loom savagely in the flashback where Sir Hugo Baskerville has his throat torn out, and later attack the tramp in a menacing silhouette on a jutting rock. The result is a cosily attractive character study-cum-whodunit, rich in red herrings (Atwill looking fishy in pebble glasses, Carradine sinister in slicked-down hair and goatee) and eccentricities (a neighbour whose mania for suing people leads him to threaten suit against someone for body-snatching when he digs up a neolithic skull). Best of all, perhaps, Holmes is off on mysterious errands for much of the time, leaving Watson in proud charge of protecting Sir Henry (Greene) from sharing his father's fate on foggy Dartmoor. Bruce is excellent throughout, but his playing of the scene where he is first frightened by a tramp on the moor, then tries to pull rank by announcing that he is the great Holmes – going into a huff when the tramp proves to *be* Holmes – is a gem. For the record, Lowry is the villain, committing the murders – while Greene romances his sister Barrie – after realizing from the family resemblance in a portrait that he is in line to inherit the Baskerville estate.

d Sidney Lanfield *p* Darryl F. Zanuck *s* Ernest Pascal *c* J. Peverell Marley *lp* Richard Greene, Basil Rathbone, Nigel Bruce, Lionel Atwill, Wendy Barrie, John Carradine, Morton Lowry

House of Fear (U) b/w 66min
May's early reputation as the German cinema's silent serial king was soon eclipsed by Fritz Lang (whose first scripts he had directed), and his undistinguished Hollywood career shows why. His laborious direction makes a dreary hash of this remake of **The Last Warning** (1929). Re-oriented towards the whodunit, though retaining the phantom apparitions that supposedly haunt a Broadway theatre where a murder has been committed and the cast has been reassembled, it drags on interminably through tiresome complications and a breathless outpouring of last-minute explanations.

d Joe May *p* Edmund Grainger *s* Peter Milne *c* Milton Krasner *lp* Irene Harvey, William Gargan, Walter Woolf King, El Brendel, Dorothy Arnold, Robert Coote

The Hunchback of Notre Dame (RKO) b/w 117min
Although not the masterpiece its reputation suggests, this version of Victor Hugo's novel has several things going for it: impressive sets, superb camerawork, elegantly stylized direction which recalls Dieterle's background in the German silents and a convincingly detailed study in grotesquerie from Laughton. Above all, it has a script which restores some of the complexity removed from the Lon Chaney version of 1923 by interweaving the plot with subtle strands of court, state and church intrigue, most importantly the sinister undercurrent of clerical lecheries represented by the remorseless pursuit of the beautiful gypsy Esmeralda (O'Hara) by Frollo (Hardwicke). As a historical pageant – a series of bustling, Breughel-like tableaux in which the beggars and tumblers, the King and courtiers, the clerics and guardsmen, even Esmeralda and her young poet (O'Brien), seem comfortably at home – the film works well. Only Laughton's Quasimodo seems a misfit, a character from nightmare dropped into reality (of a sort) and trying to find some way of belonging. The weakness of the

performance, in fact, is that Laughton keeps nudging the audience, making it aware of his own quintessential humanity, so that the character (unlike Chaney's barbaric figure) ultimately becomes a sentimental conception.

d William Dieterle *p* Pandro S. Berman *s* Sonya Levien *c* Joseph H. August *lp* Charles Laughton, Maureen O'Hara, Edmond O'Brien, Thomas Mitchell, Cedric Hardwicke, George Zucco

Return of Doctor X (WB) b/w 62min
A brisk B movie, this is not so much a sequel to **Doctor X** (1932) as an imitation of *The Walking Dead* (1936) with Bogart replacing Karloff as the executed man brought back to zombie life, this time with vampiric lusts added. Directed with some style by Sherman (his first film), but saddled with the usual lame script and stock supporting characters, the film's best moment is the first appearance of Bogart (whose performance here, his only horror movie, is wonderfully baleful), chalk-faced in pince-nez, with a white streak through his hair, clutching a white rabbit. Litel, as the doctor who brings Bogart back to life, is made up to resemble Count Zaroff/Leslie Banks in **The Most Dangerous Game** (1932).

d Vincent Sherman *p* Bryan Foy *s* Lee Katz *c* Sid Hickox *lp* Dennis Morgan, Wayne Morris, Rosemary Lane, Humphrey Bogart, John Litel, Lya Lys

Son of Frankenstein (U) b/w 95min
This starkly stylish film, which features Karloff's third and last appearance as the monster, sparked off the new spate of horror movies that ran through the early forties. Interestingly, the monster seems to be in a transitional state. Without any fuss made about how he came to be alive, Karloff is simply discovered lying on a slab in the Frankenstein vault when Ygor (Lugosi), a broken-necked shepherd who has survived a hanging for graverobbing, shows him to Frankenstein's son (Rathbone), and Rathbone is persuaded to revive him in the hope of vindicating his father. Lugosi then uses the monster to

Above: *Charles Laughton as* The Hunchback of Notre Dame.

Boris Karloff, in his last appearance as the monster, Basil Rathbone (centre) and Bela Lugosi in the stylish Son of Frankenstein.

Right: *Boris Karloff as the executioner in the bizarre* Tower of London.

murder those responsible for sending him to the gallows, which makes the monster not only a secondary character to Ygor (to the detriment of the film, although Lugosi gives one of his very best performances), but reduces him to a superhuman destructive force foreshadowing all those indestructible creatures who were to be fathered by mad doctors in the forties. Consistently enough, given that he acts as though under a hypnotic spell woven by Lugosi, Karloff's monster becomes a sort of zombie and only reveals a little of the impulse towards humanity that flickered through **Frankenstein** (1931) and flared up in **The Bride of Frankenstein** (1935) in two brief moments: once, unforgettably, when he discovers Lugosi's body and throws back his head to howl in grief; and once, more sentimentally, when Frankenstein's small son disarms him by showing no fear. The unmistakable shift is from monster as victim to monster as demon.

Yet *Son of Frankenstein* is an extremely impressive film, carefully sober (which is why Rathbone, giving a more controlled performance than Colin Clive in either of the earlier versions, seems to be acting even more hysterically in the latter stages) but saved from stiffness by a strain of dark irony centred mainly in Atwill's performance as the police inspector, who counterpoints his chilling description of how his arm was literally torn out at the roots in an earlier encounter with the monster by casually using the back of his artificial fist for sticking spare darts into during a game. Slow the film may be, but it has a kind of architectural solidity that matches the dreamlike labyrinthine massiveness of the sets (designed as a sort of realistic equivalent to UFA expressionism), and builds to a stunning climax as the monster, at bay on the brink of the sulphur pit into which he will be toppled by Rathbone, still with his foot clamped firmly on the hostage body of the latter's son, once more rips Atwill's (false) arm out by the roots.

d/p Rowland V. Lee *s* Willis Cooper *c* George Robinson *lp* Boris Karloff, Bela Lugosi, Basil Rathbone, Lionel Atwill, Josephine Hutchinson, Lionel Belmore

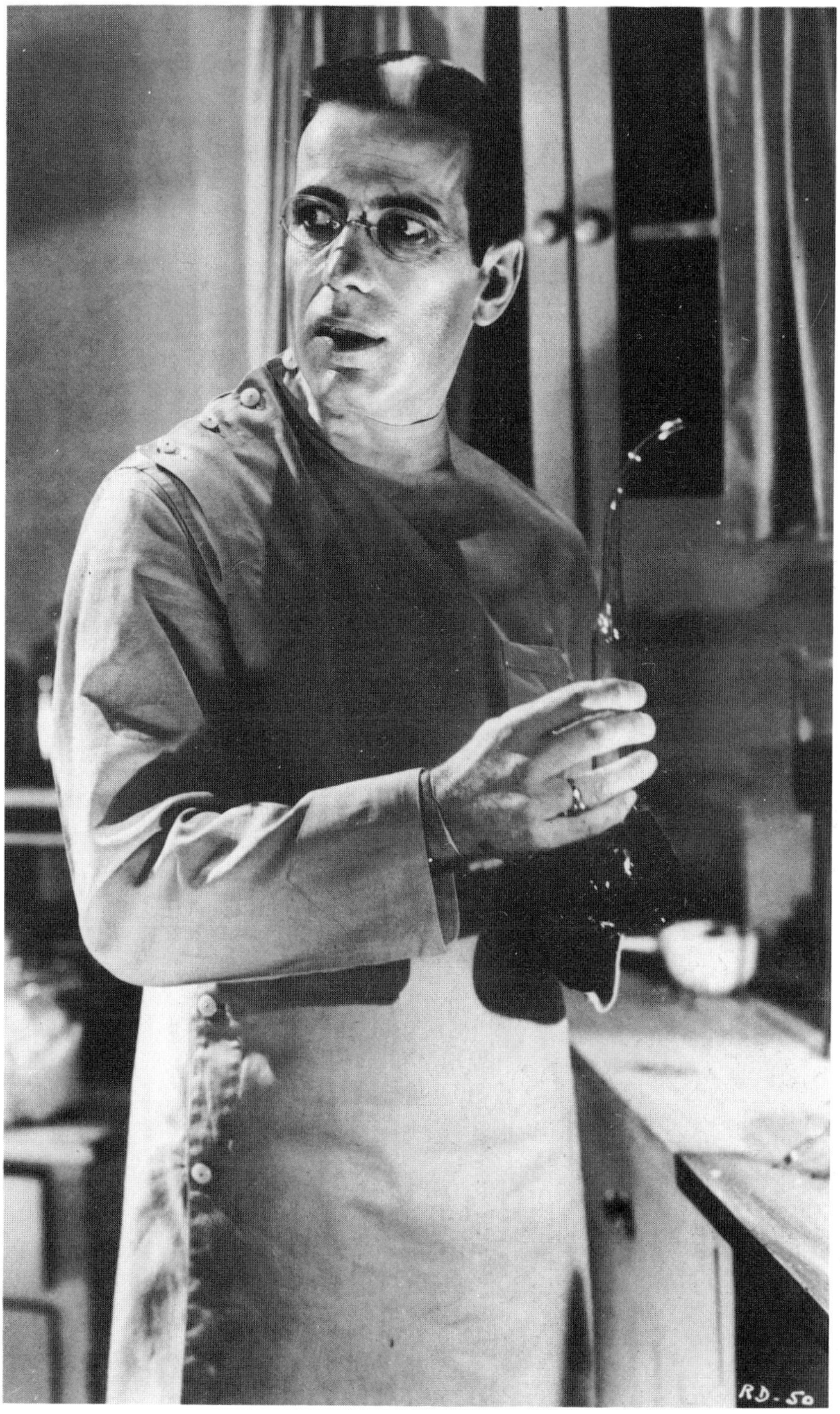

Below: *Humphrey Bogart in his only horror outing,* Return of Doctor X.

Tower of London (U) b/w 92min

Karloff, bald and club-footed, is marvellously malevolent as Mord the executioner in this historically inaccurate (loosely based on Shakespeare but with Grand Guignol replacing poetry) but vividly effective account of Richard II's murderous misdeeds. Oddly, Karloff also invites sympathy, for although he clearly delights in his work (which includes torturing prisoners, chopping off heads, and drowning Clarence in his butt of Malmsey), the implication is that his deformity has condemned him to be what he is, hidden away in the Tower like a slug beneath a stone. 'Crookback and Dragfoot,' says Richard (an equally fine performance from Rathbone) at one point, 'Misfits, eh? Well, what we lack in physical perfection we make up in brains.' Surprisingly literate within its genre-imposed limits, the script later picks up this theme of physical and intellectual horizons when Karloff pleads with the King to be allowed to leave the Tower to fight as a soldier: 'I've never killed in hot blood. It must be different, more ... more exciting. Many men are killed in battle.' There is a hint here that Mord's yearning to leave the Tower is compounded equally of intellectual curiosity, a search for new sadisms, and a wish to die.

Although made on a low budget, the film looks astonishingly handsome (even the battle scenes), thanks to direction in the same flexible yet solidly architectural style Lee brought to **Son of Frankenstein** (1939). Price, making his horror début as Clarence, took the role of Richard in **Tower of London** (1962), which though it used the same title was not a remake.

d/p Rowland V. Lee *s* Robert N. Lee *c* George Robinson *lp* Basil Rathbone, Boris Karloff, Ian Hunter, Nan Grey, Barbara O'Neil, Vincent Price

The 1940s

Horror in Limbo

If the early years of the thirties saw the production of the first classics of the American horror film, the forties, with few exceptions, continued the decline initiated in the second half of that decade. Some of the films, such as George Waggner's **The Wolf Man** (1941) and **The Picture of Dorian Gray** (1945), were decidedly superior, but for the most part the decade's films were uninspired routine monster rallies (such as **House of Frankenstein**, 1944, in which the monster met the wolfman and Dracula), saved only by the discreet charms of the likes of Evelyn Ankers and George Zucco who were in seeming perpetual attendance. The inevitable conclusion of this decline was the witless horrors of **Abbott and Costello Meet Frankenstein** (1948).

The major exception to this was the group of 11 films – most of them horror movies – produced by Val Lewton for RKO. The films themselves were uneven, those by Jacques Tourneur (**Cat People**, 1942, and **I Walked with a Zombie** and **The Leopard Man**, both 1943) being superior to those by Robert Wise (**The Curse of the Cat People**, 1944) and Mark Robson (**Isle of the Dead**, 1945), but it makes sense to talk of them together because they shared so many personnel and were conceived of by RKO as a group. The one feature all shared was a belief in shadows rather than monsters, of less rather than more. The Tourneur films, in particular, anticipated Hollywood's later borrowings from Freud, with the difference that Tourneur's movies remained delicately balanced between reason and unreason, never being reducible to crude psychologizing. Moreover, *The Leopard Man*, heavily inflected by the *film noir* in its melding of thriller and horror elements, pointed the way forward to **Psycho** (1960). In a similar fashion, Robson's fine **The Seventh Victim** (1943), with its tale of devil worship in contemporary Greewich Village, anticipates the modern fascination with the horrors of religion as represented by **The Exorcist** (1973) and the superior **Rosemary's Baby** (1968).

Another film that pointed to the future was the British **Dead of Night** (1945). The odd horror film had been made in Britain in the thirties (usually with Boris Karloff and/or Bela Lugosi starring) but these had had little impact. *Dead of Night* had more impact, in part because it followed a banning of horror films in the UK during the war. An omnibus film, a strong tradition in horror, some of the sketches were lacklustre but the episodes by Robert Hamer and Albert Cavalcanti for the first time suggested that the British film revival, when it came so shockingly in the mid-fifties, might be borne on the wings of horror.

1940

The Ape (MON) b/w 62min
This is an almost unrecognizable version of the Adam Shirk play which earlier had yielded **House of Mystery** (1934). Karloff plays yet another of his kindly old doctors, mild and droopy-moustached but the source of uneasy local speculation because he has become so obsessively devoted to his research since the death from polio of his wife and child. Desperately trying to find a cure that will benefit a crippled neighbour (Wrixon), he seizes his chance when required to treat an animal-trainer injured in a circus fire. Letting the man die so as to tap his spinal fluid for the serum he is developing, Karloff soon requires further supplies – which he gets by killing and skinning (off-screen) an ape which escaped in the fire, then dressing up in its pelt and murdering unwary passersby. He is finally gunned down, of course, but happily the girl is cured by then. Agreeably dotty (after a talkative first half) but distressingly tacky, it makes peculiarly unconvincing use of some stock circus footage.

d William Nigh *p* Scott R. Dunlap *s* Curt Siodmak, Richard Carroll *c* Harry Neumann *lp* Boris Karloff, Maris Wrixon, Gertrude Hoffman, Henry Hall, George Cleveland

Previous pages: *Lon Chaney Jnr abducts Elyse Knox in* The Mummy's Tomb *(1942), one of Universal's many formula horror films of the forties.*

Before I Hang (COL) b/w 62min
Less science fiction oriented than its Columbia companion pieces, *The Man They Could Not Hang* (1939) and *The Man With Nine Lives* (1940), this features Karloff as a benevolent old scientist working on a plasma-serum rejuvenation technique. When he is sentenced to death for a mercy killing, the prison doctor (Van Sloan) refuses to let him continue his experiments. However, he succeeds in rejuvenating himself only to turn into a killer (both inside the jail and outside when his sentence is unexpectedly commuted) because he has used the blood of a convicted murderer. Derivative and utterly predictable, the film is nevertheless cleverly muted in direction and distinguished by Karloff's usual careful characterization which never overplays the mannerisms (hand involuntarily twisting a handkerchief or massaging his neck) which betray the periods when he loses control.

d Nick Grinde *p* Wallace MacDonald *s* Robert D. Andrews *c* Benjamin Kline *lp* Boris Karloff, Evelyn Keyes, Bruce Bennett, Edward Van Sloan, Pedro de Cordoba

Boris Karloff as the benevolent old scientist in Before I Hang.

Bob Hope, Paulette Goddard and Anthony Quinn (right) in The Ghost Breakers, one of Hope's best films.

Black Friday (U) b/w 70min

Not a bad film when seen divorced from a context in which Karloff seemed to be playing nothing but a monotonous string of kindly old doctors or scientists whose well-meaning experiments go horribly wrong: *The Man They Could Not Hang* (1939), *The Man With Nine Lives* (1940), **Before I Hang** (1940), **The Ape** (1940), and *The Devil Commands* (1941). Here cast as a suavely greying doctor, he solves a moral problem – it seems unfair to let the innocent and worthier man die – when a professor of English literature (Ridges) is gravely injured by a carelessly speeding car driven by a gangster. Transferring the also injured gangster's brain to the professor, Karloff speculates interestedly on the probable psychological results of his humanitarian experiment. Predictably enough he is answered by a Jekyll and Hyde syndrome in which Ridges sometimes becomes the dead gangster, taking bloody revenge on gang members (including Lugosi) who are after the loot he had stashed away (and which Karloff also covets in order to build himself a research laboratory). In the end Karloff, who narrates the film in flashback while awaiting the electric chair, is obliged to shoot Ridges when he 'reverts' after returning to his classroom.

Although the film is standard fare, it is strikingly shot by Bredell, and Lubin's imaginative direction is enough of a reminder that he did a very sleek job on **The Phantom of the Opera** (1943) before retreating into a string of comedies starring Francis the talking mule. Lugosi, originally slated for the Ridges role, spends most of his time on the sidelines, and as a curious publicity gimmick had himself hypnotized on set for his death scene.

d Arthur Lubin *p* Burt Kelly *s* Curt Siodmak, Eric Taylor *c* Elwood Bredell *lp* Boris Karloff, Bela Lugosi, Stanley Ridges, Anne Nagel, Anne Gwynne, James Craig

The Ghost Breakers (PAR) b/w 82min

This remake of the Paul Dickey-Charles W. Goddard play, first filmed as **The Ghost Breaker** (1922), was designed to cash in on the success of **The Cat and the Canary** (1939). That film began in the middle with its old-dark-house setting, this follow-up takes rather longer to get going. Ditching the Kentucky family feud motif from *The Ghost Breaker*, it has Hope and his black servant Best, soon matching quips for the role as first coward – 'If two men come down, let the first one go, that'll be me' – making their escape from importunate gangsters. But once they are in Cuba and inveigled into accompanying Goddard to the haunted castle she has inherited, the temperature is considerably chillier than it was in *The Cat and the Canary*. The wisecracks keep flowing ('Basil Rathbone must be throwing a party', Hope remarks as a thunderstorm greets their arrival), but there is genuine menace in the zombie lurking in a tumbledown shack by the fog-laden pier (Johnson), and real flair in scenes like the discovery of Lukas' body sinisterly laid out in a coffin. This is probably Hope's best film.

d George Marshall *p* Arthur Hornblow Jnr *s* Walter de Leon *c* Charles Lang, Theodore Sparkuhl *lp* Bob Hope, Paulette Goddard, Richard Carlson, Paul Lukas, Willie Best, Anthony Quinn, Noble Johnson

The Mummy's Hand (U) b/w 67min

Livelier than **The Mummy** (1932), this is not so much a sequel as an imitation, with the mummy (now known as Kharis since Karloff's Im-Ho-Tep had finally crumbled to dust) resuscitated by an infusion of tana leaves instead of by incantation, but still seeking his reincarnated princess and exacting revenge on the desecrators of his tomb. An added element of mumbo-jumbo has the dying high priest of Karnak (Ciannelli) hand over the sacred trust of guarding the tomb to his son and disciple (Zucco), who promptly develops his own lecherous designs on the mummy's reincarnated beloved (Moran). With Zucco on hand to take care of the more mundane villainies, the mummy is free to stamp right through the film instead of casting off his grave-wrappings as Karloff had. Tyler, a veteran of countless westerns chosen to succeed Karloff because of a certain physical resemblance, brings little subtlety to his characterization but is surprisingly effective thanks to a nicely imaginative touch which has him partially paralysed by an insufficiency of tana juice: dragging one useless leg behind him as he stalks his victims with ponderous deliberation, strangling them with one monstrously powerful hand, Tyler's mummy is a genuinely baleful presence. The film itself is cheap and cheerful, padding out its already brief running time by incorporating the entire flashback sequence

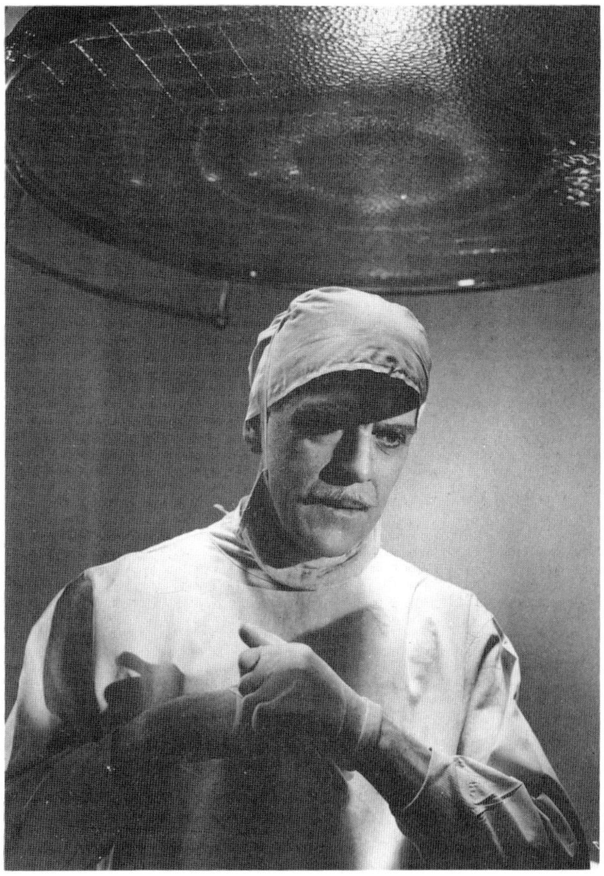

Right: Boris Karloff as yet another kindly old doctor whose experiments go wrong in Black Friday.

from *The Mummy*, lending itself a touch of visual distinction by using the temple set from James Whale's *Green Hell* (1940), and shoring up a faltering script with several borrowings, most notably a barely disguised version of the famous 'Children of the Night' speech from **Dracula** (1931).

d Christy Cabanne *p* Ben Pivar *s* Griffin Jay, Maxwell Shane *c* Elwood Bredell *lp* Dick Foran, Peggy Moran, Wallace Ford, Eduardo Ciannelli, George Zucco, Tom Tyler, Cecil Kellaway

You'll Find Out (RKO) b/w 97min
This is a routine haunted-house comedy which features the usual storm, apparitions and ape, and totally wastes its three stars as crooks trying to kill Parrish to get at her inheritance. Lugosi poses as a turbanned swami, Karloff as the family doctor and Lorre as a scientist. The most horrifying thing about the film is bandleader Kyser, taking care of the comedy and contributing five numbers.

d/p David Butler *s* J. V. Kern *c* Frank Redman *lp* Peter Lorre, Boris Karloff, Bela Lugosi, Kay Kyser, Helen Parrish, Dennis O'Keefe

1941

The Black Cat (U) b/w 70min
This has nothing to do with Poe's story except that the climax features a cat walled up in a body. A routine comedy-chiller, it has Herbert (an antique dealer) and Crawford (a real estate agent) hurrying to the Winslow estate after hearing that old Henrietta Winslow has died. She turns out to be very much alive, but not for long. While Herbert and Crawford comically try to solve the mystery of her death by poisoning, the various other members of the cast (already gathered for the reading of the will) behave suspiciously and die horribly, including Lugosi, hitherto a prime red-herring suspect as the baleful keeper of the old lady's cats. Cortez's wonderfully creepy camerawork is the highpoint of the film. Alan Ladd has a small role as Rathbone's son.

d Albert S. Rogell *p* Burt Kelly *s* Robert Lees, Fred Rinaldo, Eric Taylor, Robert Neville *c* Stanley Cortez *lp* Basil Rathbone, Hugh Herbert, Broderick Crawford, Bela Lugosi, Gale Sondergaard, Anne Gwynne, Gladys Cooper

The Devil Bat *aka* **Killer Bats**
(PRC) b/w 69min
From this point on, Lugosi's career was downhill all the way. Caricaturing even his own over-the-top conception of a mad doctor, he raises outsize bats – enlarged by a special electrical process – which he trains to attack a special scent. Much of the film is composed of endlessly repeated scenes in which Lugosi blandly hands his next victim a bottle of his patent brand of shaving lotion, stressing the malice aforethought with a sinisterly accented 'Goodbye!'. The film is, in fact, sufficiently bad as to be rather enjoyable.

A sequel, *Devil Bat's Daughter* (1946), emerged more as a mystery thriller. Minus Lugosi's Dr Carruthers but starring Rosemary La Planche as his daughter, it has a villainous psychiatrist trying to persuade her that she is a vampire. In the course of the plot, Lugosi is cleared – somewhat incredibly – of his murders in *The Devil Bat*. Though competently directed by Frank Wysbar, it has little of the strange, moody brilliance of his **Strangler of the Swamp** (1946).

d Jean Yarbrough *p* Jack Gallagher *s* John T. Neville *c* Arthur Martinelli *lp* Bela Lugosi, Suzanne Kaaren, Dave O'Brien, Hal Price, Donald Kerr, Guy Usher

Dr Jekyll and Mr Hyde (MGM) b/w 127(122, 114)min
Despite a would-be Freudian montage which emerges as risibly kinky – Tracy's Hyde as a charioteer enthusiastically whipping Bergman and Turner as his horses – this is a carefully castrated version of Stevenson's story which never even begins to match the ambiguities and the social implications of Rouben Mamoulian's 1932 version. Ringing the changes with minimal makeup, Tracy gives an honourable performance and Bergman is superb as the pathetic barmaid (no tart in this version) who loves Jekyll and is set up by Hyde as his mistress. But the film itself is solemn, ponderous and dreadfully insubstantial, a sort of perverse love story drenched in opulent MGM trimmings.

d/p Victor Fleming *s* John Lee Mahin *c* Joseph Ruttenberg *lp* Spencer Tracy, Ingrid Bergman, Lana Turner, Donald Crisp, Ian Hunter, Barton MacLane

The magnificent central set of the cheap and cheerful The Mummy's Hand.

The Face Behind the Mask (COL) b/w 69min
A marvellous little film. Not so much a horror movie as a haunting threat of horror, the film stars Lorre as an immigrant Hungarian watchmaker, barely adjusting to his new environment when his face is horribly burned in a tenement fire. Forced to wear a contoured but expressionless rubber mask that he can't pay for, lost and embittered because his appearance makes prospective employers think again – a classic shot echoes his mood as he stands contemplating suicide on a twilit dock with reflections from the water shadowing his face – he turns to crime. All that changes when he meets a blind girl (Keyes) who responds to the gentleness she senses within him. If the situation is a stock one, Florey's subtly stylized direction, Planer's superb camerawork and first-rate performances (Lorre, cleverly made up, has rarely been better) weave it into a miracle of tenderness. The payoff comes with the ending as the couple are contemplating marriage. Thinking Lorre has betrayed them, his ex-gang plant a bomb in his car. Keyes is killed and Lorre starts out on an expressionless, cold-blooded revenge.

d Robert Florey *p* Wallace MacDonald *s* Alan Vincent, Paul Jarrico *c* Franz Planer *lp* Peter Lorre, Evelyn Keyes, Don Beddoe, James Seay, George E. Stone

The Invisible Ghost (BANNER) b/w 64min
An awful film. Lugosi is the nice, ordinary doctor who thinks his wife is dead when, in fact, she's wandering around, apparently in a state of amnesia and given to staring through the window at him. She may be hypnotizing him (the script isn't entirely clear about this). At any rate, apparently not seeing her when she is there, he goes berserk and starts

strangling people. Even Lewis, to judge by the number of closeups of staring eyes, appears to have given up and gone home.

d Joseph H. Lewis *p* Sam Katzman *s* Helen Martin, Al Martin *c* Marcel le Picard *lp* Bela Lugosi, Polly Ann Young, John McGuire, Betty Compson, Clarence Muse

King of the Zombies (MON) b/w 67min
Anticipating John Carradine in **Revenge of the Zombies** (1943) but much less entertainingly, Victor (once a star in British silents and the Strong Man in **Freaks**, 1932) listlessly creates an army of black zombies on a remote island for the benefit of foreign powers. For once, with Moreland doing his usual but excellent scared black servant act, the comic relief is welcome.

d Jean Yarbrough *p* Lindsley Parsons *s* Edmund Kelso *c* Mack Stengler *lp* Dick Purcell, Joan Woodbury, Henry Victor, Mantan Moreland, John Archer

Man-Made Monster *aka* **The Electric Man** *aka* **The Atomic Monster**
(U) b/w 68(59)min
Chaney's first horror movie, originally intended as a vehicle for Boris Karloff and Bela Lugosi. Atwill gleefully hams it up as a mad electrobiologist who dreams of creating a race of living zombies. He finds his ideal guinea-pig in Chaney, the survivor of a crash into a power pylon who has turned his tolerance for electricity to account as the 'electric man' of a carnival sideshow. Atwill subjects him to ever-increasing electrical charges until he is both lethal in body and deranged in mind. Chaney, a dull actor snapped up by Universal after attracting attention as the murderously gentle Lennie in *Of Mice and Men* (1939) – doubtless in the hope that some of his father's reputation as a horror star would rub off – can make little of the role. The script, obviously derived from *The Invisible Ray* (1936), is in any case strictly machine-made, generating little suspense as Chaney is repeatedly recharged, stumps murderously around outlined by a neon halo, and is anti-climactically reduced to ashes when the rubber suit he wears as insulation is punctured on a barbed-wire fence.

Bredell's excellent camerawork lends the film more distinction than it deserves.

d George Waggner *p* Jack Bernhard *s* Joseph West *c* Elwood Bredell *lp* Lionel Atwill, Lon Chaney Jnr, Anne Nagel, Frank Albertson, Samuel S. Hinds

Below: *The two faces of Spencer Tracy in Victor Fleming's romantic version of* Dr Jekyll and Mr Hyde.

The Monster and the Girl (PAR) b/w 65(56)min
This routine mad-doctor yarn is given a certain class by Heisler's direction. Walking out of a mist to camera, Drew tells the story of her marriage to a nice young man (Paige), as a flashback slyly offers a glimpse of the shoulder holster worn by the supposed preacher (Calleia). Meanwhile a young man (Terry), framed for murder by the gang he realized was tricking his sister (Drew) into prostitution, faces execution and hysterically agrees when a Dr Parry (Zucco) asks to be allowed to use his brain for post-mortem experiment. Zucco then transplants Terry's brain into a gorilla, which proceeds to exact bloody revenge on the gang (led by Lukas). Although quite stylishly done, in particular a sequence where the ape on the rooftops stalks a gangster in the dark streets below, the characteristically arbitrary monster elements are something of a letdown after the more realistic (and unusually explicit) opening scenes detailing Drew's plight (although she gets Cameron in the end, so was presumably rescued in time). Such deficiencies are largely corrected by an exceptionally interesting cast.

d Stuart Heisler *p* Jack Moss *s* Stuart Anthony *c* Victor Milner *lp* Ellen Drew, Robert Paige, Paul Lukas, Onslow Stevens, George Zucco, Rod Cameron, Marc Lawrence, Philip Terry, Gerald Mohr, Joseph Calleia

The Smiling Ghost (WB/FIRST NATIONAL) b/w 77min
This engaging variation on **The Cat and the Canary** (1927) formula features Morris as a penniless young man hired to act as fiancé for one month to a beautiful heiress (Smith). When a member of the household is murdered in mistake for him (by a ghastly figure lurking behind a secret panel, of course), Morris learns that he is the bait to trap the 'smiling ghost' who has turned Smith into a jinxed bride by killing two previous fiancés and leaving a third (Bruce) paralysed in an iron lung. Before he can sensibly opt out, the heiress flatters him into playing Sir Galahad with a promise of marriage, much to the annoyance of a reporter (Marshall) who has fallen for him. As a classic comedy situation, the triangle is well played and contributes to the credibility of the denouement in which it emerges that Smith's selfishness is responsible for driving all her fiancés to self-destruction. Bruce, now merely simulating paralysis and embittered because Smith rejected him because he was a cripple, has been masquerading as the hideous ghost, determined that she will never marry.

Script, direction and camerawork are all surprisingly good, but it is the minor characters who give the film its edge: Hale as a private eye whose masquerade as the perfect butler slips when he relieves guests of their hats and coats ('How about the bonnet, buddy?'); Best in one of his classic scared servant roles ('I ain't afraid, but my feets ain't gonna stay around and see my body abused'); and Charles Halton as mild little great-uncle Amos, collector of shrunken heads, who keeps trying to lure the unsuspecting and rather flattered Best into his sanctum to complete his collection.

d Lewis Seiler *p* Bryan Foy *s* Kenneth Gamet, Stuart Palmer *c* Arthur Todd *lp* Wayne Morris, Brenda Marshall, Alexis Smith, Lee Patrick, Alan Hale, David Bruce, Willie Best

Spooks Run Wild (MON) b/w 62min
This is the first of a pair of horror comedies Lugosi made with the East Side Kids when his career was beginning to settle in Poverty Row. Lurking in the old dark house in his Dracula outfit as Nardo the magician (complete with dwarf assistant), Lugosi terrorizes the boys who think he is the homicidal maniac (rather surprisingly, a sex killer) reportedly on the loose. He turns out to be a red herring. The abysmal formula was slavishly repeated in *Ghosts on the Loose* (1943), except that there Lugosi was a Nazi spy safeguarding his hideout by making it appear haunted, and had already been used, minus Lugosi, by the East Side Kids in *The Ghost Creeps* (1940) – quite brightly directed by Joseph H. Lewis – and was resurrected for *Ghost Catchers* (1951).

d Phil Rosen *p* Sam Katzman *s* Carl Foreman, Charles R. Marion *c* Marcel le Picard *lp* Bela Lugosi, Dave O'Brien, Dennis Moore, Angelo Rossito, Dorothy Short, Huntz Hall, Leo Gorcey, Bobby Jordan

The Wolf Man (U) b/w 71min
Chaney's second horror movie and his first appearance in the role for which he is best remembered – no doubt because his Larry Talbot, the amiable young man controlled by evil impulses he cannot understand, relies on the actor's own rather bovine character to generate much the same sort of sympathy for dumb animals as his Lennie in *Of Mice and Men* (1939), the gentle giant who longs to love but is condemned to kill. The potentially intriguing conception of Larry Talbot as hero/villain is constantly undercut, however, by the fact that Chaney, an unimaginative actor, is unable to inject any individuality into his werewolf: incongruously covered in facial fur with fangs and canine snout yet sporting black shirt and trousers, it seems less an extension of his personality than an entirely separate entity.

The film strengthens the rather weak myth of **The Werewolf of London** (1935) by replacing the Tibetan flower with a silver-topped cane mounted with the head of a wolf and a five-pointed star, whose implications are cleverly woven through the film. The tragic circle begins when Chaney acquires the cane from the girl he is to fall in love with (Ankers) and ends when his own father (Rains) is forced to use it to beat him to death with. At its centre is the atmospheric minatory visit to a gypsy camp in the forest where he is bitten by a werewolf (Bela Lugosi, in a minor role after being slated to play the lead), warned by a fortune-teller, and then finds the pentagram symbol mysteriously imprinted over his heart.

The Wolf Man benefits from a literate script and unusually good cast, but its trump card is the superbly suspenseful atmosphere in which Valentine's camera makes virtuoso use of fog and mist to create an eerie fairytale world out of the quaint little Welsh village, the forbidding baronial hall and the gypsy encampment in a forest clearing. But Waggner makes the radical mistake of showing the werewolf – who is distinctly unhorrific since all its depradations take place off-screen or behind convenient bushes – in full view instead of hinting at some shadowy mystery as Jacques Tourneur did with Simone Simon's panther metamorphosis in **Cat People** (1942). As a result the carefully built-up suspense is almost entirely dissipated.

Universal lavished care and money on the film and were rewarded by a box-office success that revived their languishing interest in horror and sparked off their second cycle of movies in the genre.

d/p George Waggner *s* Curt Siodmak *c* Joseph Valentine *lp* Claude Rains, Lon Chaney Jnr, Ralph Bellamy, Evelyn Ankers, Warren William, Maria Ouspenskaya.

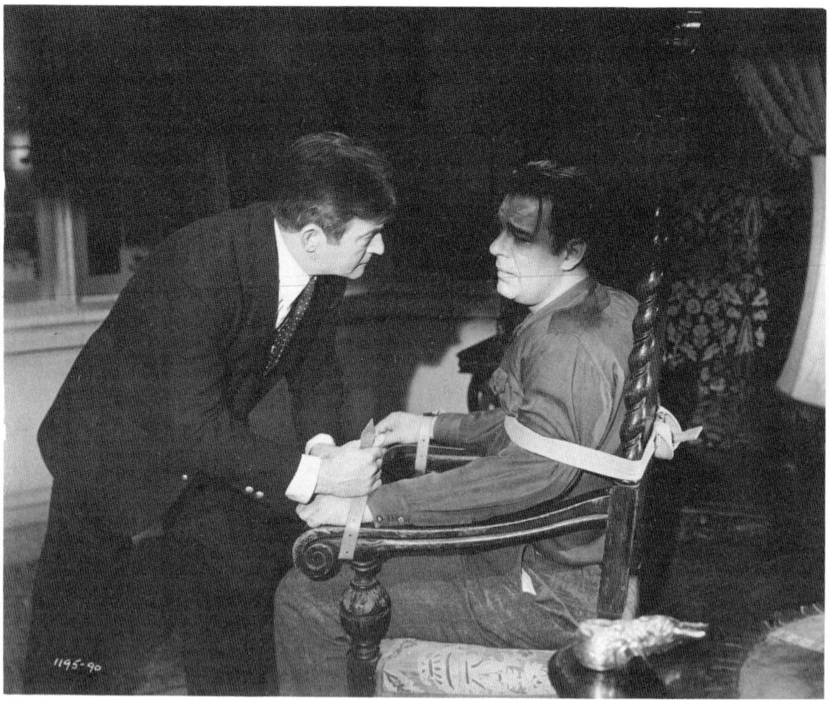

Claude Rains tries to help his son the werewolf, Lon Chaney (right), in the literate The Wolf Man.

1942

Black Dragons (MON) b/w 64min
In spite of Lugosi's claims on the publicity posters – 'Never have I worked on a story so startling or so blood-chillingly shocking' – this is a silly film. Lugosi plays the plastic surgeon sent to Japan on behalf of the Nazis to turn half-a-dozen spies into lookalikes for prominent American industrialists. The idea is murder, substitution and sabotage, but Lugosi is summarily arrested when he finishes the job. Escaping to America, he takes his revenge by killing off the substitute saboteurs one by one. With the garbled plot not exactly clarified by the fact that the plastic-surgery business is not revealed until a flashback near the end, the film is mainly a half-baked mess of screams, shadows and murkily lurking figures.

d William Nigh *p* Sam Katzman, Jack Dietz *s* Harvey H. Gates *c* Nat Reed *lp* Bela Lugosi, Joan Barclay, Clayton Moore, George Pembroke, Bob Frazer

Bowery at Midnight (MON) b/w 63min
Although no masterpiece, this is a distinct cut above the average of Lugosi's later films, no doubt because it was largely cribbed from his earlier **Dark Eyes of London** (1939). This time Lugosi is a distinguished professor whose *alter ego* runs a mission for Bowery down-and-outs as a cover for his nefarious activities. Exactly what these activities are (other than murder) never quite emerges, but the basement where he disposes of his victims is rather quaintly laid out as a cemetery complete with graves, and beneath that lies an intriguingly mysterious sub-chamber seemingly peopled by zombie ghouls. In the end, Lugosi is shoved into this pit by a disgruntled underling. It may not make too much sense, but it does have flashes of imagination.

d Wallace Fox *p* Sam Katzman, Jack Dietz *s* Gerald Schnitzer *c* Mack Stengler *lp* Bela Lugosi, John Archer, Wanda McKay, Tom Neal, Dave O'Brien, J. Farrell MacDonald

Cat People (RKO) b/w 74min
In 1942, with *Cat People*, producer Lewton inaugurated a series of modestly budgeted, extremely literate, intelligently understated horror movies – **I Walked with a Zombie, The Leopard Man, The Seventh Victim, The Ghost Ship** (all 1943), **The Curse of the Cat People** (1944) and **Bedlam** (1946)

– which should have left more of a mark on Hollywood than they did. Perhaps they were simply too delicately evocative for other film-makers to emulate. According to his own definition, Lewton's formula was simple: 'A love story, three scenes of suggested horror and one of actual violence.' Of course there is more to it than that, first and foremost the fact that a basis of ordinary, everyday reality is carefully built up to provide a correlative for the horror elements. *Cat People* is about a young New York fashion designer (the marvellously feline Simon) who falls in love and marries, but – troubled by a strange encounter which awakens her secret fear that she is descended from a medieval Balkan sect whose women turn into raging felines when their passions are roused – refuses to consummate the marriage.

The course of her obsession is vividly illustrated by the sketches she makes of the big cats at the zoo, and subsequent events, escalating from the mortal terror of a caged bird in her presence to the unseen panther claws that menace a rival for her husband's affections, are deliberately calculated to suggest that while she may indeed be undergoing metamorphosis, she may equally well be no more than a lonely, neurotic, possibly lesbian woman driven to brute violence by her obsessive fears. But the terrifying ambivalence, charged by electric detail – her enigmatic smile as her hand bats paw-like at the bird's cage; her long fingernails raking the velvet covering of a sofa in a rage – is what makes the film so arresting. Well understanding the power of suggestion, Lewton insisted on precedence being given to imagined rather than real horrors throughout the series. In a sense the whole film is predicated on suggestion, not least in the crucial encounter near the beginning between Simon and a sinister, catlike woman (Russell) whose casual glance of *recognition* in a restaurant initially triggers Simon's doubts about her own nature. The audience's sense of apprehension is given an agonizing turn of the screw by Lewton's knack of fleshing out his own phobias (in this case his fear of cats) with the traumas of others. The scene in which Simon's rival is threatened by an unseen panther while taking a dip in the basement pool was inspired by an experience in which director Tourneur once almost drowned while swimming alone at night. The sequence is made doubly terrifying by the complete vulnerability of an unclothed, unarmed swimmer. Equally nightmarish, and superbly staged by Tourneur, is an earlier scene of suggested horror in which Simon's rival is walking alone along a road through Central Park at night. The pool of light thrown by each street lamp becomes an island of safety surrounded by menacing blackness. Her hesitant footsteps seem to be echoed by stealthily padding paws and the rustle of stirring branches. The denouement, in which the anticipated doom finally materializes as a screeching feline hiss – made by the opening pneumatic doors of a bus as it pulls up alongside her – is one of the cinema's most heart-stopping moments.

The pity of *Cat People* is that Lewton and Tourneur were prevented from following through the premise that Simon is probably no more than a psychologically disturbed woman by the studio's insistence on the insertion of an unequivocal shot of a black panther.

d Jacques Tourneur *p* Val Lewton *s* DeWitt Bodeen *c* Nicholas Musuraca *lp* Simone Simon, Tom Conway, Kent Smith, Jack Holt, Jane Randolph, Elizabeth Russell

The poster for Cat People, *Jacques Tourneur's marvellous essay in evocative horror.*

The Corpse Vanishes *aka* **The Case of the Missing Brides** (MON) b/w 64min

This is a lamentably shoddy piece of work in which Lugosi lurks in a gothic castle, keeping his 80-year-old wife young and beautiful with glandular injections from a series of (presumably) virgin brides snatched from the altar after a poisonous orchid sends them into a corpse-like trance. Assisted by his servant (Urecal) and her two monstrous sons (a hideous dwarf and a half-witted giant), Lugosi keeps the bridal bodies alive in an underground vault until their glands run out. Walters is the intrepid girl reporter saved from the operating table by a combined effort from the servant and the police.

d Wallace Fox *p* Sam Katzman, Jack Dietz *s* Harvey H. Gates *c* Art Reed *lp* Bela Lugosi, Joan Barclay, Tristram Coffin, Minerva Urecal, Elizabeth Russell, Angelo Rossito

Ghost of Frankenstein (U) b/w 68min

This third sequel to **Frankenstein** (1931), the first without Karloff as the monster, despite the inadequacies of Chaney's takeover performance, is by no means a negligible film. Apparently unharmed by the bullets which finished him off in **Son of Frankenstein** (1939), Ygor the shepherd (Lugosi) digs out the also unharmed monster from the sulphur pit into which he was hurled at the end of the same film, and takes him off to see Baron Frankenstein (Hardwicke), evidently another son of the original creator. Inconsistencies – not the least of which is that the monster, having learned to talk in **The Bride of Frankenstein** (1935) and been mute in *Son of Frankenstein*, has mysteriously regained his powers of speech – aside, this opening is quite strikingly directed as the faltering monster renews his strength during an electrical storm, with the lightning recharging the electrodes in his neck. The rest of the film, graced by some delightful professional bickering as Hardwicke, who intends to dissect the monster, is persuaded by a visitation from his father's ghost to give it a 'good' brain and then maliciously doublecrossed by Atwill, who substitutes a brain from an eager donor, the evil Ygor, is more than adequate. Chaney's monster, hitherto a rather dull machine lacking any of the sympathy generated by Karloff, acquires a genuine chill as Ygor's gloatingly triumphant voice emerges from it: 'I have the strength of a hundred men! I, Ygor, will live for ever!' But, discovering that it is blind, the Ygor-monster goes berserk, and the usual conflagration ensues.

d Erle C. Kenton *p* George Waggner *s* W. Scott Darling *c* Milton Krasner, Elwood Bredell *lp* Cedric Hardwicke, Ralph Bellamy, Lionel Atwill, Bela Lugosi, Evelyn Ankers, Lon Chaney Jnr, Dwight Frye

The Mad Doctor of Market Street (U) b/w 60min

Although some strange and striking camera angles betray the presence of a director going places – to *Gun Crazy* (1949) and *The Big Combo* (1955) – there really isn't much Lewis can do with this skimpily scripted concoction. Atwill has his usual

Left: *Lon Chaney as the mummy in* The Mummy's Tomb.

field day, in what amounts to a solo showpiece, as a crazed doctor who claims to be able to raise the dead. Discredited and wanted for murder, he escapes (semi-inadvertently) to a South Sea island where he contrives to revive a comatose princess. Bursting with pride when the grateful natives (led by Johnson) respond by worshipping him as the God of Life, he turns his experimental attentions to one of his castaway companions. But unable to respond to demands that he resuscitate a drowned native, he is summarily put to death.

d Joseph H. Lewis *p* Paul Malvern *s* Al Martin *c* Jerome Ash *lp* Lionel Atwill, Una Merkel, Nat Pendleton, Claire Dodd, Anne Nagel, Noble Johnson

The Mad Monster (PNC) b/w 77min
Made in five days and looking like it, this was an attempt to cash in on the success of **The Wolf Man** (1941) from the far reaches of Poverty Row. Zucco is the standard mad doctor, infected by patriotic zeal and propounding the theory (to an audience of scientists congregating in his mind) that injections of wolf blood will create an invincible army. Experimenting on a handy farm labourer (Strange, making his horror début), he creates a hairy wolf-man who – despite the good doctor's work with a whip – promptly creates the usual mayhem and runs off with a little girl. Risible though it is, it shocked the British censor enough to ban it until 1952, and even then to insist that it should be accompanied by a disclaimer on the matter of blood transfusions.

Newfield and Zucco went on to make **Dead Men Walk** (1943) and **The Flying Serpent** (1946), in between times churning out *The Black Raven* (1943) which, for all the Poe connotations of its title, is a whodunit involving murder at the lonely inn on a stormy night.

d Sam Newfield *p* Sigmund Neufeld *s* Fred Myton *c* Jack Greenhalgh *lp* Johnny Downs, Anne Nagel, George Zucco, Glenn Strange, Mae Busch

The Mummy's Tomb (U) b/w 61min
After the success of **The Wolf Man** (1941), Universal began the thankless task of promoting Chaney as their new horror star, pushing him into all the roles made famous by Boris Karloff and Bela Lugosi. His Frankenstein's monster (**Ghost of Frankenstein**, 1942) is grotesquely overacted and his absurdly overweight mummy little better. Perhaps the weakest in the series, *The Mummy's Tomb* is a dreary re-run of **The Mummy's Hand** (1940), this time arbitrarily located in New England. Zucco, though shot three times and falling dead down a staircase at the end of *The Mummy's Hand*, reappears as the now ancient high priest handing over to his successor (Bey), who again manipulates the mummy to his own ends while the mummy again rambles in pursuit of his reincarnated love (Knox). The flashback sequence from **The Mummy** (1932) is once more trotted out, while further cost-cutting is exercised by including Zucco's 'death' scene from *The Mummy's Hand* and, for the climax, shots of villagers brandishing burning torches borrowed from **Frankenstein** (1931).

d Harold Young *p* Ben Pivar *s* Griffin Jay, Henry Sucher *c* George Robinson *lp* Lon Chaney Jnr, Dick Foran, Elyse Knox, John Hubbard, Turhan Bey, Wallace Ford, George Zucco

Night Monster *aka* **House of Mystery**
(U) b/w 73min
Morgan here plays the legless cripple who learns enough about yoga from a mysterious swami (Asther) to will himself legs (odd but serviceable) and set about murdering the doctors responsible for the amputation. Mainly a mystery with the usual sinister suspects, including Lugosi standing rather sadly on the sidelines as the butler, the film, though capably acted and serviceably directed, is routine.

d/p Ford Beebe *s* Clarence Upson Young *c* Charles Van Enger *lp* Bela Lugosi, Ralph Morgan, Lionel Atwill, Don Porter, Irene Harvey, Nils Asther, Leif Erickson

The Strange Case of Dr RX (U) b/w 68min
Although plugged as a horror movie on the posters which featured a fishy-eyed Atwill in pebble glasses (for his red-herring role as Dr Fish), this is really a comedy-thriller in which a private eye (Knowles) goes after the killer of five men, each involved in some shady business and found dead with a visiting card from the mysterious 'Doctor RX'. Fast-moving and beautifully shot for creepy effect by Bredell, it includes one of the classic horror standbys when the unlikely killer (Hinds) tries to drive Knowles mad by threatening to transplant his brain into a gorilla (the latter played by Ray 'Crash' Corrigan).

d William Nigh *p* Jack Bernhard *s* Clarence Upson Young *c* Elwood Bredell *lp* Patric Knowles, Lionel Atwill, Anne Gwynne, Mona Barrie, Paul Cavanagh, Samuel S. Hinds, Mantan Moreland

The Undying Monster *aka* **The Hammond Mystery**
(FOX) b/w 60min
A family curse is acted out in an old dark house in this atmospherically shot but otherwise stolid horror outing. In a perfunctory final sequence in which the Hammond heir (Howard), who is responsible for savaging a local wench to death, abducts his sister (Angel) and is promptly shot dead by a policeman (no charms or silver bullets necessary, apparently), the curse is revealed to be the taint of lycanthropy.

Brahm became a master of brooding Victorian melodrama with such films as *The Lodger* (1944), *Hangover Square* (1945) and *The Locket* (1946), and even invested contemporary subjects like *Guest in the House* (1944) and *The Brasher Doubloon* (1947) with the same shadowy atmosphere. Here, with a turn-of-the-century English setting, he and Ballard (with whom he collaborated on *The Lodger*) sustain the mood perfectly from a brilliant opening sequence in which a clock ominously strikes midnight, each chime punctuated by a discreet pause as the camera prowls round the great hallway of the house perched on a clifftop by the sea among gaunt, blasted trees and approached by a twisting fogbound road to pick out some significant detail. But the script, sketchily adapted from Jessie Douglas Kerruish's novel, seems to belong to another film as it labours to create a pseudo Sherlock Holmes adventure, with Ellison as a pipe-smoking Scotland Yard expert demonstrating the latest in scientific detecting techniques, and Thatcher engagingly supplying the light relief as his distaff Dr Watson.

d John Brahm *p* Bryan Foy *s* Lillie Hayward, Michel Jacoby *c* Lucien Ballard *lp* James Ellison, Heather Angel, John Howard, Bramwell Fletcher, Heather Thatcher, Aubrey Mather

1943

The Ape Man *aka* Lock Your Doors
(MON) b/w 64min
Rock-bottom even for Monogram. As directed by 'One-Shot' Beaudine, staged in cardboard sets, and overacted by all concerned with an element of self-mockery that doesn't quite make the grade, it is almost worthy of the Theatre of the Absurd. Lugosi is Dr Brewster, a scientist believed to have disappeared but actually beavering away in his basement laboratory with the doting approval of his hatchet-faced sister (Urecal). Using himself as a guinea-pig, he has for some time been experimenting with gorilla spinal fluids and is disturbed to find himself developing facial fur and a crouch. The logical answer is counter-injections of spinal fluids from lovely young bodies, but in the end the unhappy semi-simian routinely dies at the hands of the gorilla he sends out to do his killing.

d William Beaudine *p* Sam Katzman, Jack Dietz *s* Barney A. Sarecky *c* Mack Stengler *lp* Bela Lugosi, Wallace Ford, Louise Currie, Minerva Urecal, Henry Hall, Ralph Littlefield

Captive Wild Woman (U) b/w 61min
A deliriously dotty cheapie, this film also marked Carradine's first starring role as Dr Sigmund Walters, a mad surgeon specializing in endocrinology. Tempted when Ankers – who works for a fairground proprietor and whose boyfriend (Stone) is an animal trainer – brings along her ailing sister (Vickers) for a consultation, Carradine steals Stone's orang-utan and injects it with glandular extractions from Vickers. She dies, but the ape turns into a beautiful woman (Acquanetta) whom Carradine names Paula. Possessed with a strange power over animals, Acquanetta subsequently joins Stone's act, but grows increasingly jealous of his relationship with Ankers. The stress makes her go berserk and revert to her animal state. Going on alone with his act during a storm which panics the animals, Stone is saved by the ape-Paula at the cost of her own life (she has already killed Carradine). Hardly *amour fou* but quite pacily directed, it is padded out with a good deal of circus footage from a Clyde Beatty film, *The Big Cage* (1933). Acquanetta, Ankers and Stone appeared in a sequel, **Jungle Woman** (1944).

d Edward Dmytryk *p* Ben Pivar *s* Henry Sucher, Griffin Jay *c* George Robinson *lp* John Carradine, Evelyn Ankers, Acquanetta, Milburn Stone, Martha MacVicar (Vickers), Lloyd Corrigan, Fay Helm

Lon Chaney as the wolf-man in Frankenstein Meets the Wolf Man, *the first of Universal's many pairings of its monsters.*

Dead Men Walk *aka* Creature of the Devil
(PRC) b/w 64min
This was made by the same team as **The Mad Monster** (1942), just as quickly and just as tackily. Essaying a dual role, Zucco plays an adept in the black arts who returns after death as a vampire, determined to destroy his good twin. Frustrated in his attempts to get at his brother through his pretty ward (Carlisle) since she inconveniently sports a gold cross, he vampirizes several other local inhabitants before dying, along with his twin, in a fire. Frye, in his penultimate film (he died in 1943), is enjoyably on hand to repeat his role from **Dracula** (1931) as a hunchbacked assistant. Young, later a blacklisted screenwriter and an Oscar-winner for *The Defiant Ones* (1958), makes his horror début as the juvenile lead.

d Sam Newfield *p* Sigmund Neufeld *s* Fred Myton *c* Jack Greenhalgh *lp* George Zucco, Mary Carlisle, Nedrick Young, Dwight Frye, Fern Emmett, Robert Strange

Frankenstein Meets the Wolf Man (U) b/w 74min
The first of Universal's attempts to ginger up fading box-office receipts by multiplying its monsters. Lugosi at last got to play the Frankenstein monster, having missed out on the part in **Frankenstein** (1931) although, ironically, since he had originally been unhappy about playing the role silent, this monster could not speak either (although it had in **The Bride of Frankenstein**, 1935 and **Ghost of Frankenstein**, 1942). Also ironically, this is one of Lugosi's worst performances, not helped by the fact that he was now ill and stuntman Eddie Parker had to double for him through much of the film. The fact that the film was cut before release may explain at least part of the performance's embarrassing inadequacy: scenes were removed indicating that the monster was blind (as at the end of *Ghost of Frankenstein*) and that his sight was subsequently restored by Knowles. The star is, in any case, Chaney's Larry Talbot, a Byronic hero seeking death as a permanent release from lycanthropy and hoping that Frankenstein may be able to help. He finds the monster but no Frankenstein, and becoming a wolf-man again because of a meddling scientist (Knowles), fights it out with the monster until they are washed away by a dynamited dam. Competently directed (especially the beginning) but basically an unimaginative rehash, the film is definitively sunk by Lugosi's performance.

d Roy William Neill *p* George Waggner *s* Curt Siodmak *c* George Robinson *lp* Lon Chaney Jnr, Bela Lugosi, Lionel Atwill, Ilona Massey, Patric Knowles, Maria Ouspenskaya, Dwight Frye

The Ghost Ship (RKO) b/w 69min
This minor Lewton production tell the familiar tale of a jinxed ship whose captain (Dix), crushed by the weight of authority and gradually eaten away inside by malignant doubts and fears, turns into a homicidal maniac. Elegantly crafted with handsome sets, making evocative use of a sea-shanty score, and sketching a Hitchcockian transference-of-guilt theme, the film has little real horror unless one sees the giant hook which breaks loose during a storm and has to be subdued, as a monster threatening the crew.

d Mark Robson *p* Val Lewton *s* Donald Henderson Clarke *c* Nicholas Musuraca *lp* Richard Dix, Russell Wade, Edith Barrett, Ben Bard, Edmund Glover, Shelton Knaggs

I Walked with a Zombie (RKO) b/w 69min

This is a haunting nightmarishly beautiful tone poem of voodoo drums, dark moonlight and somnambulist ladies in floating white, brought to perfection by Tourneur's direction, Hunt's camerawork and Wray's dialogue. The wonderfully evocative transposition of *Jane Eyre* (loosely speaking) to the West Indies has Dee as a nurse summoned to the island of St Sebastian to look after a sick woman (Gordon), afflicted by a mysterious mental paralysis. Falling for the darkly brooding husband (Conway) but believing him still to be in love with his wife, Dee determines to take her to the voodoo ceremony, spoken of in bated breath by the servants, in the hope of a cure. In one of the cinema's great sequences, a crescendo of tracking shots and caressing dissolves orchestrated by the rustling wind and muted drums, the two women silently negotiate the terrors of the night and a giant zombie lookout (Jones), only for Dee to discover that Conway's mother (Barrett) – a missionary secretly posing as a voodoo priestess to further her own Christian ends – had in fact turned her daughter-in-law into a zombie because she threatened to break up the family by running away with her husband's alcoholic half-brother (Ellison).

The beauty of the film is that, hovering visually in precarious balance between darkness and light, nothing in it is any more clearcut than the good or evil of Barrett's motives and actions. The nebulous gulf between – established on the boat at the beginning when Conway sourly tempers Dee's delight at the beauty of the flying fish by explaining that they are leaping in terror to escape predators beneath the surface – is the keynote of the film. Aside from the transparent Dee, one never gets at the *truth* of any of the characters, only – as the calypso folksongs and carving of St Sebastian used as punctuation devices suggest – at a sense of the joy to which they aspire and the pain in which they live. Tourneur's best film, *I Walked with a Zombie* is a small masterpiece.

d Jacques Tourneur *p* Val Lewton *s* Curt Siodmak, Ardel Wray *c* J. Roy Hunt *lp* Frances Dee, Tom Conway, James Ellison, Christine Gordon, Edith Barrett, Sir Lancelot, Darby Jones

The Leopard Man (RKO) b/w 66min

Often described as a straightforward mystery thriller about a series of murders committed by a maniac killer masquerading as an escaped leopard, *The Leopard Man* was received as a disappointment after the hauntingly graceful horrors of **Cat People** (1942) and **I Walked with a Zombie** (1943) – so much so, in fact, that even Lewton and Tourneur disowned it as a miscalculation. Yet it now looks like a fascinating by-product of the then embryonic *noir* genre. As the title of Cornell Woolrich's source novel suggests (and, though truncated, it is otherwise followed with some fidelity), the leopard is merely a *black alibi*: an alibi not only for the human killer, but for the human greed, ambition and lust that preys on the world (it is no accident, for instance, that the incident which sparks off the whole affair should be a selfish publicity stunt).

Two sequences, in particular, pull the whole *noir* reference together as they trace dancer Margo's solitary walk home through the nocturnal streets after the night-club closes. The first time she takes the walk, a bravura sequence stunningly shot by de Grasse, is before the first murder; and the dark alleys, seemingly a nightmare haunt of terrors, become a friendly haven of the night, as figures lurking unseen behind dark windows and in doorways respond to the password of Margo's cheery greeting. But the second time, after the second murder has tightened the grip of fear, the streets and alleys have become a true limbo of dread, empty of all humanity save for a sinister young man in a black car (ironically, identified as the killer by fortune-telling cards) and the killer himself. Even those who fault *The Leopard Man* by comparison with *I Walked with a Zombie* grant that Margo's two walks and the passage in which a Mexican child – locked out as a punishment by an impatient mother – is killed, portrayed simply by a pool of blood seeping beneath the bolted door, are remarkable.

d Jacques Tourneur *p* Val Lewton *s* Ardel Wray *c* Robert de Grasse *lp* Dennis O'Keefe, Margo, Jean Brooks, Isabel Jewell, James Bell, Abner Biberman

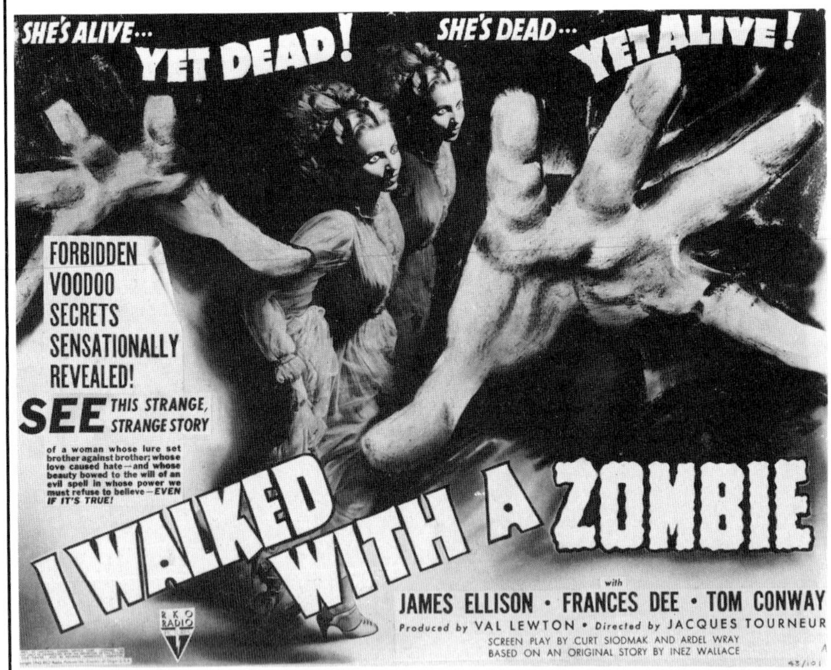

The poster from I Walked with a Zombie, *one of the undisputed masterpieces of the horror genre.*

The Mad Ghoul (U) b/w 64min

An unusually (for the period) classy B picture, thanks largely to Krasner's imaginative camerawork and excellent performances from Bruce, Zucco and Ankers, this features Zucco, at his unctuous best, as a distinguished professor who has rediscovered a gas used by the ancient Egyptians as part of a life-preserving process. Insanely jealous when he realizes that he and his young assistant (Bruce) love the same girl (Ankers), he gives Bruce a whiff of the gas, turning him into a slowly mummifying zombie. The only way to halt the process is a periodical heart transplant; so, with Bruce thinking he is merely ill, and ripe for persuasion that he ought to release Ankers from their engagement, Zucco sends him out to rob graves or murder (without any memory of what he has done). With Bruce temporarily restored by the heart thus obtained, he is allowed periodic visits to Ankers – a singer currently on tour – since Zucco hopes that she will in any case become disillusioned and turn to him. Disturbed by the change in Bruce, she turns instead to her accompanist (Bey). At last realizing what has happened, Bruce manages to give Zucco a whiff of the gas, and instead of killing Bey as ordered, commits suicide. Zucco is shot by the police while frantically trying to secure a heart from an undertaker's coffin. An unnecessarily complicated way for an ingenious mad doctor to get rid of a rival, perhaps; but Zucco, much too suave to force his attentions, contrives to suggest that the way he sees it is that he is simply giving the girl time to face the inevitable and see him as the better man. Ankers' singing voice was dubbed by Lillian Cornell.

d James P. Hogan *p* Ben Pivar *s* Brenda Weisberg, Paul Gangelin *c* Milton Krasner *lp* George Zucco, Evelyn Ankers, David Bruce, Robert Armstrong, Turhan Bey

La Mujer Sin Cabeza *aka* **The Headless Woman**
(FILMS MUNDIALES/FELIPE SUBERVIELLE; MEX) b/w 77min
English magician Bamberg took the stage name Fu Manchu, and appeared as the character in films and plays, adopting the persona popularized by Boris Karloff in **The Mask of Fu Manchu** (1932). In 1943, Bamberg wrote and starred in three pictures simultaneously: a haunted-house thriller called *El Espectro de la Novia*; a mystery adventure story about an illusionist, *El As Negro*, and this movie. All of them feature the stock characters of Fu's lazy servant, Satanas (Mendel), and the irritable cop Palomino (Sala) and were directed by ex-actor Cardona (**El Baúl Macabro**, 1936) and echo the thrillers of Feuillade and the magic of Méliès. *La Mujer Sin Cabeza* is the best of the three. Fu is suspected of murdering another magician but by using telepathy and following a trail of six women's heads modelled in wax he discovers a rival illusionist to be the culprit: his former assistant (Riquelme), who is eventually captured in a wax museum.

Bamberg exploits the cinema as a box of magic tricks to enhance his stories with supernatural overtones. His best collaboration with Cardona was *El Museo del Crimen* (1944), an entertaining detective story in which Fu glimpses, apropos of nothing, the face of a werewolf in a hotel mirror, an incident then forgotten in the rest of the movie, making it simply a playful reference to the American fantasy films they took as their model.

d/co-s René Cardona *p* Armando Espinosa *co-s* David T. Bamberg, Xavier Villaurrutia *c* Gabriel Figueroa *lp* David T. Bamberg (Fu Manchu), Manuel Mendel, Paco Fuentes, Angel T. Sala, Carlos Riquelme, Manuel Noriega, Fernando Romero, José Pando, Cuca Escobar, Alfonso Bedoya

The Mysterious Doctor (WB) b/w 57min
This is set in wartime Cornwall and features a mysterious doctor (Matthews) – actually blameless – who shows undue interest in an abandoned tinmine, which is believed to be haunted by long-dead Black Morgan, looking for his head. The headless ghost makes a somewhat absurd appearance, and several villagers are found decapitated. In the end, a Nazi, attempting to mask his subversive activities, is found to be res-ponsible. The moorland settings (both foggy and wind-swept, of course) are quite passable, and the script certainly piles on its effects: not only a headless ghost and decapitated corpses, but a sinister village idiot (Willis) and a pub landlord (Mayo) who wears a hangman's hood because his face has been disfigured by dynamite.

Claude Rains in the title role of The Phantom of the Opera.

d Ben Stoloff *p* William Jacobs *s* Richard Weil *c* Harry Sharp *lp* John Loder, Eleanor Parker, Lester Matthews, Matt Willis, Forrester Harvey, Frank Mayo

The Phantom of the Opera (U) 93min
A lush, lavish extravaganza, elegantly directed with exquisite colour camerawork, this film has been tamed too far to work as a horror movie. For one thing there are too many bouts of opera, recorded with pristine clarity but not particularly impressively, performed by Eddy and Foster. For another, reduced to a sort of avuncular mentor in a fetchingly modelled mask, Rain's Phantom (for all his supposed misdeeds) is robbed of the lunatic grandeur in which Chaney revelled throughout the later stages of the 1925 version. The chandelier sequence, curiously muffed in the earlier version, is an improvement; but the rest is mainly tasteful tedium with the unmasking scene (one of the highlights of Chaney's performance) at least better than in Hammer's 1962 remake.

d Arthur Lubin *p* George Waggner *s* Eric Taylor, Samuel Hoffenstein *c* Hal Mohr, W. Howard Greene *lp* Nelson Eddy, Susanna Foster, Claude Rains, Edgar Barrier, Leo Carrillo, Hume Cronyn

Revenge of the Zombies *aka* **The Corpse Vanished**
(MON) b/w 61min
Carradine here is superb as Dr Max Heinrich von Altermann, a mad doctor lurking in a remote mansion somewhere in the Louisiana swamplands and beavering away at producing a zombie army for the greater glory of Adolf Hitler. Simultaneously, having experimented on his dead wife and turned her into a zombie (Borg), he is now busily trying to find a cure for her. She finally leads the zombies in a revolt.

One of several low-budget programmers that followed in the wake of Jacques Tourneur's **I Walked with a Zombie** (1943), the film is lifted out of the rut by Carradine's performance and by occasional imaginative touches (notably in the laboratory scenes and the sequence where Borg's corpse is found wandering in the night). Sekely, a talented refugee from the Hungarian and German cinema, never really got much of a chance in Hollywood, but (with the aid of superlative camerawork by John Alton) made a strikingly stylish job of *Hollow Triumph* (1948).

d Steve Sekely *p* Linsley Parsons *s* Edmund Kelso, Van Norcross *c* Mack Stengler *lp* John Carradine, Robert Lowery, Veda Ann Borg, Gale Storm, Mantan Moreland, Bob Steele

The Seventh Victim (RKO) b/w 71min
Though competently directed by Robson (his first film), the strong suit of this wonderfully eerie thriller about devil-worshippers in Greenwich Village is its evocative script. So much so, that it almost matches **I Walked with a Zombie** (1943) as a film haunted by death and despair, somehow contriving to live up to the doom-laden premise of its epigraph from a poem by John Donne ('I runne to death and death meets me as fast/and all my pleasures are like yesterday'). The keynote is struck right from the start as Hunter, just graduating from pupil to teacher at a gloomy boarding school, learns that her sister has disappeared and sets off to look for her with the words of an ageing colleague ringing in her ears, begging her to have the courage not to come back, but to go out and enjoy the world before it's too late. What she finds is a room, totally empty but for a noose and a chair placed ominously beneath it, that she is told made her sister happy in some strange way. This enigma is clarified by the discovery that her sister (Brooks), condemned to death by the devil-worshippers she has betrayed by walking out on the cult, clings to her room and its noose as a kindlier refuge from the inevitable.

As Hunter pursues her search through Manhattan (studded with marvellous moments – including a premonition of the

Left: *The evocative* The Seventh Victim.

shower scene from **Psycho** (1960), the confrontation with murder on a subway, a terrifying walk home through dark streets to match the one in **Cat People**, 1942), she finds herself alone in a world of tormented souls or unhappy cynics that is to be endured rather than enjoyed. The ninth circle of hell is reached in Hunter's encounter with a consumptive prostitute (Russell) who lives next door to her sister's room and who can think of nothing but her approaching death ('I've been quiet, oh, ever so quiet. I hardly move, yet it keeps coming all the time, closer and closer'). Yet there is still one more to come, surely one of the bleakest moments in cinema, when Russell, going out on the town for one last despairing fling, hears the sinister sound of an overturning chair next door and passes on without realizing what it means.

The Seventh Victim isn't quite well directed enough to be called a masterpiece. But almost.

d Mark Robson *p* Val Lewton *s* DeWitt Bodeen, Charles O'Neal *c* Nicholas Musuraca *lp* Tom Conway, Kim Hunter, Jean Brooks, Isabel Jewell, Elizabeth Russell, Evelyn Brent, Hugh Beaumont

Son of Dracula (U) b/w 79min

Nothing in this film quite lives up to the marvellous sequence of a coffin emerging from a misty lake, with the vampire materializing from a wisp of smoke to glide ashore in his weird barque. One of the problems with the movie is that Universal's economy drive gives it a penny-pinching look (cost was the reason why Chaney's Dracula surfaces in America and is never seen in Transylvania). The other was a script stronger on character, dialogue and situation than on incident. Chaney is very much at ease in the role, looking odd, if well-fed, in suave moustache and powdered temples as he attempts (posing as Count Alucard) to establish power and wealth for himself in the New World by wooing the daughter of an aristocratic Southern family. But neither he nor Albritton bring much subtlety (or indeed passion) to the morbidly erotic side of their relationship in which she ecstatically embraces vampirism in order to share immortality with Paige, the man she really loves. On the other hand, both these deficiencies play to some extent into Siodmak's hands, and he is able to perform a sort of exercise in style: not the mature, controlled expressionism of **Spiral Staircase** (1946), but recognizably by the same hand.

d Robert Siodmak *p* Ford Beebe *s* Eric Taylor *c* George Robinson *lp* Lon Chaney Jnr, J. Edward Bromberg, Louise Albritton, Robert Paige, Evelyn Ankers, Frank Craven

1944

The Climax (U) 86min

The box-office success of **The Phantom of the Opera** (1943) inevitably spawned imitations, including this one, based on an existing play by Edward Locke, but virtually repeating the film's central plot situation. Karloff (in his first colour film) is the quiet, retiring physician of the Paris Opera House who, unknown to anyone, ten years before had strangled the woman he loved, an opera singer (Vincent), out of jealousy because she refused to give up her career. Convinced that he has met her reincarnation in a young music student (Foster) with a voice strangely like hers, he resorts to hypnotism to keep her away from other ears and eyes. His plans upset by a fellow-student who loves her (Bey), he dies in a conflagration that also consumes the embalmed body of his first love. Virtually duplicating the earlier film in its faults and virtues, it is distinguished by Karloff's carefully understated portrayal of a man obsessed.

d/p George Waggner *s* Curt Siodmak, Lynn Starling *c* Hal Mohr, W. Howard Greene *lp* Boris Karloff, Susanna Foster, Turhan Bey, Gale Sondergaard, June Vincent, Thomas Gomez

Crazy Knights *aka* **Ghost Crazy**
(MON) b/w 61min

This is the second of three witless films in which Monogram vainly tried to create a comedy team out of Gilbert, Rosenbloom and Howard (later one of the Three Stooges) – the others were *Three of a Kind* (1944) and *Trouble Chasers* (1954). The movie itself is a standard haunted-house comedy involving fake ghosts, a cemetery and a gorilla (played by Miles).

d William Beaudine *p* Sam Katzman, Jack Dietz *s* Tim Ryan *c* Marcel le Picard *lp* Billy Gilbert, Maxie Rosenbloom, Shemp Howard, Jayne Hazard, Minerva Urecal, Tim Ryan, Art Miles

Cry of the Werewolf (COL) b/w 65min

Rewarded with a leading role after her promising début in **The Return of the Vampire** (1944), Foch is a striking presence as Celeste La Tour, queen of the Troiga gypsies, a werewolf who makes her first kill to protect the name of her dead mother from whom she inherited the taint. Columbia, unfortunately, gave her little else in the way of script or direction (it was Levin's first film). The fact that the transformations occur off-screen may signal an attempt to emulate the Val Lewton style, but everything else is strictly conventional as the werewolf determinedly tries to silence not only the inquisitive young man (Crane) whose doctor father she had to kill, but his fiancée (Massen) too.

d Henry Levin *p* Wallace MacDonald *s* Griffin Jay, Charles O'Neal *c* L. W. O'Connell *lp* Nina Foch, Stephen Crane, Osa Massen, Barton MacLane, Fritz Leiber, John Abbott

The Curse of the Cat People (RKO) b/w 70min

On the face of it not so much a horror as a delicate fantasy about a lonely child who conjures up an imaginary playmate and becomes helplessly entangled in the world she creates for herself, this film takes on a much darker aspect if considered as a sequel to **Cat People**, 1942 (ideally the two films should be screened together). In the earlier film, Smith was widowed by the death of Irena (Simon); he is now married to Randolph, the girl into whose sympathetic ear he had poured his troubles about Simon's obsession that she was descended from a race of Balkan cat-women, and jealousy of whom may have provoked Simon's crisis and death. It is their child, Amy (Carter), moody, solitary, virtually ostracized by the neighbourhood children because she is different, who now lives in an imaginary world, conjuring (from photographs) the dead Simon as a playmate. There is a sense here that the curse of the cat people – the solitude that breeds despair and perhaps madness –

threatens Carter as much as it once did Simon. The menace that lies in wait for Carter seems to come not from the benevolently protective Simon, but from the 'witches' house' next door – a sinister cavern of dark shadows, fluttering curtains and creaking mysteries, beautifully evoked by Musuraca's superb chiaroscuro photography – where a half-crazed old actress (Dean) treats the deliciously terrified Carter to tea and a spirited performance of 'The Legend of Sleepy Hollow', and where her equally crazed daughter (Russell, the sinister cat-woman of *Cat People*) slinks around with feline menace because she is convinced that Carter has stolen her mother's affection from her.

The blood-and-thunder melodramatics of the old dark house and its two weird inhabitants are very carefully calculated to provide a rational, daylight terror against which the unfathomable mysteries of the night can be measured. It is those unseen nocturnal mysteries which hover over the film, giving it the same chilling smell of the pit as Henry James' *The Turn of the Screw*. A marvellous little film, *The Curse of the Cat People* is one of the least condescending and least sentimental forays ever made into what James Agee called 'the poetry and danger of childhood'.

d Robert Wise, Gunther V. Fritsch *p* Val Lewton *s* DeWitt Bodeen, (uncredited) Val Lewton *c* Nicholas Musuraca *lp* Simone Simon, Ann Carter, Kent Smith, Elizabeth Russell, Julia Dean, Jane Randolph, Sir Lancelot

The Ghost Catchers (U) b/w 69min
This is very much the same zany mixture of non-sequiturs, one-liners and nonsense gags as in *Hellzapoppin'* (1941) and *The Crazy House* (1943). Olsen and Johnson are New York night-club entertainers pressganged into helping a Southern colonel (Catlett) and his daughters (Jean and O'Driscoll) rid their house of ghosts. When exorcism to the strain of a swing band fails and a corpse turns up, things get black with all the principals walled up in the cellar. But the ghosts come to the rescue to expose the gangster villainy. Though the songs are a tiresome interruption, the special effects are surprisingly good and the incidentals (Carrillo as a mummy, Chaney as a bear, the perennially inebriated Norton as a tap-dancing ghost) are often genuinely funny.

d Edward F. Cline *p/s* Edmund L. Hartmann *c* Charles Van Enger *lp* Ole Olsen, Chic Johnson, Gloria Jean, Martha O'Driscoll, Leo Carrillo, Lon Chaney Jnr, Walter Catlett, Jack Norton

The beautiful-looking but otherwise unimaginative The Man in Half Moon Street.

House of Frankenstein (U) b/w 71min
In trying to go one better than **Frankenstein Meets the Wolf Man** (1943), which was the first of the monster rallies designed to restore horror movies to box-office favour, Universal here rather overstep the mark. So much is going on that nothing is developed and the whole film degenerates into an absurd montage of sketches. Karloff is a mad doctor with notions of outdoing Frankenstein. He and a homicidal hunchback (Naish) escape from jail, murder a travelling showman (Zucco), and take over his carnival of horrors which contains the inert Dracula (Carradine) and a manuscript which leads to Castle Frankenstein, the monster (Strange) and the Wolf Man (Chaney). All are revived, do their thing, and perish (the monster disappearing with Karloff into quicksands at the end). Really rather enjoyable in its absurdly indigestible way, it is distinguished by Robinson's camerawork and Carradine's brief but outstanding portrayal of Dracula.

d Erle C. Kenton *p* Paul Malvern *s* Edward T. Lowe *c* George Robinson *lp* Lon Chaney Jnr, Boris Karloff, John Carradine, J. Carrol Naish, George Zucco, Glenn Strange, Lionel Atwill

Jungle Woman (U) b/w 54min
Killed off at the end of **Captive Wild Woman** (1943), the orang-utan turned into sultry Acquanetta by John Carradine is brought back to life by another mad doctor (Naish) for this outing. After which, at a loss what to do next, the script simply repeats the jealousy and reversion motif from the earlier film. Poor Paula the ape-woman dies again at the end, only to be revived once more in **Jungle Captive** (1945), no longer played by Acquanetta, whose career took a nose-dive when she took to speech following her mute roles here and in *Captive Wild Woman*.

This film should not be confused with *Nabonga* (1944), released in Britain as *The Jungle Woman*: a Buster Crabbe adventure about a little girl adopted by a giant gorilla after a plane crash in Africa (and growing up to be Julie London).

d Reginald LeBorg *p* Will Cowan *s* Henry Sucher *c* Jack MacKenzie *lp* Evelyn Ankers, J. Carrol Naish, Lois Collier, Douglas Dumbrille, Acquanetta, Milburn Stone

The Man in Half Moon Street (PAR) b/w 92min
This version of Barré Lyndon's play about a man who finds the secret of (almost) eternal youth, is filmed so discreetly that the horror is entirely in the mind of the beholder. A note of civilized urbanity is struck from the outset with a society reception at which Asther, greeted by an old woman who remarks on his resemblance to his grandfather (actually himself, of course), teasingly delights and horrifies her by recounting intimate details of a long ago flirtation supposedly confided by the boastful grandfather. The measured, almost stately cadence continues with the arrival of a now elderly colleague of Asther's student days (Schuenzel), and beautifully counterpoints Schuenzel's rueful awareness of his closeness to death (instrumental in discovering the glandular transplantation process by which Asther has benefited, he himself felt it wrong to tamper with God's work) against his equally rueful awareness of the hell he has escaped. Largely by indirections, through conversations or reports studied by the baffled police, and with the solitary murder taking place off-screen, it emerges that Asther – still urbanely unable to see, as Schuenzel does, that he has become the traditional mad doctor – has for 60 years been condemned to commit a murder every six years to correct a flaw in the renewal process.

The trouble with the film, which is beautifully shot in Paramount's low-key gloss style, is that it really adds up to little more than a conventional genre yarn, and its refusal to acknowledge the shortcuts of genre convention does make for *longueurs*. But the approach pays dividends at the end, when Asther suddenly ages in the presence of his fiancée (Walker). Distressed rather than terrified, exalted by what she sees as his sacrifice to science, she confidently contemplates the future 'some time' when they will be reunited – not quite *amour fou* perhaps, but unexpectedly close. Asther's final ageing, incidentally, is to normal 80-year-old decrepitude. The Hammer remake, **The Man Who Could Cheat Death** (1958), is very different.

d Ralph M. Murphy *p* Walter MacEwen *s* Charles Kenyon *c* Henry Sharp *lp* Nils Asther, Helen Walker, Reinhold Schuenzel, Paul Cavanagh, Edmund Breon

The Monster Maker (PRC) b/w 64min

Naish is the mad scientist conducting nasty experiments in his laboratory while a giant (Strange) stands by. When his amorous overtures to McKay are rejected, he infects her father (Morgan) with acromegaly. Since Morgan is a concert pianist, the hideous deformity of face and hands that results is not good for his career; and since only Naish can cure the disease, he hopes McKay will be more reasonable. Naturally, these hopes are unfounded. Although Naish and Morgan try to bring a sharp edge of conviction to their parts, Morgan is badly let down by an appalling makeup job.

d Sam Newfield *p* Sigmund Neufeld *s* Pierre Gendron, Martin Mooney *c* Robert Cline *lp* J. Carrol Naish, Ralph Morgan, Wanda McKay, Tala Birell, Glenn Strange

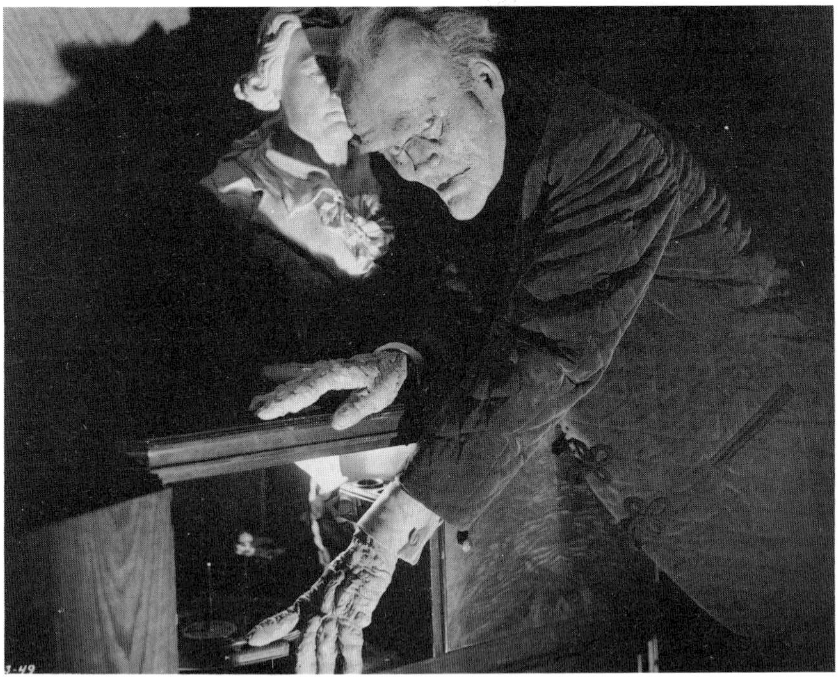

Ralph Morgan disfigured by an insane J. Carrol Naish in the lacklustre The Monster Maker.

The Mummy's Curse (U) b/w 62min

Chaney's third and last appearance as the mummy, apart from a takeoff performance in an episode for the *Route 66* teleseries (*Lizard's Leg and Owlet's Wing*, 1962). A strikingly weird opening has the Princess Anaka surfacing from her quicksand coffin when the swamp is drained by engineers. Otherwise, despite pleasantly photogenic Louisiana bayou settings, this is very much to the formula established in **The Mummy's Tomb** (1942) and **The Mummy's Ghost** (1944), with Coe as the new high priest and Christine the eternally elusive princess.

d Leslie Goodwins *p* Ben Pivar *s* Bernard Schubert *c* Virgil Miller *lp* Lon Chaney Jnr, Peter Coe, Virginia Christine, Kay Harding, Martin Kosleck, Kurt Katch

The Mummy's Ghost (U) b/w 61min

Chaney's second appearance as the mummy, with Zucco revived yet again to hand over the high priest's trust, this time to Carradine. Corners are again cut by including quotes from **The Mummy** (1932), and Kharis the mummy is once more on the trail of his princess, now exhibited in an American museum and crumbling to dust when Kharis reaches longingly for her. A touch of originality, making this a marginal improvement over **The Mummy's Tomb** (1942), has her soul reincarnated in a pretty student (Ames) outside whose window Kharis moons night after night to gaze on his beloved. But Carradine has been in lecherous pursuit with the tana juice of immortality, her hair is gradually turning white lock by lock, and when Kharis eventually carries her off in his arms – to sink together into the quicksand – she has herself become a mummy.

d Reginald LeBorg *p* Ben Pivar *s* Griffin Jay, Henry Sucher, Brenda Weisberg *c* William Sickner *lp* John Carradine, Lon Chaney Jnr, Ramsay Ames, Robert Lowery, Barton MacLane, George Zucco

Return of the Ape Man (MON) b/w 68(60)min

This companion piece to **The Ape Man** (1943) is almost as delightfully absurd, though it bears no relation plotwise. Lugosi and Carradine play a pair of scientists who contrive to revive a prehistoric ape-man (Moran) found preserved in ice. In the interests of science, Lugosi murders Carradine and transplants his brain to the creature in an attempt to humanize it. It duly becomes civilized enough to play the piano but retains an instinct for violence. After several rampages, it turns on and kills Lugosi – despite his recourse to a blow-lamp to dominate it – and perishes in flames.

d Philip Rosen *p* Sam Katzman, Jack Dietz *s* Robert Charles *c* Marcel le Picard *lp* Bela Lugosi, John Carradine, Frank Moran, Judith Gibson, Michael Ames

The Return of the Vampire (COL) b/w 69min

Playing a genuine vampire for the first time since **Dracula** (1931), Lugosi here hurries rather crossly through the part, forgetting most of the courteous social graces that made his original so memorable. His ill-humour may perhaps be partly accounted for by the fact that Columbia, keeping an eye on the success of Universal's first attempt at doubling up on their monsters with **Frankenstein Meets the Wolf Man** (1943), made him share the limelight with a somewhat unimpressive werewolf (Willis). The beginning, adventurously enough, takes place against the background of the London blitz, with Lugosi – known not as Dracula but Armand Tesla – unearthed by a stray bomb and revived when a workman removes the stake from his heart assuming it to be a chunk of shrapnel.

Thereafter, alternating between misty graveyard crypt and elegant drawing-room as the vampire mingles with unsuspecting society, the film moves sluggishly along familiar lines. The best thing about it, apart from the outstanding performances by Inescourt (as a distaff Van Helsing) and Foch (making her début as the vampire's chief victim), is the ending in which the werewolf, tired of being in thrall to the vampire, drags him into the sun as he sleeps. The last shot of Lugosi's face melting (actually a wax mould over a skeleton) was cut by the censor in Britain.

d Lew Landers *p* Sam White *s* Griffin Jay *c* John Stumar, L. W. O'Connell *lp* Bela Lugosi, Nina Foch, Frieda Inescourt, Gilbert Emery, Matt Willis, Miles Mander

La Torre de los Siete Jorobados *aka* **The Tower of the Seven Hunchbacks**

(ESPAÑA FILMS/J. FILMS; SP) b/w 90min

This darkly romantic fantasy devised by Emilio Carrere combines the world of Victor Hugo with that of Lon Chaney. The film tells of a band of hunchbacks who hole up in an underground city built centuries ago by persecuted Jews, where they perpetrate various crimes including rape. Their nefarious leader exerts a hypnotic control over the heroine, the niece of a doctor killed by the gang. Reports suggest that the movie was directed with a dose of black rather than cynical humour. The director, the Count of Berlanga de Duero, was a writer and diplomat who started making amateur movies in Hollywood where he befriended Charlie Chaplin and Douglas Fairbanks. His Spanish career dates from 1934 and yielded a number of highly regarded pictures.

Two decades later, Jesús Franco plugged into this sinister, somewhat pathological vein of Hispanic cinema – also treated in **La Corona Negra** (1950) and *Carlota* (1959) – and transformed it into a specific sex-and-sadism subgenre with his **Gritos en la Noche** (1962).

d Edgar Neville *p* Fernando Roldan *s* José Santugini *c* Henry Barreire, Perez Cubero *lp* Isabel de Pomés, Julia Lajos, Manolita Moran, Julia Pachelo, Antonio Casal, Guillermo Marin, Antonio Riquelme, Felix de Pomés, Rosario Rayo

The Uninvited (PAR) b/w 98min

A superior ghost story, *The Uninvited* stars Milland and Hussey as the brother and sister who buy a Cornish house very cheaply only to find that it's haunted by a pair of ghosts, one benevolent, the other decidedly evil. Russell is the young girl who exorcizes the evil ghost (in fact, the ghost of her mother who died in childbirth) and at the same time rids herself of her guilt. Rather too mechanically constructed to be genuinely chilling, the film's ghostly manifestations – a flower that wilts in seconds, a dog that refuses to go upstairs and a pair of doors opening for no reason – nonetheless have a real *frisson* about them.

Paramount, unsure of how to market the film, imposed several shots of ectoplasmic apparitions on director Allen to ensure that the audience knew that the supernatural (rather than Freud) was responsible. In the UK, however, the censor removed the shots of the ghosts and so the film won much praise from the critics for having the courage to make a ghost film without ghosts!

d Lewis Allen *p* Charles Brackett *s* Dodie Smith *c* Charles Lang *se* Farciot Edouart *lp* Ray Milland, Ruth Hussey, Gail Russell, Donald Crisp, Cornelia Otis Skinner, Alan Napier, Dorothy Stickney

The Voodoo Man (MON) b/w 62min

Very similar in plot to **The Corpse Vanishes** (1942), but reworked to take the success of Jacques Tourneur's superb **I Walked with a Zombie** (1943) into account, this is standard Monogram dross and rather duller than the Lugosi-Carradine-Zucco outing, **Return of the Ape Man** (1944). Lugosi is Dr Marlowe, whose wife has been a zombie for 20 years, who abducts girls in the hope of finding one on the 'same mental plane', and who wears a robe decorated with mystic symbols for his voodoo ceremonies. These attempts to transfer a life-force never manage to awaken the wife from her trance, but do succeed in making zombies of the girls. The best moments are provided by Carradine as the keeper of the basement cells where the zombie girls are imprisoned ('Hmm!' he murmurs, stroking the hair of one arrival with ominous interest, 'you're a pretty one'). Zucco helps out as a garage proprietor who steers victims into the web. When Lugosi is shot at the end, the zombies return to normal.

d William Beaudine *p* Sam Katzman, Jack Dietz *s* Robert Charles *c* Marcel le Picard *lp* Bela Lugosi, John Carradine, George Zucco, Wanda McKay, Louise Currie, Ellen Hall

Bela Lugosi, unearthed by a stray bomb in the London blitz while Matt Willis looks on in the routine The Return of the Vampire.

Weird Woman (U) b/w 63min

This is the second film in Chaney's 'Inner Sanctum' series – six extremely low-budget B movies based on novels published by Simon and Schuster which also spawned a radio series of the same title. All of them contained macabre elements, but since the stories were essentially whodunits, anything supernatural was explained away. Based on Fritz Leiber's novel *Conjure Wife*, *Weird Woman* is about a college professor (Chaney) who comes to suspect that his wife (Gwynne) is trying to summon voodoo powers to advance his career. A few stock shots of native voodoo ceremonies support the notion, but it all turns out to be the work of a jealous woman (Ankers) who murders a couple of faculty members in order to incriminate the wife who is in her way. The British remake, **Night of the Eagle** (1961), is far superior, inextricably interweaving the destructive powers of human jealousy and supernatural evil.

First and best of the 'Inner Sanctum' series was *Calling Dr Death* (1943), in which Chaney played a neurologist so hounded by a police officer who suspects him of murdering his wife that he comes to half-believe his own guilt until he employs a hypnotist to establish the truth. Thereafter the series went into a spiralling decline with *Dead Man's Eyes* (1944), *The Frozen Ghost* (1945), *Strange Confession* (1945, a remake of *The Man Who Reclaimed His Head*, 1935) and *Pillow of Death* (1945). The end of the series also signalled the termination of Chaney's Universal contract.

d Reginald LeBorg *p* Oliver Drake *s* Brenda Weisberg *c* Virgil Miller *lp* Lon Chaney Jnr, Anne Gwynne, Evelyn Ankers, Ralph Morgan, Lois Collier, Elizabeth Russell

1945

The Body Snatcher (RKO) b/w 78min

Superbly controlled and strikingly literate (to a point mistakenly criticized as excessive by several staunch admirers of Lewton's productions), *The Body Snatcher* is a magnificent reworking of Stevenson's (surprisingly flat from so accomplished a master of the macabre) short story about the moral (and murderous) clash between the infamous Dr Knox and his chief body-snatcher. Stevenson, for one thing, makes very little of Edinburgh. Lewton, on the other hand, acknowledges that the grisly shudder of body-snatching is indissolubly attached in the imagination to a dark city dominated by a castle looming out of the mists. His Edinburgh, therefore – as usual suggested rather than shown on the tight budgets at his disposal – is a patchwork of bits and pieces: sometimes solid (the terrace of the castle, a street with small boys marching proudly behind a kilted recruiting sergeant), sometimes not (the little ballad singer haunting a corner of the castle terracing, Greyfriars Bobby lying faithfully on the grave that is soon to be robbed), but always a dark, sad city of the imagination rather than of reality, a haunt of popular ballad invoked by the lines Karloff's body-snatcher croons just before killing Lugosi's would-be blackmailer ('The ruffian dogs/The hellish pair/The villain Burke/The meagre Hare ...').

Lewton (who completely rewrote MacDonald's script, only taking a pseudonymous credit at the latter's insistence), also reshuffled Stevenson's chronology and characters into an immeasurably more complex resonance. Knox, Burke and Hare are now names from the past, cunningly used to suggest a wealth of unspeakable blasphemy in the shadowy beginnings of Dr MacFarlane (Daniell) and his medical researches. Further, by elaborating the character of the body-snatcher Gray (Karloff, in the first and best of his three roles for Lewton) until he becomes a strict counterpoint to Daniell – 'a canker in my body' to be ruthlessly excized, as the latter snarls, but also the measure of his conscience and his lost virtues – Lewton turns the whole film into a subtle philosophical disquisition on the nature of good and evil.

Although commonly cited as a disappointment by comparison with Jacques Tourneur's magnificent work for Lewton on **I Walked with a Zombie** (1943), Wise's direction is actually a model of discretion and assurance, making excellent use of de Grasse's chiaroscuro lighting and managing to bring off several memorable scenes. Particularly worthy of note are Karloff's murder of the ballad singer (which takes place off-screen as the camera waits immobile at the mouth of a dark alleyway until her song is abruptly cut off), the murder of Karloff watched by a terrified cat, and the bravura of the final hallucination in a jolting carriage illuminated by bolts of lightning when Daniell starts to think that he is being haunted by Karloff's corpse.

d Robert Wise *p* Val Lewton *s* Philip MacDonald, Carlos Keith (Val Lewton) *c* Robert de Grasse *lp* Boris Karloff, Henry Daniell, Edith Atwater, Russell Wade, Rita Corday, Bela Lugosi

Dead of Night (EALING STUDIOS; GB) b/w 102(77)min
This is an overrated film, probably because it was greeted with starved enthusiasm after the moratorium on horror movies in Britain during the Second World War. The framing narrative (directed by Dearden) is excellent, introducing a genuinely oneiric quality in the sense of *déjà vu* with which an architect (Johns) drives up to a cottage he has been asked to redesign and feels he has already met the guests assembled there for a tea-party. At the prompting of a psychiatrist (Valk), each tells the story of a strange occurrence. After which, recalling having experienced all this before in a dream which ends with him strangling one of the guests, Johns starts to strangle Valk, only to be woken from a nightmare at home in bed by the telephone ringing inviting him to redesign a cottage, which he drives up to ...

The sense of a vicious circle of terror would have been much more overwhelming had the mood been sustained throughout the film. But, as in most anthology movies, the temptation to vary the diet was too strong. Hence, presumably, the inclusion of the very brief opening sketch (directed by Dearden) with its feeble joke about a cab that proves to be a hearse. Longer and more disruptive is the lewdly ribald sketch about two golfers (directed by Crichton) which is primarily an excuse for Wayne and Radford to repeat their comedy duo from *The Lady Vanishes* (1938). The other three sketches dovetail perfectly with neat variations in mood ranging from the gentle melancholy of the tale of a Christmas party at which a teenage girl (Howes) realizes she has been consoling a murdered child, to the demonic possession of a ventriloquist (Redgrave) by his dummy (both directed by Cavalcanti). The latter is perhaps the most fondly remembered episode, but it is outshone by Hamer's superb sketch about a mirror reflecting another time and place: another, much subtler tale of possession as a husband (Michael) is drawn through the looking-glass into the homicidal mania of trying to strangle his wife (Withers).

d Alberto Cavalcanti, Charles Crichton, Basil Dearden, Robert Hamer *p* Sidney Cole, John Croydon *s* John V. Barnes, Angus MacPhail, T. E. B. Clarke *c* Stan Pavey, Douglas Slocombe *lp* Mervyn Johns, Frederick Valk, Michael Redgrave, Googie Withers, Ralph Michael, Esme Percy, Sally Ann Howes, Basil Radford, Naunton Wayne

Boris Karloff as The Body Snatcher.

A Game of Death (RKO) b/w 72min
This is another version of Richard Connell's short story about a big-game hunter who has turned to human prey, more or less a copy of **The Most Dangerous Game** (1932) and incorporating footage from its climactic hunt sequence. The main difference, aside from a shift in locale to the Caribbean, is that in deference to patriotic sentiment Count Zaroff has become a German; while in deference to the prevailing concern with psychological motivation, he is no longer simply a sadist by intellectual choice, he had suffered a severe head wound which has made him homicidal. Barrier is surprisingly good in the Leslie Banks role, but like the film itself, lacks the controlled intensity of the original.

d Robert Wise *p* Herman Schlom *s* Norman Houston *c* J. Roy Hunt *lp* John Loder, Audrey Long, Edgar Barrier, Russell Wade, Jason Robards, Noble Johnson

House of Dracula (U) b/w 67min
This predictable reunion for the monsters assembled in **House of Frankenstein** (1944), has the saving grace of a slightly more coherent script. Stevens (replacing Karloff) is the benevolent doctor specializing in abnormalities who manages to cure Chaney's Wolf Man. Trying to do the same for Carradine's Dracula, he is infected by a sort of blowback during a blood transfusion, and (while Carradine dissolves in the sun) becomes a vampire who gleefully revives the Frankenstein monster (Strange). The Wolf Man, now plain Larry Talbot, shoots Stevens; a fire starts, the monster is brained, and Larry goes off to live happily ever after (in theory) with his girl Adams. The climactic fire sequence is borrowed from **Ghost of Frankenstein** (1942), and Chaney's Wolf Man went back to his old tricks in **Abbott and Costello Meet Frankenstein** (1948).

d Erle C. Kenton *p* Paul Malvern *s* George Bricker, Dwight V. Babcock *c* George Robinson *lp* Lon Chaney Jnr, Onslow Stevens, John Carradine, Lionel Atwill, Glenn Strange, Jane Adams

I Love a Mystery (COL) b/w 68min
This is the first of three films (the others are **The Devil's Mask** and **The Unknown**, both 1946) adapted from the radio series of the same name. As the title suggests, the stories were mysteries – with Bannon and Yarborough as the detective team – but distinctly ghoulish in tone. Macready plays a man living in

terror of decapitation ever since being approached by an oriental secret society with an offer to buy his head after he dies because he closely resembles their revered founder, embalmed but now deteriorating. His state of mind not eased by a man with a wooden leg who follows him round with a black bag (presumably to contain the head), or by a wife who is feigning paralysis because she hates him (and has been suborned by the society), Macready goes berserk and is decapitated in a car accident whereupon his head vanishes. Excellent performances by Macready and Foch (as the wife) are supported by an unusually clever script.

d Henry Levin *p* Wallace MacDonald *s* Charles O'Neal *c* Burnett Guffey *lp* Jim Bannon, George Macready, Nina Foch, Barton Yarborough, Carole Mathews

Isle of the Dead (RKO) b/w 72min
Based, like **Bedlam** (1946), on a painting – in this case, the eponymous work by Arnold Boecklin – *Isle of the Dead* is almost as static. Virtually nothing happens in the first half, yet a pregnantly eerie quality is sustained as a Greek general (Karloff) mournfully stalks the body-strewn battlefield (the film is set in the Balkan Wars) and is quarantined by the threat of windborne plague with a motley group, haunted by peasant superstitions of the presence of malevolent demons called vorvolakas. Suddenly, the *pièce de résistance* erupts as a woman (Emery) – established as subject to cataleptic trances – is presumed dead of plague and buried (alive, as a closeup catching a tremor about the nostrils discreetly reveals).

Robson (whose direction elsewhere is merely adequate) maintains the even tone by having the camera quietly glide through the empty tomb and up to the closed coffin. Nothing happens, only the sound of dripping water breaks the silence. The camera retreats ... and continues to retreat unblinkingly as a sudden scream and scrabbling fingernails belatedly fulfil expectation. It's a magnificent moment nothing thereafter can equal (the revived Emery, driven mad or possessed by a vorvolaka, runs amok impaling people with a trident). An impressive film.

d Mark Robson *p* Val Lewton *s* Ardel Wray, Josef Mischel *c* Jack MacKenzie *lp* Boris Karloff, Ellen Drew, Marc Cramer, Katherine Emery, Helene Thimig, Alan Napier, Jason Robards

Michael Redgrave as the ventriloquist possessed by his dummy in one of the episodes of the overrated omnibus film Dead of Night.

Jungle Captive *aka* **Wild Jungle Captive**
(U) b/w 64min
Having successfully resurrected dead rabbits, Dr Stendhal (Kruger) determines to try his hand on the body of Paula, the ape-woman killed at the end of **Jungle Woman** (1944). His monstrous assistant Moloch (the acromegalic Hatton) duly steals the body from the morgue after killing the attendant. Disappointed when the corpse revives and though turning into a beautiful woman (Lane, taking over from Acquanetta), proves to be mentally subnormal, Kruger plans to transplant the brain of his secretary (Ward). He is foiled not by the latter's fiancé (Brown), who is overpowered, but by Paula, reverting to apehood under the stress of jealousy and strangling both Kruger and Hatton before being shot down by the police. Tacky by any standards, this third adventure put an end to Paula the ape-woman's miniseries.

d Harold Young *p* Ben Pivar *s* M. Coates Webster, Dwight V. Babcock *c* Maury Gertsman *lp* Otto Kruger, Rondo Hatton, Amelita Ward, Phil Brown, Jerome Cowan, Vicky Lane

The Phantom Speaks (REP) b/w 69min
Ridges here plays the eager 'psychic scientist' who arranges for the spirit of a condemned murderer (Powers) to return and communicate with him after execution. When it does, it also seizes control of the scientist's mind, forcing him to commit revenge murders on its behalf. The film is practically a repeat performance for Ridges, since he had suffered a very similar misfortune in **Black Friday** (1940). Arlen plays a sceptical reporter to whom the scientist reveals all as he awaits execution for his crimes. Unremarkable, with the spirit's presence clumsily indicated by double exposure, the film is well acted and, oddly enough, was banned in Britain.

d John English *p* Armand Schaefer *s* John K. Butler *c* William Bradford *lp* Richard Arlen, Lynne Roberts, Stanley Ridges, Tom Powers, Jonathan Hale

The Picture of Dorian Gray
(MGM) b/w and col 110min
This is undoubtedly Lewin's best film, courtesy of Sanders' dandified cynicism as Lord Wootton, the world-weary tempter, Hatfield as the coldly snobbish and self-centred hero and Stradling's magnificent Oscar-winning cinematography. As a director, Lewin has been attacked for his earnestness and naïvety – Andrew Sarris remarked 'Lewins' clogged literary narrations and his naïve conception of refinement presume to vulgarize Wilde ... for the sake of bringing kulchur to the masses' – and indeed such films as *The Private Affairs of Bel Ami* (1947) and *Pandora and the Flying Dutchman* (1951) are a bizarre, though by no means uninteresting, mix of the merely vulgar and a literariness that at times approaches surrealism. But, in *Dorian Gray*, Lewin's gravity and sombreness are assets, giving (necessary) weight to Wilde's overly epigrammatic story and a real force to Hatfield's Jekyll and Hyde like immersion in depravity while remaining seemingly untouched by his actions.

Surprisingly, unlike Rouben Mamoulian's similarly structured **Dr Jekyll and Mr Hyde** (1932), Lewin chooses not to depict the portrait (the fixed equivalent of that film's Hyde) as Gray's *alter ego* but simply as a portrait of the evil thing that Hatfield remorselessly becomes. This gives the disclosure of the portrait (in colour, to further emphasize Hatfield's decline) a simple but satisfying climax to the film.

Lansbury, in only her third film, received her second Oscar nomination for her role as the *ingénue* cheerfully warbling 'Little Yellow Bird' without a thought of what awaits her. The other major versions of Wilde's story include *Portret Doriana Greya* (1915), Richard Oswald's incisive **Das Bildnis des Dorian Gray** (1917), and Massimo Dallamano's heavy-handed **Il Dio Chiamato Dorian** (1970).

d/s Albert Lewin *p* Pandro S. Berman *c* Harry Stradling *lp* Hurd Hatfield, George Sanders, Angela Lansbury, Donna Reed, Peter Lawford, Miles Mander

The Vampire's Ghost (REP) b/w 59min
A real shoestring shocker, which is quite unable to make anything out of a potentially intriguing story loosely derived by Leigh Brackett (a fine writer, later to work with Howard Hawks) from John Polidori's *The Vampyre*. Abbott, standing out in a more than indifferent cast, is the vampire who becomes an underworld leader spreading crime and murder through the west coast of Africa, and prevented in the nick of time from burning the heroine (Stewart) at the stake in revenge for being detected and hounded down. As directed by Selander, more at home in the B western, the action is largely taken up by milling natives, urgent tom-toms, and an extended bar-room fight.

d Lesley Selander *p* Armand Schaefer *s* John K. Butler, Leigh Brackett *c* Bud Thackery, Robert Pittack *lp* John Abbott, Peggy Stewart, Roy Barcroft, Charles Gordon, Grant Withers, Adele Mara

The Woman Who Came Back (REP) b/w 68min
This is a strikingly intelligent film about a New England woman (Kelly), granddaughter of a notorious witch-hunter, who imagines that she is the reincarnation of a witch burned at the stake 300 years previously. Obviously a disciple of the methods initiated by Val Lewton in **Cat People** (1942), Colmes works by suggestion throughout, not least in the fine opening sequence where Kelly finds herself sitting next to a strange old woman on a bus. Shortly afterwards the bus crashes into a lake, with only Kelly and the old woman's dog surviving. When all the bodies except the old woman's are recovered, Kelly's imagination gets to work, with the townsfolk feverishly following suit as the dog starts terrorizing the neighbourhood, a child falls mysteriously ill, its mother attempts suicide, and a whispering campaign gradually builds to a threat of violence against the witch. Before it all ends neatly, rationally and a trifle disappointingly, Colmes – particularly skilful in his evocation of the town's mutely growing hostility – brings off a very effective 'bus' (in the Lewton sense) when one of the witch's tormentors walks through the streets followed ominously by the tinkling of a dog's collar tag. A writer from radio, Colmes appears to have been a one-shot director.

d/p Walter Colmes *s* Dennis Cooper, Lee Willis *c* Henry Sharp *lp* Nancy Kelly, John Loder, Otto Kruger, Ruth Ford, J. Farrell MacDonald

Zombies on Broadway *aka* **Loonies on Broadway**
(RKO) b/w 68(64)min
This is probably the best of the Brown and Carney comedies, which isn't saying a great deal. The ex-vaudevillians were teamed together by RKO and featured in eight films between 1944 and 1946 in the hope that they would rival Abbott and Costello. However, their humour ran to even more cornier patter routines. Here they play a couple of New York press agents who dream up a publicity stunt announcing that the new show at Ace Miller's night-club will feature a zombie. To save their necks when the furious Miller (Leonard) is threatened with hostile radio publicity if the zombie proves to be a fake, the pair set off for the Caribbean in search of a real one. They find Lugosi, a rather weary mad doctor who contrives to inject Carney with his patent zombie serum. The effect wears off before he can be bundled on stage, but in the confusion as

Nancy Kelly who imagines herself to be The Woman Who Came Back.

Leonard attempts to make good his threat of liquidation, the gangster gets a dose of the serum instead. The fact that the film was inspired by Tourneur's **I Walked with a Zombie** (1943) is evident chiefly in that Jones and Sir Lancelot repeat their earlier roles and it reuses the same calypsos and sets.

d Gordon Douglas *p* Ben Stoloff *s* Lawrence Kimble *c* Jack MacKenzie *lp* Bela Lugosi, Wally Brown, Alan Carney, Anne Jeffreys, Sheldon Leonard, Darby Jones, Sir Lancelot

1946

The Beast with Five Fingers (WB) b/w 90(82)min
This superbly eerie film features Francen as a distinguished pianist, partially paralysed by a stroke, who lingers on in his gothic mansion in Italy surrounded by schemers (principally his secretary, Lorre), forlornly remembering his past glories as he picks out Bach on his piano with his one good hand. When he dies, leaving everything to his niece (King), Lorre is furious since he requires not only the money but access to the extensive library for his occult studies. A murder, followed by Lorre's hysterical account of a disembodied hand haunting the place with murderous intent, leads to the exhumation of Francen's body, which indeed proves to have a missing hand. All this part of the film is superb, and it is a pity that the ending, laughing away the mystery of the beast with five fingers when it is proved that Lorre was the killer all along (some studio interference here), leaves a certain sense of dissatisfaction. Florey's intention was to make it clear that the 'beast' was pure hallucination on the part of the guilt-ridden Lorre; now an occult possibility is raised only to be squashed by the ending. None of that, however, alters the fact that this is a film with a rare minatory charge.

The subjective shots of the obscenely pallid hand are as chilling as anything in cinema as it scuttles madly over the piano keys playing Bach's *Chaconne*, dislodges books as it lurks in hiding on a shelf, wriggles in frantic rage when impaled on a letter-spike and struggles furiously to get free when imprisoned in a drawer. The motifs of pianist and severed hand, not to mention the presence of a bald Lorre as in **Mad Love** (1935) – giving another marvellous performance – have led to identification of the film as one of the many variations on Maurice Renard's *Les Mains d'Orlac*. Actually it is an adaptation of William Fryer Harvey's short story *The Beast with Five Fingers*.

d Robert Florey *p* William Jacobs *s* Curt Siodmak *c* Wesley Anderson *lp* Peter Lorre, Robert Alda, Andrea King, Victor Francen, J. Carrol Naish, Charles Dingle

Bedlam (RKO) b/w 79min
This curiously pedantic film is inspired by plate 8 of Hogarth's 'The Rake's Progress' and itself evolves into tableaux which echo other Hogarth works. Though opening with the sadistic murder of a prison escapee and ending with the murder of the sadistic warder (Karloff), the action is less interesting than the historical detail, and suggests that Lewton was angling for a way out of B movies. The horror, such as it is, is sociological rather than supernatural, with Lee as an actress punished for taking indignant interest in the atrocious conditions at Bedlam (or St Mary of Bethlehem, to be exact) by being arbitrarily committed at the behest of her aristocratic 'protector' (House). Much too talkative (though the dialogue is good) and clumsily directed, it is at its best in marginalia like the death of a boy prisoner at a Vauxhall masque, asphyxiated by the gold paint in which he is costumed for the amusement of a society audience.

d/co-s Mark Robson *p* Val Lewton *co-s* Carlos Keith (Val Lewton) *c* Nicholas Musuraca *lp* Boris Karloff, Anna Lee, Billy House, Richard Fraser, Glenn Vernon, Ian Wolfe, Jason Robards

The Brute Man (PRC) b/w 58min
Though killed off at the end of **House of Horrors** (1946), Hatton's the Creeper was revived for one last film in the miniseries started by courtesy of Conan Doyle in *The Pearl of Death* (1944). This entry purports to explain how he got to be a hideous monster when a chemistry lab accident at university splashed acid in his face. From football-playing hero he turns, predictably enough, to mad killer thirsting for revenge. Equally predictably, the plot provides a blind girl (Wiley) who isn't afraid of him and who therefore touches his only soft spot. Pretty trashy by any standards, the film was actually made by Universal, who – possibly troubled by the analogy with Hatton's real-life tragedy as an averagely handsome actor turned into a monster by acromegaly – handed it down the line to PRC. Hatton, whose last film this was, died in 1946.

d Jean Yarbrough *p* Ben Pivar *s* George Bricker, M. Coates Webster *c* Maury Gertsman *lp* Rondo Hatton, Jane Adams, Tom Neal, Jan Wiley, Donald MacBride

Andrea King confronts The Beast with Five Fingers.

The Cat Creeps (U) b/w 58min
No relation to the 1930 film of the same title, this has a motley company including a reporter (Brady), his girlfriend (Collier), his photographer (Beery) and a suspect private eye (Dumbrille) foregather in an eerie old house on an island, drawn by a report that a suicide which occurred there 15 years before was really a murder. When the woman who spread the story is found murdered, mysterious nocturnal prowlings and further killings ensue until the dead woman's cat, seemingly inhabited by her soul, leads the way to the money that is the cause of all the mayhem. Disastrous attempts at humour make this lag a long way behind Kenton's fine **Island of Lost Souls** (1932), although the scenes with the cat intriguingly anticipate similar feline services performed more stylishly in *The Lost Moment* (1947) and **The Tomb of Ligeia** (1964).

d Erle C. Kenton *p* Howard Welsch *s* Edward Dein, Jerry Warner *c* George Robinson *lp* Fred Brady, Lois Collier, Paul Kelly, Douglas Dumbrille, Noah Beery Jnr, Rose Hobart

The Catman of Paris (REP) b/w 65min
Esmond is a brilliant young writer who suffers from blackouts after travelling in the mysterious Orient. Though assured otherwise by the publisher's daughter who loves him (Aubert), he becomes convinced that he must be 'the Catman' responsible for two murders which have shocked Paris. He isn't, but Wilke is. Although the cast all turn in reasonable performances, all the sinister hocus-pocus goes for very little, given leaden direction and a ridiculous pantomime makeup for the werecat: pointy ears, vampire teeth and stubbly whiskers topped off by an opera hat.

d Lesley Selander *p* Marek M. Libkov *s* Sherman L. Lowe *c* Reggie Lanning *lp* Carl Esmond, Lenore Aubert, Adele Mara, Douglas Dumbrille, Gerald Mohr, John Dehner, Robert J. Wilke

The Devil's Mask (COL) b/w 66min
The second of three films adapted from the radio series *I Love a Mystery*, this is less effective than its predecessor (**I Love a Mystery**, 1945) because it gets too entangled in the whodunit aspects of its plot. A supernumerary shrunken head turns out to belong, not to the batch brought back by an explorer from South America, but to the murdered explorer. Although the somewhat over-excited script tends to throw in everything – hypnotism, a voice from the grave, poisoned darts, a rampaging leopard – the film has its moments, notably the eerie sequence among the stuffed animals in a shop belonging to the kindly old taxidermist (Donati) who owns the leopard and who murdered the explorer because he hunted animals.

d Henry Levin *p* Wallace MacDonald *s* Charles O'Neal, Dwight V. Babcock *c* Henry Freulich *lp* Anita Louise, Jim Bannon, Michaël Duane, Mona Barrie, Barton Yarborough, Ludwig Donath

Face of Marble (MON) b/w 70min
Carradine here is the inevitable mad doctor attempting to resuscitate the dead. After successfully reviving a Great Dane which becomes semi-transparent, walks through walls and drinks blood, he experiments on a drowned sailor and his own wife (Drake). They too develop strange habits like walking through glass and also acquire rigid faces. For good measure, the film also has Rey doing some voodoo as a sinister housekeeper, and Best contributes his scared act.

d William Beaudine *p* Jeffrey Bernard *s* Michael Jacoby *c* Harry Neumann *lp* John Carradine, Claudia Drake, Robert Shayne, Maris Wrixon, Willie Best, Rosa Rey

The Flying Serpent (PRC) b/w 59min
The last of the Zucco-Newfield collaborations, this film is perhaps even more remarkable than **The Mad Monster** (1942) and **Dead Men Walk** (1943), thanks to a ludicrous monster

purporting to be the plumed serpent Quetzalcoatl. Mad archaeologist Zucco finds the creature guarding Montezuma's treasure, and contrives to train it to kill: if one of its feathers is planted on an expendable adversary, the god-bird sucks the victims blood before retrieving its property. Accompanied in flight by what sounds absurdly like a revving engine and all too clearly a prop slung about on wires, the creature occasions more giggles than chills, and the film itself looks suspiciously like a re-run of PRC's **The Devil Bat** (1941).

d Sherman Scott (Sam Newfield) *p* Sigmund Neufeld *s* John T. Neville *c* Jack Greenhalgh *lp* George Zucco, Hope Kramer, Ralph Lewis, Eddie Acuff, Wheaton Chambers, James Metcalf

Genius at Work (RKO) b/w 61min
After this dismal effort, a comedown even after **Zombies on Broadway** (1945), RKO gave up trying to promote Brown and Carney as a rival comedy team to Abbott and Costello. Here, they play the stars of a radio show who, with the help of a criminologist (Atwill), cause a stir by solving crimes on the air before the police get round to it. Their scriptwriter (Jeffreys) comes to suspect that Atwill is actually a criminal mastermind known as the Cobra. He is indeed, and strikes back by trying to kill them and initiating a bout of mayhem at his home (which comprises both torture chamber and wax museum), interrupted in the nick of time by the police. Atwill, in his last film, is his usual competent self, but Lugosi languishes dismally on the sidelines as his butler.

d Leslie Goodwins *p* Herman Schlom *s* Robert E. Kent, Monte Brice *c* Robert de Grasse *lp* Wally Brown, Alan Carney, Anne Jeffreys, Lionel Atwill, Bela Lugosi

House of Horrors *aka* **Joan Medford Is Missing**
(U) b/w 66min
After playing Gale Sondergaard's deaf-mute aide in **The Spider Woman Strikes Back** (1946), Hatton – an acromegalic who needed no makeup to play a monster – returned to his characterization as the Creeper (no longer of Hoxton) from *The Pearl of Death* (1944). Kosleck is a surrealist sculptor driven to suicidal frenzy by a malicious critic (Napier). About to throw himself into the river, he sees something crawling out of it. Delighted by the brutish creature who emerges – a notorious killer believed to have drowned – Kosleck hustles him back to his studio to use as a model, and soon discovers that the grateful Creeper is only too willing to snap the spine of anyone who crosses his benefactor. But proposing to turn the Creeper over to the police when suspicions about Napier's death come uncomfortably close to home, Kosleck himself becomes the next victim, and the Creeper is shot down by the police just as he turns his attentions to the heroine (Grey). There are glimmerings of a movie here, but the attempt is held back by Hatton's inexpressive performance and by risible dialogue.

d Jean Yarbrough *p* Ben Pivar *s* George Bricker *c* Maury Gertsman *lp* Martin Kosleck, Rondo Hatton, Kent Taylor, Virginia Grey, Alan Napier, Robert Lowery

The Mask of Diijon (PRC) b/w 73min
A quickie made with real flair, this starts off with a nice bang: Stroheim supervising a stage guillotining in which the head in the basket (belonging to his young wife, Bates) suddenly winks at him. A sleazy magician with delusions of grandeur, Stroheim's mind is less on such bits of showbiz hocus-pocus than on developing mental powers that will put him in touch with cosmic forces. That this basically means hypnotism becomes apparent when he accuses Bates (unfairly) of cheating on him with his young assistant (Wright). Becoming homicidally insane when she walks out on him and takes a job as a nightclub singer with Wright as her accompanist, he hypnotizes her and commands her to kill her lover. Although Stroheim overacts outrageously (à la Bela Lugosi) here, there is a fine payoff as Bates, in mid-song at the piano, abruptly turns to Wright, snarls, 'You'd better play "Hearts and Flowers". I'm going to kill you' and fires blanks because she has the wrong gun.

The film ends with another bang as Stroheim, trapped by the police, is decapitated when a cat trips his own guillotine illusion. Well enough directed to suggest that Stroheim might have helped out behind the camera, *The Mask of Diijon* cleverly capitalizes on its Poverty Row budget by trotting out a series of realistically shabby settings (seedy boarding-house, second-rate clubs, corner magic store and so on).

d Lew Landers *p* Max Alexander, Alfred Stern *s* Arthur St Clair, Griffin Jay *c* Jack Greenhalgh *lp* Erich von Stroheim, Jeanne Bates, William Wright, Denise Vernac, Edward Van Sloan, Mauritz Hugo

Above: *Gilbert Roland in the fantasy film* La Rebelión de los Fantasmas.

La Rebelión de los Fantasmas *aka*
The Revolt of the Ghosts
(PRODUCTION DE PELICULAS; MEX) b/w 82min
A pleasant fantasy comedy about an old house filled with famous ghosts (Chopin, Paganini, Tutankhamun, la Llorona, The Wandering Jew, Don Quixote, Caruso, etc) which is to be demolished to make room for a radio station. In contrast to European ghost comedies, which are mostly about the saving of old castles from modernization (**Fantasmi a Roma**, 1961, for example), here the script accepts the demolition of the house for the sake of progress and decrees that the ghosts will have to settle for a flat in a skyscraper like everyone else.

Roland, born Luis Antonio Damaso de Alonso in Mexico, had been a Hollywood star since the mid-twenties and continued a noteworthy career well into the sixties. Alfonso Corona Blake, later to become one of Mexico's better known fantasy directors with such films as *El Mundo de los Vampiros* (1960) and *Santo contra las Mujeres Vampiros* (1961), functioned as assistant director on this picture. The Mexican cinema of the period was rich in fantasy comedies, often taking their cue from Abbott and Costello or from *Topper* (1937)-type pictures and comics such as the young Mario Moreno (Cantinflas) or Germán Valdes (Tin Tin) made many such movies.

d/co-s Adolfo Fernandez Bustamante *p* Miguel Salkind *co-s* Enrique Castañeda, Max Aub *c* Agustin Jimenez *lp* Amanda Ledesma, Gilbert Roland, Angel Garasa, Luis G. Barreiro, Nelly Monteil, Maria Conesa, Irving 'Mister' Lee, the ballet of Coronel Basil

Right: *Rondo Hatton and Gale Sondergaard in the chilling* The Spider Woman Strikes Back.

She-Wolf of London *aka* **The Curse of the Allenbys**
(U) b/w 61min
Evidently inspired by **The Undying Monster** (1942), this feeble potboiler features yet another English family haunted by the curse of the werewolf. After several mysterious murders have occurred (one victim being a child), Lockheart comes to believe she has inherited the taint. But there is no werewolf, just a crazed killer, no atmosphere and an unbelievably bogus London setting.

d Jean Yarbrough *p* Ben Pivar *s* George Bricker *c* Maury Gertsman *lp* June Lockheart, Don Porter, Martin Kosleck, Lloyd Corrigan, Denis Hoey

The Spider Woman Strikes Back (U) b/w 59min
Quite apart from **The Hound of the Baskervilles** (1939), several of Universal's series of Sherlock Holmes mysteries starring Basil Rathbone and Nigel Bruce took in elements of horror. Two of the chilliest were *Sherlock Holmes and the Spider Woman* (1944), in which Holmes has to cope with Sondergaard's slinky lady who uses poisonous spiders and a malevolent dwarf to dispatch her enemies, and *The Pearl of Death* (1944), where he comes up against Hatton (a real-life acromegalic here playing his first horror role) as the superhumanly powerful strangler, the Hoxton Creeper. Universal's inspiration was to team Sondergaard and Hatton as a superbly sinister duo.

Joyce is the hapless heroine hired as companion to a blind woman (Sondergaard). Terrified anyway by the latter's hideous deaf-mute servant (Hatton), she soon finds more cause for alarm not only in that she is destined to be an expendable pawn in a wild scheme to regain property gambled away by Sondergaard's grandfather, but because Sondergaard and Hatton cultivate carnivorous plants which require the fresh blood of murdered girls (cows are tried first) to survive. The film goes rather off the rails towards the end, with the villainous pair ultimately perishing in a none too convincing fire, but Ivano's excellent camerawork helps to keep the rest tolerably gripping.

d Arthur Lubin *p* Howard Welsch *s* Eric Taylor *c* Paul Ivano *lp* Brenda Joyce, Gale Sondergaard, Kirby Grant, Rondo Hatton, Milburn Stone, Hobart Cavanaugh

Dorothy McGuire as the damsel in distress in the superb The Spiral Staircase.

The Spiral Staircase (RKO) b/w 83min
This is a superb thriller about a homicidal maniac whose dedication to beauty leads him to try and rid the world of maimed or disfigured women. Hitchcock couldn't have bettered the casual mastery with which the opening sequence defines not just time and place (small town, turn of the century) but the themes of voyeurism and entrapment as a carriage draws up outside a hotel, the townsfolk assemble inside for a silent picture show, and the camera lifts to a room above where a crippled girl is being watched by a hidden, malevolently glaring eye as she undresses. This first murder, discreetly executed as the girl pulls her dress over her head and we see her arms convulsively clutch in agony, introduces a note of expressionism which Siodmak uses sparingly but with unfailing elegance throughout as shadows close in on McGuire's mute, terrified heroine. Clearly destined to become the next victim as a dumb girl shut away in a gloomy old mansion where she acts as companion to a bedridden old woman (Barrymore), McGuire is unequivocally designated as such by a chilling sequence of reflections upon reflections: she pauses on the staircase to look at herself in a mirror, wryly pantomiming to herself a wish that she could talk, while seen from the viewpoint of the killer's watching eye, her face acquires an amorphous blur where the mouth should be.

Although Hollywood's current enthusiasm for Freud runs a little wild (apart from the killer's hang-up and McGuire's psychosomatic dumbness, Barrymore is a possessive mother with two weak sons trying to live up to their father's strong man image), any excesses are kept perfectly in check by Siodmak's direction, which turns different levels of the house into areas of light and shadow, not always correctly identified by McGuire as she negotiates the traumatic reef of the spiral staircase between safety and danger. The film is one of the undoubted gothic masterpieces, even if the happy ending comes a shade too pat when McGuire finds her voice in the nick of time as Brent's killer – the less suspect of the two sons but admirably cast for the role – finally corners her. Ethel Lina White's novel was remade, again as **The Spiral Staircase** in 1975.

d Robert Siodmak *p* Dore Schary *c* Mel Dinelli *c* Nicholas Musuraca *lp* Dorothy McGuire, George Brent, Ethel Barrymore, Kent Smith, Elsa Lanchester, Rhonda Fleming

Strangler of the Swamp (PRC) b/w 60min

Probably PRC's finest hour, and certainly the only film in a Hollywood condemned to lower-grade B movies that gave some measure of Wisbar's talent, this is based on Wisbar's own 1936 German film **Faehrmann Maria**, a retelling of the legend of Death and the maiden which starred Sybille Schmitz, the unforgettable victim of Carl Dreyer's **Vampyr** (1931), and carries over a fair measure of the slow, dreamy stylization the director evidently borrowed from Dreyer. La Planche takes over, rather more forgettably, as the operator of a lonely ferry in the backwoods swamplands when her grandfather is killed. Haunted by the ghost of ferryman Douglas (Middleton), hanged years before for a murder he did not commit and now returned to take revenge – those responsible for his hanging are found hanged in their turn, strangled by trailing creepers in the swamp – the superstition-ridden swamp-dwellers believe that his curse, which pertains even to descendants of the guilty, can only be ended by a life willingly sacrificed in expiation. La Planche duly offers her life to save the man she loves (Edwards, the future director in his only horror movie role); and to ensure a happy ending, though not unpleasingly, the spectre retires to its grave well satisfied by the gesture rather than the deed.

The film was shot in the studio on one set, comprising the ferryboat landing, a bit of river and a few gaunt trees with a noose hanging from one, eerily attended by a permanent ground mist and the mournful clanging of the ferry bell. The opening scenes are particularly effective, not least because no special effects are used for the spectre's appearances: Middleton simply seems to melt in and out of the shadows. The one real weakness, probably imposed on the film, is a crashingly insensitive score by Alex Steinert.

d/co-s Frank Wisbar *p* Raoul Pagel *co-s* Harold Erickson *c* James S. Brown Jnr *lp* Rosemary La Planche, Robert Barrat, Blake Edwards, Charles Middleton, Effie Parnell, Frank Conlan

The Unknown (COL) b/w 69min

This is the last, and by far the weakest, of the three films adapted from the *I Love a Mystery* radio series. Risibly inadequate, in fact, it has detectives Bannon and Yarborough pursuing a cloaked graverobber lurking around a haunted Southern mansion, while Donnell (pretty dotty herself) comes home to see her deranged mother (Morley). The first two in the series were **I Love a Mystery** (1945) – the best – and **The Devil's Mask** (1946).

d Henry Levin *p* Wallace MacDonald *s* Malcolm Stuart Boylan, Julian Harmon *c* Henry Freulich *lp* Karen Morley, Jim Bannon, Jeff Donnell, Robert Scott, Barton Yarborough

Valley of the Zombies (REP) b/w 56min

Keith is the undertaker who returns from the dead, having found (in the Valley of the Zombies) a formula which requires fresh blood to keep him going. Hypnotizing the heroine (Booth) into helping him, he for no very clear reason embalms his victims. Wearily predictable, the script seems to have exhausted its supply of wit in finding the name Ormand Murks for its mad undertaker.

d Philip Ford *p/s* Dorrell McGowan, Stuart McGowan *c* Reggie Lanning *lp* Robert Livingston, Adrian Booth, Ian Keith, Thomas Jackson, Charles Trowbridge

1948

Abbott and Costello Meet Frankenstein *aka* **Abbott and Costello Meet the Ghosts** (U) b/w 92(83)min

The Abbott and Costello flirtation with horror began with *Hold That Ghost* (1941), a routine haunted-house comedy. The first and best of the films in which they met all the classic monsters in turn, *Abbott and Costello Meet Frankenstein* is only sporadically funny, but at least the horror stars are allowed to play straight in a plot which has Lugosi's Count Dracula (his only appearance in the role apart from **Dracula**, 1931) seeking a new brain for the Frankenstein monster (Strange) and selecting Costello as donor. A mad lady doctor (Aubert) is on hand to help with the operation, and Chaney's Wolf Man emerges as the hero by frustrating Dracula's plan for world domination. Made with care and looking good, it boosted the fading Abbott and Costello career, which soon took another downward turn after a series of drearily uninventive parodies covering similar territory: *Abbott and Costello Meet the Killer, Boris Karloff* (1949, a total waste of Karloff), *Abbott and Costello Meet the Invisible Man* (1951) and *Abbott and Costello*

Below: *The poster for Republic's predictable* Valley of the Zombies.

The marvellous Shinshaku Yotsuya Kaidan.

Meet the Mummy (1955). Only *Abbott and Costello Meet Dr Jekyll and Mr Hyde* (1953) kept its head above water thanks to Karloff and fine camerawork by George Robinson.

d Charles T. Barton *p* Robert Arthur *s* John Grant, Frederic I. Rinaldo, Robert Lees *c* Charles Van Enger *lp* Bud Abbott, Lou Costello, Bela Lugosi, Lon Chaney Jnr, Glenn Strange, Lenore Aubert

The Creeper (FOX) b/w 64min
This solemn chiller about a series of cat-claw murders is pretty tepid despite the fact that pretty Wilson has convenient nightmares in which she is clawed by cats after visiting the West Indies with her father (Morgan) to collect serum for his experiments. Morgan and two laboratory assistants (Vincent and Hoffman) subsequently die in mysterious circumstances, and Wilson is saved from a similar fate by her fiancé (Baragrey). He shoots an intruder (Stevens), a doctor who has injected himself with the serum and whose hand turns into a cat's paw as he dies. Ciannelli is a real red-herring menace.

d Jean Yarbrough *p* Bernard Small, Ben Pivar *s* Maurice Tombragel *c* George Robinson *lp* Eduardo Ciannelli, June Vincent, Onslow Stevens, Ralph Morgan, Janis Wilson, David Hoffman, John Baragrey

The Fatal Night (ANGLO FILM; GB) b/w 50min
Two impoverished young Englishmen (Armstrong and Macnee) con a wealthy American acquaintance (Ferguson) into accepting a bet that he will not dare spend a night alone in a haunted room. Locked in with a candle, a match and a loaded revolver, the healthily sceptical American happily settles down to read the (thoughtfully provided) history of the haunting which tells of a gruesome murder involving two women. But when his candle blows out, his imagination starts to work, the ghastly apparitions begin, and he empties his revolver to absolutely no effect, the terror-stricken American has to be released and loses his bet. Absent on war service, the two appalled Englishmen – who had provided apparitions and loaded the revolver with blanks – learn that the American had to be committed to an asylum, hopelessly insane. Adapted from Michael Arlen's short story *A Gentleman from America* and scripted with cool and clinical detachment, the neat little yarn is all the more effective in that it makes no bones about the con from the outset, then shades gradually into areas of ambiguity where some of the macabre visions must be either real or a product of the terrified imagination. Essentially an after-dinner ghost story, it is directed with surprising restraint by Zampi, better known as a hit-or-miss specialist in zany comedy.

d/p Mario Zampi *s* Gerald Butler *c* Cedric Williams *lp* Lester Ferguson, Jean Short, Leslie Armstrong, Brenda Hogan, Patrick Macnee

1949

Shinshaku Yotsuya Kaidan *aka* **New Version of the Ghost of Yotsuya** *aka* **The Ghost of Yotsuya – New Version**
(SHOCHIKU; JAP) b/w 2 parts (86,73min)
Immediately after the Second World War when anything connected with Japanese myths and legends was stigmatized as irrational and attacked in the name of 'democratization' (ie 'modern rationalism'), in Shochiku's Kyoto studios the great Kinoshita embarked on a two-part version of Nanboku Tsuruya's famous kabuki play which dates back to 1825. The story concerns Iemon, a vagabond samurai who marries Oiwa, having killed her father, and then kills her to marry a rich heiress. Oiwa's ghost returns to drive him insane and provokes his death.

Adapting the plot to the spirit of the times, Kinoshita made Iemon (Uehara) an intelligent but unemployed hero who kills Oiwa (Tanaka) in order to marry Oume (Yamane) and to obtain work as a respectable samurai. His Iemon is remorseful and neurotic and commits suicide at the end of the film. This new interpretation tells the classic story with considerable subtlety and makes good use of seductively poetic rhythms. Uehara is typecast as the hero with demonic good looks but it is the extraordinary Tanaka, one of Mizoguchi's favourite actresses seen here in the double role of Oiwa and her sister Osode, who steals the show with her ability to convey a mixture of forcefulness and extreme sensitivity.

Kinoshita had revealed himself to be one of Japan's greatest directors with *Rikugun* (1944), an astonishingly subversive anti-militarist picture made ostensibly as militarist propaganda. He went on to make the best movie version of *Narayam Bushi Ko* (1958), a far more complex work than Imamura's version crowned at the Cannes festival in 1983. A more faithful treatment of the story of Iemon is **Tokaido Yotsuya Kaidan** (1959).

d Keisuke Kinoshita *p* Koichiro Ogura *s* Eijiro Hisaita *c* Hiroshi Kusuda *lp* Kinuyo Tanaka, Ken Uehara, Hisako Yamane, Haruko Sugimura, Choko Iida, Osamu Takizawa

The 1950s

Dracula, Frankenstein and Horror Triumphant

In the first half of the fifties, the horror film was supplanted by its near cousin the science fiction film, a genre with which horror had many elements in common, and a genre more directly suited to broaching the anxieties and fears ushered in by man's simultaneous discovery of atomic power, the Cold War and potential invasions from outer space. As those anxieties lifted slightly, the tone of the films changed until by the mid-fifties the 'creature-features' – the films devoted to monsters and monstrous aliens – increasingly took on the characteristics of the horror film. What began as a drift away from science fiction rapidly became a full-scale horror revival. 1957 was the *annus mirabile* of horror. If 1931 (the year in which Universal unleashed both **Dracula** and **Frankenstein**) saw the creation of the horror genre, 1957 saw the creation of the modern horror film.

The Curse of Frankenstein, **El Vampiro** and **I Was a Teenage Werewolf** (all released 1957), to which one can add **I Vampiri**, made in 1956 but only released internationally in 1957, each in their different way testified to the renaissance of the horror film. *Teenage Werewolf* (which was followed in 1958 by the equally bizarre **I Was a Teenage Frankenstein**), in its very title highlighted the fact that youth was the major audience for horror films, a fact that all subsequent producers would bear in mind. Henceforth, adolescents, as well as providing the major audience for horror films, would also be regularly featured on screen. *El Vampiro* was more like the Universal classics sold to American television in 1957. It and films like **La Momia Azteca** (1957) testified to older, pre-psychological notions of horror which would form a central strand in the Hispanic horror tradition. In a similar way, Jacques Tourneur's marvellous **Night of the Demon** (also 1957) harkened back to the forties and his films with Val Lewton. In complete contrast, Terence Fisher's epoch-making *The Curse of Frankenstein* (and even more so his version of **Dracula**, 1958) and Riccardo Freda's *I Vampiri* marked a radical re-orientation of horror themes. Fisher's films reinterpreted the Dracula and Frankenstein legends – giving them a sensuality that British critics found threatening – while their success at the box office inevitably lead to numerous sequels. Freda's even more flamboyant film, full of atmosphere at the expense of narrative pace, initiated a stream of Italian films, the best of which were made by his pupil, Mario Bava, in which the fantasies that underpinned so many horror films became their subject matter.

This renaissance of the horror film, seen in the steady escalation of the number of films made in the second half of the fifties, continued around the world into the sixties. By this time, despite the occasional old-fashioned piece of showmanship like William Castle's **The Tingler** (1959), amongst others, the modern horror film, even when it used traditional characters such as Dracula, bore little relation to the innocent films of the thirties.

1950

Previous pages: *Jacques Tourneur's marvellous* Night of the Demon *(1957)*.

La Corona Negra *aka* The Black Crown

(SUEVIA FILMS; SP) b/w 94min

The prestigious Argentinian director Saslavsky started his career in Spain with this adaptation of a story by Cocteau. Set in Tangier but shot in Spain, the plot concerns a woman (Felix) who loses her memory after killing her husband who was about to divorce her because of her affair with Mauricio (Gassman). The dazed murderess is befriended by a young engineer (Brazzi) but her lover catches up with her and forces her to reveal where her rich husband's jewels were hidden. Since she put them in the coffin together with the corpse, the murder is discovered but Gassman becomes the main suspect and, in a desperate bid to escape, he is killed. The ending sees the unfortunate adultress sink into madness as she embraces the dead body of the only man she really loved.

The plot is unravelled through numerous flashbacks and punctuated with dream sequences full of hallucinatory images of witches, clutching hands emerging from a grave, the black-clad widow being pursued by a dwarf in a brilliant white cemetery, and the symbolic black crown itself: the formation of ravens as they circle above a corpse. Saslavsky made other films in Europe but none justified the reputation which had preceded him on his arrival from Argentina.

d Luis Saslavsky *p* Cesareo Gonzalez *s* Miguel Mihura *c* Antonio Lopez Ballesteros, Valentin Javier *lp* Maria Felix, Rosanno Brazzi, Vittorio Gassman, José Maria Lado, Antonio Plana, Julia Caba Alba, Piéral, C. Lopez Silva, F. Fernandez

Dark Interval

(PRESENT DAY; GB) b/w 60min

A minor and rather amateur effort in the tradition of *Secret Beyond the Door* (1948), this is of interest mainly for Gilling's script which foreshadows the spate of psycho-thrillers produced by Hammer and its rivals from 1960 onwards, starting with Seth Holt's **Taste of Fear**.

The plot concerns a young bride (Marshall) who returns from her honeymoon to a creepy household and finds her husband (Osborn) is insane. There is also the knowing family doctor (Barry) and a sinister butler (Le Mesurier) who kills his revered master before poisoning himself. The movie, poorly directed, offers an unhappy mix of the conventions of melodrama, the-butler-did-it thriller and psycho-horror.

d Charles Saunders *p* Charles Reynolds *s* John Gilling *c* E. Lloyd *lp* Zena Marshall, Andrew Osborn, John Barry, John Le Mesurier, Mona Washbourne, Wallas Eaton

Vittorio Gassman (left), Rosanno Brazzi and Piéral (right) in the richly symbolic La Corona Negra.

Andrew Osborn as the mad husband in the minor Dark Interval.

En la Palma de Tu Mano *aka* **Kill Him for Me**
(PRODUCCIONES MIER Y BROOKS; MEX) b/w 90min
A few months after his performance in **El Hombre Sin Rostro** (1950), de Cordova again played a pathological killer: this time, Professor Karin, a fake medium who falls for the beautiful Ada (Palma), a cynical gold-digging murderess. She entices him into killing her ex-lover (Gay), but, when confronted with a corpse by the police, he breaks down and confesses all before realizing that the corpse wasn't that of his victim but of his own wife (Montejo) who committed suicide. Gavaldon shot the movie in high gothic style and inserted lots of scenes featuring macabre morgues, funerals, candle-lit coffins and the midnight exhumation of a body in the grounds of a deserted mansion during a thunderstorm. The picture opens with images of a nuclear blast and other 'disasters', and de Cordova's voice-over telling the audience that 'man' seems condemned to do the very things that he wanted least, which then leads to an exploration of 'man's nature' in terms of mysticism and fakery. But somewhere beyond the film's pretentious banality there are traces of a film like *Double Indemnity* (1944) treated in the gothic style, largely thanks to the enchanting but disturbing presence of Palma.

Gavaldon, who often worked with Revueltas, had an uneven career, turning out superior melodramas with Dolores del Rio (*La Otra*, 1946; *La Casa Chica*, 1949) and inferior ones, including the nationalist tearjerker *La Escondida* (1955), with Maria Felix. His American films (*The Adventures of Casanova*, 1947; *The Littlest Outlaw*, 1954) give an adequate idea of his work. His last notable fantasy movie, *Macario* (1960), was a sentimental fairytale about a poor Mexican who meets God, the devil and death, full of shots reeking of 'art' and 'meaning'.

d/co-s Roberto Gavaldon *p* Felipe Mier, Oscar Brooks *co-s* Luis Spota, José Revueltas *c* Alex Phillips *lp* Arturo de Cordova, Leticia Palma, Carmen Montejo, Ramón Gay, Consuelo Guerrero de Luna, Pascual Garcia Peña, Manuel Arvide, Lonka Becker, Victor Alcocer, Enriqueta Reza

El Hombre Sin Rostro *aka* **The Man Without a Face**
(OROFILMS; MEX) b/w 91min
Located somewhere between G. W. Pabst's *Die Buechse der Pandora* (1922) and **Psycho** (1960), this picture offers a psychoanalytical account of a Jack the Ripper figure with a split personality: he commits the crimes as his mother who, to complicate matters, appears in his dreams as a man without a face. As in his other movies (**Dos Monjes**, 1934, for example), the director uses a complicated narrative structure involving flashbacks within flashbacks and three pivotal dream sequences in a style derived from *Spellbound* (1945). The plot, told in the form of a case study report by a psychiatrist (Ferriz), concerns a doctor (de Cordova) who is disturbed by a series of vicious killings of prostitutes by a Ripper figure and consents to be analysed by Ferriz. The doctor recalls, in a further flashback, how his mother (Palou) sabotaged his love life. A dream sequence then shows how this experience provoked a negative identification with the 'mother' who proceeds to murder women guilty of provoking sexual desire in 'her' son, ie himself. The movie opens with a pre-credit sequence of a funeral procession where the man without a face is glimpsed. A later dream has him wander among statues of sexless women, enter a huge gate, descend a spiral staircase and liberate a chained-up monster which then proceeds to destroy the statues and turns into the man without a face. In the final dream, after a walk by a bloody pool, the mysterious figure turns around and is revealed to be the doctor's mother.

The director had cherished this project for 25 years, and had initially planned to produce it as a stage play. Unfortunately, the theatrical overacting, the surfeit of meaningful closeups and the relentlessly 'mysterious' score spoil the picture. He went on to make a mediocre eternal-youth fantasy, *Retorno a la Juventud* (1953) and ended a promising career with nondescript melodramas. De Cordova reprised the role of a sinister killer in **En la Palma de Tu Mano** (1950).

d/co-p/s Juan Bustillo Oro *co-p* Gonzalo Elvira *c* Jorge Stahl Jnr *lp* Arturo de Cordova, Carmen Molina, Miguel Angel Ferriz, Matilde Palou, Queta Lavat, Chela Campos, Fernando Galiana, Wolf Ruvinskis

Someone at the Door
(HAMMER; GB) b/w 85min
This is a comedy-thriller featuring a mansion riddled with sliding panels, priest-holes and sundry gothic paraphernalia, in the manner of **The Old Dark House** (1932). Medwin is the journalist who plans a scoop by murdering his wife (Owen) and discovering her body, only to find himself entangled in a jewel robbery mystery instead. The plot was taken from a stage play by Major and Dorothy Campbell Christie. Searle had directed the first Hammer effort in the creepy-mansion subgenre (*The Man in Black*, 1949) from a John Gilling script. Such gothic thrillers (including Gilling's **Dark Interval**, 1950) were the forerunners of Hammer's sixties series of psycho-horror thrillers which began with **Taste of Fear** (1960).

d Francis Searle *p* Anthony Hinds *s* A. R. Rawlinson *c* Walter Harvey *lp* Yvonne Owen, Michael Medwin, Hugh Latimer, Danny Green, Garry Marsh

1951

Bride of the Gorilla (REALART) b/w 65min
Burr, manager of a rubber plantation, kills his boss in a fight, then marries his young widow (Payton). Keeping a watchful eye on things, an old servant woman pops something in his drink which makes him act like a gorilla. Baffled by the killings that ensue, the local police chief (Chaney) eventually tracks down and kills the gorilla-man. Apart from the undeniable amusement of watching Burr labour through his transformations, this is a wearying experience set in and around an exceedingly fake jungle.

Strode makes his début as a policeman, while Herman Cohen learnt his budget-cutting trade as associate producer.

d/s Curt Siodmak *p* Jack Broder *c* Charles Van Enger *lp* Lon Chaney Jnr, Barbara Payton, Raymond Burr, Tom Conway, Paul Cavanagh, Woody Strode

Il Medium (TRANS FILM; IT) b/w 80min
Lovers of Italian opera will appreciate Menotti's film version of his own work, but filmed opera, hovering as it does uneasily between musicals and reverent art-documentaries, and having the weaknesses of both without their compensatory strengths,

is a notoriously disappointing genre for lovers of cinema. Menotti's record of the stage production, with a few exterior scenes to 'open out' the set, lapses into an over-indulgent use of closeups and an excess of decorative baroquerie. The story concerns a cruel medium (Powers) who, after years of faking seances and mistreating her young helpers, her daughter (Alberghetti), and a mute gypsy boy (Coleman), begins to feel that the forces of darkness are out to get her and senses fingers gripping her throat to choke her. The performances on the stage were, by all accounts, impressive, which in film terms means grotesquely over the top. There is no dialogue, only arias and recitative and lots of dramatic music. Cinephiles who like opera would probably prefer to buy a record. The story is not to be confused with Vernon Sewell's ghost story *The Medium* (1934).

co-d/s Gian-Carlo Menotti *co-d* Alexander Hammid *p* Walter Lowendahl *c* Enzo Serafin *lp* Marie Powers, Anna Maria Alberghetti, Leo Coleman, Belva Kibler, Beverly Dame, Donald Morgan

The Stolen Face

(EXCLUSIVE PICTURES; GB) b/w 72min

Fisher's first (and still awkwardly directed) fantasy film tells of a plastic surgeon (Henreid) who remodels the scarred face of the 'bad' Mary (MacKenzie) to make her look like his love, Alice (Scott), about to be married to a friend (Morell). Henreid then marries 'his' Scott, but she reveals herself to be as malevolent as ever. The happy ending is provided by the death of one 'Scott' and the reappearance of the other – the good one, who didn't marry Morell after all. Scott is adequate in the dual role, and Henreid is his usual prissily professional self.

With this movie, their 20th, Hammer at last settled into their familiar headquarters at Bray Studios, an elegant country house often used in later films as part of Dracula's castle. Fisher returned to the Frankenstein theme of a surgeon who creates a duplicate of his loved one in *The Four Sided Triangle* (1952).

d Terence Fisher *p* Anthony Hinds *s* Richard Landau, Martin Berkeley *c* Walter Harvey *lp* Paul Henreid, Lizabeth Scott, Andre Morell, Mary MacKenzie, John Wood, Suzan Stephen, Richard Wattis, Arnold Ridley, Russell Napier

The Strange Door (U) b/w 80min

Very much a B movie, luridly adapted from Robert Louis Stevenson's story *The Sire de Malétroit's Door*, *The Strange Door* attempts to revive the Universal style of the thirties but emerges more like a prototype for the Roger Corman Poe series that started in 1960 with **House of Usher**. Laughton goes enjoyably over-the-top as a 17th-century nobleman madly dispensing tortures and prowling the gothic castle where the rightful owner – his brother (Cavanagh), who had the temerity to marry the woman he loved – lies rotting in a dungeon with Karloff as his baleful (but sympathetic) keeper. Frustrated in his plan to complete his revenge by marrying Cavanagh's daughter to a drunken rake, Laughton throws both the daughter (Forrest) and her lover (Stapley) into her father's cell for a thunderous climax in which he starts the waterwheel mechanism that will bring the cell walls slowly crashing together. Karloff, biding his time and beautifully balancing Laughton's bravura with his quiet understatement, survives several bullet holes and stabbings long enough to ensure that Laughton's body, snared in the waterwheel, brings the mechanism grinding to a halt. Much better than its reputation suggests, the film is surprisingly imaginatively directed by Pevney, not noted for horror movies although he did direct the Lon Chaney biopic, *Man of a Thousand Faces* (1957).

d Joseph Pevney *p* Ted Richmond *s* Jerry Sackheim *c* Irving Glassberg *lp* Charles Laughton, Boris Karloff, Sally Forrest, Richard Stapley, Paul Cavanagh, Michael Pate, Alan Napier

1952

The Black Castle (U) b/w 82min

This lumbering period gothic outing features McNally (sporting a black eyepatch to signal his villainy) as an 18th-century Austrian count – first cousin to Count Zaroff of **The Most Dangerous Game** (1932) – who becomes a target for revenge for an English aristocrat (Greene) after hunting and killing two of the latter's friends as human game. Braving a moat full of alligators, a prowling leopard and the torture chambers reserved for the Count's enemies, Greene infiltrates the castle under an assumed name, falls for the Count's unhappy wife (Corday), and is thrown into a dungeon with her when discovered. Karloff, for the most part standing by looking sinister (though actually benevolent as a doctor in the Count's thrall), then takes a leaf out of *Romeo and Juliet* and administers a drug which makes the lovers appear to be dead. All but buried alive due to the Count's discovery of the plot, they are saved by the happy ending.

Despite all the ghoulish nastiness, the film is a drearily pedestrian affair with Juran (making his début as a director) handling the action as though it were one of the sword and Sinbad adventures (with Greene playing Robin Hood) for which he became known.

d Nathan Juran *p* William Alland *s* Jerry Sackheim *c* Irving Glassberg *lp* Boris Karloff, Stephen McNally, Richard Greene, Paula Corday, John Hoyt, Lon Chaney Jnr, Michael Pate

Ghost Ship (ABTCON PICTURES; GB) b/w 69min

Sewell remade his first feature (*The Medium*, 1934) no less than four times: *The Latin Quarter* (1945), *The Ghosts of Berkeley Square* (1947), *Ghost Ship* and **House of Mystery** (1961). The plot is derived from a French Grand Guignol play and involves a couple (Walsh and Court) who buy a property – here a ship, in fact director/producer Sewell's yacht – which turns out to be haunted, necessitating the intervention of a medium of some sort. The story of the property's previous occupants is told in flashback: a man murdered his wife and her lover, hiding their bodies in a water tank on board the ship. Burden is the psychic investigator who lays the ghosts and allows the happy couple to embark on their cruise. The movie's low budget visibly cramps the director's style and the film might have been more effective as a short story. But the acting and the script, though a little

Charles Laughton, as excessive as ever, in the interesting The Strange Door.

Valkoinen Peura, *one of the few Finnish horror films.*

wordy – additional dialogue is credited to Philip Thornton – are quite acceptable. Sewell's best treatment of this situation is *House of Mystery*.

d/p/s Vernon Sewell *c* Stanley Grant *lp* Dermot Walsh, Hazel Court, Hugh Burden, John Robinson, Joss Ambler, Joan Carol, Hugh Latimer, Joss Ackland, Mignon O'Doherty

Noita Palaa Elämään *aka* **The Witch** *aka* **The Witch Returns to Life**
(SONNEY; FIN) b/w 75(70)min
Made almost simultaneously with Finland's only other and best-known fantasy picture, **Valkoinen Peura** (1952), this film is based on a play by the country's leading historical novelist, Waltari, who also provided the script. It tells of an archaeologist and his wife who, by pulling a wooden stake out of a dessicated skeleton accidentally revive a witch who has been dead for 300 years. The witch, played by Mane, is a decidedly healthy-looking young girl and contrasts interestingly with the usual depictions of predatory women. However, Hällstrom, at best a routine director, fails to breathe any real life into the story and as a result the movie is rather timid.

In the late fifties, the Finnish film industry suffered a serious recession and the next generation of film-makers, who were responsible for the 'new wave' of the late sixties, appeared to have lost interest in this type of fantasy story.

d Roland af Hällstrom *s* Mika Waltari *c* Esko Toyri *lp* Mirja Mane, Tiovo Makela, Hillevi Lagerstam, Aku Korhonen, Sakari Jurkka, Helge Herala

Old Mother Riley Meets the Vampire *aka* **My Son the Vampire** *aka* **Mother Riley Meets the Vampire** *aka* **Vampire over London** *aka* **King Robot** *aka* **Mother Riley Runs Riot** *aka* **Dracula's Desire**
(RENOWN; GB) b/w 74min
The last of the long-running series of farces starring Lucan as the Irish washerwoman and his manager/wife McShane as 'her' daughter. Lugosi is the mad doctor, Van Hoosen, who dresses and behaves as a vampire should. The plot has a robot kidnap Mother Riley and pit her against Van Hoosen and the denizens of his old dark house. Immensely popular in the provinces, the film used topical fears about rent collectors and food shortages as basic comic material.

Gilling later directed some good movies for Hammer including **The Reptile** and **The Plague of the Zombies** (both 1966).

d/p John Gilling *s* Val Valentine *c* Dudley Lovell *lp* Arthur Lucan, Kitty McShane, Bela Lugosi, Dora Bryan, Hattie Jacques, Dandy Nicholls, Richard Wattis, Charles Lloyd-Pack, Graham Moffatt

Scared Stiff (WALLIS-HAZEN) b/w 108min
This remake of **The Ghost Breakers** (1940), features Martin and Lewis as nightclub entertainers on the run and Scott as the girl who has inherited a spooky island castle in the Caribbean. The scares are provided as before by loot-hunting gangsters and a lurking zombie (Lambert). With Martin replacing Bob Hope and winning the girl, Lewis more or less takes over the Willie Best role, indulging in some horrendous mugging (his salutary encounter with Frank Tashlin on *Artists and Models* (1955) was still two years away) as his fright sends him cannoning into walls. Though Marshall directs again, the result this time is a witless mess stretched very thin while Martin sings a couple of even more tired numbers (allowing Lewis, not for the first time, to do his impersonation), and Bob Hope and Bing Crosby pop up for an uncredited, unfunny guest appearance.

d George Marshall *p* Hal B. Wallis *s* Herbert Baker, Walter de Leon *c* Ernest Laszlo *lp* Dean Martin, Jerry Lewis, Lizabeth Scott, Carmen Miranda, George E. Stone, Dorothy Malone, Jack Lambert

Valkoinen Peura *aka* **The White Reindeer**
(JUNIOR FILMI; FIN) b/w 75min
Set in old Lapland, this charming tale draws on pre-Christian lore and bears remarkable similarities to American Indian mythology. The picture opens with a fairly happy couple living their pitiless exhausting lives in inhospitable surroundings which leave their cruel marks on the people who have to endure them. The woman falls under a spell and begins to live a double life: as a wife and as a man-killing reindeer, until in the end her husband kills the reindeer with cold steel. Except for the scenes involving the local shaman, the movie is underplayed and unwinds with the slow but captivating rhythms of oral literature. The beautiful Kuosmanen, who also co-wrote the script, plays the cursed woman with conviction, endowing her trans-formation scenes with an emotional power rare in films of the period, which gained the film prizes at film festivals in Cannes (1953) and Karlovy Vary (1954). The director, who doubled as editor on this film, had been one of Scandinavia's most accomplished cinematographers since the thirties. This was his début feature as director but after five more films he devoted himself to making documentaries for television.

A second Finnish witch movie, **Noita Palaa Elämään** (1952), was made almost simultaneously, but these remain the only two significant Finnish contributions to the genre to date.

d/co-s/c Erik Blomberg *co-s* Mirjami Kuosmanen *lp* Mirjami Kuosmanen, Kalervo Nissilä, Ake Lindman, Arvo Lehesmaa, Jouni Tapiola

1953

Gilbert Harding Speaks of Murder
(DANZIGER; GB) b/w 76min
One of the many omnibus films made in the early fifties which combined stories that could also be sold individually to television, a format often used by Douglas Fairbanks Jnr, as in his **Three's Company** (1953). This collection of three short murder stories introduced by TV personality Harding is notable mainly for the Barclay-scripted *Thirty Days to Die* episode in which a playwright (Gregg) plots his lethal revenge on a critic (Naismith) who gave his play a bad review. The same

plot, transposed to the world of painting, was used again in Freddie Francis's **Dr Terror's House of Horrors** (1964) and was fleshed out into a feature for **Theatre of Blood** (1973). Another episode, *The Missing Passenger*, scripted by Tabori, features two middle-aged sisters (Walsh and Davies) who keep their common ex-boyfriend (Barr) locked up in their attic for more than 20 years. Elements of this plot recur in **Fanatic** (1964) and *Three in the Attic* (1968), not to mention *The Collector* (1965) and **The Beast in the Cellar** (1970).

d Paul Dickson *p* Edward J. Danziger, Harry Lee Danziger *s* Paul Tabori, James Eastwood, Kate Barclay *c* Jack Cox *lp* Kay Walsh, Betty Ann Davies, Patrick Barr, Hubert Gregg, Lawrence Naismith, Jenny Laird, Howard Marion Crawford, Wilfred Caithness, Andrea Melandrinos

House of Wax (WB) 88min

This is one of the better 3-D films, not least because de Toth sincerely believed in the possibilities of the process (and had even written an article about it in the *Hollywood Reporter* in 1946). He brings off at least one superb sequence in which Price, as the mad sculptor who turns human corpses into wax exhibits, realizes that he has been seen committing one of his murders: his pursuit of Kirk along the gaslit streets and alleyways, with his cloaked figure towering like an angel of death or becoming monstrously foreshortened, is beautifully managed. The trouble with the film, a remake of **Mystery of the Wax Museum** (1933), is that it leaves the original script virtually intact in all its creakiness (though at least getting rid of the wisecracking girl reporter played by Glenda Farrell). It also makes the rather radical mistake of devaluing its climax – the heroine (Kirk) striking at Price's face and breaking the waxen mask – by being unable to resist showing Price's hideously blackened features earlier on.

A big success, the film made a horror star of Price. It was remade, in a sense, as **Chamber of Horrors** (1966).

d André de Toth *p* Bryan Foy *s* Crane Wilbur *c* Bert Glennon, J. Peverell Marley *lp* Vincent Price, Frank Lovejoy, Phyllis Kirk, Carolyn Jones, Paul Picerni, Charles Buchinski (Bronson)

Three's Company

(DOUGLAS FAIRBANKS JNR; GB) b/w 78min

In the early fifties, Fairbanks Jnr produced a number of omnibus movies with the intention of selling the individual stories to television. The format was fairly popular for a while (**Gilbert Harding Speaks of Murder** and *The Triangle*, both 1953; **Three Cases of Murder**, 1954) for strictly commercial reasons, but went out of style until Amicus and Freddie Francis revived it in the sixties (**Dr Terror's House of Horrors**, 1964; **Torture Garden**, 1966). This Fairbanks Jnr product is worthy of note for Fisher's first contribution, *The Surgeon*, scripted by Simmonds and Marcus, in which a surgeon (Sydney) has to operate on a man his daughter (Sellars) tried to kill. Fisher's second story, *Take a Number*, is without interest, but the third episode, directed by Saunders from Cresswell's script and based on Hester Holland's story *The Scream*, tells of a ghostly scream that inhabits a house, awaiting the murderous event that is to correspond to it. A man (Fairbanks Jnr) and his evil wife (Cummings) buy the house and respond to the scream's invitation.

Direction and acting are conventional, although at this time material made for TV still made use of cinematic techniques to convey atmosphere and suspense, with the result that these mediocre short stories are vastly superior to both the contemporary television drama and that made in the sixties.

d Terence Fisher, Charles Saunders *p* Douglas Fairbanks Jnr *s* Richard Alan Simmons, Larry Marcus, John Cresswell *c* Jimmy Wilson, Brendan Stafford *lp* Basil Sydney, Elizabeth Sellars, George Benson, Douglas Fairbanks Jnr, Constance Cummings

Left: *Vincent Price stalks the streets in* House of Wax, *one of the best of the wave of 3-D films.*

1954

The Black Forest (PRINCESS) b/w 63min

The Black Forest comes across as a sort of updated version of **The Black Castle** (1952), with Tamiroff as the delightfully named Baron von Moribund, yet another Count Zaroff imitator whose pleasure lies in hunting humans as in *The Most Dangerous Game* (1932). He also gets a sadistic kick out of tormenting his drink-sodden mistress (Garner), his gamekeeper (Buettner), and Buettner's daughter (Wischmann), over all of whom he has a hold. When a young American army officer (Howard) intrudes, falls for Wischmann, and becomes too inquisitive, Tamiroff ingeniously persuades Buettner that he may lose not only his daughter but his job. Drawing the line at murder, the gamekeeper is summarily dispatched by the increasingly demented Tamiroff, who is finally caught in one of his own mantraps and brought to justice. Shot in Europe but stagy, sluggishly directed and very wordy, it makes very little use of its location.

d/p Gene Martel *s* Joe Liss, Irve Tunick *c* Erich Claunick *lp* Akim Tamiroff, Peggy Ann Garner, Gordon Howard, Wolf Buettner, Marianne Wischmann

The Bowery Boys Meet the Monsters

(AA) b/w 65min

In addition to their haunted-house antics for Monogram (**Spooks Run Wild**, 1941, for example), the East Side Kids also fell foul of a mad doctor who tried to transplant Hall's brain to a gorilla in *Spook Busters* (1946). As the Bowery Boys they went several better, tangling with a weird family whose interests include man-eating trees (Corby), gorilla transplants (Dehner), robots (Corrigan) and vampirism (Mason). Not very amusing, but with Hall also turned into a sort of werewolf, there isn't really leisure to be bored.

d/co-s Edward Bernds *p* Ben Schwalb *co-s* Elwood Ullman *c* Harry Neumann *lp* Leo Gorcey, Huntz Hall, Lloyd Corrigan, Ellen Corby, John Dehner, Laura Mason

La Bruja *aka* The Witch

(INTERNACIONAL CINEMATOGRAFICA; MEX) b/w 90min

In this far more horror-inclined sequel to his science fiction *El Monstruo Resucitado* (1953), Urueta again opposes beauty and disfigurement. A brilliant doctor (Villarreal) who can make ugly people beautiful becomes the target of envious colleagues who destroy his laboratory. To get his revenge he takes an ugly

The routine The Bowery Boys Meet the Monsters.

woman, La Bruja – the witch – (del Valle) and makes her beautiful; he then has her kill his enemies. Eventually she falls in love with one of them and refuses to kill him. Threatened with disfigurement by acid, she tries to escape with her lover but a beggars' Tribunal of the Night, echoing Fritz Lang's *M* (1931), catches up with them. Grateful for the doctor's previous good works, they condemn the couple to death. The witch frees her lover but is stabbed in the process and, as she dies, she returns to her former unsightly self.

Urueta seems unable to decide whether to shoot this as a melodrama or as a horror movie. The makeup is crude, the transformations of the ugly to the beautiful del Valle are awkward and nobody seems to take the *Beggars' Banquet* aspects of the story seriously enough to elaborate them into a more powerful motif. The director's next effort was a horror western serial, **El Jinete Sin Cabeza** (1956), but his best work was another witchcraft story, **El Espejo de la Bruja** (1960).

d/co-s Chano Urueta *p* Sergio Kogan *co-s* Alfredo Salazar *c* Victor Herrera *se* Jorge Benavides, Antonio Bustos *lp* Lilla del Valle, Ramón Gay, Julio Villarreal, Charles Rooner, Luis Aceves Castañeda, Fernando Wagner, José Rene Ruiz (Tun Tun), Guillermo Hernandez (Lobo Negro), Guillermina Tellez Giron, Diana Ochoa

El Fantasma de la Casa Roja *aka* The Phantom of the Red House

(FILMADORA CHAPULTEPEC; MEX) b/w 90min

One of the many old-dark-house mysteries made at the time, this one provides its own variation on 'the butler did it': he merely helped the chauffeur do it. The plot puts a group of people awaiting an inheritance in an old gloomy mansion. The heroine, who goes by the delightfully unlikely name of Mercedes Benz (Aguirre), inherits the house as well as a cabaret called El Infierno, while the rest of the group, including her lover Raul Caballero (Martinez), are supposed to hunt for a hoard of gold. A detective called Diogenes Holmes (played by the comic Clavillazo) is called in, but he gets imprisoned by the masked villain who goes around knifing people. The ordinary couple, after numerous comic, murderous and musical interludes, get the property.

Delgado made most of the pictures starring Mario Morena (Cantinflas), beginning with the anarchic *El Gendarme Desconocido* (1943). He was also responsible for **Misterios de la Magia Negra** (1957).

d Miguel M. Delgado *p* Pedro Galindo *s* Maria Cristina Lesser, Ramón Perez Pelaez *c* Raúl Martinez Solares *lp* Alma Rosa Aguirre, Raúl Martinez, Antonio Espino (Clavillazo), Jorge Reyes, Guillermina Tellez Giron, Victor Alcocer, Enriqueta Reza, Conchita Gentil Arcos

The Golden Mistress (RK PRODUCTIONS) 82min

This jungle adventure has Agar and Bowie find a fabulous treasure at the bottom of a lake and have a scary time with a lost tribe called the Untamed. Shot in and around Haiti, with lots of voodoo ceremonies (courtesy of the National Folklore Theatre), it has a certain exotic interest marginal to the desultory action in which Biberman steals the idol of the title and meets a nasty voodoo end.

d/co-s Joel Judge *p* Richard Kay, Harry Rybnick *co-s* Lew Hewitt *c* William C. Thompson *lp* John Agar, Rosemary Bowie, Kiki, Abner Biberman, Andrée Marcisse

Gorilla at Large (PANORAMIC PRODUCTIONS) 94(84)min

Only four films away from the end of the 3-D boom of the fifties, and probably contributing to its demise, this is a singularly silly mystery, set in a carnival where a couple of murders bring out the suspects like flies. Trapeze artist Bancroft, disguised in a gorilla suit, is the culprit. Mitchell also gets to wear a gorilla suit since Bancroft's act consists of flying over the gorilla cage and he has to double for the dangerous brute. In the end a real gorilla (also someone in a monkey suit, but you're not supposed to realize that) carries Bancroft off to the top of the roller-coaster. She is rescued by Mitchell and has to face due process of the law. Cobb is the detective, Burr the carnival owner, and Marvin a garrulous cop.

d Harmon Jones *p* Robert L. Jacks *s* Leonard Praskins, Barney Slater *c* Lloyd Ahern *lp* Cameron Mitchell, Anne Bancroft, Lee J. Cobb, Raymond Burr, Charlotte Austin, Lee Marvin

The Mad Magician (COL) b/w and col 72min

Price is The Great Gallico, a brilliant inventor of illusions whose employer has an injunction put on him when he tries to make his stage début as a magician using his own tricks. Predictably he takes out his frustrations by putting his tormentor through the circular buzz-saw intended as a climax to his act, and madness ensues as one murder follows another until he is hoist with his latest petard: a trick coffin put through an incinerator. Though very much at home with the 1880s atmosphere, Brahm's careful direction misses out on the necessary ghoulish zest. Made in 3-D and with Price even sporting lifelike facial masks for the purposes of disguise, the whole thing is an all too obvious attempt to repeat the formula of **House of Wax** (1953).

d John Brahm *p* Bryan Foy *s* Crane Wilber *c* Bert Glennon *lp* Vincent Price, Mary Murphy, Eva Gabor, John Emery, Donald Randolph, Patrick O'Neal

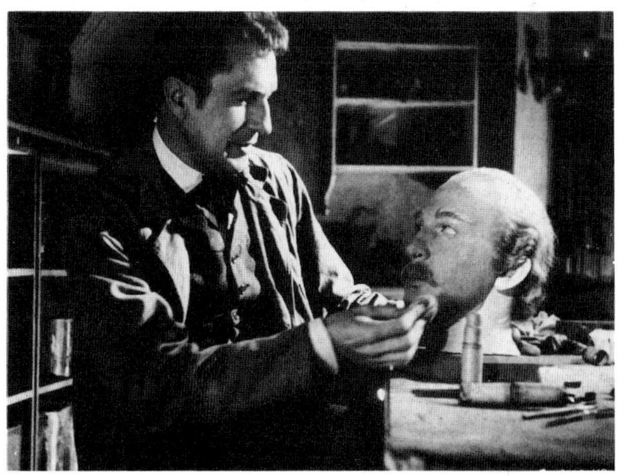

Right: *Vincent Price as* The Mad Magician.

1954

Phantom of the Rue Morgue (wb) 84min

As in **Murders in the Rue Morgue** (1932), Gemora here plays the gorilla, but this is the only resemblance between the two films. Dead girls are found with bells on their wrists; Malden (overacting like mad in the Lugosi role) works at the Paris zoo, where he has trained a gorilla to react to the tinkle of bells; and the period has been updated to around 1900 so that Dupin (Forrest) can be a Freudian psychologist whose fiancée Medina is pursued by Malden. The abysmal dialogue is full of psychoanalytical bilge, the murders are repetitive in the extreme (the best scene, paradoxically, is one in which the ape attacks a window-display dummy), and the 3-D effects are tamely restricted to the usual hail of hurled knives and clutching paws.

d Roy del Ruth *p* Henry Blanke *s* Harold Medford, James R. Webb *c* Peverell Marley *lp* Karl Malden, Claude Dauphin, Patricia Medina, Steve Forrest, Allyn McLerie, Charles Gemora

Three Cases of Murder

(WESSEX/LONDON FILMS; GB) b/w 99min

Like **Three's Company** and **Gilbert Harding Speaks of Murder** (both 1953), this is an omnibus film made with one eye on TV sales. Two of the three stories are of particular interest. The first is Toye's ingenious *In the Picture*, which uses Wilson's adaptation of a Roderick Wilkinson story about a strange painting of a deserted house. During a conversation between Pryse's painter and a Mr X (Badel), the painter finds himself being absorbed into the picture and entering the mysterious house where he falls victim to the taxidermist (Byrne) who lives there. But the real point of the story is an exploration of the artist's desire for perfection as he seeks to improve the composition of his painting in terms of a realist aesthetic which requires pictures to provide an illusion of reality. The result is a fascinating reflection on the very reality effect of images: an illusion achieved here at the cost of transforming the viewer, Pryse, into a stuffed dummy. The *Lord Mountdrago* episode, scripted by Dalrymple from a Somerset Maugham story, features Welles and Badel as political antagonists who discover that their dreams affect their opponent. They proceed to dream each other to death. Many of Maugham's stories had been used for omnibus films (*Quartet*, 1948; *Trio*, 1950), but none could boast anything like Welles' wonderfully hammy performance as Mountdrago, the imperious foreign secretary brought down by his Welsh opponent.

The omnibus format would be revived in the sixties by Amicus and Freddie Francis for a number of films including **Dr Terror's House of Horrors** (1964) and **Torture Garden** (1967) before coming fully into its own on television with Rod Serling's *Night Gallery* (1970-3).

d Wendy Toye, George More O'Ferrall, David Eady *co-p/co-s* Ian Dalrymple *co-p* Hugh Perceval *co-s* Donald Wilson, Sidney Carroll *c* Georges Perinal *lp* Alan Badel, Hugh Pryse, Leueen MacGrath, Eddie Byrne, John Salew, Orson Welles, Andre Morell, Helen Cherry, Elisabeth Sellars, John Gregson

Toto all'Inferno *aka* Toto in Hell

(EXCELSA-PONTI; IT) b/w 89min

The immensely popular Neapolitan clown made films in a wide variety of genres which, although not real parodies, combined the comic possibilities inherent in the genres themselves with his own inimitable knack for sending up human types or, better, styles of existence – an ability to do with language and gesture what Jacques Tati tried to do through gesture alone. This tale concerns Marchi (Toto), who commits suicide and winds up in hell with Satan (Buazzalli) and Belfagor (Lay), as well as with Cleopatra. Jealous of the love between Toto and Cleopatra, Satan first exiles him to an existentialist bistro, and then continues to persecute him, appearing in the guise of a policeman, a prosecutor and a judge. In the end, it is all revealed to have been a bad dream, but by then Toto's subversive humour has scored some telling anti-authoritarian points against religion, the state and conformity in general. The scenes in hell are very well done, with excellent effects, while a sequence in a circus is reminiscent of Tod Browning's **Freaks** (1932). One of the few films devised and partly co-written by Toto himself, it is among his best works. Mastrocinque, a very prolific director, signed a number of Toto's comedies as well as **La Cripta e l'Incubo** (1964) and **Un Angelo per Satana** (1966).

d/co-s Camillo Mastrocinque *p* Carlo Ponti *co-s* Toto, Alessandro Contineza, Vittorio Metz, Italo di Tuddo, Lucio Fulci, Gino Mangini *c* Aldo Tonti *se* Ditta Gatti, Serge Urbisaglia *lp* Toto, Maria Frau, Tino Buazzalli, Ubaldo Lay, Fulvia Franco, Dante Maggio, Franca Faldini

Faith Domergue as the goddess-cum-snake in the silly but enjoyable Cult of the Cobra.

1955

Cult of the Cobra (U) b/w 82(79)min

Six GIs, intruding on a secret cult of cobra-worshippers in an Indian temple, are cursed by the high priest. The revenge of the snake goddess starts that night when one of the six, all of whom are being flown home for demobilization, dies mysteriously from a snakebite. Back in New York (where all of them conveniently live), three more die in similar circumstances until only Long and Thompson are left. At first upset when his actress girlfriend (Hughes) marries Long, Thompson finds consolation in the beautiful stranger (Domergue) lurking in the apartment across the way. Becoming suspicious, Long is just in time to hurl a striking cobra out of the window, and in death its body is metamorphozed back into Domergue's. The cast is better than anything else in the film, although Metty's camerawork gives it an occasional lift.

d Francis D. Lyon *p* Howard Pine *s* Cecil Maiden, Richard Collins *c* Russell Metty *lp* Faith Domergue, Richard Long, Marshall Thompson, Kathleen Hughes, David Janssen, Jack Kelly

El Jinete Sin Cabeza *aka* **The Headless Rider**
(PRODUCCIONES UNIVERSAL; MEX) b/w 280min
This western serial, released as three features, revolves around the head of Pancho Villa which is kept in a mysterious black box and coveted by all and sundry before finally (and aptly) coming into the possession of the eponymous 'headless horseman' (Aguilar). Mysterious horsemen had figured in Mexico's first film serial, *Las Calaveras del Terror* (1943), directed by Fernando Mendez, but the picturesque motif was used in films throughout the world, from Frank Wisbar's **Faehrmann Maria** (1936) to Hammer's **Captain Clegg** (1961). The macabre aspect of this Mexican version is not the headless rider but the gimmick of devising a serial around the severed head kept in a box, which anticipates in some ways Sam Peckinpah's *Bring Me the Head of Alfredo Garcia* (1974). Except for the successful **El Espejo de la Bruja** (1960), Urueta's career remained stuck in routine adventure and fantasy material, starting with *El Monstruo Resuscitado* (1943) and ending with numerous masked-wrestler movies (*Blue Demon contra el Poder Satanico*, 1965; **Blue Demon contra los Cerebros Infernales**, 1966; and *Blue Demon contra las Diabolicas*, 1967, and others). The three features comprising this serial were entitled *El Jinete Sin Cabeza* (95 min), *La Cabeza de Pancho Villa* (94 min) and *La Marca de Satanas* (91 min).

d Chano Urueta *p* Luis Manrique *s* Ramón Obon
lp Luis Aguilar, Flor Silvestre, Crox Alvarado, Jaime Fernandez, Pascual Garcia Peña, Salvador Godinez

Notre Dame de Paris *aka* **The Hunchback of Notre Dame**
(PARIS FILMS/PANITALIA; FR,IT) scope 108(103)min
This amorphous international co-production, tarted up with some mild torture scenes involving Lollobrigida's Esmeralda, is embarrassingly awful by comparison with the Chaney (1923) and Laughton (1939) versions of Victor Hugo's *The Hunchback of Notre Dame*. Quinn (as Quasimodo) labours under slapdash makeup and doesn't made the crude dialogue of the English-dubbed version (it is difficult to imagine that Prévert had a hand in the original) any more persuasive by indulging in some weird vocal mannerisms.

d Jean Delannoy *p* Robert Hakim, Raymond Hakim *s* Jean Aurenche, Jacques Prévert *c* Michel Kelber *lp* Gina Lollobrigida, Anthony Quinn, Alain Cuny, Jean Danet, Robert Hirsch

Gina Lollobrigida and Anthony Quinn in the decidedly minor Notre Dame de Paris.

The She Creature (GOLDEN STATE) b/w 77min
This film features the first outing of the mammary monster which subsequently appeared in assorted guises in three more AIP features. When the Great Lombardi (Morris) hypnotizes his assistant (English) for his fairground act, her prehistoric former self emerges, separately incarnated as an anthropomorphic sea-monster (Blaisdell) with scales, stringy blonde hair, huge breasts, and a yen to kill. Able to control the monster through English, Morris makes a big showbiz thing of predicting its killings, sharing the ill-gotten gains with his partner (Conway). He comes to grief when English's subconscious resists the command to kill the man she loves (Fuller), and the creature turns on Morris instead.

Very much a thing of plastic and studio paste, the creature is at least more fun here than when trundled out again (with a different head) for the science fiction variation *Voodoo Woman* (1957). The original head surfaced as a prop in **How to Make a Monster** (1958), and the whole creature re-emerged as a male in **The Ghost of Dragstrip Hollow** (1959). *The She Creature* was remade, abominably and without acknowledgement, by AIP-TV as *Creature of Destruction* (1968), directed by Larry Buchanan.

d Edward L. Cahn *p* Alex Gordon *s* Lou Rusoff
c Frederick E. West *lp* Chester Morris, Maria English, Tom Conway, Cathy Downs, Lance Fuller, Paul Blaisdell

The Undead (BALBOA/AIP) b/w 71min
Though it has science fiction elements, Corman's first real (but mild) horror movie is a delightful witchcraft piece. Garland is a psychotherapist who discovers that a prostitute patient (Duncan) is the reincarnation of a witch burned at the stake. Fascinated, he contrives to go back with her to the Middle Ages where (even though it will mean changing the future) she tries to save her past self. Full of knights, beheadings, rampaging witches and Satan waving a pitchfork – all dressed up in cod Shakespearian dialogue – the film has some enterprising special effects (witch metamorphozing into cat) and nice shafts of black humour (the heroine finding herself sharing a coffin with a corpse).

d/p Roger Corman *s* Charles B. Griffith, Mark Hanna
c William Sickner *lp* Pamela Duncan, Richard Garland, Allison Hayes, Val Dufour, Richard Devon

I Vampiri *aka* **Lust of the Vampire** *aka* **The Devil's Commandment** *aka* **The Vampires**
(TITANUS/ATHENA CINEMATOGRAFICA; IT) scope 90(71)min
Freda's extraordinarily beautiful film marked the beginning of the worldwide horror renaissance and preceded all the other titles often cited in this context: Terence Fisher's **The Curse of Frankenstein** (1957), Georges Franju's **Les Yeux Sans Visage** (1959), Roger Corman's **House of Usher** (1960) and Jesús Franco's **Gritos en la Noche** (1962). Freda's approach to the Erzsebeth Bathory legend, set in contemporary Paris and featuring a mad doctor (Balpêtré) who drains the blood from young women to maintain the youth of his beloved Duchess (Canale), shows that the flowering of Italian gothic movies grew from indigenous roots and owes little to Anglo-Saxon models. If antecedents must be assigned, they would include F. W. Murnau's **Nosferatu** (1921), Fritz Lang, Italian opera and Blasetti's *La Corona di Ferro* (1941).

A sculptor by training, Freda adopted his flamboyantly romantic style at a time when Italian cinema was still struggling with the deadweight of neorealism. Overshadowed by the international reputation of his contemporaries, whose cinema of 'alienation' (*Il Grido*, 1957; *L'Avventura*, 1960) made the headlines, Freda's work has been sadly neglected. Working within the constraints of Europe's most popular film industry, and with inferior scripts, he achieved an ornate visual intensity in his best work (*Beatrice Cenci*, 1956, for example), rarely equalled by prosaic directors more preoccupied with character development than with the potential of cinema. In *I Vampiri*,

Left: *The black-cloaked Otto Reichow about to sacrifice Marsha Hunt in the erratic* Back from the Dead.

the commercial pressures are still writ large and, indeed, Freda walked off the production after ten days, allowing Bava, his cinematographer, to finish the film in a further two days. Standard-format stock shots were inserted, stretched into scope, to pad the transitions. Canale, in the role of the ageing Duchess rejuvenated by blood of the straight heroine (Guida), is photogenic; but it is Barbara Steele, noticed by Bava in some minor British films, who would come to provide the sensual presence to match the style of the oneiric *mise-en-scène* in Freda and Bava's subsequent pictures. His **L'Orribile Segreto del Dr Hichcock** (1962) would consummate the fusion of medical and gothic motifs in one of the wittiest and most disturbingly macabre works of the genre.

Ironically, this specifically Italian style of horror flopped at the box office, prompting Freda to initiate the fashion for Anglo-Saxon pseudonyms: he signed his next fantasy picture *Caltiki* (1959) as Robert Hampton, and numerous directors, actors and scenarists followed his example throughout the next two decades.

d/co-s Riccardo Freda *c/se* Mario Bava *co-s* Piero Regnoli *lp* Gianna Maria Canale, Antoine Balpêtré, Paul Muller, Carlo d'Angelo, Dario Michaelis, Wandisa Guida, Riccardo Freda, Charles Fawcett, Renato Tontini

The Werewolf (CLOVER) b/w 83(78)min

A routine quickie. Scientists Launer and Lynn experiment on Ritch with a serum intended to cure radiation poisoning, but instead turn him into a werewolf. Despite a competent performance from Ritch, the film ends in usual monster-on-the-loose style. Its only interest is in the very obvious marriage of genres at a time when horror movies were about to come back into favour after the science fiction boom of the early fifties.

d Fred F. Sears *p* Sam Katzman *s* Robert E. Kent, James B. Gordon *c* Edwin Linden *lp* Steven Ritch, Don Megowan, Joyce Holden, Eleanore Tanin, S. John Launer, George M. Lynn

1957

El Ataud del Vampiro *aka* El Retorno del Vampiro *aka* El Ataud del Muerto *aka* The Vampire's Coffin

(CINEMATOGRAFICA ABSA; MEX) b/w 86min

Six months after his successful **El Vampiro** (1957), Mendez made this somewhat chaotic but visually enchanting sequel with much the same crew and cast, again featuring the elegantly aristocratic Robles as the vampiric Count Karol de Lavud. The producer, Salazar, also returns to play the heroic Dr Enrique whose curiosity sets the plot in motion. He has Lavud's body disinterred and transported to his laboratory, but one of the graverobbers removes the stake from the Count's chest and lets him loose upon the world. The Count's lair is in a wax museum, where Maria Teresa (Montoya) gets shut into a Virgin of Nuremberg. Highlights include some effective pursuit scenes with Robles' shadow profiled on the walls (although, of course, vampires are not reflected in mirrors and therefore cannot have shadows either), especially the sequences where he menaces the heroine, Marta (Welter) in a deserted variety theatre. The picture ends with Enrique confronting the vampire in the wax museum: Lavud mocks the doctor by constantly changing himself into a bat, but Enrique eventually spears the bat, pinning it against the wall whereupon it changes back into Lavud. The US version was again 'produced' by K. Gordon Murray and 'directed' by Paul Nagle, but it would appear that no (or very little) extra material was added. Mendez' next major contribution, **Misterios de Ultratumba** (1958), was a mad-scientist movie written by Obon, while, Robles' next vampiric appearance was a self-parody, **El Castillo de los Monstruos** (1957).

d Fernando Mendez *p* Abel Salazar *s* Raúl Zenteno, Ramón Obon *c* Victor Herrera *lp* Germán Robles, Abel Salazar, Ariadna Welter, Yerye Beirute, Alicia Montoya, Guillermo Orea, Carlos Ancira

Back from the Dead

(REGAL) scope b/w 79(76)min

Although better known for his westerns, Warren made this solitary horror movie just before taking his also solitary excursion into science fiction with *The Unknown Terror* (1957). Written by Turney from her own novel *The Other One*, the cliché-ridden script is muddled, murky and a good deal less gripping. Castle plays the wife who is possessed by the spirit of her husband's first wife. Responsible is the evil Father Renall (Reichow), who heads a black magic cult and is ultimately foiled in his plans to perform a human sacrifice. Hunt, the possessed woman's sister – in effect, the heroine – gives a better performance than the circumstances warrant.

d Charles Marquis Warren *p* Robert Stadler *s* Catherine Turney *c* Ernest Haller *lp* Peggy Castle, Arthur Franz, Marsha Hunt, Marianne Stewart, Evelyn Scott, Otto Reichow

Blood of Dracula *aka* Blood Is My Heritage *aka* Blood of the Demon

(CARMEL) b/w 69min

This is a remake of the first of the teenage science-fiction cycle, **I Was a Teenage Werewolf** (1957). Like that and **I Was a Teenage Frankenstein** (1958), both films equating adolescent sex drives with monsterhood, it has Harrison as a discontented and unpopular high-school pupil turned into a vampire by her sinister chemistry mistress (Lewis), who hypnotizes her with an amulet which has occult powers. Neither so well directed as *Teenage Werewolf*, nor so well scripted as *Teenage Frankenstein*, and considerably less outrageous than either, its most striking feature is Harrison's grotesque vampire outfit, which includes chalky face, batwing eyebrows, Lugosi peak and bobbysoxer sweater.

d Herbert L. Strock *p* Herman Cohen *s* Ralph Thornton *c* Monroe P. Askins *lp* Sandra Harrison, Louise Lewis, Gail Ganley, Jerry Blaine, Malcolm Atterbury

El Castillo de los Monstruos *aka* Castle of the Monsters

(PRODUCCIONES SOTOMAYOR; MEX) b/w 90min

A routine imitation of **Abbott and Costello Meet Frankenstein** (1948), this features Clavillazo, the comic who had played the bungling detective in **El Fantasma de la Casa Roja** (1954) and a female sidekick, played by the attractive

Right: Blood of Dracula, *Herman Cohen's teenage vampire film.*

comedienne Elizondo. Their tribulations as a pair of newly-weds in a classic horror-castle include encounters with the creature of the Black Lagoon, Frankenstein's – here called Frentenstein's – monster, a mummy, a werewolf and a vampire, the latter played by Robles, the star of **El Vampiro** and **El Ataud del Vampiro** (both 1957), parodying his own performance. The prolific producer Sotomayor followed up this childish comedy with *La Nave de los Monstruos* (1959), a farce about a cowboy in a spaceship collecting monstrous creatures, and *Locura de Terror* (1960), setting the same plot in an insane asylum. A few years later, Benito Alazraki made another Abbott and Costello imitation, **Frankenstein, el Vampiro y Cia** (1961). Robles' next major performance as a vampire was as the son of Nostradamus in Federico Curiel's serial, released as four features starting with **La Maldición de Nostradamus** (1959). In Corona Blake's *El Mundo de los Vampiros* (1960), the Argentinian Guillermo Murray took over from Robles as the Count.

d Julian Soler *p* Jesús Sotomayor *s* Fernando Galiana, Carlos Orellana *c* Victor Herrera *lp* Antonio Espino (Clavillazo), Evangelina Elizondo, Germán Robles, Carlos Orellana, Guillermo Orea

Cat Girl *aka* The Cat Woman

(INSIGNIA FILMS; GB) b/w 75(67)min

A successful transposition of Tourneur's classic, **Cat People** (1942), to Britain in the fifties, this rarely screened movie symbolizes a turning point in the representation of English heroines. At first, Lenora (Shelley) seems to be yet another suffering English female – in the Virginia McKenna or Celia Johnson (*Brief Encounter*, 1945; *The Astonished Heart*, 1949) mould – as she quietly but nobly endures her husband's infatuation with another woman. David Pirie's account of what follows cannot be bettered: when her husband and his girlfriend slip into the garden one night, 'the legacy of emotion and sensuality, suppressed in countless British film heroines over the past 20 years, appears in a particularly violent and distorted form. Shaughnessy cuts to [Shelley] watching the couple on the grass, her eyes narrow and her mouth opens in startled joy as the ghostly cheetah, powered by all her repressed desire, begins to savage the lovers while she looks on in ecstasy ... there is nothing [in the movie] to equal the intensity of this first metamorphosis which marks a crucially liberating moment in British cinema.'

Other aspects of the movie – including the ending as Dr Marlowe (Ayres) runs over a cheetah with his car and discovers the body of Shelley in a shiny black mac lying in the road – are taken directly from Tourneur's masterpiece. This was Shelley's first British movie, but she soon became one of the leading fantasy actresses with **The Blood of the Vampire** (1957), **The Shadow of the Cat** (1960) and, above all, **The Gorgon** (1963) and **Dracula, Prince of Darkness** (1965).

d Alfred Shaughnessy *p* Herbert Smith *s* Lou Rusoff *s* Peter Hennessey *lp* Barbara Shelley, Robert Ayres, Kay Callard, Paddy Webster, Ernest Milton, Lilly Kann

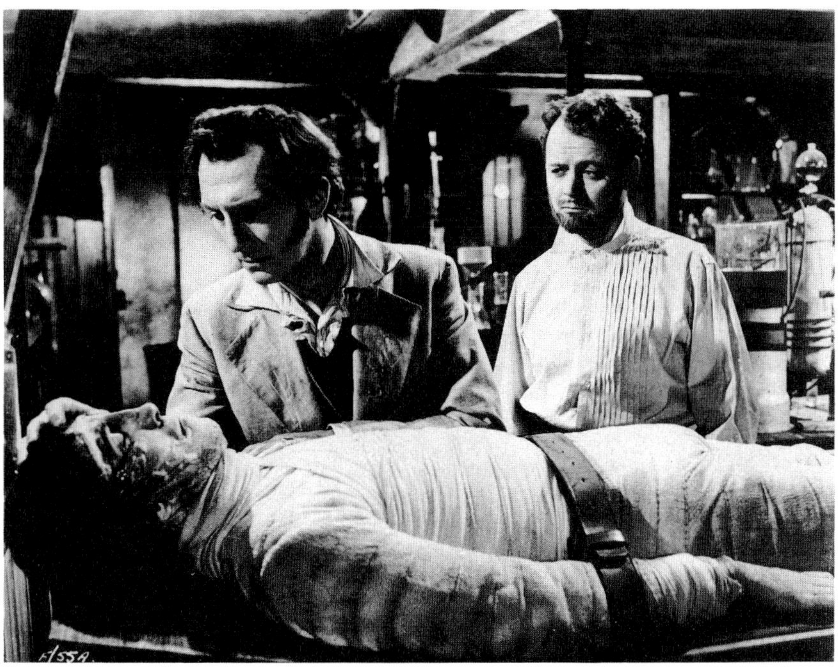

Christopher Lee as the monster and Peter Cushing as the Baron in Terence Fisher's revolutionary interpretation of the Frankenstein legend, The Curse of Frankenstein.

The Curse of Frankenstein *aka* Birth of Frankenstein

(HAMMER; GB) 82min

The breakthrough movie, not only for Hammer but for the entire genre in the postwar era. The film raised a storm of outraged protest among English newspaper critics who never dreamt that the vibrant new British cinema they had all called for would emerge from such an unexpected quarter and would be so successful, both commercially and aesthetically. Above all, it appears to have been the sensuality exuded by Fisher's movie which upset literary-minded journalists who forgot that a similar sense of outrage had greeted the publication of Lewis' *The Monk* in 1796 for much the same reason.

For copyright reasons, Hammer's makeup artist, Phil Leakey, couldn't copy Jack Pierce's designs of the creature in James Whale's **Frankenstein** (1931) and as a result the creature (Lee) looks more like Mary Shelley's original description than the image Universal had created for Boris Karloff. Because the creature is mute, Lee – in one of his best performances, although he hated the part – was forced to convey its pathetic emotional turmoil exclusively through physical gesture, hampered by the heavy makeup. But Fisher's major innovation, besides demanding that everybody play it straight – with humour but avoiding all vestiges of parody – was the character of the Baron. Cushing quickly struck the right note as the totally rational scientist so completely absorbed in his project that he excludes all other considerations. In Fisher's version of the story, the Baron and his creature are complementary figures, each embodying what the other lacks, and the relation between them constitutes the axis upon which the movie (and its sequels) turn. While the Baron seeks to create a perfected version of himself, what his creatures reflect back at him are his own moral flaws and emotional atrophy. In this sense, it is the Baron's character, played with subtle variations in successive movies, which sets the terms of the relation and not, as in Universal's movies, the creature. This also means that it was the Baron who needed to be kept alive from film to film, not the creature.

Although there are still some uncertainties in this first treatment of the story, Fisher's impeccable sense of dramatic timing and his splendid use of colour (this was the first British horror movie in colour) gave the film an operatic dimension, especially in the laboratory scenes where the Baron conducts his experiments to the accompaniment of flamboyant colour effects and weird noises, with actor and camera gliding through the scenery tracing captivating rhythms. It is worth noting that, as a myth, the Frankenstein story is the constant companion of the Dracula legend – Fisher went on to make **Dracula** (1958) one year later – each dealing with the same terms but from opposite sides of an imaginary fence. While Dracula is the disquieting survival of a feudal social order into the era of 19th-century business and scientific rationalism, Frankenstein presents the horrors of that rationalism, deploring its tendency to interfere with the old-established, religiously fixed order of things. However, in his later films (**The Revenge of Frankenstein**, 1958; **Frankenstein Created Woman**, 1966; **Frankenstein Must Be Destroyed**, 1969 and **Frankenstein and the Monster from Hell**, 1973), Fisher would give different inflections to this opposition: in the Dracula films, sexuality is associated with the return of the feudal, anti-rational repressed, whereas in his Frankenstein films, sexual deviance is the by-product of excessive rationality. In fact, Fisher's films are so rich, both in themselves and in their interconnections, that only a detailed study of his work, long overdue, could begin to do them justice.

d Terence Fisher *p* Anthony Hinds *s* Jimmy Sangster *c* Jack Asher *lp* Peter Cushing, Christopher Lee, Hazel Court, Robert Urquhart, Valerie Gaunt, Noel Hood, Michael Mulcaster, Patrick Troughton, Marjorie Hume

Daughter of Dr Jekyll

(FILM VENTURES) scope 70min

Probably best known only as a title thanks to Andrew Sarris' remark that 'anyone who loves the cinema must be moved by *Daughter of Dr Jekyll*', Ulmer's contribution to the Jekyll/Hyde myth is the most unorthodox treatment of Stevenson's theme to date. The bizarrely heterogenous storyline has Janet Smith (Talbott) arrive in England to claim an inheritance from a father she never knew. His former guardian Shields reveals that her father was none other than Dr Jekyll and when a number of killings occur Talbott falls under suspicion. The real villain, however, turns out to be Shields himself who had obtained the secret of metamorphosis from Dr Jekyll and now periodically turns into a werewolf. He is eventually dispatched by the angry villagers with a stake through the heart. Ulmer's direction is as hypnotic as ever but producer Pollexfen's script leaves him little room for genuine creativity.

The final shot, which shows the werewolf alive and well and promising to return suggests the film was conceived as the first of a possible series, but this never materialized. When shown on American television some of the film's frames were double printed to stretch out the action, and Talbott's nightmare was augmented with footage from *Frankenstein 1970* (1958).

d Edgar G. Ulmer *p/s* Jack Pollexfen *c* John F. Warren *lp* John Agar, Gloria Talbott, Arthur Shields, John Dierkes, Martha Wentworth, Mollie McCart

The Disembodied (AA) b/w 66min

The silly jungle saga of Tonda (Hayes), who does not love her doctor husband (Weingraf) and secretly gets her thrills as a native voodoo queen. When visitors arrive, she falls for one (Burke) and tries to persuade him to kill her husband since her voodoo has failed to do the trick (though apparently powerful enough to effect an overnight cure when another of the visitors is mauled by a lion: she cuts a native's heart out and the mauling promptly heals, though with a confusing side-effect of personality transfer). When Burke baulks at murder, Hayes sets him up as a voodoo sacrifice, but is herself killed by the dead native's grieving mate.

d Walter Grauman *p* Ben Schwalb *s* Jack Townley *c* Harry Neumann *lp* Paul Burke, Allison Hayes, John E. Weingraf, Eugenia Paul, Joel Marston

I Was a Teenage Werewolf

(SUNSET PRODUCTIONS) b/w 76min

One of the most famous movie titles of all time, this was the first feature of Fowler, who went on to make the science fiction *I Married a Monster from Outer Space* (1958). Raw-meat-loving teenager Landon is sent to psychiatrist Bissell in an attempt to cure his psychotic rages. Bissell, however, is crazy and believes that mankind can only be saved from atomic war by an enforced return to primitive times. To this end, he injects Landon with a mysterious serum, hypnotizes him and watches the startling results. Thornton's script and Fowler's surprisingly witty direction have Landon behave like a fully fledged werewolf and butcher all those he comes into contact with, including Bissell, before being killed by cop Phillips.

d Gene Fowler Jnr *p* Herman Cohen *s* Ralph Thornton *c* Joseph La Shelle *lp* Michael Landon, Yvonne Lime, Whit Bissell, Tony Marshall, Dawn Richard, Barney Phillips

Kaidan Kasanegafuchi *aka* Ghost Story – The Kanane Swamp *aka* The Ghost of Kasane *aka* The Depths

(SHINTOHO; JAP) scope 60min

With his rather odd vampire movie *Kyuketsuki Ga* (1956), the veteran Nakagawa embarked on a series of nine horror movies called Kaidan Eiga (literally, ghost story films). This, his first major contribution to the genre, was taken from the celebrated 19th-century bard Encho Sanyutei. Its two-tier construction starts with a samurai's murder of a blind masseur. Haunted by his victim, the samurai accidentally kills his wife and then commits suicide. The second part concerns his adopted son who causes the suicide of the masseur's daughter, a samisen teacher, because he rejects her when he falls for one of her students. She haunts the lovers until the young man kills his beloved and then throws himself into the Kasane swamp. By all accounts the result was a haunting movie with some extraordinarily powerful passages such as the classic scene in an inn where the two lovers take refuge and are served three cups of tea, the waitress gently asking what the 'third' lady desires. Although the lovesick ghost doesn't appear in the scene, it remained famous for its sinisterly glacial atmosphere. The story, originally called *Shinkei Kasanegufuchi*, had been filmed before by the great Mizoguchi as **Kyoren no Onna Shisho** (1926) as well as by Hachiro Ogura in 1937. Yasuda remade the picture in 1970.

Nakagawa's next major feature was a baneneko mono (a story with a ghostly cat), *Borei Kaibyo Yashiki* (1958); he then

The bizarre Daughter of Dr Jekyll, *Edgar Ulmer's contribution to the Jekyll and Hyde cycle.*

Nadia Haro Oliva and her assistant, Carlos Ancira, in the ludicrous Misterios de la Magia Negra.

turned to a hilariously odd vampire picture, **Onna Kyuketsuki** (1959).

d Nobuo Nakagawa *p* Mitsugu Okura *s* Yasunori Kawauchi *c* Yoshimi Hirano *lp* Katsuko Wakasugi, Takashi Wada, Tetsuro Tamba, Noriko Kitazawa, Kikuko Hanaoka

La Maldición de la Momia Azteca *aka* **The Curse of the Aztec Mummy**
(CINEMATOGRAFICA CALDERON; MEX) b/w 65min
Shot immediately after **La Momia Azteca** (1957) with the same crew and cast, this sequel sees the evil Dr Krupp (Castañeda) once again in pursuit of the Aztec jewels adorning Xochitl's corpse. He has Flor (Arenas) kidnapped and hypnotizes her in his laboratory to force her to reveal the location of the treasure, which, as Xochitl's reincarnation, she must know. Aided by bandits led by El Tierno (Martinez), he is again opposed by Arenas's lover (Gay) and his assistant (Alvarado) as well as by Popoca, the warrior mummy guarding Xochitl's tomb. Alvarado also doubles as superhero, donning a mask and turning into the wrestler El Angel. After a number of comic-strip adventures, the mummy locks Castañeda in the room of Death with a few hundred vipers while he retires to his own tomb with the recovered jewels. The heroes escape again by brandishing a crucifix to keep the mummy in check, confirming the Aztec warrior's odd susceptibility to Christian symbolism – which perhaps reminds him of the cruelties of the crucifix-brandishing conquistadores (easily on a par with the blood-thirstiness of the Aztecs). Although not nearly as accomplished as Steven Spielberg's expensively shot adventure films, Portillo's efforts, shot on a shoestring in two weeks, can be seen as less objectionably racist than the Indiana Jones tales. He went on to make a third mummy movie without a break in the production schedule, **La Momia Azteca vs el Robot Humano** (1957). The English version of this film was prepared by K. Gordon Murray.

d Rafael Portillo *p/co-s* Guillermo Calderon *co-s* Alfredo Salazar *c* Enrique Wallace *lp* Ramón Gay, Rosita Arenas, Crox Alvarado, Luis Acevas Castañeda, Arturo Martinez, Emma Roldan, Guillermo Hernandez (Lobo Negro), Jesus 'Murcielago' Velazquez, Enrique Llanes, Alejandro Cruz

Misterios de la Magia Negra *aka* **La Magia Negra** *aka* **Mysteries of Black Magic** *aka* **Return from the Beyond**
(ALFA FILMS/SERGIO KOGAN; MEX) b/w 87min
Released in 1958, Delgado's picture contains some high camp footage of Haro Oliva as a witch declaiming ludicrous incantations amid a cast so rigid they look like jerky puppets. The plot has Haro Oliva, the reincarnation of a 15th-century witch now appearing as a stage magician, pitted against professor Tejada (Riquelme), whose daughter (Parga) is the woman in peril; her lover (Monti) is the hero. In a crypt, Haro Oliva and her assistant (Ancira) keep the revered body of their contemporary warlock-master whose sexual jealousy triggers the climax as the witch falls for Monti and abducts him. The warlock returns from the grave and while the demonic lovers have their lethal tiff, the hero and his girlfriend escape from the crypt. The effects are rudimentary and the script's possibilities (a witch performing her tricks on stage as a spectacle could have yielded some nice cinematic parallels) wasted as Delgado opts for a crude melodramatic approach devoid of humour and beset with decidedly anti-semitic overtones.

d Miguel M. Delgado *p* Sergio Kogan *s* Ulises Petit de Murat *c* Victor Herrera *se* Antonio Neira *lp* Nadia Haro Oliva, Carlos Riquelme, Aldo Monti, Lulu (Lourdes) Parga, Angelines Fernandez, Carlos Ancira, Ada Carrasco, Elodia Hernandez, Diana Ochoa, Elvira Lodi

La Momia Azteca *aka* **Attack of the Mayan Mummy** *aka* **La Momia** *aka* **The Mummy Strikes** *aka* **The Mummy**
(CINEMATOGRAFICA CALDERON; MEX) b/w 80min
Understandably, Mexican versions of the mummy don't have their foundations in English forays into Egypt to plunder the tombs of the Pharaohs, but used their own history which had been destroyed by the Spanish conquest and repressed since then. Aztec motifs had been used before (as in *El Signo de la Muerte*, 1939, for example), but Portillo's Aztec mummy series is the best-known elaboration of them, appropriately triggered off by one of the shadier examples of American scientific research, the Bridey Murphy reincarnation fraud. One of the 'researchers' involved, Dr Joseph Barkley, even acted as consultant to this fairytale.

Dr Almada (Gay) expounds his theories of regression to previous lives by hypnosis which he then applies to his lover, Flor (Arenas). She once was Xochitl, ritually killed for an illicit affair with the warrior Popoca who was then buried alive to guard the amulet and bracelet on Xochitl's corpse. The two pieces of jewellery are the key to the location of the Aztec's treasure. Gay and his helper (Alvarado) steal the jewels and thus reactivate Popoca who mistakes Flor for his lover and tries to re-enact the ritual killing. The 'good' doctor is opposed by the evil, masked Dr Krupp (Castañeda) who calls himself El Murcielago (the bat). In the end, the goodies escape while the mummy is kept in check vampire-style by a crucifix before being blown up with dynamite. Popoca returned in two more Portillo films, **La Maldición de la Momia Azteca** and **La Momia Azteca vs el Robot Humano** (both 1957).

d Rafael Portillo *p/co-s* Guillermo Calderon *co-s* Alfredo Salazar *c* Enrique Wallace *lp* Ramón Gay, Rosita Arenas, Crox Alvarado, Luis Aceves Castañeda, Arturo Martinez, Jorge Mondragon, Angel di Stefani, Guillermo Hernandez (Lobo Negro), Emma Roldan, Jesús 'Murcielago' Velazquez

La Momia Azteca vs el Robot Humano *aka* **El Robot Humano** *aka* **The Robot vs the Aztec Mummy**
(CINEMATOGRAFICA CALDERON; MEX) b/w 65min
The third and final Portillo Aztec mummy movie (after **La Momia Azteca** and **La Maldición de la Momia Azteca**, both 1957). The evil Dr Krupp (Castañeda), having escaped from the room of Death's vipers where he had been left at the end of the previous film, now tries to hypnotize Flor (Arenas) at a distance to force her to reveal the location of the Aztec treasure guarded by the mummy of Popoca, the warrior lover of Xochitl, a previous incarnation of Arenas. In order to eliminate the powerful Popoca, Castañeda constructs a robot with a human brain and limbs of steel, a sort of bionic man. Nevertheless, Popoca destroys the creature and after the sacred

jewels belonging to Xochitl have been returned to him, he retires into his pyramid. The hero, Almada (Gay) has Castañeda and his bandits led by El Tierno (Martinez), arrested.

All three features were shot within two months, although this last one wasn't released until 1958. Portillo was no stranger to such extraordinary production schedules, having made three musicals at the same time a year earlier, in 1956, also for producer Calderon. Like *La Maldición*, this picture was anglicized by K. Gordon Murray for his own distribution company and he changed the producer's name to William C. Stell. The Aztec mummy made a brief reappearance in **Las Luchadoras contra la Momia** (1964).

d Rafael Portillo *p/co-s* Guillermo Calderon *co-s* Alfredo Salazar *c* Enrique Wallace *lp* Ramón Gay, Rosita Arenas, Crox Alvarado, Luis Aceves Castañeda, Arturo Martinez, Salvador Lozano, Guillermo Hernandez (Lobo Negro), Jesús 'Murcielago' Velazquez, Enrique Llanes, Firpo Segura

Night of the Demon *aka* Curse of the Demon *aka* The Haunted

(SABRE; GB) b/w 82min

Shot at exactly the same time as Terence Fisher's **The Curse of Frankenstein** (1957), this brilliant adaptation of M. R. James' *Casting the Runes* is related more to Tourneur's American work than to the British horror renaissance. It tells of Dr Holden (Andrews), an American psychologist, who is asked by Joanna (Cummings) to look into the death of her father (Denham). The mysterious Dr Karswell (MacGinnis), a specialist in the occult, had been threatened by the professor and now he predicts that Andrews will die within four days. It emerges that whoever possesses a small piece of parchment meets with a horrible fate, and when the sceptical Andrews is at last convinced that he is in serious danger, he manages to pass the scroll back to MacGinnis in a train and the occultist falls victim to the demon.

Tourneur, who excelled at films that staged the eruption of repressed desires, made the classic horror movies **Cat People** (1942) and **I Walked with a Zombie** (1943) and an equally effective *film noir*, *Out of the Past* (1947). Here his extraordinary placing and handling of the camera imbue seemingly ordinary surroundings with a brooding sense of menace. The trees, objects or simply unlit areas darkly obtruding in the foreground suggest the presence of implacable forces waiting to pounce on vulnerable, isolated figures. Some suspense scenes, perfectly timed and staged, stand out as models of their kind: the shots of a car with blazing headlights speeding through the night, filmed from behind a cluster of trees; the sudden storm at the children's party presided over by the villain dressed up as a clown; or Andrews' growing panic as he walks through the woods after a visit to the necromancer. The intensely rhythmic opening sequences, intended to set a tone of impending doom, were ruined by the distributor's insistence on the need for early shock effects, but the rest of the movie is an object lesson in atmospheric horror.

The impact of Fisher's work opened up a different direction for British and American horror, but the best of the Italian black and white movies – directed by Riccardo Freda, Mario Bava and Antonio Margheriti – can be seen as flamboyant extensions of Tourneur's quietly sinister pictorial style.

d Jacques Tourneur *p* Frank Beviss *s* Charles Bennett, Hal E. Chester *c* Ted Scaife *lp* Dana Andrews, Peggy Cummings, Niall MacGinnis, Athene Seyler, Maurice Denham, Ewan Roberts, Brian Wilde, Liam Redmond, Peter Elliott, Reginald Beckwith

Pharaoh's Curse

(BEL-AIR) b/w 66(63)min

Neise and Brewster head an archaeological expedition into the Valley of the Kings with tediously predictable results. Warned by a mysterious Arab girl (Rodann) against desecrating the tomb of a royal priest, the fanatical Neise ignores her and opens the sarcophagus. When an incision is made in the mummy's wrappings, the spirit of the Arab girl's brother (Guillot) is impelled by a curse to enter the body. Coming to life and gradually crumbling as it decimates the expedition, it is eventually sealed into the tomb along with Neise, killed by falling rocks. The film is ill-written and lamentably directed.

d Lee Sholem *p* Howard W. Koch *s* Richard Landau *c* William Margulies *lp* Mark Dana, Ziva Rodann, Diane Brewster, George Neise, Kurt Katch, Alvaro Guillot

Teenage Zombies

(GOVERNOR) b/w 73min

In this dismal concoction four water-skiing teenagers are taken prisoner on a seemingly deserted island by an ape-man who delivers them to a mad lady doctor (Victor) working on a nerve gas that will turn human beings into mindless slaves (world domination is her ultimate design). Friends alert the sheriff (Concannon) who, it turns out, is supplying her with suitable subjects but they manage to escape anyway and a zombie (Niles) who has already undergone treatment destroys the laboratory. Supposedly tongue-in-cheek, it was made in 1957 but not released until three years later, rather missing out on Herman Cohen's teenage horror cycle spearheaded by **Blood of Dracula** and **I Was a Teenage Werewolf** (both 1957).

d/p Jerry Warren *s* Jacques Licotier *c* Allen Chandler *lp* Don Sullivan, Katherine Victor, Steve Conte, Raul Pepper, Nan Green, Chuck Niles, Mike Concannon

The Vampire *aka* Mark of the Vampire

(GRAMERCY) b/w 75min

This is the first of two films in which Landres and Fielder tried to demystify the vampire legend. Less successful than **The Return of Dracula** (1958), it works as a simple Jekyll and Hyde variation with Beal as a doctor who inadvertently takes a pill from a bottle belonging to a colleague who had been doing research on vampire bats. They prove to be habit-forming, but only after two murders and an attack on his nurse (Gray) does Beal realize that the pills turn him into a vampire and that he himself is the killer. Predictable and rather dull, the film undercuts its own rationalist-scientific approach – with small town replacing gothic castle – by having Beal transform into a

Dana Andrews as the rationalist confounded by the shadows of necromancy in Jacques Tourneur's classic Night of the Demon.

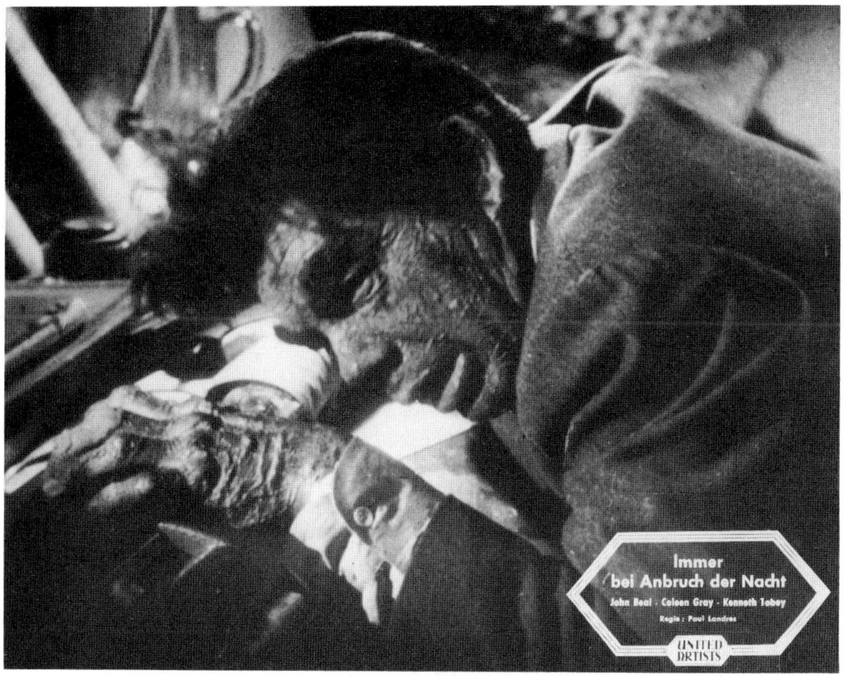

John Beal as the scientist who discovers blood is addictive in The Vampire.

wrinkled, shaggy monster-man.

d Paul Landres *p* Jules V. Levy, Arthur Gardner *s* Pat Fielder *c* Jack McKenzie *lp* John Beal, Coleen Gray, Kenneth Tobey, Lydia Reed, Dabbs Greer

El Vampiro *aka* **The Vampire**
(CINEMATOGRAFICA ABSA; MEX) b/w 95(84)min
Mendez, primarily a director of adventure melodramas, had shown considerable promise with *El Ladrón de Cadaveres* (1956) before making this classic Mexican horror movie which introduced Robles as a worthy rival of Christopher Lee. Produced a year before Terence Fisher's **Dracula** (1958), Mendez' tale refers back to Browning's **Dracula** (1931) and Murnau's **Nosferatu** (1921) rather than to Bram Stoker. The plot, devised by Obon, the writer of the macabre western serial **El Jinete Sin Cabeza** (1956), as the Hungarian Count Karol de Lavud (Robles) arrive in Mexico's Sierra Negra where he buys a property known as the Sicomoros, inhabited by the lugubrious Eloisa (Montejo), Emilio (Jimenez) and Maria Teresa (Montoya). The latter is being buried when her niece, Marta (Welter) and a doctor, Enrique (Salazar) arrive. Robles vampirizes Salazar and abducts Welter, but is pursued through subterranean crypts by Enrique who eventually stakes the Count, thus reducing Montejo to dust as well. Montoya, infected by vampirism but not really dead yet, intervenes at various stages to save the young couple.

The story is familiar, but Mendez' direction, although hampered by a restricted budget, is effective, making expert use of choreographic camera movements, especially for subtly surprising re-framings. Swirling fog abounds and the special effects, including the absence of reflections in mirrors while the objects manipulated by vampires appear to float in the air, are convincingly achieved. The transformation of vampires into bats is done by judiciously timed editing and a good use of the soundtrack: in one scene, two vampires continue their dialogue uninterrupted as they become bats, creating a sense of continuity in spite of the abrupt cut marking the change from human to animal. Robles acts the Count with distinction and menace, expertly handling the obligatory cape, while Montejo is excellent in the role of a passionate but frustrated spinster for whom vampirism comes as a sensual liberation. The intense funereal lyricism achieved by Mendez in this picture was sadly lacking in his sequel, **El Ataud del Vampiro** (1957). The English version of Mendez' classic, released in 1968 with some 20 good minutes missing, and about nine bad ones added, was provided by Paul Nagle for K. Gordon Murray, the distributor and adaptor of the Aztec mummy series. Additional scenes featured Dick Barker, Edward Tucker and Lydia Melon. Tucker was in fact Robles' American pseudonym.

d Fernando Mendez *p* Abel Salazar *s* Ramón Obon *c* Rosalio Solano *lp* Germán Robles, Abel Salazar, Ariadna Welter, Carmen Montego, José Luis Jimenez, Mercedes Soler, Alicia Montoya, José Chavez, Julio Daneri, Margarito Luna

Womaneater (FORTRESS FILMS; GB) b/w 71min
Another improbable shocker from the team responsible for *The Man Without a Body* (1957). Moran (Coulouris), a mad scientist, has a carnivorous tree with tentacle-like branches which eats women, preferably young ones. In exchange for the food, the tree supplies the doctor with a liquid that restores life to the dead. When he resuscitates his deceased housekeeper, she turns out to be insane too and causes the usual conflagration that brings everything to an end. Direction, acting and scripting are all equally questionable and totally lack the inspired silliness required to get away with such a motif, best seen in Roger Corman's **The Little Shop of Horrors** (1960) with its carnivorous piece of flora. The idea of the vampiric tree was later revived by Ernest von Theumer in **La Isla della Meurte** (1966). Saunders' movie is notable mainly for a fleeting appearance of the lovely Dawn, soon to star in the Franco-Brazilian smash-hit *Orfeo Negro* (1959).

d Charles Saunders *p* Guido Coen *s* Brandon Fleming *c* Ernest Palmer *lp* George Coulouris, Vera Day, Joy Webster, Peter Wayn, Jimmy Vaughan, Sara Leighton, Joyce Grenfell, Maxwell Foster, Marpessa Dawn

Zombies of Mora Tau *aka* **The Dead That Walk**
(CLOVER PRODUCTIONS) b/w 70min
Producer Katzman was the veteran of innumerable terrible B movies, not least Bela Lugosi's encounters with the East Side Kids in **Spooks Run Wild** (1941) and *Ghosts on the Loose* (1943), by the time he turned to this silly tale of adventurers diving for a sunken treasure of diamonds off the African coast and finding it guarded by amphibious zombies. Cahn does his best, staging a couple of more or less creepy voodoo rituals, but the underwater special effects are abysmal, and the acting little better.

d Edward L. Cahn *p* Sam Katzman *s* Raymond T. Marcus *c* Benjamin H. Kline *lp* Gregg Palmer, Allison Hayes, Autumn Russell, Joel Ashley, Morris Ankrum

1958

The Bat (LIBERTY/AA) b/w 80(78)min
This is a remake of the Mary Roberts Rinehart-Avery Hopwood play previously filmed under the same title in 1926 and as **The Bat Whispers** (1930). As though aware that the hoary formula of prowling maniac, hidden loot and beleaguered household would no longer hold water, the script adds a real bat to terrorize the ladies while trying to hype the Bat's murderous activities a little more by giving him a clawed hand with which to rip jugular veins. Promising performances by Moorehead as the spinster mystery-writer who solves the case, and Price as the principal suspect who does his share of killing and loot-hunting before being killed by the Bat (Gordon), are nipped in the bud by Wilbur's ponderous direction.

d/s Crane Wilbur *p* C. J. Tevlin *c* Joseph Biroc *lp* Vincent Price, Agnes Moorehead, John Sutton, Gavin Gordon, Lenita Lane, Elaine Edwards

The Blood of the Vampire
(TEMPEAN; GB) 85min
Following her success in **Cat Girl** (1957), Shelley played the female lead in this superior British horror movie about an

anaemic Dr Callistratus (Wolfit) freshly raised from the dead, who takes control of an insane asylum. He uses the inmates to replenish his blood supply, forcing a young doctor (Ball) and a dumb, one-eyed hunchback (Maddern) to assist him. Shelley plays Ball's girlfriend intent on helping him to escape, but in a highly suggestive scene filmed in colours worthy of Mario Bava, she and her lover are caught and chained to the wall in the mad vampire's dungeon. The hunchback baulks at strapping Shelley on to the operating table and attacks his master instead, allowing the lovers to escape. Wolfit, in hot pursuit, is torn to shreds by his own pack of dogs.

The Berman and Baker team's first horror effort, this was followed by *The Trollenberg Terror* and **Jack the Ripper** (both 1958), **The Flesh and the Fiends** and the *The Hellfire Club* (both 1959). They, rather than Hammer, manufactured strengthened versions of their films for export, leaving the heavily bowdlerized ones to Britain – a practice which earned them an enthusiastic following on the continent. This was probably the routine Cass's best movie. Once thought lost, prints have now recently resurfaced in America.

d Henry Cass *p* Robert S. Baker, Monty Berman *s* Jimmy Sangster *c* Geoffrey Seaholm *lp* Donald Wolfit, Vincent Ball, Barbara Shelley, Victor Maddern, William Devlin, Andrew Faulds, Bryan Coleman, John Le Mesurier, Milton Reid

The Bride and the Beast

(AA) b/w 78min

The notoriously inept Wood (of **Night of the Ghouls**, 1959, fame) provided the script for this preposterous film about a big-game hunter's wife (Austin) who feels strangely attracted when a gorilla makes advances on her wedding night in the jungle. Under hypnosis after her astonished husband (Fuller) shoots the animal and consults a doctor, she reveals herself to be the reincarnation of an ape. Subsequently kidnapped by a huge gorilla while on safari, she attacks Fuller when he tries to rescue her. Comprising mostly a mix of stock shots, mock jungle and stilted dialogue, the film does offer the hilariously bizarre spectacle of the heroine in filmy nightdress being embraced by Calvert in a gorilla suit.

d/p Adrian Weiss *s* Edward D. Wood Jnr *c* Roland Price *lp* Charlotte Austin, Lance Fuller, Johnny Roth, Steve Calvert, William Justine

Corridors of Blood *aka* Doctor from Seven Dials

(PRODUCERS ASSOCIATES; GB) b/w 86min

Shot back-to-back with **Grip of the Strangler** (1958) by the Croydon-Day-Karloff team, but far gorier, this film anticipates aspects of Jesús Franco's **Gritos en la Noche** (1962) and Riccardo Freda's **L'Orribile Segreto del Dr Hichcock** (1962). Day's film, however, is more unpalatably sadistic in that it fails to engage with the intensely sexual components of the desire to stage and watch such proceedings. *Corridors* merely chronicles in detail a succession of surgical operations mostly performed without anaesthetic and achieving nothing but the systematic mutilation of the victims. As such, it is an extremely puritanical spectacle in which sadism substitutes for sex, repressing the complex unconscious links between them. In Freda's movie, or in Mario Bava's **Sei Donne per l'Assassino** (1964), the links between sexuality, sadism and cinematic representation are the very subject of the films, enmeshing viewers in an oneiric delirium. There are moments in Franco's otherwise sensationalist work which achieve similar effects. But this British team appears to lack both the cultural awareness and the cinematic intelligence to understand either their medium or their subject matter.

d Robert Day *p* John Croydon *s* Jean Scott Rogers *s* Geoffrey Faithfull *lp* Boris Karloff, Betta St John, Christopher Lee, Adrienne Corri, Francis Matthews, Francis de Wolff, Finlay Currie, Nigel Green, Charles Lloyd-Pack

Curse of the Faceless Man

(VOGUE) b/w 66min

A huge calcified figure found buried near Pompeii is sent to an American museum, demonstrating en route that life persists by strangling the lorry driver transporting it, and also figuring in a premonitory dream experienced by a pretty artist (Edwards) whose boyfriend (Anderson) is the museum's scientific adviser. Research indicates that 2000 years ago it lived as Quintilius, an Etruscan slave-gladiator who loved the daughter of a Roman senator; and since the plot is little more than an ingenious reworking of **The Mummy** (1932) – substituting a golem figure vaguely modernistic in design – it isn't long before the hapless heroine is under threat. Tolerably gripping thanks to a lucidly economical script by Bixby (a short-story writer of uncommon wit, oddly neglected by Hollywood), the script has a neat twist at the end when the creature (Bryant) heads for the sea with Edwards in his arms (only to dissolve in the water), evidently under the impression that he is saving his beloved from the eruption of Vesuvius that buried Pompeii.

d Edward L. Cahn *p* Robert E. Kent *s* Jerome Bixby *c* Kenneth Peach *lp* Richard Anderson, Elaine Edwards, Adele Mara, Luis Van Rooten, Gary Moore, Bob Bryant

Dracula *aka* Horror of Dracula

(HAMMER; GB) 82min

In marked contrast to the crepuscular romanticism of F. W. Murnau's **Nosferatu** (1921) and Carl Dreyer's oneiric **Vampyr** (1931), the theatricality that had marred much of Tod Browning's **Dracula** (1931) and the fascinating flamboyance characteristic of Riccardo Freda's work in Italy (**I Vampiri**, 1956), Fisher deployed a poetic, subtly ironic, realism for this epoch-making movie, which marked the first significantly *British* cinematic interpretation of the myth. His Dracula is the 19th-century equivalent of James Bond – a man with all the qualities, power and pleasures the petty bourgeoisie guiltily pines for, a lurid representation of the aristocracy in the same way that the then current figure of the teenage hoodlum was a lurid representation of the working class as seen through the same eyes. Part of the extraordinary force of Fisher's film can be attributed to its deep roots in British history where the aristocracy is a caste with considerable power, mostly exercised behind closed doors, which it should have lost long ago but which nevertheless survives as a burden voluntarily assumed by the 19th-century English middle class which was neither rational nor strong enough to get rid of it. This aristocracy

The enthralled Carol Marsh awaiting her nightly visitation from Christopher Lee in Terence Fisher's epoch-making Dracula.

Boris Karloff – hunter and hunted – in the enigmatic Grip of the Strangler.

survives still, long after its apparent death, feeding upon the desires and expectations of status-craving merchants and administrators.

Such is the fantasy represented in historical terms by the seductive, but frighteningly powerful Count. The key sequence in Fisher's movie, in this respect, occurs when Van Helsing (Cushing) and Arthur (Gough) are outside guarding the home while Dracula, living in the basement and thus already inside, spends the night with Gough's wife, Mina (Stribling). Fisher also played down Dracula's foreign ancestry: there are no long voyages from Transylvania to England since the Castle and the Holmwood residence are within riding distance of each other – a money-saving alteration of the novel with felicitous thematic consequences, making Dracula a domestic English phenomenon. Accurately tuning into the political unconscious of the English middle class, the film was nevertheless acclaimed – and condemned – for the way it conveyed the erotic aspects of the vampire's relationship with his female victims, especially in the scenes in which Lucy (Marsh) readies herself, somewhat apprehensively but with real sensuality, for the Count's nightly visits. The most disturbing aspect of it all, vociferously objected to by some critics, is that the sadistically brutal actions are performed by the representatives of Christian morality: they are the ones who brutally drive the stake into the flesh of sexually aroused women, heedless of their screams and the gushing blood, mercilessly driving pleasure and life out of their bodies and leaving only the dry, shrivelled remains of unsightly hags.

The acting of the most famous horror duo in film history – Cushing and Lee – is impeccable, as is that of the female protagonists. But it is Fisher's uncanny sense of atmosphere, rhythm and colour, his poetic ellipses – the swirling autumn leaves outside Lucy's window indicating Dracula's arrival, for example – and his knack of building sequences in parallel action converging into a shot that binds the two actions together in one frame composed in depth, which makes this one of the most enthralling films made in Britain.

Having disposed of Dracula rather drastically by reducing him to dust, blown away as the final credits roll, and with Lee refusing to play Dracula again for fear of becoming typecast, Hammer's next vampire movie, **The Brides of Dracula** (1960), was a disappointment. It would be nine years before Fisher and Lee combined again to produce a worthy sequel, **Dracula, Prince of Darkness** (1965).

A South Korean imitation of Fisher's movie, entitled *Ahkea Kkots* (1961) was made by Yongmin Lee.

d Terence Fisher *p* Anthony Hinds *s* Jimmy Sangster *c* Jack Asher *lp* Peter Cushing, Christopher Lee, Michael Gough, Melissa Stribling, Carol Marsh, Valerie Gaunt, Miles Malleson, John Van Eyssen, Charles Lloyd-Pack

Frankenstein's Daughter *aka* **She Monster of the Night**
(LAYTON/ASTOR) b/w 85min
This is a decidedly shoddy teenage monster movie. Murphy is a descendant of Frankenstein who secretly tests a new drug, actually developed by the elderly scientist he works for (Locher), on the latter's niece (Knight). While the bewildered Knight goes on nocturnal prowls, Murphy and the half-witted gardener (Barzell) kill a girl (Todd) and attempt to re-model her as a superior female. Annoyed when the result is a monster, Murphy decides to try again with Knight because she has spurned his advances. Weighed down with the usual scenes of teenage partying, the film eventually ends with a routine conflagration when the required running time has been reached.

d Richard E. Cunha *p* Marc Frederic *s* H. E. Barrie *c* Meredith Nicholson *lp* John Ashley, Sandra Knight, Donald Murphy, Sally Todd, Harold Lloyd Jnr, Wolfe Barzell, Felix Locher

Grip of the Strangler *aka* **The Haunted Strangler**
(PRODUCERS ASSOCIATES; GB) b/w 81(78)min
This is an interesting, though poorly paced and constructed, attempt to convey some of the everyday horror that permeated Victorian society. The movie opens with a public hanging in the presence of a callous crowd which treats the event as an entertaining sideshow. Karloff plays the part of a novelist who investigates the case of the Haymarket Strangler, hanged for five gruesome murders, because he suspects the real murderer, a Dr Tennant, was never caught. However, he discovers that he himself is the vanished insane Dr Tennant, and he continues the murders until he is shot on the grave of the man wrongly hanged for his crimes. At times succeeding in depicting a typically English capacity for brutality and the repressive effects of the prevailing social order, the movie loses itself in the absurdly contrived plot and endless chases. The monochrome photography strains for realist effects as if unaware that an improbable story about a psychopath needs a high degree of stylization in order to direct attention to irrational forces that are invisible to the eye of a documentary camera.

The script was adapted from Read's story *Stranglehold*. Croydon had produced *Fiend Without a Face* (1957), a minor science fiction effort about creatures fed by atomic energy requiring a nearby American plant to be shut down. But the companion piece to *Grip* was another Croydon-Day-Karloff combination, **Corridors of Blood** (1958).

d Robert Day *p* John Croydon *s* Jan Read, John C. Cooper *c* Lionel Banes *lp* Boris Karloff, Tim Turner, Jean Kent, Vera Day, Elizabeth Allan, Anthony Dawson, Diane Aubrey, Dorothy Gordon

El Hombre y el Monstruo *aka* **The Man and the Monster**
(CINEMATOGRAFICA ABSA; MEX) b/w 90(78)min
This adaptation of Stevenson's Jekyll and Hyde story substitutes art for science, thus neatly turning the Victorian story's values inside out while retaining the same narrative structure. A pianist, Alejandra (Roth) acquires the manuscript of an enchantingly beautiful piece of music and becomes very successful. The envious Samuel (Rambal) kills her and keeps her mummified body at home in a niche before which he plays the piano opus in question. As he plays he is transformed into a werewolf-like Mr Hyde and only the touch of his mother's hand returns him to normality. To make amends he trains the young Laura (Roth again) to become a pianist. The climax sees Laura perform the fated piano concert under Rambal's direction, and when he changes into his hairy self, he is shot

dead. The touch of his mother (Guilmain) changes the hairy cadaver back to Rambal's 'decent' appearance.

In this story, art no longer represents man's finer feelings but his bestial side, which is contained only by the familiar, safely everyday maternal touch. The picture provides an involuntary but apt parody of Stevenson's story but is spoiled by the director's overblown melodramatic approach. Salazar, the producer, plays the hero, a concert promoter who winds up with the spoils of the drama, when the successful score becomes his property.

d Rafael Baledon *p* Abel Salazar *s* Raúl Zenteno, Alfredo Salazar *c* Raúl Martinez Solares *lp* Enrique Rabal, Abel Salazar, Martha Roth, Ofelia Guilmain, Anita Blanch, José Chavez, Carlos Suarez, Maricarmen Vela

The Hound of the Baskervilles

(HAMMER; GB) 85min

This is the definitive version to date of Conan Doyle's classic, first filmed in Germany as **Der Hund von Baskerville** (1914). Holmes, like Van Helsing, is a perfect figure for a Fisher film: he is the incarnation of reason, living in a world still shaped by superstition and prejudice. Cushing, in one of his finest performances, embodies this contradiction perfectly in a story that combines a legend of a family curse and fabulous cruelty, with the detective's superbly Victorian confidence in logic and reason. Establishing the tone with a darkly romantic sequence in which vicious aristocrats torment a young girl, Fisher moves to Baker Street where Holmes, Watson (Morell) and Dr Mortimer (de Wolff) start the investigation into the death of Sir Charles and the dangers awaiting Sir Henry Baskerville (Lee). Fittingly, for a Fisher film, the driving force of evil turns out to be a wildly passionate woman, Cecile (Landi), whose hatred for the Baskervilles is equal to their legendary cruelty and animates the nightmarish hound. From this perspective the fear which Holmes is called upon to exorcize is that the aristocracy's victims and their bastard offspring will take revenge, end their reign and seize their property. The price Sir Henry pays to hang on to his property is that his lover, the demonic Cecile, is sucked into the swamp. The happy ending sees him alive and well but facing a lonely, sterile future.

Fisher's evocation of the uncanny atmosphere surrounding Holmes, and Baskerville Hall and the moors, aided by Asher's wonderfully muted Technicolor photography, skilfully relies upon precise editing and a dramatic compositional style which gives the movie a spellbinding rhythm. The success of the film prompted Sangster to write *The Hellfire Club* (1959) for the brazenly exploitative producer-director team, Monty Berman and Robert Baker.

d Terence Fisher *p* Anthony Hinds, Michael Carreras *s* Peter Bryan *c* Jack Asher *lp* Peter Cushing, Christopher Lee, Andre Morell, Marla Landi, Miles Malleson, David Oxley, Francis de Wolff, Ewen Solon, John Le Mesurier, Judi Moyens

How to Make a Monster (AIP) b/w 73min

As though aware that he was on to a shortlived good thing with his teenage horror cycle, Cohen appended this behind-the-scenes footnote to **I Was a Teenage Werewolf** (1957) and **I Was a Teenage Frankenstein** (1958). Harris plays a makeup man, 25 years a specialist in horror movies, who goes berserk when the new studio bosses decide to switch to musicals. Using special doped makeup on the final horror production, he hypnotizes the young actors – Conway playing the Monster as in *Teenage Frankenstein*, Clarke as the werewolf – into murdering the moguls, then tries to dispose of them in caveman guise. Dismally routine in the main, the film is given a certain historical fascination by the backstage setting and litter of old props from AIP movies, including the head of the female horror from **The She Creature** (1956).

d Herbert L. Strock *p/co-s* Herman Cohen *co-s* Kenneth Langtry *c* Maury Gertzman *lp* Robert H. Harris, Paul Brinegar, Gary Conway, Gary Clarke, Walter Reed

I Was a Teenage Frankenstein

(SANTA ROSA PRODUCTIONS) b/w and col 74(72)min

In this quickly mounted follow-up to **I Was a Teenage Werewolf** (1957) Bissell as the versatile scientist assembles a human body from an assortment of different cadavers. Kandel's quirky screenplay is surprisingly effective, particularly when the young face of a kidnapped teenager is grafted on to the monstrous head. Bizarrely, the body is then dismantled before crating for shipment to England, whereupon the monster (Conway) naturally protests, kills Bissell and goes on the rampage. The excellent makeup helps the credibility of the sewn-together cadaver and the film bursts into glorious colour for the climax in which the monster is electrocuted by a power board.

One of the mini-series of teenage films that followed in the wake of *Teeenage Werewolf*, the film remains watchable because Kandel's script (though not Strock's direction, which is pedestrian) has an element of parody about it.

d Herbert L. Strock *p* Herman Cohen *s* Kenneth Langtry (Aben Kandel) *c* Lothrop Worth *lp* Whit Bissell, Phyllis Coates, Robert Burton, Gary Conway, George Lynn, John Cliff

Jack the Ripper *aka* The Return of Jack the Ripper

(MIDCENTURY; GB) b/w 88(84)min

This routine, somewhat stagebound thriller exploiting the Ripper murders was made by the Baker/Berman team at the time they were attempting to challenge Hammer's supremacy in the export market with **The Blood of the Vampire** (1958), *The Hellfire Club* and **The Flesh and the Fiends** (both 1959). Their policy of manufacturing specially strong versions of their films for export, considerably weakens the force of several of their movies, this one included. The narrative has an American detective (Patterson) who helps the Yard's man (Byrne) to stop the long, realistically shown list of murders perpetrated in the usual foggy streets by a surgeon crazed by venereal disease and intent on cutting the 'malignant virus' of prostitution out of the social fabric. The love interest is supplied by McDowall and the red herrings by her surgeon-father (Le Mesurier).

Left: *Sherlock Holmes and Dr Watson as portrayed by Andre Morell (left) and Peter Cushing in* The Hound of the Baskervilles.

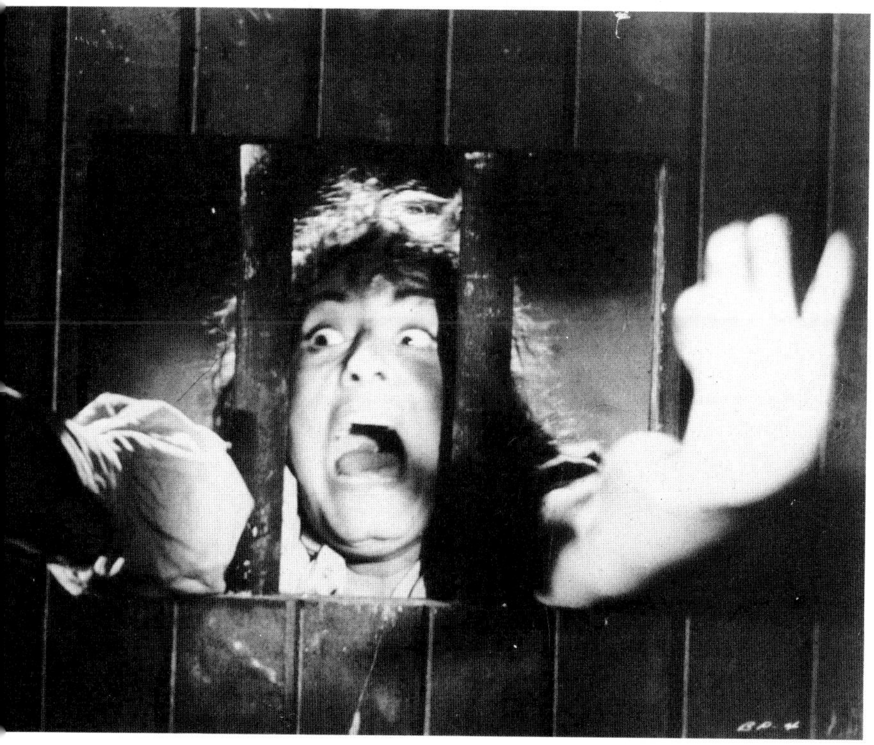

The melodramatic Misterios de Ultratumba.

As a Ripper film, this is a respectable effort that can stand alongside Zbonek's **Das Ungeheuer von London City** (1964), Madrid's **Jack el Destripador de Londres** (1971), **A Study in Terror** (1965) and half-a-dozen others. But the best treatments of the story in the sound cinema are Bob Clark's *Murder by Decree* (1979) and Peter Sasdy's **Hands of the Ripper** (1971).

d/p/c Robert S. Baker, Monty Berman *s* Jimmy Sangster *lp* Lee Patterson, Eddie Byrne, Betty McDowall, Ewen Solon, John LeMesurier, George Rose, Barbara Burke, Philip Leaver

Macabre (AA) b/w 73min
The horror début of Castle who, after 15 years directing second features (forgotten but not entirely forgettable: *The Whistler* and *The Mark of the Whistler*, both 1944, are competently handled), developed ambitions to usurp Hitchcock's title as the master of suspense but succeeded only in becoming the king of showmen. Here he ingeniously tried to drum up business by taking out a Lloyds of London insurance policy whereby anybody who died during the screening – of fright rather than natural causes – would receive $1000. Despite the hearses and fake nurses who prowled at premières, Lloyds had little to fear from the film.

Based on Theo Durrant's *The Marble Forest*, a novel actually written chapter by chapter by a dozen Californian members of the Mystery Writers of America, the script seems as much of a collaborative effort. When his sister-in-law's death follows suspiciously on that of his wife, Dr Barrett (Prince) finds his patients deserting him; and when his daughter disappears, supposedly buried alive by a madman, his frantic search of the cemetery reveals freshly turned earth around most of the graves. Predominantly set in undertaker's office and foggy graveyard, all this is tolerably effective. But the atmosphere is considerably thinned by a series of flashbacks laboriously explaining the reasons various other members of the cast have for hating the doctor, followed by a crude doubletake (borrowed from H. G. Clouzot's *Les Diaboliques*, 1955) revealing that the doctor had engineered the whole thing, having murdered both women for their money and now attempting to frighten his wealthy father-in-law to death.

d/p William Castle *s* Robb White *c* Carl E. Guthrie *lp* William Prince, Jim Backus, Jacqueline Scott, Christine White, Philip Tonge, Ellen Corby

The Man Who Could Cheat Death
(HAMMER; GB) 83min
This rather awkward variation on the Dorian Gray motif has Diffring as a surgeon who manages to retain his youth with ten-yearly operations and regular doses of a luminous green potion. The intervening years are spent making statues of beautiful women. Lee is the man who finally refuses to operate and thus causes Diffring to disintegrate and die in a fire started by his disfigured ex-model (Lawrence) while Lee's girlfriend, Janine (Court) is rescued from the mad surgeon's dungeon-laboratory. Though based on Barré Lyndon's play, filmed by Ralph Murphy under its original title, **The Man in Half Moon Street** (1944), the script is perfunctory. A few setpieces emphasizing physicality betray Fisher's hand, but the movie remains a minor item in his work, although it looks like one of Hammer's more lavish productions. Diffring was a more effectively disturbing surgeon in **Circus of Horrors** (1959), while Lee simply walks through his part.

d Terence Fisher *p* Michael Carreras *s* Jimmy Sangster *c* Jack Asher *se* Les Bowie *lp* Anton Diffring, Hazel Court, Christopher Lee, Arnold Marle, Delphi Lawrence, Francis de Wolff, Michael Ripper, Gerda Larsen

Misterios de Ultratumba *aka* **The Black Pit of Dr M** *aka* **Mysteries from Beyond the Grave**
(ALAMEDA FILMS; MEX) b/w 82(71)min
Following on from his two successful classic movies, **El Vampiro** and **El Ataud del Vampiro** (both 1957), Mendez directed this macabre zombie story which anticipates the tenor of many Spanish pictures of the sixties. Two doctors working at an insane asylum make a pact: when one dies, he will return to tell the other about life after death. Dr Aldama (Raxel) dies and his colleague, Dr Mazali (Bertrand) arranges a seance to force Raxel to stick to their bargain. The ominous message that comes back is that Bertrand will learn everything about the hereafter within three months. Whereupon he is accused of murder, found guilty and executed, only to rise from the grave in possession of a disfigured body (Ancira). He seeks out Raxel's daughter (Cortes) and is about to throw acid on to her face, in order to make her as unsightly as he is, when her lover (Santos) saves the day by transforming the zombie into a human torch.

Mendez stirs the conventions of melodrama, mad-scientist movies and funereal lyricism (especially in the impressive return from the grave sequence) into a confusing mixture which is too heterogeneous to be effective.

d Fernando Mendez *p* Alfredo Ripstein Jnr, Cesar Santos Galindo *s* Ramón Obon *c* Victor Herrera *lp* Gaston Santos, Rafael Bertrand, Mapita Cortes, Carlos Ancira, Carolina Barret, Luis Aragon, Beatriz Aguirre, Antonio Raxel, Lupe Carriles

The Return of Dracula *aka* **The Fantastic Disappearing Man** *aka* **The Curse of Dracula**
(GRAMERCY) b/w and col 77min
Learning from the mistakes of **The Vampire** (1957), Landres and Fielder began here with a traditional gothic motif before bringing their vampire into the everyday world. Wielding crucifixes, a priest and attendant police exhume Dracula's coffin, but it proves to be empty. The action then cuts to a railway station in Transylvania where an emigrating artist bids his parents farewell, boards a train and settles beside a solitary traveller muffled behind a newspaper. The train starts and the stranger peeps sinisterly over his paper. The camera cuts from the artist's sudden anguished expression to a shot of the train arriving in a small Southern Californian town as homey as apple pie where Dracula (the admirable Lederer) masquerades as the artist to insinuate himself into the home of the latter's New World cousins: mom, teenage daughter (plus high-school date), and junior with pet kitten which is soon found dead in a pool of blood.

Although Lederer takes on the appearance of a wolf or a curl of mist as he perpetrates his horrors, our abiding view of him is not as a monster but as a human being, indeed one as disarmingly suave as Uncle Charlie in Hitchcock's *Shadow of a Doubt* (1943). It's an intelligent conception for a B movie, with just a shade of the master's thriller touch to the patient pursuit of the vampire by an investigator from the Department of Immigration. McKenzie's camerawork – notably a scene where the investigator, about to leave by train, suddenly sees a woman in white seemingly materialize on the edge of the woods on the other side of the tracks – on occasion reveals a flair worthy of Georges Franju.

d Paul Landres *p* Jules V. Levy, Arthur Gardner *s* Pat Fielder *c* Jack McKenzie *lp* Francis Lederer, Norma Eberhardt, Ray Stricklyn, Jimmie Baird, John Wengraf, Virginia Vincent

The Revenge of Frankenstein

(HAMMER; GB) 89min

The sequel to Fisher's **The Curse of Frankenstein** (1957), this opens with a brilliantly innovative narrative trick by which the Baron (Cushing) escapes the guillotine as he and an accomplice manage to have the priest sent to perform the last rites decapitated in his place. The Baron, alias Dr Victor Stein, is next seen in charge of a hospital for the poor where he also uses patients' limbs to create a new synthetic man, Karl (Gwynn). The subtle alteration of the Baron's character, compared to the previous film, consists of the introduction of a genuinely compassionate dimension into his scientific obsession: he creates the creature in order to give his crippled assistant a healthy new body. But his work is ruined, first by a brutal janitor (Woodbridge) who mercilessly beats Gwynn whose body then starts to twist back into its original shape while he develops cannibalistic tendencies, then by the hospital patients who stupidly turn on their benefactor, making the Baron a martyr to ignorance and prejudice. In an extraordinary scene, Gwynn, painfully reverting to his monstrous shape, crashes through the french windows at a fashionable party and drags himself towards Cushing with a pitiful cry for help. In that scene it is the vicious and bigoted 'old world' which is designated as the villain while Frankenstein, though misguided, is clearly a positive force for progress. It is Fisher's and Cushing's achievement that the value of the Baron's character has thus been reversed while, as a character, he remained consistent enough to be a credible continuation of the coldly maniacal scientist of *The Curse*. In the end, the Baron dies on the operating table, having given his colleague, Hans (Matthews) instructions about how to transplant his brain into an artificially created body which he kept in a glass cage. The result is a 'creature' that looks exactly like Cushing, and shortly afterwards, a Dr Frank establishes a practice in London. The doctor has become his own creation.

Asher's gloriously saturated Technicolor photography helps to make this one of the most complex and intelligent treatments of the story to date. The next instalment in the story was Freddie Francis' **The Evil of Frankenstein** (1964), a far less successful effort.

d Terence Fisher *p* Anthony Hinds *s* Jimmy Sangster, H. Hurford Janes *c* Jack Asher *lp* Peter Cushing, Michael Gwynn, Francis Matthews, Eunice Gayson, John Welsh, George Woodbridge, Lionel Jeffries, Oscar Quitak, Richard Wordsworth, Michael Ripper

The Screaming Skull

(MADERA) b/w 68min

The Screaming Skull features Hudson as the man who sets about driving his bride (Webber) insane by manipulating skulls purporting to belong to his dead first wife all over the old dark Southern mansion and grounds. Crosby's camerawork is superb, and there are some nicely macabre moments (birds screeching all around, grinning skulls popping out of a dark pool). But having just returned from a mental home after a nervous breakdown, the wife is rather too ripe a case for terrorization, while the husband's retribution at the teeth of one of a horde of screaming (and apparently genuinely ghostly) skulls is not exactly convincing. Nicol, an actor here directing for the first time, lets the action spin out much too slackly, dissipating the grasp of moody tension he displayed in his unpretentiously excellent war movie, *Three Came Back* (1960).

d Alex Nicol *p/s* John Kneubuhl *c* Floyd Crosby *lp* John Hudson, Peggy Webber, Tom Johnson, Russ Conway, Alex Nicol

She Demons

(SCREENCRAFT/ASTOR) b/w 80(77)min

This incredible piece of schlock features four shipwreck survivors who find themselves on an uncharted island where a Nazi war criminal (Anders) is experimenting on girls to try to restore his wife's (Tana) scarred face. With each failure the victims are left looking gruesome and developing animal tendencies. Their bikini-clad bodies, needless to say, are left fulsomely intact. In the end, American bombers inadvertently use the island for target practice, causing a volcanic eruption which enables the intruders to get away: a needless extravagance since a shove would have sent the sets tumbling.

d/co-s Richard E. Cunha *p* Arthur A. Jacobs *co-s* H. E. Barrie *c* Meredith Nicholson *lp* Irish McCalla, Tod Griffin, Victor Sen Yung, Rudolph Anders, Leni Tana

The Spaniard's Curse

(WENTWORTH FILMS; GB) b/w 80min

This inept film is based on Edith Pargiter's novel *The Assize of the Dying*, apparently an old Spanish curse invoked by people wrongly sentenced to death. A man (Digman) is convicted of murder and uses the curse, after which those associated with the conviction start to die. In the end, it emerges that a real-life murderer was the culprit after all. Although photographed by Grant, who achieved sensational images for Terence Fisher, the movie is a flat and poorly directed programme filler.

d Ralph Kemplen *p* Roger Proudlock *s* Kenneth Hyde *c* Arthur Grant *lp* Tony Wright, Lee Patterson, Michael Hordern, Susan Beaumont, Basil Dignam, Ralph Truman, Henry Oscar, Olga Dickie

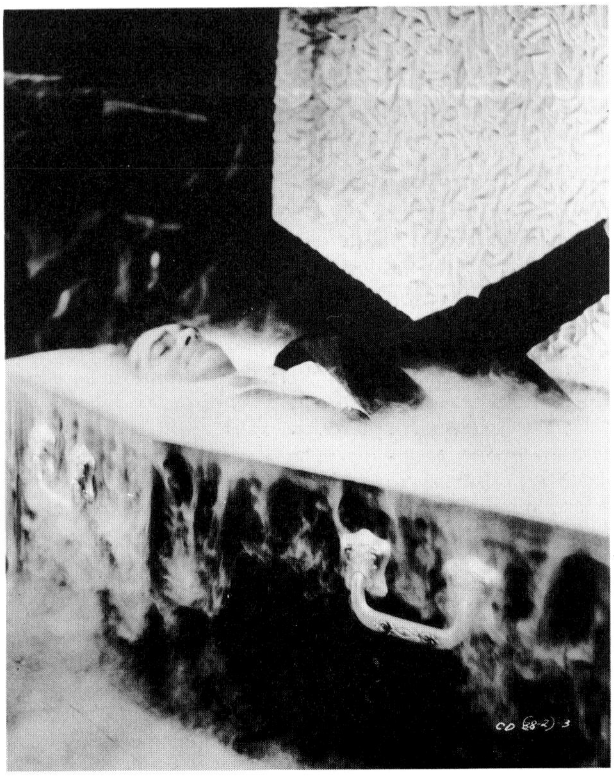

Francis Lederer as the Count in the impressive The Return of Dracula.

Lon Chaney as a Mexican werewolf in the slapdash La Casa del Terror.

The Thing That Couldn't Die (U) b/w 69min
Low-grade horrors set on a California ranch. Kearney is a pretty water-diviner gifted with ESP and therefore credited with satanic powers. With her rod she unearths a chest containing the severed head of a sailor, a member of Magellan's crew executed for devil-worship and buried by Sir Francis Drake in 1579. According to legend, the torso was buried separately, and with the head exercising an evil hypnotic influence over the ranch-dwellers, Kearney locates the second chest. When head and body are brought together, the thing proves vulnerable to a talisman and crumbles to dust. The result is made even more ludicrous by the mumbling head's Lugosi-like staring eyes.

d/p Will Cowan *s* David Duncan *c* Russell Metty
lp William Reynolds, Andra Martin, Carolyn Kearney, Jeffrey Stone, Robin Hughes

1959

Ama no Bakemono Yashiki *aka* **The Haunted Cave** *aka* **Girl Divers from Spook Mansion**
(SHINTOHO; JAP) b/w scope 82min
A minor Kaidan Eiga (ghost story) produced at Shintoho by one of Nakagawa's less inspired colleagues shortly before the studio went bankrupt, this film tells of the young Yumi (Mihara) whose family treasure lies deep in the sea, buried by an earthquake. Members of her family are mysteriously killed and the ghost of her sister emerges from one of the traditional ghost-producing sites in Japanese folktales: the bottom of a well (as in Nagisha Oshima's *Ai no Borei*, 1979). It appears that a deep cave gives access to the treasure and a group of criminals seek to appropriate the loot, but Yumi, her friend Kyoko and a detective, aided by the ghost, prevent the robbery and punish the culprits. The main interest of this banal ghost story resides in the quaintly titillating scenes of the two young women in their prudish diving outfits. Magatani's second horror picture of the year, **Kyuju-Kyuhonme no Kimusume** (1959), provided an odd mixture of modern teenage melodrama and rural Japan's brutally superstitious practices.

d Morihei Magatani *p* Mitsugu Okura *s* Akira Sugimoto, Nao Akatsukasa *c* Kagai Okado *lp* Yoko Mihara, Bunta Sugawara, Reiko Sato, Masayo Banri, Yoichi Numata

Beast from Haunted Cave
(FILMGROUP) b/w 75(67)min
Hellman's first film, this is a routine Roger Corman programmer which shows only traces of the talent that emerged so strikingly in *The Shooting* and *Ride in the Whirlwind* (both 1966). A standard creature-feature, it has a gangster (Wolff), his alcoholic girl (Carol) and two aides guided to their mountain hideout by a ski instructor (Forest), after they have robbed a mine. At this point the explosion they used to create a diversion releases a monster hitherto presumed to be purely legendary. Tracking down and decimating the group, the monster (Robinson) is killed by a flare pistol when a snowstorm forces the survivors to shelter in the cave where the monster's victims are stored in giant cocoons. But the monster itself, a sort of perambulating cobweb cabbage, is hardly an exciting rare species.

d Monte Hellman *p* Gene Corman *s* Charles Griffith *c* Andy Costikyan *lp* Michael Forest, Sheila Carol, Frank Wolff, Wally Campo, Chris Robinson, Richard Sinatra

A Bucket of Blood (AIP) b/w 66min
This is a marvellous little film which takes some delightful sideswipes at beatnik pretensions (Allen Ginsberg is hilariously caricatured) and breathes rude life into a story that neither **Mystery of the Wax Museum** (1933) nor **House of Wax** (1953) was quite able to animate. Miller, almost a mascot in early Corman movies, is wonderfully deadpan as the half-witted waiter at a beatnik coffee shop who yearns to emulate the poets and painters he serves. His wish is gratified when he accidentally kills the landlady's cat by impaling it on a knife. Shamefacedly trying to conceal the evidence by covering the contorted body with clay, he sees it hailed as a work of genius. Having found his style, he carries it to new heights of creativity by moulding human bodies, more or less accidentally murdered. Wittily inventive – the decapitation of a carpenter with a circular saw leads to a bust as a change from full-length studies – his career comes to a sad and untimely end when a fingernail is spotted beneath the clay, and his last creative act is to turn himself into a clay model of a hanged man.

d/p Roger Corman *s* Charles B. Griffith *c* Jack Marquette *lp* Dick Miller, Barboura Morris, Anthony Carbone, Julian Burton, John Brinkley, Ed Nelson

La Casa del Terror *aka* **The Face of the Screaming Werewolf** *aka* **La Casa del Vampiro**
(DIANA FILMS; MEX) b/w 85(60)min
While Mario Morena (Cantinflas) was seeking his fortune in Hollywood, Valdes (Tin Tan) was Mexico's most popular and prolific film comic. He made a spoof musical called *El Fantasma de la Opereta* (1959) with the sumptuous Ana Luisa Peluffo and immediately went on to star in this mediocre comedy notable mainly for the presence of Lon Chaney Jnr as the werewolf. A mad scientist robs graves for his resurrection experiments and the failures are put in a wax museum, unbeknownst to its absent-minded caretaker, Tin Tan. A thunderstorm helps the scientist to put life back into a mummy (Chaney) which turns out to have suffered from lycanthropy and reverts to its unsavoury practices. When the werewolf (makeup by Ramón Juarez), abducts Tin Tan's lover (Varela), he confronts the monster on the rooftops and triggers the fire that burns the werewolf, the scientist and the laboratory.

The picture is slapdash rather than slapstick, with banal erotic dream sequences and musical interludes to further spoil the rhythm of a story that requires a relentless pace and expert timing in order to work at all. The Mexican version was produced by the great Fuentes's son who continued the family business as a producer and distributor, while the US release print, severely cut, was supervised by Jerry Warren. The American print anglicized the credits, calling the director Gilbert Solar, changing Varela to Landa Varle and Barron to D. W. Barron. The Mexican version was released in 1960, the

US one in 1965. Tin Tan's next fantasy farce was *El Espectro de Televicentro* (1959).

d/co-s Gilberto Martinez Solares *p/co-s* Fernando de Fuentes Jnr *co-s* Juan Garcia *c* Raúl Martinez Solares *lp* Germán Valdes (Tin Tan), Lon Chaney Jnr, Yolanda Varela, Yerye Beirute, Oscar Ortiz de Pinedo, Consuela Guerrero de Luna, Alfredo Wally Barron, Agustin Fernandez

Ch'ien-nu Yu-Hin *aka* Enchanted Shadow *aka* Soul of a Beautiful Girl

(SHAW BROTHERS; HONG KONG) 85min

Released in 1960, this vivid ghost story by ex-designer Li Hanxiang was based on a tale from Pu Songling's classic Ming dynasty anthology, *Strange Stories from a Chinese Studio*, previously mined by Tao Qin for *Love with a Ghost* (1954) and subsequently by Bao Fang for **Hua Pi** (1966). The plot has a young scholar (Lei) encounter a lovely girl (Le Di) in a temple where he spends the night. She seems determined to seduce him, but gradually he realizes that she is a ghost intent on setting him up to be killed by her evil aunt (Dong), who also is a ghost. Only his moral fortitude saves him from their spectral clutches and finally destroys the persecutory female.

Generally regarded as the director's best work of the period before he broke with Shaw and set up his own company in Taipei in 1963-4, the film's skilful and well-paced direction is further enhanced by Ho Lu-Ying's colour cinematography. The whole is a lovely mood piece mixing romance and horror. Shortly before leaving Taiwan, the prolific director contributed an episode to the omnibus movie **Hsi Nou Ai Lueh** (1970). He later returned to Shaw to become their main contract director. The female lead, Le Di, achieved stardom with this performance and was subsequently featured in the Chinese version of *The Phantom of the Opera*, **Ye Ban Ge Sheng** (1961).

d Li Hanxiang (Li Han Hsiang) *p* Yuan Quifeng *s* Wang Yueh-ting *c* Ho Lu-Ying *lp* Le Di (Betty Lo Tih), Zhano Lei, Yang Zhiqing (Yang Chih-Ching)

Circus of Horrors

(ANGLO AMALGAMATED; GB) scope 91(88)min

Anglo Amalgamated followed up their success with Crabtree's **Horrors of the Black Museum** (1959) – a sensationalist exploitation of coyly shot violence arranged in the manner of an advertising catalogue – with this equally exploitative example of cultural conservatism set in a circus where performers meet with lethal accidents in full view of an audience hungry for gory thrills. Diffring plays the plastic surgeon who compulsively collects disfigured women and operates on them while running an one-ring circus. As he grows tired of his creatures, he arranges accidents for them: a knife-throwing act goes wrong and the scantily dressed target receives the knife in her body; an acrobat falls to her death and, in addition, his beloved Melissa (Romain), the lion-tamer, is torn to shreds during a performance. Diffring himself is finally killed by his first surgical patient-lover-victim (Wilde) in front of the circus's Temple of Beauty.

Repeating the structure of *Horrors*, *Circus* opens with a gruesome shock sequence as Wilde removes the bandages covering her face prematurely. From then on, the bizarre excitement Diffring conveys in the presence of disfigured women and the use of the circus as an attraction which, like the film, allegedly trades on the expectation of mutilation or the grotesque, show Hayers to be in control of the macabre or sexy aspects of the spectacle. But the sequences linking those attractions together, such as the police investigations of the murder, are flat and lifeless. Michael Powell – whose extraordinary **Peeping Tom** (1960) was made for the same company – achieved a far more powerful and, ironically, less conservative movie by avoiding the hypocritical moralism inherent in both *Horrors* and *Circus*, something neither Hayers nor Crabtree were good enough film-makers to do. Hayers' one respectable movie, **Night of the Eagle** (1961) was a professional, but failed, attempt to equal Jacques Tourneur's **Night of the Demon** (1957). The executive producer, Herman Cohen, later presided over another circus horror, this time starring Joan Crawford, **Berserk** (1967).

d Sidney Hayers *p* Julian Wintle, Leslie Parkyn *s* George Baxt *c* Douglas Slocombe *lp* Anton Diffring, Yvonne Monlaur, Donald Pleasance, Jany Hylton, Yvonne Romain, Erika Remberg, Vanda Hudson, Colette Wilde, Kenneth Griffith

Curse of the Undead *aka* Mark of the West

(U) b/w 79min

The first vampire western, this sorry film drags to the predictable conclusion of a shootout between the Spanish vampire (Pate) and Preacher Dan (Fleming), who has taken the precaution of loading a bullet with a cross on it. The silly gimmick was only marginally less tiresome when spoofed in **Billy the Kid vs Dracula** (1965).

d/co-s Edward Dein *p* Joseph Gershenson *co-s* Mildred Dein *c* Ellis Carter *lp* Eric Fleming, Michael Pate, Kathleen Crowley, John Hoyt, Bruce Gordon, Edward Binns

The Devil's Hand *aka* The Naked Goddess *aka* Witchcraft *aka* Live to Love

(CROWN INTERNATIONAL PICTURES) 71min

This is a cheaply made and rather cramped production from the director of **The Ghost of Dragstrip Hollow** (1959) with which it compares distinctly unfavourably. After repeatedly dreaming about the beautiful Bianca (Christian), Rick (Alda) discovers that she really exists when, by means of strange powers, she summons him to her. Through her he is initiated into a cult which worships the devil god Gamba and indulges in human sacrifice.

The film was the last one Broadway star Alda (the father of writer/actor/director Alan) made before quitting America for Rome and 15 years of European co-productions.

d William J. Hole Jnr *p* Alvin K. Bubis *s* Jo Heims *c* Meredith Nicholson *lp* Linda Christian, Robert Alda, Neil Hamilton, Ariadne Welter, Gene Craft, Jennie Carman, Julie Scott, Diana Spears

Beauty and the Beast in Sidney Hayer's sensationalist Circus of Horrors.

Peter Cushing greets his niece June Laverick in Flesh and the Fiends.

The Flesh and the Fiends *aka* Mania *aka* The Fiendish Ghouls *aka* Psycho Killers

(TRIAD; GB) b/w scope 97(87,74)min

Gilling's effective version of the dealings between the Scottish pioneer of surgery, Dr Know (Cushing), and the bodysnatchers Burke and Hare (Rose and Pleasance), marked his return to the genre after directing the first British vampire movie, **Old Mother Riley Meets the Vampire** (1952) and a science fantasy, *The Gamma People* (1956). Cushing's Knox is a coldly determined scientist, rather like his Frankenstein, for whom the ends justify the means and is nearly disgraced when it emerges that he turned a blind eye to the bodysnatchers' efforts to increase the supply of corpses by killing local down-and-outs. Caught after the murder of a prostitute (Whitelaw), Hare turns King's evidence to escape the gallows and Knox is forced to justify himself before a medical tribunal. Burke is hanged, Hare is lynched by an outraged mob who burn out his eyes, and Knox goes on to become one of Edinburgh's most renowned surgeons. Gilling's rather stereotypical and studio-bound depiction of Edinburgh in the 1820s, with its grim slums and seedy taverns, shot in starkly contrasted, sharp-edged black and white images, provides an appropriate atmosphere. Pleasance and Rose tend to ham it up with fake accents, but otherwise the acting, especially Whitelaw's sinuous prostitute and Cushing's dignified scientist, is nicely straightforward without a hint of self-parody.

Producers Baker and Berman were responsible for a short series of horror movies including **Blood of the Vampire** and **Jack the Ripper** (both 1958) and the entertaining horror spoof, **What a Carve-Up!** (1961), but their work never seriously challenged the domination of Hammer. This story was later remade as **Burke and Hare** (1971).

d/co-s John Gilling *co-p* Robert S. Baker *co-p/c* Monty Berman *co-s* Leon Griffiths *lp* Peter Cushing, June Laverick, Donald Pleasance, George Rose, Dermot Walsh, Billie Whitelaw, Renee Houston, John Cairney, Melvyn Hayes, June Powell

The Four Skulls of Jonathan Drake

(VOGUE) b/w 70min

A preposterous but undeniably lively confection in which Richards is the sceptical policeman required to investigate a murder within a family cursed 180 years ago when an ancestor massacred a tribe of headhunters in Ecuador. Of two surviving brothers coming up to the age for decapitation stipulated by the curse, one (Cavanagh) has already died, and his head has turned up as per tradition in the family vault. The other (Franz) survives a murderous attack by an Ecuadorian zombie (Wexler), whereupon Richards' investigation leads to Dr Zurich (Daniell), a Swiss anthropologist whose hobby is head-shrinking. It emerges that Zurich, who died 180 years ago, is really the Ecuadorian witch-doctor using Zurich's head as a disguise. Zurich kidnaps Franz's daughter French as a lever to get at her father but, by summoning voodoo powers to help him, Franz decapitates Zurich, who crumbles to dust.

Cahn's direction is pedestrian, but he manipulates the paraphernalia of skulls and shrunken heads to eerie effect, while Daniell and Wexler (the latter's zombie unnervingly boasting the sewn lips of a shrunken head) make superbly sinister presences.

d Edward L. Cahn *p* Robert E. Kent *s* Orville H. Hampton *c* Maury Gertsman *lp* Eduard Franz, Valerie French, Henry Daniell, Grant Richards, Paul Cavanagh, Paul Wexler

The Ghost of Dragstrip Hollow (AIP) b/w 65min

The death throes of the teenage-horror cycle, this is an inane, virtually plotless mixture of haunted house, hot-rodders and rock'n'roll. Forced by cash difficulties to vacate their club, a group of drag-racing teenagers and their girls find alternative premises in an abandoned house. The usual scares, caused by a parrot and a monster, among other things are explained at a Halloween party when the monster – Blaisdell in his costume from **The She Creature** (1956) but without the mammary appendages – is discovered to be an unhappy actor frustrated because (à la **How to Make a Monster**, 1958) he doesn't get to play in monster movies any more.

d William Hole Jnr *p/s* Lou Rusoff *c* Gilbert Warrenton *lp* Jody Fair, Martin Braddock, Russ Bender, Leon Tyler, Elaine Dupont, Paul Blaisdell

The Headless Ghost

(MERTON PARK; GB) b/w scope 61min

An undemanding ghost comedy about three holidaying American students who meet a friendly spirit (Revill) in Ambrose Castle who asks them to help an executed ancestor recover his head, which would quieten the castle's restless spectres. Somewhat similar to **Fantasmi a Roma** (1961) or **Das Spukschloss im Spessart** (1960), Scott's movie has the merit of preceding both of them. A specialist in slight comedies and tame exploitation movies, Scott's best work was the Hammer-produced **Captain Clegg** (1961), although *Panic in Madame Tussauds* (1948) had its atmospheric moments.

d Peter Graham Scott *p* Jack Greenwood *s* Kenneth Langtry, Herman Cohen *c* John Wiles *lp* Richard Lyon, Clive Revill, Liliane Sottane, David Rose, Jack Allen, Alexander Archdale, Carl Bernard

Right: *Hot Rod meets horror in the inane* The Ghost of Dragstrip Hollow.

1959

Horrors of the Black Museum

(ANGLO AMALGAMATED/HERMAN COHEN; GB)
scope 95(81)min

In the late fifties, the only British companies that challenged Hammer's supremacy in the horror stakes were the Berman/Baker team with, for example, **The Blood of the Vampire** and **Jack the Ripper** (both 1958), and Cohen's Anglo-American operation which had been responsible for **I Was a Teenage Werewolf** (1957) and **I Was a Teenage Frankenstein** (1958) before launching a London-based assault on the market with this picture and **Circus of Horrors** (1959).

Black Museum tells of a cynical crime-obsessed writer (Gough) who induces his assistant (Curnow) to commit a series of morbidly staged murders which he then writes up into novels avidly bought by a sensation-hungry public. The Grand Guignol spectacle opens with a pair of trick binoculars gouging out the eyes of a young woman and finishes at a funfair with Curnow leaping from a great height, knife first, plunging it in to Gough's heart – the ultimate fairground attraction. The Gainsbrough veteran Crabtree, director of the mildly interesting science fiction story, *Fiend Without a Face* (1957), makes effective use of colour and the scope format, revelling in the depiction of a catalogue of horror clichés, especially when such items can be salted with locker-room notions of sexuality. The irony of such a movie, clearly demonstrated by the cinematic intelligence underpinning **Peeping Tom** (1960) – made for the same company – is that the very reference to the sado-voyeuristic components inherent in the relation between viewers and spectacle also necessarily reveals the way film-makers conceptualize that relationship. By proposing such a trivial conception of the relationship, *Horrors* reveals its profound cultural conservatism.

Predictably, the outrage of the critics was reserved for one of the most intelligent treatments of the subject, *Peeping Tom*. The hallucinatory lyricism of Riccardo Freda (**I Vampiri**, 1956; **L'Orribile Segreto del Dr Hichcock**, 1962) or Mario Bava (**Sei Donne per l'Assassino**, 1964; **La Maschera del Demonio**, 1960) was too alien to English traditions of commercial storytelling for it to be taken seriously enough to have an impact. In England, only Hammer – and there, mostly Fisher – managed to find the right mix of visual intelligence and dramatic-novelistic complexity to produce a consistently innovative popular cinema deeply rooted in indigenous cultural traditions. Neither the Berman/Baker nor the Cohen productions, nor indeed the Tigon or Amicus productions of the sixties could match Hammer's achievement in spite of their occasionally felicitous pictures.

d Arthur Crabtree *p* Jack Greenwood *s* Aben Kandel (Kenneth Langtry), Herman Cohen *c* Desmond Dickinson *lp* Michael Gough, Graham Curnow, June Cunningham, Shirley Ann Field, Geoffrey Keen, Gerald Andersen, Beatric Varley, Nora Gordon, John Warwick

The House on Haunted Hill

(AA) b/w 75min

Efficient, considerably boosted by Price's sinisterly genial performance, and quite enjoyable in its oldfashioned horror-comedy way, Castle's follow-up to **Macabre** (1958) has a plot which seems like one of his own promotional gimmicks. An eccentric millionaire (Price) rents an old house – the scene of seven murders – so that his wife (Ohmart) can throw a haunted-house party. By offering $10,000 to anyone who will spend the night there, he attracts five guests who are assailed by skeletal apparitions, blood dripping from the ceiling, a witch, a suicide, a severed head and a vat of acid in the cellar. Plotting Price's death with her lover (Marshal), a psychiatrist present because he is supposedly studying hysteria, Ohmart tires to ensure that he is shot by one of the pistols he had thoughtfully supplied the guests with (packaged in miniature coffins). 'Emergo', Castle's gimmick here – 'More startling than 3-D' – was simply a skeleton on wires trundled out over the audience when Price turns the tables on wife and lover and tumbles them into the vat of acid that makes for instant skeletons.

Michael Gough and one of his victims in the, then, shocking Horrors of the Black Museum.

d/p William Castle *s* Robb White *c* Carl E. Guthrie *lp* Vincent Price, Carol Ohmart, Richard Long, Alan Marshal, Elisha Cook Jnr, Carolyn Craig

Kyuju-Kyuhonme no Kimusume *aka* The Blood Sword of the 99th Virgin

(SHINTOHO; JAP) b/w scope 82min

Shot in the same year as Magatani's **Ama no Bakemono Yashiki** (1959), this picture offers an interesting confrontation between modern Japan, represented by lively teenagers, and the remnants of a brutally susperstitious rural community in the north of the country. The villagers conduct magic sword-tempering rituals that require the blood of virgins. In a secret underground room, the police discover 98 swords and on top of the mountain, the skeletons of a great many young women. To fulfil a pledge to the local deity, the villagers abduct women holidaying in the area, kill them as they hang upside down from a tree and gather their blood in a large vessel: their ancestors had promised the gods 99 swords tempered with the blood of virgins and the movie recounts what happens to the manufacture of the last sword. The climax sees the investigating policeman's daughter, kidnapped by the local yokels, dangling upsidedown from the fateful tree as the last ritual gets underway. Although the script is decidedly shaky, Magatani occasionally succeeds in creating weird images worthy of such an outlandish fantasy.

d Morihei Magatani *p* Mitsugu Okura *s* Susumu Takahira, Jiro Fujishima *c* Kagai Okado *lp* Bunta Namiji Matsuura

La Maldición de Nostradamus *aka* The Curse of Nostradamus

(ESTUDIOS AMERICA; MEX) b/w 77min

In between **El Ataud del Vampiro** (1957) and the next major Mexican movie, **El Mundo de los Vampiros** (1960), Robles starred in a serial of 12 25-minute instalments, which were re-edited and released as four features between August 1961 and April 1963. This was the first. The plot begins with Duran (Soler) denouncing superstitious beliefs in vampires while in a forest, the vampiric Nostradamus Jnr (Robles) visits the tomb of his father. The vampire challenges Duran not only to believe in the supernatural but to rehabilitate the reputation of his illustrious father, the 16th-century occultist. The subsequent episodes chronicle the various misdeeds of Nostradamus who notifies Soler by letter in advance of every crime, knowing the professor won't call the police because that would imply giving credence to vampirism. In the first feature, Nostradamus causes one of Soler's colleagues to be buried alive; he mockingly invites Soler to shoot him and changes into a bat; he hypnotically forces another professor to commit a murder and finally abducts Soler's daughter (Alvarado). Soler and his assistant (Aleman) save her while the vampire flees through a warren of underground tunnels, avoiding Soler's silver bullets

The second film, *Nostradamus y el Destructor de Monstrous* sees the vampire make use of a criminal he subjected to his will, while Soler defends himself by means of an apparatus which emits soundwaves harmful to bats. In *Nostradamus el Genio de las Tinieblas*, the vampire falls in love and the professor steals the ashes of the old Nostradamus from the crypt in the forest. In the final film, *La Sangre de Nostradamus*, the vampire is pursued by police armed with silver bullets but in the end he is staked like a good vampire should be.

In all four films (Curiel's début features), he shows himself to be a worthy successor to Feuillade. He skilfully uses editing effects to emphasize the commanding presence of the vampire and endows the pictures with the force and atmosphere of the best of the silent mystery of thrillers (such as Fritz Lang's *Spione*, 1928), managing to overcome the excruciating banality of the dialogue with an enchantingly archaic image track. Juan Bustillo Oro's *Nostradamus* (1936), although it deals with the occultist, was an historical epic and cannot be regarded as a precursor of Curiel's use of the character.

d/co-s Federico Curiel *p* Victor Parra *co-s* Carlos Enrique Tabaoda, Alfredo Ruanova *c* Fernando Alvarez Garces (Colin) *lp* Germán Robles, Julio Aleman, Domingo Soler, Aurora Alvarado, Manuel Vergara (Manver), Manuel Casanueva, Manuel Donde, Roberto Araya, Patricia de Morelos, Fernando Curiel

The Monster of Piedras Blancas

(VANWICK) b/w 71min

This crude echo of *The Creature from the Black Lagoon* (1954) features a remarkably similar scaly marine monster (played by producer Kevan) which lives in a cave at the foot of some cliffs on the Pacific Ocean. Superstitiously fed by lighthouse-keeper Harmon, who suspects it is after his daughter (Carmen), it finally emerges after much talkative preamble to tear off a few heads, throw the keeper to his death, and finally topple from the lighthouse after frantic pursuit by the sheriff (Lewis), a doctor (Tremayne), and a biologist (Sullivan) in love with the daughter.

d Irvin Berwick *p* Jack Kevan *s* C. Haile Chace *c* Philip Lathrop *lp* Les Tremayne, Forrest Lewis, John Harmon, Jeanne Carmen, Don Sullivan

The Mummy *aka* Terror of the Mummy

(HAMMER; GB) 88(75)min

After Hammer bought up the rights to all the old Universal horror movies, they re-launched the whole catalogue of monsters, one after the other, carefully varying the themes to avoid saturating the market with any single motif. Thus after Frankenstein and Dracula, Fisher turned to the mummy before going on to the werewolf (1960) and **The Phantom of the Opera** (1962).

The plot has Lee as Kharis, an Egyptian priest mutilated and executed for loving the Queen Anaka (Furneaux). When the Queen's tomb is desecrated by a team of Egyptologists, led by Aylmer, the priest comes back to life to protect her and destroy the vandals, but he recognizes the wife of Aylmer's son (Cushing) as the exact lookalike of his own long-lost lover and his passion again brings about his destruction.

Fisher's surrealist use of colour, at its most unforgettable in the nightmarish scenes of the mummy's death in the swamps

La Maldición de Nostradamus, *Federico Curiel's imaginative reinterpretaion of the Nostradamus myth.*

Christopher Lee rises from the swamp in The Mummy.

and in the opening sequence set in ancient Egypt, together with his unnerving sense of camera position and cutting, give the movie a genuinely macabre poetry never achieved in mummy films before or since. At this time, Hammer's movies were still made in Technicolor, which gave them warmly saturated colours which Fisher and his cameramen moulded into a distinctive style, markedly different from such non-Hammer movies as **Horrors of the Black Museum** or **Circus of Horrors** (both 1959). From **The Phantom of the Opera** (1962) until the late sixties, Hammer switched to Eastmancolor but maintained their style until faster filmstock was introduced, making the images disintegrate and destroying the tone and brilliance of their colours. *The Mummy* was not a remake of Freund's 1932 film, but it incorporated elements of **The Mummy's Hand** (1940) and **The Mummy's Tomb** (1942). The inspiration for the story dated back to Lord Caernarvon and Howard Carter's opening up of Tutankhamun's tomb in 1923, followed by the Caernarvon's mysterious death.

d Terence Fisher *p* Michael Carreras *s* Jimmy Sangster *c* Jack Asher *se* Les Bowie *lp* Peter Cushing, Christopher Lee, Yvonne Furneaux, Eddie Byrne, Felix Aylmer, George Pastell, Raymond Huntley, John Stuart, Michael Ropper

Die Nackte und der Satan *aka* **The Head** *aka* **Head for the Devil** *aka* **The Screaming Head**
(RAPID FILM/WOLFGANG HARTWIG/PRISMA FILM/TRANSLUX; WG) 92min
This is a surreal variation of Curt Siodmak's oft-filmed novel *Donovan's Brain.* Professor Abel (Simon) invents a serum that can keep a dog's severed head alive. His mad disciple, Dr Ood (Frank) then uses the serum to keep Simon's own severed head in working order after a heart transplant has gone wrong. The extraordinary, multi-chinned head of Simon is kept on a glass slab wired up with electrodes and bathed in vile green or cold blue lights, pleading to be allowed to die. Dr Ood also grafts the head of his beautiful but hunchbacked nurse (Kernke) on to the desirable body of a stripper (Maybach) in an attempt to fashion his ideal love object.

Trivas, a Russian *émigré*, had collaborated with Pabst in the twenties and was best known for his pacifist movie, *Niemandsland* (1931). After working in France and in the USA, where he furnished the script for the worst film Buster Keaton ever appeared in (*El Moderno Barba Azul*, shot in Mexico in 1946), he returned to Germany. This tongue-in-cheek horror movie, employing the talents of his old friends Simon and Hermann Warm – one of the designers of **Das Cabinet des Dr Caligari** (1919) – was a celebration of that return.

d/s Victor Trivas *p* Wolfgang Hartwig *c* George Krause, Otto Reinwald, Kurt Rendel *se* Theodor Nischwitz *lp* Michel Simon, Horst Frank, Karin Kernke, Christiane Maybach, Paul Dahlke, Barbara Valentin

Night of the Ghouls *aka* **Revenge of the Dead**
(EDWARD D. WOOD/ATOMIC) b/w 60min
Wood has been much touted as the most inept film-maker of all time – a label that is probably true. But his perverse films have an indefinable something: the disarmingly vulnerable sincerity of *Glen or Glenda?* (1953), for instance, in which a home

movie/neorealist account of a transvestite's mental torments is intercut with shots of Bela Lugosi madly cackling 'Bevare! Bevare! Ze story must be told' in a necromancer's laboratory; or simply an ineffable weirdness as in the meaningless footage, repeated again and again in *Plan 9 from Outer Space* (1956), of Lugosi entering a forest clearing, looking round, and departing again. *Night of the Ghouls*, which opens with TV prophet Criswell arising from his coffin to warn of monsters who are to be pitied and monsters who are to be despised, is as inept as anything Wood ever made.

A fake medium (Duncan), aided by an equally fake spirit (Hansen) and a huge monster (Johnson), goes about his business of conning people into believing he can contact their dead. Accidentally, however, he resusciates some corpses and is buried alive by the ghoulish zombies while the beatnik Vampira gleefully cavorts as (apparently) a real spirit. Grotesque, literally incoherent nonsense, yet like other Wood films it has moments when – all proportions maintained – one is faced by the sort of hallucinating disorientation systematized by Carl Dreyer's **Vampyr** (1931).

d/p/s Edward D. Wood Jnr *lp* Criswell, Tor Johnson, Keene Duncan, Valda Hansen, Maila 'Vampira' Nurmi

Onna Kyuketsuki *aka* **The Woman Vampire** *aka* **The Male Vampire** *aka* **Vampire Man**
(SHINTOHO; JAP) b/w scope 98min
Japan's main practitioner of Kaidan Eiga (ghost story films), Nakagawa, made this rather weak picture at a time when he was turning out four or five features a year. The main problem is the script which has difficulty transposing the Christian European vampire myth to Japan, even though there are many bloodsucking creatures in traditional Japanses ghost stories. Nakagawa had tried his hand at European style horror before, with his *Kyuketsuki Ga* (1956) – in which a vampire turns into a moth instead of a bat – but here he opts for a truly chaotic pot-pourri. Niwako (Mihara), the descendant of a 300-year-old christian family and the wife of an atomic scientist, is kidnapped by a vampire (Amachi) and taken to his underground castle. Apparently, the vampire had survived by feeding off the family's virgins, but in Mihara's case, he is ready to overlook her marital status. Also, this Japanese vampire is unable to bear the light of the moon, wields a western-style duelling sword and is attended by a dwarf, a witch and a bald wrestler. To break down Mihara's resistance, Amachi changes her into a wax doll, but eventually she is rescued by her husband and daughter who bring along the police. The vampire's castle is destroyed as its cache of gunpowder explodes.

Amachi was well known at the time for playing villains with demonic good looks and he was typecast in that part in Nakagawa's masterful **Tokaido Yotsuya Kaidan** (1959). Mihara was the house star for fantasy pictures, appearing in Magatani's two features **Ama no Bakemono Yashiki** and **Kyuju-Kyuhonme no Kimusume** (both 1959).

d Nobuo Nakagawa *p* Mitsuga Okura *s* Shin Nakazawa, Katsuyoshi Nakatsu *c* Yoshimi Hirano *lp* Shigeru Amachi, Yoko Mihara, Keinosuke Wada, Junko Ikeuchi

Horst Frank (left), Karin Kernke and Michel Simon in the surreal Die Nackte und der Satan.

The Stranglers of Bombay *aka* **The Strangler of Bengal**
(HAMMER; GB) scope 81(76)min
Fisher's first Hammer horror film without Jimmy Sangster as writer meshes sex and terror to an unprecedented degree in a colonial fantasy chronicling both the callousness of British rule in India and the amazed culture-shock when a mirror image of their own murderous greed is presented to them with equally high-sounding moral-religious justification. Set in British East India company territory in the 1820s, the film has Rolfe as the officer who discovers the Thuggee cult dedicated to robbing and strangling fellow Indians not devoted to Kali-worship. In the face of the utter indifference of a snobbish fellow officer (Cuthbertson), Rolfe resigns and pursues his detection activities, escaping execution twice and ultimately eliminating the local adepts after they have wiped out a rich caravan and the English soldiers guarding it. Fisher takes the opportunity to stage some of his nastiest scenes as the sect mutilates and kills two of its renegade members, including his second cutting out of the tongue scene that year (the first one was in the opening sequence of **The Mummy**). The deepest impression, however, is left by Devereux's portrayal of a lascivious Indian girl watching excitedly as Rolfe's spreadeagled body is approached by a poisonous snake or gloating over two freshly blinded victims grovelling at her feet. Whereas other members of the cast play fanatics of one sort or another, she manages to convey the passionate excitement that can accompany the twisted but liberating explosion of revenge after decades of poverty and repression.

In many ways, the Thuggee can be seen as created by the colonial power in its own image, rather like Frankenstein's monster. But since the movie presents this perspective through English eyes, the results are deeply disturbing for their racist implications and suggest that nothing had been learned from colonialism in the intervening century-and-a-half. A sequel of sorts was provided by Anthony Bushell with **The Terror of the Tongs** (1960), which transports the action to Hong Kong. Previous Thug movies had included two Italian-German efforts co-directed by Gian Paolo Callegari and the American Ralph Murphy, *La Vendetta dei Thugs* (1952) and *I Misteri della Jungla Nera* (1954), both starring Lex Barker.

d Terence Fisher *p* Anthony Hinds *s* David S. Goodman *c* Arthur Grant *se* Les Bowie *lp* Guy Rolfe, Allan Cuthbertson, Andrew Cruickshank, George Pastell, Marne Maitland, Tutte Lemkow, Jan Holden, Marie Devereux, David Spenser

Tempi Duri per i Vampiri *aka* **Uncle Was a Vampire** *aka* **Hard Times for Vampires** *aka* **Hard Times for Dracula** *aka* **My Uncle the Vampire**
(MAXIMA FILM/CEI INCOM/MONTFLOUR FILM; IT)
scope 85min
In this outing Lee, fresh from his first Hammer successes, parodies his most famous role. He plays the old time vampire, Baron Rodrigo, who passes on his nocturnal habits to his nephew, Count Osvaldo (Rascel), an indebted aristocrat who sells his castle to a hotelier and accepts the job of porter in it. Now Rascel, much to his annoyance, has to get up every night and attack the (mostly female) guests in their beds. His efforts

to get rid of the troublesome Baron all fail and only a loving kiss from the beautiful gardner, Lilliana (Koscina) breaks the spell, suggesting physical love can cure anything. Rascal's imitation of Lugosi and the emphasis on scantily dressed young women may be faintly entertaining but Lee's talents are wasted as the ancestral vampire. The film shows that without the popular Neapolitan comic Toto, Steno's comedies become simple routine farces.

d Steno (Stefano Vanzina) *p* Mario Cecchi Gori *s* Edoardo Anton, Dino Verde, Alessandro Continenza *c* Marco Scarpelli *lp* Renato Rascel, Sylvia Koscina, Christopher Lee, Lia Zoppelli, Kay Fisher, Susanna Loret, Antie Geerk, Franco Scandurra

Terror Is a Man

(LYNN-ROMERO/PREMIERE PRODUCTIONS; US, PHII`
b/w 89(76)min

It is fitting that the two main figures in the Filipino fantasy cinema should have co-directed this movie which sparked off a series of cheap American co-produced horror items. The story is a variation on H. G. Wells' *The Island of Dr Moreau* with Derr playing the shipwrecked victim washed ashore on the remote island of Dr Girard (Lederer). Lederer captures a tiger and, after some 200 operations, changes it into something resembling a man (Carlos), to the dismay of Mrs Girard, played by the improbably opulent Thyssen. She then gravitates towards Derr but is kidnapped by the monster. Eventually, the creature hurls its creator over a cliff and is shot by the moronic-looking hero who gets the doctor's widow as his reward.

By playing it straight, regardless of the silliness of the plot and the risible dialogues, the directors manage to imbue the scenes with a rough dignity, often missing from their 'knowing' American counterparts. Lederer, fresh from the unfortunate **The Return of Dracula** (1958), easily outplays his fellow performers. The duo's next directorial contribution to the genre was *Brides of Blood* (1965). De Leon went on to make **The Blood Drinkers** (1966) and **Curse of the Vampires** (1970) on his own, while Romero directed *Beast of Blood* (1969) and **The Beast of the Yellow Night** (1970) as solo efforts.

co-d Gerardo de Leon *co-d/co-p* Eddie Romero *co-p* Kane Lynn *s* Harry Paul Harber *c* Emmanuel I. Rojas *lp* Francis Lederer, Greta Thyssen, Richard Derr, Oscar Keesee, Lilia Duran, Peyton Keesee, Flory Carlos

Le Testament du Docteur Cordelier *aka* Experiment in Evil *aka* The Doctor's Horrible Experiment

(RTF/SOFIRAD/COMPAGNIE JEAN RENOIR) b/w 95(74)min

Made for television but released to cinemas, this reworking of Stevenson's Jekyll and Hyde theme obviously attracted Renoir for two reasons. One was the chance to revisit the nihilistic tramp of *Boudu Sauvé des Eaux* (1932) and explore the joyous anarchy which comes when the bonds of conventional morality are loosed. The other was to give Barrault a role which would offer full scope to his talents as actor and mime. The focal point of the movie is, therefore, the moment when Barrault's dignified Dr Cordelier turns into the bestial Monsieur Oplae and rushes into the streets to explore his freedom, darting in on his victims for sudden, vicious attacks and insolently twirling his cane like a drum-majorette as he melts away in search of new targets for his sadism.

Prancing, twitching, moving with the animal grace of a dancer, Barrault is magnificent, creating an extraordinary chimera whose intrusion into the Paris streets lends them an unsettling air of menace. Yet, there are *longueurs*, because scenes are allowed to run on longer than planned because Renoir was enjoying Barrault's invention. The result is a certain lack of balance, a sense that Barrault's performance is less a characterization than a bravura exercise in technique.

d/p/s Jean Renoir *c* Georges Leclerc *lp* Jean-Louis Barrault, Micheline Gary, Michel Vitold, Teddy Bilis, Jean Topart

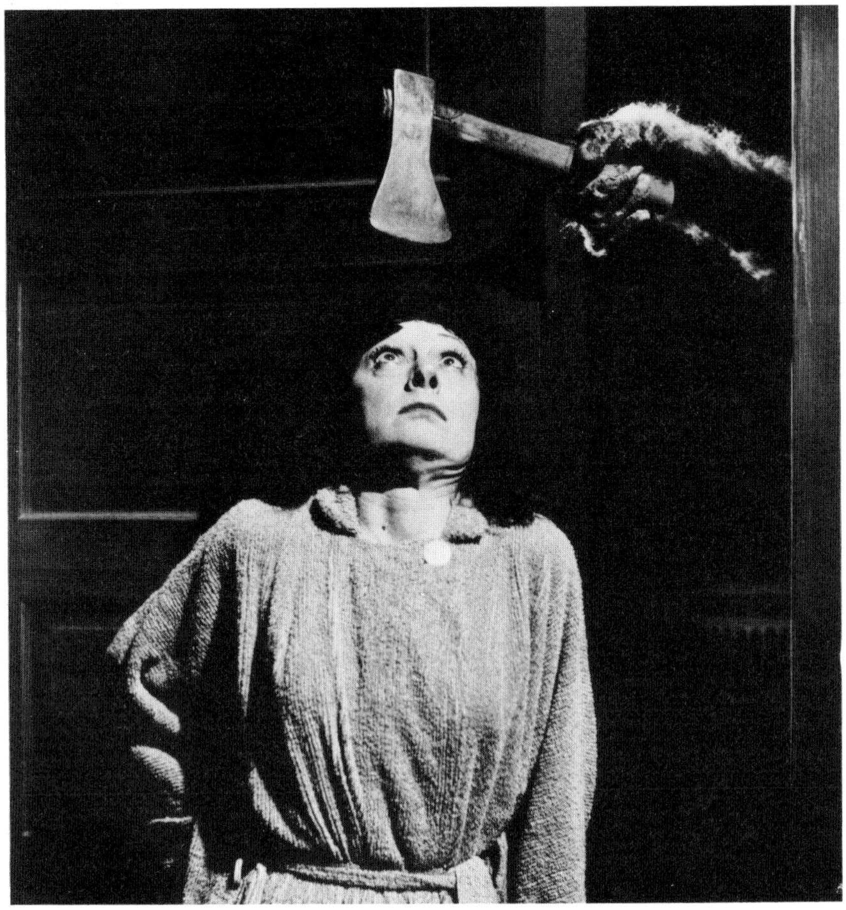

Judith Evelyn under threat in William Castle's cheerfully vulgar The Tingler.

The Tingler

(WILLIAM CASTLE PRODUCTIONS) b/w 82min

This is Castle's best film, although much of the credit belongs to White for his ingenious (and remarkably well written) script, which sets out from the intriguing notion of Price as a doctor who has come to suspect that fear causes a centipede-like organism to grow in the body until it shatters the spine and causes death. Conducting research with his young assistant (Hickman) who is in love with his daughter (Cutts), he tries to use himself as a guinea-pig only to realize (as he amiably remarks) that 'you can't just say boo!'. But he does establish (the film's second great notion – the isolation of the primal scream) that screaming is the safety valve draining off tension and keeping the tingler from growing since it is no longer fed by fear. Summoned by a man (Coolidge) to treat his sick wife (Evelyn), Price realizes that she, being deaf-and-dumb and therefore unable to scream, is the perfect subject for his experiments. Before he can start, Evelyn is frightened to death by horrible apparitions – including an arm emerging from a blood-filled bath – in the apartment above the cinema specializing in silent movies (the film's third great notion) which she and her husband run. Unaware that Coolidge has deliberately provoked his wife's death, Price obtains permission to operate. He indeed finds a tingler – a scaly, scuttling organism which grips the nerves and for once offers a credibly shuddery movie monster – but it escapes and sows screaming panic in the cinema.

Castle's innate vulgarity is apparent here and there, notably in the crudely distorted images of a sequence where Price experiments on himself with drugs, and in a cheap shock climax where, after the tingler has been recaptured and restored to Evelyn's body to die, the guilt-ridden Coolidge sees the corpse come menacingly back to life. To be fair to Castle, however, he does do justice to White's ideas in the admirable scene where the tingler gets loose among a cinema audience watching, of all things, Henry King's tranquilly rustic silent, *Tol'able David* (1921). His promotional gimmicks, much inferior to the film itself, included the 'Percepto' process: certain seats wired to give the occupants a mild electric tingle; a momentary blank screen when the movie's projectionist is killed by the tingler, accompanied by an announcement advising the audience to scream for their lives; and a red tint suffusing the screen when Evelyn is faced by bath-taps running blood. Castle's eager encouragement of audience participation found its natural conclusion in the later phenomenon attending *The Rocky Horror Picture Show* (1975).

d/p William Castle *s* Robb White *c* Wilfred M. Cline *lp* Vincent Price, Judith Evelyn, Darryl Hickman, Patricia Cutts, Philip Coolidge, Pamela Lincoln

Tokaido Yotsuya Kaidan *aka* **The Ghost of Yotsuya** *aka* **Ghost Story of Yotsuya in Tokaido**
(SHINTOHO; JAP) scope 96min
Nanboku Tsuruya's kabuki play, written in 1825, had been adapted by the great Kinoshita (**Shinshaku Yotsuya Kaidan**, 1949), but Nakagawa's version is the classic interpretation of the tale. The plot revolves around the vagabond samurai Iemon (Amachi) who kills a respectable samurai and then marries the man's daughter, Oiwa (Wakasuki) with a promise to avenge her father's death. Greed drives him to trap him wife into adultery, then to poison and murder her and her lover, thereby freeing himself to marry a rich heiress, Oume (Ikeuchi). The corpses of Oiwa, hideously disfigured by the poison, and that of the bald would-be lover, with a deep red gash down the middle of his face, are nailed to a piece of wood and dumped in a swamp, but both return on Iemon's wedding night to haunt him, driving him to kill his new bride and her entire family. Insanely slashing away at the ghosts – which are invisible to the rest of the cast – he is also challenged by Oiwa's sister (Kitazawa) and brother, seeking to revenge her. In the end, Iemon succumbs in a frenzy of hallucinatory panic by the swamp.

The lamp carrier Naosuke (Emi) – a lower class figure, representing the baser aspects of Iemon's character – plays a key role in the tragedy, egging him on and murdering on his behalf. In this way, Naosuke operates on the same narrative level as the ghosts which, in traditional Japanese fashion, embody the moral outrages committed by the protagonists and are visible only to the guilty ones. Strictly speaking, Naosuke and the ghosts are no more than figures representing aspects of Iemon's character, rather than psychological beings in the western sense. This makes the traditional notions of character as understood in western fictions inapplicable to Nakagawa's Kaidan Eiga (**Jigoku**, 1960; *Borei Kaibyo Yashiki*, 1958), which dramatize the Japanese concept of karma: that fate is the accumulated effects of one's own actions and that eventually it will confront the individual as an external force relentlessly acting upon him/her.

The appearances of the ghosts, alternating with the intrusion of both real and imaginary scenes, are powerfully staged, and announced by a dimming of the light, wild bursts of music and deliriously stylized colours. This stylization of the narrative, explicitly announced as theatrical in the pre-credit sequence showing a curtain opening to reveal a stage readied for the performance, gains a great deal from Haruyasu Kurosawa's designs. Although the script has a tendency to meander, the horror scenes are eerily poetic as well as suitably gruesome – the corpses surfacing in the swamp amidst bright red foam, a hand emerging from the soil to claw at Iemon's legs, and so on – and confirm Nakagawa's status as Japan's foremost horror director. Amachi, typecast as the villain, is no match for the phlegmatic Tatsuya who played the part in Shiro Toyoda's version, **Yotsuya Kaidan** (1965). Mori used the action film star Sato for his remake **Yotsuya Kaidan – Oiwa no Borei** (1969). Other versions include the silent cinema master Ito's *Shinpan Yotsuya Kaidan* (1928), Masaki Mori's *Yotsuya Kaidan* (1956) and Misumi's identically titled picture of 1959.

d Nobuo Nakagawa *p* Mitsugu Okura *s* Masayoshi Onuki, Yoshihiro Ishikawa *c* Tadashi Nishimoto *lp* Shigeru Amachi, Noriko Kitazawa, Katsuko Wakasuki, Shintaro Emi, Ryusburo Nakamura, Junko Ikeuchi, Jun Otomo

Edith Scob as the disfigured embodiment of innocence in Georges Franju's masterful Les Yeux Sans Visage.

Les Yeux Sans Visage *aka* **Eyes Without a Face** *aka* **The Horror Chamber of Dr Faustus**
(CHAMPS ELYSEES-LUX; FR) b/w 95(84)min
With the camera looking unblinkingly on as one scene opens with a scalpel tracing a bloody line on a girl's face, preparatory to the removal of a section of facial tissue for a skin graft, *Les Yeux Sans Visage* has some claim, along with **Psycho** (1960), to co-paternity of the splatter genre. Yet, there is nothing gratuitous about the shot as used by Franju; indeed it is essential to the film in that it offers a first intimation of the intolerable, pointless pain inflicted by a surgeon (Brasseur) in his repeated and invariably doomed attempts to restore her beauty to the daughter (Scob) whose face was destroyed in a car-crash, and who ultimately rebels to put an end to his experiments. Although the plot is as wildly fantastic as anything Hollywood ever dreamed up for Boris Karloff or Bela Lugosi, Franju invests it with a weird poetry in which the influence of Cocteau is unmistakable (scenes, for instance, in which Scob drifts through the house in a waxen mask of eerie beauty). 'The more you touch on mystery, the more important it is to be realistic', Cocteau once said in discussing his hatred of poetic effects; and the mysterious breath of poetry which surges through *Les Yeux Sans Visage* comes precisely because Franju coaxes a hard, insistent realism out of his fantasy material.

In the sterilized sleaziness of the morgue where Brasseur identifies an unknown corpse as his daughter so that the police will assume her to be dead; in the breezy normality of the street outside the Sorbonne where his assistant (Valli) awaits her students victims; in the cool callousness of the skin-grafting sequences; and in details like the sickening thud of the scalpel which Scob finally plunges into Valli's neck, Franju builds a solid springboard for the extraordinary final sequence. Lit by an incandescent flame of beauty, terror and madness, the victim turns on the torturer, looses the dogs on her vivisectionist father, and wanders free through the night, her disfigured face seen only by the dogs at her feet and the dove on her shoulder.

d/co-s Georges Franju *p* Jules Borkon *co-s* Jean Redon, Claude Sautet, Pierre Boileau, Thomas Narcejac *c* Eugen Schuefftan (Shufftan) *lp* Pierre Brasseur, Alida Valli, Edith Scob, Juliette Mayniel, Béatrice Altariba

The 1960s

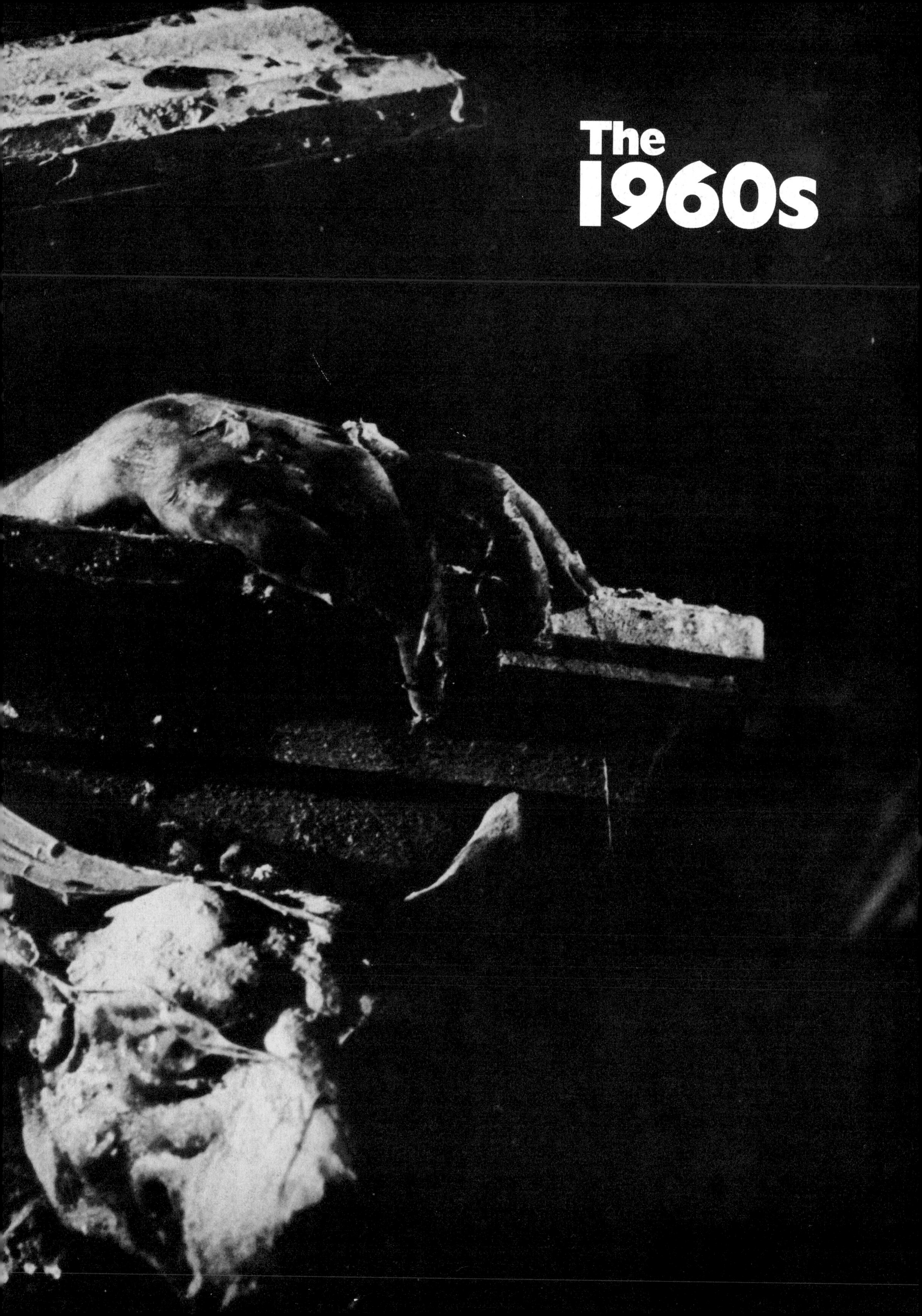

The Horror Film Goes International

If the horror film had been revived in the fifties, in the sixties it flourished. In America, Roger Corman began his series of adaptations of the works of Edgar Allan Poe with the magnificent **House of Usher** (1960), while films like **Onibaba** and **Kwaidan** (both 1964) revealed to the West the violent Japanese horror tradition. In Italy, Mario Bava commenced his explorations of perverse sexuality with the delirious **La Maschera del Demonio** (1960), while in Spain, Jesús Franco's gruesome **Gritos en la Noche** (1962) initiated a stream of similarly inclined medical-horror films in which surgical dismemberment and violence to women's bodies took the place of sex, still the mainstay of vampire movies. This latter strand also quickly surfaced, in a pared-down fashion, in America in the 'splatter movies' of Herschell Gordon Lewis, among others, with **Blood Feast** (1963), the early examples of which, in their own gory way, were as much exercises in *Grand Guignol* as **Whatever Happened to Baby Jane?** (1962) and its numerous clones.

The speed with which horror regenerated itself as a genre around the world can be seen in the emergence of a new breed of horror stars (Vincent Price, Peter Cushing, Christopher Lee and Barbara Steele) whose careers, like those of Bela Lugosi and Boris Karloff, were both advanced and limited by their association with the genre. The decade also saw would-be parodies such as **Carry on Screaming** (1966) – which failed because they didn't take into account just how close to parody so many horror films were – and the proliferation of subgenres like Jacinto Molina's seeming endless werewolf saga that began with **La Marco del Hombre Lobo** (1967) and the Mexican films devoted to the exploits of masked wrestlers Santo and the Blue Demon. More significant were the sex-vampire films, first brought to the screen by Jean Rollin in 1967 with **Le Viol du Vampire**. He was swiftly overtaken by Hammer in the seventies – the studio's last creative burst before its decline into mediocrity featured sex-vampires.

These trends notwithstanding, the decade is best summed up by four film-makers, Alfred Hitchcock, Roman Polanksi, Michael Powell and George Romero, whose work both defined the horror film in the sixties and pointed to the future. Romero's **Night of the Living Dead** (1968) marked the death of the vampire and the arrival of the zombie as the central figure of the horror film. Similarly, though Hitchcock's **Psycho** (1960) quickly spawned imitations from the likes of William Castle (**Homicidal**, 1961) and Hammer (**Taste of Fear**, 1960), its true significance would only emerge in the seventies at the head of a new tradition of American horror film-making which took for its subject the family. Powell's **Peeping Tom** (1960) had little direct influence but it remains the classic film about film-making and the fantasies that underpin our fascination with the cinema. Polanski's three films, **Repulsion** (1965), **Dance of the Vampires** (1967) and **Rosemary's Baby** (1968), neatly mark the stages of the horror film's evolution throughout the decade. The first is an art film cum female version of *Psycho*, the second as intelligent a genre film as one could wish for and the last, with its big budget, the forerunner of the 'respectable' religious-horror films which would have their, albeit brief, day in the seventies.

1960

Agatha – Lass das Morden Sein *aka* **Agatha – Stop the Murders**
(FILMAUFBAU; WG) b/w 99min
A comedy about a beautiful writer of bloodthirsty crime novels (von Koczian) who becomes the victim of a hoax when Brent (Wussow) invites her to his country mansion and stages a gruesome charade with the help of a firm of undertakers. Essentially a misogynistic love story riddled with horror imagery as the level-headed male reveals the successful authoress to be a frightened little girl, the film failed at the box office because it was overshadowed by the equally inane **Das Spukschloss im Spessart** (1960), released at the same time.

d/co-s Dietrich Haugh *co-s* Franz Geiger, Stefan Gommermann, Franz Marischka, Eva Nager, Franz M. Schilder, Wolfgang Schnitzler *c* Guenther Senftleben
lp Johanna von Koczian, Klausjuergen Wussow, Elisabeth Flickenschildt, Peter Vogel, Hans Dieter Zeidler, Karl Lieffen

L'Amante del Vampiro *aka* **The Vampire and the Ballerina** *aka* **The Dancer and the Vampire** *aka* **The Vampire's Lover**
(CONSORZIO ITALIANO FILMS; IT) b/w 86(78)min
The unimaginative plot of this quickie trying to cash in on Riccardo Freda's **I Vampiri** (1956) and the Hammer horror movies revolves around two young ballet dancers Luisa (Remy) and Francesca (Gloriani) who take refuge one stormy night in an old castle inhabited by a vampire countess (Rolando) and her domineering vampire servant (Brandi). A great deal of footage of people wandering through dark forests pads out a badly acted and directed movie which verges on sexploitation. Brandi also starred as the vampire in the more frankly sexy **L'Ultima Preda del Vampiro** (1960). Polselli's next effort, **Il Mostro dell'Opera** (1964), contained some good sequences but also degenerated into a potboiler and his later work was both more sadistic and more sexploitative.

d/co-s Renato Polselli *p* Bruno Bolognesi *co-s* Giuseppe Pellegrini, Ernesto Gastaldi *c* Angelo Balstrocchi
se Leopoldo Rosi, Raffaele del Monte *lp* Helene Remy, Tina Gloriani, Maria Luisa Rolando, Walter Brandi, Isarco Ravaioli, John Turner

Previous pages: Dr Terror's House of Horrors *(1964), one of the many omnibus movies of the sixties.*

Walter Brandi as the butler cum vampire in L'Amante del Vampiro, *a quickie Italian imitation of Riccardo Freda's seminal* I Vampiri *(1956).*

The atmospheric City of the Dead.

The Brides of Dracula

(HAMMER; GB) 85min

After his classic performance as the Count in Fisher's **Dracula** (1958), Christopher Lee refused to play the part again for fear of becoming typecast. In order to cash in on its string of box-office hits, therefore, Hammer resorted to this odd tale without a Count which features Peel as Baron Meinster, the elderly vampire under house arrest in the ancestral castle. His mother (Hunt) protects and provides victims for him until Van Helsing (Cushing) takes up the challenge and saves French teacher Marianne (Monlaur) as she is about to marry the young vampire. Although Peel, who looks like a young mod in Transylvanian garb, is a poor stand-in for the Count, the movie has some good scenes, including one in which the old sorceress, playing midwife, helpfully removes some earth while whispering encouragements to the vampire trying to break out of her grave. The climax sees Cushing, bitten by the vampire, removing the infectious mark by burning his own neck with a white-hot branding iron before arranging the arms of a moonlit windmill so as to cast the shadow of a cross on to Peel. Fisher's direction is effective, with his customary lingering camera movements, but the overall result is decidedly uneven.

Cushing didn't play the part of Van Helsing again for 12 years, until **Dracula AD 1972** (1972), **The Legend of the Seven Golden Vampires** and **The Satanic Rites of Dracula** (both 1973). Lee returned to the series in 1965 for the marvellous **Dracula, Prince of Darkness** (1965).

d Terence Fisher *p* Anthony Hinds *s* Jimmy Sangster, Peter Bryan, Edward Percy *c* Jack Asher *se* Sydney Pearson *lp* Peter Cushing, David Peel, Martita Hunt, Yvonne Monlaur, Miles Malleson, Mona Washbourne, Michael Ripper, Henry Oscar, Andree Melly

City of the Dead *aka* Horror Hotel

(VULCAN/AMICUS; GB) b/w 76min

Baxt, the scenarist of Sidney Hayers' **Circus of Horrors** (1959), here provides a script that combines the **Psycho** (1960) gimmick of killing the apparent heroine at the beginning of the movie, with elements of the Salem witches' story. The resulting film is reminiscent in some ways of Jacques Tourneur's work in the forties. The plot has Professor Driscoll (Lee) send Nan (Stevenson), one of his students, to Whitewood in Massachusetts to research local legends of witchcraft. In the decaying village, she is used as a human sacrifice by a coven presided over by Lee himself and a resurrected witch (Jessel) who now runs the local inn. In fact, the whole village is full of zombie-like creatures dedicated to unspeakable rites as they wander through the swirling night mists dressed in monkish habits. They are eventually eliminated by Nan's boyfriend (Naylor) brandishing a cross as he dies with a knife in his back. Although cheaply made, studio-bound and short on complexity, the film has a beautifully eerie Lovecraftian atmosphere. Baxt later collaborated with Richard Matheson on Hayers' only other watchable movie, **Night of the Eagle** (1961).

This was the first – and uncredited – production in England of American *émigré* Subotsky, who soon after took over as head of Hammer's only rival in the horror business, Amicus. Moxey eventually emigrated to the United States where he became a better than average director of fantasy films for television.

d John Moxey *co-p* Donald Taylor *co-p/co-s* Milton Subotsky *co-s* George Baxt *c* Desmond Dickinson *se* Cliff Richardson *lp* Patricia Jessel, Christopher Lee, Betta St John, Dennis Lotis, Venetia Stevenson, Valentine Dyall, Ann Beach, Tom Naylor, Fred Johnson

The Curse of the Werewolf *aka* The Wolfman

(HAMMER; GB) 91min

After **The Two Faces of Dr Jekyll** (1960), Fisher returned to the same territory with this hauntingly romantic adaptation of Guy Endore's novel *The Werewolf of Paris*, first published in 1933. This time, the complementary evils of puritanism and cruel perversity are firmly rooted in a notion of social, as opposed to metaphysical, evil. In 18th-century Spain, a beggar is imprisoned by an aristocrat (Dawson) and left to rot. Ten years later, when the pustule-faced Marquis is refused by a mute servant girl (Romain), she is thrown into the same dungeon and raped by the insanely degenerated beggar. She escapes, kills her master and attempts suicide. Saved by a doctor (Evans), she bears a child, Leon (Reed), who is adopted and lovingly raised to adulthood until a caricature of love, presented by a prostitute, triggers off Leon's werewolf side. In love with Cristina (Feller), Leon dreads that his baser instincts will destroy her, but discovers that her loving presence actually stops him turning into a beast. The tragedy is sparked off when her bigoted father locks him up, thereby separating him from his beloved. The desperate creature breaks loose and, pursued

Right: *Peter Cushing as the rational Van Helsing under attack in* The Brides of Dracula.

by a yowling mob, tries to escape across the rooftops until it is trapped in a clocktower and shot by its adoptive father.

In many ways, *Curse*, released in 1961, can be seen as a companion to Fisher's **The Gorgon** (1963), each film presenting one side of the contradictory forces animating Fisher's movies: *Curse* is a meditation on the ravages caused by an unfettered patriarchy with the sons paying for the sins of the fathers, while *The Gorgon* presents the petrifying fear inspired by the manless matriarch. While the latter film is given the shape and tone of a dream, *Curse* is firmly anchored in the social order: the real villain is the vile aristocrat and the order he represents, a world in which love is caricatured or forbidden and where compassion has no place.

The film has a classic circular construction, with church bells opening and closing the tragedy. But these religious symbols are peculiarly ironic since throughout the movie, the werewolf and Jesus are linked in mocking parallels, including their birth on Christmas Day. The elegiac film works on many levels through richly evocative scenes, which detract somewhat from Fisher's usually tight narrative pacing. Reed's portrayal of the werewolf is well controlled and is probably the actor's best performance to date. Roy Ashton, Hammer's makeup specialist, excelled himself with his creation of the unsightly Marquis, a far more frightening figure than the werewolf. Mitchell, later to become a popular TV comedian, appears briefly as Pepe, a stereotyped 'ordinary' Spaniard.

d Terence Fisher *p* Anthony Hinds *s* John Elder (Anthony Hinds) *c* Arthur Grant *se* Les Bowie *lp* Oliver Reed, Yvonne Romain, Catherine Feller, Clifford Evans, Anthony Dawson, Josephine Llewellyn, Richard Wordsworth, Warren Mitchell, Michael Ripper, Peter Sallis

Oliver Reed rampant in The Curse of the Werewolf.

Doctor Blood's Coffin

(CARALAN; GB) 82min

A crude shocker (in the manner of **Corridors of Blood**, 1958) with an inane plot, this film simply piles up shots of bloody surgery and decayed flesh, on the assumption that vivisection or a heart transplant performed in a disused Cornish tin-mine are sufficient to tap into audiences' unconscious fears or taboo fantasies. The story concerns a surgically inclined father (Hunter) and son (Moore), the latter trying to impress their widowed receptionist (Court) by exhuming her husband (Stockman) and putting a living heart into his corpse. The kindest possible comment about Juran's story and script, adapted by Kelly and Miller, is poverty-stricken. Films like this testify to the brilliance of Terence Fisher's conception of the Frankenstein character.

The Canadian director, Furie, later made a name for himself by coating his movies (*The Ipcress File*, 1965; *The Appaloosa*, 1966) with a superficial flashiness.

d Sidney J. Furie *p* George Fowler *s* Jerry Juran, James Kelly, Peter Miller *c* Stephen Dade *lp* Kieron Moore, Ian Hunter, Hazel Court, Gerald C. Lawson, Kenneth J. Warren, Paul Stockman, Fred Johnson, Andy Alston

Left: *The resurrected Paul Stockman in Sidney J. Furie's crude shocker,* Doctor Blood's Coffin.

El Espejo de la Bruja *aka* Cuentos de Brujas *aka* The Witch's Mirror

(CINEMATOGRAFICA ABSA; MEX) b/w 84(75)min

This is Urueta's best-made movie, largely thanks to Stahl's good trick photography, and combines the story of Snow White with surgical motifs. In the 19th century, a witch, Sara (Corona), who uses her magic mirror to warn her god-daughter, Elena (de Marco), against Dr Eduardo (Calvo), the latter's husband. In spite of her evocation of the demon Adonai, however, Calvo poisons his victim and marries Deborah (Arenas). Corona gets her revenge by making de Marco's ghost appear in a mirror at which Arenas is sitting: the terrified Calvo throws an oil lamp at her, setting fire to and disfiguring his new wife's face and hands. Promising to restore her beauty, he then uses the corpses of young women to provide her with skin and the hands of a pianist who had been buried alive. But Corona substitutes one of de Marco's hands, which, against Arenas's will, eventually plunges a pair of scissors into her husband's body.

The story is told with many well-executed effects, including a piano that plays by itself, flowers that wilt suddenly, the appearance of a demonic cat and, above all, the many spectral manifestations in the mirror. Arena, the heroine of Portillo's Aztec mummy films, is excellent in a role which again requires her to suggest that she is taken over by an alien force as her hands take on a life of their own, trying to strangle her husband and playing a taboo piece of music on the piano. Adding to the picture's interest is the introduction of a benevolent witch who uses her satanic powers against a ruthlessly oppressive husband and wife-killer, in marked contrast to Urueta's woman-hating **La Bruja** (1954), which also revolved around the motifs of beauty and disfigurement. Perhaps this novel approach was due to the scenarists Taboada and Ruanova, whose inventiveness had been demonstrated in the Nostradamus serial, **La Maldición de Nostradamus** (1959) and its sequels.

d/co-s Chano Urueta *p* Abel Salazar *co-s* Alfredo Ruanova, Carlos Enrique Taboada *c* Jorge Stahl Jnr *lp* Rosita Arenas, Armando Calvo, Isabela Corona, Dina de Marco, Carlos Nieto, Wally Barron

Et Mourir de Plaisir *aka* Blood and Roses

(FILMS E.G.E./DOCUMENTO FILM; FR,IT)
scope 87(85,74)min

This adaptation of Sheridan LeFanu's *Carmilla* – like the rest of Vadim's early work before his soft-porn persona came to the fore – flatters to deceive. Clearly intended as an art-house horror movie, it aims for a dreamily languorous rhythm which never quite manages to overcome the obstacles posed by stilted performances (Ferrer in particular), bathetic dialogue, and direction too prosaic to achieve the necessary intensity.

Predictably enough, Vadim highlights the lesbian implications behind Carmilla's choice of the Karnstein bride as the favoured object of her vampiric attentions (implications elided in Dreyer's much looser adaptation of the LeFanu story, **Vampyr**, 1931); and he equally predictably manages to sensationalize the resulting erotic tension in the byplay between Annette Vadim and Martinelli. The film, in fact, emerges as a pretty crude assemblage of discordant elements which fails to integrate the elements of myth with the modern setting. What flair it has is almost entirely due to Cocteau (whose influence is felt throughout to the point of plagiarism) and to Renoir's camerawork, which contrives some striking – colour draining from the screen to highlight the vivid splash of blood on Carmilla's white dress; the dream sequence in which Martinelli's loss of blood to the vampire is reflected by the pallid red tint – though not particularly subtle, effects.

d/co-s Roger Vadim *p* Raymond Eger *co-s* Claude Brule, Claude Martin, Roger Vailland *c* Claude Renoir *lp* Mel Ferrer, Elsa Martinelli, Annette Vadim, Jacques-René Chauffard, Marc Allégret

The Hands of Orlac *aka* Les Mains d'Orlac *aka* Hands of a Strangler

(RIVIERA INTERNATIONAL/PENDENNIS; GB,FR)
b/w 105(95)min

Maurice Renard was France's leading science-fantasy author of the early 20th century but, ironically, his weakest book became his best-known work and was filmed twice before – as **Orlacs Haende** (1924) with the brilliant Conrad Veidt as Orlac; **Mad Love** (1935) with Colin Clive as Orlac and Lorre as the mad doctor – and once after – **Hands of a Stranger** (1962) – this Anglo-French version, released in 1962 and starring Ferrer as the pianist who requires a new pair of hands after a plane crash. Professor Volchett (Wolfit) performs the operation asked for by Ferrer's fiancée, the wealthy Louise (Saint Simon). Convinced that his hands belong to an executed strangler and are becoming uncontrollable, Ferrer flees his house and gets involved with a stage magician (Lee) who attempts to blackmail him. Betrayed by his assistant (Carrel), Lee gets his revenge by sticking real swords into a cabinet containing Carrel during his act, changing the spectators' applause into shrieks as they see the blood seeping out of it. Ferrer is then reunited with his fiancée and it is revealed that the previous user of his hands had been innocent of the crimes for which he was executed.

Greville was a talented director who had learned his craft with E. A. Dupont and René Clair in France, and had directed Lee before in *Beat Girl* (1960), which may account for the way the film improves when he enters the story. But Ferrer is too lightweight an actor for the role of a neurotic who fears his hands may be enacting his secret wishes, and the whole movie suffers from this central weakness, allowing Lee, who should be a secondary figure, to steal the show. Co-producer Taylor also contributed additional English dialogue and renowned jazz musician Claude Bolling provides an effective score. The movie was made in English and French versions simultaneously, with an identical cast, except for Antoine Balpêtré in the role of the professor. The French version was shot by Jacques Lemare.

d/co-s Edmond T. Greville *p* Steven Pallos, Donald Taylor *co-s* John Baines *c* Desmond Dickinson *lp* Mel Ferrer, Christopher Lee, Danny Carrel, Lucille Saint Simon, Felix Aylmer, Basil Sydney, Donald Wolfit, Donald Pleasance, David Peel, Peter Reynolds, Campbell Singer

Mel Ferrer as the pianist who can't control his hands in The Hands of Orlac, *the third film version of Maurice Renard's novel.*

The House in Marsh Road *aka* The Invisible Creature

(ETERNAL; GB) b/w 70min

This is a rather tame supernatural thriller based on a Lawrence Meynell story from Tully, a veteran of medium- and low-budget British programme fillers. The plot concerns a surly book reviewer (Wright) and his mistress (Dorne) who plan to murder his wife (Dainton), but she is saved by the poltergeist who inhabits an old house that she inherited. The ghost also appears to be responsible for the house catching fire during a storm, trapping the adulterous couple in the flames.

d Montgomery Tully *p/s* Maurice J. Wilson *c* James Harvey *lp* Tony Wright, Patricia Dainton, Sandra Dorne, Derek Aylward, Sam Kydd, Llewellyn Rees, Anita Sharp Bolster, Roddy Hughes, Geoffrey Denton, Olive Sloane

House of Usher *aka* The Fall of the House of Usher

(ALTA VISTA/AIP) scope 80min

With American horror stagnating in an endless round of men in monster suits towards the end of the fifties, Hammer took the lead by going back to the classic figures of Frankenstein and Dracula, additionally upping the budgets and employing colour. Whereupon Corman went even further back to Poe, throwing in CinemaScope, and adding the bonus of colour used expressively rather than (primarily) decoratively.

The result was a minor masterpiece, surprisingly faithful to Poe as it tells the story of Roderick Usher (Price), his fears for the sanity of his sister Madeline (Fahey), her burial alive while in a cataleptic trance, and the fall of the house of Usher as she returns to exact revenge on her brother. Price, in a magnificent performance, gives the film its tone, grand in manner and gesture yet secretly sickening from some inner corruption: an incestuous desire (as Crosby's probing, hesitating, incessantly agitated camera subtly suggests) which has communicated itself to the house that has locked them within a familial passion and which is itself crumbling under the same deadweight of decadence. A magnificently *coherent* film that is often dismissed as pure decoration, it shows a remarkable care for detail. When Fahey's suitor (Damon) first enters the room in which Price has virtually imprisoned himself, for instance, he is wearing blue, a splash of vivid life that jars against the crimson worn by Price and echoed throughout the furnishings: the colour of blood (and perhaps the guilt that already stains Price's mind) when Fahey returns from the grave to claim him in her bloodstained funeral shroud.

The style established here – a fusion of Corman's direction, Matheson's script, Crosby's camerawork and Daniel Haller's sets – was to be carried over, virtually unchanged but with varying success, in a series of Poe films: **The Pit and the Pendulum**, **Premature Burial** and **Tales of Terror** (all 1961), **The Raven**, **The Terror** and **The Haunted Palace** (all 1963), **The Masque of the Red Death** and **The Tomb of Ligeia** (1964).

d/p Roger Corman *s* Richard Matheson *c* Floyd Crosby
lp Vincent Price, Myrna Fahey, Mark Damon, Harry Ellerbe

Jigoku *aka* Hell *aka* The Sinners to Hell

(SHINTOHO; JAP) scope 100min

Like most directors in the commercial Japanese cinema at the time, Nakagawa usually made three or four features a year. In 1960, however, he only made two to enable him to concentrate on this film – the pivotal work of his career – which summarizes his moral-religious philosophy. Set in a theological faculty of a university, the plot focuses on two characters, the quiet but indecisive Shiro (Amachi) and the mephistophelean Tamura (Numata). When they become involved in a manslaughter, their own process of dying is beset by visions of a Dante-esque journey through hell according to the lore of Japanese Buddhism. They witness gruesome tortures such as skinning alive, the gouging of eyes and other, even longer term, discomforts. Dispensing with the rules of verisimilitude, the film operates like a moral fable: the demonic Numata suddenly appears in various locations, acting as the link between the world of the living and that of the dead and thus, like the Japanese notion of karma, binding the two inextricably together. In many ways, the characters function as they would in Western medieval morality plays, with Amachi representing both 'incest' – with his sister/lover Sachiko (Mitsuya) – and 'complicity', while others represent 'injustice', 'drunkenness', 'corruption', 'egotism', 'lust', and so on. The credit sequence functions as a summary of the movie as a whole: over the lurid graphics of the title, Nakagawa dubbed the sounds of city life, nightclub music, a film studio, an ambulance or police siren and other sounds forming a symphonic texture to represent human desire and follies, but by adding images of naked women to the credits, sexuality becomes the driving force to perdition, a point all major religions in the world seem to agree upon.

The overtly allegorical dimension of this epic picture, although generating an interestingly fragmented narrative, also detracts somewhat from the force of karma as represented in Nakagawa's classic **Tokaido Yotsuya Kaidan** (1959), which also starred Amachi. There, the moral implications of certain actions were returned to the perpetrator in the shape of ghosts, thereby avoiding the simplistic split between here and a nightmarish hereafter. Haryasu Kurosawa, the designer of the previous film, also provided the at times abstract setting for *Jigoku*. Particularly noteworthy are the poetic designs for the shores of the river of death while other effects are primarily achieved through eerie lighting and use of colour filters to bathe isolated bits of action marked off from a black or monochrome background. This picture is not to be confused with Shiro Toyoda's beautiful adaptation of the Akutagawa story **Jigokuhen** (1969), although Tatsumi Kumashiro did remake Nakagawa's film (**Jigoku**, 1981). Shortly after Nakagawa's film was released, the production company, Shintoho, collapsed.

Vincent Price, by the sixties a central icon of the horror film, with Mark Damon in House of Usher, *the first of Roger Corman's adaptations of the stories of Edgar Allan Poe.*

d/co-s Nobuo Nakagawa *p* Mitsugu Okura *co-s* Ichiro Miyagawa *c* Mamoru Morita *lp* Shigeru Amachi, Yoichi Numata, Torahiko Nakamura, Fumiko Miyata, Ukato Mitsuya, Hiroshi Hayashi, Kimie Tokudaiji, Akiko Yamashita, Jun Otomo

Kaibyo Otamage-Ike *aka* The Ghost of Otamage-Ike

(SHINTOHO; JAP) scope 75min

Shot when Shintoho, the studio base of Japan's Kaidan Eiga master Nobuo Nakagawa, was about to go bankrupt, this second-rate bakeneko mono (cat ghost story) repeats the motifs and plot structure of Nakagawa's beautiful *Borei Kaibyo Yashiki* (1958) which Ishikawa and Fujishima had also scripted. When a young woman (Kitazawa) is harassed by a white-haired old woman who also appears as a cat, it emerges that she is the descendant of a bailiff who, in the distant past, murdered a lord's entire family in front of their beloved cat. The cat then went on to haunt the bailiff's family through the years, and ends up assaulting the film's modern-day heroine. Acted by members of the studio's regular troupe, including the stunning Kitazawa who had played the vengeful sister in Nakagawa's **Tokaido Yotsuya Kaidan** (1959), and the company's brylcremed leading males, the picture's main asset is Kawasaki's expert photography.

d/co-s Yoshihiro Ishikawa *p* Mitsugu Okura *co-s* Jiro Fujishima *c* Kikuzo Kawasaki *lp* Shozaburo Date, Noriko Kitazawa, Yoichi Numata, Namiji Matsuura

The Little Shop of Horrors

(SANTA CLARA/FILMGROUP) b/w 70min

Surely the best horror-comedy ever made in two days. Although its plot looks suspiciously like an adaptation of John Collier's short story *Green Thoughts*, even down to the denouement of the plant's buds opening to reveal the reflected faces of its victims, the film is a more-or-less remake of **A Bucket of Blood** (1959) with Haze again the dim-witted florist's assistant looking for bodies to feed his body, in this case a carnivorous plant he has developed.

Not to be taken seriously for an instant with its snappish cries of 'Feed me!' and its delicate digestive habits (gunmen go down well but the guns are regurgitated with a reproachful belch), the monster plant is irresistibly tatty, starting life as what looks suspiciously like two halves of an avocado potted with a fringe of greenery, and ending it unashamedly as a thing of shreds and patches. Corman's inventiveness is magnificently in evidence in the way he gets round the starvation budget either by flaunting it (the tacky florist's shop decorated with crude hand-lettered signs announcing 'Lots plants cheap' or '40% off everything') or ignoring it by shooting on location (the first murder in the railway yards, the Wellesian chase in a factory yard stacked high with endless rows of rubber tyres). The Jewish humour is occasionally stretched a little thin, but whenever this happens Corman soon switches to one of his inexhaustible supply of splendid comic characters like the manic dentist drilling his blues away at the expense of his patients ('Hurt? Good, you ain't felt nothing yet') who meets his match in Nicholson's super-masochist ('No novocaine, it dulls the senses').

Irresistible, far more so than the 1986 remake.

d/p Roger Corman *s* Charles B. Griffith *c* Arch Dalzell *lp* Jonathan Haze, Jackie Joseph, Mel Welles, Myrtle Vail, Dick Miller, Jack Nicholson

La Marca del Muerto *aka* Creatures of the Walking Dead

(ALAMEDA FILMS; MEX) b/w 80(74)min

A routine rejuvenation picture which exploits its female cast members for additional (although tame, when compared to Jesús Franco's work in Spain or even **L'Amante del Vampiro** (1960) in Italy) sexual thrills. The picture begins in 1890 with the hanging of a Dr Malthus (Casanova) for killing young women whose blood, mixed with a potion of his own invention, he injected into his heart to acquire eternal youth. Years later the doctor's great-grandson, Gonzalo (Casanova again) and his fiancée, Rosa (Furio), come to live in their ancestor's castle, discover the old man's mummy, laboratory and notes and repeat the experiments, using the blood of a maid (Alvarado). Old Malthus revives and clamours for more blood which Gonzalo refuses to supply, leading the wizened old doctor, made up by Armando Meyer, to turn his bloody attentions to Furio. This causes serious disagreement in the family and leads to the customary conflagration.

Cortes' customary pedestrian direction – evidenced in numerous inane comedies starring his wife, Mapy Cortes, or Germán Valdes (Tin Tan) (*El Espectro de Televicentro*, *El Fantasma de la Opereta*, both 1959) – fails to endow the banal story with the sense of patriarchal perversion it so badly needs. The US version was prepared by Jerry Warren with additional footage shot by Richard Wallace, special effects by Nicolas Reye and extra cast members listed as Rock Madison, Ann Wells, Willard Gross, George Todd, Bruno Ve Sota and Katherine Victor. The American print listed director Cortes as Frederick Corte.

d/co-s Fernando Cortes *p* Cesar Santos Galindo, Alfredo Ripstein Jnr *co-s* José Maria Fernandez Unsain, Alfredo Varela Jnr *c* José Ortiz Ramos *lp* Fernando Casanova, Sonia Furio, Pedro de Aguillon, Aurora Alvarado, Rosa Maria Gallardo, Hortensia Santoveña, Edmundo Crispino, Guillermo Cramer

Barbara Steele in the Mario Bava's chilling masterpiece, La Maschera del Demonio.

La Maschera del Demonio *aka* Black Sunday *aka* The Demon's Mask *aka* Revenge of the Vampire *aka* House of Fright *aka* Masque du Demon

(GALATEA FILMS/JOLLY FILMS; IT, FR) b/w 84min

Bava's first (and best) film as a solo director, this also launched Steele's career as the ultimate horror actress. An experienced cameraman, Bava had shot and co-directed Riccardo Freda's beautiful **I Vampiri** (1956) and here he extends the flamboyantly romantic style they had developed and adds his own prowling camera movements and stylish art direction. Loosely based on Gogol's *The Vij*, this superb film tells of Princess Asa (Steele), killed as a witch in a brutal opening sequence, which culminates in the fixing of a spiked devil-mask on to her face as a punishment for her adultery, labelled 'witchcraft' by the local inquisitor, her brother. Two centuries later, she and her lover (Dominici) return from the crypt to destroy the descendants of her cursed family.

The film's highlights include the laborious resurrection of Dominici as he slowly claws his way out of his grave and lumbers off into the night; the slow-motion shot of a ghostly hearse driving through the forest and the vampirizing of Katia (Steele) by Asa as she rejuvenates herself. Steele's double role as the virginal Katia and the sexual witch, whose body is marked by the stigmata of unholy penetrations suggestively presents the only two options allowed for women in such religious imagery: madonna or whore. The movie derives its lyrical force and indeed its sense of horror from the knowledge that a woman's sexuality cannot be eliminated and will return, bearing the scars of the violence with which it was repressed, to challenge the order of things. The ultimate threat, according to the movie's narrative logic, is signalled at the end: the possible merger of Asa and Katia into one single image. Only religion (the cross) and cutting keep the two apart. Rarely has guilty sexuality, transformed into a fascinating fear of women, been represented as explicitly.

Bava continued to make chillingly perverse movies in which males desperately tried to eradicate desire – expressed as femininity – thus destroying themselves. These include **La Frusta e il Corpo** (1963) and **Sei Donne per l'Assassino** (1964). After the splendid **Ercole a Centro della Terra** (1961), in which the hero literally must overcome the fear of death before he can 'know' his lover, Bava shot Freda's classic, **L'Orribile Segreto del Dr Hichcock** (1962), before continuing his own career in horror with the disappointing **I Tre Volti della Paura** (1963). The American version of *La Maschera*, atrociously dubbed and with a ponderous score by Les Baxter, was the responsibility of Lee Kresel.

d/co-s/co-c/se Mario Bava *p* Massimo de Rita *co-s* Ennio de Concini, Marcello Coscia, Mario Serandrei *co-c* Ubaldo Terzano *lp* Barbara Steele, John Richardson, Ivo Garrani, Andrea Cecchi, Arturo Dominici, Enrico Olivieri, Clara Bindi, Antonio Pierfederici, Tino Bianchi, Germana Dominici

Il Mio Amico Jeckyll *aka* **My Friend Jeckyll** *aka* **My Pal Dr Jeckyll**
(CINEMATOGRAFICA MARINO GIROLAMI/CEI INCOM; IT) b/w 100min
In this Jekyll and Hyde comedy the ugly Professor Fabius (Vianello) transfers his personality into the body of Giacinto (Tognazzi), a teacher in a girls' school. Every time the transformation takes place, Tognazzi becomes a lecher trying to organize orgies with the girls. When his secret is discovered, Vianello agrees to transfer his personality into the body of a chimp at the zoo. As a crazy comedy using the props and settings of horror movies, it is a tolerably competent effort on a par with the British *Carry On* series. Girolami specialized in comedies and musicals but never excelled at any genre, and eventually turned to crude sexploitation movies.

d/p/co-s Marino Girolami *co-s* Giulio Scarnicci, Carlo Veo, Tarabusi *c* Luciano Trasatti *lp* Ugo Tognazzi, Raimondo Vianello, Abbe Lane, Carlo Croccolo

Il Mulino delle Donne di Pietra *aka* **Mill of the Stone Women** *aka* **Horror of the Stone Women** *aka* **The Horrible Mill Women** *aka* **Mill of the Stone Maidens** *aka* **Drops of Blood**
(VANGUARD FILM/FARO FILM/EXPLORER FILM/CEC; IT, FR) scope 95(63)min
This is an oddly international picture: a Franco-Italian co-production with a German villain (Preiss, soon to become identified with the role of Dr Mabuse in a number of German thrillers), set in Holland and based on a Flemish tale. After Mario Bava's **La Maschera del Demonio** (1960), Ferroni's film is the most notable successor to Riccardo Freda's **I Vampiri** (1956) of its year (although it also borrows liberally from silent German films and especially from Terence Fisher, to whom the film is dedicated).

The plot, taken from *Flemish Tales* by Peter Van Weigen, has an art student, Hans von Arnim (Brice), discover a windmill with a carillon and statues of women in strange poses. Professor Wahl (Preiss) uses the mill to drain women of the blood he needs to inject into his dying daughter (Gabel), transforming their corpses into the statues that have made the mill famous. The film contains genuinely nightmarish scenes as Preiss goes about his macabre task in hideously beautiful surroundings, littered with severed limbs, mutilated corpses and the bodies of petrified women.

Ferroni became better known as Calvin Jackson Padget, director of Italian westerns. *Il Mulino* is by far his best work, even foreshadowing in some ways Freda's masterpiece, **L'Orribile Segreto del Dr Hichcock** (1962). He later (briefly) returned to the genre with **La Notte dei Diavoli** (1972), an extended version of the Wurdalak story used in Bava's **I Tre Volti della Paura** (1963).

d/co-s Giorgio Ferroni *p* Gianpaolo Bigazzi, Lucien Vittet *co-s* Remigio del Grosso, Ugo Liberatore, Giorgio Stegani *c* Pierludovico Pavoni *lp* Pierre Brice, Wolfgang Preiss, Scilla Gabel, Dany Carrel, Liana Orfei, Marco Guglielmi, Herbert Boehme, Olga Solbelli

El Mundo de los Vampiros *aka* **World of the Vampires**
(CINEMATOGRAFICA ABSA; MEX) b/w 85min
This rather poor picture works on the assumption that vampires are particularly sensitive to soundwaves, an idea introduced in Federico Curiel's *Nostradamus y el Destructor de Monstruos* (1959). The film opens with the rising of the vampire, Sergio Sotubai (Murray), who glides through his cobweb-ridden castle and, in a subterranean vault, plays an organ with pipes made of human bones and skulls, while in the forest above a jeep is stopped by a cloud of smoke that turns into a horde of vampires. They tie one of the jeep's female occupants to a sacrificial altar while Murray intones the movie's plot over her body: he must avenge his family by destroying that of Professor Kolman (Baviera), who happens to have two attractive young nieces (Fournier and Bauman). The vampire's opponent is Rodolfo (Garces), an expert occultist, who uses the soundwaves' theory instead of crucifixes. The climactic scenes in Murray's castle where he is about to vampirize the heroine sees Garces destroy the attendant bloodsuckers by playing a special tune on Murray's organ but, since the canny Murray had protected himself with earplugs, Garces has to push him into a pit full of wooden stakes. Other unconventional motifs include the suggestion that the life of a vampire gradually turns people into hairy werewolf-like beings, courtesy of Elda Loza's makeup, indicating that in this fantasy both vampirism and lycanthropy are seen as the uninhibited acting-out of forbidden desires, and thus as somehow equivalent to each other.

The next serious Mexican vampire film was **La Invasión de los Vampiros** (1961), again starring Bauman, with Carlos Agosti as Count Frankenhausen.

d Alfonso Corona Blake *p* Abel Salazar *s* Paul Zenteno, Ramón Obon *c* Jack Draper *lp* Guillermo Murray, Mauricio Garces, Erna Martha Bauman, Silvia Fournier, José Baviera, Mari Carmen Vela, Wally Barron, Alicia Moreno, Carlos Nieto

Wolfgang Preiss surrounded by the petrified bodies he has created in the impressive Il Mulino delle Donne di Pietra.

Muñecos Infernales *aka* **The Curse of the Doll People** *aka* **Devil Doll Men**
(CINEMATOGRAFICA CALDERON; MEX) b/w 85(83)min
This routine, but well-directed, story features the acting out of a voodoo curse on a group of people who steal a Haitian doll. One after the other, the unsuspecting and irresponsible tourists, paying no attention to one of their female friends, Karina (Quintana), a specialist in occultism, are killed by demonic living dolls and a weird-looking zombie controlled by the evil voodoo priest Zandor (Bulnes). In the end, Bulnes is tracked to his basement lair where, frightened by Quintana's crucifix, he causes the predictable climactic conflagration. The little dolls stalking the corridors looking for their designated victims exude the required atmosphere of menace, although the script and the final appearance of a long-haired Bulnes

dressed in a black robe decorated with a gigantic white snake are disappointing.

Alazraki had made a significant impact with his début film, *Raices* (1953), but his career developed very unevenly veering from abjectly sentimental melodramas and Tin Tan farces to **Frankenstein, el Vampiro y Cia** (1961) and masked-wrestler epics, including *Santo contra los Zombies* and the melodramatic **Espiritismo** (both 1961).

d Benito Alazraki *p* Pedro A. Calderon, Guillermo Calderon *s* Alfredo Salazar *c* Enrique Wallace *lp* Elvira Quintana, Ramón Gay, Roberto G. Rivera, Quintin Bulnes, Alfonso Arnold, Jorge Mondragon, Xavier Loya, Nora Veryan, Luis Aragon

Obras Maestras del Terror *aka* **The Master of Horror** *aka* **Short Stories of Terror** *aka* **Masterworks of Terror** *aka* **Masterpieces of Horror**

(ARGENTINA SONO FILM; ARG) b/w 115(61)min

A year before Roger Corman's **Tales of Terror** (1961), the Argentinian Carreras brothers produced this collection of Poe stories which covers much the same territory. They include three fairly faithful adaptations of *The Facts in the Case of Mr Valdemar* (1843), *The Cask of Amontillado* (1846) and *The Tell Tale Heart* (1843). The framing story uses a bored French maid who, on a stormy night, reads Poe's tales. After the third tale she closes the book, goes into the kitchen, sees a mouse and faints.

The American release print – supervised by Jack H. Harris, and appearing in 1965 – removed *The Tell Tale Heart*, thereby reducing the film's running time quite drastically. Another Argentinian omnibus movie, **El Demonio en la Sangre** (1964) uses the *Heart* story again, but introduces significant modifications to the plot. Carreras was a well-known commercial director whose credits include *El Fantasma de la Opereta* (1955), a black-comedy version of **The Phantom of the Opera** (1925, 1943, 1962).

d Enrique Carreras *p* Nicolas Carreras *s* Luis Penafiel *c* Amerigo Hoss *lp* Narcisco Ibañez Menta, Carlos Estrada, Iñez Moreno, Narcisco Ibañez Serrador, Mercedes Carreras, Lilian Valmar

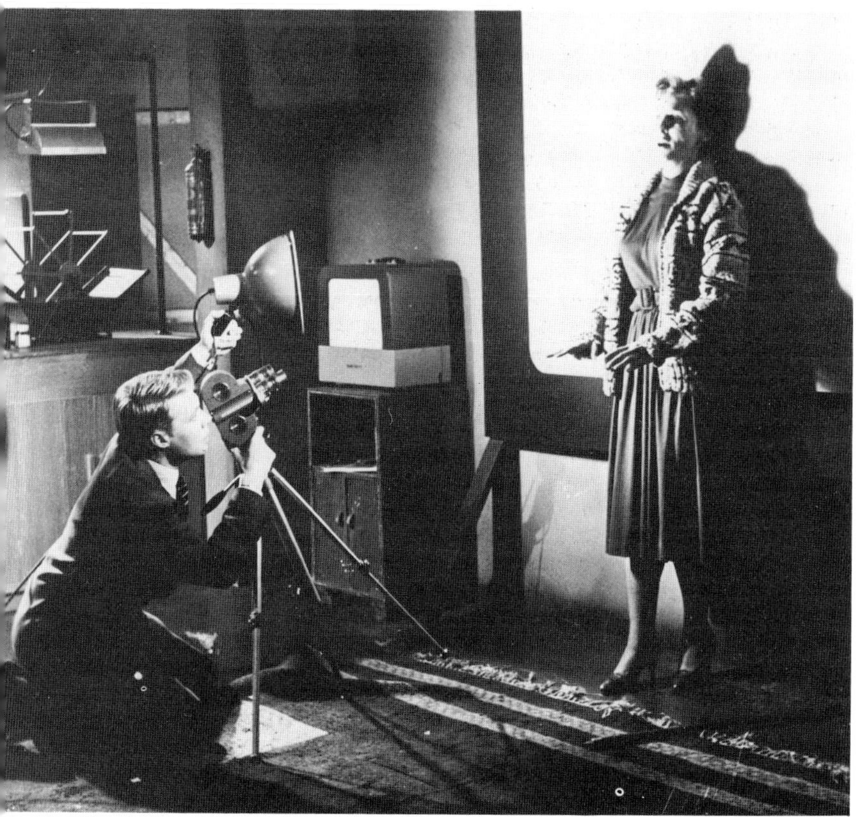

Carl Boehm, cameraman-voyeur and murderer in Michael Powell's Peeping Tom, *one of the best and most disturbing films to be made in Britain.*

Orlak, el Infierno de Frankenstein *aka* **Orlak the Hell of Frankenstein** *aka* **El Infierno de Frankenstein** *aka* **The Hell of Frankenstein**

(FILMADORA INDEPENDIENTE; MEX) b/w 103min

This is one of the relatively few Mexican versions of the Frankenstein legend, though the creature appeared many times in comedies (such as **El Castillo de los Monstruos** (1958) and **Frankenstein, el Vampiro y Cia**, 1961) or as a guest star in masked-wrestler movies such as **Santo contra la Hija de Frankenstein** (1971). At the turn of the century, Jaime (Cordero), convicted for body-snatching (and not for witchcraft, as in Hammer's more historically pertinent interpretations of the legend), while sharing a cell with Frankenstein (Soler) gains control of the Doctor's creature called Orlak (also played by Cordero) and supplies it with blood. Orlak, which the script tells us means invincible in ancient Dalmatian, has a metal skeleton powered by electricity and is remote-controlled and able to speak. Wearing a sombrero and a black cape, Orlak prowls the streets carrying out Jaime's revenge, killing those who convicted him as well as his former lover, a cabaret singer (de Castilla). Jaime and Orlak are both in love with Elvira (Dorantes) and the monster abducts her in a classic beauty-and-the-beast sequence before eventually turning against his master and rival.

Frankenstein's laboratory clearly shows the limitations imposed by the shoestring budget and whatever interest the picture has is probably due to Taboada and Ruanova's uncanny ability to fill their labyrinthine plots with invention and keep things going at breakneck speed, as in **La Maldición de Nostradamus** (1959) or **El Espejo de la Bruja** (1960). The picture was shot at America Studios, licensed only to produce shorts and newsreels, while feature-film production was reserved for a rival union based at the prestigious Churubusco-Azteca studios. Film-makers at America Studios – including ex-matinée idol Baledon – circumvented this restriction by shooting films in episodes which could then be combined and released as a feature. Made in four episodes and shot in less than three weeks, the film confirms Baledon's reputation as an extremely fast worker.

d/p Rafael Baledon *s* Alfredo Ruanova, Carlos Enrique Tobaoda *c* Fernando Alvarez Garces (Colin) *lp* Joaquin Cordero, Armando Calvo, Andres Soler, Rosa de Castilla, Irma Dorantes, Tedro de Aguillon, David Reynoso, Carlos Incira, Carlos Nieto, Antonio Raxel

Peeping Tom

(MICHAEL POWELL THEATRE; GB) 109(86)min

Released shortly before **Psycho** (1960), both movies provoked a torrent of abuse in the English press, partly, no doubt, because they are among the most complex and intelligent films ever made about the cinema and bring us face to face with the unspeakable but indispensable desires without which cinema would not exist. Powell's film is the most direct representation to date of the specifically scopophilic relationship that binds viewer and spectacle together in the cinema.

The film is structured around Mark Lewis (Boehm), a young voyeur-director-cameraman obsessed with filming the most intense emotion imaginable as it registers on the faces of desirable women. To this end, he devises a contraption that is the cinema's answer to the look of the mythical Gorgon or Medusa: a 16mm camera mounted on a tripod of which one leg is a spike which, extended horizontally, penetrates and transfixes his victims who witness their own death as it is reflected back at them in a parabolic mirror clipped on to the camera. The chinese-box structure allows us to watch the image of a film-maker filmically penetrating the object of his desire while he, and we, watch her looking at her own image, unsettlingly splitting the audience's identification process as we – and he – are both in the position of aggressor and victim, at both ends of the sado-masochistic spectrum. To prevent any avenue of escape or defence, Powell also introduces subjective camera techniques for his soft-porn images, and, later, when the police have discovered his victims, links Boehm's obsession with exactly the kind of images viewers seek in 'normal' cinema: scenes showing attractive women, action, emotion, investigations, drama – although each is somehow turned back upon the audience, the porn model is revealed to be scarred, for example. Powell surrounds this *mise-en-scène* of cinema-in-action with a history (Boehm's father, played by Powell himself, transmitting in the course of his experiments on the effects of fear on his young son an intense desire to observe things not usually seen) and a future, which is impossible or unacceptable: Boehm promises his innocent girlfriend (Massey) never to film her, which causes him to turn his lethal contraption on himself. The only weakness is in the script, which burdens the movie with the emphatic and superfluous symbolism represented by Massey's blind mother (Audley).

Peeping Tom remains one of the supreme achievements of the British cinema – and of cinema in general.

d/p Michael Powell *s* Leo Marks *c* Otto Heller *lp* Carl (Karlheinz) Boehm, Anna Massey, Maxine Audley, Moira Shearer, Esmond Knight, Shirley Anne Field, Jack Watson, Nigel Davenport, Miles Malleson, Michael Powell

Psycho (PAR) b/w 109min

In the early sixties, horror films began to make regular appearances on the box-office charts. People who had previously looked upon gothic horrors and Grand Guignol as beneath contempt flocked to see *Psycho* and **What Ever Happened to Baby Jane?** (1962). Looking back at the phenomenal success of *Psycho*, however, it seems evident that the film was something of a watershed. Where horror movies had normally either distanced their preoccupations by masking them in guises borrowed from fairytale and gothic fantasy, or presented them directly through a heightened realism, Hitchcock sought a more visceral effect. He achieved it, firstly, by making his heroine (Leigh) – the identification figure whom the audience confidently expects to win through to the end – fall victim to the mother-fixated killer (Perkins) at a disorientingly early stage of the plot; and secondly, by presenting the murder in graphic detail that seems to show everything (while in fact showing very little).

Although much more than the sum of its parts – the ultimate in old-dark-house movies, it leaves cosy notions as to the twin healing properties of psychoanalysis and mom's apple pie in some disarray – it was the gleeful relish of the murder which undoubtedly spawned the splatter movies. But few of Hitchcock's successors can match either his uncanny technical skill or the diabolically mocking wit that makes *Psycho* so irresistible (the analogy between Perkins and the stuffed birds; the agonizing pause before the tell-tale car finally sinks with a slurp; the derisive snook cocked at psychiatry by the crafty calculation of Perkins' final line, 'They'll see and they'll say, Why, she wouldn't even hurt a fly') and still quite capable of jangling the nerves after umpteen viewings.

Perkins reprised his role in the sequel, **Psycho II** (1983).

d/p Alfred Hitchcock *s* Joseph Stefano *c* John L. Russell *lp* Anthony Perkins, Janet Leigh, Vera Miles, John Gavin, Martin Balsam, John McIntyre

Der Raecher *aka* **The Avenger**

(KURT ULRICH FILM; WG) b/w 100min

This is a well-crafted psycho-thriller set in England, in which the killer, assisted by a gorilla-like servant, decapitates his victims and sends their heads through the mail. Michael Brixan (Drache) is brought in by Scotland Yard to solve the murders, which involves saving a film actress (van Bergen) on location in southern England from the madman. Except for the odd image vaguely evoking silent German 'shadow' films, this is a routine contribution to the informal series of German thrillers of the period set in the UK (**Die Toten Augen von London**, 1961; *Der Wuerger von Tower*, 1961 and so on). Kinski's cameo as a misanthropic film director is worthy of note.

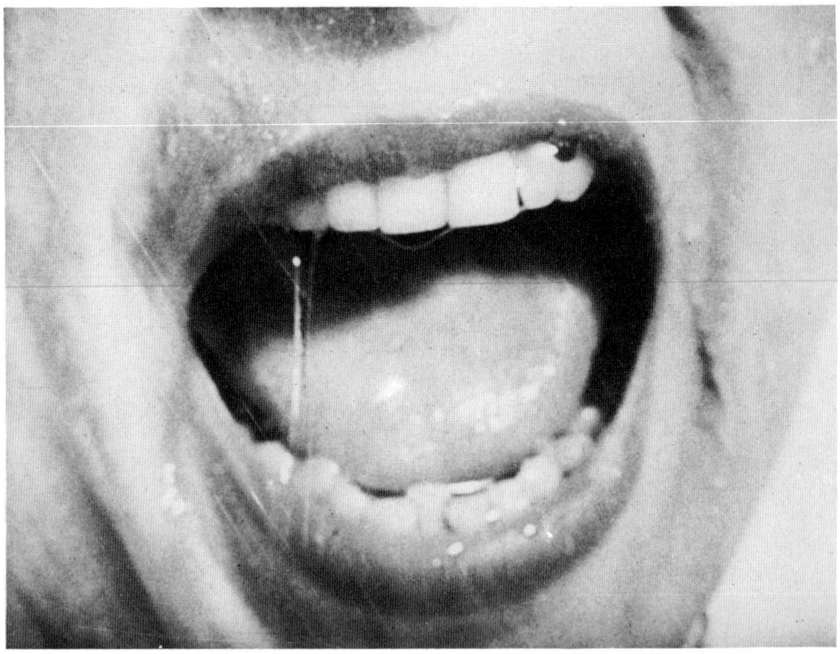

Psycho, *the most influential horror film of modern times.*

d Karl Anton *p* Kurt Ulrich *s* Dr G. Kampendonk, R. Cartier *c* Willi Sohm *lp* Heinz Drache, Ingrid van Bergen, Benno Sterzengbach, Ina Duscha, Ludwig Linkmann, Klaus Kinski

Seddok – l'Erede di Satana *aka* **Atom Age Vampire**

(LION'S FILM; IT) b/w 105(87)min

This is a poor imitation of Georges Franju's classic **Les Yeux Sans Visage** (1959) with elements of Poe's short story *The Murders in the Rue Morgue* thrown in for good measure. Lupo plays the doctor trying restore the face of Loret with materials taken from the bodies of living women. A side-effect of his formula is that the serum also causes hideous disfiguration after a while, which forces him to keep reinjecting his victims and allows the narrative to repeat its 'horror' moments a number of times. Moreover, by injecting himself, he can turn into a monster at will and pretend that his crimes were in fact committed by an escaped gorilla. Only the last scene gives an indication of what the film might have become if more intelligently handled: unable to prevent himself from turning into a monster, he helplessly moans 'I love you' as his beloved watches the transfiguration.

Majano was a competent director of radio and television plays, but his film work remains flat and conventional in spite of the odd redeeming scene. An export version of *Seddok* disguised Majano's name under the pseudonym of Richard McNamara and added a John Hart to the script credits.

d/co-s Anton Giulio Majano *p* Mario Bava *co-s* Pierre Monviso, Gino de Santis, Alberto Bevilacqua *c* Aldo Giordani *se* Ugo Amadoro, Euclide Santoli *lp* Alberto Lupo, Susanne Loret, Sergio Fantoni, Franca Parisi Strahl, Ivo Garrani, Andrea Scotti, Rina Franchetti

The Snake Woman *aka* **The Terror of the Snake Woman**

(CARALAN; GB) b/w 68min

An inept shocker from the team that was responsible for **Doctor Blood's Coffin** (1960), this film rehearses the motifs that John Gilling later used in the wonderfully weird **The Reptile** (1966). In the 1890s, the repeated injection of snake venom administered by Dr Adderson (Cazabon) to his wife, results in their daughter, Atheris (Travers), becoming a cobra. A Scotland Yard man (McCarthy) sent to investigate a spate of mysterious deaths by snakebite and the wild rumours of a snake-woman roaming the moors, clears up the puzzle when he notices that Travers responds to the sound of a snake-charmer's flute. He kills the cobra which promptly reassumes the shape of the unfortunate young woman. Travers, seen briefly as one of the victims in Michael Powell's **Peeping Tom** (1960), isn't even given the opportunity to try and convey the sensuality which Jacqueline Pearce so mesmerically achieves in Gilling's film. Amateurishly directed, the film fails in all departments.

d Sidney J. Furie *p* George Fowler *s* Orville Hampton *c* Stephen Dade *lp* John McCarthy, Susan Travers, Geoffrey Denton, Arnold Marle, Elsie Wagstaff, John Cazabon, Frances Bennett, Hugh Moxey

Das Spukschloss im Spessart *aka* The Haunted Castle *aka* The Spook Castle of Spessart

(GEORG WITT FILM; WG) 105min

A broad comedy set in a haunted castle, where the ghosts of a gang of thieves emerge to create comic mischief and help the lady of the manor, Countess Charlotte (Pulver), solve her financial problems. Hoffmann, the son of cameraman Carl Hoffmann, was a thoroughly undistinguished director who, as a fascist, got his break as a film-maker when self-respecting directors had left the country. He made several Spessart farces between 1958 and 1967. Because of some vapid songs and cabaret numbers, the movie was promoted as a 'grusical', best translated as a 'horrical'. Hailed at the time as a major success, its reputation for technical competence is mainly due to Anders' camerawork. As a ghost comedy, it never achieves the lightness of touch and amiable eccentricity of Pietrangeli's **Fantasmi a Roma** (1961).

d Kurt Hoffmann *p* Georg Witt *s* Guenther Neumann, Heinz Pauck *c* Guenther Anders *se* Theodor Nischwitz *lp* Liselotte Pulver, Heinz Baumann, Hubert von Meyerinck, Curt Bois, Elsa Wagner, Hans Clarin, Veronika Fritz, Ernst Waldow, Hanne Wieder

Susan Strasberg in Taste of Fear, *one of the first, and best, of Hammer's imitations of Alfred Hitchcock's* Psycho *(1960).*

Taste of Fear *aka* Scream of Fear

(HAMMER; GB) b/w 81min

After the success of **Psycho** (1960), Hammer launched a series of psycho-thrillers, starting with this contrived but excellently directed Holt movie, which also marks Sangster's production début. The script, as usual with Sangster, is a mechanical piece of suspense-mongering, which sacrifices logic and verisimilitude to achieve the mandatory number of shocks and 'twists' at the end. The movie opens with Strasberg's dead body being fished out of a lake, and then cuts to her, apparently alive in a wheelchair, in a villa on the French Riviera, where she is visiting her stepmother (Todd). She appears to see the dead body of her father a number of times, which makes her fear she is going insane. The chauffeur (Lewis) helps her look for the body and an attending doctor (Lee) acts in a suitably mysterious way. In the end, Lewis and Todd are revealed as the guilty couple who send Strasberg over a cliff in a runaway car, but find her back, alive, the next day when it emerges that she isn't the dead man's daughter but her lookalike friend come – assisted by the doctor – to find out what happened to her father.

Strasberg, daughter of the famous acting teacher, Lee Strasberg, acquits herself well, as do the rest of the cast, but the picture's main asset is Holt's canny direction which, skilfully assisted by Slocombe's photography, expertly builds up the mood of incipient insanity. Hammer's subsequent efforts in this vein – **Maniac** and **Paranoiac** (both 1962), **Nightmare** (1963), **Hysteria** (1964), **The Nanny** (1965) and **Crescendo** (1969) – were, in the main, disappointing. Narizzano's **Fanatic** (1964), together with Holt's opener, are easily the most captivating of the series.

d Seth Holt *p/s* Jimmy Sangster *c* Douglas Slocombe *lp* Susan Strasberg, Ann Todd, Christopher Lee, Leonard Sachs, Anne Blake, John Serrett, Fred Johnson

The Tell-Tale Heart *aka* Panic

(THE DANZIGERS; GB) b/w 78min

Directed with some flair by Morris – an otherwise routine director of thrillers – this film, together with *The Fall of the House of Usher* (1948), is one of the few British adaptations of Poe. Edgar (Payne), a shy loner with a limp, is encouraged by his philandering friend Carl (Walsh) to make contact with a pretty woman (Corri) who lives across the road. Hopelessly in love, Payne is shattered when he observes his girl and his best friend together. He murders Walsh and puts him under the floorboards, but is pursued by the dead man's heartbeat which eventually turns him into a crazed wreck, at which point he awakens, looks out of the window and sees a young woman moving into the house opposite. With the exception of the ending – which is cribbed from **Dead of Night** (1945) and repeated numerous times, including in **Corruption** (1967) – the sense of growing hysteria is well rendered as various apparently innocent objects such as a clock or a dripping tap echo and intensify the relentless heartbeat invading Payne's world.

d Ernest Morris *p* Edward J. Danziger, Harry Lee Danziger *s* Brian Clemens, Elden Howard *c* Jimmy Wilson *lp* Lawrence Payne, Adrienne Corri, Dermot Walsh, Selma Vaz Diaz, John Scott, John Martin, Annette Carell, Rosemary Rotheray, Suzanne Fuller, Yvonne Buckingham

The Terror of the Tongs *aka* Terror of the Hatchet Men

(HAMMER/MERLIN; GB) 79min

Following their successful exercise in cruelty and terror, **The Stranglers of Bombay** (1959), Hammer repeated the gimmick but changed the locale for this film to Hong Kong, where Chung King (Lee) is the grim leader of the Red Dragon Tong which runs foul of *Boys' Own* colonial hero, Captain Jackson (Toone). Although flatly directed by ex-actor Bushell, the film includes some bloodletting but the real violence is in Lee's performance and the way he asks the captive Jackson, 'Have you ever had your bones scraped?', for example. Maitland, who had played the chief villain in *Stranglers*, here reappears as

a mere beggar, making way for Lee whose commanding presence as an evil Chinese secured him the role of Fu Manchu in Don Sharp's **The Face of Fu Manchu** (1965) and in the series that followed. Kwouk later made his name as Peter Sellers' valet in the *Pink Panther* series.

d Anthony Bushell *p* Kenneth Hyman *s* Jimmy Sangster *c* Arthur Grant *lp* Geoffrey Toone, Christopher Lee, Yvonne Monlaur, Bert Kwouk, Marie Burke, Brian Worth, Barbara Brown, Marne Maitland, Milton Reid, Roger Delgado

Tormented (CHEVIOT) b/w 75min
The attempt at an *amour fou* theme makes this film more 'adult' than most of Gordon's epics but just as tacky. Carlson, a jazz pianist engaged to the wealthy Sanders, is initially pleased when his mistress (Reding) falls to her death from a lighthouse. Her corpse is never found, however, and haunts the faithless Carlson, who is driven to one murder and falls to his death from the same lighthouse while attempting a second. In death the two corpses are found intertwined. The result is a totally routine display of crawling hands, ghostly footprints, floating head and sinister superimpositions, although the first appearance of Reding's corpse – smothered in and then becoming seaweed – is quite effective.

d/co-p Bert I. Gordon *co-p* Joe Steinberg *s* George Worthing Yates *c* Ernest Laszlo *lp* Richard Carlson, Juli Reding, Lugene Sanders, Susan Gordon, Joe Turkel

The Two Faces of Dr Jekyll *aka* **House of Fright** *aka* **Jekyll's Inferno**
(HAMMER; GB) scope 88(80)min
Fisher here continues his exploration of the ambiguous attractions of 'evil', which he equates with indulgence of sexual desire unfettered by moral codes. He adapts a procedure reminiscent of his beautiful classic **Dracula** (1958): instead of presenting 'evil' in the shape of an unsightly monster, he gives it the shape of a smooth, urbane and seductive man-about-town. Massie plays both the bearded Jekyll and the clean-shaven, amoral charmer, Hyde, in one of the most intelligent adaptations of Stevenson's Victorian tale. In a powerful scene announcing a motif worked out with more complexity in **Frankenstein Must Be Destroyed** (1969), Hyde visits and rapes his own (Jekyll's) wife (Addams), driving her to suicide as a punishment for her flirtation with his best friend (Lee). Violated in the scarlet dressing-room of Hyde's dancer-lover (Marla), she kills herself as Marla wakes up in Jekyll's bed but in Hyde's arms; later Marla dies in Mrs Jekyll's nightgown to confirm that the women's personalities have been exchanged in parallel with the Jekyll/Hyde split. Lee, as Mrs Jekyll's lover, meets his death crushed by the snake which Hyde's mistress used in her strip-dancing act. In the end, the pitiful figure of an exhausted and aged Jekyll, drained of his drive to live (ie Hyde), is reduced to a sobbing wreck.

Massie's acting isn't as strong as it should be, but Lee, Marla and, especially, Kossoff as Jekyll's wise confidant provide excellent performances while Fisher's direction obviously delights in depicting the sins of the flesh – especially when their flavour can be heightened with a dash of moral horror (the American version was severely censored). Reed, seen here briefly in a strong-man act, starred in Fisher's next major exploration of the Jekyll/Hyde motif: **The Curse of the Werewolf** (1960).

d Terence Fisher *p* Michael Carreras, Anthony Nelson Keys *s* Wolf Mankowitz *c* Jack Asher *se* Les Bowie *lp* Paul Massie, Dawn Addams, Christopher Lee, Norma Marla, Joy Webster, David Kossoff, Francis de Wolff, Oliver Reed, Magda Miller

L'Ultima Preda del Vampiro *aka* **The Last Victim of the Vampire** *aka* **The Last Prey of the Vampire** *aka* **The Vampire's Last Victim** *aka* **Desires of the Vampire** *aka* **Daughters of the Vampire** *aka* **The Playgirls and the Vampire** *aka* **Curse of the Vampire**
(NORD FILM ITALIANA; IT) b/w 85(66)min
Following on from **L'Amante del Vampiro** (1960), Regnoli's tale of five showgirls and two male companions who take refuge in Count Kernassy's (Brandi) castle, improves on its predecessor mainly by featuring more undressed young women. The twist in the story is that Brandi plays a double role: the good Count Kernassy and his vampiric ancestor, which allows him to destroy himself while saving the heroine, Vera (Rocco). The film abounds with shots of (admittedly beautiful) naked women, with closeups of legs, calves, ankles, thighs, breasts and so on. As such it can be seen as a precursor of Rollin's sexy vampire movies. Although there are a few memorable scenes, such as the naked Giovannini, transformed into a vampire, facing her victim, most of the movie is carelessly photographed. The ending, with the vampire disintegrating as the sunlight streams through the suddenly opened curtains, is a poor imitation of Terence Fisher's **Dracula** (1958).

Regnoli was a film journalist for an ultra-Catholic paper before turning to a career as a scenarist (on Riccardo Freda's **I Vampiri**, 1956) and a routine director of adventure and sexploitation movies. One Italian production catalogue lists Aldo Greci as the cameraman.

d/s Piero Regnoli *p* Tiziano Longo *c* Ugo Brunelli *lp* Walter Brandi, Lyla Rocco, Maria Giovannini, Tilde Damiani, Corinne Fontaine, Erika di Centa, Marisa Quattrini, Alfredo Rizzo

Left: *Christopher Lee (right) in* The Terror of the Tongs.

The crawling hand from Bert I. Gordon's Tormented.

L'Ultima Preda del Vampiro, *Piero Regnoli's sexy follow-up to* L'Amante del Vampiro *(1960)*.

1961

El Barón del Terror *aka* **The Brainiac**
(CINEMATOGRAFICA ABSA; MEX) b/w 85(80)min
This film was shot a month before, and has the same narrative structure as, the same team's disappointing **La Cabeza Vivente** (1961). The action starts in 1661 with Baron Vitelius (Salazar) laughing at the Mexican inquisition's torturers and cursing their families while his helper, Miranda (Rojo), mysteriously escapes. Three centuries later, Reynaldo (Rojo again) and his lover Victoria (Gallardo), a descendant of one of the inquisitors, witness the appearance of a comet which falls to earth and turns into a hairy creature with a sinuous, forked tongue, pointy ears and arms that end in pincers: the dreaded Vitelius. The monster, who kills people by kissing them and then snaking his lizard-like tongue into their heads to slurp out their brains – keeping some of the sticky grey mess in an urn for occasional snacks – eventually gets round to eliminating the descendants of his torturers. This includes a scene in which he hypnotically compels a father (Robles) to watch him do his slurping on the man's daughter (Bellini), before he's finally destroyed by a flame thrower.

The perverse script is filmed rather primitively, but the mischievous enthusiasm with which the scenarist concocted the outrageous tale does communicate itself. Welter, Robles' victim in **El Vampiro** (1957) and its sequel, makes a cameo appearance as a prostitute who succumbs to the baron's tongue. It is worth noting that the brain eater is played by the producer, who reserved minor but heroic parts for himself in other pictures (**El Hombro y el Monstruo**, 1958, for example in which he plays the policeman who brings the narrative to a close).

Together with **El Espejo de la Bruja** (1960), this is Urueta's weirdest picture.

d Chano Urueta *p* Abel Salazar *s* Adolfo Torres Portillo, Federico Curiel *c* José Ortiz Ramos *se* Juan Muñoz Ravelo *lp* Abel Salazar, Ruben Rojo, Rosa Maria Gallardo, Germán Robles, Luis Aragon, Mauricio Garces, René Cardona, Ariadna Welter, Federico Curiel, Roxana Bellini

Bloodlust (CINEGRAF) b/w 68min
A wretched misuse of the Richard Connell story which inspired the marvellous **The Most Dangerous Game** (1932). Tricked out for the times, it has Leslie Bank's proud sadist, now known as Dr Balleau (Graff), as a dismal pervert pursuing teenagers whose bodies he stores in glass tanks.

d/p/s Ralph Brooke *c* Richard E. Cunha *lp* Wilton Graff, Lilyan Chauvin, Robert Reed, June Kenny, Joan Lora

La Cabeza Vivente *aka* **El Ojo de la Muerte** *aka* **The Living Head**
(CINEMATOGRAFICA ABSA; MEX) b/w 79(75)min
Continuing the example set by Rafael Portillo's **La Momia Azteca** (1957), this picture exploits Mexico's rich and bloody pre-conquest history. The film opens with the ritual beheading of chief Acatl (Garces) and the burial alive of priestess Xochiquetzal (Peluffo) and then shifts to the present day as Professor Mueller (Robles) and his team discover their tomb. The similarity with Egyptian mummy movies is extended as Robles removes the ring of death from the priestess and gives it to his daughter Marta (Peluffo again) who could be the dead woman's twin. He also takes Acatl's head with him in a box and later finds out that Marta's fiancé is the double of the Aztec chief (Garces again). The amazingly healthy and muscular-looking mummy of a priest (Cramer) supervises the revenge against the graverobbers. The story bears a remarkable resemblance to that of Seth Holt's **Blood from the Mummy's Tomb** (1971), but Urueta's direction remains predictable and flat. Mexican critics commented on the film's racist overtones, pointing to a tourist-board notion of Aztec culture, with the recourse to a European name for the professor, and the extreme naïvety the picture attributes to its audience.

A month earlier, the same team of film-makers had produced the weird **El Barón del Terror** (1961), but, with the exception of **El Espejo de la Bruja** (1960), Urueta's work remains undistinguished.

d Chano Urueta *p* Abel Salazar *s* Federico Curiel, Adolfo Torres Portillo *c* José Ortiz Ramos *se* Juan Muñoz Ravelo *lp* Ana Luisa Peluffo, Germán Robles, Mauricio Garces, Abel Salazar, Guillermo Cramer, Antonio Raxel, Eric del Castillo, Salvador Lozano, Alvaro Matute

Captain Clegg *aka* **Night Creatures** *aka* **Dr Syn**
(HAMMER/MAJOR; GB) 81min
The stars of Terence Fisher's **The Curse of the Werewolf** (1960) are reunited in this smugglers' story set in 18th-century England, with Reed and Romain as the romantic leads joined by Cushing as the ruthless pirate, Captain Clegg, who leads the villagers by night on their smuggling raids and serves as their innocuous vicar by day. The highlights of the movie are the appearance of ghostly, luminous night-riders haunting the misty swamps and causing enough fear for the smugglers to ply their trade relatively undisturbed, until Captain Collier (Allen) of the English army puts a stop to it all and unmasks Cushing. The result is the best movie in Scott's undistinguished career which included **The Headless Ghost** (1959), *Panic in Madame Tussaud's* (1948) and contributions to *The Avengers* teleseries.

MacGowran, one of Samuel Beckett's favourite actors and the lead in Roman Polanski's **Dance of the Vampires** (1967), has a brief cameo as a man frightened by the phantom creatures. The picture was released in 1962.

d Peter Graham Scott *p* John Temple-Smith *s* John Elder (Anthony Hinds), Barbara S. Harper *c* Arthur Grant *se* Les Bowie *lp* Peter Cushing, Oliver Reed, Yvonne Romain, Patrick Allen, Michael Ripper, Martin Benson, Derek Francis, Milton Reid, Jack MacGowran

Creature from the Haunted Sea
(FILMGROUP) b/w 63min
This is a horror-comedy in the same vein as **A Bucket of Blood** (1959) and **The Little Shop of Horrors** (1960), but not nearly so funny as either. Carbone plays a gangster who plans to help the loyalist cause after a revolution in a certain Caribbean island. As a cover for his shady plans, which involve getting rid of the crew of his boat, he invents a sea monster to take the blame. But a real sea monster (looking tacky enough to be the figment of his imagination) shows up and devours practically

the entire cast. Shot in Puerto Rico as an afterthought following the filming of *The Last Woman on Earth* and *Battle of Blood Island* (both 1960), its shows every sign of haste and the cast simply isn't up to it.

d/p Roger Corman *s* Charles B. Griffith *c* Jacques Marquette *lp* Anthony Carbone, Betsy Jones-Moreland, Edward Wain, Edmundo Rivera-Alvarez, Robert Bean

The Dead One (MARDI GRAS) scope 71min
This is an abominably acted, scripted and directed attempt to use the voodoo motif. Nudie-specialist Mahon starts his film with a tour of New Orleans' strip-joints where MacKay and his bride (Ormond), en route for the family plantation where they plan to honeymoon, pick up a bellydancer. A cousin (Davis), furious because the marriage means that she loses the plantation, summons voodoo powers to resuscitate her dead brother (Kelley) but the zombie kills Myrick in mistake for Ormond and then disintegrates in the sun while the police shoot the voodoo princess.

Before becoming one of the first sex-movie tycoons, Mahon was Errol Flynn's agent. As such he directed the star's last film – which Flynn also co-produced, scripted and narrated – *Cuban Rebel Girls* (1959) which also featured MacKay.

d/p/s Barry Mahon *c* Mark Dennes *lp* John MacKay, Linda Ormond, Monica Davis, Clyde Kelley, Darlene Myrick

Enchenme al Vampiro *aka* **Bring Me the Vampire**
(ESTUDIOS AMERICA; MEX) b/w 100min
This fairly innovative horror comedy on the old-dark-house theme was made in three episodes and has a group of people, all failures in their field of endeavour, summoned to Black Castle in the hope of inheriting a fortune. In the second episode, the plot gathers pace as the group learn that they are supposed to stay in the sinister castle for a month while murders, disappearing corpses and other grisly events constantly incite them to flee. At the end of the third episode, it appears that Carlos (Mantequilla), the disinherited brother of the lord of the manor, is the mad murderer who pretended to be a vampire to scare off his rivals.

The follow-up feature, also made in three episodes and released as *La Casa de los Espantos*, has the aspiring inheritors return, much against their will, to the castle because Mantequilla was unable to find the treasure. In the midst of further unnerving events with hooded spectres, animated skeletons, a disembodied talking head on a plate and spiritualist seances, the group find that some high-tension cables wrapped around the place prevent their escape. In the end, it emerges that nobody really died as everything had been staged by the resident intellectual in order to 'shock' the failures into acquiring some self-confidence. This having been accomplished, everybody leaves quite happily. All six episodes were released as two features in 1963.

Mario Bava's gothic peplum, Ercole al Centro della Terra.

The German-born Crevenna's Mexican début as director, *Adam, Eva y el Diablo* (1955) had also starred Soto (Mantequilla), but his later work, including a remake of Léontine Sagan's *Maedchen in Uniform* (1931) called *Muchachas de Uniforme* and Ibsen's *The Dolls' House, Casa de Muñecas* (1953), verged on melodramatic 'quality' cinema. His best work in the genre, a six-part serial released as two features, *Rostro Infernal* and *La Huella Macabra* (both 1962), was followed by more routine efforts, including *Las Bestias del Terror* (1972) and *La Dinastia de Dracula* (1978).

d Alfredo E. Crevenna *p/co-s* Mario Garcia Camberos *co-s* Alfredo Ruanova *c* Fernando Alvarez Garces (Colin) *lp* Fernando Soto (Mantequilla), Joaquin Garcia Vargas (Borolas), Alfonso 'Pompin' Iglesias, José Jasso, Roberto Cobo (Calambres), Maria Eugenia San Martin, Carlos Riquelme, Yerye Beirute, Hortensia Santoveña, Lulu Parga

Ercole al Centro della Terra *aka* **Hercules at the Centre of the Earth** *aka* **Hercules in the Centre of the Earth** *aka* **Hercules in the Haunted World** *aka* **Hercules vs the Vampires** *aka* **The Vampires vs Hercules** *aka* **With Hercules to the Centre of the Earth**
(SPA CINEMATOGRAFICA; IT) scope 91(73)min
Bava's gothic imagination and superb sense of colour transform this scrappily scripted offering into a nightmarish delight, with violent clashes of bright reds, blues and greens in eerie settings. The fairytale plot has Hercules (Park) retrieve the golden apple from the island of the Hesperides and a magic stone from Hades in order to cure the insane Deianira (Ruffo), held under the influence of the demonic Lico (Lee), the agent of Hell. The homosexual pleasure afforded by the spectacle of scantily clad musclemen takes second place to the glorious *mise-en-scène* of the horrors of hell and the mythic island of the Hesperides, which is shrouded in eternal night. The appearance of a monstrous Procrustes and the ghouls emerging from their dank, cave tombs to menace the hero are scenes worthy of Lovecraft.

This excellent picture is not to be confused with the interesting **Maciste contro il Vampiro** (1961), nor with Riccardo Freda's disappointing **Maciste all'Inferno** (1962), neither of which manages to transcend the handicaps presented by the musclemen, who must be seen being 'strong' – usually by throwing heavy weights around. One of the scenarists, Tessari, became one of the better directors of Italian westerns,

Left: *Linda Ormond under threat in the awful* The Dead One.

while Bava devoted most of his career to horror and sub-Hitchcockian thrillers such as *La Ragazza che Sapeva Troppo* (1962).

d/co-s/c/se Mario Bava *p* Achille Piazzi *co-s* Duccio Tessari, Alessandro Continenza, Franco Prosperi *lp* Reg Park, Christopher Lee, Leonora Ruffo, Giorgio Ardisson, Marisa Belli, Ida Galli, Ely Draco, Grazia Collodi, Franco Giacobini, Mino Doro

Espiritismo *aka* **Spiritism**
(CINEMATOGRAFICA CALDERON; MEX) b/w 90(85)min
This middle-class drama is notable mainly for revealing an abyss of spiritual poverty. A bourgeois household asks Satan to help out with the mortgage. Predictably, it is the wife (Veryan) who achieves contact with the devil and receives the necessary funds when her son dies in an accident and she can claim his life insurance. Although the son's lousy business sense and general irresponsibility were the cause of the family's penury, Veryan dutifully dies on hearing of his death and the father (Jimenez) goes insane. The story, told in flashback, is framed by scenes in which the distraught father tells the events to a priest. In the insecure middle-class world evoked, defaulting on the mortgage is a disaster of cosmic proportions, partly no doubt because being declassed in Mexico raises the spectre of shanty towns and backbreaking manual labour – the lot of most Mexicans. Alazraki went on to direct a silly comedy for the same producer, **Frankenstein, el Vampiro y Cia** (1961).

d Benito Alazraki *p/co-s* Guillermo Calderon *co-s* Rafael Garcia Travesi *c* Enrique Wallace *lp* José Luis Jimenez, Alicia Caro, Nora Veryan, Beatrice Aguirre, Carmelita Gonzalez, Antonio Bravo, Augusto Benedico, Jorge Mondragon, Maria Eugenia San Martin, René Cardona Jnr

Fantasmi a Roma *aka* **Ghosts in Rome** *aka* **Phantom Lovers**
(LUX FILMS/VIDES/GALATEA; IT) 100min
This pleasant, amiable ghost comedy set in an old dark house is far superior to the German box-office success **Das Spukschloss im Spessart** (1960) which uses the same motifs. When the aristocratic lord of the manor (Mastroianni) is blown up by his water heater, he joins his castle's ghosts to prevent the sale of his property to newly rich property developers. The film is professionally directed and the cast looks as if they are enjoying themselves while Rotunno, one of Visconti's regular cinematographers, provides the excellent photography and the beautifully timed movements of the white-, blue- and silver-tinted ghosts.

Pietrangeli, a minor figure in the sixties, had qualified as a doctor before becoming a critic for Italy's most prestigious film journal, *Bianco e Nero*. He excelled at light comedy and the Italian equivalent of 'women's pictures' – this film is a somewhat unusual item in his filmography. Co-scenarist Scola later became a leading Italian comedy director and achieved international recognition with *Una Giornata Particolare* (1977).

d/co-s Antonio Pietrangeli *p* Franco Cristaldi *co-s* Ennio Flaiano, Sergio Amidei, Ettore Scola, Ruggero Maccuri *c* Giuseppe Rotunno *lp* Marcello Mastroianni, Vittorio Gassman, Belinda Lee, Sandro Milo (Alexandra Marini), Eduardo de Filippo, Tino Buazzelli, Claudio Gora, Franca Marzi, Ida Galli, Lilla Brignone

Jean Arless threatens Eugenie Leontovich in William Castle's Homicidal.

Frankenstein, el Vampiro y Cia
(CINEMATOGRAFICA CALDERON; MEX) b/w 80min
Like **El Castillo de los Monstrous** (1957), *La Nave de los Monstruos* (1959) and *Locura de Terror* (1960), this movie, released in 1962, is an Abbott and Costello type farce starring 'Loco' Valdes. Valdes and Jasso deliver wax replicas of Frankenstein's creature and of a vampire (Bulnes) to a typical horror castle, but the cargo comes alive. The most credible of the incidents has Bulnes try to persuade a female doctor (Veryan) to put Valdes's brain into the Frankenstein creature's body and then send the creature to conquer the United States. The wolfman also makes an appearance.

Alazraki's reputation is largely based on his neorealist *Raices* (1953), a melodrama in the style of Vittorio de Sica, but in the light of the director's subsequent work, claims that the excellence of *Raices* was due primarily to the brilliant cameraman Walter Reuther and to the innovative producer Manuel Barbachano, seem well justified. Alazraki's **Muñecos Infernales** (1960) boasted few effective scenes, but neither this picture nor **Espiritismo** (1960) nor *Santo contra los Zombies* (1961) betrays any real talent.

d Benito Alazraki *p* Guillermo Calderon *s* Alfredo Salazar *c* Enrique Wallace *lp* Manuel Loco Valdes, José Jasso, Joaquin Garcia Vargas (Borolas), Martha Elena Cervantes, Nora Veryan, Roberto G. Rivera, Quintin Bulnes, Jorge Mondragon, Antonio Bravo

Homicidal
(WILLIAM CASTLE PRODUCTIONS) b/w 87min
Marking time after **The Tingler** (1959), Castle decorated *Thirteen Ghosts* (1960), a mildly macabre fantasy thriller set in a haunted house, with a gimmick called 'Illusion-O': audiences were issued with tinted glasses known as 'ghost viewers' with one red eyepiece through which the ghosts could be seen and a blue one through which they could not. Having made a start with a walk-on appearance in *Thirteen Ghosts*, with this film he further aped Alfred Hitchcock by making a clumsy personal appearance in a prologue to introduce what purports to be based on a real-life Scandinavian murder case but looks suspiciously like a reworking of **Psycho** (1960).

The film starts intriguingly enough as a young blonde called Emily (Arless) pays a startled bellboy (Rust) to become her husband for a day. Subsequently stabbing the justice of the peace who married her under the name of Miriam, she heads for a gloomy mansion owned by Warren, a mysterious young man who lives as something of a recluse following a childhood tyrannized by his now-dead father, and startles Warren's half-sister Miriam (Breslin) by announcing that she and Warren are married. Warren's old nurse (Leontovich), now paralysed and speechless, is clearly terrified of Emily; and when Miriam's fiancée (Corbett) uncovers evidence linking Emily to the JP's death, the horrified Miriam confides in Warren while her fiancé goes for the police. At which point, with Leontovich decapitated before she can reveal the truth, Emily – surprise, surprise, unless you've seen *Psycho* – pulls off her wig to reveal that she is Warren. It works well enough as a coarse shocker, but the garbled explanation of how Emily was brought up as a boy and had to get rid of Miriam to safeguard his/her inheritance, is a good deal less than persuasive, as is Arless's performance (she is particularly ludicrous in drag). In place of the *Psycho* ruling that no one would be allowed in after the film had begun, Castle introduced a 'fright break' two minutes before the end of the film: a pause during which anyone too frightened to stay could leave and have the price of admission refunded.

d/p William Castle *s* Robb White *c* Burnett Guffey
lp Glenn Corbett, Patricia Breslin, Jean Arless, Eugenie Leontovich, Richard Rust

House of Mystery

(INDEPENDENT ARTISTS; GB) b/w 56min
This is Sewell's fifth and final version of the plot with which he had made his directorial début – in *The Medium* (1934) – and, after the uneven **Ghost Ship** (1952), here he goes back to the more appropriate haunted-house setting. An enigmatic old woman tells a young couple (Hines and Wilde) inquiring about a house that the previous occupants (Newman and Kaufmann) had been plagued by eerie happenings including lights going on and off and the ghostly image of a man appearing in the living-room and on the TV screen. They had summoned a medium (Gordon) and a psychic investigator (Urquhart) who, in a nicely underplayed and rather ambiguous seance, found that the evil vibrations animating the house's living-room stemmed from the grisly events that had occurred before their purchase: an insane electrical engineer (Dyneley) – who even used his cat for experimental purposes – had wired up the living-room so that his wife and her lover (Hylton and Merivale) would be electrocuted if they touched anything. As the old woman finishes her narrative, she fades away, leaving the young couple standing in the middle of the lethal living-room. Sewell handles the complex flashback structure with considerable skill, and there is no padding to divert attention from the gradual intensification of the suspense up to the unnerving ending.

Sewell's subsequent work (**The Blood Beast Terror**, 1967; **The Curse of the Crimson Altar**, 1968) was both more ambitious and less successful, although both films extended the thematic motif of neurotic but still sane men being driven over the edge by perverse, insatiable women.

The picture's title is, to say the least, unoriginal, having been used before for entirely different stories, in 1934, 1938 and 1939. A French play *L'Angoisse*, by Pierre Mills and C. Vylars, was cited as the film's source.

d/s Vernon Sewell *p* Julian Wintle, Leslie Parkyn *c* Ernest Steward *lp* Jane Hylton, Peter Dyneley, Nanette Newman, Maurice Kaufmann, Colin Gordon, Molly Urquhart, John Merivale, Ronald Hines, Colette Wilde

The Innocents *aka* Suspense

(FOX/ACHILLES; GB) b/w scope 99min
A highly praised, somewhat academic rendering of Henry James' classic *The Turn of the Screw* (1898), a literary *tour de force* which leaves the status of the narrated events completely undecidable. Since a film must work with actual images and cannot leave it open whether something is seen or not, the sensed presence of the passionate Quint (Wyngarde) and Miss Jessel (Jessop), whose influence after death on two children, Miles (Stephens) and Flora (Franklin), provides the central enigma, is transformed into ghostly apparitions hallucinated by the repressed spinster-governess, Miss Giddens (Kerr). The film thus presents the very psychological narrative which James' writing painstakingly invalidated and avoided.

Deborah Kerr and Martin Stephens in Jack Clayton's somewhat academic version of Henry James' The Turn of the Screw, The Innocents.

The script tends towards a study in the psychopathology of bigotry, as Kerr's repressed sexual urges invade and transmogrify the world she inhabits. Although she has the best of intentions, she ends up terrorizing the children, convinced they are guilty of the delusions she imposed upon them. Some of the sequences seem heavily influenced by the successful Hammer movies, especially the nocturnal storm and the appearances of Wyngarde on a tower, surrounded by bats, and behind a window.

The luscious cinematography of Francis (soon to become a prolific director of competently shot but mostly routine horror movies, including **Vengeance** and **Paranoiac**, both 1962) is enhanced by Georges Auric's characteristically atmospheric score. Kerr's performance is remarkable and largely rescues the movie from Clayton's rather heavy-handed approach. A penchant for images that are ever so pregnant with meaning ruined many of his films (eg *Our Mother's House*, 1967 and *The Pumpkin Eater*, 1964) and characterizes his work as archetypal English 'art cinema'. That said, compared to Michael Winner's remake of the story, **The Nightcomers** (1971), Clayton's version is a model of sensitivity and taste.

d/p Jack Clayton *s* William Archibald, Truman Capote, John Mortimer *c* Freddie Francis *lp* Deborah Kerr, Martin Stephens, Pamela Franklin, Megs Jenkins, Michael Redgrave, Peter Wyngarde, Clythie Jessop, Isla Cameron, Eric Woodburn

La Invasión de los Vampiros *aka* La Invasión de los Muertos *aka* The Invasion of the Vampires

(INTERNACIONAL SONO FILMS/TELE TALIA FILMS; MEX)
b/w 100(78)min
Mexico's first serious vampire picture since *El Mundo de los Vampiros* (1960) is as confused as its predecessor, freely mixing Teutonic and Castillian elements with an idiosyncratic use of vampire conventions as it pits occultist Dr Albaran (del Rio) against Count Frankenhausen (Agosti) and his daughter Brunilda (Bauman). To Bauman's astonishment, the Count is soon revealed to be a vampire and the doctor uses acid distilled from black garlic to combat the Count, who changes into a bat before being pinned against the wall with a stake. But then all the Count's former victims come alive and, led by the Count's ex-wife, Frau Hildegarde (Moss), besiege the village. The doctor again uses his black garlic potion to inject the vampires and liberate the village before going off with his prize, Bauman.

Transgressing all the genre's conventions, the vampires who come alive on their master's demise wander about with stakes still firmly implanted in their hearts, providing a ludicrous climax to the mixed-up script.

Director Morayta was one of a number of Spanish *émigrés* working in Mexico from the early forties onwards. The group included Jaime Salvador, José Diaz Morales and Luis Buñuel. With the exception of Buñuel, all were thoroughly average film-makers.

The US release version of *Invasion* was prepared as usual by K. Gordon Murray's distribution outfit. The next Frankenhausen picture was Morayta's *El Vampiro Sangriento* (1962), shot simultaneously with Alfonso Corona Blake's *Santo vs las Mujeres Vampiro* (1962).

d/s Miguel Morayta *p* Rafael Perez Grovas *c* Raúl Martinez Solares *lp* Erna Martha Bauman, Rafael del Rio, Carlos Agosti, Tito Junco, Fernando Soto (Mantequilla), Berta Moss, David Reynoso, Enrique Garcia Alvarez

Maciste contro il Vampiro *aka* Goliath and the Vampires *aka* The Vampires *aka* Goliath and the Island of Vampires *aka* Maciste against the Vampires *aka* Maciste vs the Vampire

(AMBROSIANA CINEMATOGRAFICA; IT) scope 92min

Although less hallucinatory than Mario Bava's **Ercole al Centro della Terra** (1961), this Gentilhomo-Corbucci collaboration makes up in violence what it lacks in style. The story revolves around the confrontation between Maciste (Scott), called Goliath in English-language versions, and Kobrak (Celano), a translucent-black-robed vampire who controls an army of faceless robots. Maciste's helper is Kurtik (Sernas), the pretty leader of the subterranean Blue Men, his girlfriend is again played by Ruffo and Canale is predatory female. The ending has the vampire assume the shape of Scott, thus making the final duet a confrontation between Scott and himself. Some of the violent scenes – such as the impaling of a slave on a bed of spikes – are well done, and the army of faceless robots battling with Blue Men on the banks of a river makes a picturesque sequence.

co-d/co-s Sergio Corbucci *co-d* Giacomo Gentilhomo *p* Paolo Moffa *co-s* Duccio Tessari *c* Alvaro Mancori *lp* Gordon Scott, Gianna Maria Canale, Leonora Ruffo, Annabella Incontrera, Guido Celano, Jacques Sernas, Rocco Vitolazzi, Mario Feliciani

The banalities of The Mask.

La Maldición de la Llorona *aka* La Casa Embrujuda *aka* The Curse of the Crying Woman

(CINEMATOGRAFICA ABSA; MEX) b/w 80(74)min

This film attempts to incorporate the specifically Mexican ghost of the wailing mother, la Llorona, into the classic gothic conventions of the horror story. The pre-credit sequence sets the tone. A zoom singles out a suitably anguished Llorona (Bustamante), watching a carriage pass through a nocturnal forest: one of the passengers is telling of the horrible murders that occurred in the area when a fierce-looking man, played by the archvillain specialist Moctezuma, jumps on to the coach, stabs the driver and kills the passengers, driving over the inanimate body of a woman (Julissa) to the accompaniment of Bustamente's wailing.

The rest of the picture chronicles the adventures of Salazar and Arenas as they fall prey to the vampiric Macedo – who is set on resuscitating Bustamente, now a mummified corpse in a dank crypt – and her husband (Lucero), a disfigured homicidal maniac. The adventures include torture, ghostly apparitions, hypnotic domination and many deaths before the couple escape and Macedo is murdered by Lucero.

The most impressive part of the film is a flashback in negative, recalling Murnau's **Nosferatu** (1921), to fill in la Llorona's history. This switch to negative, however, also betrays the fundamental incompatibility of the anglo-saxon gothic and Mexican *mater dolorosa* – exemplified by **La Llorona** (1933), *La Herencia de la Llorona* (1946), *El Grito de la Muerte* (1958), for example – traditions. Arenas's performance as the victim, a role she repeated in the three Aztec mummy films and in **El Espejo de la Bruja** (1960), is competent.

d Rafael Baledon *p* Abel Salazar *s* Fernando Galiana *c* José Ortiz Ramos *se* Juan Muñoz Ravelo *lp* Rosita Arenas, Abel Salazar, Rita Macedo, Carlos Lopez Moctezuma, Enrique Lucero, Mario Sevilla, Julissa de Llano, Roy Fletcher, Arturo Corona, Victorio Blanco

The Man in the Back Seat

(INDEPENDENT ARTISTS; GB) b/w 57min

This is a well-crafted thriller about a pair of petty criminals, Frank (Faulkner) and Tony (Nesbitt), who find themselves saddled with the unconscious, dying bookie they robbed. Tension is built up somewhat mechanically as they try – and fail – to get rid of him until finally the weaker and increasingly nervous Faulkner, hallucinating that their victim's body is sitting bolt upright behind them in the car, causes them to crash, killing Nesbitt and enabling the police to arrest a totally crazed Faulkner. Sewell, who excelled at ghost stories such as *Latin Quarter* (1945), starts the picture as an average thriller and gradually pushes it over the edge into the realm of the psychotic. The rear-view mirror scenes which concretize the body's menacing presence are particularly skilfully handled and provide a model for similar scenes in Don Sharp's **Witchcraft** (1964), in which a witch materializes in the back seat of cars. Wintle and Parkyn also financed Sewell's best film, **House of Mystery** (1961).

d Vernon Sewell *p* Julian Wintle, Leslie Parkyn *s* Malcolm Hulke, Eric Paice *c* Reginald Wyver *lp* Derren Nesbitt, Keith Faulkner, Carol White, Harry Locke

The Mask *aka* The Eyes of Hell

(ROFFMAN-TAYLOR; CAN) b/w and col 95(80)min

Ancient so-called primitive objects exerting a hypnotic fascination and able to dislocate established systems of belief are a recurrent fantasy motif, as shown by **The Skull** (1965) and in numerous mummy films. However, here the mask is simply wheeled on in order to precipitate a succession of arbitrary murders of women. Donning the mask produces a series of hallucinatory visions which are supposed to reveal 'the key to evil in men's minds' and to trigger uncontrollably homicidal behaviour – 3-D effects in about 15 minutes of colour footage signify the hallucinations. But these, although credited to the

great Vorkapich, a montage expert and experimental film-maker, are totally predictable, with flashes of flame supposedly shooting over the audience's heads alternating with cuts to mouldering corpses in the tradition of amusement park ghost trains. Some exhibitors gave viewers a mask to put on whenever a character in the fiction did so, no doubt realizing that viewers needed extra incentives to keep watching.

d/p Julian Roffman *s* Frank Taubes, Sandy Haber *c* Herbert S. Alpert *se* Slavko Vorkapich, Herman S. Townley, James B. Gordon *lp* Paul Stevens, Claudette Nevins, Bill Walker, Anne Collings, Martin Lavutt, Leo Leyden, Eleanor Beecroft, William Bryden, Stephen Appleby, Nancy Island

Mr Sardonicus

(WILLIAM CASTLE PRODUCTIONS) b/w 89min

This is one of Castle's brighter films, though it borrows shamelessly from **The Man Who Laughs** (1928), probably because it's far better scripted than his usual efforts. Rolfe is the 19th-century central European aristocrat whose face is permanently set in a hideous grimace – like the clown Gwynplaine in Paul Leni's film – from the shock of seeing the skeleton of his father move while Rolfe was excavating the grave in search of a valuable lottery ticket. Having failed to find a cure in the experiments conducted by his servant (Homolka, having great fun in the basement torture chamber liberally applying leeches to a wench's face), Rolfe blackmails a distinguished English surgeon (Lewis) into taking his case by threatening to mutilate Dalton, once the doctor's sweetheart but now in his clutches. Lewis succeeds in reducing the grin to normality by shock treatment, only for the frenzied Rolfe to realize that now his mouth won't open at all at which point, having already introduced the film à la Hitchcock, Castle brought in his gimmick: a pause for a 'punishment poll' in which the audience is asked to choose between alternative endings according to whether they feel Sardonicus has suffered enough or not. After which Sardonicus is invariably left to starve to death by a gleeful Homolka.

d/p William Castle *s* Ray Russell *c* Burnett Guffey *lp* Oscar Homolka, Ronald Lewis, Audrey Dalton, Guy Rolfe, Vladimir Sokoloff, Erika Peters

The Naked Witch *aka* The Naked Temptress

(MISHKIN) 80(60)min

Between 1963 and 1973 Milligan made 23 films and along with Herschell Gordon Lewis, Al Adamson and Ted V. Mikels rates as one of the more prolific and consistent directors at the Z level of gore exploitation. His output includes at least 11 horror films and 12 sexploitation efforts, all made on budgets which even Lewis would have found cramping. Often thought of (and written of) as English, on account of the fact that several of his films were made and set in Britain and featured actors with English accents, Milligan is in fact a resident of Staten Island and made most of his films there before buying an Off-Broadway theatre. His English period pieces reflect an interest in costumes and, in fact, he worked in the garment industry before buying his first 16mm camera and making his first movie.

His films, if not exactly immediately recognizable, do exhibit certain common traits: the period settings, for example, a 'homemade' feel in terms of costumes and other production values, often grainy 16mm blow-up photography and elements of camp humour. Contrary to popular belief, Milligan's films are not all graphically gory, and certainly nowhere near the Lewis level of hyperbole. *The Naked Witch* was his first horror film, and made for veteran New York exploitation distributor Mishkin. Shot in around eight or nine days in Mannesquan, New Jersey for $7500 and released in 1964, the film concerns a witch executed in the 19th century who comes back to life when a student removes the stake through her heart. He then falls under her spell. In 1967 the film was re-released with an extra 20 minutes added.

d/c Andy Milligan *p* William Mishkin *s* Clay Guss *lp* Beth Porter, Robert Burgos, Lee Forbes

Night of the Eagle *aka* Burn, Witch, Burn

(INDEPENDENT ARTISTS; GB) b/w 87min

Hayers' only watchable movie is a well-crafted occultism story in the tradition of Jacques Tourneur's **Night of the Demon** (1957). A sceptical psychology professor, Norman (Wyngarde) becomes involved, largely through his wife, Tansy (Blair), in a harrowing series of events which culminate in a scene in the crypt of a remote cemetery where he is forced to reclaim his wife from the powers of darkness with magic incantations in a powerful scene worthy of Terence Fisher's **The Devil Rides Out** (1967). The forces of evil have been unleashed by a jealous faculty wife, Flora (Johnston), and they eventually attack the professor directly, in the shape of a giant stone eagle come to life, which swoops down on him in his lecture hall. Johnston gets her just deserts as the statue crashes down on her as she leaves the school.

Based on Fritz Leiber's book, *Conjure Wife*, the movie's three scenarists provide a flawed but effectively constructed plot allowing Hayers to concentrate on visual effects achieved through judicious framing and camera movement. The gradual accumulation of harbingers of doom – from the aftermath of a bridge party when Blair discovers a witch doll strapped to a chair, to the eerie churchyard sequence and the attack of a possessed Blair on her husband – is particularly impressive.

Left: *Guy Rolfe (right) as* Mr Sardonicus.

The Pit and the Pendulum *and Vincent Price.*

Ray Milland and Hazel Court in Premature Burial.

None of Hayers' other pictures before or after this one confirmed the talent shown here, which suggests that the particular chemistry at work in this collaboration with Matheson, Beaumont and Leiber could be responsible for the film's undoubted quality. In addition, the expertise of executive producers, Julian Wintle and Leslie Parkyn, who also oversaw Vernon Sewell's best work that same year, may have worked as the necessary congenial catalyst for the collaborative venture.

d Sidney Hayers *p* Albert Fennell *s* Charles Beaumont, Richard Matheson, George Baxt *c* Reginald Wyver
lp Peter Wyngarde, Janet Blair, Margaret Johnston, Anthony Nicholls, Colin Gordon, Kathleen Byron, Reginald Beckwith, Norman Bird, Judith Scott

Night Tide (VIRGO) b/w 95(84)min
Harrington's first feature, this features Hopper as a lonely sailor on leave in Little Venice. At the amusement pier he meets a young Greek girl (Lawson) who earns her living posing as a mermaid in a tank, and despite warnings of mysterious drownings associated with her, falls in love. One night, believing herself to be a siren who must return to the sea people, she has to be rescued by Hopper from drowning. Subsequently attempting to drown him, she swims out to sea and disappears, whereupon he finds her dead body on display in the tank.

Clearly inspired by **Cat People** (1942), following Val Lewton's principles by having a vividly realistic setting (the tawdry pier and funfairs) and providing a rational explanation for most of the mystery (the girl's adoptive father planted the siren story in her mind), it is both clumsy and tentative and strikingly atmospheric. More of a fantasy than a horror movie perhaps, the film does make darkly minatory use of its dream sequences (the mermaid nightmarishly metamorphozing into an octopus) and the recurrent motif of the mysterious woman in black whose appearances frighten the girl.

d/s Curtis Harrington *p* Aram Kantarian *c* Vilis Lapenieks, Floyd Crosby *lp* Dennis Hopper, Linda Lawson, Gavin Muir, Luana Anders, Marjorie Eaton

The Pit and the Pendulum
(ALTA VISTA/AIP) scope 85(80)min
Conceived and executed in very much the same style as **House of Usher** (1960) by precisely the same team, this is marginally less successful. A much freer rendition of Poe, it again has a visitor (Kerr) arriving at a gloomy castle (in Spain), this time to inquire about his sister (Steele), and again finding Price (his brother-in-law) in a state of agitation: his wife, it transpires, died in the castle torture chamber (which had fascinated her ever since she learned that Price had seen his father entomb his mother alive there after killing her lover). Now, haunted by the sound of his wife's voice in his room, Price fears that she too was entombed alive.

The trouble with the film is that although the plot is coherent enough, it doesn't quite cohere. Where *House of Usher* sustained its mood evenly as the ineluctable machinery of doom worked itself out, *The Pit and the Pendulum* not only has more action, it has to incorporate a somewhat disruptive subplot whereby Steele turns out to be merely faking death in a plot concocted with her lover (Carbone) to drive her husband mad. On the other hand, the sexual motif is again beautifully worked out through the confusion of guilts as Price, already identifying his wife as his mother, begins to turn into his father. If Price's performance is noticeably more extravagant than in the earlier film, this is offset (or matched) by the markedly greater fluidity of camera movement. *House of Usher* seemed a little unsure of how to cope with the rush of action as Madeline returned from the grave; *The Pit and the Pendulum* has no such hesitations. From the great sequence in which Steele lures Price down into the crypt to the finale (Steele sealed into an iron maiden, the pendulum in motion, Price tumbling into the pit), its action is terrific.

d/p Roger Corman *s* Richard Matheson *c* Floyd Crosby
lp Vincent Price, Barbara Steele, John Kerr, Luana Anders, Anthony Carbone

Premature Burial (SANTA CLARA/AIP) pv 81min
This is the third and weakest film in Corman's Poe cycle. Imagination plays happily with the idea of Vincent Price, as the man driven by a terror of premature burial, proudly showing off the efficiency of the do-it-yourself coffin-kit he has thoughtfully provided to ensure every conceivable escape route should the worst happen. Milland simply does not have the necessary flamboyance (or the vulnerability) Price would have brought to the role. As though aware of this, Corman relies too heavily on the gloomy graveyards, gothic mansions, swirling ground-fogs, bats, candelabra and opulent spiderwebs that had been elaborated in **House of Usher** (1960) and **The Pit and the Pendulum** (1961). The best sequence in the film is Milland's hallucinatory vision of being buried alive, which starts with the screen going dark and the soundtrack registering only the pounding of his heartbeat. The rest, over-indulging in shock cuts as Milland is buried alive while in a cataleptic trance and takes berserk revenge when secretly exhumed in the interests of scientific experiment, is superior routine.

d/p Roger Corman *s* Charles Beaumont, Ray Russell
c Floyd Crosby *lp* Ray Milland, Hazel Court, Richard Ney, Heather Angel, Alan Napier, John Dierkes, Dick Miller

The Shadow of the Cat (BHP; GB) b/w 79min
As a sustained stylistic exercise, this is one of Gilling's best pictures. It tells of a black cat, the only witness to the killing of its mistress (Lacey) by her husband (Morell) and two servants (Jackson and Crawford). The cat, a vengeful presence reminding the murderers of their heinous act, is presented as a relentless force persecuting and eventually provoking the death of the villains as well as of the three venal relatives they summon to help get rid of the animal (Warner, Lucas and Godsell). The happy ending sees the only survivor, the old woman's favourite niece (Shelley), inherit all the money – but her friend (Phillips), a local journalist, is ready to share her legacy. If the story is totally predictable, Gilling adeptly uses his camera to suggest the cat's active persecutory role, even resorting to subjective shots from the animal's point-of-view and changing the shape of the image to convey the cat's slant-eyed vision.

1961

After **The Flesh and the Fiends** (1959), Gilling was hired by Hammer, where he did his best work (**The Reptile**, 1966). Although the production credits give BHP as the company responsible for this film, it is a Hammer movie shot at Bray Studios with excellent art direction by Bernard Robinson and moody photography by Grant. The picture also boasts a good score by Mikis Theodorakis in his pre-*Zorba the Greek* (1964) days. The vengeful-cat motif was used again in Rich's **Eye of the Cat** (1969) and in Tyburn's first horror movie, **Persecution** (1973) providing further variations on Poe's story filmed as **The Black Cat** in the United States (1934, 1941) and as one of the stories in the German omnibus film **Unheimliche Geschichten** (1919, 1932).

d John Gilling *p* Jon Pennington *s* George Baxt *c* Arthur Grant *lp* William Lucas, Barbara Shelley, Andre Morell, Conrad Phillips, Alan Wheatley, Vanda Godsell, Richard Warner, Freda Jackson, Andrew Crawford, Catherine Lacey

Tales of Terror (ALTA VISTA/AIP) scope 90min

Corman's fourth Poe film, this is a portmanteau of three stories with Price starring in each and partnered by Lorre in the second and Rathbone in the third. The first, *Morella*, is in many ways perfection, and echoes the incest motif of **House of Usher** (1960) in its tale of a young woman (Pierce), embittered and dying, who returns home (having been banished when her mother died giving birth) to find her father (Price) a lonely alcoholic brooding over the mummified body of his wife. Done with great delicacy as the triangular web of love and hatred conjures the dead woman's vengeful spirit (Gage), it's only fault is that the prowling camera, swirling mists and final conflagration confer a certain sense of *déjà vu*.

The Black Cat, incorporating Poe's story *The Cask of Amontillado*, essays a vein of sardonic humour that would be explored more fully in **The Raven** (1963). The episode has many superb moments, not least the wine-tasting with Lorre getting increasingly drunk, his hallucination of the cat eating his head, and the maniacally funny rage with which he proceeds to exact revenge on his faithless wife (Jameson) and friend (Price), with the black cat of course walled up with them. *The Facts of the Case of M. Valdeman* is cruder, but has fine performances from Price as the dying old man and Rathbone as the scheming mesmerist who persuades him to undergo hypnotism as he dies. It also has a wonderfully ghoulish denouement with Rathbone dying of fright in the clutches of the horribly liquefying Price.

d/p Roger Corman *s* Richard Matheson *c* Floyd Crosby *lp* Vincent Price, Peter Lorre, Basil Rathbone, Debra Paget, Joyce Jameson, Maggie Pierce, Leona Gage

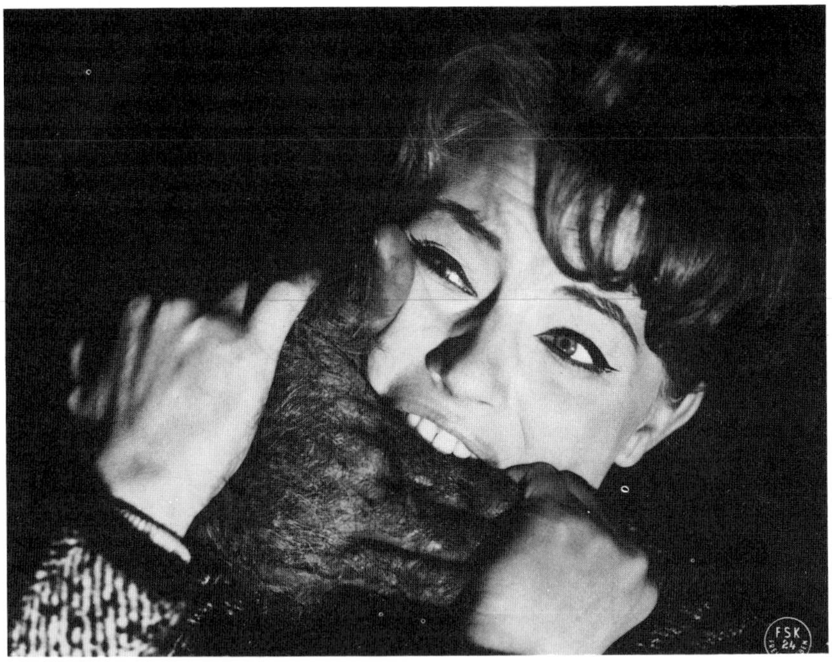

Karin Baal in distress in Die Toten Augen von London.

Terror in the Haunted House *aka* My World Dies Screaming (OMECC) b/w 84(76)min

A verbose slice of cut-price psychology devoted to the well-worn theme of the husband who tries to drive his wife mad. Or so it seems when, after a subjective camera prologue in which heroine O'Donnell talks to a psychiatrist about her recurring nightmare involving an old mansion, she is whisked off as a newlywed to what proves to be that self-same house by her husband (Mohr). But despite his heavily suspicious behaviour, Mohr is not responsible for the terrors that greet her, including the death of caretaker Qualen; he is merely trying to shock her out of a childhood trauma when she saw his family being axed to death in the attic. The shock of being forced into the attic by her loving husband does indeed bring her memory back, just as the film essays its own pathetic shock by producing another insane axe-murderer (Ching).

The sole interest of the film is that, actually shot in 1958, it employed a process grandly called Psychorama: the horror was supposedly enhanced by words or images subliminally superimposed on the screen. Subliminal techniques, as used by advertisers to 'persuade' cinemagoers to buy their products, were banned in 1961.

d Harold Daniels *p* William S. Edwards *s* Robert C. Dennis *c* Frederick E. West *lp* Gerald Mohr, Cathy O'Donnell, William Ching, John Qualen, Barry Bernard

Die Toten Augen von London *aka* Geheimnisse von London *aka* The Dark Eyes of London *aka* The Dead Eyes of London

(RIALTO FILM; WG) b/w 104(95)min

Edgar Wallace's *The Testament of Gordon Stuart* had been filmed before as **Dark Eyes of London** (1939) with Bela Lugosi as the mad director of an institution for the blind who uses the residents as medical guinea pigs. The evil Reverend Dearborn (Borsche) here uses his victims to assassinate London's lonely millionaires. The murders, committed by zombie-like creatures and shown in explicit (for the period) detail, are solved by Fuchsberger, the hero of a number of German Wallace adaptations. The picture features a menacing performance by the theatre-trained Berlin actor Kinski, later to achieve fame in the films of Werner Herzog, including **Nosferatu: Phantom der Nacht** (1979). The imposing hulk of Berber gives added weight to the lethal human automaton and, as in *Arzt ohne Gewissen* (1959), Baal continues to frequent the lunatic fringe of the medical profession. Vohrer continued to churn out sensational thrillers in Germany's Wallace series

Left: *Andre Morell (right) with Andrew Crawford and corpse in the imaginative* The Shadow of the Cat.

throughout the sixties, including *Die Tuer mit den Sieben Schloessern* (1961), *Der Moench mit der Peitsche* (1967), and *Der Hund von Blackwood Castle* (1968).

d Alfred Vohrer *p* Herbert Sennewald *c* Karl Loeb *lp* Joachim Fuchsberger, Karin Baal (Blauermel), Dieter Borsche, Klaus Kinski, Ady Berber, Wolfgang Lukschy

What a Carve-Up! *aka* **No Place like Homicide**
(NEW WORLD; GB) b/w 88min
One of the first and best British horror spoofs (a subgenre which also includes **Carry On Screaming** and **The Wrong Box**, both 1966), *What a Carve-Up!* is loosely based on Frank King and Leonard Hines' story *The Ghoul*, which was filmed 'straight' in 1933. Ernie Broughton (Connor), a proofreader of horror stories, and Syd (James) become involved in an old-dark-house adventure which decimates the Broughton family. All the horror-thriller clichés are passed in revue: the sinister visitor (Pleasance), a mad family living in a place called Blackshaw Towers on the Yorkshire Moors, a club-footed butler (Gough), a masked killer and plenty of thunderstorms and fog. With the exception of the brief guest appearance of Adam Faith, Jackson – a veteran from the British documentary school – skilfully keeps the movie finely balanced between crazy comedy and horror with witty camera angles and judicious cutting. This is arguably the Baker and Berman team's best film after **The Blood of the Vampire** (1958) and **The Flesh and the Fiends** (1959).

d Pat Jackson *co-p/c* Monty Berman *co-p* Robert S. Baker *s* Ray Cooney, Tony Hilton *lp* Kenneth Connor, Sidney James, Shirley Eaton, Donald Pleasance, Esma Cannon, Dennis Price, Michael Gough, Michael Gwynn, Valerie Taylor, George Woodbridge

Ye Bang Ge Sheng *aka* **Midnightmare**
(SHAW BROTHERS; HONG KONG) 97min
Clearly based on **The Phantom of the Opera** (1925, 1943), this film was made at the time when Shaw was developing its aesthetic of artifice, the creation of a mythological world using lush studio sets and costumes. The story tells of a warlord's daughter, Li, who falls in love with Song, a revolutionary actor in Republican China. Song is arrested but on his release, his face is badly scarred in an acid attack by an angry official. Unable to act and reluctant to see his lover again, Song secludes himself in the disused wing of an old theatre and spreads the news that he has died. People believe him to be a ghost, but years later he is befriended by a young actor whom he helps and uses as a messenger to contact Li again. Song finally avenges himself on the official who maimed him but he is drowned during the struggle.

Glynis Johns in Roger Kay's ridiculous adaptation of Robert Weine's classic 1919 film, The Cabinet of Dr Caligari.

The film is notable for the appearance of Le Di, an actress of considerable promise who achieved stardom in 1959 with *Enchanting Shadows* and went on to some top productions including *The Love Eterne* (1963) and King Hu's first feature, *Sons of the Good Earth* (1965). She founded the Gold Eagle Film Company with her brother Lei Zhan and director Yuan Quifeng. They made a number of martial arts films which proved to be unsuccessful and the company failed. Le Di committed suicide in 1968 at the age of 31.

d/s Yuan Quifeng *p* Run Run Shaw *lp* Le Di (Betty Loh Tih), Zhou Lai, Fang Li, Zhang Chong

1962

The Cabinet of Caligari
(LIPPERT/FOX) scope b/w 105(103)min
Not so much a remake of Robert Wiene's **Das Cabinet des Dr Caligari** (1919) as 'suggested' by it, with Bloch's script churning out indigestible chunks of his inimitable dime-store psychology. When her car breaks down on a lonely road, Johns is put up for the night by Dr Caligari (O'Herlihy), the suave, sinister owner of a large house nearby. Preparing to bid Caligari a grateful farewell as she leaves the next morning but shocked by the suggestive postcards he shows her, she finds herself drugged and held prisoner. Nightmarish experiences follow as she is spied on by Caligari in her bath, almost stabs a handsome man she thinks is the voyeur, witnesses a brutal murder, is terrorized by a huge dog, and on the advice of the handsome man, accuses Caligari of impotence while flaunting her naked body before him. Under the influence of cumulative shocks, she eventually realizes that the handsome man *is* Caligari, that she is suffering from sexual repression, and that she is under treatment in a mental home.

Bloch's first screenplay, after providing the source material for **Psycho** (1960), comes complete with distorted sets, much higher lunacy, and a striking performance from O'Herlihy. The result is perversely fascinating.

d/p Roger Kay *s* Robert Bloch *c* John Russell *lp* Dan O'Herlihy, Glynis Johns, Estelle Winwood, Vicki Trickett, J. Pat O'Malley

Carnival of Souls (HARCOURT) b/w 80(75)min
Hilligoss is drowned in an accident during a drag-race but reappears and drives off to a new job as church organist in a small Utah town. There, haunted by strange hallucinations involving a man with a dead face (Harvey), feeling cut off from the world and thought crazy by the people she meets, she feels drawn to a derelict amusement park where the man of her hallucination escorts her into a dance of the dead in the ballroom. Meanwhile, police back at the scene of the accident find her corpse. Insufferably portentous, the script harks back to those expressionistic dramas which solemnly debated this life and the next with heavy-breathing dialogue ('You cannot live in isolation from the human race, you know'). Yet Harvey's direction has a weird flair, sometimes suggesting a throwback to the silent days and drawing a kind of awkward honesty out of the amateurish actors. The film is a real curiosity with strikingly used locations, in particular the derelict amusement park isolated among mudflats, its machinery rusting and its vast ballroom still hung with dusty streamers.

d/p Herk Harvey *s* John Clifford *c* Maurice Prather *lp* Candace Hilligoss, Frances Fiest, Sidney Berger, Art Ellison, Herk Harvey

Gritos en la Noche *aka* **The Awful Dr Orloff** *aka* **Cries in the Night**
(HISPAMER; SP) b/w 88(80)min
The initiator of an entire subgenre mixing horror and medical science fiction motifs in a gory way which borders on the pornographic, *Gritos en la Noche* builds on the traditions of fifties Mexican horror and science fiction films and codifies

those traditions into a generic formula. Based on the novel by David Kuhne (one of Franco's many pseudonyms), the film tells the story of Dr Orloff (Vernon) who compulsively drains young women of blood and attempts to graft their skin on to his daughter's disfigured face (echoing **Les Yeux Sans Visage**, 1959). He is aided by a lecherous blind hunchback, Morpho (Valle), who matches his master's sadism and also disposes of the bodies. The film lingers on the naked bodies as Vernon uses his scalpel on them and as Morpho explores their figures as they lie chained in the doctor's dungeon laboratory.

In essence a sick combination of Jack the Ripper set at the turn of the century, with Vernon stalking the foggy backstreets in search of victims, and Terence Fisher's Hammer films of the late fifties, the film's mixture of eroticism and sadistic surgery seemed to strike a chord with its audiences. The peculiarly Hispanic subgenre, dominated by the visually surreal, excessively visceral, but often lazily filmed, works of Franco, flourished for more than a decade and includes such films as **El Secreto del Dr Orloff** (1964) and **Besame Monstruo** (1967).

d/s Jesús Franco *p* Serge Newman, Leo Lax *c* Godofredo Pacheco *lp* Howard Vernon, Conrado San Martin, Perla Cristal, Diana Lorys, Riccardo Valle, Maria Silva, Mara Laso, Felix Dafauce, Faustino Comejo

Hands of a Stranger (AA) b/w 86(73)min

In this worthy but dull, uncredited adaptation of Maurice Renard's novel *Les Mains d'Orlac*, Stapleton is the pianist whose hands are mutilated in an accident and Lukather the surgeon who grafts on the hands of a murdered man. Unlike Peter Lorre's much more entertaining Dr Gogol in **Mad Love** (1935), Lukather is no mad villain. Cast as the romantic interest, he falls for the pianist's sister (Harvey) while the pianist is left to his own psychological devices. Rather unconvincingly going mad because his new hands refuse to obey his desultory attempts to play the piano, he promptly resolves to kill everyone connected with the operation. Sally Kellerman has a small part (her second) as a nurse.

d/co-p/s Newton Arnold *co-p* Michael du Pont *c* Henry Cronjager *lp* Paul Lukather, Joan Harvey, James Stapleton. Irish McCalla, Ted Otis, Michael du Pont

Kiss of the Vampire *aka* **Kiss of Evil**

(HAMMER; GB) 88min

In between **Dracula** (1958) and **Dracula, Prince of Darkness** (1965), while Lee refused to play the Count, Hammer continued their vampire series without Dracula. **The Brides of Dracula** (1960) and this, Sharp's first major movie, were the uneven results. Set in turn-of-the-century Bavaria, the script has Ravna (Willman), a local lord, gather his disciples to his castle for vampiric orgies. His opponent, introduced in a pre-credit sequence which shows him ferociously staking his own daughter (Black), is the dour, black-clothed Professor Zimmer (Evans), the representative of an austere and ruthless puritanism that is merely the other side of the vampiric coin. Although shot within Hammer's by now established stylistic conventions, Sharp achieves some remarkable scenes as the newly married Marianne (Daniel) is drawn into Willman's circle during a bizarre party full of figures in bird masks reminiscent of Georges Franju's *Judex* (1963). The ending, in which hordes of bats attack the vampire's white-robed disciples trapped in a magic circle, evokes Hitchcock's *The Birds* (1963), although both *Judex* and *The Birds* were shot after Sharp's film but released before it. Only a veiled reference to *The Lady Vanishes* (1938), as the very existence of the disappeared Marianne is denied by scared villagers, suggests these similarities were not accidental and point to the common interests of the film-makers involved. Indeed, when the film was screened on American television, this patchwork effect was further strengthened by the inclusion of shots taken from **The Evil of Frankenstein** (1964) and extra scenes featuring Carl Esmond.

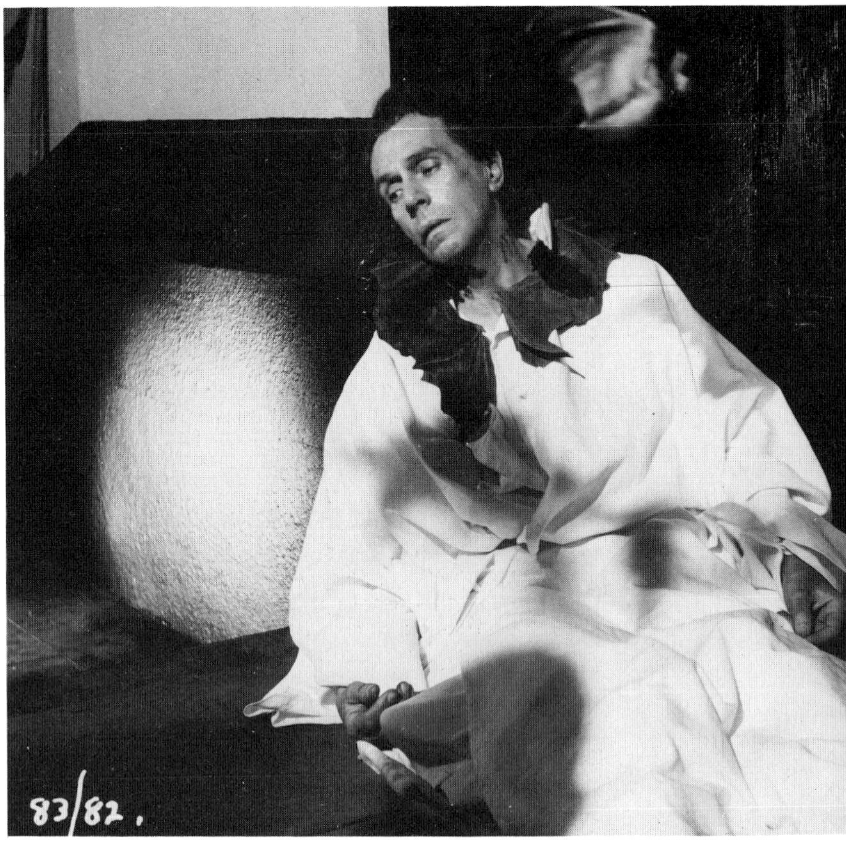

Noel Willman, the master vampire of Kiss of the Vampire, *meets his end.*

Sharp's ability to use his settings, including a beautifully photographed Bavarian wood, the sinister castle and a deserted inn, demonstrates his talent for *mise-en-scène*, the hallmark of his subsequent films, including **Rasputin – The Mad Monk** and **The Face of Fu Manchu** (both 1965).

d Don Sharp *p* Anthony Hinds *s* John Elder (Anthony Hinds) *c* Alan Hume *se* Les Bowie *lp* Clifford Evans, Noel Willman, Jennifer Daniel, Edward de Souza, Barry Warren, Isobel Black, Peter Madden, Vera Cook, Margaret Read, Elisabeth Valentine, Olga Dickie

Lycanthropus *aka* **Werewolf in a Girl's Dormitory** *aka* **I Married a Werewolf** *aka* **Bei Vollmond Mord** *aka* **Monster among the Girls** *aka* **The Ghoul in School** *aka* **Ghoul in a Girl's Dormitory**

(ROYAL FILM; IT, AUSTRIA) b/w 83(81)min

This professionally made, decently acted but incompetently scripted movie, has Lowens as the werewolf director of a women's reform school and O'Connor as the mistress who blackmails and murders to protect his guilty secret. The script awkwardly tries to divert suspicion on to a newly arrived teacher (Schell), formerly a doctor who killed a patient suspected of lycanthropy. The gothic ambience of the isolated mansion and its grounds are adequately rendered and, except for the dialogue, the film is passable. The American version inserted a sequence in which Marilyn Stewart and Frank Owens sing a rock and roll number entitled 'The Ghoul in School'.

Heusch started his career as a director with a creditable science fiction effort, *La Morte Viene dallo Spazio* (1959), but his greatest achievement is the film version of Pasolini's novel about down-and-outs in Rome, *Una Vita Violenta* (1962).

d Richard Benson (Paolo Heusch) *p* Jack Forrest (Guido Giambartolomei) *s* Julian Berry (Ernesto Gastaldi) *c* George Patrick *lp* Barbara Lass, Carl Schell, Curt Lowens, Maurice Marsac, Maureen O'Connor, Mary McNeeran, Grace Neame, Alan Collins (Luciano Pigozzi), Anni Steinert, Joseph Mercer

Maciste all'Inferno *aka* **Maciste in Hell** *aka* **The Witch's Curse**
(PANDA FILM/INDUSTRIA CINEMATOGRAFICA ITALIANA; IT) scope 90(78)min
One of Freda's most disappointing films, this opens with an obvious but poorly executed imitation of the first scenes of Mario Bava's **La Maschera del Demonio** (1960). Freda chronicles the adventures of Maciste (Morris) as he goes to the underworld to find the witch (Chanel) in order to remove a curse from her descendant (Silenti). The picture is spoiled by bad cutting, worse special effects and a ludicrous setting: a 'Scotland' with pine trees, a terraced city and houses with whitewashed walls. Morris's acting is limited to hurling boulders and, to reach the minimum running time, scenes from Maciste's previous adventures are inserted. The film's only point of interest is strictly anecdotal: the prestigious English film journalist and promoter of things Italian, John Francis Lane, appears briefly as a coachman.

Some sources suggest this was a remake of Brignone's *Maciste all'Inferno* (1927), but the two films share nothing but their title. Although Freda had made peplums before (*I Giganti della Tessaglia* and *Maciste alla Corte del Gran Khan*, for example), this cheapie appears to have been made with so little thought that it borders on dishonesty, especially since this was no fallow period for Freda's talent: **L'Orrible Segreto del Dr Hichcock**, his masterpiece, was made in the same year, 1962.

d Riccardo Freda *p* Luigi Carpentieri, Ermanno Donati *s* Oreste Biancoli, Piero Pierotti, Ennio de Concini, Eddy H. Given (Ermanno Donati) *c* Riccardo Pallotini *se* Serge Urbisaglia *lp* Kirk Morris, Helene Chanel, Vira Silenti, Andrea Bosic, Angelo Zanolli, John Karlson

Maniac (HAMMER; GB) b/w 86min
This is the second of Hammer's horror-thrillers made in the wake of **Psycho** (1960) – the first was **Taste of Fear** (1960). The typical Sangster script, a mechanical structure with the traditional surprise ending as just one more arbitrary device to close the narrative when a respectable running time has been reached, tells of an American painter, Geoff (Mathews), who becomes involved with the perfidious Eve (Gray) whose husband has been imprisoned for murdering with an oxy-acetylene torch the man who raped their daughter (Brousse). After numerous familiar twists including a corpse that keeps turning up, mistaken identity, a seemingly haunted shed and grossly planted red herrings suggesting the mad torchman has returned, the culprit turns out to be Gray's accomplice and lover (Houston) trying to build a new life for the adulterous couple. The French Camargue setting is virtually wasted, and suspense is reduced to a few sensationalist images of a blowtorch approaching the hero's face. Carreras' best film is the arresting *The Lost Continent* (1968).

Maniac was released in 1963 on a double bill with Joseph Losey's magnificent *The Damned* (1961) which Columbia delayed releasing for some two years.

d Michael Carreras *p/s* Jimmy Sangster *c* Wilkie Cooper *lp* Kerwin Mathews, Nadia Gray, Donald Houston, Liliane Brousse, Norman Bird, George Pastell, Jerold Wells, Arnold Diamond

Barbara Steele in Riccardo Freda's hymn to necrophilia, L'Orribile Segreto del Dr Hichcock.

L'Orribile Segreto del Dr Hichcock *aka* **The Terrible Secret of Dr Hichcock** *aka* **The Horrible Dr Hichcock** *aka* **The Terror of Dr Hichcock** *aka* **Raptus**
(PANDA FILM; IT) scope 88(76)min
Freda's hymn to necrophilia, *L'Orribile Segreto del Dr Hichcock* is also his gothic masterpiece, a macabre poem as perverse, powerful and fascinating in form as Poe's best work. In a gloomy English mansion in 1885, Dr Hichcock (Flemyng) injects his wife, Margareta (Vianello), with an overdose of anaesthetic to make her simulate death during a sex game. Having buried her, he returns years later with a new wife, Cynthia (Steele), only to find the withered body of an insane Vianello, who was buried alive, returning to reclaim her lover. Steele gets caught in the *amour fou* which links the doctor and his first wife: he even attempts to drain her blood in order to restore Vianello's youth. As indicated by the title, the film abounds with references to the great Alfred: *Suspicion*'s poisoned glass of milk, *Jamaica Inn*'s skull in the bed and *Rebecca*'s fascinating portrait. But its morbid oneirism, deployed with a perfect control of colour, rhythm and atmosphere, brilliantly integrates such play with fragments of film history into its compelling fantasy texture. In addition, the reference to Hitchcock is not simply playful: Alfred's 'horrible' secret – his uncanny knack for constructing a cinema that traces the contours of the desire for sexual looking that underpins cinephilia – also animates Freda's fantasy.

The visual motif that carries the narrative – the controlling and investigating look at the female body with all the anxieties that it generates – is enhanced by Freda's inspired orchestration of light, which not only delights in gazing at the image but imprints the disturbing pleasures of looking on the very surface – the skin – of the movie, which functions as a beautiful deathmask. It is this figure of beauty as the sublimated appearance of death which is so vividly captured by Steele's screen image: the face stretched around the contours of her skull, the eyes and mouth that both invite and mockingly defy the desire to go beyond, to exhaust desire in transgressing its acceptable limits. The face of Steele (which is probably how Norman Bates remembers his mother in **Psycho**, 1960) explains why her mere presence suffices to trigger the perverse but fundamental and pleasurable fantasies that form the raw material of the horror genre itself and why her image, more than any other, is the emblem and fetish of the genre.

d Robert Hampton (Riccardo Freda) *p* Louis Mann (Luigi Carpentieri, Ermanno Donati) *s* Julyan Berry (Ernesto Gastaldi) *c* Donald Green (Raffaele Masciocchi) *lp* Robert Flemyng, Barbara Steele, Teresa Fitzgerald (Maria Teresa Vianello), Montgomery Glenn (Silvano Tranquili), Harriet White, Spencer Williams

Paranoiac (HAMMER; GB) b/w 80min
This is the third and most representative of Hammer's horror-thrillers that began with Seth Holt's interesting **Taste of Fear** (1960), and was followed by Michael Carreras' tame **Maniac** (1962). The plot has Eleanor (Scott) believe she's going mad because she glimpses her brother, Tony (Davion), presumed dead. When Davion materializes, she believes she's going even

crazier because she falls in love with her own brother, until he confesses to being an impostor trying to unmask a mad murderer, who turns out to be her real brother, Simon (Reed), aided by Aunt Harriet (Burrell). The actors perform fairly credibly on the basis of an impossible script which merely passes the time with red herrings until the usual 'twists' at the end provide ample excuse for shock cuts and general hysteria. Francis's direction is professional, relying heavily on Grant's expert camerawork and Elisabeth Lutyens' effective score. The film was released in 1963 and followed by the slightly less crudely shocking **Nightmare** (1963) and the lacklustre **Hysteria** (1964).

d Freddie Francis *p* Anthony Hinds *s* Jimmy Sangster *c* Arthur Grant *se* Les Bowie, Kit West *lp* Janette Scott, Oliver Reed, Alexander Davion, Sheila Burrell, Liliane Brousse, Maurice Denham, Colin Tapley

The Phantom of the Opera

(HAMMER; GB) scope 84min

Fisher's most romantic movie is closer to Gaston Leroux's original story than either of the previous film versions (1925, 1943). The obligatory shock elements are largely delegated to the phantom's misshapen servant (Wilson), which puts the story's emphasis on the tragic love of the composer/phantom (Lom) for the opera singer Christine (Sears, dubbed by Pat Clark for the singing). The movie's climax is neither the famous chandelier scene nor the unmasking but the image of the lonely phantom watching the triumphant performance of Sears as Joan of Arc, silently crying as he is overcome with emotion, an effect heightened by Edwin Astley's dramatic score.

Hammer's most expensive production at the time it was made, the film was designed as a major first-run release, rather than as part of a double bill. In spite of some nods to the traditional Hammer audience (a stabbing in the eye, a hanged man bursting through the stage curtain, the phantom's underground lair), the film failed at the box office, apparently because the phantom was portrayed too sympathetically. Except for the jarring performance of Gough as the malicious impresario who steals Lom's opera and also causes his disfigurement, the movie is an intense love story, acted with great sensitivity by Lom and Sears, and brilliantly filmed by Fisher. It is ironic that one of his best movies should have been the reason for his temporary fall from grace.

d Terence Fisher *p* Anthony Hinds *s* John Elder (Anthony Hinds) *c* Arthur Grant *se* Les Bowie *lp* Herbert Lom, Michael Gough, Heather Sears, Edward de Souza, Thorley Walters, Michael Ripper, Miriam Karlin, Miles Malleson, Marne Maitland, Renee Houston, Ian Wilson

Tower of London (ADMIRAL PICTURES) b/w 79min

Less interesting thematically than Rowland V. Lee's **Tower of London** (1939), since the removal of the club-footed executioner as a parallel to Richard Crookback also removes the preoccupation with elective as opposed to predetermined villainies, this film is, however, equally enjoyable. Corman aims less at Grand Guignol and more at Poe-inspired black comedy, letting his gently prowling camera play happily over dank corridors, sweating walls hung with torches, cobwebby secret passages and creaking portcullises. Price makes a very creditable stab at a sub-Shakespearean Crookback, visually splendid but with his vocal intonations occasionally lapsing into parody that is broader than, say, the fiendishly funny afterthought with which, after locking a victim's head into an iron mask, he absently drops a rat in as well. The opening scenes, graced by dialogue as literate as in the 1939 version, are particularly good; but towards the end convention begins to take over as Richard descends into raving madness and the horrid hallucinations multiply. The Battle of Bosworth, disappointingly, is stock footage, possibly from the 1939 version.

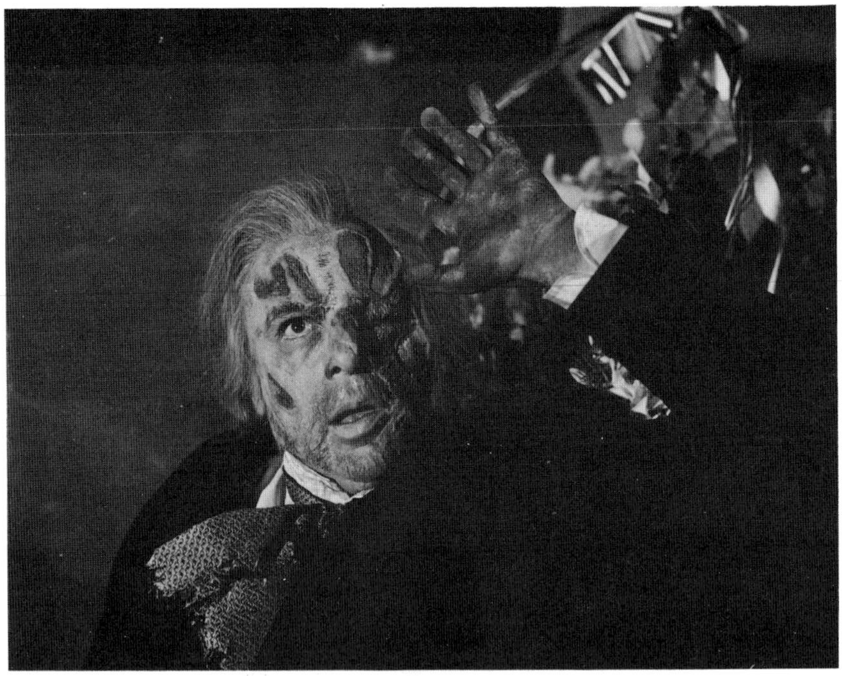

Herbert Lom as The Phantom of the Opera.

d Roger Corman *p* Gene Corman *s* Leo V. Gordon, F. Amos Powell, James B. Gordon *c* Arch R. Dalzell *lp* Vincent Price, Joan Freeman, Richard McCauly, Michael Pate, Justice Watson, Sandra Knight

Vengeance *aka* The Brain *aka* Ein Toter Sucht Seinen Moerder *aka* Over My Dead Body

(CCC/RAYMOND STROSS; GB, WG) b/w 83min

Apart from his uncredited collaboration on *The Day of the Triffids* (1962), this was cameraman Francis's first outing as a fantasy director. One of the many films derived from Curt Siodmak's *Donovan's Brain*, it tells of two doctors, Corrie and Shears (van Eyck and Lee) who save the brain of a planecrash victim. Van Eyck comes under the brain's hypnotic influence and becomes instrumental in its search for vengeance against those who plotted to cause the crash. Lee eventually switches off the current to the brain and van Eyck goes on to find the murderer. Francis manages to create some genuinely eerie images, but the script's unhappy mixture of horror, science fiction and straightforward crime investigation preclude the creation of a consistent atmosphere. The cameos of such excellent character actors as Miles Malleson and Jack MacGowran enliven many individual scenes.

d Freddie Francis *p* Raymond Stross *s* Robert Stewart, Philip Mackie *c* Bob Huke *lp* Peter van Eyck, Bernard Lee, Ann Heywood, Cecil Parker, Irene Richmond, Allan Cuthbertson, Kenneth Kendall, George A. Cooper, Siegfried Lowitz

What Ever Happened to Baby Jane?

(WB/ASSOCIATES AND ALDRICH) b/w 133min

The main claim to fame of this luridly oldfashioned melodrama is that the superbly uninhibited performances by Crawford and (especially) Davis encouraged other ageing or fading stars to try the horror field. Taking the project on at a lowpoint in his career, Aldrich directs with a crude energy that is very effective but leaves no room for the ambivalences usual in his work. The plot is a model of the kind of duplicity with which scriptwriters seek to please. A prologue (set in 1917) establishes child star Baby Jane as a spoiled brat, demanding and receiving adulation while her elder sister Blanche looks on with helpless jealousy. A second prologue (1935) reveals that while Jane's career languished, Blanche became a star until crippled in a car accident involving both sisters in deliberately unspecified roles.

The action proper (dated 'Yesterday') sees Blanche (Crawford), confined to a wheelchair, looked after with a grudging devotion by Jane (Davis), who comes to see her sister as an obstacle in her grotesque plan to stage a comeback in her Baby Jane persona, and begins to mete out Cold Comfort punishments, culminating in murder. So contrived are the situations, so extreme the expressions of Blanche's long-suffering sweetness and Jane's escalating madness, that the last-minute revelation – Jane was tricked into believing she crippled her sister while drunk; Blanche was at the wheel and crashed in an attempt to run Jane down – emerges as little more than a conventionally ingenious plot twist. The pity of it is that there is more to the theme than just gothic fireworks, especially given the catalytic presence of Buono – a third monster, the grotesquely obese, petulantly infantile pianist hired as accompanist for Jane's comeback – who should (but doesn't quite) focus the tangle of perverted maternal/sexual jealousies that have encrusted around the sisters since childhood. Highly enjoyable, even so.

The Aldrich company produced two companion pieces: **Hush ... Hush, Sweet Charlotte** (1963) and **What Ever Happened to Aunt Alice?** (1969). Henry Farrell, author of the novel on which *What Ever Happened to Baby Jane?* was based, and co-scriptwriter of *Hush ... Hush, Sweet Charlotte*, followed up with scripts in much the same horror-nostalgia vein: **What's the Matter With Helen?** and **Whoever Slew Auntie Roo?** (both 1972), and for TV, *How Awful About Allan* (1970).

d/p Robert Aldrich *s* Lukas Heller *c* Ernest Haller
lp Bette Davis, Joan Crawford, Victor Buono, Anna Lee, Maidie Norman

Xi Xuefu *aka* **Vampire Woman**
(ZHONG LIAN; HONG KONG) b/w 97min
Li Tie's highly emotive indictment of feudalism – which prevailed in China up to the victory of the revolution in 1949 – makes its point by introducing horror imagery into the basically melodramatic plot. A daughter-in-law (Bai Yang) is victimized by her husband's family which orders her baby to be removed from her and handed to a servant. One night, a woman is seen sucking the baby's blood and a medium is called in. The 'vampire' is revealed to be Bai Yang and she is buried alive. In the end, the truth emerges: when Bai Yang's sister-in-law (Rong Xiaoyi) got married, her former lover (Jiang Zhongping) killed her husband and became the family's servant intent on destroying them. The 'vampire' incident was merely Bai Yang trying to save her baby, poisoned by the evil Jiang.

Joan Crawford as the helpless Blanche tormented by Bette Davis in Robert Aldrich's luridly successful melodrama, What Ever Happened to Baby Jane?

The picture is infused with a sense of eeriness, which is further emphasized by Ju Ren's score using organ music and ominously shadowy images add conviction to the allegations of sorcery and vampirism. Chu Yuan reworked the plot in his *The Mad Woman* (1964), but he engineered a starker ending: instead of a happy family scene, he ended the movie with the feudal patriarch lost and lonely in his dilapidated and empty ancestral hall. Li Tie made well over 100 features and is considered to be one of the three most outstanding Cantonese directors of the fifties, together with Qin Jian and Li Chenfeng. The production company, Zhong Lian, is also known as Chung Luen.

d Li Tie *p* Zhu Ziqui *s* Cheng Gang *c* Wei Haifeng
lp Bai Yang (Bak Yin), Zhang Huoyou (Cheng Wo-Yau), Huang Manli (Wong Manlee), Rong Xiaoyi, Jiang Zhongping (Keung Chung-ping)

1963

Beauty and the Beast (HARVARD) 77(74)min
Cahn's last film, completed the year before he died in 1963, this is a modest, somewhat stiff, but quite attractively staged version of Perrault's fairytale. Despite the occasional nods in the direction of horror – notably a posse of villagers brandishing torches as in **Frankenstein** (1931) – there is nothing horrific about it, nor is there intended to be. It warrants inclusion here because the curse which condemns hero Damon to be a beast by night transforms him into a werewolf. The distinct resemblance to Lon Chaney Jnr in **The Wolf Man** (1941) is hardly surprising since Jack Pierce conceived the makeup for both characters.

d Edward L. Cahn *p* Robert E. Kent *s* George Bruce, Orville H. Hampton *c* Gilbert Warrenton *lp* Joyce Taylor, Mark Damon, Eduard Franz, Michael Pate, Merry Anders

Black Zoo (AA) scope 88min
Gough here is the owner of a private zoo in Los Angeles whose brain snaps under pressure from property developers determined to take over the site. A member of the 'true believers' – a cult of animal worshippers who believe in soul transference between beasts and men – he solves his problem by using his strange power over animals to have one of his lions kill the speculator (Cowan). On to a good idea, he similarly disposes of a keeper who misuses an animal (Cook) and an agent (Grey) who threatens to lure his wife away with the offer of a circus job. When his wife (Cooper) finally decides to leave him, he tries to dispatch her too. But this provokes his son (Lauren) – mute since childhood after seeing his mother (Gough's first wife) killed by a lion at his father's order – and he is forced to kill the berserk Gough. Ineptly scripted, ploddingly directed, wildly overacted by Gough (who looks more than a little ridiculous wearing his tigerskin rug-robe), it has nowhere near the same charge as the very similar **Murders in the Zoo** (1933). But Crosby's camerawork is excellent, and no film that has the wit to include a scene in which Gough ushers a lion, a tiger, a black panther and a cougar into his sitting-room, installs them on couches and easy chairs, and solemnly indulges then with a lullaby on the organ, can be all bad.

d Robert Gordon *p/co-s* Herman Cohen *co-s* Aben Kandel *c* Floyd Crosby *lp* Michael Gough, Jeanne Cooper, Rod Lauren, Virginia Grey, Elisha Cook Jnr, Jerome Cowan

Blood Feast
(DAVID F. FRIEDMAN/HERSCHELL G. LEWIS PRODUCTIONS) 75(61)min
Blood Feast is the very first splatter movie. As its creator, Herschell Gordon Lewis, put it '*Blood Feast* was the first picture of its type. I've often compared it with a Walt Whitman poem – it's no good but it's the first of its type'. Before this, Lewis was a director of low-budget, soft-core sex films but as, in the early sixties, nudity and simulated sex were beginning to

creep into mainstream Hollywood products, he and his partner Friedman decided to move in a different direction. Impressed by the success of Hammer films and **Psycho** (1960 – and its many imitators – they chose what one might call hard-core gore. As Lewis himself put it: 'there were a whole series of taboos that I set out deliberately to violate. There were no effects such as exploding uniforms, which Sam Peckinpah brought out later, that we could hope to match. We couldn't match production values. We didn't have name actors and actresses. What could we do, then, to justify our pictures? The answer was that we could provide effects, however crudely drawn, that nobody else would dare to do'.

Blood Feast was shot in Miami in nine days and cost less than $70,000. Trashed by the critics (one of whom called it 'amateur night at the butcher's shop') and mauled by several State censorship boards, the film was Lewis' first huge commercial success, his biggest hit ever, and set new standards in on-screen bloodletting. The plot has an Egyptian caterer who is preparing a 'blood feast' in order to bring to life an Egyptian love goddess. For this he needs the members and organs of various young girls, so we see a woman having her brains scooped out on a deserted beach, another having both legs amputated in a bath, a heart removed and the cutting out of a tongue. The film inaugurated a whole series of Lewis movies in which young women are chopped up and eviscerated in ever more bizarre and gruesome fashion, reaching the heights of hyperbole in **The Wizard of Gore** (1968) and **The Gore Gore Girls** (1971), and paved the way for the likes of George Romero and Tobe Hooper. John Waters paid homage to Lewis in **Multiple Maniacs** (1969) and the director's trash aesthetics seem to have struck a deep chord in the punk sensibility.

With increasing numbers of articles (and a book) appearing, Lewis' films are doing big business on video in the United States (all are banned in Britain in any form) and there are constant rumours of the director re-emerging to make *Blood Feast II* or *Gore Feast*. Lewis himself is refreshingly frank about his own work; as he put it, 'after *Blood Feast* and **2000 Maniacs** (1964) a sophistication/erosion process set in. Motion picture audiences were delightfully childlike in their early 1960s reactions, compared with the brutally critical evaluation they make in the 1980s. It's our fault (if we can call it a fault) as producers, because we've generated this reaction by our own recognition that, having seen an effect before, the theatre-goer will demand a greater excess from us in order to be shocked again. So as the target develops a tolerance, we must serve up greater and greater dosages. It's hardly sensitive of us, but it *is* sensible'.

Cheap, crude and undeniably (though far from 'believably') gruesome, Lewis' films inspire wildly divergent responses veering from camp adulation, intellectual curiosity to bitter hostility. As for the director himself, told that he had been categorized as 'a subject for further research' by the magazine *Cahiers du Cinéma* he replied 'that's what they say about cancer'.

d/co-p/c/se Herschell Gordon Lewis *co-p* David F. Friedman, Stanford S. Kohlberg *s* Allison Louise Downe *lp* Thomas Wood, Mal Arnold, Connie Mason, Scott H. Hall, Lyn Bolton, Toni Calvert, Gene Courtier

A Comedy of Terrors

(ALTA VISTA/AIP) scope 88(83)min

Surprisingly heavily directed by Tourneur, Matheson's parodic script (more farcical than his much wittier one for **The Raven**, 1963) never really gets off the ground. Price and Lorre overplay rather desperately as a drunken undertaker and his craven assistant who bunglingly try to drum up business by creating their own candidates for burial. Karloff has virtually nothing to do (but does it well) as Price's senile father-in-law, always on the verge of being poisoned but innocently contriving to do the poisoning. The best moments come from Rathbone as one of the prospective victims, a would-be Shakespearian actor subject to catalepsy who keeps getting coffined and uncoffined, endlessly and aptly reciting the Bard's immortal words all the while. The sets, by Daniel Haller, are attractive.

d Jacques Tourneur *p* James H. Nicholson, Samuel Z. Arkoff *s* Richard Matheson *c* Floyd Crosby *lp* Vincent Price, Peter Lorre, Boris Karloff, Basil Rathbone, Joe E. Brown, Joyce Jameson

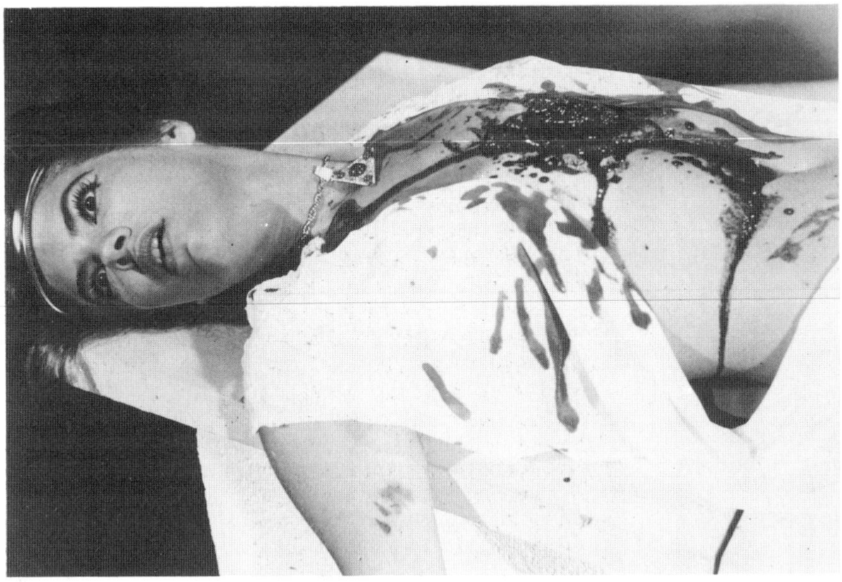

Herschell Gordon Lewis' Blood Feast, *the very first splatter movie.*

The Curse of the Living Corpse

(DEAL FILMS) b/w 84(78)min

Morbidly afraid of a premature burial, a tyrannical millionaire promises retribution in his will against his grasping family should he be buried alive. After his death and consignment to the family vault, a hooded figure stalks by night, the maid is found murdered, and various family deaths occur in the manner provided for in the will, each taking account of the victim's most secret fear: by disfigurement (Milli), fire (Waren) and drowning (Hartman). Although the tomb is found to be empty (until filled by the body of a murdered servant), common avarice rather than supernatural revenge turns out to lie behind the crimes.

An early gore movie – its best moment has the maid's severed head served up on a breakfast tray – it is evidently intended as a straightfaced parody of the old-dark-house school (complete with secret panels and watching eyes), but is so laboriously directed that it emerges as creakily oldfashioned melodrama. Scheider, in his début, gives one of the better performances in an indifferent cast.

d/p/s Del Tenney *c* Richard L. Hilliard *lp* Helen Waren, Roy Scheider, Margot Hartman, Robert Milli, Hugh Franklin, Candace Hilligoss

Delitto allo Specchio *aka* Sex Party

(PT CINEMATOGRAFICA/ROC; IT, FR) b/w 77min

This whodunit is enlivened by Barrymore's unlikely performance as a clairvoyant who, at a party in a castle, foretells various events, including the death of Serena (Lualdi). When the guests find themselves isolated and locked in a castle with a menacingly imbecilic servant, they panic. Lualdi executes a very unimpressive dance and Barrymore, far better in **Roma contra Roma** (1963), seems to lose interest in the proceedings as soon as he arrives on the scene. The result, a disappointingly missed opportunity to make a claustrophobic chiller, was the director's only film.

co-d/co-p/co-s Jean Josipovici *co-d* Ambroglio Molteni *co-p* Pasquale Tagliaferri *co-s* Giorgio Stegani *c* Rafaele Masciocchi *lp* Antonella Lualdi, Gloria Milland, John Drew Barrymore, Michel Lemoine, Maria Valdemarin, Luisa Rivelli

Dementia 13 *aka* **The Haunted and the Hunted**
(FILMGROUP) b/w 81(73)min
Coppola's official first feature (having previously been involved with exploitation films and done some tinkering for Corman) and one senses the presence of a director right from the moody opening sequence: night, Anders and her husband in a boat arguing about money, he suddenly dies of a heart attack, she dumps him in the lake, and music still drifts up from the transistor that went with him.

The film itself is a piece of high gothic melodrama set in and around an Irish castle where the family still mourn a drowned child and Anders sees a way to get rich by pretending to be in communication with the dead child. Preparing a demonstration, she sinks some dolls in the lake. She is then brutally axed to death; and the dolls later float eerily to the surface. Everybody gives the impression of being mad (elder brother Campbell wanders around with an oxyacetylene torch, but then he is a sculptor; others behave even more oddly), but it is younger brother (Patton) who commits the very nasty axe murders, having also been responsible for his little sister's death. The weakness of the film is in the script, which gives every sign of having been bundled together at the last minute; which, since the opportunity to make the film came from a characteristic Corman decision to make additional use of existing cast and facilities, it was.

d/s Francis Ford Coppola *p* Roger Corman *c* Charles Hannawalt *lp* William Campbell, Luana Anders, Bart Patton, Mary Mitchell, Patrick Magee, Barbara Dowling

Devil Doll (GALAWORLDFILM/GORDON FILMS; GB,US) b/w 80(70)min
This is a lacklustre adaptation of Frederick E. Smith's story about a hypnotist and ventriloquist (Halliday) who kills his partner and then transfers the man's soul into a dummy. However, when Halliday attempts to do the same with Romain's soul, which he intends to lodge in a female dummy, the original dummy and Romain's boyfriend (Sylvester) stop him. The ventriloquist's dummy motif is virtually guaranteed to make for compelling scenes, as in **Dead of Night** (1945), but Shonteff and company still manage to botch it up with a surfeit of TV closeups, crude editing and flatly monotonous acting. *Devil Doll* was not released until 1965, after the same team's **Curse of Simba** (1964), an incompetently made piece of racism.

d Lindsay Shonteff *p* Kenneth Rive *s* George Barclay, Lance Z. Hargreaves *c* Gerald Gibbs *lp* Bryant Halliday, William Sylvester, Yvonne Romain, Sandra Dorne, Karel Stepanek, Francis de Wolff

Luana Anders in Dementia 13, *Francis Ford Coppola's official first feature.*

Diary of a Madman (ADMIRAL) 96min
In this amalgam of several Guy de Maupassant stories – principally 'The Horla' – Price plays a respected French magistrate who, on a visit to the condemned cell, is attacked by and inadvertently kills a murderer frenziedly attempting to explain that he has been possessed by an evil spirit which drives him to kill. Possessed in his turn, Price is tormented by ghostly manifestations involving a picture of his dead wife and child and wakes from a trance to find he has butchered a pet canary. Then, after reviving a therapeutic interest in sculpture on the advice of his doctor, he finds himself impelled to kill the duplicitous model (Kovack) he falls in love with as she poses for him. The sequence in which Price returns to his studio, oblivious of the murder, and follows a trail of blood up the stairs to be confronted by Kovack's severed head glaring at him from within his bust of her, is splendidly macabre. Script and direction, however, are for the most part little more than serviceable, lamely presenting the 'Horla' as a prosaic off-screen voice, making heavy weather of the device of the explanatory diary left by the madman as he immolates himself with the evil spirit, and resorting to a battery of shoddy tricks (including a bar of green light shakily superimposed over the eyes of the Horla's victims).

Price and the charming Kovack apart, the film's most attractive feature is the cheap but effective set design provided by Daniel Haller, Roger Corman's regular art director before himself turning director with **Monster of Terror** (1965).

d Reginald LeBorg *p/s* Robert E. Kent *c* Ellis W. Carter *lp* Vincent Price, Nancy Kovack, Chris Warfield, Elaine Devry, Stephen Roberts

La Frusta e il Corpo *aka* **Incubo** *aka* **What** *aka* **The Whip and the Body** *aka* **The Body and the Whip** *aka* **Night Is the Phantom** *aka* **The Way and the Body** *aka* **Son of Satan** *aka* **The Whip and the Flesh**
(VOX FILM/LEONO FILM/FRANCINOR/PIP; IT, FR) 92(77)min
Lee once said that this inspired sado-masochistic fantasy is the best of his Italian films. The central figure is Nevenka (Lavi), the wife of Christian (Stella), the lover of her brother-in-law, Kurt (Lee), and the mistress of their father (Ardow). Lee's passion is to whip her violently, which she suffers with mixed feelings. After she kills Lee, signs of his ghostly presence proliferate (mainly on the soundtrack) while she continues to experience intense nightly flagellations as Lee's demonic laughter reverberates through the castle. In the end she kills herself with the dagger she used to kill her two lovers, father and son, slashing at Lee's fantasized presence in front of the incomprehending eyes of her husband.

Although overly reliant on the zoom lens, Bava creates an uncannily sensuous atmosphere, especially when he trains his camera on Lavi, obsessively detailing her face as desire, pleasure and pain mingle in a hallucinatory erotic delirium. Lee represents a notion of maleness which requires him to see the signs of his potency reflected in the intensity of Lavi's reactions. But in so doing he also inevitably comes face to face with his own radical insufficiency: to the extent that Lavi's reactions can also be seen as signifying her pleasure, she reduces him to a function of *her* desire. This deadly dialectic in which each reduces the other to different functions in their respective fantasies (an asymmetrical dialectic because Lavi acts by refusing to be reduced to a mirror for Lee) comes to an end when the dagger she plunges into the body of her lovers also comes to penetrate her own body, closing the circuit. The disturbing aspect of the movie is that this death wish is played out, in relation to the camera, from a perspective which becomes identified with the dead Lee, the ghostly and cruelly perverted off-screen watcher. Although cheaply made, Bava's film is a far more telling and honest representation of the murkier sides of the desire for cinema – visual pleasure and the sado-masochistic process involved in *amour fou* – than the crude exploitation of these motifs in pictures such as *The Night Porter* (1973). Unfortunately the film has been screened mostly

in a savagely mutilated version, reducing it to a vaguely sexy but totally incoherent potboiler. In its original form it is an extraordinary, impressive achievement.

Lavi, an Israeli actress who worked in many countries, is best known for her performances in *Il Demonio* (1963) and *Lord Jim* (1965) but, in Bava's film, her presence makes up for Barbara Steele's absence.

d John M. Old (Mario Bava) *p* John Oscar (Elio Scardamaglia) *s* Julian Berry (Ernesto Gastaldi), Robert Hugo (Ugo Guerra), Martin Hardy (Luciano Martino) *c* David Hamilton (Ubaldo Terzano) *lp* Christopher Lee, Daliah Lavi, Tony Kendall (Luciano Stella), Harriet White, Isli Oberon, Alan Collins (Luciano Pigozzi), Jacques Herlin, Dean Ardow (Gustavo de Nardo)

The Gorgon (HAMMER; GB) scope 83min
This eerily poetic evocation of an archetypal image to represent the fear of the female sex was one of Fisher's favourite movies. Released in 1964, it tells of a mysterious figure, Megara, who haunts a small German village and inhabits Fisher's dankest and most uncannily empty castle, literally petrifying all who gaze upon her. Goodliffe is the sceptical professor who investigates while his son (Pasco), in love with his father's companion, Carla (Shelley), slowly begins to realize that the terrifying creature is none other than his beloved. He withstands an attack by his sword-wielding father who wants to stop his son's desire to know the forbidden woman, and finally faces the horrifying image, solving the mystery but losing his love in the same instant.

The pervasive fantasy of the phallic mother is so logically and consistently enacted that even a psychoanalytic interpretation could not be more explicit. In spite of some awkward effects (the badly animated snakes in the gorgon's hair, her severed head bouncing down the steps), the movie's overall impact remains unnervingly powerful as it brilliantly presents one of the fundamental nightmare images of our culture, something even most horror films (**Alien**, 1979, for example) shy away from, preferring to cloak the monstrous mother-figure in less easily recognizable shapes. This is Fisher's most dreamlike and bewitching work, perfectly acted by all concerned – including a cameo performance by Lee as the outsider who understands the unconscious forces at play in the Goodliffe-Pasco-Shelley family romance but is powerless to prevent the protagonists acting out their compulsions to the bitter end.

d Terence Fisher *p* Anthony Nelson Keys *s* John Gilling *c* Michael Reed *se* Syd Pearson *lp* Peter Cushing, Christopher Lee, Richard Pasco, Barbara Shelley, Michael Goodliffe, Patrick Troughton, Jack Watson, Jeremy Longhurst, Tony Gilpin, Prudence Hyman

The Haunted Palace (ALTA VISTA/AIP) scope 85min
This rich but flawed film was Corman's attempt to break fresh ground after the five Edgar Allan Poe adaptations from **House of Usher** (1960) to **The Terror** (1963). Although the title is borrowed from a Poe poem, the script is adapted from H. P. Lovecraft's novel *The Case of Charles Dexter Ward*, with Price as the man who arrives in the New England village of Arkham to claim the palatial mansion that was once the domain of his great-great-grandfather, a black magician burned alive 110 years before after placing a curse of vengeance on the village. Surprised by the hostility which greets his arrival and by the strangely deformed people to be seen in the village, Price finds a portrait of his ancestor (his exact double) exercising an increasingly baleful influence on him, until he finally becomes an instrument executing his ancestor's evil plan of creating a race of mutants who will enable the dark powers (a favourite Lovecraft theme) to return and rule the earth.

With this call to the dark powers hovering tellingly in the background, the film has a real narrative drive as the ancestor takes time out from his main purpose to set about resuscitating his dead wife, wreaking vengeance on the descendants of the villagers who burned him and preparing to sacrifice Price's wife (Paget) to the lecherous four-armed thing lurking in the underground vaults. There is real menace, too, in a scene where the mutants converge on Price and Paget in the village square in an attempt to frighten them away. Ultimately, though, with Daniel Haller's art direction creating much the same ambience as in *House of Usher* – the slightly musty colours, the echoing passages hung with cobwebs and shadows, the exteriors perpetually shrouded in ground fogs – *The Haunted Palace* becomes another of Poe's constructs of the mind. Lovecraft's cosmic vision of domination by evil, altogether more tangible than Poe's nightmarish explorations of guilty fears and desires, perhaps needed to be set in a more demonstrably real world, such as Corman discovered for **The Tomb of Ligeia** (1964).

Left: *Claire Bloom and Julie Harris in Robert Wise's* The Haunting.

Prudence Hyman about to lose her head in *The Gorgon.*

Vincent Price explores The Haunted Palace *with Lon Chaney Jnr.*

d/p Roger Corman *s* Charles Beaumont *s* Floyd Crosby *lp* Vincent Price, Debra Paget, Lon Chaney Jnr, John Dierkes, Leo Gordon, Elisha Cook Jnr

The Haunting

(ARGYLE ENTERPRISES; GB) b/w scope 112min

Wise, a good professional but never a great director, made his first movie (**The Curse of the Cat People**, 1944) under the guidance of Jacques Tourneur's favourite producer, Val Lewton. Having learned from the Tourneur-Lewton movies that horror is a matter of suggestion, he goes all out in this picture to make sure his suggestions are noticed. Based on the Shirley Jackson novel, *The Haunting of Hill House*, the story itself is fairly conventional: an empty house near Boston, reputedly haunted, is investigated by an anthropologist, Dr Markway (Johnson) and two psychic women, one a study in repression (Harris), the other with ESP (Bloom). There are plenty of mysterious noises and poltergeist phenomena in the house which has a surfeit of corridors, a spiral staircase and no right angles anywhere. Events come to a head when Mrs Markway (Maxwell) arrives and goes to sleep in the room where the fearful phenomena appear to be generated, the nursery. Next, her face suddenly appears in a skylight frightening Harris, and then she flits across Harris's path as she drives away, causing the car to crash with fatal results. Apparently, Maxwell had been frightened by weird noises and got lost in the warren of corridors.

With an over-emphatic sound and music track and plenty of distorting lenses, the film soon becomes a ponderous affair and whatever atmosphere it creates is due mainly to Boulton's cinematography, the special effects and excellent acting from Harris and especially Bloom, even though the script presents her lesbianism as somehow equally unnatural as Harris's susceptibility to ghosts. It is small wonder that a script which conceives lesbianism in such bigoted terms also designates the nursery as the wellspring of all horror and a married, maternal figure (Maxwell) as the woman-in-white who causes the sensitive Harris's death. In the end, what haunts the movie is precisely the notion that lesbianism is somehow unnatural and horrifying. Wise's next excursion into the genre was **Audrey Rose** (1977).

d/p Robert Wise *s* Nelson Gidding *c* David Boulton *se* Tom Howard *lp* Julie Harris, Claire Bloom, Richard Johnson, Russ Tamblyn, Lois Maxwell, Fay Compton, Rosalie Crutchley, Valentine Dyall, Diane Clare

The Horror of It All

(LIPPERT-ASSOCIATED PRODUCERS; GB) b/w 75min

After the commercial failure of Hammer's most expensive project, **The Phantom of the Opera** (1962), Fisher spent some years in the wilderness directing science fiction stories, including *The Night of the Big Heat* (1964) and *Island of Terror* (1965). This uninspiring horror parody, released in England three years after its production, was also part of Fisher's penance. Patterned on William Castle's **The Old Dark House** (1963), the plot has American salesman Jack Robinson (Boone) pursue Cynthia (Rogers) to her ancestral mansion where he discovers an eccentric set of characters, including her long-nailed vampire sister (Melly), a madman locked in the basement (Duncan), a loony inventor (Bligh), the head of the family who speaks in Lugosi-like tones (Dyall) and a crazy actor who fakes his own death (Price).

This format is only feasible if carried by an established comedy team with its own following and able to play with the disjointed gags and genre conventions and is best suited to television, as shown by the success of *The Munsters* teleseries. Fisher's sense of black humour does not lend itself to such a farcical romp with cartoon characters. Boone, the clean-cut, crooning answer to Elvis Presley, wrote and performed the title song.

d Terence Fisher *p* Robert L. Lippert *s* Ray Russell *c* Arthur Lavis *lp* Pat Boone, Erica Rogers, Dennis Price, Andree Melly, Valentine Dyall, Jack Bligh, Archie Duncan, Erik Chitty

House of the Damned

(ASSOCIATED PRODUCERS) scope b/w 63min

A standard haunted-house movie with Foster as an architect invited to make a survey of a castle leased to a retired circus showman who has disappeared. He, his wife (Anders) and a couple of friends are subjected to a flurry of mysterious happenings which culminate in the discovery of a seemingly decapitated body. These turn out to have been perpetrated by a family of freaks, hiding in the dungeons and resorting to old tricks in a desperate attempt to avoid being thrown out of their home following the sudden death of the showman. As directed by Dexter, who made his small mark in the sixties with a series of intelligently handled B movies like *Womanhunt* (1961), *The Purple Hills* (1961) and *Harbor Lights* (1963), the old formula comes up fresh with a disarmingly touching twist at the end when the unmasked monsters – mostly genuine freaks – have to make up their minds to face the outside world again. The film features an early appearance by Richard Kiel, who later achieved fame as Jaws in the James Bond series.

d/p Maury Dexter *s* Harry Spalding *c* John Nickolaus Jnr *lp* Ronald Foster, Merry Anders, Richard Crane, Erika Peters, Georgia Schmidt

Nightmare

(HAMMER; GB) b/w scope 82min

This is Francis's second contribution to Hammer's series of horror-thrillers inspired by Alfred Hitchcock's **Psycho** (1960). As with **Paranoiac** (1962), he was saddled with a mechanical Sangster script in which people attempt to drive a woman insane. In an old house, Henry (Knight) and Grace (Redmond) stage grisly apparitions to drive Janet (Linden), who fears insanity since she saw her mother kill her father, to murder Knight's wife. The scheme succeeds and Linden is sent to the asylum, but then Redmond falls prey to similar hallucinations and she and Knight start fighting. A teacher, Mary Lewis (played by Bruce who was Carl Boehm's first victim in **Peeping Tom**, 1960), and the chauffeur (Cooper) solve the charade and expose the criminals.

Francis's direction is professional and he makes good use of starkly contrasted black and white images which are particularly suited to the ghostly appearances of a woman-in-white played by Jessop, previously seen as Miss Jessel in **The Innocents** (1961). Francis's next entry in the series, **Hysteria** (1964), was the weakest.

d Freddie Francis *p/s* Jimmy Sangster *c* John Wilcox *se* Les Bowie *lp* David Knight, Moira Redmond, Jennie Linden, Brenda Bruce, George A. Cooper, Irene Richmond, Clytie Jessop, John Welsh

The Nutty Professor

(JERRY LEWIS ENTERPRISES/PAR) 107min

A horror movie only by association, but containing a brilliantly realized idea – analogous to the Hyde-Jekyll reversal in Hammer's **The Two Faces of Dr Jekyll** (1960) – whereby Lewis's buck-toothed old sad sack of a professor is transformed by potion into a greasily and synthetically odious crooner. The monsters of the pop world are punctured here with a venomous skill that easily outshines the crude humour and facile campery of **Phantom of the Paradise** (1974). The result is probably Lewis's best film.

d/co-s Jerry Lewis *p* Ernest D. Glucksman*co-s* Bill Richmond *c* W. Wallace Kelley *lp* Jerry Lewis, Stella Stevens, Del Moore, Kathleen Freeman, Howard Morris

The Old Dark House

(HAMMER; GB, US) b/w and col 86(77)min

So outrageously bad that it becomes enjoyable, this film – which bears little resemblance to James Whale's classic **The Old Dark House** (1932) – has a dreary American (Poston) visit his distant relatives at Femm Manor. The denizens are all rather eccentric, and include the twins Casper and Jasper (Bull), one in his coffin and the other expecting to die any moment; their mother (Grenfell), dedicated to knitting; Morley as a gun-obsessed uncle and Johns as another uncle intent on building an ark; their homicidally puritanical father (Green); the pretty Cecily (Scott) and the sexy Morgana (Fielding). The family are condemned to live in the manor on pain of losing their share of the family fortune. Scott begins to murder one after the other until Poston blows her up, which leaves him with Fielding, the patriarch, and the ark-building uncle.

Castle is better known for his cynical approach to the provision of thrills (he wired up the audience's seats for **The Tingler**, 1959) and his brazen translations of Hitchcock's techniques into crude but effective shockers, an example later followed by Brian de Palma. This adaptation of J. B. Priestley's *Benighted* should be compared to such pictures as **Carry On Screaming** (1966) for its good-humoured sense of the macabre to be fully appreciated. The backgrounds to the credits were drawn by Charles Addams, whose cartoons later inspired the popular teleseries *The Addams Family*. The American release prints of this picture were in black and white while the British release in 1968 used the Technicolor version and eliminated many humorous sequences.

d/co-p William Castle *co-p* Anthony Hinds *s* Robert Dillon *c* Arthur Grant *se* Les Bowie *lp* Tom Poston, Fenella Fielding, Janette Scott, Robert Morley, Joyce Grenfell, Mervyn Johns, Peter Bull, Danny Green

The Raven (ALTA VISTA/AIP) pv 86min

The fifth in Corman's Poe series has less to do with Poe than with an excuse to assemble Karloff, Lorre and (particularly memorably) Price as a riotous trio of rival magicians, with Karloff being ganged up on because he had pinched Price's wife and turned Lorre into a raven. Although the settings and decorations look reminiscent of earlier films in the series, *The Raven* makes it clear from the outset that self-parody is the name of the game: a raven flies in at the window and Price, seeking information as to the whereabouts of his wife, is greeted with a 'How the hell should *I* know' in Lorre's unmistakable rasping snarl. Matheson's script keeps the wit flowing nicely for a while, with Price recoiling fastidiously from the catalogue of ingredients required for transforming ravens back into humans ('Entrails of *troubled* horse?'), or Lorre's muttered 'Where else?' as Price explains that he keeps his wife's corpse in a coffin in the living room. Then comes a lengthy patch in which both horror and humour are sparse, before picking up again for the final duel of magicians, which is both wittily and imaginatively staged.

d/p Roger Corman *s* Richard Matheson *c* Floyd Crosby *lp* Vincent Price, Peter Lorre, Boris Karloff, Hazel Court, Jack Nicholson, Olive Sturgess

Roma contra Roma *aka* War of the Zombies *aka* Night Star – Goddess of Electra

(GALATEA FILMS; IT) scope 105(95)min

This is a minor contribution to the horror-peplum hybrid genre of which Mario Bava's **Ercole al Centro della Terra** (1961) is the most successful example. Here, a crazy magician, Aderbal (Barrymore) in the service of a bloodthirsty goddess resuscitates an army of Roman soldiers and launches the zombie horde in a bid for world power. Pogany and art director Giovannini provide some genuinely arresting scenes, including Aderbal's underground cave with a golden idol shrouded in whirling mist and a servant girl, Rhama (Galli), roaming through the forest looking like someone who strayed from a Bava set. Vari was never more than a routine director and editor of second-rate box-office fodder, but with the right collaborators, his movies occasionally contained impressive sequences, as in the first half of this effort, released in 1964 and scripted from an outline furnished by the producers.

d Giuseppe Vari *p* Ferrucio de Martino, Massimo de Rita *s* Piero Pierotti, Marcello Sartarelli *c* Gabor Pogany *se* Ugo Amadoro *lp* John Drew Barrymore, Susy Andersen, Ettore Manni, Ida Galli, Mino Doro, Philippe Hersent, Matilde Calman

Lo Spettro *aka* The Ghost *aka* The Spectre

(PANDA FILMS; IT) scope 93min

Freda's follow-up to the sublime **L'Orribile Segreto del Dr Hichcock** (1962), again features the mortiferous beauty of Steele as Margareta who, with the aid of her lover (Baldwin), kills her husband, Dr Hichcock (Elliott). Elliott is faking, however, and returns to drive his wife insane by injecting her with a paralysing drug and making her await death in total immobility. He then drinks the poison with which she had intended to commit suicide and dies before the eyes of the motionless Steele, her face distorted by a macabre grin.

Freda dispenses with any reference to the supernatural to make the fantasies enacted more palatable, possibly because the dominant force in play is no longer a morbid and perverse

When is a corpse not a corpse?: Nightmare.

Jacqueline Soussard in a scene from I Tre Volte della Paura, *Mario Bava's contribution to the omnibus cycle.*

passion but simply greed. Free reign is given to a delirious, black romanticism as the camera roams through eerily lit corridors, orchestrating astonishing colour compositions, creating a fantasy texture in which lyrical excess clashes with formal classicism and making narrative and spatial coherence fragment under its pressure. As in *L'Orribile Segreto*, Freda succeeds in giving the film extra force by making it turn on the motif of the petrifying wish/fear to see the forbidden. Steele is driven mad by her inability to see either her husband's presence or his hidden jewels, and when all is revealed to her, only her eyes remain alive as she – like the viewer, transfixed by the nightmarish spectacle – witnesses with the gaze of an insane medusa the desired death of her husband.

d/co-s Robert Hampton (Riccardo Freda) *p* Louis Mann (Luigi Carpentieri, Ermanno Donati) *co-s* Robert Davidson *c* Donald Green (Raffaele Masciocchi) *lp* Barbara Steele, Peter Baldwin, Leonard Elliott (Elio Jotta), Harriet White, Raoul H. Newman (Umberto Raho), Charles Kechler, Reginald Price, Carol Bennet

The Terror (FILMGROUP/AIP) 81min
Characteristically, having brought **The Raven** (1963) in a couple of days under schedule and with Karloff owing two days work, Corman decided to make another movie during those two days (plus the succeeding weekend). At least five people helped out with the direction (Francis Coppola, Monte Hellman, Jack Hill, Dennis Jacob and Nicholson) without giving the film any more than the usual low-budget quota of rough edges; and since the script was evidently more or less improvised, the film benefits to the extent of several striking silent passages (notably the beautifully shot scenes of Nicholson wandering along the seashore and in the forest).

An officer in the Napoleonic armies, lost somewhere on the Baltic coast, Nicholson is searching for a mysterious girl he met on the shore. He is directed to the castle of Baron Lippe (Karloff), who has been mourning the death of his wife for 20 years. The dead wife and the girl sought by the lovelorn Nicholson are of course one, as we discover after teasing complications and before she disintegrates messily in Nicholson's arms. An honorary member of the Poe cycle by virtue of its necrophiliac theme, the film is likeable but indifferently acted (Karloff excepted) and lacking in any sort of compulsion. It is the film showing at the drive-in cinema in **Targets** (1968).

d/p Roger Corman *s* Leo Gordon, Jack Hill *c* John M. Nickolaus Jnr *lp* Boris Karloff, Jack Nicholson, Sandra Knight, Dick Miller, Jonathan Haze

I Tre Volti della Paura *aka* **Black Sabbath** *aka* **The Three Faces of Fear** *aka* **Black Christmas** *aka* **The Three Faces of Terror**
(GALATEA FILMS/EMMEPI CINEMATOGRAFICA/SOCIETE CINEMATOGRAPHIQUE LYRE; IT, FR) 100(95)min
After the impressive *La Ragazza che Sapeva Troppo* (1962), Bava essayed a mixture of psycho-thriller and horror for this offering composed of three different stories linked by Karloff as master of ceremonies. *The Drop of Water* is adapted from Chekhov's tale about a nurse (Soussard) who steals a ring from the corpse of a clairvoyant but, back at home, a dripping tap heralds the appearance of the woman's ghost which scares her to death. In *The Telephone*, based on a Howard Snyder story, a prostitute, Rosy (Mercier) is terrorized by phone calls from a man and asks a friend, Mary (Alfonzi), to stay with her. When the man breaks in, he mistakenly kills Mary and Rosy stabs him to death, but the phone calls start again. *The Wurdalak*, the most substantial episode, is adapted from a story by Alexei Tolstoy. Gorca (Karloff) is a Wurdalak – a Russian species of vampire – who gradually infects all members of his family. When the hero (Damon) takes his daughter (Andersen) away, Karloff finds them and infects her too. During the lovers' next embrace, she turns from an icy corpse into a vampire and kills Damon who thus joins her in the realm of the undead.

Although the first two stories are basically atmospheric thrillers with a sting in the tail, the final one has some remarkably effective scenes, achieved largely through framing, lighting and camera movement. It is a stylistic exercise rather than a serious horror movie: the narratives seem to function as mere pretexts for the creation of atmosphere and setpieces. The American release replaced Roberto Nicolosi's music with a Les Baxter score, and some sources name Ugo Guerra as co-scenarist. Bava's **La Frusta e il Corpo** (1963) proved a far more satisfyingly perverse achievement, as would his **Terrore nello Spazio** (1965).

d/co-s Mario Bava *p* Paolo Mercuri *co-s* Marcello Fondata, Alberto Bevilacqua *c* Ubaldo Terzano *lp* Michele Mercier, Lydia Alfonsi, Gustavo de Nardo; Boris Karloff, Susy Andersen, Mark Damon, Glauco Onorato, Rika Dialina; Jacqueline Pierreux (Jacqueline Soussard), Milly Monti, Harriet White, Gustavo de Nardo

Twice Told Tales (ADMIRAL PICTURES) 119min
This omnibus film features three stories from Nathaniel Hawthorne, although only the first is from the collection *Twice Told Tales*. This is *Dr Heidegger's Experiment* in which Dr Heidegger (Cabot) and his friend (Price) discover an elixir of youth which makes them young again and restores to life Dr Heidegger's fiancée (Blanchard) – for a while, at least. The second, *Dr Rapaccini's Daughter* (from *Mosses from an Old Manse*) concerns a Paduan scientist who has discovered a way of preserving his daughter's virginity – by injecting a poison into her veins which is so strong that she destroys every living thing which she touches. In *The House of the Seven Gables* (a full-length book in itself) Price searches for a rumoured hidden fortune in his haunted ancestral home but meets only ghosts and, finally, his own death.

Presumably an attempt to do for Hawthorne what **Tales of Terror** (1961, also starring Price) did for Poe, *Twice Told Tales* is effectively creepy and Price's performance in the third tale is even an improvement on his *The House of the Seven Gables* (1940). However, production values – miniature work and makeup – leave something to be desired in places.

d Sidney Salkow *p/s* Robert E. Kent *c* Ellis W. Carter *se* Milton Olsen *lp* Vincent Price; Sebastian Cabot, Mari Blanchard; Brett Halsey, Abraham Sofaer, Joyce Taylor, Edith Evanson; Beverly Garland, Richard Denning, Jacqueline de Wit, Floyd Simmons, Gene Roth

La Vergine di Norimberga *aka* **The Virgin of Nuremberg** *aka* **Horror Castle** *aka* **The Castle of Terror** *aka* **Terror Castle**

(ATLANTICA CINEMATOGRAFICA; IT) scope 83(70)min

Elaborating on Roger Corman's **The Pit and the Pendulum** (1961) as well as on Mario Bava's **La Maschera del Demonio** (1960), Margheriti's film is based on a novel by Frank Bogart. Mary (Podesta) is the young bride of a German aristocrat (Rivière) threatened by the gruesome contraption in the castle's torture dungeon. In spite of the obviously Italian landscape, the dialogue sets the story in Germany, where the lord of the manor (Valentin), wearing a hood to hide his skull-like appearance and rendered insane by Nazi tormentors, hides deep in the castle's bowels, periodically emerging to put the torture chamber, and especially the spiked 'virgin', to use. In an interesting reversal of the standard cliché, Lee plays the part of a hideously disfigured servant who turns out to be a benevolent character. The script and the dialogue are ludicrous, but the extraordinary cruelty of the film – like the rat cage placed over a woman's face, with predictably terrifying consequences – soon chokes the temptation to laugh and the effective special effects arranged by Margheriti himself make for some impressive scenes.

Margheriti was a more consistent but also less inspired director than Bava; his best work in the genre came later with such gothic period pieces, shot in black and white, as **La Danza Macabra** (1964) and **I Lunghi Capelli della Morte** (1964), both starring the unique Barbara Steele. The English-language version of this film was credited to Richard McNamara, a name also cited as responsible for the export version of Majano's **Seddok – l'Erede di Satana** (1961).

d/co-s/se Anthony Dawson (Antonio Margheriti) *p* Marco Vicario *co-s* Edmond T. Greville, Gastad Green (Ernesto Gastaldi) *c* Richard Palton (Riccardo Pallotini) *lp* Rosana Podesta, Georges Rivière, Christopher Lee, Jim Dolen, Anna delli Uberti, Luigi Severini, Luciana Milone, Mirko Valentin, Patrick Walton, Lucille Saint-Simon

Left: *Mirko Valentin in the crude but powerful* La Vergine di Norimberga.

1964

The Black Torment (COMPTON/TEKLI FILM; GB) 85min

This is a crude British attempt to match the Italian horror movies of the period. The sloppily constructed plot is set in 1780 and tells of Sir Richard Fordyce (Turner) who returns to his castle under suspicion of rape, murder and witchcraft. After ghostly goings-on, including a banging window, apparitions of his first wife in the garden and on horseback and a mute, paralytic grandfather hanging from a chandelier, it emerges that Turner has a demented twin brother who has been unleashed by his living-in sister-in-law (Lynn) and her cousin (Arne). The film's tone is set in a pre-credit sequence showing a young woman (Ronay) running through the woods trying to escape a murderous rapist. The cutting is predictable, the sound grossly over-emphatic, the colour ugly and the tension non-existent. Sears, so effective in Fisher's **The Phantom of the Opera** (1962), is miscast as Turner's new bride.

The same team was later responsible for **Corruption** (1967), a crudely exploitational concoction of horror, sex and surgery, highly derivative of Jesús Franco's Spanish work. Pictures like these underline the extraordinary achievement of Roman Polanski who made **Repulsion** (1965) for the same company. A similar story, without the ghostly trappings, was made by José Luis Merino as **Ivanna** (1971).

d/p Robert Hartford-Davis *s* Donald Ford, Derek Ford *c* Peter Newbrook *lp* Heather Sears, John Turner, Ann Lynn, Peter Arne, Francis de Wolff, Edina Ronay, Raymond Huntley, Patrick Troughton, Annette Whiteley, Joseph Tomelty

Il Castello dei Morti Vivi *aka* **Castle of the Living Dead** *aka* **Le Château des Morts Vivants** *aka* **Crypt of Horror**

(SERENA FILM/FRANCINOR; IT,FR) b/w 90(85)min

This is the film in which the immense talent of Reeves is revealed for the first time. Although credited to Ricci, the movie was in fact directed by Keifer with Reeves initially doing second-unit work. His work was so impressive, however, that he was invited to enlarge his contribution.

The plot involves a mad Count Draco (Lee) who immortalizes people by embalming them. One failed exper-iment results in a grotesque witchlike woman (Sutherland, who also plays the part of a sergeant), while another produces the motionless, slowly decaying body of Draco's wife as she lies on a bed in a cobwebbed room, fixed in a position which forces her to stare glassy-eyed into a mirror. The scenes with Lee, the basement laboratory littered with the remnants of mummification research, and most of the story for that matter are presented unimaginatively. But from the appearance of Lee's scythe-wielding servant (Valentin) and the energetic dwarf (de Martino) who protects the threatened heroine (Germani), the film shifts into a different gear, achieving some genuinely disturbing scenes such as the duel between the dwarf and the coachman in a garden with decaying statues. On the basis of his work on this film, the producer invited Reeves to make a cheap feature called **La Sorella di Satana** (1965), which inaugurated his brief directorial career.

d Herbert Wise (Luciano Ricci), (uncredited) Warren Keifer *p* Paul Maslansky *s* Warren Keifer, (uncredited) Michael Reeves *c* Aldo Tonti *lp* Christopher Lee, Gaia Germani, Philippe Leroy, Mirko Valentin, Antonio de Martino, Donald Sutherland, Jacques Stanislawski, Luciano Pigozzi

Catacombs *aka* **The Woman Who Wouldn't Die**

(PARROCH/MCCALLUM; GB) b/w 90min

The first film of Berlin-born Hessler, this is a minor thriller with macabre overtones about a gigolo (Merrill) who kills his rich wife (Cookson) but then finds her haunting him until he falls to his death, when it is revealed that his two accomplices, the lovely Alice (Merrow) and the rich wife's secretary

A shot from one of Michael Reeves' (uncredited) sequences of Il Castello dei Morti Vivi.

(McCallum), double-crossed him. The plot is routine, involving a corpse buried in the potting shed and ghostly happenings arranged to drive the duped killer insane, but the direction is quietly effective and gives a foretaste of the bravura sequences Hessler was to achieve in his later, very uneven but consistently interesting, work such as **The Oblong Box** and **Scream and Scream Again** (both 1969). The movie, based on a novel by Jay Bennett and produced by Robert Lippert's habitual partner, wasn't released until 1967.

d Gordon Hessler *p* Jack Parsons *s* Dan Mainwaring *c* Arthur Lavis *lp* Gary Merrill, Jane Merrow, Georgina Cookson, Neil McCallum, Rachel Thomas, Jack Train, Frederick Piper

Cien Gritos de Terror *aka* One Hundred Cries of Terror

(MEXICO FILMS; MEX) b/w 85min

Obon, one of the better scenarists of Mexican gothic movies (whose work includes **El Vampiro**, 1957; **Misterios de Ultratumba**, 1958; and **La Loba**, 1964) made his directorial début with this feature in which he adapts two of his own Poe-inspired stories. The first, *Panico*, tells of a man (Cordero) who conspires with his lover (Montesco) to terrorize his wife (Welter) to death. In their lugubrious house, weird shrieks and spectral appearances seem to do the trick, but Welter's corpse vanishes, after which Montesco is plagued by ghostly phenomena engineered by Welter who only pretended to be a wildly staring corpse. Montesco eventually turns on her lover and kills him before falling to her death, leaving Welter the triumphant survivor. The second story, *Miedo Supremo*, has a doctor (de Hoyos) visit a cemetery where he witnesses a burial and accidentally gets locked into a crypt. Eerie noises and wailing alert him to the fact that the recent burial victim had been interred prematurely while suffering an epileptic fit. He frees her but the experience has unhinged her mind and he is forced to strangle her in self-defence. He then puts her back into the coffin and in the morning, liberated from the crypt, he leaves, secure in the knowledge that nobody will ever find out that he committed a murder.

With this film Obon reveals himself to be a capable director, enjoying the creation of sinisterly gothic atmospheres and injecting the proceedings with a macabre sense of humour sorely lacking in most Mexican horror pictures. The film was released in 1965.

d/s Ramón Obon *p* Antonio del Castillo, Gerardo Welter *c* Agustin Martinez Solares *lp* Joaquin Cordero, Ariadna Welter, Ofelia Montesco, Jorge Martinez de Hoyos, Alicia Caro

Color me Blood Red

(FRIEDMAN-LEWIS/BOX OFFICE SPECTACULARS) 74min

This was the last of Lewis' unofficial 'gore trilogy', which also includes **Blood Feast** (1963) and **2000 Maniacs** (1964). A near relation to Corman's **A Bucket of Blood** (1959), the film features a mad artist who murders to obtain materials for his gruesome pictures – just the right shade of red pigment. Interestingly, the story of an artist forced into greater and greater excesses by the success of his work has certain parallels with Lewis' own career, although in fact *Color Me Blood Red* is less gruesome than its predecessors. This film marked the end of Lewis' partnership with David Friedman who went to Hollywood to produce a series of soft-core sexploitation movies. Lewis, meanwhile, turned his attention to other areas of exploitation cinema for a while, before returning to gore with **The Wizard of Gore** (1968) and **The Gore Gore Girls** (1971).

d/s/c Herschell Gordon Lewis *p* David F. Friedman *lp* Don Joseph, Candi Conder, Scott H. Hall, Elyn Warner, Patricia Lee, Jerome Eden, Jim Jaekel

La Cripta e l'Incubo *aka* La Maldición de los Karnstein *aka* Crypt of Horror *aka* Terror in the Crypt *aka* The Karnstein Curse *aka* La Maledizione dei Karnstein *aka* The Crypt of the Vampire *aka* The Vampire's Crypt *aka* Karnstein *aka* The Crypt and the Nightmare *aka* Carmilla *aka* The Curse of the Karnsteins

(MEC CINEMATOGRAFICA/HISPAMER FILMS; IT,SP) b/w scope 84min

This is a flaccid rendering of Sheridan LeFanu's *Carmilla*, which had previously been adapted by Carl Dreyer (**Vampyr**, 1931), and Roger Vadim (**Et Mourir de Plaisir**, 1960). Count Ludwig von Karnstein (Lee) is worried about a curse on his family which says that the evil witch Sheena will eventually be reincarnated in one of his descendants. Although it appears that his daughter, Laura (Ambessi), is the witch, her friend Lyuba (Quaglia) is revealed to be the reincarnation. The crepuscular atmosphere with candlelit interiors, the obligatory crypt and, on stormy nights, a bell tolling in a ruined church, lack the bite of a genuinely perverse force while all attempts at eroticism are foiled by the bovine incomprehension of the participants. Mastrocinque's next horror film, **Un Angelo per Satana** (1966), benefited from the presence of Barbara Steele.

d Thomas Miller (Camillo Mastrocinque) *p* William Mulligan *s* Julian Berry (Ernesto Gastaldi), Robert Bohr (Bruno Valeri), Maria del Carmen, Martinez Ramón, José L. Monter *c* Julio Ortas, Giuseppe Acquari *lp* Audrey Amber (Adriana Ambessi), Christopher Lee, Ursula Davis (Pier Ana Quaglia), José Campos, Nela Conjiu, Vera Valmont, José Villasante, Angel Milland (Angela Minervini)

The Curse of the Mummy's Tomb

(HAMMER; GB) scope 81min

The mummy story was never an easy myth to film effectively, and Terence Fisher's *tour de force* (**The Mummy**, 1959) with its inventive staging and surreal colours was not an easy act to follow for a producer who had only directed one horror film before (**Maniac**, 1962). Mindful of Hammer's American market, Carreras delivers a contrived and pedestrian picture about an American showman (Clark) who plans to take Ra-Antef's mummy (Owen, made up by Roy Ashton) on tour as a sensational sideshow against the advice of an Egyptian played by Pastell, repeating his red-fezzed performance from Fisher's picture. The love interest is provided by Howard and Roland, the latter also being coveted by the villain, Morgan, who turns out to be the mummy's brother and killer cursed with immortality. In spite of a catalogue of murders, the script and structure of the movie are so muddled that no tension can be generated. The only effective moments are contained in two scenes, one where a heavy steel door closes, severing Morgan's hand and the final sequence in London's sewers where the ancient Egyptian brothers destroy each other while Roland – dressed in the obligatory fashion for swooning women being carried by monsters: a flowing, diaphanous nightdress and gown – looks on.

Carreras later redeemed himself with *The Lost Continent* (1968) and he also finished **Blood from the Mummy's Tomb** (1971) after Seth Holt died during production. Hammer's next contribution to Egyptology was John Gilling's **The Mummy's Shroud** (1966).

d/p Michael Carreras *s* Henry Younger (Anthony Hinds) *c* Otto Heller *lp* Terence Morgan, Ronald Howard, Fred Clark, Jeanne Roland, George Pastell, Jack Gwillim, Dickie Owen, John Paul, Michael Ripper, Harold Goodwin

Curse of Simba *aka* Curse of the Voodoo *aka* Lion Man *aka* Voodoo Blood Death

(GALAWORLDFILMS/GORDON FILMS; GB, US) b/w 77(61)min

In this crudely racist voodoo story big-game hunter Mike (Halliday) is tortured telepathically for having killed a lion. It appears that the only way to stop a black African's angry retaliation against the hunter's arrogant intrusion and 'sport' is to kill him, which Halliday does by running him over in his jeep. The result is little but a string of clichés that staggers from TV closeup to TV closeup with paralysing incompetence. Shonteff, an ex-television director, made the equally atrocious **Devil Doll** (1963), also starring the less than exciting Halliday.

d Lindsay Shonteff *p* Kenneth Rive *s* Tony O'Grady, Leigh Vance *c* Gerald Gibbs *lp* Bryant Halliday, Dennis Price, Lisa Daniely, Mary Kerridge, Ronald Leigh Hunt, Jean Lodge

La Danza Macabra *aka* Terrore *aka* La Danse Macabre *aka* La Lunga Notte del Terrore *aka* Castle of Blood *aka* Castle of Terror *aka* The Long Night of Terror *aka* Tombs of Horror *aka* Coffin of Terror *aka* Dimensions in Death

(VULSINIA FILM/JOLLY FILM/LEO LAX FILM/ULYSEE FILM; IT,FR) b/w 87(82)min

After a brief excursion into 'art' cinema (Fellini's *8½*, 1963), Steele returned to the genre that suited her appearance best, though she never again recaptured the delirious intensity of her performances in the movies of Riccardo Freda (**L'Orribile Segreto del Dr Hichcock**, 1962) or Mario Bava (**La Maschera del Demonio**, 1960). Claimed to be based on a story by Poe, this film tells the tale of a man, Alan (Rivière), challenged to spend the night in a haunted castle where he finds himself involved in a macabre series of crimes of passion re-enacted by ghosts. The central figure of these happenings is Elizabeth (Steele) who appears to be a real person until she falls into a well and later re-appears, together with all the other ghosts. Realizing they are after his blood, Rivière tries to escape with Steele's apparent help. In their final embrace, her face turns into a grinning skull as he flees the castle, only to be impaled in a spiked gate, where he is found the next morning by his challenger, who calmly and coolly collects his bet from the corpse's wallet.

Margheriti's direction is wonderfully atmospheric, with long, meandering sequence shots and perfectly executed gothic imagery. Unfortunately the Roz Ortolani score is grossly over-emphatic and the English dubbing ruins whatever virtues the spoken words may have had. Margheriti directed a number of picturesque movies such as **La Vergine di Norimberga** (1963) and **I Lunghi Capelli della Morte** (1964) but, although aesthetically pleasing, his work never reaches the levels of disturbing perversity achieved by Bava, partly because he never allows the pathology of cinematic voyeurism to displace completely a film's narrative pretext, which both reduces the intensity of his imagery and heightens the defects in his scripts. He later remade this film as **Nella Stretta Morsa del Ragno** (1970).

co-d Anthony Dawson (Antonio Margheriti) *co-d/co-s* Gordon Wilson Jnr (Sergio Corbucci) *p* Frank Belty (Marco Vicario), Walter Sarch (Giovanni Addessi) *co-s* Jean Grimaud (Gianni Grimaldi) *c* Richard Kramer (Riccardo Pallotini) *lp* Barbara Steele, George Rivière, Margaret Robsahn, Sylvia Sorente, Henry Kruger, Montgomery Glenn (Silvano Tranquili), Raoul H. Newman (Umberto Raho)

El Demonio en la Sangre *aka* Demon in the Blood

(SERGIO KOGAN; ARG) b/w 102(75)min

Mujica's first feature, *El Centroforward Murio al Amanecer* (1959) had been a promising fantasy movie about a rich man who acquires a soccer star for his collection of precious objects, rather like one might buy a famous painting. But this omnibus movie, although technically competent, is disappointing. Three different stories are used to illustrate how people can stray into evil ways. The first features a mortally wounded black boxer who fantasizes being hypnotized by his manager and finds himself compelled to kill all those who were kind to him. The second tale recounts a version of Poe's *The Tell-Tale Heart*, with a murdered wife returning to plague her husband and his mistress. The last story rehearses the banal motif of a mysterious stranger intruding upon a couple and seducing the bored wife of the blinkered husband. The acting (including that of Ruvinskis, better known as Neutron in the Mexican masked-wrestler series) is routinely hammy. Some Poe stories, including *The Tell-Tale Heart*, had been filmed before in Argentina as part of the omnibus film **Obras Maestras del Terror** (1960).

d René Mujica *p* Sergio Kogan *s* Augusto Roa Bastosa, Tomas Eloy Martinez *c* Ricardo Younis, Oscar Nelli *lp* Rosita Quintana, Ubaldo Martinez, Ernesto Blanco, Arturo Garcia Buhr, Wolf Ruvinskis, Lidia Lamaison, Graciela Dufau

Dr Terror's House of Horrors

(AMICUS; GB) scope 98min

This is the first of Francis's omnibus movies, and revives a format pioneered in Germany with *Hoffmanns Erzaehlungen*

Barbara Steele's triumphant return to the horror film, La Danza Macabra, *directed with verve by Antonio Margheriti.*

Christopher Lee assailed by the hand of the painter he ran over in Freddie Francis' Dr Terror's House of Horrors.

(1911, 1916, 1923), and often used by Douglas Fairbanks Jnr in the fifties (**Three's Company**, 1953) as well as by Italian directors in the early sixties. The picture comprises five stories linked by the framing device of Cushing's seedy, mittened Death (alias Dr Schreck) telling five people in a railway carriage their unhappy fortunes. McCallum is killed by a female werewolf (Howells); a creeping vine envelops the house of Freeman and Bell; Castle is the trumpet player who is punished for having stolen voodoo music; Lee is the pompous art critic pursued and blinded by the amputated hand of a painter (Gough) he ran down in his car; and Sutherland, in his pre-*MASH* (1970) days, finds himself convicted for the murder of his vampire wife (Jayne) because the friend he had asked for advice and help (Adrian) turns out to be a vampire also and lets Sutherland take the blame because 'there isn't room for two doctors and two vampires in a small town'. With the exception of the poorly acted and racist voodoo sequence, the movie is better than average, and odd scenes are very impressive.

Francis was a fine cameraman (he photographed Jack Clayton's **The Innocents**, 1961, and Karel Reisz's **Night Must Fall**, 1964), but as a director his work was rarely anything other than routine, professional but never inspired. He was responsible for a number of horror omnibus movies, including **Torture Garden** (1967) and **Tales from the Crypt** (1972).

d Freddie Francis *co-p/s* Milton Subotsky *co-p* Max J. Rosenberg *c* Alan Hume *lp* Peter Cushing; Neil McCallum, Ursula Howells, Peter Madden; Alan Freeman, Ann Bell, Bernard Lee, Jeremy Kemp; Roy Castle, Kenny Lynch, Tubby Hayes; Christopher Lee, Michael Gough, Isla Blair; Donald Sutherland, Max Adrian, Jennifer Jayne, Irene Richmond

The Evil of Frankenstein (HAMMER; GB) 86min

After making **The Curse of Frankenstein** (1957) and **The Revenge of Frankenstein** (1958) in close succession, six years elapsed before Hammer returned to the character for this third movie. Since Terence Fisher had been responsible for the commercial failure of **The Phantom of the Opera** (1962), the direction here was entrusted to Francis, Britain's second but far less inspired horror specialist. Having come to an agreement with Universal, Hammer abandoned the Phil Leakey-Fisher conception of the monster and reverted to a pale imitation of the design Jack Pierce had used for Boris Karloff, here concocted by Roy Ashton. The narrative does not connect with *The Revenge* and a flashback explaining the plot's prehistory also ignores the *The Curse* and harks back instead to the motifs of **Frankenstein Meets the Wolf Man** (1943), with the creature (Kingston) being discovered preserved in an ice cave near the Baron's ancestral castle in Karlstaad.

The plot involves a hypnotist (Woodthorpe) who uses the creature for his own ends. The Baron (Cushing) manages to re-establish his control over the creature, aided by his assistant (Eles) and a mute girl (Wild). The creature gets drunk on brandy and chloroform to cause the usual conflagration at the end. The movie is tedious, amateurishly scripted and, except for Cushing's deadpan professionalism, hammily acted. The American television presentation of the movie was padded with an extra sequence showing the mute girl's childhood encounter with the creature and, later, the US TV version of Hammer's **Kiss of the Vampire** (1962) was similarly padded with shots from this movie.

The principal merit of this instalment is that it emphasizes Fisher's originality and directorial abilities which are confirmed by Hammer's next contribution to the series, **Frankenstein Created Woman** (1966).

d Freddie Francis *p* Anthony Hinds *s* John Elder (Anthony Hinds) *c* John Wilcox *se* Les Bowie *lp* Peter Cushing, Peter Woodthorpe, Kiwi Kingston, Duncan Lamont, Sandor Eles, Katy Wild, David Hutcheson
US TV sequence: William Phipps, Steven Geray, Maria Palmer

Fanatic *aka* Die! Die! My Darling
(HAMMER/SEVEN ARTS; GB) 98min

This enjoyable, though uneven, picture centres on the mad Mrs Trefoile, extravagantly played by a Bankhead determined to best Bette Davis's Baby Jane. Convinced that her dead son's visiting ex-fiancée, Patricia (Powers), has come home to stay, she becomes increasingly unhinged at Powers' efforts to leave the old mansion and locks her in the attic where she is starved and subjected to interminable Bible readings. Powers' change from mild amusement to sheer terror and Bankhead's development from eccentricity to homicidal mania are handled with consummate skill by the two actresses. Unfortunately, Narizzano shared with his Canadian compatriot Sydney Furie a tendency to lapse into gratuitous baroqueries. Matheson's script, based on Anne Blaisdell's novel *Nightmare*, gives some suitably ironic lines to Bankhead, provides ample opportunity for gory goings-on in cellars and contains a nicely menacing part for Vaughan as the lecherous servant out to kill Bankhead, a performance foreshadowing Vaughan's contribution to Sam Peckinpah's *Straw Dogs* (1971). Sutherland, a familiar figure in British horror movies of the period (**Dr Terror's House of Horrors**, 1964, for example) is very convincing in the role of an imbecile gardener. The movie was part of Hammer's series of post-**Psycho** (1960) horror-thrillers initiated by Seth Holt's **Taste of Fear** (1960).

d Silvio Narizzano *p* Anthony Hinds *s* Richard Matheson *c* Arthur Ibbetson *lp* Tallulah Bankhead, Stefanie Powers, Peter Vaughan, Maurice Kaufman, Yootha Joyce, Donald Sutherland

The Flesh Eaters (VULCAN PRODUCTIONS) 92(88)min

This highly watchable piece of gory horror-comic fantasy has a group of travellers stranded on an island inhabited by a sinister marine biologist (Kosleck), who has been cultivating tiny, glowing flesh-eating marine creatures. Eventually his electrical experiments produce two sea monsters.

The film is carried along with tremendous verve and pace and a good deal of imagination: the organisms were created by scratching the film with pins and the monsters are remarkably convincing. The film is full of off-beat compositions and includes a shot from inside the second monster's head during the climactic battle (a scene which is in black and white, for some reason, in the British print). Kosleck is probably best known as a forties Universal heavy and played Goebbels at least three times. Notable hard-core director Radley Metzger was the editor.

d/co-p Jack Curtis *co-p* Terry Curtis *co-p/s* Arnold Drake *c* Carson Davidson *se* Roy Benson *lp* Martin Kosleck, Rita Morley, Byron Sanders, Ray Tudor, Barbara Wilkin

Der Fluch der Gruenen Augen *aka* Cave of the Living Dead *aka* The Curse of the Green Eyes *aka* Night of the Vampires

(OBJEKTIV/TRIGLAV; WG, YUG) b/w 89(81)min

This film is even worse than Ratony's *Das Geheimnis der Gelben Narzissen* (1961), possibly because this time the director was also responsible for the storyline. Inspector Doren (Hoven) investigates the death of some women near the caves that extend under the castle of the local vampire, Professor Adelsberg (Preiss). The bone of contention between the policeman and the vampire is Karin (Field), the professor's secretary who gets vampirized but is cured by her lover while the villain turns into a skeleton before exploding. The male lead, Hoven, an associate of Jesús Franco, also distinguished himself as Germany's most sickeningly sadistic sexploitation director with his **Hexen Geschandet und zu Tode Gequaelt** (1972) and **Hexen bis aufs Blut Gequaelt** (1969).

d Akos von Ratony *p* Richard Gordon *s* C. von Rock *c* Hrvoj Saric *lp* Adrian Hoven, Carl Moehner, Erika Remberg, Wolfgang Preiss, Emmerich Schrenck, John Kitzmiller, Vida Juvan, Stane Sever

Der Hexer *aka* The Mysterious Magician *aka* The Wizard *aka* The Squeaker

(RIALTO FILM/PREBEN PHILIPSEN; WG) b/w scope 90min

Vohrer's professional adaptation of Edgar Wallace's popular novel was the 17th in Rialto's series of Wallace movies. Here the ending of the novel was modified in order to keep the identity of the main character secret and prepare the way for the sequel, *Neues vom Hexer* (1965), made by the same team. The story has the murderous squeaker return from Australia to pre-empt Scotland Yard's investigation into the murder of his sister, the secretary of a shady lawyer. The one-man death squad escapes, still shrouded in mystery.

Whereas previous series of Wallace adaptations had concentrated on the detective elements of the stories, the German series strongly emphasized the horrific and atmospheric sides of the tales, taking their cue from the psycho-thrillers then in vogue and from the prestigious German tradition exemplified by Fritz Lang's work, his Mabuse films in particular. Nearly all these Wallace movies feature old dark houses with phantom-like masked marauders emerging from hidden passageways, or Jack the Ripper settings in a romantically stylized East End of London (which, in the German image of the city, merges with Soho). Vohrer, one of the most prolific contributors to the series, also made **Die Toten Augen von London** (1961), *Der Bueckliges von Soho* (1966) and *Der Tuer mit den Sieben Schlossern* (1962), among others.

d Alfred Vohrer *p* Horst Wendlandt *s* Herbert Reinecker *c* Karl Loeb *lp* Joachim Fuchsberger, Heinz Drache, Sophie Hardy, Siegfried Lowitz, Ann Savo, Margot Trooger, Eddie Arent

Hysteria (HAMMER; GB) b/w 85min

Following the success of **Psycho** (1960), Hammer launched a series of horror-thrillers, beginning with Seth Holt's **Taste of Fear** (1960) and including **Maniac** (1962), **Fanatic** (1964) and Francis's three titles, **Paranoiac** (1962), **Nightmare** (1963) and *Hysteria*, the last and weakest of his contributions. Sangster's mechanical script about an amnesia victim (Webber) who hires a detective (Denham) to recover his identity, is routinely directed, with Francis relying on shock cuts and bouts of hallucinations to generate a sense of creeping insanity. Hammer added **The Nanny** (1965), *The Anniversary* (1967) and **Crescendo** (1969) to the series before abandoning the vein of macabre melodrama, while Francis extended his series of tepid thrillers with **Psychopath** (1965), made for Amicus.

d Freddie Francis *p/s* Jimmy Sangster *c* John Wilcox *lp* Robert Webber, Lelia Goldoni, Maurice Denham, Anthony Newlands, Jennifer Jayne, Peter Woodthorpe

I Eat Your Skin *aka* Zombies

(DEL TENNEY PRODUCTIONS) b/w 81min

When producer Jerry Gross needed a co-feature for **I Drink Your Blood** (1971) he bought a seven-year-old unreleased black and white film *Voodoo Blood Bath* (1964), directed by Del Tenney of *Horror of Party Beach* (1964) fame, re-titled it and put out a double-feature programme advertised as 'Two great blood horrors to rip out your guts'.

The story concerns Dr Biladeau (Stanton) who lives on a tropical island and attempts to derive a serum to cure cancer from the local plants. Unfortunately, the side-effects of his experiments have produced a large number of zombies whom plantation owner Coy plans to use to take over the world. No skin is eaten.

d/p/s Del Tenney *c* François Farkas *se* Guy del Rosso *lp* William Joyce, Heather Hewitt, Betty Hyatt Linton, Dan Stephenson, Walter Coy, Robert Stanton

The Incredibly Strange Creatures Who Stopped Living and Became Crazy Mixed up Zombies!!! *aka* Teenage Psycho Meets Bloody Mary

(MORGAN/STECKLER PRODUCTION) 81min

This is the best known (even if only by the title) of an intriguing group of horror films directed by Steckler, who also appeared in various exploitation movies (including his own) under the pseudonym Cash Flagg. His career began as a cameraman on *World's Greatest Sinner* (1961), an underground classic with a soundtrack by Frank Zappa, and continued as a director on such films as *Wild Guitar* (1961), *The Thrill Killers* (1964), and *The Lemon Grove Kids Meet the Monsters* (1966). One of Steckler's promotional ploys was to have fully made up members of his films' casts jump out from behind the screen at key moments during performances and abduct members of the audience, a technique he began with *Incredibly Strange Creatures*.

The first monster musical, the film centres on a Long Beach amusement park at which Madame Estrella (O'Hara), a gypsy fortune-teller, hypnotizes patrons, disfigures them with acid

Brett O'Hara (centre) in one of the genre's best titles, if not films: The Incredibly Strange Creatures Who Stopped Living and Became Crazy Mixed Up Zombies.

Kwaidan, *one of the few Japanese horror films to be screened in the West.*

and keeps them as freaks in cages. When she hypnotizes beatnik Jerry (Steckler) he embarks on a killing spree and is followed by the rest of the monsters, who break loose during a dance number and kill everyone in sight. The film began life when Steckler got together with three choreographers who had a large number of lavish costumes, plus a cast of dancers eager for work, left over from a show they had done at the Moulin Rouge, Hollywood. Together they choreographed what would later become the film's musical numbers and performed them live before the prospective backer, who was sufficiently impressed to support the project, which cost a mere $38,000. That it looks like it cost a good deal more is due not simply to the professionalism of the cast but also to the excellence of the photography, which is credited to Mascelli (the author of the classic handbook on cinematography) but also includes (uncredited) contributions from Laszlo Kovacs and Vilmos Zsigmond, both of whom began their careers in the exploitation field. Tight direction and editing also make the most of the shoestring budget so that, all in all, the film (unusually) delivers as much as it promises.

d/p Ray Dennis Steckler *s* Gene Pollock, Robert Silliphant, E. M. Kevke *c* Joseph V. Mascelli *lp* Cash Flagg (Ray Dennis Steckler), Brett O'Hara, Carolyn Brandt, Atlas King, Sharon Walsh, Madison Clarke, Erina Enyo, Jack Brady, Toni Camel, Neil Stillman

Kwaidan *aka* **Ghost Stories** *aka* **Weird Tales**
(NINJIN CLUB/BUNGEI; JAP) scope 164(125)min
Arriving in the West together with **Onibaba** (1964) at the Cannes film festival of 1965, this picture was enthusiastically received for its formal beauties (though it didn't escape the suspicion of having been made especially for Western consumption, with its stress on picturesque aspects of local colour and a slow rhythm thought to please non-Japanese viewers).

The script adapts traditional stories as collected and retold by American Lafcadio Hearn in his *Kwaidan – Stories and Studies of Strange Things*, first published in 1904. As a stylistic exercise, with each tale placed in a different season of the year, the movie contains some astonishingly beautiful sequences. *Kurokami*, taken from Hearn's *Shadowings* opens the film. It tells the story of a young samurai (Mikuni) who leaves his wife (Aratama) but eventually returns to his home and finds it dilapidated, although his wife appears exactly as he left her. They spend the night in a passionate reconciliation but the next morning he wakes up with a corpse in his arms, her long black hair entwining itself around him until he dies of shock. The plot is similar to Akinari Ueda's story which Mizoguchi had incorporated into his *Ugetsu Monogatari* (1953), but Kobayashi's treatment is both slower to get to the point and cruder when it gets there. *Chawan no Nak* has the samurai (Ganemon Nakamura) drink a cup of tea in which he sees the reflection of someone else's face (Nakaya) whose personality then comes to haunt him. The most spectacular story, *Miminashi Hoichi no Hanashi* tells of a blind biwa player (Katsuo Nakamura) who recites the saga of the Heike clan's defeat in a sea battle with the Taira clan. Summoned to go and perform his song for a nobleman, it emerges that his audience is the ghostly army of defeated soldiers. To protect the musician, a priest paints holy texts on his body but forgets to cover the ears which are then torn off by the ghosts. A fourth tale, *Yukionna*, about a beautiful woman spectre who lures people to a snowy death was removed from the Western release prints and later circulated as a short.

The movie is notable mainly for its eye-catching colour compositions, in particular in the stylized sea battle against a scarlet sky which ends with the Heike clan's women drowning themselves in a blood red sea, their robes forlornly floating behind them, and the tombstones changing into a ghostly assembly of warriors waiting for the musician's performance. Although over-rated, the picture – which was a flop in Japan – looks wonderful and has an effective score by one of Japan's most original film-music composers, Toru Takemitsu.

d Masaki Kobayashi *p* Shigeru Wakatsuki *s* Yoko Mizuki *c* Yoshio Miyajima *lp* Rentaro Mikuni, Michiyo Aratama, Ganemon Nakamura, Noboru Nakaya, Katsuo Nakamura, Takashi Shimura, Tetsuro Tamba, Keiko Kishi, Tatsuya Nakadai

La Loba *aka* **Los Horrores del Bosque Negro** *aka* **Los Misterios de Bosque Negro** *aka* **The She Wolf**
(PRODUCCIONES SOTOMAYOR; MEX) b/w 85min
Baledon's quickie is too busy adding such gore as the removal of intestines or manglings by dogs to the traditional Mexican horror product to take the opportunity to make an original contribution to the genre, by presenting a love story between two werewolves. The opening sequence shows, with relentlessly insistent music, a werewolf emerging from a tomb and killing two people before disappearing into a house down its chimney. The story that follows features Lisandro (Cordero), a young doctor specializing in lycanthropy cases, who collaborates with the weird family of Dr Fernandez (Moreno) – wife Dominguez, daughter de Hoyos, mute little girl, ominous servant Alvarado – and another young woman (Roel), a specially trained werewolf-hunting dog and its mistress (Murayama). In spite of numerous red herrings, it becomes evident that there is something seriously wrong with de Hoyos, since her parents keep locking her up in her room and are terrified when Cordero asks to marry her. First Cordero is seen committing some lycanthropic acts, but then, before the terrified little girl's eyes, de Hoyos also has a transformation scene and is let out of her locked room by the servant. In the end, the dog and the doctor's assistant (Cañedo) kill both werewolves who die in each other's arms. Only the picture's closing sequence gives an idea of what it might have become in more capable hands. Ludicrous makeup and a story that requires every night to have a full moon and exhausts itself in detours, effectively kill whatever good ideas the scenarist may have devised.

d Rafael Baledon *p* Jesús Sotomayor *s* Ramón Obon *c* Raúl Martinez Solares *lp* Kitty de Hoyos, Joaquin Cordero, José Elias Moreno, Columena Dominguez, Roberto Cañedo, Noé Murayama, Crox Alvarado, Maria Roel, Ramon Bugarini, Hortensia Santoveña

Las Luchadoras contra la Momia *aka* The Wrestling Woman vs the Aztec Mummy

(CINEMATOGRAFICA CALDERON; MEX) b/w 77min

In this typical outing las Luchadoras – a group of rather appealing looking female wrestlers led by Loreat (Velazquez) and Rubi (Campbell) – take on a gang of criminals in search of an Aztec treasure. The gang leaders, called Fujita and Mao, go around murdering, abducting and hypnotically controlling young women, at one point even sending two male wrestlers to confront the heroines in the ring. The chase finally leads to the tomb of Xochitl, the Aztec Princess, guarded by the mummy of Tezomoc, a warrior. Tezomoc loses his temper when the orientals steal a medallion from the princess's body and he kills them, destroying the entire pyramid in the process.

Although the movie is shot as an old-style children's serial, the recourse to the well-established pornographic subgenre of wrestling women suggests that the film-makers assumed their audience to be infantile adults, an assumption shared by the makers of *Santo contra las Mujeres Vampiro* (1962) and a great many other 'adult' wrestler movies which increasingly dwelt on sexy, screaming women. Las Luchadoras, who had made their first appearence in *El Medico Asesino* (1962), returned to battle in *Las Lobas del Ring* (1964), *Las Mujeres Panteras* (1966) and, with different actresses, in **Las Luchadoras contra el Robot Asesino** (1969).

d René Cardona *p/co-s* Guillermo Calderon *co-s* Alfredo Salazar *c* Ezequiel Carrasco *lp* Lorena Velazquez, Elisabeth Campbell, Armando Silvestre, Maria Eugenia San Martin, Chucho Salinas, Ramón Bugarini, Victor Velaquez, Ton-La Tapatia, Irma Gonzalez, Chabela Romero

I Lunghi Capelli della Morte *aka* The Long Hair of Death

(CINEGAI; IT) b/w 100(96)min

In spite of a perfunctory script, this, Margheriti's second film with Steele (the first was **La Danza Macabra**, 1964) is equally atmospheric and contains some very impressive sequences. Set in the early 16th century, the movie begins in **La Maschera del Demonio** (1960) territory as the wife of Count Humbolt (Rafferty) is burnt at the stake falsely accused of a murder committed by the Count's son, Kurt (Ardisson). Her agonies are witnessed by her two daughters, Helen (Steele) and Lizabeth (Zalewska). Rafferty also kills Steele but she returns from the dead – in a splendid scene in which a thunderbolt splits her tomb to reveal her worm-eaten face – making Rafferty die of fright. There are some fine shots of a white-robed Zalewska wandering through the medieval castle with shafts of light falling from high windows, and Steele's presence alone suffices to lift any such fantasy well above the average, especially when her role combines eroticism and vengeful menace directed against brutally callous men.

Margheriti went on to make a series of science fiction movies, including the beautiful *Il Pianeta Errante* (1966), before his career degenerated into routine exploitation thrillers and camp parodies such as **Il Mostro E in Tavola ... Barone Frankenstein** and **Dracula Cerca Sangue di Vergine e ... Mori di Sete** (both 1973), two mediocre efforts often credited to Paul Morrissey.

d Anthony Dawson (Antonio Margheriti) *p* Felice Testa Gay *s* Robert Bohr (Bruno Valeri), Julian Berry (Ernesto Gastaldi) *c* Richard Thierry (Riccardo Pallotini) *lp* Barbara Steele, Giorgio Ardisson, Halina Zalewska, Robert Rains, Jean Rafferty (Giuliano Raffaelli), Laureen Nuyen (Laura Nucci), John Carey, Jeffrey Darcy

The Masque of the Red Death

(ALTA VISTA/ANGLO AMALGAMATED; GB) scope 90(84)min

The seventh in Corman's Poe cycle, this might not be the best (that is probably **The Tomb of Ligeia**, 1964), but it's certainly the most ambitious. Price plays Prospero, devil-worshipping prince of a small Italian province in the 12th century, a practised sadist confined to the sanctuary of his castle with his aristocratic guests while the plague rages outside. Inside, all is revelry and cruelty until, during the great masque which crowns Price's entertainment, Death enters the dance and the guests succumb one by one to the plague. Initially, its most striking feature is that there is no sign of the hazily filtered colour effects which tactfully conceal decorative limitations in the American Poe films. Here the colour is brilliantly sharp and clear, and Corman makes the most of the solid, exquisitely wrought sets and costumes permitted by a (comparatively) high budget, whether introducing the lovely mosaic flooring of the castle in a reflective overhead shot as Price paces slowly across it, or dazzling the eye with sudden changes from white to yellow, purple and black by tracking Asher (the innocent being unwillingly instructed in the mysteries of diabolism by Price) as she runs through a series of four adjoining rooms, each designed in a different colour motif. More importantly, the film is graced by an uncommonly intelligent script which probes the concept of diabolism with considerable subtlety, even though the black-magic scenes (six minutes worth) were censored out before release.

Where most films of this nature tend simply to pile on the blood, here there is a genuine chill of intellectual evil because Price, initiating tortures with a characteristic air of sadistic glee, also conveys a genuine philosophical curiosity as to the unknown territories into which his quest for evil may lead him. One readily believes in this world of his, where good and evil are not merely words but ideas to be tested and perhaps found wanting. At times, in fact, the film is reminiscent of Ingmar Bergman's *The Seventh Seal* (1956) in its intellectual probings, in its figuration of Death, and in the conception of the final sequence (although the masque itself was diminished by production difficulties).

d Roger Corman *p* George Willoughby *s* Charles Beaumont, R. Wright Campbell *c* Nicolas Roeg *lp* Vincent Price, Hazel Court, Jane Asher, David Weston, Patrick Magee, Skip Martin

Moonshine Mountain

(HERSCHELL G. LEWIS PRODUCTIONS) b/w 90min

If Lewis left the nudie field because less strict censorship of sex scenes meant that Hollywood was stealing his audience, the director was also forced to abandon gore for a while because, after **Blood Feast** (1963) had caught them unawares, the censorship authorities were now lying in wait for further

The vengeful Barbara Steele in I Lunghi Capelli della Morte.

The arrival of the plague in Roger Corman's The Masque of the Red Death.

excesses. Censorship problems may well explain why **2000 Maniacs** (1964) was financially less successful than its technically inferior predecessor. Nonetheless *Moonshine Mountain*, a 'good ole boy' hillbilly epic about a successful country and western singer who goes back to his Carolina roots in search of fresh inspiration and becomes involved in a moonshine racket, is still a great deal more gory than most other films in the backwoods' genre and features some particularly nasty murders by and axe and explosion.

d/p/c Herschell Gordon Lewis *s* Charles Glore *lp* Chuck Scott, Adam Sorg, Jeffrey Allen, Bonnie Hinson, Carmen Sotir, Ben Moore, Pat Patterson, Mark Douglas, Karin March, Gretchen Eisner

Il Mostro dell'Opera *aka* **Il Vampiro dell'Opera** *aka* **The Vampire of the Opera** *aka* **The Monster of the Opera** (NIF; IT) b/w 80min

A year after finishing **L'Amante del Vampiro** (1960), Polselli started to make a movie entitled *Il Vampiro dell'Opera*, which was eventually finished and released in 1964 as *Il Mostro dell'Opera*. Loosely based on Gaston Leroux's *Phantom*, the story opens well with a group of actors entering a disused opera house and becoming increasingly edgy as they begin to sense its uncanny atmosphere. A woman follows a mysterious stranger into the basement and disappears only to return as an enchantingly disturbing vampire. The rest of the picture chronicles her seductions of the women and then of the men in the group, limping on to the predictable final conflagration. When tension building has to give way to delivering shocks in the film's second half, Polselli seems to lose interest and allows the movie to degenerate into a routine sexploitation effort. He went on to make many more sexploitation films, including **Riti Magie Neri e Segrete Orge del Trecento** (1973), usually hiding under the pseudonym Ralph Brown.

d/s Renato Polselli *lp* John McDouglas (Giuseppe Addobbati), Vittoria Prada, Marc Marian (Marco Mariani), Barbara Howard, Catla Cavelli

Night Must Fall (MGM; GB) b/w 99min

With the proceeds of the successful *Tom Jones* (1963), Finney repaid Reisz for *Saturday Night and Sunday Morning* (1960) by producing and starring in this leaden adaptation of Emlyn Williams' old theatrical warhorse, previously – and better – filmed by Richard Thorpe in 1937. While the play endows the contents of the mad axeman's cherished box with some mystery, Reisz's version has Danny (Finney) wielding the axe from the start and there is little subtlety in his relation with the resultant severed head. Trading on the stereotype of the virile, working-class lad established in English 'realist' movies and plays after *Look Back in Anger* (1956), Finney seduces all the women in sight, cannily playing whatever role they expect from him. The direction is imitative (of early Jean-Luc Godard), flashy and empty, uncertain whether to go for 'art' or exploitation. The movie's only redeeming feature is the camerawork of Francis, whose crisp images endow the film with a sense of danger.

d/co-p Karel Reisz *co-p* Albert Finney *s* Clive Exton *c* Freddie Francis *lp* Albert Finney, Mona Washbourne, Susan Hampshire, Sheila Hancock, Michael Medwin, Joe Gladwin, John Gill, Martin Wyldeck

The Night Walker (CASTLE PICTURES) b/w 86min

This ludicrously contrived shocker sees Castle once again trying to be Hitchcock. The plot has a blind electronics engineer (Rorke) accuse his wife (Stanwyck) of being unfaithful with his solicitor (Taylor) because she talks in her sleep about a lover. Rorke is then blown up in an explosion and haunts Stanwyck's dreams, which seem to spill over into a nightmarish reality, with a dream lover (Bochner) materializing and on one occasion taking her to a chapel to be married by a waxwork priest (before waxwork witnesses) and where she sees her husband with his face horribly burned. After more frights and a murder, it turns out that Bochner, a private eye hired by her husband before his death, has blackmail in mind. Taylor, after her money and trying to drive her mad by posing as her husband wearing a mask, kills Bochner but falls to his death before he can deal with her. Shoddy stuff despite Stanwyck's sterling performance, the film is pompously prefaced by a lecture on the meaning of dreams.

d/p William Castle *s* Robert Bloch *c* Harold Stine *lp* Barbara Stanwyck, Robert Taylor, Hayden Rorke, Lloyd Bochner, Rochelle Hudson

Onibaba *aka* **The Hole** *aka* **The Demon** *aka* **Devil Woman** (KINDAI EIGA KYOKAI/ TOKYO EIGA; JAP) b/w scope 104min

Shindo's film was the first Japanese picture with horrific elements to achieve a wide distribution in the West. His arty *Hadaka no Shima* (1961) had been widely acclaimed, but *Onibaba*'s success was due more to its reputation as 'the most nude, sexiest pic to be unveiled in New York so far', as *Variety* put it in 1965.

Shindo, a prolific scenarist and director stemming from peasant stock, had made melodramas, one of which, *Genbaku no Ko* (1952), about the children of Hiroshima, had been banned by the Americans in Japan. *Onibaba* is a period drama told resolutely from a peasant point-of-view and thus runs counter to the many period movies presenting samurai in a heroic light. Set in the 16th century, the story tells of an elderly woman (Otowa) and her daughter-in-law (Yoshimura) who live by killing fleeing soldiers and selling their armour. One night their swamp dwelling is visited by a samurai (Uno) with a demonic mask. The mother kills him, removes the mask – revealing a putrefied face – and puts it on to frighten her daughter-in-law out of an affair with a neighbour, Hachi (Sato). In the end, it requires vigorous hammer blows to dislodge the feudal mask of superstition from Otowa's face, which has become a festering mess. The marshy plain, overgrown with waving weeds, the demon-masked stranger following Otowa on a moonlit night and the opening sequence tracing the flight of two soldiers through the reeds by showing only the ripples on the surface of the field until the women's glittering spears suddenly stab out of the darkness at them, are staged and photographed with consummate mastery. Otowa and Yoshimura provide tremendously powerful performances as they convey the destitute peasant women's fierce vitality and determination to survive in a society laid waste by its aristocratic rulers. Otowa, a regular in Shindo's films since 1952 and a partner in his independent production company, also appeared in the companion piece to *Onibaba*, **Yabu no Naka Kuroneko** (1968).

d/p/s Kaneto Shindo *c* Kiyomi Kuroda *lp* Nobuko Otowa, Jitsuko Yoshimura, Kei Sato, Jukichi Uno, Taiji Tonoyama

El Secreto del Dr Orloff *aka* Dr Orloff's Monster *aka* The Secret of Dr Orloff *aka* Mistresses of Dr Jekyll *aka* Brides of Dr Jekyll *aka* Dr Jekyll's Mistress

(COOPERATIVA CINEMATOGRAFICA/LEO FILMS; SP) 88min

Franco's first sequel to **Gritos en la Noche** (1962), this only has a few tenuous links with the previous picture. A disciple of a Dr Orloff (no relation to the doctor who got killed in *Gritos*) called Fisherman (Arroita-Jauregui) develops a way of teleguiding people through a radio beam. Angered by an adulterous relationship between his wife (Cristal) and his brother (Blanco), he kills and transforms his brother into a radio-controlled zombie whom he makes kill a number of women, including Cristal. The heroine, played by Spaak, is the zombie's daughter. She alerts the police and, when the doctor orders the zombie/her father to kill her, vestiges of paternal love blow the zombie's fuses and he turns on his master before disappearing into the woods. The ending sees the zombie enticed into the village square, with his daughter as bait, and destroyed.

Combining clichés and ponderous dialogue with flamboyant bits of gothic *mise-en-scène* and a decided tendency to slip in to sexploitation long before Hammer or Italian productions took that route, Franco here concocts a mixture characteristic of his work until the late sixties. After his remake of Stoker's classic tale, **El Conde Dracula** (1970), he turned virtually exclusively to sadistic sex movies often in a horror setting. Like *Gritos* and *La Mano de un Hombre Muerto* (1962), this film was accompanied by the publication of a novel under Franco's pen name David Kuhne. Some sources credit the film to Jess Franck and add a Nick Franck as co-scenarist.

Franco used the same plot device in his next film, **Miss Muerte** (1965) and also featured teleguided robots in his best film of the period, *Cartes sur Table* (1966).

d/s Jesús Franco *c* Alfonso Nieva *lp* Agnes Spaak, Hugh White (Hugo Blanco), Marcelo Arroita-Jauregui, Perla Cristal, Pastor Serrador, Luisa Sala, José Rubio, Daniel Blumer

Sei Donne per l'Assassino *aka* Blood and Black Lace *aka* Six Femmes pour l'Assassin *aka* Blutige Seide *aka* Fashion House of Death *aka* Six Women for the Murderer

(EMMEPI CINEMATOGRAFICA/PRODUCTIONS GEORGES DE BEAUREGARD/TOP FILM/MONARCHIA FILMS; IT,FR,WG) 90(85)min

With **La Maschera del Demonio** (1960), **Ercole al Centro della Terra** (1961) and **La Frusta e il Corpo** (1963), Bava joined Terence Fisher and Roger Corman as one of the leading artists in the horror genre. But where Fisher's films were imbued with mythical overtones and Corman's with socio-historical ones, Bava's work operates almost exclusively on the level of cinematic style. His films are as plotless and scriptless as it is possible for non-avant-garde cinema to be, using the strict minimum necessary to motivate the *mise-en-scène* of lusciously flamboyant sado-voyeuristic operas. In this picture the audience is no longer asked to care about who gets killed – the title announces and summarizes the action – and the killer, in his featureless mask, is merely the faceless representative of the male spectator as he stalks, one after the other, a series of women guilty of nothing less than provoking desire.

The movie is set in a fashion house run by Bartok – it is her business to make women desirable – which also acts as a front for a drug ring. A man (Mitchell), attempting to control this empire of senses, ends up cruelly destroying the women models and is killed himself in the process. The Grand Guignol theatre of the unconscious, writing in flaming red and deathly green what most movies decently hide behind believable scenarios and well-rounded characters, allows its chilling perversity to seep into every square inch of the screen as the female victims are persecuted and violently killed in a fantasy that doesn't allow real women any place at all. Killer and victims become dream figures enacting a scenario of male phobias turning upon the desperate (because impossible) attempt to eliminate the disturbances caused by desire within men. In this film, women represent the desiring side of men, and the misogyny is a sign of male self-hatred triggered by panic at the very existence of male desire. Later sadistic-terror films such as **The Texas Chainsaw Massacre** (1974) are careful to let viewers off the hook by making their killers into sub- or superhuman killers or deviants. Here, Bava dispenses with hypocrisy as the killer's face is reduced to a blank screen offering no comforting resistance for projective identifications by the male spectators, and representing a menacing 'every man' for female viewers. *Sei Donne* is a genuinely disturbing movie, but it is also a demonic ceremony visualizing the pathological dimensions inherent in the cinematic spectacle itself, confronting us with a sado-voyeuristic delirium that simultaneously fascinates and repels. Of Bava's subsequent giallo terror-thrillers initiated by *La Ragazza che Sapevo Troppo* (1962) none except **Ecologia del Delitto** (1971) reach this level of intensity. *Sei Donne* was made both in Italian and English versions, the latter's production being supervised by Lou Moss.

d/co-s Mario Bava *p* Massimo Patrizi, Alfred Mirabel (Alfredo Mirabile) *co-s* Marcello Fondato, Joe (Giuseppe) Barilla *c* Herman Tarzana (Ubaldo Terzano) *lp* Eva Bartok, Cameron Mitchell, Thomas Reiner, Ariana Gorini, Mary Arden, Lea Kruger, Claudia Dantes, Harriet White, Nadia Anty, Heidi Stroh

Strait-Jacket

(WILLIAM CASTLE PRODUCTIONS) b/w 93(89)min

Castle's flow of tacky gimmicks, begun with **Macabre** (1958), was brought to an end by the protestations of exasperated cinema managers, so here he contents himself with imitating Robert Aldrich's highly successful ploy of plunging Joan Crawford and Bette Davis into the horrors of **What Ever Happened to Baby Jane?** (1962). Hence Crawford here is an axe-murderess, released from an asylum 20 years after she killed her husband and his lover in front of her small daughter, who repairs to the farm where the daughter (Baker) now lives

Nobuko Otowa in the demonic mask of Onibaba.

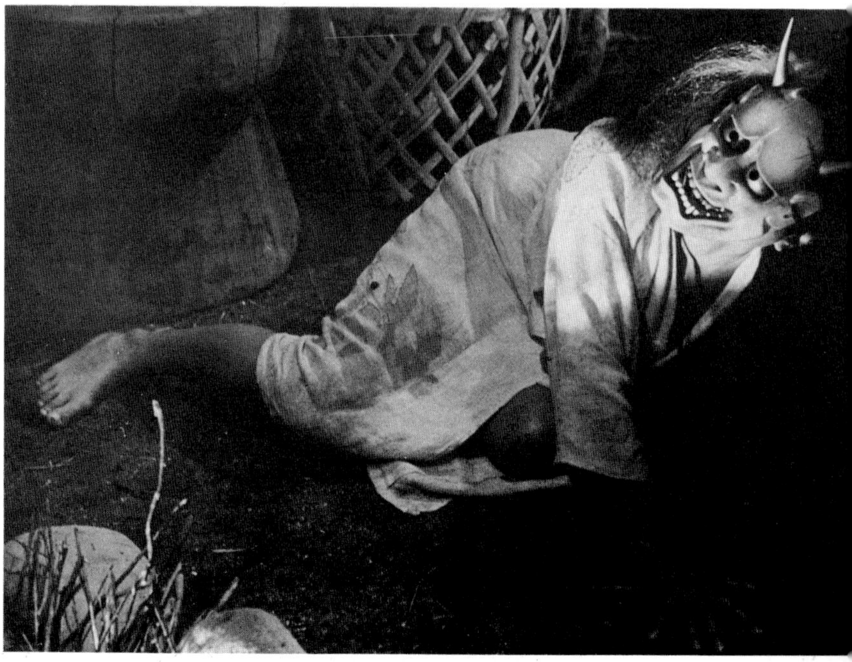

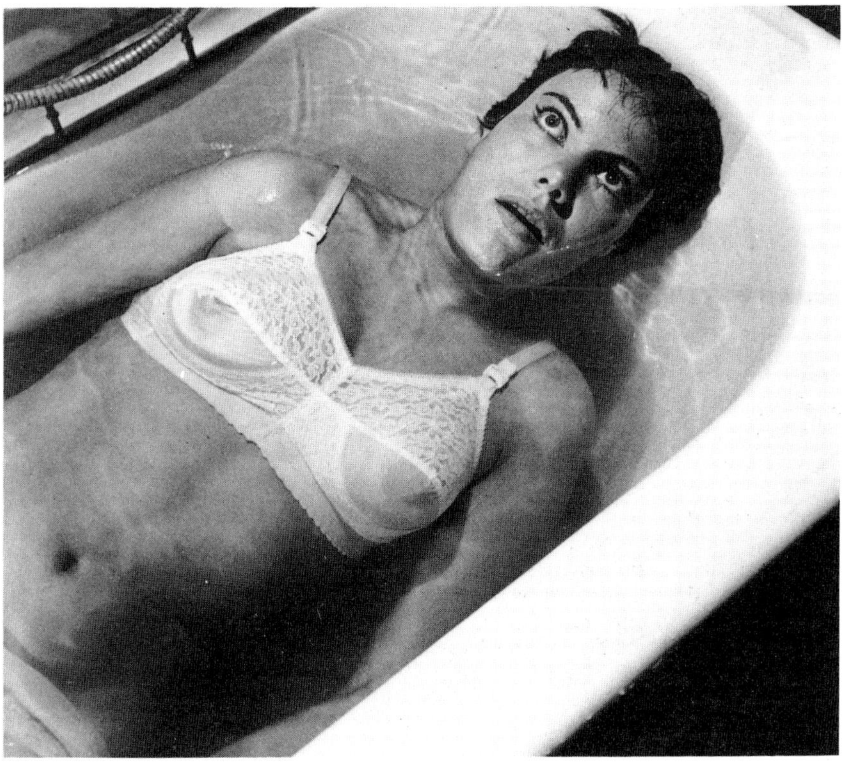

Claudia Dantes, one of the many corpses that populate Sei Donne per l'Assassino, *Mario Bava's chilling essay in sexual perversity.*

with her aunt and uncle. Believing herself sane but suffering from nightmares and very visible stress (toying with knives and sharp instruments), she is soon disabused by terrifying hallucinations, followed by a series of axe murders. All have been perpetrated by Baker to get rid of her boyfriend's disapproving parents in the knowledge that Crawford would be blamed, especially if driven insane by the 'hallucinations'.

As empty of psychology as it is of wit or style, the film is of interest only in offering an absurd parody of Crawford's image and mannerisms. Despite the traumas she suffered and is suffering, she still fights her way tooth and nail, she's still a woman who has been around (laconically striking a match on a gramophone record), and she still stuns handsome young men (one is suitably abashed when confronted by her after a quick change from prison black to flowered print, jangling bracelets and sultry wig). Most archetypal of all and a *sine qua non* for later Crawford, is the organ blast of self-sacrificial mother love with which the film ends as, together at last, mother shepherds daughter off to the asylum where she will take charge.

d/p William Castle *s* Robert Bloch *c* Arthur Arling
lp Joan Crawford, Diane Baker, Leif Erickson, Howard St John, Rochelle Hudson, George Kennedy

The Tomb of Ligeia

(ALTA VISTA/AIP; GB) scope 81min

This, the last entry in Corman's Poe cycle which began with **House of Usher** (1960) and his last horror movie to date, sees him on familiar territory. Price's Verden Fell lurks behind the dark glasses in the gloomy vastness of his gothic abbey home (1821 vintage), wrestling hopefully and fearfully with his obsessive conviction that his wife is not really dead. A black cat squalls, the dead woman's eyes open in the coffin, and the possession of his usurping second wife by the restless spirit of the first (both played by Shepherd) is soon under way.

Yet the very fact that it was shot on location instead of in studio sets, using an old Norfolk abbey as Price's home, gives the film a markedly different tone, a tangible solidity to add to the psychological subtlety: it is as though one were watching Poe filtered though the gothic melodrama of a *Jane Eyre* and reaching – with the perfectly legitimate yet somehow anachronistic dark glasses affected by Price acting as a bridge – forward to the very different kinds of obsession and possession in Hitchcock's *Vertigo* (1958). Although the final sequence returns a little disappointingly to formula (the blinding of Price, the destruction of the abbey by fire as he is enfolded in the bloody embrace of his dead wife), the rest of the film is superbly structured around the conception of him as a man both wilfully blinding himself to the truth and tempted to pry into forbidden mysteries. Hidden behind dark glasses, exposed when these are stolen, and finally scratched out, Price's eyes (a recurring motif with Corman) are crucial to the film's vision. One of the most rivetingly bizarre sequences has him simultaneously seeing and not seeing as the black cat, carrying the purloined glasses, lures the beautiful Lady Rowena up the stairway leading to the abbey belltower. What Price sees is the danger to Rowena, trapped on the narrow ledge at the top of stairway as the great bell starts to swing; what he does not see is that, with this bell leading straight to the wedding bells, his marriage to Rowena will give dead Ligeia the foothold she needs for a vengeful return.

d Roger Corman *p* Pat Green *s* Robert Towne *c* Arthur Grant *lp* Vincent Price, Elizabeth Shepherd, John Westbrook, Oliver Johnston, Derek Francis, Richard Vernon

Two on a Guillotine (WB) pv b/w 107(84)min

This is one of those silly shockers involving dead men who are not really dead. By the terms of her father's will, Stevens has to spend the night alone in his house if she is to inherit the estate. A stage magician driven mad when he accidentally cut off his wife's head while performing an illusion, the father (Romero) also promises in the will to return from the dead, instructing that his body be handcuffed to the utmost. Return he does and, mistaking Stevens for her mother (she plays both parts), straps her to the trick guillotine, determined to atone for his earlier lapse by demonstrating his skill. Leavitt's camera lingers effectively on the clutter of weird illusions and magician's props that litter the house, but apart from one bizarre scene – the reading of the will from the stage of the deserted Hollywood Bowl – the film is strictly routine.

d/p William Conrad *s* Henry Slesar, John Kneubuhl *c* Sam Leavitt *lp* Connie Stevens, Dean Jones, Cesar Romero, Parley Baer, Virginia Gregg, Connie Gilchrist

2000 Maniacs

(FRIEDMAN-LEWIS PRODUCTIONS) 88(75)min

A gore variation on *Brigadoon* (1954), *2000 Maniacs* was made to exploit the obviously lucrative market revealed by the success of **Blood Feast** (1963). It tells the story of a small Southern town ravaged by Union troops during the Civil War which magically reappears 100 years later to wreak its revenge on six tourists visiting from the North. Described by Lewis as 'the one picture we really took pains on', it may not have the 'tremendous production values' claimed by its maker but, technically, it's undeniably an advance on *Blood Feast*, with a

Right: *Vincent Price administering to Elizabeth Shepherd in Roger Corman's* The Tomb of Ligeia, *the last of his Edgar Allan Poe adaptations.*

more literate script, varied and attractive locations (St Cloud, Florida, now the site of Disneyworld), reasonable acting and a relatively mobile camera. It's still extremely gory, however, moving through a tourist having a thumb and then an arm chopped off, cannibalism, a man dismembered by being tied to horses which gallop off in different directions and the famous scene of a man being rolled downhill in a barrel lined with spikes.

d/s/c Herschell Gordon Lewis *p* David F. Friedman *lp* Connie Mason, Thomas Wood, Jeffrey Allen, Ben Moore, Shelby Livingston, Vincent Santo, Gary Bakeman, Mark Douglas, Michael Korb

Das Ungeheuer von London City *aka* The Monster of London City

(CCC FILMKUNST; WG) b/w scope 87min

With this Jack the Ripper story based on a novel by Bryan (the son of Edgar) Wallace the rival Wallace series produced by Brauner came to an end, leaving the field free for the Rialto produced series which continued for another eight years. While Richard Sand (Felmy) plays Jack the Ripper on the stage of the Edgar Allen Poe Theatre in Whitechapel, someone starts murdering women in the neighbourhood, raising the question of the influence of violent theatre on the crime rate. The real culprit turns out to be a friend of the actor, Dr Greely (Schoenherr). This poor contribution to the series was furnished by the same team that made *Der Henker von London* (1963). These German adaptations, following on from the British series produced in the thirties, helped to make Wallace the most filmed author ever, with more than 150 screen adaptations to his credit. The scenarist Stemmle, also a director in his own right, is best known as an authority on crime stories. Zbonek was an Austrian film journalist turned director, but his films proved as routinely insipid as his criticism.

d Edwin Zbonek *p* Artur Brauner *s* Robert A. Stemmle *c* Siegfried Hold *lp* Marianne Koch, Hansjoerg Felmy, Dietmar Schoenherr, Hans Nielsen, Chariklia Baxevanos, Fritz Tillman, Walter Pfeil, Kai Fischer

Where Has Poor Mickey Gone?

(LEDECK-INDIGO PRODUCTIONS; GB) b/w 59min

Only Ottilie Patterson's performance of the title song and the appearance by Mitchell four years before he became a popular television star as the obnoxious Alf Garnett in *Till Death Us Do Part* are of interest in this inept exploitation quickie about a teenage gang, led by Mick (Malcolm), who invade the basement workshop of a stage magician (Mitchell) who manages to make his tormentors disappear with a magic cabinet. Levy later made the science fiction film, *The Body Stealers* (1969).

d/p Gerry Levy *s* Peter Marcus *c* Alan Pudney *lp* Warren Mitchell, John Malcolm, Raymond Armstrong, John Challis, Christopher Robbie, Karol Hagar, Joseph Cook, Philip Newman

Witchcraft *aka* Witch and Warlock

(LIPPERT; GB) b/w 79min

Fresh from the uneven but impressive **Kiss of the Vampire** (1962), Sharp turned out this effectively staged tale of ancient, legitimate resentments being released as a bulldozer churns up a cemetery. The developer, Bill Lanier (Hedley) belongs to a family that in the 17th century persecuted and cheated the Whitlock family out of their property, burying Vanessa (Rees) alive in the bargain. Now, she returns to get her family's revenge. Her contemporary descendants are played by Chaney Jnr and Clare. The climax involves the rescue of Hedley's wife (Dixon) from a black mass and the destruction of the Whitlock family by pouring boiling oil over them. The main effects include the appearance of Rees in the back of cars, causing fatal accidents, and the environment of the aged Malvina Lanier (Ney), the old woman in Hedley's attic who knows all about family curses. Among pleasingly understated performances, Ney's hamminess and Chaney's blustering provide discordant elements, but Sharp managed to turn this Poverty Row effort into a very well made movie with a particularly good beginning. Sharp's strong point, besides being able to direct action – a rare talent in British cinema – is the way he can make a set or a location come alive and assume an importance almost equal to that of the actors. The context in which he places the actions specified in the script bring additional reverberations to the story in a manner reminiscent of Vincente Minnelli's use of décor. This aspect of his work often saved bad scripts and is most in evidence in his best movie to date, **The Face of Fu Manchu** (1965).

Yvette Rees as the malevolent witch in Don Sharp's better than average Witchcraft.

d Don Sharp *p* Robert Lippert, Jack Parsons *s* Harry Spalding *c* Arthur Lavis *lp* Jack Hedley, Jill Dixon, Marie Ney, David Weston, Lon Chaney Jnr, Diane Clare, Viola Keats, Yvette Rees

1965

Amanti d'Oltretomba *aka* The Faceless Monster *aka* Nightmare Castle *aka* Orgasmo *aka* Lovers Beyond the Tomb *aka* Night of the Doomed

(EMMECI CINEMATOGRAFICA; IT) b/w 105(73)min

Less a horror film than a well intentioned, but bad, love poem addressed to Steele, this picture's complicated plot is simply strung together to allow us to see her being lustful, tortured, disfigured, sleeping, walking, fainting, loving, afraid, and so on. Completely structured around her presence, the film has her in two roles: the hot-blooded, dark-haired Muriel Hampton, caught in the act with her lover David (Battaglia) by her husband Stephen (Miller) who viciously tortures and kills her, and the innocent, blonde Jenny, Muriel's half-sister, driven insane by Miller and gradually taken over by the vengeful ghost of Muriel. The film seems frozen in its fetishistic contemplation of Steele, an impression underlined by Ennio Morricone's repetitive score. It appears that directors unable to use Steele's uncanny beauty for the kind of horror films that are also designed to churn up the viewer's relation to cinematic fantasies *per se* (**L'Orribile Segreto del Dr Hichcock**, 1962; **La Maschera del Demonio**, 1960), were simply overwhelmed by the force of her image, making their films disintegrate into superficial picture albums.

d/p/co-s Allan Grunewald (Mario Caiano) *co-s* Fabio de Agostini *c* Enzo Barboni *lp* Barbara Steele, Paul Muller, Helga Liné, Laurence Clift, John McDouglas (Giuseppe Addobbati), Rik Battaglia

Atacan las Brujas *aka* **Santo en la Casa de las Brujas** *aka* **Santo Ataca las Brujas** *aka* **Santo Attacks the Witches**
(FILMICA VERGARA; MEX) b/w 90min
Huerta, the Silver Masked wrestler, fresh from his adventures with the strangler (*Santo vs el Estrangulador* and *Santo contra el Espectro*, both 1963), here confronts a reincarnation of the 17th-century witch Mayra (played by Velazquez, who had also appeared in **Las Luchadoras contra la Momia**, 1964). Velazquez bewitches Ofelia (San Martin) so her lover (Bugarini) invokes the wrestler's help to stop San Martin being used as a human sacrifice in the spring festival. After numerous adventures involving the use of protective crucifixes, sequestrations in dank caves and a fight with demon serpents – and sundry other creatures – in a cemetery, Santo saves the world and the witches perish in a fire.

The film was released in 1968 after the same team's next three-episode feature combined into a single movie, *El Hacha Diabolica* (1965), in which Santo confronts a vampire, the Black Mask and his magic axe. Santo's next encounters with vampires were **Santo y el Tesoro de Dracula** (1968) and **La Venganza de las Mujeres Vampiro** (1969).

d José Diaz Morales *p* Luís Enrique Vergara *s* Rafael Gracia Travesi, Fernando Oses *c* Alfredo Uribe *lp* Santo (Rodolfo Guzmán Huerta), Lorena Velazquez, Ramón Bugarini, Maria Eugenia San Martin, Edaena Ruiz, Fernando Oses, Altia Michel, Crox Alvarado, Mary Montiel, Guillermo Hernandez (Lobo Negro)

The Beach Girls and the Monster *aka* **Monster from the Surf** (US FILMS) b/w and col 70min
This is a plodding attempt by Hall, a former sarong king of *The Hurricane* (1937) and *South of Pago Pago* (1940) fame, to get into the rebellious youth/beach-party syndrome. In the opening sequence, a girl is killed on the beach by a seaweedy, pointy-headed relative of *The Creature from the Black Lagoon* (1954). This turns out to be Hall, an oceanographer who dresses up as a sea-monster whom he blames for his problems (work-shy son won't follow in his footsteps, wife plays around). The colour sequence is stock footage of surfing in Hawaii, the bongo music is by Frank Sinatra Jnr, and there is a car-chase to end it all.

d Jon Hall *p* Edward Janis *s* Joan Gardner *c* Dale Davis *lp* Jon Hall, Sue Casey, Walker Edmiston, Arnold Lessing, Elaine Dupont

Billy the Kid vs Dracula
(CIRCLE PRODUCTIONS) 89(73)min
This film features not merely a vampire in the old West, as in **Curse of the Undead** (1959), but Count Dracula himself. Carradine, who last played the role in **House of Dracula** (1945), looks a bit fragile but overacts heartily in compensation. The spoofing is probably intentional, but it isn't always easy to tell. Courtney is the reformed Billy who saves Plowman from becoming Dracula's latest bride.

The movie is so awful that, along with its stablemate **Jesse James Meets Frankenstein's Daughter** (1966), it has achieved cult status.

d William Beaudine *p* Carroll Case *s* Carl K. Hittleman *c* Lothrop Worth *lp* John Carradine, Chuck Courtney, Melinda Plowman, Virginia Christine, Olive Carey, Harry Carey Jnr

Il Boia Scarlatto *aka* **Il Castello di Artena** *aka* **The Scarlet Hangman** *aka* **The Crimson Executioner** *aka* **The Red Hangman** *aka* **Bloody Pit of Horror**
(MBS CINEMATOGRAFICA/INTERNATIONAL ENTERTAINMENT/RALPH ZUCKER; IT,US) scope 80(74)min
This exploitation outing is a classic example of repressed homosexuality transformed into sadistic aggression towards women. Ex-Mr Universe Hargitay plays a crazed ex-actor totally preoccupied with his narcissism until a writer (Brandi), his chaste fiancée (Baratto) and some photographic models invade his castle. When the scantily dressed models are readied for some scary pictures in the dungeon's torture chamber, Hargitay assumes the personality of a masked, bare-chested executioner wearing a broad leather belt, a medallion on a chain and revealing tights. He proceeds to subject the women to medieval tortures and only the writer and his girlfriend escape the carnage. Presumably she is spared because, unlike the models whose erotic underwear betrays a certain amount of sexual experience and makes them 'fair game' for the torturer, she never takes off her clothes, proving she is the type of girl one marries.

Judging by the character Hargitay plays and the prominence accorded to his well-oiled, hairless torso, the viewer is invited to derive pleasure from contemplating the male body but the trouble such homo-erotic pleasures provoke for the supposedly macho viewer is diverted towards sadistic aggression against women who thus come to function as detour and safety valve within a circuit of homosexual narcissism established between the male viewer and Mr Universe. Desire, with all its connotations of femininity, is here only evoked to be ostentatiously eliminated as woman after woman is killed, culminating with impeccable fantasy logic in the emergence of a safely conventional couple at the end of the movie. The effects are crude, the direction primitive and the whole of interest only as a case study to illustrate a theory of cinema-as-fantasy in psychoanalytic terms.

Director Pupillo was also responsible for the film's distribution, under his pseudonym Ralph Zucker.

d Max Hunter (Massimo Pupillo) *p* Francesco Merli *s* Robert Christmas (Roberto Natale), Robert McLorin (Romano Migliorini) *c* John Collins (Luciano Trasatti) *lp* Mickey Hargitay, Walter Brandt (Brandi), Louise Barrett (Luisa Baratto), Ralph Zucker (Massimo Pupillo), Alfred Rice (Alfredo Rizzo), Femi Martin (Eufemia Benussi), Rita Klein, Barbara Nelli, Moha Tahi, Nick Angel (Nando Angelini)

Devils of Darkness (PLANET; GB) 90min
This is the first British vampire movie in a contemporary setting, possibly because the shoestring production lacked the means to hire a studio. Count Sinistre (Noel) plays the vampire preying on British holidaymakers in a Breton village. Sylvester is the straight hero who puts an end to Noel's career and rescues the love-sex interest (Reed). Comfort, a cameraman turned director, never even achieved the modest professionalism of, say, Freddie Francis. He finished his undistinguished career, which included *Daughter of Darkness* (1945) and *The Ugly Ducking* (1959), in television.

d Lance Comfort *p* Tom Blakeley *s* Lyn Fairhurst *c* Reg Wyer *lp* William Sylvester, Hubert Noel, Tracey Reed, Carole Gray, Diana Decker, Rona Anderson, Peter Illing, Gerald Heinz

Amanti d'Oltretomba, *one of the many fetishistic hymns to Barbara Steele.*

La Donna del Lago *aka* **The Possessed**
(BCR PRODUZIONE/INSTITUTE LUCE; IT) b/w 90(82)min
This is a hopelessly inept cross between Hammer's psycho-horrors (**Nightmare**, 1963, for example) and Antonioni-style existential anguish movies. Baldwin, in search of the deceased Lisi in a small Italian village, stumbles upon a collection of people in an advanced state of alienation, a condition he also falls prey to himself. The sick mind that causes the death of nearly all the principal characters predictably belongs to a young woman: the blood-spattered Cortese is discovered in a shock ending to have viciously either drowned or meat-axed her father's lovers, her brothers and, eventually, her beloved father as well. As Baldwin leaves, the police are searching for her body in the nearby lake.

Full of shots of actors staring vacantly into the distance and ponderously self-conscious camera movements, the movie also sports showy editing which positively oozes meaning. A depressing example of direction that fails to understand anything about either art cinema or the horror genre, it deservedly remained Rossellini's only directorial effort.

d/co-s Luigi Bazzoni, Franco Rossellini *p* Manolo Bolognini *co-s* Giulio Questi *c* Leonida Barboni *lp* Peter Baldwin, Virna Lisi, Salvo Randone, Valentina Cortese, Pia Lindstrom, Philippe Leroy, Piero Anchisi

Dracula, Prince of Darkness *aka* **Disciple of Dracula** *aka* **Revenge of Dracula** *aka* **The Bloody Scream of Dracula** (HAMMER; GB) scope 90min
After the sublime **Dracula** (1958), Lee refused to play the Count for nearly ten years – with one unfortunate exception, **Tempi Duri per i Vampiri** (1959) – while he established himself as the leading European horror actor by appearing in such extraordinary movies as **La Frusta e il Corpo** (1963) and continued to play non-vampiric parts in Hammer films (**The Mummy**, 1959; **The Gorgon**, 1963). This return to his most famous role was greeted with mixed feelings, largely because Fisher opted for an unsettling combination of graphically gruesome violence and lusciously poetic atmosphere, which gives the movie a sense of stylish formalism and invites an appreciation of the way the story is told, rather than taking the more direct, 'innocent' approach of *Dracula*.

A group of travellers arrives at Castle Dracula where the Count's servant (Latham) revives his master by hanging Alan (Tingwell) upsidedown over the tomb containing Dracula's ashes and draining the blood from him. The scene is one of hallucinatory beauty as bright colours and swirling mist emphasize the overwhelming physicality of the ritual which allows Tingwell's lifeblood to be released as pure energy making Dracula swell into a blood-gorged body dedicated to the pursuit of sensual pleasure. The female martyrs to pleasure (Farmer and Shelley) are subjected to horrible violence by the forces of religion represented by Father Sandor (Keir). Fisher's prowling camera effectively sustains the movie's disturbing atmosphere while the story pays more attention to characterization than to shock effects. Keir's no-nonsense personality, dismissing a fellow monk as a superstitious fool, in particular, is a worthy substitute for Van Helsing.

Shelley gives probably the best performance of her career as the straightlaced Helen who is transformed into a demoniacally sensual woman, staked/raped by the monks with fearful brutality.

d Terence Fisher *p* Anthony Nelson Keys *s* John Samson, John Elder (Anthony Hinds) *c* Michael Reed *se* Bowie Films *lp* Christopher Lee, Andrew Keir, Barbara Shelley, Francis Matthews, Suzan Farmer, Charles Tingwell, Thorley Walters, Philip Latham

The Face of Fu Manchu *aka* **The Mask of Fu Manchu**
(HALLUM PRODUCTIONS; GB) scope 96(94)min
Starting with an eerily filmed beheading, moving through colourful chemical warfare experiments and mysteriously hypnotic trances, this movie culminates in a tunnel under the Thames where Fu Manchu (Lee) executes a female servant by drowning her in a glass cage. The plot, loosely based on Sax Rohmer's characters, is merely an excuse for Sharp to string together excellently staged scenes in wonderfully atmospheric surroundings. In this picture, Rohmer's *Boys' Own* fantasy of the yellow peril is distilled into its essence: Fu Manchu is less a demonic criminal than the incarnation of all that is thought to be alien, and therefore threatening, to Imperial England (ironically, the movie's force is due in no small degree of the Dublin and Kilmainham jail locations). Green, in his best performance ever, is perfect as the phlegmatic but ruthless public-school product, Nayland Smith, for whom London's docklands are as exotically dangerous as Fu Manchu's Tibetan lair. It is also interesting to note that the supreme villainy attributed to the evil oriental, employing the world's leading scientists in secret establishments where they develop a toxic substance of which a minute quantity suffices to exterminate an entire village, bears an uncanny resemblance to projects developed in well-known British and American military installations. Except for the unconvincingly made up non-orientals cast as Chinese, the picture is skilfully made and far outclasses its literary source. Intended as the first in a series, Sharp's act proved difficult to follow. Even his own follow-up, **The Brides of Fu Manchu** (1966) failed to match this enchanting opener.

d Don Sharp *p* Oliver A. Unger, Harry Alan Towers *s* Peter Welbeck (Harry Alan Towers) *c* Ernest Steward *lp* Christopher Lee, Nigel Green, James Robertson-Justice, Howard Marion Crawford, Tsai Chin, Joachim Fuchsberger, Karin Dor, Walter Rilla, Harry Brogan, Poulet Tu

Above: *Christopher Lee's return to his most famous role*, Dracula, Prince of Darkness.

Hush ... Hush Sweet Charlotte
(ASSOCIATES AND ALDRICH) b/w 134(132)min
'It's not often we have a homicide and can't find the victim's head or hands', mutters the sheriff rather crossly, referring to a particularly nasty murder by meat chopper. Thirty-seven years later, locked away in the now crumbling Louisiana mansion, the scene of the murder she is supposed to have committed, and half-crazed with grief and haunted by memories, Davis is driven over the brink by person or persons unknown for a variety of motives.

The film is a shameless follow-up to the phenomenally successful **What Ever Happened to Baby Jane?** (1962), and although second helpings are almost by definition less satisfactory, Davis has a habit of tearing definitions to pieces. First glimpsed during the prologue, screaming 'I could kill you' as her lover mutters his excuses, she roars into the film proper by grabbing a shotgun, rushing to a balcony, and threatening to shoot the men who have come to bulldoze her garden. After that there's no holding her as she croons love songs to herself by night, ferociously bullies everyone in sight, or steals out to put flowers on her father's grave like a child at her first party. As in *Baby Jane*, her control over the character's bewildering shifts of mood is a superb *tour de force*. And, as if Davis weren't enough, there's also Moorehead, revelling in her best part since Aunty Fanny in *The Magnificent Ambersons* (1942) as a slatternly, devoted housekeeper, wearing what appears to be a dishmop instead of hair, stumping crossly about muttering glorious imprecations. There's Astor as a black widow, discreetly dying as she pours out tea on the verandah; and there's de Havilland as a vampirishly sweet-tempered cousin. Aldrich's contribution to the Grand Guignol is mainly a matter of telegraphing the shocks and letting the ladies get on with it, but Biroc's camerawork is ravishing.

d/p Robert Aldrich *s* Henry Farrell, Lukas Heller *c* Joseph Biroc *lp* Bette Davis, Olivia de Havilland, Joseph Cotten, Agnes Moorehead, Cecil Kellaway, Victor Buono, Mary Astor

Kaidan Katame no Otoko *aka* Ghost of the One Eyed Man *aka* Curse of the One Eyed Corpse

(TOEI; JAP) b/w scope 84min

Following on from Sato's **Kaidan Semushi Otoko** (1965), this film repeats the plot device of gathering a group of people together in a ghostly mansion and then having each meet a violent death. A disfigured body is found by a river and identified as that of a rich businessman, Koichiro (Nakamura). His relatives, who all participated in a plot to murder him, gather in the house to divide the spoils but Koichiro isn't really dead and he returns, systematically driving all his nearest and dearest to their graves either by murdering them or terrorizing them into committing suicide. The end sees the lonely but satisfied Koichiro set off in a small boat, leaving the sinister house and all the bodies behind. Although not as visually entertaining at Sato's imitation of the Mario Bava style of gothic horror, the film is competently handled by Kobayashi, one of Toei's routine house directors who had been responsible for *Tomei Kaijin* and *Kubinashi Otoko* (both 1958).

Kaidan Semushi Otoko, *an unusually Italianate Japanese horror outing.*

d Tsuneo Kobayashi *p* Hiroshi Okawa *s* Hajime Takaiwa, Ichiro Miyagawa *c* Noboru Takanashi *lp* Akira Nishimura, Sanae Nakahara, Kikuko Hojo, Masao Mishima, Yusuke Kawazu

Kaidan Semushi Otoko *aka* House of Terrors *aka* The Ghost of the Hunchback

(TOEI; JAP) b/w scope 81min

This variation on themes elaborated in Italian horror movies tells of a mansion which is inhabited by ghosts and managed by a hunchbacked caretaker. When a doctor, his assistant and his young niece ignore the hunchback's warnings and install themselves in the place, they are all horribly killed. The hunchback, who had become attached to the young woman, is driven insane by the nocturnal happenings, sets fire to the house and perishes in the flames.

With lighting and costumes modelled on the gothic films of Maria Bava and Antonio Margheriti, the prolific B-picture director Sato achieves some well-composed images although the tricky angles and gruesome sequences do not compensate for the film's imitative aspects and rudimentary script. A follow-up feature, **Kaidan Katame no Otoko** (1965), which repeats both the style and the basic situation of Sato's film, was shot immediately afterwards by Tsuneo Kobayashi. Sato went on to make the routine science fiction story *Kaitei Daisenso* (1966) and the interesting but wordy *Kyuketsuki Gokemidoro* (1968).

d Hajime Sato *p* Hiroshi Okawa *s* Hajime Takaiwa *c* Shoe Nishikawa *lp* Akira Nishimura, Yuko Kusunoki, Yoko Hayama, Masumi Harakawa, Shinjiro Ebara

Miss Muerte *aka* The Diabolical Dr Z *aka* Dans les Griffes du Maniaque *aka* Miss Death *aka* Miss Death and Dr Z

(HESPERIA FILMS/SPEVA FILMS/CINE ALLIANCE; SP, FR) b/w scope 90(86)min

Carriere, Buñuel's regular collaborator (the pair worked together on *Belle du Jour*, 1966) helped adapt the novel by David Kuhne (Franco) on which this second sequel to **Gritos en la Noche** (1962) is based. When von Zimmer (Escribano) dies from a heart attack after his mind-control research has been rejected, his daughter Irma (Karr) avenges him, using an exotic dancer with long fingernails (Blain) as her murder tool.

Franco's work offers a classic example of how the nightmare side of phallocratic fantasies can produce sick but sometimes effective cinema with beautifully stylized imagery, with women as both the victims and the perpetrators of sadistic aggression. Here the exercise involves an apparatus that sinks huge needles deep into the flesh of its victims to perform a sort of moral acupuncture therapy, and Karr's horrid mutilation of another woman. The bland hero (Montes) also gets strapped to the penetration device before being rescued by the police. Stylistically, the stark black and white of the opening sequence featuring a prison escape in a thunderstorm and the many shots of corridors, spiral staircases, and Karr's doll-filled room which contrasts with the deadly caress of her nails, imbue the movie with a coldly disturbing sensuality. Unfortunately, Franco's films rarely achieve the intensity of fully fledged cinematic delirium, as in Mario Bava's work, nor do they become pathological case studies, in the style of the films of José Mojica Marins. Instead, his work often has the distance associated with a cynically exploitative attitude which easily degenerates into a mechanical stringing together of exploitative scenes. This picture seems poised between nightmare and crude sensationalism, lacking the sadistic exuberance of *Gritos en la Noche* but not yet a callous exploitation of sadism, as in his numerous women-in-prison movies (such as *Frauengefaengnis*, 1976). Some sources credit this picture to Henri Baum, one of Franco's many pseudonyms. Under the alias Frank Hollman, Franco returned to the same motifs with **Mrs Hyde** (1970).

d/co-s Jesús Franco *p* Serge Silberman, Michel Safra *co-s* Jean Claude Carriere *c* Alejandro Ulloa *lp* Howard Vernon, Mabel Karr, Estella Blain, Fernando Montes, Antonio J. Escribano, Guy Mairesse, Lucia Prado, Ana Castor, Marcelo Arroita

Monster of Terror *aka* **Die, Monster, Die** *aka* **The House at the End of the World**
(ALTA VISTA; GB, US) scope 81min
This disappointing adaptation of H. P. Lovecraft's *The Colour out of Space* (1927) proves that it takes a good director rather than a good art director to turn atmospheric settings into an effective movie. Having provided excellent décors for a great many Roger Corman movies, including his Edgar Allan Poe adaptations, Heller's first directorial effort relies exclusively on the evocative power of eerie settings. Adams' approach to the Witley house in Arkham is reminiscent of studio-scapes designed for Corman's **House of Usher** (1960); the disfigured old woman (Jackson) hidden behind a gauze veil; Nahum's (Karloff) mysterious cellar with its green glowing light and a greenhouse with hideous mutants all seem to promise a film that never really materializes. The idea that radiation from a fallen meteorite is responsible for the physical disintegration of both people and ecology is too prosaically handled, making the narrative hesitate between science fiction and horror, an indecision aggravated by wooden acting and a static script.

Haller tried filming Lovecraft again, with **The Dunwich Horror** (1969), but the results were even more disappointing.

d Daniel Haller *p* Pat Green *s* Jerry Sohl *c* Paul Beeson *se* Wally Veevers, Ernie Sullivan *lp* Boris Karloff, Nick Adams, Suzan Farmer, Freda Jackson, Terence de Marney, Patrick Magee, Leslie Dwyer, Paul Farrell

Il Mostro di Venezia *aka* **The Embalmer** *aka* **The Monster of Venice**
(GONDOLA FILM; IT) b/w 85(80)min
Tavella's second and last feature, this is a routine potboiler which revolves around a few interesting ideas. The monster appears as a frogman emerging from Venetian canals to abduct women whom he kills and stuffs for his collection of white-robed, mock-classic statues ranged in niches along the walls of his underground lair. Out of his aquatic gear, the monster dons a monk's habit and a skull mask. Whenever he targets a beautiful, likely addition to his collection, the film freezes the frame, allowing the viewer a few seconds to enjoy the aesthetic-fetishistic pleasure which the psychopath seeks to extend by keeping the women as motionless figures for him to contemplate at this leisure. Most of the movie is padded with tourist-board imagery of Venice and other pointless sequences. Only the ending offers more moments of interest as the heroine, trapped in the subterranean crypts, encounters not only the statues but also a series of cobwebbed, disintegrating mummies with grinning skulls. The movie was butchered by censors and distributors alike on its release in 1967.

d/co-s Dino Tavella *p* Christian Marvel *co-s* G. Muretta *c* Mario Parapetti *lp* Maureen Lidgard Brown, Gin Mart, Luciano Gasper, Anita Todesco, Alcide Gazzotto, Alba Brotto, Elmo Caruso, Viki del Castillo, Carlo Russo, Paola Vaccari

The Nanny (HAMMER; GB) b/w 93min
The second (after **Taste of Fear**, 1960) of the underrated Holt's contributions to Hammer's series of post-**Psycho** (1960) horror thrillers – although this title derives equally from Robert Aldrich's **What Ever Happened to Baby Jane?** (1962). Davis plays Nanny to ten-year-old Joey (Dix). Adapted from an Evelyn Piper novel, both script and direction revolve around her performance which, for once, is understated and quietly effective. Holt excellently captures the chilly arrogance and the petty eccentricities of Nanny's employers, while Dix gives a fine performance as the spoilt public-school brat who, even if he didn't actually drown his sister and poison his mother, would be quite capable of doing so. Craig, here the ineffectual mother, later did her best work in TV sitcoms and, ironically enough, starred in a (disappointing) teleseries in which she played a nanny.

d Seth Holt *p/s* Jimmy Sangster *c* Harry Waxman *lp* Bette Davis, Wendy Craig, Jill Bennett, James Villiers, William Dix, Pamela Franklin, Maurice Denham, Jack Watling, Alfred Burke

Corpse, doll and Psychopath.

Psychopath *aka* **Schizoid**
(AMICUS; GB) scope 83min
Amicus, Hammer's principal competitor in the sixties, got their house director to extend Hammer's series of psychological thrillers, which had included Francis's **Paranoiac** (1962), **Nightmare** (1963) and **Hysteria** (1964), with this cliché-ridden Bloch script. Wymark, investigating a series of vicious murders in which each time a doll was left on the site of the crime, is led to the wheelchair-bound widow (Johnson) of a German industrialist and her son (Standing). She lives surrounded by an enormous collection of dolls and eventually reduces her son to a grotesquely rouged doll, sitting in a high chair moaning 'mamma'. As in the far better-known script for **Psycho** (1960), the mother is the evil-doer, rising from her invalid's chair wielding a knife. Johnson's acting and her environment are stereotypically psychopathic, destroying whatever suspense may have been intended, but Wymark is more restrained than usual and Huxtable, as the daughter of one of the murder victims, has an engaging way of conveying vulnerability and courage, a quality later put to better effect in the uneven **Scream and Scream Again** (1970). The colours seem to have been ruined in the laboratory, and except for a suitably shocking opening sequence depicting a long-drawn-out murder, and an effective chase scene in a deserted boathouse, Francis's direction has little to recommend it.

d Freddie Francis *p* Max J. Rosenberg, Milton Subotsky *s* Robert Bloch *c* John Wilcox *se* Ted Samuels *lp* Patrick Wymark, Margaret Johnson, John Standing, Alexander Knox, Judy Huxtable, Thorley Walters, Don Borisenko, Robert Crewdson, Colin Gordon

Rasputin – The Mad Monk *aka* **The Mad Monk**
(HAMMER; GB) scope 92min
Although primarily a highly melodramatic account of the vigorous monk's doings at the tsar's court, Lee's towering presence and performance transform the charlatan into the incarnation of a supernatural evil who echoes Dracula's hypnotic powers and gargantuan erotic appetites. Shelley, as the tsarina's (Asherson) lady-in-waiting, seduced and driven to suicide by Rasputin, adds further vampiric overtones to the proceedings. The final murder, arranged by the monk's drunken, jealous rival at court, Dr Zargo (Pasco), is staged in a grandly gothic manner, from Lee's consumption of the poisoned chocolates, to his excited pacing around the room while the conspirators cower in the shadows, and his prolonged death agonies until he is thrown off the castle wall by the dying Zargo.

Sharp's usually astute sense of *mise-en-scène* comes to life in the riotous inn scenes and for the climax, but he fails to come to grips with the obscene decadence of a Russian court inhabited by cruelly bigoted throwbacks to the Middle Ages. He proved himself more at ease with a straightforwardly mythical character like Fu Manchu (**The Face of Fu Manchu**, 1965) or with the legends of evil rooted in the more familiar social order of Western Europe (**Kiss of the Vampire**, 1962; **Witchcraft**, 1964).

Further films about Rasputin include Pierre Chenal's *L'Ultimo Zar* (1960), Georges Combret's *Rasputin* (1953) and Robert Hossein's *J'Ai Tué Raspoutine* (1967).

d Don Sharp *p* Anthony Nelson Keys *s* John Elder (Anthony Hinds) *c* Michael Reed *lp* Christopher Lee, Barbara Shelley, Richard Pasco, Francis Matthews, Dinsdale Landen, Suzan Farmer, Renee Asherson, Joss Ackland, Derek Francis

Repulsion (COMPTON/TEKLI; GB) b/w 104min
This, Polanski's first English-language film, was produced by a fellow Pole and boasts a Chico Hamilton score. It tells of a Belgian girl, Carol Ledoux (Deneuve), whose sexual repressions erupt in the form of persecutory fantasies which drive her to murder and eventually catatonia. The breakdown is triggered by her sister Helen (Furneaux) going on holiday with Michael (Hendry), leaving Deneuve alone in a flat invaded by hallucinations: rooms grow vast and are distorted in perspective, walls yawn apart with rending cracks, solid plaster softens to take the imprint of her hand and turns into cloying mud from which hands reach out to claw her as she passes. When her boyfriend, worried by her refusal to let him in, breaks down the door, she bludgeons him to death with a candle-holder and stores his body in the bath. After a few days, flies gather around the corpse. The landlord tries to force his attentions on her and is slashed to death with a razor. When Furneaux and Hendry return, Deneuve is lying inert, staring eyes wide open, on the floor surrounded by a flat in chaos and two rotting cadavers.

Although Polanski's first feature, *Noz w Wodzie* (1962) had gained him an international reputation, it also caused some ripples at home and forced him abroad, where he found it difficult to get funds for his productions. Gutowski, who was involved with sexploitation and horror movies, commissioned this genre film and it is a mark of Polanski's supreme talent that he not only adapted to commercial requirements but achieved a marvellous film doing so. Although flawed – the dialogue, in particular, suffers from Polanski's imperfect knowledge of and feel for the language at that time – *Repulsion* sets up the major lines of force that structure the whole of his work: a cinema that relentlessly questions the relation of fascination between the viewer and an audiovisual spectacle. He plays a complex game with audience expectations, identification, perceptions and generic conventions, simultaneously fascinating and unsettling the viewer, exploring the fundamental fantasies, desires and anxieties at stake in our relationship with cinema as spectacle. In this respect Polanski (with Alfred Hitchcock and Fritz Lang) is one of the very few cineastes to not only succeed in addressing these issues in the context of commercial cinema, but whose explorations are astonishing in their intelligence.

d/co-s Roman Polanski *p* Gene Gutowski *co-s Gerard Brach* *c* Gilbert Taylor *lp* Catherine Deneuve, Yvonne Furneaux, Ian Hendry, John Fraser, Patrick Wymark, Renee Houston, James Villiers, Valerie Taylor

Catherine Deneuve as the psychotic girl in Roman Polanski's marvellous Repulsion.

The Skull (AMICUS; GB) scope 90(83)min
American producers Subotsky and Rosenberg with house director Francis established Amicus as a credible alternative to Hammer in the mid-sixties, with such films as **Dr Terror's House of Horrors** (1964), **The Psychopath** (1965), **The Deadly Bees** (1966) and **Torture Garden** (1967). This picture, although seriously flawed, together with the last episode of *Torture Garden*, is their best work. It tells of a collector, Professor Maitland (Cushing), who feels compelled to acquire the Marquis de Sade's skull in spite of dire warnings from a fellow collector (Lee) who claims the object has evil powers. Cushing falls under the skull's spell and begins to hallucinate, barely avoiding stabbing his wife (Bennett). Next morning, he is found with his throat torn out.

The opening sequence, establishing the skull's history, is professionally shot but betrays an appalling ignorance about de Sade: to associate the marquis with black magic is a sign of cultural barbarism unthinkingly taken over from Robert Bloch's original story published in 1945. But given their preposterous premise, the movie manages to build up a disturbing atmosphere, leaving it open as to whether the skull does have evil powers or whether it merely stimulates its possessor's unconscious anxieties and desires. Francis overdoes his camera movements, inserting too many point-of-view shots from within the skull, detracting from their effectiveness. Most of the credit for the film's success should go to Bill Constable and Scott Slimon for their claustrophobic sets which expertly convey the barely contained pathological tendencies of a manic collector of occult bric-à-brac.

d Freddie Francis *co-p/s* Milton Subotsky *co-p* Max J. Rosenberg *c* John Wilcox *se* Ted Samuels *lp* Peter Cushing, Christopher Lee, Jill Bennett, Patrick Wymark, Michael Gough, Nigel Green, George Coulouris, Patrick Magee, Peter Woodthorpe

Left: *Barbara Windsor, one of Jack the Ripper's victims in the routine* A Study in Terror.

La Sorella di Satana *aka* **The Revenge of the Blood Beast** *aka* **The She Beast** *aka* **Satan's Sister**
(LEITH FILMS; IT) scope 76min
A cheap and untidy film which nevertheless contains scenes of enormous power and betrays Reeves' genuine talent. On the strength of his contribution to **Il Castello dei Morti Vivi** (1964), Reeves was given a script – which he thoroughly overhauled – a meagre budget, and four days of Steele's time. In spite of these daunting limitations, including the use of a second unit to save time, he delivers an impressive movie.

Two hundred years after the unsightly witch Vardella was viciously killed by the godfearing people of a Transylvanian village, an English couple on holiday, Philip (Ogilvy) and Veronica (Steele) crash their car and the witch re-emerges in possession of Veronica. When the vengeful Vardella has been exorcized, Veronica reappears as herself, but she ominously remarks at the end of the film: 'I'll be back.'

The flashback sequence introducing Vardella is one of the film's highlights, prefiguring the equally effective beginning of Reeves' **The Witchfinder General** (1968): a boy runs through a menacing but beautiful evening landscape and bursts into the church summoning the help of the priest and his congregation. Carrying flickering torches, they sweep out of the chapel through the night towards a yawning black cave where a decomposing hand betrays Vardella's presence. The subsequent impaling and ducking of the witch, as the priest intones his litany surrounded by villagers impassively watching the excruciating agonies they inflict on the witch, stands as a key scene in the whole of Reeves' work: for him, the ghastly evil unleashed on people by dark forces affects victims and executioners alike, united in a common bestiality and reflecting the potential for a nightmarish cruelty inherent in all human irrationality. The second-unit's contribution, including some scenes with a motorcyclist, merely pad out the story and bring it up to feature length. Steele's role is minimal and some facile jokes further impair the atmosphere, but the movie clearly shows what Reeves might have been able to achieve with adequate resources.

d Michael Reeves *p* Paul Maslansky *s* Michael Byron (Michael Reeves) *c* G. Gengarelli *lp* Barbara Steele, Ian Ogilvy, John Karlsen, Mel Welles (Ernst von Theumer), Jay Riley, Richard Watson, Ed Randolph

A Study in Terror *aka* **Sherlock Holmes Grosster Fall**
(COMPTON/TEKLI/SIR NIGEL; GB, WG) 95min
A substandard Holmes adventure based on Conan Doyle's *Fog* which pits the detective (Neville) against Jack the Ripper (Fraser). Hill tries hard to enliven the proceedings with shock-cut murders and the introduction of an aristocratic prostitute whose face has been scarred by acid (Corri) but the excellent cast is wasted on a misguided effort by a sexploitation company (Compton) to establish itself in the quality horror market after their success with Roman Polanski's **Repulsion** (1965). Alex Vetchinsky's art direction provides a suitable setting, but the film's mixture of theatrical, actorly performances and crude shock-horror techniques make it inept rather than uneven, something the film-makers must have realized as the movie constantly seems about to turn to self-parody.

d James Hill *p* Henry E. Lester *s* Donald Ford, Derek Ford *c* Desmond Dickinson *se* Wally Veevers *lp* John Nevill, Donald Houston, John Fraser, Anthony Quayle, Barbara Windsor, Robert Morley, Adrienne Corri, Frank Finlay, Judi Dench, Cecil Parker

Terrore nello Spazio *aka* **Terror en el Espacio** *aka* **Planet of Blood** *aka* **Demon Planet** *aka* **The Haunted Planet** *aka* **The Planet of Terror** *aka* **Terror in Space** *aka* **The Outlawed Planet** *aka* **The Planet of the Damned** *aka* **Planet of the Vampires**
(ITALIAN INTERNATIONAL/CASTILLA CINEMATOGRAFICA; IT,SP) scope 88(86)min
Bava's object lesson in how to make a sensational science fiction-horror movie on a shoestring foreshadows, and in many ways outclasses, **Alien** (1979), especially when the unequal financial resources of the two films are taken into account. The story, adapted from Renato Pestriniero's *Night of Twenty-One Hours*, concerns the occupants of two spaceships that land on a strange planet where they find the remains of an alien species. The aliens vampirically take possession of the crews. Lack of funds forced Bava to cloak his set in swirling, brightly coloured fog, but the sheer inventiveness of the movie – in particular the sequences in which the vampires rise from their surreal tombs in billowing, translucent shrouds, and corpses decay in an eerie landscape animated by restless streaks of colour and disquieting sounds – is astonishing. In a typical sting in the tail ending, Bava has the vampirized astronauts land on a blue-green planet: earth. Like his **Ercole al Centro della Terra** (1961), this is a perfectly achieved blend of two genres.

Antonio Margheriti tried a similar blend with *I Criminali della Galassia* and *I Diafanoidi Vengono dallo Spazio* (both 1965), but didn't match the hallucinatory beauty of Bava's images. The acting by Sullivan and his Brazilian co-star, Bengel, is professional. The English-language version, slightly shortened, was supervised by Ib Melchior.

d/co-s Mario Bava *p* Fulvio Lucisano *co-s* Callisto Cosulich, Alberto Bevilacqua, Antonio Roman, Rafael J. Salvia *c* Antonio Rinaldi *lp* Barry Sullivan, Norma Bengel, Angel Aranda, Evi Morandi, Fernando Villena, Ivan Rassimov, Rico Boido, Massimo Righi, Stelio Candelli, Mario Morales

Un Vampiro para Dos *aka* **A Vampire for Two**
(BELMAR; SP) b/w scope 85min
The idea of a Spanish 'guest worker' couple (Morales and Lopez Vazquez) being vampirized by their aristocratic German employers could have yielded an interesting comedy but in this film script and direction opt for a broad farce rather than corrosive satire. The Spanish servants eventually escape Baron von Rosenthal (Gomez) and his bloodsucking family and return to their native country. On its release, the picture already looked about ten years out of date and in spite of the awkward references to Hammer movies, it seems to belong more to the fifties era of television sitcom, a format in which the popular Spanish comedy duo felt more at home. Lopez Vazquez was one of Spain's most prolific comic actors, appearing in such classics as Ferreri's *El Pisito* (1958) and *El Cochecito* (1961) and Berlanga's *Placido* (1960) and *El Verdugo* (1964). Lazanga was a veteran director of routinely commercial material including *Niebla y Sol* (1951), which testified to a sense of pictorial composition absent from this film.

d/co-s Pedro Lazanga Sabater *co-s* José Maria Palacio *c* Eloy Molla *lp* Gracita Morales, José Luis Lopez Vazquez, Fernando Fernan Gomez, Trini Alonso, Goyo Lebreros, José Oyas

Yotsuya Kaidan *aka* Illusion of Blood *aka* The Ghost of Yotsuya

(TOKYO EIGA; JAP) scope 190(107)min

Although Kobayashi's **Kwaidan** (1964) had been a commercial disaster in Japan, Toyoda, using a similarly stylized approach but applying it to the Japanese cinema's most popular ghost story, achieved an astonishing movie that rivals Nakagawa's classic **Tokaido Yotsuya Kaidan** (1959). Adapting Nanboku Tsuruya's kabuki play of 1825, the veteran Toyoda presents Iemon (Nakadai) as an obsessive character, propelled from crime to bloody crime with a remorseless logic. Disposing of his wife Oiwa (Okada) he marries the richer Oume (Ozora) while his partner in evil, Naosuke (Nakamura), gets together with Oiwa's sister (Ikeuchil, who had played Oume in Nakagawa's version). But the vengeful ghost of Oiwa returns to drive Iemon insane in the picture's gloriously stylish climax which adds scurrying rats to the ghostly snakes and cadavers plaguing the ambitious and greedy samurai. The eerie electronic score by Toru Takemitsu, the brilliant colour cinematography and the excellent acting by the distinguished cast combine with Toyoda's confident direction to produce an enchanting movie.

Nakadai had become internationally famous through his appearances in a series of Kobayashi movies (*Ningen no Joken*, 1959-61; *Seppuku*, 1962) and Kurosawa's *Yojimbo* (1961). Here he uses his coolly intense acting style to marvellous effect, giving even greater impact to his sudden explosions of hideous violence. Okada specialized in playing amorous young women opposite immature men with mother hang-ups. Other notable versions of the story were directed by the great Kinoshita (**Shinshaku Yotsuya Kaidan**, 1949), Issei Mori (1969), Masaki Mori (1956) and Kenji Misumi (1959). The classic silent version of the tale is *Shinpan Yotsuya Kaidan* (1928), directed by Ito. Toyoda's picture was released in 1966. He returned to the genre with the excellent **Jigokuhen** (1969).

d Shiro Toyoda *p* Ichiro Sato *s* Toshiro Yamuzi *c* Hiroshi Murai *lp* Tatsuya Nakadai, Mariko Okada, Junko Ikeuchi, Kanzaburo Nakamura, Mayumi Ozora, Keiko Awaji, Eitaro Ozawa, Masao Mishima, Yasushi Nagata

Pier Ana Quaglia (right) and Barbara Steele in the last of her major horror outings, Un Angelo per Satana.

1966

Un Angelo per Satana *aka* An Angel for Satan

(DISCOBOLO CINEMATOGRAFICA; IT) b/w 93(88)min

Steele here (as in **La Maschera del Demonio**, 1960 and **Amanti d'Oltretomba**, 1965) plays a double role, as the simultaneously doe-eyed and perverse Harriet, the latter possessed by the spirit of Belinda, represented in the movie by an ancient statue recovered from a pond. The hero is a young artist (Steffen), hired to restore the statue, while the villain is the Count of Montebruno (Gora), egged on by a malevolent Ilda (Berti), who hypnotizes Harriet to cause her Jekyll and Hyde transformations. Mastrocinque's stylish adaptation of Luigi Emmanuele's story and Steele's performance are excellent, enhancing the dreamily melancholic atmosphere of the house and its grounds, dominated by the mysterious lake. Although the picture has its share of violence and rape, the overall impression is one of a poetic, somehow slow-moving rhythm animating the unfolding of a crepuscular image.

After this film, Steele's brief but glorious career went into a decline. It was also Mastrocinque's last horror film after a prolific career directing many Toto movies, including **Toto all'Inferno** (1954), as well as the disappointing **La Cripta e l'Incubo** (1964).

d/co-s Camillo Mastrocinque *p* Liliana Biancini, Giuliano Simonetti *co-s* Giuseppe Mangione *c* Giuseppe Acquari *se* Antonio Ricci *lp* Barbara Steele, Anthony Steffen (Antonio de Teffé), Claudio Gora, Ursula Davis (Pier Ana Quaglia), Aldo Berti, Maureen Melrose (Marina Berti), Vassili Karamesinis, Betty Delon

The Black Cat

(FALCON INTERNATIONAL) b/w 77(69)min

Cheaply made and indifferently acted, this loose adaptation of Poe's story begins quite engagingly with Frost, more or less an alcoholic, being given a first wedding anniversary gift of a black cat by his wife (Baker) and formally introducing it to his menagerie of monkeys and parrots with champagne for all. Eventually becoming so devoted to the cat that he neglects his wife, he hangs it, having come to believe – after drunkenly gouging one of its eyes out when it scratches him – that it's the reincarnation of the dead father he hated. After this, the film goes steadily downhill as Frost's house mysteriously burns down, he assaults his lawyer on finding it was uninsured, is committed to a sanatorium, and returns saddled with a stray black cat (also one-eyed) and nightmares which lead him to kill his wife in mistake for the cat and wall her up in the cellar (along with the cat, whose telltale miaow alerts the police).

The Poe atmosphere, frayed by Hoffman's uncertain direction and pacing (a protracted and totally unnecessary nightclub sequence; absurd melodramatics in the lawyer's office and sanatorium), is finally dissipated by explicit gore in the manner of **Blood Feast** (1963): the cat's eye cut out, a decapitation and an axe splitting a skull.

d/s Harold Hoffman *p* Patrick Sims *c* Walter Schenk *lp* Robert Frost, Robyn Baker, Sadie French, Scotty McKay, George R. Russell

Blood Bath *aka* Track of the Vampire

(AIP) b/w 80(69)min

Cheap and crude, with echoes of a dozen movies ranging from **Mystery of the Wax Museum** (1933) to **A Bucket of Blood** (1959), this film isn't unenjoyable. Campbell plays an artist of Italian origin living in Venice, California who believes he is a reincarnation of his 15th-century ancestor, an artist burned at the stake as a vampire. His mania leads him to stalk girls, starting with a friend of the dancer he loves (Mathes) and believes to be a reincarnation like himself. Luring the girls to his studio (in the bell-tower), he dips them in a vat of molten wax, then paints their bodies. In the end the victims inexplicably return to life to take their revenge. Some of the confusion may be explained by the fact that when Hill was fired (by Roger Corman), Rothman took over, and part of original brief was to find some way of incorporating footage from a Yugoslavian film Corman had bought the rights to.

co-d/p/co-s Jack Hill *co-d/co-s* Stephanie Rothman *c* Alfred Taylor *lp* William Campbell, Marissa Mathes, Lori Saunders, Sandra Knight, Jonathan Haze

The Blood Drinkers *aka* **Vampire People**
(CIRIO H. SANTIAGO PRODUCTIONS; PHIL)
b/w and col 87(75)min
After his adaptation of H. G. Wells' novel *Island of Dr Moreau*, **Terror Is a Man** (1959), de Leon turned for this film to central European vampire mythology. With a story developed by Rico Omagap and a refreshingly straightforward approach, he manages to bring out the legend's social implications, in a way that most Anglo-American horror movies avoid.

Marco (Remy), a bald-headed aristocrat whose lover Christine (Fuentes) is dying, comes to a small village to get the healthy blood and heart of his lover's twin sister Charita. With the help of a bat and two associates, the sexy Tanya (Montez) and a hunchbacked dwarf, he lords it over the village until a young traveller (Fernandez) saves Charita by rousing the local priest, police and villagers against the despotic bloodsucker and his allies. Armed with burning crosses and flares to turn the night into day, they hunt down the vampires in the forest and stake them, but Remy escapes and Montez, unable to live without him, commits suicide.

Although the editing is jerky and the English dubbing perfunctory, de Leon makes good use of emotive red and blue sequences to punctuate the black and white film. The film also features an interesting fight between the hero and the vampire in which the villain annoys his opponent by constantly rendering himself invisible. De Leon and his colleague Eddi Romero went on to collaborate with Roger Corman on cheap exploitation movies like *Women in Cages* or *The Big Doll House* (both 1971) as well as co-directing *Brides of Blood* (1965) and *The Mad Doctor of Blood Island* (1968).

d Gerardo de Leon *p* Danilo Santiago *s* Cesar Amigo *c* Felip Sacdalan *se* Hilario Brothers *lp* Amalia Fuentes, Ronald Remy, Eddie Fernandez, Eva Montez, Celia Rodriguez, Paquito Salcedo, Jess Roma, Felisa Salcedo, Renato Robles, Vicky Velazquez

Blue Demon contra Cerebros Infernales *aka* **Blue Demon vs El Crimen** *aka* **Cerebro Infernal** *aka* **Blue Demon vs the Infernal Brain**
(ESTUDIOS AMERICA/CINEMATOGRAFICA RA; MEX) 85min
Having just tackled wrestling spider-women in *Arañas Infernales* (1966), the blue-trousered hulk (Cruz) who uses a mask to hide his 'masculine ugliness', as one Mexican critic aptly put it, here comes to grips with a gang of diabolical women led by Angely. They try to compensate for their no doubt equally natural feminine lack of intelligence by extracting brain matter from prominent male intellectuals such as scientific geniuses and wrestlers. The script, penned by ex-wrestler Oses, entrusts the operations to Dr Sanders (Junco), Angely's accomplice and co-ruler of a band of female zombielike slaves. Policeman Reynoso and his lover (Martin) dispose of the villains with the help of the heroic welterweight.

One of Blue Demon's particular characteristics – an invention no doubt prompted by scenarists working on the Santo films – is his silence: the ex-railway employee of Monterey hardly ever speaks a word, preferring to express himself via muscular reflexes rather than through speech, though admittedly, in his own ponderous way, he is a more elegant mover than most of his rivals. His next assignment, also supervised by Urueta, was against more evil women, *Blue Demon contra las Diabolicas* (1967) before he teamed up with his rival in *Santo contra Blue Demon en la Atlantida* and *Santo y Blue Demon contra los Monstrous* (both 1968).

Amalia Fuentes and Eva Montez in the Philippines' production, The Blood Drinkers.

d Chano Urueta *p* Rafael Perez Grovas *s* Antonio Orellana, Fernando Oses *c* Alfredo Uribe *lp* Blue Demon (Alejandro Cruz), David Reynoso, Ana Martin, Victor Junco, Barbara Angely, Noé Murayama, Dagoberto Rodriguez

The Brides of Fu Manchu *aka* **Die Dreizehn Sklavinnen des Dr Fu Manchu**
(HALLAM PRODUCTIONS/FU MANCHU FILMS; GB,WG)
scope 94(91)min
After the success of **The Face of Fu Manchu** (1965), and the commanding performances by Lee as the evil oriental and Nigel Green as his ruthless opponent, Sharp's follow-up adopts a similarly freewheeling approach but the result is far less successful. The hopelessly convoluted plot, built around Fu Manchu's kidnapping of a series of young women in order to blackmail the influential males connected with them, proved too badly constructed to allow the effectively staged setpieces to develop, making the movie disintegrate into a great many banal scenes and a few brief hallucinatory moments. The sets are still well chosen and designed, but the scenes unwind at breakneck pace – as if Sharp were anxious to finish the project – in marked contrast to the earlier film in which he had lingered lovingly over particularly atmospheric sequences. Also, Wilmer is closer to Sax Rohmer's original, one-dimensional Nayland Smith, a pale reflection of Green's energetic public-school bully. In the end, with the Foreign Legion's attack on Fu's north African temple and a subsequent explosion, the echoes of the Bond films become too intrusive.

With the next instalment, *The Vengeance of Fu Manchu* (1967), partly shot in Hong Kong by Jeremy Summers, the series rapidly degenerated into *Boys' Own* adventure stories with racist overtones, until Jesús Franco's **El Castello de Fu Manchu** (1968) finally obliterated all traces of Sharp's excellent start with clumsily introduced scenes of sadism and blatantly exploitative nudity. Towers wrote the script, using his customary pseudonym Peter Welbeck.

d Don Sharp *p/s* Harry Alan Towers *c* Ernest Steward *lp* Christopher Lee, Douglas Wilmer, Marie Versini, Heinz Drache, Howard Marion Crawford, Tsai Chin, Roger Hanin, Kenneth Fortescue, Joseph Fuerst, Carole Gray

Carry On Screaming *aka* **Carry On Vampire**
(ANGLO AMALGAMATED; GB) 97min
Rogers and Thomas's popular Carry On farces started in 1958, continued relentlessly into the seventies and now have been

accorded Disney status on British television, with choice extracts being strung together to make a series of TV programmes. Predictably, their pre-adolescent lavatorial approach to comedy also tried to exploit the popularity of Hammer's movies. The sketches, loosely connected into a script, feature a zombie professor, Dr Watt (Williams), his vampire sister (Fielding), a Frankensteinish creature, Odbodd (Clegg), a mummy (Blake), a wax-museum type cauldron that vitrifies women who are then sold as window dummies and a pair of silly policemen (Corbett and Butterworth). The acting is of the usual 'adults putting on a funny show for children' variety, with the exception of Corbett's performance which is atrocious even by these amateurish standards. Only Fielding's voice, a parody of Joan Greenwood's extraordinary nose-and-throat noises, prevents this depressing effort from being utterly irredeemable.

d Gerald Thomas *p* Peter Rogers *s* Talbot Rothwell *c* Alan Hume *lp* Kenneth Williams, Fenella Fielding, Harry H. Corbett, Joan Sims, Jim Dale, Charles Hawtrey, Peter Butterworth, Bernard Bresslaw, Tom Clegg, Dennis Blake

Chamber of Horrors (WB) 100(81)min
This was originally made as a pilot for a projected teleseries based on **House of Wax** (1953) which was to feature Danova and Hyde-White as amateur criminologists and owners of a wax museum in Baltimore (the setting of *House of Wax*). Considered too shocking for transmission, it was expanded into a film. The additions unfortunately include a 'fear flasher' and a 'horror horn', designed to warn audiences when proceedings are going to be too horrible to watch. Nevertheless, the film boasts an excellent performance by O'Neal as a homicidal maniac who gets things off to a promising start by forcing a preacher to marry him to the girl he has just strangled. Arrested and sentenced to death thanks to the efforts of Danova, he escapes by jumping off a train after cutting off his own manacled hand. Presumed dead, he is immortalized in the museum as 'the Baltimore Strangler'. Very much alive, though, and armed with a wooden hand which can be fitted with an awesome array of knives and cleavers, he sets out for vengeance. Some arrestingly lurid moments, though – not least O'Neal being impaled on the hook of his own wax image as he is about to finish off Danova – are undermined by the TV format and the silly gimmicks.

d/p Hy Averback *s* Stephen Kandel *c* Richard Kline *lp* Patric O'Neal, Cesare Danova, Wilfrid Hyde-White, Laura Devon, Patrice Wymore, Suzy Parker, Tony Curtis

Daimajin, *a Japanese golem film.*

Cinque Tombe per un Medium *aka* **The Tombs of Horror** *aka* **Terror Creatures from the Grave** *aka* **Five Graves for a Medium** *aka* **Coffin of Terror**
(MBS CINEMATOGRAFICA/GIA CINEMATOGRAFICA/ INTERNATIONAL ENTERTAINMENT CORP; IT,US)
b/w scope 90(83)min
This, Pupillo's directorial début, is an effective, professionally made vehicle for Steele. She is Cleo, the widow of the occultist Dr Hauff, a man who summons medieval creatures buried around his castle to avenge his murder. A lawyer (Brandi) discovers that Steele, his employer (Garrone) and other victims of the plague-spreading zombies were all guilty and escapes with the only innocent resident, Corinne (Mitchell), as purifying rain exorcizes the evil spell. The supernatural atmosphere is competently orchestrated with clear, luminous photography, aided by the turn-of-the-century setting. The erratic script doesn't give Steele much to do except look mysterious and perfidious, but her very presence considerably enhances the film's pictorial beauty.

Pupillo had started his career as a child actor and worked his way through the technical grades in film and television. He went on to direct **Il Boia Scarlatto** (1965) and *La Vendetta di Lady Morgan* (1966), but neither fulfilled the promise shown here, which suggests that this achievement may best be credited to the excellent cameraman, di Palma.

d/co-p Ralph Zucker (Massimo Pupillo) *co-p* Frank Merle *s* Roberto Natale, Romano Migliorine *c* Charles Brown (Carlo di Palma) *lp* Barbara Steele, Walter Brandt (Walter Brandi), Marilyn Mitchell (Mirella Maravidi), Alfred Rice (Alfredo Rizzo), Richard Garret (Riccardo Garrone), Alan Collins (Luciano Pigozzi), Tilde Till, Ennio Balbo

Il Cuarto Chino *aka* **The Chinese Room**
(FAMOUS PLAYERS/CLASA FILMS MUNDIALES/SAGITARIO FILMS; MEX, US) 95min
Zugsmith, maverick producer of Douglas Sirk's *Written on the Wind* (1956) and Orson Welles' *Touch of Evil* (1958) and director of such surreal classics as *Sex Kittens Go to College* (1960) and *Confessions of an Opium Eater* (1962), produced this adaptation of Vivian Connell's long-banned sensationalist novel, substituting Mexican mushrooms for the more traditional opium. The central character is Rivas, a dissolute drug addict who regularly retires to his secret 'Chinese Room' presided over by an enigmatic Buddha statue courtesy of art director Manuel Fontanals. He is surrounded by a demented wife (Campbell), a club-footed secretary (Torné, who also visits the hidden room to forget her infirmity) and a servant, Consuleo (Ortiz) whose unrequited love for the hero once pushed her into a suicide attempt. Dr Saluby (Murray) comes to try and cure the various members of the strange household with unorthodox measures like hypnosis and leaves mysterious notes around which drive the hero further into dementia. A fake hanging, complicated sexual relations leading to unwanted pregnancies, madness and erotic as well as nightmarish dream sequences further enliven the virtually plotless but hallucinatory picture.

The result is a rare, weirdly enchanting and perverse potboiler released in 1968 and a worthy addition to Zugsmith's extraordinary filmography.

d/s Albert Zugsmith *p* Felip Subervielle, Rafael Lebrija *c* Gabriel Figueroa *lp* Guillermo Murray, Elisabeth Campbell, Carlos Rivas, Germán Robles, Regina Torné, Gloria Leticia Ortiz, Carlos East, Jorge Rado, Felix Gonzales

Daimajin *aka* **Majin** *aka* **Majin the Monster of Terror** *aka* **Majin The Hideous Idol** *aka* **The Devil Got Angry** *aka* **The Vengeance of the Monster**
(DAIEI; JAP) scope 86min
Majin is a Japanese equivalent of the golem: a gigantic warrior statue which can be roused, like his Jewish counterpart, to come to the defence of the people against tyrannical despots.

Set in the 18th century, the story begins as a conventional period action movie. The nobleman Samanosuke (Gomi) usurps power in the region by killing the local lord and enslaving the population. The lord's children, Korosa (Takada) and Tadafumi (Aoyama) escape and hide for a decade on the mountain where Majin rests, contained in the form of a statue. On the children's return to their village, all efforts to counter the cruel rule of the usurper fail but when Gomi also kills a priestess and sends his men to destroy Majin, the statue comes to life as the earth shakes and cracks open. The giant then destroys the tyrant's castle and pins the villain to a wall, transfixing him with a huge spike.

A mixture of Kaiju Eiga (monster movie) and Jidai Geki (historical drama), Yasuda's picture remains a hybrid although it was sufficiently successful to spawn two sequels, **Daimajin Ikaru** and **Daimajin Gyakushu** (both 1966). Kuroda's special effects, mostly process work in the last third of the movie, are expertly achieved and generally integrate the rubber-clad Majin well into the sequences. Yasuda, a routine director, later excelled himself with the highly entertaining **Yokai Hyaku Monogatari** (1968), a Kaidan movie also scripted by Yoshida and starring Tanaka.

d Kimiyoshi Yasuda *p* Masaichi Nagata *s* Tetsuro Yoshida *c* Fujio Morita *se* Yoshiyuki Kuroda *lp* Miwa Takada, Yoshihiko Aoyama, Jun Fujimaki, Ryutaro Gomi, Tatsuo Endo

Daimajin Gyakushu *aka* Majin Strikes Again *aka* The Return of Majin

(DAIEI; JAP) scope 80min

The third and final film about the giant warrior god in full samurai regalia, Majin, *Daimajin Gyakushu* opens with a traditional Kaiju Eiga (monster movie) cataclysm: an earthquake and a flood, fires and crumpled houses. This time, Majin rescues three children from the clutches of the tyrannical villain who lords it over the village. Kuroda's special effects are a match for Tsuburaya's work at the Toho studios, although he had less occasion to practise his skills. Like Misumi, the director of the previous Majin picture, **Daimajin Ikaru** (1966), Mori also contributed a film, **Yotsuya Kaidan – Oiwa no Borei** (1969), to the ghost-story genre, although he specialized in period adventure movies. Special effects' man Kuroda also graduated to directing and was responsible for the spectacular **Yokai Daisenso** (1968), a mixture of the Kaidan and Kaiju Eiga genres.

d Issei Mori *p* Masaichi Nagata *s* Tetsuo Yoshida *c* Fujio Morita, Hiroshi Imai *se* Yoshiyuki Kuroda *lp* Hideki Ninomiya, Masahide Kizuka, Shinji Hori, Shiei Iizuka, Muneyuki Nagatomo

Daimajin Ikaru *aka* The Return of the Majin *aka* The Return of the Giant Majin

(DAIEI; JAP) scope 79min

This sequel to **Daimajin** (1966) starts with Majin losing its temper when a giant effigy of it is destroyed by villains. From its base in the middle of a lake, Majin wreaks havoc, until the heroine's tears, falling into the lake, persuade it to go home. Though so obviously a rubber-suited actor, Majin is quite impressive and the scene of it clearing a path through the water is reminiscent of Cecil B. DeMille's *Ten Commandments* (1956). With Issei Mori's third instalment of Majin's adventures, **Daimajin Gyakushu** (1966), confusingly given the same English-language title (*The Return of the Majin*) in an American trade review, the series came to an end.

Misumi was a routine director of programme fillers and contributed a few fantasy films including a version of *Yotsuya Kaidan* (1959) made in the same year as Nakagawa's classic treatment of that popular ghost story, **Tokaido Yotsuya Kaidan** (1959). The highpoint of his career was the extraordinary **Kozure Ookami** (1972) and its sequels, mind-bogglingly violent surrealist operas which can be regarded as the filmic equivalents of Lautréamont's *Chants de Maldoror*.

Left: *David Niven prepares to be sacrificed in the silly* Eye of the Devil.

Below: *Brazilian director José Mojica Marins, surely one of the most bizarre personalities of the cinema, in the role of Zé do Caizao in the surreal* Esta Noite Encarnarei no Teu Cadaver.

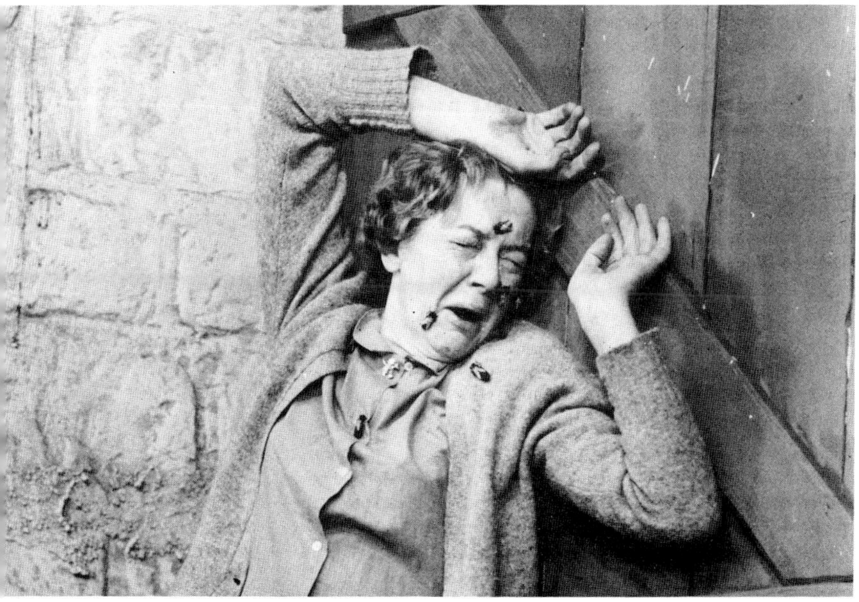

The routine The Deadly Bees.

d Kenji Misumi *p* Masaichi Nagata *s* Tetsuo Yoshida *c* Fujio Morita *se* Yoshiyuki Kuroda *lp* Kojiro Hongo, Shiho Fujimura, Tara Fujimura, Taro Murui, Jutaro Hojo, Takashi Kanda

The Deadly Bees (AMICUS; GB) 123(83)min
A lacklustre adaptation of H. F. Heard's novel, *A Taste of Honey*, this is one of Francis's worst films. Even the removal of 40 minutes from the original can't disguise that the film is obviously derived from *The Birds* (1963). Vicki (Leigh), a tired pop singer, takes a holiday on a remote farm where she encounters a surly beekeeper (Doleman) and an ever-so friendly one (Finlay). There is talk of a deadly strain of bees being developed, and suspicion is aroused by the bloody corpses of a dog and a woman (Finn) who have been stung to death. When Leigh is attacked in her room – in a scene reminiscent of Tippi Hedren's ordeal in *The Birds* – she seeks refuge with the nice beekeeper, who predictably turns out to be the nasty one. There she manages to turn the stinging creatures against their creator.

Although the colours are pleasant and the faces of the bees' victims suitably horrific, the script's red herrings are so obvious and the direction so tame that the movie falls hopelessly flat. In fact, bees never did provide good horror material, as is borne out by *The Swarm* (1978) and *Invasion of the Bee Girls* (1973).

d Freddie Francis *p* Max J. Rosenberg, Milton Subotsky *s* Robert Bloch, Anthony Marriott *c* John Wilcox *se* Michael Collins *lp* Suzanna Leigh, Frank Finlay, Guy Doleman, Catherine Finn, John Harvey, Michael Ripper, Katy Wild, Michael Gwynn, Tim Barrett

Death Curse of Tartu
(FALCON PRODUCTIONS) 87(85)min
Down in the Florida Everglades a Seminole witch-doctor stirs. Legend says he will return to wreak vengeance on anyone who disturbs his grave, so a group of archaeology students do and he does. Materializing variously as alligator, snake, shark or Indian brave (Hobart) to destroy his enemies, he is finally swallowed up in quicksands. Sadly Grefe makes little of the fact that the avenging spirit is an Indian, the one interesting feature of the plot. The result is a routine outing that lacks even the verve of William Girdler's similarly motivated **The Manitou** (1977).

d/s William Grefe *p* Joseph Fink, Juan Hidalgo-Gato *c* Julio Chavez *lp* Fred Pinero, Babette Sherril, Mayra Christine, Sherman Hayes, Doug Hobart

Esta Noite Encarnarei no Teu Cadaver *aka* **Tonight I Will Paint in Flesh Colour** *aka* **Tonight I Will Make Your Corpse Turn Red**
(IBERIA FILMES; BRAZIL) b/w and col 105min
Based in São Paulo, Marins embarked on a controversial career as a director with the, as yet, unreleased *Sentença de Deus* in the early sixties. He organized his own studio in an abandoned synagogue and achieved notoriety with nightmarishly sadistic, brutally pathological horror movies featuring amateur performers often recruited from the city's sub-proletariat. At the heart of these fantasies stands Zé do Caizao (literally, Joseph the Grave), a megalomaniac master of ceremonies played by Marins himself. The character was established in the cheap, nasty and successful *A Meia Noite Levarei Sua Alma* (1965) and in this picture, its follow-up.

The story simply provides an excuse to indulge in an endless orgy of gore and torture, which produces the occasional surreal scene but more often leaves an impression of a very sick man's home movies. In search of an ideal woman worthy of bearing his child, the mad Zé abducts a series of women and subjects them to hideous forms of suffering. Most of his victims fail to impress him and are killed, while the one who manages to survive the torture and the horrors dies in childbirth. Sinking into a psychotic delirium, he then goes totally berserk in a frenzy of barbarous carnage.

The film is barely watchable as its 'amateur' actors are subjected to attacks of live poisonous spiders, are thrown into real snakepits, have their heads crushed in a press, and so on. Nonetheless, the shoestring production exudes a genuine sense of madness both in its imaginings and in the treatment of its participants, with the eccentric, seemingly out-of-control staging veering from the pathological to the surreal. The climactic scenes offer bloodcurdling visions of hell: a cave filled with crucified, near-naked men and women, some upsidedown, others arranged in irregularly angled diagonals, or the ice cave with denuded, frost-covered bodies merging with the crudely fashioned white (plaster) walls and pillars while Zé attacks them with heinous savagery. Marins' next released picture (some were banned by the censors) extended the series with **O Estranho Mundo de Zé do Caixao** (1968) and his **Delirios de um Amoral** (1978) included scenes from these and earlier Zé do Caixao pictures.

d/p/co-s José Mojica Marins *co-s* Aldenora de Sá Pôrto *c* Giorgio Attili *lp* José Mojica Marins, Tina Wohlers, Nadia Freitas, Tania Mendoça, Mina Monte, Esmeralda Ruchel, Roque Rodrigues, Lya Lagutte, Carmen Marins, Antonio Fracari

Eye of the Devil (FILMWAYS; GB) b/w 90min
This is an inane – though well-photographed – story about an occult rite which requires the head of a wine-growing family (Niven) to be sacrificed when the vineyards fail. Based on Philip Loraine's *Day of the Arrow*, the movie has its characters wandering or riding about exchanging meaningful glances, with various notables of the British theatre tucked away in remote corners of the château. The occult brotherhood – 12 hooded figures parading through the grounds – does produce some picturesque images, but the awkward attempts to evoke echoes of **The Innocents** (1961), with Kerr looking mystified and two youngsters (Tate and Hemmings) behaving ever so oddly, fail miserably.

d J. Lee Thompson *p* Martin Ransohoff, John Calley *s* Robin Estridge, Dennis Murphy *c* Erwin Hillier *lp* Deborah Kerr, David Niven, Donald Pleasance, Flora Robson, Emlyn Williams, Sharon Tate, David Hemmings, John Le Mesurier, Edward Mulhare

Frankenstein Created Woman *aka* **Frankenstein Made Woman** (HAMMER/SEVEN ARTS; GB) 86min
Fisher's third and Hammer's fourth contribution to the series forgets **The Evil of Frankenstein** (1964) and takes up the

dynamic established in **The Revenge of Frankenstein** (1958). After his painful experiences with ignorant and bigoted people, the Baron (Cushing) has become more embittered against society and consequently more 'inhuman' and self-absorbed. Also, realizing that immortality cannot be achieved by manufacturing synthetic bodies which always end up behaving irrationally, in direct opposition to his own beliefs, the Baron shifts his attention to the problem of 'soul' transplants. He transfers the soul – an incandescent mass briefly trapped in a magnetic field – of the decapitated Hans (Morris) into the body of his crippled lover, Christina (Denberg).

The movie is structured as a pattern of symmetrical inversions and echoes. The first half starts with the double ritual of horror as a father is guillotined before the eyes of his son and then the son's decapitation is witnessed by his lover, while the second half, contained between Christina's two suicides by drowning, is punctuated by two rituals of pleasure as she seduces and gruesomely kills Hans's tormentors. These flamboyant explosions of violence mingled with pleasure and death are bound together by the Baron's calm but relentless experimentation, filmed in tenderly muted Technicolor, which culminate in the ironic poetry of the ending as Cushing watches Denberg's body being carried along in a mountain river and, with a shrug of the shoulders, turns away, providing what must be the most understated ending ever for a horror movie.

Crammed with felicitous directorial touches, the movie contains a splendidly characteristic scene which summarizes Fisher's conception of the Baron's character. Appearing as a witness in court, Cushing casually and with an air of amused condescension fingers a few pages of the Bible. But this dismissive attitude towards religious myth doesn't prevent him believing in the physical existence of the soul. Such a scene forms the counterpart to Van Helsing's impatience with narrowly positivist attitudes that are blind to the notion of vampirism: the Baron is a scientist who still accepts a religious world, the Professor is a religious figure who already inhabits the rationalist world. Enhanced by admirably controlled acting, especially by Cushing, his colleague (Walters) and Denberg, this is the best of Hammer's Frankenstein movies. Fisher's next contribution, **Frankenstein Must Be Destroyed** (1969), continued the personality-transfer motif and boasted some remarkable scenes but the overall effect was less intensely oneiric.

d Terence Fisher *p* Anthony Nelson Keys *s* John Elder (Anthony Hinds) *c* Arthur Grant *se* Les Bowie *lp* Peter Cushing, Susan Denberg, Thorley Walters, Robert Morris, Duncan Lamont, Peter Blythe, Alan MacNaughton, Peter Madden, Barry Warren, Derek Fowlds

The Gruesome Twosome

(MAYFLOWER PRODUCTIONS) 72min

With this effort, released in 1967, Lewis returned to the gore genre in which he had made his name. According to Lewis himself 'it's about a little old woman who runs a wig shop. And her idiot son who lives in the basement gives her the makings to make these wigs. On one side of the house she has rooms for rent and on the other side of the house she has wigs for sale. All these young girls, naturally, come in, rent a room, are promptly scalped by the idiot son, and the wigs are made'.

From here on in, Lewis' films become ever more violent, presumably reflecting changing standards of censorship and acceptability. *The Gruesome Twosome* itself contains a scalping with a butcher's knife, a throat being slit with an electric carving knife and a disembowelling. As Krough and McCarty put it in their book on Lewis 'these scenes of scalping and dismemberment are the epitome of Herschell Lewis' gore effects. They are authentic looking to an unbelievable degree and are shot in unblinking closeups with a minimum of cutaways, and represent the very best in pre-Dick Smith and Tom Savini gore makeups'. Nonetheless, the film was clearly intended by Lewis to be a black comedy, as is made clear in two bizarre scenes (shot after the editing was completed to bring the picture up to feature length): in one a young couple go to a drive-in and watch a parody of a foreign art movie, whilst a prologue has a conversation between two styrofoam heads with cutout paper faces stuck on them.

d/p/c Herschell Gordon Lewis *s* Allison Louise Downe *lp* Elizabeth David, Chris Martel, Gretchen Welles, Rodney Bedell

The Hand of Night *aka* The Beast of Morocco

(ASSOCIATED BRITISH PATHE; GB) 73min

An awkward attempt to combine the mummy and Dracula legends, this is a sweaty story about a Moroccan vampire princess (Gur) who nightly entices the hero (Sylvester) into the fairytale Moorish palace which, by day, is an ancient ruin. Clare, as Sylvester's girlfriend, decorously submits to the usual indignities as she is abducted by Omar, the vampire's servant (de Marney), and staked out in the desert. Reputed to be the great granddaughter of Buffalo Bill, she started out well as a fantasy actress in Robert Wise's **The Haunting** (1963) and Don Sharp's **Witchcraft** (1964) but her career stalled with John Gilling's **The Plague of the Zombies** (1966) where she was overshadowed by Jacqueline Pearce.

d Frederic Goode *p* Harry Field *s* Bruce Stewart *c* William Jordan *se* Biographic Films *lp* William Sylvester, Alizia Gur, Diane Clare, Edward Underdown, Terence de Marney, William Dexter, Sylvia Marriott, Angela Lovell

Hua Pi *aka* The Painted Skin

(FENG HUANG FILM CO; HONG KONG) 86min

The 17th-century collection of short stories *Strange Tales from a Chinese Studio* had provided the source material for a number of Hong Kong films, including Tao Qin's *Love with a Ghost* (1954) and Li Hanxiang's *Enchanting Shadows* (1959). *Hua Pi* is a fairly straightforward adaptation which mixes the fantastic and the melancholic in its tale of two brothers from Shanxi province. The elder is a scholar who falls in love with a beauty who is revealed to be a ghost wearing the painted skin of a beautiful woman. The ghost is liquidated by the younger brother, a skilled martial artist, when it threatens the scholar's marriage and the stability of the family.

Made at the time of the emerging neo-martial arts cinema spearheaded by King Hu's *Come Drink with Me* (1965), the film

Left: Frankenstein Created Woman: *Peter Cushing and* Playboy *model Susan Denberg.*

The inept La Isla de la Muerta.

does show traces of cashing in on that trend. Bao Fang acted in a number of classic films – *Sorrows of a Forbidden City* (1948) and *The Soul of China* (1948) among them – before directing his first feature in 1964. Most of his career has been connected with the so-called 'left-wing' film companies (those oriented towards the People's Republic of China), including Feng Huang for which he has directed at least 18 features.

d/s Bao Fang *lp* Gao Yuan, Zhu Hong, Chen Juanjuan, Wang Wu

El Imperio de Dracula *aka* **Las Mujeres de Dracula** *aka* **Sinfonia del Más Alla** *aka* **The Empire of Dracula**
(FILMICA VERGARA; MEX) scope 90min
This, the first Mexican horror film in colour, tells a traditional tale of a dying mother who sends her son Luís (del Campo) to Castle Draculstein to avenge his father who was killed by the vampire (del Castillo). After the usual tribulations with a reluctant coachman, the young man and his female companions (including Villa as his wife) arrive at the castle where Igor, the servant, resuscitates the Count in a manner inspired by Terence Fisher's **Dracula, Prince of Darkness** (1965): he positions an abducted woman above the ash-filled tomb and plunges a dagger into her allowing the blood to cascade into the tomb. The rest of the picture chronicles the vampirizing of del Campo's female friends and the abduction of his wife before the Count gets stabbed with a wooden cross. The coda details the killing of Igor, pursued on horseback by del Campo, and the use of the cross against the remaining female vampire. Following both Hammer's lead and the general trends of the contemporary commercial cinema, the movie emphasizes eroticism whenever the opportunity arises.

The interesting variation offered by the story is that while the vampire is explicitly designated as a threat to patriarchy (the narrative is motivated by the killing of the hero's father) this threat is most clearly represented, not by a lubricious Count, but by the voracious sexuality of the vampire woman whose destruction is the effective climax of the film: it is her sexuality which is presented as the ultimate menace, thus undercutting the implications of the Dracula myth as shaped by Bram Stoker and Fisher in Great Britain and substituting a more directly sexual politic relevant to the pathologically macho aspects of Mexican popular culture. The picture, released in 1967, was the first serious engagement with the Dracula myth in Mexico since the two Frankenhausen movies, **La Invasión de los Vampiros** (1961) and *El Conde Frankhausen* (1962).

d Federico Curiel *p* Luís Enrique Vergara *s* Ramón Obon Jnr *c* Alfredo Uribe *lp* Eric del Castillo, Cesar del Campo, Lucha Villa, Ethel Carrillo, Rebeca Inturbide, Altia Michel, Gigi Monet, Raúl Ferrer, Victor Alcoce, Fernando Oses

Incubus (DAYSTAR) 78min
Directed by the creator of *The Outer Limits* and starring Shatner in his last pre-Captain Kirk feature, *Incubus* is also the first feature film – horror or otherwise – with dialogue entirely in Esperanto; it has English subtitles for the uninitiated. Set in the mythical land of Nomen Tuum, the allegorical and symbolic story revolves around Marc (Shatner), a representative of the powers of good, who is tempted by the powers of evil when they send a beautiful succubus (Ames) to seduce him. She, however, falls in love with him and in revenge an incubus (Milos) is sent to rape Shatner's sister Arndis (Atman).

The use of Esperanto, described by Stevens as a language 'at once imaginary and universal, out of time and space' clearly points to the film's aspirations as a parable along the lines of C. S. Lewis' *Voyage to Venus* but it is also interesting to note that it was first conceived around the personae of Ames and Milos, both of whom clearly fascinated Stevens. Intriguingly the latter (actually called Milos Milosevicz) lived out his demonic role here in real life by killing his lover Barbara Rooney (wife of Mickey) and then committing suicide. *Incubus* was shot at Big Sur which is strikingly captured by Hall, who photographed Stevens' earlier films *Private Property* (1960) and *Hero's Island* (1962), as well as several episodes of *The Outer Limits*.

d/s Leslie Stevens *p* Anthony M. Taylor *c* Conrad Hall *lp* William Shatner, Allyson Ames, Eloise Hart, Robert Fortier, Ann Atman, Milos Milos

Las Isla de la Muerte *aka* **Das Geheimnis der Todeninsel** *aka* **Bloodsuckers** *aka* **The Island of the Doomed** *aka* **Death Island** *aka* **The Maneaters of Hydra** *aka* **Island of the Dead**
(ORBITA/TEFI; SP,WG) scope 88(79)min
Released in 1967, this is a cheap shocker about a vampiric tree created by Baron von Weser (Mitchell) in his island mansion's garden of carnivorous plants. The tourists who visit the island off the Italian coast are repelled by vegetarian dishes that taste like meat before they fall victim to the bloodthirsty tree. The climax sees Beth (Montes) embraced by the slurping thing's serpent-like tentacles while her lover (Martin) takes an axe to them. This prompts the Baron to intervene but he falls prey to his creation. The direction is token and the movie's only watchable scene is the latterday Eve's reunion with the tree in the Baron's obscene garden of Eden followed by the surreal image of the profusely bleeding tree. Von Theumer later achieved some notoriety with the perverse **La Figlia di Frankenstein** (1971).

d/co-s Mel Welles (Ernst von Theumer) *p* George Ferrer (Ernst von Theumer) *co-s* Ira Meltcher, Stephen Schmidt *c* Cecilio Paniagua *lp* Cameron Mitchell, Elisa Montes, George Martin, Kay Fisher, Matilde (Muñoz) Sampedro, Ralph (Rolf von) Naukoff, Hermann Nehlson, Mike Brendel, Riccardo Valle

Jesse James Meets Frankenstein's Daughter
(CIRCLE PRODUCTIONS) 82min
Like its companion piece **Billy the Kid vs Dracula** (1965), a crude attempt to marry the horror and western genres. To be strictly accurate, it is Frankenstein's grand-daughter (Onyx) who meets Jesse James (Lupton) when, after conducting some experiments in a Mexican village, she transplants an artificial brain created by her ancestor into Jesse's muscular but moronic sidekick (Bolder). As hopeless as the earlier film, it would be unbearable but for Onyx, who makes a richly overripe, querulously kinky prima donna out of the mad scientist. Beaudine's last film, it makes a not entirely inappropriate coda to a prolific career down among the Bs.

d William Beaudine *p* Carroll Case *s* Carl K. Hittleman *c* Lothrop Worth *lp* John Lupton, Cal Bolder, Narda Onyx, Estelita, Steven Geray, Jim Davis

Kairyu Daikessen *aka* **Grand Duel in Magic** *aka* **The Magic Serpent** *aka* **Froggo and Droggo**
(TOEI; JAP) scope 86min
A cross between a costume drama, monster movie and fairytale, this rather crudely acted but colourful fantasy owes much to Seiji Yada's art direction and the inventiveness of Mokuami Kawatake's original story. An evil nobleman (Amatsu) usurps power by killing the lord of his clan, but the lord's son (Matsukata), having become a master of the occult arts, later returns and kills the villain who also turns out to be the long-lost father of his lover (Ogawa). The climactic sequence consists of a duel between the hero and an evil magician in the service of the villain. The hero conjures up a fire-spitting horned toad while his antagonist fields an equally fiery dragon. Their fight destroys the castle on the shores of the picturesque lake Biwa and unleashes a tornado before the heroine intervenes by throwing a hairpin at the dragon. Since this object belonged to her grandmother, a spider-woman, a giant spider appears who, with a flash of blinding light, breaks all the magic spells. Back in human form, the hero then kills his opponent with a sword, whereupon he and his love are carried off by a giant eagle.

d Tetsuya Yamauchi *p* Hiroshi Okawa *s* Masaru Igami *c* Motonari Washio *lp* Hiroki Matsutaka, Tomoko Ogawa, Ryutaro Otomo, Bin Amatsu, Nobuo Kaneko

La Lama nel Corpo *aka* **The Murder Clinic** *aka* **The Knife in the Body** *aka* **The Blade in the Body** *aka* **Les Nuits de l'Epouvante** (LEONE FILM/ ORPHEE PRODUCTIONS; IT,FR) scope 87(75)min
Scardamaglia here manages to create some eye-catching images despite Gastaldi's lazy script based on Robert Williams' *The Knife in the Body*. The picture multiplies scenes featuring a hooded razor-slashing killer and screaming women in a claustrophobic clinic at the turn of the century. The old deformed woman in the attic (Maurin) and the doctor working on skin grafts (Berger) motifs are used again, with the extra twist that the manic killer turns out to be the doctor's jealous and invalid wife (Young). The victims include a blackmailer, Giselle (Prevost), a lunatic patient (Dean) and Mary (Wilson), who escapes to provide the happy end after the good doctor's relations have been disposed of.

Although nowhere near as deliriously lyrical as Riccardo Freda, Mario Bava or even Antonio Margheriti's work, the film does show some flair in the editing, as stifling, candlelit interiors alternate with airy, verdant exteriors.

co-d/p Michael Hamilton (Elio Scardamaglia) *co-d* Domenico de Felice *s* Julian Berry (Ernesto Gastaldi), Martin Hardy (Luciano Martino) *c* Mark Lane (Marcello Masciocchi) *lp* William Berger, Françoise Prevost, Mary Young, Barbara Wilson, Delphine Maurin, Max Dean (Massimo Righi), Harriet White, Philippe Hersent

Libido (NUCLEO FILM; IT) b/w 85min
This pretentious movie revolves around a boy, Christian (Giannini), who witnessed his mad father kill his mistress in a mirror-filled room. When he returns to the patriarchal villa with his bride, Helene (Boschero), and another couple, Paul and Brigitte (Pigozzi and Maryl), strange happenings suggest his father, thought to have thrown himself off a cliff, may still be around. By the time it emerges that the women are scheming to lay their hands on his inheritance, Giannini has become insane and repeats the acts of his father, leaving Maryl to die in the mirror room before jumping off a cliff. The self-consciously arty direction kills whatever suspense the story might have provided as it relentlessly rolls on to its predictable climax. The plot, provided by Maryl, could have given rise to an eccentric revenge story by the woman for the mad patriarch's crime, but instead it purveys the usual image of lethally greedy women.

d/s Julian Berry (Ernesto Gastaldi), Victor Storff (Vittorio Salerno) *c* Ramón Garron (Romolo Garroni) *lp* Dominique Boschero, Mara Maryl (Maria Chianetta), John Charlie Johns (Giancarlo Giannini), Alan Collins (Luciano Pigozzi)

La Lunga Notte di Veronique *aka* **But You Were Dead** *aka* **Veronique's Long Night**
(MERCURFILM ITALIANA; IT) 79min
This slow, laboured ghost story features Rigazzi as the woman who makes a suicide pact with a Count (Poggi) which he fails to keep. Her revenge is to seduce his orphaned grandson (Morrison) and frighten him into committing suicide by feigning a lethal accident while resisting his embrace. Additional interest is provided by the old Count's young companion (Gajoni) who also makes a play for the unfortunate hero.

Vernuccio, who started his career as a propagandist during the Second World War and went on to make features in his native Egypt before returning to Italy, is best known for his Dino Buzzati adaptation, *Un Amore* (1966). However, this one-man production shows him to be incapable of shedding his documentary past, inserting explanatory flashbacks at every opportunity.

d/co-s/c Gianni Vernuccio *p* Oscar Righini *co-s* Enzo Ferraris *lp* Alex Morrison, Alba Rigazzi, Walter Poggi, Cristina Gajoni, Tony Bellani, Gianni Ruben, Marco Righini, Charlie Poleski

The Mummy's Shroud (HAMMER; GB) 84min
Hammer's third entry in their mummy series continued the downward slide from Fisher's **The Mummy** (1959), initiated by Michael Carreras' follow-up, **The Curse of the Mummy's Tomb** (1964). Set in 1920, the film tells of an archaeological team, led by Morell and financed by the egomaniac Phillips, who fall foul of Prem (Powell), the guardian mummy of a young pharaoh's tomb. The mummy is revived by a demented Arab (Delgado), after which some gory murders punctuate the lacklustre script based on a plot devised by John Elder (Anthony Hinds). One of the team, Claire (Kimberley) ends the story by mumbling a few magic words she learnt from a Haitian soothsayer (Lacey) and the mummy crumbles into dust in a scene cribbed from Fisher's **Dracula** (1958). The prologue also echoes Fisher's introduction to the mummy, sketching the events that led to the pharaoh's burial 4000 years earlier. In

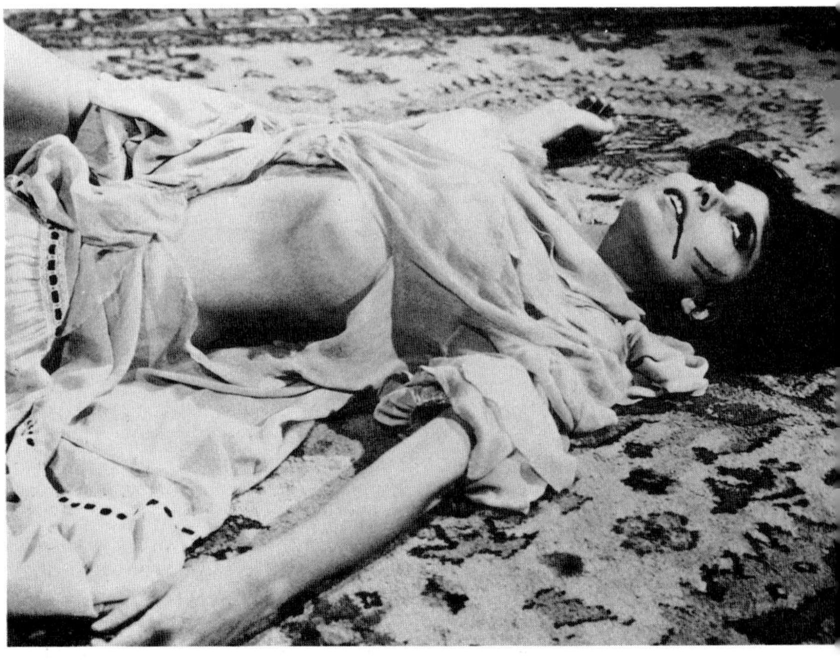

Maria Chianetta dead in Libido.

A typical moment of shock from The Mummy's Shroud.

between these two borrowings from the master, there is little of interest except perhaps the pleasantly over-the-top performances of Lacey as the toothless hag and Ripper as the venal but ineffectual agent of the expedition's glory-seeking sponsor.

Hammer's next contribution to the series was the far better **Blood from the Mummy's Tomb** (1971).

d/s John Gilling *p* Anthony Nelson Keys *c* Arthur Grant *se* Bowie Films *lp* John Phillips, Andre Morell, David Buck, Elisabeth Sellars, Maggie Kimberley, Michael Ripper, Richard Warner, Roger Delgado, Catherine Lacey, Dickie Owen, Eddie Powell

Munster Go Home! (U) 96(86)min

Munster Go Home! proves an exception to the usual rule that half-hour television sitcoms do not translate too well into big-screen, feature-length films. The Munster family gather for the reading of Herman's (Gwynne) uncle's will and discover that he has inherited an estate in England. Visiting their new acquisition, the clan are met by their cousins Lady Effigie (Gingold) and her children Freddie and Grace (Thomas and Arnold), none of whom are too pleased to see them and attempt to scare them away with a whole series of apparitions and weird happenings. The Munsters, however, are all delighted. Eventually they discover the reason for their frosty reception: Munster Hall is being used as the centre of a counterfeiting ring.

Well paced and with excellent Technicolor photography, the film features the entire TV cast with the exception of Watson – one of four different actresses who filled the role at different times – as Marilyn. The film concludes with a wild car chase through the English countryside, with Gwynne driving his Dragula, a custom-built, coffin-shaped car. The regular cast's professional polish and panache is ably augmented by Gingold and Thomas who enter full-bloodedly into the spirit of the enterprise. A minor entry, but charming nonetheless, far better than the awful telefilm *The Munster's Revenge* (1981).

d Earl Bellamy *co-p/co-s* Joe Connelly, Bob Mosher *co-s* George Tibbles *c* Benjamin H. Kline *lp* Fred Gwynne, Yvonne De Carlo, Al Lewis, Butch Patrick, Debbie Watson, Terry-Thomas, Hermione Gingold, Jeanne Arnold, Robert Pine, Maria Lennard

Naked Evil (GIBRALTAR FILMS; GB) b/w 79min

Black actors have precious few job opportunities in Britain and they cannot be blamed for participating in this example of racist sensationalism about evil voodoo practices in a fictitious English town called Middlehampton. Based on John Manchip White's play *The Obi*, the film tells of a malicious caretaker, Amazon (Ford), who uses a poor student (Saunders) to distribute homemade obis: bottles containing soil from graves, cockerel feathers and an evil spirit that kills its recipient. The action is set in a university hostel for black students whose director (Dignam) is gruesomely killed, and although Ford is found hanged, the hostel secretary (Ainley) becomes possessed and needs to be exorcized by the unimaginatively named priest, Goodman (Pooley). A police inspector (Coleman) is also involved, but in the end it appears that the black menace hasn't been eliminated yet as Ford, presumed dead, can be seen still lumbering through the bushes. Directed without the slightest trace of irony, it is a tiresomely offensive film exploiting the *Boys' Own* black bogeyman stereotype, even though some of 'them' may appear to be decent chaps.

d/s Stanley Goulder *p* Michael F. Johnson *c* Geoffrey Faithfull *lp* Anthony Ainley, Basil Dignam, Brylo Ford, Richard Coleman, George A. Saunders, Olaf Pooley, Suzanne Neve, Ronald Bridges, Pearl Prescod, Carmen Munroe, Bari Johnson

Operazione Paura *aka* **Curse of the Dead** *aka* **Kill, Baby, Kill** *aka* **Curse of the Living Dead** *aka* **Operation Fear**

(FUL FILMS; IT) 85(75)min

Bava's last major gothic, as opposed to terror, movie, this is also one of his – and therefore one of the genre's – best pictures. The ghost of a young girl, left to bleed to death by feasting villagers, takes her revenge on the village, acting through the aged Baroness Graps (Vivaldi), hidden away in a desolate villa amid candles and black lace curtains. The corpses of her victims all have gold coins embedded in their hearts, the work of a local black-robed witch, Ruth (Dali), surging mysteriously out of the night as she fights evil represented by a golden-haired little girl dressed in white.

The narrative is carried by Dr Eswai (Rossi-Stuart) and his assistant, Monica (Blanc) as they investigate the macabre happenings. With exquisite colours and a prowling camera lovingly gliding through a moss-laden village beset by swirling mists, through dusty corridors and sombre, cobwebbed rooms, as black cats and shadowy figures steal through the graveyard fog, Bava weaves his magic cinematic skills, calling up the frightened faces of villagers anxiously awaiting the sounds of a tolling bell and childish laughter. With the exception of the inversion of the conventional depictions of good and evil, this is one of Bava's least perverse pictures. The many conflicting images of 'woman' which his films usually condense into a single, hallucinatory female figure are here dispersed across different characters: the chillingly innocent child; the decrepit old baroness; the black but good maternal witch and the pretty young medical student. The erotic charge inherent in cinema – which Bava usually presents through the *mise-en-scène* of sado-voyeuristic fantasies barely constrained by a narrative structure reduced to its most rudimentary motifs – is here displaced on to the deliriously stylized, flamboyantly romantic imagery and enhanced by an eerily poetic soundtrack.

With the exception of *Diabolik* (1967), Bava's later work tended to degenerate into facile, mechanical effect-seeking with a lazy reliance on the zoom lens (*Il Rosso Segno della Follia*, 1969, for example, and **Cinque Bambole per la Luna di**

Agosto, 1970) although **Ecologia del Delitto** (1971) recalls the extraordinarily disturbing fascination of his best work.

d/co-s Mario Bava *p* Nando Pisani, Luciano Catenacci *co-s* Romano Migliorini, Roberto Natale *c* Romano Rinaldi *lp* Erica Blanc (Enrica Bianchi Colombatto), Giacomo Rossi-Stuart, Fabienne Dali, Gianna Vivaldi, Piero Lulli, Max Lawrence, Giuseppe Addobbati, Franca Domonici, Micaela Esdra

Picture Mommy Dead
(EMBASSY/BERKELEY) 88(82)min
Another film fashionably bolstered by slipping stars, this also provided a first starring role for director Gordon's daughter Susan as the girl returning home after three years in a sanatorium, still traumatized by memories of the mysterious death of her mother (Gabor) in a fire. Father (Ameche) is remarried to her governess (Hyer), who behaves like the proverbial wicked stepmother, trying to have her recommitted (so as to collect her inheritance) and murdering the scarred handyman (Reed) with a steel hook when he tries to interfere. Hyer is then strangled by Ameche, who confesses that he also murdered Gabor because of her infidelities with the handyman. Re-traumatized but happy to be alone with her father, Susan sets fire to the house and waits with him for the arrival of the police. The result is typical Gordon trash, enlivened by a few crude shock effects and competent performances.

d/p Bert I. Gordon *s* Robert Sherman *c* Ellsworth Fredricks *lp* Don Ameche, Martha Hyer, Susan Gordon, Zsa Zsa Gabor, Maxwell Reed, Wendell Corey, Signe Hasso

The Plague of the Zombies *aka* **The Zombie** *aka* **The Zombies**
(SEVEN ARTS/HAMMER; GB) 91min
Gilling, a veteran scenarist and director, made the first British vampire movie since the Second World War, **Old Mother Riley Meets the Vampire** (1952). Hammer hired him on the basis of **The Flesh and the Fiends** (1959), and he produced his best work for the studio – the script for **The Gorgon** (1963), some energetic swashbucklers and two very effective horror titles, shot back-to-back late in 1965: *The Plague of the Zombies* and **The Reptile** (1966), both set in Cornwall and intended, but never released, as a double bill.

Morell is the professor who investigates a mysterious epidemic in a Cornish village, which turns out to be the work of the local squire (Carson) who practices voodoo, creating zombies, to work his tin-mine. Gilling achieves some visually stunning moments, including the local doctor's (Williams) chillingly green nightmare vision of a graveyard with dead fingers clawing their way through the heaving mounds of earth as rotting corpses emerge in an often quoted resurrection sequence (**The Return of Count Yorga** and **Fright**, both 1971). The moral and political tone is set early on in a well-judged scene in which a picturesque, redcoated hunting party is seen careering through a funeral procession, knocking over the coffin. The scene neatly demonstrates that it is aristocratic arrogance and callousness that is responsible for the evil that infects the village. Pearce is excellent as the fascinating Alice who is 'saved' from zombie-hood by being decapitated, but Clare, reputed to be Buffalo Bill's great granddaughter, seems bland and out of place. Pearce went on to give an outstanding performance in *The Reptile*.

d John Gilling *p* Anthony Nelson Keys *s* Peter Bryan *c* Arthur Grant *se* Bowie Films *lp* Andre Morrell, Diane Clare, Jacqueline Pearce, John Carson, Brook Williams, Michael Ripper, Alex Davion, Marcus Hammond, Roy Royston

The Reptile (HAMMER; GB) 91min
Shot back-to-back with **The Plague of the Zombies** (1966) in late 1965, *The Reptile* uses the same late-19th-century Cornish setting and also concerns a hideously corrupting disease carried by aristocrats with a colonial past. The movie opens to the incongruously spellbinding sounds of an eastern flute while Gilling, with slow deliberation, introduces us to the Franklyn mansion, the windows of which are always lit when there is a death. The story concerns the fraught relationship between the weak but proud Dr Franklyn (Willman) and his daughter Anna (Pearce), the victim and embodiment of her father's guilty desires. Having yielded to the temptations of forbidden knowledge in Malaya, Willman has caused his daughter to become a lascivious creature who, aroused by emotional as well as physical heat, turns into a snake-woman. Gilling manages some wonderfully sensuous scenes: Pearce becoming entranced at a musical evening, beginning to sway in response to the compelling eastern rhythms; her body writhing on a bed to the accompaniment of her Malay master/servant's (Maitland) chanting; and Willman's desperate disgust at his daughter's bed with her discarded green skin and nightgown. In her few appearances as herself, Pearce offers a gloriously sensual performance which, together with Gilling's controlled direction and alluring imagery, constitutes the highlight of the uneven, but cinematically seductive, picture.

The Reptile is far superior to Sidney Furie's treatment of the same theme in **The Snake Woman** (1960), and, together with his first Hammer movie, **The Shadow of the Cat** (1961), is Gilling's best work.

d John Gilling *p* Anthony Nelson Keys *s* John Elder (Anthony Hinds) *c* Arthur Grant *se* Bowie Films *lp* Jacqueline Pearce, Noel Willman, Jennifer Daniel, Ray Barrett, Michael Ripper, John Laurie, Marne Maitland, Charles Lloyd-Pack, George Woodbridge, David Baron

She Freak (SONNEY-FRIEDMAN) 87min
A loose adaptation of **Freaks** (1932). Brennan, tired of waitressing, goes to work with a travelling carnival, marries the boss (McKinney) for his money, and carries on with her lover (Raymond). Alerted to the situation by a dwarf (Silla), McKinney gets killed in a showdown and Raymond is jailed. Brennan inherits the carnival but, since she can't stand freaks, she fires the dwarf. The freaks gang up and mutilate her (somehow managing to turn one half of her into a B-movie

Left: *Jacqueline Pearce is* The Reptile *in John Gilling's marvellous film.*

The Plague of the Zombies, *John Gilling's companion piece to* The Reptile *(1966).*

werewolf with vampire fangs and a globular eye). Although meretriciously directed with none of the humanity of Tod Browning's version (Friedman had previously produced **Blood Feast**, 1963; **Colour Me Blood Red**; and **2000 Maniacs**, both 1964), the general air of sleaziness does convey something of the feel of a freak show.

d Byron Mabe *p/s* David F. Friedman *c* Bill Troiano *lp* Claire Brennan, Lee Raymond, Lynn Courtney, Bill McKinney, Van Teen, Felix Silla

The Shuttered Room (TROY/SCHENCK; GB) 99min
Set in New England but shot in Britain, this story inspired by H. P. Lovecraft and August Derleth is notable as the début of Greene, a once promising director. The plot centres on Susannah (Lynley) who returns to her childhood home with her husband Mike (Young). The return stirs memories of a repressed traumatic event, whose menace is represented by Reed – repeating his role from *The Damned* (1962) – who persecutes Lynley and triggers the final conflagration. The dreadful secret, locked in the shuttered room guarded by an old aunt (Robson), is Lynley's demented and disfigured twin sister.

The script is uninspired, the acting stereotypical and the dialogue feeble, but Greene manages to create suspenseful moments through a judicious use of subjective camera, showing the terrified victims backing away from the lens. Unfortunately, except for the competently made *The Strange Affair* (1968), his subsequent films were thoroughly average.

d David Greene *p* Phillip Hazelton *s* D. B. Ledrow, Nathaniel Tanchuck *c* Ken Hodges *lp* Carol Lynley, Gig Young, Flora Robson, Oliver Reed, William Devlin, Judith Arthy, Bernard Kay, Robert Cawdron, Celia Hewitt

Solo un Ataud *aka* **Only a Coffin** *aka* **The Orgies of Dr Orloff**
(PC SANTOS ALCOCER/PC HISPAMER; SP) b/w scope 89min
Although Enrique Jarnes was credited with the original story for this movie, the murkily shot horror-thriller is simply an updated version of **The Cat and the Canary** (1927) with a few modifications. A man who is about to die (Vernon) assembles all his relatives at his old castle. The old patriarch is found dead in a coffin with a knife in this chest and, predictably, the rest of the cast begin to suffer similar fates before the decomposing culprit is discovered. Vernon is best known for his collaborations with Jesús Franco, including **Gritos en la Noche** (1962). Here he acquits himself honourably largely by staying out of the frame as much as possible. A few extra scenes with naked women appear to have been inserted for obviously commercial reasons.

Franco himself later made an official version of *The Cat and the Canary*, entitled **La Noche de los Asesinos** (1974).

d/p/s Santos Alcocer *c* Emilio Foriscot *lp* Danielle Godet, Howard Vernon, Maria Saavedra, Adolfo Arles, José Bastida, Tota Alba, Rosa Yarza, Mary Leyva, José Maria Seoane

La Sombra del Murcielago *aka* **The Shadow of the Bat**
(FILMICA VERGARA; MEX) b/w 90min
The wrestler Velazquez, nicknamed El Murcielago (the Bat), wrote this story to provide himself with a starring role. He plays a monstrously disfigured wrestler who surrounds himself with four equally ugly acolytes and imprisons young women in the dungeons of his ominous castle, hoping to force his amorous attentions upon them. The ugly group also abduct other wrestlers to provide their master with opponents who, when vanquished in the private ring, are dropped into a cave full either of rats or bats. The screaming heroine (Romero) is rescued by her lover (Fernandez) who calls in Blue Demon to the rescue.

Curiel fell ill during the production and, assisted by Fernando Rivero, Vergara finished the film which was released in 1968. The same Vergara-Curiel team went on to make **El Imperio de Dracula** (1966) from a script by Ramón Obon few months later. Without scripts by either Obon or Alfredo Ruanova, as in **La Maldición de Nostradamus** (1959) and its sequels, Curiel's work lost much of its interest. *La Sombra* was shot, as usual, at the Estudios America in the form of three episodes designed to be combined into one feature, since feature film production as such was reserved for the rival union based at the Churubusco-Azteca studios.

d Federico Curiel *p* Luís Enrique Vergara *s* Jesús 'Murcielago' Velazquez *lp* Blue Demon (Alejandro Cruz), Jaime Fernandez, Martha Romero, Fernando Oses, Jesús 'Murcielago' Velaquez

Something Weird
(HUR-LEW PRODUCTIONS INC) b/w 83min
One of Lewis' most obscure films, this features McCabe as a man whose face is horribly scarred in an electrical accident, which also leaves him with extra sensory powers. He is then visited by Lee, an ugly witch who offers to restore his face if he will become her lover. He agrees, and then goes on to become a famous psychic. Eventually he is investigated by ESP expert Brooker who falls for Lee. Brooker kills McCabe but is later horribly burned in an accident and Lee offers him the same deal that she offered McCabe ...

The picture was released in 1967.

d/c Herschell Gordon Lewis *p/s* James F. Hurley *lp* Tony McCabe, Elizabeth Lee, William Brooker

La Strega in Amore *aka* **The Witch** *aka* **Aura** *aka* **The Witch in Love** *aka* **The Strange Obsession**
(ARCO FILM; IT) b/w 103min
In between neorealist inspired movies like *La Isola di Arturo* (1962) and jaundiced looks at corrupt state officers (*Confessione di un Commissario di Polizia*, 1971), Damiani made some virulently misogynist pictures including this contribution to the horror genre. Based on the Mexican Carlos Fuentes' novel, *Aura*, published in 1962, the story posits the questionable thesis that men can only relate to each other satisfactorily when women are destroyed. The fantasy used to illustrate this proposition has a historian, Sergio (Johnson), who must get rid of his predecessor, Fabrizio (Volonte), if he is to stay on at a palace editing the salacious memoirs of a deceased general. The general's wizened widow, Consuelo (Ferrati) is also a witch and assumes the appearance of the beautiful Aura (Schiaffino) in order to pit the men against each other, inciting Johnson to

murder Volonte. When the historian discovers that Consuelo and Aura are the same person and he learns that he is to be replaced, he burns the witch. In spite of professional shooting and acting, the picture remains a depressingly bigoted and woman-hating effort.

d/co-s Damiano Damiani *p* Alfredo Bini *co-s* Ugo Liberatore *c* Leonida Barboni *lp* Rosanna Schiaffino, Richard Johnson, Sarah Ferrati, Gian Maria Volonte, Margherita Guzzinati

Theatre of Death *aka* **The Blood Fiend** *aka* **The Female Fiend**
(PENNEA PRODUCTIONS; GB) scope 91(88)min
This potentially interesting, excellently photographed story about necrophilia in a Grand Guignol setting is wasted by unimaginative direction. Darvas (Lee) is a lugubrious stage director of horrid spectacles who indulges in mesmeric exercises on the side. While his theatre of death plays to packed audiences, his ward, Nicole (Till), commits vampiric murders. After Lee, who functions as the movie's red herring, is found dead, Till's room-mate Dani (Goldoni) discovers her friend's vampirism and triggers the final confrontation between the two women which takes place underneath the stage and ends when, as part of the voodoo dance performed on the boards, a spear is plunged through the floor into Till. The beautiful Goldoni, best known for her part in John Cassavetes' *Shadows* (1961), animates the screen whenever she appears, but the horror paraphernalia, including sliding panels, a cobwebbed chamber and a figure scuttling around in a black cloak, is routinely used.

d Samuel Gallu *p* Michael Smedley-Aston *s* Ellis Kadison, Roger Marshall *c* Gilbert Taylor *lp* Christopher Lee, Lelia Goldoni, Jenny Till, Julian Glover, Ivor Dean, Evelyn Laye, Joseph Fuerst

The Vulture *aka* **Manutara**
(HOMERIC/ILIAD/FILM FINANCIAL; GB, US, CAN) 91min
This tame variation on *The Fly* (1958) ranks somewhere alongside the moth of **The Blood Beast Terror** (1967). Tamiroff is the scientist whose experiment with a matter-transmitter succeeds in changing him into a knobbly-kneed vulture with a human head and arms. The story, set in Cornwall, also involves the legend of a Spanish sailor and his pet vulture, buried alive as a witch in the 18th century, which accounts for the vulture's animosity towards the Stroud family, descendants of the man responsible for this brutish act. This was the last film of Huntington's long and consistently undistinguished career. Filmed in colour, it was released in black and white in the America for New Year 1966.

d/p/s Lawrence Huntington *c* Stephen Dade *lp* Robert Hutton, Akim Tamiroff, Broderick Crawford, Diane Clare, Philip Friend, Annette Carell, Patrick Holt, Edward Caddick

The Witches *aka* **The Devil's Own**
(HAMMER; GB) 91min
Compared to Don Sharp's quietly effective **Witchcraft** (1964), Frankel's film offers a more conventional, less resonant treatment of the witchcraft motif in its tale of Gwen (Fontaine) who, traumatized by a voodoo priest in Africa, returns to England as headmistress of a private school run by Alan (McCowan) and his sister Stephanie (Walsh). She finds herself driven to another breakdown, is forcibly initiated into a coven and has to kill the demonic Walsh before being able to lead a quiet life with the kinky McCowan who likes dressing up as a priest and arranges his private study as a church with taped organ music.

In his adaptation of the novel by Peter Curtis (Nora Loftis), Kneale, best known as the author of the *Quatermass* teleseries and films, provides a script which trades on the usual racist and sexist stereotypes, with blacks, women and children as the weak-minded people who are particularly vulnerable to the forces of evil. Walsh's powerful performance as the witch can't overcome the basic design of her character: as an idealist child-oriented teacher she is presented as ready to sacrifice an innocent child in her care in order to further her ambition of improving the world. She – not her near-psychotic brother with religious obsessions – is the symbol of evil, and it takes a self-sacrificing woman to restore the world to order by putting an end to her sinister attempts to change it.

d Cyril Frankel *p* Anthony Nelson Keys *s* Nigel Kneale *c* Arthur Grant *lp* Joan Fontaine, Kay Walsh, Alec McCowan, Ingrid Brett, Martin Stephens, Duncan Lamont, Gwen Ffrangcon-Davies, Leonard Rossiter, Michele Dotrice, Viola Keats

The Wrong Box (SALAMANDER; GB) 110min
This swinging sixties attempt to recapture the flavour of an Ealing black comedy revolves around two elderly brothers (Mills and Richardson) and their family, all deceiving each other to try and become the last survivor and collect a fortune. The plot, derived from R. L. Stevenson and Lloyd Osbourne's charmingly absurd satire on upper-class greed, has a dutiful grandson (Caine) and two perfidious cousins (Moore and Cook) become entangled in murderous schemes as they attempt to dispose of both real and apparent corpses. With an all-star cast, some were bound to hit the right note: Sellars as the cat-ridden venal doctor, or Lemkow as the Bournemouth Strangler, knitting away madly in the corner of railway carriage and Richardson as the excruciatingly boring brother oblivious to the attempts on his life made by his apoplectic sibling are the film's highlights. But script and direction appear intent on treating the story like a TV sitcom – but not *MASH* which co-writer Gelbart went on to co-produce – without the canned laughter, wheeling in one guest star after another, cramming each scene with music-hall gags regardless of the overall dynamic and necessary comic timing. The Victorian period setting is bungled, with television aerials in evidence, and, unable to achieve an effective filmic structure, the movie resorts to quaint or explanatory intertitles.

d/p Bryan Forbes *s* Larry Gelbart, Burt Shevelane *c* Gerry Turpin *lp* John Mills, Ralph Richardson, Michael Caine, Peter Cook, Dudley Moore, Tony Hancock, Nanette Newman, Peter Sellers, Wilfrid Lawson, Tutte Lemkow

Joan Fontaine, victim of The Witches.

Peter Cushing as the surgeon who dreams of restoring Sue Lloyd's face in *Corruption*, a gory potboiler.

1967

Berserk *aka* **Circus of Blood** *aka* **Circus of Terror**
(HERMAN COHEN PRODUCTIONS; GB) 96min
This badly scripted shocker is designed as a vehicle for Crawford, who sports a black leotard, scarlet tailcoat and top hat in her role as the tyrannical mother/owner of a circus. The story merely fills the gaps between some sensational murders: Gough's head is nailed to a tent post, Dors is sawn in half and Hardin is knifed and falls on a bed of spikes. That the homicidal maniac should turn out to be Crawford's daughter, played by 17-year-old Geeson, merely confirms that the movie's central fantasy is the anxiety generated by the figure of the sexually threatening mother, an image tailormade for the star. The required running time is achieved by showing various acts of Billy Smart's organization going through their routine, a grand parade and other padding devices.

d Jim O'Connolly *p/co-s* Herman Cohen *co-s* Aben Kandel *c* Desmond Dickinson *lp* Joan Crawford, Ty Hardin, Diana Dors, Michael Gough, Judy Geeson, Robert Hardy, Geoffrey Keen, Sydney Taffler, Philip Madoc, Milton Reid

Besame Monstruo *aka* **Kiss Me Monster** *aka* **Castle of the Doomed** (AQUILA FILM ENTERPRISES/FILMS MONTANA; SP,WG) 79(77)min
Badly shot, hastily put together, and borrowing liberally from such Hammer movies as **The Revenge of Frankenstein** (1958), this is the weakest of Franco's three pictures for Aquila. Although shot back-to-back with **Rote Lippen** (1967), the film uses a more conventional gothic setting – an isolated castle complete with dungeons and a monstrous apelike creature locked in a glass cage – for its routine series of gory experiments carried out on (mostly naked) women. As with *Rote Lippen*, the original story was attributed to K. H. Manchen.

Franco went on to make **Necronomicon** (1967), by far the best of the Aquila series, while his team and sets were borrowed by the actor-producer Hoven to make a sex and horror quickie under the pseudonym Percy G. Parker, **Im Schloss der Bluten Begierde** (1967).

d/s Jesús Franco *p* Pier A. Caminnecci, Adrian Hoven *c* Jorge Herrero *lp* Janine Reynaud, Rossana Yanni, Adrian Hoven, Michel Lemoine, Chris Howland, Carlos Mendi

The Blood Beast Terror *aka* **The Vampire Beast Craves Blood** *aka* **Blood Beast from Hell** *aka* **The Deathshead Vampire**
(TIGON BRITISH; GB) 88min
Although Sewell was Britain's veteran director of supernatural thrillers (*The Medium*, 1934; *Latin Quarter*, 1945; **Ghost Ship**, 1952; **House of Mystery**, 1961 – all versions of the same story), this tale of a young woman (Ventham) who periodically turns into a bloodthirsty death's-head moth, is disappointing. Professor Mallinger (Flemyng) feeds Ventham while trying to concoct a mate for her in a laboratory hidden away in a nearby country house. The entomological mystery is solved by Quennell (Cushing) while his daughter (Howard) is rescued through the predictable expedient of attracting the lethal moth to a fire. The settings are quaintly rural 19th-century England but the direction never overcomes the lazy accumulation of horror clichés that passes for a script.

Sewell's decline continued with **The Curse of the Crimson Altar** (1968), a cynical piece of exploitation.

d Vernon Sewell *p* Tony Tenser, Arnold L. Miller *s* Peter Bryan *c* Stanley A. Long *se* Roger Dicken *lp* Peter Cushing, Robert Flemying, Wanda Ventham, Vanessa Howard, David Griffin, Roy Hudd, Russell Napier, Kevin Stoney

El Coleccionista de Cadaveres *aka* **Cauldron of Blood** *aka* **Blind Man's Buff** *aka* **The Corpse Collectors** *aka* **Death Comes from the Dark** *aka* **The Shrinking Corpse**
(HISPAMER/ROBERT D. WEINBACH PRODUCTIONS; SP,US) scope 97(87)min
Following his **Solo un Ataud** (1966), the undistinguished Alcocer was hired for this belated American 'runaway' production released in 1971. Karloff (in a role originally intended for Claude Rains before he fell ill) plays a blind sculptor who uses skeletons as the basis for his unorthodox artworks. Unbeknownst to him, his wife Tania (Lindfors, miscast as a leather fetishist and whip-wielding killer) and her lover (Rojo) provide the skeletons by murdering people and dumping them into an acid bath they keep in a basement laboratory. A journalist (Aumont) and his girlfriend (Monteros) are the straight couple who trigger the climax after their friend Helga (Zurakowska) has been given the acid treatment. Karloff kills his wife and hurls himself on to the rocks below his mansion.

The most famous elaborations of the motif of an artist using murder victims as the basis for artworks are **House of Wax** (1953) and **A Bucket of Blood** (1959). Other titles using the same basic idea include **Games**, **Rote Lippen** (both 1967), **The Crucible of Terror** (1971) and Gordon Hessler's telefilm *Scream Pretty Peggy* (1973).

d/co-s Edward Mann (Santos Alcocer) *p* Robert D. Weinbach *co-s* John Melson, José Luis Bayonas *c* Francisco Sempere *se* Thierry Pathé *lp* Boris Karloff, Viveca Lindfors, Jean-Pierre Aumont, Jacqui Speed, Rosenda Monteros, Dianik Zurakowska, Ruben Rojo, Milo Quesada, Mercedes Rojo, Mary Lou Palermo

Corruption *aka* **Carnage**
(TITAN; GB) 91min
This crude exploitative cocktail announces the gory potboilers which became so popular on video in the early eighties. Although there had been British plastic-surgery thrillers before (including Terence Fisher's **The Stolen Face**, 1951), this is a poor imitation of the Hispanic variety of medical science fiction (**Gritos en la Noche** or *La Cara del Terror*, both 1962), leavened with elements of Jack the Ripper, *Penthouse* magazine and distant echoes of **Dead of Night** (1945). A surgeon (Cushing) dreams he has to keep restoring the scarred face of his lover (Lloyd) by resorting to the murder and decapitation of women until in a grand climax everybody is killed, at which point he wakes up and takes Lloyd to a party where he begins to

live the very beginning of his dreams. Including sex and teenage gangs as well as gory surgery, the movie also features such subtle details as a severed head wrapped in a polythene bag and stored in the fridge.

O'Mara, here the heroine's sister, later became a minor attraction in Hammer's **The Vampire Lovers** and **The Horror of Frankenstein** (both 1970), before graduating to TV soap operas. The same team was responsible for an equally crude failed imitation of Italian horror movies, **The Black Torment** (1964).

d Robert Hartford-Davis *p/c* Peter Newbrook *s* Donald Ford, Derek Ford *se* Mike Albrechtsen *lp* Peter Cushing, Sue Lloyd, Noel Trevarthen, Kate O'Mara, David Lodge, Anthony Booth, Vanessa Howard, Wendy Varnals

Dance of the Vampires *aka* The Fearless Vampire Killers; Or Pardon Me, But Your Teeth Are in My Neck *aka* The Vampire Killers

(CADRE FILMS/FILMWAYS; GB) scope 107(91)min

Often described as a spoof, Polanski's enchanting reworking of his favourite Hammer movies is, in fact, an encounter between horror and crazy comedy set in the world of fairytales. The film is an astounding cinematic *tour de force* that is funny, chilling and intensely lyrical at the same time and shows that the generally accepted wisdom that horror shall either be played straight or become a comedy, is false since both jokes and anxiety are rooted in the same soil of unconscious desires and combine to generate the sense of the uncanny. The resulting movie is one of the very few perfectly achieved examples of the uncanny, delicately poised between the familiar and weird.

Highlights include the image of Abronsius (MacGowran) crossing the icy parapet of Count Von Krolock's (Mayne) castle, gesturing stiffly like a demented puppet but evoking Nosferatu's figure in the process; the vampirizing of Sarah (Tate) in the inn, combining burlesque with the lyrical image of snow falling on a patch of scarlet blood; and the eerily stately minuet danced by the gruesome aristocratic corpses which ends abruptly in front of a huge mirror which remains empty but for the reflections of the three interloping humans – a dreamlike sequence hesitating between nightmare and farce, preventing the viewer from simply opting for one or the other.

The plot itself is familiar enough: Professor Abronsius and his assistant, Alfred (Polanski) arrive in Transylvania and discover the castle of the vampire, protected by the hunchbacked servant Koukol (Downes). They try to stake the vampires and rescue everybody's object of desire, Tate, but instead flee while Tate vampirizes a willing Polanski in the back of the sleigh and MacGowran unwittingly carries the couple's evil pleasures back to civilization, there to spread across the world. Polanski, MacGowran and Bass, as the Jewish innkeeper, are brilliant amid a generally excellent cast. The other credits, no doubt inspired by Polanski's intelligence and unrivalled eye for the right setting, are equally impressive,

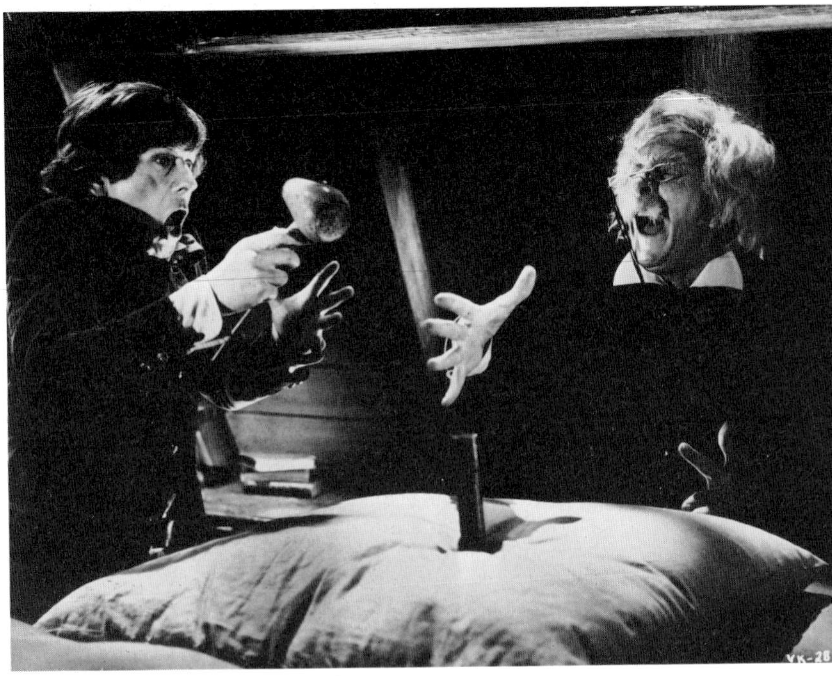

Roman Polanski and Jack MacGowran as the inept vampire killers in the marvellous Dance of the Vampires.

with Krzysztof Komeda providing the most innovative and haunting score ever devised for a horror movie.

Officially a co-production between Polanski's Cadre Films, represented by Gutowski, and Filmways, the film was butchered for its American distribution by British-based American executive producer, Martin Ransohoff, who added an animated credit sequence, slicing away 16 minutes and re-dubbing some voices. The US print with the silly title, *The Fearless Vampire Killers or Pardon Me But Your Teeth Are in My Neck*, was rightly repudiated by Polanski who asked for the removal of his name from the credits.

d/co-s Roman Polanski *p* Gene Gutowski *co-s* Gerard Brach *c* Douglas Slocombe *lp* Jack MacGowran, Roman Polanski, Sharon Tate, Alfie Bass, Jessie Robins, Ferdy Mayne, Iain Quarrier, Terry Downes, Fiona Lewis, Ronald Lacey

The Devil Rides Out *aka* The Devil's Bride

(HAMMER; GB) 95min

After the fallow period that followed from the commercial failure of **The Phantom of the Opera** (1962) – a three-year interlude in which only **The Gorgon** (1963) stands out – Fisher finished his career with five impressive movies of which *The Devil Rides Out* is the most accomplished. It explicitly stages the basic Manichaeistic conflict that animates all of his work as the two complementary notions of superstition/belief are pitted against each other. The Duc de Richleau (Lee) and Mocata (Gray), each know far too much about the other for their positions to be seen as anything other than positive and negative aspects of the same thing. They play a relay game in which the souls of Simon (Mower) and the eerily beautiful Tanith (Arrighi) are the stakes. The real climax of the film is a long night spent in a magic circle while the forces of evil do their worst. After that, the rescue of Arrighi from a satanist ritual is a foregone conclusion.

Fisher builds his atmosphere with uncannily precise editing, a marvellously controlled camera style and, above all, through an astonishingly sophisticated use of colour schemes, summarized in the image of the dazed Arrighi standing motionless in the swirl of a sabbath, dressed in a white robe splattered with intensely red blood. Set around 1925, the attention to period detail, which extend to objects, dress and cars, evokes a world in which Fantomas might still be active, a sense reinforced by the rigorously linear, almost serial-like structure of Matheson's script which considerably improves

Left: *Christopher Lee, Patrick Mower, Sarah Lawson and Paul Eddington seek sanctuary in the magic circle in Terence Fisher's magisterial* The Devil Rides Out.

Dennis Wheatley's original story. Intended as the first film in a Wheatley series, only *The Lost Continent* (1968) followed before Hammer abandoned the series following the commercial failure of both movies.

d Terence Fisher *p* Anthony Nelson Keys *s* Richard Matheson *c* Arthur Grant *se* Michael Stainer-Hutchins *lp* Christopher Lee, Charles Gray, Nike Arrighi, Leon Greene, Patrick Mower, Gwen Ffrangcon-Davies, Sarah Lawson, Paul Eddington

Games (U) scope 100min

A genuinely bizarre piece of gamesmanship, *Games* opens with a horsedrawn cab pulling up outside an imposing mansion in a dusky Manhattan street. A cadaverous elderly man (fleetingly reminiscent of the gaslit villains of Patrick Hamilton or Mrs Belloc Lowndes) emerges and enters an antique household of mahogany, lacquer and suits of armour where the one discordant note is a pop-art painting figuring prominently on the wall. The sense of disorientation continues as he strolls into a drawing-room where a flamboyant entertainment of Victorian galvanism and mesmerism is succeeded by a pinball machine funfair with a guest triumphantly ringing up the prize-winning death's head. The party ends on a note of weary decadence with the host (Caan) reclining voluptuously on furs, toying with a crimson rose as his wife (Ross) covers him with kisses: happily married but bored, they are wealthy enough to indulge their eccentricities in a round of games and parties in a home partially furnished from her heirlooms and his collection of Americana.

Into this décor, trailing tarot cards and a romantically doom-laden past of concentration camps and lovers dying at dawn, comes the enigmatic Signoret, who fits snugly in as the missing cast member without whom the play of death and sexuality cannot begin in earnest. Introducing the couple to the delights of Russian roulette, Signoret switches the games on to more dangerous sado-masochistic ground as a delivery boy (Stroud) is co-opted as a player, inadvertently shot and turned into a plaster-cast statue. At this point, unfortunately, the script turns into *Les Diaboliques* (1955), with Caan and Signoret revealed as being in league to drive Ross mad (for her money). Harrington directs the hash of horror stand-bys – bumps in the night, self-propelled elevators, perambulating corpses with one eye gruesomely shot away – with a good deal of verve and flair, but it disappoints after the subtle ambiguities of the first half.

d Curtis Harrington *p* George Edwards *s* Gene Kearney *c* William A. Fraker *lp* Simone Signoret, James Caan, Katharine Ross, Don Stroud, Kent Smith, Estelle Winwood

Hiroku Onna-ro *aka* **Ona Niko** *aka* **Women's Prison**

(DAIEI; JAP) b/w scope 75min

The gory violence and bone-crushing realism of respected Japanese classics like Kobayashi's *Seppuku* (1962) or Kurosawa's *Aka Hige* (1965), in combination with the quantitatively most important genre of Japanese production, soft-core sexploitation, spawned a uniquely gruesome sub-genre which chronicles sexual tortures but draws them out into feature-length fantasies. Its undisputed master, Wakamatsu (*Kabe no Naka no Himegoto*, 1963; *Taiji ga Mitsuryo Suru Toki*, 1966; **Okasaretu Byuakui**, 1967; *Riyu Naki Boko-Gendai Seihanzua Zekkyohen*, 1969) also directed a feature simply entitled *Gomon Hyakunenshi* (1975). The commercial companies practised the genre as well, with Teruo Ishii's **Tokugawa Onna Keibatsushi** (1968) and this picture by Inoue.

The narrative excuse used for the film's non-stop sexual violence is the imprisonment of a young woman (Yasuda) in the 18th century on suspicion of murder. The film dwells on her painful experiences and graphically portrays her stepfather being tortured to death. As an added twist, her main tormentor in prison is later revealed to be her long-lost sister. Unlike American sex-and-gore movie-makers like Michael and Roberta Findlay, Andy Milligan and Herschell Gordon Lewis, Japanese practitioners rarely slip into the torture-for-fun-and-profit attitude signalled by the American directors by means of gross special effects, tongue-in-cheek crudeness and high-school standards of acting. As a result, their stylish and 'straight' cruelty films are at times unbearable to watch, simply because they avoid the cultural conservatism of their American colleagues who denigrate their audiences and refuse to take responsibility for the unpalatable fantasies they exploit. Inoue's film, which banks on the troubled pleasures of going beyond the bearable, proved one of Japan's biggest box-office hits of the season.

d Akira Inoue *p* Masaichi Nagata *s* Shozaburo Asai *c* Yasukazu Takemura *lp* Michiyo Yasuda, Sanae Nakahara, Shigako Shimegi, Mayumi Nigisa, Machiko Hasegawa, Sei Hiraizumi, Fumio Watanabe

Histoires Extraordinaires *aka* **Tales of Mystery** *aka* **Spirits of the Dead**

(FILMS MARCEAU/COCINOR/PEA CINEMATOGRAFICA; FR, IT) 121min

Three more unlikely allies on an anthology of Poe stories than Vadim, Malle and Fellini are difficult to imagine, and the results of the collaboration are predictably uneven (and remote from Poe). Adapting *Metzengerstein*, Vadim's imagination seems to have exhausted itself on the teasing perversity of casting Jane and Peter Fonda as the decadent countess and the object of her frustrated passions. Shot with an ugly reliance on zooms, the episode is little more than an excuse for some titillating orgies and a bit of demonic galloping by the black stallion animated by the young man's spirit after she inadvertently incinerates him. Malle's version of *William Wilson*, with Delon as an Austrian army lieutenant whose sadistic impulses are repeatedly curbed by the intervention of a mysterious double, is not uninteresting. The elaborations to the story are both intelligent and precise (Bardot re-doubling in a dual role; the card game with the players in masks to conceal their dissembling), but it finally emerges as too skeletally brief to be really persuasive.

The best episode is Fellini's version of *Never Bet the Devil Your Head*, with Stamp as a drink- and drug-sodden English film star visiting Rome to appear in a spaghetti western and to collect the new Ferrari promised as a bonus. Trailing the usual cast of clowns and grotesques as Stamp uncooperatively submits to the inevitable circus of interviews and celebrity appearances – always haunted by the presence of a strange little girl who finally gets a new ball to play with when he is decapitated at the wheel of his new car – the episode is pure Fellini.

Right: *Katharine Ross, James Caan and Simone Signoret (left to right) play* Games, *in Curtis Harrington's witty horror outing.*

An earlier *Histoires Extraordinaires* (1949) leavened two Poe stories (*The Tell-Tale Heart*, *The Cask of Amontillado*) with an adaptation of Thomas de Quincey's *Murder Considered as One of the Fine Arts*. Aiming at black comedy rather than horror and rather ponderously directed by Jean Faurez, it is distinguished chiefly by a witty performance from Jules Berry, partnered by the lugubrious Fernand Ledoux, in *The Cask of Amontillado*.

d/co-s Roger Vadim, Louis Malle, Federico Fellini
co-s Pascal Cousin, Daniel Boulanger, Bernardino Zapponi
c Claude Renoir, Tonino delli Colli, Giuseppe Rotunno
lp Jane Fonda, Peter Fonda, Alain Delon, Brigitte Bardot, Terence Stamp

Im Schloss der Bluten Begierde *aka* **Castle of Lust** *aka* **Castle of Bloody Lust** *aka* **The Castle of Unholy Desires** *aka* **In the Castle of Bloody Lust**
(AQUILA FILM ENTERPRISES; WG) 80min
Giving Jesús Franco a brief rest from his Aquila productions, Hoven borrowed most of his cast and crew and made this exceedingly wordy period horror fantasy. Set in a lugubrious castle, the story concerns the Count von Saxon (Vernon) and his family curse. One of his ancestors had killed his lover and used her blood to save his daughter (Butenuth) who had been raped. This act caused him to be beheaded. Three centuries later, the current Count finds himself in a similar situation. A baron (Lemoine) rapes Elena (Berndorff) and the Count kills Lemoine's lover (Butenuth again) to save Berndorff by means of a heart transplant. But after the delicate operation, he clumsily kills her by accident. He then murders the baron and finally commits suicide.

Hoven went on to direct two extremely nasty witch-hunting pictures, **Hexen bis aufs Blut Gequaelt** (1969) and **Hexen Geschandet und zu Tode Gequaelt** (1972).

d/co-s Percy G. Parker (Adrian Hoven) *p* Pier A. Caminnecci *co-s* Eric Martin Schnitzler *c* Jorge Herrero, Franz Hofer *lp* Howard Vernon, Elvira Berndorff, Claudia Butenuth, Janine Reynaud, Jan Hendricks, Michel Lemoine, Pier A. Caminnecci, Vladimir Medar

It *aka* **The Curse of the Golem** *aka* **Anger of the Golem**
(SEVEN ARTS/GOLDSTAR; GB) 97(95)min
Released as the top of a double bill with Leder's *The Frozen Dead* (1966), this rather silly attempt to revive the golem legend in a movie designed for the US campus market, becomes decidedly sinister when, all in good fun, a 'small' atom bomb is dropped on a country estate to destroy the creature, unsuccessfully as it turns out. McDowall plays the ineffectual Pimm who discovers how to activate a mysterious pointy-headed statue identified by an American expert called Perkins (Maxwell) as the famous 16th-century Prague golem. Mother's-boy Pimm – whose live-in companion is the mummified body of his mother – becomes a megalomaniac, ordering the creature to destroy Hammersmith bridge just for the hell of it and then using it to abduct his girlfriend, Ellen (Hasworth), who has become more interested in the virile American expert. In the end, Pimm and his house are pulverized by a nuclear blast but the creature wearily lumbers off into the sea. With obvious references to **Psycho** (1960) and to Wegener's German classic, **Der Golem: Wie Er in die Welt Kam** (1920), and with its infantile hero, the movie offers a confused mixture of horror and comedy, succeeding in doing justice to neither tendency. Production values and cinematography are acceptable though erratic, especially in scenes requiring special effects, but the animation of the scraggy creature is well done. The director's name is sometimes given as Leger, while the cinematographer has been listed as David Bolton or Davis Boulton.

d/p/s Herbert J. Leder *c* David Boulton *lp* Roddy McDowall, Jill Haworth, Paul Maxwell, Noel Trevarthen, Ian McCulloch, Ernest Clark, Aubrey Richards, Allan Sellers

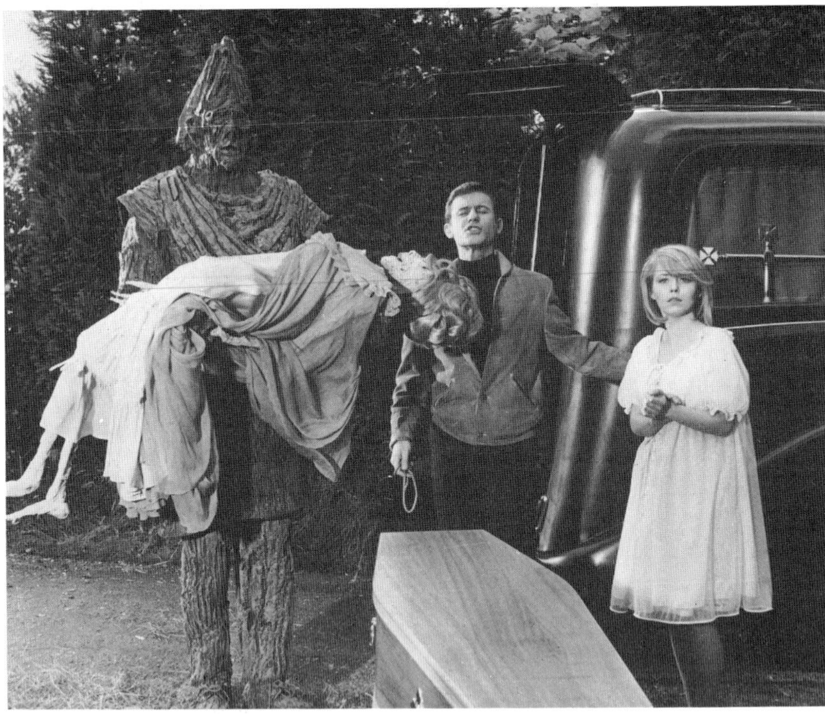

Allan Sellers, Roddy McDowall (centre) and Jill Haworth in the atrocious It.

La Marca del Hombre Lobo *aka* **Frankenstein's Bloody Terror** *aka* **Hell's Creatures** *aka* **The Mark of the Wolfman** *aka* **El Hombre Lobo** *aka* **The Vampire of Dr Dracula** *aka* **The Wolfman of Count Dracula**
(MAXPER; SP) scope 133(78)min
Molina's début as the werewolf Count Waldemar Daninsky, a role he would play a dozen times or more, tells us that he is a descendant of the lycanthropic Count Imre Wolfstein, called upon to kill his ancestor when gypsies remove the silver cross from the old man's tomb. In the process, he is fatally infected. The weird Hungarian couple who try to cure him, Professor Mialhov (Ugarte) and his wife Wandessa (Yanni), turn out to be vampires too but the film's hero and heroine (Zurakowska and Manzanaque) befriend the werewolf and, after he has killed the vampires as well as the couple's parents, Zurakowska shoots him with a silver bullet and, wounded by the dying werewolf, she dies with him.

Although the vampiric motifs of the badly scripted story don't mesh well with the rest of the plot, they nevertheless account for the film's few striking images, such as the vampire couple's arrival at a desolate looking, foggy railway station at night and the smoke clearing from the platform to reveal them standing motionless, waiting. The rest is uninspiringly photographed routine fare, although the script idea that the werewolf can only be killed by someone who loves him could have yielded some nicely black romantic scenes.

A 3-D version was released as well as a 70mm copy, but the best-known print is the adulterated, dubbed and re-cut version under the direction of F. Neumann, which gives the cast anglicized names and credits Eguiluz as Henry Egan. The distributor of the American version was committed to releasing a Frankenstein picture he had advertised and he inserted a new credit sequence: over a series of drawings which showed by means of dissolves the Frankenstein monster changing into a werewolf, a voice-over explained that the Frankenstein family had been infected by lycanthropy and was now called Wolfenstein. The rest of the picture was the severely cut and re-edited version of the Spanish original.

Molina, a weightlifter in a circus when Eguiluz recruited him for this picture, went on to become Spain's most important horror scenarist and actor (and later director). His subsequent Daninsky films include **Las Noches del Hombre Lobo** (1968), **El Hombro que Vino de Ummo** (1969), **La Noche de Walpurgis** (1970) and **La Furia del Hombre Lobo** (1971).

d/p Enrique L. Eguiluz *s* Jacinto Molina *c* Emilio Foriscot *lp* Paul Naschy (Jacinto Molina), Diane Konopka (Dianik Zurakowska), Julian Ugarte, Rossana Yanni, Michael Manz (Manuel Manzanaque), Joseph Morton (José Nieto), Carl Casara (Carlos Casaravilla), Anita Avery (Aurora de Alba), Gilbert Granger (Gualberto Galban), Victoriano Lopez

Necronomicon *aka* **Getraeumte Stunden** *aka* **Succubus**

(AQUILA FILM ENTERPRISES; WG) 91(82)min

In a break in his domestic Spanish career – which included second-unit work on Orson Welles' *Campañadas a Medianoche* (1966), and the seven collaborations with Harry Alan Towers, initiated with **El Castillo de Fu Manchu** (1968) – Franco made three pictures, all starring Reynaud, for the Munich-based Aquila company: **Rote Lippen**, **Besame Monstruo** and *Necronomicon* (all 1967). *Necronomicon* is the best film largely because Franco abandoned his tiresome over-use of the zoom lens and opted for a more fluid, occasionally even languorous, camera style.

The story alternates dream and reality to the point where both merge into a fantasy scenario chronicling a sado-masochistic obsession. The nightclub performer Lorna (Reynaud) does an S-M act in which she tortures and makes love to a chained couple before pretending to kill them. Apparently under the influence of a mysterious stranger (Vernon) who may have 'created' her, she is increasing overwhelmed by visions of the past and outlandishly nightmarish but also romantic visions of castles by the sea. She seems to close an act with a real murder as well as killing her girlfriend during an orgy at which people refer to her as Countess. In the end, her male lover (Taylor) tries to have her killed but she turns up again in his bed and knifes him to death while making love. She is then seen walking towards a castle with her stranger. The movie completely blurs the borderlines between the various levels of the narrative and succeeds in making Reynaud an oneiric creature condensing desire and death in to a single figure. Franco returned to the character in the more sexploitative **Les Possedées du Diable** (1974). The excellent photography is enhanced by an intelligent jazz score provided by Friedrich Gulda and arranged by Jerry van Rooyen. The film was shot in Berlin and Lisbon and Fritz Lang has said that this was the first erotic film he had seen all the way through because it was a beautiful piece of cinema.

Janine Reynaud in Jesús Franco's sado-masochistic Necronomicon, *one of the best looking and most interesting of the prolific director's films.*

d Jess Frank (Jesús Franco *co-p/s* Pier A. Caminnecci *co-p* Adrian Hoven *c* Franz Lederle, Georg (Jorge) Herrero *lp* Janine Reynaud, Jack Taylor, Howard Vernon, Michel Lemoine, Nathalie Nort, Pier A. Caminnecci, Adrian Hoven, Rosanna Yanni, Chris Howland, Amerigo Coimbra

Okasaretu Byuakui *aka* **Violated Angels** *aka* **Violated Women**

(WAKAMATSU PRODUCTIONS; JAP) b/w and col 58(57)min

The deliriously sado-masochistic films of Nagisa Oshima's protégé Takashi Ito, better known as Wakamatsu, derive much of their power from the desperate panic at, and fascination for, a descent into psychosis. As the male 'heroes' seek to possess female bodies to the point of merging with them, they also mutilate and destroy their objects of desire in an effort to rejoin some mystical essence of femininity beyond the 'surface' femininity offered by 'real' women who only evoke the irrevocably lost 'ideal' woman – the pre-oedipal mother – forever unattainable since she exists only as an unconscious fantasy. In common with ultra-leftist groups that turned to terrorism and other irrational cultural and political practices, Wakamatsu conflates the psychopathology of psychosis and its utopian fantasy of dissolution into an oceanic-maternal space (the lost paradise) with revolutionary politics.

This short feature, said to have been shot within a week of news of a notorious massacre of nurses in Chicago by a madman, opens with routinely commercial porn images, followed by a boy (Kara) incestuously discharging his weapon into the sea (as the historian Neil Burch pointed out, the Japanese character for 'sea' contains within it a recognizable variant of the character 'mother'). Kara is invited to a nurse's dormitory to watch a drawn-out, repetitious session of lesbian lovemaking. He responds by suddenly shooting the protagonists, followed by a long, sadistic sequence depicting the women moaning in shock. The rest of the picture, chronicling the boy's demented sexual cruelty, constantly repeats the same sexual rhythm of repetitious gesture, sudden outburst and panting subsidence.

Shot mostly in black and white, the film erupts into colour as the head nurse (Koyanagi) is confronted with the flayed body of a young colleague. The shot theatricalizes the movie by clearly showing the red paint daubed on to the victim's body. In the end, the psychotic boy, naked and surrounded by a circle of corpses, curls up into the lap of the youngest nurse (Sakamoto), at which point idyllic images of childish joy interrupt the film, followed by black and white shots of the police arriving on the scene – from which the young nurse, in keeping with the film's fantasy logic, has vanished. An epilogue shows stills signifying student rebellion and police repression.

Wakamatsu, who stems from peasant stock in remote northern Japan, made his name as a director of soft-core sex films. With the encouragement of Oshima, whose *Ai no Corrida* (1976) he eventually produced, he developed into one of the *'cinéaste maudit'* figures of the cinema, and has connections with the lunatic fringes of both Japanese and Palestinian terrorist groups. This film, his most powerful work to date, forms a companion piece to Pasolini's *Salo* (1975) and Tsui Hark's original version of *Diyi Leixing Weixian* (1980). Wakamatsu depicts the logical conclusion of the notion that unbridled sexual activity is a legitimate 'revolt' against sexual/political alienation. Pasolini splits the same notion into two aspects: positive unbridled sexuality is relegated to a prehistoric never-never-land while its alienated manifestations are equated with fascism. Tsui Hark's extraordinary film, structurally analogous to Wakamatsu's, offers the most complex and intelligent account of violent rage, refusing to privilege sexuality and grounding demented violence firmly in socio-historical conditions of oppression and frustration.

d/p/co-s Koji Wakamatsu *co-s* Masao Adachi, Juro Kara *c* Hideo Ito *lp* Juro Kara, Michiko Sakamoto, Heiko Koyanagi

Rote Lippen *aka* **Sadisterotica** *aka* **El Caso de las dos Bellezas** *aka* **Red Lips** *aka* **The Case of the Two Beauties** (AQUILA FILM ENTERPRISES/FILMS MONTANA; WG,SP) 92(79)min
This is the first of three films Franco made for the Munich-based Aquila company, all of which starred Reynaud; the others are **Besame Monstruo** and **Necronomicon** (both 1967). Here Reynaud is a private eye who uses the imprint of her rouged lips as a trademark. Together with her equally seductive female sidekick (Yanni) she pursues an eyepatch-wearing artist (Hoven) who abducts young women and sketches them while they are being killed by his brutish ape-man assistant. He then transforms them into statues by encasing the bodies in plaster, **A Bucket of Blood** (1959) style. Franco exceeds the usual limitation of soft-core porn with an emphasis on the sadistic component of his voyeur-artist's obsession, which accounts for the 13 missing minutes from the German release print. As usual with Franco, the dialogue here is both relentless and risible, although Jerry van Rooyen's score restores some interest to the German soundtrack. The picture was released in 1969.

A regular Franco collaborator, Hoven added direction to his producing and acting functions with **Im Schloss der Bluten Begierde** (1967) and the sickeningly exploitative **Hexen Geschandet und zu Tode Gequaelt** (1972).

d/co-s Jess Frank (Jesús Franco) *p* Pier A. Caminnecci, Adrian Hoven *co-s* G. G. Hoffmann *c* Jorge Herrero *lp* Janine Reynaud, Rossana Yanni, Adrian Hoven, Michel Lemoine, Chris Howland, Alexander Engel, Marcelo Arroita-Jauregui, Jesús Franco

Die Schlangengrube und das Pendel *aka* **The Blood Demon** *aka* **The Snake Pit** *aka* **The Torture Chamber of Dr Sadism** *aka* **The Snake Pit and the Pendulum** *aka* **The Torture Room**
(CONSTANTIN FILM; WG) scope 85(75)min
Repeating their collaboration on *Die Unsichtbaren Krallen des Dr Mabuse* (1961), the Reinl-Dor-Barker team was here reinforced by Lee for this exceedingly free adaptation of Poe's *The Pit and the Pendulum*. Count Regula (Lee) is about to consume his 13th virgin (Dor, Reinl's wife) in order to retain his eternal youth when she is saved by Barker. Just enough elements of the plot and characters of the Poe story are retained to keep the film commercially viable, but the whole point and force of the movie is the presentation of oneiric, genuinely disturbing perverse images. Eerily lit tableaux and nightmarishly disjointed scenes set in caves, secret passages, a forest garlanded with hanging corpses and hands emerging from trees, a chamber of horrors populated with the frozen bodies of naked, bloodless women, all combine to achieve a powerful sense of delirium. Needless to say, the narrative collapses under the pressure of the accumulation of images. Whatever the reason for this (bad cutting, lackadaisical scripting or the censor's scissors), memorable moments are achieved in the imagination of the less savoury desires and fantasies mobilized by the cinematic spectacle itself. If the cinematography had been up to, say, Mario Bava's standards, this movie could have become a surreal masterpiece. The psychotic films of the Brazilian José Mojica Marins (**Esta Noite Encarnarei no Teu Cadaver**, 1966) are some of the few examples to achieve a similarly intense depiction of unfettered delirium, burning images into the memory of viewers while the rest of the pictures vanish into deserved oblivion.

d Harald Reinl *p* Wolfgang Kuehnlenz *s* Manfred R. Koehler *c* Ernst W. Kalinke *se* Erwin Lange, Theo Nischwitz *lp* Lex Barker, Karin Dor, Christopher Lee, Carl Lange, Christiane Ruecker, Vladimir Medar, Dieter Eppler

The Sorcerers (TIGON/CURTWELL/GLOBAL; GB) 85min
Reeves' second feature, based on John Burke's novel, also marked the emergence of Tigon as specialists in horror. The plot features a drab, elderly couple, Dr Marcus Monsarrat (Karloff) and his wife Estelle (Lacey) who possess a device that enables them to impose through telepathy their fantasies on people and allows them to experience the sensations felt by their subjects. They take control of a teenager (Ogilvy) and have him live out the excitements which the staid lower-middle-class couple associate with contemporary youth: violence and sex. The brilliance of the script is that it works simultaneously on many different levels: as a metaphor for cinema, with the couple, like the spectators, vicariously experiencing the fantasies acted out on their behalf; as an astute depiction of the tabloid society's lurid stereotype of youth, deriving its thrills from the awful things it imagines youth to be up to; as yet another typically Reevesian account of how quickly 'decent' people surrender to their worst impulses, and so on, with each register reinforcing the others to produce a disturbingly powerful effect even though from a strictly cinematic point-of-view, the movie isn't as fascinatingly realized as **The Witchfinder General** (1968) or even the best scenes of **La Sorella di Satana** (1965). However, as an idea, Reeves' film rivals the brilliance and intelligence of **Peeping Tom** (1960).

Left: *Ian Ogilvy lives out the sexual and violent fantasies of Boris Karloff and Catherine Lacey in Michael Reeves' impressive* The Sorcerers.

d/co-s Michael Reeves *p* Arnold L. Miller, Patrick Curtis, Tony Tenser *co-s* Tom Baker *c* Stanley Long *lp* Boris Karloff, Catherine Lacey, Ian Ogilvy, Susan George, Elisabeth Ercy, Victor Henry, Dani Sheridan, Ivor Dean

A Taste of Blood *aka* **The Secret of Dr Alucard**
(CREATIVE FILM ENTERPRISES INC) 120min
This film marked Lewis' return to gore after a temporary foray into various other areas of the exploitation field. In terms of length, an epic by Lewis standards, it also boasted sufficiently high production values for the director to feel able to use it as an audition to make films for Roger Corman. However, although Corman was suitably impressed, Lewis was dissatisfied with the deal he was subsequently offered and decided to carry on on his own.

The Black Cat, *1934*

The Innocents, *1961*

King Kong, *1933*

The Phantom of the Opera, *1943*

The Curse of Frankenstein, *1957*

What Ever Happened to Baby Jane?, *1962*

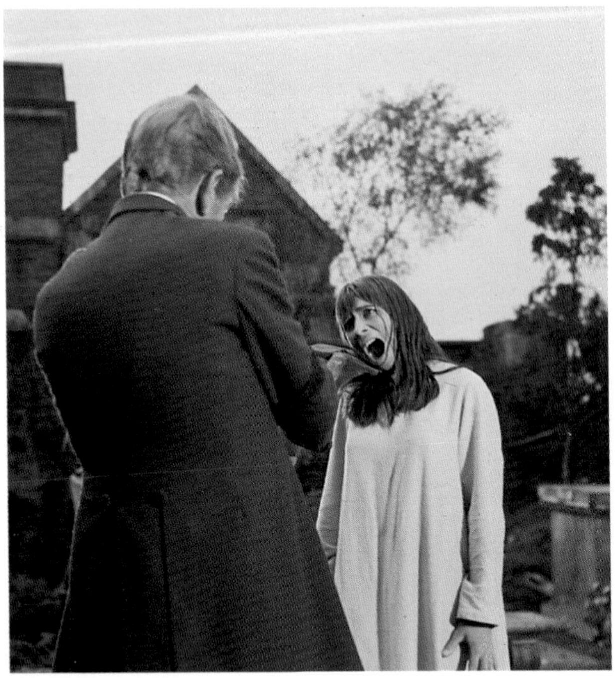
The Plague of the Zombies, *1966*

The Curse of Frankenstein, *1957*

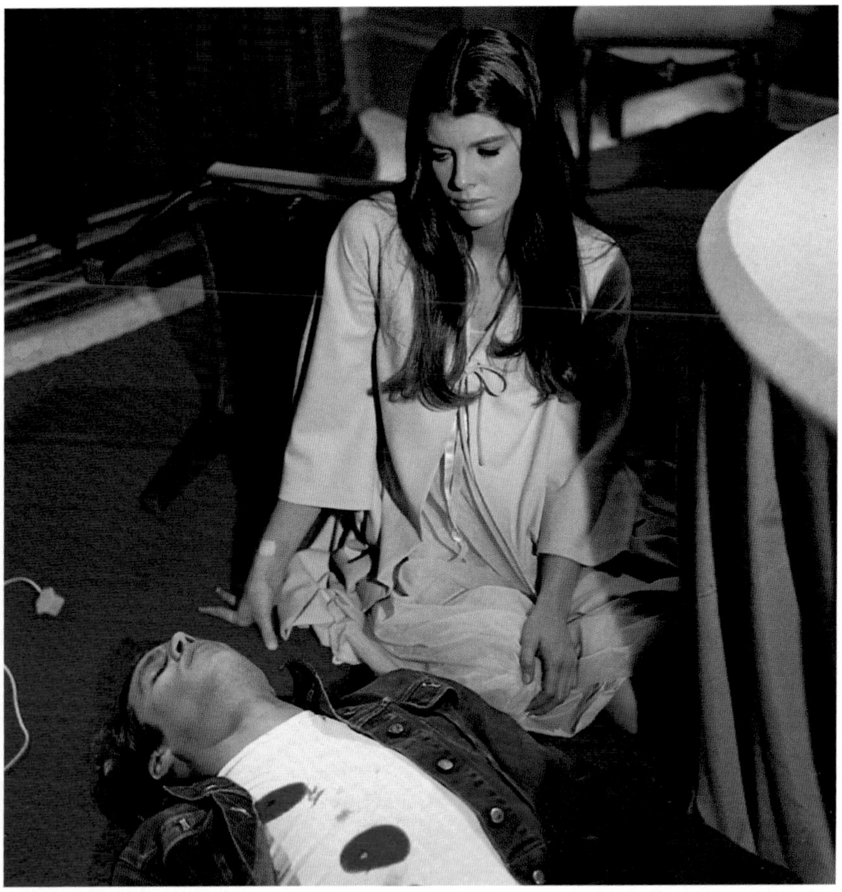

Games, *1967*

Games, *1967*

Berserk, *1967*

Dance of the Vampires, *1967*

The Devil Rides Out, *1967*

Dance of the Vampires, *1967*

The House That Dripped Blood, *1970*

Rosemary's Baby, *1968*

The Horror of Frankenstein, *1970*

The Devils, *1971*

The Abominable Dr Phibes, *1971*

Twins of Evil, *1971*

Tales from the Crypt, *1972*

Theatre of Blood, *1973*

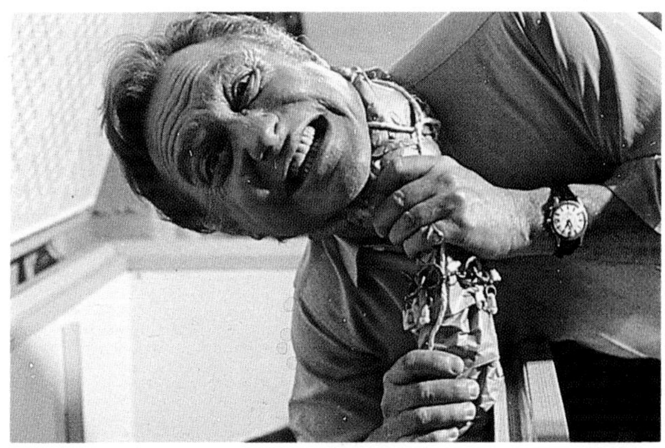

Asylum, *1972*

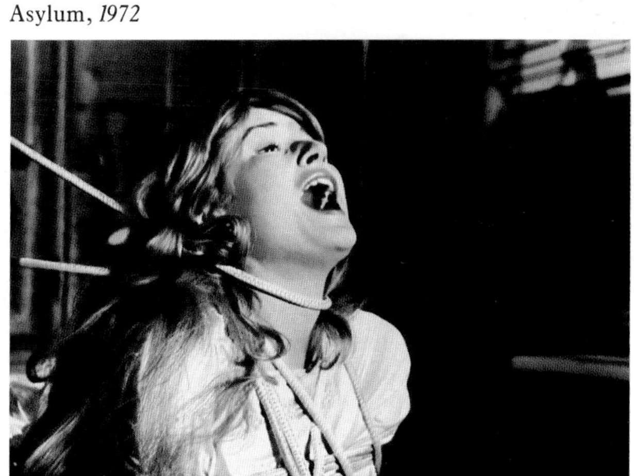

The Nightcomers, *1971*

The Other, *1972*

Nosferatu, *1978*

Carrie, *1976*

Jaws, *1975*

The Omen, *1976*

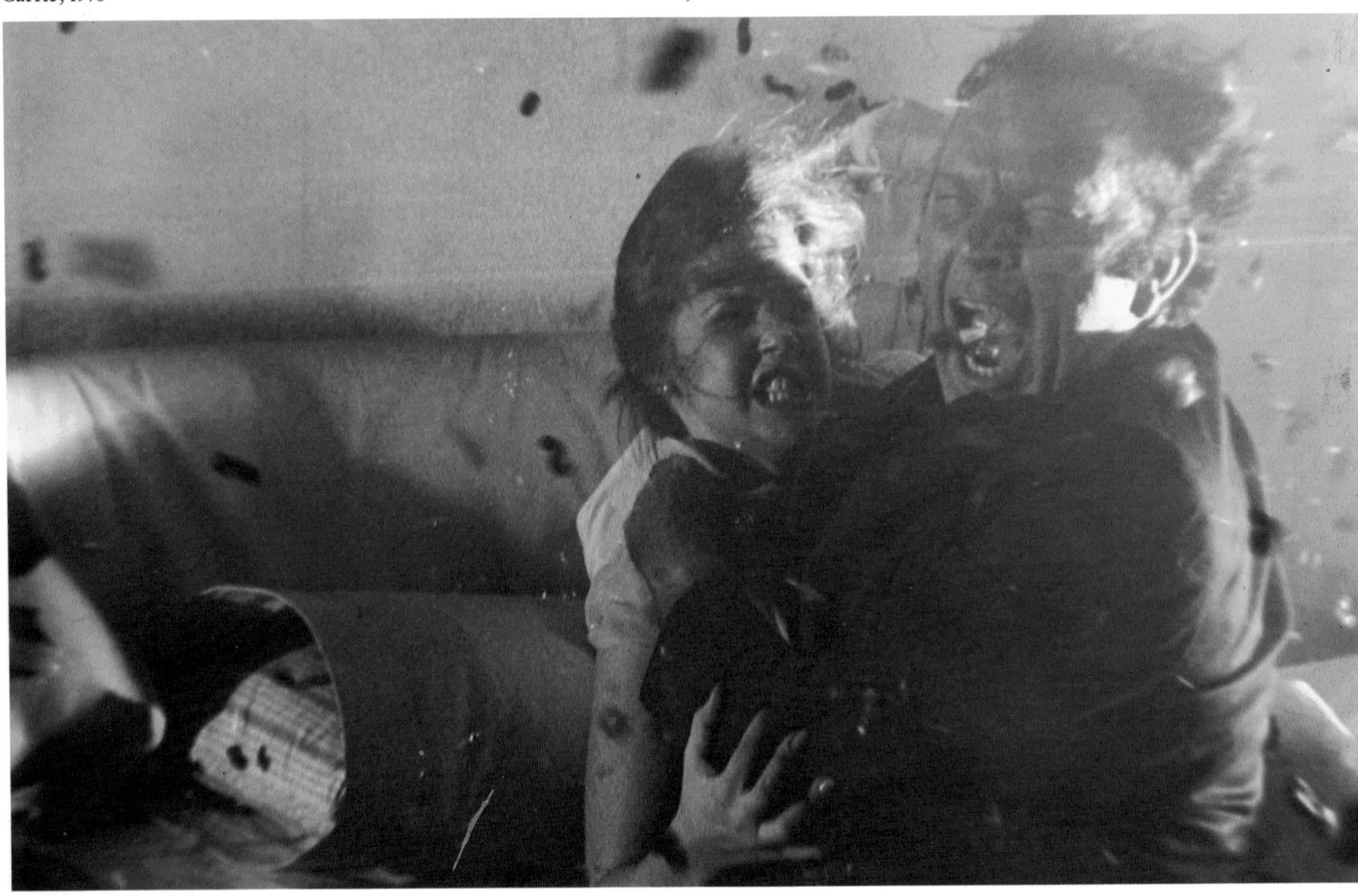

Exorcist II: The Heretic, *1977*

Audrey Rose, *1977*

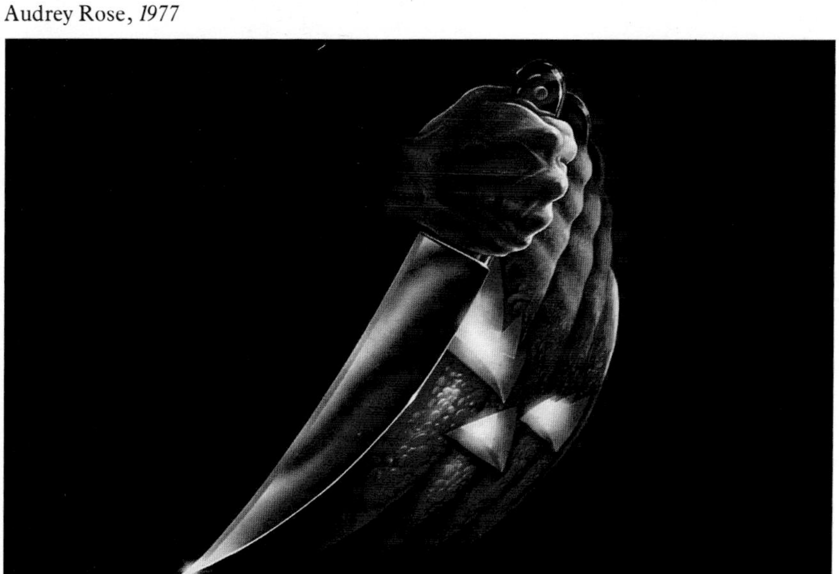

Halloween, *1978*

Picnic at Hanging Rock, *1975*

The Watcher in the Woods, *1982*

Dracula, *1979*

The Fog, *1979*

The Howling, *1980*

He Knows You're Alone, *1980*

Wolfen, *1981*

Poltergeist, *1982*

Christine, *1982*

Psycho II, *1983*

The Keep, *1984*

The Company of Wolves, *1984*

Blue Velvet, *1986*

The Stepfather, *1986*

A Nightmare on Elm Street IV, *1988*

Angel Heart, *1987*

Misery, *1991*

The Addams Family, *1991*

The Lawnmower Man, *1992*

The story has Rogers receive two ancient bottles of Slivovitz in a mysterious package from England along with instructions to drink it in a toast to a long-dead ancestor. Soon he's sleeping during the day and prowling about at night. He decides to visit England, where he discovers that he is the descendant of Count Dracula and has been chosen to wreak vengeance on Dracula's executioners. On his return to America, he becomes a fully fledged vampire and is finally destroyed by being staked by Dr Howard Helsing (Schlesinger). If hardly 'the *Gone With the Wind* of gore' as one critic has suggested, *A Taste of Blood* is nonetheless considerably more elaborate than most of Lewis' films, with varied and often quite impressive locations and particularly atmospheric photography in some of the night-time exteriors.

d/p Herschell Gordon Lewis *s* Donald Stanford *c* Andy Romanoff *lp* Bill Rogers, Elizabeth Wilkinson, Thomas Wood, Otto Schlesinger, Eleanor Vaill, Lawrence Tobin, Ted Schell, Herschell Gordon Lewis, Dolores Carlos, Sidney Jay

Torture Garden (AMICUS; GB) 93min
Francis's workmanlike professionalism is here enhanced by Bloch's adaptations of his own stories. The result is an omnibus movie far better than Francis's **Dr Terror's House of Horrors** (1964) and an improvement on previous Francis-Bloch collaborations such as **The Skull** and **Psychopath** (both 1965) or the execrable **The Deadly Bees** (1966). Bloch's stories (*Enoch*, *Terror over Hollywood*, *Mr Steinway* and *The Man Who Collected Poe*) are strung together by the device of having five visitors to a fairground enter the sideshow of Dr Diabolo (Meredith) who promises to reveal where their secret desires may lead them. Williams (Bryant) finds himself murdering a rich uncle (Denham) and falling prey to the dead man's cat which eats human heads; as Carla (Adams) tries to sleep her way to Hollywood stardom, she discovers the screen idols are in fact metal automatons animated by their own brains, a fate that befalls her too as she achieves success to the adoring cries of her fans: 'Isn't she a doll ... a living doll?'; and while interviewing a famous pianist (Standing) Dorothy (Ewing) is driven to her death by a grand piano animated by the jealously possessive spirit of the artist's mother, a story that activates the sinister undertones of the Liberace-type persona.

The final – and best – episode has Wyatt (Palance), an obsessive Poe fan kill Canning (Cushing) to acquire his fabulous collection of Poe memorabilia, including an unpublished manuscript. It emerges that Cushing had managed to resurrect Poe and hold the cobwebbed figure (Wallace) prisoner in a macabre basement crypt. Palance frees Poe, setting fire to the place, and gleefully perishes alongside his idol in the flames. The fifth visitor (Ripper) kills Diabolo and everybody flees from the show, but Palance returns, discovering that Diabolo has staged his own murder and is in fact no mere fairground charlatan ...

Jack Palance and Peter Cushing in The Man Who Collected Poe *episode, the best one, from* Torture Garden.

As a gothic exercise with ex-cameraman Francis creating four enjoyable variations in style, from the shocker with the cat to the moody atmospherics of the mother-obsessed pianist with echoes of Bloch's best known family romance, **Psycho** (1960), the film works well. Palance is particularly impressive as the manic collector, excitedly fondling the treasures he cannot buy and chuckling with delight at each new horror as he finds himself becoming part of the Poe legend – even a character in Poe's 'last' story.

d Freddie Francis *p* Max J. Rosenberg, Milton Subotsky *s* Robert Bloch *c* Norman Warwick *lp* Burgess Meredith, Jack Palance, Peter Cushing, Michael Bryant, Maurice Denham, Robert Hutton, Beverly Adams, Barbara Ewing, John Standing, Michael Ripper

The Undertaker and His Pals (EOLA) 60min
Like Herschell Gordon Lewis with humour (of a kind), *The Undertaker and His Pals* is an extremely black comedy which often featured in triple bills with **The Corpse Grinders** (1971) and *The Embalmer* (1965). The film's tone is perhaps best summed up by the original poster which promised 'a macabre story of two motorcycle riding, knife-wielding, shiv-shoving, eye-gouging, arm-twisting, chain-lashing, scalpel-flashing, acid-throwing, gun-shooting, bone-breaking pathological nuts and their pal the undertaker'. In other words, a couple of bikers murder women to provide business for an undertaker who gives trading stamps to his customers. Bits of the victims are then served up in a diner as 'leg of lamb' (by a Miss Lamb).

d/p David C. Graham *s* Tom Swicegood *c* Andrew Janczak *lp* Ray Dennis, Warrene Ott, Rad Fulton, Robert Lowery, Marty Friedman, Sally Frei, Rick Cooper, Charles Fox, Karen Ciral, Ryck Rydon

Le Viol du Vampire *aka* **Les Femmes Vampires** *aka* **La Reine des Vampires** *aka* **Queen of the Vampires** *aka* **Vampire Women** *aka* **The Rape of the Vampire**
(LES FILMS ABC/SAM SELSKY; FR) b/w 100min
The only consistently interesting director of horror films working in France, Rollin imbues his films with a sense of surrealist cinephilia that transforms them into a series of striking, poetic images at the expense of narrative coherence and weaves a highly decorative fetishistic eroticism into the stylized compositions, which are often reminiscent of comic-strip art. He also avoids the adolescent sniggering that tends to spoil Hammer's efforts in this direction (**Lust for a Vampire**, 1970, for example).

Having made a few short films, Rollin was asked to supply a half-hour sexy film to accompany an hour-long American vampire film acquired by a French distributor. He was then asked to add another hour to his short, so that it could be released as a feature. Made on a shoestring with a group of mainly non-professional friends, the film's plot is extremely fragmented and melodramatic, full of quotes, in-jokes and setpieces with over-the-top lines and bizarre imagery such a a naked woman in a convertible, a blind man playing skittles, a wedding in a theatre, nude women with jars of blood, and so on. The ending, which echoes Frank Borzage's *A Farewell to Arms* (1932), has the hero standing in the Place de la Bastille cradling his wife's corpse in his arms while reciting passages from Rollin's favourite author, Gaston Leroux. The acting is purposefully flat, reducing the bodies and voices of the cast to formal elements rather than supports for pseudo-realistic 'characters' – a strategy that would mark all his films and often draw accusations of 'bad direction of actors'. In fact, his films refuse to give characterization any priority over visuals and rhythm.

The famous comic-strip artist Druillet, who also designed Rollin's posters, and the sculptor Deville make brief appearances. While this first effort was still somewhat amateurish, his next movies (**La Vampire Nue**, 1969; **Le Frisson des Vampires**, 1970; **Requiem pour un Vampire**, 1971) quickly established him as an original, obsessively lyrical and typically French director. These films were all made for his own production company, ABC, often with American producer Selsky.

d/co-p/s Jean Rollin *co-p* Sam Selsky *c* Guy Leblond, Antoine Harispé *lp* Bernard Letrou, Solange Pradel, Ursule Pauly, Nicole Romain, Catherine Devil, Jacqueline Sieger, Ariane Sapriel, Marquis Polho, Barbara Girard

1968

Anybody Anyway (SHB) 79(71)min

After their car has run out of petrol two young girls stay the night at the mysterious hilltop mansion of a Mr Bradley and his sister Mina. They soon discover they are prisoners, and are to be used as subjects in Bradley's 'scientific experiments' to find a perfect love mate. A mixture of old-dark-house horrors and sexual goings-on, *Anybody Anyway* is effectively suspenseful and climaxes in a Corman-esque conflagration further enlivened by the appearance of the re-animated corpses of Bradley's previous victims.

d/s Charles Romine *p* Stanley H. Brasloff *c* Victor Petrashevic *lp* Joyce Denner, Eve Reeves, Daniel Garth, Ivan Hagar, Irene Lawrence, Andrea Beatrice, Allan Michaels, Madeline le Roux, Michael Lawrence, Christina Piroska

El Bosque del Lobo *aka* El Bosque de Ancines *aka* The Wolf Forest *aka* The Ancines Woods *aka* The Wolfman of Galicia *aka* The Wolf's Forest

(AMBOTO; SP) 90min

This is an impressively photographed but slow-moving story about an epileptic peddlar (Lopez Velazquez) who lures 11 women into the Ancines woods in Galicia and kills them, with the result that the locals come to regard him as a werewolf. He is eventually caught in a wolf's trap. Based on a novel by Carlos Martinez Barbeto and drawing heavily on Galician folktales, the young Basque director manages to deliver a mood piece notable mainly for the revelation of popular comedian Lopez Velazquez (**Un Vampiro para Dos**, 1965) as an accomplished dramatic actor.

An ex-film critic, Olea had graduated from film school with a fantasy story, *Anabel* (1964), later filmed by Joseph Losey as *Secret Ceremony* (1968). His knack for mixing historical vignettes with a downbeat, social realist approach was also much in evidence in his *La Casa Sin Fronteras* (1972), a mordant allegory about a powerful Catholic institution. His best work, *Tormento* (1974), is unfortunately less well known than *El Bosque*, which received awards at the Chicago and Valladolid festivals.

d Pedro Olea *p* Jesús Sanchez, Imanol Olea *s* Juan Antonio Porto *c* Aurelio G. Larraya *lp* José Lopez Velazquez, Amparo Soler Leal, Antonio Casas, Nuria Torray, Alfredo Mayo, John Steiner

La Camara del Terror *aka* The Fear Chamber

(FILMICA VERGARA; MEX) 91(85)min

This silly story about a primeval, lapidary monster that feeds on a substance which frightened women are supposed to secrete in their bloodstreams was one of the four Mexican features which incorporate footage with Karloff shot in Hollywood shortly before his death. The unhappy production circumstances were the same as those which prevailed for **La Muerte Viviente** (1968) as well as the science fiction *La Invasión Siniestra* and **Serenata Macabra** (both 1968). The title of this movie refers to the room arranged by Dr Mantell (Karloff) to scare female victims before he draws their blood. Much of the film's action is concerned with the greedy doings of secondary characters while Karloff is supposed to be ill. His daughter (Julissa) and her lover (East) go on holiday, leaving Helga (Vega) and her mad hunchback (Beirute) to supervise the project. The living stone extracted from a volcano is their coveted object and they feed it with yet more victims (mostly striptease performers) until the 'stone' becomes a creature with tentacles. The climax has Karloff and his family return to the mansion and reverse the computer programme of the creature's life-support system, thus reducing it back to a stone.

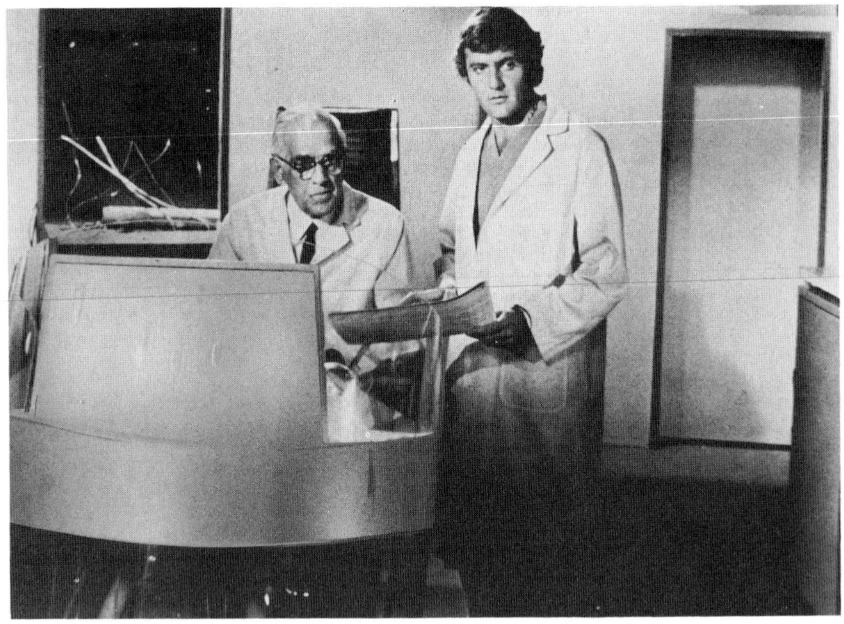

La Camara del Terror, *an unworthy end to Boris Karloff's career.*

The threadbare narrative and virtually non-existent direction emphasize that the film's reason for existence is simply to convert images of frightened women into box-office revenue. Even so, the sadism and eroticism are so ineptly staged that even these scenes fall completely flat. It is worth noting that the evil Vega's three assistants are a hunchback, a dwarf and an Arab, providing a clear example that the equation between physical and mental or moral blemishes so pervasive in films (and literature) is part of a racist way of thinking which here equates being an Arab with being a hunchback or a dwarf.

d Juan Ibañez, Jack Hill *p/co-s* Luis Enrique Vergara *co-s* Jack Hill *c* Raúl Dominguez, Austin McKinney *se* Enrique Gordillo *lp* Boris Karloff, Julissa, Carlos East, Isela Vega, Yerye Beirute, Eva Muller, Sandra Chavez, Rafael Muñoz (Santanon), Pamela Rosas, Fuensanta

El Castillo de Fu Manchu *aka* The Castle of Fu Manchu *aka* Die Folterkammer des Dr Fu Manchu *aka* Il Castello di Fu Manchu *aka* Fu Manchu's Castle *aka* Assignment Istanbul

(TILMA/TERRA FILMKUNST/ITALIAN INTERNATIONAL; SP,IT,WG) scope 92(86)min

Having finished his series for the German Aquila company with the interesting **Necronomicon** (1967), shot largely in Turkey, Franco went on to collaborate with Harry Alan Towers for seven pictures starting with this Fu Manchu title, also shot in Turkey. The previous Fu Manchu outing (*The Vengeance of Fu Manchu*, 1967) had been a straightforward thriller with a little added cruelty and was shot in Hong Kong by Jeremy Summers. With Franco the series degenerated even further.

Here the fiendish oriental is holed up in Istanbul and tries to turn the South Atlantic into an ice flow. This involves a makeshift heart transplant operation on Dr Herakles (Re), performed in insanitary conditions by Curt (Stoll) and his assistant (Perschy). The familiar faces of Greene, Crawford and Tsai Chin appear again as Nayland Smith, Dr Petrie and Lee's slinky sidekick Lin Tang, although Lee himself doesn't have much to do.

Franco and Towers continued their collaboration beyond the two Fu Manchu pictures with *Justine* (1968), **Venus in Furs** and **El Processo de las Brujas** (both 1969), **De Sade 70** and **El Conde Dracula** (both 1970).

d Jess Frank (Jesús Franco) *p* Harry Alan Towers, Jesús Balcazar *s* Manfred Barthel, Peter Welbeck (Harry Alan Towers) *c* Manuel Merino *lp* Christopher Lee, Tsai Chin, Richard Greene, Howard Marion-Crawford, Guenther Stoll, Maria Perschy, Rosalba Neri, José Manuel Martin, Gustavo Re, Werner Aprelat

The Curse of the Crimson Altar *aka* The Crimson Cult *aka* The Crimson Altar *aka* The Reincarnation *aka* Spirit of the Dead

(TIGON BRITISH/AMERICAN INTERNATIONAL; GB) 89(81)min
Shot in the house of W. S. Gilbert (of Gilbert and Sullivan fame), which was reputed to be haunted since the owner's death by drowning in 1911, this is of minor interest as the only time Lee, Karloff and Steele appeared in the same movie, although bizarrely they have no scenes together. It was also the wheelchair-ridden Karloff's last British picture.

Coquillon, the talented cinematographer of Michael Reeves' **The Witchfinder General** (1968), devised all kinds of innovative ways of lighting the house and achieves results superior to many studio-lit productions. Unfortunately the script, in spite of its (uncredited) derivation from August Derleth's *Dreams in the Witch House*, merely offers a catalogue of exploitable scenes, including a threatened multiple rape as youngsters in a car pursue a young woman, the sadistic whipping of a naked woman tied on a sacrificial altar and a drugs-and-sex orgy.

The complicated temporal structure of the story is confused rather than genuinely complex. Robert (Eden), in search of his vanished brother, stumbles upon a coven led by the civilized-looking Morley (Lee) who is enacting the revenge of Lavinia (Steele), his witch ancestor burned in the 17th century. Eden falls prey to vivid dreams of Steele, in which her face is painted green, and she has blood-red lips and sports a golden ram headpiece adorned with peacock feathers. The climax has Lee set fire to his own house, and as he's consumed by the flames, he changes into Steele. Karloff plays a local witchcraft expert who rescues the hero and his love (Wetherell). Image by image, the movie is very watchable, but as a whole it is a testament to Tigon's crudely exploitative approach to horror.

d Vernon Sewell *p* Louis M. Heyward *s* Mervyn Haisman, Henry Lincoln, Gerry Levy *c* Johnny Coquillon *lp* Boris Karloff, Christopher Lee, Barbara Steele, Mark Eden, Virginia Wetherell, Rupert Davies, Michael Gough, Rosemarie Reede, Derek Tansley, Michele Warren

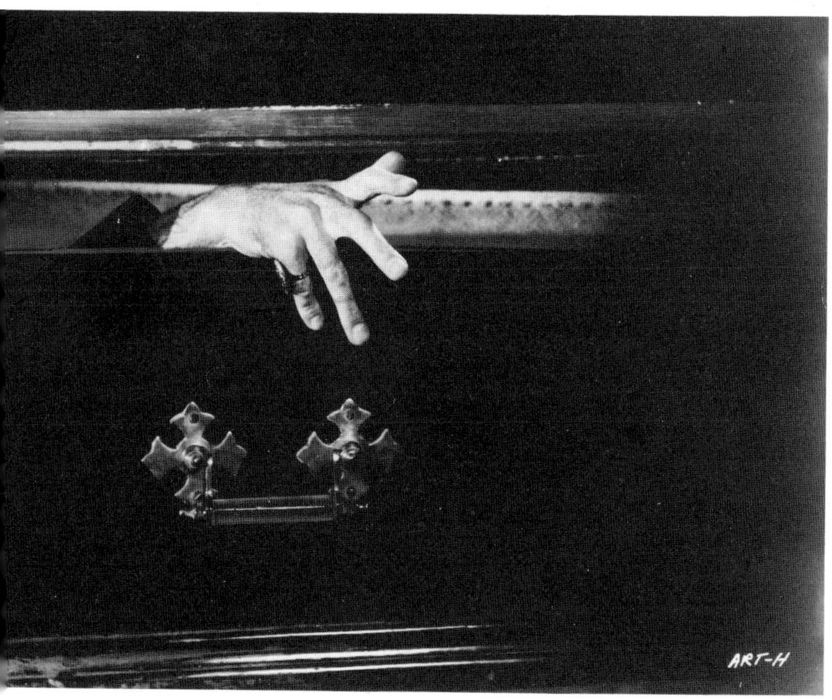

Dracula Has Risen from the Grave, Freddie Francis's workmanlike contribution to Hammer's Dracula series.

Dracula Has Risen from the Grave *aka* Dracula's Revenge

(HAMMER; GB) 92min
Excluding the aberrant **The Brides of Dracula** (1960), this was the third of Hammer's series starring Lee as the Count. Fisher had imposed his own particular dark romanticism on **Dracula** (1958) and **Dracula, Prince of Darkness** (1965) but, sadly, Hammer handed over the third instalment to the workmanlike Francis, who proceeded to string together largely arbitrary – though occasionally well composed and atmospheric – scenes and considerably increased the sex element for its own sake regardless of how such scenes related to the vampire story.

The movie starts out well with two priests fighting their way through a storm up to the looming castle to fix a golden cross to its gate. As one of them falls through the ice that covers the Count's body (he had fallen into the water at the end of his previous outing), the blood of the priest's wounds revives the vampire. The monsignor (Davis) becomes his main antagonist as he enslaves Zena (Ewing) and lusts after Maria (Carlson), scampering over the rooftops like Judex in order to reach her window. He abducts her and forces her to remove the cross barring entry to his castle and to throw it into an abyss. Shortly after, the Count is pushed into the same abyss and impaled on the fateful crucifix. Ewing is excellent as the waitress dying with an expression of satisfied lust, but by the same token, the glow of repressed sensuality appropriate to Dracula's Victorian victims and so expertly conveyed in Fisher's movies, is totally lost by Francis.

Peter Sasdy was the next director to take a hand in the series with **Taste the Blood of Dracula** (1969).

d Freddie Francis *p* Aida Young *s* John Elder (Anthony Hinds) *c* Arthur Grant *se* Frank George *lp* Christopher Lee, Rupert Davies, Veronica Carlson, Barbara Ewing, Barry Andrews, Ewan Hooper, Michael Ripper, Marion Mathie

Enigma de Muerte

(FILMICA VERGARA; MEX) 89min
The second of Carradine's Mexican pictures for Vergara – the prolific producer responsible for Boris Karloff's last movies – has him play the demented boss of a Nazi cell, given to dressing up as a clown and performing in a travelling circus. His opponent is the masked wrestler Mil Mascaras. Carradine eventually perishes in a gas oven of his own design. He encountered Mil Mascaras again in Curiel and Vergara's next picture, *Las Vampiras* (1968), where he played the leader of a pack of vampires. The same producer used the Hollywood veteran at the beginning and end of his **Pacto Diabolico** (1968) in a manner reminiscent of Karloff's brief appearance in **Serenata Macabra** (1968).

Besides the wrestlers del Castillo and Frankenstein, it is worth noting the presence of Vega in the cast: she became the only Latin American woman director of horror films with **Las Amantes del Señor de la Noche** (1983).

d Federico Curiel *p* Luis Enrique Vergara *s* Ramón Obon *c* Alfredo Uribe *lp* John Carradine, Mil Mascaras, Maria Duval, Isela Vega, Victor Junco, David Silva, Erik del Castillo, Altia Michel, Nathaniel Frankenstein

O Estranho Mundo de Zé do Caixao *aka* The Strange World of Zé do Caixao

(IBERIA FILMS; BRAZIL) b/w 80min
After the disturbing **Esta Noite Encarnarei no Teu Cadaver** (1966) and his contribution to the omnibus movie **Trilogia de**

Terror (1968), Marins here again features his megalomaniac *alter ego*, Zé de Caixao. This time, the brutally sadistic Zé merges with the image of the director as he presides over the framing of three different stories. One tells of a doll-maker (Cacador) who uses real human eyes. The second episode features a hunchbacked sex maniac (Michel) obsessed by a girl (Bruzzi) who ignores him but dies on her wedding day, giving the monstrous creature the opportunity to dig up her body and consummate his passion. The last story reverts to Marins' usual terrain as he hideously tortures a couple (de Souza and Reis) to prove the triumph of instinct over reason. The production is amateurish, the narrative sloppy and disjointed and the acting unmentionable as the film wallows in rape, necrophilia and visceral savagery, predictably accompanied by the 'hero' (Marins) indulging in infantile posturing and routine blasphemy.

Marins also published a comic strip and his films have often been compared to horror comics, but such a reference overlooks the fact that comic-strip imagery requires a degree of stylization and attention to design. His films rarely betray any such concerns as cheapness and speed appear to win out over aesthetics and professionalism every time. Watching his work is distinctly disturbing, not simply because of the activities depicted, but because his films convey an overwhelming sense of looking at a genuine psychopath's private fantasies, pathetically proffered as a plea for help to which viewers are unable to respond. His next offering, the unreleased *O Ritual dos Sadicos* (1970), extended the quasi-documentary chronicling of mental illness and he regressed even further to a regime of infantile megalomania with *Finis Hominis* (1970) in which the director plays a mad but 'inspired' saviour of the world performing miracles, and its sequel with the same character, **Quando os Deuses Adormecem** (1971).

d/co-p/s José Mojica Marins *co-p* Jorge Michel Sakeis *c* Giorgio Attili *lp* José Mojica Marins, Luiz Sergio Person, Rosalvo Cacador, Jorge Michel, Iris Bruzzi, Osvaldo de Souza, Nidi Reis

Fu Manchu y el Beso de la Muerte *aka* **The Blood of Fu Manchu** *aka* **Kiss and Kill** *aka* **Der Todeskuss des Dr Fu Manchu** *aka* **Fu Manchu and the Kiss of Death** *aka* **Fu Manchu and the Keys of Death**
(TERRA FILMKUNST/ADA FILMS/UDASTEX FILMS/ TOWERS OF LONDON; SP,WG,US,GB) scope 92(61)min

This is the fifth and final title of Lee's Fu Manchu series initiated by Don Sharp's **The Face of Fu Manchu** (1965). It was shot in Madrid and Brazil, and has as its gimmick ten young women who have been injected with a poison which causes anyone who kisses them to go blind and slowly die. Nayland Smith (Greene) becomes the victim of the Black Widow (Eaton) but he is saved with a blood transfusion from Carmen (Kahn). The main plot, involving some sadistic tortures, features a Brazilian bandit (Palacios), Dr Petrie (Crawford) and Smith's agent in South America (George) as well as an amorous nurse, played by Rohm, one of Franco's favourite sadean actresses (**Venus in Furs**, 1969; **De Sade 70**, 1970). Eventually, Fu's Amazonian lair is blown up to the accompaniment of the familiar voice-over promise: 'The world shall hear from me again', although this wasn't until *The Fiendish Plot of Dr Fu Manchu* (1980) with Peter Sellers in the starring role.

Franco's direction fails to achieve any sense of menace, even from the Amazonian jungle which looks like a local park shot in ugly green and brown colours. His tiresome reliance on the zoom lens is much in evidence, but it is difficult to assess a film of which one third has been removed, making it totally incomprehensible: characters inexplicably vanish, casually turning up again midway through a later scene. The script is the work of Franco and Towers, the latter using his customary Welbeck pseudonym. The German version was prepared by Manfred Koehler.

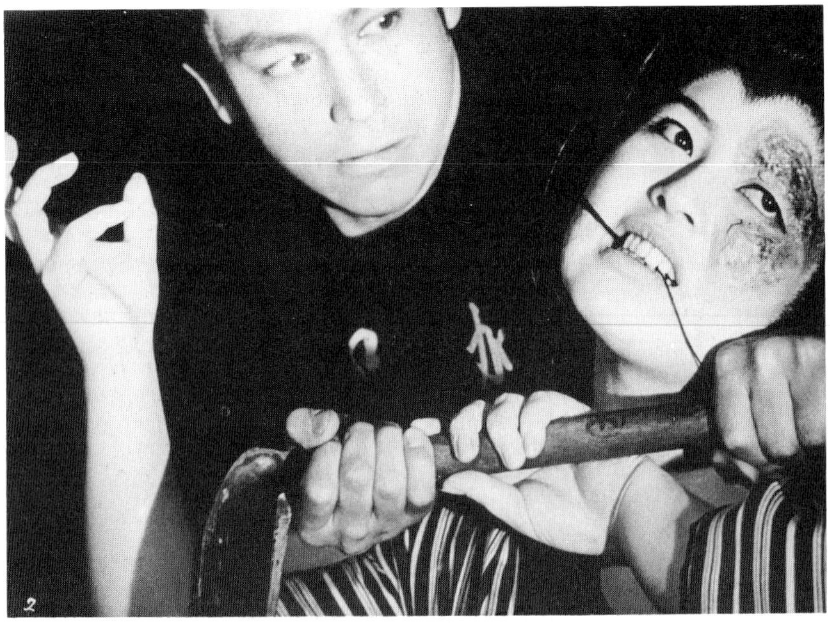

Kaidan Zankoku Monogatari: *a Japanese family romance of murder, mutilation, passion and incest.*

d/co-s Jess Frank (Jesús Franco) *p* Harry Alan Towers *co- s* Peter Welbeck (Harry Alan Towers) *c* Manuel Merino *lp* Christopher Lee, Richard Greene, Howard Marion-Crawford, Goetz George, Maria Rohm, Shirley Eaton, Riccardo Palacios, Tsai Chin, Loni von Friedl, Frances Kahn

Kaidan Botandoro *aka* **A Tale of Peonies and Lanterns** *aka* **A Ghost Story of Peonies and Stone Lanterns** *aka* **The Bride from Hades** *aka* **Botandoro** *aka* **The Bride from Hell** *aka* **Ghost Beauty** *aka* **My Bride Is a Ghost** (DAIEI; JAP) scope 89min

This is one of the enchantingly funereal love poems which were the speciality of Yoda, Mizoguchi's favourite scenarist. Adapting a popular legend, previously filmed by Akira Nobuchi (*Botandoro*, 1955), Yoda recounts the familiar Kaidan of a man (Hongo) who falls in love with a beautiful young woman (Akaza) during the O-Bon festival (the festival of the dead, which was also the time when most horror films were released in Japan). His servant (Nishimura) and a local priest (Shimura) both warn the hero that the woman is a ghost, and even she admits to being one, but she pleads to be allowed to stay with him one more night. Since he genuinely loves her, he agrees. After a long night, while the villagers bang their drums and float a myriad of candles – symbolizing dead souls – down the river, he is found dead with a female skeleton in his arms.

Shimura, best known for his masterful performances in Kurosawa's pictures (*Ikiru*, 1952, for example) strikes exactly the right note as the worried, slightly awestruck priest and Yamamoto, better known for such anti-militarist movies as *Shinku Chitai* (1952), directs this stylish poem with a delicate lyricism not usually associated with his work. A few years later, the story was also used as the basis for a soft-core sex film by Chusei Sone, *Seidan Botandoro* (1972).

d Satsuo Yamamoto *p* Masaichi Nagata *s* Yoshitaka Yoda *c* Chishi Makiura *lp* Kojiro Hongo, Miyoko Akaza, Michiko Otsuka, Mayuni Ogawa, Ko Nishimura, Takashi Shimura

Kaidan Yukigoro *aka* **Yukionna** *aka* **Snow Ghost** *aka* **Woman of the Snow** *aka* **Ghost of the Snow Girl Prostitute** (DAIEI; JAP) scope 80min

Previously filmed as one of the stories in Kobayashi's **Kwaidan** (1964), but cut from Western release prints of that film, this popular legend tells of a snow spirit, Yukionna (Fujimura), who falls in love with a young man (Ishihama). Cursed to lure men to their deaths with her unearthly beauty, she nevertheless spares a young sculptor on condition that he never mentions their encounter. Later he marries and has a child with a woman called Yuki. When he breaks his vow, it is revealed that Yuki is the snow woman and must now kill him after all. Love for her baby prevents her from doing so and she vanishes.

The thinly veiled incest story is an interesting variation of the legend of Oedipus' marriage: the happiness of the union depends not just on the man's ignorance but on his silence – his agreement to repress the fact that he married a stand-in for the remote and forbidden object of his desire – whereas the woman knows that what is at stake in this repression is her very existence as an autonomous person. When the ghostly game of substitution is revealed, the hero should go away and tear out his eyes. However, in this Japanese version, the maternal love proves to be the undoing of the mother as she sacrifices herself for the happiness of her boy child, in line with the pattern of relations so vividly depicted in a great many of Mizoguchi's films. An updated version of the tale was filmed by Susume Hani, *Aido* (1969) and, arguably, in Hollywood as *Carnal Knowledge* (1971), where a woman of ice is reduced to a masturbation fantasy.

Tanaka went on to make the more horrific **Hiroku Kaibyoden** (1969).

d Tokuzo Tanaka *p* Masaichi Nagate *s* Fuji Yakiro *c* Chishi Makiura *lp* Shino Fujimura, Akira Ishihama, Machiko Hasegawa, Taketoshi Naito, Mizuho Suzuki, Fujio Suga, Sachiko Murase

Kaidan Zankoku Monogatari *aka* Curse of the Blood *aka* Cruel Ghost Legend

(SHOCHIKU; JAP) b/w scope 126(88)min

This harrowingly gruesome and macabre story derived from Rensaburo Shibata's tale, recounts a family curse in all senses of the term. The plot proceeds in three phases: a poor samurai (Tomura) kills a blind moneylender (Kaneko) and sets the curse in motion as the victim's ghost drives the killer insane, causing him to murder his wife and then commit suicide. The blind man's daughter, also the lover of one of Tomura's sons (Tamura) is accidentally killed and, crazed with grief, the boy takes to a life of crime. The third movement is inaugurated by the samurai's second son (Kawazu). While courting a music teacher, played by Kawaguchi, he is seduced by the evil Sakurai, who poisons her rival. As always in the Kaidan genre, this disfigures the victim who is subsequently killed by her suitor before he flees with his *femme fatale*.

At this point, the story starts working up to its climax: the fleeing brother finds the severed head of his criminal sibling and is haunted by the ghost of the woman he killed, which drives him to murder his lover. In addition, his mother reveals that his dead lover was also his half-sister. The family curse ends when he murders the old woman (his father's lover) before committing suicide. Shibata's original story combined motifs from various well-known ghost stories (including **Kyoren no Onna Shisho**, 1926), but Hase's frenetic direction gives this family romance of murder, mutilation, passion and incest a power all its own.

d Kazuo Hase *p* Tsuneo Kosumi *s* Masahige Narusawa *c* Kenji Maruyama *lp* Matsuhiro Tomura, Nobuo Kaneko, Masakazu Tamura, Yunusuke Kawazu, Hiroko Sakurai, Saeda Kazaguchi, Masumi Harukawa, Yukie Kagawa, Eizo Kitamura

Kyuketsu Dokurosen *aka* Living Skeleton

(SHOCHIKU; JAP) b/w scope 81min

A ghost-ship story without ghosts, this picture centres on the ship's necrophiliac doctor. Two men (Okada and Kaneko) murder the crew of a ship and steal its gold cargo. Later, the sister of one of the victims (Matsuoka in a double role) discovers the corpse-ridden ship and takes revenge by luring the two killers back on board. There they find the ship's doctor who survived by feeding off the cadavers, which turned him into a hideously vampiric creature. While he attaches himself to one of the villains, the young woman assumes the appearance of her sister's ghost and scares the other villain to death, after which the horrid denizens of the ship disappear. A rather unsuccessful attempt to merge the Western legend of the Flying Dutchman with the motifs of the Kaidan genre, the film achieves some watchable sequences largely because of the picture's format: even a routine and average film can look good in black and white scope.

d Hiroshi Matsuno *p* Shiro Kido *s* Kikuma Shimoizaka, Kyuzo Kobayashi *c* Masayuki Kato *lp* Kikko Matsuoka, Akira Nishimura, Masumi Okada, Nobuo Kaneko, Yasunori Irikawa

The Mad Doctor of Blood Island

(HEMISPHERE PRODUCTIONS; US,PHIL) 86(83)min

Having barely recovered from the ravages caused by radio-active fallout, mutants and a limb-tearing monster (detailed in the science fiction film, *Brides of Blood*, 1968), the inhabitants of Blood Island now discover in their midst a mad scientist experimenting with a chlorophyll drug in order to achieve eternal youth. However, his guinea pig – his lover's husband – turns into a green monster who eventually causes the laboratory to go up in flames. The film offers an enthusiastic mixture of the Frankenstein, zombie and Dr Moreau motifs but tends to slip up into an over-indulgent use of the zoom lens. Since Beverly Hill's demise in the arms of the previous movie's creature, the sexual activity on the island seems to be limited to ogling bathing beauties. The ugly greenish tint that pervades the imagery may be appropriate in this context, but the slapdash approach to acting, narration and camera are beyond redemption.

For their next ventures, the two directors parted company, Romero delivering *Beast of Blood* (1969) and **The Beast of the Yellow Night** (1970), de Leon returning to the vampire motif he had used in **The Blood Drinkers** (1966) for his **Curse of the Vampires** (1970).

co-d/p Eddie Romero *co-d* Gerardo de Leon *s* Reuben Candy *c* Justo Paulino *lp* John Ashley, Angelique Pettyjohn, Ronald Remy, Alicia Alonso, Bruno Punzalan, Quiel Mendoza, Alfonso Carvajel, Tita Muñoz

Malenka – La Nipote del Vampiro *aka* Malenka – La Sobrina del Vampiro *aka* La Nipote del Vampiro *aka* Malenka *aka* The Niece of the Vampire *aka* The Vampire's Niece *aka* Fangs of the Living Dead

(TRITON FILMINDUSTRIA/VICTORY FILMS/COBRA FILMS/FELIX; SP,IT) scope 94min

In this routine low-budget effort Ugarte, fresh from his role as a vampire in **La Marca del Hombre Lobo** (1967), again plays a bloodsucker, this time as lord of a castle inherited by his niece Silvia (Ekberg). He explains to her that she is the reincarnation of Malenka, a nun accused of witchcraft years earlier and burnt by the villagers. Upset by these revelations, Ekberg breaks with her fiancé (Medici), but when he turns up anyway, she cannot bring herself to kill him. Ugarte is then revealed to be the villain of the piece: he staged elaborate vampirizations in the region and tried to convince Ekberg that she was a witch in order to make her renounce her inheritance.

This is the first contribution to the genre of de Ossorio – best known for his effective blind-dead series which started with **La Noche del Terror Ciego** (1971) – and some of his sequences come perilously close to parody. Ekberg's career in fantasy pictures started with *Abbott and Costello Go to Mars* (1953) where she played a Venusian guard. Since then, her career stagnated as director after director used her opulent figure as the stereotype of the European dumb blonde.

d/s Amando de Ossorio *c* Fulvio Testi *lp* Anita Ekberg, Julian Ugarte, John Hamilton (Gianni Medici), Diana Lorys, Audrey Ambert (Adriana Ambesi), Maria Luisa de Benedictus, Rosanna Yanni, Carlos Casarvilla, Paul Muller

Mantis in Lace *aka* Lila

(BOX OFFICE INTERNATIONAL) 73min

Managing to cram a psycho-killer, drugs and nudity all into one movie, *Mantis in Lace* is the cautionary tale of a topless go-go dancer who drops too much acid, lures men to a candlelit warehouse with promises of sex and then kills them with various garden implements whilst hallucinating that they are giant insects, bunches of bananas (!) and so on. Like a number of low-budget movies made around this time, the film is distinguished mainly by Kovacs' photography. Director Rotsler was, with the likes of Barry Mahon, one of the first sex movie tycoons.

d William Rotsler *p/s* Sanford White *c* Leslie (Laszlo) Kovacs *lp* Susan Stewart, Steve Vincent, M. K. Evans, Pat Barrington, Vic Lance

La Muerte Viviente *aka* La Isla de los Muertos *aka* Isle of the Snake People *aka* Island of the Snake People *aka* Snake People

(FILMICA VERGARA; MEX) 89min

Towards the end of his life, Karloff, hardly able to move because of his painful illness, agreed to appear in four films to be produced by the prolific Vergara who had done a similar deal with John Carradine (**Pacto Diabolico**, *La Señora de la Muerte*, both 1968). The deal required all scenes involving Karloff to be shot in Hollywood. Having rejected the scripts sent by Vergara, Karloff accepted the rewrites by Hill, a fellow client of Karloff's lawyer. Hill proceeded to try and shoot the material but disagreements about casting, logistical and contractual difficulties extended the planned three-weeks shooting into four weeks and a lot of extra costs which caused the productions to be halted in 1968. The footage appears to have been returned to Mexico where more problems arose following Vergara's death. However, in 1971, the films appeared in Mexico in versions which, according to Hill, bore little resemblance to the original scripts. Extra shots requiring Karloff, who died in 1969, were made with a stand-in, Jerry Petty. The other three pictures involved were **La Camara del Terror**, the science fiction *La Invasión Siniestra* and **Serenata Macabra** (all 1968). All were credited to Ibañez and the US release prints give co-direction and script credits to Hill.

La Muerte Viviente recounts the adventures of Captain LaBiche (Bertrand) on the island of Kulabai where he tries to put a stop to the activities of the mad scientist Count Karl von Molder (Karloff), the man who also presides over cannibalistic voodoo rites in a cave, disguised as the satanic priest Damballah. Bertrand gets bitten by a cobra and the heroes (Julissa and East) escape when the island's volcano explodes. Mexican prints also omit the name of McKinney who shot the footage with Karloff. His scenes are routinely handled but the additional Mexican scenes dwell lovingly on the extravagantly exotic satanic revelries. Ibañez, who had just scored a box-office hit with his first feature, a sensationalist social drama about teenage hoodlums, is best remembered for his respected experimental theatre productions.

co-d John (Juan) Ibañez *co-d/co-s* Jack Hill *p/co-s* Henry Verg (Enrique Vergara) *c* Raúl Dominguez, Austin McKinney *se* Ross Hahn *lp* Boris Karloff, Julissa, Charles (Carlos) East, Ralph Bertan (Raphael Bertrand), Tongolele (Yolanda Montes), Rafael Muñoz (Santanon), Quintin Bulnes, July Marichael, Yolanda Duhalt

Night of the Living Dead (IMAGE TEN) b/w 96min

An assured début, *Night of the Living Dead* was made on a minuscule budget over several weekends by Romero and a group of film-makers in Pittsburg. The film's power lies in the way the basic plot – radiation fallout from an abortive rocket launch revives and zombieizes corpses, turning them into mindless killers – is carried through to its conclusion with ruthless logic and subtle irony, on the way deflating every cliché it throws up. Thus, to take just two examples, the hero (Jones) does everything right but to no avail, while the heroine (O'Dea), once immobilized by shock, remains so throughout the rest of the film.

Romero's genius lies in the way he builds up tension throughout the film – as the zombies grow in number, seemingly unstoppable – until the sense of terror becomes all-consuming, intensified by the speed with which his characters collapse under the stress of their new-found situation. The film's final irony, the shooting of Jones in mistake for a gun-crazy member of the public, is similar in tone to that of *Easy Rider* (1969).

The film's success (almost singlehandedly) spawned vast numbers of mutations as, in the seventies, zombies of all nations stalked the screens.

d/c George A. Romero *p* Russell Steiner, Karl Hardman *s* John A. Russo *lp* Judith O'Dea, Duane Jones, Karl Hardman, Keith Wayne, Judith Ridley, Marilyn Eastman

Las Noches del Hombre Lobo *aka* Nights of the Werewolf (KIN FILMS; SP,FR) scope 82min

This rarely seen combination of Jesús Franco-type surgical and werewolf motifs – a sequel to the equally unhappy attempt to combine vampires and werewolves, **La Marca del Hombre Lobo** (1967) – again features Molina as Daninsky. This time out, he seeks help from a mad scientist who uses the unhappy lycanthrope to get rid of hostile colleagues. Molina eventually, however, goes berserk and kills the scientist before meeting his own end.

Sources give conflicting information about the film. Although shot in Paris, there is no record of its release in France and director Govar is not listed in any of the production catalogues as ever having made another picture, which suggests he may have used a pseudonym. For his next appearance as Count Waldemar Daninsky (*Los Monstrous del Terror*, 1969), Molina figured merely as one item in a catalogue of familiar horror creatures, but he returned to more conventional story material with **La Noche de Walpurgis** (1970) and with the subsequent titles of the series from **La Furia del Hombre Lobo** and **Dr Jeckill y el Hombre Lobo** (both 1971) to **El Retorno del Hombre Lobo** (1980) and **La Bestia y la Espada Magica** (1983).

d/co-s René Govar *co-s* Jacinto Molina, Carlos Belario *lp* Paul Naschy (Jacinto Molina), Monique Brainvillé, Hélène Vatelle, Peter Beaumont

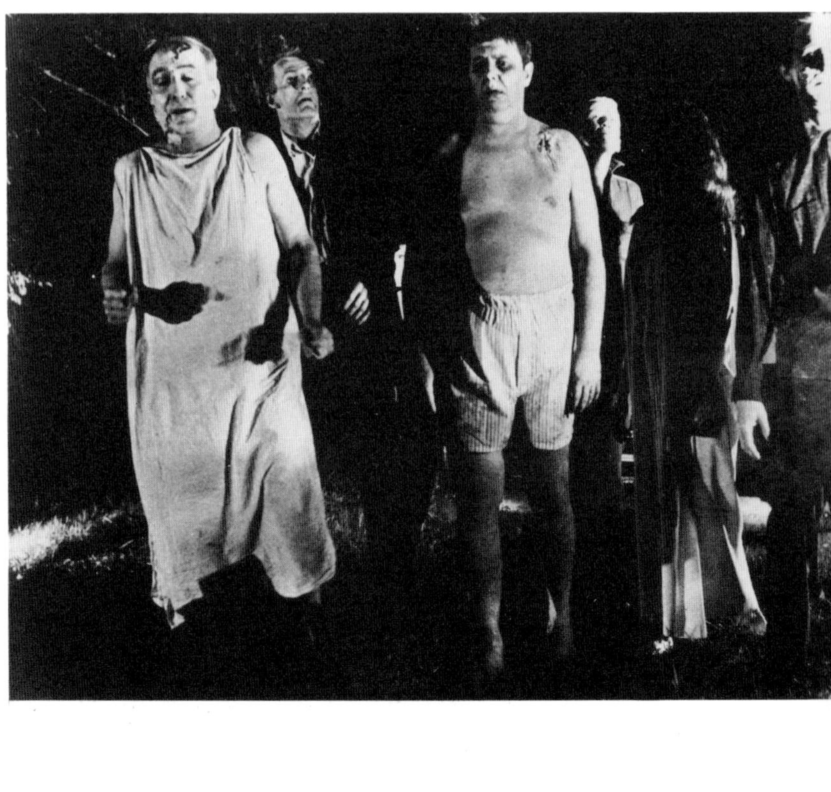

Night of the Living Dead, *the film that brought new life to the zombie subgenre.*

The expectant satanists awaiting Rosemary's Baby.

result that Farrow's journey of discovery is a shared experience between victim and viewer. Polanski's grip on his audience's involvement is perfectly illustrated by the scene where Farrow, firmly convinced by now in the existence of witchcraft, visits a psychiatrist who not only doesn't believe her but also questions her sanity. The audience, having been as certain as she was, is suddenly riddled with doubt because of her half-hysterical description of events and the psychiatrist's persuasive rationale, but instead of abandoning belief in her find themselves *willing* her explanation to be the correct one, because if Farrow's perceptions are tinged with madness, then they have similarly misjudged her experiences.

Many subtle devices are employed to involve the viewer. In the scene in which Rosemary is overcome by the pain she has described as burning like wire, for example, Polanski cuts to a shot of raindrops streaming down the windowpanes: the effect is like a physical jolt as one feels the wires of pain torturing her. The film's style is deliberately naturalistic, using familiar, everyday locations (telephone boxes, kitchens) as its tools of terror. Less importantly, but nevertheless essential to ensure implicit suspension of disbelief in an otherwise ludicrous set of circumstances, *Rosemary's Baby* is one of the few films (**Night of the Demon**, 1957, is another) where the artefacts and rituals of witchcraft are given credibility and where its practitioners are virtually free of caricature: the unreal, for a short while, becomes reality.

d/s Roman Polanski *p* William Castle *c* William Fraker *lp* Mia Farrow, John Cassavetes, Ruth Gordon, Sidney Blackmer, Maurice Evans, Ralph Bellamy

Pacto Diabolico *aka* Diabolical Pact *aka* The Pact with the Devil

(FILMICA VERGARA; MEX) 85min

The last of Carradine's quartet of Vergara-produced Mexican movies (the others are *La Señora Muerte*, **Enigma de Muerte** and *Las Vampiras*, all 1968) is a variant on the Jekyll and Hyde motif. As a mad scientist obsessed with rejuvenation, he extracts a special substance from the retina of a man condemned to death to use on himself. Although the logic of such an operation is a little baffling, it does allow the producer to replace the American star with a cheaper, unknown Mexican actor (Alvarez) for most of the movie, as the 'rejuvenated' Carradine. The emaciated figure of the star re-materializes at the end when it emerges that the medical benefits of the operation are not long lasting and, in despair, the scientist hurls himself into a furnace. Carradine's next Latin American adventure was Moctezuma's **Mary, Mary, Bloody Mary** (1975).

d Jaime Salvador *p* Luis Enrique Vergara *s* Ramón Obon Jnr, Adolfo Torres Portillo *c* Alfredo Uribe *lp* John Carradine, Regina Torné, Miguel Angel Alvarez, Isela Vega, Guillermo Zetima, Andres Garcia, Laura Ferlo, Gloria Munguia, Silvia Villalobos

Rosemary's Baby

(PAR/WILLIAM CASTLE PRODUCTIONS) 136min

When they move into a new apartment block, Rosemary and Guy Woodhouse (Farrow and Cassavetes) are adopted by their neighbours the Castavets (Gordon and Blackmer), whose kindly attentions border on the intrusive. Conceiving after a vivid dream of being raped by a horned beast, Farrow experiences constant violent pain during her pregnancy, and concurrent events – combined with the weird circle of visitors at the neighbours' – convince her that she is the victim of a satanists' plot. When she wakes after a drugged birth, she is told that her child was born dead. Still drugged, she enters the Castavet apartment to find the entire coven taking part in a satanic rite and is both fascinated and repelled by the strange eyes of the baby she finds there.

Polanski's achievement in *Rosemary's Baby* is to have taken Ira Levin's fairly ingenious, somewhat oldfashioned horror-chiller and, while remaining faithful to the source material, to have transformed it into an absorbingly tense study of an isolated, frightened woman struggling to retain her sanity as the terrifying nature of her situation is revealed. The novel's interior monologue structure has been jettisoned, with the

Santo y el Tesoro de Dracula *aka* El Tesoro de Dracula *aka* Santo en el Tesoro de Dracula *aka* Santo contra Dracula *aka* El Vampiro y el Sexo *aka* Santo and Dracula's Treasure

(CINEMATOGRAFICA CALDERON; MEX) 81min

Cardona made two Santo pictures in quick succession, *El Tesoro de Montezuma* (1968) and this Dracula movie featuring Agosti in a role familiar from **La Invasión de los Vampiros** (1961) and *El Conde Frankenhausen* (1962). The story proceeds in two movements: first a scientist's daughter, Luisa (Noel) uses a time machine and ends up being vampirized by the Count. Santo, who witnessed the events on a TV monitor in his Batman-style secret laboratory, follows her, locates the Count's treasure and, in spite of a masked villain's opposition, destroys both the vampire and his treasure, but is unable to save the unfortunate Noel. As usual for the period, the movie is flavoured with plenty of comic-strip violence, bare-breasted women and repeated freestyle wrestling bouts and, as with **Las Luchadoras contra el Robot Asesino** (1969), a sexier version was prepared for the export market under the title *El Vampiro y el Sexo*.

Santo's next outing had him confront the opponents from his most insanely entertaining adventure in **La Vengenza de las Mujeres Vampiro** (1969) before he teamed up again with Blue Demon for an epic encounter in *Santo y Blue Demon contra Dracula y el Hombre Lobo* (1970).

d René Cardona *p* Guillermo Calderon *s* Alfredo Salazar *c* Raúl Martinez Solares *lp* Santo (Rodolfo Guzman Huerta), Noelia Noel, Aldo Monti, Carlos Agosti, Alberto Rojas, Roberto Rivera, Jorge Mondragon, Pili Gonzalez, Fernando Mendoza, Gina Moret

Satanik

(RODIACINES/COPERNICES; IT, SP) scope 80min

Like Mario Bava's *Diabolik* (1967), Vivarelli – better known for his soft-core sex pictures and the fantasy **Il Dio Serpente** (1970) – here makes use of the title of a popular Italian comic strip, this time featuring an evil heroine. Marnie (Konopka) is an 'ugly' female who kills her scientist employer, drinks his youth and beauty potion and embarks on a career of seduction and murder, although she needs regular of the magic potion, as in *La Cara del Terror* (1963). She also becomes a notorious cabaret performer, but when the police finally track her down she has reverted back to her monstrous appearance. That said, the film is a routine potboiler derived from gangster clichés, science fiction and horror movies with the odd musical number thrown and totally lacking in style.

d Piero Vivarelli *p* Romano Mussolini *s* Eduardo M. Brochero *c* Silvano Ippoliti *lp* Magda Konopka, Julio Pena, Armando Calvo, Umberto Raho, Luigi Montini, Mimma Ippoliti, Antonio Pica, Isarco Ravioli, Luis de Tejada

Serenata Macabra *aka* **House of Evil**
(FILMICA VERGARA; MEX) 90min
As in **La Camara del Terror**, *La Invasión Siniestra* and **La Muerte Viviente** (all 1968), Karloff only appears briefly to set up the story and at the end of the picture to provide the climax, while the rest of the movie meanders along with the Mexican cast residing in an old castle awaiting their inheritance, being eliminated by toy automatons. The excessively wordy movie strings together a number of clichés, from the mysterious organ playing which precedes the murders to the patriarch who didn't really die in the final conflagration. The effects are crude and limited to a few eyeless corpses and actors pretending to be animated toy statues.

co-d Juan Ibañez *co-d/co-s* Jack Hill *p/co-s* Luis Enrique Vergara *c* Raúl Dominguez, Austin McKinney *se* Enrique Gordillo *lp* Boris Karloff, Julissa, Andres Garcia, Angel Espinosa (Ferrusquilla), Beatriz Baz, Quintin Bulnes, Manuel Alvarado, Carmen Vega, Felipe Flores, Fernando Saucedo

Targets (SATICOY) 90(80)min
Bogdanovich's first official film – he'd earlier pseudonymously directed the additional sequences which, together with the special effects' footage Roger Corman cannibalized from *Planeta Burg* (1962), comprised *Voyage to the Planet of Prehistoric Women* (1962) – this is less a horror movie than a reflection on the nature of horror. Bogdanovich's script interweaves two parallel stories. In one, Byron Orlok (Karloff), a veteran horror star, tells his director (Bogdanovich) he intends to retire, insisting that he is growing old and out of date, more of a joke than a menace to audiences in his traditional role as monster or mad magician. (As he talks, he is watching a TV re-run of Howard Hawks' *The Criminal Code*, 1931, in which Karloff plays a prison trusty who kills an informer.) In the other, Bobby Thompson (O'Kelly), an apparently normal and unassuming young man, happily married and with sensible, prosperous parents, suddenly gives way to his obsession with guns. He shoots his wife and mother and a delivery boy, fills a kitbag with guns and ammunition, climbs to the top of a gas-tower overlooking the freeway, and begins to snipe at passing cars.

Bogdanovich illustrates the disparity between the two kinds of terror, with the modern horror shown not as stalking dark nights and cobwebby castles, but as dispassionately invading crowded streets, neat suburban homes and public places. Perhaps the most horrifying thing about O'Kelly's story is its sense of hygiene: the prim way he tidies up the family living-room after his killings; the dazzlingly fresh white paint on the gas-tower where he lays out his armoury in obsessively neat rows; the indifference on the highway until it finally dawns that what is happening is more than merely a normal accident rate. But at the end old and new are fused in a magnificent *coup de théâtre* to touch a genuinely raw, modern nerve. Taking refuge in a drive-in movie theatre, the psychopath begins to snipe at the audience from behind the huge screen where, as the panic-stricken audience becomes trapped in a hopeless traffic jam, Byron Orlok towers gloatingly in his latest role as a mad magician (actually Karloff in Roger Corman's **The Terror**, 1963).

d/p/s Peter Bogdanovich *c* Laszlo Kovacs *lp* Boris Karloff, Tim O'Kelly, Nancy Hsueh, James Brown, Peter Bogdanovich

Left: *Tim O'Kelly as the all-American killer in* Targets, *Peter Bogdanovich's assured (official) directorial debut.*

Tokugawa Onna Keibatsushi *aka* **The Joys of Torture** *aka* **Criminal Women**
(TOEI; JAP) scope 96min
This, Toei's most notable contribution to the sex and torture movies popular in the Japanese film industry – although the censors vigorously removed all explicit depictions of sex – is very much in the mould of Daiei's successful **Hiroku Onna-ro** (1967) and Wakamatsu's films. The movie consists of three different stories, starting with a 17th-century tale of a woman (Tachibana) arrested on suspicion of murder and incest with her mentally retarded brother (Yoshida). The second story is set in a temple with bald-headed nuns. Reiho (Kagawa), the abbess, forces a monk (Hayachi) to watch the young nun he loves being tortured. The lovers later commit suicide together and the jealous abbess, who had her own designs on the monk, is crucified. The last story concerns a sadist (Watanabe) who criticizes the work of a famous tattoo artist (Koike) and offers to demonstrate what a woman's face really looks like under extreme agony. In the end, it is the face of the sadist in his death-throes which the artist sketches, a narrative motif recalling not just **Peeping Tom** (1960) but also **Jigokuhen** (1969), Tanaka's *Joro Semejigoku* (1975), Oshima's *Amakusa Shiro Tokisada* (1962), and many others.

This motif is part of a wider aesthetic preoccupation with the link between violence, pleasure and intensity of emotion, which is one of the acknowledged aims of art itself and leads to the fantasy of the best work of art being the work that condenses the most intense physical and emotional experiences in the one image, whether these be orgasm and death or the fantasy union of both, as in Wakamatsu's **Okasaretu Byuakui** (1967). Ishii, who had learned his craft as an assistant of Mikio Naruse, made a number of action and cruelty pictures for Toei, but his most notable horror movie is **Kyofu Kikei Ningen** (1969).

d/co-s Teruo Ishii *p* Hiroshi Okawa *co-s* Misao Arai *c* Motonari Washio *lp* Masumi Tachibana, Teruo Yoshida, Fumio Watanabe, Asao Koike, Yukie Kagawa

Trilogia de Terror *aka* **Trilogy of Terror**
(PRODUCTORA NACIONAL DE FILMES/PRODUÇOES CINEMATOGRAFICAS GALASY/FRANCO BRASILEIRA; BRAZIL) scope 99min
Based, like the Brazilian **Incrivel, Fantastico, Extraordinario** (1969), on a radio series, this is an omnibus movie with three directors fashioning their own screenplays from stories supplied by Marins. The first, *Pesadelo Macabro*, tells of a man who fears being buried alive and resorts to macumba to cure himself. When one night he sees his girlfriend being raped, he suffers a cataleptic fit and is promptly buried alive. In *O Acordo*, a prostitute-mother makes a deal with the devil to force a marriage between her daughter and the village boss. In the

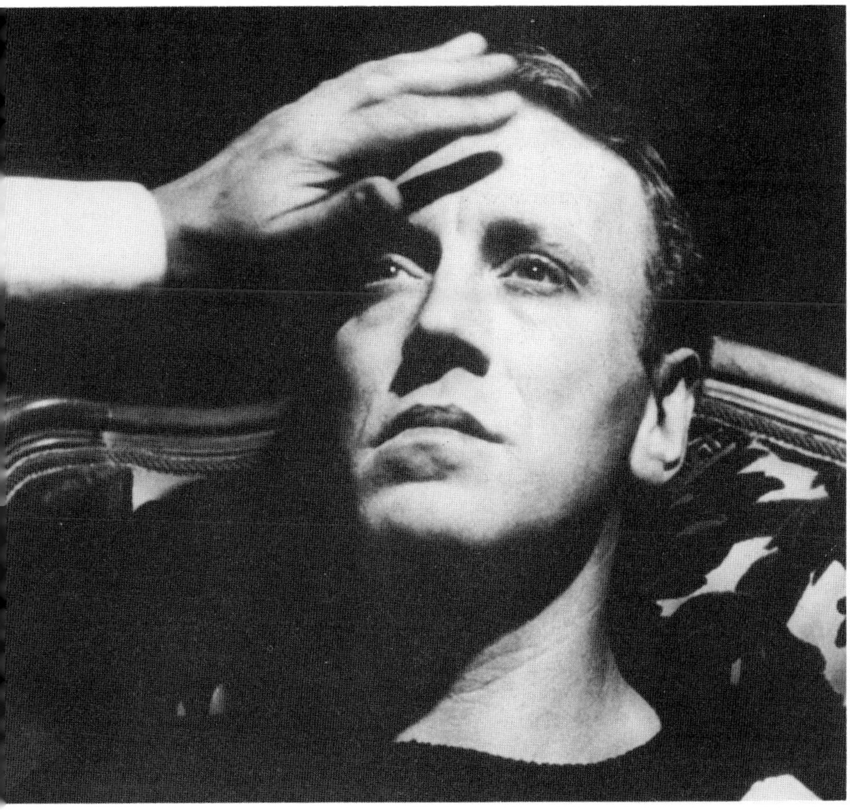

Max von Sydow under pressure in Vargtimmen.

last story, a boy finds a dead soldier in the bushes and eventually his father decides to confront those responsible for the killing: phantom guerrillas. The picture ends with an ambiguous call to arms, implicitly acknowledging that the military regime in Brazil generated a veritable army of ghostly guerrillas.

Spanish-born Marins made pornochanchadas (a peculiarly Brazilian form of sexploitation movie) under the pseudonym J. Avelar. Brazil's most prominent and prolific director of horror movies (**O Estranho Mundo do Zé do Caixao**, 1968; **Esta Noite Encarnarei no Teu Cadaver**, 1966), he has also played something of a Roger Corman role in Brazil, supporting new directors.

Pesadelo Macabro: *d/s* José Mojica Marins *c* George Attil (Giorgio Attili) *lp* Vany Miller, Mario Lima, Ingrid Holt, Nelson Gasparini
O Acordo: *d/s* Ozualdo Candeias *c* Peter Overbeck *lp* Lucy Rangel, Regina Celia, Alex Ronay, Durvalino de Souza
Rocissao dos Mortos: *d/s* Luiz Sergio Person *c* Oswaldo de Oliveira *lp* Lima Duarte, Cacilda Lanuza, Waldir Guedes, Lenoir Bittencourt

Twisted Nerve (CHARTER FILMS; GB) 118min
Although presented as a thriller in the mould of **Psycho** (1960), complete with a Bernard Herrmann score, this inept film is memorable only as the first British splatter movie. Mrs Durnley (Calvert) has one mongoloid child and transmitted a damaged chromosome to her second son, Martin (Bennett), who as a result is a homicidal maniac who occasionally pretends to be a six-year-old child. He murders his stepfather (Finlay) with a pair of scissors for insisting that he get a job, and he axes his landlady (Whitelaw) for making sexual advances to him. Telltale signs of the dangerously violent lunatic at large include reading comics in public and Kraft-Ebbing under the bed-clothes. In the end he also turns on Susan (Mills), who took a friendly interest in him, but a large number of coincidences result in her being rescued by the police in the nick of time.

Blaming mongolism for the hero's homicidal mania aroused such indignation that the makers found it necessary to add an introduction denying such a link, simultaneously revealing their total ignorance about the very thing they had just filmed. In addition, the film-makers hypocritically include some speeches deploring a current trend towards sex and violence, betraying a cultural conservatism which despises the very audiences it vociferously tries to create and exploit.

d/co-s Roy Boulting *p* George W. George, Frank Granat *co-s* Leo Marks, Roger Marshall *c* Harry Waxman *lp* Hywel Bennett, Hayley Mills, Billie Whitelaw, Frank Finlay, Barry Foster, Salmaan Peer, Thorley Walters, Gretchen Franklin, Russell Napier, Phyllis Calvert

Vargtimmen *aka* **Hour of the Wolf**
(SVENSK FILMINDUSTRI; SW) b/w 89min
Bergman explained his title as referring to the time between night and dawn, a time when most people die, most births occur and nightmares are most vivid. This is the time he chooses as the setting for his most visually striking, even hallucinatory, movie to date, in which he extends some of the motifs outlined in *Persona* (1966).

While holidaying on a remote island, the painter Borg (von Sydow) admits to his wife Alma (Ullmann) that he lives in terror of the dark and shows her his sketchbook which contains pictures of monstrous bird-men and insect demons. Ullmann secretly reads his diary and discovers that his former mistress, Veronica (Thulin), is on the island too. While her jealousy and his neuroses increase, they attend a dinner at the nearby castle of Baron von Markens (Josephson) where they appear to be humiliated. Von Sydow tries to shoot Ullmann to remove the pressure of her jealousy and return to the castle, now a labyrinth with his demonic hosts mocking and tormenting him as he attempts to make love to Thulin, who he discovers lying corpselike on a bier. Eventually, he is seen disappearing into a swamp, pursued by his bird-man-demons.

As (nearly) always, Bergman's film is less about 'great existential problems' than about people unable to see further than the ends of their noses who have all the time in the world to concentrate on their favourite (and only) view. Nevertheless, in this gothic fantasy Bergman keeps his hero's morbid obsessions under perfect control, allowing them to grow like a cancer from the menacing calm at the beginning through the whispered fears of the night to the full-blooded terrors of the end, the whole imaginatively photographed and orchestrated into an absorbing dream. A movie like *Vargtimmen* allows us to glimpse what a Bergman might have achieved had he worked under the same constraints as, say, Mario Bava, or indeed what a Bava might have achieved if allowed to work with Bergman's resources and creative control.

d/s Ingmar Bergman *p* Lars-Owe Carlberg *c* Sven Nykvist *se* Evald Andersson *lp* Max von Sydow, Liv Ullmann, Ingrid Thulin, Erland Josephson, Gertrud Fridh, Gudrun Brost, Bertil Anderberg, Georg Rydeberg, Ulf Johanson, Naima Wifstrand

Witchfinder General *aka* **The Conqueror Worm**
(TIGON; GB) 87min
Reeves' best (and unfortunately also his last) film, this centres on the black-robed figure of Price's cynically religious maniac. Taking advantage of the social dislocation of the English Civil War, he instigates a reign of macabre and bloody terror as he roams the country instigating witch-hunts both for profit and pleasure. As in **La Sorella di Satana** (1965), the tone is set by the opening sequence of a coldly vicious execution of a woman accused of witchcraft: she is brutally dragged screaming across a windswept landscape, while a priest pitilessly mouths sanctimonious litanies, and hanged from a gibbet hastily erected on a desolate hill.

The emotional triggers of the action are provided by a Cromwellian soldier (Ogilvy) and his bride, Sara (Dwyer), who fall prey to Price's pathological cruelty. The torture and degradation inflicted by the witchfinder is part of an evil that pervades the social fabric itself, chronicled coolly in all its unsavoury details by Reeves' camera. The colours of death and decay imbue the movie with a muted but eerie intensity, relentlessly building up to the explosion of unconsionable violence as Ogilvy, driven into a frenzy by the spectacle of his wife being tortured, breaks his chains and ruthlessly hacks his tormentor to pieces until a horrified friend intervenes and finishes Price's bloody hulk off with a bullet.

The film aroused an outcry about violence, but rarely has violence been used so legitimately: Reeves shows a man who sets out to rid society of a deeply ingrained evil that has become an accepted part of daily living. He has himself become so infected by it that the purging process duplicates the insanity against which it is deployed. Shortly after making this film, barely 25 years old, Reeves died.

d/co-s Michael Reeves *co-p* Tony Tenser, Arnold L. Miller *co-p/co-s* Louis M. Heyward *co-s* Tom Baker *c* Johnny Coquillon *se* Roger Dicken *lp* Vincent Price, Ian Ogilvy, Hilary Dwyer, Rupert Davies, Robert Russell, Patrick Wymark, Wilfrid Brambell, Michael Beint

The Wizard of Gore (MAYFLOWER PICTURES INC) 96min

Shot in 1968 but released in 1970, this was Lewis' penultimate gore film and reaches gruesome heights/depths. However, the film itself is actually surprisingly self-reflective and playful, a kind of gore version the old art-movie staple theme, illusion versus reality. Montag the Magician (Sager) performs bizarre mutilation tricks on stage on the bodies of female volunteers. All appear to be OK at the time but within an hour of leaving the theatre what appeared to be an illusion has become a reality. Local TV personality Cler and her boyfriend Ratay decide to investigate, and discover that much of Sager's trickery relies on hypnotism. Sager tries to kill Cler but before he can do so is apparently killed by Ratay. Later, however, Ratay peels away his face, revealing himself to be the magician, and proceeds to rip out Cler's guts. She, however, simply laughs, telling him she too has magical powers and transports them both back to the beginning of the film, in which Montag commits his bloody acts on stage watched by a sceptical Cler and Ratay in the audience.

d/p/co-se Herschell Gordon Lewis *s* Allen Kahn *c* Alex Ameri (Eskandar Ameripoor), Daniel Krogh *co-se* Allison Louise Downe, Robert Lewis *lp* Ray Sager, Judy Cler, Wayne Ratay, Phil Laurensen, Jim Rau, John Elliot, Don Alexander

Yabu no Naka Kuroneko *aka* **Kuroneko**
(KINDAI EIGA KYOKAI/NIHON EIGA SHINSHA; JAP)
b/w scope 99min

This is the more frankly horrific companion piece to the same team's better-known **Onibaba** (1964). In the 12th century, an elderly woman, again played by Otowa, and her daughter-in-law (Taichi) are raped and killed by samurai, but they return as ghosts able to change into cats and sworn to kill all samurai they meet. When a heroic warrior, played by Nakamura, a famed kabuki actor, is dispatched to get rid of the two deadly women-cats, he discovers they are his mother and wife. Although Taichi has killed all her victims by tearing out their throats, she can't bring herself to do the same to her own husband and, the spell broken, she returns voluntarily to the horrors of hell. He has to confront his mother, however, and cuts off her arm (which becomes a cat's paw the woman carries between her teeth). Apparently victorious, he is found dead the next day with a black cat prowling around him.

The picture fluctuates wildly from beautiful poetic imagery to gross shock effects and unimaginative repetitions, betraying a surprising and damaging indifference to the narrative rhythm of the story. Wonderful images include the splendid shot of the great gateway with the shimmering figure of the ghost high on the parapet to lure unwary samurai, and the women somersaulting high above their intended victims as they ride through the forest, rendered in the most impressive format invented to date: black and white scope. In contrast to the unevenness of the visuals, the soundtrack presents a virtuoso mixture of Hikaru Hayashi's score and natural sounds recorded by Tetsuo Ohashi. Shigeo Kobayashi's makeup of the spectral figures and the gruesome wounds they inflict also deserves credit. However, as so often with Shindo's work both as a director and as a scenarist, the main interest of the narrative resides in the way it differs from the standard genre formula. Here, as in *Onibaba*, the ghostly figures are less intent on avenging a particular crime than the socially sanctioned brutality of a class, indeed of an entire social system, against its weakest members.

d/s Kaneto Shindo *p* Nobuyo Horiba, Setsuo Noto, Kazuo Kuwahara *c* Kiyomi Kuroda *lp* Nobuko Otowa, Kiwako Taichi, Kichiemon Nakamura, Kei Sato, Hideo Kanze, Rokko Toura, Taiji Tonoyama

Yokai Daisenso *aka* **Spook Warfare** *aka* **Ghosts on Parade** (DAIEI; JAP) scope 79min

In the face of *Kaiju Shoshingeki* (1968) – Inoshiro Honda's Kaiju Eiga (monster movie) for Toho, which featured all the studio's monsters, Daiei, not really having a repertory of ghosts of draw upon, replied with this spectacular Kaidan (ghost story) which mobilizes an army of local Japanese ghosts to defeat an alien (safely Babylonian) horror called Daimon. The tale is set in the 18th century when the issue of Japan's commercial relations with the outside world was coming to the forefront of external Japanese politics, while internally, the growing power of the merchant class was beginning to cause stress within the feudal society – problems not unrelated to the kinds of stresses that prevailed in post-1945 Japan.

The governor of Izu and his daughter (Kawasaki) are fishing when a storm breaks and Daimon, a monstrous skull-bedecked giant who once ruled Babylon, emerges, sucks all the kindly governor's blood, occupies his body and starts to reign as a tyrant. A native water-spirit realizes what has happened and summons his local demon friends to fight the foreign occupier, but they are defeated. A valiant retainer (Aoyama) of the former governor tries to kill Daimon by shooting an arrow into his eye, but still the thing survives. Only the massed forces of all the native spirits of the islands eventually succeed in driving out the monstrous foreigner. Directed by Daiei's special effects expert (who had worked on **Daimajin**, 1966), the picture has numerous impressive sequences which make use of special lighting techniques, process work and colour filters, while minimizing the number of scale models that often mar the work of Toho's special effects' master, Eiji Tsuburaya.

Vincent Price as the cynical religious maniac in The Witchfinder General, *the last film made by the talented Michael Reeves.*

The impressive Yokai Daisenso.

d Yoshiyuki Kuroda *p* Masaichi Nagata *s* Tetsuro Yoshida *c* Hiroshi Imai *lp* Yoshihiko Aoyama, Akane Kawasaki, Osamu Okawa, Tomoo Uchida, Hajime Kimura, Takashi Kanda

Yokai Hyaku Monogatari *aka* **The Hundred Monsters** *aka* **The Hundred Ghost Stories**
(DAIEI; JAP) scope 79min
This highly entertaining picture weaves together the motifs of sex, storytelling, pleasure and fear in a manner reminiscent of *A Thousand and One Nights*. The differences are that, here, the stories impede sexual activity instead of binding the sexual partners together, and provoke death rather than forestalling it. A rich property developer changes a shrine into a brothel and opens his new establishment with a special performance by the local storyteller who narrates the famous 'One Hundred Monster Collection', a series of tales about ghosts and other frightening creatures. Everyone is so captivated that they neglect to perform the required exorcism ceremony which usually concludes such a show. The result is that the 100 ghosts evoked by the narrator's words erupt into the brothel, frightening the prostitutes and their customers alike. In the end, the owner mistakenly kills his assistant and commits suicide by plunging himself on to his sword.

The movie offers a weird tapestry of horrific spectres as the film-makers exhaust themselves devising a myriad of creatures in different shapes and sizes. One particularly successful one is the snake-woman who strangles her unfaithful husband with her exceedingly long, rubbery neck. Other inventive sequences include an 'umbrella ghost', (a drawing of a one-legged creature with one eye and a very long tongue come to life) and the ending in which the horde of misshapen ghosts leave a cadaver-ridden brothel in a wildly frantic but utterly silent procession. Yasuda, one of Daiei's house directors, made **Daimajin** (1966), and numerous adventure films and other genre products, but this energetically conducted film, together with **Kaidan Kasanegafuchi** (1970) remain his best work.

d Kimiyoshi Yasuda *p* Masaichi Nagata *s* Tetsuo Yoshida *c* Yasukazu Takemura *lp* Jun Fujimaki, Miwa Takada, Mikiko Tsubouchi, Takashi Kanda, Ryutaro Gomi, Yoshio Yoshida

Zhi Mo Nu *aka* **The Leech Girl** *aka* **Elephant Wife**
(KAN YUNG; HONG KONG) scope 93min
The 'family romance' or melodrama is one of the cornerstones of Chinese cinema whether overseas or on the mainland. In this film, a farmer's daughter falls in love with the village chief's son, unaware that he is her brother. The presence of an elephant, whom the farmer believes to be the girl's father, appears to protect the family. However, a witch-doctor plans to prevent the union of the two youngsters by forcing the girl to eat poisonous leeches, a diet which drives her temporarily insane and causes her to become infested with leeches. Believing her to be an evil creature, the chief has her tortured. The underlying motifs of the animal and the human as the demarcations between them begin to be blurred provide an unsettling dimension to the picture which is most effectively used when magic is invoked to prevent the elephants from rescuing the girl. The most intriguing aspects of the film unfortunately are undercut by the film's final revelation that the heroine's fiancé was not her brother after all but an adopted cousin, allowing the marriage to go ahead and disappointingly providing a far less effective ending than the elephants could have engineered.

d Jin Weng, Lin Yixiu *p* Hui Qiang *s* Lin Huangkum *c* Oi Shingle *lp* Ma Shayue, Jin Luhua, Wang Kunseng

1969

Blood of Dracula's Castle *aka* **Dracula's Castle**
(A AND E FILM CORP) 84min
A variation on the Dracula legend from prolific Z movie director Adamson, who was probably best known for *Dracula vs Frankenstein* (1971), *Satan's Sadists* (1969) and *The Female Bunch* (1969), which was shot on the Manson ranch and was the last released film of Lon Chaney Jnr. Here Count and Countess Townsend (D'Arcy and Raymond – although Jayne Mansfield was slated to star), who are in fact Count and Countess Dracula, living in a castle in the Mojave desert, are waited on by their butler George (Carradine) who keeps their cellar well stocked with victims. Things hot up, however, with the arrival of a werewolf and then a young couple who claim to have inherited the estate.

As an attempt to update the Dracula myth to present-day America, *Blood of Dracula's Castle* is simply too forced and badly done to be successful, though is fairly gruesome for its time. A sequel, *Dracula's Coffin*, was planned but never filmed.

d/co-p Al Adamson, Jean Hewitt *co-p/s* Rex Carlton *c* Laszlo Kovacs *lp* John Carradine, Paula Raymond, Alex D'Arcy, Robert Dix, Ray Young, Vicki Volante, John Cardos, Kent Osborne

Contronatura *aka* **Schreie in der Nacht** *aka* **The Unnaturals**
(CCC/EDO CINEMATOGRAFICA/SUPER INTERNATIONAL PICTURES; IT, WG) scope 84min
After the banal psycho whodunit set in a girl's school, *Nude … si Muore* (1968), Margheriti, in a lean period, concocted this routine tale, set in England in the thirties, of a group of travellers, all with murky pasts, seeking refuge in an old mansion inhabited by a weird old woman and her son, both devoted spiritualists. The old woman, in a trance during a seance, reveals the horrible crimes committed by her guests, which include incest and murder. It turns out that the spiritualists are in fact ghosts returning from the beyond to bring retribution: they unleash a flood which drowns everybody.

The storm which forces the group to turn to the old house and the atmospheric rooms and corridors vaguely recall the Margheriti of **I Lunghi Capelli della Morte** (1964), but the picture never comes alive in spite of the presence of Koch. The rest of the acting, as in his **Nella Stretta Morsa del Ragno** (1970) or **La Morte negli Occhi del Gatto** (1973), is unbearably wooden.

d/co-s Anthony Dawson (Antonio Margheriti) *co-s* Hannes Dahlberg *c* Riccardo Pallottini *lp* Joachim Fuchsberger, Marianne Koch, Dominique Boschero, Claudio Camaso, Alan Collins (Luciano Pigozzi), Marianne Leibl, Marco Morelli, Helga Anders

1969

The Corpse *aka* **Crucible of Horror** *aka* **The Velvet House** (LONDON CANNON/ABACUS; GB) 90min
This psycho-thriller features Gough as the tyrannical husband and father, murdered by his wife (Mitchell) and daughter (Gurney), whose corpse re-emerges, first nailed in a crate, then swinging from a rope in the attic, attacks his daughter and finally, as if nothing had happened, resumes his place at the head of the table, leaving his wife staring dementedly into space as the film ends. Scripted by an actor – he plays the part of a nosy neighbour – the movie is primarily an actor's exercise in registering various types of fear, from nervousness to terror via anxiety and shock while the narrative abandons any pretense of verisimilitude. Ritelis fails to shake off some bad television habits including an excessive reliance on closeups of meaningful details and erratic focus-pulling. Although the story is remarkably similar to that of *Fragment of Fear* (1969), which was shot almost concurrently, this picture could be seen as an allegory indicating that killing a patriarch doesn't eliminate patriarchy.

d Viktors Ritelis *p* Gabrielle Beaumont *s* Olaf Pooley *c* John Mackey *lp* Michael Gough, Yvonne Mitchell, Sharon Gurney, Simon Gough, Olaf Pooley, David Butler, Mary Hignett, Nicholas Jones

Crescendo (HAMMER; GB) 95min
By the late sixties, Hammer's post-**Psycho** (1960) thrillers, initiated by Seth Holt's **Taste of Fear** (1960), were showing signs of exhaustion as Sangster's scripts became more schematic than ever. For this outing Hammer yet again adopted the traditional British ploy of interesting US distributors by casting an American heroine. Susan (Powers) visits a villa in southern France where she encounters a widow (Scott), her invalid and heroin-addicted son, paralysed from the waist down (Olson) and the maid who administers to his needs (Lapotaire). When the maid is murdered, Powers is drawn into the circle by the scheming widow while her son suffers nightmares of being killed. The traditional shock ending is obtained by the lazy script device of revealing the existence of an insane twin brother for whom Powers had been destined. In spite of the collaboration of Shaughnessy (the director of **Cat Girl**, 1957), the script is so contrived that Gibson is reduced to injecting a number of sex scenes to keep viewers interested. His next efforts – *Goodbye Gemini* (1970) and **Dracula AD 1972** (1972) – proved equally disappointing.

d Alan Gibson *p* Michael Carreras *s* Jimmy Sangster, Alfred Shaughnessy *c* Paul Beeson *lp* Stefanie Powers, James Olson, Margaretta Scott, Jane Lapotaire, Joss Ackland, Kirsten Betts

The Dunwich Horror (AIP) 90(86)min
Haller's second attempt at filming H. P. Lovecraft, this is much more successful than **Monster of Terror** (1965) at capturing the idiosyncratic antiquarian-book flavour of his horrors. Derived principally from his pet occult volume, *The Necronomicon*, the film centres on Stockwell's mad plan to restore the ancient powers to their former evil dominion over the world – a plan which calls, not unappealingly, for the sacrifice of Dee in a fertility rite. Although murky secrets haunt the Stockwell home (a great-grandfather hanged as a demon, a semi-demented grandfather pottering about, a monstrous twin brother kept locked away), Haller manages for the most part to escape the Roger Corman-Poe influence. One of the strengths of the film is that it attempts (though not always successfully) to root the action in the normality of a sleepy university town. The other is that, as in Jacques Tourneur's **Night of the Demon** (1957), the evil power (represented by the monster twin) is glimpsed once, but is otherwise evoked by a rushing wind, the thud of a beating heart and the cry of gulls, and in one magnificent shot seems to darken the whole face of the earth as the camera catches a shadow rippling on a stretch of water. Less pleasing, but symptomatic of the time, is Haller's occasional recourse to vaguely psychedelic effects to enhance the mood.

d Daniel Haller *p* James H. Nicholson, Samuel Z. Arkoff *s* Curtis Lee Hanson, Henry Rosenbaum, Ronald Silkosky *c* Richard C. Glouner *lp* Sandra Dee, Dean Stockwell, Ed Begley, Sam Jaffe, Lloyd Bochner

Eye of the Cat
(JOSEPH M. SCHENCK ENTERPRISES/U) 102(99)min
Sarrazin here plays an aelurophobe with a taste for macabre jokes who is persuaded by a pretty girl (Hunnicutt) to murder his invalid aunt (Parker) for her money. Terrified by a cat apparently spying on them, Sarrazin accidentally electrocutes it, then returns to the home he had previously walked out of because his aunt showed a more than normal interest in him, leaving his disgruntled brother (Henry) to look after her. He is horrified to find the place overrun with cats, but in deference to his phobia Parker promises to get rid of them, cut them out of her will, and make a new one in his favour. Secretly in league to get rid of both Sarrazin and Parker, Hunnicutt and Henry use the cats to frighten Sarrazin into a catatonic state, then set about Parker's murder. They are foiled partly because Sarrazin had been merely pretending to play along with the murder, and partly because the watchful cats – led by the vengeful spirit of the electrocuted one – take a hand and tear Hunnicutt to pieces.

The busy plotful of phobias and perversions was concocted by Stefano (who scripted **Psycho**, 1960), and has some superbly menacing felines trained by Ray Berwick (who trained the birds for *The Birds*, 1963). But Rich is no Hitchcock, and though extravagantly enjoyable with excellent performances, the film never quite brings off its notion of the house as a family hell in which the characters are trapped by a grim charade of their own devising.

d David Lowell Rich *c* Bernard Schwartz, Philip Hazelton *s* Joseph Stefano *c* Russell Metty, Ellsworth Fredricks *lp* Michael Sarrazin, Gayle Hunnicutt, Eleanor Parker, Tim Henry, Laurence Naismith

Frankenstein Must Be Destroyed
(HAMMER; GB) scope 97min
The title of Hammer's fifth film in their Frankenstein series betrays a certain impatience with the character of the Baron, again played by Cushing. Society's callous bigotry and vicious injustices having ruined all his fundamentally noble efforts, chronicled in Fisher's previous four outings, starting with **The**

Sandra Dee about to be sacrificed in Daniel Haller's interesting The Dunwich Horror.

The cats attack Gayle Hunnicutt in Eye of the Cat.

Curse of Frankenstein (1957), and *Frankenstein Must Be Destroyed* sees the Baron not merely embittered but downright misanthropic. He is now the monster and his creature merely a pathetically unhappy victim, a development clearly signalled in the opening sequence as a hideous creature peels off its rubber mask to reveal the face of Cushing.

He transplants the brain of the brilliant but insane Dr Brandt (Pravda) into the body of the benign Dr Richter (Jones), ruthlessly blackmailing Anna (Carlson) and Karl (Ward) into assisting him. With cruelly deliberate misogyny, he rapes her 'for discipline' and thus triggers his own destruction as the traumatized Carlson knifes the unfortunate creature as he stumbles towards her, mistaking his desperate pleas for help as another sexual attack. Then, in one of Fisher' s most powerful scenes, Jones drags himself home where, his mind encased in an alien body, he cries as he watches his wife (Audley) sleeping before trying to explain what happened, pathetically hiding behind a screen to prepare her for his unsightly appearance. The final scene sees Jones, whose mental agonies have turned into a burning hatred for his 'creator', carrying the Baron back into his blazing house.

Thematically, this story devised by Nelson Keys was the end of the Baron's adventures as conceived by Fisher. Hammer's next film in the series, **The Horror of Frankenstein** (1970), was a clumsily misjudged self-parody, proving they didn't know where to go next. Fisher himself provided the sinister coda with his last film, **Frankenstein and the Monster from Hell** (1973).

d Terence Fisher *p* Anthony Nelson Keys *s* Bert Batt *c* Arthur Grant *se* Studio Locations Ltd *lp* Peter Cushing, Veronica Carlson, Freddie Jones, Simon Ward, Thorley Walters, Maxine Audley, George Pravda, Geoffrey Bayldon, Harold Goodwin, Colette O'Neil

The Ghastly Ones *aka* Blood Rites

(JER PICTURES) 81min

The Ghastly Ones, which concerns a number of grisly murders which occur when a family gathers to await the reading of a will, was Milligan's first film in the Victorian, period-horror mode (though as usual it was filmed on Staten Island). Apart from his interest in costumes (which he always made himself) Milligan had another reason for setting his films in the past: 'most things are retitled and sent out again and again. If you do a costume setting, it can be reissued and reissued and reissued and you can't tell what year it was made'. (However, in the case of this film the decidedly sixties hairstyles give the game away!)

With hangings, disembowellings by pitchfork and axe, and a maniac who devours live rabbits (though some of this is hard to make out given the lighting and grainy photography), *The Ghastly Ones* is among Milligan's more gruesome works and has been banned in Britain as a 'video nasty'. Milligan subsequently remade the film in 1972 as *Legacy of Blood*.

d/p/co-s/c Andy Milligan *co-s* Hal Sherwood *lp* Don Williams, Veronica Radburn, Maggie Rogers

Una Hacha para la Luna de Miel *aka* Il Rosso Segno della Follia *aka* Blood Brides *aka* An Axe for the Honeymoon *aka* A Hatchet for the Honeymoon *aka* The Red Sign of Madness *aka* Un'Accetta per la Luna di Miele

(PAN LATINA FILMS/MERCURY FILMS; SP,IT) scope 93(83)min

After the stylish comic-strip movie *Diabolik* (1967), Bava's work stagnated for a while as he sought to recapture the intensely cinematic perversity of his giallo films like **Sei Donne per l'Assassino** (1964). This picture features Forsyth as a stereotypical handsome macho, except that he is impotent with his wife (Betti) and compulsively axes women in bridal gowns to death. As a rich fashion designer, he even keeps a special room filled with female dummies dressed up as virginal brides, exactly the way mamma would like them to look. The narrative is grotesquely oedipal: with every murder he remembers an extra detail of childhood trauma involving a stairway, a keyhole and the killing of his mother. In spite of the police's interest in him, he attempts a final killing, that of his lover (Lassander), in order to gain complete recall of the half-remembered scene which, predictably, reveals him to be guilty of matricide.

The movie provides a richly revealing account of a classic 'lover boy's' maternal hangups, and as such could be read as a critique of the filmic presentation of romantic male stars in melodramas, and of all those who identify with them. Unfortunately, except for the occasional stunningly beautiful fetishistic image, the movie's mechanical narrative, crude voice-over technique and abuse of the zoom lens dilute and damage its attempt to establish an equation between narrative as fantasy and cinema itself as a fantasy process. As in **Psycho** (1960), the hero ends up insane, condemned to be perpetually accompanied by the ghostly presence of his mother image which here is that of his shrewish wife who is also his mother, and as such the one woman he can't make love to.

The companion pieces to this gory tale are **Ecologia del Delitto** (1971) and **Cinque Bambole per la Luna d'Agosto** (1970).

d/co-s/co-c Mario Bava *p* Manuel Cano Sanciriaco *co-s* Santiago Moncada, Mario Musy *co-c* Antonio Rinaldi *lp* Stephen Forsyth, Dagmar Lassander, Laura Betti, Jesús Puente, Femi (Eufemia) Benussi, Antonia Mas, Alan Collins (Luciano Pigozzi), Gerard Tichy, Fortunato Pasquale, Veronica Llimera

The Haunted House of Horror *aka* The Dark *aka* Horror House

(TIGON BRITISH/AIP; GB) 92(79)min

This tediously scripted and indifferently acted outing stars Avalon, fresh from his beach movie adventures, as a callow youth out for kicks in swinging London. Richard (Barnes) suggests it might be fun for the gang to visit a haunted house he used to play in. There, one of the gang is found slaughtered. A nosy policeman (Price) prompts their return to the house where Barnes reverts to his psychotic personality during the full moon and kills Avalon before the police arrive. The result is a routine youth movie with added gore.

The film's only, and decidedly minor, point of interest is an early appearance by O'Sullivan, who soon began a career in British TV comedy. Armstrong subsequently tried to improve his commercial fortunes by directing an outright sadistic sexploitation movie in Germany (**Hexen bis aufs Blut Gequaelt**, 1969).

d/s Michael Armstrong *p* Louis M. Heyward *c* Jack Atcheler *se* Arthur Beavis *lp* Frankie Avalon, Jill Haworth, Dennis Price, Julian Barnes, Mark Wynter, Richard O'Sullivan, Gina Warwick, Robin Stewart, Carol Dilworth

Hexen bis aufs Blut Gequaelt *aka* Brenn Hexe Brenn *aka* Mark of the Devil *aka* Austria 1700 *aka* Satan

(HIFI STEREO 70; WG) 97(90)min

This grotesquely sadistic sex movie released in 1970, uses witchcraft trials as an excuse to depict, at length, the torture of women. Set in 18th-century Austria, the plot opens with a peasant turned witch-hunter, Albino (Nalder), persecuting a waitress, Vanessa (Vuco). A young baron (Kier) rescues her but then runs foul of his mentor (Lom), a witchfinder who copes with his impotence by torturing women. In the end, the villagers rebel and when Lom helps Nalder escape, they hang Kier instead, leaving Vuco to mourn by his corpse.

Taking off from Michael Reeves' **The Witchfinder General** (1968), the picture devotes extensive footage to tortures: tongue pincers are used on a woman (Fuchs), as are thumbscrews, nails to probe for the Devil's spot, whipping posts, racks, fingers are cut off, and so on. The production was designed by one of Jesús Franco's collaborators, Hoven, an actor turned producer and director and who aimed the film squarely at the American sex-and-gore market. The British director, fresh from the exploitative *The Haunted House of Horror* (1969), served the producer well. Lom's witchfinder doesn't match Price's but then he isn't called upon to function as a complex historical figure either. Although the film's cynical promotional campaign ran into trouble in the United States, it proved successful enough for Hoven to make an even more obnoxious sequel inspired by Ken Russell's **The Devils** (1971), **Hexen Geschandet und zu Tode Gequaelt** (1972). Both films feature Nalder, also a Franco acolyte, best known for his part as the murderer in Hitchcock's *The Man Who Knew Too Much* (1955).

d Michael Armstrong *p* Adrian Hoven *s* Sergio Cassner, Percy Parker (Adrian Hoven) *c* Ernst W. Aklinke *lp* Herbert Lom, Udo Kier, Olivera Vuco, Reginald Nalder, Herbert Fuchs, Michael Maien, Ingeborg Schoener, Gaby Fuchs, Dorothea Carrera, Adrian Hoven

Hiroku Kaibyoden *aka* The Haunted Castle

(DAIEI; JAP) scope 83min

Tanaka filmed this well-known bakeneko mono (cat ghost-story) about the vengeful cat of Nabeshima with the same stylishly brooding elegance he had displayed in his funereal love story, **Kaidan Yukigoro** (1968). The plot is set in the genre's favourite era, the 18th century, and tells of the sense of terror that pervades the castle of Lord Nabeshima (Uenoyama) as a night creature kills members of his entourage, makes him ill and also eats the goldfish in his pond. The ghost-cat, able to take the form of a sharp-fanged woman with long white hair, is a result of Uenoyama's murder of the castle's former lord. The dispossessed lord's sister (Kamei) committed suicide and her cat lapped up her blood and, by the same token, her thirst for revenge. A samurai (Hongo) discovers that the cat has also taken possession of the lord's favourite mistress (Kobayashi), but eventually succeeds in killing the spectre by transfixing it with a sword.

The movie remains stuck halfway between Nakagawa's brilliant *Borei Kaibyo Yashiki* (1958) and Shindo's **Yabu no Naka Kuroneko** (1968) which transfers the traditional family context of such stories on to a broader historical canvas of social injustice. Although visually seductive, the film never quite reaches the level of generality and abstraction required to make his characters representative of the forces at play in feudal society, so that the movie seems uncomfortably poised between the two options. The story had also been filmed by Kunio Watanabe as *Nabeshima Kaibyoden* (1949).

d Tokuzo Tanaka *p* Masaichi Nagata *s* Shozaburo Asai *c* Hiroshi Imai *lp* Kojiro Hongo, Naomi Kobayashi, Mitsuyo Kamei, Matsuhiro Toura, Koichi Uenoyama, Akane Kawasaki, Natsuke Oka, Ikuko Mori

El Hombre que Vino de Ummo *aka* Dracula versus Frankenstein *aka* Frankenstein *aka* Dracula Jagt Frankenstein *aka* Assignment Terror *aka* The Man Who Came from Ummo *aka* Los Monstruos del Terror

(PRODUCCIONES JAIME PRADES/EICHBERG FILM/INTERNATIONAL JAGUAR; SP,IT,WG) scope 89(81)min

Rennie – in a pale imitation of his best-known role, the alien in *The Day the Earth Stood Still* (1951) – here plays Dr Odo Warnoff, an alien from Ummo who settles in a Transylvanian castle whence he plans to conquer the earth. The bodies of Dr Kirian (Hill) and the lab assistant Maleva (Dor) are revived to help him. The plan involves unleashing the world's legendary monsters on to the population: Dracula, the Frankenstein monster, a mummy and Count Waldemar Daninsky, the werewolf (Molina). Unfortunately for the alien, love rears its head and Dor falls for the werewolf who then kills his fellow monsters before being shot (and thus cured) by his lover while the castle and its alien occupant go up in flames. The cast's gallery of creatures locked in the basement, and the abducted women, contrast favourably with the tatty scientific paraphernalia reduced to banks of flashing lightbulbs. Shot in six days, the film's main interest appears to be in the repeated shots of women's faces as they undergo torture by soundwaves.

For his next outing, Molina returned to more familiar territory with **La Noche de Walpurgis** (1970). Demichelli's film is not to be confused with Jesús Franco's **Dracula contra Frankenstein** (1972) nor with Al Adamson's *Dracula vs Frankenstein* (1971). The anglicized version of this film was prepared by Peter Riethof.

d Tulio Demichelli *p* Jaime Prades *s* Jacinto Molina *c* Godofredo Pacheco *se* Antonio Molina *lp* Michael Rennie, Karen Dor, Craig Hill, Paul Naschy (Jacinto Molina), Paty Shepard, Angel del Pozo, Ella Gessler, Peter Damon, Manuel de Blas, Gene Reyes

Incrivel, Fantastico, Extraordinario *aka* Incredible, Fantastic, Extraordinary

(C. ADOLPHO CHADLER PRODUÇOES CINEMATOGRAFICAS; BRAZIL) scope 90min

A spin-off from a popular Brazilian radio series, this pedestrian film contains four short stories. The first episode, *A Ajuda*, tells of a woman (Clara) who pleads with a motorist (Farney) to save her son after a bad car-crash, in which she died. The next story, *O Sonho*, has a hooded schoolgirl predict the deaths of her classmates, but also foresee her own imminent death of a heart attack. The third one, *A Volta*, tells of a widow (Rocha), who is haunted to death by the guilty knowledge of having killed her husband. The final episode, *O Coveiro*, shows a gravedigger (Sabag) who dies of fright as the corpse he is robbing appears to grab him. Da Costa is a minor director, producer, scenarist and actor who worked in Hollywood and in Europe. He also produced *O Impossivel Acoutece* (1970), directing the episode based on a story by Richard Matheson (uncredited), *Disappearing Act*, which had been used for a *Twilight Zone* TV episode in 1959, entitled *And When the Sky Was Opened*.

d/p/co-s Adolpho Chadler (Cicero Adolpho Vitorio da Costa) *co-s* René Martin *c* Roberto Pace *lp* Cyll Farney, Sonia Clara, Glauce Rocha, Fabio Sabag, Wanda Oliver, Big Jones, Marcia Tania, Alzira Silva, Nira Clara

Isabella Duchessa dei Diavoli
aka **Isabel Duchess of the Devils**
(CINESECOLO/INDIEF/HAPE FILM; IT,MON) scope 86min
The Italian sadistic sex comic strip, 'Isabella', was started in 1966 by Alessandro Angiolini. Each story, published as a separate paperback, has Isabella or another woman captured and tortured before the villain is defeated. This is the only film derived from the popular strip and confronts the heroine (Skay) with Baron von Nutter (Williams), the man she saw murder her parents. Returning to 'her' castle which the Baron usurped, she cuts off his nose and an ear, prompting the villain to hide his features behind a leather mask. She is then captured and, as so often in Isabella's adventures, subjected to an inquisitorial torture session. In the end, she escapes, as does the Baron, thereby opening the way for a sequel.

The prolific Bruno is the less talented brother of the equally prolific Sergio Corbucci who co-directed **La Danza Macabra** (1964) with Antonio Margheriti, but excelled in the Italian western genre. Bruno's directorial career started in 1965 and consists exclusively of potboilers.

d Bruno Corbucci *s* Giorgio Cavedon, Mario Amendola, Elisabeth Forster *c* Fausto Zuccoli *lp* Brigitte Skay, Tino Scotti, Mimmo Palmara, Fred Williams, Emina de Witt, Salvatore Borgese, Mario Novelli, Renato Baldini, Enzo Andronico

Jigokuhen *aka* **Portrait of Hell** *aka*
A Story of Hell *aka* **The Hell Screen**
(TOHO; JAP) scope 95min
Published in 1918, Ryonosuke Akutagawa'a classic short story chronicled an 11th-century painter's obsession with creating a perfect work of art, even going so far as seeing his own daughter burned alive to achieve perfection. The veteran Toyoda changed the original story by making the painter a Korean (Nakadai) and his powerful aristocratic patron (Nakamura) a cultural boor. The plot has Nakamura take the painter's daughter (Naito), saying he will give her back in exchange for a painting of paradise. The artist, seeing only horror and misery around him, offers to paint a picture of hell with, as the centrepiece, the image of a burning carriage, preferably with the lord inside it. Nakamura then chains Naito to the carriage's seat and insists on an apology. Mistakenly counting on the lord's lust for Naito, Nakadai refuses and is forced to watch his daughter being burned alive. Realizing that hell is where he is in fact living – that is, feudal Japan – the Korean artist finishes the picture and hangs himself, while the lord, driven insane by the powerful impact of the painting which shows him in the carriage, eventually perishes in his burning palace.

Toyoda transformed the story into a corrosive attack on the widespread anti-Korean racism in Japan, deflating Japanese feelings of superiority in the process. Unfortunately, Nakadai's excellent performance as the haughty painter can't obscure the fact that the part should have been played by a Korean actor. Nevertheless, this fine film, one of Toyoda's last, together with his version of the often filmed **Yotsuya Kaidan** (1965), must be counted among the director's best work. A similar theme, transposed to a rural Italian setting, informs Pupi Avati's **La Casa delle Finestre che Ridono** (1976), the best and most innovative European horror picture of the late seventies.

d Shiro Toyoda *p* Tatsuo Matsuoka *s* Toshio Yasumi *c* Kazuo Yamada *lp* Tatsuya Nakadai, Kinnosuke Nakamura, Yoko Naito, Toshio Oide, Hideo Yamamoto, Kichiro Nakamura, Masanobu Okubo, Masao Yamafuki, Ikio Sawamara, Kumeko Otoba

Jonathan – Vampiren Sterben Nicht *aka* **Jonathan**
(IDUNA FILM; WG) 103(100)min
Sold as an anti-fascist vampire movie, this free adaptation of Bram Stoker's novel offers a confused political allegory covered with a glossy lacquer of bright colours and ponderously arty imagery and betrays a fundamental incomprehension both of fascism and of the Dracula myth. The Count (Krumm) is a Hitler lookalike who, with blackshirted associates, terrorizes a peasant village on the North Sea coast. Led by a professor (von Schab), some students aided by the locals plan an uprising and

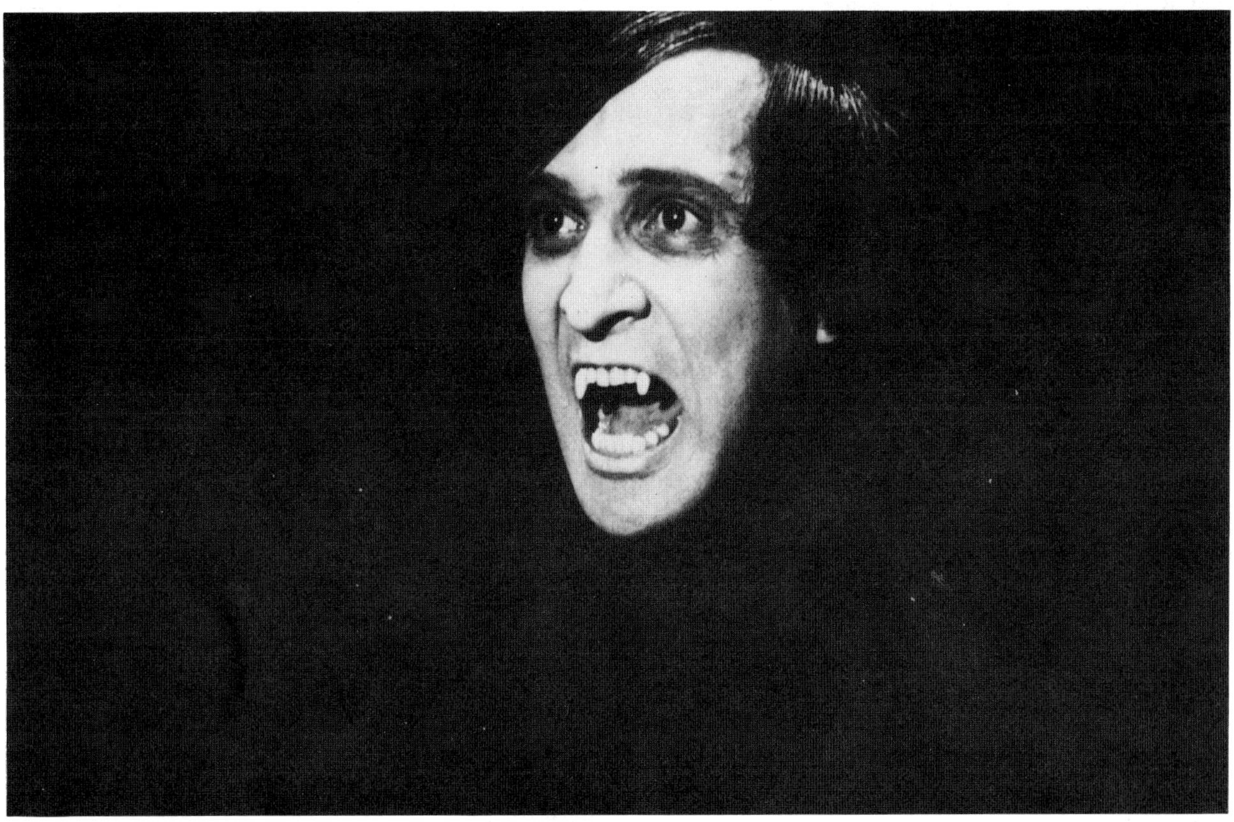

Hitler as a vampire: Jonathan.

dispatch Jonathan (Jung) to the castle by the sea to rouse the prisoners to join the revolt which eventually drives the vampire horde, gathered for a gala party, into the sea.

Sadly, the allegory falls flat since, from a historical point-of-view, the Count represents the survival of feudal remnants in a bourgeois state and cannot be made to symbolize popularist fascism. Consequently, the script meanders through setpieces desperately signalling 'totalitarianism' in general. The heavy-handed direction and slow-motion, ever-so meaningful acting transform the movie into a series of pretty and gory pictures interrupted by cynically crude bits of narrative and periodic shots of white-robed women swanning around on staircases and in other unlikely places. Stock characters populate the story: the professor, the slow-witted Jonathan, decomposing corpses, timorous villagers, a hunchback drooling over a collection of religious paraphernalia and a masochistic maiden who, in a scene cribbed from one of Hammer's weakest innovations, drinks from an open wound in the Count's chest.

The movie proved difficult to sell and extra scenes with sex and gore were added. Geissendoerfer's first feature – after an early career in TV – the film parallels that of his contemporary, Niklaus Schilling (**Nachtschatten**, 1972) as an attempt to break into the world of lucrative exploitation cinema by trading on the reputation and look of the European art movie. Geissendoerfer went on to try various genre formulas before over-reaching himself by attempting something more than routinely commercial gloss, *Der Zauberberg* (1981). His vampire movie is mainly notable as an early stylistic exercise of Mueller, later to achieve fame as cinematographer for Wim Wenders.

d/s Hans W. Geissendoerfer *p* Ullrich Steffen *c* Robbi Mueller *lp* Juergen Jung, Paul Albert Krumm, Hertha von Walter, Oscar von Schab, Hans-Dieter Jendreyko, Eleonore Schminke, Ilona Grubel, Ulrike Luderer, Thomas Astan, Ilse Kunkele, Arthur Brauss

Kyofu Kikei Ningen *aka* Horror of a Deformed Man *aka* The Horror of Malformed Men

(TOEI; JAP) scope 99min

Like Masumura's **Moju** (1969), Ishii's film is based on a story by Rampo Edogawa, Japan's leading horror film story-writer. However, in this instance, Edogawa appears to have borrowed liberally from H. G. Wells' novel *The Island of Dr Moreau*. A medical student (Yoshida) finds he has been trained as a surgeon to assist his mad, ugly, web-fingered father who conducts medical experiments on a remote island where he lives with his wife (Aoi). When Yoshida arrives on the island, he encounters Siamese twins, hunchbacks and a collection of freaks. But in contrast to Dr Moreau, old Kamoda surrounds himself with such creatures in order to drown his own ugliness. When he learns that one of his trusted retainers (Koike) and a female relative (Kagawa) have been murdering their way towards the front of the inheritance queue, he kills them and then isolates himself even further by biting off his tongue.

Although this is Ishii's principal horror movie, combining elements from the action and cruelty films he made for Toei, his talents as a director were better suited to the short-story format as his sadistic omnibus movie **Tokugawa Onna Keibatsushi** (1968) shows. His next horror picture, **Kaidan Noboriryu** (1970) was made for a rival company, Nikkatsu.

d/co-s Teruo Ishii *p* Hiroshi Okawa *co-s* Masahiro Kakefuda *c* Shigeru Akatsuka *lp* Teruo Yoshida, Minoru Oki, Asao Koike, Yuki Kagawa, Mitsuko Aoi, Teruko Yumi, Michiko Obata

Las Luchadoras contra el Robot Asesino *aka* El Robot Asesino *aka* El Asesino Loco y el Sexo *aka* Sex Monster *aka* Wrestling Women vs the Murdering Robot

(CINEMATOGRAFICA CALDERON; MEX) 73(80)min

The Luchadoras fifth adventure has a different cast of women from those who had been involved in **Las Luchadoras contra la Momia** (1964). Here, they are pitted against the villainy of a Dr Orlac (Cordero) – star of **Orlak, el Infierno de Frankenstein** (1960) – who abducts various scientists and, of course, women, to construct an army of robots. The wrestlers Gaby (Torné) and Gema (Reyes), with their lovers (Lechuga and Agosti) destroy his workplace, but the doctor returns to the attack by capturing their friend Berta (Chaves) and using his main monster, Carfax (Cepeda) to challenge Torné in the ring. The evildoers are unmasked and thrown off a cliff.

Following the practice established with **Santo y el Tesoro de Dracula** (1968), Cardona made two versions, one for general consumption and an additional one with extra sex, nudity and sadism, released as *El Asesino Loco y el Sexo*, with a cast list referring to Hector Lechug and Regine Thorne, for the American sex market.

d René Cardona *p* Guillermo Calderon *s* Alfredo Salazar *c* Raúl Martinez Solares *lp* Joaquin Cordero, Regina Torné, Malu Reyes, Ector Lechuga, Carlos Agosti, Gerardo Cepeda, Gloria Chaves, Genaro Moreno, Pascual Garcia Peña, Leo Herrera

Moju *aka* The Blind Beast

(DAIEI; JAP) scope 84(80)min

This grotesquely fetishistic tale derived from a story by Japan's leading horror writer, Rampo Edogawa, was directed by the father of the Japanese new wave of the sixties. A blind sculptor, Michio (Funakoshi), with help from his mother (Sengoku), kidnaps a young model, Aki (Midori) and locks her up in a room decorated with large blow-ups of various parts of the female anatomy: one wall has nothing but photographs of eyes, one wall has lips, one has breasts, and so on. Gradually, Midori succumbs to the room's weird atmosphere and to the blind sculptor's tactile perversities. Imprisonment in the darkened room causes her to become blind as well, whereupon both enter into a deliriously sado-masochistic relationship which involves biting, whipping, cutting, until, in the escalating tactile frenzy, she agrees to become the 'perfect statue': he takes a meat cleaver and hacks off her arms and legs and reduces her body to a phallic lump. The psychotic Funakoshi then dissolves himself into maternal darkness by committing suicide.

Considered to be one of Masumura's most outrageous pictures and foreshadowing Oshima's *Ai no Corrida* (1976), the film's horror is grounded in the obscene immediacy with which it figures some of cinema's most fundamental fantasies: the image as source of erotic gratification; the fictional world evoked as a darkened, enclosed fantasy box. It exposes the foundation of scopophilia upon the very impossibility of tactile contact with an object of desire, the look substituting for touch, graphically and ironically represented in the film by a sightless couple wallowing in an orgy of touch which somehow never quite reaches what it looks for and the fetishization of the female body which underpins the star image. In fact, after the scene has been set and motifs announced in the opening sequences (Midori responds as Funakoshi caresses a statue she modelled for), the narrative virtually comes to a stop as a repetitiously oneiric logic takes over, replaying with increasing desperation the impossibility of conveying touch through sight. The only element that spoils this otherwise impeccably nightmarish picture is the superfluous dialogue.

d Yasuzo Masumura *p* Masaichi Nagata *s* Yoshio Shirasoka *c* Setsuo Kobayashi *lp* Eiji Funakoshi, Mako Midori, Noriko Sengoku

Multiple Maniacs

(FILM-MAKERS CO-OP) 94min

As much an 'underground' movie as a horror film, *Multiple Maniacs* owes as much to the Warhol aesthetic as to Herschell Gordon Lewis, to whose **2000 Maniacs** (1964) Waters' title pays obvious homage. As Waters himself put it, 'I discovered his monstrous trilogy **Blood Feast**, **2000 Maniacs** and **Colour Me Blood Red** at my local drive-in. And when I saw the

Eiji Funakoshi as the blind sculptor and Mako Midori as the model he kidnaps in the deliriously fetishistic Moju.

teenage couples hopping from their cars to vomit, I knew I had found a director after my own heart'. But as well as relating backwards to Warhol, the film also relates forward to the punk sensibility which was to 'discover' Lewis. As Waters put it: 'during the late sixties I felt like a fish out of water. As the rest of my generation babbled about peace and love I stood back, puzzled, and fantasized about the beginning of the "hate generation". Woodstock was the last straw. Sitting in the mud with a bunch of naked hippies and their illegitimate children and listening to Joan Baez was hardly my idea of a good time. Violence was this generation's sacrilege, so I wanted to make a film that would glorify carnage and mayhem for laughs ... I always referred to *Multiple Maniacs* as my "celluloid atrocity". Even though it's technically primitive and the actors sometimes forget their lines, it's still my favourite of all my films. I like its meanness and harsh documentary look'.

The making of the film also coincided with the Manson murders, and before Manson was revealed as the guilty party Waters wanted to have the film's star, Divine, take credit for the murders during the film. As the director put it 'we wanted to "scare the world", just like the unheard-of Manson family, but we used a movie camera instead of deadly weapons'. The film centres on the havoc wreaked on Baltimore (Waters' home town) when Lady Divine's Cavalcade of Perversions – a travelling show whose patrons are trapped, robbed and occasionally murdered by the Lady herself – arrives. The women who staff the show are modelled on the amazing trio in Russ Meyer's *Faster Pussycat! Kill! Kill!* (1965). Though pretty gross and *outré*, *Multiple Maniacs* is actually better when read about in Waters' autobiography *Shock Value* than when seen on screen (in the case of Lewis, precisely the reverse is the case).

The film was originally made in 16mm.

d/p/s/c John Waters *lp* Divine, David Lochary, Mink Stole, Cookie Mueller, Mary Vivian Pearce, Edith Massey, Susan Lowe

Night after Night (DUDLEY BIRCH FILMS; GB) 88min

This sleazy film extends a scene in Lindsay Anderson's *If ...* (1968) into a whole movie. May is the stern judge who turns out to be a Jack the Ripper figure in his spare time, murdering scores of women, including the wife (Marlowe) of the policeman (Wynne) who unmasks him in the end. Anderson's facile indignation – the judge getting his bottom whipped in chambers – is here elaborated further, providing the judge with a secret room full of kinky photographs and equipment where he dons leather gear and a wig. The cast also features a clerk of the court (Scully) who reads pornography and a rapist (Sumpter) whose main function is to be a red herring. Force's direction is crude, the script silly and the picture tedious.

d Lewis J. Force *p* James Mellor *c* Dail Ambler *s* Douglas Hill *lp* Jack May, Justine Lord, Gilbert Wynne, Linda Marlowe, Terry Scully, Donald Sumpter, Peter Forbes-Robertson, Jacqueline Clerk, Carol Haddon, April Harlow

Night of Bloody Horror

(CINEMA IV/TASTE OF BLOOD INC) 89(87)min

Very much an imitation of **Psycho** (1960), *Night of Bloody Horror* has Wesley (McRaney) prone to blackouts since accidentally killing his brother Jonathan as a child. When his girlfriends start to die violent deaths McRaney becomes a prime suspect and, on account of his blackouts, is unable to clear himself. Eventually the culprit is revealed to be his mother Agatha (Hendricks), who is trying to punish him for the childhood accident and who now keeps the mummified corpses of the dead child and husband (who committed suicide after the tragedy) concealed in her sanctum.

Filmed in 16mm 'Violent Vision' in New Orleans, and fairly gruesome for its time (eye gouging, axeing, meat-cleaver mutilations), the film is beset with flashy stylistic pretensions (green whorls denoting blackouts, superimpositions, montages of stills, split-screen, shock-cuts, and so on) that perfectly match the cheap, crude psychology underlying the script.

d/p/co-s Joy N. Houck Jnr *co-s/c* Robert A. Weaver *lp* Gerald McRaney, Gaye Yellen, Evelyn Hendricks, Herbert Nelson, Lisa Dameron, Charlotte White, Nicholous R. Krieger, Michael Anthony, Burt Robert, Gordon Ogden

Nightmare in Wax *aka* **Crimes in the Wax Museum**
(A AND E FILM CORP) 91min
Vince Renard (Mitchell), a makeup artist at Paragon Studios until he had a fight with studio boss Max Black (Kroeger) which left him scarred for life, now owns a wax museum famed for its lifelike figures, four of whom represent Paragon players who have mysteriously disappeared. It transpires that Mitchell embalmed the players alive, and is waiting his chance to add Kroeger and his fiancée (Helm) to the collection. Eventually the 'waxworks' are restored to a semblance of life and force Mitchell into a vat of boiling wax.

Filmed at the Movieland Wax Museum in Los Angeles, *Nightmare in Wax* does its best with the limited wax-museum theme and builds to an effective enough climax. However, the overall impression is one of time-spinning and the film is no match for either **Mystery of the Wax Museum** (1933) or **House of Wax** (1953).

d Bud Townsend *p* Martin B. Cohen *s* Rex Carlton *c* Glen Smith *lp* Cameron Mitchell, Anne Helm, Scott Brady, Barry Kroeger, Victoria Carrol, Phillip Baird, Johnny Cardos, Hollis Morrison, James Forrest

The Oblong Box (AIP; GB) scope 91min
This picture was begun by Michael Reeves, who died during the production, and completed, with honourable results, by Hessler. The script, officially derived from Edgar Allan Poe's *Premature Burial*, but actually closer to Kipling's *The Mark of the Beast*, is a somewhat contrived combination of Burke and Hare with echoes of Jack the Ripper and *The Phantom of the Opera*. The most interesting aspect is that, as in **The Reptile** (1966) and **The Mummy** (1959), yet again, like a guilty conscience, the evils of British colonialism come home to haunt and destroy its perpetrators. Sir Edward Markham (Williamson) is horribly disfigured by Africans as retribution for his brother, Julian's (Price), nonchalant murder of a black child. Held prisoner in the gloomy family mansion, Williamson escapes by feigning death, but is double-crossed and buried alive. Graverobbers deliver his coffin to Dr Neuhartt (Lee) and Williamson blackmails the doctor into sheltering him while, cloaked in a scarlet mask, he embarks on a vicious revenge spree as he becomes increasingly demented. Before dying, he bites his brother's hand, transmitting a ghastly disease.

The film, which features the first co-starring appearance by Lee and Price, is surprisingly effective, though over-elaborate, and is excellently photographed by Coquillon. Christopher Wicking, the writer of Hessler's next movie (**Scream and Scream Again**, 1969), completed the script written by Huntington, a veteran director of below-average movies including *Tower of Terror* (1941) and **The Vulture** (1966), who died in 1968.

d/p Gordon Hessler *s* Lawrence Huntington *c* John Coquillon *lp* Vincent Price, Christopher Lee, Alastair Williamson, Hilary Dwyer, Peter Arne, Harry Baird, Rupert Davies, Sally Geeson, Carl Rigg, Maxwell Shaw, Uta Levka

El Processo de las Brujas *aka* **El Juez Sangriento** *aka* **Il Trono di Fuoco** *aka* **Der Hexentoeter von Blackmoor** *aka* **The Bloody Judge** *aka* **The Witch Killer of Blackmoor** *aka* **Night of the Blood Monster** *aka* **Throne of the Blood Monster** *aka* **The Witches Trial** *aka* **The Trial of the Witches**
(PRODIMEX FILMS/FENIX FILMS/TERRA FILMKUNST; SP,IT,WG) scope 98(82)min
Franco's version of Michael Reeves' **The Witchfinder General** (1968) features Lee as the notorious 17th-century Lord Chancellor, Judge Jeffreys, a dissolute and depraved character who mercilessly persecuted 'witches' and presided over judicial slaughter on behalf of James II. The plot mixes rebellion, torture and romance as Seften (Hass) falls in love with Charity (Rohm), the sister of a woman (Schell) burnt at the stake. When the Monmouth rebellion fails, Rohm ends up in Jeffreys' clutches and submits to his demands to save her lover. But the perfidious Judge and his assistant (Quesada) keep her prisoner anyway. Eventually, William of Orange's victory puts an end to Jeffreys' reign and Quesada is gruesomely killed by his former victims. Apparently, extra torture scenes were inserted after Lee's departure from the film, which may account for the movie's lack of structure and rhythm. Lee is good as the complex but vicious central figure, but the additional scenes together with Franco's insistent use of the zoom lens spoil the picture.

Franco shot six features in the year 1969-70, including **Venus in Furs**, **De Sade 70** and **El Conde Dracula** (both 1970), all produced by Towers. Some sources list George Sanders and Pier Angeli among the cast, but they didn't participate in the film as released. Franco again featured Judge Jeffreys in his **Les Démons** (1972).

d/co-s Jesús Franco *p* Harry Alan Towers *co-s* E. Colombo, Peter Welbeck (Harry Alan Towers) *c* Manuel Merino *lp* Christopher Lee, Maria Schell, Maria Rohm, Hans Hass, Leo Genn, Margaret Lee, Howard Vernon, Dennis Price, Milo Quesada, Diana Lorys

La Residencia *aka* **The House That Screamed** *aka* **The Boarding School**
(ANABEL FILMS; SP) scope 104(76)min
Like **Psycho** (1960), this glossily produced effort, set in a French boarding school for difficult girls, concentrates on the mother-son relationship of a pair of psychopaths. Fourneau (Palmer) keeps admonishing her son, Luis (Moulder Brown) not to get involved with the girls and to save himself for someone more 'decent' like herself. The literal-minded son proceeds to kill the women he feels attracted to and, alone in his laboratory, uses what he takes to be his victim's 'good bits' to construct, Frankenstein-fashion, his ideal woman. When his mother discovers his hobby and the array of dead women, he locks her in with his creation.

The Oblong Box, *begun by Michael Reeves and completed by Gordon Hessler after Reeves' death.*

The offensively misogynist La Residencia.

Besides the gorily shot slasher murders, a subplot involving a sadistic headgirl (Maude), and flagellations – usually followed by prayer sessions – visited upon a newcomer (Galbo) were inserted for extra box-office appeal. These scenes are only tenuously linked to the story of Moulder Brown, in that he's a peeping tom too. The glossy veneer of the movie masks a cynically sexploitative approach, making it more offensively misogynist than Jesús Franco's sadean pictures which do not seek to cloak sexploitation under a veneer of art respectability and gestures towards psychological 'realism'.

d Narcisco Ibañez Serrador *p* Arturo Gonzalez *s* Luis Verna Penafiel *c* Manuel Berenguer *lp* Lilli Palmer, Christina Galbo, John Moulder Brown, Mary Maude, Candida Losada, Tomas Blanco, Pauline Challoner, Maribel Martin, Conchita Paredes

Scream and Scream Again *aka* **Screamer**
(AIP/AMICUS; GB) scope 95min
Fritz Lang praised Hessler's third, but first major, horror movie, possibly because the depiction of an impersonal, highly technological Big Brother state is reminiscent of Lang's own *Spione* (1927), *Metropolis* (1926) and Mabuse films, and the persistent cop who finds but who can't defeat the evil at the top, is familiar from *The Big Heat* (1953). But such praise is not entirely justified by the confused script, based on Peter Saxon's novel, *The Disorientated Man*, which deals with a group of humanoids taking over European governments. The naïvely paranoid politics of the script are made irrelevant by the fragmentation of the narrative threads, which break the film up into some effectively staged but isolated fantasy sequences, anticipating the shock sequences later adopted by splatter movies. Ironically and probably unintentionally, the plot deals with the growth of totalitarian control systems stitching society up into a seamless whole while the film as a narrative structure speaks of utter disintegration and loss of control, reflected even in the motifs of organ transplants and amputations strewn across the story.

Dr Browning (Price), a mad scientist, conducts the operations in his modern clinic with an acid vat nearby to dispose of any unwanted transplants. One of his creatures (Gothard) goes berserk and commits grisly vampiric murders, thereby attracting the attention of the police. The pathologist, Sorel (Mathews), outlives the climactic slaughter as Price and Konratz (Jones), a foreign humanoid who wishes to keep the group's activities secret at all costs, get dunked in the acid vats only to find that the chief of British intelligence, Fremont (Lee), is a humanoid too. The film's best sequence is the excitingly shot chase – during which Gothard tears off his own hand to escape from handcuffs – that culminates in his self-destruction as he dives into the ever-present vat of acid. The opening sets the tone with apparently unrelated scenes: a brutal rape and vampiric murder, a young man who keeps waking up in a hospital to find yet another of his limbs missing, and a foreign politician dying. Each sequence is well handled, but they remain separate incidents. Unlike **The Sorcerers** (1967), which successfully mixed horror and science fiction, Hessler's picture works more like a patchwork of motifs derived from different genres, as if the tendency towards disintegration also affected the generic framework at a time when the Hammer horror style seemed to have run its course, and the body-in-pieces fantasy of gore movies hadn't yet caught hold of the genre.

Shot by the excellent cinematographer of **The Witchfinder General** (1968), this was the only picture which united Price, Lee and Cushing, although the latter had very little screentime. Hessler's next film, **Cry of the Banshee** (1970), confirmed the director's flair for individual shots but inability to come to grips with the complexities of an extended fantasy process; his best work in the genre is **Murders in the Rue Morgue** (1971).

d Gordon Hessler *p* Max J. Rosenberg, Milton Subotsky *c* Christopher Wicking *c* John Coquillon *lp* Vincent Price, Christopher Lee, Peter Cushing, Alfred Marks, Christopher Matthews, Anthony Newlands, Peter Sallis, David Lodge, Uta Levka, Judy Bloom, Marshall Jones, Michael Gothard, Yutte Stensgaard, Julian Holloway

Um Sonho de Vampiros *aka* **A Vampire's Dream**
(SER-CINE; BRAZIL) 80min
Cavalcanti's second feature tries to offer a carnivalesque equivalent of Roman Polanski's **The Dance of the Vampires** (1967). Dr Pan (Ankito), a nonentity, is visited by Death and given the choice between dying or becoming a vampire. Opting for a vampire's life which allows him to indulge all his dreams of power, he proceeds to vampirize all the city's notables including the vicar, a soldier, a factory owner, and so on, and

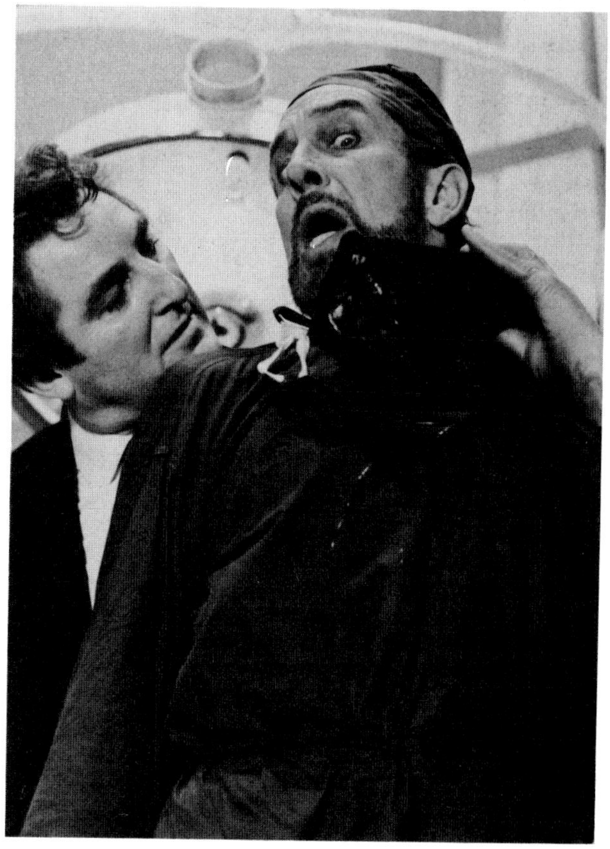

Right: *The impressive* Scream and Scream Again.

orgiastic pandemonium takes hold of the town. A young couple (Chermoni and Costa) provide the focus for audience identification as they try to escape the vampiric advances made to them. Played as a grotesque comedy, the picture loses whatever satiric thrust it may have had and disintegrates into a succession of exuberantly played, usually sexist and rarely funny gags. Direction and cinematography are equally inhibited, as is Carlos Prieto's makeup of the undead.

d/p/s Ibere Cavalcanti *c* Renato Neumann *lp* Ankito, Irma Alvarez, Janet Chermoni, Sonelia Costa, Augusto Mala Filho, Robson Bob, Janira Santiago, Zuza Curi, Tuna Espinheira, Jorge Dias, Simon Khouri

Taste the Blood of Dracula

(HAMMER; GB) scope 95min

A year after **Dracula Has Risen from the Grave** (1968), Hammer produced this intriguing tale which for the first time locates Dracula squarely within the culture that codified the legend, Victorian England. It tells of the depraved Lord Courtley (Bates – a poor substitute for Cushing, though soon to become Hammer's leading man), possessor of the Count's relics in a phial of dried blood, who resurrects Dracula (Lee) in a prolonged, dramatically shot ritual in a derelict church. The three Victorian gentlemen (Keen, Carson and Sallis), out for fun and getting more than they bargained for, flee the church, leaving the corpse of Bates behind. The Count revenges the death of his servant by seducing the insipid children of the three (Corlan, Hayden and Blair) and having them kill their own hypocritical fathers, making this the first Dracula film since Fisher launched the series which explicitly designates the Count as standing for the forces that threaten the laboriously constructed ideal of the Victorian family; he represents an aristocratic, spendthrift notion of sexuality which must be repressed if the family is to survive. The Count's fascinating powers transform the two nauseating daughters into passionately sensual creatures, writhing in ecstasy on their idol's tombstone and gleefully staking the man who came to stake the vampire. Dracula is destroyed as he cuts himself slashing the cobwebbed church's stained-glass windows which feature a cross.

This was the Hungarian-born Sasdy's first feature, though he had done successful work in TV, and suggested that a worthy successor to Fisher might have been found. His flamboyant romanticism, luscious colours and elegantly stylish camera movements and placings promised well. His next films (**Countess Dracula**, 1970 and **Hands of the Ripper**, 1971) confirmed him as one of the few directors working in Britain who prized cinematic values over literary ones. Unfortunately, his later work (such as **I Don't Want to Be Born**, 1975) has been disappointing.

Dracula's next outing was the tired **The Scars of Dracula** (1970).

d Peter Sasdy *p* Aida Young *s* John Elder (Anthony Hinds) *c* Arthur Grant *se* Les Bowie *lp* Christopher Lee, Linda Hayden, Isla Blair, Anthony Corlan, Geoffrey Keen, Peter Sallis, John Carson, Ralph Bates, Michael Ripper

La Vampire Nue *aka* The Naked Vampire

(LES FILMS ABC; FR) 90(79)min

After the promising, but far from perfect, **Le Viol du Vampire**(1967), Rollin made this, his second vampire fantasy, in colour. The convoluted storyline, reminiscent of the silent serials he admired, mixes elements of horror and science fiction. The hero (Martin) becomes involved with a young woman dressed in diaphanous robes. This leads to adventures with a sect given to performing suicide rituals, a group of vampires in an old castle, men wearing deer and bird masks, women wearing spikey ornaments on their nipples, and so on. The film's visual highlights include shots of nightlit streets which evoke the paintings of André Delvaux, or tableaux à la Max Ernst (a strong influence on Rollin) often using spotlights to achieve vivid contrasts and shadowy outlines, as well as backlighting to make women's dresses translucent. The picture is most fascinating if seen as an intensely fetishistic but luscious play of textures punctuated by beautifully stylized, extravagantly romantic comic-strip compositions chronicling the obsessions of a guiltily catholic voyeur, wallowing in a sense of perversion and sin. Unfortunately, the narrative pace slows after a while, thereby also diminishing the impact of the pop aesthetics. The acting is still refreshingly one-dimensional, as befits comic-strip characters, and doesn't interfere with the moments of visual delight scattered throughout the movie. His next film, **Le Frisson des Vampires** (1970) adopted a more conventional plot.

d/p/co-s Jean Rollin *co-s* S. H. Mosti *c* Jean-Jacques Remon *lp* Oliver Martin, Maurice Lemaitre, Caroline Cartier, Ly Letrong, Bernard Musson, Jean Aron, Michel Delahaye, Ursule Pauly, Nicole Isimat, Christine François

Christopher Lee surrounded by his loving acolytes, Linda Hayden and Isla Blair, in Taste the Blood of Dracula.

La Venganza de las Mujeres Vampiro *aka* Santo en la Venganza de las Mujeres Vampiro *aka* The Vengeance of the Vampire Women

(CINEMATOGRAFICA FLAMA/PELICULAS LATINOAMERICANAS; MEX) 90min

Curiel's efforts here fail to recapture the weirdly fascinating narrative delirium of Alfonso Corona Blake's *Santo contra las Mujeres Vampiro* (1962). The vampire countess Mayra (Romand), the hulk's arch-enemy because he happens to be the last descendant of the man who impaled her Transylvanian ancestors in 1630, is revived by the mad Dr Brancor (Junco). While she recruits an army of both sexes, he concocts a creature, Frankenstein-fashion, called Razos (Leon). Santo saves an attractive journalist, Papi (Lazareno) from a fate worse than death, takes Leon apart and terminates Junco by blowing up his laboratory before burning and staking the vampires.

By this time, Santo's films had become more 'adult' in their iconography, although most of his outings were still aimed at a childish audience. His next opponents in the horror genre included a return engagement with Dracula in *Santo y Blue*

Demon contra Dracula y el Hombre Lobo (1970), a bout with several monstrous creatures in *Santo contra los Asesinos de Otros Mundos* (1971), two encounters with mummies, *Santo contra las Momias* and *La Venganza de la Momia* (both 1971) and one with another threatening female, **Santo contra la Hija de Frankenstein** (1971). Huerta, who had started his career as a film star in the fifties, is said to have been replaced by his son is the more energetic fight scenes, although a Brazilian source suggests that Eric del Castillo, the vampire of **El Imperio de Dracula** (1966), played Santo in at least one of the series.

d Federico Curiel *p/co-s* Garcia Besne *co-s* Fernando Oses *c* José Ortiz Ramos *lp* Santo (Rodolfo Guzmán Huerta), Aldo Monti, Norma Lazareno, Gina Romand, Victor Junco, Patricia Ferrer, Carlos Suarez, Alfonso Munguia, Yolanda Ponce, Nathaniel Leon (Frankenstein)

Venus in Furs *aka* Black Angel *aka* Paroxismus *aka* Puo una Morta Rivivere per Amore? *aka* Venuz im Pelz

(TOWERS OF LONDON/TERRA FILMKUNST/CINEPRODUZIONI ASSOCIATE; GB,IT,WG) 86min

The late sixties saw three versions of Sacher Masoch's infamous book, all called *Venus in Furs*: Joe Marzano's US version (1967), an Italo-German one by Massimo Dallamano (1968) and Franco's, which is by far the best. With a slow, dreamlike style reminiscent of **Necronomicon** (1967), the film tells the story of a jazz trumpet player (Darren) who finds the naked, mutilated body of Wanda (Rohm) washed ashore on a Turkish beach. He seems to recall, or fantasize, having seen her as the victim of a sadistic trio (Kinski, Price and Lee) in an isolated mansion, finishing their cruel orgy with a necrophiliac finale. Darren tries to escape his obsession by fleeing to Rio where he takes up with a singer (McNair), but Rohm, nude except for a silver mink, panties and stockings, appears again and causes the death of her tormentors. Darren eventually follows her to a cemetery where she disappears, leaving the mink lying on her grave. As in *Necronomicon*, the constant merging of dream and reality with oneiric slow-motion shots and fluid camera movements, transitions and superimpositions, works very well and is shattered only by the crude money-saving inserts of tourist-board shots. Similarly, Darren's voice-over narration and dialogue lines are a constant irritant.

German and Italian prints credit Hans B. Billian, a genuine German director whose name Franco sometimes borrowed when there was German production money involved, as director. The jazz score was contributed by Manfred Mann and Mike Hugg. The Italian version, in black and white, was adapted by Bruno Leder, Carlo Fadda and Milo G. Cuccia.

d/co-s Jess (Jesús) Franco *p* Harry Alan Towers *co-s* Malvin Wald *c* Angelo Lotti *se* Howard A. Anderson *lp* Maria Rohm, James Darren, Barbara McNair, Klaus Kinski, Dennis Price, Margaret Lee, Paul Mueller, Jesús Franco, Adolfo Lastretti, Mirella Pamphili

What Ever Happened to Aunt Alice?

(ASSOCIATES AND ALDRICH/PALOMAR PICTURES) 101min

This third slice of Grand Guignol from the Aldrich company, despite the title, is closer in spirit to **Hush ... Hush Sweet Charlotte** (1965) than to **What Ever Happened to Baby Jane?** (1962). Page is terrific as a crazed *grande dame*, left only a stamp album when her husband dies, who solves the problem of living up to her station by murdering a succession of housekeepers and appropriating their savings. She meets her match when Gordon takes the job, looking for a missing colleague (Dunnock). It's not that she doesn't manage another murder (she does), but that Gordon gives her a fine run for her money in the extravagance stakes. Not particularly well directed but admirably uncluttered and done with ghoulish relish, the film boasts fine camerawork by Biroc, who makes a memorable image of Page's garden blooming in the Arizona desert, each tree fertilized by a body beneath.

d Lee H. Katzin *p* Robert Aldrich *s* Theodore Apstein *c* Joseph Biroc *lp* Geraldine Page, Ruth Gordon, Rosemary Forsyth, Robert Fuller, Mildred Dunnock, Joan Huntington

Yotsuya Kaidan – Oiwa no Borei *aka* The Curse of the Ghosts

(DAIEI; JAP) scope 94min

Previous film versions of Tsuruya's kabuki play, including Nakagawa's **Tokaido Yotsuya Kaidan** (1959), Kinoshita's **Shinshaku Yotsuya Kaidan** (1949) and Toyoda's **Yotsuya Kaidan** (1965), had offered varying approaches to the central character, the vagabond samurai Iemon. Mori locates his Iemon (Sato) explicitly in the context of a wantonly autocratic regime: the beautiful Oiwa (Inano) is married to Iemon and her sister Osode (Mikage) is betrothed to another samurai (Aoyama), but her entire family is reduced to poverty when the shogunate arbitrarily disbands their lord's clan, forcing the two men to take to the road in search of new employers. Arranging for the daughter of a rich merchant to be attacked so that he may rescue her and enter the employ of her father, Iemon finds the lady falling in love with him. Encouraged by the merchant, he then trades his samurai honour for wealth and decides to poison his wife. Her ghost returns to drive Iemon insane, setting him off on a murderous rampage until he succumbs to the attacks of Mikage and her husband. The final sequences in the swamp as the ghost harasses the sword-wielding Iemon achieve the required hallucinatory effect although Sato, a martial arts actor, can't match the demonic intensity brought to the part by Nakadai in Toyoda's version.

d Issei Mori *p* Masaichi Nagata *s* Kinya Naoi *c* Senkichiro Takeda *lp* Kei Sato, Kazuko Inano, Yoshihiko Aoyama, Kyoko Mikage, Shoji Kobayashi, Sonosuke Sawamura

Ruth Gordon prepares to sell her life dearly in What Ever Happened to Aunt Alice?

The 1970s

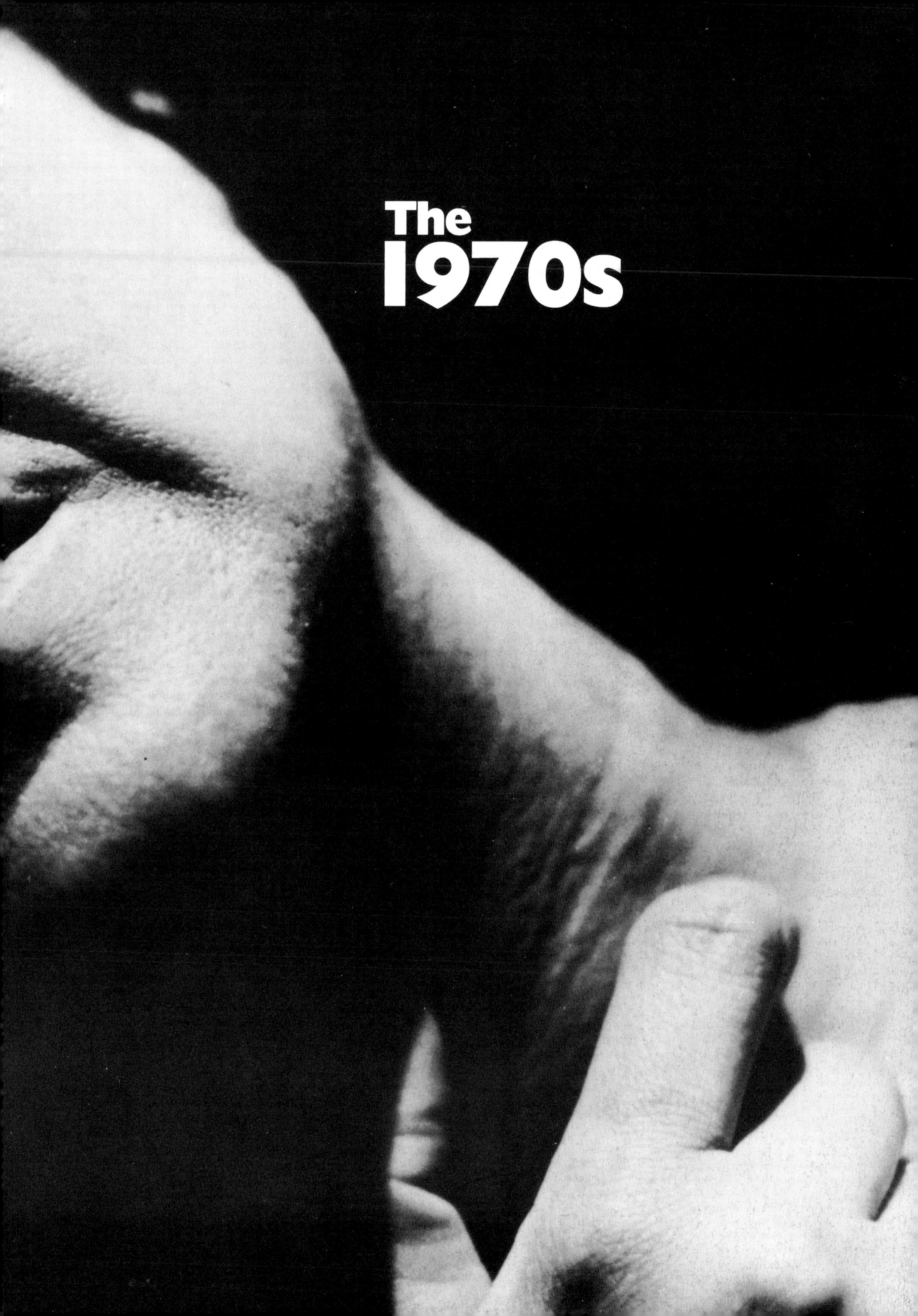

Big and Small Budgets, Horror Goes Up and Down Market

In the twenties and early thirties, the horror film had achieved a degree of respectability. Since then, notwithstanding the genre's renaissance in the sixties, Hollywood had frowned on it and accordingly rarely committed big names or budgets to horror movies. All this changed following the enormous success of **Rosemary's Baby** (1968). Interestingly, most of the big budget films, such as **The Exorcist** (1973) and **The Omen** (1976) and their various sequels, were highly conservative in tone. Studiedly respectable, they approached horror from a religious perspective, literally playing on their audience's loss of faith (though in comparison to **La Casa dalle Finestre che Ridono**, 1976, their concern with religion was shallow to say the least). However, this didn't stop them delivering highly realistic, and decidedly gory, shock sequences whose major difference to similar scenes in exploitation films was that exploitation directors had to make do with unknowns rather than stars.

The other difference, of course, was that few of the exploitation films had any informing context beyond the theme of women/girls-in-peril that made its first appearence in Dario Argento's psycho-slasher movie **L'Uccello dalle Piume di Cristallo** (1970) and reached its climax in John Carpenter's superior **Halloween** (1978) – which in turn spawned a slew of American teenagers-in-peril movies. These disturbing films were closely modelled on Alfred Hitchcock's **Psycho** (1960), though in the case of Argento and his followers the influence of Hitchcock-imitator William Castle seems stronger. In a similar manner, just as the up-market success of *The Exorcist* spawned several sequels and imitations, so the slew of down-market European zombie/cannibal movies were all derived from George Romero's **Night of the Living Dead** (1968).

By far the most significant strand of horror film-making in the seventies was the genuinely subversive strain of American rural gothic films, best represented by the influential **The Texas Chainsaw Massacre** (1974) and **The Hills Have Eyes** (1977). In contrast to the conservatism of both the big budget and pure exploitation shockers, these films marked the first radical break in the development of the American horror film and, as the debate about 'video nasties' made clear, in doing so re-discovered the power of the horror film to shock and amaze audiences.

1970

Previous pages: *The visceral horror of the seventies:* Schizo *(1976).*

The Beast in the Cellar *aka* Are You Dying, Young Man? *aka* Young Man, I Think You're Dying

(TIGON BRITISH/LEANDER FILMS; GB) 101(87)min

In marked contrast to the classic *Arsenic and Old Lace* (1944), TV scenarist turned director Kelly plays the notion of a pair of sweet but gruesome old ladies (Reid and Robson) for real gore. Having immured their brother (Havard) in the cellar to prevent him from going to war in the thirties, when he goes mad, breaks through an outside wall and embarks on a series of savagely brutal killings, they are forced to attempt to cover up the results, which they do with a chillingly callous impassivity. The mechanics of suspense are deployed with routine efficiency and a homage to **Nosferatu** (1921) is attempted with a shot of a talon's shadow on the wall as the 'thing' in the cellar lurks behind the banisters, but the atmosphere is dissipated by the laboured performances, a badly constructed script which pointlessly elaborates the simplest encounters and the perfunctory introduction of sniggering bawdiness in the barn to boost the picture's box-office appeal.

d/s James Kelly *p* Graham Harris *c* Harry Waxman, Desmond Dickinson *lp* Beryl Reid, Flora Robson, Tessa Wyatt, John Hamill, T. P. McKenna, David Dodimead, Christopher Chittell, Peter Craze, Dafydd Havard, Vernon Dobtcheff

Beast of the Yellow Night

(FOUR ASSOCIATES PRODUCTION; PHIL) scope 87min

In this offbeat version of the Jekyll and Hyde story, the Devil saves Ashley from death on condition that he becomes his disciple and a guinea pig to a group of satanists: upon the death of each man, he is to inherit that person's evil characteristics, thus gradually becoming a condensation of different people's unpleasant sides. This also makes him look somewhat unsightly as he goes about killing prostitutes. An encounter with a blind man who confesses that his torment is precisely the possession of a soul instead of the lack of one, leads to Ashley's salvation. However, Ashley isn't a sufficiently good actor to convey the complexities of a character that is supposed to be a collection of different personalities while Romero's direction does not provide the necessary relief from the cod theology and the pedestrian action.

d/co-p/s Eddie Romero *co-p* John Ashley *lp* John Ashley, Mary Wilcox, Eddie Garcia, Leopoldo Salcedo, Ken Metcalf, Vic Diaz, Andres Centenera

Flora Robson (left) and Beryl Reid as the little old ladies who cover up for their brother, The Beast in the Cellar.

unrelenting. Amid the welter of thoroughly unpalatable characters, Grahame as the orphanage superintendent is awesome in her matter-of-fact portrayal of human depravity.

d Philip Gilbert *co-p/s* Gil Lasky *co-p* Ed Carlin *c* Paul Hipp *lp* Gloria Grahame, Melody Patterson, Milton Selzer, Len Lesser, Vic Tayback, Terri Messina, Ronald Taft, Dennis Christopher, Peter Armstrong, Maggie Corey

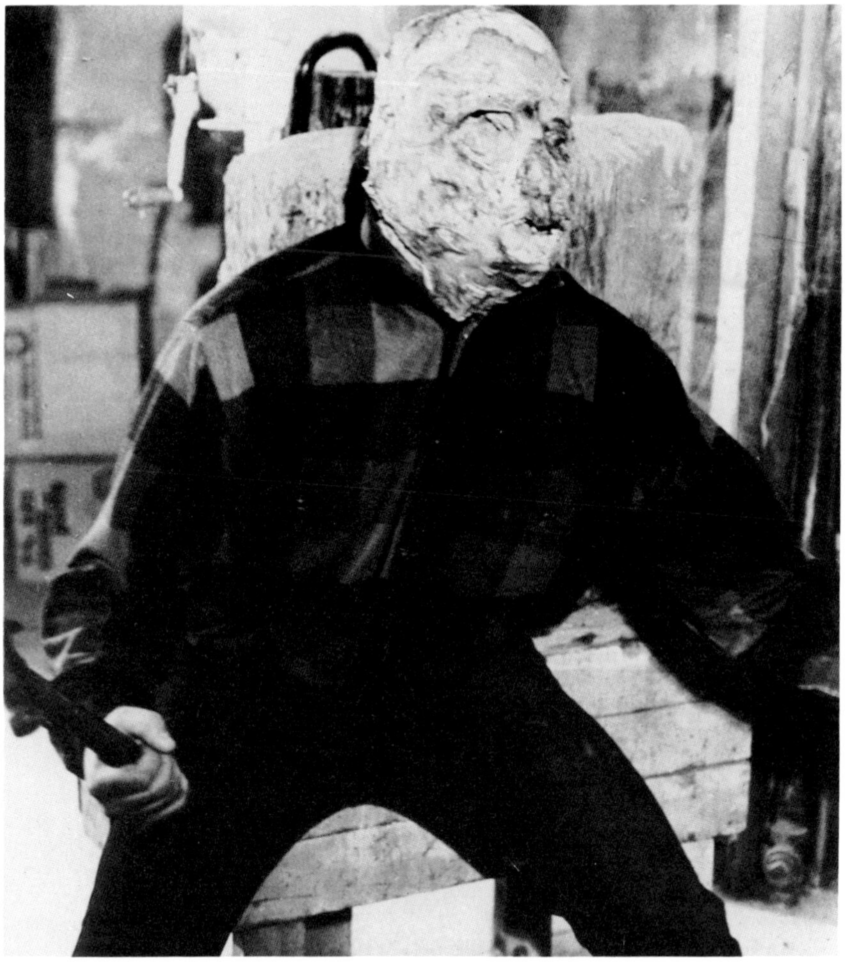

Above: Blood and Lace, *one of the most graphic American horror films of the seventies.*

Beiss Mich, Liebling *aka* **Bite Me Darling**
(NEW ART FILM; WG) 102(85)min
This moronic sex comedy features a postman (Jordan) with a limitless ability to make love and a psychiatrist who grows fangs out of frustration since women seem to prefer the postman's way of treating their problems. The happy ending is provided by Renzi who puts a stop to the proceedings by marrying the hero. Foernbacher specialized in this sort of entertainment and merely introduced vampirism as a desperate gimmick to vary the usual gropings. Fuchs brings a modicum of enthusiasm to his part as the postman's grumbling boss. The German cinema repeated the soft-core Dracula formula with **Graf Dracula Beisst Jetzt in Oberbayern** (1979), which was called originally *Dracula Sucks* in English until the makers became aware of Philip Marshak's hard-core movie starring Jamie Gillis with the same title.

d/p/co-s Helmut Foernbacher *co-s* Martin Roda Becher, W. H. Riedl *c* Igor Luther *lp* Patrick Jordan, Herbert Fuchs, Eva Renzi, Dieter Augustin, Brigitte Skay, Ralf Wolter, Were Frydtberg, Barbara Valentin, Hannsi Linder, Frederick Pressel

Blood and Lace
(CONTEMPORARY FILM-MAKERS/CARLIN CO) 87min
The daughter of a murdered prostitute is sent to an orphanage which, unbeknown to the authorities is run by two brutal sadists who murder those of their charges who try to run away and store their bodies in the freezer. For its time remarkably graphic and unrelenting, *Blood and Lace* has been compared favourably with de Sade for its unflinching, unrelieved catalogue of psychopathology which includes incest, starvation, death by hammer blows, blackmail, rape and torture. An atmosphere of stark, one-dimensional gloom prevails, and the attack on the hypocrisy of small-town America is absolutely

Bloodthirsty Butchers (MISHKIN) 79min
While Milligan was in London making **The Body Beneath** (1970) for Cinemania he also made *Bloodthirsty Butchers* and *Curse of the Full Moon* on 16mm for his old producer, Mishkin. Basically a retelling of the Sweeney Todd story – with Keller in the Todd role – this is one of Milligan's best-known films and is probably his most explicitly gory work, though apparently Mishkin cut out some of the more gruesome scenes.

d/co-s/c Andy Milligan *p* William Mishkin *co-s* John Borske *lp* John Miranda, Annabella Wood, Berwick Kaller

Chi o Suu Ningyo *aka* **Yureiyashiki no Kyofu-Chi Wo Suu Ningyo** *aka* **The Night of the Vampire**
(TOHO; JAP) scope 71min
With this picture Toho made a bid to take over the Kaidan Eiga genre from the Daiei studio which was going bankrupt. The film starts with Kazuhiko (Nakamura) disappearing while visiting his lover, Yuko (Kobayashi) in her old mansion. His sister, Keiko (Matsuo) and her friend (Nakao) go to investigate. Seeing Kobayashi wandering in the garden at night, they also discover she is supposed to have died long ago. In a flashback, the story of the family curse unfolds, including the rape of Kobayashi's mother at the end of the war by Dr Yamaguchi (Usami) and the subsequent birth of the unfortunate Kobayashi. Later, her mother made a pact with the devil to ensure the child's survival after an accident, but she survives only as an undead vampire intent on taking revenge against a world that treated her unkindly. In the end she attacks Matsuo but kills her own father in the process, breaking the spell and causing her body to crumble into dust.

Yamamoto manages to achieve a few atmospheric scenes but his attempt at a mixture of Japanese ghost-story elements and the Judeo-Christian vampire myth doesn't really work. His next movie, **Chi o Suu Me** (1971), was a straightforward Dracula tale.

d Michio Yamamoto *p* Tomoyuki Tanaka, Fumio Tanaka *s* Ei Ogawa, Hiroshi Nagano *c* Kazutami Hara *lp* Kayo Matsuo, Akira Nakao, Yukiko Kobayashi, Yoko Minazake, Atsuo Nakamura, Junya Usami, Itaru Takashima, Sachio Sakai, Jun Hamamura, Kinzo Sekiguchi

Cinque Bambole per la Luna d'Agosto *aka* **Five Dolls for an August Moon**
(PRODUZIONI ATLAS CINEMATOGRAFICA; IT) 88(81)min
Saddled with the plot of *The Ten Little Niggers*, which he hated, Bava shows his disinterest by allowing the story to degenerate into incomprehensibility. An inventor, a series of potential investors, their wives, lovers and servants gather in a castle by a beach where they are killed off. Most of the bodies wind up in the deep freeze wrapped in plastic bags and hung amid other chunks of meat. Bava relieves the boredom with some weird, excellently composed images – the sudden emergence of a man wearing a golden, scarlet plumed demon mask, a glittering silvery stole being slowly dragged through a room by a mysterious hand – and the murders are picturesque and testify to his stylish sense of colour.

The companion pieces to this picture are the virtually plotless **Ecologia del Delitto** (1971) and the grotesquely oedipal **Una Hacha para la Luna de Miel** (1969). At this time, the giallo films Bava had perfected with **Sei Donne per l'Assassino** (1964) had become international big business in the formula codified by his disciple, Dario Argento.

d Mario Bava *p* Luigi Alessi *s* Mario di Nardo *c* Antonio Rinaldi *lp* Ira Fuerstenberg, Edwige Fenech, William Berger, Howard Ross (Renato Rossini), Helena Ronée, Justine Gall (Edy Galleani), Edith Meloni, Teodoro Corra, Mauro Bosco

El Conde Dracula *aka* **Count Dracula** *aka* **Nachts Wenn Dracula Erwacht** *aka* **Il Conte Dracula** *aka* **Bram Stoker's Count Dracula** *aka* **Dracula 71** *aka* **The Nights of Dracula**

(FENIX FILMS/CORONA FILMPRODUKTION/FILMAR COMPAGNIA CINEMATOGRAFICA/TOWERS OF LONDON; SP,IT,WG)
scope 98(86)min

Promoted as the first faithful adaptation of Stoker's novel, this is a bitter disappointment. The film is set in Budapest and the Count (Lee) is eventually destroyed by peasants who set fire to his coffin. Dracula is depicted as a moustachioed Magyar who grows younger as he imbibes blood, but there the resemblance with Stoker's character ends. The settings are Mediterranean, the dialogue is stilted and the relentless zooms together with the repetition of identical cutaway shots ruin the picture's rhythm and atmosphere. Inept day for night shooting, cardboard rocks bouncing about and desultory squirts of red paint accompanying the staking of vampires push the venture into involuntary parody. Only Kinski's manic portrayal of Renfield provides some watchable moments. Even the director admitted the film didn't live up to his expectations. The movie's credits vary according to different sources: Cuccia and Fadda apparently adapted the story together with Towers and Franco, with Dietmar Behnke listed as responsible for the dialogue. Finochi's participation seems to relate more to the Italian version and the considerably shorter Spanish version credits Bruno Mattei as editor instead of Derek Parsons.

Franco returned to the vampire motif a number of times; his films on the subject include **Vampyros Lesbos** (1970), **Dracula contra Frankenstein** and *La Fille de Dracula* (both 1972). The Spanish avant-garde film-maker Pedro Portabella was granted access to the sets used for *El Conde Dracula* and produced a far more interesting documentary fantasy, also starring Lee, called *Vampir* (1971): a poetic meditation on the vampire genre itself, made as a silent film and sonorized with a fascinatingly incongruous soundtrack combining contemporary noises with Lee's voice-over reading the passages in which Stoker describes the Count's death. Portabella's film revels in images of decay, evoking dim memories of images glimpsed in the vaults of dusty archives. Lee was also the subject of Portabella's *El Umbracle* (1970), a fantasy poem about the actor with Lee reciting *The Raven*, singing excerpts from Berlioz's *The Damnation of Faust* and wandering about in a Barcelona transformed into a dream city.

d/co-s Jesús Franco *p* Harry Alan Towers *co-s* Peter Welbeck (Harry Alan Towers), Augusto Finochi, Carlo Fadda, Milo G. Cuccia *c* Manuel Merino *se* Sergio Pagoni *lp* Christopher Lee, Herbert Lom, Klaus Kinski, Frederick Williams, Maria Rohm, Soledad Miranda, Jack Taylor, Teresa Gimpera, Paul Mueller

Count Yorga, Vampire

(ERICA PRODUCTIONS/AMERICAN INTERNATIONAL) 90min

This movie set in contemporary Los Angeles adopts a manner at once offbeat and strangely matter of fact. Yorga (Quarry) holds seances in his mansion as a means of bringing women under his control, and the plot proceeds along traditional lines as two women (Anders and Lang) successively fall under the Count's malign spell and a sympathetic doctor (Perry) and Anders' boyfriend (Macready) eventually brave Yorga's stronghold and put an end to the count and to Lang, now his chief disciple. Perry falls victim to the vampires, but Macready manages to rescue Anders. However, in a predictable but nicely timed twist ending, she turns on him to reveal that she too is a vampire. The low-key treatment offsets authentically nasty moments like that in which Lang is discovered devouring a cat, and Quarry – who later appeared with Vincent Price in **Dr Phibes Rises Again** and **Madhouse** (both 1974) – cuts a commanding figure. The producer is the son of veteran actor George Macready, who provides the film's narration. A sequel, **The Return of Count Yorga** (1971), followed quickly.

d/s Bob Kelljan *p* Michael Macready *c* Arch Archambault *se* James Tannenbaum *lp* Robert Quarry, Roger Perry, Donna Anders, Judith Lang, Michael Murphy, Michael Macready, Edward Walsh, Julie Conners, Paul Hansen, Marsha Jordan

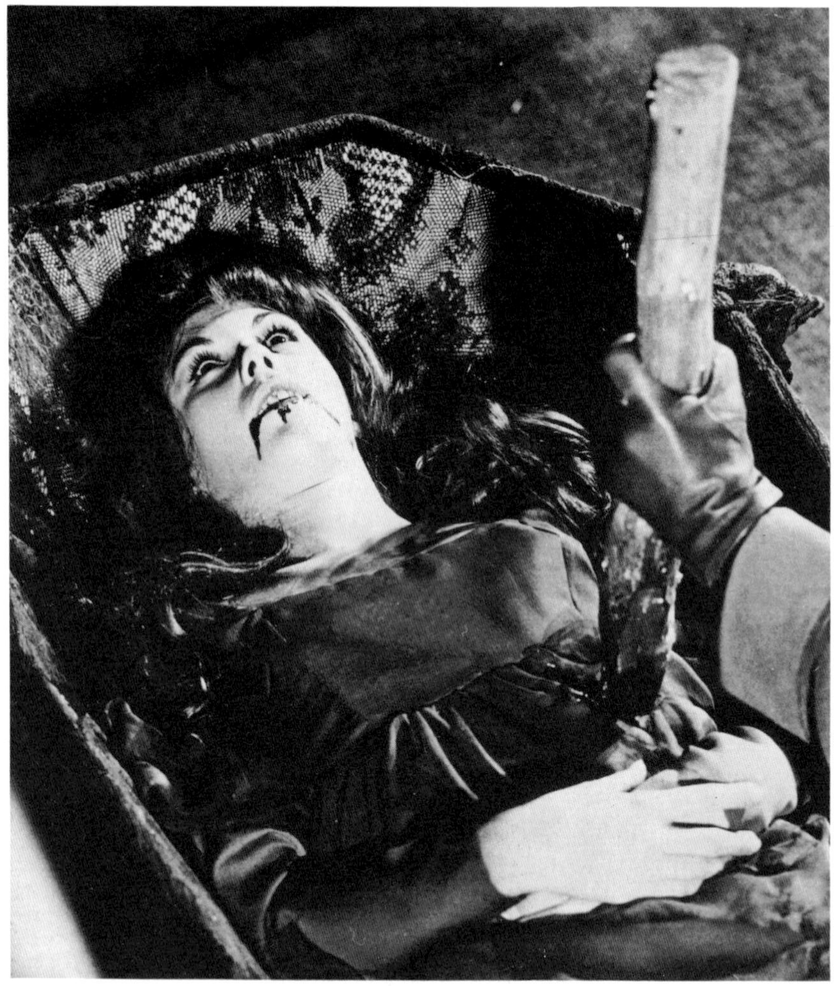

Above: *A traditional scene from the inept* El Conde Dracula.

Countess Dracula (HAMMER; GB) 93min

Sasdy's second film confirms the promise of his début, **Taste the Blood of Dracula** (1969). In extending his exploration of horror motifs in terms of the relations between adults and their children, he made pictures which were far superior to his respectably realist contemporaries' efforts in the same area, such as Ken Loach's *Family Life* (1971). Using Valentine Penrose's book, *The Bloody Countess*, Sasdy, Paal and Gabriel Ronay devised a story about the Hungarian widow Countess Elizabeth (Pitt) who discovers that bathing in virgins' blood restores her youth. Aided by a servant (Green) and her old nanny (Collier) she kidnaps her own daughter, Ilona (Down) and takes on her identity to seduce a young hussar, Toth (Eles). Eventually, her lover discovers the unpalatable truth but, unable to tear himself away, the wedding plans proceed and culminate in the harrowing scene of Pitt reverting to her hideously withered self, desperately slashing at her daughter to be able to shower in her rejuvenating blood but killing Eles instead. The movie ends with the crazed, lonely old hag being immured in her room, mutely gazing into a mirror. Green is excellent as the fiery major domo, hopelessly in love with his cruel mistress, and Arrighi, the uncannily beautiful heroine of

The Devil Rides Out (1967), makes a welcome, though brief, appearance as a gypsy girl.

Pitt is particularly good in a difficult part, vividly conveying the tragic ambivalence of the Countess's all-consuming desire for youth, prepared to absorb the lifeblood of her own child in order to live a life of passion again. Sasdy's depiction of an older generation prepared to destroy its children out of jealousy, and in frustration at the waste of their own lives, achieves a complexity and poignancy absent from the schematically naïve treatments this theme receives in 'serious' plays and films. He skilfully deploys the austere sets, playing with contrasts between sickly green hues and bright, crystalline colours, cleverly seizing on the opportunities afforded by a stylized genre to create richly evocative images and carry the unconscious fantasies that texture the movie. His next picture, **Hands of the Ripper** (1971) rehearsed the father-daughter relationship in cruelly symbolic terms, but after that, poor scripts and uncongenial production circumstances blighted his career (*Doomwatch*, 1972; *Welcome to Blood City*, 1977). Many other pictures referred to the Countess Bathory, but only José Grau's **Ceremonia Sangrienta** (1972) at times achieves a degree of visual intensity to rival Sasdy's classic version.

d Peter Sasdy *p* Alexander Paal *s* Jeremy Paul *c* Kenneth Talbot *se* Bert Luxford *lp* Ingrid Pitt, Nigel Green, Sandor Eles, Maurice Denham, Patience Collier, Peter Jeffrey, Lesley-Anne Down, Leon Lissek, Nike Arrighi, Charles Farrell

Ingrid Pitt as Countess Dracula, *Peter Sasdy's imaginative rendition of the legend of the Countess Bathory.*

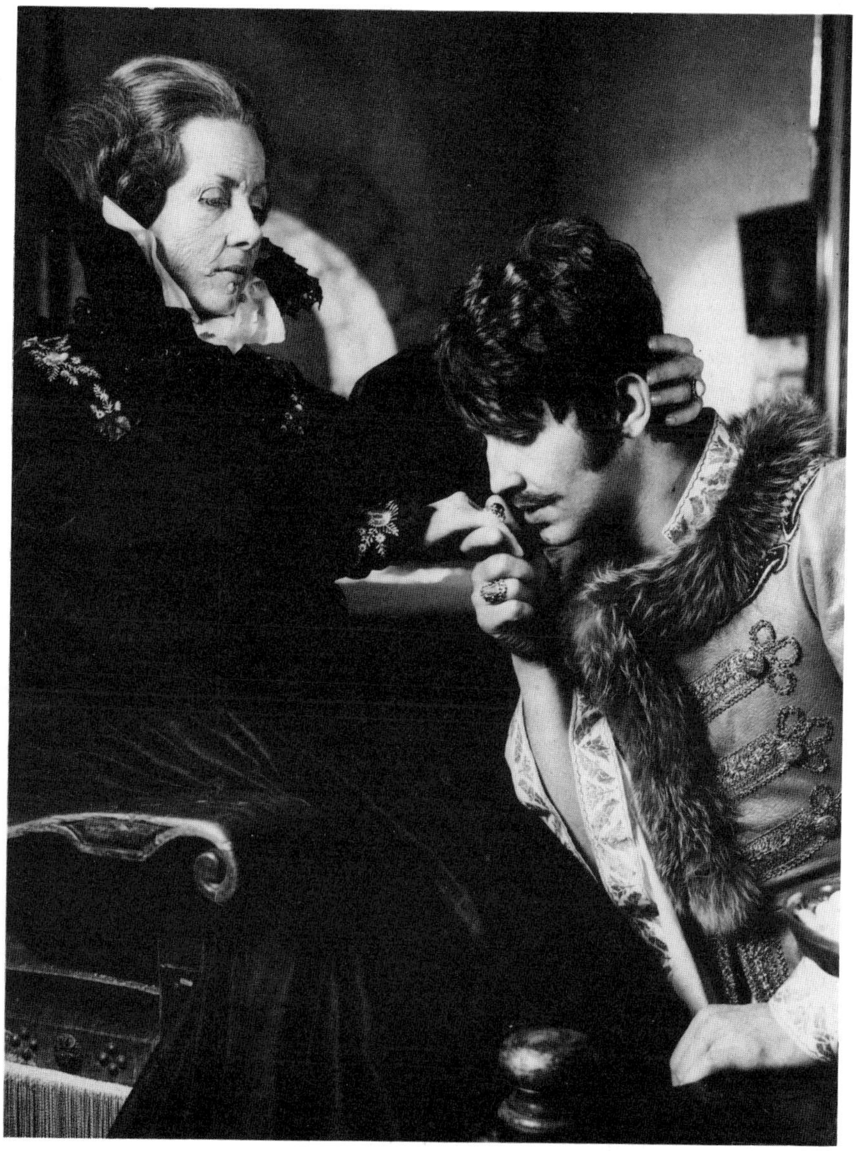

Cry of the Banshee

(AMERICAN INTERNATIONAL; GB) scope 87min

Witchcraft raises its head in the 16th century and is ruthlessly hunted by an English magistrate (Price), only for the old religion to fight back by sending an avenging spirit (Mower) into the heart of the magistrate's household to destroy him in this, the weakest of the collaborations between Wicking and Hessler (**The Oblong Box** and **Scream and Scream Again**, both 1969). Only in the location scenes does Hessler create a sense of haunting evil. Elsewhere, the film exploits whatever opportunities for violence are provided by its theme: women are stripped, one is burnt alive, a head is blown off, there is a massacre, and so on. The blame for all this is put on the high priestess of a local coven, Oona (Bergner) who gets her throat slit. The film ends with a quintessentially generic scene in which the coach containing Price and his slain family is driven through the forest with none other than the avenger himself in the driver's seat. Dwyer, who had been Price's victim in **The Witchfinder General** (1968) and in *The Oblong Box*, is effective as the magistrate's daughter whose sexual favours enable the 'groom' to penetrate the household. Price performs with professional aplomb and only those who remember Bergner's sugary performances of the late twenties and early thirties will appreciate the nicely sacrilegious aspect of casting her as Oona and cutting her throat.

d/p Gordon Hessler *s* Chris Wicking, Tim Kelly *c* John Coquillon *lp* Vincent Price, Elisabeth Bergner, Hilary Dwyer, Essy Persson, Patrick Mower, Sally Geeson, Pamela Fairbrother, Hugh Griffith, Marshall Jones, Michael Elphick, Robert Hutton

Curse of the Vampires *aka* Creatures of Evil

(SCEPTRE INDUSTRIES; US,PHIL) 90(82)min

De Leon again features Fuentes (star of **The Blood Drinkers**, 1966) in this, his second vampire movie to be resolutely set in a family context. Leonora (Fuentes) and her brother (Garcia) arrive at their father's estate. The revelations that follow the line 'what's going on behind the wall in papa's room?' initiate a family drama worthy of Greek tragedy. Mama (Walter) is banished to the basement crypt for being a vampire, which causes Fuentes to break her engagement with Vasquez. Garcia is vampirized by his mother before his father manages to stake her. The brother then seeks to vampirize his sister, manages to kill her fiancé and marries the fiancé's sister, having vampirized her as well. Fuentes digs up the corpse of her lover, to make sure that he is well and truly dead, but his ghost turns up to save her from her brother's incestuous bloodlust and thus liberates her from the family curse. While a procession of villagers, carrying statues of a blood-red-lipped madonna approaches the mansion, the ghost kneels by the bed of his lover, her face twisted in a lustful frenzy since she has been bitten by Garcia after all, and prays. This then causes a crucifix to materialize which plunges itself into her breast, allowing the lovers to be united in the hereafter.

As a story of family relations, the script cannot be improved, except perhaps in the dialogue. The director – or the processing – uses garish colours in his contrasting of a sentimental but intense religiosity with the opposite side of the sacred coin: vampirism as sex, or vice versa. The film doesn't distinguish between licit and illicit sex as marital, premarital and incestuous relations are all presented as equally sinful. Only when 'the flesh' has been eliminated and the lovers are safely dead, can a 'pure' union be consummated. In this way, de Leon's film enacts in a raw and direct manner, rarely matched by more 'knowing' films, what amounts to an analysis of the sexual and religious (if there is a significant difference) fantasies that underpin the vampire legend.

d Gerardo de Leon *p* Amalia Muhlach *s* Ben Fello, Pierre L. Salas *c* Mike Accion *lp* Amalia Fuentes, Eddie Garcia, Romeo Vasques, Mary Walter, Johnny Monteiro, Rosario del Pilar, Francisco Cruz, Quiel Mendoza, Paquito Salcedo

De Sade 70 *aka* **Eugenie – The Story of Her Journey into Perversion** *aka* **Philosophy in the Boudoir** *aka* **Die Jungfrau und die Peitsche**
(VIDEO-TEL INTERNATIONAL PRODUCTIONS; WG)
scope 91min
Franco's first reference to the works of de Sade, *Justine* (1968), was little but a sexy costume drama, but his second effort, again produced by Towers, was a more disturbing achievement. The circular narrative, echoing **Dead of Night** (1945), tells the story of Eugenie (Liljedahl) who spends a weekend on the island retreat of Madame St Ange (Rohm) and her stepbrother, Mirvel (Taylor) where she takes part in the practices of a sadistic cult presided over by Dolmance (Lee). The drugged Liljedahl is subjected to sexual torture and humiliation involving dungeons, chains, whips and so on. Later she is told her experiences were only a dream, but she doesn't believe it and murders her tormentors. When it appears that she has woken up from her 'nightmare', she receives an invitation to go and spend a weekend on St Ange's island....

Less pretentious than other de Sade films (Cy Enfield's *De Sade*, 1969; Pierson's *Justine*, 1970; Scandellari's *La Philosophie dans le Boudoir*, 1969), this does benefit from Franco's ability to convey something of the obsessively repetitious narrative structure that distantly evokes de Sade's writing. Lee said that he had been unaware of the kind of film he had participated in and asked that his name be removed from the credits, but he consented to collaborate with Franco again on their next film, **El Conde Dracula** (1970). A Spanish version of *De Sade 70*, possibly the result of a co-production deal, is credited to Jesús Balcazar's company with the script attributed to Welbeck, Towers' customary pseudonym. Franco went on to make *Eugenie* (1970), starring Soledad Miranda.

d/co-s Jesús Franco *p/co-s* Harry Alan Towers *c* Manuel Merino *lp* Marie Liljedahl, Maria Rohm, Christopher Lee, Jack Taylor, Nino Korda, Herbert Fuchs, Paul Mueller, Margaret Lee, Kathy Lagarde, Anney Kablan

Il Dio Chiamato Dorian *aka* **Das Bildnis des Dorian Gray** *aka* **The Evils of Dorian Gray**
(TERRA FILMKUNST/SARGON FILM/TOWERS OF LONDON; IT,WG) 98min
Set in an Italian gutter-press version of swinging London, Dallamano's film is a hopelessly inept treatment of Wilde's story. Its attempt to give body to Wilde's hints of unmentionable vice is pathetic: a shot of a hairy masculine arm soaping Dorian's back in the shower. For the most part, the picture offers excruciatingly bad acting, worse dubbing and tired sexploitation imagery. Compared to Hurd Hatfield's performance in the masterly film by Albert Lewin, **The Picture of Dorian Gray** (1945), Berger appears a poor amateur as he and Todd seem to compete with each other to try and produce the most embarrassing performance ever. Even the climactic revelation of the monstrous image is undramatic since the viewer has been shown it many times throughout the last half-hour of the movie.

d/co-s Massimo Dallamano *p* Harry Alan Towers *co-s* Marcello Costa *c* Otello Spila *lp* Helmut Berger, Richard Todd, Herbert Lom, Marie Liljedahl, Margaret Lee, Maria Rohm, Beryl Cunningham, Isa Miranda, Eleonora Rossi Drago, Renato Romano

Il Dio Serpente *aka* **The Snake God** *aka* **The God Snake** *aka* **The Serpent God**
(FINARCO; IT) scope 89(80)min
Filmed in Venezuela and Colombia, this interesting movie offers a pleasant variation on traditional voodoo motifs. An Italian woman (Cassini) is told by her black friend (Cunningham) about the Caribbean love god Jambaya who appears in the form of a snake. By the end of the movie, Cassini has decided to give herself to Jambaya while Cunningham departs with her white friend's ex-lover, establishing a neat symmetry between their respective fantasies of exoticism. After a slow start in which the usual stereotypes are set in place, the picture comes alive as it takes off into fantasy and begins to combine the traditional motifs into new configurations. The highlight is the nocturnal ritual with the naked Cassini and her serpent, which takes on human form only at the very last moment before the union is consummated. The film seems calculated to outrage catholic conservatism and although many of its images confirm romantically surrealist notions of female sexuality, it also achieves an enchantingly perverse oneirism and sensuality rare in cheap potboilers. In comparison director Vivarelli's **Satanik** (1968) is a routine outing at best.

d/co-s Piero Vivarelli *p* Alfredo Bini *co-s* Ottavio Alessi *c* Benito Frattari *lp* Nadia Cassini, Beryl Cunningham, Galeazzo Bentivoglio, Arnaldo Palacios, Juana Sobreda, Claudio Trionfi

Flesh Feast
(VIKING INTERNATIONAL PICTURES; CAN) 72min
Apart from *Footsteps in the Snow* (1966), an obscure feature made in Montreal, this was Lake's first film in 22 years (she also co-produced it). Cheaply made and in one or two scenes extremely gruesome it does not even feature in some of Lake's filmographies though is mentioned in her autobiography, *Veronica*. The plot features Lake as Elaine, a scientist and concentration camp survivor, who experiments with restoring youth with the aid of flesh-eating maggots which get rid of old skin tissue. She is asked to operate on the leader of a forthcoming world revolution but when she discovers, on the operating table, that this is no less than Adolf Hitler she turns him over live to the maggots.

d/co-p Brad F. Ginter *co-p* Veronica Lake *s/c* Thomas Casey *se* Doug Hobart *lp* Veronica Lake, Phil Philbin, Heather Hughes, Martha Mischon, Yanka Mann, Dian Wilhite, Chris Martell

Le Frisson des Vampires *aka* **Sex and the Vampire** *aka* **The Terror of the Vampires** *aka* **Vampire Thrills**
(LES FILMS ABC/FILMS MODERNES; FR) 90(72)min
With echoes of Don Sharp's **Kiss of the Vampire** (1962), Rollin's third surreal vampire fairytale relies on a rather conventional plot structure. A honeymooning couple (Julien and Durand) find themselves a medieval castle inhabited by

David Prowse as the monster, with the busty Kate O'Mara in the lacklustre The Horror of Frankenstein.

Thayer David and Roger Davis in House of Dark Shadows, *the first of a couple of features developed by Dan Curtis from the* Dark Shadows *teleseries.*

two caftan-wearing ageing hippies (Delahaye and Robiolles, who later became a film-maker too) and the mistress they share (Nancel). At the stroke of midnight, the gorgeous vampire Dominique emerges from a grandfather clock and proceeds to subject everybody to her seductive charms. She also makes the bride her victim in a sensuous cemetery scene. Nancel is sadistically killed by the jealous Dominique before she too perishes frantically trying to suck blood from her own arm. The vampiric hippies then concentrate their lustful activities on Julien until the morning sun puts an end to the lethally erotic proceedings by destroying them.

The hallucinatory appearance of Dominique out of the clock is the highlight of the movie, but there are many other visually impressive moments: the bright red blood of a dove spilling on to a coffin, the macabre sensuality of contrasting the texture of a naked woman's skin with that of cold stone as she lies on the lid of a massive tomb, the eerie, violent clash of bright colours conveying a bizarre, ritualistic sadism underpinning both the lesbian and the heterosexual encounters.

The dialogue, co-written by Monique Natan, is both cryptic and banal while the cast seem to have been left to their own devices, which means they often strike a jarring note. With his next film, **Requiem pour un Vampire** (1971), Rollin achieved a more deliriously lyrical sadean poem, although still hampered by the severe financial restrictions imposed upon his work since **Le Viol du Vampire** (1967).

d/p/s Jean Rollin *c* Jean-Jacques Renon *lp* Sandra Julien, Dominique, Nicole Nancel, Michel Delahaye, Jacques Robiolles, Marie-Pierre Tricot, Kuelan, Jean-Marie Durand

Gebissen Wird nur Nachts *aka* Happening der Vampire *aka* The Vampire Happening

(AQUILA FILM ENTERPRISES; WG) 102(97)min

This minor German vampire comedy, like Roger Vadim's **Et Mourir de Plaisir** (1960), is a tribute to the beauties of its leading actress, in this case, amateur producer Caminnecci's wife, Dagermark, the celebrated beauty who starred in *Elvira Madigan* (1967). However, the picture fails to convey any sensuality other than that exuded by Dagermark herself. Even the orgies staged in an old pseudo-Balkan castle are routine. The plot concerns a Hollywood beauty who resembles her vampiric grandmother and begins to act accordingly.

Like his *Das Verraetertor* (1964), this was another unhappy venture – at least as far as the results were concerned – into Germany by Francis. The title role is played by the luckless Mayne, parodying his performance in Polanski's **Dance of the Vampires** (1967). The film was released in 1971.

d Freddie Francis *p* Pier A. Caminnecci *s* August Rieger, Karl Heinz Hummel *c* Gerard Vandenberg *lp* Pia Dagermark, Thomas Hunter, Ingrid van Bergen, Ferdy Mayne, Lyvia Bauer, Joachim Kemmer, Daria Damer, Yvor Murillo

The Horror of Frankenstein

(HAMMER/EMI; GB) 95min

Terence Fisher's masterly **Frankenstein Must Be Destroyed** (1969) clearly showed the series had to come to an end if it was to avoid the degeneration that had befallen the old Universal movies. Unfortunately, Hammer itself precipitated that embarrassing development by getting Sangster to make this crude parody. The grossness and flatfooted acting of this picture, written and directed by the man who had written Fisher's original masterpiece, confirms Fisher's directorial brilliance beyond a shadow of a doubt.

The plot has Victor Frankenstein (Bates, playing the Baron as a philandering lout) dispose of his father and engage in building a creature (Prowse) while bedding his busty housekeeper (O'Mara). Gore is provided by a series of murders, including the electrocution of Bates's best friend (James), the killing of a professor (Archard), the father of Bates's girlfriend (Carlson), the immersing in acid of a graverobber (Price) and sundry misdeeds perpetrated by the creature. The end has a little girl accidentally destroy the creature with acid as it lies hidden in an empty vat while the police interrogate Bates. Released in a double bill with **The Scars of Dracula** (1970), this Hammer programme symbolized the end of the great British gothic cinema.

d/p/co-s Jimmy Sangster *co-s* Jeremy Burnham *c* Moray Grant *lp* Ralph Bates, Kate O'Mara, Graham James, Veronica Carlson, Bernard Archard, Dennis Price, Joan Rice, David Prowse

House of Dark Shadows (MGM) 97min

The popular daytime teleseries *Dark Shadows* was so successful that it prompted producer Curtis to make two full length features from it, of which this is the first. It was followed by the less interesting **Night of Dark Shadows** (1971).

The films feature a number of the regular series cast, including Bennett, some repeating their TV roles. Freed from television censorship restrictions, Curtis is able to inject more sex and gore into his subject than usual. Here, 18th-century vampire Barnabus Collins (Frid) is accidentally released from his coffin in the crypt of Collinwood, Maine. He introduces himself as a cousin from England and proceeds to go on the rampage. Playing, design and photography all achieve consistently high standards, and Curtis gives the conventions new force and resonance through a simple trust in their original power. The climax is particularly effective. Smith used exactly the same makeup on Frid as he did on Dustin Hoffmann in *Little Big Man* (1970).

d/p Dan Curtis *s* Sam Hall, Gordon Russell *c* Arthur Ornitz *se* Dick Smith, Robert Layden *lp* Jonathan Frid, Joan Bennett, Roger Davis, Grayson Hall, Kathryn Leigh Scott, Nancy Barrett, John Carlen, Thayer David, Louis Edmonds, Donald Brice

The House That Dripped Blood

(AMICUS; GB) scope 102(101)min

Appearing midway through Amicus's series of omnibus movies (**Torture Garden**, 1967; **Tales from the Crypt**, 1972), the film recounts four tales derived from stories by Bloch. Each tale centres on the inhabitants of a house that seems 'blighted'.

Method for Murder involves a writer (Elliott) who moves into the house in order to complete a horror story involving an insane strangler, only to find the character (Adams) taking him over. The story has a double twist ending revealing a plot to drive the writer insane. *Waxworks*, originally published in 1939, tells of a stockbroker (Cushing) obsessed with the Salome figure in a local wax museum whose head winds up gracing her platter when the jealous proprietor (Morris) kills him. *Sweets to the Sweet* from *Weird Tales* sees Lee maniacally trying to prevent his daughter (Franks) from following in her witch-mother's footsteps but his actions only serve to drive her towards the forbidden practices: her nanny (Porter) catches her sticking pins in an effigy of her father, causing Lee acute discomfort. While the other episodes are entertaining, this one evokes a genuinely emotional basis for evil within family relationships. The final tale, *The Cloak*, a story published in *From Unknown Worlds*, returns the film to its previous level of effective whimsicality: an opening shot of a skull on a copy of Lotte Eisner's *The Haunted Screen*, a narrator named Stoker, bookshelves crammed with copies of Poe, Hoffmann, Hawthorne, Mary Shelley and so on. A veteran horror star (Pertwee) buys a cloak that changes its wearer into a vampire. When his leading lady (Pitt) dons the garment, he becomes her victim. The comic aspects are amiable and the dialogue mercifully remains this side of camp. This was Duffel's feature film début after a career in TV (*The Avengers*, *Journey to the Unknown*). However, his film career never took off and eventually he returned to TV where he directed the colonial soap opera *The Far Pavilions* (1984). Amicus's next omnibus movie, **Asylum** (1972) again adapted Bloch's stories.

d Peter Duffel *p* Max J. Rosenberg, Milton Subotsky *s* Robert Bloch *c* Ray Parslow *lp* Denholm Elliott, Joanna Lumley, Tom Adams, Robert Lang; Peter Cushing, Joss Ackland, Wolfe Morris; Christopher Lee, Nyree Dawn Porter, Chloe Franks; Jon Pertwee, Ingrid Pitt, John Bennett

Hsi Nou Ai Lueh *aka* Four Moods

(YANG CHIAO-BLUE SKY; TAIWAN) scope 140min

This Taipei-based production presents four different stories, each by a different director, rather like **Pastel de Sangre** (1971) and some British omnibus movies of the fifties such as **Three's Company** (1953). The first one, called *Joy*, is the often-told tale of a young man who spends the night with a ghost. When he wants to repeat the experience, another woman turns up to claim him for Death which he appears to love so much. The second story is a traditional martial arts sketch, but the third one returns to the fantasy theme. Called *Sorrow*, it tells of a man who returns from prison to find his family have been massacred by the Lan clan, but since his enemies are dead as well, he cannot do his duty by taking revenge. He takes up with a young woman living nearby in an isolated house but when she finds him desecrating the Lan's tombs, she returns to her own grave among the Lan clan, leaving the distraught hero in front of a tombstone on which the inscription begins to bleed. The final episode is a comic tale as the ghost of a drunkard is given a chance to redeem himself. The direction varies in quality but the first tale, almost entirely silent, and the third one with its beautifully eery funereal locations and surreal ending, are striking achievements.

co-d/s Li Hanxiang *co-d* Bai Ching-Zue, Hoo Ching-chuen, Lu Shing *c* Ling Tsan-Ting, Lai Chen-ing, Chang Yong-Shu *lp* Tseng Chang, Yue Yang, Liu Ming, Chang Kuo-chuin; O Wei, Chang Mei-Yao, Hang Su; Lee Li Hua, Yang Chiung, Sue Shiang-ling, Chiang Ching

I, Monster (AMICUS; GB) 75min

Of the three directorial talents that emerged during Hammer's final years, Peter Sykes was the most professional, Peter Sasdy the most flamboyantly brilliant and Weeks perenially promising. This, his first feature, a reworking of the Jekyll and Hyde story, is both stylish and restrained, lyrical and scrupulously realist in its Victorian period detail. Lee plays Dr Marlowe who administers an inhibition-relieving drug to himself, thereby revealing an ugly *alter ego* called Blake who becomes more and more ugly with each change until he becomes a pathetic, frightened animal. As he tries to kill his solicitor friend (Cushing), he catches fire in the struggle and falls to his death, whereupon the unsightly creature changes back into the dignified Marlowe.

Weeks was severely hampered by both an obviously shoestring budget and having to begin shooting a 3-D process which was eventually abandoned. His next effort, *Sir Gawain and the Green Knight* (1972), achieved a mythic dimension, but the film still lacked narrative and structural control, as did his **Ghost Story** (1974).

d Stephen Weeks *co-p/s* Milton Subotsky *co-p* Max J. Rosenberg *c* Moray Grant *lp* Christopher Lee, Peter Cushing, Mike Raven, Richard Hurndall, George Merritt, Kenneth J. Warren, Susan Jameson, Marjie Lawrence, Aimee Delamain

Lokis, *one of the few Eastern European forays into the horror genre.*

Incense for the Damned *aka* Bloodsuckers

(LUCINDA FILMS/TITAN INTERNATIONAL; GB) scope 87(83)min

This fairly faithful adaptation of Simon Raven's modern vampire novel, *Doctors Wear Scarlet*, tells of the foreign secretary's son (Mower), an Oxford don with a girlfriend aptly called Penelope (Hinde). The plot has him fall under a pagan spell of the sensual Greek woman (Hassall) who leads him astray into black magic rites and satanism and, ultimately, vampirism and death. The film bravely tries to convey that vampirism is not a supernatural phenomenon but a sexual disturbance related to impotence. It gradually shifts from chase thriller as Mower is pursued by embassy officials (Macnee) and friends (Davion and Sekka), to horror, climaxing in the cross-cutting of a bunch of scarlet-robed dons greedily devouring food while in his room Mower vampirizes his lover, the principal's daughter. Unfortunately, the subversive potential of the story remains unrealized as the movie wastes time on depictions of 'hippy' decadence with clichéd psychedelic effects, badly timed chase sequences and facile oppositions between alleged Greek paganism and the genteelly repressive Oxford cricket pitch. The production suffered long delays and problems resulting in the director removing his name from the credits, presumably because of the vampire-staking scenes which contradicted the picture's basic premise of vampirism as nervous illness. Hassall is quite convincingly sensuous but Cushing has little to do as the domineering principal but look sinister.

d Michael Burrowes (Robert Hartford-Davis) *p* Graham Harris *s* Julian More *c* Desmond Dickinson *lp* Patrick Mower, Peter Cushing, Patrick Macnee, Imogen Hassall, Alex Davion, Johnny Sekka, Madeline Hinde, Edward Woodward, David Lodge, Valerie Van Ost

Kaidan Kasanegafuchi *aka* **The Masseur's Curse** *aka* **Horror of an Ugly Woman**
(DAIEI; JAP) scope 82min
This is a routine remake of Nakagawa's classic version of Sanyutei's story filmed in 1957 and remade once before by Yasuda (1960), with a few sex scenes added for the new generation of film-viewers. Having come to collect a debt, the blind masseur Soetsu (Ishiyama) is paid in kind by the wife of a dissolute samurai (Date). The samurai catches them in the act and kills both of them, dumping their bodies in the local swamp. The pair return as ghosts causing their killer to commit suicide and his daughter (Oka) to disappear. In the second phase of the story, the blind man's daughter and the samurai's son get together, but when her face is scalded by boiling water, she turns into a hideous creature. The ending has Oka reappear on the scene and form an incestuous and murderous triangle, setting the scene for a predictably violent ending. Although not as inventive as his **Yokai Hyaku Monogatari** (1968), Yasuda here acquits himself reasonably well. This was the last horror picture to be released by Daiei before they went bankrupt.

d Kimiyoshi Yasuda *p* Masaichi Nagata *s* Shozaburo Asai *c* Tsuchimoto Hayashi *lp* Ritsu Ishiyama, Saburo Date, Maya Kitajima, Reiko Kasahara, Matsuko Oka, Ryuko Minagami, Takumi Shinjo, Kenjiro Ishiyama

Kaidan Noboriryu *aka* **The Blind Woman's Curse** *aka* **The Haunted Life of a Dragon-Tattooed Lass** *aka* **Tattooed Swordswoman**
(NIKKATSU; JAP) scope 85min
This bakeneko mono (cat ghost story) is unusual in that the cat doesn't represent a dead person. A female gangster and swordsman Akemi (Kaji) kills a rival boss and accidentally blinds his daughter Aiko (Tokuda), only for Tokuda to bring home to Kaji the nefarious results of her actions, particularly when one of her own henchmen hangs himself with a curse inscribed in his body. She teams up with the vagabond samurai (Sato) and gets into trouble with another gang which killed her uncle, whose ghost later intervenes to save the samurai's life. The climax is provided by the blind Tokuda who has become an expert knife thrower: she turns out to be the samurai's sister and confronts Kaji in a sword duel.

The direction is routine, and occasionally borders on the ludicrous – as when mean-looking yakuza appear coiffed with bowler hats and flat caps. As he had already shown with **Kyofu Kikei Ningen** (1969), Ishii's talents didn't stretch as far as the horror genre.

d/co-s Teruo Ishii *p* Hideo Koi, Shiro Sasaki *co-s* Yoshida Sone *c* Shigeru Kitazumi *lp* Mieko Kaji, Hoki Tokuda, Makoto Sato, Yoko Takagi, Hideo Sunazuka, Toru Abe, Yuzo Halumi, Yoshi Kato

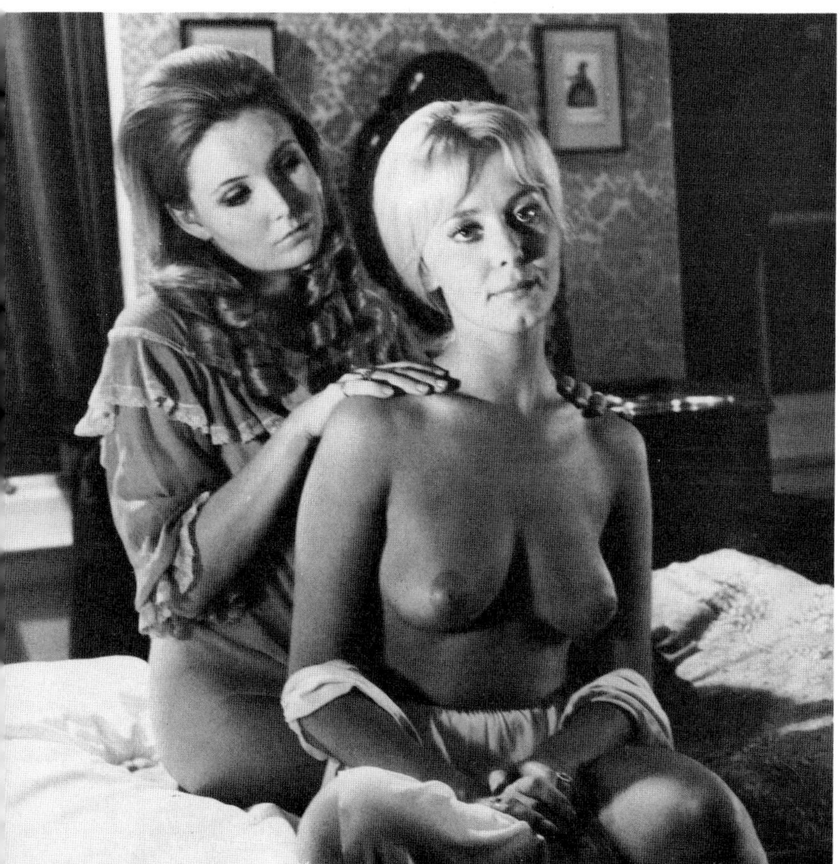

Yutte Stensgaard as the blonde vampire with Pippa Steele in Lust for a Vampire, *Hammer's sequel to* The Vampire Lovers *(1970).*

Lokis *aka* **The Bear** (TOR; POL) 100min
An extremely skilful adaptation of Prosper Mérimée's story *Professor Wittembach's Manuscript*, about a young man (Duriasz) whose mother was carried off by a bear on her wedding day, and who broods morosely about the possibility that he is a were-bear until finally he cuts his bride's throat on their wedding night and disappears into the forest. Told largely from the point-of-view of the professor (Fetting) who arrives to study some manuscripts and among them finds an account of the mother's abduction, the film does perhaps overdo the brooding, but is engaging nevertheless, shot in richly muted colours that suggest a Hammer horror without the emphasis on graphic violence. One of the few Eastern European film-makers to show an interest in the genre, Majewski adapted another Mérimée horror story (*La Vénus d'Ile*) for television although much of his work falls into the area of fantasy.

d/s Janusz Majewski *c* Stefan Matyjaskiewicz *lp* Józef Duriasz, Edmund Fetting, Gustaw Lutkiewicz, Malgorzata Braunek, Zofia Mrozowska

Lust for a Vampire *aka* **To Love a Vampire**
(HAMMER; GB) 95min
This is the second of Hammer's Karnstein trilogy of films derived from Sheridan LeFanu's *Carmilla*, which began with **The Vampire Lovers** (1970) and ended with **Twins of Evil** (1971). Unfortunately, while LeFanu's story was an excellent variation on its French model, Théophile Gauthier's *La Morte Amoureuse*, Sangster's effort is only a ludicrously adolescent imitation of Rollin's erotic vampire movies (**Le Viol du Vampire**, 1967; **La Vampire Nue**, 1969).

The story, set in 1870, tells of the ravages perpetrated by Mircalla Karnstein (Stensgaard) in a girls' finishing school adjacent to the castle's grounds. The victims also include two male teachers, the unctuously creepy Giles (Bates) and a writer, Richard (Johnson) who enjoys Stensgaard's favours until the school is burnt down by the outraged villagers and a falling beam accidentally stakes her. Studded with repetitive zooms and erratic colour cinematography, Sangster's direction seems embarrassed by the very sensuality the movie seeks to exploit, spoiling passionate scenes with mockingly inappropriate songs on the soundtrack and lapsing into sniggering locker-room jokes. Most of the women, and especially Stensgaard, set about conveying a delightfully passionate sense of perversion with refreshing conviction, evoking what the picture might have become in the hands of film-makers not intimidated by the powerful sexual charge exuded by the actresses.

d Jimmy Sangster *p* Harry Fine, Michael Style *s* Tudor Gates *c* David Muir *lp* Yutte Stensgaard, Suzanna Leigh, Ralph Bates, Michael Johnson, Barbara Jefford, Mike Raven, Helen Christie, Pippa Steel, David Healy

The Man Who Haunted Himself

(EXCALIBUR FILMS/ABP; GB) 94min
In an effort to regenerate the British film industry, ABP launched a batch of films including this effort by the once interesting Dearden, who died shortly afterwards. A tired re-hash of thriller clichés of a bygone era, it tells of the businessman Pelham (Moore) who, one evening, suffers a car accident and wakes up to find his more extrovert double has been released and taken over the old Pelham's life, moving into his house and marital bed. Old Pelham, now superfluous, eventually goes mad and crashes his car, with more lasting effects. The picture is very dull, which fits Moore's style and range of acting perfectly, while Jones, hamming it up as an eccentric psychiatrist, provides light relief and tips the film into crazy comedy. The effects, particularly when both Pelhams have to appear in the same frame, are extremely awkward. Considering that Dearden's work was interesting for its uncanny Englishness, it seems appropriate, although unfortunate, that his last film should confirm the bankruptcy of the classic English cinema epitomized by films like **Dead of Night** (1945). The script was derived from Anthony Armstrong's story *The Strange Case of Mr Pelham.*

d/co-s Basil Dearden *p/co-s* Michael Relph *c* Tony Spratling *lp* Roger Moore, Hildegard Neil, Olga Georges-Picot, Anton Rodgers, Freddie Jones, Thorley Walters, John Carson, John Welsh, Charles Lloyd-Pack

Mrs Hyde *aka* Sie Toetete in Extase

(TELECINE/FENIX FILMS; SP,WG) 77min
Returning to the territory of his earlier **Miss Muerte** (1965), in this sadistic sexploitation thriller Franco presents a lethal female (Miranda) intent on avenging the wrongs suffered by her father (Williams), a doctor who experimented with human embryos but whose work was condemned by the medical establishment, causing him to commit suicide. The daughter kills those she holds responsible: three male doctors and one female one become her victims before she puts her father's dead body next to her in a car and drives off a cliff. The plot concentrates on the four deadly encounters, mixing sex and blood as she seduces and castrates her male victims. The rather perfunctory direction may be due to its director's workrate: Franco made eight feature films in 1970, as well as numerous soft-porn thrillers such as *Der Teufel Kam aus Akasuka* and *Der Todesraecher von Soho*, which was released in 1972. Both were unorthodox efforts to compete with the successful German Edgar Wallace series of movies which was just coming to an end. In France, the credits of Franco's picture were added to an anonymously made French hard-core film entitled *Sylvia dans l'Extase*.

d/s Frank Hollmann (Jesús Franco) *p* Arturo Marcos *c* Manuel Merino *lp* Susan Korda (Soledad Miranda), Fred Williams, Ewa Stroemberg, Paul Mueller, Howard Vernon, Horst Tappert

Mumsy Nanny Sonny and Girly *aka* Girly

(RONALD J. KAHN; GB) scope 101min
This whimsically ghoulish horror melodrama needed either more ghoul and guignol or more of the deliberate grotesquerie of something like *The Munsters* teleseries. Set in a country estate inhabited by a saccharine, Disney-like family, whose speciality is kidnapping and murder, the film follows the decline of the family when one of their victims (Bryant) begins to play sexual games of his own with the eponymous mumsy (Howells), daughter (Howard) and nanny (Heywood). As a result the son and the nanny meet their death.

The mind-game resonances of Pasolini's *Teorema* (1968) sit uncomfortably in the context. The fey ghoulish premise of the narrative based on Maisie Mosco's play, has adults pretending to be wayward and malevolent inhabitants of the nursery, a dimension underscored by the characters' names, but this also precludes any development of the potentially satirical aspects of the material and Comport's script remains on the level of a slightly eccentric farce instead of the anarchic explosion of familial stereotypes it might have been.

d Freddie Francis *p* Ronald J. Kahn *s* Brian Comport *c* David Muir *lp* Michael Bryant, Ursula Howells, Pat Heywood, Vanessa Howard, Howard Trevor, Robert Swann, Imogen Hassall, Michael Ripper, Hugh Armstrong

Nella Stretta Morsa del Ragno *aka* Dracula im Schloss des Schreckens *aka* Prisonnier de l'Araignée *aka* In the Grip of the Spider *aka* Web of the Spider *aka* Edgar Poe chez les Morts Vivants *aka* E Venne l'Alba ... Ma Tinto di Rosse

(PRODUZIONE DC7/PARIS CANNES PRODUCTIONS/ TERRA FILMKUNST; IT,WG,FR) 102(93,76)min
Margheriti's faithful remake of his own **La Danza Macabra** (1964) features Mercier in the Barbara Steele role. This free adaptation of Poe's story, set in 19th-century England, opens inside a pub with a sceptical American journalist, Foster (Franciosa), interviewing Poe himself (Kinski) and taking up the challenge to spend All Souls' Night in Lord Blackwood's Villa Providence. The unnerving events he witnesses in the decrepit manor with the customary dank crypts and squeaky doors, billowing curtains and flickering candles, not to mention the bloodsucking murders and apparent resurrections which culminate in the ghostly horde assailing the shattered journalist and driving him to try and escape but he is finally killed, impaled on the iron gate to the property. Ortolani's score is as intrusive as in the original version and the presence of Kinski doesn't compensate for the absence of Steele, but the camerawork is pleasant, and helps make the film one of Italy's last classic gothic movies before gore and sex drastically changed the genre, as in Margheriti's own **Dracula Cerca Sangue di Vergine e ... Mori di Sete** (1973), attributed to Paul Morrissey largely for publicity reasons and American sales.

d Anthony Dawson (Antonio Margheriti) *p* Giovanni Addessi *s* Bruno Corbucci, Giovanni Grimaldi *c* Sandro Mancori, Memmo Mancori *lp* Anthony Franciosa, Michele Mercier, Peter Carsten, Silvano Tranquilli, Karin Field, Raf Baldassare, Klaus Kinski, Irina Meleva, Paolo Goslino, Enrico Osterman

Roger Moore as The Man Who Haunted Himself.

Robert Swann, the butt of one the sillier games that comprise Mumsy Nanny Sonny and Girly.

La Noche de Walpurgis *aka* **Shadow of the Werewolf** *aka* **The Werewolf's Shadow** *aka* **The Werewolf versus the Vampire Women** *aka* **Nacht der Vampire** *aka* **The Black Harvest of Countess Dracula**
(HIFI STEREO 70/PLATA FILMS; SP, WG) scope 86min
After **Las Noches del Hombre Lobo** (1968) and **El Hombre que Vino de Ummo** (1969), Molina returned to the familiar territory of **La Marca del Hombre Lobo** (1967), as Count Waldemar the reluctant werewolf whose fate it is to be destroyed by someone who loves him, pitted this time against Countess Waldessa (originally Rossana Yanni's creation but henceforth mostly Shepard). When doctors extract the silver bullet from Molina's corpse, he revives, dispatches his rescuers and returns to his lonely castle. Two young female students arrive in search of the vampiric Waldessa's tomb and they are joined by Molina who wishes to find the silver cross with which the Countess was staked. Repeating a scene from Bava's **La Maschera del Demonio** (1960), one of the women cuts herself and drips blood on to the Countess's face, reactivating her. She bites one of the women and abducts the other one, saving her for a satanic ritual on Walpurgis Night. Daninsky, in his werewolf persona, saves her and, as custom demands, is killed by her.

Padded with a dozen or so deaths, the story shows scant regard for the genre's conventions as vampires wander about in broad daylight and are confused with witches while their victims magically recover. The Countess's death is cribbed from Fisher's **Dracula** (1958), except that the progressive decomposition of the corpse includes a scene in which maggots work at the speed of light.

The very incoherence of the narrative suggests that the appeal of the Waldemar-werewolf character is due to a more subconscious fantasy logic requiring the presence of a few basic motifs such as the physically repulsive but basically lovable, lonely hero, and a split representation of 'woman': a bad, vengeful female and a good, caring one who is prepared to sacrifice herself for the beastly boy-man. Molina continued his werewolf career with **La Furia del Hombre Lobo** (1971), **El Retorno de Walpurgis** (1973), **La Maldición de la Bestia** (1975) and others. Klimovsky's zoom-ridden direction is as insipid as his early work in Spain and Argentina. He often worked with Molina (**Dr Jeckill y el Hombre Lobo**, 1971; **La Rebellión de las Muertas**, 1972; *Planeta Ciego*, 1975).

d Leon Klimovsky *p* Salvadore Romero *s* Jacinto Molina, Hans Munkel *c* Leopoldo Villaseñor *se* Antonio Molina *lp* Paul Naschy (Jacinto Molina), Paty Shepard, Gaby Fuchs, Barbara Capell, Andrew Reese (Andres Resino), Julio Pena, Yelena Samarina, José Marco, Barta Barri

Satan's Skin *aka* **Blood on Satan's Claw**
(TIGON BRITISH/CHILTON FILMS; GB) 93min
Starting with a ploughman's discovery of a rotting half-man half-beast in his field, the film proceeds to chronicle the effect on the local community of the evil emanations of the monstrous devil figure. A young girl, Angel (Hayden) becomes its main vehicle as she leads the village children into a devil-worship cult which spreads through the 17th-century community like the plague, providing narrative excuses for scenes of witch hunts, satanism, mutilation and rape as well as an interesting sequence in which Hayden seduces a priest in his own church. More violent than its model, Michael Reeves' brilliant **The Witchfinder General** (1968), Haggard's picture collapses into gory but well-shot sensationalism, depicting the villagers as ignorant yokels and sadistic fiends while lingering lovingly on torture and brutality, including the arbitrarily inserted scene detailing the surgical removal of devil's skin from a girl's leg. The American television print censored some of the cruder and nuder scenes by darkening the offending shots, including the climactic satanic orgy during which the local judge (Wymark) impales Satan, in slow motion, on his blessed sword. Hayden gives a stronger performance than in **Taste the Blood of Dracula** (1969), but neither her presence nor that of Wymark, who played Cromwell in Reeves' film, are sufficient to counteract the picture's exploitative approach, even though the director manages to cloak this under excellently stylized imagery.

d Piers Haggard *p* Peter L. Andrews, Malcolm B. Heyworth *s* Robert Wynne-Simmons *c* Dick Bush *lp* Linda Hayden, Barry Andrews, Patrick Wymark, Avice Landon, Simon Williams, Tamara Ustinov, Michele Dotrice, James Hayter, Anthony Ainley

The Scars of Dracula (HAMMER/EMI; GB) 96min
After Peter Sasdy's exciting **Taste of Blood of Dracula** (1969), which reinterpreted the Dracula myth by concentrating on the story's relation to Victorian society, Hammer went back to Stoker's novel and its mid-European setting for fresh inspiration. They also tried to increase the film's commercial appeal by cynically inserting extra nudity and pointlessly sadistic scenes, such as Dracula (Lee) stabbing his mistress (Hempel) to death and whipping his crippled servant (Troughton). The plot has a disagreeable youth (Matthews) blunder into the Count's castle, allowing some of the scenes of Harker's arrival and first night to be replayed before he is killed. The youth's lover (Hanley), brother (Waterman) and the local priest (Gwynn) follow Matthews to the castle. The

Right: *Paty Shepard (right) as Countess Waldessa in* La Noche de Walpurgis, *one of Jacinto Molina's many werewolf outings.*

Left: *Joe Cornelius as the ice-age troglodyte in* Trog.

priest is gruesomely killed by bats and Waterman fights Lee over Hanley on the battlements before Lee is struck by lightning and falls in flames from the castle's turret. The result is an unhappy mixture of interesting scenes, such as the shot of Dracula crawling lizard-like down the wall of his castle, and crudely exploitative sequences betraying utter contempt for the audiences Hammer catered for. Baker's direction is heavy-handed, the score is far too emphatic and the acting – except for Hempel's sensuousness and Lee's customary professionalism – dogged rather than intense.

Up until the late sixties, Hammer had carefully avoided releasing Dracula films in quick succession, but the pressure to make money faster led to the series being speeded up. Thus, the studio began to produce a new Dracula every year, in addition to numerous other vampire pictures (**The Vampire Lovers, Lust for a Vampire** and **Countess Dracula**, all 1970). The next instalments featured increasingly desperate measures to re-kindle the series' commercial appeal, but to no avail. With **Dracula AD 1972** (1972) and **The Satanic Rites of Dracula** (1973), the series of seven Lee-Dracula movies came to an end.

d Roy Ward Baker *p* Aida Young *s* John Elder (Anthony Hinds) *c* Moray Grant *lp* Christopher Lee, Jenny Hanley, Dennis Waterman, Christopher Matthews, Anoushka Hempel, Patrick Troughton, Michael Gwynn, Wendy Hamilton, Delia Lindsay, Michael Ripper

Torture Dungeon

(MISHKIN/CONSTITUTION) 80 min

Filmed in 'dripping blood colour', this is Milligan's most gory and effect-filled work after **Bloodthirsty Butchers** (1970). The story has the evil Duke of Norfolk torturing and murdering various successors to the throne of medieval England and includes such scenes as pitchfork impalement and torture by silver skewers and rattlesnakes. Some of the makeup is actually quite effective, especially is the scenes featuring rotting corpses.

d/co-s/c Andy Milligan *p* William Mishkin *co-s* John Borske *se* Walter Terry *lp* Jeremy Mishkin, Susan Cassidy

Trog (HERMAN COHEN PRODUCTIONS; GB) 93(91)min

This film takes its title from its monstrous protagonist, an ice-age troglodyte discovered in an unexplored cave. Tension develops between the demands of scientific knowledge represented by investigating anthropologist Crawford (in one of her few sympathetic roles at the end of her career), and the newshounds and locals who both terrorize and are terrorized by the creature, played by Cornelius in Charles Parker's makeup. Some scenes echo **King Kong** (1933) and James Whale's **Frankenstein** (1931) but the picture's principal – though awkwardly assimilated – point of reference appears to be François Truffaut's *L'Enfant Sauvage* (1969). Kandel's script was based on a story provided by the distinguished Hammer alumni, Peter Bryan and John Gilling, director of the fascinating **The Reptile** (1966), but the motifs of the noble savage versus both the positive and the negative aspects of civilization remain undeveloped and lack conviction under Francis's routine direction. Electrodes fixed to the creature's brain provide an opportunity to conjure up prehistoric 'memories' represented by sequences taken from Irwin Allen's *The Animal World* (1956).

d Freddie Francis *p* Herman Cohen *s* Aben Kandel *c* Desmond Dickinson *lp* Joan Crawford, Michael Gough, Bernard Kay, David Griffin, Kim Braden, Joe Cornelius, John (Mark) Hamill, Thorley Walters, Rona Newton-John, Robert Hutton

L'Uccello dalle Piume di Cristallo *aka* The Gallery Murders *aka* The Bird with the Crystal Plumage *aka* The Bird with the Glass Feathers *aka* Das Geheimnis der Schwarzen Handschuhe

(CCC/SEDA SPETTACOLI; IT,WG) scope 98(94)min

Alfred Hitchcock had deployed a superbly sophisticated form of narrative premissed on the multiple functions of the look in cinema, involving viewers in a complex play of seeing which simultaneously motivated the characters, propelled the narrative and displayed the foundations of cinema as a voyeuristic spectacle. In Italy, Mario Bava had stripped away much of the narrative, reducing it to the minimum pretext required to feed the desire for looking, stressing the sexual components of the fantasies thus generated. In this way he cut Hitchcock's play of looking loose from its narrative moorings and tended to drift into visual delirium. In the United States, William Castle adopted the opposite strategy of reducing Hitchcock's manner to a set of techniques for audience manipulation. With this psycho-slasher picture, Argento hit upon the formula for a super-efficient entertainment cinema by amplifying Castle's strategy still further, punctuating it with moments of visual flamboyance derived from Bava and holding the concoction together with a superficial, tongue-in-cheek narrative studded with eccentric bits of character acting. In this way, Argento's first feature initiated the trend towards transforming cinema into an effective machine for dispensing emotional shocks, a trend that would absorb the physical horror of George Romero's **Night of the Living Dead** (1968) and the mindless irrationalism of William Friedkin's **The Exorcist** (1973) and produce the splatter genre exemplified by David Cronenberg's **Scanners** (1981) or Samuel Raimi's **The Evil Dead** (1982).

L'Uccello, derived (uncredited) from Frederic Brown's *The Screaming Mimi*, has Sam (Musante) on a visit to an art gallery, witness a slasher attack involving Monica (Renzi). After numerous more slasher attacks on women and attempts

A French poster for Dario Argento's influential psycho-slasher movie, L'Uccello dalle Piume di Cristallo.

ring me the head of . The Vampire *overs: Peter Cushing ith Ingrid Pitt in the rst of Hammer's trio of sbian vampire movies.*

on the lives of Musante and his lover, Julia (Kendall), it emerges that the initial scene was not an attack on Renzi but her attempt to kill her husband (Raho). As in Castle's **Homicidal** (1961) and Brian de Palma's **Dressed to Kill** (1980), the psycho slasher's masculine appearance throughout the movie turns out to be an illusion, allowing for a shock ending by suddenly reversing, on the basis of the flimsiest of psychological excuses, the killer's gender. Argento makes clever use of suspense devices, such as the lights going out during a young woman's ascent of a staircase and having her proceed by matchlight (expertly filmed by Storaro), the screaming Kendall trapped in a room while the killer hacks his/her way through the door, a scene repeated in **The Shining** (1980), and so on. As part of the narrative tying these scenes together, Argento proposes some engaging cameos such as the harrassed but humorous police commissioner (Salerno), a stammering pimp (Adorf) and other eccentric character parts. Ennio Morricone's repetitively insistent score both stresses the mechanical aspects of the movie's suspense machinery and effectively cues the viewer's desired response. Storaro's images are impressive, although full recognition of his Bava-like ability to create fascinating images did not come until *Apocalypse Now* (1979). Argento pushed his shock formula further in *Il Gatto a Nove Code* (1970) and **Quattro Mosche di Velluto Grigio** (1971), eliminating more and more plot with each outing, until by the time of **Profondo Rosso** (1975), **Suspiria** (1976) and **Inferno** (1980) the films were pure shock-machines.

d/s Dario Argento *p* Salvatore Argento *c* Vittorio Storaro *lp* Tony Musante, Suzy Kendall, Eva Renzi, Umberto Raho, Enrico Maria Salerno, Mario Adorf, Renato Romano, Werner Peters, Raf Valenti

The Vampire Lovers (HAMMER/AIP; GB) 91(88)min

In competition with Jean Rollin's peculiarly sub-surrealist erotic vampire pictures and building on their own drift towards sexier notions of vampirism (such as **Taste the Blood of Dracula**, 1969), Hammer embarked on a trilogy derived from Sheridan LeFanu's *Carmilla*. This first instalment features Mircalla (Pitt), the beautiful member of the Karnstein family which escaped destruction by vampire hunter Baron Hartog (Wilmer). She vampirizes the young Laura (Steele), daughter of General Spielsdorf (Cushing), Emma (Smith) and then, in quick succession, Emma's doctor (Mayne), governess (O'Mara) and butler (Hall). Cushing and Wilmer eventually destroy her by staking and decapitation.

The direction shows signs of confusion, veering from an eerily poetic pre-credit sequence to insipid soft-core scenes punctuated by realistically shot Grand Guignol. Pitt is excellent as the sensuous lesbian resented by the various patriarchs whose daughters become her lovers, and Cushing is convincing as the puritanical father capable of extraordinary violence. Unfortunately the film doesn't really explore the contrast between the deliriously passionate sexuality of the young women and the anxious puritanism of the fathers, as both script and direction seem to shrink back from the story's implications, suggesting a typically English unease with luscious eroticism, which too often makes the picture collapse into restrained, but insipid, girlie magazine imagery. Hammer's next Karnstein movie, **Lust for a Vampire** (1970), went even further in this direction.

d Roy Ward Baker *p* Harry Fine, Michael Style *s* Tudor Gates *c* Moray Grant *lp* Ingrid Pitt, Pippa Steele, Madeleine Smith, Peter Cushing, George Cole, Dawn Addams, Kate O'Mara, Douglas Wilmer, Ferdy Mayne, Harvey Hall

El Vampiro de la Autopista *aka* **The Vampire of the Highway** *aka* **The Horrible Sexy Vampire**
(CINEFILMS; SP) scope 91(89)min

Direction, script and acting which all verge on the incompetent make this nudie vampire film set in a Black Forest castle worse than average. The last of the Von Winninger family, Count Oblensky (Wohlfahrt) and his lover (Loran) come to take possession of their inheritance, which requires them to spend the night in the cursed castle which has been the focus of evil goings-on for centuries, due to the activities of the occasionally invisible Baron von Winninger, a vampire. The action is restricted to the vampire's endlessly repeated attacks on anonymous women as they come out of the shower, go to bed, and so on – in fact, as soon as a woman undresses, an attack can be expected. The castle's atmosphere is largely provided by the repetition of a hollow-laughter track at regular intervals. The rest consists of static, overwritten dialogue scenes.

d/s Jim Delavena (José Luis Madrid) *p* Al Peppard *c* Francis Madur (Francisco Madurga) *lp* Waldemar Wohlfahrt, Patricia Loran, Luis Iduni, Adela Tauler, Joe Camroy (Anastasio Campoy), Barta Barry, Victor Davis, Mary Trovar, Joseph Marco, Susan Carvasal

Vampyros Lesbos *aka* **Die Erbin des Dracula** *aka* **Las Vampiras** *aka* **Lesbian Vampires** *aka* **El Signo del Vampiro** *aka* **The Sign of the Vampire** *aka* **The Heritage of Dracula**
(CCC TELECINE/FENIX FILMS; SP,WG) 92min

Franco's sexy, rather sadistic horror movie combines the Countess Dracula motifs with elements of Sheridan LeFanu's *Carmilla* and Bram Stoker's *Dracula's Guest*. Competing with Hammer's drift into Franco territory (**The Vampire Lovers** and **Lust for a Vampire**, both 1970; **Twins of Evil**, 1971), Franco tells of the Count's descendant, a beautiful woman called Nadina (Miranda) who lives on an isolated island. She entices young women to her abode and does what she has to in order to remain young forever. The Spanish version was relatively tame, but the German one, signed with the transparent pseudonym Franco Manera, contained many salacious scenes of lesbianism and bloodsucking. Unfortunately, the slapdash direction complete with irritating tics such as relentlessly repeated zooms, was further hampered by the notoriously inane script which includes such lines as: 'Can you give me any information about a Count Dracula and his family?'

After the series of films produced by Harry Alan Towers, from **El Castillo de Fu Manchu** (1968) to **El Conde Dracula** (1970), mostly starring Maria Rohm, Franco's German thrillers, and horror movies revolved around Miranda, who brought her own brand of sensuality to such diverse figures as the cruel killer in **Mrs Hyde** and the Sadean victim in *Eugenie* (both 1970). Shot in 1970, in Turkey, the film was released in Germany in 1971, while the Spanish version was premièred in 1974.

d/co-s Franco Manera (Jesús Franco) *p* Arturo Marcos *co-s* Jaime Chavarri *c* Manuel Merino *lp* Susan Korda (Soledad Miranda), Dennis Price, Ewa Stroemberg, Paul Mueller, Hiedrun Kussin, Victor Feldman, Jesús Franco, Michael Berling

Virgin Witch (UNIVISTA; GB) 89(85)min

Compared with Hammer's foray into the sex and horror subgenre with **The Vampire Lovers** and **Lust for a Vampire** (both 1970), this nudie by ex-stuntman Austin, although bearing the marks of a shoestring budget, emerges as a far less embarrassed picture and avoids the sniggering approach to sex which mars the Hammer films. The conventional plot has two young women, Betty and Christine (Ann and Vicky Michelle) encounter the lesbian head of a model agency, Sybil (Haines), whose country mansion is the headquarters of a witches' coven run by her husband (Hallett). The two women become involved in satanic rituals, including an atmospherically shot torchlit initiation ceremony culminating in a coupling with a fake Satan. In spite of the tabloid press association of lesbianism with demonic perversions, the charged relationship between Haines and Vicky Michelle is presented with some skill. Even the obligatory heavy-breathing sequences fail to dispel the film's overall suggestion of an intense but repressed sexuality desperately struggling for expression and escaping the control of the male protagonists who are forced into trickery to achieve their prosaic goals. Unfortunately, the shooting and editing of the rest of the picture is below par. Austin went on to direct numerous fantasy programmes for television as well as the unfortunate *Doctor Maniac* (1973).

d Ray Austin *p* Ralph Solomons *s* Klaus Vogel *c* Gerald Moss *lp* Ann Michelle, Vicky Michelle, Keith Buckley, Patricia Haines, James Chase, Paula Wright, Christopher Strain, Neil Hallett, Esme Smythe, Garth Watkins

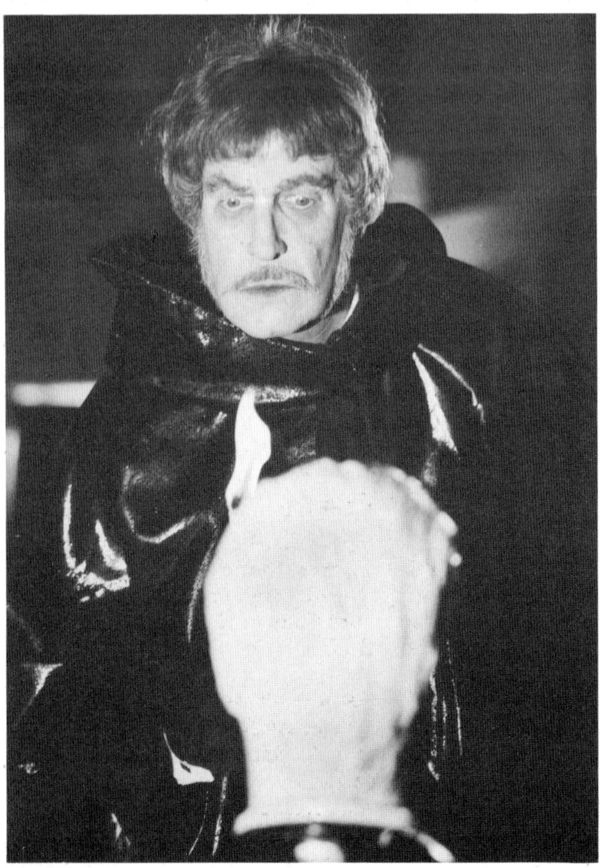

1971

The Abominable Dr Phibes (AIP; GB) 94min

This cross between the standard psycho-killer plot and *The Phantom of the Opera* demonstrates that the genre's third major phase (the German twenties, Hollywood's thirties and the sixties in many countries) was running out of steam and heading for a mutation, a dynamic more clearly represented in Terence Fisher's **Frankenstein and the Monster from Hell** (1973). Described in *Variety* as an 'anachronistic period horror musical camp fantasy', it tells of Dr Phibes (Price), atrociously maimed in a car-crash and now able to speak only through an electronic gadget in his neck, who still plays the organ wonderfully. The plot has him kill the doctors who failed to save his wife's life in surgery. His revenge is modelled on the Old Testament's ten curses unleashed upon Egypt: his first victim is stung by bees, producing swellings reminiscent of the curse of boils; the second is killed by bats, and so on. Brian Eatwell's lavish and expensive art deco sets are wasted by the picture's crassly undergraduate approach, going for easy laughs rather than exploring the potential of the grotesque variations on generic clichés which the script and casting seem to promise. Price, in his 100th feature, is deprived of his most characteristic instrument, his voice. A sequel followed in 1972, **Dr Phibes Rises Again**.

d Robert Fuest *p* Louis M. Heyward, Ron Dunas *s* James Whiton, William Goldstein *c* Norman Warwick *se* George Blackwell *lp* Vincent Price, Joseph Cotten, Hugh Griffith, Terry-Thomas, Virginia North, Aubrey Woods, Susan Travers, Peter Gilmore, Caroline Munro, John Laurie

Las Amantes del Diablo

(LACT INTERNATIONAL FILMS/PRODIMEX FILMS; SP,IT) 90min

Bogged down with lengthy tourist-board footage of the Spanish holiday resort of Marbella, this slow-moving picture sees Elorietta attempting to compete with Jesús Franco in the sex-horror stakes. Dr Nescu (Santoni) is a seductive practitioner of black magic and sadism. His sensuous assistant (Gimpera) recruits the female victims whom Santoni then dresses up as his mother before killing and storing them in a Hindu sarcophagus installed as decoration in his castle. The heroine (Nell), in search of her sister, falls under Santoni's hypnotic spell and is prepared as the sacrificial victim for a black mass whereupon Gimpera turns on her master because she feels attracted to the heroine. He kills her, the heroine kills him and, when the crisis is over, the police arrive to end the story more formally.

Santoni, who also produced the picture, cast his ex-wife (Diaz) and another well-known Spanish socialite, de Mora, in minor roles, destroying much of the picture's credibility for Spanish audiences by reducing it to an ostentatious home movie. He repeated the part of a satanic seducer in **Ceremonia Sangrienta** (1972), which was released a year before *Las Amantes*.

d Joe Lacy (José Maria Elorietta *p* Espartaco Santoni *s* José Luis Navarro, Michael Skaife (Miguel Madrid) *c* Emmanuele di Cola *lp* Espartaco Santoni, Krista Nell, Teresa Gimpera, Carla Conti, Veronica Lujan, Thomas Moore (Enio Girolami), Jaime de Mora, Maruja Diaz, Julio Pena, Luis Villa

Blood from the Mummy's Tomb

(HAMMER/EMI; GB) 94min

Holt, one of Britain's more talented directors, died during the production of this film and Michael Carreras took over for the final week, honourably acquitting himself of a difficult task since the picture attempted a radical rethinking of the awkward mummy subgenre. The script spends a long time constructing a credibly menacing world around an evil deity and offers an interesting exploration of the moral issues involved in releasing another power for evil into a 'real' world which is itself depicted in a decidedly jaundiced manner. Appropriately, the picture

Left: *Vincent Price as* The Abominable Dr Phibes.

Derren Nesbitt and Glynn Edwards as Burke and Hare.

centres on the twin themes of sexuality and parent-child relationships, with a father (Keir) whose quest for knowledge unleashes the power of darkness. As the mummified queen Tera is discovered, his wife dies in childbirth and the father's sin is visited on the daughter, Margaret (Leon), who becomes the vehicle for the mummy's power. The script also has the sense to eliminate the insipid hero (Edwards) early on, concentrating on the strange enchantment that befalls Leon when her father places Tera's ring on her finger, and the desperate fascination exerted by the evil Egyptian queen. When the father mutilates Tera's body to break the spell, the whole ancestral home collapses upon him while, in hospital, the catastrophe's sole survivor, Leon, awakens swathed in bandages.

Holt, ably assisted by Wicking's script (which was adapted from Bram Stoker's *Jewel of the Seven Stars*), plays the film for hypnotic fascination rather than for shock value. Leon is excellent in the dual role of mummy and daughter, making the scarcity of her appearances in fantasy film all the more regrettable. Wicking, fresh from scripting Gordon Hessler's **The Oblong Box** and **Scream and Scream Again** (both 1969), went on to provide the story for one of Hammer's best sexy horror movies, **Demons of the Mind** (1971).

d Seth Holt, (uncredited) Michael Carreras *p* Howard Brandy *s* Christopher Wicking *c* Arthur Grant *se* Michael Collins *lp* Andrew Keir, Valerie Leon, James Villiers, Hugh Burden, Rosalie Crutchley, Aubrey Morris, David Markham, James Cossins, Tamara Ustinov, Penelope Holt

Blood of Ghastly Horror *aka* The Fiend with the Electronic Brain *aka* Psycho-a-Go-Go

(HEMISPHERE) 87min

A prolific exploitation director, Adamson had shown that he was not above cannibalizing his own and others' films with **Horror of the Blood Monsters** (1970). He repeats the formula here. This film originally began life in 1965 as *Psycho-a-Go-Go* and was about jewel thieves using a war-scarred Vietnam vet as a kind of robot. New scenes were added in 1969 and it was released as *The Fiend with the Electronic Brain*. In 1971 more scenes still were added, and the title changed again to *Blood of Ghastly Horror*. By this time the plot had changed considerably, and the film as released features a doctor unleashing a zombie to avenge his son who was destroyed by another doctor's 'artificial brain component'.

Perhaps the most interesting thing about Adamson's films is that several of them are early examples of the work of ace cameramen Laszlo Kovacs (*Close Encounters of the Third Kind*, 1977) and Zsigmond (*Heaven's Gate*, 1980).

d/p Al Adamson *s* Dick Poston, Chris Martino, Sam Sherman *c* Vilmos Zsigmond *se* Lee James *lp* Regina Carol, Roy Morton, Tracey Robbins, Kent Taylor, John Carradine, Tommy Kirk

Burke and Hare

(KENNETH SHIPMAN PRODUCTIONS/ARMITAGE; GB) 91min

A simple-minded exploitative version of the dealings of a medical pioneer, Dr Knox (Andrews), with the homicidal graverobbers (Nesbitt and Edwards) – here depicted as a couple of thick but greedy Irishmen. Much time is wasted inserting supposedly sexy scenes in equally phoney 19th-century Edinburgh brothels and the acting, especially involving the duo's pushy wives (Shenderey and Joyce), is played for broad comedy instead of incongruous horror, as in John Gilling's flawed but interesting **The Flesh and the Fiends** (1960). Stensgaard, an effective Mircalla in **Lust for a Vampire** (1970), is here reduced to a piece of meat tailor-made for the killers, while Andrews hams it up, gleefully carving into bodies during anatomy lessons.

Sewell had made some memorable fantasy movies in black and white (including **House of Mystery**, 1961) but from the mid-sixties onwards his career nosedived. The title song is performed by The Scaffold.

d Vernon Sewell *p* Guido Coen *s* Ernie Bradford *c* Desmond Dickinson *se* Pat Moore *lp* Harry Andrews, Derren Nesbitt, Glynn Edwards, Dee Shenderey, Yootha Joyce, Françoise Pascal, Alan Tucker, Paul Greaves, Yutte Stensgaard, Joan Carol

Cannibal Girls

(SCARY PICTURES PRODUCTIONS; CAN) 84(82)min

A young couple's car breaks down in the remote town of Farnhamville. Here they learn of the legend of the Cannibal Girls and decide to visit the farmhouse, now a restaurant, where the girls supposedly once lived. They are the only customers and are served by their host the Reverend Alex St John (Ulrich), and three beautiful waitresses. Since a maniac is rumoured to be at large they stay the night, only to discover that the legend is indeed true, and that the crazed Reverend has introduced the entire neighbourhood to the delights of cannibalism.

Shot on a tiny budget and under difficult circumstances, *Cannibal Girls* was one of Reitman's earliest directorial efforts: after this film's success he went on to produce David Cronenberg's *Shivers* (1975) and *The Brood* (1976) and thence to direct *Meatballs* (1979), *Stripes* (1981) and **Ghostbusters** (1984). Though quite gruesome in places, the film is more amusing than horrific, thanks largely to excellent improvised comic performances from Levy and Martin as the young couple. As in **Chamber of Horrors** (1966) a buzzer sounds to warn the audiences of impending scenes of horror, whilst a chime announces the all-clear.

d/co-p/co-s Ivan Reitman *co-p/co-s* Daniel Goldberg *co-s* Robert Sandler *c* Robert Saad *se* Richard Whyte, Michael Lotosky *lp* Eugene Levy, Andrea Martin, Ronald Ulrich, Randall Carpenter, Bonnie Neilson, Mira Pawluk, Bob McHeady, Alan Gordon, Allan Price

Chi o Suu Me *aka* Noroi no Yakata-Chi Wo Suu *aka* Lake of Death *aka* Bloodthirsty Eyes *aka* Dracula's Lust for Blood *aka* Japula

(TOHO; JAP) scope 82(79)min

This is the first major Dracula movie in Japan since Nakagawa's disappointing **Onna Kyuketsuki** (1965). A young woman painter, Akiko (Fujita), and her sister Natsuko (Emi)

live in a lakeside house and become entangled in strange goings-on. Natsuko's medical boyfriend (Takahashi) starts getting exsanguinated women to treat and finds his lover becoming pale and distant as well. Fujita remembers her childhood nightmares, which start to return in her paintings, about a mysterious old house where she saw a bloody-lipped vampire with fierce, penetrating eyes and discovers the place really exists and houses a gaunt stranger with fangs and golden eyes (Kishida). A diary found by an old woman's corpse reveals that the mansion's owners had emigrated from Transylvania to escape the vampire's curse but they couldn't prevent their son becoming one. As if on cue, Kishida and the vampirized Emi emerge to attack Fujita and the young doctor, but the corpse intervenes to make the vampire (her son) fall on to a sword, after which the classic ending of Terence Fisher's **Dracula** (1958) is replayed. Yamamoto and his art director, Shuichi Ikuno, stuck close to the iconography established by Hammer, adding their own elegantly cool, pastel-coloured stylization. Good timing and compositions combined with Kishida's fairly restrained acting, for most of the picture, help to make this an interesting movie.

Daiei studios, the main producer of horror films at the time, went bankrupt in 1970, and with Yamamoto's films Toho made a bid for control of the market, hoping to add the Kaidan monopoly to their domination of the Kaiju Eiga (monster movies) thanks to the work of Inoshira Honda. Yamamoto's first vampire movie, **Chi o Suu Ningyo** (1970) had been well received and he went on to make a third, **Chi o Suu Bara** (1975), a silly story about a couple of vampires running a girls' school.

d Michio Yamamoto *p* Fumio Tanaka *s* Ei Ogawa, Katsu Takeura *c* Rokuro Nishigaki *lp* Mori Kishida, Midori Fujita, Osahide Takahashi, Sanae Emi, Kaku Takashina, Hideji Ohtaki, Tadao Fumi, Mika Katsuragi, Tatsuo Matsushita, Fusako Tachibana

The Corpse Grinders (CG PRODUCTIONS) 72(62)min
An endearingly ramshackle exercise in bad taste, *The Corpse Grinders* features Mitchell and Foster as the proprietors of a cat-food firm who find their sales booming after they push a sleeping partner into the meat-grinder when he proposes to withdraw his backing. To meet the demand for that particular mix, they turn first to the local gravedigger (Ball), and then employ a house strangler. The local cats, unfortunately, begin to develop tigerish tendencies on their new diet. Not particularly well staged or acted (to put it mildly), the film nevertheless has moments that Roger Corman might have been proud of. A poster for the cat food with the new ingredient, for example, bears the legend 'For cats who like people'. Equally delightful is a sequence (cut by absurd demand of the British censor) in which victims – still decorously clad in their underwear – fed into the perilously wobbly papier-mâché grinders emerge from the other end as sausagemeat, pink for girls and brown for boys.

d/p Ted V. Mikels *s* Arch Hall, Joseph L. Cranston *c* Bill Anneman *lp* Sean Kenney, Monika Kelly, Sanford Mitchell, J. Byron Foster, Warren Ball

The Crucible of Terror (GLENDALE; GB) 91min
This pleasantly eccentric variation on the house-of-wax theme features Raven as an irascible sculptor who pours molten bronze over women's bodies to produce saleable statues. Most of the picture is taken up with the steamy goings-on in the sculptor's Cornish cottage as people tiptoe from one bedroom to another while a mad killer decimates the occupants of the house. For its climax, the picture shifts into a dreamlike atmosphere, with the mad artist mixing multicoloured concoctions in his cave studio suffused with the glow of the menacing furnace. As he is about to turn the leading lady, Millie (Maude), into a sculpture, she reveals herself to be possessed by the spirit of his first victim, a Japanese girl (Lay), and kills him as she did the others in the picture.

A onetime disc-jockey, Raven is miscast but he struggles gamely, while the others in the cast, including Bolam (better known as a TV sitcom star), seem to enjoy hamming it up in the beautiful Cornish locations. This was the director's first feature, while Newbrook, doubling here as executive producer and cameraman, went on to direct the respectable **The Asphyx** and **The Disciple of Death** (both 1972).

d/co-s Ted Hooker *p/co-s* Tom Parkinson *c* Peter Newbrook *lp* Mike Raven, Mary Maude, James Bolam, Ronald Lacey, Betty Alberge, John Arnatt, Beth Morris, Judy Matheson, Melissa Stribling, Me Me Lay

Las Crueles *aka* **The Exquisite Cadaver** *aka* **El Cadaver Exquisito** *aka* **The Cruel Ones**
(FILMS MONTANA; SP) scope 108(100)min
Gonzalo Suarez, the well-known writer and director of such arty fantasy films as *Aoom*, *El Extraño Caso del Dr Fausto* (both 1969), and *Paranda* (1977), provided the story upon which Aranda based this workmanlike, but at times pleasantly

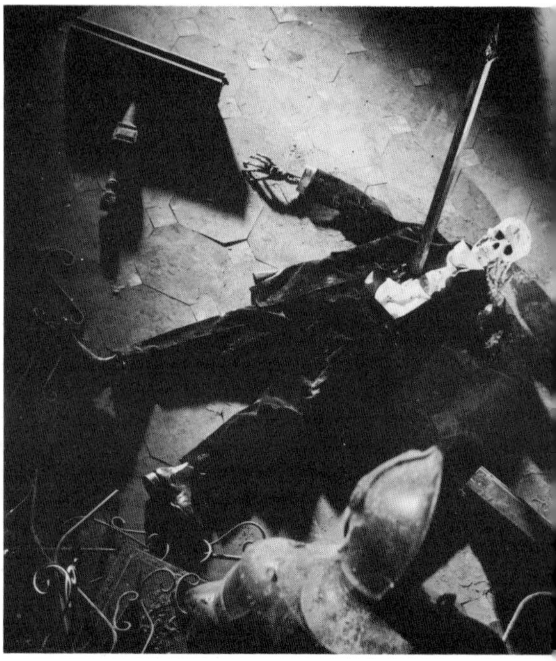

Before and after: the classic ending of Terence Fisher's Dracula *replayed in the interesting* Chi o Suu Me.

Ava Gardner in the erratic but compelling The Devil's Widow.

macabre, picture. After being jilted by her husband (Estrada), Esther (Matheson) tries to commit suicide, but eventually takes up with a lesbian, Parker (Capucine) before finally overdosing. Capucine, bent on revenging her lover's death, entices the husband to her house and shows him Matheson's corpse in the fridge. Then she starts to mail to him things associated with Matheson – a dress, a dead turtle – before getting round to pieces of her body, beginning with a severed hand and ending with a severed head. She completes her revenge by breaking up the man's new marriage.

The idea of driving an 'ordinary' macho male around the bend by confronting him with morbid reminders of the effects of his callous egocentricity is promising, especially since poetic justice is meted out by a woman whose sexual proclivities make her a particularly threatening figure for the macho stereotype. Unfortunately, the story is told as a terror-thriller from the man's point-of-view, inviting the audience to share his horrified reactions and to condemn a perverted psychopath's persecution of a basically nice fellow. The Catalan director, who shot the picture in English, went on to make *La Novia Ensangrentada* (1972), another film focusing on lesbian relations.

d/co-s Vincente Aranada *co-s* Antonio Rabinad *c* Juan Amoros *lp* Carlos Estrada, Capucine, Judy Matheson, Teresa Gimpera, Alicia Tomos, José Maria Blanco

Il Delitto del Diavolo *aka* **Le Régine** *aka* **Queens of Evil** *aka* **Les Sorcières du Bord du Lac**
(FLAVIA CINEMATOGRAFICA/CARLTON FILM EXPORT/ LABRADOR FILM; IT,FR) 91(85)min
Cervi, producer of Antonioni's *Deserto Rosso* (1964) and the Bertolucci-Pasolini picture *La Commare Secca* (1962), turned director in 1968. This film, his second feature, offers a gloomy fairytale of the European hippy era. The devil, a wealthy bourgeois driving a Rolls Royce, deplores modern motorbike-riding youth's imperviousness to oldfashioned notions of sin and guilt. He arranges for a boy (Lovelock) to get involved with three eccentric women who share a house. He becomes their lover and when he eventually decides to abandon his quest for personal freedom and settle down with them, they kill him. The devil then appears to congratulate them and to send them on their way in search of a new victim. Although presenting the bourgeoisie and women as the two biggest threats to male youth's sense of freedom – a widespread notion at the time within youth-culture – the movie's unsettling atmosphere endows many sequences with a genuine sense of style.

d/co-s Tonino Cervi *p* Raoul Katz *co-s* Antonio Benedetti, Antonio Troisio *c* Sergio d'Offizi *lp* Haydee Politoff, Raymond Lovelock, Evelyn Stewart (Ida Galli), Silvia Monti, Gianni Santuccio, Guido Alberti

Demons of the Mind *aka* **Blood Will Have Blood**
(HAMMER/FRANK GODWIN PRODUCTIONS; GB) 89min
The sins-of-the-fathers motif – making the elder generation's neuroses responsible for the younger one's reprehensible behaviour – is a popular but double-edged theme in a large number of horror movies of this period, ranging from Michael Reeves' complex **The Sorcerers** (1967) to the simplistic **The Beast in the Cellar** (1970).

This movie is set in the 19th century and has Elisabeth (Hills, in the role originally intended for pop singer Marianne Faithfull) escape from the custody of her elders and spend some idyllic times with her lover, Carl (Jones) before being returned to the oppressive care of her father (Hardy), living in his gloomy baronial mansion. The Baron is maniacally severe with his daughter and son (Briant), convinced they are afflicted by the family's strain of insanity. In fact, the savage violence unleashed on the local village and, in a gruesomely bloody finale, on the family itself results from the projection of his own unconscious fantasies on to his son who is thus driven to an orgy of murders. The villagers stop the mayhem by plunging a burning cross into the Baron's gut, leaving Hills and Jones to provide the happy ending.

Shot with all the classic horror paraphernalia, from the doom-laden mansion to the torch-wielding villagers and swaying carriages with frightened coachmen, the picture shows that ex-television director Sykes was ready to take his place alongside Peter Sasdy in Hammer's second generation of horror stylists. But whereas Sasdy succeeded in making some extraordinary movies (**Countess Dracula**, 1970; **Hands of the Ripper**, 1971) before being reduced to hackwork, Sykes's career stagnated. The result was a number of powerfully orchestrated sequences in otherwise routine or poor films (**Venom**, 1971; **The House in Nightmare Park**, 1973; **To the Devil a Daughter**, 1976) which never really matched this first impressive achievement.

d Peter Sykes *p* Frank Godwin *s* Christopher Wicking *c* Arthur Grant *lp* Paul Jones, Gillian Hills, Robert Hardy, Michael Hordern, Patrick Magee, Shane Briant, Yvonne Mitchell, Virginia Wetherell, Kenneth J. Warren, Thomas Heathcote

The Devil's Widow *aka* **Tam Lin** *aka* **The Devil's Woman** (WINKAST; GB) scope 106min
This oddly uneven but watchable picture has an unhappy production history. Shot in 1969, but shelved when Commonwealth United collapsed, AIP unsuccessfully tried to chop the material into exploitable shape. McDowall returned to the film and finished post-production work in 1971.

The story's beginning is clichéd as the middle-aged Mrs Cazaret (Gardner) and her retinue leave swinging London for her Scottish manor. Her favourite, Tom (McShane) falls in love with the local minister's daughter, Janet (Beacham), although warned by Gardner's secretary (Wattis) that the old lady will not be jilted. Designated the victim in a game of murders, and suffering from drug-induced hallucinations, McShane runs for his life through the misty forest, pursued by a pack of imaginary hounds of hell in a sequence worthy of **The Most Dangerous Game** (1932). After the boring opening and the syrupy freeze-frame depiction of McShane and Beacham's blossoming romance, McDowall's direction, together with inspired dialogue alluding to Robert Burns' *The Ballad of Tamlin* – about a young man held in thrall to the queen of the fairies – begin to bring the picture to life. Impressive sequences include Beacham impulsively fortifying herself with the purchase of a yellow rose before trying to obtain an abortion, and other touches flesh out the characters. Equally well done is the gradual build-up of a broodingly enigmatic sense of menace that culminates in Gardner's appearance sporting a glittering devil mask as McShane is turned into a panic-stricken prey, making the final part of the picture delightfully inventive. The depiction of Gardner as a near-carnivorous den-mother surrounded by homosexual goons points to the repressed aspects of the fantasy scenario which underpin both plot and imagery, but the film's overall effect is strangely compelling.

d Roddy McDowall *p* Alan Ladd Jnr *s* William Spier *c* Willy Williams *lp* Ava Gardner, Ian McShane, Richard Wattis, Cyril Cusack, Stephanie Beacham, David Whitman, Sinead Cusack, Joanna Lumley, Jenny Hanley, Madeline Smith

The Devils

(RUSSO PRODUCTIONS/WB; GB) scope 111min

With this picture, Russell matches the crassly exploitative Adrian Hoven's similar **Hexen Bis aufs Blut Gequaelt** (1969). The plot offers a version of Aldous Huxley's *The Devils of Loudun* (1952) as adapted for the stage by John Whiting. A priest, Grandier (Reed), supports the King of France against Richelieu's plans to strip the aristocracy of its powers. But Russell isn't interested in the cleric's reactionary politics. Instead, he paints Reed as a victim of sexually repressive forces represented most vividly – and predictably – by a woman unaware that her 'natural' hysterical tendencies are being manipulated to political ends by an agent of the Cardinal. The mother superior, deprived of ways of expressing her natural lewdness, is played by Redgrave and the cynical exorcist who manipulates the women's essential masochism in order to get rid of the philandering priest by Gothard. The film soon degenerates into an orgy of torture applied to both men and women while, for extra effect and additional symbolic weight, the country is shown as ravaged by an outbreak of the plague. In the end, what remains of Reed is burnt alive.

Throughout the film, Russell indulges his predilection for camp imagery and his virulent contempt of women, so much so that his bombastic grandiloquence keeps generating images that recall 19th-century equivalents of Mills and Boon romances as revised through the spectacles of cheap Italian sadistic comic strips (**Isabella Duchessa dei Diavoli**, 1969). What Russell's films depict is far less horrifying than their implicit demand that the viewer share their risible notion of what constitutes 'art'.

d/co-p/s Ken Russell *co-p* Robert H. Solo *c* David Watkins *lp* Oliver Reed, Vanessa Redgrave, Dudley Sutton, Max Adrian, Gemma Jones, Murray Melvin, Michael Gothard, Georgina Hale, Christopher Logue, Andrew Faulds

Dr Jeckill y el Hombre Lobo *aka* Dr Jekyll y el Hombre Lobo *aka* Doctor Jekyll and the Werewolf *aka* Dr Jekyll and the Wolfman

(ARTURO GONZALEZ; SP) scope 96(85)min

The sixth adventure of Waldemar Daninsky (Molina) picks up on the resemblance between the Mr Hyde of both Rouben Mamoulian's and Victor Fleming's **Dr Jekyll and Mr Hyde** (1932 and 1941). Molina's story has him subjected to the ministrations of a Dr Jeckill (Taylor) which releases his Mr Hyde who does the nightspots of London's Soho in top-hat and cloak, indulging in much the same villainies as his Victorian ancestor, and competing with the wolfman for Waldemar's personality. The blonde heroine (Corrigan), who seeks to help him, is foiled by the dark-haired assistant (Miller) who goes mad and kills the good doctor, and is killed in her turn by Hyde who then proceeds to turn into a fully fledged werewolf before being terminated by his lover. In spite of a 70mm format, the innovation of a triple personality as the central character and a final shot cribbed from Cocteau's *L'Eternel Retour* (1943), the pedestrian direction, aggravated by atrocious dubbing, make this a thoroughly routine contribution. Molina's next outings as Daninsky were **El Retorno de Walpurgis** (1973), **La Maldición de la Bestia** (1975) and **El Retorno del Hombre Lobo** (1980).

d Leon Klimovsky *p* Arturo Gonzalez *s* Jacinto Molina *c* Francisco Fraile *lp* Paul Naschy (Jacinto Molina), Shirley Corrigan, Jack Taylor, Mirtha Miller, Barta Barri, Luis Induni

Dr Jekyll and Sister Hyde

(HAMMER/EMI; GB) 97min

The idea of recasting the Jekyll and Hyde story in a tale of transexual change runs the risk of being modishly sensational, but Baker's sensibly solid direction for the most part avoids cheap laughs and plays it admirably straight. The trouble comes with the script: the evil side of Jekyll (Bates) is represented by a sensuous woman (Beswick) who is also made responsible for the Jack the Ripper killings as the doctor needs female hormones to conduct his experiments and takes to murdering prostitutes for the purpose. However, whereas Terence Fisher's **The Two Faces of Dr Jekyll** (1961) was genuinely subversive, this picture unthinkingly proposes the cliché that a sensual woman is all that Victorian morality claimed her to be: the darkly transgressive forces of untamed nature which, unchecked by the bounds of civilization, becomes evil incarnate. That said, the complexity of the motif itself produces ingeniously ironic touches, including the proposition that a transexual identity is maintained only at the price of eliminating women. Accordingly, the notion of femininity represented by Hyde is very much a male caricature. Beswick's performance as Hyde is nicely judged, clearly bringing out the fetishistic aspects that characterize her appearance as a male fantasy. Although there are a few attempts to explore the complexities of sexual-identity fantasies further, as in the scene where Jekyll feels driven to make a pass at his girlfriend's brother who is in fact Hyde's lover, the movie's narrative efficiency mitigates against a more courageous exploration of the motif's possible ramifications. The obligatory gory murders and the use of Burke and Hare-type graverobbers betray some of the commercial and generic constraints the film was unable to overcome. In the end, and in spite of the excellent technical credits, Baker's picture fails largely through lack of courage or imagination as it anxiously tries to close the pandora's box opened up by the story's interesting initial idea.

Ken Russell's hysterical film version of John Whiting's play, The Devils.

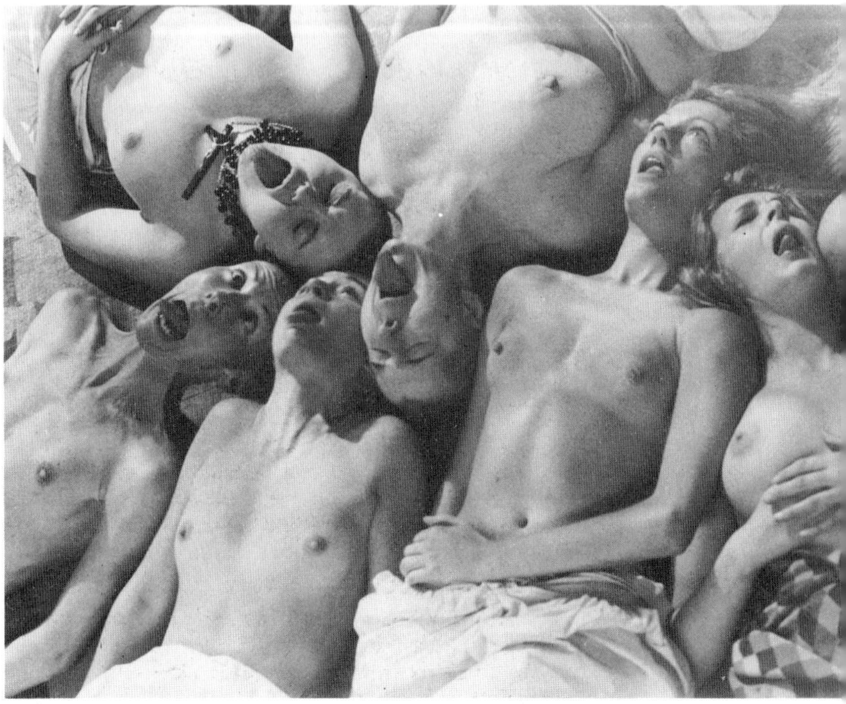

d Roy Ward Baker *co-p/s* Brian Clemens *co-p* Albert Fennell *c* Norman Warwick *lp* Ralph Bates, Martine Beswick, Gerald Sim, Lewis Fiander, Dorothy Alison, Neil Wilson, Ivor Dean, Susan Broderick, Virginia Wetherell

Ecologia del Delitto *aka* **Antefatto** *aka* **Reazione a Catena** *aka* **The Ecology of a Crime** *aka* **Before the Fact** *aka* **Twitch of the Death Nerve** *aka* **Carnage** *aka* **Bloodbath Bay of Blood**

(NUOVA LINEA CINEMATOGRAFICA; IT) scope 90(76)min

Bava's humorously titled picture anticipates the psycho-gore explosion of the late seventies with its chain-reaction scenario offering 13 murders like so many stanzas in a funeral chant. Two lovers are skewered on a spear that suddenly shoots up through the bed, a woman's face is split by an axe, a wheelchair-ridden woman (Miranda) is garrotted, a man is repeatedly knifed low in the belly, and so on. But Bava's film is different from those of his followers in his refusal to psychologize his Grand Guignol operas: the plot simply acknowledges desire for possession as sufficient motive to drive the picture from one scene to the next (all the killings revolve around attempts to possess a lovely piece of real estate, a desirable 'scene'). Neither does he resort, on this occasion, to the traditional psycho-killer figure as the killings are carried out by various characters, with the final murders committed as a form of child's play: the two surviving murderers are playfully shot dead by their own two children.

Unfortunately, Bava doesn't quite manage to get rid of all vestiges of characterization or 'psychological realism' so the film falls short of being the symphony of violence it might have become in a non-commercial context. Nevertheless, he does achieve some striking images, including a woman swimming in a lake who bumps into floating corpse, and the blue and grey colours of the misty landscapes. Zooms, no doubt programmed by the imperative to work quickly, spoil some scenes that cried out for Bava's particularly fluid use of camera movement which were so much in evidence in **Operazione Paura** (1966). It is worth noting the presence in the cast of Miranda, the star of Ophuls' masterly *La Signora di Tutti* (1934).

d/co-s/co-c Mario Bava *p* Giuseppe Zaccariello *co-s* Joseph McLee (Giuseppe Zaccariello), Filippo Ottoni, Dardano Sacchetti, Franco Barberi *co-c* Antonio Rinaldi *lp* Claudine Auger, Luigi Pistilli, Claudio Volonte, Anna Maria Rosati, Laura Betti, Chris Avram, Brigitte Skay, Isa Miranda, Leopoldo Trieste, Paola Rubens

Escalofrio Diabolico *aka* **Diabolical Shudder**

(ABC; SP) 85min

This film was shot in the feudal castle used for Miguel Madrid's **Necrophagus** (1971) and concerns an evil man, played by Martin in his directorial début, who keeps his half-brother chained in a dungeon and attempts to expedite the death of his demented mother while a bunch of hooded satanists roam the castle's cellars preparing rituals requiring human sacrifices. The luckless half-brother's fiancée (Shepard) chooses to spend her vacation in this household and, predictably, is selected as the next sacrificial victim. The happy ending/bloodbath sees the half-brother break loose and machine-gun the satanists, rescuing his lover from the altar, while the police arrive in time to shoot the villain who falls to his death from the battlements. With total disregard for consistency, the picture mixes jet travel and the gothic, candlelit castle reverberating to the sounds of clanging chains and shrieks. For his first stint behind the camera, Martin was helped by Elorietta with whom he had made a number of action movies.

d/p/co-s George (Jorge) Martin *co-s* Daniel Ceballos, Joe de Lacy (José Maria Elorietta) *c* Alfonso Nieva *lp* George (Jorge) Martin, Paty Shepard, Silvana Sandoval, Marta Monterrey, Cris Huerta, José Villasante, Antonio Vidal Molina, Rosario Royo

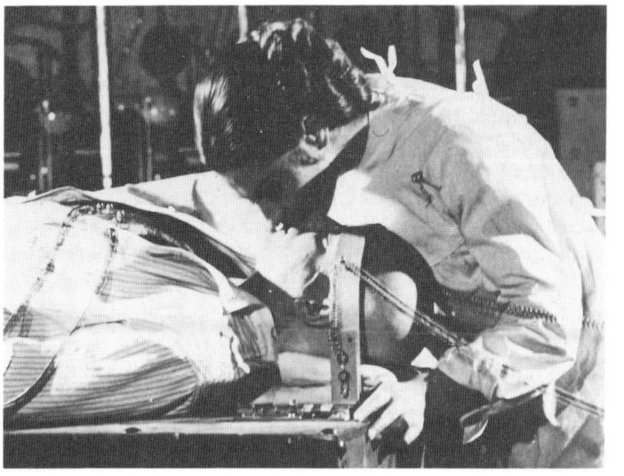

Right: *The monster as toyboy:* La Figlia di Frankenstein.

The Fiend *aka* **Beware the Brethren** *aka* **Beware of the Brethren**

(WORLD ARTS MEDIA; GB) scope 98(87)min

After his unhappy experience with the interesting but severely flawed **Incense for the Damned** (1970), Hartford-Davis filmed this tale about a bizarre religious sect which indulges its unsavoury forms of religious terrorism in the suburbs of London, at the home of Birdie (Todd) and her psychotic son (Beckley). The son, raised in the brutalizing religious atmosphere and fixated on his diabetic mother, is a security guard who does missionary work on the side: he kills prostitutes to save them from sin, records the act and plays the tapes back to himself at home. Todd is concerned that he shouldn't have soiled himself coming into contact with sexually active women. When the sect's minister (Magee) insists on removing artificial elements like medicine for diabetes from the house, the dutiful son nails the minister to the cross of his own chapel. Hinde plays the district nurse and Leith her journalist sister who investigate the goings-on in suburbia. Whatever opportunities the script may have offered to examine the chilling ramifications of lunatic sects or psychotic mother-son relationships, or even the cinematic perversities of homicidal voyeurism, are lost in the series of ugly, rapid closeups to signal 'key' sequences.

d/p Robert Hartford-Davis *s* Brian Comport *c* Desmond Dickinson *lp* Ann Todd, Tony Beckley, Patrick Magee, Madeline Hinde, Percy Herbert, Suzannah Leigh, David Lodge, Ronald Allen, Janet Wild, Diana Chappell, Maxine Barrie

La Figlia di Frankenstein *aka* **Lady Frankenstein** *aka* **Madame Frankenstein**

(CONDOR INTERNATIONAL; IT) scope 99(85)min

Stressing crudely visceral details and nudity, this poor imitation of Hammer's Frankenstein movies spares Cotten, who plays the Baron, by killing him off early on. The central figure is Tania (Neri), his daughter, a qualified surgeon who concocts a creature with Cotten but then improves her technique by putting a friend's brain into the body of a good-looking stable boy, thus creating an ideal, well-endowed lover. Unfortunately, as the torch-wielding villagers burst into the castle at the end of the movie, they find her falling victim to her lover's all too vigorous attentions.

d/p Mel Welles (Ernst von Theumer) *s* Edward di Lorenzo *c* Richard Pallotin (Riccardo Pallotini) *se* CIPA *lp* Joseph Cotten, Sara Bay (Rosalba Neri), Mickey Hargitay, Paul Mueller, Paul Whiteman, Herbert Fuchs, Renata Kashe, Ada Pometti, Lorenzo Terzon

Fright (FANTALE FILMS; GB) 87min

An openly sexploitative film in which George plays a young woman who finds herself terrorized by the homicidal ex-husband (Bannen) of a friend (Blackman), who escapes from the local asylum and returns home one dark night to exact revenge. The film manages to mobilize both mental illness and the notion of woman as automatic victim, sexual and otherwise, for the generation of shock and suspense, while suggesting some sympathy for the male maniac. Collinson's direction is full of inserted closeups and over-familiar shots of a telephone looming in the foreground. He also appropriates one of John Gilling's best sequences by showing the cemetery sequence from **The Plague of the Zombies** (1966) on a television. Gates's awkward script and the demand for instant shocks leaves the solid cast little room for manoeuvre. Collinson also directed **Straight on Till Morning** (1972) for Hammer in a similarly brutish fashion. The British prototype for this kind of picture was not **Psycho** (1960), but the inept **The Twisted Nerve** (1968).

d Peter Collinson *p* Harry Fine, Michael Style *s* Tudor Gates *c* Ian Wilson *lp* Susan George, Honor Blackman, Ian Bannen, John Gregson, George Cole, Dennis Waterman, Tara Collinson, Maurice Kaufman, Michael Brennan, Roger Lloyd Pack

La Furia del Hombre Lobo *aka* **The Fury of the Wolfman** (MAXPER; SP) scope 85min

Molina's fifth werewolf movie takes up the motifs of his second outing, **Las Noches del Hombre Lobo** (1968). This time, Count Waldemar Daninsky (Molina) seeks the help of a female doctor (Cristal) who is still bitter because he once jilted her in favour of Erika (Lujan). She gets Waldemar to bite his beloved, turning her into a werewolf as well. But instead of this producing a perfectly suited couple and satisfying Cristal's revenge, all three feel unhappy and end up getting killed. Weakly directed and unintentionally funny, the film benefits from the delightful visual presence of the Argentinian-born Cristal, who makes up, in part, for the ridiculous dialogue. As usual, Molina devised and scripted the story as well as acting the lead, making the series effectively his work. His next outing as Daninsky was **Dr Jeckill y el Hombre Lobo** (1971).

d José Maria Zabalza *s* Jacinto Molina *c* Leopoldo Villaseñor *lp* Paul Naschy (Jacinto Molina), Perla Cristal, Veronica Lujan, Mark Stevens, Michel Rivers

The Gore Gore Girls *aka* **Blood Orgy** (LEWIS MOTION PICTURE ENTERPRISES) 90min

Released in 1974, this was Lewis' last gore film and indeed his last feature as a director. Here a private investigator (Kress) tries to solve the murder of a series of go-go girls with the help of local newspaper reporter Farrell. Undoubtedly Lewis' most extreme movie, this includes scenes in which a victim has her face repeatedly smashed into a mirror, another in which a girl's mutilated buttocks are rubbed with salt, a hot iron applied to a face, a head shoved into a pan of boiling oil and, most notorious of all, a scene in which a girl's nipples are cut off and one breast gushes forth chocolate milk.

Put thus, or looked at only via stills, the film sounds totally depraved and obscene. However, Lewis' films have to be seen and not read about to be fully appreciated and, paradoxically, it is precisely at their most extreme (and so *obviously* self-parodic) that they become least unpleasant. As John McCarty puts it in *Splatter Movies*, Lewis' excesses 'defuse these films of their psychological grimness, turning them into exercises in outrageousness and absurdity. If it were not for this sense of their own absurdity, in fact, Lewis' films would be little more than Nazi death camp films re-staged as entertainment'. Lewis' films have about as little to do with 'realism' of any kind as Tom and Jerry.

d/p/co-se Herschell Gordon Lewis *s* Alan J. Dachman *c* Alex Ameri (Eskandar Ameripoor) *co-se* Allison Louise Downe, Robert Lewis *lp* Frank Kress, Amy Farrell, Hedda Lubin, Russ Badger, Nora Alexis, Phil Laurenson, Frank Rice, Ray Sager, Henny Youngman

Hands of the Ripper (HAMMER; GB) 85min

Hungarian-born Sasdy's third and best film to date is an object lesson in suspense timing and confirms the promise shown in **Taste the Blood of Dracula** (1969). Anna (Rees) witnesses her father, Jack the Ripper, gorily kill her mother, after which he kisses his daughter and flees. Later, whenever light reflections and an embrace coincide, Anna goes into a trance-like state and stabs whoever embraces her. A psychiatrist (Porter) knows of her leanings but ignores the actual triggering mechanism. Trying to cure her, he instead gets drawn into covering up for her murders until he himself becomes her victim. The climax occurs in St Paul's Cathedral where the mortally wounded doctor calls to Rees who is threatening another young woman (Merrow) in the whispering gallery: Rees jumps down on to his paternal body, their blood mingling as they lie dead, framed by a circular pattern on the cathedral's floor.

The incestuous desires imprinted in the young girl's mind in the shape of a mortiferous kind of penetration are echoed by the psychiatrist's desire for her, as he obsessively tries to penetrate her mind, fascinated but blind to the perversity of the ties that bind them until they find each other in a macabre union. Sasdy uses the two-phase trigger, an embrace followed by a reflected light shimmering in her eyes, with consummate skill, finding a different and surprising staging for each killing in a sophisticated cat-and-mouse game with the viewer's expectations. In addition, he adds a disturbing sensuality to the proceedings, heightened by the glorious colours and the enchanting beauty of Rees. The picture is perhaps most interestingly seen as Sasdy's reply to Michael Powell's **Peeping Tom** (1960), putting a woman in Mark's position as the victim of the father's perversion, prey to a compulsion to translate expressions of love into spectacularly staged lethal penetrations. Formal aspects of Sasdy's film, too, reinforce the parallels between the two films. These include the use of specifically cinematic devices such as the complex play upon the nexus of looks both within the movie and at the image. Unfortunately, Sasdy's later work didn't match the strangely overwhelming power exuded by this movie but he showed himself to be an extremely talented cineaste with *Hands of the Ripper*, arguably the last masterpiece produced by Hammer.

d Peter Sasdy *p* Aida Young *s* L. W. Davidson *c* Kenneth Talbot *se* Cliff Gulley *lp* Eric Porter, Angharad Rees, Jane Merrow, Keith Bell, Derek Godfrey, Dora Bryan, Marjorie Rhodes, Lynda Baron, Norman Bird, Margaret Rawlings

Susan George terrorized by Ian Bannen in Fright.

Eric Porter as the psychiatrist with one of the victims in Peter Sasdy's marvellous Hands of the Ripper.

Hanno Cambiato Faccia *aka* **They've Changed Faces** *aka* **They Have Changed Their Faces** *aka* **They Have Changed Their Face** (FILMSETTANTA; IT) 90min

Like Hammer's **Dracula AD 1972** (1972), ex-critic Farina's début feature offers an updated – although more overtly allegorical – version of the Dracula legend. Nosferatu (Celi) is the boss of a Fiat-type enterprise who summons a young man (Disperati) to his mansion and offers him a directorship if the employee is prepared to become a ruthless exploiter of people. In the end, a revolt against the 'unacceptable face' of capitalism fails, as does an attempt to kill the boss, and the hero takes his rightful place among the 'undead' executives.

Alternating humour and leaden symbolism, the movie is noteworthy mainly for confirming Fisher's more intelligently oblique approach to the story's contemporary relevance, making Dracula not a representative of modern capital but of antiquated, feudal power structures which anachronistically persist within advanced capitalist societies and feed on its fantasies. Farina went on to make **Baba Yaga** (1973), an adaptation of Guido Crepax's fetishistic comic strip.

d/co-s Corrado Farina *co-s* Giulio Berrute *c* Aiace Parlini *lp* Adolfo Celi, Giuliano Disperati, Geraldine Hooper, Francesca Modigliani, Amadeo Tommasi, Rosalba Bongiovanni, Pio Buscaglione, Salvadore Cantagalli

O Homem Lobo *aka* **The Werewolf**
(PINHEIRO FILMES; BRAZIL) 91min

In this cheap film, Rossi blames paternal neglect for lycanthropy among the younger generation. The father in question, a professor (Braga), is provided with excuses: he has a terribly possessive wife (Cerine) and his son, Roberto (played by the director), was adopted – his mother died in childbirth – and sent to a boarding school where, with the onset of adolescence, the boy began to grow into a werewolf. Roberto indulges his cravings in such a way that suspicion always falls on his father, who accepts the blame until he is forced to face up to his responsibilities and sets out to discipline his son, armed with a gun and a silver bullet. This call for fathers to reassert their authority over wives and sons sells its macho message with long sequences showing scantily dressed women in the woods being attacked by the director-werewolf. A more interesting Brazilian werewolf picture was made by Elyseu Visconti Cavalleiro, **O Lobisomem** (1974). São Paulo based Rossi returned to the theme of paternal authority four years later with **Seduzidas pelo Demonio** (1975).

d/s Raffaele Rossi *p* José Pinheiro de Carvalho *c* Antonio Bonacin Thomé *lp* Raffaele Rossi, Claudia Cerine, Lino Braga, Juliana Pitelli, Tony Cardi, Osmano Cardoso

I Drink Your Blood
(JERRY GROSS PRODUCTIONS) 83(73)min

I Drink Your Blood had all the makings of another **Night of the Living Dead** (1968) or **The Texas Chainsaw Massacre** (1974) but, unfortunately, threatened with an X rating by the MPAA (apparently this was one of the very few times when a film was threatened with an X on account of violence rather than sex), the film was extensively cut and re-edited and 10 minutes of new footage were added. The plot has a group of hippies who are also into satanism give LSD to an old man. In revenge, his son injects the blood of a rabid dog into meat pies and gives them to the hippies. They become rabid, killing each other and the inhabitants of a nearby town, spreading the disease further in the process. As the film now stands what looks like it might have been a raw, ferocious thriller has become a frustrating exercise in splicing, incessantly building up to scenes of bone-crushing horror and violence which never actually happen. As one American reviewer put it: '... any picture which actually visualizes one of the prime youth nightmares of our time – a horde of literally rabid, axe-wielding hard-hats hunting down members of the younger generation – must have some claim to redeeming social value.'

d/s David Durston *p* Jerry Gross *c* Jacques Demarecaux *lp* Bhaskar, Jadine Wong, Ronda Fultz, Elizabeth Marner-Brooks, George Patterson, Riley Mills, Iris Brooks, John Damon, Richard Bowler, Tyde Kierney

Jack el Destripador de Londres *aka* **Jack the Ripper** *aka* **Jack the Mangler of London**
(CINEFILMS/INTERNATIONAL APOLLO; SP,IT) scope 87min

This lacklustre update of the Ripper story, released in 1972, transfers the maniac's activities from Whitechapel to Soho. When a mysterious figure starts knifing prostitutes, the police make the connection with the Ripper's old methods, except that his modern guise also slices bits off the body to keep as mementoes: a hand, eyes, an ear, and so on. Suspicion first falls on Bruno (Molina), then on an effete aristocrat, but in the end the investigating detective's own assistant is revealed to be the villain. When he is discovered amidst his collection of physical memorabilia in the basement of a country house, Molina turns up to kill the maniac with his own disembowelling stiletto. The direction is unimaginative, staging killing after monotonously repeated identically shot killing. Jesús Franco's version, **Jack the Ripper** (1976), with Klaus Kinski, managed to make the story disturbingly chilling again, but the best sound version to date remains **Murder By Decree** (1979).

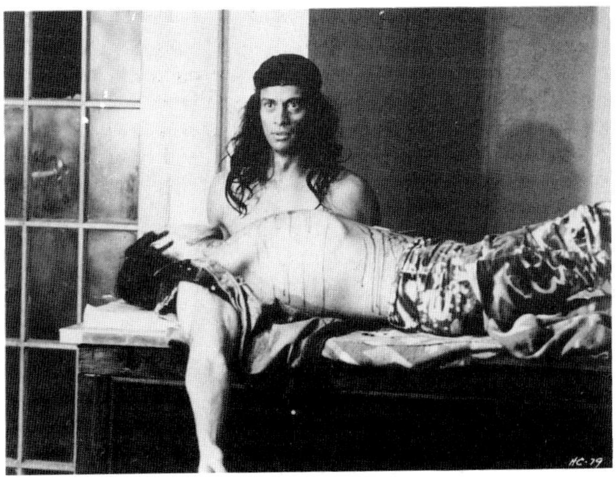

Right: *Two of the rabid hippies in the gory* I Drink Your Blood.

d/p/co-s José Luis Madrid *co-s* Jacinto Molina, Sandro Contineza *c* Diego Uberda *se* Antonio Molina *lp* Paul Naschy (Jacinto Molina), Patricia Loran, Rensso Mariñano, Andres Resino, Orquidea de Santis, Franco Borelli, Irene Mir, Victor Iregua

Let's Scare Jessica to Death (PAR) 89min
A poetic and persuasive film, this borrows from both the gothic and post-**Night of the Living Dead** (1968) traditions to depict the death of the love generation as a group of dropouts find rural America less than accommodating.

Jessica (Lampert), newly released from a sanatorium and not cured of her fascination with death, joins her husband (Heyman) and his ageing hippie friend (Connor) on an apple farm where they hope to establish themselves. There they meet Emily (Costello), a young squatter, who resembles a Victorian vampire girl who was drowned in a nearby lake, and the hostile townsfolk, all of whom seem to bear recent wounds and shamble about like senile ghouls. As Jessica's paranoia grows, her hallucinations take over the film's reality, and Hancock stages several truly terrifying sequences, charging the lovely settings with an air of unease and paying off with a combination of the ghastly and the surreal as everyone becomes a monster while Jessica's fragile psyche fractures. One confrontation between Jessica and Emily, in which a playful swimming expedition turns nasty, is capped with the extraordinary image of the ghost girl submerging while wearing a modern bathing suit only to bob up moments later in a soaked nineteenth-century wedding dress. Directed with eerie brilliance, this goes beyond the banality of an is-it-all-in-her-mind? game. It is one of the cinema's greatest ghost stories.

d John Hancock *p* Charles B. Moss Jr, William Badalto *s* Norman Jones, Ralph Rose *c* Bob Baldwin *lp* Zohra Lampert, Barton Heyman, Mariclare Costello, Kevin Connor, Gretchen Corbett

La Llamada del Vampiro *aka* **Aquellarre de Vampiros** *aka* **The Curse of the Vampyr**
(LACY FILMS/SESENA/ARCO FILMS; SP) 102(88)min
An atmospheric (though amateurishly acted) vampire story released in 1973, this tells of a woman doctor (Lacy) and her assistant Erika (Sorel) who are invited by Carl von Rysselbert (Ney), the son of a dying baron, to stay in his sinister mansion by a lake. Ney and Sorel become lovers, but under the influence of the full moon, he vampirizes her and later attacks the doctor as well. One night villagers see Sorel rising from the lake in response to Ney's call. The place only returns to normal after Ney has been staked and Lacy has left the area. Although made for Spanish domestic consumption, the film had a limited circulation in other European countries.

Elorietta specialized in action pictures and had helped one of his regular stars, Jorge Martin, with his directorial début **Escalofrio Diabolico** (1971). His other horror films include **Las Amantes del Diablo** (1971) and **El Espectro del Terror** (1972).

d/co-s Joseph de Lacy (José Maria Elorietta) *p* Riccardo Vazquez *co-s* Enrique Gonzalez Macho *c* Juan Ruiz Romero *lp* Beatriz Lacy, Nicholas Ney, Ines Skorpio, Diana Sorel, Loretta Martin, Loli (Loretta) Tovar, José Villasante, Antonio Jimenez Escribano, Rosario Royo

Una Lucertola con la Pelle di Donna *aka* **A Lizard in a Woman's Skin** *aka* **Schizoid** *aka* **Una Lugartija con Piel de Mujer** *aka* **Le Vénin de la Peur**
(INTERNATIONAL APOLLO/LES FILMS CORONA/ATLANTIDA FILMS; IT,SP,FR) scope 105(95)min
Following the example of Dario Argento, who infused his crime thrillers with sex and horror elements, Fulci's tale of a woman (Bolkan) whose nightmarish fantasies begin to turn into reality, liberally draws on gory and gothic imagery. Together with the claustrophobic motifs characteristic of Fulci's movies (**Sette Note in Nero**, 1977; **Il Gatto Nero**, 1981), the most memorable images are in the dream sequences designed by Rambaldi: whimpering dogs with their stomachs cut open, swarms of bloodthirsty bats, a row of silently screaming, eyeless cadavers, and so on. For the most part, however, the frenetic zooming and zip-panning serve only as reminders of the emptiness of both the imagery and the story. Baker appears as a policeman in one of his rare, invariably disastrous, excursions into Italian movies. Fulci eventually achieved some notoriety with imitations of George Romero's films such as **Zombi 2** (1979).

d/co-s Lucio Fulci *p* Edmondo Amati *co-s* Roberto Gianviti, José Luis Martinez Molla, André Tranche *c* Luigi Kuveiller *se* Carlo Rambaldi *lp* Florinda Bolkan (José Soara Bulco), Stanley Baker, Jean Sorel, Leo Genn, Silvia Monti, Anita Strindberg, Georges Rigaud, Alberto de Mendoza, Mike Kennedy, Edy Gall (Galleani)

O Macabro Dr Scivano
(NATUS PRODUÇOES CINEMATOGRAFICAS; BRAZIL) b/w 72min
Promoted as the first Brazilian science fiction film, this is in fact far closer to a horror cheapie. The plot tells of Dr Scivano (Calhado), a failed politician, who returns to his village where he becomes an object of ridicule. Dabbling in macumba, he receives a piece of gold each night from a ghostly figure and thus becomes rich. One night he turns into a vampire and starts preying upon the local women until he is killed and reduced to ashes in front of a crucifix (echoing Terence Fisher's famous ending of **Dracula** (1958), which was also repeated in the Japanese **Chi o Suu Me** (1971) and numerous other pictures). Taking its cue from **Psycho** (1960), the film ends with a psychologist discussing the case of Dr Scivano and diagnosing him as paranoid, which, according to the experts in the film, is confirmed when they discover a shop-window mannequin in his bed. For publicity purposes, the co-director and star of the film adopted the name Scivano in the castlist, imitating José Mojica Marin's gimmick of appearing in public as Zé do Caixao, the central character of many of his most unpalatable films.

co-d/co-p/co-s/co-c Raúl Calhado *co-d* Rosalvo Cacador *co-p* Faustino Correia Campos, Laercio Silva *co-c* Wanderley Silva *se* Josef Reindl *lp* Edmundo Scivano (Raúl Calhado), Luis Leme, Oswaldo de Souza, Henricao (Henrique Filipe), Lauro Sawaya, Genesio Aladim, Ester Brasil, Cleber Holanda

Las Melancolicas *aka* **Women of Doom** *aka* **Exorcism's Daughter** (DAURO FILMS; SP) 110(93)min
This courageous but flawed political fable made in fascist Spain and drawing on *Marat-Sade* (1966) and on the libertarian overtones of the late sixties anti-psychiatry movement, suffered by being released and promoted in the wake of **The Exorcist** (1973). Set in an asylum for insane women, ruled by a military-style dictator (Rabal) who nostalgically looks back on his role in the Spanish Civil War, the story chronicles the disappointing efforts of a progressive psychoanalyst (Santoni) to re-connect with the healthy forces that caused the inmates to go mad. His efforts are impeded by the institution's governors and by the townspeople, who accuse him of sexual improprieties and witchcraft. His endeavours are concentrated on Tania (Gade), a young woman terrified by dolls and shoes. After some setbacks, he discovers her state of shock was caused by witnessing her mother, allegedly possessed by the devil, being exorcized and killed in the process. In the Spanish context, where the Catholic establishment described 'reds' as being possessed by the devil, this traumatic memory constitutes a barely veiled allusion to the outcome of the Civil War. In the end, the doctor leads a procession to the village square and bitterly accuses the townspeople of hypocrisy. This seals his fate and he is forced to leave, assuring Gade that he will return when he has found an effective way to free her. In the

Left: *Barbara Parkins with her labrador, complete with human mask, in the bizarre* The Mephisto Waltz.

meantime the asylum's dictator dons his military regalia and continues his brutal regime.

The director gave his own name to the idealistic doctor and quotes freely from Jean Vigo (a pillow fight in slow motion) and Luis Buñuel (insects, a dramatic bell-tower scene), but even these obvious pointers fell on blind eyes as the picture was sold on the basis of a brief exorcism scene and the women-in-prison motif. Aured, assistant director on this film, went on to make violent exploitation pictures such as *Los Frios Senderos del Crimen* and **El Espanto Surge de la Tumba** (both 1972).

d/s Rafael Moreno Alba *p* Espartaco Santoni *c* Mario Pacheco *lp* Analia Gade, Francisco Rabal, Espartaco Santoni, Maria Asquerino, José Vivo, Yelena Samarina, Maria Vico, Eulalia del Pino, Pilar Bardem, Victor Israel

The Mephisto Waltz

(QM PRODUCTIONS/FOX) 115(109)min

This complicated occult tangle has the soul of a dying pianist (Juergens) transferred to an unwitting younger one (Alda), while the soul of Alda's wife (Bisset) – after nightmare revelations of satanic influences concerning her child – vengefully transfers itself after suicide to Juergens' incestuous lover (Parkins). Adapted from a novel by Fred Mustard Stewart, the film is basically **Rosemary's Baby** (1968) and **The Hands of Orlac** (1925) amalgamated into a muddy brew of diabolism and perversion, blood transfusions and transferences of personality. Here and there Wendkos manages to bring off some bizarre effects – a dog trotting round in a human mask, for instance – but it is all too perfunctory to rouse much interest.

d Paul Wendkos *p* Quinn Martin *s* Ben Maddow *c* William W. Spencer *lp* Alan Alda, Jacqueline Bisset, Barbara Parkins, Bradford Dillman, Curd Juergens, William Windom

Muñeca Reina

(CINEMATOGRAFICA MARCO POLO; MEX) scope 90min

A lyrical ghost story based on a tale by Carlos Fuentes, this movie recounts a man's growing obsession with a female fantasy figure. When he is about to get married, Rocha falls prey to a morbid nostalgia for his youthful ambition to become a writer. In this state, the image of a child called Amilamia (Brambila) comes to haunt him with sweet persistence. Trying to find out as much as he can about her, he locates the house where she lived, interrogates her parents (Bravo and Souza) and learns that she died and that her mummified body is preserved in the basement of the house. Gradually, his fascination transforms the child into a young woman (Medina) with whom he enters into an intense relationship to the annoyance of his fiancée (Rojo). In the end, he is totally overwhelmed by his fantasy love life, abandoning all social ties and degenerating into a ghost himself.

This auspicious début by Olhovich made him part of the so-called renovation of the Mexican cinema in the early seventies. On his return from Moscow's prestigious film school, he taught at the University of Film Studies (CUEC) in Mexico City.

d/co-s Sergio Olhovich *p* Leopoldo Silva, Marco Silva *co-s* Eduardo Lujan *c* Alex Phillips Jnr *lp* Ofelia Medina, Enrique Rocha, Helena Rojo, Antonio Bravo, Pilar Souza, Carlos Cortes, Leopoldo Silva, Marco Silva, Mario Casillas, Rocio Brambila

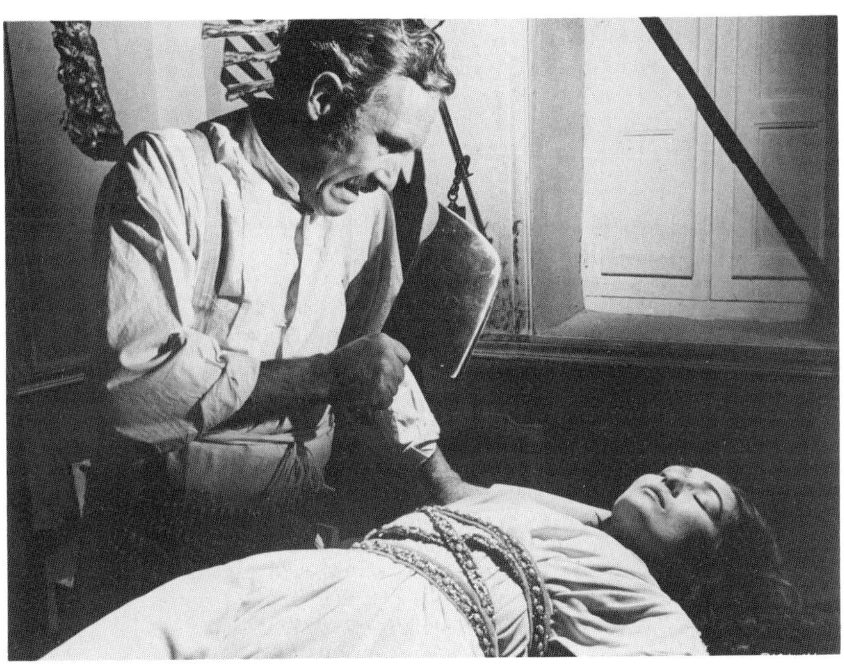

The superior Murders in the Rue Morgue.

Murders in the Rue Morgue (AIP) 87min

After their interesting collaboration on **Scream and Scream Again** (1969), Wicking and Hessler appear to have their complex narrative games better under control in this film, although the alleged 'front office' interference still mars the picture. The plot is a basic revenge story – a disfigured actor returns to execute his persecutors – but the story is told in an intriguingly layered form which ultimately comes to represent the movement of fantasy itself, with its constant shifts from one level to another.

Charron (Robards) and his company perform Poe's story on the stage. His wife, the actress Madeleine (Kaufmann) is prey to recurrent nightmares (boringly shot with the predictable colour filters) which reverberate into her life as a performer; the accident that befell Marot (Lom) – Kaufmann threw vitriol in his face – occurred on stage and is revealed to have been staged by Robards. Lom then acts out a fake suicide and returns, disfigured, to avenge himself. But his revenge also takes the form of an enactment of Kaufmann's nightmare, until, at the film's climax, he falls to his death on the stage of the theatre but still overcomes even that barrier between fantasy (play) and reality by returning from the dead to invade Kaufmann's world, driven by his deliriously intense passion for her.

It is appropriate that a movie with constantly shifting references to performance and fantasy should itself be staged as a carefully designed costume (melo)drama, adhering to the conventions of the genre, with pseudo-historical personages such as Vidocq (Celi), while also obediently rehearsing the familiar, traditional moments of the Grand Guignol story, the evocation of the Beauty and the Beast motif of Poe's story, the beheading of Robards on stage, referring to French judicial practice, and so on. In this way the boundaries between fantasy and reality are totally blurred, suggesting they cannot be distinguished since each is shaped under the determining pressures of the other. Perhaps the film's greatest achievement is that it manages to convey this fundamental insight without falling into the paranoid delirium of *Scream and Scream Again*. This allows the film's final sequences to be lifted to the level of surrealist poetry. The performances of Robards, Celi, Palmer and Lom, each with their distinctive theatrical style, further enriches this sophisticated play upon the mechanisms of spectacle and representation itself. The result is Hessler's finest achievement to date.

d Gordon Hessler *p* Louis M. Heyward *s* Christopher Wicking, Henry Slesar *c* Manuel Berenguer *lp* Jason Robards, Herbert Lom, Christine Kaufmann, Adolfo Celi, Lilli Palmer, Maria Perschy, Michael Dunn, José Calvo, Peter Arne, Werner Umberg

Myonuriui Han *aka* The Ghost

(DAE YANG FILM; ROK) scope 88min

Park is the principal, and often most stylish, South Korean horror director, approaching the traditional tales in period settings with an aesthetic which recalls (for Westerners, anyway) the Japanese Kaidan movies: bright, saturated blue, red and green colours with white-robed female spectres and exaggerated, fairytale-type acting. This picture consists of two stories. The first tells of a young bride who, when captured by bandits, bites off her tongue and bleeds to death, whereupon she appears as a ghost enticing her husband to follow her into the realm of the dead. The second story is rooted in the social conditions of a feudal, landowning society with its own problems of family lineage and the transmission of property. A rich scholar whose wife is barren takes a concubine for breeding purposes, but his wife locks the newcomer away and murders her immediately after she has given birth, pretending the concubine's child is her own. The girl's ghost returns to haunt the household and drive the jealous villainess insane. A similar story was used by Kim In Soo for his **Huphyokwi Yanyo** (1981). Park's subsequent pictures include the beautifully stylized **Two Women from the Nether World** (1982) and the poetic possession story **Manryongui Kok** (1980).

d Park Yoon Kyo *s* Choi Jin *c* Koo Moon Suk *lp* Yoon Mira, Paek Il Sub, Sa Miya

Necrophagus *aka* **El Descuartizador de Binbrook** *aka* **Graveyard of Horror**
(FILMS INTERNACIONALES; SP) scope 88min
Madrid, co-scenarist of **Las Amantes del Diablo** (1971), wrote and made his début film with a team of relative newcomers. Set in Scotland, it tells of Michael (Curran) who returns home to find that his wife died in childbirth. Suspecting foul play, he digs up her coffin which is empty, as are the other graves in the cemetery. His brother, a famous scientist, experimenting with drugs that cause mutations, has vanished as well. But then the earth begins to move and heave, a pair of claws break through the soil, followed by an ugly-looking monster, and it emerges that the scientist brother had succumbed to the effects of one of his drugs and been buried for months while corpses were fed to him.

Since the direction is amateurish, the acting wooden and the script confused, one can only conclude that it was Nieva's Eastmancolor cinematography which won the film first prize at the 1971 Festival of the Cine de Terror at Sitges. The castle featured in the film was re-used for Martin's **Escalofrio Diabolico** (1971). Madrid's next contribution to the genre was **El Asesino de Muñecas** (1974).

d/s Michael Skaife (Miguel Madrid) *p* Tony Recoder *c* Alfonso Nieva *se* Medina *lp* Bill Curran, Beatriz Lacy, Victor Israel, Frank Braña, Yocasta Grey, Catherine Ellison, Marisa Shiero, J. R. Clark, Antonio Escribano

The Night Digger *aka* **The Road Builder**
(YONGESTREET/TACITUS; GB) 110min
The imaginative author of fantasy and children's stories, Dahl, used Joy Crowley's *Nest in a Falling Tree* as a basis for the script of this old-dark-house chamber-horror piece. A gothic mansion is inhabited by a blind, domineering old lady (Brown) and her frustrated, middle-aged daughter (Neal). The plot chronicles their encounter with a charming but psychopathic handyman played by Clay in his film début. However, the script signally fails to renew the formulaic material and histrionic acting, especially by Brown, is used to make up for the story's lack of inventiveness.

d Alastair Reid *p* Norman S. Powell, Alan D. Courtney *s* Roald Dahl *c* Alex Thomson *lp* Patricia Neal, Pamela Brown, Nicholas Clay, Jean Anderson, Yootha Joyce, Peter Sallis, Brigit Forsyth, Graham Crowden, Diana Patrick

Night Hair Child (LEANDER FILM; GB) 89min
Louis Malle's *Le Souffle au Coeur* (1971) treated the motif of a child's pubertal incest fantasies in a glossily melodramatic way. Kelly's film offers a paranoid and rather cowardly version of the theme, by substituting a stepmother (Ekland) for the real thing, and making the husband/father (Krueger) a naïve dimwit and the child (Lester) a fully fledged murderous psychotic. These safeguards allow the picture, mostly shot in Spain, to concentrate on its real business of stringing together luridly voyeuristic shots, providing titillating child-sex scenes – rendered acceptable by passing them off as the imaginings of a sick brain – and turning the mother into an even sicker person who finally frees herself from the boy's attentions by luring him into a fatal car accident. The potentially interesting exploration of the sexual pathology of the family in terms of the unconscious fantasies at play in the family romance is thus transformed into a misogynistic sexploitation picture which offers the audience what it is supposed to crave while hypocritically condemning as 'sick' the very fantasies and images the film seeks to convert into box-office cash.

d James Kelly *p* Graham Harris *s* Trevor Preston *c* Luis Cuadrado, Harry Waxman *lp* Mark Lester, Britt Ekland, Hardy Krueger, Lilli Palmer, Harry Andrews, Conchita Montez, Collette Jack

The cemetery, a classic sequence of the traditional horror film, Night of Dark Shadows.

Night of Dark Shadows *aka* **Curse of Dark Shadows**
(DAN CURTIS PRODUCTIONS/MGM) 97min
This is a follow-up to **House of Dark Shadows** (1970) which in turn was based on America's first day-time teleseries to feature the supernatural, *Dark Shadows*. Like *House* produced and directed by Curtis, who also produced the original teleseries and featuring several of the original players of both the series and the first film, this uses the same setting and family, but with a new storyline. Here, Quentin Collins (Selby) inherits a crumbling New England mansion, Collinwood. After a while begins to feel himself possessed by the spirit of his ancestor Charles (Selby again) and a whole series of supernatural evils begin. That said, the film is considerably less interesting than its predecessor, its only real asset being its splendidly spooky setting – the sumptuous Hudson River gothic mansion at Tarrytown NY, once owned by rubber baron Jay Gould.

d/p/co-s Dan Curtis *co-s* Sam Hall *c* Richard Shore *lp* David Selby, Lara Parker, Kate Jackson, Grayson Hall, John Karlen, Nancy Barrett, James Storm, Diana Millay, Christopher Pennock, Thayer David

The Nightcomers
(SCIMITAR/ELLIOTT KASTNER-JAY KANTER-ALAN LADD JNR PRODUCTIONS; GB) 96min
Like people clinging to a flat-earth theory, the makers of this picture apparently still believed in the long-discredited notions

of 'psychological' literary criticism which mistakes the literary constructs known as 'characters' for real people. They compounded this backwardness by selecting Henry James' *The Turn of the Screw* for such a treatment, ignoring the very point of James' 'undecidable' story and providing a banal 'explanation' of the very things James chose not to explain.

According to this picture, Quint (Brando) and Jessell (Beacham) were a pair of crude perverts, and the children (Harvey and Ellis) imitated some of their habits. When Beacham wants to leave, the children kill her and then shoot an arrow into Brando. At the end, a newly recruited governess (Palk) arrives. The poverty-stricken direction endearingly persists in failing to find a suitable camera position throughout the film and, in desperation, uses the zoom lens to point out the 'significant' bits in virtually every shot. Entering into the spirit of the movie, Brando performs like a clownish parody of himself, nearly (but not quite) succeeding in transforming the film into crazy comedy.

d/p Michael Winner *s* Michael Hastings *c* Robert Paynter *lp* Marlon Brando, Stephanie Beacham, Thora Hird, Harry Andrews, Verna Harvey, Christopher Ellis, Anna Palk

La Noche del Terror Ciego *aka* **Tombs of the Blind Dead** *aka* **La Noche de la Muerta Ciega** *aka* **Crypt of the Blind Dead** *aka* **Night of the Blind Dead**

(PLATA FILMS/INTERFILME; SP,PORT) scope 93(86)min

In spite of an uneven script, which occasionally lurches into cynical commercialism, as in the flashback to lesbian fumblings in a girls' school, this is a well made and effective horror product. The basic idea is that the cruel Templars, executed in the 13th century and their corpses left for the crows to pick out their eyes, rise from their graves in search of blood. Since they have no eyes, they locate their victims by sound only. After introducing the Templars with some grisly 13th-century torture scenes – often cut from release prints – the plot has a group of youngsters stray into a dilapidated monastery. At night, the graveyard comes alive, withered hands burst through the heaving earth and mouldering, caped bodies lumber through the foggy cemetery, mount upon ghostly horses and ride off in slow motion. The cadaverous Templars are shown in all their gory details – courtesy of José Luis Campos' makeup – as they move in on the sound of their screaming and panting victims, draining them of blood.

The structuring of the narrative, as in the juxtaposition of a rape with the rising of the undead, clarifies the nature of the fantasy at stake in the movie: the emergence of the sightless clerical knights is provoked by sexual desire and is therefore, according to religious logic, presented as a punishment for sexuality, especially that of women. The putrefying zombies and the bloodless corpses of their victims are what remains after people have been drained of desire, with brutal violence substituting for sex. The ending sees the only surviving heroine, who jumped on to a passing train, followed by hordes of zombies, arrive at a station, totally crazed among the slaughtered passengers, about to spread the scourge of puritanism across the rest of the world. The picture spawned three sequels: **El Ataque de los Muertos Sin Ojos** and **El Buque Maldito** (both 1973), and **La Noche de los Gaviotas** (1975).

d/s Amando de Osorio *p* Salvadore Romero *c* Pablo Ripoll *se* Julio Garcia Soria *lp* Oscar Burner, Lone Fleming, Maria Silva, José Telman, Helen Hay (Maria Elena Arpon), Juan Cortes, Rufino Ingles, Veronica Limera

Marlon Brando and Stephanie Beacham consummate their strange love in the overblown The Nightcomers.

La Notte che Evelyn Usci dalla Tomba *aka* **The Night Evelyn Came out of the Grave** *aka* **The Night She Arose from the Tomb** *aka* **The Night that Evelyn Left the Tomb**

(PHOENIX CINEMATOGRAFICA; IT) scope 103(88)min

This sexy psycho-horror story briefly and unconvincingly trespasses into Jesús Franco territory. An unbalanced English lord (de Teffé), given to whipping prostitutes in his castle's dungeon, finds his wife's corpse rising from the grave to drive him insane. However, the ghost is simply his second wife (Malfatti) scheming to inherit his wealth, but she is poisoned by her lover (Murdock) who is having an affair with Susan (Bianchi), one of the flagellating lord's victims at the beginning of the movie. The plot meanders on in this fashion, turning victims into tormentors and vice versa until a respectable running time has been achieved. The picture's main assets, the physical charms of Bianchi, were nearly all removed by the censor. In a sequence where a dying Malfatti confronts Bianchi, the emphatically edited closeups à la Sergio Leone reveal that the director was more at home making Italian westerns under the alias Hal Brady. His next horror effort also featured Malfatti, **La Dama Rossa Uccide Sette Volte** (1972).

d/co-s Emilio P. Miraglia *co-s* Fabio Pittoru, Massimo Felisatti *c* Gastone di Giovanni *lp* Anthony Steffen (Antonio de Teffé), Erika Blanc (Enrica Bianchi Colombatto), Marina Malfatti, Rod Murdock, Giacomo Rossi Stuart, Umberto Raho, Roberto Maldera

La Notte dei Dannati *aka* **Night of the Damned**

(PRIMAX; IT) scope 90(87)min

An unusually engaging movie about a reincarnated witch who seeks vengeance against the family of her aristocratic husband who sentenced her to death long before. The classically constructed tale starts in Sherlock Holmes fashion, with a pipe-smoking detective (Brice), closer to Poe's Auguste Dupin than to Conan Doyle's hero, who receives a letter asking for help. The ending sees the detective saving his own wife (Viotti) from the witch by smashing the urn containing the original witch's ashes and thus causing her reincarnation to shrivel into dust. As well as introducing an understated sense of humour, Ratti deploys a few Hitchcock-type effects such as the fleeting superimposition of a skull on to a dying man's face. The detective comes across as a somewhat dimwitted poseur, which is appropriate in a genre which, by definition, refuses rational explanations.

Ratti, a minor director of exploitative fare, is best known for his respectable biopic *Eleonora Duse* (1974) and an effective evocation of fascism, *Dieci Italiani per un Tedesca* (1962).

d Peter Rush (Filippo Walter Maria Ratti) *p* Nicola Addario, Lucio Carnemolla *s* Aldo Marcovecchio *c* Girolamo la Rosa *se* Rino Carboni *lp* Pierre Brice, Patrizia Viotti, Angelo de Leo, Mario Carra, Antonio Pavan, Daniele d'Agostini, Irio Fantini, Carla Mancici

L'Occhio nel Labirinto *aka* **Blood**
(TRANSEURO FILM/TV13; IT,WG) 94min
Caiano, best known for directing Barbara Steele in **Amanti d'Oltretomba** (1965), here tells an unlikely story of a woman (Dexter) who dreams that her psychiatrist-lover (Frank) is brutally slain by a knife-wielding fiend. Persecuted by this vision, which includes a nightmarish, white-corridored labyrinth dominated by a huge eye, she enlists the help of a gangster (Celi) who lives in a castle with a range of dissolute characters presided over by Valli. After an obligatory LSD trip and some sadistic sex thrills in the basement, it is revealed that the heroine is a schizophrenic and that she is in fact the fiendish slasher, a performance she repeats on her gangster friend.

With the exception of a few well-designed scenes and the shock discovery of a severed head in the fridge, the movie is constructed on sanctimoniously hypocritical premises: the moral of the story is that, below the surface, all women are mad. No matter how inoffensive and victimized they may appear to be, at any moment they can turn into homicidal maniacs, especially when they come into contact with drugs that release their 'inner selves'. The male hoodlum, on the other hand, is presented as a little eccentric but basically a victim who fully deserves our empathy.

d/co-s Mario Caiano *p* Nello Santi, Hans Pfluger *co-s* Antonio Saguera, Horst Hachler *c* Giovanni Ciarlo *se* De Rossi Sforza *lp* Rosemary Dexter, Adolfo Celi, Horst Frank, Alida Valli, Franco Ressel, Benjamin Lev, Michael Maien, Sybil Danning, Gigi Rizzi

Octaman *aka* **Octa-Man** (FILMERS GUILD) 90min
This film is a return to the world of aquatic monsters for the co-scriptwriter of *The Creature from the Black Lagoon* (1954), here making his dismal directorial début. Designed by George Barr, the creature was actually constructed by Rick Baker. Baker later co-created the gallery of aliens in the famous cantina sequence of *Star Wars* (1977), and won an Oscar for his makeup on **An American Werewolf in London** (1981). However, the creature in the monster suit (it walks on two feet and has four arms plus two appendages) is ridiculous. It has the usual yen for the heroine, and the rest is padded out with endless footage of the same set of caves being explored.

d/co-p Harry Essex *co-p* Joel Freeman *s* Leigh Chapman *c* Robert Caramico *lp* Kerwin Mathews, Pier Angeli, Jeff Morrow, David Essex, Jerome Guardino

La Plus Longue Nuit du Diable *aka* **Au Service du Diable** *aka* **La Notte Piu Lunga del Diavolo** *aka* **La Terrificante Notte del Demonio** *aka* **The Devil's Nightmare** *aka* **The Devil's Longest Night**
(DELFINO FILM/CETELCI; BEL,IT) scope 95(87)min
A surprisingly well-shot story, this combines the clichéd situation of the family curse and the travellers stranded in an aristocratic mansion with the folkloric theme of the seven deadly sins. The curse is on the family of Baron von Rumberg (Servais): the eldest daughter in each generation shall be an agent of the devil. Seven travellers, directed to the house by a man in black – the devil (Emilfork) – spend the night and are killed by a ghastly woman (Blanc) exactly when each commits the particular sin they represent. Made up to resemble Barbara Steele, Blanc is revealed to be the product of an illicit affair between the Baron's elder brother and the housekeeper, which makes her the carrier of the curse. The murders follow each other with relentless predictability as one is decapitated, one falls on a bed of spikes, and so on. The direction telegraphs the violent climaxes, dissipating the suspense.

One of the elaborate shocks that form the backbone of Dario Argento's Quattro Mosche di Velluto Grigio.

Brismée had taught at a film school in Brussels. This was his first feature and benefited from technical advice of the French commercial director André Hunnebelle.

d/co-s Jean Brismée *p/co-s* Charles Lecocq *co-s* Patrice Rhomm, André Hunnebelle *c* André Goeffers *lp* Erika Blanc (Enrica Bianchi Colombatto), Jean Servais, Daniel Emilfork, Jacques Monseau, Ivana Novak, Shirley Corrigan, Colette Emmanuelle, Lorenzo Terzon, Lucien Raimbourg, Christian Maillet

Quando os Deuses Adormecem
(NELSON TEIXEIRA MENDES PRODUCTORA E DISTRIBUIDORA DE FILMS; BRAZIL) 82min
Marins' second exercise in mock-religious infantile megalomania stars himself as the admittedly insane but powerful, miracle-performing Messiah first featured in *Finis Hominis* (1971). The gods go to sleep and evil – manifested in the form of a sex epidemic and primitively occult practices in the cities' poor quarters – rules the world. Finis Hominis is sent to prevent human sacrifices and restore moral law and order, which he does before returning whence he came, an insane asylum. After the gruesome torture and mutilation pictures in which he starred as Zé do Caixao, Marins' two Finis Hominis movies present blatant reparation fantasies with himself as the saviour of the world, revealing (and in a way pathetically designating) where he speaks from: the site of madness. In his next Zé do Caixao film, **O Exorcismo Negro** (1974), Marins dramatized the complementarity of Zé and Finis by playing a double role: himself, using his real name, and his *alter ego*, Zé.

d/co-s José Mojica Marins *p* Nelson Teixeira Mendes *co-s* Rubens Francisco Luchetti *c* Edward Freund *lp* José Mojica Marins, Andrea Eryan, Amires Paranhos, Sabrina Marquezinha, Walter Portela, Rosalvo Cacador, Nivaldo Lima, Alzinete Santana

Quattro Mosche di Velluto Grigio *aka* **Four Flies on Gray Velvet** *aka* **Four Patches of Grey Velvet** *aka* **Four Flies on Grey Velvet** *aka* **Quatre Mouches de Velours Gris**
(SEDA SPETTACOLI/MARIANNE PRODUCTIONS; IT,FR)
scope 105(94)min
After the successful **L'Uccello dalle Piume di Cristallo** (1970) and the banal thriller *Il Gatto a Nove Code* (1970), Argento's third movie shows him refining his commercially efficient

shock-machine view of cinema. Here he tells the story of a drummer (Brandon) whose acquaintances are viciously murdered by – predictably, in an Argento movie – a mysterious figure who turns out to be his wife (Farmer). With the flimsiest of narratives, the director concocts long sequences playing cat and mouse with the viewer and eventually offers release in brutally violent explosions of female aggression, intensified by Morricone's obsessive score and plenty of shrieking. The technique is most evident in a scene where a terrified woman hides in a cupboard while the killer passes by; she then creeps away in the dark only to be suddenly attacked by a figure jumping out of the shadows. The procedure is mechanical but effective and was later used by John Carpenter for his finale in **Halloween** (1979). Having set the terms for a new psycho-slasher genre acceptable to mainstream cinema, Argento then followed its commercial impetus into the splatter genre with **Profondo Rosso** (1975), **Suspiria** (1977) and **Inferno** (1979).

d/co-s Dario Argento *p* Salvatore Argento *co-s* Luigi Cozzi, Mario Foglietti *c* Franco di Giacomo *lp* Michael Brandon, Mimsy Farmer, Jean-Pierre Marielle, Francine Racette, Bud Spencer (Carlo Pedersoli), Calisto Calisti, Marisa Fabbri, Oreste Lionello, Costanza Spada

Reflection of Fear *aka* **Labyrinth** *aka* **Autumn Child** (COL) 89min

In this, former cinematographer Fraker's second directorial feature (after the magnificent western, *Monte Walsh*, 1970), Locke is the adolescent kept secluded from the outside world by her mother (Ure) and grandmother (Hasso) on a large country estate. When, after an absence of ten years her father (Shaw) returns to ask for a divorce so that he can marry Kellerman, Locke develops a strong love for him and an obsessive hatred for her mother and grandmother, who are brutally murdered by an apparently male intruder. After Kellerman too is attacked, Shaw pursues the assailant only to discover it is Locke, who is in fact a boy, brought up from birth as if she were a girl, by a mother who is obsessed with a lifelong hatred of men.

Shelved for two years after completion, the film was drastically cut to qualify for a PG rating. In spite of excellent acting and camerawork *Reflection of Fear* comes across as a heavy-handed and ponderous imitation of **Psycho** (1960).

d William A. Fraker *p* Howard B. Jaffe *s* Edward Hume, Lewis John Carlino *c* Laszlo Kovacs *lp* Robert Shaw, Sally Kellerman, Mary Ure, Sondra Locke, Signe Hasso, Mitchell Ryan, Gordon DeVol, Gordon Anderson, Victoria Risk, Leonard John Crofoot

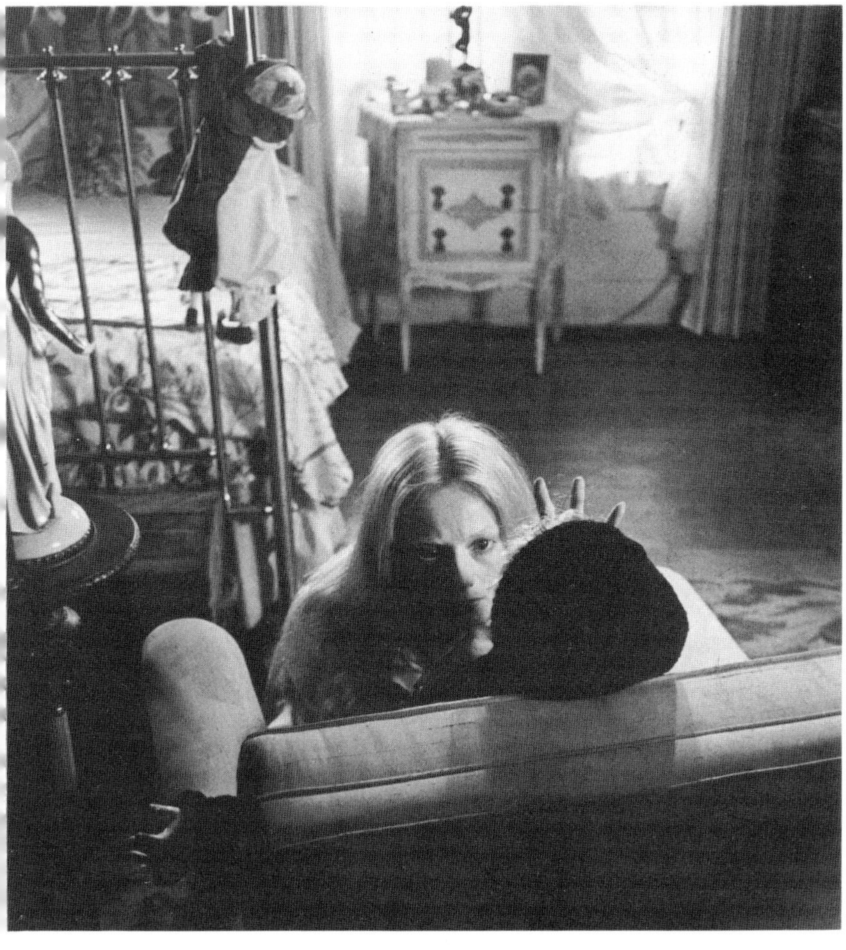

Sondra Locke in a sequence from the sadly mutilated Reflection of Fear.

Requiem pour un Vampire *aka* **Vierges et Vampires** *aka* **Sex Vampires** *aka* **Requiem for a Vampire** *aka* **Virgins and Vampires** *aka* **The Virgins and the Vampires** *aka* **Caged Virgins** *aka* **The Crazed Vampire**

(LES FILMS ABC; FR) 95min

Rollin's fourth sex-vampire film in a row achieved some splendidly morbid imagery, largely through his skilful use of spotlights and bright colours, while the stylized sadean sex scenes add their own dimension of obsessive intensity. Characterization and narrative are kept to a minimum, emphasizing the film's status as a fantasy chronicling some of the (at times) misogynist erotic motifs underpinning French surrealism – the feeding ground of Rollin's imagination. As in Hans Bellmer's photographs, the bodies of the actors and especially of the actresses are reduced to formal elements, to sexual signs upon which and into which the phantasmatic drives are carved out. In this respect, Rollin's films anticipate the sadism used by Alain Robbe-Grillet in his films.

The rudimentary story has two women on the run seek shelter in an ominous castle where they fall prey to a sadistic vampire. Obviously shot on a shoestring, the sex scenes look as if they were inserted as autonomous fragments, probably to ensure success at the box office. But within these terms, they are beautifully achieved comic-strip nightmares which give a shape to the perverse flipside of catholicism grafted on to traditional male oedipal anxieties. With its dank cemetery, a gallery of hooded skeletons, bizarre rooms and slithery vaults, the picture comes close to Lovecraft – except that its sexual components are more graphically presented. With long periods devoid of dialogue, this is one of Rollin's most lyrical films, surpassed only by his **Lévres de Sang** (1975). For his next film, **La Rose de Fèr** (1973), he produced a horror version of Romeo and Juliet set in a cemetery.

d/co-p/s Jean Rollin *co-p* Sam Selsky *c* Renan Polles *lp* Marie-Pierre Castel, Mireille Dargent, Philippe Gaste, Louise Dhour, Dominique, Michel Delesalle, Dominique Toussaint, Paul Biscaglia, Olivier François, Antoine Mausin

The Return of Count Yorga

(AMERICAN INTERNATIONAL/PEPPERTREE) 97min

A sequel to **Count Yorga, Vampire** (1970), involving many of the same personnel, but clearly made with a bigger budget. The style is also more expansive and expressionist, starting off with an elaborate sequence in a graveyard, where a horde of ghouls make their appearance, and proceeding to a fancy-dress party at which half the men present seem to be rigged out as Draculas. The narrative design is broadly similar to that of the earlier film, with Yorga (Quarry) using powers of hypnosis to gain control of the heroine (Hartley), though having her family killed by his vassals. Her fiancé (Perry) starts an investigation and eventually persuades the police to search Yorga's mansion. This leads to a running battle with the vampires ensconsed there, at the conclusion of which Perry hurls Quarry to his doom from a balcony. However, in an inversion of the ending of *Count Yorga, Vampire*, he is revealed, in the fade-out clinch with Hartley, to have been vampirized. The film is uneven, and some of the dialogue awkward but the actors all perform well and the result is quite distinctive. The producer's father, George Macready, has a minor role as a professor.

d/co-s Robert (Bob) Kelljan *p* Michael Macready
co-s Yvonne Wilder *c* Bill Butler *se* Roger George
lp Robert Quarry, Mariette Hartley, Roger Perry, Yvonne Wilder, Tom Toner, Rudy de Luca, Walter Brooks, Craig Nelson, Karen Huston, Paul Hansen

Revenge *aka* **Terror from Under the House**
(PETER ROGERS PRODUCTIONS; GB) 89min
A ghoulish sensationalist melodrama. When a north country publican's ten-year-old daughter is raped and murdered, her father (Booth) kidnaps a suspicious recluse (Griffith) in order to force a confession. He attacks him and leaves him for dead in the pub's cellar. The man is not dead, however, and the family are unable to either kill him or set him free. His presence affects the whole family, leading to drink, impotence and incestuous assault. The twist comes when the man, having been released, proves to be the child rapist after all. The film mobilizes brutality and sex as a way of sustaining interest in its tangled web of familial relationships and its gallery of crudely drawn characters. Only Collins (as the publican's wife) manages her role with a modicum of flair.

The film's executive producer is best known for his interminable series of *Carry On* pictures while Hayers, who once made an interesting film, **Night of the Eagle** (1962), seems unable to overcome his long years of working in television. This picture is not to be confused with Jud Taylor's telefilm, *Revenge* (1971), starring Shelley Winters.

d Sidney Hayers *p* George H. Brown *s* John Kruse
c Ken Hodges *lp* Joan Collins, James Booth, Ray Barrett, Sinead Cusack, Tom Marshall, Kenneth Griffith, Zuleika Robson, Donald Morley, Barry Andrews

La Rouge aux Lèvres *aka* **Daughters of Darkness** *aka* **The Promise of Red Lips** *aka* **The Red Lips** *aka* **Erzebeth** *aka* **Blut an den Lippen**
(SHOWKING/CINEVOG/MAYA FILMS/ROXY FILMS; BEL,FR,WG) 87min
The specifically Belgian variety of surrealism with its quietly uncanny, absurdist humour, and fascination for comic-strip narratives in settings that wear normality like a sheen spawned two extraordinary film-makers, André Delvaux and Kuemel. The latter's second feature imagines an out-of-season seaside resort visited by Countess Bathory (Seyrig) and her companion (Rau) where they become involved with a couple (Ouimet and Karlen). Pervading the deserted Ostend hotel with her presence, dressed à la Dietrich in the thirties, Seyrig provokes an erotic malaise which leads to bloody deaths. As she and the young bride drive away, sunlight suddenly hits their car and they crash, leaving the Countess hanging impaled on a tree branch. The stunningly shot picture is riddled with echoes of Kuemel's master, Sternberg. The script proceeds with comic-strip tableaux, frozen in their fetishistic splendour but also destroying whatever narrative coherence, if any, may have been intended. The gory deaths feature razors and broken glass and inundate the screen with bright scarlet to match Seyrig's lips and counterpoint the deep blues and vibrant whites that mark the other scenes. Kuemel's next picture, **Malpertuis** (1972) only occasionally achieved such flamboyant visuals. With art direction by Françoise Hardy, the picture combines eerie poetry with elements of camp parody, skilfully avoiding a collapse into either option and produces an unsettlingly intelligent film which sadly wasn't well received by any of the established audiences for art cinema, horror or camp movies.

d/co-s Harry Kuemel *p* Paul Collet, Alain Guillaume
co-s Pierre Drouot *c* Eddy van der Enden *lp* Delphine Seyrig, John Karlen, Daniele Ouimet, Andrea Rau, Paul Esser, Georges Jamin, Joris Collet, Fons Rademakers

Left: *Delphine Seyrig and Daniele Ouimet in Harry Kuemel's seductive essay in surrealism,* La Rouge aux Lèvres.

The Sabbat of the Black Cat
(RALPH LAWRENCE MARSDEN; AUST) 80min
This one-man venture, shot on a part-time basis on 16mm and partly funded by the Experimental Film and Television Fund, used the Poe story as the inspiration for what is the first attempt at indigenously Australian gothic film-making. The plot has a young man who accidentally stumbles upon a witches' sabbat spending the rest of the movie being persecuted by a black cat. The Melbourne-based operation used an abandoned gold-mining settlement in Victoria for its professionally handled location work. Made for about $7000 Australian, the feature received a brief public run at the Melbourne Coop Cinema in 1973. Marsden, who graduated from TV commercials subsequently worked for an Australian TV before emigrating to the UK.

d/p/s/c Ralph Lawrence Marsden *lp* Ralph Lawrence Marsden, Barbara Brighton, Tracey Tombs, David Bingham, Jim Fitch, Babylon Dance Troupe

Santo contra la Hija de Frankenstein *aka* **La Hija de Frankenstein** *aka* **Santo vs Frankenstein's Daughter** *aka* **The Daughter of Frankenstein**
(CINEMATOGRAFICA CALDERON; MEX) 97min
Delgado was responsible for such insipid pictures as *Santo y Blue Demon contra Dracula y el Hombre Lobo* (1971), **El Fantasma de la Casa Roja** (1954) and the unfunny parody of wrestler movies, *El Superflaco* (1967). This routine picture sees the silver-masked hulk, having defeated a Frankenstein creature called Ursus, taking on the scientist's daughter

Joan Collins, Tom Marshall (left) and James Booth in a scene from Revenge.

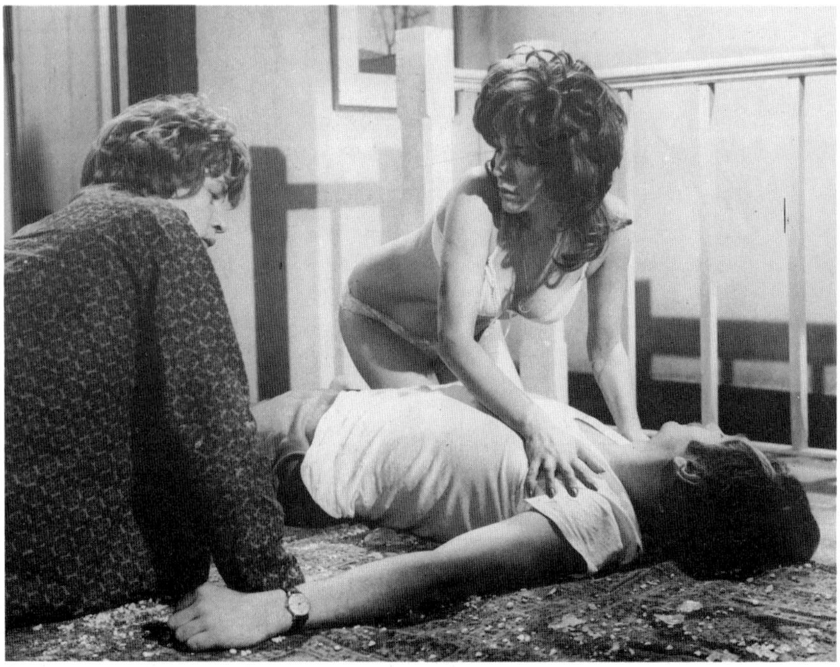

Above: *Kirsten Lindholm in danger in* Twins of Evil, *the last and best of Hammer's Karnstein trilogy of films.*

(Romand). She is a villainous female who uses corpses and young women's blood to concoct a youth elixir. To extend the life of the potion, she tries to obtain the blood of an extraordinary man – Santo – and to this end kidnaps Fuentes and transforms her aunt into a withered mummy (Gallardo) but Santo hangs on to his 'powerful' blood and liberates the women. The name Ursus recalls the superhero detective of the silent Italian cinema, a figure that later gave rise to the Hercules character in the peplum genre.

Santo's next adventure saw him terminate, in his customary brutal fashion, a group of lepers in René Cardona's *Santo contra los Jinetes del Terror* (1972). He was, however, again involved in his favourite world of mad surgery in Rafael Romero Marchent's *Santo contra el Doctor Muerte* (1973).

d Miguel M. Delgado *p* Guillermo Calderon *s* Fernando Oses *c* Raúl Martinez Solares *lp* Santo (Rodolfo Guzmán Huerta), Gina Romand, Roberto Cañedo, Carlos Agosti, Sonia Fuentes, Lucy Gallardo, Jorge Casanova

Il Strangolatore di Vienna *aka* **Der Wuerger Kommt auf Leisen Socken** *aka* **The Strangler of Vienna** *aka* **The Mad Butcher** *aka* **The Mad Butcher of Vienna** *aka* **The Vienna Strangler** *aka* **Meat Is Meat**

(REGINA/HI-FI/NEPTUNIA; IT,WG) 83min

A macabre comedy inspired by the grisly Fritz Haarman murders which also influenced Lang's *M* (1931) and Lommel's **Zaertlichkeit der Woelfe** (1973). Promoted in Germany as a *Kanniballade*, the story is set in a stuffy Vienna where Otto (Buono) produces succulent sausages by putting his wife (Field) in the meat grinder. To keep up the supply of his widely appreciated and lucrative delicacy, he proceeds to turn more female victims into minced meat until a police inspector (Ireland) finds buttons and brooches in the sausages served in the police canteen. A reporter (Harris) and his girlfriend also narrowly escape the mad butcher's clutches.

Zurli, who also worked under the pseudonym Albert Moore, specialized in parodies of popular genre products with films like *E Mezzanotte ... Butta Giu il Cadavere* (1966) and *Silenzio: si Uccide* (1976).

d Guido Zurli *p* Harry Hope, Eugenio Corso *s* Charles Ross, Enzo Gicca *c* Enrico Betti *lp* Victor Buono, Karin Field, Brad Harris, John Ireland, Franca Polcelli, Hannsi Linder, Sybil Martin, Arthur Mann, Carl Stearns, Michael Turner

La Tarantola dal Ventre Nero *aka* **The Black Belly of the Tarantula** *aka* **The Black Bellied Tarantula** *aka* **La Tarentule au Ventre Noir**

(DA MA PRODUZIONE/PAC; IT,FR) 89(88)min

Cavara's emphatically mannerist movie scripted by its producer has both eyes firmly set on the US sex-and-violence market. A blind masseur (Marano) in a beauty salon is also a latterday Jack the Ripper. The climax of the story is his attack on the wife (Sandrelli), of the investigating policeman (Giannini). The film's title refers to the way a wasp kills a tarantula by administering a paralysing sting before ripping open its belly, a *modus operandi* similar to the sex maniac's, who penetrates his victims' bodies with an acupuncture needle before embarking on bloody surgery, the whole shot with gleeful sadism and wallowing in the obviously sexual overtones of the murders. Only Auger as the blackmailing owner of the beauty salon and Bach's cameo as one of the luckless victims stand out in this meretricious picture with a facile Morricone score. Cavara remained best known as co-director of the infamously racist exploitation movie *Mondo Cane* (1962) and its equally obnoxious sequels.

d Paolo Cavara *p/co-s* Marcello Danon *co-s* Lucile Laks *c* Marcello Gatti *lp* Giancarlo Giannini, Claudine Auger, Barbara Bach, Barbara Bouchet, Stefania Sandrelli, Rossella Falk, Ezio Marano, Annabella Incontrera, Silvano Tranquili, Ana Salea

Twins of Evil *aka* **The Gemini Twins** *aka* **Virgin Vampires** *aka* **Twins of Dracula**

(HAMMER; GB) 87min

This is the third, last and best of Hammer's Karnstein trilogy, the first two films in which were **The Vampire Lovers** and **Lust for a Vampire** (both 1970). The plot opposes the puritanical witch-hunter, Weil (Cushing) and the vampiric Count Karnstein (Thomas), battling over the fate of the *Playboy* centrefold Collinson twins, one of whom is vampirized while the other is the lady-in-distress who provides the happy end when she is rescued by the local beau (Warbeck). The vampiric twin is decapitated, the Count axes his puritanical antagonist to pieces and is then reduced to a putrid mess when his heart is pierced by a lance.

The conflict between puritanism and the Count's lecherous excesses is echoed in Roy Stanhard's excellently designed sets in which Cushing's austere surroundings are stylishly counterpointed by the flamboyantly gothic castle and its lusciously funereal colours, swirling mists and flickering candlelight. The Count's inadvertent resuscitation of Carmilla/Mircalla (Keith) is one of the film's beautifully poetic highlights: the ethereal hooded shape of the young woman rises from a tomb and floats silently towards the terrified descendant. Vampire films often turn on the motif of the sexually active and therefore menacing woman versus the virginal love object, an opposition both confirmed and undercut by the use of identical twins caught between two equally lethal forms of neurosis: merciless repression and unbridled indulgence. In his later work for Disney, Hough never matched the directorial skills deployed here.

d John Hough *p* Harry Fine, Michael Style *s* Tudor Gates *c* Dick Bush *se* Bert Luxford *lp* Peter Cushing, Madeleine Collinson, Mary Collinson, Dennis Price, Kathleen Byron, Damien Thomas, Harvey Hall, David Warbeck, Isobel Black, Luan Peters, Kirsten Lindholm

Vampire Circus (HAMMER; GB) 87min

Young's best feature combines the circus setting (previously used in **Circus of Horrors**, 1959, and **Berserk**, 1967) with the vampire motif to good effect for half the picture. In 1825 the mysterious Circus of Nights appears in a Serbian village cut off from the world by an outbreak of the plague, and corpses start being found drained of blood. The vampire performers are able to change into animals which results in some spectacular scenes as trapeze artists become bats in mid-act to the uncomprehending applause of the backward villagers. The circus also sports a mirror maze in which victims glimpse their impending death. Eventually, the hero (Brown) decapitates the vampire leader (Tayman) and brings the movie to an end, although not until we have been treated to the obligatory abduction of the heroine (Frederick) and the usual quota of sex for horror films of this period. Halfway through, the movie runs out of steam, halfheartedly justifying the proliferation of sex scenes with ludicrous lines and desperately multiplying cross-brandishing climaxes to breathe life into the proceedings.

The script was based on a story devised by the producer in collaboration with George Baxt, the scenarist of *Circus of Horrors*.

d Robert Young *p* Wilbur Stark *s* Judson Kinberg *c* Moray Grant *se* Les Bowie *lp* Adrienne Corri, Lawrence Payne, Thorley Walters, John Moulder Brown, Robert Tayman, Lynne Frederick, Elisabeth Seal, Anthony Corlan, Richard Owens, David Prowse

The Velvet Vampire *aka* **The Waking Hour**
(NEW WORLD) 80(79)min

One of the few horror movies to be directed by a woman – other examples are **Monster** (1980) and **The Slumber Party Massacre** (1982) – this is a visually inventive film which makes excellent use of strikingly shot Californian locations to lend an air of incongruity to its tale of a lady vampire (Yarnall) stalking her prey among the West Coast culturati. However, apart from being indifferently acted, the film suffers from a rudimentary narrative.

The vampire invites a fashionable young couple (Blodgett and Miles) to weekend at her desert home. In between vampirizing males who cross her path, she takes the couple to visit a nearby mine, where, while she attempts to seduce Blodgett, the unfortunate Miles is bitten by a snake. In an amusing twist on expectations, Yarnall saves her by sucking out the poison. Yarnall succeeds in vampirizing Blodgett, and

Shelley Winters (right) and Debbie Reynolds in Curtis Harrington's What's the matter with Helen?

when Miles – who has herself been attracted to Yarnall – discovers her husband's body, she rushes into the desert, and succeeds in returning to Los Angeles, though with Yarnall in pursuit. In an arresting finale, Yarnall meets fate on the streets of Los Angeles when Miles threatens her with crosses, then causes her to shed the protective clothing which protects her from the sun's destructive rays. Despite the film's reputation, it is difficult to perceive any particularly feminist slant on the proceedings.

d/co-s Stephanie Rothman *p/co-s* Charles S. Swartz *co-s* Maurice Jules *c* Daniel Lacambre *lp* Sherry Miles, Michael Blodgett, Celeste Yarnall, Paul Prokop, Gene Shane, Jerry Daniels, Sandy Ward, Bob Tessler, Chris Woodley

Venom *aka* **The Legend of Spider Forest**
(CUPID/ACTION PLUS PRODUCTIONS; GB) scope 91(79)min

After an auspicious horror début with **Demons of the Mind** (1971), Sykes confirmed his talent with this rather striking film based on a story by Stephen Collins. The plot concerns a tourist (Brent) in Bavaria who comes across a mysterious but very attractive woman (Arneric) reputed to be a spider goddess who brings death to all who come close to her. After some detours involving murderous villagers (Allen and Newark), nocturnal threats, buzzing electric saws and brandished axes, Brent eventually persuades Arneric to take him home with her. Her guardian (Vivian) lives in a large, lugubrious mansion where her Nazi father (Soall) experiments with a nerve drug developed from spider's venom. The climax sees the villagers and the Nazis destroy each other, with Arneric throwing herself into the flames that are consuming her father. Brent and Arneric are personable characters and Sykes brings off several sequences of nicely sustained menace even though inopportune zooms tend to destroy the carefully built-up atmosphere. Sykes, whose subsequent films continued to suffer from the same handicap, deserved better.

d Peter Sykes *p* Michael Pearson, Kenneth Rowles *s* Donald Ford, Derek Ford *c* Peter Jessop *se* Roy Whybrow *lp* Simon Brent, Neda Arneric, Derek Newar, Sheila Allen, Gerard Heinz, Gertan Klauber, Bette Vivian, Terence Soall

Left: *The snake dance from* Vampire Circus.

Werewolves on Wheels

(SOUTHSTREET PRODUCTIONS) 85min

In spite of possessing one of the greatest schlock titles in movie history, *Werewolves on Wheels* is decidedly disappointing. The plot has the Devil's Advocates, a group of Hells Angels, visit a monastery inhabited by devil-worshipping, black-robed monks. When the monks try to persuade one of the bikers, (Anderson) to offer herself to Satan, the gang trash the monastery and leave. However, Anderson is now possessed and at night turns into a werewolf, killing the gang members one by one.

The main problem is that the film is simply too much of a generic hodge-podge, and does not really impress as either a biker or werewolf movie (particularly as we don't really get a good glimpse of a werewolf until far too near the end). On the other hand, it does contain some amusing, clearly improvised sequences, moves along at a zippy pace and has some excellently atmospheric photography from Mankovsky. Sixties music fiends will note the presence of Barry ('Eve of Destruction') McGuire as Scarf.

d/co-s Michel Levesque *p* Paul Lewis *co-s* David M. Kaufman *c* Isadore Mankovsky *lp* Stephen Oliver, Severn Darden, D. J. Anderson, Deuce Berry, William Gray, Gray Johnson, Owen Orr, Anna Lynn Brown, Leonard Rogel

What's the Matter with Helen?

(FILMWAYS/RAYMAX) 101min

Harrington, most of whose horror movies have been made for TV – more's the pity, since he brings a rare cinematic culture to his work – here bedecks a script by Farrell (author of the novel on which **What Ever Happened to Baby Jane?**, 1962, was based and co-scriptwriter of **Hush ... Hush, Sweet Charlotte**, 1965) with some brilliantly realized Hollywood memorabilia of the thirties. The period is beautifully set by a newsreel of Roosevelt promising his New Deal which merges imperceptibly into fake footage of a sensational murder trial which leaves two teenage boys in jail and their mothers trying to remake their lives. Haunted by anonymous phone calls from an asthmatic avenger, they flee to Hollywood, where one (Reynolds) sets up a talent school for aspiring Shirley Temples, while the other (Winters), Bible in hand, starts to brood about divine retribution.

At this point, a dark, asthmatic stranger (MacLiammoir, impeccably sinister in the Lugosi manner) enters, seeking a job as voice teacher, and with him come all manner of joys for the film buff. Reynolds, deciding that she is cut out to be another Jean Harlow, thereafter sports only genuine Harlow gowns and a platinum bleach. Dallying with a millionaire who brings her gardenias ('Oh! Joan Crawford's favourite!'), she performs a languid tango à la Valentino. And her moppet pupils put on a show which includes a hallucinating resurrection of Shirley Temple's 'Animal Crackers', an obscenely accurate pastiche of Mae West, and one of those tap-dancing chorus lines paying homage to Uncle Sam. Winters, meanwhile, ever more deeply enmeshed in guilt and terror, rushes off to an evangelical temple, only to find a magnificently mordant Moorehead holding the pulpit and hustling her sinners to the collection box with all possible speed. It blows up, by way of some time-honoured shocks, into a hugely entertaining and gory ending which remembers to pay homage not only to horror but to Hollywood.

Harrington and Winters went on to make **Whoever Slew Auntie Roo?** (1971).

d Curtis Harrington *p* George Edwards, James C. Pratt *s* Henry Farrell *c* Lucien Ballard *lp* Debbie Reynolds, Shelley Winters, Michael MacLiammoir, Dennis Weaver, Agnes Moorehead

Bruce Davison and friends threaten a terrified Ernest Borgnine in Willard.

Whoever Slew Auntie Roo? *aka* Who Slew Auntie Roo? *aka* Gingerbread House

(AIP/HEMDALE; GB) 91min

Weird thrillers about predatory mother figures such as **What Ever Happened to Baby Jane?** (1962) or **Hush Hush Sweet Charlotte** (1965) proved a congenial format for Harrington's type of fairytales, which often involve such ogres (**Queen of Blood**, 1966; **Games**, 1967; **What's the Matter with Helen?**, 1971).

This updated version of Hansel and Gretel, devised by David Osborn and with additional dialogue by Gavin Lambert, commences with the batty old Rosie (Winters), affectionately known as Auntie Roo, who keeps the skeleton of her dead daughter in a coffin in her huge, cavernous mansion. Gradually, the movie shifts to the point-of-view of the two orphans (Lester and Franks) she takes under her wing. Events begin to be seen primarily through the little boy's eyes making Auntie an increasingly menacing figure until she is locked into a cupboard by the children who then set fire to it and leave, taking the 'treasure', her jewels, with them. Harrington tends to overdo the Grand Guignol sequences, as in the attic scenes where the orphans discover the professional equipment of Roo's late husband, a stage magician, to which is added an even more arbitrary sequence in which a servant terrifies them by pretending to be a ghost. However, the relationship between Roo and the youngsters is handled well, her kindness to the somewhat sinisterly naïve children being tinged with deeply neurotic overtones to prepare the ground for the changeover to the horrid ogre imagined by the little boy and lead to the gruesome climax.

Harrington had made a few experimental shorts in France before this British AIP release, but his career as a fantasy director was started by Roger Corman (**Night Tide**, 1963) in Hollywood.

d Curtis Harrington *p* Samuel Z. Arkoff, James H. Nicholson *s* Robert Blees, James Sangster *c* Desmond Dickinson *lp* Shelley Winters, Mark Lester, Chloe Franks, Ralph Richardson, Lionel Jeffries, Hugh Griffith, Rosalie Crutchley, Pat Heywood, Judy Cornwell, Michael Gothard

Willard

(BING CROSBY PRODUCTIONS) 95 min

Davison here is Willard, a withdrawn young man of many resentments, not at least against his nagging mother (Lanchester), and his ruthless boss (Borgnine) whom he suspects of engineering his father's death to gain control of the family business. Told by Lanchester to get rid of the rats lurking around their dilapidated old mansion, Davison instead becomes fascinated by them. Gradually managing to train them to do his bidding, he starts by using them to help him commit a robbery and ends by setting them on Borgnine. Finally falling in love (with Locke), he decides to get rid of the rats, but they forestall him in a carnivorous revenge.

With its old dark house and domineering mother, the films sets out very much like an echo of **Psycho** (1960), but scriptwriter Ralston (adapting his own novel) saw it as a 'rat morality play'. Consequently there are acres of 'serious' plotting and motivation to get through, and when the horrors do come, they are very tame indeed. Settling for facile effects like the cut-in shot of rats tearing at a piece of raw meat while supposedly demolishing Borgnine, Mann gradually drives what might have been an intriguing film pretty much into the ground, although Davison's performance is excellent.

The film's box-office success dictated a sequel, **Ben** (1972).

d Daniel Mann *p* Mort Briskin *s* Gilbert A. Ralston *c* Robert B. Hauser *lp* Bruce Davison, Ernest Borgnine, Elsa Lanchester, Sandra Locke, Michael Dante, J. Pat O'Malley

1972

The Asphyx (GLENDALE; GB) scope 99(98)min
A somewhat wordy though sensitive retelling of the fable about the man who labours to make himself immortal only to find he is left with nothing but sadness to endure for eternity. Adapted from an idea supplied by Christina and Lawrence Beers, the film, set in 1875, uses the emergent art of photography and the invention of cinematography as the catalysts for the appearance and identification of the asphyx: the spirit of death which according to Greek mythology hovers about a person in moments of mortal peril. The central character, Hugo (Stephens) identifies it as a black shape on a cine film – achieved by means of animation effects – showing accidental deaths. Aided by his daughter (Lapotaire) and her lover (Powell), he conducts a series of experiments to try and trap his asphyx, which would make him immortal. He submits to a slow electrocution which produces the desired result only by chance. His daughter also tries the procedure but she fails and dies, causing Powell to commit suicide, which leaves the lonely Stephens to meditate on his misfortunes for all eternity.

Although John Stoll's art direction, the acting and Young's camerawork in Todd-AO are excellent, the static nature of the script fails to generate any of the cerebral excitement the theme demands, and leaves various contradictions and loopholes which hamper credibility. Newbrook is also responsible for the interesting **Disciple of Death** (1972).

d Peter Newbrook *p* John Brittany *s* Brian Comfort *c* Freddie Young *se* Ted Samuels *lp* Robert Stephens, Robert Powell, Jane Lapotaire, Alex Scott, Ralph Arless, Fiona Walker, Terry Scully, John Lawrence, David Grey, Tony Caunter

Asylum *aka* **House of Crazies**
(AMICUS/HARBOUR PRODUCTIONS; GB) scope 88(80)min
Although individual items in previous Amicus productions of Bloch's tales – **Torture Garden** (1967) and **The House That Dripped Blood** (1970), for example – were often more ingenious, this picture hit on a felicitous linking device. Dr Martin (Powell) arrives at an asylum that looks more like a gothic castle. Dr Rutherford (Magee) and an odd butler/orderly (Bayldon) receive him with a challenge: one of the doctors has gone mad and it is the newcomer's task to tell the doctor from the patients. This device leads into three stories and a Grand Guignol finale in which the whole situation is provided with a convincing twist ending. *Frozen Fear* has Parkins narrate her encounter with a dismembered but living corpse; *The Weird Tailor*, the weakest story, tells of a magic suit that brings a dummy to life. *Lucy Comes to Stay* recalls **Psycho** (1960) as Rampling recounts how her friend Lucy (Ekland) murdered her family, but then the 'Lucy' personality takes over Rampling who turns into a homicidal maniac. The climax, *Mannikins of Horror*, features Lom who makes homunculi that end up stabbing Magee to death just as the young newcomer has decided that he doesn't want the job. He is then strangled by the butler/orderly, and the position taken over by the demented Dr Starr he was looking for.

Robert Powell (centre) embarks on the search for eternity in The Asphyx.

The sick sketches set in the bleakly oppressive confines of madhouse cells, dark corridors and cavernous halls are well handled, underplaying the black humour most uncharacteristically. The excellent cast, including Powell's first appearance in a genuine horror film, give the picture more power than any of Ward Baker's previous efforts. His next picture, **Fengriffen** (1973), was a disappointment.

d Roy Ward Baker *p* Max J. Rosenberg, Milton Subotsky *s* Robert Bloch *c* Denys Coop *se* Ernie Sullivan *lp* Patrick Magee, Robert Powell, Geoffrey Bayldon; Barbara Parkins, Sylvia Syms, Richard Todd; Peter Cushing, Carry Morse, Ana Firbank; Britt Ekland, Charlotte Rampling, James Villiers, Megs Jenkins; Herbert Lom

Asylum of Satan (STUDIO ONE) 80min
Dr Spector, a devil's disciple who also runs a mental asylum, offers one of his young charges to his master. Unfortunately, she is not a virgin, as required, and – quite literally – all hell breaks loose. A very low-budget film whose special effects, including axe-chopped bodies, a mechanical snake and the final apparition of the devil, leave a good deal to be desired, *Asylum of Satan* is interesting only as the first feature directed by Girdler (who went on to make **Abby**, 1974; *Day of the Animals*, 1977; and **The Manitou**, 1977). He died in 1978 in the Philippines whilst scouting locations for a new horror film.

d/s William Girdler *p* J. Patrick Kelly III *c* William L. Asman *lp* Charles Kissinger, Carla Borelli, Nick Jolly, Sherry Stein

Ben (BING CROSBY PRODUCTIONS) 94min
A sequel to **Willard** (1970), whose climactic sequence is reprised under this film's opening titles, *Ben* takes up the story as the rat army move out into the city and set up home in a storm-drain system. Ben, their leader, is discovered on a foraging trip by a small boy (Montgomery); the child makes a pet of the rodent and is eventually taken by Ben to the rats' hideout. Meanwhile, the rats' scavenging activities are causing a panic but the police prove unable to trace the creatures. Eventually, the boy's mother (Murphy) finds Ben with her son and alerts the police. The child refuses to disclose the rats' whereabouts to investigating cop Campanella but subsequently

the rats' abode is uncovered anyway and Montgomery's attempt to warn the animals is thwarted. Ben survives, though, and at the last is seen making his way to Montgomery and being nursed back to health. The ending is sentimental but affecting, and the film as a whole is pieced together with considerable efficiency.

Aided by Metty's camerawork, crime-movie veteran Karlson responds with pointed economy to the sequences elaborating the police investigation, and the colloquies between Campanella and a sardonic reporter (O'Connell) are invested with a formulary kind of conviction. The episode in which Montgomery penetrates Ben's subterranean dwelling, to be confronted by what seems like hundreds of rodents, is bought off with an understatement calculated to be disconcerting.

The film's title song is performed by Michael Jackson.

d Phil Karlson *p* Mort Briskin *s* Gilbert A. Ralston *c* Russell Metty *se* Bud David *lp* Lee Harcourt Montgomery, Arthur O'Connell, Joseph Campanella, Rosemary Murphy, Meredith Baxter, Kaz Garras, Paul Carr, Kenneth Tobey, Norman Alden, Richard Van Fleet

Blacula (AMERICAN INTERNATIONAL) 93min
Attempting to yoke the horror film with the appeal of the blaxploitation movies of the early seventies – notably crime pictures like *Shaft* (1971) – *Blacula* emerges as a largely unenterprising 'gimmick' movie. In a prologue set in 1815, an African prince (Marshall) visits Count Dracula (Macaulay) with the somewhat eccentric purpose of enlisting his help in combatting the slave trade, but instead is vampirized and imprisoned in a coffin. Back in the present, the coffin is sent to Los Angeles after Dracula's castle is ransacked by two antique dealers, and Blacula duly goes on the rampage in between attempts to seduce a woman (McGee) who appears to be the reincarnation of his lost wife. The concluding passages move the film closer to police-thriller territory as Blacula is tracked down at his lair in a factory; finally, after his lover has been staked to death, Blacula suicidally strays into the sunlight and crumbles to dust. Besides not making use of the protagonists' blackness for any purpose of social or philosophical provocation, the film is dully scripted and for the most part flatly directed. The central character was resurrected for **Scream, Blacula, Scream** in 1973.

d William Crain *p* Joseph T. Naar *s* Joan Torres, Raymond Koenig *c* John Stevens *se* Roger George *lp* William Marshall, Vonetta McGee, Denise Nicholas, Gordon Pinsent, Thalmus Rasulala, Charles Macaulay, Emily Yancy, Ted Harris, Rick Metzler, Logan Field

ne of the homunculi in e 'Mannikins of orror' episode from sylum.

Blood Orgy of the She Devils
(GEMINI/OCCULT) 73min
Blood Orgy of the She Devils was written, produced and directed by Ted V. Mikels, a member of the Herschell Gordon Lewis/Al Adamson school of low-budget horror/exploitation. Probably best known as the director of the inimitable **The Corpse Grinders** (1971) and *Astro Zombies* (1965), he also distributed **The Undertaker and His Pals** (1967) and *The Worm Eaters* (1975), and his 14 films to date also cover such diverse genres as musical comedy, soft-core sexploitation and action-adventure. Less deliberately ludicrous and sleazy than *The Corpse Grinders*, *Blood Orgy of the She Devils* nevertheless found it hard to get advertising space in the newspapers on account of the title. The plot has Mara (Zaborin), queen of the witches, lead her coven of beautiful young girls in ritual sacrifices of male victims. The film, which includes reincarnation and witch-burning motifs, climaxes in Zaborin, allegedly 'evil incarnate', being destroyed.

d/p/s Ted V. Mikels *c* Anthony Salinas *se* Lee James *lp* Lila Zaborin, Tom Pace, Leslie McRae, Victor Izay, William Bagdad

Blood Waters of Dr Z *aka* **ZaAT** *aka* **Hydra**
(CAPITAL/BARTON) 100min
Despite stiff competition from William Grefé's *Death Curse of Tartu* (1966) and *Sting of Death* (1966), this has the dubious distinction of being the most boring monster movie ever made in Florida. Misanthropic mad scientist Grauer doses himself with 'ZaAT', 'the formula they all laughed at', and turns into a bulbous-headed amphibian with a shaggy, baggy suit. Black marine biologist Cruse, redneck sheriff Galloway and two government agents (Dickerson, Ringhaver) investigate a series of murders which appear to have been perpetrated by catfish and trace them back to the monster. Much of the film appears to have been shot silent, with a ranting voice-over and plentiful stock music failing to disguise the time-wasting tedium of the monster's very slow wanderings. The ending is downbeat, with most of the good guys dead or wounded and the heroine, dosed with the ZaAT formula, following the monster into the sea to populate the world with similar creatures. To stretch this charade out the film drags in some irrelevant hippie singalongs and a lot of marine life footage.

d/p Don Barton *co-s* Lee Laren *co-s/se* Ron Kivett *c* Jack McGowan *lp* Marshall Grauer, Dave Dickerson, Gerald Cruse, Paul Galloway, Wade Popwell, Sanna Ringhaver

Captain Kronos – Vampire Hunter *aka* **Kronos** *aka* **Vampire Castle** *aka* **Captain Kronus – Vampire Hunter**
(HAMMER; GB) 91min
Desperately looking for a new angle for their series of vampire movies, Hammer entrusted this spoof to TV comedy specialist Clemens, thus uniting in the one film the company's two major threads: horror and TV spin-offs. Set in the early 19th century, the film opens like a western gone wrong with its blond, caped superhero (Janson) astride a horse, his saddle embellished with an ornate K, and accompanied by a hunchbacked sidekick and a rickety wagon driven by professor Grost (Cater). The trio are professional vampire hunters on their way to investigate a village where young women suddenly die of old age. Kronos

picks up Carla (Munro) on the way, discovers the vampire to be the middle-aged lady of the manor (Ventham) who covered her youthful face with a mask, and defeats her and her resurrected husband with a magic sword before riding off into the distance in search of more vampires to fight.

Clemens mixes a variety of genres, from adventure serial to Grand Guignol, with a rocky, grainy, freewheeling camera style derived from his experience in television. Numerous frame-within-the-frame compositions suggest an unease with the large-screen format and give the film the feel of a series of sketches spun out way beyond breaking point, although there are some funny moments and lines. Acting honours go to Hendry's hired killer, Carson's doctor who gets the vampire bug and Munro as the hero's love interest. The movie, which stayed on the shelf for two years, was a flop on its release in 1974.

d/co-p/s Brian Clemens *co-p* Albert Fennell *c* Ian Wilson *lp* Horst Janson, John Carson, Caroline Munro, John Cater, Shane Briant, Ian Hendry, Wanda Ventham, Lois Daine, Caroline Villers

Ceremonia Sangrienta *aka* **The Female Butcher** *aka* **The Legend of Blood Castle** *aka* **Countess Dracula** *aka* **Lady Dracula** *aka* **Bloody Ceremony** *aka* **Le Vergini Cavalcano la Morte**

(X FILMS/LUIS FILMS; SP,IT) scope 102(87)min

With Peter Sasdy's **Countess Dracula** (1970) this is the classic interpretation of the legend associated with Erszebet Bathory. Set in a 17th-century Hungarian village, the movie opens with the ritual exhumation of a suspected vampire who is then officially decapitated in public. But the crimes that ravage the area continue. The local count, Karl (Santoni), commits suicide but returns as a vampire who also supplies his wife, Elisabeth (Bose) with victims in whose blood she bathes to keep her youthful appearance.

With its brilliant cinematography and energetically innovative *mise-en-scène*, this is one of Spain's best horror pictures of the period. Grau's expert direction and the disturbing presence of Italy's 1947 beauty queen, Bose, who graced Antonioni's early films, combine to increase the hideously macabre atmosphere exuded by a picture that wallows in torture and blood. Although promoted as based on contemporary trial records, the film seems to shrink back from the full horror of Bathory's character – a pitfall avoided by Sasdy – and most of the gory doings are delegated to Karl. More interestingly, Grau relates the aristocratic couple's inhuman cruelty to the equally monstrous cruelty practised by the authorities and superstitious villagers in the name of religion.

Grau is a Catalan who studied at the Centro Sperimentale in Rome and worked as a critic and a documentarist before becoming assistant to Riccardo Freda, Sergio Leone and Luis Berlanga and breaking into directing with *Noche de Verano* (1962). He went on to make the much appreciated **No Profanar el Sueño de los Muertos** (1974) but later began churning out a series of straight sex-and-violence movies, including *La Trastienda* (1975) and *Cartas de Amor de una Monja* (1978).

d/co-s Jorge Grau *p* José Maria Gonzalez Sinde *co-s* Juan Tebor, Sandro Continenza *c* Fernando Arribas *lp* Lucia Bose, Ewa Aulin, Espartaco Santoni, Ana Farra, Franca Grey, Silvano Tranquili, Lola Gaos, Angel Memendes, Enrico Vico

La Corrupción de Chris Miller *aka* **The Corruption of Chris Miller** *aka* **Sisters of Corruption**

(XAVIER ARMET; SP) scope 115(107)min

The most interesting aspect of this film is the casting of child star Marisol as Chris, a mad woman traumatized by having been raped as a child by a weightlifter. Considering Jacinto Molina, an ex-weightlifter, was the undisputed king of Spanish fantasy cinema, it might seem that Bardem was saying something about the condition of Spanish cinema in general.

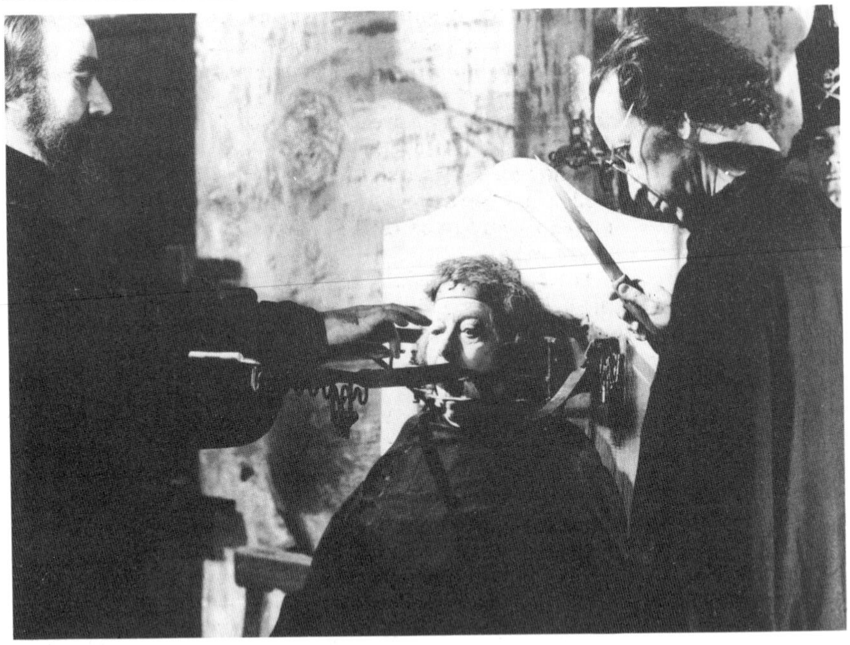

Ceremonia Sangrienta, *one of Spain's best horror films and with Peter Sasdy's* Countess Dracula *(1970), the classic interpretation of the legends associated with Erszebet Bathory.*

However, the film itself is routine: Chris's stepmother (Seberg) encourages the child's murderously hysterical fits as revenge against her ex-husband, Chris's father. A drifter (Stokes) arrives on the scene and becomes the lover of both women while the region is buzzing with news of sensational murders committed by a figure dressed as a monk and wielding a sickle. After gorily stabbing the drifter to death in a prolonged scene, they discover he wasn't the killer when a local aristocrat is caught in the act so they bury their common lover in a roadworks, but the pea pods he had in his knapsack start sprouting and break through a crack in the newly laid tarmac.

d Juan Antonio Bardem *p* Xavier Armet *s* Santiago Moncada *c* Juan Gelpi *se* Antonio Parra, Antonio Bueno *lp* Jean Seberg, Marisol, Barry Stokes, Perla Cristal, Rudy Gaebel, Gerard Tichy, Antonio Vidal Molina, Juan Bardem, Gustavo Re, Antonio Parra

La Corta Notte delle Bambole di Vetro *aka* **Malastrana**

(JADRAN FILM/DIETER GEISSLER FILM/DORIA CINEMATOGRAFICA; IT,WG,YUG) scope 92(90)min

Lado's clever début feature, constructed in the vein of Gordon Hessler's **Scream and Scream Again** (1969), reveals him to be a director of considerable power. The first part of the movie sets up a clichéd cold-war story with an American journalist (Sorel) discovering the brainwashing experiments of a mad professor in Prague. But the story really takes off when he is captured and put in a cataleptic state by the professor. Apparently dead, though his mind is still very much alive, his body is stored in a deep freeze until it is wheeled out and dissected in an anatomy class. The second, decidedly chilling, part of the movie is told with excellent control and a flair for covering up the holes in the narrative by playing cat-and-mouse with audience expectations. Lado's subsequent work confirmed his professionalism with such effective shockers as *L'Ultimo Treno della Notte* (1975) and *L'Umanoide* (1979).

d/s Aldo Lado *p* Dieter Geissler *lp* Jean Sorel, Ingrid Thulin, Mario Adorf, Barbara Bach, Jeurgen Drews, Fabian Sovagovic

The Creeping Flesh

(TIGON BRITISH/WORLD FILM SERVICES; GB) scope 91min

After a brief foray in Germany, Francis returned to England to make this entertaining rumination about what should be done with the severed finger of a malevolent skeleton which, when it comes into contact with moisture, swells and becomes fleshy.

Cushing is the scientist who inoculates his daughter (Heilbron) with the essence of evil which – predictably, considering this essence has been shown to be phallus-derived – causes her to become convulsed with sensuality. The parable about sex-and-the-Victorian-family ends with patriarch Cushing imprisoned in an asylum run by his brother (Lee), while his wife and daughter are both stigmatized as demented. In the meantime, Heilbron – sexuality incarnate, courtesy of Roy Ashton's makeup – stalks the country in the form of a black-hooded putrifying mess.

Using a cool style, with many medium and long shots, Francis gives the picture a sense of desolation and bleakness appropriate to the kind of 'decency' that must be accepted if the events recounted are to be viewed as disturbingly evil. The result is Francis's most complex and revealing picture, achieving exactly the right tone for such a depressing fable about 'Englishness'. The contemporary relevance of the story was brought out by critic Robin Wood: 'The film suffers from the somewhat squalid bourgeois morality which afflicts so much British (and other) popular art: the equation with evil of all displays of energy or overt sexuality, the consequent implication that all expressions of spontaneous vitality must be ruthlessly punished.'

d Freddie Francis *p* Michael Redbourne *s* Peter Spencely, Jonathan Rumbold *c* Norman Warwick *lp* Peter Cushing, Christopher Lee, Lorna Heilbron, George Benson, Kenneth J. Warren, Michael Ripper, Duncan Lamont, Jenny Runacre, Harry Locke, Hedger Wallace

The Curse of Bigfoot

(GOLD KEY TV/UNIVERSAL ENTERTAINMENT) 87min

This early entry in the Bigfoot cycle is an attempt to resurrect footage from a never-released early sixties movie in which the creature that menaces students on a field trip is not Bigfoot but a mummified monster who may be the missing link.

Bigfoot, America's home-grown yeti, has been featured in a long list of mainly dirt-cheap movies, often hokey semi-documentaries. These include *Big Foot* (1971), **Legend of Boggy Creek** (1972), *The Beast and the Vixens* (1973), *Shriek of the Mutilated* (1974), *The Mysterious Monsters* (1975), *Panic in the Wilderness* (1975), *Bigfoot – Man or Beast?* (1975), *In Search of Bigfoot* (1976), *Snowbeast* (1977), *Sasquatch* (1977), *Manbeast! Myth or Monster* (1978), *Return to Boggy Creek* (1978) and *Revenge of Bigfoot* (1979).

Peter Cushing and the malevolent skeleton in The Creeping Flesh.

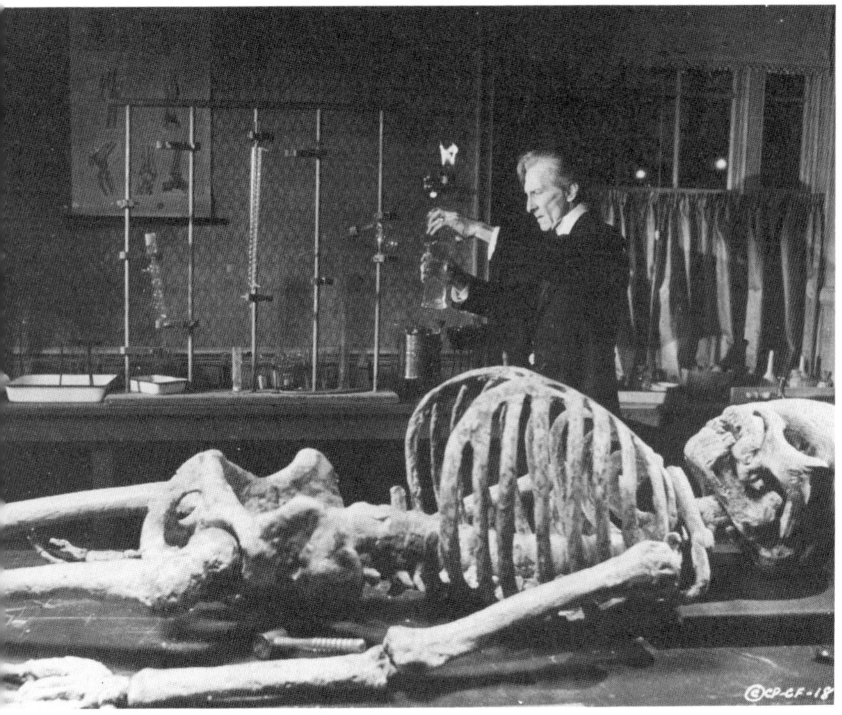

d Don Fields *p/s* J. T. Fields *lp* William Simonsen, Robert Clymire, Jan Swihart, Ken Kloepfer

Cu'un Sae Han Nyo *aka* The Revengeful Ghost

(THE CENTURY COMPANY; ROK) scope 90min

The spectral revenge of a wronged woman is the staple element in the plots of a great many Korean – and Japanese – horror movies (**Myonuriui Han**, 1971; **Wolnyoui Han** and **Yo**, both 1980; **Mangryongui Wechingturesu**, 1981). Here a young woman whose lover has been forced to marry into a rich family is murdered by her father to keep the love affair a secret. She returns to haunt her lover and his new wife, luring them to the cave where she was killed in order to consummate her revenge. Ahn, who later shot **Mangryongui Kok** (1980), achieves strikingly poetic effects with his camera, but the picture's highlight remains the macabre scene in the skeleton-infested cave.

d/p Im Won Sik *s* Kim Sung Yub *c* Ahn Chang Bok *lp* Oh Soomi, Yoon Yang Ha, Woo Yun Yung, Lee Nakh Oon

La Dama Rossa Uccide Sette Volte *aka* The Red Queen Kills Seven Times

(PHOENIX CINEMATOGRAFICA/ROMANO FILM/TRAIAN BOERU; IT,WG) 98min

In this follow-up to the sexploitative **La Notte che Evelyn Usci dalla Tomba** (1971), Miraglia stresses the gothic rather than sex elements. The story, set almost entirely in an old castle, concerns a family curse, represented in a painting, which decrees that every 100 years one daughter will kill her sister. A female figure in a red cape, looking like the woman in the painting, wanders about the place giving people heart-attacks. She appears to be one of the two sisters, except that the other one thought that she had killed and buried her in the subterranean vaults. Since the Lady in Red was supposed to have been stabbed seven times, the legend requires her to kill seven times and the corpses – mainly of women in the fashion business – pile up. The ending has the caped Lady in Red, awaiting the heroine (Bouchet) in the dank caves of the castle, eliminated when another villain floods the vaults before the heroine can escape with her lover (Pagliai). The convoluted script is performed by a cast who look like refugees from an aftershave ad, while the rest is routine terror-thriller stuff.

d/co-s Emilio P. Miraglia *co-s* Fabio Pittorru *c* Alberto Spagnoli *lp* Barbara Bouchet (Gutcher), Marina Malfatti, Ugo Pagliai, Maria Pia Giancaro, Marino Masé, Fabrizio Moresco, Sybil Danning, Nino Korda, Rudolph Schuendler

Dark Places

(SEDGLED/GLENBEIGH; GB) scope 91min

Sharp's calmly professional direction of this pedestrian old-dark-house script is the only notable feature of the movie. Hardy is the man who looks for a hidden hoard of money in the grisly manor of Marr's Grove. A doctor (Lee), his sister (Collins) and a solicitor (Lom) do their best to scare him away, but he gradually becomes possessed by the house's previous owner who murdered his own wife and children after they killed his lover. In the end, and unsurprisingly, Hardy is discovered to be a madman, as he strangles Collins and pickaxes Lee. The money is found behind a wall in a niche which also harbours four mouldering corpses. Sharp resists the temptation to go over the top and manages a few shocks very well (Hardy hacking a hole in a wall and releasing fluttering bats, for example), but it all remains a somewhat mechanical effort. The picture was released in 1973.

d Don Sharp *p* James Hannah Jnr *s* Ed Brennan, Joseph Van Winkle *c* Ernest Steward *lp* Christopher Lee, Robert Hardy, Joan Collins, Herbert Lom, Jane Birkin, Carleton Hobbs, Jennifer Thanisch, Michael McVey, Jean Marsh, Linda Gray

1972

Daughters of Satan

(A AND S PRODUCTIONS; US,PHIL) scope 90(86)min

This is one of the weakest of the Filipino horror pictures of the period (which include **Night of the Cobra Woman**, 1972; **Curse of the Vampires**, 1970; and **Patayin Mo Sa Sindak si Barbara**, 1973). A painting of three witches being burned at the stake is bought by Selleck whose wife appears to be the twin of one of the figures. Gradually she is taken over by another personality and begins to attack her husband, a remote descendant of the witchfinder responsible for the depicted scene. In the end, she and two other reincarnated witches (Guthrie and Paraluman) drug Selleck and drive his car over a cliff but he survives only to be stabbed by his demonic wife. In addition to inane dialogue, the story devised by John Bushelman is padded with repeated zooms into the painting, some irrelevant scenes with a demonic black dog and endless but fruitless attempts to conjure up 'atmosphere' by resorting to big closeups or aimlessly roving camera movements around the couple's house. With Selleck (soon to make his name in the *Magnum* teleseries) in the lead, the picture looks more like a Californian soap opera intercut with footage from Manila that could have been ordered by telephone.

d Hollingsworth Morse *p* Aubrey Schenk *s* John C. Higgins *c* Nonong Rasca *lp* Tom Selleck, Barra Grant, Toni Phelps Guthrie, Paraluman, Vic Silayan, Vic Diaz, Gina Laforteza, Paquito Salcedo

Dead of Night *aka* The Night Walk *aka* Deathdream *aka* The Night Andy Came Home

(NIGHT WALK LTD/IMPACT QUADRANT FILMS; CAN) 90(89)min

This is an unpretentiously effective film which turns the zombie theme to unexpected contemporary use in its story of a soldier (Backus) who returns from combat – unspecified, although the film was made during the Vietnam war – to a reunion with his family in their small-town home. His father (Marley) grows suspicious of the boy's conduct and it eventually emerges that Backus is one of the walking dead and will disintegrate without a supply of blood, for which he kills the family doctor (Forsythe). More murders ensue as Backus does indeed start to disintegrate – the sight of him causes Marley to commit suicide – and in a wild finale the boy's mother (Carlin), still refusing to reject her son, drives with him to the cemetery, where he has already dug himself a grave, before the police can close in on him. The script avoids spurious moralizing but quite sharply sketches in the undercurrents of tension within the apparently model middle-class home. As in the more conventional **Black Christmas** (1974), Clark's direction is efficient and cleancut. Scenarist Ormsby also took charge of the makeup effects, with Tom Savini.

d/p Bob Clark *s* Alan Ormsby *c* Jack McGowan *lp* Lynn Carlin, John Marley, Richard Backus, Henderson Forsythe, Anya Ormsby, Jane Daly, Michael Mazes, Arthur Bradley

Dead People *aka* Messiah of Evil *aka* The Second Coming *aka* Revenge of the Screaming Dead *aka* Return of the Living Dead

(V/M PRODUCTIONS) 89min

Katz and Huyck made *Dead People* just before writing and working on *American Graffiti* (1973). The film nods fairly heavily in the direction of **Night of the Living Dead** (1968), as some of the alternative titles suggest, but the story of Arletty (Hill) who visits a small California town in search of her surrealist painter father only to discover a colony of rampaging zombies is executed with a good deal of imaginative stylistic panache and is actually relatively restrained (in comparison to similar zombie films) in terms of bloodletting.

d/co-s William Huyck *p/co-s* Gloria Katz *c* Stephen Katz *lp* Michael Greer, Marianna Hill, Joy Bang, Anitra Ford, Royal Dano, Elisha Cook Jnr

Death Line, *Gary Sherman's assured directorial debut.*

Dear Dead Delilah

(A JACK H. MUSIC PRESENTATION) 90(75)min

This rather weak attempt at Southern gothic was filmed in Nashville and features Moorehead as Delilah, a domineering, wheelchair-ridden matriarch, who regally presides over her decaying Southern mansion. Fearing that she is close to death, she tells her family that her eccentric father buried $600,000 in the grounds, and that whoever finds it can keep it. During the frantic search that follows the family are decimated by a series of axe murders. Director/scriptwriter Farris went on to write **The Fury** (1978).

Producer Clement is much better known as a songwriter ('Ballad of a Teenage Queen') and record producer, in which capacity he worked with Johnny Cash and Charley Pride, country music's first black superstar, among others.

d/s John Farris *p* Jack Clement *c* William R. Johnson *lp* Agnes Moorehead, Will Geer, Michael Ansara, Patricia Carmichael, Dennis Patrick, Anne Meacham, Robert Gentry, Elizabeth Eis, Ruth Baker, Ann Gibbs

Death Line *aka* Raw Meat

(KL PRODUCTIONS; GB) 87min

Based on a story devised by the director himself, this is an extraordinary début film which offers a uniquely successful blend of repulsive physical terror and sensitive compassion for its gruesome hero (Armstrong), a plague-ridden cannibal living deep below the ground, but tenderly concerned about the equally unsightly, pregnant woman (Turner) who shares his horrifying dwelling amid stacks of rotting, half-consumed corpses. The creature periodically emerges, through long abandoned tunnels, into the Russell Square underground station looking for consumable stragglers. The ingenuous motivation for the creature's existence is a cave-in during the construction of a new underground station in 1892, which buried many people alive. The assumption is that the people not only survived in their claustrophobic hell, but also reproduced themselves. In the end, the man abducts a young woman (Gurney) as a replacement for his deceased wife, causing her lover (Ladd) to pursue him through the subterranean warren, saving his girlfriend and, in a state of near hysteria, viciously kicking the pathetic creature's head in, whereupon the police (Pleasance) arrive to discover the charnel-house world. One of Sherman's major achievements is the subtly achieved shift from revulsion to sympathy for the monstrous cannibal, with his macabre cry of 'Mind the Doors', in a pivotal camera movement which begins with a rat nibbling at a bloody arm and takes in the nightmarishly decomposing bodies, but also reveals the creature solicitously bending over the dying woman, and goes on to complete the picture of the man's world, ending on the arm again. During the course of this one scene, the whole mood has changed from one of physical terror to tragedy, from a statement about human degradation to one of the persistence of tenderness in the most appalling material conditions.

Sherman's next film, *Dead and Buried* (1981), was a more pessimistic affair, suggesting that George Romero-type zombies are a cop-out fantasy since small-town America is populated by ordinary-looking but equally deadly zombies anyway.

d Gary Sherman *p* Paul Maslansky *s* Ceri Jones *c* Alex Thomson *se* John Horton *lp* Donald Pleasance, David Ladd, Sharon Gurney, Christopher Lee, Hugh Armstrong, Norman Rossington, June Turner, James Cossins

The Deathmaster

(R. F. PRODUCTIONS/WORLD ENTERTAINMENT) 88(75)min

Quarry (of **Count Yorga, Vampire**, 1970 and **The Return of Count Yorga**, 1971 fame) here plays a long-haired vampire washed up in his coffin on a beach in southern California. After this moderately striking beginning (though not a patch on its model, **Son of Dracula**, 1943), the film settles down to become embarassingly dated as he becomes guru to a band of hippies – which, in an effort to be slightly more modern, includes a kung fu fighter – who form a sort of Manson cult. Technically, the movie is inadequate in all departments.

d Ray Danton *p* Fred Sadoff *s* R. L. Grove *c* Wilmer C. Butler *lp* Robert Quarry, Bill Ewing, Brenda Dickson, John Fiedler, Betty Ann Rees

Les Démons *aka* Os Demonios *aka* The Demons *aka* Les Démons du Sexe *aka* The Sex Demons

(INTERFILME/COMPTOIR FRANÇAIS DU FILM; FR,PORT) 116(94)min

Returning to the themes of **El Processo de las Brujas** (1969), Franco here again features the notorious witch-hunter Judge Jeffreys (Foster) in a story adapted from his own pulp novel, published under his customary pen name David Kuhne. The 'Bloody Judge' and his companions, Lady de Winter (Field) and Renfield (Dalbes), are cursed by a witch they condemn to the stake. The angels of vengeance, her daughters Margaret (Nichols) and Kathleen (Gibert) are discovered in a nunnery where they indulge in erotic fantasies, allegedly under the influence of the devil. At various times the women are captured and tortured but they nevertheless seduce everyone in sight, including Mother Superior (Thomas) – who commits suicide – and their male as well as female pursuers. Gibert perfects a lethal kiss which turns her partners into skeletons, and thus allows her to dispose of the villains. Condemned to burn, as a last favour, she kills the judge with her withering kiss before being consumed by the flames. Mostly shown in severely truncated prints, the carelessly staged picture nevertheless avoids the ponderous pretentiousness of its model, Ken Russell's **The Devils** (1971) and approaches the sex scenes with a gusto totally alien to English petty sensationalism. But the over-abundant use of zooms moving in and out of female crotches mars this perverted fairytale. The director returned to the witchcraft motif with **Les Possedées du Diable** (1974), his best effort in the subgenre.

d/s Clifford Brown (Jesús Franco) *p* Victor de Costa *c* Raoul Artigot *lp* Anne Libert (Josiane Gibert), Britt Nichols, Howard Vernon, Alberto Dalbes, Karin Field, John Foster, Luis Barboo, Doris Thomas

imon Raven tears out e heart of Virginia 'etherell in the erratic isciple of Death.

Disciple of Death

(HERITAGE/CHROMAGE; GB) 84min

This film was made soon after **The Crucible of Terror** (1971) by some of the participants in that film. Set in 18th-century Cornwall, the story features the revival of the Stranger (Raven), a demon from hell, by two lovers accidentally spilling a drop of blood on to his grave. The Stranger's task is to find a virgin who is prepared to sacrifice herself willingly and readily to spend the rest of eternity with the unsavoury zombie and, naturally, his search involves a series of grisly killings. Concentrating primarily on gory effects, such as the ritual tearing out of the spreadeagled Wetherell's heart and wringing it out like a sponge to fill a cup with blood, the movie's outrageously visceral scenes seem tongue-in-cheek, and push it towards black comedy, wittingly or not. The intentionally comic passages involving a Jewish cabbalist (Amer) are well handled even if the jokes are a little basic ('Trinity, schminity – this is none of your Christian schmitters, this is your kosher Yiddisher magic'). The photography is functional and there are a few inspired shots, usually the ones without dialogue or action. The makeup, the work of Frank Turner, is acceptable within the limits of an obviously shoestring production.

d/co-p/co-s Tom Parkinson *co-p/co-s* Chuston Fairman *c* William Brayne *lp* Simon Raven, Marguerite Hardiman, Ronald Lacey, Virginia Wetherell, Stephen Bradley, Nicholas Amer, George Belbin

Dr Phibes Rises Again

(AIP; GB) 89min

In this sequel to **The Abominable Dr Phibes** (1971), Price and his mute assistant Vulnavia (Kemp) set about the obsessive task of restoring life to his wife, killed through alleged medical incompetence. Phibes himself is resurrected thanks to a preordained conjunction of the planets which enables his cadaver automatically to be pumped full of blood. He then systematically eliminates all the helpers of his main antagonist (Quarry), using different forms of cruelty on each occasion.

Fuest and his scenarist obviously enjoyed working with the characters originally created by James Whiton and William Goldstein, and his previous experience directing *The Avengers* teleseries had prepared him well for this knowing, camp, art-deco play with generic conventions. The pleasures of the film consist in the balance of ghoulish humour: the macabre ends dreamed up for opponents, the phlegmatic exchanges of lines and Brian Eatwell's deliberately over-the-top art direction, which matches Price's grand theatricality. Quarry, fresh from his successful portrayal of **Count Yorga, Vampire** (1970) provides a suitably devious foil for Price's supervillain.

d/co-s Robert Fuest *p* Louis M. Heyward *co-s* Robert Blees *c* Alex Thompson *lp* Vincent Price, Robert Quarry, Valli Kemp, Fiona Lewis, Peter Cushing, Beryl Reid, Terry-Thomas, Hugh Griffith, Peter Jeffrey, Caroline Munro

Dracula AD 1972 *aka* **Dracula Chelsea 72** *aka* **Dracula Chases the Mini Girls** *aka* **Dracula Today**
(HAMMER; GB) 95(98)min
For the most part Hammer were fairly inventive and conscientious in their attempts to rework their mythic material, as in **Twins of Evil** (1971), **The Legend of the Seven Golden Vampires** (1973) and **Blood from the Mummy's Tomb** (1971). With this picture they followed a particularly post-sixties dead end by resurrecting the Count in the vacuously trendy context of a so-called youth movie set in fashionable swinging London. Houghton, who also scripted *The Legend of the Seven Golden Vampires*, lapsed into camping up the script with silly lines ('She's a bit drained ...') while Cushing bravely continues his deadpan interpretation of Van Helsing Jnr, with the result that his performance sits incongruously in a vacuum. Lee's role is almost totally reduced to the vampiric act itself and the direction contents itself with getting from one scene to the next without fuss or inspiration.

Dracula's next Hammer-sponsored outing, **The Satanic Rites of Dracula** (1973), which is only marginally more interesting, brought Hammer's famous series to an inglorious end. The American version of Gibson's movie added a three-minute commercial featuring a Dracula impersonator who invited the audience to join the Dracula Society and took them personally through the oath of membership.

d Alan Gibson *p* Josephine Douglas *s* Don Houghton *c* Richard Bush *se* Les Bowie *lp* Christopher Lee, Peter Cushing, Stephanie Beacham, Michael Coles, Christopher Neame, William Ellis, Marsha Hunt, Caroline Munro, Janet Key, Michael Kitchin

Dracula contra Frankenstein *aka* **Dracula Prisonnier de Frankenstein** *aka* **Dracula Against Frankenstein** *aka* **Dracula contra el Dr Frankenstein** *aka* **Dracula vs Frankenstein** *aka* **Satana contra Dr Exortio** *aka* **The Erotic Rites of Frankenstein**
(FENIX/COMPTOIR FRANÇAIS DU FILM; SP,FR)
scope 87(85)min
After his initial Spanish and German work, which included **Necronomicon** (1967), and the series of Harry Alan Towers productions, Franco briefly returned to Germany before embarking on a number of French movies of which this is one. It offers a catalogue of horror elements together with some stylish scenes strung together by a ludicrous storyline. Jonathan (Dalbes) stakes Dracula (Vernon) but Frankenstein (Price) and his mute servant Morpho (Barboo) use a female singer's blood to restore the Count, thereby becoming masters of a horde of vampires. The Baron's creature (Bilbao) attacks Dalbes but he's nursed back to health by a gypsy witch (Francis). Aided by a werewolf (Brandy) he again tackles the Baron, but to no avail. Eventually, the Baron turns on his own vampire slaves and kills the Count and his companion (Nichols), escaping the conflagration when Dalbes and the gypsies set fire to the castle. The narrative doesn't make sense; Frankenstein drives about in a limousine while Dracula uses an oldfashioned carriage, making the picture hover uneasily between comedy and fantasy. Highlights include Morpho's necrophiliac onslaught on the exsanguinated corpse of Gibert before she is cremated, and various comic-strip-type scenes of gore. The puffed-up body of the ill-looking Price contrasts unfavourably with Peter Cushing's personification of reason.

Franco continued in this vein with **Les Expériences Erotiques de Frankenstein** and **A Filha de Dracula** (both 1972) as well as a considerable number of often sadistic soft-porn movies to which he generally added hard-core scenes later if the producer requested it.

Caroline Munro in the disappointing Dracula AD 1972.

d/s Jesús Franco *p* Robert de Nesle, Arturo Marcos *c* José Climent *lp* Dennis Price, Howard Vernon, Alberto Dalbes, Britt Nichols, Anne Libert (Josiane Gibert), Fernando Bilbao, Mary Francis, Brandy, Luis Barboo, Genevieve Delori

El Espanto Surge de la Tumba *aka* **Horror Rises from the Tomb** (PROFILMES; SP) scope 88min
This gory film was presided over by Molina, Spain's leading horror practitioner. A knight (Molina) is decapitated while his wife, suspended upsidedown and naked, is forced to watch before being cut in two herself. In modern France and Spain, the knight's curse comes into effect when descendants of the protagonists, Hugo (Molina) and Maurice (Winner) and their girlfriends (Cohen and Liné) return to their ancestral home in search of the knight's head, allegedly buried there. Subsequent events, triggered by the malignant head, involve a robber (Ciges) who uses a sickle to decapitate a housemaid (Cantudo), the reunification of the knight's head and body, the resuscitation of his wife in the shape of Suriani, many decapitations, a group of zombies rising out of a lake, a seduction scene in which Suriani rips the flesh off her lover's back and hysterical exorcism fits when a talisman is applied to the demonic figures.

Aured's début echoes the opening scenes of **The Witchfinder General** (1968) but then appears to treat each scene as an individual event disconnected from the rest of the story, going for maximum shock effect each time. The acting is hyperbolic and reminiscent of Grand Guignol melodrama. Aured and Molina collaborated again on **La Venganza de la Momia, El Retorno de Walpurgis** and **Los Ojos Azules de la Munēca Rota** (all 1973). The settings were provided by a specialist in the genre, Gumersindo Andres.

d Carlos Aured *p* Ricardo Muñez Suay, José Antonio Perez Giner *s* Jacinto Molina *c* Manuel Merino *lp* Paul Naschy (Jacinto Molina), Emma Cohen, Vic Winner (Victor Alcazar), Helga Liné, Betsabe Ruiz, Maria José Cantudo, Cristina Suriani, Julio Peña, Luis Ciges, Francisco Llinas, Juan Cazalilla

El Espectro del Terror
(LACY INTERNACIONAL FILMS; SP) scope 93min
After **La Llamada del Vampiro** and **Las Amantes del Diablo** (both 1971), the prolific Elorietta wrote, produced and directed this terror picture in an attempt to imitate the successes of Mario Bava and Dario Argento's brand of women-

in-peril stories. The film features a sadistic sex maniac who kills air hostesses and dissolves their corpses in an acid bath. One particular hostess (Perschy), who is also the investigating policeman's fiancée, becomes the psychopath's main target but she eventually kills her tormentor. The script merely strings together clichés of the genre while bombastic music by Javier Elorietta signals when the film is supposed to be suspenseful – in fact, it's never more than sensationalist.

d/p/s Joe Lacy (José Maria Elorietta) *c* Pablo Ripoll *lp* Maria Perschy, Aramis Ney, Betsabe Ruiz, Sancho Garcia, May Oliver (Maritza Olivares), Victor Alcazar, Ernesto Vanes, Titania Clement

Les Expériences Erotiques de Frankenstein *aka* La Maldición de Frankenstein *aka* La Malédiction de Frankenstein

(COMPTOIR FRANÇAIS DU FILM/FERRIX; FR,SP) scope 90min
Following on from **Dracula contra Frankenstein** (1972), this film opens with the arrival of Melissa (Gibert), a bird-woman created by Cagliostro (Vernon), and her servant (Barboo) at the castle of Frankenstein (Price). Breaking into the Baron's laboratory, she tears him limb from limb while her servant disposes of the Baron's assistant (Franco) and kidnaps the creature (Bilbao) the Baron had manufactured. They take the creature back to their master who uses it to abduct women who have to submit to his peculiar desires before being killed in order to furnish the bits the Cagliostro requires to build a 'perfect woman'. Frankenstein's daughter (Nichols) is also captured and prepared for a ritual mating with the creature, but the proceedings are interrupted by the hero (Dalbes). The film's title is misleading since the erotic experiences which occupy a considerable amount of screentime are in fact those of Cagliostro, the Baron having been killed in the first reel. Highlights, apparently culled from Italian 'adult' comics, include Barboo and Savon, tied back to back and lying on a spiked tabletop, being whipped for Vernon's pleasure and the weirdly effective blind bird-woman, naked except for some plumage, who savagely scratches and bites people to death. The cast and sets are almost identical to those of *Dracula contra Frankenstein* and the shooting style, relying on a relentless use of the zoom lens, betrays the indecent haste with which the production was thrown together. Except for occasional scenes translating castration anxieties into genuinely nightmarish images, the film remains a slapdash quickie.

Franco went on to make **A Filha de Dracula** (1972), starting the fourth period of his career (after the first Spanish, then German and then Harry Alan Towers productions) with a trilogy in the style of Hammer's Karnstein films, except that the scripts cohere only on the fantasy level and substitute fully fledged erotic sadism for the English films' embarrassed prurience. Daniel J. White, who appears briefly as an actor, was better known as one of Franco's regular music composers. The film also features the début of Lina Romay, who went on to star in more than 30 Franco pictures, as a gypsy in a scene missing from most release prints.

d/s Jesús Franco *p* Victor de Costa *c* Raoul Artigot *lp* Howard Vernon, Anne Libert (Josiane Gibert), Dennis Price, Britt Nichols, Alberto Dalbes, Luis Barboo, Fred Harrison (Fernando Bilbao), Beatriz Savon, Jesús Franco

Peter Cushing as the deranged headmaster in Fear in the Night.

Fear in the Night (HAMMER; GB) 85min

Returning to the plot device of the scheming lovers he had used in **Taste of Fear** (1960), scenarist Sangster's third directorial effort (following **The Horror of Frankenstein** and **Lust for a Vampire**, both 1970) is a competent though still mechanically constructed psycho-thriller. Peggy (Geeson) is the victim of a plot by her lover, a prep school teacher (Bates) and the headmaster's wife (Collins) to get her to murder the old, mentally deranged headmaster (Cushing) who has never recovered from a tragic fire that devasted his school and left him with an artificial arm. He resorts to playing tapes with school sounds to animate the deserted buildings, and appears to be persecuting Geeson who escapes various attacks. Given a shotgun to protect herself, she appears to shoot the headmaster, but the elaborate plot misfires as the intended victim proves to be one step ahead of the plotters. The best scene is the credit sequence in which the camera roams through the school's grounds and discovers the gently swaying body of a hanged man ...

d/p/co-s Jimmy Sangster *co-s* Michael Syson *c* Arthur Grant *lp* Judy Geeson, Peter Cushing, Joan Collins, Ralph Bates, Gillian Lind, James Cossins, John Brown, Brian Grellis

A Filha de Dracula *aka* La Fille de Dracula

(INTERFILME/COMPTOIR FRANÇAIS DU FILM; FR,PORT) 90min
This cheaply made quickie completes a trilogy, with **Dracula contra Frankenstein** and **Les Expériences Erotiques de Frankenstein** (both 1972), made with almost identical casts and sets. The story tells how, after Dracula has been killed, a dying old woman reveals to her daughter, Maria Karnstein (Nichols) that she is a descendant of the Count. When the obligatory lesbian and heterosexual nude sucking scenes have taken place, the two remaining vampires are destroyed, one by a stake through the skull, one by fire.

The hastily shot production is among Franco's weakest efforts. The relentlessly prolific director went on to make **Les Démons** (1972) and a number of sex films often starring Lina Romay who, after Janine Reynaud, Maria Rohm, Soledad Miranda and Nichols, became the director's fifth and longest serving fetish actress. She had starred in his most stylish film, **Necronomicon** (1967) and enlivened *La Comtesse Noire* (1973) as well as the extraordinary fantasy **Les Possedées du Diable** (1974).

d/s Jesús Franco *p* Victor de Costa *c* José Climent *lp* Britt Nichols, Anne Libert (Josiane Gibert), Howard Vernon, Alberto Dalbes, Luis Barboo, Daniel J. White, Jesús Franco

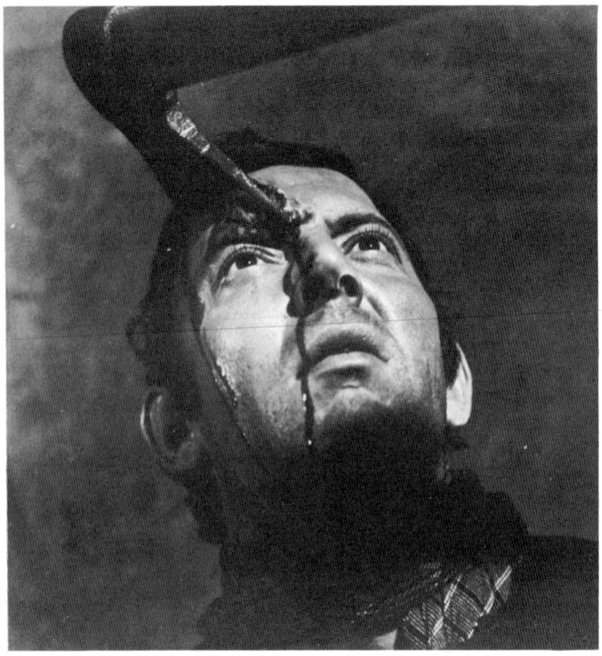

The Flesh and Blood Show

(PETER WALKER-HERITAGE LTD; GB) 96min

Although this film has a window dressing of sexploitation and some misjudged humour, it retains a degree of charm, no doubt due to Jessop, who had directed **Cat Girl** (1957). The quaintly Agatha Christie-like plot and characters are set in an ever-so-English locale: a dilapidated old theatre in a seaside resort. A company of actors arrive to rehearse a Grand Guignol play for an employer (Barr) none of them has met. The unseen employer turns out to be a maniac, an ex-leading actor whose hatred for the profession has festered ever since he murdered his wife and her lover by entombing them following a performance of *Othello*. The film then chronicles the maniac's decimation of the troup. Burdened with a ludicrously ineffective 3-D conclusion, Walker's tawdry direction nearly smothers Shaughnessy's mildly interesting script. His collaboration with the ex-critic David MacGillivray (**Frightmare**, 1974; *House of Whipcord*, 1974) resulted in sadistic sexploitation movies which have little of the rigour of such Japanese examples of the genre as **Moju** (1969) or **Okasaretu Byuakui** (1967).

d/p Peter Walker *s* Alfred Shaughnessy *c* Peter Jessop *lp* Jenny Hanley, Ray Brooks, Luan Peters, Judy Matheson, Candace Glendinning, Robin Askwith, Tristan Rogers, Penny Meredith, Patrick Barr, Peter Walker

The Folks at Red Wolf Inn *aka* Terror at Red Wolf Inn *aka* Terror House

(A RED WOLF PRESENTATION) 90(83)min

Like **Cannibal Girls** (1972) and, to a lesser extent, the wonderful **Death Line** (1972), *The Folks at Red Wolf Inn* mixes cannibalism and comedy together surprisingly effectively, coming across as something of a gory variation on *Arsenic and Old Lace* (1941). Gillin is the young student on holiday at the inn run by two nice old people (Jackson and Space), who have a mentally retarded grandson (Neilson). After two of the guests disappear, Gillin discovers that her genial hosts are in fact cannibals. Thanks mainly to excellent playing by the cast and a fair amount of genuine wit, as opposed to gross humour, the film actually works as that most difficult of generic hybrids, the horror comedy, even though the final credits role in the form of a menu.

d Bud Townsend *p* Michael Macready *s* Allen J. Actor *c* John McNichol *lp* Linda Gillin, John Neilson, Mary Jackson, Arthur Space

Las Garras de Lorelei *aka* When the Screaming Stops *aka* The Lorelei's Grasp

(C.C. ASTRO/PROFILMES; SP) scope 102min

A low-budget quickie from the director of the successful **La Noche del Terror Ciego** (1971), this film is loosely based on the Rhineland legend of Lorelei with additional elements taken from the Nibelungen myth. Lorelei (Liné) is a siren living in a gothic cave near the Rhine who occasionally turns into a scaly creature that attacks young women and rips out their hearts to ensure her own survival. A hunter, appropriately called Sigurd (Stella), is hired by a girls' boarding school to put an end to the bloody menace. He becomes involved with the siren but eventually kills her with a steel blade forged from the mythic Siegfried's sword given to him by the local mad scientist (Menendez).

Apart from the detailed depictions of the siren's cardiac operations and a few scenes in her cave, the film is amateurishly directed and, seemingly, unable to make up its mind whether it is a horror film or a mythic fairytale. The English title echoed the alternative title of **Fengriffen** (1973), *And Now the Screaming Starts*.

d/s Amando de Ossorio *p* José Antonio Perez Giner *c* Miguel F. Mila *se* Alfredo Segoviono *lp* Tony Kendall (Luciano Stella), Helga Liné, Silvia Tortosa, Loretta Tovar, Luis Induin, José Theman, Angel Menendez, Luis Barboo

Do Gaz Jameen ke Neeche *aka* Crime Does Not Pay

(RAMSAY FILMS; INDIA) scope 141min

The Ramsay family, autonomous producers working in Hindi since 1955, virtually monopolized the despised horror genre in India in the seventies. As indigenous horror motifs tended to be elaborated in terms of melodramatic ghost stories or as mythological tales, the few horror movies comparable to Western examples were in fact hybrid pictures introducing zombies and other monstrous creatures into the traditional formats of the commercial Hindi film industry, including its obligatory musical interludes. This film tells of a perfidious woman who, with the aid of her uncle, marries a rich young man, kills and buries him, but finds her enjoyment of his wealth spoiled when a chemical compound revives the husband's cadaver, allowing it to return from the grave to take revenge. The Ramsays' first venture into horror, *Ek Nanhi Munni Ladki Thi* (1970) had been a box-office disaster, and this, their second attempt, ran into censorship trouble which severely restricted its audiences. But it proved successful enough for them to continue in this vein with *Andhera* (1975), **Darwasa** (1978) and many others, making them the undisputed specialists in this area.

d R. Tulsi Ramsay, Shyam Ramsay *p* F. V. Ramsay *s* Kumar Ramsay *c* Ganga Ramsay, Keshu Ramsay *lp* Surendra Kumar, Pooja, Imtiaz, Shobhana, Satyendra Kapoo, Smita Mayank, Habib, Dhumal

El Gran Amor del Conde Dracula *aka* Dracula's Great Love *aka* Cemetery Girls *aka* Dracula's Virgin Lovers

(JANUS FILMS/EVA FILMS; SP) 91(83)min

After Jesús Franco's attempt at a faithful adaptation of Bram Stoker's novel, **El Conde Dracula** (1970) and Leon Klimovsky's **La Saga de los Dracula** (1972), Aguirre directed this elegiac version with Molina – whose short, stout stature as an ex-weightlifter was much better suited to his numerous impersonations of a werewolf – as the Count. The story is set in 1870 and tells of a Mr Wendell (Molina) who turns out to be the Count and vampirizes a group of travellers who take shelter in a dilapidated nursing home near his castle. In love with one of them (Politoff), he decides to abstain from her blood, preferring to wait for her consent. Besides, he needs a willing victim to follow him into the realm of the undead if his dead daughter is to be regenerated. Since Politoff refuses him, the distraught Count buries his daughter and stabs a stake into his own heart.

Left: *One of the many victims of* El Gran Amor del Conde Dracula.

Although the film is seriously marred by the obviously Mediterranean setting and by bad day-for-night shooting, Aguirre nevertheless achieves some lovely scenes as the vampire women wonder through the corridors and participate in occult rituals. Molina's indecently healthy presence detracts from the required perversity of the sex scenes, but something of the interesting basic idea does come through into the *mise-en-scène*. Aguirre's other film with Molina, **El Jorobado de la Morgue** (1972) was more impressive cinematically. Politoff had achieved some notoriety in Eric Rohmer's *La Collectionneuse* (1967) but was miscast, like Molina, in this picture where she simply plays the role of egocentric dimwit which had made her famous. The film was released in 1975, by which time the sex scenes looked decidedly prudish.

d/co-s Javier Aguirre *p* Francisco Lara Polop *co-s* Jacinto Molina, Alberto Insua *c* Raúl Perez Cubero *se* Pablo Perez *lp* Paul Naschy (Jacinto Molina), Haydée Politoff, Rossana Yanni, Mirta Miller, Vic Winner (Victor Alcazar), Ingrid Garbo, Julio Peña, Alvaro de Luna, José M. Martin, Susan Latur

Guru das Siete Cidades

(GURU PRODUÇOES CINEMATOGRAFICAS; BRAZIL) 85min

This misogynist black-magic story proposes the hardly novel 'moral' that those who do evil will be destroyed by it. The wife (Medeiros) of a millionaire becomes involved with a group of hippies led by a Manson-type guru (Terceiro) who indulge in black-magic sessions and wander about in picturesque monk's garb with hoods. Since their rituals require human sacrifices, she proposes her husband as a victim. When he has been murdered, the group choose her as their next sacrificial victim. Peddling its moral lesson as a hypocritical cover for a luridly sensational sexploitation movie, the picture proposes the usual gutter-press clichés of menacingly dissolute 'youth', treacherously gold-digging women and other 'silent majority' stereotypes in order to make a quick profit out of the Tate murders. The cinematography by Silva is, as usual, excellent.

d/s Carlos Bini *p* José Pinheiro de Carvalho *c* Helio Silva *lp* Rejane Medeiros, Angelito Mello, Paulo Ramos, Otavio Terceiro, Rosangela Alves, Wilson Grey, Roberto Bustamente, Antonio Severo Neta

One of the many torture scenes from Hexen Geschandet und zu Tode Gequaelt.

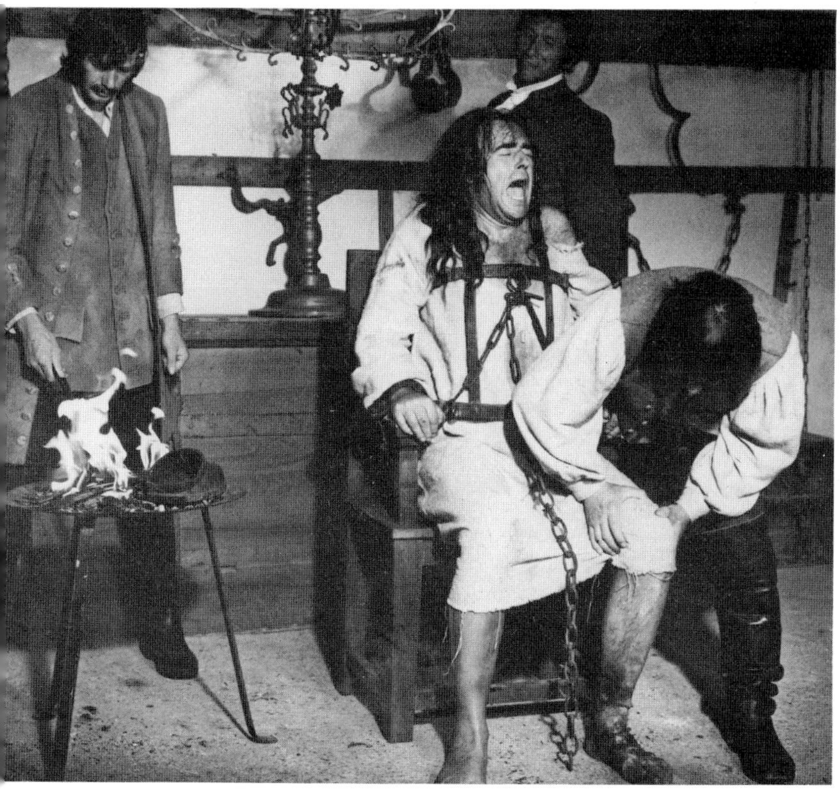

Hexen Geschandet und zu Tode Gequaelt *aka* Mark of the Devil, Part 2

(TV 13; WG) 90(88)min

This is less a sequel than a rehash of the profitable ingredients of **Hexen bis aufs Blut Gequaelt** (1969). This time the witchfinder (Diffring) and his helper (Nalder) kill Count Alex (Hoven) and try to get hold of the aristocrat's fortune by torturing his young widow (Blanc). She eventually escapes with her son. A sadistic sex film, it borrows imagery from Ken Russell's **The Devils** (1971) and features extended scenes in which nearly or totally nude women have their bodies pierced, torn, impaled, whipped, stretched, and so on, and lots of blood and added bone-crunching sounds for the entertainment of its intended audience.

Both Hoven's films are extreme examples of cultural conservatism, feigning disapproval of the perversions they portray for monetary gain while condemning the assumed bloodlust and other forms of moral degeneration attributed to the consumers of such spectacles. Rather than explore the links between sexuality, sadism and cinema as a spectacle, these films simply deploy gross brutality in a fantasy regime that poses emaciated and broken female bodies as ideal images of women and the rippling muscles of the 'macho' man as the ideal of masculinity. This trend culminated, not in the Herschell Gordon Lewis gore movies but in the Nazi medical-camp films of Don Edmonds, *Ilsa – She Wolf of the SS* (1974) and its sequels and imitations.

d/p/s Adrian Hoven *c* Ernst W. Kalinke *lp* Jean-Pierre Zola, Erica Blanc (Enrica Bianchi Colombatto), Anton Diffring, Reginald Nalder, Percy Parker (Adrian Hoven), Lukas Ammann, Astrid Kilian, Ellen Umlauf, Rosy-Rosy

Invasion of the Blood Farmers

(NMD) 80min

This excellent early example of schlock cinema, directed by Adlum (who was also responsible for **Shriek of the Mutilated**, 1974), concerns an upstate New York druid cult searching the hillbilly valley of Jefferson for a rare blood type in order to resurrect their queen in time for a ritualistic blood feast.

Deliberately sleazy and phoney and featuring lashings of hyberbolic gore and queasy humour, the film was financed for less than $40,000, raised by Adlum on the (resonantly suggestive) title alone whilst he was working at the magazine *Cashbox*, where he met scriptwriter Kelleher. A life-long devotee of B movies and occasional rock publicist, Kelleher has also written a book about the Plasmatics rock group, led by onetime hard-core porn star Wendy O. Williams. Their stage act, which involves blowing up cars, wielding chainsaws and destroying TVs with sledge hammers, has its roots in precisely the same trash aesthetic as schlock cinema like *Invasion of the Blood Farmers*.

d/p/co-s Ed Adlum *co-s* Ed Kelleher *lp* Norman Kelly, Cynthia Fleming, Tanna Hunter, Bruce Detrick, Jack Neubeck, Warren D'Oyly-Rhind

Jack's Wife *aka* Hungry Wives *aka* Season of the Witch

(LATENT IMAGE) 130(89)min

After the success of **Night of the Living Dead** (1968), 'money just fell out of the trees' according to Romero. But, instead of giving audiences more of the same, he seized the opportunity to make other kinds of films that interested him. First came *There's Always Vanilla* (1971) and then *Jack's Wife*, which was cut from its original 130 minutes and retitled by the distributor. Feeling insecure and suffering from nightmares as she approaches 40, White refuses to believe her psychiatrist (Fisher) when he tells her that her dreams are simply expressions of her dissatisfaction with life. She becomes interested in a witches' coven led by Greenwald and one day when her husband Jack (Thunhurst) returns home unexpectedly she mistakes him for the prowler of her dreams and shoots him. She is then received into the coven and feels cured of her nightmares and anxieties.

Romero's own personal favourite of his first four films, *Jack's Wife* was described by its maker as 'a feminist film' and by one critic as 'torn between genre and art'. Certainly the overall effect is of a film not quite sure where it's going, with overtones of horror allied to a strange, experimental almost Bergmanesque aura. With its rational, demystificatory approach to witchcraft and black-magic lore, it is perhaps best considered as an interesting, if uneven, dry run for Romero's masterpiece **Martin** (1976).

d/s/c George A. Romero *p* Nancy M. Romero *se* Rege Survinski *lp* Jan White, Ray Laine, Anne Muffly, Joedda McClain, Bill Thunhurst, Neil Fisher, Esther Lapidus, Dan Mallinger, Ken Peters, Virginia Greenwald

El Jorobado de la Morgue *aka* **The Hunchback of the Morgue**

(JANUS FILM/EVA FILMS; SP) scope 87(80)min

Molina's most interesting (although far from perfect) films of the period – **El Gran Amor del Conde Dracula** (1972) and this, as macabre as the former tried to be lyrical – were both directed by Aguirre. Molina is Gotho, a moronic hunchback employed in a hospital morgue and hopelessly in love with Arpon, who suffers from TB. When she dies, he axes the medical students who wish to dissect her body and hides her in an underground crypt. In a hallucinatory scene he discovers her corpse being eaten away by rats and he fights them off with a torch in an extremely realistic passage shot without special effects, which caused the actor to be bitten many times and to convey real pain and panic. A mad biologist (Dalbes) promises to restore her to life in exchange for a supply of cadavers – later live bodies – to feed to a creature he has created. Soon Molina's underground world becomes a nightmarish charnel house packed with rotting corpses. Eventually, realizing he is only being used, he releases a sympathetic psychiatrist (Yanni) and her fellow prisoners intended as food for the creature, kills the beast and its creator and falls into a cauldron full of acid. The *tour de force* with the rats and the many gruesome activities of the hunchback earned Molina the best acting award at the Paris convention of fantastic cinema in 1973.

The Basque Aguirre also made crude comedies and effective thrillers such as *El Asesino Esta entre los Trece* (1973), starring Paty Shepard, Molina's companion in a number of werewolf pictures. But alongside his frankly commercial work, he also pursued a career as Spain's foremost experimental cineaste along with the Catalan Pedro Portabella. His *Anti-Cine* manifesto was published in 1972. Producer Lara also directed films, including the impressive **La Mansión de la Niebla** (1972).

d/co-s Javier Aguirre *p* Francisco Lara Polop *co-s* Jacinto Molina, Alberto S. Insua *c* Raúl Perez Cubero *se* Pablo Perez *lp* Paul Naschy (Jacinto Molina), Rossana Yanni, Alberto Dalbes, Maria Perschy, Vic Winner (Victor Alcazar), Manuel de Blas, Angel Menendez, Antonio Pica, Elena Arpon, Susan Taff, Kinito

Kosure Ookami – Ko Wo Kashi Ude Kashi Tsukatsuru *aka* **Kozure Ohkami** *aka* **Sword of Vengeance** *aka* **Lightning Swords of Death**

(KATSU PRODUCTIONS; JAP) scope 83(81)min

With this excellent, exceedingly violent film based on his own storyline, Misumi initiated a series of movies built around the character of Itto (Wakayama), the man who performs the decapitations at the climax of seppuku rituals for the Tokugawa shogunate. A professional executioner for over a decade, he has become a brutalized killing machine. His last job is the decapitation of an aristocratic child. A victim of court intrigue by a jealous colleague who has also killed his wife, Itto retaliates and becomes a fugitive, surviving as a travelling killer. He offers his baby son (Tomikawa) the choice between a ball and a sword, fully prepared to kill the infant if the wrong choice should be made. When the child takes the sword, Itto fashions a baby carriage with lethal accessories and the two set out on the road, slaughtering their enemies (the jealous villain's men as well as the shogun's killers) and becoming folk heroes in the process. Misumi builds his picture around explosions of unconscionable violence, going out of his way to make the killings as gruesomely spectacular as possible. However, in this first episode he is still primarily concerned with establishing the terms of the situation and the characters. With the second movie, released three months later, he was no longer hampered by such preliminaries and produced a surreal opera of violence of delirious intensity and beauty.

Tomisaburo Wakayama in action in the delirious Kosure Ookami-Sanzu no Kawa no Ubagurama.

The series was designed by actor-producer Katsu as a vehicle to turn his brother, Wakayama, into a star, a goal that was achieved beyond all expectation. The relative awkwardness of this first instalment and the disappointment of the third one, *Kosure Ookami – Shinikase no Mukau Ubagurma* (1972), may be due to the censor's intervention: the feature released third was intended to be the first in the series but, although it was shot in 1969, its release was delayed for three years by the censor, and finally appeared minus two major fight scenes. This meant that the second film had to reiterate the basic situation and open the series.

d Kenji Misumi *p* Shintaro Katsu *s* Kazuo Koike, Gohseki Kojima *c* Chishi Makiura *lp* Tomisabruo Wakayama, Tomoko Mayama, Fumio Watanabe, Shigeru Tsuyuguchi, Akihiro Tomikawa, Yunosuke Ito, Yomiso Kato, Asao Uchida, Keiko Fujita, Saburo Date

Kosure Ookami – Sanzu no Kawa no Ubagurama *aka* **Kozure Ohkmi n. 2** *aka* **Baby Cart at the River Styx** *aka* **Shogun Assassin**

(KATSU PRODUCTIONS; JAP) scope 85(81)min

The second in the Itto series, released three months after the first episode, this is a brilliant, stylized, eerie opera of violence and the closest cinematic equivalent to date of Lautréamont's *Chants de Maldoror*. From the first images, heads are split and blood showers the scene as Itto (Wakayama), the hired killer pushing his equally lethal infant son (Tomikawa) around in a multi-purpose pram, disposes of his assailants. The carriage is a sadean vehicle, able to launch volleys of spears and to sprout blades that chop off legs below the knees.

The film is structured like a Hong Kong martial arts movie and numerous other traditional picaresque narratives and features a succession of ever fiercer battles with increasingly dangerous opponents. Itto's main rival in this film is a woman,

Sayaka (Matsuo), the leader of a gang of female killers. She is introduced in a fight in which she dismembers her male opponent, calmly nails his bloody trunk to the floor and cuts off his head. As the bodies disintegrate into their constitutent parts, a process filmed in hallucinatory crystalline colours, the language on the soundtrack also fragments into obsessive onomatopeias, the film no longer depicting the fantasy of the body-in-pieces but becoming part of that fantasy texture itself, transforming the body of the film in a manner that recalls Wakamatsu's *Okasaretu Byuakui* (1967), a film structured according to the rhythm of the sex act.

Misumi conjures up imagery that stuns the senses: hands with steel claws gouge into eyes, heads explode, bodies are split from head to navel, all under the imperturbable gaze of the little boy (and the viewer) who occasionally intervenes to save his father. In one extraordinarily beautiful scene, one of Itto's prospective antagonists is shown alone in an expanse of sand dunes. Suddenly he plunges his steel-gloved hands into the sand and tears a screaming head out of the ground, frantically rushing about repeating the act until hordes of fighters rise up out of the sand, ready for a battle that will turn the desert red. In the end, the three super-villains (Oooki, Arata and Kishida) – one with a club, one with a mailed fist and one with steel claws – are killed by Itto. Only Sayaka remains but she appears to commit suicide.

In contrast to American or Italian gore movies, Misumi deploys an astonishing pictorial sense which is not subordinated to audience manipulation through editing or blatant character-identification devices. The aesthetics of the image and of the ritualistically, though energetically enacted, carnage become more important than the story and elevate the film on to the level of painfully intense poetry. The next two instalments could not improve on this masterpiece and, at best, the series stagnated before it was finally transferred to television. Misumi directed the third film, *Kosure Ookami – Shinikaze ni Mukai Ubaguruma* (1972) and the fourth, *Kosure Ookami – Meifu* (1973), after which Buichi Saito contributed number five, *Kosure Ookami – Oya no Kokoro Kono Kokoro* (1973). In 1980, Roger Corman's New World company released an American version of *Kosure Ookami – Sanzu No Kawa no Ubaguruma* called *Shogun Assassin*, produced by David Weisman and 'directed' by Robert Houston, with an electronic soundtrack by Mark Lindsay, once the singer with Paul Revere and the Raiders, which included 12 minutes from the first film in the series. It featured a badly dubbed soundtrack narrating the events from the child's point-of-view. Itto's voice was equally badly dubbed by the director Lamont Johnson.

The decidedly uncomfortable dinner in Wes Craven's influential The Last House on the Left.

d Kenji Misumi *p* Shintaro Katsu *s* Kazuo Koike *c* Chishi Makiura *lp* Tomisaburo Wakayama, Akihiro Tomikawa, Kayo Matsuo, Minoru Ooki, Mori Kishida, Shogen Arata, Shoki Kobayashi, Reiko Kasahara, Yukari Wakayama, Yuriko Mishima

The Last House on the Left *aka* Krug and Company *aka* Sex Crime of the Century

(THE NIGHT COMPANY) 91(85)min

After working together on the pseudo-documentary porno film, *Together* (1970), which was extremely successful commercially, relative newcomers Cunningham and Craven were given $90,000 by their delighted backers and told to go and make a 'knock-down, drag-out horror movie'. The result was *The Last House on the Left*, which raised a storm of controversy (some scenes were reportedly cut for the sake of an R rating, but this is a film about which legends abound) and millions of dollars at the box office. Cunningham and Craven went on to make **Friday the 13th** (1980) and **The Hills Have Eyes** (1977) respectively. Meanwhile, a host of opportunistic retitlings resulted in the likes of *The New House on the Left* (1978) and *Last House on the Left II* (1978).

The story concerns two teenage girls (Grantheim and Cassel) who, on their way to a rock concert, stop to buy some dope. The dealers are Hess and Lincoln (two escaped sex murderers), Hess's girlfriend (Rain) and his drug-addicted son (Sheffier). He lures the girls back to the gang's hideout where they beat and rape Grantheim. The next day the gang set out with them by car for the Canadian border. When the car breaks down in some woods the girls attempt to escape and are killed by the gang. Then, in a bizarre plot twist (in fact borrowed from Ingmar Bergman's *The Virgin Spring*, 1960) the gang take refuge in the house of Cassel's parents (St James and Carr). When they find out that they are in fact entertaining their daughter's murders the parents wreak a terrible revenge, descending to horrific levels of brutality in the attempt, just as the gang attempt to pass themselves of as insurance salesmen and solid members of the bourgeoisie.

Last House has been the subject of so much invective on the one hand and fulsome praise (mainly from Robin Wood) on the other, that it's hard not to lapse into either simply defending or attacking the film. It's certainly extremely gruesome, but it must be said that the violence is never presented in a romanticized (à la Sam Peckinpah) or simply pyrotechnic (body-count) fashion – which is why it's so shocking. As Craven himself put it: '*Last House* was really a reaction on my part to the violence around us, specifically to the Vietnam war. I spent a lot of time on the streets protesting the war, and I wanted to show how violence affects people. It blew away all the clichés of handling violence. Before that violence had been neat and tidy: I made it painful and protracted and shocking and very human. And I made the people who were doing the killing very human.' This, again, gives the film an extremely disturbing quality, for the characters never cease to be recognizably human, like de-romanticized Bonnie and Clydes who, at the climax of the disembowelling of Rain, clearly feel disgust at what they have done. (It should be pointed out that Hess as Krug makes a horribly convincing psychopath, a role he recreated with even greater force in the not dissimilar *The House on the Edge of the Park*, 1981.) The unmannered acting, the lack of posturing, the attentive ear for dialogue and nuance, the refusal to resort to *Friday the 13th* style special effects' wizardry for the gruesome scenes all help to explain the film's peculiarly upsetting ambience.

It has been argued that the film displays a puritanism every bit as oppressive as the more recent women-in-jeopardy series (what might be called the '*Don't* cycle'): when the girls meet their killers they are trying to score some dope on their way to a gig by a band called Bloodlust who are renowned for their on-stage violence, and one girl's bedroom is plastered with posters of early seventies parental hate figure Mick Jagger. This reading is borne out by the advertising campaign mounted by the film's producers in the wake of widespread criticism of the film, part of which read: 'Violence and bestiality are not condoned in *The Last House on the Left* – far from it! The movie makes a plea for an end to all the senseless violence and inhuman cruelty that has become so much a part of the times in which we live .... This fact is already borne out by the number of parents who have taken their daughters to see the film. These parents regard this movie as a perfect deterrent to this type of behaviour.'

d/s Wes Craven *p* Sean S. Cunningham *c* Victor Hurwitz *lp* David Hess, Lucy Grantheim, Sandra Cassel, Marc Sheffier, Jeramie Rain, Fred Lincoln, Gaylord St James, Cynthia Carr, Ada Washington

The Legend of Boggy Creek
(PIERCE-LEDWELL PRODUCTIONS) scope 90min
'This is a true story', Pierce's film announces, and the pity of it is that it could have been a fascinating documentary about 'the Fouke monster', since it uses the laconically drawling inhabitants of Fouke, Arkansas (pop. 350) to recount sightings of the three-toed, gorilla-like giant hopefully identified as a Sasquatch (the shy woods' folk of Indian legend). Veracity, however, isn't the strong suit of Pierce, a sort of perennial home-movie maker who turned directly to schlock with **The Town That Dreaded Sundown** (1977). Here his documentary reconstructions are not only tarted up with glimpses of the monster, but a man-in-a-gorilla-suit monster at that, looking and behaving exactly as if it had just walked out of some Monogram or PRC horror. Just to make matters worse, what seems like half the running time is devoted to luridly lyrical, travelogue shots of the beauties of nature.

d/p/c Charles B. Pierce *s* Earl E. Smith *lp* Willie E. Smith, John P. Hixon, John W. Oates, Jeff Crabtree, Buddy Crabtree

Lisa e il Diavolo *aka* **Il Diavolo e i Morti** *aka* **El Diablo se Lleva a los Muertos** *aka* **La Casa dell'Esorcismo** *aka* **Lisa and the Devil** *aka* **The Devil and the Dead** *aka* **The House of Exorcism** *aka* **Lise e il Diavolo**
(EUROAMERICA/TECISA/ROXY; IT,SP,WG)
scope 98(93,91)min
Toward the end of his career, the works of the master of funereal lyricism became difficult to see. Either they remained unreleased (as *Cani Arrabbiati*, 1974) or appeared in hopelessly adulterated forms. This picture is particularly difficult to reconstruct: it consists of the remnants of the Bava film intercut with an endlessly repetitive imitation of **The Exorcist** (1973), shot in one room with Robert Alda as the grimacing priest and Sommer vomiting toads, swearing and causing objects to fly about the room. These additional scenes bear no relation whatsoever to Bava's film in which Alda doesn't even appear. The new film was released as *La Casa dell'Esorcismo* and ran for 93 minutes, which means that about 20 minutes must have been cut out of Bava's film, 15 or so of which were then replaced with the vomiting scenes which not only destroy the rhythm of Bava's picture but no doubt also remove the most poetic sequences since they wouldn't contribute to the action. This butchery seems to be the work of Leone, who 'produced' and 'scripted' the new version.

According to the Spanish critics who saw the original, Bava's film was a hauntingly beautiful poem about decay and death. It tells of the hallucinatory experiences of Lisa (Sommer) who recognizes a wax dummy as her double and encounters a man (Savalas) who resembles the image of the devil in a painting which fascinates her. She flees and finds herself stranded in an isolated mansion peopled with putrefying corpses and weird characters including the lollipop-sucking Savalas as the butler. There she learns that she is the double of the owner's unfaithful, deceased lover whose corpse is kept in a vegetation-infested room, while a blind matriarch (Valli) imbues the house with her neurotic presence. Some murders follow and she escapes to an airport. On the plane, the pilot turns out to be Savalas again. (The doctored version ends with a bolt of lightning which liquidates the priest.)

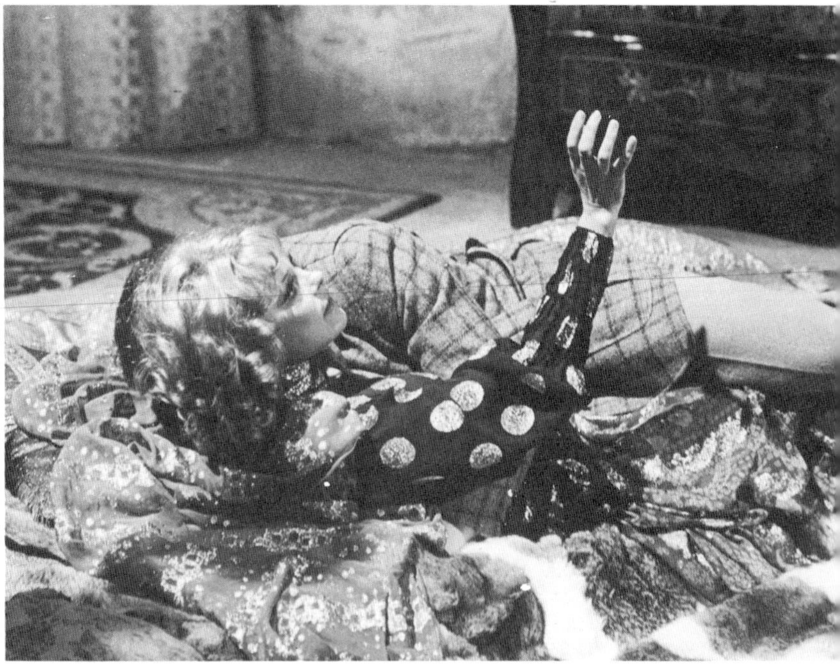

Elke Sommer in Mario Bava's dreamlike Lisa e il Diavolo.

The overwhelmingly morbid sense of necrophilia exuded by the movie, with Bava's camera lovingly caressing draperies and corpses, is punctuated by flamboyantly eerie exterior night scenes in which the director's morbid romanticism achieves intensely beautiful effects. His most impressive scene of necrophilia remains in all versions of the movie: the hero makes love to the fainted Sommer while the bed is shared by the decomposing corpse of his former lover. Produced in 1972 and shown at Cannes that year, the film was released later as *Il Diavolo e i Morti* (1973) and then re-released, in the butchered version, as *La Casa dell'Esorcismo* (1975), with direction credited to Mickey Lion, one of Bava's lesser known pseudonyms, the scenario to Leone and Alberto Cittini, and the special effects to Franco Tocci.

d/co-s Mario Bava *p* Alfred Leone *co-s* Roberto Natale, Giorgio Manlini *c* Cecilio Paniagua *lp* Elke Sommer, Telly Savalas, Sylva Koscina, Alida Valli, Alessio Orano, Gabriele Tinti, Eduardo Fajardo, Carmen Silva, Franz von Treuberg, Espartaco Santoni

Madhouse *aka* **The Revenge of Dr Death**
(AMICUS/AIP; GB,US) 92(89)min
Labouring under an unsuitable title, this adaptation of Angus Hall's *Devilday* sets out to mine two rich thematic seams. One is that of an actor, Toombes (Price), who finds himself pursued by his old screen creation, the monstrous Dr Death. Barely recovered from a mental breakdown, he quickly becomes the centre of a series of gruesome Dr Death-like murders, culminating in an attack upon himself by a figure in the Dr Death costume. The second strand is provided by the confrontation of two horror styles: AIP-Corman veteran Price is the object of a complicated revenge plot devised by Hammer-Fisher's Cushing, playing a TV scenarist. The final scene has Price being obliged to assume Cushing's screen identity before he can play the role he himself had made famous.

Although Price and Cushing had appeared together before (**Scream and Scream Again**, 1969; **Dr Phibes Rises Again**, 1972), this story offered an opportunity to give their interplay an extra dimension. Instead both Price's flamboyance and Cushing's cool, more introverted style are simply used – often as the subject for facile in-jokes – but never explored in Clark's competent but humdrum direction. The film was released in 1973.

Right: *Susan Hampshire as the Gorgon and Mathieu Carrière as the unsuspecting sailor who enters the surreal world of* Malpertuis.

d Jim Clark *p* Max J. Rosenberg, Milton Subotsky *s* Greg Morrison, Ken Levinson *c* Ray Parslow *se* Kerss and Spencer *lp* Vincent Price, Peter Cushing, Robert Quarry, Adrienne Corri, Natasha Pyne, Michael Parkinson, Linda Hayden, Harry Dennen

Malpertuis *aka* **Malpertuis: Histoire d'une Maison Maudite** *aka* **The Legend of Doom House**
(SOFIDOC/SOCIETE D'EXPANSION DU SPECTACLE/ARTISTES ASSOCIES/ARTEMIS; BEL,FR,WG) 110(124)min
After his stylish vampire movie *Les Lèvres Rouges* (1971), Kuemel spent the most lavish budget ever accorded a Belgian director in this adaptation of Jean Ray's brilliantly weird novel about an old seadog (Welles) who discovers the gods of ancient Greece, exhausted by centuries of neglect but still alive. He captures them and, with the help of a taxidermist (Janssens), sews them into human skins. Now they live as somewhat drab petit bourgeois characters in a large old house in Ghent. Their stuffy ordinariness, however, is literally only skin deep, and the somewhat seedy and repressed characters turn into grotesque demons around whom parallel worlds open up like yawning abysses. Three spinsters embody the furies; Lampernisse (Cassel) is chained at the bottom of a stairwell and lives in fear of an eagle that periodically swoops down to eat his liver; a beautiful woman (Hampshire) is the fearful gorgon, and so on. The house itself, named after the fox's lair in a popular folktale, also exudes an uncanny aura and contains a 'living' room that needs feeding. Into this demented world, presided over from his bed by the dying patriarch, strays a young sailor (the somewhat bland Carrière) who falls in love with the gorgon and ends up as a stone statue.

The movie is exhilaratingly shot in glorious colours, but whereas Ray's novel succeeded in fusing the idea of Greek gods with the musty, obscurely perverse world of the tawdry characters' existence by endowing the details of that everyday existence with an uncanny intensity that escalates into nightmarish absurdity, the film opts for flamboyant fantasy from the start and thus loses the horror generated by the coexistence of two incompatible worlds. In spite of Hampshire and Carrière's inappropriate performances, the Antwerp comic Janssens and Bouquet as a dirty old man strike the right note of incongruousness. The adaptation, authored by a Belgian fantasy writer, fails to do justice to Ray's only novel written over a dozen years earlier but published in 1943. Ray, one of Raymond Jean Marie de Kremer's many psudonyms, is one of the 20th century's most brilliant fantasy writers, perhaps best known for his Harry Dickson stories which Alain Resnais wanted to film. His unique style and savoury language weave a literary spell which doesn't translate easily to the screen. Only one other feature was based on his work, Jean Pierre Mocky's *La Grande Frousse* (1964), which had a similarly unfortunate production history, and was re-released in a re-edited version in the early seventies.

d Harry Kuemel *p* Paul Laffargue, Rita Laffargue *s* Jean Ferry *c* Gerry Fisher *se* M. Bernard *lp* Orson Welles, Mathieu Carrière, Susan Hampshire, Jean-Pierre Cassel, Sylvie Vartan, Michel Bouquet, Charles Janssens, Daniel Pilon, Dora van der Groen, Walter Rilla

Adrienne Corri in the humdrum Madhouse.

The Man With Two Heads *aka* **Dr Jekyll and Mr Blood**
(MISHKIN) 80min
Not to be confused with *The Thing With Two Heads* (1972) or *The Incredible Two Headed Transplant* (1971), this bizarre outing is a variation on the Dr Jekyll and Mr Hyde theme. Set in London in 1835 and filmed in England, the story concerns Jekyll's attempts to control the evil in people by isolating parts of their brains. Unfortunately, the serum with which he injects himself calls forth his terrible *alter ego*, Mr Blood.

d/s/c Andy Milligan *lp* Denis de Marne, Julia Stratton, Gay Feld, Jacqueline Lawrence, Berwick Kaler, Bryan Southcombe, Jennifer Summerfield

La Mansión de la Locura *aka* **Dr Tarr's Torture Dungeon** *aka* **House of Madness** *aka* **The Mansion of Madness** *aka* **The System of Dr Tarr and Professor Feather**
(PRODUCCIONES PRISMA; MEX) 88min
Combining Poe's story with elements of Peter Newbrook's *Marat-Sade*, filmed by Peter Weiss in 1966, and adeptly playing on its absurdly carnivalesque aspects, Moctezuma's second feature signals the emergence of a major new Mexican fantasy director. Set in early 19th-century France, the film has a journalist (Hansel) visit an asylum and eventually discover that a madman (Brook) has taken it over, having impersonated the doctor and his staff. The love interest introduced into the tale revolves around Sherman, the real psychiatrist's daughter rescued by the hero after some weird and violent happenings as the inmates are allowed to act out their compulsions, which involve a corn-eating chicken man, a Lady Godiva and a whole gallery of menacing characters.

An experienced theatre and television director, Moctezuma handles the shifts between gothic horror – the mysterious apparitions in the castle's grounds – and the humorously sinister and erotic chaos in the asylum with considerable skill. From the solarized colour sequences that open the film to the garish grotesqueries at the end, the cinematography effectively situates the picture in a no man's land between the comic and the uncanny. The director's love of comic strips and surrealism is plainly in evidence, not least in the use of Brook, one of Buñuel's favourite actors, and in the stylized play with generic conventions which echoes Jodorowsky's *El Topo* (1971), which he produced. His next feature was the American co-production **Mary, Mary, Bloody Mary** (1974).

d/co-s Juan Lopez Moctezuma *p* Roberto Viskin *co-s* Carlos Illescas *c* Rafael Corkidi *lp* Claudio Brook, Arturo Hanse, Ellen Sherman, Martin Lasalle, David Silva, Robert Dumont

La Mansión de la Niebla *aka* Quando Marta Urlo nella Tomba *aka* Murder Mansion

(MUNDIAL FILM/TRITONE FILMINDUSTRIA; SP,IT) scope 103(86)min

The early seventies were the heyday of Spanish horror with many young directors getting their first chance to make films. Lara's début as a director was more auspicious than that of either Jorge Martin (**La Escalofrio Diabolico**, 1971) or José Maria Oliveira (*Las Flores del Miedo*, 1972). Patterned on the best work of Mario Bava and Antonio Margheriti in the gothic tradition, his atmospheric terror picture achieves its effects with excellent cinematography, which overcomes both the script and the acting. Adapting the Catalan scenarist Blain's own story, the film tells of a bike-riding couple (Resino and Nardi), lost in the fog, who encounter a terrified woman (Gade) near an apparently haunted cemetery that surrounds a mysterious mansion. The trio shelter in the house and become embroiled in horrific events in the castle's gloomy rooms and eerie underground tunnels. The gimmick is that Gade's husband (Fajardo) staged the spectral phenomena in order to drive her insane. He succeeds but she then kills him while, at dawn, Resino and Nardi escape the fog-shrouded mansion.

Lara went on to make the effective thrillers *Cebo para una Adolescente* (1973) and *Perversion* (1974) before his work degenerated into routine sexploitation material (*Virilidad a la Española*, 1975). He also produced Javier Aguirre's two interesting pictures, **El Jorobado de la Morgue** and **El Gran Amor del Conde Dracula** (both 1972).

d/p Francisco Lara Polop *s* Luis G. de Blain, Antonio Troisio *c* Guillermo Mancori *lp* Analia Gade, Andres Resino, Anna Lisa Nardi, Evelyn Stewart (Ida Galli), Franco Fantasia, Eduardo Fajardo, Alberto Dalbes, Ingrid Garbo, Yelena Samarina, George Rigaud

Le Moine *aka* The Monk

(MAYA FILMS/COMACICO/INTERNATIONAL PRODUCTIONS/PERI PRODUCTIONS/TRITONE CINEMATOGRAFICA/STUDIO FILMS; FR) 92(90)min

Scripted by Buñuel, who had long wanted to film M. G. Lewis' classic gothic novel (first published in 1796), *The Monk* was eventually filmed by Buñuel's long-time admirer, the surrealist critic Kyrou. Sadly, the result is an exercise in academic surrealism.

Set in the Middle Ages, *Le Moine* tells of Father Ambrosio (Nero) and his lethal passion for a novice who turns out to be a diabolical seductress (Delon), leading him to perdition by delivering to him the virginal Antonia (De Santis) whom he keeps in a dungeon and rapes. The depraved monk escapes the wrath of the Inquisition by making a pact with the devil. In the end he walks away a free man to the mocking applause of an off-screen flock. Kyrou's direction is flat and uninspired, without any sense of pace or dramatic construction and, although Vierny's photography is clear and professional, the acting of the rather starry cast is somewhat strained. Little is left of what Buñuel might have wanted to make of the script, except for the general anti-clerical theme and the occasionally effectively staged contrast between Ambrosio's unhealthy attitudes towards sex and the surrounding countryside positively buzzing with the sounds of life.

d Ado Kyrou *p* Henri Lange *s* Luis Buñuel, Jean-Claude Carrière *c* Sacha Vierny *lp* Franco Nero, Nathalie Delon, Nicol Williamson, Nadja Tiller, Eliana de Santis, Elisabeth Wiener, Denis Manuel, Agnes Capri, Maria Machado

El Monte de las Brujas *aka* Witches Mountain

(AZOR; SP) 100(90)min

Cinematographer Artigot (**Les Démons**, 1972) borrows heavily from Jesús Franco (for whom he worked regularly) in this tale of a photographer (Caffari) who treks to a desolate area to do a report on witches. He and his girlfriend (Shepard) spend some time in the expected gloomy castle inhabited by a coven of witches, where she finds herself selected as the next sacrificial victim. She escapes only to splatter her skull on the rocks as she jumps off a cliff. Returning home in the belief that he has destroyed the women, Caffari finds them, led by one of his ex-lovers (Randall), in his flat. In spite of Sempere's brave efforts to imbue the landscapes with a sense of menace, Artigot's concentration on the orchestration of sexploitative scenes is at the expense of the narrative and atomspheric aspects of the picture. The film comes alive only for a brief moment when a demonic child mysteriously materializes on the photographer's snaps; for the rest, the picture stumbles from situation to situation, all of which allow the display of women in sexual activity or as victims of gory doings.

d/p/s Raoul Artigot *c* Ramon Sempere *lp* Paty Shepard, John Caffari, Monica Randall

Morbo *aka* Morbidness

(BOCACCIO FILMES; SP) 95(85)min

Suarez was one of Spain's leading novelists before he turned to the cinema and embarked on an undistinguished series of movies which varied from the pretentious to the whimsical. These include *Ditirambo* (1967), *El Extraño Caso del Doctor Fausto* (1969) and the mystical flop, *Aoom* (1970), which was destroyed after some unsuccessful festival screenings. This picture tries to engage with established generic forms. A couple of newlyweds in a trailer stumble on such disquieting events as an old, wheelchair-ridden woman (Vico) sitting in an old ruin,

Left: *Franco Nero as* Le Moine, *with Nathalie Delon, in Ado Kyrou's academic version of M. G. Lewis's classic gothic novel* The Monk.

Orson Welles as the occult toymaker with Pamela Franklin and Michael Ontkean in Necromancy.

dressed in a bridal gown. After murdering a passerby (Pollard) and Vico, they dump the bodies and drive off into a marriage based upon a better understanding of each other's characters. Belen is pleasant to watch but her husband (Manuel, a well-known folk singer, which accounts for the presence of Bob Dylan on the soundtrack) remains a one-dimensional figure.

d/p/co-s Gonzalo Suarez *co-s* Juan Cueto Alas *c* Juan Amoros *lp* Ana Belen, Victor Manuel, Michael J. Pollard, Maria Vico

Nachtschatten *aka* **Nightshade**
(VISUAL PRODUKTION; WG) 96min
This is the first, pretentiously arty feature – it was even shot in 16mm – by one of the few directors to successfully imbue his glossy exploitation movies with echoes of the pictorial fetishism characteristic of much of the 'new German cinema'. The story revolves around a woman (Hart) suspected of having killed her husband. She lives in an isolated farm on the Lueneburger moors where she is visited by a man (van Dreelen) who could be the twin of the vanished husband. As she slots him into the dead man's shoes, he is drawn into her world and the story culminates in death as he sinks into a swamp and she overdoses. The twist is that the viewer is supposed to believe that the man's death could also be a memory or a fantasy scene. However, the picture quickly exhausts itself with mannered editing, nervous camera movements and Schilling's leaden direction of his actors.

d/s Niklas Schilling *c* Ingo Hamer *lp* Elke Hart, John van Dreelen, Ella Timmermann, Max Kruegel

Necromancy (ZENITH INTERNATIONAL) 82min
Not dissimilar in theme to **Halloween III: Season of the Witch** (1983), *Necromancy* is distinguished mainly by the presence of Welles and Franklin (of **The Legend of Hell House**, 1973, fame), atmospheric use of its Los Gatos locations and first-rate production values that belie the relative paucity of the budget. Unfortunately, however, various scenes (including a good deal of nudity) were excized for a PG rating in the States and this gives the film a choppy, disjointed feel.

Hoping that a change of scene will help his wife Lori (Franklin) recover from the loss of her baby, Frank Brandon (Ontkean) accepts a new job working for toy manufacturer Mr Cato (Welles) in the town of Lilith. After a while, however, they discover that Welles is manufacturing not toys but occult instruments, and that she is the intended victim of an experiment in necromancy by which Welles hopes to bring his dead son back to life.

d/p/s Bert I. Gordon *c* Winton Hoch *se* William ('Dutch') Vanderbyl *lp* Orson Welles, Pamela Franklin, Lee Purcell, Michael Ontkean, Harvey Jason, Lisa James, Sue Bernard, Terry Quinn

Neither the Sea nor the Sand
(TIGON BRITISH; GB) 94min
Scripted from his own novel by Honeycombe, better known as a television newsreader, *Neither the Sea nor the Sand* essays the gothic theme of life after death but is too coy and reticent to be convincing. The heroine (Hampshire) embarks on an extramarital affair during a stay in Jersey, then remains there with her lover (Petrovitch). Subsequently he 'dies' of a heart attack but appears to his lover still to be alive. The romantic agony entails his brother (Finlay) accusing Hampshire of sorcery, then being killed in a car-crash through the agency of the 'dead' man. Finally Hampshire and Petrovitch wade off into the sea together. The mysticism requires an altogether more heightened mood to be persuasive: the 'overpowering' relationship between the two principals is dramatized mainly in some seaside-postcard imagery of bicycling about the sights of Jersey and romping on the beach. Stilted dialogue and Petrovitch's weak performance are no help either.

d Fred Burnley *p* Jack Smith, Peter Fetterman *s* Gordon Honeycombe *c* David Muir *lp* Susan Hampshire, Frank Finlay, Michael Petrovitch, Jack Lambert, Michael Craze, David Garth, Anthony Booth

Night of the Cobra Woman *aka* **Movini's Venom**
(NEW WORLD; US,PHIL) 85min
Ex-Warhol acolyte and experimental film-maker Mayer was one of the many young directors who broke into features via America's most successful film school: Roger Corman's productions. Shot in Manila as part of a co-production deal with Corman, this off-beat movie bears no relation to Robert Siodmak's kitschy classic *Cobra Woman* (1944). In search of the legendary fire-ring cobra, Joanna (Bang) allows her boyfriend Duff (Garrett) to wander off looking for the jungle princess Lena (Clark) who possesses a snake whose venom is supposed to bestow eternal youth upon its users. Clark and Garrett become lovers and Bang only narrowly escapes with her life when she intrudes upon their steamy affair. The lovers discover that passionate sex is required to stimulate the immortality drug and Garrett, exhausted by Clark's demands, begins to supply her with a series of partners, all of whom shrivel into skeletons soon after. Eventually, the venom overwhelms Clark who turns into a snake and Garrett agrees to be sacrificed to her.

Meyer wisely tries to play the preposterous story straight without destroying the sexually delirious *amour fou* tale with camp and knowing nudges. The jungle scenes with live snakes are impressive, but the patchy script veers from the inventive (severed pieces of snakes turn into yet more snakes) to the implausible (as the cobra woman unceremoniously stuffs her discarded skin into a handbag as if it were dirty underwear). The music is mercifully kept to a minimum and occasionally the snake motifs rival those of the genre's classic, **The Reptile** (1966). Another Philippines-based production about a snake cult, *The Golden Viper* (1983), features Eartha Kitt as the priestess.

d/co-s Andrew Meyer *co-p/co-s* Kerry Magness *co-p* Harvey Marks *c* Nonong Rasca *se* Felling Hilario *lp* Marlene Clark, Joy Bang, Roger Garrett, Slash Marks, Vic Diaz

La Noche de los Mil Gatos *aka* **The Night of the Thousand Cats** (AVANT FILMS; MEX) scope 92(90)min
The philandering hero (Stiglitz) of this picture lives in an isolated castle near Acapulco where he keeps a pitful of cats who survive on daily rations of human flesh, and an ugly servant (Cepeda) with whom he plays chess. Stiglitz makes

regular forays into the city, using a helicopter or motorbike, to pick up attractive young women. He brings them to his castle, makes love with them, decapitates them, feeds them to the cats and keeps their severed heads in jars on a shelf. When one of his potential victims puts up some resistance as he tries to strangle her, she throws a spear which accidentally releases the horde of cannibalistic pets and, while she escapes, the hero is devoured in his turn. Cardona Jnr achieves some impressive sequences at the beginning of the movie, detailing the maniac's sick surroundings, but the killings are unimaginative and repetitive while the expeditions into Acapulco are riddled with tourist-board imagery. That said, there are times when Phillips' cinematography evokes the macabre lyricism he generated for Olhovich's *La Muñeca Reina* (1974).

d/co-s René Cardona Jnr *p* Mario Z. Zacaria *co-s* Mario Marzac *c* Alex Phillips Jnr *lp* Hugo Stiglitz, Gerardo Cepeda, Anjanette Comer, Zulma Faiad, Christa Linder, Tereza Velasquez, Barbara Angel

Non si Sevizia un Paperino *aka* **Don't Torture the Duckling** (MEDUSA; IT) scope 110(90)min

Following the trend towards bloodier supernatural giallo movies exemplified by Dario Argento's work, Fulci tries here to find a new angle on an old plot by setting the action in Italy's rural south. The narrative is carried by a series of child killings which, after an outbreak of mass hysteria that results in the brutal killing of a gypsy woman (Bolkan), turn out to have been committed by a young priest with homosexual tendencies, allegedly in an effort to save the youngsters from having to come into contact with the 'plague' of sexuality. Fulci wallows in gutter-press stereotypes: the people of the Mediterranean south, especially its women, are retarded and prone to mass hysteria; female sexuality is malignant (a woman from the city parades her nudity in front of children); children are 'innocent'; peasants are cruel and superstitious, and so on. Such platitudes are taken for granted, sensationalized and peppered with scenes of horrendous violence: eyeless children, decapitated animals, split skulls, screeching mobs, magic dolls transfixed with pins. In contrast to Fleischmann's *Jagdszenen aus Niederbayern* (1969), Fulci's picture refuses to put rural cretinism in the historical and social context that gives it meaning, thus ending up with a racist tract himself. The only point of interest in this mid-career Fulci effort is his use of the flat rural landscape to create a sense of agoraphobia, which is pursued in his later movies in terms of claustrophobia.

d Lucio Fulci *p* Felice Calaiacono, Franco Puccioni *s* Gianfranco Clerici, Roberto Cianviti *c* Sergio d'Offizi *lp* Florinda Bolkan (José Soara Bulco), Barbara Bouchet (Gutcher), Thomas Milian, Irene Papas, Marco Porel, George Wilson, Antonello Campodifiori, Ugo d'Alessio

Nothing but the Night *aka* **The Resurrection Syndicate** (CHARLEMAGNE PRODUCTIONS; GB) 90min

This is the first film made by Charlemagne, Lee and Nelson-Keys' production company. Based on a novel by John Blackburn, the story provides a demonic variation on John Wyndham's *Village of the Damned*, filmed in 1960, with the children of an orphanage on a remote Scottish island as the strangely possessed murderous creatures led by Mary (Strong), the daughter of a prostitute and murderess (Dors). Colonel Bingham (Lee) investigates the deaths of the orphanage's trustees with the help of a pathologist (Cushing) and a journalist (Brown). Suspecting Dors of threatening her daughter's life, Lee discovers – in the only genuinely well-conducted scene of the picture – that the dummy burned on the bonfire is in fact Dors. As the satanic children possessed by the spirits of dead adults try to drag Lee into the bonfire, Strong is showered with burning debris by a passing helicopter and she plunges to her death in the sea. The children, in a trance-like state, following suit.

A hopelessly confused script and silly dialogue seriously damage the film, with Sasdy only occasionally showing what a brilliant director he can be. Lee and Cushing play their parts in a suitable deadpan manner, while the late Dors camps up her role as red herring. Shot immediately after the science fiction outing, *Doomwatch* (1972), the film was released early in 1973, just before **The Exorcist** (1973) turned possessed children into a major box-office draw.

d Peter Sasdy *p* Anthony Nelson-Keys *s* Brian Hayes *c* Kenneth Talbot *se* Les Bowie *lp* Christopher Lee, Peter Cushing, Diana Dors, Georgia Brown, Keith Barron, Gwynneth Strong, Fulton MacKay, John Robinson, Shelagh Fraser, Duncan Lamont

La Notte dei Diavoli *aka* **Night of the Devils** *aka* **La Noche de los Diablos** (FILMES CINEMATOGRAFICA/DUE CINEMATOGRAFICA/COPERNICES; IT,SP) scope 91(88)min

Whereas Ferroni had achieved some genuinely memorable scenes in his **Il Mulino delle Donne di Pietra** (1960), his extended version of Alex Tolstoy's story *The Wurdalak* – previously filmed by Mario Bava as part of **I Tre Volti della Paura** (1963) – this reworking of the story is a disappointment. The tale of a young man, Nicola (Garko), who becomes involved with a peasant family infected by vampirism, ignores the story's use of oblique methods for building the overwhelming sense of menace that pervades the family's

La Novia Ensangretada, *one of the many 'lesbian' horror films nominally derived from Sheridan LeFanu's* Carmilla.

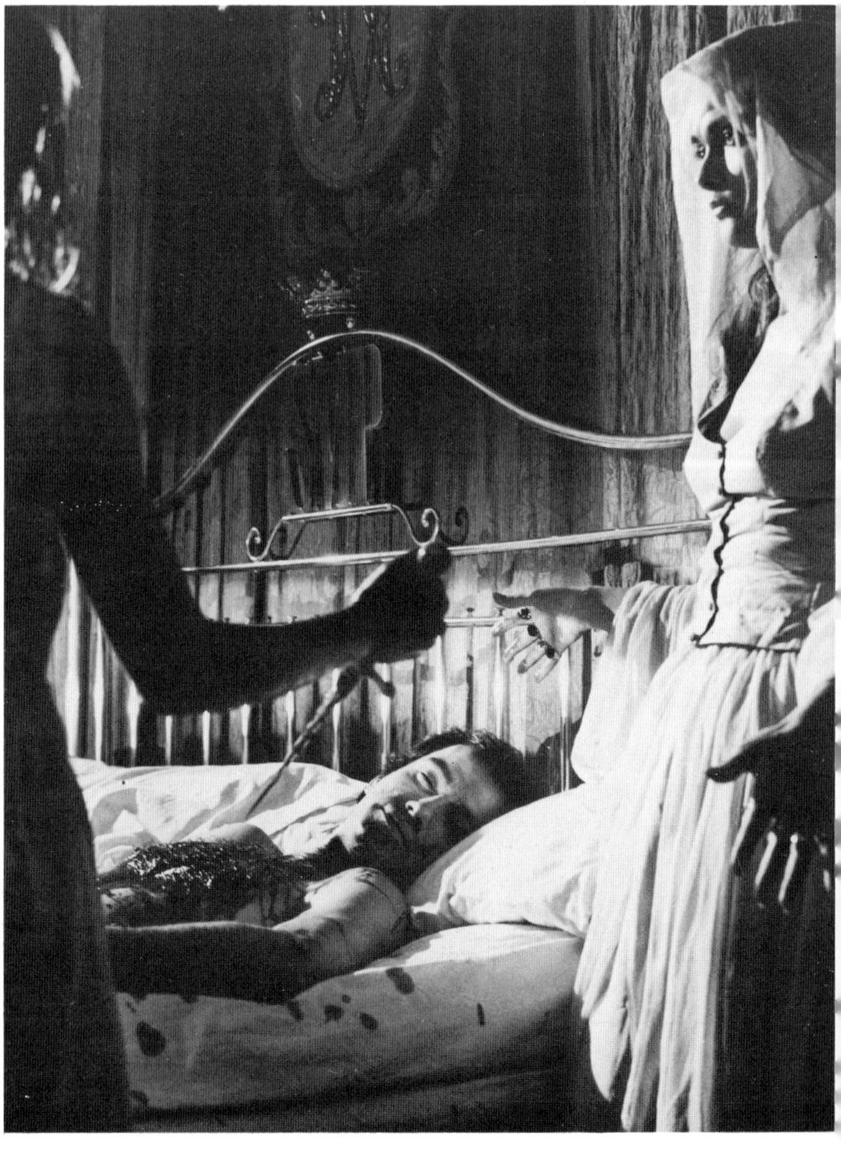

The mini-skirted Elke Sommer in danger in Mario Bava's Gli Orrori del Castello di Norimberga.

residence as the patriarch returns from an unsuccessful attempt to stake a witch. Instead, Ferroni's movie staggers from one explicitly gory scene to the next, zooming with abandon and repeating inserts of decomposing cadavers into what otherwise would have been a most effective sequence: Garko's desperate flight by car through a forest pursued by a horde of creatures straight out of George Romero's **Night of the Living Dead** (1968). The cut from a worm-eaten head to that of Garko wired up to medical machinery in hospital is a promising opening but the rest of the picture fails to live up to it. In the end, the crazed Garko stakes his beloved Sdenka (Belli) when she visits him in hospital after his ordeal, believing her to be a vampire like the rest of her family. This error allows the film to end on an ambiguous note: perhaps the whole story was imagined by a paranoid madman.

d Giorgio Ferroni *p* Luigi Mariani *s* Romano Migliorini, Giambattista Mussetto, Eduardo M. Brochero *c* Manuel Berenguer *se* Rambaldi *lp* Gianni Garko, Agostina Belli, Mark Roberts, Cinzia de Carlos, Teresa Gimpera, Umberto Raho, William Vanders, Luis Suarez

La Novia Ensangretada *aka* **The Blood Splattered Bride** *aka* **'Til Death Us Do Part**
(MORGANA FILMS; SP) 102(95)min
Repeating the motifs of lesbianism Aranda had introduced in **Las Crueles** (1971), but with more emphasis on sadism and sex, the nominal source of this film is Sheridan LeFanu's novella *Carmilla*, which had earlier provided the impetus for Carl Dreyer's **Vampyr** (1931) and Roger Vadim's **Et Mourir de Plaisir** (1960). It is closer in spirit to the latter film but never quite matches it in visual elaboration or glossy expertise. Martin plays a frigid young newlywed and Bastedo (first seen, inexplicably, buried up to her neck in the sand) an enigmatic figure who proves to be a vampire. In a frenzied finale, heavily censored in British and American release versions, the awkwardly related tale ends with Martin's husband (Andreu) seeing off both women by tearing out their hearts, a clear indication that the fantasy at stake is the 'macho' man's anxiety in the face of lesbianism – a threat the audience is invited to share.

d/s Vicente Aranda *p* José Lopez Moreno *c* Fernando Arribas *se* Antonio Molina *lp* Simon Andreu, Maribel Martin, Alexandra Bastedo, Dean Selmier, Monserrat Julio, Angel Lombarte, Maria Rosa Rodriguez

La Orgia de los Muertos *aka* **La Orgia dei Morti** *aka* **Bracula the Terror of the Living Dead**
(PREODIMEX/PETRUKA FILMS; SP,IT) 97min
A rather lively routine European horror movie. Set in the Carpathians in the 19th century, the eventful plot crams in a sinister doctor (Titchy), trying to harness 'nebula electricity' in order to resurrect the dead, and the usual crypts and secret passages. Igor is finally decapitated in a struggle with the hero (Rosi) but only after a tremendous effort in which he contrives to wrench a knife from his own heart to attack his adversary. The zombies whom the doctor creates and who finally, in time-honoured fashion, see him off, are quite persuasive, the narrative is briskly handled and Molina, a ubiquitous presence in Spanish movies since **La Marca del Hombre Lobo** (1967), plays with appropriate gusto.

d/co-s José Luis Merino *p* Ramón Plana *co-s* Enrico Columbo *c* Modesto Rizzolo *lp* Stan Cooper (Stelvio Rosi), Dianik Zurakowska, Maria Pia Conte, Paul Naschy (Jacinto Molina), Pasquale Basile, Gerard Tichy, Aurora de Alba, Charles Quiney

Gli Orrori del Castello di Norimberga *aka* **Baron Blood** *aka* **Chamber of Tortures** *aka* **The Blood Baron** *aka* **The Thirst of Baron Blood** *aka* **The Torture Chamber of Baron Blood**
(EURO INTERNATIONAL FILMS/DIETER GEISSLER; IT,WG) 92(90)min
This film tells of a student, Peter von Kleist (Cantafora) and his mini-skirted lover Eva (Sommer) who resuscitate Baron von Kleist (Cotten), a 16th-century warlock nicknamed the Bloody Baron. After his initial traumatic appearance, the Baron disguises himself as the wheelchair-ridden purchaser of his own medieval castle where he indulges his cruellest fantasies in the renovated torture chamber and decorates the towers with impaled, very human-looking figures. Cantafora and Sommer eventually fall into his hands but a magic amulet causes all the Baron's victims to rise from the dead and vent their gruesome revenge on him.

Shot mostly on location in Austria immediately after Bava's unfortunate experiences with **Lisa e il Diavolo** (1972) for the same producer, the film contains many excellent sequences in spite of the obtrusive zooms: a caped figure pursuing Sommer through foggy streets in an old city; and the hideous Baron's encounter with a little girl (played by the blue-eyed Emmi, who went on to make her mark in Italian exorcism movies as well as in Dario Argento's **Profondo Rosso**, 1975). With the exception of a few minutes of decidedly gory thrills, removed from the US print, the picture's style and tone evoke the Italian films of the early sixties and don't match the deliriously funereal excesses of *Lisa e il Diavolo*. After a straight thriller, the as yet unreleased (*Cani Arrabbiati*, 1974), Bava made his last feature for the cinema, **Shock (Transfer Suspense Hypnos)** (1977), a horror symphony which outclasses **The Omen** (1976) while anticipating the inferior **The Amityville Horror** (1979). The American version of this film replaced Stelvio Cipriani's score with one by Les Baxter.

d/co-s Mario Bava *p* Alfred Leone *co-s* Vincent Forte, William A. Bairn (Willibald Eser) *c* Antonio Rinaldi *se* Franco Tocci *lp* Joseph Cotten, Elke Sommer, Antonio Cantafora, Massimo Girotti, Alan Collins (Luciano Pigozzi), Dieter Tressler, Humi (Umberto) Raho, Rada Rassimov, Nicoletta Emmi

The Other (REX-BENCHMARK PRODUCTIONS) 100min
Though released only briefly in Britain, *The Other* is an exceptionally imaginative horror film in the Jacques Tourneur-Val Lewton vein. Low on gore but high on suggestion, the film revolves around a small rural community of the thirties in which Niles (Chris Udvarnoky) maintains a fantasy that his dead twin brother Holland (Martin Udvarnoky) is in fact still alive. His Russian-born grandmother (Hagen) teaches him a

strange game of projection whereby he is able to imagine himself living out the experiences of the other. When a mysterious series of killings occurs, and Udvarnoky asserts that his brother was responsible, Hagen tries to stop him playing the projection game but it is too late and the killings continue.

Mulligan's work is shot through with portraits of disturbed adolescence and childhood and *The Other* comes across as a fascinating mixture of his earlier *To Kill a Mockingbird* (1962) crossed with Jack Clayton's **The Innocents** (1961). The film is photographed with all the lushness of *Summer of '42* (1971), also directed by Mulligan and photographed by Surtees.

d/p Robert Mulligan *c* Robert L. Surtees *s* Thomas Tryon *lp* Uta Hagen, Diana Muldaur, Chris Udvarnoky, Martin Udvarnoky, Norma Connolly, Victor French, Loretta Leversee, Lou Frizzell, Portia Nelson, Jenny Sullivan

El Paese del Sesso Selvaggio *aka* Mondo Cannibale *aka* Deep River Savages

(ROAS PRODUZIONI/MEDUSA; IT) 94min

Following his exploitative horror-thriller, *Das Raetsel des Silbernen Halbmonds* (1972), the prolific Lenzi continued trying to turn gore and sex into cash with this racist fantasy which shows what *Apocalypse Now* (1979) hints at: the irredeemable savagery of south-east Asian natives who nevertheless have to bow to white supremacy and make an English adventurer their divine leader. The picture dwells on extended scenes of torture and introduces cannibalism which was rapidly becoming a central motif in horror movies (as a means of conveying Europeans' terror at the prospect of Third World people fighting back against the invasion of their territory?). Here, an English photographer (Rassimov) in the jungles of Thailand and Burma witnesses 'primitive sexual rites' and other bloodthirsty nightmares before being forced to marry the chief's daughter (Me Me Lay) and becoming chief himself. Follow-ups include **Ultimo Mondo Cannibale** (1976), again featuring the ex-TV presenter Lay, and **La Montagna del Dio Cannibale** (1978).

d Umberto Lenzi *p* M. G. Rossi *s* Francesco Barilli, Massimo d'Avack *c* Riccardo Pallottini *lp* Ivan Rassimov, Me Me Lay, Pratitsak Singhara, Sulallewan Suwantat, Ong Ard, Prapas Chindang, Tuan Tevan

Panico en el Transiberiano *aka* Horror Express *aka* Panic in the Trans-Siberian Train

(GRANADE FILMS/BENMAR PRODUCTION; SP,GB) 90(88)min

Set around 1900, this film starts in China when the arrogant Professor Saxton (Lee) boards the train with a crate containing what he believes to be the remains of the missing link: a monster, in fact alive, whose eyes glow red and boil the brains of whomever looks at it as it absorbs their intelligence. It also turns its victims into zombies possessed by its personality. The usual group of eccentric figures include Lee's scientific rival, Dr Wells (Cushing), Countess Irina (Tortosa) and her husband (Rigaud), a beautiful spy (Liné), a Rasputin-type monk (de Mendoza) and a cossack (Savalas) who joins the train later but quickly falls victim to the beast. The plot gathers speed as more and more people are turned into zombies until the train is full of them whereupon the English heroes succeed in uncoupling the infested carriages which plunge over a cliff while their own wagon comes to a halt on the edge of a precipice.

This combination of *Murder on the Orient Express* (1974) and **La Noche del Terror Ciego** (1971) gets away with its unlikely story through the fast speed of the action and some nicely humorous passages such as Lee and Cushing, accused of being callous monsters, protesting 'But we are English!'. The picture was given the best screenplay award at the Sitges festival in 1972, presumably for the way it enthusiastically piles incident upon incident, relentlessly driving the narrative as if both the story and its setting were powered by a locomotive. Other contributions by Martin included *Hipnosis* (1962), and **Una Vela Para el Diablo** (1973).

d/p/co-s Gene Martin (Eugenio Martin) *co-s* Arnaud d'Usseau *c* Alejandro Ulloa *lp* Christopher Lee, Peter Cushing, Helga Liné, Silvia Tortosa, Telly Savalas, George Rigaud, Alberto de Mendoza, Angel de Pozo, Julio Peña, Jose Jaspé

Please Don't Eat My Mother! *aka* Hungry Pets *aka* GLUMP *aka* Please Release My Mother *aka* Please Not My Mother

(HARRY H. NOVAK PRODUCTIONS) 98min

Henry Fudd (Kartalian) is a middle-aged virgin who lives with his domineering mother and finds sexual pleasure in voyeurism. One day he finds a talking female plant in a flower shop and takes it home where it eventually develops a voracious appetite for human flesh. Basically a remake of **The Little Shop of Horrors** (1960) with the addition of some soft-core, the film is actually a rather engaging, well-made black comedy.

d/p Carl Monson *c* Jack Beckett *se* Harry Woolman *lp* Buck Kartalian, Rene Bond, Alicia Friedland, Lyn Lundgren, Dash Fremont, Flora Wiese, David Curtis

Poor Albert and Little Annie *aka* I Dismember Mama

(ROMAL FILMS) 78min

Albert (Hall) escapes from a sanatorium in order to punish his rich mother who sent him there and cut him off from his inheritance. A twisted misogynist, he feels the need to kill various 'impure' (ie sexually attractive) women until he falls for the nine-year-old daughter of his mother's housekeeper. Morbid and bleak rather than gruesome, the tone of the film is perhaps best summed up by one of Hall's proverbs 'what good is breeding if all it ever results in is a multiplication of worms?', or the detective's (Mullavey) solution to psychotics' problems 'give 'em a nice pill'. Hall is impressive as the outwardly calm but inwardly deranged killer, but otherwise – except for a well-staged finale in a warehouse full of mannikins – the low budget tends to show.

Mullavey went on to star in *Mary Hartman, Mary Hartman* and director Leder made the 3-D *A.P.E.* (1976).

d Paul Leder *p* Leon Roth *s* William Norton *c* William Swenning *lp* Zooey Hall, Geri Reishl, Joanne Moore Jordan, Greg Mullavey, Marlene Tracy, Frank Whiteman, Elaine Partnow, Rosella Olson, Robert Christopher

The 'thing' at work in Eugenio Martin's engaging Panico en el Transiberiano.

Christopher Plummer in search of The Pyx.

promise of sex (peep holes in walls, black leather gear, the doll, and so on) but remains a meretricious exploitation exercise in spite of the occasional inventive variation (removed by the British censor) on standard generic scenes.

d Paul Bartel *p* Gene Corman *s* Philip Kearney, Les Rendelstein *c* Andrew Davis *lp* Ayn Ruymen, Lucille Benson, John Ventantonio, Laurie Main, Stanley Livingstone, Charles Woolf, Len Travis, Dorothy Neumann, Gene Simms

The Pyx (HOST-ROHAR PRODUCTIONS; CAN) pv 111min
A policier with supernatural trimmings filmed on location in Montreal, *The Pyx* is an ambitious but somewhat portentous film. The title refers to the container used for carrying the host in the celebration of mass, and the movie begins as a prostitute (Black) falls from a high balcony with a pyx clutched in her hand. Two hard-boiled detectives (Plummer and Pilon) pursue an inquiry, which eventually leads, via Black's sinister madame (Brind'Amour) and the lonely homosexual (Haig) – Black's confidant – to a highly placed businessman (Roux) who proves to be a practitioner of the black mass and who pushed Black to her death during a sacrilegious rite; in the last sequence, Roux goads Plummer into shooting him dead.

Despite atmospheric widescreen camerawork, the film suffers from the slow pace and somewhat awkwardly constructed narrative: the action unfolds partly in flashbacks, but these are randomly interpolated rather than arising from the detectives' inquiries. The acting is excellent: Roux is a cleverly understated figure of menace, Plummer is effectively cast against type, and Black – who is heard on the soundtrack singing three of her own songs, one of which takes its lyric from the Song of Solomon – is admirable. Overall, however, a feeling persists that Hart, who earlier won praise for the very different, American-made *Bus Riley's Back in Town* (1965), overloads his material with religio-cultural nuances it cannot properly sustain.

d Harvey Hart *p* Maxine Samuels, Julian Roffman *s* Robert Schlitt *c* René Verzier *lp* Christopher Plummer, Karen Black, Jean-Louis Roux, Donald Pilon, Yvette Brind'Amour, Jacques Godin, Terry Haig, Lee Broker, Robin Gammell, Louise Rinfret

The Possession of Joel Delaney
(ITC/HAWORTH) 108(105)min
MacLaine here plays a wealthy New York divorcee who is beastly to her Puerto Rican maid (Colon) and is rewarded by a surfeit of horrors when her brother Joel (King), on whom she dotes in more than a sisterly fashion, becomes possessed by the spirit of a Puerto Rican sex-murderer. There is no real connection between the two Puerto Ricans but this does not prevent the film offering some slick moralizing which suggests that white New Yorkers shouldn't be beastly to their less privileged neighbours. That said, however, a couple of decapitations (Trentham and Powell the victims), some mumbo-jumbo in which shrieking Puerto Ricans try to exorcize the demon, and the climax in which MacLaine and her children are tortured at knife-point by the spirit of racial vengeance, point to the alarmist message which reads 'Keep New York White'. Hussein's direction is glossy but sluggish and producer Poll had his name removed from the credits.

d Waris Hussein *p* Martin Poll *s* Matt Robinson, Grimes Grice *c* Arthur J. Ornitz *lp* Shirley MacLaine, Perry King, Michael Hordern, Lovelady Powell, Barbara Trentham, Miriam Colon

Private Parts (PENELOPE PRODUCTIONS) 87(82)min
A graduate of the Corman school of exploitation quickies, Bartel tends to use comedy as a way of denigrating both his films (*Deathrace 2000*, 1975; *Eating Raoul*, 1982; *Not for Publication*, 1984) and his audience. The result, writ large in this early feature, is a hodge-podge of generic clichés and often facile gags ostentatiously designed to please the titillation market while suggesting that it's all just for fun-and-money and that the director is capable of far better stuff.

Set in a ramshackle boarding house run by Aunt Martha (Benson), the story has a girl (Ruymen) get involved with a kinky photographer (Ventantonio) who turns out to be the landlady's daughter forced to grown up as a man. 'He' keeps a lifesize inflatable doll in his room, fills it with Ruymen's dirty bathwater and makes love to it by means of a syringe filled with red liquid. 'He' also murders people in conventional psycho-killer fashion before the heroine disposes of him, triggering a psychotic attack from 'his' mother. The picture ends, quite arbitrarily, with a demented Ruymen assuming the personality of Aunt Martha. With numerous references to **Psycho** and **Peeping Tom** (both 1960) and to the homosexual motifs of *Midnight Cowboy* (1969), the picture mainly trades on the

The Rats Are Coming! The Werewolves Are Here *aka* **Curse of the Full Moon** (MISHKIN) 92min
This lacklustre 16mm outing was originally shot in England as *Curse of the Full Moon* for Milligan's old producer Mishkin while Milligan was trying to sort out the Cinemania deal that produced **The Body Beneath** (1970). The original film concerned a family of lycanthropes and was only about 67 minutes long. When **Willard** (1971) was released, Mishkin decided to bring the film up to feature length by inserting some scenes with rats and so a whole subplot featuring a girl who raises man-eating rats was tacked on. These additional scenes were shot in Milligan's home area of Staten Island.

d/s/c Andy Milligan *p* William Mishkin *se* Lois Marsh *lp* Hope Stansbury, Jacqueline Skarvellis, Berwick Kaler, Noel Collins

La Rebellión de las Muertas *aka* **La Vendetta dei Morti Viventi** *aka* **Vengeance of the Zombies** *aka* **Revolt of the Dead Ones** *aka* **The Rebellion of the Dead Women**
(PROFILMES/PROMOFILMS; SP,IT) 99(85)min
This routine quickie has its origins in Terence Fisher's **The Stranglers of Bombay** (1959). A young English woman living in Benares becomes prey to nightmares in which she sees acquaintances being killed. Subsequently, they do indeed get murdered. Learning that her family inherited a curse dating back to colonial times, she seeks refuge with a mystic of the Krishna cult and becomes involved in weird rites until it turns out that the cult leader's brother is the villain, making use of an army of zombies to carry out the ancestral curse until the

psychologist hero (Alcazar) puts a stop to things. Hamfisted direction ruins most scenes, including the resurrection of the zombies, and the script misses every opportunity to elaborate on the revenge-of-the-colonized overtones which fuel English gothic movies like **The Reptile** and **The Plague of the Zombies** (both 1966).

d Leon Klimovsky *p* José Antonio Perez Giner *s* Jacinto Molina *c* Francisco Sanchez *lp* Paul Naschy (Jacinto Molina), Vic Winner (Victor Alcazar), Romy, Mirta Miller, Maria Kosti, Aurora de Alba, Antonio Pica

La Rose de Fèr *aka* **La Nuit de Cimetière**
(LES FILMS ABC; FR) 85(81)min
After the sadean **Requiem pour un Vampire** (1971), Rollin essayed a funereal poem largely devoid of sex, except for a tastefully handled dream sequence. Two young lovers (Pascal and Dupont) meet in Amiens' lovely old cemetery and get locked in. The pair frantically try to escape but in vain. Terrified, Pascal causes her boyfriend to suffocate in a tomb. She then abandons herself to a hysterical dance on the gravestones until, exhausted, she joins her dead lover in his crypt. In the morning, an old woman passes by, shuts the crypt and deposits a bunch of flowers by its side. The movie counterposes adolescent passion to the decaying surroundings reeking of death but by spinning out to feature length a situation that would have made a wonderful short film, most of its lyrical intensity and emotional effect are dissipated. This was Rollin's most ambitiously arty movie and it proved a resounding flop upon its release in 1973. After a brief but inglorious excursion into straight pornography (*Jeunes Filles Impudiques*, 1973) with Joelle Coeur, he returned to more familiar terrain with the impressive **Les Démoniaques** (1973) again starring Coeur.

d/co-p/co-s Jean Rollin *co-p* Sam Selsky, Pierre Letovsky *co-s* Maurice Lemaitre *c* Jean-Jacques Renon *lp* Françoise Pascal, Pierre Dupont, Mireille Dargent, Nathalie Perrey

La Saga de los Dracula *aka* **The Saga of the Draculas** *aka* **Dracula's Saga** *aka* **The Saga of Dracula**
(PROFILMES; SP) scope 102(91)min
Made at the same time as **El Gran Amor del Conde Dracula** (1972), this odd story about the Count's family could have used the same title. Set in contemporary Hungary, the picture recounts how the pregnant Berta (Saenz) and her husband (Isbert) arrive at the castle of her grandfather, the Count. The flirty husband soon gets distracted by the many beautiful women that roam around the place while Saenz is well looked after since she carries the aristocrat's offspring. It emerges that the family has become degenerate through inbreeding, so every effort is made to ensure the 'health' of the impending extra vampire. But when Saenz discovers that the wine she is served at mealtimes is in fact blood, she is repelled by the prospect, kills her newly born infant and stakes the entire family. Mortally wounded by the caretaker (Ibañez-Menta), she falls over her baby's body, which begins to suck her blood. The script and the acting could have yielded a good comedy in the Polanski style, but in spite of Gumersindo Andres's excellent sets, Klimovsky only succeeds in making the picture entertaining rather than stimulatingly insane.

d Leon Klimovsky *p* José Antonio Perez Giner *s* Lazarus Kaplan *c* Francisco Sanchez *lp* Tina Saenz, Tony Isbert, Helga Liné, Narcisco Ibañez-Menta, Cristiana Suriani, Maria Kost, J. J. Paladino, Betsabe Ruiz, Luis Ciges

Margot Kidder with knife, the instrument of horror in the seventies and eighties, in the marvellous Sisters.

Left: *The silly* La Rebellión de las Muertas.

La Semana del Asesino *aka* **The Apartment on the 13th Floor** *aka* **Cannibal Man**
(TRUCHADO FILMS; SP) 120(98)min
This film, like **Una Vela Para el Diablo** (1973), locates the trigger for psychotic behaviour in socially pervasive hypocrisy and bigotry which, ironically, earned *La Semana del Asesino* an official ban as a 'video nasty' in Britain. A brutalized young man (Parra) employed in a slaughterhouse – which provides the expected bloody mood-setting scenes – loses his patience with a cab driver who objects to petting in the backseat and kills him. Next day, to silence his fiancée's recriminations, he throttles her during a perversely erotic, extended kiss. On Wednesday, his brother pays the penalty for discovering the girl's corpse under the bed; next day, the brother's fiancée's throat is cut. On Friday her father is killed by a meatcleaver in the face, on Saturday he rests but on Sunday a prostitute becomes his last victim. The pile of decomposing bodies attracts too many flies, prompting Parra to try and dispose of the cadavers in a meatgrinder. The ending is unexpected, interesting and weak at the same time: a homosexual young man who witnessed the carnage from a nearby window contacts the killer and offers to help bury the bodies. Burnt out, the killer cannot bring himself to murder the only being who seems to love him in spite of his faults, and he turns himself in to the police.

The fetid atmosphere in the villain's room is underlined by a remarkably appropriate score from Fernando Garcia Morcillo. But the solution of the movie, although sensitively handled and a tricky motif to introduce to catholic Spain, remains inadequate because it merely ends up reinforcing the notion that homosexuals have a special affinity with psychotic killers. Similarly, the *Cannibal Man* title is particularly misleading since that practice isn't even mentioned in the picture.

Director Iglesia went on to make the science fiction story, *Una Gota de Sangre para Morir Amando* a year later. In that film he suggests that an attempt at the rehabilitation of a degenerate humanity is a utopian wish.

d/s Eloy de la Iglesia *p* Joe Truchado *c* Raoul Artigot *lp* Vicente Parra, Emma Cohen, Eusebio Poncela, Vicky Lagos, Ismael Merlo, Charlie Bravo, Rafael Hernandez, Lola Herrera, Valentin Tornos

Sette Scialli di Seta Gialla *aka* **The Crimes of the Black Cat**
(CAPITOLINA PRODUZIONE; IT) scope 108(98)min
Pastore's minor horror-thriller is enhanced by quotes from **Psycho**'s (1960) shower murder scene and sub-Mario Bava effects due chiefly to Mancori's camera and Alberto Boccianti's art direction. A number of people are slain and a blind composer (de Teffé) with a flat full of tape-recorders and editolas becomes the 'wrong man' who must seek to clear himself by exposing the real villain. The killings are mostly done by a black cat whose claws have been poisoned with curare. The final revelations involve a husband (Stuart) trying to shield his hideously disfigured and homicidal wife, and the death of the composer's lover (Koscina). Memorable scenes include a corpse found propped up under a huge perspex dome and a hooded lady stalking the streets like something out of *Orphée* (1950). Unfortunately, the wildly pulsating zooms and heavy-handed editing effects preclude the sustained mood necessary to elevate the film from being a 'mere' entertainment.

Chris Robinson with pets in the amiable, if silly, Stanley.

d/co-s Sergio Pastore *p* Edmondo Amati *co-s* Alessandro Continenza, Giovanni Simonelli *c* Guglielmo Mancori *se* Eugenio Ascani, Renato Marinelli *lp* Anthony Steffen (Antonio de Teffé), Sylva Koscina, Giacomo Rossi Stuart, Jeannette Len, Renato de Carmine, Umberto Raho, Annabella Incontrera, Shirley Corrigan, Romano Malaspina

Sexy Cat (TITANIC FILMS; SP) scope 87(83)min
Actor Tabernero's directorial début seems to be derived from Alain Jessua's *Jeu de Massacre* (1967). It tells of a film company's bad luck when they decide to film the adventures of a comic-strip character called Sexy Cat with Zurakowska in the lead. A mysterious killer unleashes a poisonous snake in her apartment while she is in the shower and a series of slasher killings bedevil the production. The culprit is shown to be a woman in the early part of the film, but reversing Dario Argento's gimmick and reconnecting with the **Psycho** (1960) and **Homicidal** (1961) plot devices, 'she' is finally revealed to be a comic-mad boy previously seen confined to a wheelchair. He is cornered and decapitated by a piece of machinery in a junkyard. Tabernero continued his horror career with the self-explanatory *Terror Cannibal* (1981).

d/p/s Julio Perez Tabernero *c* Alfonso Nieva *lp* Dianik Zurakowska, Germán Cobos, Lone Fleming, Monica Kolpek, Maria Villa, Emilio Laguna, Antonio Vidal Molina

Sisters *aka* **Blood Sisters**
(PRESSMAN-WILLIAMS ENTERPRISES) 92min
Grace (Salt) witnesses one of her neighbours dying from the effect of stab wounds and, exasperated by police inefficiency at investigating the murder, follows up the case herself with the help of private eye, Durning. She eventually discovers that the murderer was one of a pair of Siamese twins (Kidder) who, when approached by a man, is invaded by the murderous personality of the twin who died in the operation to separate them.

This was the film that first brought de Palma to public attention. Hailed as a homage to the art of Alfred Hitchcock and by one reviewer as a 'really radical feminist film', *Sisters* actually seems less and less like either the more one sees of both Hitchcock and de Palma. Increasingly de Palma seems to be merely imitating Hitchcock or mechanically repeating his various devices – here, for example, he 'borrows' the personality-transference theme from **Psycho** (1960), and the early killing-off of a sympathetic audience-identification figure and the witness of a murder through binoculars from *Rear Window* (1954). De Palma's later films invite the opinion that *Sisters* is simply another invocation of mysterious female destructiveness, albeit a highly convoluted and stylish one. That said, however, the use of split screen (a very un-Hitchcockian device) is both inventive and imaginative, and Kidder's hallucination sequence is genuinely disturbing and one of the most powerful things de Palma has ever done. The film also benefits from an excellent score from Bernard Herrmann.

d/co-s Brian de Palma *p* Edward R. Pressman *co-s* Louisa Rose *c* Gregory Sandor *lp* Margot Kidder, Jennifer Salt, Charles Durning, Bill Finley, Lisle Wilson, Barnard Hughes, Mary Davenport, Dolph Sweet

Stanley (CROWN INTERNATIONAL) 106(96)min
Robinson is the Seminole Indian, disturbed by his experiences in Vietnam, who withdraws to a shack in the Florida Everglades, with his two pet rattlesnakes for company. Needless to say, when people start bugging him (usually by abusing snakes in various ways), he uses the snakes to strike back, and once even bites someone to death himself. There is a certain splendour to some of the notions here, notably a scene in which Robinson proudly informs his rattlesnakes, one gaily sporting a garland of flowers about its neck, that they are about to become a mummy and a daddy but the film is played

completely straight and the script demonstrates its deadly seriousness with a mess of turgid dialogue about racial prejudice, human greed and so forth. Given dreary direction and amateurish performances (Robinson excepted), the result is routine horror, with the snakes proving even blander in their role as menace than the rats of **Willard** (1971).

d/p William Grefé *s* Gary Crutcher *c* Cliff Poland
lp Chris Robinson, Alex Rocco, Steve Alaimo, Susan Carroll, Gary Crutcher

Straight on till Morning

(HAMMER; GB) scope 96min
A routine madman-on-the-loose, woman-in-jeopardy movie in much the same vein as Collinson's earlier **Fright** (1971). Here Tushingham plays another variation on her *Taste of Honey* (1961) role as an innocent Liverpudlian who arrives in London complete with an attitude to relationships that reads like a swinging sixties rewrite of a Mills and Boon romance. She becomes pregnant and her dream lover (Briant) turns out to be a psychotic who has already murdered several women. There is a calculated reference to **Peeping Tom** (1960) in a sequence in which Briant regales his latest victim with tape-recordings of his previous exploits. The direction is meretriciously geared to easy shock – a stock feature of all Collinson's films – and again a good cast, including the under-used Bell, is wasted in this throwback to Hammer's post-**Psycho** (1960) series of horror-thrillers that began with Seth Holt's **Taste of Fear** (1960).

d Peter Collinson *p* Michael Carreras *s* Michael Peacock
c Brian Probyn *lp* Rita Tushingham, Shane Briant, Tom Bell, Annie Ross, Katya Wyeth, James Bolam, Claire Kelly, Harold Berens, John Clive, Mavis Villiers

Tales from the Crypt

(AMICUS/METROMEDIA PRODUCERS COMPANY; GB) 92min
Amicus here extend their series of omnibus movies initiated with **Dr Terror's House of Horrors** (1964) and **Torture Garden** (1967) with an atmospheric collection adapted from the controversial horror comics of William Gaines. The framing story has a group of characters visit catacombs and encounter the hooded crypt keeper (Richardson) who offers them a vision of their future – which turns out to be a re-run of their past before their final descent into hell, a trick deployed again in the sequel, **Vault of Horror** (1973). The first story, *And All Through the House*, has Collins murder her husband (Boddey) but then find herself stalked by a maniac (MacGreevey), only for her little daughter (Franks) to sweetly open the door for him as he's dressed up as Father Christmas. *Reflection of Death* tells of a man (Hendry) punished for leaving his wife and family to join his mistress (Grant): he is killed in a car crash and becomes a hideously scarred walking corpse but this is revealed to be a dream as he wakes up in the car, just in time to become aware of an impending crash. These two cautionary tales which warn against infringing conventional family life, are followed by an admonishment about neighbourliness, *Poetic Justice*, in which a kindly old widower (Cushing), driven to suicide by a heartless neighbour (Phillips), returns from the grave to rip out the offensive neighbour's heart. *Wish You Were Here* tells of a thoughtless wife (Murray) who is granted three wishes: her wish for money causes the death of her husband (Greene), her wish for her husband results in the return of a zombie and her wish for his eternal life condemns the man to perpetual agonies as the embalming fluid eats into his guts. The final and most gory tale has the callous director (Patrick) of a home for the blind fall prey to his victims' revenge: as they rise from their beds and relentlessly shuffle towards him, he is forced to choose between being savaged by his dog or going down a long dark corridor lined with razor blades.

Francis's direction, although professional, is rarely inspired and adds little to the conservative black humour except efficiently staged shocks at the end of each story.

Nigel Patrick confronts a corridor of terror in Tales from the Crypt.

d Freddie Francis *co-p* Max J. Rosenberg *co-p/s* Milton Subotsky *c* Norman Warwick *lp* Ralph Richardson, Geoffrey Bayldon; Joan Collins, Martin Boddey, Chloë Franks, Oliver MacGreevey; Ian Hendry, Susan Denny, Angie Grant; Peter Cushing, Robin Phillips, David Markham, Robert Hutton; Richard Greene, Barbara Murray, Roy Dotrice; Nigel Patrick, Patrick Magee, Harry Locks

Tower of Evil *aka* Horror of Snape Island

(GRENADIE FILMS/FANFARE; GB,US) 89(85)min
Based on a story by George Baxt – writer of **Circus of Horrors** (1959) and **Vampire Circus** (1971) – this film opens with an American girl (Glendenning) taken to a mental hospital in a state of shock, suspected of slaughtering her companions. Fishermen discover one mutilated cadaver and another one impaled on an ancient Phoenician spear. A private investigator (Halliday) and a team of archaeologists (intrigued by the spear) arrive but the murders continue. The prime suspects are now a crazed lighthouse-keeper presumed dead, his wife – a rotting corpse sitting in a rocking chair – and an equally demented son (McBride) who is revealed to be the real villain. There are the broadest hints of fairly widespread insanity in the isolated community, while a subplot with a Phoenician temple is brought in to distribute red herrings. The film is decorated with incongruous and self-conscious nudity as if to hedge its distributional bets. The dialogue is uncomfortable and it is not surprising, despite O'Connolly's vigorous handling of the murders and the mayhem, that the performances are unconvincing.

d/s Jim O'Connolly *p* Richard Gordon *c* Desmond Dickinson *lp* Bryant Halliday, Jill Haworth, Anna Palk, William Lucas, Anthony Valentine, Candace Glendenning, Mark McBride, Jack Watson, Mark Edwards, Dennis Price

Il Tuo Vizio E una Stanza Chiusa e Solo Io ne Ho la Chiave *aka* **Your Vice Is a Closed Room and Only I Have the Key** *aka* **Excite Me**
(LEA FILM; IT) 96min
After the insipid Roman Polanski imitation **Tutti i Colori del Buio** (1972), Martino continued his series of soft-core thrillers with this weak echo of Poe's *The Black Cat*, apparently set in an old mansion on the Cornish coast. An over-emotional couple indulge in marital warfare, which includes several murders of mistresses and servants. The wife (Fenech), in a fit of rage, grabs a pair of scissors and gouges out an eye of her husband's beloved cat. She also discovers his plan to murder her and beats him to it, burying him in the grave he had prepared for her. In the end, cat noises from behind the cellar wall reveal the whereabouts of the bricked-up cadaver.

Fenech, who had worked with Martino before, tries to give some credibility to the maniacal wife but the inane script, with its crude introduction of a bisexual hippy (Strindberg) to underline the protagonists' degeneracy as she beds both partners, as well as some facetious references to the women's movement, makes this a crassly exploitative effort. The sledgehammer style of direction, with repetitive shots of the cat and of the main characters relentlessly emoting in closeup, reduces the proceedings to a tiresome domestic drama larded with Grand Guignol effects. Martino continued in this vein with **I Corpi Presentano Tracce di Violenza Carnale** (1973).

d Sergio Martino *p* Luciano Martino *s* Ernesto Gastaldi, Adriano Bolzone, Sauro Scavolini *c* Giancarlo Ferrando *lp* Edwige Fenech, Anita Strindberg, Luigi Pistilli, Ivan Rassimov, Franco Nebbia, Riccardo Salvino, Angela la Vorgna, Enrica Bonaccorti

Tutti i Colori del Buio *aka* **Todos los Colores de la Oscuridad** *aka* **They're Coming to Get You** *aka* **Una Stranha Orchidea con Cinque Gocce di Sangue**
(LEA FILM/NATIONAL/CINEMATOGRAFICA/CC ASTRO; IT,SP) scope 99(90)min
Clearly derived from Roman Polanski's **Repulsion** (1965) rather than Hammer's terror-thrillers of the sixties, Santiago Moncada's story tells of a woman, Jane (Fenech), traumatized as a child when she witnessed her mother's murder. Prey to persecution mania, she seeks help from a psychiatrist (Rigaud) to get rid of the notion that a man (Rassimov) is trying to kill her. A mysterious woman offers to cure her by means of black magic, but the participation in satanic rituals only aggravates her condition until she realizes that her fears are not delusions but unpleasant reality. At this point, her husband (Hilton) intervenes and it is revealed that the whole thing was a plan concocted by her sister as a means of inheriting the family fortune. The direction is ploddingly obvious, rehearsing all the motifs of the creeping-paranoia subgenre, as one would expect from a director who slavishly followed whatever sensationalist genre was currently successful at the box office, be it giallo-thrillers, sadistic women-in-peril movies or cannibal pictures such as **La Montagna del Dio Cannibale** (1978).

d Sergio Martino *p* Mino Loy, Luciano Martino *s* Ernesto Gastaldi, Sauro Scavolini *c* Giancarlo Ferrando, Miguel F. Mila *lp* Edwige Fenech, Georg Hilton, Ivan Rassimov, Julian Ugarte, George Rigaud, Maria Cumani Quasimodo, Susan Scott (Nieves Navarro), Marina Malfatti

Below: *Jill Haworth in danger in* Tower of Evil.

Who Fears the Devil? *aka* **The Ballad of Hillbilly John**
(TWO'S COMPANY) 89min
This is a clumsy but attractive distillation from Manly Wade Wellman's superb collection of Appalachian folktales, *Who Fears the Devil?*. Although it attempts to make too much of hero Silver John (Capers), a ballad singer who fights the devil and his minions with his silver-strung guitar, and gets a little too Capra-esque for comfort towards the end when he saves some black workers from exploitation by plantation bosses (and is last seen ambling towards the Capitol in Washington), the opening sequences are impressive. The matter-of-fact folksy tone is captured to perfection as a mysterious mountebank (Darden) appears in his caravan to help Capers find the Spanish pieces of eight that will string his conjure guitar, and as Capers' grandpappy (Pyle) comes to grief in his peppery attempt to call out the Devil and face him down. Newland also strikes exactly the right *faux-naïf* touch, too, with the monsters (including the delightfully absurd, pterodactyl-like ugly bird) that strew Capers' path, and the superbly shot locations in backwoods North Carolina. It's a pity that the music, otherwise pleasant enough as rock-tinged country and western, is a shade too modern to fit the bill.

d John Newland *p* Barney Rosenzweig *s* Melvin Levy *c* Flemming Olsen *lp* Hedge Capers, Severn Darden, Sharon Henesy, Denver Pyle, Susan Strasberg, Harris Yulin, R. G. Armstrong

1973

Al Otro Lado del Espejo *aka* **Ultratumba** *aka* **Le Miroir Obscène** *aka* **Inside a Dark Mirror** *aka* **Outre-Tombe** *aka* **Inceste** *aka* **Beyond the Grave**
(ORFEO PRODUCTIONS/COMPTOIR FRANÇAIS DU FILM; SP,FR) scope 99min
This minor psycho-thriller with added sex scenes was released virtually without publicity four years after its production but nevertheless earned its female star (Cohen) considerable acclaim in Spain. She plays a young woman whose father commits suicide under mysterious circumstances. His ghostly presence pursues and torments her and drives her first to murder and insanity and then to suicide herself. Cohen's performance as a neurotic sinking into paranoia and eventual psychosis is enhanced by the competent contributions of the talented Brion and Lemaire as well as those of Franco regulars Vernon, Romay, Arno and Broquet (Arno's sister). Understandably (but not excusably), since he made 12 features in 1973, Franco's direction is somewhat perfunctory. Besides this picture, **Plaisir à Trois**, **La Comtesse Perverse** and **Les Avaleuses**, he also made two sexy muscleman films in 1973 and a number of porn and suspense features. Some sources credit the cinematography of *Al Otro Lado* to Gerard Brissaud.

d/co-s Jesús Franco *p* José Maria Forque, Robert de Nesle *co-s* Nicole Guetard *c* Antonio Millan *lp* Emma Cohen, Robert Woods, Philippe Lemaire, Françoise Brion, Howard Vernon, Ramiro Oliveros, Lina Romay, Alice Arno (Marie-France Broquet), Chantal Broquet

1973

Arnold

(FENADY ASSOCIATES/BING CROSBY PRODUCTIONS) 95min

A tiresome attempt at horror-comedy from the producer and director of **Terror of the Wax Museum** (1973). The eponymous eccentric (Stuart) refers in his will to a secret hoard of gold. His relatives scheme to discover its whereabouts but in doing so meet a variety of macabre ends: his ex-wife (Wallis) is killed with poisoned face-cream, his brother (McDowall) squeezed to death by a suit, and his widow (Stevens) and an ambiguous lawyer (Granger) by a shower cubicle that contrives to crush its occupants to death. Finally, Arnold's sister (Lanchester) finds the gold in the family crypt, only to be entombed alive in it. Murray scripted the ingenious spoof-thriller, *It's Only Money* (1963), but this movie falls squarely between the stools of parody and pastiche.

d George Fenady *p* Andrew J. Fenady *s* Jameson Brewer, John Fenton Murray *c* William Jurgenson *lp* Stella Stevens, Farley Granger, Elsa Lanchester, Roddy MacDowall, Shani Wallis, Victor Buono, Patric Knowles, John McGiver, Bernard Fox, Jamie Farr

El Ataque de los Muertos Sin Ojos *aka* The Return of the Evil Dead

(ANCLA CENTURY FILMS; SP) 91(87)min

The follow-up to **La Noche del Terror Ciego** (1971) again features the mouldering, slow-moving corpses of the sightless Knights Templar who locate their victims by sound. During the annual celebrations of the massacre of the Templars in the Middle Ages, they rise up and occupy a village. The survivors of their first attack, holed up in a church, try various sorties but they nearly all meet a gruesome fate at the zombies' hands. The script follows the formula of the original movie fairly closely, including the obligatory attempted rape scene (by Braña of Roy), slow-motion shots of the zombies on horseback and the escape of the hero (Stella), here accompanied by two women (Roy and Tovar). The end echoes *The Birds* (1963) as the survivors move gingerly through the ranks of the zombies which, caught in the first rays of the sun, begin to crumble into dust.

The next instalment, **El Buque Maldito** (1974), shifts the action to a nautical setting while **La Noche de los Gaviotas** (1975) brings the zombies back to the beach. Both sequels sought to increase the amount of gore, but the pictures derive their main impact from the eerie figures themselves and the way they move, effects that are enhanced by a judicious use of shock cuts, as in the lengthy escape scene undertaken by the village idiot and a young woman through an underground passage, only to find the zombies waiting for them at the other end. As in *La Noche del Terror Ciego*, de Ossorio took charge of makeup and special effects himself.

d/s/se Amando de Ossorio *p* Ramón Plana *c* Miguel F. Mila *lp* Tony Kendall (Luciano Stella), Esther Ray (Esperanza Roy), Fernando Sancho, Lone Fleming, Frank Blake (Frank Braña), Loretta Tovar, José Canalejas

Les Avaleuses *aka* La Comtesse Noire *aka* La Comtesse aux Seins Nus *aka* Jacula *aka* Yacula *aka* Sicarius – The Midnight Party *aka* The Last Thrill

(GENERAL FILMS/EUROCINE; FR,BEL) scope 101(59)min

Possibly because the central character is a mute vampire with an equally mute servant (Barboo), this variation on *Deep Throat* (1972) is one of Franco's best contributions to the genre, outclassing by far **El Conde Dracula** and **Vampyros Lesbos** (both 1970). Shot largely in Portugal, the story features Countess Irina Karlstein (Romay) who fellates her male lovers to death, and kills her female partners in a similar way. Eventually she falls in love with Taylor, whose penis she bites off after an idyllic session in a forest, and, in an extraordinary dreamlike ending, she drowns herself in a bath of blood in order to rejoin her beloved in the realm of the dead. Freed of the need to fill his central characters' mouths with dialogue, Franco achieves some of his best scenes since **Miss Muerte** (1965) and **Necronomicon** (1967). The gothic settings are well lit and filmed with unusual care and the many and varied erotic scenes, dwelling on the familiar dungeons and torture chambers with scantily clad women in chains (Arancio and Watican), convey an intensely morbid sensuality. As well as directing, scripting, editing and photographing the film, Franco plays the part of Dr Roberts, who, with the help of the blind Dr Orloff – played by fantasy film critic and historian Bouyxou – uncovers the Countess's vampiric activities.

The British release print is missing half the footage, while in Europe three versions were circulated: a horror film without much sex under the title *La Comtesse Noire*; a mixture of horror and sex called *The Bare Breasted Countess* and a hard-core sex movie without much horror called *Les Avaleuses*. The credits of the different versions vary considerably, suggesting that extra scenes were inserted for specific national releases. In Italy the film was credited to Peter Kerr and its script to David Kuhne, both pseudonyms used by Franco. Charles Matton used a similar oral sex and vampirism motif in his *Spermula* (1975).

d J. P. Johnson (Jesús Franco) *p* Marius Lesoeur, Pierre Querut *s* P. Belair or David Kuhne (both Jesús Franco), Gerard Brissaud *lp* Lina Romay, Alice Arno (Marie-France Broquet), Jack Taylor, Monica Swinn, Jess Franck (Jesús Franco), Luis Barboo, Jean-Pierre Bouyxou, Raymond Hardy (Ramon Ardid), Gilda Arancio, Anna Watican

Carrol Baker (centre) and Isabelle de Funès in Baba Yaga, *which was derived from the sado-masochistic comic strips of Guido Crepax.*

Baba Yaga *aka* Devil's Witch

(14 LUGLIO CINEMATOGRAFICA/PRODUCTIONS SIMONE ALLOUCHE; IT,FR) scope 90min

After his heavy-handed vampire allegory **Hanno Cambiato Faccia** (1971), ex-critic Farina turned to the sado-fetishistic comic strips of Guido Crepax for inspiration. The daughter of the popular French comedian Louis de Funès plays the archetypal Crepax heroine, Valentina, a photographer who becomes fascinated by a thin, black-clad woman (Baker) and gets drawn into her witchlike dreamworld. Imprisoned in a sinister castle where she's whipped and sexually abused, de Funès is only released when her boyfriend breaks into her nightmare (or fantasy) and, by destroying a mysterious doll, also kills the witch.

Farina alleged that about 20 minutes were removed from the picture by the producers who eliminated all the politically

Right: *Kerwin Mathews as* The Boy Who Called Werewolf.

'relevant' bits of dialogue. What remains is a tame, albeit tastefully executed sado-masochistic fantasy – which is more than can be said for Bruno Corbucci's adaptation of a more frankly pornographic comic strip, **Isabella Duchessa dei Diavoli** (1969).

d/s Corrado Farina *p* Simone Allouche *c* Alace Parolin *lp* Isabelle de Funès, Carrol Baker, George Eastman (Luigi Montefiori), Ely Galleani, Daniela Balzaretti, Mario M. Giorgetti, Angela Covello, Cesarina Amendola

Blackenstein *aka* Black Frankenstein

(FRISCO PRODUCTIONS) 92 min

Like **Blacula** (1972) and **Dr Black, Mr Hyde** (1976), *Blackenstein* is one of blaxploitation cinema's several forays into the horror genre. Interestingly, the film also invokes the Vietnam trauma in its story of a soldier who is crippled by an exploding mine and has an arm and a leg graft carried out on him by Dr Frankenstein (Hart), his girlfriend's boss. Unfortunately, the doctor's butler has designs on the same girl and sabotages the operation, turning the soldier into a rampaging monster. The movie also features a large number of girls having their shirts ripped open, Renay (of *Desperate Living*, 1977, fame), and, rather extraordinarily, some special effects work by Kenneth Strickfaden, who made the electronic gadgetry for the original Universal Frankenstein movies.

d William A. Levey *p/s* Frank R. Saletri *lp* John Hart, Ivory Stone, Andrea King, Liz Renay, Roosevelt Jackson, Joe de Sue, Nick Bolin, Cardella di Milo, James Cousar, Marva Farmer

The Boy Who Cried Werewolf (RKF/U) 93min

Although it boasts a cute title, this film about a 12-year-boy (Sealey) who sees a werewolf and finds that nobody will believe him, doesn't really work, partly because Juran and Mathews (as Sealey's father) seem unable to shake off their pasts in juvenile adventure films (they were responsible for *The Seventh Voyage of Sinbad*, 1958, and *Jack the Giant Killer*, 1962). When Mathews gets bitten fighting off what he thought was a human attacker, and when he begins to feel the old urge, he gets Sealey to lock him in but mother lets him out again. The film has one nice sequence (in which a group of Jesus freaks stage an exorcism as a sort of tourist attraction, forming a pentagon which Mathews finds to his embarrassment he cannot enter) and one nice joke (when Mathews abruptly returns to human form with the rising sun, and the leader of the freaks, Homel, yelps in ecstasy under the impression that God has inspired him to cast out a demon). The rest, however, consists solely of stilted dialogue and thumping shocks, the latter rather muffled by the fact that the werewolf puffing through the forest is oddly reminiscent of Walt Disney's Pluto.

d Nathan H. Juran *p* Aaron Rosenberg *s* Bob Homel *c* Michael P. Joyce *lp* Kerwin Mathews, Elaine Devry, Scott Sealey, Robert J. Wilke, Bob Homel

One of the macabre jokes of La Campana del Infierno.

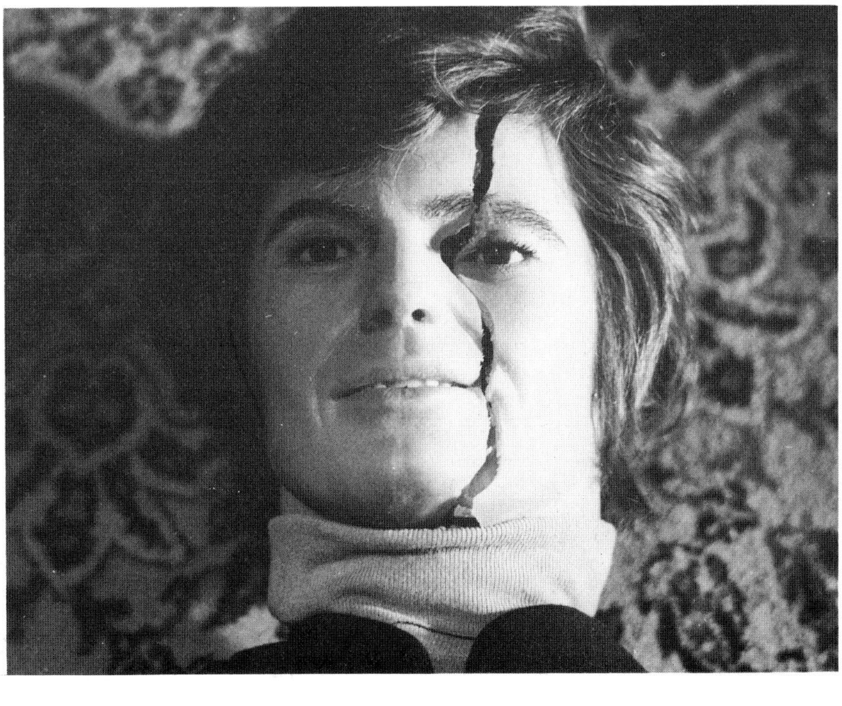

La Campana del Infierno *aka* The Bell of Hell *aka* A Bell from Hell

(HESPERIA/FILMS DE LA BEOTIE; SP,FR) scope 106(97)min

One of the few excellently crafted psycho-horrors to emerge from Spain, this movie is on a par with Seth Holt's **Taste of Fear** (1960). Juan (Verley) returns from an asylum to take revenge on the aunt (Lindfors) and her three daughters (Martin, Gimeno and Betzner) who had him locked away as a psychopath in the hope of gaining his inheritance. He smears honey over his sleeping aunt's face before releasing a swarm of bees and frightens the three daughters by dragging them into a basement arranged as a slaughterhouse. These macabre 'jokes' go awry when Pedro (Mayo), a friend of the now swollen-faced Lindfors locks Verley in a clocktower with a bell rope around his neck to await the tower's inaugural ceremony next day. After the ceremony, which includes the ringing of the bell, Mayo sees a light in Verley's room and, when he goes to investigate, posthumous evidence of the young psychotic's weird sense of humour proves to be his undoing.

Director Hill, who fell from the bell tower and died on the last day of shooting, manages to keep Verley's character thoroughly ambiguous, never quite dispelling the fear that he really is a psychotic even though he is offered as an identification figure for the audience among his villainously self-centred and greedy relatives. Hill's corrosive anti-clerical humour is reminiscent of Luis Buñuel and Saki, whose story *The Open Window* (1912) is quoted in the picture. His premature death was a genuine loss for the Spanish cinema. The picture was finished by the prestigious Juan Antonio Bardem.

d/p Claudio Guerin Hill *s* Santiago Moncada *c* Manuel Rojas *se* Manuel Baquero *lp* Renaud Verley, Viveca Lindfors, Alfredo Mayo, Maribel Martin, Nuria Gimeno, Christine Betzner, Saturno Cerra, Nicole Vesperini, Erasmo Pascual, Susana Latour

The Case of the Full Moon Murders *aka* The Case of the Smiling Stiffs

(LOBSTER ENTERPRISES/DANA FILMS) 74(62)min

A beautiful vampire who causes death by fellatio, leaving her victims in a state of happy erection, is the sort of idea which needs a little wit to round it out. What it gets in this hard-core joke, designed as a *Dragnet* parody with a couple of Miami detectives investigating the mysterious murders, is dismal schoolboy smut. Walker is the vampire, killed by Reems (of *Deep Throat*, 1972) with his 'stake'.

d/p Sean S. Cunningham *s* Bud Talbot, Jerry Hayling *c* Gus Graham *lp* Fred Lincoln, Ron Browne, Cathy Walker, Harry Reems, Sheila Stuart

Il Castello della Paura *aka* **Terror** *aka* **Il Castello delle Donne Maledette** *aka* **The House of Freaks** *aka* **Frankenstein's Castle of Freaks** *aka* **Terror Castle** *aka* **The Monsters of Dr Frankenstein**
(CLASSIC FILMS INTERNATIONAL; IT) 89min
Made at the same time as **Il Mostro E in Tavola ... Barone Frankenstein** (1973), this film has Count Frankenstein (Brazzi) – in fact, a routine mad scientist – with the help of a malevolent dwarf (Dunn), a hunchback and other misfits, put a brain into a backward hulk called Goliath. The dwarf is expelled from the castle and enlists the aid of Ook the Neanderthal Man, played by Lugosi – no relation. In the ensuing carnage, everyone is killed. The inept movie recalls the antics of the Kuchar brothers and their 'underground' fantasy epics made in home-movie style, with Ook sporting a pair of tennis shorts underneath his hairy disguise. Randall's career, which started with such nude films as *Searching for Venus* (1963), also included the Japanese-Thai co-production *Krokodil* (1977) and a sexploitation version of Robinson Crusoe called *Never on Friday* (1977).

d/s Robert H. Oliver *p* Dick Randall *lp* Rosanno Brazzi, Michael Dunn, Edmund Purdom, Christiane Royce, Boris Lugosi, Gordon Mitchell, Alan Collins (Luciano Pigozzi), Xiro Papas, Loren Ewing, Lewis Garfield

Children Shouldn't Play with Dead Things
(GENENI PRODUCTIONS) 87min
Five young actors and their company director Alan (Ormsby) come by boat to a lonely burial island off the east coast of the United States, wher Ormsby wants to dig up a fresh corpse and try to raise the dead. The rites appear to fail but once the troupe have retreated to a cottage on the island the dead awaken and wreak terrible vengeance on the desecrators of their tombs.

This was Clark's second feature (and first horror movie) and on the strength of this, he and co-scriptwriter Ormsby were able to raise the money for the excellent *The Night Walk* (1973). Clark then turned in two more excellent horror films in **Black Christmas** (1974) and **Murder by Decree** (1978) while Ormsby directed the superb **Deranged** (1974) and wrote **Cat People** (1982).

Made for $70,000 in 14 days *Children* was financed by Clark and featured a number of his college friends. The film became a minor cult hit, cashing in on the success of **Night of the Living Dead** (1968), to which it adds a leavening of black (if occasionally rather self-conscious) humour. Considering the budget and the numbers of actors involved, the special effects (by Ormsby himself) are surprisingly effective.

d/co-p/co-s Benjamin (Bob) Clark *co-p* Gary Goch *co-s/se* Alan Ormsby *c* Jack McGowan *lp* Jeffrey Gillen, Paul Cronin, Roy Engleman, Bob Filep, Bruce Solomon, Alecs Baird, Seth Sklarey

La Comtesse Perverse *aka* **Les Chasses de la Comtesse Zaroff** *aka* **La Comtesse Zaroff** *aka* **Les Croqueuses** *aka* **The Evil Countess**
(COMPTOIR FRANÇAIS DU FILM; FR) 88min
Shot in Portugal back to back with **Plaisir à Trois** (1973), this is a sadistic – although humorous – version of **The Most Dangerous Game** (1932) and, though allegedly based on a 15th-century Spanish manuscript by Abel Alazred, was in fact was scripted by the prolific Franco himself. The narrative, which is set in a weird mansion on a remote island, has Moira (Busselier) and Bod (Woods) hunt people and deliver them to the cruel perversities of Sylvia (Romay), Count Zaroff (Vernon) and Ivanna (Arno), who also appears as a naked huntress. When Romay turns her sadistic attentions to Busselier, Woods kills her with an arrow. Fairly hard-core erotic scenes with Arno, Busselier and Swinn have been removed from most prints and replaced with about 10 minutes of anodyne footage, breaking whatever rhythm or atmosphere the original picture may have had. In keeping with the fashion of the period, some flesh-eating shots are included, and the bright colours and settings and Romay's presence considerably enhance the sense of morbid sexuality and incipient madness.

Franco next projects were **Al Otro Lado del Espejo** (1973, one of his best acted movies) and two sexy muscleman films, *Maciste Contre la Reine des Amazones* and *Les Exploits Erotiques de Maciste dans l'Atlantide* (both 1973), starring Wal Davis (Waldemar Wohlfahrt), Arno and her sister Chantal. Franco further exploited the cannibalism motif in his *Mondo Cannibale* (1979) featuring Shirley Knight, Candy Coster (Romay) and Pamela Stanford, but his sickest cannibal scenes occur in *Greta – Haus Ohne Maenner* (1977), starring Dyanne Thorne, Romay and Busselier.

d/s Clifford Brown (Jesús Franco) *p* Robert de Nesle *c* Gerard Brissaud, Antonio Millan *lp* Lina Romay, Kali Hansa, Alice Arno (Marie-France Broquet), Robert Woods, Howard Vernon, Tanya Busselier, Monica Swinn

I Corpi Presentano Tracce di Violenza Carnale *aka* **Torso** *aka* **The Bodies Bear Traces of Carnal Violence** (CC CHAMPION; IT) 90(86)min
The United States had to wait until **The Texas Chainsaw Massacre** (1974) before gory cannibal movies became part of mainstream cinema, and until **Halloween** (1978) before adolescents became the standard victims of homicidal maniacs acting out Moral Majority revenge fantasies against a youth that was, if not actually drug-sodden and violently anarchic, at least in favour of premarital sex, feminism and other forms of

Suzy Kendall in the gory I Corpi Presentano Tracce di Violenza Carnale.

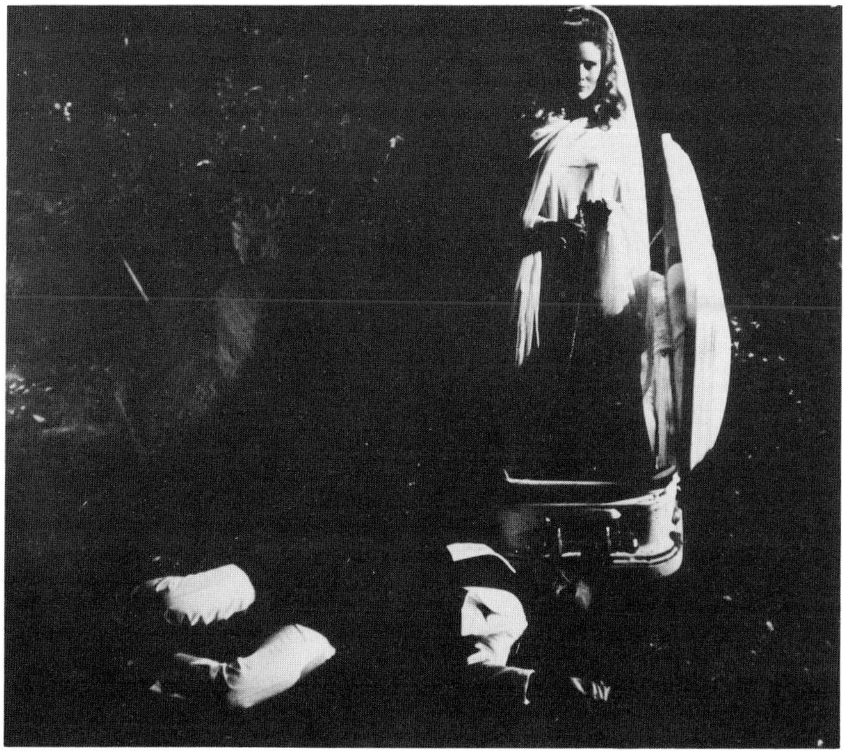

Jo Morrow arises from her coffin, her life restored by Dr Death: Seeker of Souls.

moral turpitude. Europe anticipated this trend with its variations on Jack the Ripper and in the Italian giallo movies perfected by Dario Argento (**L'Uccello dalle Piume di Cristallo**, 1970, for example). Martino's sub-Argento efforts include this film about a hooded hacksaw maniac (Richardson) slashing and dismembering college girls.

There is a disturbing similarity between the killer's treatment of female bodies, cutting off the limbs, and the director's use of the frame's edges to sever legs from bodies or to 'cut out' naked female torsos. Significantly, the actual dismembering is not shown (the cutting in the story is substituted by the cutting of the story) and only an explicit eye-gouging remains for us to see. Virtually unwatchable except for Ferrando's excellent landscape photography and the beauties of both Kendall and Aumont, the movie trades on the thrill of destroying just such beautiful women.

d/co-s Sergio Martino *p* Carlo Ponti *co-s* Ernesto Gastaldi *c* Giancarlo Ferrando *lp* Suzy Kendall, Tina Aumont, Luc Merenda, John Richardson, Angela Covello, Carla Brait, Cristiana Airoldi, Patrizia Adiutori, Roberto Bisacco

Les Démoniaques *aka* Les Diablesses *aka* Deux Vierges pour Satan *aka* Tina, la Naufrageuse Perverse *aka* Demoniacs

(LES FILMS ABC/NORDIA FILMS/GENERAL FILMS; FR,BEL) 100min

Set on the Belgian coast in a small village at the turn of the century, *Les Démoniaques* slides from scrappily shot sex scenes to enchantingly beautiful and cruelly poetic scenes and back to bombastic banality. The meandering plot has two women (Burr and Hermenier) washed ashore only to fall into the hands of a brutal shipwrecking gang led by the seductive Tina (Coeur) and her lover (Rico). The women are raped and left for dead, but reappear as spectres in a dingy tavern before seeking refuge in an old abbey where they make a pact with the devil (Zimovir), acquiring supernatural powers to carry out their revenge. In the end, they're captured by the gang and crucified to the remains of wrecked ships as the waves rise to engulf them and their tormentors.

The voluptuous Coeur, star of Rollin's previous movie, the hard-core *Jeunes Filles Impudiques* (1973), sheds her clothes too frequently, but some of the scenes, such as those in the old tavern run by the weird, singing and fortune-telling Louise (Dhour) and the final scenes among the skeletal remains of dead ships, are genuinely hallucinatory achievements. The dialogue is frankly unrealistic and the acting characteristically non-descript while Pierre Raph's emphatic score spoils many sequences. The level of delirium sustained in **Requiem pour un Vampire** (1971) is reached only intermittently, making the picture somewhat uneven. Before going on to make another horror picture, arguably his best (**Lèvres de Sang**, 1975), Rollin finished a second potboiler under the pseudonym Michel Gentil, *Douces Pénétrations* (1975), starring Jesús Franco regular Tanya Busselier.

d/s Jean Rollin *p* Lionel Wallman *c* Jean-Jacques Renon *lp* Joelle Coeur, Patricia Hermenier, Lieva Burr (Lieve Baekelmans), John Rico, Isabelle Copejans, Mireille Dargent, Louise Dhour, Paul Biscaglia, Misha Zimovir

Don't Look Now (BRITISH LION) scope 110min

Adapted from Daphne du Maurier's novella, this is virtually an art-house version of a Dario Argento giallo film.

Art historian Sutherland is in Venice with his wife (Christie) to supervise the restoration of a church, and recover from the trauma-inducing death of their daughter in a drowning accident. Christie is drawn to a pair of English spinster sisters, one of whom (Mason) is a psychic who claims to be in contact with the girl, while Sutherland keeps glimpsing a small figure in a red raincoat whom he takes for his daughter's ghost. When Christie briefly returns to England, Sutherland sees her with the spinsters taking part in a Venetian funeral. When she returns, Sutherland pursues the apparition in red and confronts not the dead girl but a homicidal dwarf. Bleeding to death, he realizes that the foreseen funeral is his own. Roeg's mosaic approach to screen time (a love-making session is intercut with the couple prosaically getting dressed afterwards) makes even matter-of-fact scenes magical and threatening. The film proved influential within the genre, notably on Argento's **Profondo Rosso** (1975) and Richard Loncraine's **Full Circle** (1976).

d Nicolas Roeg *p* Peter Katz *s* Allan Scott, Chris Bryant *c* Anthony Richmond *lp* Julie Christie, Donald Sutherland, Hilary Mason, Adelina Poerio, Leopoldo Trieste, Clelia Matania, Massimo Serato

Dr Death: Seeker of Souls

(FREEDOM ARTS PICTURES) 89min

In his efforts to revivify his wife Laura (Morrow) who was killed in a car accident, Fred Saunders (Coe) visits Dr Death (Considine) who claims to have transferred his own soul down through the centuries via a number of bodies. He offers to revive Morrow's corpse with another woman's soul and murders numerous women for the purpose, but to no avail. If read as an outrageously black necrophiliac comedy *Dr Death* is bizarrely funny in an absurdist fashion, and an effective satire on California cultism with the oily Dr Death as a kind of L. Ron Hubbard figure. Considering the low budget, the special effects are quite good, but the film's tone is best judged by the note which Considine sends to Coe along with the severed head of his latest victim – 'this is to let you know that I'm still trying' – and by the fact that his initial demonstration features Moe Howard, one of the Three Stooges, in his last screen role.

d/p Eddie Saeta *s* Sal Ponti *c* Kent Wakeford, Emil Oster *se* Siegfried Geike *lp* John Considine, Barry Coe, Cheryl Miller, Stewart Moss, Leon Askin, Jo Morrow, Florence Marly, Sivi Aberg, Jim Boles, Athena Lorde

Dracula *aka* Bram Stoker's Dracula

(DAN CURTIS PRODUCTIONS/UNIVERSAL; US,GB) 120(98)min

Curtis specialized in adapting horror classics for TV – his credits include *The Strange Case of Dr Jekyll and Mr Hyde* (1968), *The Picture of Dorian Gray* (1973), *The Turn of the Screw*

(1974) and *Dead of Night* (1977) – and this, his version of *Dracula*, is far more interesting than the previous attempt (by the BBC in 1970, with Denholm Elliott as the Count) to bring the character to the small screen. The familiar story, with only minor alterations, is enlivened by the depiction of the Count as a figure generated by the conventions of cheap 19th-century literature, with Palance as the simultaneously fascinating and repulsive villain/hero straight out of macabre melodramatic penny dreadfuls, the 'high romanticism' equivalents of current teledrama. Palance dwarfs the rest of the cast, which includes Davenport as Van Helsing, the man who stakes the sensuous Lucy (Lewis) together with the somewhat insipid hero (Ward), and Horner as Mina, who is saved in the end as Dracula dies with a spear thrust into his heart.

Unfortunately, in an effort to compensate for the subtler, more cinematic ways of building atmosphere which cannot make their full impact on a small screen constantly invaded by adverts and viewed with far less concentration, the direction over-relies on zooms and other hamfisted devices to make its point. The film was released theatrically, drastically cut to 98 minutes, but is totally unsuited to the big screen. Curtis revealed himself a more professional film-maker with **House of Dark Shadows** (1970) and **Burnt Offerings** (1976).

Other TV Draculas include John Carradine (*Matinee Theatre*, 1956) and Louis Jourdan in Philip Savill's *Count Dracula* (1978).

d/p Dan Curtis *s* Richard Matheson *c* Oswald Morris *se* Kit West *lp* Jack Palance, Simon Ward, Nigel Davenport, Fiona Lewis, Pamela Brown, Penelope Horner, Murray Brown, Virginia Wetherell, Sarah Douglas, Barbara Lindley

Dracula Cerca Sangue di Vergine e ... Mori di Sete *aka* Dracula Vuole Vivere: Cerca Sangue di Vergina *aka* Blood for Dracula *aka* Andy Warhol's Young Dracula *aka* Andy Warhol's Dracula

(CC CHAMPION/JEAN YANNE-JEAN PIERRE RASSAM PRODUCTION; IT,FR) scope 103(90)min

In this companion piece to **Il Mostro E in Tavola** (1973), Margheriti seems to have paid more attention to the picture's setting and tone than in his previous collaboration with Morrissey (one of Andy Warhol's acolytes, usually credited with a vague 'supervisory' function on this film). Kier's Dracula needs virginal blood like drug addicts need a fix. Unable to find any virgins in his native Romania, the emaciated vampire and his trusted servant (Juerging) travel to Catholic Italy in search of consumable women and become the guests of a family of impoverished aristocrats presided over by de Sica. However, the heroic gardener (Dallesandro), who is also prone to mouthing American undergraduate ideas of revolutionary slogans, infects the blood of all available women, including the family's 14-year-old daughter, with his sexual activities. Starved of his fix, Dracula collapses into a vomiting heap in the bathroom every time he sucks 'impure' blood and, in the end, the gardener takes an axe to the Count and reduces him to a bloody stump before staking him.

The story is silly and the sexual motifs suggest, with the usual tongue-in-cheek safeguards, that women are both disgusting and terrifying. But Margheriti, credited as director in Italian sources, occasionally gets away with a visual gag (Dracula grooming himself in front of a mirror which casts no reflection) and his effective use of the decadent décor provided by the rapidly putrefying villa saves the picture. Acting honors go to Polanski for his cameo as a belligerent peasant, while de Sica is excellent in the role of the pompous but mercenary aristocratic patriarch.

co-d Anthony Dawson (Antonio Margheriti) *p* Andrew Braunsberg *co-d/s* Paul Morrissey *c* Luigi Kuveiller *se* Carlo Rimbaldi, Roberto Arcangeli *lp* Udo Kier, Vittorio de Sica, Joe Dallesandro, Maxime McKendry, Arno Juerging, Milena Vukotic, Dominique Darel, Stefania Casini, Silvia Dioniso, Roman Polanski

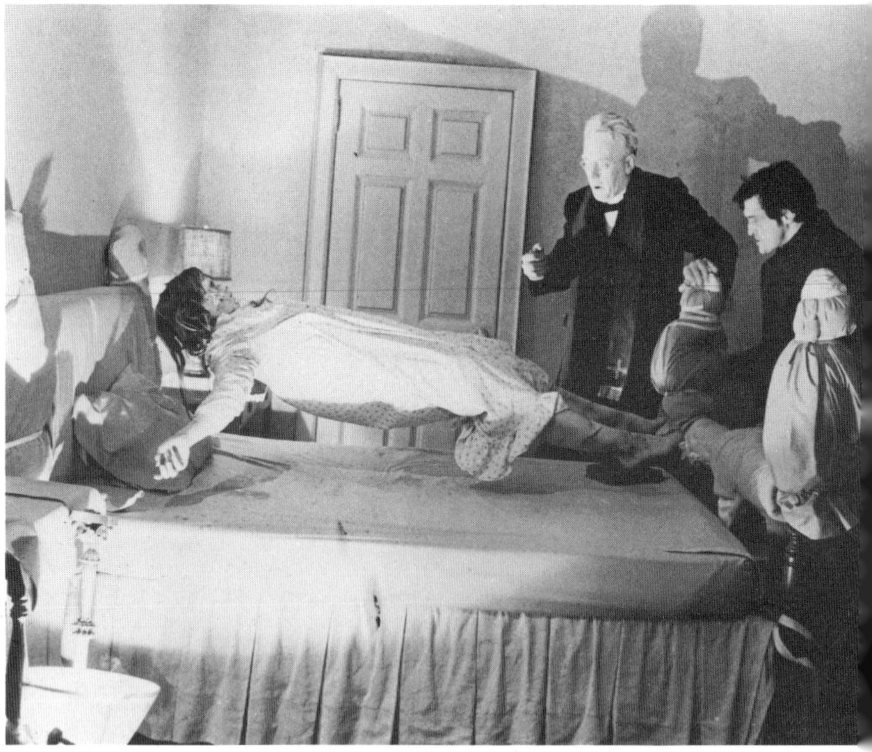

Horror goes big budget: The Exorcist.

The Exorcist

(HOYA PRODUCTIONS/WB) 122min

In retrospect it is hardly surprising that *The Exorcist* became the most commercially successful horror movie ever made. The film cunningly tweaked a sensitive contemporary nerve. There but for the grace of God, many a parent anxiously contemplating the mystery of precocious rebellion must have sighed as the 12-year-old child (Blair) is possessed of a demon; and when that demon provokes the child to piss on the parental carpet, vomit green bile over a priest and masturbate violently with a crucifix, many a teenager must have applauded and envied the inventive daring. All this, religion and big-budget respectability too!

What *is* surprising is that the film, so patently hoping to be taken as more than just another slice of blood-and-thunder horror was indeed taken seriously by reverend gentlemen and media personages who talk solemnly about 'the social and religious phenomenon' that the film represented. Actually, the 'serious' side of the film – represented chiefly by the spiritual torments of Father Karras (Miller) a Jesuit who loses his faith but takes the sins of the world on his shoulders by calling upon the demon to enter his body when the attempt at exorcism seems doomed to failure – is about as profound as the religious conviction in a DeMille biblical epic.

By far the best of the film comes around the middle, where it can forget about significance and concentrate on the chills. There is a hair-raising moment when, almost at the edge of perception, one realizes that the possessed child's head has turned round much too far for human possibility (the effect is repeated later, centrescreen and rather absurdly this time, with the head turning full circle like an owl's). Even more horrifying, perhaps, are the elaborate and endless medical tests to which the unfortunate child is submitted, with the ghastly ritual of encephalograms and spinals shot to look like a refined form of torture. Beside these scenes, the messier aspects of the possession (the vomited bile, the self-inflicted wounds) look all to much like routine paint and makeup jobs; but enjoyed by millions who normally wouldn't be seen dead at a horror movie, they undoubtedly sparked off the special effects boom of the past ten years.

Mercedes McCambridge provides the demon's hoarsely mocking voice and Eileen Smith doubled for Blair in the vomiting scenes.

d William Friedkin *p/s* William Peter Blatty *c* Owen Roizman, Billy Williams *lp* Ellen Burstyn, Max von Sydow, Lee J. Cobb, Jack MacGowran, Jason Miller, Kitty Winn, Linda Blair

Fengriffen *aka* **And Now the Screaming Starts** *aka* **I Have No Mouth But I Must Scream** *aka* **Bride of Fengriffen** *aka* **The Screaming Starts**
(AMICUS; GB) 87min
Amicus temporarily abandoned its string of omnibus movies (**Tales from the Crypt**, 1972; **The House that Dripped Blood**, 1970) for this grisly tale about the Fengriffen family curse in which a disembodied hand avenges a Fengriffen ancestor's rape of a servant's virgin bride. The curse is visited on Charles and his pregnant bride (Oglivy and Beacham) until Dr Pope (Cushing) diagnoses the cause of the supernatural goings-on. The mechanical script merely repeats the narrative structure of *The Hound of the Baskervilles*, replacing the hound with the hand and focusing on a woman for added sexual titillation. The picture misses a good opportunity to explore the sinister implications of the class conflict that underpins the drama as the sons and daughters of the aristocracy have to pay the price for their father's callous 'use' of a servant's body. Instead, the picture merely engineers a series of shocks linked by the almost incessant screaming of the heroine, although camerawork and excellent art direction – by Tony Curtis and Fred Carter – make it quite a luscious-looking movie if watched with the soundtrack switched off. As for the sins-of-the-fathers theme, Peter Sykes' **Demons of the Mind** (1971) tackles the subject with considerably more flair and sophistication. This film and **The Beast Must Die** (1974) conclusively demonstrate that Amicus's talents do not lie in the production of single-plot features.

d Roy Ward Baker *p* Milton Subotsky, Max J. Rosenberg *s* Roger Marshall *c* Denys Coop *lp* Peter Cushing, Ian Ogilvy, Stephanie Beacham, Herbert Lom, Patrick Magee, Guy Rolfe, Geoffrey Crutchley, Rosalie Crutchley, Janet Key, Gillian Lind

Frankenstein 1980 *aka* **Mosaico** *aka* **Frankenstein**
(MGD FILM; IT) scope 96min
Less overtly erotic than **La Figlia di Frankenstein** (1971) or even *Frankenstein all'Italiana* (1976), this is a conventional quickie in which a monster called Mosaico (Papas) runs amok looking for spare parts and slaughters nearly the entire cast, including its creator, Dr Albrechtstein (Mitchell). The trigger for the mayhem is that the creature's various bits of body begin to be rejected by the brain. In the meantime, the victims – who include a female butcher, a prostitute, a professor, his assistant, a ballerina, a tramp, a courting couple and a man watching a car race – meet their ends in various brutal scenes as the direction staggers from one setpiece to another with relentless predictability. The film was released in the Italian provinces only, although it later surfaced in Brazil. Many of the cast prudently hide behind difficult to trace pseudonyms.

d/co-s Mario Mancini *p* Benedetto Graziani *co-s* Ferdinando di Leoni *c* Emilio Varriano *lp* John Richardson, Renato Romano, Xiro Papas, Gordon Mitchell, Dalila Parker, Bob Fix, Gigi Bonos, Lemmy Carson, Dada Galotti, Marco Mariani

David Prowse contemplates beauty in Terence Fisher's exemplary Frankenstein and the Monster from Hell.

Frankenstein and the Monster from Hell
(HAMMER; GB) scope 93(85)min
Fisher's fifth and Hammer's seventh Frankenstein picture, shot in 1972, is a pivotal work in the genre, both confirming the end of a period and announcing the mutated form that would come to dominate seventies fantasies. The emphatically titled **Frankenstein Must Be Destroyed** (1969) signalled the close of the gothic horror era dominated by the complex Dracula-Frankenstein mirror image: the Count representing the survival of feudalism in a society ostensibly professing rationalism, the Baron the premature emergence of social engineering and science in a society still dominated by feudal conceptions. Dracula erupts into a society that refuses the demonic while Frankenstein is accused of sorcery in a society that refuses science. Subsequently, the genre's fantasy regime mutated to a more paranoid form figuring not the mythical transition to a 'rational' social order – which is itself a myth, as the films demonstrate – but the fearful vision of that social order's disintegration as the body politic is distorted and exploded by either too much or not enough 'control': the apocalyptic body-in-pieces fantasy.

Fisher, who died shortly after finishing this film, set the entire story within the walls of an asylum, with the Baron (Cushing), apparently a prisoner but in fact its master, wielding unchallenged authority over staff and inmates, using some of the latter for his private body-building work. He is presented as a somewhat brutish cultural boor, guffawing at a bad joke, unable to solve maths problems or to appreciate music. His hands, burnt in **Frankenstein Created Woman** (1966), are useless for surgery. With the help of an equally unpleasant but younger surgeon (Briant), incarcerated for following in the Baron's footsteps, a creature is assembled using the gigantic body of an insane murderer, the brain of a musical and mathematical genius, the hands of a sculptor and various bits from other people. The resultant creature (Prowse) is a neurotic monster, torn between the conflicting aspects of 'himself' – a highly intelligent and artistic person imprisoned in a neanderthal hulk – which gives rise to some incongruously surreal scenes, such as the hulk solving complicated mathematical equations on a blackboard. In the end, this inner conflict is transposed into the narrative structure itself as the inmates fall upon this 'torn' creature and tear it to bits, the horror of 'unnatural assembly' being superceded by the body-in-pieces fantasy, here presented as still contained within the walls of a prison but soon unleashed upon the world at large in the movies of David Cronenberg and George Romero.

Fisher's film is shot in uncharacteristically cold colours and at an almost clinical distance. The Baron, soberly underplayed by Cushing, repeats his experiments almost out of habit rather than conviction since there is no longer an 'outside world' he wants to persuade of the benefits of science: officially the scandal of Frankenstein is dead and he has now become a famous scientist whose reputation far exceeds the world he rules. The film also delineates with glaring clarity the marginal erotic component of the Frankenstein story in the figure of the mute Sarah, also referred to as Angel (Smith). She represents the reproductive function assigned to the female in this scenario: rendered mute by her father's sexual attack upon her, she is then called upon to mother the progeny of the Baron's creation. Through her, the dimension of filiation is added to the myth of creation symbolized by the men's work. Prowse had played the creature before in Hammer's risible **The Horror of Frankenstein** (1970) but his best remembered appearances belong to the post-Dracula/Frankenstein era: he was Darth Vader in the *Star Wars* (1977) saga, a science fiction version of the control/disintegration fantasy.

d Terence Fisher *p* Roy Skeggs *s* John Elder (Anthony Hinds) *c* Brian Probyn *se* Les Bowie *lp* Peter Cushing, Shane Briant, Madeline Smith, Bernard Lee, David Prowse, Charles Lloyd-Pack, Patrick Troughton, Sydney Bromley, John Stratton

Frankenstein: The True Story *aka* Dr Frankenstein

(U/NBC; GB) 190(123)min

Originally produced as a three-hour TV spectacular, this shortened version of *Frankenstein: The True Story* was released theatrically. The film was promoted as a faithful adaptation of Mary Shelley's novel and recounts how the doctor (Whiting) with assistance from Clervel (McCallum) produces a beautiful-looking creature (Sarrazin). Soon, however, the creature begins to turn ugly in all senses of the term whereupon Whiting is blackmailed by the villain of the story, Dr Polidori (Mason) into creating a mate for the creature, Prima (Seymour). When Seymour is presented to polite society at a ball, the male creature rushes in and beheads her in a spiteful effort to destroy beauty. In the end, it kills Whiting's wife (Paget) and Mason before causing an ice avalanche that buries the creature and its creator.

Far less concerned with the horrific aspects of the story, Smight's movie concentrates, as did Shelley, on the metaphysical melodrama which opposes beauty and ugliness, good and evil, science and faith. As a result, the film is very literary, relying primarily on the acting skills of the cast of stars rather than on the cinematic abilities of the director. The theatrically released version dispenses with a lot of the wordy psychological teledrama footage, but the film remains trapped in its wastefully expansive, fundamentally uncinematic television format with the camera following the characters rather than weaving its own spells.

d Jack Smight *p* Hunt Stromberg *s* Christopher Isherwood, Don Bachardy *c* Arthur Ibbetson *se* Roy Whybrow *lp* James Mason, Leonard Whiting, Michael Sarrazin, David McCallum, Jane Seymour, Nicola Paget, Michael Wilding, Clarissa Kaye, Agnes Moorehead, Margaret Leighton

From Beyond the Grave *aka* The Undead *aka* Tales from Beyond the Grave *aka* Tales from the Beyond *aka* The Creatures

(AMICUS; GB) 98min

The seventh in a long series of omnibus movies produced by Amicus – its most noteworthy precursors were **Torture Garden** (1967) and **The House That Dripped Blood** (1970) – this film contains four stories based on the work of R. Chetwynd-Hayes (whose work also provided the basis for **The Monster Club**, 1980) within a contrived linking framework set in a sinister East End antique shop, of which Cushing plays the proprietor. The first episode entails a malign mirror, whose 'prisoner' Warner becomes. In the second, an ex-army officer (Bannen) is caught up in black magic by a sinister match-seller (Pleasance). The third story, semi-humorous in style, involves a well-off couple (Carmichael and Porter) becoming the victims of an 'elemental' or invisible demon. The last episode concerns an oak door, bought by Ogilvy, which 'converts' the room in which it is installed into the scene of its macabre earlier existence. Despite enthusiastic playing from the star cast, only the second episode is distinctive; the last is reminiscent of, but wholly inferior to, the haunted mirror episode of **Dead of Night** (1945). This was the first film directed by Connor, who went on to make the engaging **Motel Hell** (1980).

d Kevin Connor *p* Max J. Rosenberg, Milton Subotsky *s* Robin Clarke, Raymond Christodoulou *c* Alan Hume *se* Alan Bryce *lp* Peter Cushing; David Warner, Rosalind Ayres; Ian Bannen, Donald Pleasance, Angela Pleasance, Diana Dors; Margaret Leighton, Ian Carmichael, Nyree Dawn Porter; Ian Ogilvy, Lesley-Anne Down, Jack Watson

Ganja and Hess *aka* Double Possession *aka* Blood Couple

(KELLY JORDAN ENTERPRISES) 110(78)min

Until it was cut, retitled and re-released in 1975, *Ganja and Hess* was, along with *Lord Shango* (1975), one of the most interesting black movies produced by Hollywood, and a far cry indeed from such blaxploitation fare as **Blacula** (1972) and **Blackenstein** (1973). Like *Lord Shango*, the film is clearly and seriously concerned with black culture, and in particular the opposition between black spiritual roots and an imposed western/Christian culture. The story concerns a black anthropologist (Jones) who is studying the ancient black culture of Myrthia which disappeared when it was destroyed by a transmittable amoebic parasite that was addicted to blood. In the course of his research he is stabbed with a Myrthian dagger by his assistant (Gunn, the film's writer and director) who then kills himself. Jones discovers that he has become both addicted to blood and resistant to death.

This is a film of astonishing richness of sound (part revival spiritual, part African folkways track), rhythm, colour (Gunn

Below: *Tessa Dahl wields the meatcleaver in* Happy Mother's Day ... Love George.

Mike Combs and Hilarie Thompson in the atmospheric *Hex*.

is also a painter) and subversive sensual power. Like Christopher Lee in Hammer's Dracula films, Jones is clearly the film's hero, its centre of vitality. But here blood becomes more than just a symbol of life; it is an atavistic reminder of the indestructibility of the black race, of a suppressed but not destroyed African heritage. After his infection with the Myrthian virus Jones becomes like a black god, inverting Christian symbols and myths and invoking rich, plenitudinous sensuality that is the very reverse of western puritanism. Nor is this simply a hymn to black virility, since Jones' persona is perfectly counterbalanced by the presence of the quite stunning Clark (who has featured in various Russ Meyer films) as Ganja Meda, Gunn's wife.

d/s Bill Gunn *p* Chiz Schultz *c* James E. Hinton *lp* Duane Jones, Marlene Clark, Bill Gunn, Sam Waymon, Leonard Jackson, Candece Tarplay, Richard Harrow, John Hoffmeister, Betty Barney, Mabel King

Happy Mother's Day ... Love, George *aka* **Run, Stranger, Run**
(TAUREAN FILMS) 90min
This film, the directorial début of actor McGavin – made after his brilliant teleseries *Kolchak, the Night Stalker* was cancelled – comes across a as a kind of horror version of *Peyton Place*. Howard arrives in a tranquil New England fishing village to a generally hostile reception, which turns even less friendly when he announces that he's come to try and discover the identity of his father. In spite of an emotional reunion with his mother (Leachman), she refuses to divulge his father's name, and as Howard continues his search alone, he begins to uncover a nest of vampires in his birthplace. Meanwhile the community is startled by the brutal unsolved slayings of four men.

The movie is aided by a strong cast which includes Neal as Howard's aunt, Dahl as her daughter (in fact, her daughter in real life) and Darin, in his last starring role before dying in December 1973 following open-heart surgery, and Lassally's striking photography of the Nova Scotia locations.

d/p Darren McGavin *s* Robert Clouse *c* Walter Lassally *lp* Patricia Neal, Cloris Leachman, Bobby Darin, Tessa Dahl, Ron Howard, Kathi Browne, Joe Mascolo, Simon Oakland, Thayer David, Gale Garnett

Hex (FOX) 93min
A curious off-beat movie, *Hex* crosses elements of the bike film with those of the post-western and the supernatural tale. Set in Nebraska in 1919, the picture starts with the arrival in a small town of a six early motorcyclists, who claim to be making their way to California. Ill feeling develops, and the group take refuge at a farm run by two sisters (Herazo and Thompson). When one of the bikers (Busey) attempts to rape Thompson, Herazo conjures up powers inherited from her Indian father, causing Busey to be savaged to death by an owl. After the girlfriend (Cook) of the group's leader (Carradine) becomes jealous of Herazo, she is also killed by a spell. Further deaths (Glenn, Walker) ensue, before an ambiguously happy ending, in which one of the two remaining cyclists (Combs) opts to stay with Thompson, while Herazo heads for a new life with an understandably bemused Carradine. The film scarcely succeeds in welding its disparate components together, but still makes a distinctive, atmospheric impression. The story credit is shared by Vernon Zimmerman, who went on to direct **Fade to Black** (1980).

d/co-s Leo Garen *p* Clark Paylow *co-s* Steve Katz *c* Charles Rosher Jnr *lp* Keith Carradine, Tina Herazo, Hilarie Thompson, Mike Combs, Scott Glenn, Gary Busey, Robert Walker, Doria Cook, Dan Haggerty, Iggie Wolfington

Horror Hospital *aka* **Computer Killers**
(NOTEWORTHY FILMS; GB) 91(88)min
Eccentric independent distributor Balch, a former collaborator with William S. Burroughs, had parodied sexploitation quickies in his *Secrets of Sex* (1970), and managed to combine parody with black humour while avoiding campness. This film repeats that same tightrope act in its story of a songwriter fed up with the music scene who goes for a rest at the health clinic of Dr Storm (Gough). The narrative unfolds around a series of setpieces: a decapitation, taps running with blood, experimental lobotomies, and so on, and the cast of clinic's inmates is unusually broad – a cripple, a dwarf, a gang of bike boys, a former brothel keeper and the generically inevitable prowling monster, subsequently revealed to be the disfigured doctor himself. Balch's direction plays the genre's conventions to the hilt, even pushing them beyond their usual limits into the realm of macabre gore movies, anticipating the visceral 'nasties' of the late seventies, and his characters are stereotypes, to be relished for their sheer outrageousness. The sheer vitality of the enterprise, however, ensures that the film's low budget and inherent predictability don't cause it to drown in the drab mediocrity that characterizes the work of, say, Pete Walker or Norman J. Warren.

d/co-s Antony Balch *p* Richard Gordon *co-s* Alan Watson *c* David McDonald *lp* Michael Gough, Robin Askwith, Vanessa Shaw, Ellen Pollock, Skip Martin, Dennis Price, Kurt Christian, Kenneth Benda, Barbara Wendy

The House in Nightmare Park *aka* **Nightmare Park**
(ASSOCIATED LONDON FILMS/EXTONATION; GB) 95min
Howerd's vaudeville comedy requires the giggling complicity of a live audience. On film, the limits of his range as a comic actor are painfully obvious, making him a buffoon instead of a comic, a pitfall Bob Hope skilfully managed to avoid in his **The Cat and the Canary** (1939), the model for Sykes' film. In 1907, a ham actor (Howerd) is invited to perform in an eerie stately home and discovers he is the heir to the family fortune while

corpses pile up around him. With **Demons of the Mind** (1971) Sykes had shown himself an interesting director but here, in spite of laudable and noticeable efforts to lift the picture by playing some scenes for genuine suspense and excitement, Howerd's dogged staginess remained an insuperable handicap.

d Peter Sykes *p/s* Clive Exton, Terry Nation *c* Ian Wilson *lp* Frankie Howerd, Ray Milland, Hugh Burden, Kenneth Griffith, John Bennett, Rosalie Crutchley, Ruth Dunning, Elizabeth MacLennan, Aimee Delamain, Peter Munt

Inki

(BAYERISCHER RUNDFUNK/BARBARA MOORSE WORKSHOP; WG) b/w 93min

In this feature adapted from a story by Ludovico Maria Sinistra, American expatriate Moorse rehearses the standard clichés of a sensitive woman (Bender) who feels alienated, becomes schizophrenic and fantasizes a macho male called Inki into existence. When Inki (Waldron – who had appeared as a brutish stud in *Flesh*, 1968) beats her up, she turns on the people who mistakenly try to help her through her crisis and affirms her autonomy by killing them. She ends up toasting herself and presumably her 'dream-lover'-persecutor with champagne. The infantile script turns the picture into a pubertal *angst* fantasy, assuming young women must be hypersensitive creatures but, being women, must also hanker after big bad wolf-men and the awkward, relentlessly meaningful acting and photography do nothing to lift the film.

d/s George Moorse *p* Barbara Moorse *c* Gerard Vandenberg *lp* Angelika Bender, Dieter Schidor, Louis Waldron, Alexander McDonald

The Legend of Hell House

(ACADEMY PICTURES; GB) 94min

Matheson's disappointing adaptation of his own novel, *Hell House*, concerns the corpse (Gough) of a mad millionaire which generates evil forces from his tomb in the walls of his mansion's chapel. During his life he had indulged in painful perversions that included the amputation of his own limbs in order to replace them with artificial ones endowing him with a more imposing stature. The hauntings are investigated by psychics, most of whom die in the process. A physicist (Revill), his wife (Hunnicutt), a medium (Franklin) and the sole survivor of a previous investigation (McDowall) are handsomely paid to try and resolve the house's secret once more. After the routine manifestations of telekinesis, apparitions and so on – including the deaths of the physicist and the medium – the owner's corpse is discovered in its leaden mausoleum.

Hough had shown himself a capable genre director with **Twins of Evil** (1971) but in spite of some atmospheric sequences, the film doesn't overcome the script's failure to establish the necessary conflict between science and occultism, relying instead on a mechanical succession of spectacularly staged shocks. As a result, the impact of the climactic revelations about the mad millionaire's perversions are an anticlimax because they are inadequately prepared. This picture was executive producer James H. Nicholson's first independent venture following his departure from AIP.

d John Hough *p* Albert Fennell, Norman T. Herman *s* Richard Matheson *c* Alan Hume *se* Roy Whybrow *lp* Pamela Franklin, Roddy McDowall, Clive Revill, Gayle Hunnicutt, Roland Culver, Peter Bowles, Michael Gough

The Legend of the Seven Golden Vampires

aka **Dracula and the Seven Golden Vampires** *aka* **The Seven Brothers Meet Dracula**

(HAMMER/SHAW BROTHERS; GB,HONG KONG) scope 110(89)min

When Christopher Lee refused to appear in any further Dracula pictures after **The Satanic Rites of Dracula** (1973), Forbes-Robertson took over the role for this flawed but interesting result of the marriage between Hammer and Shaw. Successful and evocative sequences such as the rising of the undead, the annihilation of Dracula's Chinese disciple, a simultaneous vampire staking and suicide, stand out amid routine and misconceived material which fails to understand the role of hand-to-hand combat in the martial arts' genre, though some fights are effectively choreographed by Liu Chia-Liang, who went on to become a prominent director of martial arts' movies himself. At times the fights achieve the familiar sense of apotheosis through pain essential to the genre, but unfortunately the tournament aspects of the fights are played for jarring realism. The combat with the vampires, in particular, fails to build progessively from level to level of struggle and the script loses any sense of direction, faltering over the simplest sequences. Cushing is unflappable in the Van Helsing role, here tracking his old adversary to a village in China where he links up with his Chinese opposite number, played by Shaw veteran Chiang, in the double role of Hsu Tien-an, the old man who destroyed the seventh vampire and his son, Hsu Ching. Finally, Cushing confronts Dracula alone.

Baker's direction fails to make anything of the differences between the filmic traditions that fed Hammer's gothic style and the Shaw brothers' choreographed martial adventures, attempting instead to meld them together. With a more inspired approach, this picture might have opened up a vast new thematic as well as stylistic range for horror films.

Chiang had just set up his own production company but he returned to Shaw for this one-off project to help the Hong Kong studio's effort to exploit the success of Bruce Lee's films in the West.

d Roy Ward Baker *co-p/s* Don Houghton *co-p* Vee King Shaw *c* John Wilcox, Roy Ford *se* Les Bowie *lp* Peter Cushing, David Chiang, Julie Ege, Shih Szu, Robin Stewart, Robert Hanna, John Forbes-Robertson, Chan Shen, James Ma

Roddy McDowall in danger in the over-rated The Legend of Hell House.

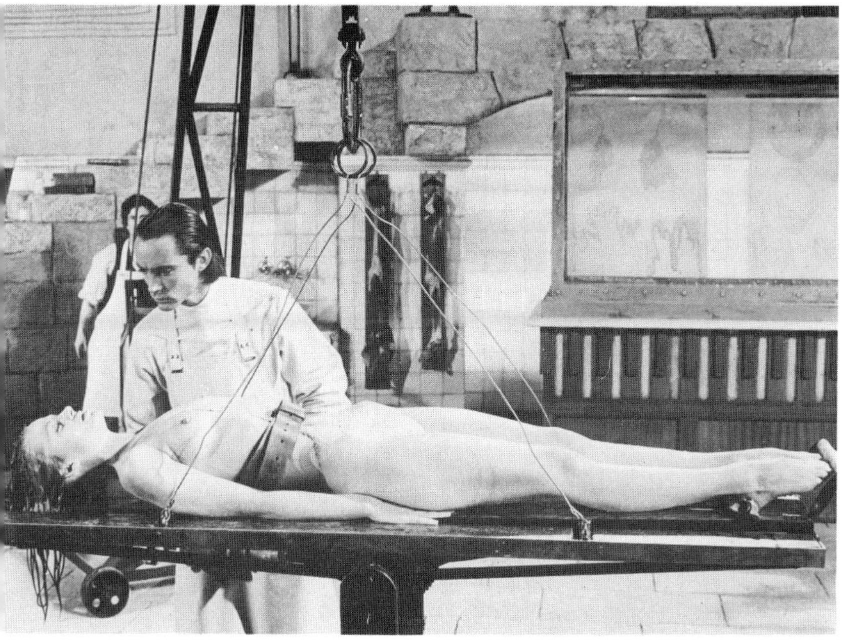

Udo Kier inspects his latest creation in Il Mostro E in Tavola... Barone Frankenstein.

The Legendary Curse of Lemora *aka* Lemora – Lady Dracula *aka* Lemora – A Child's Tale of the Supernatural

(BLACKFERN) 90min

In rural America in the 1920s Lila (Smith), the 13-year-old daughter of fugitive gangster Alvin Lee (Whitton) is living with the puritanical Reverend Mueller (Blackburn) when she receives a mysterious letter from a woman named Lemora (Gilb) who tells her that her father is staying with her and is close to death. On her way to visit him, she is menaced by various subhuman creatures (in fact, members of a coven of the undead) and when she arrives Gilb attempts to initiate her into the delights of vampirism.

An interesting addition to the vampire subgenre, *Lemora* is nothing less than a subversive fairytale for adults, a cross between *Daughters of Darkness* (1971) and *Valerie and Her Week of Wonders* (1970) leavened with a fierce anti-Catholicism that recalls not only **Communion** (1976) but also the works of Luis Buñuel (and which won it a condemned rating from the Catholic Film Board in the United States). Although the scenes with Lemora's forest-dwelling zombies are fairly gruesome, the film is, above all, a work of oneiric suggestion and (incidentally) considerable eroticism which details in a most imaginative fashion and with scant regard for conventional ethics the sentimental/sensual education of a young girl. Particularly impressive is the way in which Blackburn's elaborate yet meticulous *mise-en-scène* captures the essential amorality and mysteriousness of the world of childhood. Blackburn later went on to co-write *Eating Raoul* (1982), another amoral tale.

d/co-s Richard Blackburn *p/co-s* Robert Fern *c* Robert Caramico *se* Byrd Holland *lp* Lesley Gilb, Cheryl Smith, William Whitton, Steve Johnson, Hy Pyke, Maxine Ballantyne, Parker West, Richard Blackburn, Charla Hall, John Drury

La Morte negli Occhi del Gatto *aka* Corringa *aka* Seven Dead in the Cat's Eyes

(STARKISS-FALCON INTERNATIONAL/CAPITOL FILMS/ROXY FILM; IT,FR,WG) scope 96(93)min

Margheriti, once a promising imitator of Mario Bava with **La Danza Macabra** (1964) and **I Lunghi Capelli della Morte** (1965), was on familiar terrain with this horror-thriller set in a sinister old castle with endless corridors, dank subterranean vaults with rotting corpses eaten by rats and surrounded by a foggy cemetery. The plot concerns an ancient curse that suggests the castle's matriarch changes into a giant cat, and has a group of relatives after an inheritance gather in the ominous setting. In spite of plenty of gore, including seven murders, the tale refuses to get off the ground and looks like an Edgar Wallace thriller enhanced by gothic imagery. European scandal-sheet couple Gainsbourg – as the detective on duty – and Birkin (better known for their sexy pop songs) try their best but both are overshadowed by the hammy performance of veteran villain Diffring as a malevolent doctor. Margheriti's direction looks tired as he goes through the appropriate routines without conviction and allows even the action scenes to fall flat, with the only atmospherics generated by Riz Ortolani's score.

Margheriti's next major contributions to the genre were a collaboration with ex-Warhol acolyte Paul Morrissey, **Il Mostro E in Tavola ... Barone Frankenstein**, and **Dracula Cerca Sangue di Vergine e Mori di Sete** (both 1973).

d/co-s Anthony Dawson (Antonio Margheriti) *co-s* Giovanni Simonelli *c* Carlo Carlini *lp* Jane Birkin, Serge Gainsbourg, Anton Diffring, Venantino Venantini, Françoise Christophe, Hiram Keller, Dana Ghia

Il Mostro E in Tavola ... Barone Frankenstein *aka* Carne per Frankenstein *aka* Flesh for Frankenstein *aka* Andy Warhol's Frankenstein *aka* Frankenstein *aka* The Frankenstein Experiment *aka* Warhol's Frankenstein *aka* Up Frankenstein *aka* The Devil and Dr Frankenstein

(CC CHAMPION/CARLO PONTI-JEAN YANNE-JEAN PIERRE RASSAM PRODUCTION; IT,FR) 95(87)min

Anglo-Saxon sources credit ex-Warhol associate Morrissey as director of both this picture and its companion piece featuring Kier as Dracula (**Dracula Cerca Sangue**, 1973) but, according to Italian sources Margheriti directed both pictures with Morrissey providing scripts and a 'supervisory' role. Judging by the Warhol factory's cavalier attitude towards directing and the use of Warhol's name as a publicity gimmick, the Italian version of the credits, with their clear implication that Morrissey's presence may have animated the picture but that it was directed by Margheriti, seems the most likely one. However, it must be admitted that there is little to choose between a declining Margheriti and a Morrissey graduating into crass commercialism.

The story, devised by Morrissey, allows the actors to spin out a few lines of camp dialogue across the entire movie. The main characters, the Baron (Kier) and his moronic assistant (Jeurging), are both obsessed with disembowelling people. Around them revolve the Baron's nymphomaniac sister and lover (Van Vooren), a parody of the already parodic Neri in **La Figlia di Frankenstein** (1971), a randy shepherd (Dallesandro) and the two 'creatures' (Mancini and Zelenovic) concocted by the Baron as the start of his planned Serbian master race. The action, shot in Arch Oboler's Spacevision process to achieve acceptable 3-D effects of gushing entrails, consists mostly of copulations and disembowellings and features tons of intestines slithering in gallons of blood, turning the movie into a slightly up-market version of the Herschell Gordon Lewis gore pictures. Highlights include the often quoted line, 'You can't say that you know life until you've fucked death in the gall bladder', and the ending as the strung-up Dallesandro, in a room littered with bits of dead bodies, sees the Baron's two children advancing towards him, scalpels at the ready. The whole movie exudes an amateurish and exploitative atmosphere, which is hypocritically masked by a tongue-in-cheek tone designed to absolve film-makers and viewers alike from blame for indulging in this cynically venal spectacle of macho brutality.

d Anthony Dawson (Antonio Margheriti) *p* Andrew Braunsberg *s* Paul Morrissey *c* Luigi Kuveiller *se* Carlo Rambaldi, Roberto Arcangeli *lp* Udo Kier, Monique Van Vooren, Joe Dallesandro, Carlo Mancini, Arno Juerging, Srdjan Zelenovic, Dalila di Lazzarro, Cristina Gaioni, Marco Liofredi, Nicoletta Elmi

1973

Los Muertos, la Carne y el Diablo *aka* The Dead, the Devil and the Flesh

(OLIVEIRA FILMS; SP) 87min

Apparently undeterred by the failure of **Las Flores del Miedo** (1972), Oliveira went on to produce this anxiety-ridden picture which exudes both fear of women and self-pity. A novelist (Estrada) cannot persuade his free-thinking wife (Wright) to share his conversion to catholicism. Predictably, she pays the price for her ungodly insistence on sexual autonomy and is murdered by her lover. When one night the writer seeks shelter in a monastery, his wife's ghost appears and taunts him with her apparently enjoyable evil sexual ways. The victimized artist perishes during his attempt to confront the demonic woman, succumbing to her malevolent power. Although the script is weak, the movie manages to convey the feelings of religious bigotry and sin with a fair degree of conviction.

d/s José Maria Oliveira *p* José Lopez Moreno *c* Francisco Fraile *lp* Carlos Estrada, Patricia Wright, Emiliano Redondo, Milo Quesada, Adriano Dominguez, Manuel de Blas, Max Heatherley, Dennis Vaughan, José Maria Blanco, Antonio Mayans

The Night God Screamed *aka* Scream

(LASKY-CARLIN) 85(80)min

Unfortunately, the great title of this film hides an indifferent movie about a group of fanatical Jesus freaks (led by Sugich) who strike a blow against 'commercialized' religion by crucifying a preacher (Nicol). With Sugich and two followers sentenced to death on evidence furnished by the preacher's widow (Crain), the latter is tricked – with tragic consequences – by bored teenagers into thinking she is the victim of a bloody revenge plan. Then the real night of vengeance starts. No Joan Crawford, Crain has difficulty sustaining interest in a role which chiefly requires her to maintain a state of terror while being assaulted by a non-stop bag of horrors. The film in any case is a hoary old collection of grinning skull masks, rattling doorknobs, unseen presences and bloody stabbings, not made any more palatable by its opportunistic reminders of the Manson murders.

d Lee Madden *co-p* Ed Carlin *co-p/s* Gil Lasky *c* Stephen Larner *lp* Jeanne Crain, Alex Nicol, Daniel Spelling, Michael Sugich, Barbara Hancock

La Noche de los Brujos *aka* The Night of the Sorcerers

(PROFILMES/HESPERIA; SP) 95(83)min

In contrast to his successful **La Noche del Terror Ciego** (1971) and its sequels, de Ossorio also made a number of perfunctory quickies trading on a mixture of gore and sex, including **Las Garras de Lorelei** (1972) and this racist fantasy shot in Portugal but set in the African jungle. The picture opens with comic-strip blacks ripping the clothes off a white woman, putting her on an altar and chopping off her head in a sorcery ritual dedicated to a demonic leopard god, only for the British army to arrive and massacre all the blacks, whereupon the woman's severed head comes alive again and screams. The film's actual plot has an expedition venture into the area a few years later and one of its members (Tovar) come across a group of vampiric witches dressed in leopard-skin bikinis. It emerges that they are the victims of previous ritual decapitations who come to life again in the night. Graphic violence and plentiful soft-core sex cannot relieve the tedium as guide Andreu and mestizo woman Hansa escape the routine slaughter.

d/s Amando de Ossorio *p* José Antonio Perez Giner, Luis Laso Moreno *c* Francisco Sanchez *lp* Simon Andreu, Jack Taylor, Lorena Tower (Loretta Tovar), Maria Kosti, Kali Hansa, Joseph (José) Thelman, Barbara King

Los Ojos Azules de la Muñeca Rota *aka* The Blue Eyes of the Broken Doll *aka* House of the Psychotic Women *aka* House of Doom

(PROFILMES; SP) 91(85)min

Aured's fourth film with Molina (after **El Espanto Surge de la Tumba**, 1972; **El Retorno de Walpurgis** and **La Venganza de la Momia**, both 1973) features the podgy ex-weightlifter in one of his few non-monster roles of the period. An ex-convict, he is employed by three mad sisters in an eerie house on top of a hill. Lorys suffers from erotomania and seems intent on exhausting him sexually; Leon has a synthetic hand and Perschy appears to be confined to a wheelchair, which, according to the rules of the genre (à la **Psychopath**, 1965, for example, or **Sexy Cat**, 1972) means that she's a mad murderess. Numerous corpses of blue-eyed, blonde, young women, heads severed and eyes gouged out, litter the story. Made on a shoestring, Aured plays the explicit gore and sex angles for all they are worth, endlessly repeating the women-in-peril motif and throwing in the slaughter of a pig for good measure.

A comparison between this movie and, say, Mario Bava's **Sei Donne per l'Assassino** (1964) shows clearly the difference between a fantasy engaging with the murky substrata of male desire for cinema and a hypocritical use of sadism to cover up a petrifying fear of women.

d Carlos Aured *p* José Antonio Perez Giner *s* Jack (Jacinto) Molina *c* Francisco Sanchez *lp* Paul Naschy (Jacinto Molina), Diana Lorys, Maria Perschy, Eva Leon, Eduardo Calvo, Ines Morales, Antonio Pica, Luis Ciges

Patayin Mo Sa Sindak si Barbara *aka* Kill Barbara with Panic

(ROSAS PRODUCTIONS; PHIL) 96min

Like Gerardo de Leon's **Curse of the Vampires** (1970), Castillo's picture writes large what most Western fantasy movies wrap up in various disguises. In this demonic-possession story devised by the director, religious paraphernalia are largely dispensed to allow for a less contorted treatment of hysteria and to more clearly designate the central dynamic of the neuroses at stake in this type of fantasy scenario: sexual jealousy which is, precisely, a matter of possessiveness.

A young woman commits suicide after vowing revenge against her unfaithful husband (Rivero) and his lover (Roces). The rest of the movie chronicles the ghost's chilling, often gorily physical, persecution of her victims. Although unevenly scripted with wordy and overly sentimental passages, the *mise-en-scène* of the action is effective and easily matches **The Exorcist** (1973) while the movie's approach to the motif of possession is far more intelligent than William Friedkin's.

Castillo is one of the Filipino cinema's most interesting characters. Originally a writer of comic strips, he initiated the 'bomb' genre – the Philippine equivalent of Italy's giallo movies – with the controversial *Nympha* (1970), which ended

Left: *Eva Leon offers a helping hand in* Los Ojos Azules de la Muñeca Rota.

Lana Turner in Persecution.

with a nauseatingly graphic depiction of a backstreet abortion and intercut a prayer scene with a lovemaking one, the heroine achieving absolution exactly when the lovers outside her window achieve their climax. He essayed various genres and eventually received international recognition with *Burlesk Queen* (1977), which was acknowledged as the best Filipino film of that year.

d Celso ad Castillo *s* Mike Makiling *c* Ricardo Remias *lp* Susan Roces, Dante Rivero, Rosanna Ortiz

Persecution *aka* **The Terror of Sheba**
(TYBURN; GB) 96(92)min
Following in the footsteps of Bette Davis and Joan Crawford, Turner has a go at playing a demented mother in this, Tyburn's first production. Having been crippled by her husband (Allen) for an affair with Howard, which resulted in a son (Bates), Turner kills her husband and mistreats her son, as a result of which the boy kills his pet cat. As an adult, Bates marries Janie (Farmer), but their son is stifled in a cot by a cat. In addition, Turner pays a prostitute (Georges-Picot) to break up the marriage. After Farmer trips over a cat and falls to her death, Bates goes insane and, imagining he is throttling a cat, murders his mother who has just realized that it wasn't her husband who pushed her down a flight of stairs, but her lover and that she killed the wrong man.

Although Turner's presence lifts the film and Talbot's cinematography is excellent, the script is so contrived that Chaffey appears to have given up any hope of breathing life into the silly psychodrama. The direction concentrates instead on trying to suggest some feline devilishness, evoking echoes of John Gilling's **The Shadow of the Cat** (1961). Tyburn's next effort, **The Ghoul** (1974), was a slight improvement.

d Don Chaffey *p* Kevin Francis *s* Robert B. Hutton, Rosemary Wooten, Frederick Warner *c* Kenneth Talbot *lp* Lana Turner, Ralph Bates, Olga Georges-Picot, Trevor Howard, Patrick Allen, Suzanne Farmer, Mark Weavers

Plaisir à Trois *aka* **Les Inassouvies n. 2** *aka* **How to Seduce a Virgin**
(COMPTOIR FRANÇAIS DU FILM; FR) 80(64)min
The nightmarish scene of a cellar full of young women's bodies frozen in postures of terror and death, was used to great effect in Harald Reinl's **Die Schlangengrube und das Pendel** (1967) and in José Mojica Marins' **Esta Noite Encarnarei no Teu Cadaver** (1966). Franco uses the image equally well but can only build a tedious porn quickie around it. A woman, Martine (Arno) is released from an asylum and returns home to her 'museum' of petrified women. Together with her husband (Woods) she plans to add Cecile (Busselier) to the collection but she becomes the victim instead as Busselier and Woods strap her to a table and inject her with embalming fluid before leaving together on a world cruise. The hard-core version contains more and cruder zooms into women's crotches as well as endless grind and groan sequences. The film, which was shot in Portugal back to back with **La Comtesse Perverse** (1973), has none of the stylish approach of **Les Avaleuses** (1973) or **Necronomicon** (1967), for example.

d Clifford Brown (Jesús Franco) *p* Robert de Nesle *s* Jesús Franco Manera, Alain Petit *c* Gerard Brissaud *lp* Alice Arno (Marie-France Broquet), Robert Woods, Tanya Busselier, Howard Vernon, Alfred Baillou, Lina Romay

Il Plenilunio delle Vergine *aka* **Full Moon of the Virgins** *aka* **The Devil's Wedding Night** *aka* **Countess Dracula**
(VIRGINIA CINEMATOGRAFICA; IT) scope 85min
Neri, seen in all her physical splendours seducing the creature in **La Figlia di Frankenstein** (1971), again apologizes for her acting with plenty of nude scenes in this vampiric potboiler. An archaeologist (Damon) and his twin brother learn that the legendary ring of the Nibelungen is to be found in Transylvania. The less intelligent of the twins rashly travels to the local castle where he falls into the busy hands of Countess de Vries (Neri). His slightly smarter brother arrives to find his thoroughly vampirized twin residing in a coffin. The climax is provided by the (commercially convenient) legend that the ring attracts all the local virgins to the castle where they fall victim to the Countess's bloody rituals. The archaeologist destroys all the women, bringing sex and the film to an end, but not before a cadaverous hand has reached out from the grave to grab the ring deposited on the vampirized brother's tomb.

Damon, older and portlier than he was in Roger Corman's **House of Usher** (1960), bravely tries to compete with Neri's more eye-catching activities, but not even by playing two parts can he shift the focus of attention away from her, especially since the murky photography makes all but the most blatantly voyeuristic scenes almost unwatchable. One of the demonic figures, Papas, went on to play Frankenstein's creature in Mario Mancini's only feature, **Frankenstein 1980** (1973).

d Paolo Solvay (Luigi Batzella) *p/co-s* Ralph Zucker (Massimo Pupillo) *co-s* Alan M. Harris (Walter Bigari) *c* Aristide Massaccesi *lp* Sara Bay (Rosalba Neri), Mark Damon, Frances Davis (Francesca Romana Davila), Miriam Barrios (Esmeralda Barros), Stan Papps (Xiro Papas), Sergio Pislar, Stefano Oppedisano, A. Getty

El Retorno de Walpurgis *aka* **Curse of the Devil** *aka* **The Return of Walpurgis** *aka* **The Black Harvest of Countess Dracula**
(LOYUS FILMS/PRODUCCIONES ESCORPION; SP) 87(84)min
Continuing the motifs of **La Noche de Walpurgis** (1970), the seventh outing of Waldemar Daninsky (Molina) as the wolf-

man begins in ancient Hungary where the satanic Countess Elisabeth (Shepard) curses the family of the local inquisitor (Molina) as she is burned at the stake. Centuries later, Molina shoots a werewolf and reactivates the curse, invoked by a gypsy witch. A beautiful girl (Olivares) is sent to seduce and infect him with werewolf virus in a curious role reversal which exonerates the male hero whose beastly desires become a simple response to female sexual aggression. Molina then goes on the rampage during each successive full moon until his lover (Falcon), warned by Waldemar's mother figure and trusted domestic servant (Farra), plunges a dagger fashioned from a silver cross into his body, extinguishing both his lusts and his life. The original sin of sexual desire has not been liquidated however: she goes on to bear his child and the film ends as she visits her husband's grave together with the child while the full moon rises ominously behind them over the cemetery.

While it gives the werewolf legend a more catholic inflection, the movie is also bloodier, sexier and more atmospheric than Molina's previous lycanthropy films (**La Marca del Hombre Lobo**, 1967, for example). Aured, Klimovsky's assistant on *La Noche de Walpurgis*, had directed Molina before in the sadistic **El Espanto Surge de la Tumba** (1972), a better effort than his terror movie **Los Ojos Azules de la Muñeca Rota (1973).**

d Carlos Aured *p* Luis Mendez *s* Jack Moll (Jacinto Molina) *c* Frank (Francisco) Sanchez *se* Paul Percy *lp* Paul Naschy (Jacinto Molina), Faye (Fabiola) Falcon, Vinc Molina (Antonio Vidal Molina), May Oliver (Maritza Olivares), Maria Silva, Ana Farra, Eduardo Calvo, Patty Shepard, Santiago Rivero, Ines Morales

Riti Magie Nere e Segrete Orge del Trecento *aka* The Reincarnation of Isabel *aka* The Ghastly Orgies of Count Dracula *aka* The Horrible Orgies of Count Dracula *aka* Black Magic Rites – Reincarnations

(GRP; IT) scope 100(90)min

This, Polselli's most gothically and sexually sadistic horror effort, has satanic rites conducted in an ancient castle's underground vaults with the aim of reviving a witch who was killed 400 years ago. The rites involve slaughtering seven naked virgins dazed by their experiences during demonic orgies but, when the ritual is interrupted by one of the women's lovers, the satanists turn into vampires, eventually exhausting the patience of the local villagers who retaliate by crucifying, stoning and burning the witches. Hargitay, the former Mr Universe husband of Jayne Mansfield, also starred in the sadistic **Il Boia Scarlatto** (1965). Compared with Polselli's tame nudie **L'Amante del Vampire** (1960), this picture suggests that the director had finally mustered the courage to let his violent sex fantasies rip but his directorial skills simply aren't good enough to translate them into good cinema: the events in the vaults are stagy and the acting remains awkwardly amateurish. Shot in 1973, the movie wasn't released until 1976.

d/s Ralph Brown (Renato Polselli) *c* Ugo Brunelli *lp* Mickey Hargitay, Rita Calderon, Max Dorian, Consolata Moschera, Marcello Bonini, W. Darni

The Satanic Rites of Dracula *aka* Count Dracula and his Vampire Bride *aka* Dracula Is Dead ... and Well and Living in London

(HAMMER; GB) 87min

The team responsible for the unfortunate **Dracula AD 1972** (1972) try and fail again with this story, in which the Count (Lee) is a Howard Hughes tycoon figure living in the penthouse of a huge office block, until Van Helsing (Cushing) tracks him down. The central gimmick is that Dracula is about to spread plague throughout the world by means of a bacteriological strain developed by Dr Keeley (Jones). The plot also involves the kidnapping of Cushing's daughter (Lumley), Dracula's country house with its James Bond-like security and the climactic burning of the place while various pillars of society enslaved by the Count perish after exposure to the lethal disease.

With this film, Lee said goodbye to Hammer's Dracula series, while Cushing reprised his Van Helsing role in the odd **The Legend of the Seven Golden Vampires** (1973). Although there were some isolated attempts to rework the legend's original formulation, future Dracula movies tended to be either camp parodies or mere injections of vampirism into gore or sex movies (**Dracula Cerca Sangue di Vergine e ... Mori di Sete**, 1973; *Dracula Sucks* or **Mama Dracula**, both 1979).

The picture confirms that the Dracula myth is unsuitable to convey the anxieties attendant on the use of monopoly capitalism but is rooted in the 'unnatural' survival of feudal forces into the capitalist era. The notion that property developers or business moguls are bloodsuckers is too shallow a metaphor to sustain the complexity of the phenomenon condensed in the vampire myth, and the series died from atrophy, to be replaced by disaster movies, cannibalism and body-in-pieces fantasies such as **Frightmare** (1974) and efficient elaborations of the film-as-shock-dispenser formula typified by the work of Dario Argento after **L'Uccello dalle Piume di Cristallo** (1969).

d Alan Gibson *p* Roy Skeggs *s* Don Houghton *c* Brian Probyn *se* Les Bowie *lp* Christopher Lee, Peter Cushing, Joanna Lumley, Michael Coles, Freddie Jones, William Franklyn, Richard Vernon, Patrick Barr, Barbara Yu Ling

Scream and Die *aka* Psycho Sex Fiend *aka* The House That Vanished

(BLACKWATER FILM PRODUCTIONS; GB) 99(85)min

Spanish sexploitation director Larraz made two notable movies in the sex-and-horror subgenre, **Vampyres** and **Symptoms** (both 1974). This picture, however, in spite of a few arty echoes

Below: *The silly* The Satanic Rites of Dracula.

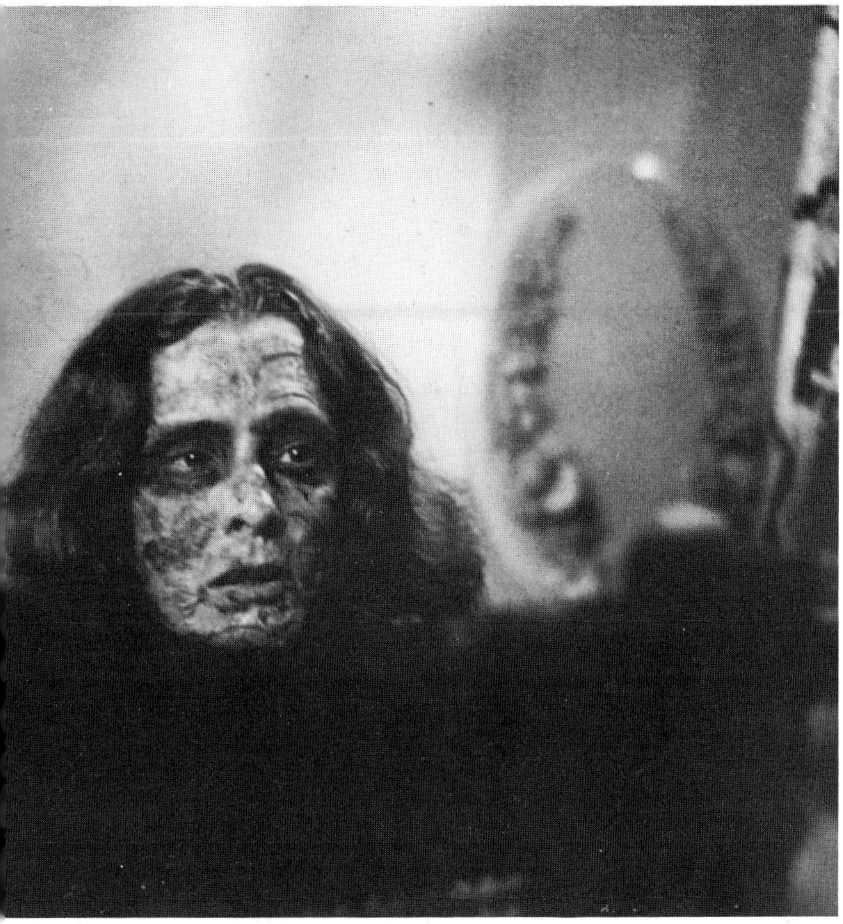

Anne Meachum disfigured in Seizure.

of Joseph Losey, is just another sexploitation effort. Women are shown making love, getting out of bed or into the bath, and the same tawdry approach is applied to the psycho-killer, shown only as a man in a black coat and black leather gloves. The woman in peril is Allan, the sexy Matheson is the victim of rape and murder and the villain, predictably the 'sweetest' of boyfriends up to the climax of the picture, is Lanchbury, a young man kept under the domineering thumb of his aunt. In the end, urged to kill Allan by his jealously possesive aunt (Walker), he turns on her instead, getting in a few stabs before the police arrive. The absurdest of red herrings is provided by a neighbour who wears a black coat and gloves even indoors. The only truly effective scenes are those with a collection of birds kept in the basement, their fluttering wings nightmarishly intruding upon the heroine's dreams.

d Joseph (José Ramon) Larraz *p* Diana Daubeney *s* Derek Ford *s* Trevor Wrenn *lp* Andrea Allan, Karl Lanchbury, Maggie Walker, Peter Forbes-Robertson, Judy Matheson, Annabella Wood, Alex Leppard, Lawrence Keane, Daphne Lea

Scream, Blacula, Scream
(AMERICAN INTERNATIONAL) 96min
A sequel to **Blacula** (1972) by the director of **Count Yorga, Vampire** (1970), which, in common with both films, sets down a latterday vampire in modern America. This time round, the bones of Blacula (again played by Marshall) are found by an adherent (Lawson) of an American voodoo society. The latter is duly vampirized and becomes Blacula's slave. Subsequently, leaving a trail of victims behind him, Blacula becomes fixated upon a woman (Grier) whom he believes will help him restore peace to his soul. This is to be achieved during a voodoo ceremony, but the ceremony is interrupted by the police and after a wild affray, Grier dispatches Blacula by the novel means of driving a stake into a voodoo doll replica of him. This and a few other moments of invention (the narcissistic Lawson is horrified to find that as a vampire he can no longer admire himself in the mirror) are not enough to offset a prevailing air of threadbare conventionality.

d Bob Kelljan *p* Joseph T. Naar *s* Joan Torres, Raymond Koenig, Maurice Jules *c* Isidore Mankofsky *se* Jack de Bron *lp* William Marshall, Pam Grier, Michael Conrad, Don Mitchell, Richard Lawson, Lynne Moody, Bernie Hamilton, Barbara Rhoades, Beverly Gill, Don Blackman

Seizure (INTERCONTINENTAL INDUSTRIES/ QUEEN OF EVIL; CAN) 94min
The first feature by the future scriptwriter of *Midnight Express* (1978) and director of **The Hand** (1981), this is a half-baked hotch-potch of ideas borrowed from a dozen other movies which looks a little like a malevolent segment from TV's *Fantasy Island*. Frid plays a writer specializing in supernatural themes who invites six weekend guests, announcing (after himself being frightened by a face at the window and the death of his dog) that he has dreamed that they are to be joined by three figments of his imagination. These materialize (from the novel he is working on) as the Queen of Evil (Beswick), a giant black executioner (Baker), and an evil dwarf (Villechaize), inaugurating a series of games, contests and conflicts. With each guest in turn having met a horrible fate and Frid himself threatened through his family, he wakes to find it was all a nightmare – but a nightmare that is continuing in reality (as in **Dead of Night**, 1945), and he dies of a heart attack. The script appears to be straining to say something about the creative imagination, but exactly what never emerges from the indifferently staged muddle which is distinguished only by Frid's performance.

d/co-s Oliver Stone *p* Garrard Glenn, Jeffrey Kapelman *co-s* Edward Mann *c* Roger Racine *lp* Jonathan Frid, Martine Beswick, Joe Sirola, Christina Pickles, Hervé Villechaize, Troy Donahue, Henry Baker, Anne Meachum

The Severed Arm
(MEDIA CINEMA/MEDIA TREND) 92(83)min
Trapped for two weeks by a rock fall, a group of six amateur pot-holers decide that only cannibalism can save them and draw lots to decide who will begin by donating an arm. Dennis loses, but almost immediately the operation is over, help arrives. He vows revenge, and five years later the original group members start to meet violent deaths. Despite a final promising launch into Grand Guignol of the **What Ever Happened to Baby Jane?** (1962) variety, *The Severed Arm* is a fairly average post-**Psycho** (1960) pre-**Halloween** (1978) vengeful-maniac-on-the-loose movie distinguished only by a relatively high level of gore for the period.

d/co-s Thomas S. Alderman *p* Gary Adelman *co-s* Darrel Presnell, Larry Alexander, Marc B. Rand *c* Bob Maxwell *se* Martin Varno *lp* Deborah Walley, Paul Carr, David G. Cannon, Vincent Martorano, Roy Dennis, Marvin Kaplan, John Crawford, Bob Guthrie, George Dann

Silent Night Bloody Night *aka* **Night of the Dark Full Moon** *aka* **Death House**
(CANNON) 88min
This convoluted, atmospheric and (at times) extremely gruesome movie features O'Neal as a lawyer who arrives in a small town to sell his client's house for a knockdown sum to the town council. O'Neal and his girlfriend spend the night in the house, once an asylum, and are killed. It emerges that when the original owner of the asylum found that the doctors were little better than the inmates, he released all the patients who, after initially going on the rampage, settled down and are now the town's citizens. The events of the past, however, are still not fully played out, and the ex-inmates are picked off one by one by an unseen hand. The flashbacks to the asylum's history are played out by underground movie alumni Ondine, Smith, Brown and Darling.

d/co-s Theodore Gershuny *co-p/co-s* Jeffrey Konvitz *co-p* Amy Artzi *co-s* Ira Teller *c* Adam Giffard *lp* Patrick O'Neal, John Carradine, Walter Abel, James Patterson, Mary Woronov, Astrid Herren, Candy Darling, Ondine, Tally Brown, Jack Smith

Tales That Witness Madness

(WORLD FILM SERVICES; GB) 90min

After **Asylum** (1972), Roy Ward Baker's contribution to the long-running series of Amicus omnibus movies, Francis made this black comedy using the same format and setting. In the framing narrative, psychiatrist Pleasance tries to convince a sceptical Hawkins (in his final screen appearance and dubbed by Charles Gray) of a new theory. This involves recounting the case histories of four of the asylum's inmates. *Mr Tiger* is about a boy (Lewis) who gets an invisible tiger to kill his bickering parents, Brown and Houston. *Penny Farthing* features antique dealer McEnery who gets propelled into the past by a spinning bicycle wheel and, under the quizzical eye of his Uncle Albert's (Forsyth) ever-changing portrait, causes the death of his lover (Kendall). *Mel* is the name of a living tree acquired by Jayston and hated by his wife (Collins). In a nice twist ending to the tale, the tree disposes of Collins. *Luau* stars Novak – who replaced Rita Hayworth shortly after production started – as the literary agent of a diabolical author (Petrovich) who uses her precocious daughter (Tamm) as a sacrifice to revive his dead mother (Segal). The episode culminates in a Hawaiian feast at which the guests unwittingly consume human flesh. The picture closes with Pleasance being locked up and Hawkins being mauled by an invisible tiger.

The script – by actress Jayne – avoids farce and develops a nicely deadpan style of humour which is ably sustained by the excellent cast in which only Novak appears unable to hit the right note.

d Freddie Francis *p* Norman Priggen *s* Jay Fairbank (Jennifer Jayne) *c* Norman Warwick *lp* Donald Pleasance, Jack Hawkins; Russell Lewis, Georgia Brown, Donald Houston; Suzy Kendall, Peter McEnery, Frank Forsyth, Beth Morris; Michael Jayston, Joan Collins; Kim Novak, Michael Petrovich, Mary Tamm, Zohra Segal, Lesley Nunnerley

Terror Circus *aka* Barn of the Naked Dead

(CMC-PACIFIC) 86min

A young man whose mother deserted him as a child captures young women and chains them up in his barn, treating them like animals and training them to take part in a bizarre circus act which he dreams of producing. They also fall victim to his father who has been turned into a rampaging monster by H-bomb testing in the surrounding desert. Apart from the potential anti-nuke note, *Terror Circus* is surprisingly gross for the time: considering its low budget the special effects are occasionally quite striking. Director Rudolph later became the most interesting of Robert Altman's many protégés.

d Alan Rudolph *p* Gerald Cormier *s* Roman Valenti *c* E. Lynn *se* Byrd Holland, Douglas White *lp* Andrew Prine, Manuella Theiss, Sherry Alberoni, Gyl Roland, Al Cormier, Chuck Niles, Gil Lamb, Sheila Bromley

Terror in the Wax Museum

(BING CROSBY PRODUCTIONS/FENADY ASSOCIATES) 94min

In Victorian London the night before Claude Dupree (Carradine) is due to sell his waxworks exhibition of notorious murderers to New York showman Amos Burns (Crawford), he is apparently murdered by his model of Jack the Ripper. Before Carradine's niece (Shelby) and her guardian (Lanchester) can complete the deal with Crawford, he too is found murdered with one of the museum's weapons. The killer is revealed to be Hayward who runs the pub next door and, knowing that Carradine's fortune is hidden among the exhibits, is attempting to stop the exhibition leaving the country. Milland is the museum's manager and sculptor.

The imaginative story idea and an excellent cast (including Carradine in what he claims to be his 415th film! – 250 is a more likely number) is wasted by poor and unimaginative direction and writing, although both the score and the production design are excellent. Particularly aggravating in some scenes is the 'models' inability to stand still!

d George Fenady *p/co-s* Andrew J. Fenady *co-s* Jameson Brewer *c* William Jurgenson *lp* Ray Milland, Elsa Lanchester, Broderick Crawford, Maurice Evans, John Carradine, Nicole Shelby, Louis Hayward, Shani Wallis, Patric Knowles, Mark W. Edwards, Lisa Lu

Theatre of Blood *aka* Much Ado About Murder

(CINEMAN; GB) 104(102)min

A supposed dead Shakespearian actor (Price) returns to take lethal revenge on eight members of the Critics' Circle who denied him the Best Actor Award and arranges the murders so that they correspond to the plays in which his performances were slated. He claims a pound of flesh from Andrews, saws off Lowe's head, makes Hawkins kill his own wife, arranges a fencing duel with Hendry and then threatens to blind him unless he hands over the coveted prize in a deserted church, a place to which he is enticed by Price's devoted daughter (Rigg). Replaying motifs from **The Abominable Dr Phibes** (1971), the film is notable chiefly for offering Price a role which enables him to give full reign to his particularly gothic style of acting. In fact, Price's virtuosity lends the demented actor a dignity missing from the Phibes character, while fully bearing out the critics' judgement that he is a hopeless ham whose style of performance belongs on a provincial Victorian stage. The direction skilfully exploits the possibilities of the mobile camera to avoid theatricality. The sequence in which a crowd of crazed meths drinkers round on their hapless victim, in particular, is an effective piece of Grand Guignol, as are some of the more outlandish executions. The plot soon begins to take second place to the spectacle of the excellent cast going through its paces on the basis of a decidedly over-the-top script. The gore is suitably grotesque and the film includes a nicely irreverent scene for English dog lovers: Price kills Morley by forcing him to eat his pet poodles – only the choice of corgis could have improved the scene.

d Douglas Hickox *p* John Kohn, Stanley Mann *s* Anthony Greville-Bell *c* Wolfgang Suschitzky *lp* Vincent Price, Diana Rigg, Ian Hendry, Harry Andrews, Coral Browne, Robert Coote, Jack Hawkins, Michael Hordern, Arthur Lowe, Robert Morley

Joan Collins confronts the tree that has won her husband's affections in one of the stories in the elegant Tales That Witness Madness.

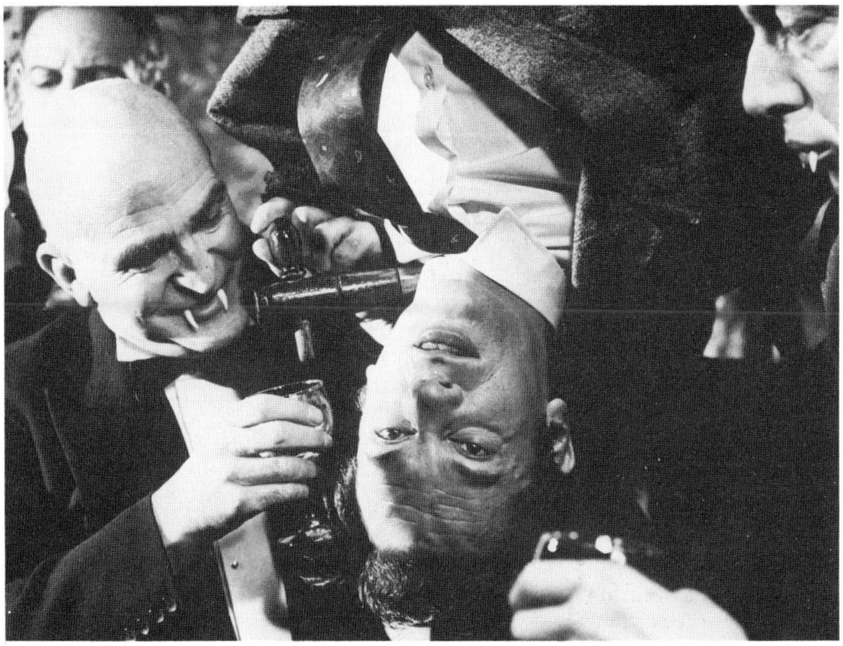

Daniel Massey finds himself on tap in the routine Vault of Horror.

La Tumba de la Isla Maldita *aka* **Vampire Woman** *aka* **Crypt of the Living Dead** *aka* **Young Hannah, Queen of the Vampires** *aka* **Vampire Women** *aka* **Hannah, Queen of the Vampires**
(ORBITA FILMS; SP) 99(83)min
The opening of the tomb of Hannah (Gimpera), the beautiful vampire bride of Louis VII, buried alive on Vampire Island after the King's return from the Crusades, leads to gruesome events. Amateur archaeologists Prine and Damon provoke the vampire's renewed thirst for blood and she proceeds to do her worst, attacking the villagers, either vampirizing them or assaulting them werewolf fashion. Damon, a frustrated artist, worships Gimpera in the ruins of her tomb until he's eliminated by the locals. Prine stakes the queen and leaves with the heroine, a schoolteacher (Shepard), but it appears that one of her pupils has been infected and is likely to continue justifying the island's reputation.

Scenes of graphic violence punctuate the movie and culminate in the images of Gimpera set alight with an oil lamp and staked with the camera chronicling in detail the disintegration of her body and face into an unsightly mess. Script and dialogue are both rudimentary, but Gimpera and Damon – who pursued a moderately successful career as an actor in Europe before becoming a producer – are credible tragic lovers. The picture was re-directed for American distribution with additional footage produced by Wolf Schmidt and Lou Shaw, and re-scripted by Shaw.

d Ray Danton *s* Julio Salvador *c* Juan Gelpi *se* Antonio Molina *lp* Andrew Prine, Mark Damon, Teresa Gimpera, Patty Shepard, Frank Braña, Daniel Martin, Ihsan Genik, Mariano Rey

Vault of Horror *aka* **Further Tales from the Crypt**
(AMICUS/METROMEDIA PRODUCERS CO; GB) 86min
Like its predecessor, **Tales from the Crypt** (1972), Amicus's sixth omnibus movie is based on the horror comics of Al Feldstein and William Gaines, banned in the fifties after a successfully orchestrated wave of moral panic and anti-American populism in Britain, even though many of the comic stories were themselves intensely critical of the McCarthy witch-hunts. However, the stories included in this collection are selected for their shock effects rather than their politics. *Midnight Mess* tells of a man (Massey) who murders his sister (Massey) and goes to dinner in a restaurant filled with vampires. He is 'unmasked' when a curtain is suddenly pulled away revealing a huge mirror in which only he is reflected. *The Neat Job* is a sketch about an obsessively fussy man (Terry-Thomas) who drives his wife (Johns) round the bend: she kills him and keeps the dissected bits of his corpse in neatly labelled jars. *This Trick'll Kill You* concerns a couple of magicians (Jurgens and Addams) who murder a rival (Hilton) to obtain a rope trick which eventually kills them. *Bargain in Death* recounts an insurance fraud gone wrong: a man (Craig) fakes death with drugs hoping his friend (Judd) will disinter him later, but he is double-crossed and a gravedigger (Mullard) accidentally 'damages' the pretend corpse's head while trying to sell it to medical students as an anatomical specimen. *Drawn and Quartered* returns to the embittered artist motif: voodoo enables a painter (Baker) to make his paintings come true. This allows him to disfigure, blind and mutilate a trio who cheated him but when someone accidentally spills turpentine on his self-portrait the painting begins to run and he is run over by a truck.

The awkwardly handled framing story has the five main protagonists trapped in a basement room. Each recounts a recurring dream which turns out to be a past experience they are condemned to relive every night since they are in fact dead and the basement is a cemetery. Whereas Francis often managed to inject some atmosphere into his Amicus omnibus movies, Baker's flat direction can't overcome the lengthy and plodding expository scenes, making this the least interesting of the series in spite of the excellent photography and Tony Curtis's pleasing sets.

d Roy Ward Baker *co-p/s* Milton Subotsky *co-p* Max J. Rosenberg *c* Denys Coop *lp* Daniel Massey, Anna Massey, Michael Pratt; Terry-Thomas, Glynis Johns, John Forbes-Robertson; Curt Jurgens, Dawn Addams, Jasmina Hilton; Michael Craig, Edward Judd, Arthur Mullard; Tom Baker, Denholm Elliott, Terence Alexander, John Witty

Una Vela Para el Diablo *aka* **A Candle for the Devil** *aka* **Nightmare Hotel** *aka* **It Happened at Nightmare Inn**
(VERGA FILMS/MERCOFILMS/VEZAFILMS; SP) 92(84)min
This picture from Martin (director of the energetic **Panico en el Transiberiano**, 1972, and the thriller **Sobrenatural**, 1980) is set in a small Spanish village, where two sisters, one (Bautista) dominant and malevolent, the other (Roy) meek, run the local hotel. Driven mad by sexual frustration, Bautista develops a religious mania which causes her to kill, with knives and meat-cleavers, those women whose morals she disapproves of. The

Right: *Nicole Shelby discovers Broderick Crawford plus sword in* Terror in the Wax Museum.

hacked up bodies are stored in urns in the hotel's basement and eventually provoke a bout of food poisoning. The investigations are conducted by a young English tourist (Geeson), in search of her sister, who is saved by the police from the axe-wielding Bautista in the nick of time. Punctuated by crudely obvious shots of boys furtively ogling girls, Bautista ogling bathing little boys, villagers ogling scantily dressed tourists, and so on, the plot's coherence as a parable about the poisonous effects of catholic bigotry, treated in the manner of a slasher movie, is pushed into the background as the conventions of the genre take over. Aguayo's camera spends too long lingering on knives, axes, and lumps of raw meat to allow the characters to develop beyond the usual stereotypes and, with the exception of the odd location shot which echoes Aguayo's work for Luis Buñuel on *Tristana* (1970) and the brave efforts of the cast, the picture remains cliché-ridden.

d/co-s Eugene (Eugenio) Martin *p* José Lopez Moreno *co-s* Antonio Fos *c* José Fernandez Aguayo *se* Pablo Perez *lp* Judy Geeson, Aurora Bautista, Esperanza Roy, Vic Winner (Victor Alcazar), Lone Fleming, Blanca Estrada, Loretta Tovar, Julia Montserrat, Fernando Hilbeck

La Venganza de la Momia *aka* **The Mummy's Vengeance** *aka* **The Mummy's Revenge** *aka* **The Vengeance of the Mummy**
(LOTUS FILMS/SARA FILMS; SP) scope 91min
After the commercial success of their collaboration on **El Espanto Surge de la Tumba** (1972), Aured and Molina made three more features: **El Retorno de Walpurgis**, **Los Ojos Azules de la Muñeca Rota** (both 1973) and this mummy picture. Like Gilling's **The Mummy's Shroud** (1966), Molina's script starts in ancient Egypt where the cruel Pharaoh Amen-Ho-Tep (Molina) and his skimpily dressed queen (Liné) slash the throats of young women to drink their blood. Mummified alive for their crimes, they are disturbed by an English Egyptologist (Taylor) and a mysterious Arab, Oseth Bey (Molina again) who revives the sadistic Pharaoh. With the mummy on the rampage, the film stumbles from one gory scene to the next, with closeups of hands and heads being crushed, women's faces slashed and throats cut until the require running time has been achieved, whereupon the Englishman burns the mummy. The capable art direction of Gumersindo Andres maximizes the movie's obviously shoestring budget, but whereas Fisher's creature, played by the imposing and ascetic figure of Lee, had been motivated by and victimized for his passionate love for a beautiful woman, Molina's stout weightlifter's physique, combined with a rapidly misogynist script, transforms the mummy into a moronic butcher.

d Carlos Aured *s* Jacinto Molina *c* Francisco Sanchez *lp* Paul Naschy (Jacinto Molina), Jack Taylor, Maria Silva, Helga Liné, Eduardo Calvo, Luis Davila, Luis Gaspar, Celia Cruz, Rina Ottolina

Vera, un Cuento Cruel (ETNOS FILMS; SP) 95min
This atmospheric adaptation of Villiers de l'Isle Adam's story marks the début of Molina, Spain's second woman director who is as talented but not as well known as Pilar Miró.

A man (Humphreys) become a recluse after the death of his young bride. In spite of help offered by a woman friend, he never leaves his domain, where his only companion is a trusted servant (Fernan Gomez) who was also deeply in love with his deceased mistress. The man's disturbed mental state begins to affect his servant who, enlisting the help of the female friend, locks his master into the dead woman's crypt and then poisons his accomplice. The short story is spun into an effective funereal moodpiece reminiscent of Roger Corman's **House of Usher** (1960). The film also marks the acting début of the two children of Lucia Bose, but it is the cinematography and Fernan Gomez's performance which sustain interest in the picture despite its thin storyline.

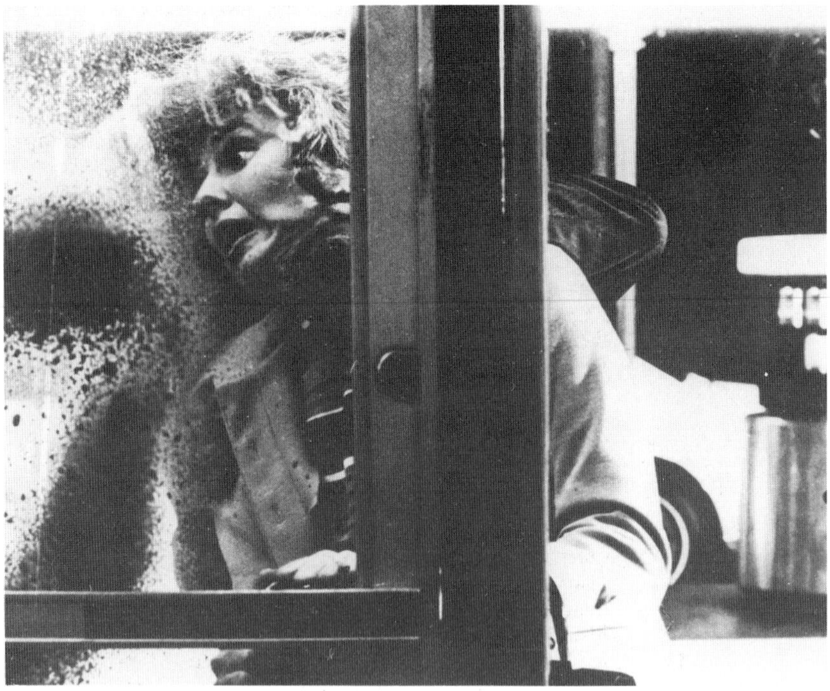

Above: *Dean Stockwell as* The Werewolf of Washington.

Molina's next feature, *Función de Noche* (1981) confirmed her potential as a major film-maker.

d/co-s Josefina Molina Roig *co-s* José Samano *c* José Luis Alcaine *lp* Mel Humphreys, Victor Valverde, Julieta Serrano, Fernando Fernan Gomez, Silvia Vivo, José Vivo, Alfredo Mayo, Luis Ciges

Voices (MORDEN PRODUCTIONS; GB) 91min
Based on a play by Richard Lotz, this ghost story never succeeds in leaving its stage origins behind. The plot turns on the mental instability of the leading female character (Hunnicutt), a woman who lost her son in a boating accident. She first attempts to kill herself and then agrees to accompany her husband (Hemmings), a writer, to an isolated and decrepit country mansion for a rest. After a near fatal crash in the fog they arrive at the house where she begins to hear the voices of a ghostly family which inhabits the place. When her husband hears them as well, he rushes out of the house while she begins to see the apparitions. In a typical twist ending which smacks of a theatrical coup, it is revealed that Hunnicutt and Hemmings are themselves the ghosts while the voices and apparitions belong to the family living in the house.

Although Billington's direction is plodding, there are some half-hearted attempts at stylishness in the bleached colours and the pale makeup, but the film remains a teleplay padded out to feature length. As usual in this type of story, a propensity towards mental instability is assumed to be a self-evident natural aspect of the female psyche.

d Kevin Billington *p/co-s* Robert Enders *co-s* George Kirgo *c* Geoffrey Unsworth *lp* Gayle Hunnicutt, David Hemmings, Lynn Farleigh, Russell Lewis, Eva Griffiths, Adam Bridge, Peggy Ann Clifford

Welcome to Arrow Beach *aka* **Tender Flesh**
(BRUT PRODUCTIONS) 99(95,84)min
After escaping from a car-crash teenage hitch-hiker Foster wanders on to deserted Arrow Beach where she meets a photographer (Harvey) who lives nearby with his sister (Pettet) and who offers her a bed for the night. Unknown to Foster, Harvey has developed a taste for human flesh as a result of having to eat three of his comrades when their bomber crashed on a deserted Pacific island during the Korean War. She manages to escape, but the police disbelieve her and she is forced to expose Harvey on her own.

An unfortunate and unfitting swan song for Harvey, *Welcome to Arrow Beach* was briefly distributed by Warner Brothers in 1973 but virtually disowned by them and the re-released in 1976 by the original producers, Brut, with 15 minutes of cuts and the exploitation title *Tender Flesh* (to make matters more confusing, the British censor cut the original too). Harvey seems strained and remote and the film's style is mainly flat and functional, punctuated by jarring jump cuts and inane inserts.

d/p Laurence Harvey *p* Jack Cushingham *s* Wallace C. Bennett, Jack Gross Jnr *c* Gerald Perry Finnerman *lp* Laurence Harvey, Joanna Pettet, Stuart Whitman, John Ireland, Meg Foster, Gloria le Roy, Dody Heath, David Macklin, Elizabeth St Clair, Robert Luccier

The Werewolf of Washington (MILLCO) 90min

This neat topical joke seized on the Watergate affair to literalize the horrors of the White House by imagining a presidential aide roaming its precincts with nefarious intent after being bitten by a werewolf during a side trip to Hungary. Apart from one excellent scene where the werewolf-aide (a superb performance from Stockwell) clambers all over an overturned telephone booth frantically scrabbling to get at the screaming victim inside, Ginsberg handles the horror motif rather drearily in a vague pastiche of the Universal style. But his script has its moments, notably a scene in which the president's daughter (House), amorously importuning Stockwell at the wrong moment (he is about to metamorphoze), imperiously cries 'Will you please not bark at me?' while he tries to lock himself into a lavatory and his despairing pleas of 'Out! Out!' tail away into a mournful canine howl. It also toys profitably with the whole notion of a political cover-up, with a po-faced psychiatrist assuring the unhappy werewolf that his secret is better kept dark ('There's no doubt the press would seize on your present tragedy to discredit the President'), and the President himself (McGuire) blandly refusing to credit the evidence of his own ears and eyes. Nonetheless, it remains essentially a one-joke film, tending to fall flat (as in the sequence involving Dunn as a mad-dwarf scientist) whenever it tries to broaden its satire.

d/s Milton Moses Ginsberg *p* Nina Schulman *c* Bob Baldwin *lp* Dean Stockwell, Biff McGuire, Clifton James, Jane House, Beeson Carroll, Michael Dunn

The inventive The Wicker Man.

The Wicker Man (BRITISH LION; GB) 102(86)min

The screenplay by Shaffer, who had previously authored *Sleuth* (1972) is the strong suit of *The Wicker Man*. Like its predecessor, it plays ingeniously upon the conventions of the mystery thriller, here inflected toward those of the Hammer horror movie – a reference confirmed by the presence of Hammer veterans Lee and Pitt. The setting, handsomely visualized by Waxman's camerawork, is a remote island on the west coast of Scotland. An upright police officer (Woodward) arrives to investigate the case of a missing child and is greeted with hostility by the peculiar locals, though one of them (Ekland) makes an open attempt to seduce him. The squire (Lee) is ostensibly helpful and speaks of the islanders' worship of the gods of nature as arising from their dependance on the soil. The detective becomes convinced that the missing girl is to be a human sacrifice at the island's May Day rites but he has been led into an elaborate trap; he, an adult male virgin, is the sacrifice the islanders had in mind, and as the film ends he is burned alive inside the island's giant 'wicker man' totem.

The film not only recapitulates, in more expansive vein, the themes of several Hammer movies of the sixties but anticipates those of several subsequent British pictures, notably **Satan's Slave** (1976). It operates, however, at a considerably more sophisticated level and must rank among the most inventive recent British contributions to the genre.

d Robin Hardy *p* Peter Snell *s* Anthony Shaffer *c* Harry Waxman *lp* Edward Woodward, Christopher Lee, Britt Ekland, Ingrid Pitt, Diane Cilento, Walter Carr, Lesley Mackie, Lindsay Kemp, Irene Sunters, Geraldine Cowper

Zaertlichkeit der Voelfe *aka* **The Tenderness of Wolves** (TANGO FILM; WG) 87min

This is a neo-expressionist rendering of the case of Fritz Haarman: a paedophiliac homosexual rapist and vampire who killed some 25 boys in pre-Hitler Germany. A professional police informer, Haarman (Raab) also sold the flesh of his victims on the black market. Made by the Fassbinder troupe and including a performance by the master himself in a suitably seedy role, the film abounds with skilfully composed tributes to **Nosferatu** (1921) and to Fritz Lang's *M* (1931). Raab's face and smile even evoke Peter Lorre while his bald head and pointed ears are a reminder of Max Schreck. The discovery of bones along a riverbank and mutilated corpses floating in the water eventually lead to Raab's capture. Excessively aetheticized images give an overwhelming and suffocating portrayal of the world of petty criminals, decadent nightlife, squalor and hunger in depression-torn Germany.

The film is a fascinating but extremely macabre poem from which some particularly gruesome but effective tableaux – the bald Raab's face as he is disturbed in a deathly orgy, his mouth smeared with blood, for example, or the low-angle shot of the vampire on the bridge, motionless between two dead trees – remain imprinted in the memory.

d Ulli Lommel *p* Rainer Werner Fassbinder *s* Kurt Raab *c* Jurgen Jorges *lp* Kurt Raab, Jeff Roden, Margit Carstensen, Wolfgang Schreck, Rainer Werner Fassbinder, Ingrid Caven

Left: L'Anticristo, *one of the many imitations of* The Exorcist *(1973).*

1974

Abby (MID-AMERICA PICTURES) 89min
Marshall, the vampire from **Blacula** (1972), turns bishop in this feeble, blasphemous blaxploitation parody of **The Exorcist** (1973). Speed is the unhappy bishop's daughter-in-law, possessed by a demon of sexuality unleashed in a backlot version of Africa before moving to Kentucky.

d/co-p William Girdler *co-p* Mike Henry *co-p/s* Gordon Cornell Layne *c* William Asman *lp* William Marshall, Carol Speed, Terry Carter, Austin Stocker, Juanita Moore

L'Anticristo *aka* **The Antichrist** *aka* **The Tempter**
(CAPITOLINA PRODUZIONI CINEMATOGRAFICHE; IT)
scope 112(96)min
Following his first horror effort, *Horror* (1963), de Martino made a series of westerns and gangster pictures before returning to the genre with this imitation of **The Exorcist** (1973). Though it has a slightly more intelligent storyline than its model, it very soon degenerates into anti-intellectual obscurantism. The young daughter (Gravina) of an Italian prince (Ferrer) is possessed by the spirit of one of the family's black sheep, a medieval ancestor burned at the stake for witchcraft. In terms of the lurid details of the demonic possession, however, the film is close to its model: there is the same vomiting of green bile, the same levitation and flying furniture. But, predictably, they are not staged with comparable resources and rely heavily on Morricone's score to achieve their effects. The climax is set in the Coliseum in Rome – the symbol of Italy's glorious heritage – with the heroine eventually being freed from the devil by embracing a large crucifix.

Coulouris plays the exorcist and it is sad to see him and such fine character actors as Valli and Kennedy wasted in supporting roles. Much of the camerawork (or the print) appears out of focus and the editing is erratic. There is also the by now familiar scene of a copulation with an invisible partner, allowing viewers direct access, unimpeded by the sight of hairy buttocks, to Gravina's body. In this respect, de Martino's movie is less hypocritical than the American film with its small-town notions of sins and thrills undermining traditional middle-class family values. His **Holocaust 2000** (1977) was an imitation of **The Omen** (1976).

d/co-s Alberto de Martino *p* Edmondo Amati *co-s* Gianfranco Clerici, Vincenzo Mannino *c* Aristide Massaccesi *lp* George Coulouris, Mel Ferrer, Carla Gravina, Arthur Kennedy, Alida Valli, Umberto Orsini, Anita Strindberg, Mario Scaccia, Ernesto Colli, Remo Girone

El Asesino de Muñecas
(HURACAN FILMS; SP) scope 103min
A classic Hispanic tale of surgical horror set in contemporary Barcelona, this film concerns the psychotic activities of a young man, Paul (Rocha), the son of the gardener who tends the grounds of a wealthy duchess's palace. Living in a strange room surrounded by dolls and mannequins, he kills courting couples who use the park and, wearing a wig and a mask, subjects them to outlandish surgical practices. The story also suggests that his pathological sexuality is the result of the duchess's hold over him – making the movie an unsavoury version of *Lady Chatterley's Lover*. Rocha tries to transfer his affections to the duchess's daughter (de Santy), but his homicidal compulsions get the better of him and the film ends with the customary conflagration. Madrid's direction, improved since his **Necrophagus** (1971), occasionally achieves some surprising effects as he chronicles the boy's necrophilia in revolting detail. It is worth mentioning that most of the female characters here remain dressed while the boyish hero has numerous nude scenes.

d/s Michael Skaife (Miguel Madrid) *p* Jacinto Ferrer Bayarri *c* Pablo Ripoll *lp* David Rocha, Inma de Santy, Helga Liné, Elisenda Ribas, Lupe Rocha, Antonio Molina, Maria Condal, Alejandro del Rio, Susana Taber, Indio Gonzalez

The Beast Must Die
(AMICUS; GB) 93min
A contrived variation on the standard country-house whodunit in which a rich eccentric (Lockhart) invites a group of guests to his mansion riddled with closed-circuit TV cameras. Each guest is connected with a strange death and one of them is thought to be a werewolf, whose unmasking is supposed to provide the host with an unusual prey for a hunting party. Taking a leaf from William Castle's book of manipulative showmanship, the film is introduced by a prologue informing the audience that they are the detectives invited to discover the identity of the werewolf on the basis of clues scattered across the picture. Towards the end, the film stops and asks the viewers whether they have succeeded before finally revealing the solution of the riddle. The script rather lazily offers clues in the guise of long treatises on werewolf folklore, wheeling on a Dr Lundgren (Cushing) for the purpose. Predictably, each guest comes under scrutiny and red herrings are liberally distributed destroying whatever echoes of **The Most Dangerous Game** (1932) the story might have afforded.

As they had shown with **Fengriffen** (1973), Amicus's talents did not lie in the area of single-plot features, even though John Stoll's art direction and the camerawork combine to offer decidedly watchable images. The original story by James Blish, *There Shall Be No Darkness*, was published in the *Witches Three* collection which also included the first publication of Fritz Leiber's *Conjure Wife*, later filmed as **Night of the Eagle** (1961).

d Paul Annett *p* Max J. Rosenberg, Milton Subotsky *s* Michael Winder *c* Jack Hildyard *se* Ted Samuels *lp* Calvin Lockhart, Peter Cushing, Charles Gray, Anton Diffring, Marlene Clark, Ciaran Madden, Tom Chadbon, Michael Gambon, Sam Mansaray, Andrew Lodge

Black Christmas
(FILM FUNDING/VISION IV/FAMOUS PLAYERS/CANADIAN FILM DEVELOPMENT CORP; CAN) 97min
This efficient horror-thriller predates **Halloween** (1978) but rehearses very similar motifs in an old-dark-house setting with

a twist: the house is the sorority house at a Canadian college, where a number of young girls are about to embark on their Christmas party ignorant of the maniac (Dullea) in the room upstairs. As usual in such plots, the maniac's activities are directed against girls/women guilty of an interest in sex, which awakens the 'uncontrollably' psychotic drives of the harmless-looking hero/madman. The mechanics of the plot are deployed with considerable skill: obscene phone calls which in the end are revealed to emerge from within the house itself; subjective camera sequences signifying the maniac on the prowl; various noises off-screen; the retreat into the basement of a girl-in-peril and the false ending where the characters are allowed to breathe a sigh of relief only find the final horror is still to come.

Kidder, with Brian de Palma's **Sisters** (1972) behind her and a wider audience for her Lois Lane in *Superman* (1978) to come, plays one of the sorority girls.

d/co-p Robert Clark *co-p* Gerry Arbeid *s* Roy Moore *c* Reginald Morris *lp* Olivia Hussey, Keir Dullea, Margot Kidder, Andrea Martin, John Saxon, Marian Waldman, Art Hindle, Lunne Griffin, James Edmond, Douglas McGrath

Blood (BRYANSTON KENT) 74min

This film starts from the interesting premise that, in 1984, the son of the wolfman marries Dracula's daughter. The pair then move to Staten Island and start to experiment with carnivorous plants.

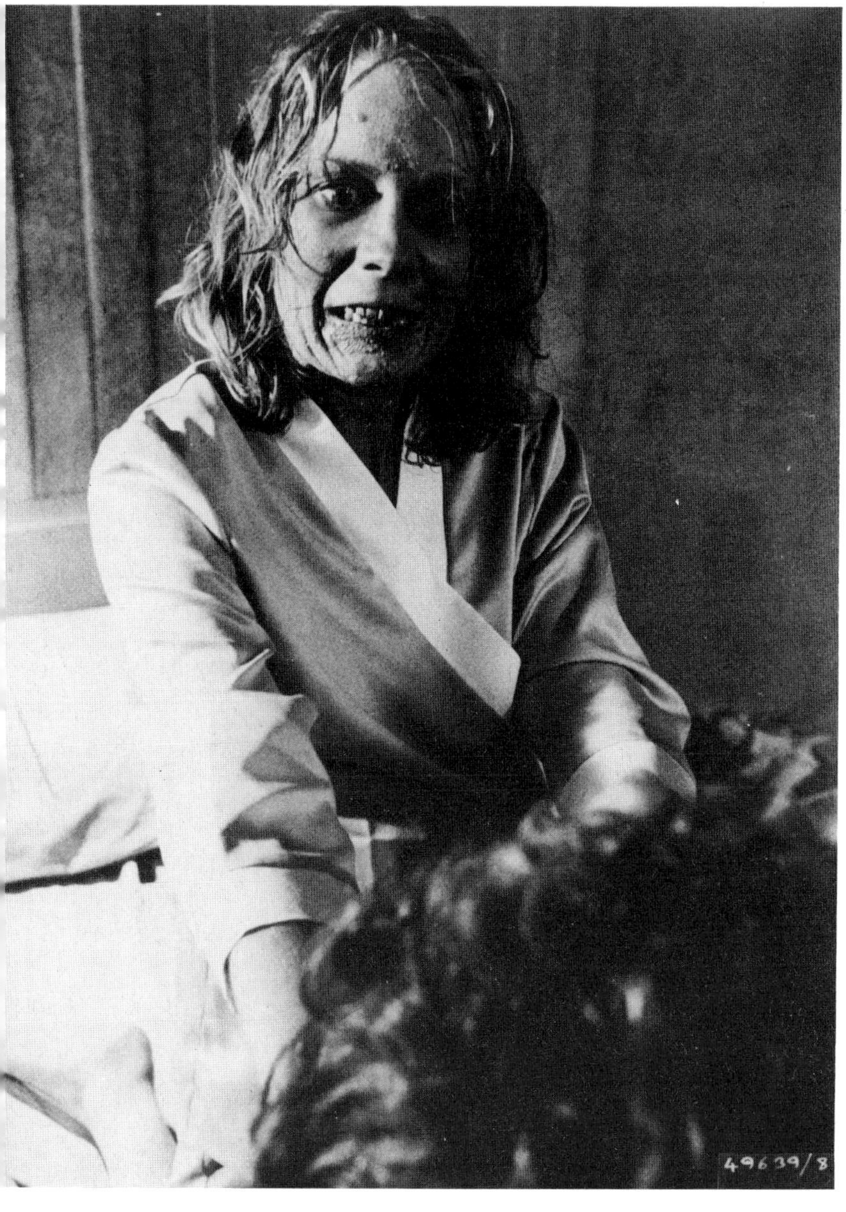

Juliet Mills in Chi Sei?, *an unimaginative combination of* Rosemary's Baby *(1968) and* The Exorcist *(1973).*

Milligan's last horror film before he moved on to pornography, shot in 10 days and costing $20,000 – an almost princely sum by Milligan standards – the film marks the end of an *oeuvre* which can justly be called '*maudit*'. Though hardly fascinating, Milligan's work is better than most reference works will allow and his horror movies do not actually fall within the sexploitation genre, as is frequently suggested. If for nothing else Milligan deserves recognition as virtually a one-man production crew – it was this that enabled him to make films on budgets that were minuscule even by Z-movie standards. He himself has said: 'I wrote my own scripts, did my own camera work, did my own stills, fitted all my own costumes and did all the sets, basically, with one or two people helping me. One person could basically do all the stuff. It wasn't ego, it was necessity.'

d/s/c Andy Milligan *p* Walter Kent *lp* Allen Berendt, Hope Stansbury, Eve Crosby, Patti Gaul, Pamela Adams

El Buque Maldito *aka* La Noche del Buque Maldito *aka* Horror of the Zombies *aka* The Ghost Galleon

(ANCLA CENTURY/BELEN FILMS; SP) 106(85)min

Foreshadowing such films as **Death Ship** (1980) and **The Fog** (1979), de Ossorio followed his successful **El Ataque de Los Muertos Sin Ojos** (1973) with this ghostly-galleon story. Investigating the disappearance of some models, three women and three men board the weird ship and find it inhabited by hooded zombies who proceed to tear the bikini-clad women to pieces before turning their attention to the men. One of the men escapes and reaches the shore, only to find the cowled figures rising from the surf and lumbering on to the beach to finish him off. The movie is capably handled and the gory action fast paced and sustained by a regular succession of professionally shot shocks. Torre de la Fuente's art direction creates an atmospheric nautical setting spoiled only by the ineptly shot burning of a model to represent a ship at sea.

While continuing to exploit the zombie wave with another blind-dead movie (**La Noche de los Gaviotas**, 1975), de Ossorio also contributed to the series of exorcism pictures with **La Endemoniada** (1974).

d/s Amando de Ossorio *c* Raul Artigot *lp* Maria Perschy, Jack Taylor, Carlos Lemos, Blanca Estrada, Barbara Rey, Manuel de Blas, Margarita Merino

Chi Sei? *aka* Beyond the Door *aka* The Devil Within Her *aka* Who?

(A. ERRE CINEMATOGRAFICA; IT) 109(100)min

In spite of the silly story and inept direction, this film was a huge success in America. The plot combines **Rosemary's Baby** (1968) with **The Exorcist** (1973) as Jessica (Mills), the wife of a record producer (Lavia) living in San Francisco, pays for an extramarital affair with a man called Dimitri (Johnson). Since Johnson is single and promiscuous, the arch-conservative fantasy makes him a satanist while Jessica's apparent inability to content herself with being a good mother leads to the expected consequences: vomiting gallons of pea soup, levitation, swearing in a deep voice, being nasty to her husband and turning her head through the obligatory 360 degrees. Beginning with a black screen and a voice-over haranguing the audience about the reality of the unseen, the film moves towards the unwatchable as Johnson energetically hammers away at Jessica's stomach in order to speed up the emergence of the child from between her legs – which, of course, such a film can't bear to show since the entire fantasy edifice is premised on the notion that female sexuality is too unbearable to contemplate. As exorcism movies go, Mario Bava's stylish **Shock (Transfer Suspense Hypnos)** (1977, which was in fact entitled *Beyond the Door II* in some territories) or even the crassly sexploitative **L'Ossessa** (1974) are infinitely preferable both to this Italian effort and to its American models, mainly because they manage to portray the links between sex and hysteria without prurient hypocrisy.

co-d/co-s Oliver Hellman (Sonia Assonitis) *co-d/co-s/c* Richard Barrett (Roberto d'Ettore Piazzoli) *p* Ovidio G. Assonitis, Giorgio C. Rossi *co-s* Antonio Troisio, Giorgio Marini Aldo Crudo *se* Donn Davison, Wally Gentleman (Gentilomo) *lp* Juliet Mills, Richard Johnson, Gabriele Lavia, Nino Segurini, Elisabeth Turner, Carla Mancini, Barbara Fiorini, David Cilin Jnr, Joan Acti, Vittorio Fanfoni

Craze *aka* **The Infernal Idol**
(HARBOR-HERMAN COHEN PRODUCTIONS; GB) 96min
A wheezing antique dealer (Palance) who dabbles in witchcraft believes that providing an idol he possesses with human sacrifices will help him stay financially solvent. As is only too common in such films, women with a semblance of sexual autonomy are automatically regarded as 'loose' and therefore legitimate targets for maniacs. Accordingly, the dealer kills two of them (Kendall and Ege) with impunity before committing the mistake of dispatching a 'decent' woman, his aunt (Evans), whereupon the police (Jayston and Howard) catch up with him. The film was made by the team responsible for **Trog** (1970).

d Freddie Francis *p/co-s* Herman Cohen *co-s* Aben Kandel (Kenneth Langtry) *c* John Wilcox *lp* Jack Palance, Diana Dors, Julie Ege, Edith Evans, Hugh Griffith, Trevor Howard, Michael Jayston, Suzy Kendall, Martin Potter

Deranged (KARR INTERNATIONAL) 82(80)min
Like **Psycho** (1960) and **The Texas Chainsaw Massacre** (1974), *Deranged* is based on the true story of the 'Wisconsin ghoul' Ed Gein (who was imprisoned for life for his crimes and died only in 1984). Though the film does not stick exactly to the facts of the case, its story of Ezra Cobb who mummifies his mother's body when she dies and then takes home other bodies to keep her company, before turning to murder and wearing the flayed skin of his victims, is true in its essentials. Annoyingly punctuated by the pontifications ('perhaps we can learn from it' and so on) of an on-screen narrator à la *Phenix City Story* (1955), the film is nonetheless an excellent and imaginative reconstruction of the private world of a maniac. Gillen and Ormsby succeed in creating a bizarre, self-contained universe in which the grossest horrors nevertheless have a certain crazy logic, thanks to Blossom's superbly serene performance as a childlike 'innocent', totally unequipped to deal with everyday life in a normal fashion. The scenes in which he tells his neighbours about his fantasies and drops hints about his activities to a generally disinterested and disbelieving audience have a blackly comic edge.

Accordingly, although the film eschews the relentless kinetic drive of Tobe Hooper's *The Texas Chainsaw Massacre*, its setpieces – a seance, a chase through the woods, and the mummified corpses around the dinner table – are as effective as anything that its slicker contemporary can offer.

co-d/co-s/co-se Alan Ormsby *co-d/co-s* Jeff Gillen *p* Tom Karr *c* Jack McGowan *co-se* Tom Savini, Jerome Bergson *lp* Roberts Blossom, Cosette Lee, Robert Warner, Marcia Diamond, Brian Sneage, Robert McHeady, Micki Moore, Pat Orr, Marion Waldman

La Endemoniada *aka* **El Poder de las Tinieblas** *aka* **Demon Witch Child**
(RICHARD FILMS; SP) 99(88)min
Released a week before Juan Bosch's **Exorcismo** (1974), this picture is also a variation on William Friedkin's blockbuster. An old woman accused of witchcraft possesses the nine-year-old daughter of the politician who imprisoned her. The child, occasionally taking on the appearance of the old hag, becomes sexually precocious, presides over satanic rituals and experiences grotesque fits. She disposes of various people by demonic means and in the final confrontation between good and evil (which takes place by the old witch's tomb) the exorcist-priest triumphs. The result is a banal conservative picture affecting the high moral tone of a sensationalist scandal sheet which exploits irrationalist bigotry while providing consumers with the very thrills it pretends to condemn. The director's next efforts were the fourth (and last to date) instalment of his blind-dead series, **La Noche de los Gaviotas** (1975) and the competent **El Buque Maldito** (1974).

Dame Edith Evans awaits her fate in the inept Craze.

d/s Amando de Ossorio *c* Vicente Minaya *lp* Julian Mateos, Marian Salgado, Lone Fleming, Maria Kosti, Fernando Sancho, Angel del Pozo, Tota Alba, Roberto Camardiel, Daniel Martin

Enigma para Demonios
(C. H. CHRISTENSEN PRODUÇOES; BRAZIL) 99min
In this psycho-thriller in the style of Hammer's **Taste of Fear** (1960), Lafond is the heroine who, returning home after her child has died, learns of the death of her parents in mysterious circumstances. At her uncle's house, she encounters a friend of the family, the enigmatic Jurema (Barbosa). After a visit to the cemetery where she picks a rose, Lafond is persecuted by menacing phone calls which eventually drive her insane. The cause of the diabolic phenomena is revealed to be Barbosa, who is trying to get the family inheritance. The unimaginative script, which is derived from Carlos Drummond de Andrade's *Flor, Telefone, Moça*, is enhanced by excellent location photography in Belo Horizonte and Ouro Preto.

d/p/co-s Carlos Hugo Christensen *co-s* Origines Lessa *c* Antonio Gonçalves *lp* Monique Lafond, Luiz Fernando Ianelli, Barbosa, Licia Maggi, Rodolfo Arena, Mario Brasini, Daniel Carvalho, Jotta Barroso, Gerry Dias

Exorcismo (PROFILMES; SP) 98(92)min
In the race to rip off William Friedkin's smug blockbuster, the Catalonian veteran Bosch was beaten at the post by Amando de Ossorio's **La Endemoniada** (1974) by one week. Bosch recounts how a deceased father who resented his wife's infidelity returns as a sadistic demon to possess his daughter. She turns into a homicidal maniac, behaves badly and gets exorcized by an Anglican specialist in demonology (Molina) who exiles the evil spirit into the 'mind' of a dog. Following Friedkin's example, Bosch concocted a tract on behalf of the most obnoxious members of 'the silent majority': the possessed 'innocent' exemplifies evil by using uncouth language, being disrespectful towards her mother and associating with a rebellious youth corrupted by drugs, luxury and laziness. The ultimate horror of these exorcism pictures is that any deviation from a suffocatingly oppressive familial and moral order is

presented as undiluted evil to be combatted with the most drastic of measures. In effect, a refusal to conform to bigotry becomes the work of the devil (which, ideologically, bears remarkable similarity to the Nazi depiction of satanic Jews).

d/co-s Juan Bosch *co-s* Jacinto Molina *c* Francisco Sanchez *lp* Paul Naschy (Jacinto Molina), Maria Perschy, Maria Kosti, Grace Mills, Jorge Torras, Marta Avile, Roger Leveder

O Exorcismo Negro

(CINEDISTRI; BRAZIL) b/w 100min

The director's *alter ego*, Zé do Caixao, established as a psychopath in *A Meia Noite Levarei Sua Alma* and **Esta Noite Encarnarei no Teu Cadaver** (both 1966), was changed to a mad messiah in 1971 with *Finis Hominis* and **Quando os Deuses Adormecem** (both 1971). With this black-magic picture, he dramatizes the conflict and the complementarity between these two figures by pitting himself, playing a film director called José Mojica Marins, against the evil Zé, his own fantasy creation (Marins again). The plot has the director go to a friend's house to write a script and his arrival trigger strange and violent happenings among his hosts. Lucia (Gomide), the wife of Alvaro (Stuart), makes a pact with a witch (Kosmo) while others behave as if possessed by the devil. In a torture chamber, a Black Mass is enacted to exorcize the evil influences. The ritual culminates in a savage duel between Marins and Zé. Although obviously seeking to cash in on the recent exorcism boom, Marins nevertheless continued to produce quasi-documentaries thinly disguised as fiction, chronicling the successive phases and crises of an insane person here explicitly designated as himself. The change from sadistic psychopath (Zé) to Messiah (Finis Hominis) to split personality could be seen as evidence that his therapy-through-film-making was achieving some positive results. Subsequent films would bear this out since Marins graduated to cheap, fairly conventional horror movies no longer testifying to a relentless and uncontainable descent into psychosis such as **A Estranha Hospedaria dos Prazeres** (1976).

d/co-s José Mojica Marins *p* Anibal Massaini Neto *co-s* Adriano Stuart, Rubens Luchetti *c* Antonio Meliande *lp* José Mojica Marins, Jofre Suares, Walter Stuart, Georgia Gomide, Adriano Stuart, Wanda Kosmo, Alcione Mazzeo

The mummified family in Deranged, *Jeff Gillen and Alan Ormsby's imaginative reworking of the story of Ed Gein, whose life also provided the source material for* Psycho *(1960) and* The Texas Chainsaw Massacre *(1974).*

Flavia la Monaca Musulmana *aka* Flavia la Nonne Musulmane *aka* Flavia Priestess of Violence *aka* The Rebel Nun

(PAC/ROC; FR,IT) 99(95)min

Although Mingozzi was a respected director of documentaries (he made *Michelangelo Antonioni*, 1965, for example) this is anything but a respectable exploitation of women's liberation motifs. Set in the 15th century, the film tells of a woman, Flavia (Bolkan), forcibly imprisoned in a nunnery by her father. There she is further alienated from Italy's macho society when she witnesses a brutal rape and a hysterical orgy of the Tarantula sect, which is followed by sadistic punishments. First, she tries to escape with a Jewish friend, then, when the Muslims invade Italy, she takes the opportunity to join forces with them and pursues her own bloody revenge against those who wronged her while the Muslims abandon themselves to uninhibited carnage. When they leave, she is captured by a mob which proceeds to skin her alive. Other choice bits of violence include beheadings, a convent courtyard festooned with bloody cadavers and broken bodies, a spear crashing into a man's crotch, and so on, all filmed in a deceptively luscious style.

The references to Flavia's rebellion against patriarchy in the 15th century are wildly anachronistic and betray a cynical – if not ignorant – approach. A female director might wish to express anger in a similarly brutalized manner (for example, Marleen Gorris' *De Stilte Rond Christine M.*, 1982) but Mingozzi's movie banks on the saleability of sexual sadism and derives its force from the graphic depiction of mutilation culminating in the nauseating flaying at the end.

d/p/co-s Gianfranco Mingozzi *co-s* Raniero di Giovambattista, Sergio Tau, Francesca Vieltri, Fabrizio Onofri, Bruno di Geronimo *c* Alfio Contini *lp* Florinda Bolkan, Maria Casares, Claudio Cassinelli, Spiros Focas, Diego Michelotti, Jill Pratt, Raika Juri, Antony Corlan

Frightmare

(PETE WALKER (HERITAGE) LTD; GB) b/w 86min

It would appear that the collaboration with scenarist McGillivray (who appears as a young doctor in this film) marked a decisive change for Walker, previously a director of insipid sexploitation movies. After the sadistic *House of Whipcord* (1974), he made this gore picture about a couple of psychotic cannibals (Davies and Keith) living on an English farm after their release from the asylum. Their daughter, Debbi (Butcher), rapidly changes from a demented woman into a homicidal maniac and joins with her mother in an attack on her half-sister (Fairfax), having first disposed of the psychiatrist (Greenwood) who came to investigate. The demented mother, forcefully played by Keith, is shown tearing her victims to bits with an electrical drill before eating the raw flesh. The flimsy narrative is simply an excuse to link the numerous gory sequences.

Together with the American and Italian examples of the genre, of which **The Texas Chainsaw Massacre** (1974) is the most stylish to date, these gore movies signalled a profound shift in the fantasies underpinning the horror genre. The oedipal problems of castration and the enigma of sexual difference which had structured countless film scripts in the fifties and sixties with their images of surgery and lethal sexuality, came to be replaced from the mid-seventies onwards, and in parallel with the disaster movie epidemic, by horror movies centering on the more regressive body-in-pieces fantasy, harking back to earliest infancy. But whereas this fantasy had a social grounding in America after the catastrophe of Vietnam had torn the country apart and Watergate had uncovered degeneracy hidden beneath the symbol of American unity and power, the European gore movies merely imitated their American models, cynically trying to cash in on the phenomenon. Previously, gore had been an underground activity (as in the work of Herschell Gordon Lewis) or a sign of a director's inability to produce a decent horror thriller (eg **Twisted Nerve**, 1968). From the mid-seventies onwards, invulnerable superheroes and their negative images, victims with their bodies torn to pieces (and their in-between figure: the Romero-type zombie simultaneously invulnerable and in tatters) were actively cultivated as a subgenre in their own right.

d/p Peter Walker *s* David McGillivray *c* Peter Jessop
lp Rupert Davies, Sheila Keith, Deborah Fairfax, Paul Greenwood, Kim Butcher, Fiona Curzon, John Yule, Tricia Mortimer, Pamela Farbrother, David McGillivray

The Gardener *aka* **Seeds of Evil**
(KKI FILMS) 81min
This is the film in which Dallesandro turns into a tree. Shot in Puerto Rico, the story features Dallesandro as a gardener who grows plants that kill people. A bizarre mixture of sexual melodrama and transformational horror, the film fails to work on either level and the special effects, in particular, are laughable. The movie is interesting as Dallesandro's first starring assignment away from the Warhol factory but any would-be horror movie which can be described (by *Variety*) as 'merely pleasant' is surely way off course.

d/s Jim Kay *p* Tony Belletier *c* Michael Zingale
lp Katherine Houghton, Joe Dallesandro, Rita Gam, James Congdon, Theodorina Bello

Ghost Story *aka* **Asylum of Blood**
(STEPHEN WEEKS COMPANY; GB) 89min
After **I, Monster** (1970) and *Sir Gawain and the Green Knight* (1972), Weeks' third movie is a promise of achievements to come. Shot in Tamil Nadu but set in England in the thirties, the story tells of McFayden (Melvin), Duller (Mackerall) and Talbot (Dann), who are invited to test whether an ancestral mansion is haunted or not. Duller soon leaves since his equipment fails to pick up ghostly manifestations, but Talbot, under the influence of an enigmatic doll, begins to see or dream disturbing scenes: a man (Lawson) signs his sister, Sophy (Faithfull), over to an insane asylum; the breakout by the inmates who kill the director-doctor (Bate); Faithfull stabbing her brother to death whereupon Talbot is strangled by the doll which has been plaguing him. McFayden drives away from the house but in the back seat a trunk springs open and the hand of a doll emerges ....

In effect, a commercial version of *Céline et Julie Vont en Bâteau* (1974), the film suffers from unexceptional special effects and a fatal sense of dislocation as the horrors of incest and madness fail to surface sufficiently centrally as they are relayed through the appearance of the string-pulled doll. That said, the movie as a whole, especially when the music of Ron Geesing, the sets of Peter Young and the cinematography are allowed a free reign, is far superior to John Irvin's identically titled 1981 movie. Weeks' film also boasts a welcome cameo by Shelley as the asylum's matron.

d/p/co-s Stephen Weeks *co-s* Rosemary Sutcliffe *c* Peter Hurst *lp* Larry Dann, Murray Melvin, Vivian Mackerall, Marianne Faithfull, Anthony Bate, Penelope Keith, Leigh Lawson, Sally Grace, Barbara Shelley

The Ghoul *aka* **The Thing in the Attic**
(TYBURN FILM PRODUCTIONS; GB) scope 88(87)min
Tyburn followed up their début picture (**Persecution**, 1973) with this equally disappointing concoction devised by Hammer stalwards Hinds and Francis, produced by Francis Jnr and featuring some familiar Hammer faces. Cushing is the defrocked priest living with a guilty secret: a compulsively cannibalistic son (Henderson) locked away in the attic. This taint on his family is connected with his stay in India, suggesting the corrupting effects of colonialism – a motif often used in Hammer films, including **The Reptile** (1966) and the various mummy pictures – but this film seems intent on marginalizing such implications in favour of whatever shock-horror scenes can be generated around its bloody and degenerate monster. This lack of attention to the experience of empire shifts the focus towards Cushing's moral dilemma as he is torn between the roles of father, jailer and executioner. The result is that the Indian motifs represented by idols and an evil servant (Watford) are left without a context and thus engender the other aspect of colonialism: racism. In spite of the determined use of swirling mist and other traditional generic imagery, the fragmented script and endless shots of legs descending stairs, as well as the predictably bloody finale, make this a deeply flawed movie lacking the persuasiveness of, for example, **The Creeping Flesh** (1972).

Francis Snr and Jnr teamed up again with Cushing and Hinds for Tyburn's next, even more disappointing, film, **Legend of the Werewolf** (1974). Both these pictures were released in 1975. The ghoul's makeup was devised by Roy Ashton, another member of the Hammer family.

Don Henderson points his jewelled dagger at Alexandra Bastedo in The Ghoul.

d Freddie Francis *p* Kevin Francis *s* John Elder (Anthony Hinds) *c* John Wilcox *lp* Peter Cushing, John Hurt, Gwen Watford, Alexandra Bastedo, Veronica Carlson, Don Henderson, Ian McCulloch, Stuart Bevan

Gu Jing You Hun *aka* **Ghost in the Mirror**
(DIYI FILMS; TAIWAN) scope 104min
The scholar who falls in love with the beauty, who may be a ghost or an illusion, is a common theme in Chinese literature and has been adapted to the cinema many times. In Song Cunshou's variation, a scholar sets out to fulfil his sacred promise to copy out all the Buddhist scriptures if his mother is cured of her illness. In his secluded house, however, he encounters a beautiful ghost who is controlled by an evil dragon. The scholar helps the beauty escape this fate by reincarnating her through the use of a mirror but the dragon attacks and eventually cracks the mirror, thereby killing the beauty.

One of Taiwan's most distinguished horror films, in a cinema more renowned for its impressive melodramas, *Gu Jing You Hun* is played, not surprisingly, as as oedipal drama with the director using the scholar's devotion to his mother and the suggestion of the paternal dragon as essential parts of his narrative. The film is visually stylish, from the ghost's first appearance, traditionally as an image in a well, to the scholar's

Right: *David Rintoul as the wolf-child turned werewolf in* Legend of the Werewolf.

attempts to prevent the dragon from entering his study by pasting texts of Buddhist scriptures around the walls. The only jarring element is the representation of the dragon itself, which looks as stiff and artificial as the papier mâché from which it appears to have been fashioned.

d Song Cunshou *p* Huang Zhuhan *s* Zhang Yongxiang *lp* Lin Qingxia (Lin Chinghsia), Shi Jun, Gu Wenzong, Zhang Bingyu

Homebodies (CIC) 96min
With a cast composed of elderly and little known actors, no sex, and a relatively low gore quota, *Homebodies* might at first seem to have little going for it in the horror stakes. What its story of a group of old people who, faced with eviction from their comfortable but old Cincinnati apartment building by an urban renewal programme, take the desperate step of eliminating their evictors, can boast, however, are topnotch production values (on what appears to be a modest budget), an inventive script which manages to combine grisly black humour, gripping suspense and genuine pathos, crisp direction and superb character performances all round. The film was actually shot while Cincinnati was undergoing an urban renewal programme and Mankofsky's cinematography of the wrecked cityscape is wonderfully atmospheric.

Director Yust had previously produced the witty black comedy *Pretty Poison* (1968).

d/co-s Larry Yust *p* Marshall Backlar *co-s* Howard Kaminsky, Bennett Sims *c* Isidore Mankofsky *lp* Peter Brocco, Frances Fuller, William Hansen, Ruth McDevitt, Paula Trueman, Ian Wolfe, Linda Marsh, Douglas Fowley, Kenneth Tobey, Wesley Lau

The intriguing Homebodies.

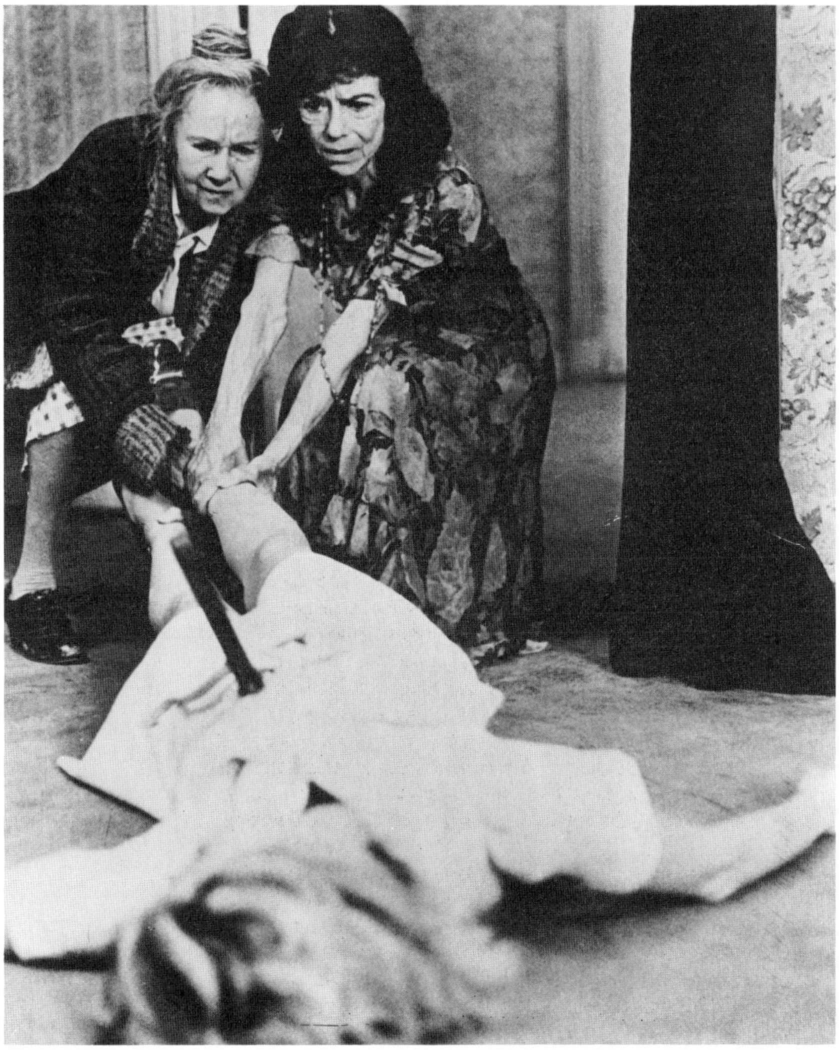

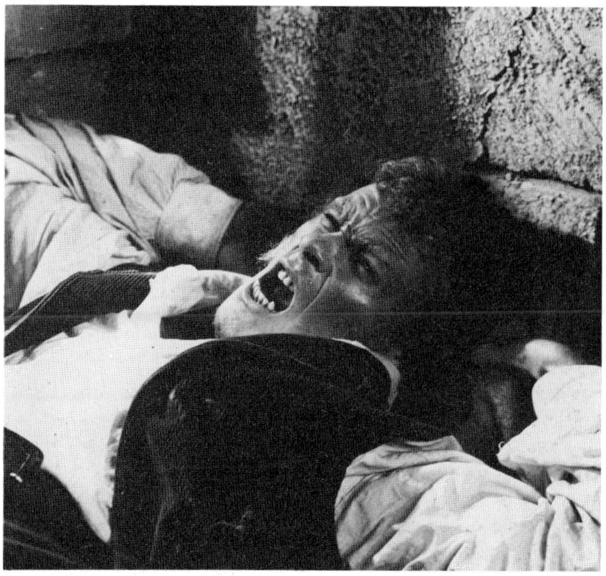

House of the Seven Corpses
(TCA PRODUCTIONS) 90min
During the shooting of a horror film in a haunted house with a violent history, the star, Gayle (Domergue, of *This Island Earth*, 1955, fame) reads from the Tibetan Book of the Dead and causes the dead to rise and wreak havoc. The idea of having a horror movie revolve around the making of a horror movie is not new, but it has rarely been carried off so successfully as here. Although of the horrific scenes do not occur until very close to the end (which also boasts a genuinely surprising twist), the film manages to sustain an extremely tense, fraught atmosphere throughout, and the scenes detailing the making of the film-within-the-film, while interesting in themselves, don't distract from the narrative's main theme.

d/co-p/co-s Paul Harrison *co-p* Paul Lewis *co-s* Thomas J. Kelly *c* Don Jones *lp* John Ireland, John Carradine, Faith Domergue, Charles Macauley, Carol Wells, Jerry Strickler

Legend of the Werewolf (TYBURN; GB) scope 90min
Although scripted by Hinds, who had written Terence Fisher's **The Curse of the Werewolf** (1960), *Legend* is a disappointment. In the mid-19th century a wolf-child grows up with a travelling showman (Griffith) and becomes a werewolf (Rintoul) who makes his making a living as a zoo-keeper in Paris. On discovering that his beloved (Dalby) is a whore he vents his anger on the well-to-do clients of a brothel, eventually getting trapped in the sewers by the police pathologist (Cushing) and a detective (Gryff) where he succumbs to the silver bullets.

The simplistic story signals the werewolf's attacks with frantic subjective camera movements and red filters, while Paris is represented by poorly designed sets decorated with signs in cod French. The dialogue is riddled with incredibly silly lines like 'I'm a countryman from the Massif Central district'. The film was the third Tyburn production released in 1975, with **Persecution** (1973) and **The Ghoul** (1974). Unfortunately, only *The Ghoul* contains any moderately interesting sequences and traditional generic imagery. The production of *Legend* is chronicled in one of the few English film books devoted to a single movie, *Making Legend of the Werewolf* by Edward Buscombe.

The werewolf makeup was the responsibility of Graham Freeborn.

d Freddie Francis *p* Kevin Francis *s* John Elder (Anthony Hinds) *c* John Wilcox *se* Charles Staffell *lp* Peter Cushing, Ron Moody, Hugh Griffith, Lynn Dalby, David Rintoul, Roy Castle, Stefan Gryff, Renee Houston, Marjorie Yates, Norman Mitchell

1974

O Lobisomem (ELYSEU VISCONTI; BRAZIL) 75min
The second feature of Visconti Cavalleiro (better known as a maker of shorts, his first full-length film, *Os Monstros de Babaloo*, 1970, was never released), this experimental horror film freely borrows its central figure from Bram Stoker, although calling the fanged hero a werewolf instead of Dracula. An eccentric millionaire (Grey) becomes a werewolf and presides over a bloodsucking congregation in a forest. His reign of seduction and terror is stopped by the sudden emergence of the forces of good in the shape of a white-robed figure of justice. Although chaotic, the film is one of Brazil's better lycanthropy movies, when compared with Rossi's **O Homem Lobo** (1971) or the black comedy **Quem Tem Medo de Lobisomem** (1974).

d/p/s/c Elyseu Visconti Cavalleiro *lp* Wilson Grey, Suzana de Moraes, Paulo Villaça, Jack de Castro, Jacira Silva, Andre Valli

Macchie Solari *aka* **Autopsy**
(CLODIO CINEMATOGRAFICA; IT) scope 125min
Before his better known sex comedy, *Frankenstein all'Italiana* (1975), Crispino made a rather unusual Italian western *John il Bastardo* (1968) and some giallo movies, the peculiarly Italian mixture of thriller, sexploitation and horror/terror conventions initiated by Mario Bava's *La Ragazza che Sapeva Troppo* (1962) and elaborated into a major commercial formula by Dario Argento. His *L'Etrusco Uccide Ancora* (1972), with its suggestion of a homicidal Etruscan deity, used some catacomb imagery to give the thriller plot an atmosphere reminiscent of the better German Edgar Wallace adaptations. This picture stresses the sex far more and takes Crispino on to Bava's necrophiliac terrain.

The story spins out the usual cliché of a woman (Farmer) propelled into mortiferous fantasies by her repressed sexuality, a plot best handled in Roman Polanski's **Repulsion** (1965). In spite of rumours that sunspots are responsible for a wave of suicides and other odd events, the narrative concentrates on motifs of cruelty – a visit to the police's chamber of horrors, decomposing flesh – all allegedly relating to the heroine's frigidity. The basic underlying fantasy that structures the movie is simply that women who are not swept off their feet by crudely macho advances must be insane, perverted, or, as in this case, both.

d/co-s Armando Crispino *p* Leonardo Pescarolo *co-s* Lucio Battistrada *c* Carlo Carlini *lp* Mimsy Farmer, Barry Primus, Ray Lovelock, Angela Goodwin, Massimo Serato, Carlo Cattaneo, Gaby Wagner

Mary, Mary, Bloody Mary
(TRANSLOR FILMS/PROA FILMS; US,MEX) 101(91)min
An ex-theatre director and actor, as well as radio presenter of jazz programmes, Moctezuma followed his successful **La Mansión de la Locura** (1972) with this rather disappointing bisexual vampire thriller before returning to the full-blown gothic with **Alucarda** (1975). Here, Mary (Ferrare) is an artist (and thus, according to the conventional portrayal of intellectuals in such fantasies, a perverted maniac) in the habit of stabbing unsuspecting victims of both sexes in the neck and drinking their blood. Soon she discovers she has competition from another bloodsucker: her vampiric father (Carradine), presumed dead but in fact only disfigured by fire. He has returned to try and kill his wayward daughter to rescue her from vampirism, but she gets the better of him and kills both him and her male lover (Young) in the picture's bloodsoaked finale. The sex interest is represented primarily by Ferrare's lesbian encounter with Greta (Rojo). The original plot was provided by Don Rico and Don Henderson, but although Moctezuma shows some visual flair in a number of the sequences, he doesn't appear to have been capable of overcoming its crushing banality. With his next film, *Alucarda*, he took a more active hand in the script and devised a story that offered greater scope for his baroque sense of stylization.

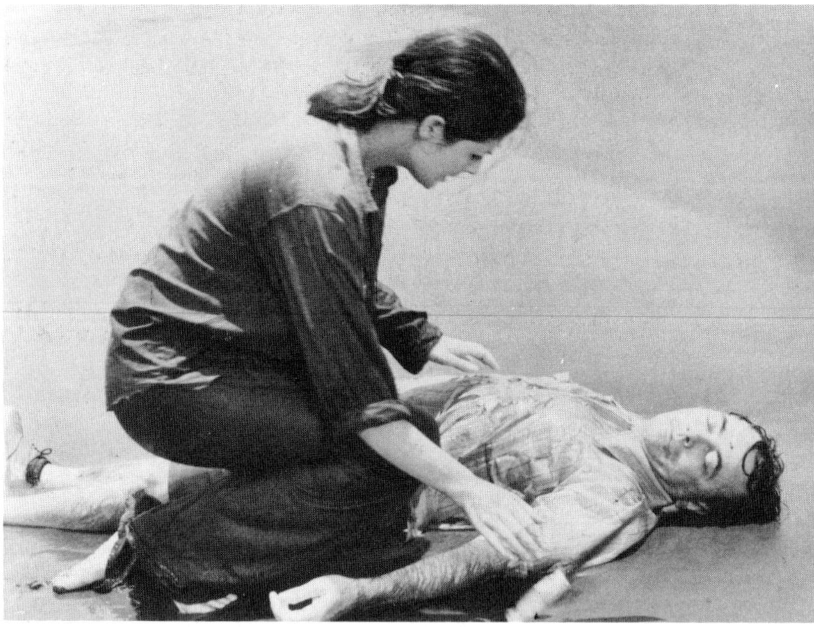

The disappointing Mary, Mary, Bloody Mary.

d Juan Moctezuma *p* Robert Yamin, Henri Bollinger *s* Malcolm Marmorstein *c* Miguel Garzon *lp* Christina Ferrare, John Carradine, David Young, Helena Rojo, Arturo Hansel, Enrique Lucero, Susan Kamini

Il Medaglione Insanguinato *aka* **The Cursed Medallion** *aka* **The Night Child**
(MAGDALENA PRODUZIONE/ITALIAN INTERNATIONAL; IT) scope 95(92)min
A routine demonic-child story. A British TV director and widower (Johnson) travels to Spoleto with his pubescent daughter, Emily (Elmi) to research demonic paintings. One particular painting, showing the death of a woman before the eyes of a child wearing the same medallion Emily received as a present from her father, begins to exert its nefarious influence. The climax comes as Elmi slashes the painting and then, knife in hand, rushes into her father's arms. The incestual overtones of the script are left unexplored while the movie is liberally padded with tourist-board imagery of the (admittedly beautiful) Spoleto region. Kedrova's appearance is suitably witchlike but the rest of the cast simply sit around looking anguished. Stelvio Cipriani's score helpfully signals the bits that are supposed to be suspenseful. Some sources credit a young Jan Hartmann as co-scenarist.
d/co-s Massimo Dallamano *p* William C. Reich, Fulvio Lucisano *co-s* Franco Marotta, Laura Toscano *c* Franco delli Colli *lp* Richard Johnson, Nicole Elmi, Joanna Cassidy, Evelyne Stewart (Ida Galli), Lila Kedrova, Edmund Purdom

No Profanar el Sueño de los Muertos *aka* **Fin de Semana para los Muertos** *aka* **Non sì Deve Profanare il Sonno dei Morti** *aka* **The Living Dead at the Manchester Morgue** *aka* **Breakfast at the Manchester Morgue** *aka* **Don't Open the Window**
(STAR FILMS/FLAMINIA PRODUXIONI; SP,IT) 93min
After **Ceremonia Sangrienta** (1972) and a thriller, *Pena de Meurte* (1973), Grau made this, his best-known movie, which, promoted as the first horror film with stereophonic sound, combines aspects of George Romero's **Night of the Living Dead** (1968) with ecological motifs. The government's new agricultural pest-control machine, working with ultrasonic waves, has an unfortunate side-effect: it revives the dead who then by the simple process of anointing the eyelids of fellow corpses with blood, rapidly increase their number. The hero, George (Lovelock), has more trouble staying out of the hands of a brutal cop (Kennedy) than from the zombies, and when he sees his girlfriend (Galbo) eaten in a hospital, overcome by a

horde of the undead on a cannibalistic spree, he destroys the creatures by fire but is shot by the cop for his pains. In the end, the audience is invited to identify with the zombified Lovelock as he returns to get the policeman.

Although made with some humour and a flair for maximizing the effectiveness of individual sequences, the naïvety of the film's politics make the narrative inconsistent. Starting with shots of desensitized rush-hour crowds, inviting audiences to share the horror of a zombified commuter existence, the movie then shifts into paranoia directed at both the police and the zombies, and ends with the reversal of its initial premise: only a zombie can defeat the fascist policeman, that is only he can become the activist hero. The picture was awarded a prize at the Sitges festival.

d Jorge Grau *p* Edmondo Amati *s* Sandro Continenza, Marcello Coscia, Miguel Rubio, Juan Cobos *c* Francisco Sempere *se* Giannetto de Rossi, Luciano Bird *lp* Ray Lovelock, Cristina Galbo, Arthur Kennedy, Aldo Massasso, Giorgio Trestini, Roberto Posse, Jeanine Mestre, José Ruiz Lifante, Fernando Hilbeck, Isabel Mestre

La Noche de los Asesinos (FENIX FILM; SP) 88min

After the busiest year of his prolific career in which he made one feature per month, Franco took time off to concoct this thoroughly average adaptation of *The Cat and the Canary*, best filmed by Paul Leni in 1927. An old man is murdered in his castle and the relatives gather for the reading of his will. One by one, starting with his wife who discovered the body and supervised the burial, they're killed in various exotic ways. Although there are murmurs of an ancient curse, it emerges that the old man had been buried alive. Wearing a mask, he proceeds to eliminate the clan gathered in his castle in order to make sure his property is left to the youngest members of the family.

A few years earlier, Santos Alcocer had made a similar picture, **Solo un Ataud** (1966) starring Howard Vernon, Franco's collaborator on more than 30 films but absent from this one. Franco's movie was allegedly based on Edgar Allan Poe's *Premature Burial*, but the story bears little resemblance to the classic. Some sources cite Xavier Perzeopulos as cinematographer.

d/s Jess Franck (Jesús Franco) *p* Arturo Marcos *c* Javier Perez Zofio *lp* William Berger, Alberto Dalbes, Evelyn Scott (Deher), Lina Romay, Maribel Hidalgo, Helene Samarina, Antonio Mayans

The dead arise in the atnospheric No Profanar el Sueño de los Muertos.

Le Nosferat ou les Eaux Glacées du Calcul Egoïste
(LES FILMS DU GROUPE DE CHAMBRE; BEL) 100min

A well-meaning adaptation by the director of his own play, shot on 16mm and blown up to 35mm, which purports to construct a Brechtian parable with songs, newsreel inserts, and so on, all set pre-Second World War. The plot telescopes the figures of Jack the Ripper and Nosferatu into a single, unsavoury character who symbolizes the pathological currents which produced the perverted idealism of fascism. The young bourgeois hypocrite terrorizes prostitutes as part of a crusade to purify the body politic of unhealthy elements. The picture's politics are exceedingly naïve and its references to Brecht are limited to a profoundly anti-Brechtian, mechanical application of so-called alienation devices and the use of popular culture stereotypes: references to vampirism as he drinks the blood of the female victims, the psycho family setting, and so on. In the tradition of paranoid-student films, Rabinowicz also takes lines from Nazi speeches and murderers' confessions to put into the mouth of his antihero. Cinematically, some nice images are achieved here and there, which make the result look like an inarticulate sketch for Ulli Lommel's **Zaertlichkeit der Woelfe** (1973).

d/co-s Maurice Rabinowicz *co-s* Yvette Michelems *c* Jean-Jacques Mathy *lp* Veronique Peynet, Maïté Nahyr, Martine Bertrand, Guy Pion, Quentin Milo

L'Ossessa *aka* **The Sexorcist**
(TIBERIA FILM INTERNATIONAL; IT) 87(86)min

Gariazzo, the director of incoherent variations of current American cops and robbers movies such as *La Mano Spietata della Legge* (1973) and Italian westerns, here offers a frankly sexploitative imitation of **The Exorcist** (1973). The heroine, a painter (Carnacina), is a little more mature than her counterpart in William Friedkin's movie and is burdened with a mother (Love) given to indulging in sado-masochistic practices, to the great discomfort and possibly envy of her frustrated daughter. In this respect, the movie is preferable to Friedkin's provincial bigotry in that it at least renders more explicit the hysterical processes which religion translates into demonic possession. The climax though is on the same lines with the demon which is said to possess the young woman being exorcized by a priest (Pistilli) at the cost of his own life. But here too Gariazzo indicates quite clearly that the real conflict is between sexual desire and religious repression since the priest dies not only overcoming 'the demon' but, more importantly, his own lust for the heroine. Special effects, such as flaming crucifixes, a raging storm, and the heroine being nailed to a cross, are used extensively but lack conviction, as does the direction which merely exploits the sex scenes rather than elaborating upon their relationship with religious practices.

d/co-s Mario Gariazzo *p* Riccardo Romano, Paulo Azzoni *co-s* Ambogio Molteni *c* Carlo Carlini *se* Paulo Ricci *lp* Stella Carnacina, Chris Avram, Lucretia Love, Luigi Pistilli, Ivan Rassimov, Gabriele Tinti, Umberto Raho, Giuseppe Addobbati, Piero Gerlini, Elisa Mantellini

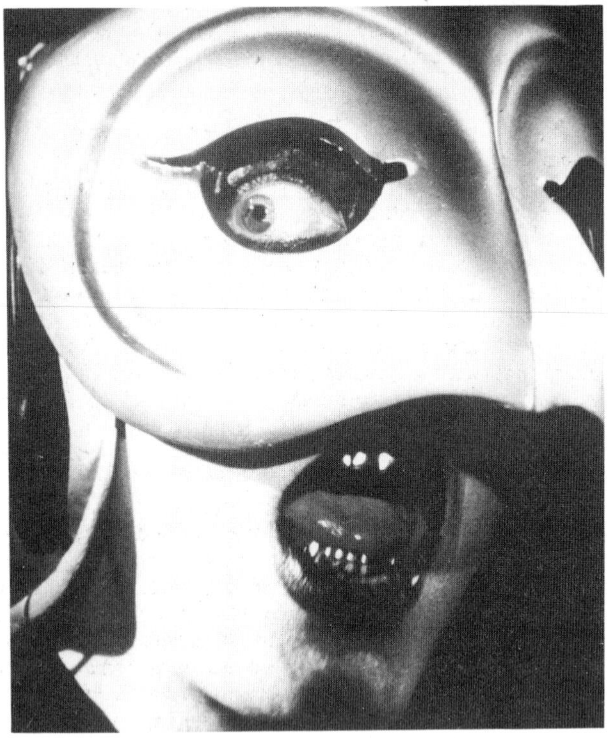

Left: *William Finley as the* Phantom of the Paradise.

Phantom of the Paradise

(PRESSMAN WILLIAMS) 91min

De Palma, who made the psychological horror movie **Sisters** (1972) and went on to direct such films as **Carrie** (1976) and **The Fury** (1978), here attempts a mating of pastiche horror and rock opera. (The film appeared the year before Ken Russell's *Tommy*, 1975.) As the title implies, the picture is partly a modern variation on **The Phantom of the Opera** (1925, 1943, 1962) – to be precise of the two later versions, which feature a composer cheated of recognition by an unscrupulous impresario – but also has elements of the Faust legend and **The Picture of Dorian Gray** (1945). The composer here (Finley) has written a rock opera on the Faust theme; a song from it is stolen by the all-powerful impresario Swan (Williams), who has the hapless composer framed on a drugs charge. The latter escapes from jail bent on vengeance, but is presumed dead in an accident after breaking into Williams' record factory. In fact he is alive, but hideously disfigured; masked and looking vaguely like a giant bird he sets himself to sabotaging the mogul's rock palace, the Paradise. Eventually, after it emerges that Williams has made a pact with the Devil that will allow him to remain eternally young, a violent climax is reached in which both men die in the course of a spectacular concert at the Paradise, an intended – though thwarted – feature of which was to have been the assassination at Williams' behest of the singer (Harper) whom he had selected for his bride. This last development points to the increasing incoherence of the plotline, and to the film's inability to make much headway in satirizing or illuminating its 'mythic' components. It is certainly realized with tremendous energy, but this in itself, manifested in a non-stop succession of tricks and tropes, ultimately becomes self-defeating.

d/s Brian de Palma *p* Edward R. Pressman *c* Larry Pizer *se* Greg Auer *lp* Paul Williams, Jessica Harper, William Finley, George Memmoli, Gerrit Graham, Gene Gross, Henry Calvert, Bobby Birkenfeld, Carol O'Leary

Les Possedées du Diable *aka* Lorna l'Exorciste *aka* Les Possedées du Démon

(COMPTOIR FRANÇAIS DU FILM; FR) 90min

By resuscitating the succubus of **Necronomicon** (1967), Franco produced one of his most revolting pictures to date. Patrick (Delorme) and Marianna (Parent) have a daughter Linda (Romay) who is claimed by his ex-lover, the satanic Lorna (Stanford). Horrified by his wife's sex, which disgorges black spidery creatures, Delorme realizes Stanford has cast an evil spell on them. He takes a gun and kills her and her servant (Vernon) but not before she has subjected the virginal Romay to a gruesome coupling with a huge dildo, thereby transmitting her satanic powers to the young woman. When Delorme returns from his murderous escapade, Romay seduces him before taking a knife and slashing her father's throat. The spiders emerging from between Parent's legs and Stanford licking the blood off the artificial phallus she used on Romay constitute the pathological but effective highlights of the picture, achieving a nauseating depiction of male castration anxieties. Even Franco's merciless use of the zoom lens seems justified in this context, making the vision of these images simultaneously more painful and inescapable.

This movie and **Les Avaleuses** (1973) are the last interesting films of the prolific Franco who continued to direct dozens of sex and horror movies including *Sexorcismes* (1974, his first hard-core porn picture), **Die Saege des Todes** (1981), and numerous women-in-prison films, usually starring Romay (who also appeared under the pseudonym Candy Coster).

d/s Clifford Brown (Jesús Franco) *p* Robert de Nesle *c* Gerard Brissaud *lp* Lina Romay, Pamela Stanford, Guy Delorme, Jacqueline Parent, Howard Vernon, Jesús Franco

Qiu Deng Ye Yu *aka* All in a Dim Cold Night

(FENG GUAN FILM; TAIWAN) scope 92min

This stylish picture manages to combine the conventions of the horror film with social criticism. A rich landowner seduces Qiu, the daughter of one of his tenants, but then reneges on his promise to marry her, even though she is pregnant. Instead he intends to marry a wealthy heiress. One cold night, he refuses to give shelter to Qiu and her newborn son who consequently freeze to death. The landowner's wife commits suicide after their wedding night and he sees instead Qiu lying in his bed. Haunted by her, he finally meets his death by drowning. The script is patchy and makes liberal use of coincidences, like a fortuitously falling oil lamp that burns the charms that keep Qiu's ghost locked in her tomb and triggering the picture's climactic ending.

d/s Yao Fengpan *p* Liu Guanjun *c* Lai Zhengying *lp* Qin Meng, Yue Yang, Jin Lingai

Quem Tem Medo de Lobisomem

(IPANEMA/CIRCUS/R. F. FARIA; BRAZIL) 92min

This oddly unsettling movie starts with two men (Faria and Nercessian) setting out to investigate legends of the supernatural. They team up with Iracema (Amado), a woman looking for husband, and install themselves in an abandoned farm only to be taken prisoner by a family with six daughters and a son. All the daughters, each in their own way, seduce the two adventurers who try to escape while Amado marries the only son and seventh child who, according to legend, can change into a werewolf. The violent death of the two heroes involves a vampire and a mad chase. Faria's fourth feature and starring himself, the film treats its horror fantasies with considerable (although at times heavy-handed) humour, and echoes the often gruesome exuberance of the films of Joaquin Pedro de Andrade.

d/co-p/s Reginaldo Faria *co-p* Mauricio Nabuco, Orlando Bonfim *c* José Medeiros *se* Wilmar Menezes, Geraldo José *lp* Reginaldo Faria, Stepan Nercessian, Camila Amado, Carlos Kroeber, Christina Aché, Fatima Freire, Fabiola Fracaroli, Griselda Padilha, Ana Maria Accurso, Elisa Fernandes

Shanks *aka* Shock (PAR) 93min

The last film directed by Castle, this imaginative and amusing story hovers uneasily between horror, black comedy and sentiment. The story features French mime artist Marceau as Shanks, a put-upon deaf-mute puppeteer working for an old scientist (Marceau again) who shows him how to make dead animals move by means of electric currents. When the old man dies he discovers that human corpses too can be re-animated and starts to use the technique as a means of avenging himself on those who have abused him throughout his life. Although the rape and murder of Shanks' only friend, a young girl (Eilbacher), seems curiously out of place, the film's production values are excellent, Marceau is compulsively watchable and the score by Alex North (father of producer Steve) was nominated for an Oscar.

d William Castle *p* Steven North *s* Ranald Graham *c* Jospeh Biroc *lp* Marcel Marceau, Tsilla Chelton, Philippe Clay, Cindy Eilbacher, Larry Bishop, Don Calfa, Giff Manard, Mondo, Phil Adams, Helena Kallianiotes

Shriek of the Mutilated *aka* **Mutilated**
(AM FILMS) 92min
This film has a college professor ask four of his students to go to Boot Island with him to capture a yeti. On the island, the team meet another doctor and his mute Indian servant Laughing Crow. After two of the students have been killed by a big white hairy beast, the two remaining discover that the two doctors are the leaders of the Vauderi cannibal cult who use the yeti story simply as a means of luring the unsuspecting to the island.

The second (and last) feature of the Adlum/Kelleher team – who were also responsible for **Invasion of the Blood Farmers** (1972) – this is a slightly more elaborate, higher budget affair, described by scriptwriter Kelleher as 'a more intellectual film. We tried to have a plot, we went for characterization. It's a more atmospheric movie. It's to my way of thinking the better film, the better written film, but it does not have the visceral, gut-grabbing impact of *Blood Farmers. Shriek of the Mutilated* has more cerebral violence, it comes from your caring about the characters and what happens to them. It was directed by Michael Findlay ... I met him during *Blood Farmers*, he was assistant director or something, and he was certainly involved with the editing'. Findlay, in fact, was a one-time sexploitation director and one of the inventors of the 3-D process used in *Carne per Frankenstein* (1974). He was killed in an accident on top of the Pan Am building shortly after making the infamous **Snuff** (1974).

The poster for Snuff *which was promoted as featuring real on-camera torture and killings.*

d Michael Findlay *p/co-s* Ed Adlum *c* Roberta Findlay *co-s* Ed Kelleher *lp* Alan Brock, Jennifer Stock, Tawm Ellis, Darcy Brown, Michael Harris, Morton Jacobs

Snuff *aka* **The Slaughter**
(MICHAEL FINDLAY/MONARCH RELEASING CORP; US,ARG)
82min
Clever promotion turned this incompetent gore quickie into one of the most controversial movies ever. The New York-based exploitation specialists Michael and Roberta Findlay raised money for a gore film to be shot in Argentina called *The Slaughter*. The script, described as 'really awful, it made no sense' by Roberta Findlay herself, tried to cash in on the Manson murders and had Argentinian women, obeying a male leader, massacre a pregnant actress and her friends. The results were so bad that the picture stayed on the shelf until Allan Shackleton of Monarch arranged to tack on a four-minute sequence in which a woman is brutally and systematically mutilated, dismembered and disembowelled. The publicity gimmick was to suggest that this sequence was a piece of cinema verité, to withhold credits of the film and to launch it to the accompaniment of vociferous protests by fictitious decency groups. The trick worked and the film made a substantial amount of money before it was eventually withdrawn. With virtually no nudity, the incoherent effort works strictly as a spectacle of amateurishly staged violence using animal entrails and crude effects in the style of Herschell Gordon Lewis' films.

Michael Findlay was later decapitated in a gruesome helicopter accident on the top of the Pan Am building in New York, while Roberta went on to make numerous sexploitation and porn films, including *Angel Number 9* (1977). The publicity surrounding the release of *Snuff* in 1976 spawned two tamer efforts exploiting the same title: a Brazilian thriller by Claudio Cunha, *Victimas do Prazer – Snuff* (1977) and a German film starring Claudia Fielers (1976).

co-d/p/s Michael Findlay *co-d/c* Roberta Findlay

The Spectre of Edgar Allan Poe
(CINTEL PRODUCTIONS) 86min
In early-19th-century America, Lenore (Grover), beloved of Edgar Allan Poe (Walker), is accidentally buried alive, and although she is rescued, remains in a semi-catatonic state. Poe's close friend Dr Adam Forrest (Drake) recommends that she be taken to a private asylum run by Dr Grimaldi (Romero) and his wife Lisa (Ohmart). Here Poe himself is treated to a series of nightmarish experiences and finally discovers that Romero is carrying out bizarre human experiments and Ohmart is a murderous psychopath. Though purporting to show how Poe's mind was affected by the strange fate of his first love, *The Spectre of Edgar Allan Poe* bears little relation to the facts of his life; unfortunately, however, it's not especially interesting as fantasy either, except for the scenes in a flooded cellar infested with snakes. Production values are relatively high, but direction, script and acting (especially that of a woefully miscast Romero) are dull. Indeed so unhorrific was the film that it was awarded a PG rating in the United States.

d/p/co-s Mohy Quandour *co-s* Kenneth Hartford, Denton Foxx *c* Robert Birchall *se* Byrd Holland *lp* Robert Walker, Mary Grover, Cesar Romero, Tom Drake, Carol Ohmart, Marsha Mae Jones, Frank Packard, Mario Milano, Karen Hartford, Dennis Fimple

Sugar Hill *aka* **Voodoo Girl** (AIP) 91min
When her boyfriend, the owner of the Club Haiti, is beaten to death by a gang of white racketeers, Diana 'Sugar' Hill (Bey) enters into a pact with Baron Samedi (Colley): in return for her body he summons up an army of zombies who wipe out the gang one by one.

The result is a brisk and efficient 'blaxploitation' horror movie with an intriguing historico-political resonance: the avenging zombies are slaves who died during the voyage from

Guinea in the 17th century and were buried still in their shackles. They arise 300 years later to avenge themselves on contemporary white exploitation and racism as represented by the white mafiosi. Their resurrection from their mouldy graves, cobwebbed, blank-eyed and plastered with mud and leaves, carries a real *frisson* and seems to nod in the direction of the excellent **The Plague of the Zombies** (1966).

d Paul Maslansky *p* Elliot Schick *s* Tim Kelley, Alvin Kazak, Maurice Jules *c* Bob Jessup *se* Roy L. Downey *lp* Marki Bey, Robert Quarry, Don Pedro Colley, Richard Lawson, Betty Anne Rees, Zara Culley, Larry D. Johnson, Charles Robinson, Rick Hagood, Ed Geldhart

Symptoms *aka* The Blood Virgin

(FINITION; GB) scope 91(80)min

Possibly remembering the impact made by Roman Polanski's **Repulsion** (1965), Britain entered this picture by an *émigré* Spanish director at the 1974 Cannes festival. Pleasance gives a convincing performance as Helen, a repressed but pathologically jealous lesbian who invites a friend, Ann (Heilbron) to come and stay at her dilapidated old house in the country. The place appears to be haunted by Cora (Mailleux), a previous house guest. As the sinister-looking gardener (Vaughan) prowls in the woods and Heilbron's boyfriend starts to become a nuisance tension builds to the bloody finale: one night Heilbron investigates noises in the attic and is stabbed to death by Pleasance who settles the corpse in an armchair. She then kills the boyfriend and Vaughan who has discovered Mailleux's body in the lake. The ending sees Pleasance in a catatonic state, surrounded by the three slaughtered bodies.

Stylistically, the low-budget picture is striking and Larraz makes excellently eerie use of the English landscape and the house. Rapid montage sequences juxtapose fragments of dreams, memories and contemporary scenes while a sparse, strongly rhythmic dialogue conveys the disturbing undertones of the women's relationship. But the fantasy of lesbianism as a pathological phenomenon clearly signals that Larraz is presenting a decidedly male-anxiety scenario, a tendency confirmed in his compellingly erotic **Vampyres** (1974). As such, the picture is less about a lesbian relationship than a representation of a panicky attempt to exorcize – and thus to recognize – the very notion of a female sexuality distinct from and irreducible to men's definition of it. As in Freda and Bava's **Lo Spettro** (1963), the heroine isn't eliminated but neither can the autonomy of her desires be acknowledged, presenting the narrative with a hopeless contradiction which leaves her, literally, frozen into paralysis at the end of the picture.

d/co-s Joseph (José) Larraz *p* Jean Dupuis *co-s* Stanley Miller *c* Trevor Wrenn *lp* Angela Pleasance, Lorna Heilbron, Peter Vaughan, Ronald O'Neil, Nancy Nevinson, Marie-Paul Mailleux, Michael Grady, Raymond Huntley

The Texas Chainsaw Massacre

(A VORTEX/HENKEL/HOOPER PRODUCTION) 83min

On account of its garishly schlocky title and its undeniable ability to deliver the goods, *The Texas Chainsaw Massacre* is one of the seventies most notorious horror films and perhaps *the* emblematic so-called 'splatter' movie. Though showcased at the London Film Festival in 1975, the film was refused a certificate by the British Board of Film Censors. After the unjust dismissal of **Eaten Alive** (1976), Hooper went on to make the excellent **The Funhouse** (1981) and to hit the big time with the rather less impressive **Poltergeist** (1982).

Based, like **Psycho** (1960) and the tremendous **Deranged** (1974), on the case of Ed Gein, the film is, above all else, extremely well made, and it is this that gives its story of a group of young friends terrorized and murdered by a houseful of maniacs in rural Texas its undoubted visceral power and lifts it above the level of so many of its rivals in the low-budget schlock-horror stakes. Every bit as unrelenting as **Night of the Living Dead** (1968), *The Texas Chainsaw Massacre* knows how to use both camera and editing to sweep up the spectator into the holocaust on the screen – this is precisely the opposite of the clinical, almost surgical, horror of, say, David Cronenberg. In fact Hooper, like Fritz Lang, knows exactly what *not* to show, and realizes that much of the power of horror lies in suggestion rather than overt gore – there is, surprisingly, little overt bloodletting in the film. Particularly effective, too, are the apocalyptic rumblings and roarings of the unsettling, *musique concrète* score by Hooper and Wayne Bell, which lend an even more nightmarish tone to the bizarre proceedings.

Gunnar Hansen as Leatherface in the seminal The Texas Chainsaw Massacre.

It has to be admitted that in its treatment of the only survivor, Sally (Burns), the film takes the woman-as-victim syndrome to quite hyperbolic lengths but on the other hand the narrative's driving oppositions – between the 'good' and 'bad' families, between 'civilization' and the wilderness – open up the interesting possibility of a reading in which the 'bad' family can be seen not only as the ultimate degeneration of the pioneers who have succumbed to the dark forces of the wilderness, but also as a macabre parallel to the 'good' family who are the products of 'getting ahead' – the very process which destroyed the American frontier. Instead of James Fenimore Cooper's noble Leatherstocking we have the insane Leatherface who hunts, not animals, but people, and with a chainsaw. The hunter's pursuit of his quarry for food has become perverted into that institution of mass butchery, the slaughterhouse (the 'bad' family is in the meat business though as Hooper puts it the film is about 'crazy retarded people going beyond the line between animal and human'). As critic Tony Williams has put it: '... like the dark world of the subconscious, the oppressed emerge to take revenge for their exploitation .... The hunter has turned from clearing the wilderness on behalf of a society which will make him obsolete to take revenge on those representatives of material affluence who have been responsible for the destruction and repression that the American ideal has achieved throughout its ideological existence.'

d/p/co-s Tobe Hooper *co-s* Kim Henkel *c* Daniel Pearl *se* Dorothy Pearl, Lynn Lockwood, W. E. Barnes *lp* Marilyn Burns, Allen Danziger, Paul A. Partain, William Vail, Teri McMinn, Edwin Neal, Jim Siedow, Gunnar Hansen, John Dugan

Vampira *aka* **Old Dracula** *aka* **Vampirella** *aka* **Vampir**

(WORLD FILM SERVICES; GB) 88min

This desperately strained attempt at a comic marriage of vampire conventions and a return visit to sixties-style 'swinging London', is as much beside the point as the 'straight' attempt to do the same thing in **Dracula AD 1972** (1972). The script has Dracula (Niven, sadly traduced) coming to London in search of a rare type of blood for Vampira, his wife (Graves), and taking over the mind of a writer (Henson) to lead him to suitable donors. The oddest, and most objectionably stupid, aspect of the proceedings is that transfusion of the wrong blood type converts Vampira and later (after she bites him) Dracula himself into negros. The humour exudes an aura of stale farce as the film-makers laboriously try to update a fifties comedy format by introducing more bosomy females and modish references to race.

d Clive Donner *p* Jack H. Wiener *s* Jeremy Lloyd *c* Tony Richmond *lp* David Niven, Peter Bayliss, Teresa Graves, Nicky Henson, Jennie Linden, Bernard Bresslaw, Linda Hayden, Veronica Carlson, Freddie Jones, Frank Thornton

Vampyres *aka* **Daughters of Dracula** *aka* **Vampyres – Daughters of Darkness** *aka* **The Vampyre Orgy**

(ESSAY FILMS; GB) scope 87(84)min

This is one of the very rare treatments of vampirism as an explicitly male fantasy in which the women are simultaneously objects of terror and intoxicatingly desirable. Two young women vampires (Morris and Anulka) living in a decaying mansion lure passersby into their lair to use them up within one night. However one of their victims, Brown, and Morris fall madly in love with each other and he decides to stay, fully aware of his lover's vampirism. Becoming weaker and weaker after each successively orgiastic night, he eventually asks a couple in a nearby caravan to take him to hospital. The women exsanguinate the couple but Brown is saved by the dawn. Both sex and the (other) bloodthirsty activities are depicted with exuberant explicitness achieving a hallucinatory eroticism which, in spite of an obvious low budget and grainy images, genuinely succeeds in conveying the ambiguities in the *amour fou* of loving and being loved to death. The scenes with the camping couple irritatingly spoil what could have become, together with Mario Bava's **La Frusta e il Corpo** (1963), a masterpiece of erotic fantasy.

Nothing in the director's work, except perhaps **Symptoms** (1974) pointed to his ability to achieve such a unique, though flawed, picture. The majority of his films were and continued to be cheaply sensational, often sexploitative material: *Whirlpool* (1969), **Scream and Die** (1973), **Estigma** (1981) and **Los Ritos Sexuales del Diablo** (1982). Only **La Momia Nacional** (1981) extended his bizarre pictorial sense.

d Joseph (José) Larraz *p* Brian Smedley-Aston *s* Diana Daubeney *c* Harry Waxman *lp* Marianne Morris, Anulka, Murray Brown, Brian Deacon, Sally Faulkner, Bessie Love, Michael Byrne, Carl Lanchberry, Elliot Sullivan

Marianne Morris and Anulka as the vampires seeking a resting place as dawn breaks in the genuinely erotic Vampyres.

Whispers of Fear

(SIDELINE PRODUCTIONS; GB) scope 73min

A throwback to the Hammer psycho-thrillers of the early sixties. The ineptly told story concerns a young woman (Hindley) who arrives in a Welsh village to close up the isolated house she has inherited from her mother. She is assailed by her long-repressed resentments against her mother and begins to hallucinate strange noises and men attacking her as she rapidly sinks into psychosis. In a scene borrowed from **Repulsion** (1965), a man delivering a message is stabbed to death. In the end, the house's maternal associations prove too much and she retreats to a shed in a demented stupor. Virtually the same story is treated with far greater flair in Egill Edvardsson's **Husid** (1982).

d/s Harry Bromley Davenport *p* Ian Merrick *c* Joe Mangine *lp* Ika Hindley, Charles Seely, William Jones, Johnny Johnson, Carlo Davis, Alan Williams, Les King, Elwyn Rees

Yin-Yang Chieh *aka* **Blood Reincarnation**

(FONG MING COMPANY; HONG KONG) scope 99min

The actor Yang Chun, who stars in the third and final story of this excellent omnibus movie, and his wife Yu Feng-Chih, co-produced the film. Each tale is directed in a different style and each has its own tone, ranging from aggressive goriness to poetic classicism via comedy. *The Treasure* is a hysterically visceral tale shot with frantic camera and editing styles. A man (Shih) and his pregnant wife (Huang) double-cross and murder an old woman (Chi) over a pot of treasure which in fact merely contains human bones. Huang's child, born amidst screams of pain, is possessed by the old woman's spirit and promptly kills its father. *The Wanton* switches to a comic mode with Meng parodying her own roles in sexploitation movies. A factory boss (Chiang) is nailed into a chest and dumped into a river by his wife (Meng) and her lover (Yu). Returning as a water spirit, he causes acute anguish to his rival with broad gags such as keeping his rival's urine flowing inexhaustibly, until in the end the faithless couple turn on each other. The third, longest and most stylish story, *Lau Tin Sok*, tells of an acupuncturist, Lau (Yang), who is summoned to treat a rich man's wife. The wife's lover, frightened that his relationship will be disclosed, kills her but manages to blame the murder on the acupuncturist, who is executed. But a friend has taught him the 'blood reincarnation' spell which allows Yang's ghost to return and clear up outstanding matters in the next seven days. During that time he finishes writing a text book and tells his sad story to a government man before liquefying into a pool of blood. The villain is duly punished and reincarnated as a pig.

The inordinately prolific director, who made six or more features a year, had started his career in 1969 in Taiwan under the wing of Li Hanxiang. His pictures, understandably uneven, often contain stylish sequences and testify to a bizarre inventiveness close to the spirit of surrealism.

d/s Ting Shan-Hsi *p* Yu Feng-Chih *c* Chen Ching-Chu *lp* Shih Tien, Shirley Huang (Huang Sha-li), Chi Shih-Ying; Chiang Nan, Meng Li, Yu Yang (Henry Yue Young); Yang Chun, Tang Pao-Yun, Ou-Yang Sha-Fei, Chi Lien-Kui, Chang Pei-Shan, Li Yun-Chung, Wang Ting

1974

Young Frankenstein

(GRUSKOFF/VENTURE FILMS/CROSSBOW PRODUCTIONS/JOUER)
b/w 108(106)min

Young Frankenstein begins on a dark and stormy night, with the camera panning lovingly over a torchlit courtyard, zooming slowly in to a dusty window, and dissolving as the clock strikes midnight into a caressing inspection of the gothic inscription on a coffin reposing within a dank and doom-laden crypt. A brilliant pastiche of the horror film's studied quest for atmospherics, the sequence suggests that Brooks knows his genre and intends to use it. That illusion is dashed all too soon – despite the reappearance of Kenneth Strickfaden's original designs for Frankenstein's laboratory equipment – as Frederick Frankenstein (Wilder), grandson of the infamous Baron Victor, becomes involved in a repeat experiment on the monster.

Anything goes even more frantically than it did in *Blazing Saddles* (1974), in a ragbag jumble of slapdash smut, grotesquely unfunny mugging from the abysmal Feldman, and mildly funny parodies that have nothing to do with horror movies. The pity of it is that two sequences not only come very close to brilliance, they also show the path a really good parody might have taken. One is the monster's game of throwing flowers into the water with the little girl, staged in the same tender, fragile charm as in James Whale's **Frankenstein** (1931), but in which, as the little girl wails 'Oh dear, nothing left, what shall we throw in now?', the monster turns to stare knowingly but doubtfully at the camera: he too has seen the movie. The other is the monster's encounter with the blind hermit (Hackman) who, in trying to be hospitable to his new friend, accidentally pours soup over him, showers him with wine and splinters of glass in drinking his health, and finally drives him out gibbering with terror and rage after setting fire to him in mistake for a cigar. In both these sequences, Brooks extends the spirit of the originals, confounds expectations, and creates a sort of poetry of his own very much in keeping with the spirit of **The Bride of Frankenstein** (1935). There is also a delightful scene in which the monster and his creator – top-hatted, white-tied and tailed – do their best to do a Fred Astaire on 'Puttin' on the Ritz', with the monster bellowing a marvellous phonetic equivalent to the lyrics. Boyle as the monster is in fact one of the undiluted pleasures of the film (and the only actor ever to suggest that he might play the part as well as Karloff). The other is Hirschfeld's lovingly and cleverly pastiched black-and-white photography.

d/co-s Mel Brooks *p* Michael Gruskoff *co-s* Gene Wilder *c* Gerald Hirschfeld *lp* Gene Wilder, Peter Boyle, Marty Feldman, Madeline Kahn, Cloris Leachman, Gene Hackman, Teri Garr

Above: *Shall we dance? – Gene Wilder and Peter Boyle in Mel Brooks'* Young Frankenstein.

1975

Alucarda (FILMS 75/YUMA FILMS; MEX) 90min

After the routinely exploitative **Mary, Mary, Bloody Mary** (1974) Moctezuma embarked on this bloody tale which chronicles the nightmarish anxieties of a catholic macho man – anxieties provoked by the idea of sexuality in general and lesbianism in particular. Justine (Kamini) – an oblique reference to de Sade's heroine – lives in a monastery and comes under the spell of a venomous little witch called Alucarda (Romero). Together they indulge in unclean practices such as sorcery, aided and protected by Dr Oszek (Brook, who also appears as a warlock and a hunchback). The hooded monks, led by Father Lazaro (Silva), try to exorcize Justine and persecute the evil ones who infected their congregation with sensuality. This only results in her apparent death, followed by an explosion of infernal phenomena, climaxing in a festival of blood, screaming and fire that includes as one of the visual highlights of the picture the sudden resurrection of Justine as she emerges from a blood-filled tomb.

The claustrophobic settings give Moctezuma ample opportunity to indulge his predilection for baroque composition and eerie atmosphere, thereby redeeming the silly script with an impressive image track, which is enhanced by Gavira's special sound effects and Cruz's expert lighting. Promoted as the first instalment of a series dealing with witchcraft, no sequel appears to have been produced as yet. Though he must be regarded as Mexico's leading fantasy director with a genuine talent for creating poisonously enveloping worlds, Moctezuma's major claim to fame remains his adventurous decision to produce Jodorowski's surreal fantasy *El Topo* (1971).

d/co-s Juan Lopez Moctezuma *p* Eduardo Moreno, Max Guefen *co-s* Yolanda L. Moctezuma, Alexis T. Arroyo *c* Xavier Cruz *se* Gonzalo Gavira *lp* Tina Romero, Susana Kamini, Claudio Brook, David Silva, Lily Garza, Martin Lasalle, Adriana Roel, Betty Catania

Il Cavaliere Costante Nicosia Demoniaco Ovvero Dracula in Brianza *aka* Dracula in the Provinces

(CORALTA CINEMATOGRAFICA; IT) 100min

Fulci, best known today for his gory zombie movies (**Zombi 2**, 1979; **Paura nella Citta dei Morti Viventi**, 1980), started his career in 1959 with a long list of comedies. His work began to shift nearer the gothic thriller with *L'Una sull'Altra* and *Beatrice Cenci* (both 1971). This Dracula spoof, which stars the Sicilian comic Buzzanca and is co-scripted by Avati (who himself developed into a major horror director with **La Casa dalle Finestre che Ridono**, 1976) confirmed the change to his new specialization. Buzzanca plays an entrepreneur who gets bitten by Dragulescu (Steiner) on a trip to Romania. Fearing he has been 'infected' by homosexuality, he becomes depressed and desperately tries to regain his macho powers. In the process, he discovers by accident that the consumption of blood makes all his troubles disappear. Reconciled to being a vampire, he organizes a blood bank in his factory with every worker contributing to its constant replenishment. While the labour relations' aspect of the story is more to the point than in the overtly symbolic **Hanno Cambiato Faccia** (1971), the movie's assumption that its audience will share the view that homosexuality is both terrifying and ludicrous reeks of retarded rural catholicism. The script is extremely garrulous and works like a sitcom rather than a cinematic crazy comedy. Ingrassia, who starred in many of Fulci's earlier comedies, makes an appearance as an old Sicilian warlock while Orfei participates in some of the kinkier sex scenes.

d/co-s Lucio Fulci *p* R. Marini *co-s* Pupi Avati, Bruno Corbucci, Mario Amendola *c* Sergio Salvati *lp* Lando Buzzanca, Sylva Koscina, Christa Linder, Moira Orfei, Rossano Brazzi, Valentina Cortese, Ciccio Ingrassia, John Steiner, Grazia Spadaro, Giancarlo Rossi

Chi o Suu Bara *aka* **The Evil of Dracula**

(TOHO; JAP) scope 87min

After making two vampire movies for Toho (**Chi o Suu Ningyo**, 1970 and **Chi o Suu Me**, 1971) Yamamoto and his scenarists appeared to have run out of interesting ways of treating the subject, and turned for inspiration to Sheridan LeFanu's *Carmilla*, although this film also – all too obviously – follows the example of Hammer's **Lust for a Vampire** (1970). The principal (Tanaka) of a school and his wife, like all the school's directors before them, are said to be the descendants of Dracula but, because they live a frugal life, they consume only one or two female pupils per year. Nevertheless, the establishment's doctor gets suspicious when he continually has to treat students who faint during class and finds fang marks on their breasts and warns the new psychology teacher (Kurosawa), but pays with his life when he attempts to catch the principal in the act. Having learnt the full story from his predecessor, now incarcerated in an asylum, the teacher destroys the vampire couple by ramming a red-hot poker into the principal's heart, causing both bloodsuckers to decompose into skeletons.

This ludicrous anti-authoritarian youth movie sadly spelled the end of a once promising series.

d Michio Yamamoto *p* Fumio Tanaka *s* Ei Ogawa, Masaru Takasue *c* Katsumi Hara *lp* Toshio Kurosawa, Mariko Mochizuki, Shin Kishida, Hunie Tanaka, Katsuhiko Sasaki, Mio Ota, Mika Katsuragi, Tetsuko Aramaki, Yunosuke Ito

Ernest Borgnine as the satanist in The Devil's Rain.

La Cruz del Diablo *aka* **The Devil's Cross**

(BULNES; SP) 96min

Gilling's best movie before he retired as a director (and settled in Spain) was also the first Spanish feature to be directed by a non-Hispanic foreigner and a special ministerial permit was needed to overrule the union's objections. The bad feelings aroused by this action may have something to do with the picture's virtual disappearance since its opening in March 1975.

The narrative is derived from stories by the great 19th-century *poète maudit*, Gustavo Adolfo Becquer, whose work had previously been used for Antonio del Amo's *El Huesped de las Tinieblas* (1949). The hero (Marsillac) is a writer fascinated by mysterious folk legends, as was Becquer himself. Gradually, he loses his grip on reality and believes himself to be possessed by the devil. He tries to break the spell through his love for an ideal woman (Sevilla), but she turns out to be part of the problem, and his world disintegrates into a nightmare. Through a dream sequence, showing the medieval Templars' sect, the movie came to be associated with Amando de Ossorio's blind-dead series. Gilling's direction is as effective and intriguing as at the time of his best Hammer movies (**The Reptile** and **The Plague of the Zombies**, both 1966), even though he hadn't made a film since **The Mummy's Shroud** (1967).

d John Gilling *s* Juan José Porto, Jacinto Molina *c* Fernando Arribas *se* Pablo Perez *lp* Carmen Sevilla, Adolfo Marsillac, Emma Cohen, Fernando Sancho, Eduardo Fajardo, Monica Randall, Ramiro Oliveros, Tony Isbert

Deafula (SIGNSCOPE) b/w 90min

A routine low-budget vampire movie, with Wechsberg the theology student who periodically grows fangs, develops a thirst and becomes Deafula, having been infected before birth by Count Dracula himself (Holmstrom). Eventually trapped in a church, he expires under the weight of religious symbolism. As a curiosity, however, *Deafula* is unique: it was filmed entirely in deaf-and-dumb sign language (though with a voice-over commentary providing a literal translation) by a director who was responsible for America's first TV newscast in sign language.

d/s Peter Wechsberg *p* Gary R. Holmstrom *lp* Peter Wechsberg, James Randall, Dudley Hemstreet, Lee Darrel, Gary R. Holmstrom

The Devil's Rain

(SANDY HOWARD PRODUCTIONS) 86min

Borgnine here plays the leader of a satanist cult who operate out of a ghost town and liquidate (literally) anyone getting in their way. He's the reincarnation of a 17th-century witch burned at the stake, and is is looking for a book containing the names of people promised to the devil and without which he cannot deliver their souls. Having found it, he has all the souls in a bottle, but someone breaks it and the coven all melt into puddles of sticky goo. Although script, direction and acting are all desperately stilted, the special effects, including the transformation of Borgnine into a horned demon, are fairly impressive. The film was shot in Todd-AO 35, but released in most territories in standard format.

d Robert Fuest *p* James V. Cullen, Michael S. Glick *s* Gabe Essoe, James Ashton, Gerald Hopman *c* Alex Phillips Jnr *lp* Ernest Borgnine, Eddie Albert, Ida Lupino, William Shatner, Keenan Wynn, Tom Skerritt

Exposé *aka* **The House on Straw Hill** *aka* **Trauma**
(NORFOLD INTERNATIONAL PICTURES; GB) 117(82)min
With the producer of José Larraz's sex-and-horror movie, **Vampyres** (1974), and a director-writer who had made a TV documentary about sexploitation movies for the BBC, a great deal could have been expected from this collaboration. The story combines classic psycho-thriller and sex motifs: a writer (Kier) and his lover (Richmond) are joined by a secretary (Hayden). Caught masturbating by two boys who proceed to rape her, Hayden calmly blows them away with their own shotgun. She next seduces both Richmond and Kier, stabs the housekeeper (Smart), kills Richmond and is about to terminate Kier when one of the rapists, a horrible barely alive bloody mess, enters the picture to stab Hayden to death. The film ends with Kier, a hysterical wreck, surrounded by gore-covered cadavers. The motivation for all this mayhem is that Kier's bestselling novel had in fact been written by Hayden's husband who committed suicide. Neither gory enough for the psycho market nor sexy enough for the soft-porn market, the film sits uncomfortably in between the two stools, although this could be due to the censor's intervention which removed about 30 minutes. Only the violent nightmares that plague Kier given an indication of the direction the picture could have pursued to better overall effect.

d/s James Kenelm Clarke *p* Brian Smedley-Aston *c* Denis Lewiston *lp* Udo Kier, Linda Hayden, Fiona Richmond, Patsy Smart, Vic Armstrong, Karl Howman, Sydney Knight

El Extraño Amor de los Vampiros *aka* **La Noche de los Vampiros** *aka* **Los Vampiros También Duermen**
(RICHARD FILMS; SP) scope 91min
This picture is often confused with Klimovsky's **La Orgia de los Vampiros** (1972). Before returning to his string of collaborations with Jacinto Molina with *Planeta Ciego* (1975), the Argentinian-born director made this sexploitative quickie about a young woman (Cohen, who made her name in Jesús Franco's **Al Otro Lado del Espejo**, 1973) who falls in love with an aristocrat (Ballesteros). After their one night stand, she senses his calling out to her and she goes to his sinisterly mysterious castle peopled by vampires. Orgiastic scenes follow and, in spite of her efforts to protect her lover, disapproving villagers along with her own father put an end to the unseemly goings-on, killing her in the process. The vampire eventually commits suicide, as he did in **El Gran Amor del Conde Dracula** (1972). In less exclusively commercial hands, the story might have become a delirious love poem, but Klimovsky ignores the subtler aspects of the relationship and goes for the usual shock-horror effects leavened with sex.

d Leon Klimovsky *s* Juan José Daza, Carlos Pumares, Juan José Porto *c* Miguel Mila *lp* Emma Cohen, Carlos Ballesteros, Vicky Lusson, Rafael Hernandez, Barta Barry, Mari Paz Pondal, Roberto Camardiel

Forvandlingen *aka* **Metamorphosis**
(SVENSKA FILMINSTITUTET; SW)
b/w and col scope 88(85)min
This is an overly academic but visually impressive version of Kafka's famous early short story *Die Verwandlung* about a man (Schildt) who wakes up one morning to find he has turned into a giant beetle. The horror and disgust at his own physical existence experienced by the central character are reflected in the reactions of those around him. In the end, utterly miserable and lonely after even his sensitive sister (Karlsson) – she plays the violin – turns away from him, he commits suicide. Whereas Kafka's expert and bizarre language games constituted the backbone of his profoundly uncinematic story, Dvorak and his fellow refugees from Czechoslovakia try to compensate by using exceedingly stylish and mobile black-and-white camerawork, punctuated with fantasy sequences in colour, but still fail to overcome the fundamentally static nature of the situation. The beetle was the creation of special effects' man Krecik.

The simple brutalities of Pete Walker's House of Mortal Sin.

d/co-s Ivo Dvorak *p* Bengt Forslund *co-s* Lars Foressell *c* Jiri Tirl, Lasse Karlsson, Roland Steiner *se* Eugen Krecik *lp* Peter Schildt, Ernst Guenther, Gunn Wallgren, Per Oscarsson, Ingalill Karlsson, Jan Blomberg, Augustin Benka, Claire Wikholm

House of Mortal Sin *aka* **The Confessional**
(PETE WALKER-HERITAGE-LTD; GB) 104min
With this picture the Walker-McGillivray team tried to do for the Catholic church what their **Frightmare** (1974) had done for the family and *House of Whipcord* (1974) for prisons: adopt a brutally cynical approach loosely related to sixties, anti-authoritarian ideologies and ruthlessly exploit the theme for all the gore and sex it can possibly yield within a commercially saleable format.

Producer/director Walker himself devised this tale of a sex-mad, homicidal priest (Sharp) and a heroine in peril (Penhaligon). The film-makers amuse themselves by turning all the traditional paraphernalia of salvation into tools for blackmail and murder: the priest keeps a tape-recorder in his confessional, uses his rosary to strangle a woman (Beacham), administers a poisonous communion wafer to his old mother and manages to kill a man with a flaming incense burner. For added box-office appeal, the grotesque violence is fleshed out with arbitrary evocations of blighted sexual liaisons. However, the direction remains hamfisted, the performances unfocused rather than maniacal and the script woefully contrived.

d/p Pete Walker *s* David McGillivray *c* Peter Jessop *lp* Anthony Sharp, Susan Penhaligon, Stephanie Beacham, Sheila Keith, Norman Eshley, Hilda Barry, Stuart Bevan, Mervyn Johns, Julia McCarthy, Kim Butcher

I Don't Want to Be Born *aka* **The Monster** *aka* **The Baby** *aka* **The Devil Within Her** *aka* **Sharon's Baby**
(UNICAPITAL; GB) 94min
This potentially interesting variation on the exorcism and demon-baby motifs is ruined by a bad script and lackadaisical direction. Having first encouraged, then rejected, the advances of a dwarf (Claydon) in the strip club where she works, Lucy (Collins) finds that her baby – which she fears may be the result of an affair with the seedy owner of the strip club (Steiner) – is possessed. Both factors are clearly blamed on her own sexual peccadilloes she is duly punished as the dwarf, after a long delay to allow for the gruesome murders of her husband (Bates) and a doctor (Pleasance), eventually kills her too. The happy ending is provided by the sexless nun Albana (Atkins) performing a boringly routine exorcism, intercut with the dwarf's death in the middle of his stage act. Sasdy and most of the cast seem to have lost interest quite early in the proceedings, although there is the occasional echo of the director's cinematic flair shown so impressively in **Countess Dracula** (1970) and **Hands of the Ripper** (1971).

d Peter Sasdy *p* Norma Corney *s* Stanley Price *c* Kenneth Talbot *se* Bert Luxford *lp* Joan Collins, Eileen Atkins, Donald Pleasance, Ralph Bates, Caroline Munro, Hilary Mag, John Steiner, George Claydon, Janet Key, Judy Buxton

Inn of the Damned
(TERRYROD PRODUCTIONS; AUST) 125(110)min
Bourke specialized in low-budget potboilers aimed at the American exploitation market. This awkward cross between an Australian western and a psycho-killer picture is set in 1896 in the impressive Gippsland region, here reduced to picturesque, tourist-board scenery for a rudimentary plot. A sleazy coach stop is run by a deranged woman (Anderson) and her bloodthirsty husband (Furst), driven over the edge when their children are murdered by an escaped convict (Quilter). Anyone who stays at the inn disappears.

Joan Collins as the mother who gives birth to a 'possessed' baby with Eileen Atkins whose exorcism finally saves the day in the confused I Don't Want to Be Born.

Direction and script are routinely bland, failing to blend the two genres. Compared with David Cronenberg's uniquely pathological science fiction fantasies – made in a territory similarly colonized by the culture industry of the United States – Bourke's drab picture constitutes a depressing attempt to please the colonizers' assumed tastes and it was rewarded with condescending pats on the back, which didn't prevent the film from sinking immediately into the glut of the US video fodder. He pushed the sexploitation elements of this effort a bit further in **Lady, Stay Dead** (1982), but the results remained remarkably similar.

d/co-p/s Terry Bourke *co-p* Rod Hay *c* Brian Probyn *lp* Judith Anderson, Alex Cord, Michael Craig, Joseph Furst, Tony Bonner, John Meillon, Robert Quilter, Carla Hoogeveen, Linda Brown

El Inquisidor *aka* **The Inquisitor**
(INDUSTRIA ANDINA DEL CINE/MARLO; PERU,ARG) 90min
This potentially interesting story, with its unusual role for witches, was elaborated into a film marred by the traditional misogyny which presents women as at their deadliest when a man enters them during lovemaking. The woman doctor in charge of an asylum takes some of the inmates, including one with inquisitorial fantasies, to an old castle where they are supposed to administer justice to a bunch of sinners. She selected the unsuspecting sinners very carefully, making sure she stood to gain a considerable amount from their deaths. However, two of the guests, both beautiful young women, are real witches who invoke the help of Satan to return the evil doctor's evil in kind, which results in the deaths of the scheming doctor and her accomplices. Zubarry, the *grande dame* of Argentinian fantasy movies who appeared in Soffici's *El Extraño Caso del Hombre y la Bestia* (1951) as well as in numerous melodramas, makes a welcome return to the genre.

d Bernardo Arias *s* Gustavo Ghirardi *c* Carlos Bonnatti, Pedro Marcialetti *se* Roberto Combi *lp* Maria Aurelia Bisutti, Dulio Marzio, Olga Zubarry, Elena Sedova

Jaws (U) pv 125min
In 1972, in *Duel*, Spielberg turned a petrol tanker lumbering along the highway into a nightmarish Jungian archetype. Although sharks – to judge by the phenomenal success of *Jaws* and the countless imitations it spawned – occupy an even more privileged place of terror in the collective unconscious, Spielberg this time was hampered by the pretensions which linger in Benchley's adaptation of his own bestseller. The peaceful little Long Island holiday resort just happens to be preparing for the 4 July influx as the Great White claims its first two victims. When the mayor (Hamilton) overrules the police chief (Scheider) about closing the beaches, arguing that panic measures will jeopardize the town's summer prosperity, the stage is set for an Ibsenish social conflict. No conflict materializes, however, since the mayor proves to be little more than a straw dummy, and the police chief is soon more preoccupied with personal problems arising from his morbid fear of the sea. Instead, the film turns to Herman Melville for inspiration and drags in an old man of the sea (Shaw) who offers his services as a shark hunter but is really seeking a showdown with his own Moby Dick. Nevertheless, despite these hesitations, the film remains remarkably gripping.

In the brilliant opening sequence – a solitary moonlight bathe by the first victim – Spielberg sets up a *frisson* which keeps the nerves jangling nicely as one wonders with the foreboding police chief which of the holidaymakers on the crowded beach will be the first to venture into the surf, or as one seems to glimpse a suspicious shadow just as the lookout cheerfully signals that all is clear for bathers. The last third of the film, claustrophobically set on the small boat in which three men set out to hunt the shark and going into fascinating detail about the techniques of shark fishing, is even better. Here, with the monster making its electrifying first appearance and the camera unnervingly suggesting that the hunters may in fact be the hunted, *Jaws* leaves bestselling considerations behind and rejoins Jung – even if the monster's rubber origins become all too evident.

d Steven Spielberg *p* Richard D. Zanuck, David Brown
s Peter Benchley, Carl Gottlieb *c* Bill Butler
lp Roy Scheider, Robert Shaw, Richard Dreyfuss, Lorraine Gary, Murray Hamilton

El Jovencito Dracula
(LOS FILMS DEL MEDITERRANEO; SP) scope 95min
Although a first feature made with obviously limited means, this ingenious comedy offers a welcome variation on the Dracula-Van Helsing relationship. Summoned to Transylvania on the death of the last Count Dracula to attend the reading of the will, young Jonathan Dracula (Benpar), a student of vampirology at the university of Venice, encounters Mina Harker and her friend Lucy. Van Helsing's latest descendant has become the local mayor and is intent on wiping out all traces of the Dracula family by acquiring their castle and turning it into a tourist attraction. With the help of the faithful family servant Renfield, young Jonathan is able to foil these entrepreneurial schemes and, accepting his familial responsibilities, he becomes the incarnation of the prestigious Count. The opposition between the aristocratic youth's dedication to sensual enjoyment and the stuffy greediness of the mayor could have been explored further, to elaborate on the conflict between aristocracy and bourgeoisie which both Stoker and Terence Fisher placed at the heart of the Dracula myth. However, Parra tends to go for easy laughs allowing a potentially fascinating critique of the myth to disintegrate into broad farce. The film nevertheless remains far more interesting than the burlesque *El Pobrecito Draculin* (1976).

d/p/co-s Carlos Benpar (Carlos Benito Parra) *co-s* José Domenech, Patricio Raoran *c* Tomas Pladevall *lp* Carlos Benpar (Carlos Benito Parra), Susanna Estrada, Victor Israel, Marina Ferri, Veronica Miriel, Norma Kerr

Kun Pi *aka* **Kan Pi** *aka* **Pregnant by a Ghost**
(FIVE STARS PRODUCTION; THAI) scope 110min
Both the coyly melodramatic and the gory horror elements of this post-**Exorcist** (1973) movie are typical of Thai contributions to the genre in this period, although this film is perhaps not quite as gruesome as some. As so often in Asian horror films (**Curse of the Vampires**, 1970 and **Patayin Mo Sa Sindak si Barbara**, 1973, for example), the neurotic fantasies underpinning the script are represented with more explicit candour than is the case in their Western counterparts. While **Rosemary's Baby** (1968) required satan as a father and *The Exorcist* prudishly cloaked the sexual implications of the 'possession' of a body, here the process is shown directly: during a rainstorm, Narin (Sripatimakul) and Kata (Lieh) shelter in a cave where they make love. During the act, a 'demon' takes over Lieh's personality and Sripatimakul finds herself pregnant with a demonic child. Lieh, one of the Shaw brothers' action stars, is here cast against type as the romantic hero. The story was provided by Sumon Sirima.

d/s Rom Bunnag *p* Kiat Iempungpon *c* Wang Yonglong
lp Lo Lieh, Runglawan Sripatimakul, Krung Sriwilao, Wantana Bunbanterng, Fang Ye, Lak Apichart

The Last Victim *aka* **Forced Entry**
(PRODUCTIONS TWO) 83(79)min
The only real interest in this poorly photographed and edited film is in the skeletons in the closets of Roberts and Allen. Originally released in 1975, the film was reissued in 1980 as *Forced Entry* in the wake of the success of both women. The rudimentary plot features Max as Carl, the gas station attendant who seems to be the typical boy-next-door but is, in fact, a habitual rapist and murderer. The opening in which, *film noir* fashion, Max drives through the city streets violently sounding off against 'whores' is quite in keeping with the slow-motion rapes and murders that follow, climaxing in the lengthy terrorizing of a young housewife (Roberts).

d/co-p/s Jim Sots *co-p* Henry Scarpelli *c* Aaron Kleinman
lp Tanya Roberts, Ron Max, Nancy Allen, Robin Leslie, Michelle Miles

The terrors of the deep: Jaws.

Leonor (ARCADIE PRODUCTIONS/FILMS 66/URANUS/GOYA FILMS/TRANSEUROPA FILMS; SP, FR, IT) 100min
This early-19th-century tale, attributed to one of Poe's admired authors, Ludwig Tieck, is one of the rare stories of the period to feature a female vampire. Buñuel, the son of the great Luis, changed it from a macabre folktale into a gothic *amour fou* movie about a 14th-century knight (Piccoli) who is so obsessed with his deceased wife, Leonor (Ullmann) that, in spite of his remarriage to Catherine (Mutti), he moves into the vault of his castle to live near his beloved's tomb, and makes a pact with the Devil to bring her back to life. Although the resurrected Leonor turns out to be a plague-carrying vampire, wreaking havoc in the area, the knight remains devoted to her until, pursued by the vengeful villagers, they finally die together by drowning in the moat. In spite of the impressive colour photography, the movie's funereal lyricism fails to achieve the degree of delirium the story requires, and the film remains stuck somewhere in the area between Roger Corman's Poe movies and Mario Bava's **Operazione Paura** (1966). The acting is generally excellent and Ennio Morricone's characteristically obsessive score enhances the picture.

d/co-s Juan Buñuel *co-s* Philippe Nuridzany, Pierre Maintigneux, Jean Claude Carrière, Clement Biddle Wood
c Luciano Tovoli *lp* Michel Piccoli, Liv Ullmann, Ornella Mutti, Antonio Ferrandis, José Maria Caffarel, Angel del Pozo

Lèvres de Sang
(OFF PRODUCTION/SCORPION 5/NORDIA FILMS; FR) 90min
With this beautifully macabre poem, Rollin delivered his best work since **Le Frisson des Vampires** (1970) and **Requiem**

pour un Vampire (1971) and the film remains his most impressive work to date. It tells of a young man, played by Philippe (who also co-authored the script) who has visions, perhaps memories, of an old castle and an ethereal woman in white (Briand). He becomes increasingly obsessed by her and she appears to him as a spectral figure in a dark cinema, leading him to the Montmartre cemetery and causing him to open coffins and release a horde of female vampires on the city. Eventually he finds his way to a dank dungeon where his family are gathered round a coffin. His mother tells him to destroy the once beautiful girl buried there and so put an end to the family curse. Mad love, however, triumphs and the man finally gets together with Briand, who turns out to be his sister, ceremonially entombed by his mother for vampirizing his father.

This is Rollin's most explicit oedipal fantasy with the unattainable, virginal but mysteriously sensual woman in white as the keeper, together with the mother, of the family's darkly sensual secrets. In many ways also his most oneiric and technically accomplished visual poem, the film proved a flop at the box-office in the sex-and-horror circuit, satisfying neither market. Some of the images, such as the naked woman draped in a mauve cloak lying in the dunes by the ruins of a seaside castle, help make this one of the best surrealist pictures in the genre. Before embarking on a series of pornographic quickies, Rollin again attempted a sex-and-horror picture, this time with hard-core sequences, **Phantasmes** (1975).

d/co-s Jean Rollin *p* Jean-Marc Ghanassia *co-s* Jean-Lou Philippe *lp* Jean-Lou Philippe, Anne Briand, Nathalie Perrey, Willy Braque, Paul Biscaglia, Cathy Castel, Pony Castel, Martine Grimaud, Anita Berglund, Claudine Béccarie, Mireille Dargent, Hélène Maguin

The Love Butcher (A DESERT PRODUCTION) 83min

Not released until 1982, *The Love Butcher* is interesting in that whilst its production pre-dates the stalk-'n'-slash craze, its ironic tongue-in-cheek script actually highlights and parodies the gross misogyny of the subgenre. The film's central character is Caleb (Stern), a balding crippled gardener constantly mistreated by his female suburban Los Angeles employers. Whenever he is insulted or dismissed he returns as his handsome virile *alter ego* 'brother' Lester, who seduces and kills the offenders with various gardening tools, after first delivering a tirade about how they emasculate men and deserve to die. What makes the low-budget feature particularly parodic is its combination of self-consciously 'arty' techniques (flashy slow-motion inserts and ludicrous cross-cutting) with ridiculous dialogue.

co-d Mikel Angel *co-d/co-s/co-c* Don Jones *p* Gary Williams, Micky Belski *co-s* James Evergreen *co-c* Austin McKinney *lp* Erik Stern, Kay Neer, Jeremiah Beecher, Edward Roehm, Robin Sherwood

La Noche de los Gaviotas, *the third in the bizarre series of films featuring the hooded, eyeless Knights Templar zombies.*

La Maldición de la Bestia *aka* **Night of the Howling Beast** *aka* **The Werewolf and the Yeti**

(PROFILMES; SP) scope 95min

This sequel to **El Retorno de Walpurgis** (1973), was Molina's eighth film as Waldemar Daninsky, the reluctant werewolf, in a series initiated by **La Marca del Hombre Lobo** (1967). The picture opens with views of London, incongruously accompanied by strains of 'Scotland the Brave' on the soundtrack. Waldemar joins an expedition to Tibet in search of the yeti. While exploring the mountains, he strays into a cave inhabited by two exotic women with whom he spends some enjoyable moments before discovering them eating his guide. Bitten by one of his eccentric lovers, Waldemar turns into a werewolf. After a series of adventures including an ambush by armed bandits, capture by the wicked Saga Khan, seduction by an evil princess, torture and magic, Waldemar eventually rescues the heroine (Mills) and is cured by a wise monk. The encounter with the yeti, delayed to the last moments of the movie, is anti-climactic in the extreme.

By the mid-seventies, the veteran Catalan director's career was going from bad to worse – that is, from female Tarzan movies (*Klima, Reina de las Amazonas*, 1975) to soft-core efforts. Molina's next adventure as the werewolf was **El Retorno del Hombre Lobo** (1980), which he directed himself.

d Miguel Iglesias Bonns *s* Jacinto Molina *c* Tomas Pladevall *lp* Paul Naschy (Jacinto Molina), Grace Mills, Castillo Escalona, Silvia Solar, Gil Vidal, Luis Induni

Meatcleaver Massacre *aka* **Hollywood Meatcleaver Massacre** *aka* **Revenge of the Dead**

(FOREST FILM PRODUCTIONS) 87min

When intruders raid his home, leaving him paralysed and brain damaged and his wife and children dead, Professor Cantrell (Habif), a specialist in the occult, summons a demon, Meraki, to avenge him. The result is a poor man's **The Exorcist** (1973), a muddled mixture of artiness and amateurishness with a prologue spoken by Lee in a vain attempt to give the film some cachet.

d Evan Lee *p/co-s* Ray Atherton *co-s* Keith Burns *c* Guerdon Trueblood *lp* Christopher Lee, Larry Justin, J. Arthur Craig, James Habif, Robert Clark, Doug Senior, Bob Meed, Alisa Beaton, Pat Nagel, Woody Wise

La Noche de los Gaviotas *aka* **Night of the Seagulls**

(PROFILMES/ANCLA CENTURY; SP) 85min

After their nautical excursion in **El Buque Maldito** (1974), de Ossorio's hooded zombies returned to the shore for another instalment in the series initiated by **La Noche del Terror Ciego** (1971). Here the eyeless Templar zombies preside over nightly sacrifices of white-robed virgins who are left tied to a rock on the beach by the villagers' black-clad wives. The rituals, announced by the eerie tolling of a bell, are in honour of the Templars, hideous idol: a sea monster. The heroes are a doctor and his wife (Petit and Kosti) who eventually destroy the idol in spite of the fierce opposition of the undead knights. The ending sees the zombies again crumble to dust.

The beach scenes are particularly atmospherically photographed, but at this stage in the series, the zombies themselves have become too familiar to inspire much terror as they shuffle about, and the pictures are forced to compensate by introducing other macabre imagery – the ghostly processions on the beach, a lugubrious castle and the idol itself. Although pleasant enough to watch, the movie's narrative rhythm, previously totally dominated by the tension between the slow-moving zombies and the frantic behaviour of their victims, is thrown out of gear and many scenes begin to drag. As usual, de Ossorio supervised the special effects and the makeup himself. The next and final instalment of the saga, **La Cruz del Diablo** (1975), seems to have disappeared almost as soon as it was released in Spain.

d/s/se Amando de Ossorio *c* Francisco Sanchez *lp* Victor Petit, Maria Kosti, Sandra Mozarowsky, Julie James, Julia Saly, José Antonio Calvo

Phantasmes *aka* Phantasmes Pornographiques *aka* Once Upon a Virgin

(LES FILMS ABC/IMPEX FILMS; FR) 88(49)min

Released in 1976, this attempt by Rollin to wed horror to pornography proved a mistake on all fronts. The carelessly directed story brings three women to an ancient castle inhabited by a mysterious pervert who talks about his dead wife and locks up the three visitors. After the obligatory orgy with an arbitrary collection of guests, it emerges that the lord of the manor is evil incarnate and must subject the one he loves to hideous tortures. Rather improbably, she consents to being used in this way and so dies. The film ends where it began with a new female visitor being shown a photograph of the maniac's 'dead wife' as he tells the same old story. Some scenes, including the first lovemaking session involving a coffin in a chapel, suggest Rollin tried to do his best but soon lost interest.

His next pictures, directed under the pseudonym Michel Gentil, were all straight pornography. Only with the Romero-inspired **Les Raisins de la Mort** (1978) did he return to the French horror series he had initiated with **Le Viol du Vampire** (1967).

d/s Jean Rollin *p* André Samarq, Jean-Paul Bride *c* Allinh *lp* Mylène d'Antes, Jean-Louis Vattier, Rachel Mhas, Marlene Myller, Monica Swinn, Catherine Castel, Pony Castel, Marie-Pierre Castel, Jean Rollin, Jean-Pierre Bouyxou

Picnic at Hanging Rock

(PICNIC PRODUCTIONS/BEF FILM DISTRIBUTORS/SOUTH AUSTRALIAN FILM CORP/AFC; AUST) scope 115min

By art-cinema standards, this is a visually pleasing film which illustrates in sunlight, soft focus and nicely framed landscapes Joan Lindsay's rather clichéd sentimental novel about a favourite psychological myth: the emergence of sexuality. In order to sustain this myth, it is necessary to equate childhood with 'innocence' and adulthood with more or less guilty 'knowledge'. *Picnic at Hanging Rock* provides a story frozen in this mythical moment of transition, its schoolgirls still absorbed in a worship of the beauties of intact maidenhood but presented as ripe for violation (as the perceptive Australian writer Meaghan Morris has described it). The narrative situation – there is very little plot – is a turn-of-the century girls' school outing. Like innumerable other awakening-sex movies, the picture starts in an educational institution but, in a characteristically Australian development, it then moves towards a sexed representation of nature as the rock becomes invested with decidedly phallic overtones (an Australian equivalent of the snake in the apple tree). The narrative proceeds to chart a series of oppositions: masculine/feminine, Australia/Europe, vulgarity/cultivation using such stereotypical figures as the fat girl, the orphan, the French mistress, the sensuous dark-haired girl (Vallis) and the ethereal blonde one (Lambert). Some deaths occur, but we are never told exactly what happened and why, suggesting that the drama is played out on a more metaphorical level: the blonde is chosen by the rock – the phallic but somehow pure force of nature – and this takes her beyond the impure physicality of this world as the young girls vanish into nature's embrace.

The film's lyricism and its peculiarly Australian deployment of a sexed concept of raw nature, reinforced by Georg Zamphir's pan-pipe score, set Weir's effort apart from other, grosser schoolboy/girl fantasies that use the rituals of educational institutions as mere excuses to ogle teenage girls or, more rarely, boys. Weir's macho nature mysticism also underpinned his violent science fiction fantasy, *The Cars That Ate Paris* (1974) and gave racist overtones to his *The Last Wave* (1977) where 'nature' was symbolized by an Aboriginal man.

Innocence preserved: Picnic at Hanging Rock.

d Peter Weir *p* Hal McElroy, Jim McElroy *s* Cliff Green *c* Russell Boyd *lp* Rachel Roberts, Dominic Guard, Anne Lambert, Jane Vallis, Helen Morse, Jacki Weaver, Vivean Gray, Kirsty Child, Karen Robson

The Premonition (GALAXY FILMS) 90min

This is a film which bears favourable comparison with such earlier moodpieces such as **Night Tide** (1961) and **Carnival of Souls** (1962). Sheri and Miles Bennett (Farrell and Bell) live in a small Mississippi town with their adopted daughter (Brisebois). One day, her real mother (Barber) arrives and tries to kidnap her. She fails, and is later murdered by a demonic clown (Lynch) in a visiting carnival. Meanwhile Farrell starts to suffer from terrible nightmares and feels that Barber is threatening her and Brisebois from beyond the grave.

Strange, complex and haunting, in the Val Lewton tradition, the film draws its effect largely from suggestion as opposed to blatant horrors. Eerie and atmospheric, *The Premonition* is also graced with excellent performances, by Farrell who brings to her role the same kind of controlled hysteria she exhibited to such effect in *It's Alive* (1974), Lynch who portrays unbalanced evil as effectively as in *Scarecrow* (1973) and *The Seven Ups* (1973), and Barber as the insane, obsessed mother.

d/p/co-s Robert Allen Schnitzer *co-s* Anthony Mahon *c* Victor C. Milt *lp* Sharon Farrell, Edward Bell, Jeff Corey, Chitra Neogy, Richard Lynch, Ellen Barber, Danielle Brisebois, Rosemary McNamara, Roy White

Profondo Rosso *aka* Deep Red *aka* Dripping Deep Red *aka* The Sabre Tooth Tiger

(SEDA SPETTACOLI; IT) 104(98)min

Argento's filmic debts are not only to his mentor, Mario Bava, and to American crime writers like Fredric Brown, but also to the Italian western and its elaborate choreographies of violent death. He acknowledged that debt by giving Bud Spencer a small part in **Quattro Mosche di Velluto Grigio** (1971). *Profondo Rosso* too can be seen as an extended dance of death supported by a flimsy plot.

After the death of a medium (Meril) who 'saw' the event shortly before the axe-wielding killer burst through the door,

Right: *The jagged histrionics of* Profondo Rosso.

Hemmings and journalist Nicolodi – Argento's wife – become involve in, and start to investigate, a series of murders, which lead them to a psychotic piano player (Lavia) and his demented mother (Calamai). The quest starts (à la *Blow Up*, 1967) with Hemmings witnessing a murder and ends as Calamai is decapitated by a descending elevator. Along the way, a corpse has been found bricked up and a fresco depicting a strange murder, a nursery rhyme and the masturbatory fantasy of teeth being knocked out has taken the plot into the world of childhood and pre-oedipal psychopathology. The narrative is structured through a series of elaborate doubling devices – each death is 'rhymed' with a scene prefiguring the event and Argento makes great use of mirrors – and climaxes in a double ending (false/real murderer; son/mother) one of which involves a man being run over by two cars. There are several further references to other films and filmic conventions scattered through the narrative. Argento's jagged cutting and predilection for weird camera angles are much in evidence and give the movie a disturbingly unbalanced rhythm in which banal, over-written scenes suddenly give way to an eerily shot interior or location, or to a gruesome setpiece executed for maximum shock effect.

Profondo Rosso is a transitional work in Argento's career. Having finished the trilogy of psycho-thrillers which began with **L'Uccello dalle Piume di Cristallo** (1970), he directed a period drama, *Le Cinque Giornate* (1973), before returning to the horror-thriller format with this series of Grand Guignol sketches. This picture, however, also prefigures his irrationalist splatter movies of the late seventies.

d/co-s Dario Argento *p* Claudio Argento, Salvatore Argento *co-s* Bernardino Zapponi *c* Luigi Kuveiller *se* Germano Natali, Carlo Rambaldi, Guicar *lp* David Hemmings, Daria Nicolodi, Gabriele Lavia, Macha Meril, Clara Calamai, Glauco Mauri, Eros Pagni, Giuliana Calandria, Nicoletta Elmi

Quien Puedo Matar a un Niño? *aka* **Who Can Kill a Child?** *aka* **Would You Kill a Child?** *aka* **Death Is Child's Play** *aka* **Island of Death** *aka* **Island of the Damned**
(PENTA FILMS/MANUEL SALVADOR; SP) scope 112(105)min
After his **La Residencia** (1969), the Uruguayan-born director provided this equally dubious but again effectively staged

Innocence defiled: the demonic children of Quien Puedo Matar a un Niño?

contribution to the demonic-children subgenre. Extending the motifs treated by Peter Sasdy in **Nothing but the Night** (1972), the story has a couple of English tourists (Ransome and Fiander) arrive on an isolated island apparently devoid of adults. As they begin to discover the mutilated corpses of adults, they begin to realize what happened: the innocent-looking children massacred all the adults, exploiting the adults' reluctance to defend themselves by killing children. In the end, Fiander escapes the machine-gunning children but is shot himself by a passing coastguard vessel which mistakes him for a psychopathic child killer. This opens the way for the mortiferous infants to invade the mainland where they can increase their numbers with impunity.

The credit sequence is accompanied by images, removed from some release prints, of children as victims of wars and other 'adult'-initiated catastrophes like famines. This is supposed to provide the plot, which is derived from Juan José Plans' novel *El Juego* (*The Game*), with its moral justification. But this humanist approach is soon revealed to be hypocritical as the film goes on to equate abortion with infanticide and as we begin to realize that the basic plot is taken from Hitchcock's *The Birds* (1963) with children substituting for the animal forces of nature. As in *La Residencia*, the director proves himself an expert in conservative politics able to exploit the very 'taboo' thrills (killing kids) which are self-righteously denounced. In the end, the picture's message appears to be that turbulent and disrespectful children should be dealt with most severely and that protecting them is a mistake. Much of the film's emotional power is again due to Waldo de los Rios' score and to Ibañez' skilful use of ellipses.

d Narcisco Ibañez Serrador *p* Manuel Perez *s* Luis Penafiel (Narcisco Ibañez Serrador) *c* José Luis Alcaine *se* Sixto Rincoin *lp* Lewis Fiander, Prunella Ransome, Maria Durille, Lourdes de la Camara, Roberto Nauta, Javier de la Camara, Luis Mateos, José Luis Romero

Race With the Devil (SABER/MASLANSKY) 88min
Cruising through Texas in a luxurious motor home en route to a skiing holiday, Fonda, Oates and their wives (Swit and Parker) are horrified witnesses to a sort of witches' sabbath in which a girl is sacrificed according to Aztec rites. With the sheriff of the next town (Armstrong) pouring scorn on their story, they soon find themselves in headlong flight from what appears to be a general conspiracy. Done with more subtlety, the film might have carried a charge similar to **Night of the Living Dead** (1968), with the citizens of America's most reactionary state as its mindless villains. Starrett, however, is more concerned with the violence which escalates unsubtly into an absurd holocaust on the highway, with bullets and cars flying in all directions. Directing with stolid obviousness, and hampered by weak dialogue and characterizations (the women scream, the men

face manfully up to the challenge), he settles for a routine chase thriller which completely fails to live up to the promise of a credit sequence which uses a nocturnal highway, a gaunt hanging tree and racing clouds to brilliantly ominous effect.

d Jack Starrett *p/co-s* Wes Bishop *co-s* Lee Frost *c* Robert Jessup *lp* Peter Fonda, Warren Oates, Loretta Swit, Lara Parker, R. G. Armstrong

The Reincarnation of Peter Proud
(BING CROSBY PRODUCTIONS) 104min
This is a ludicrous attempt to extract some psychological horror from the situation of a young history lecturer (Sarrazin) who comes to believe he is the reincarnation of a murdered man. Tracing the place where the death occurred – a small Massachusetts town back in 1946 – he goes there, meets the dead man's daughter (O'Neill), and falls for her. But while trying to exorcize his dream of the past, he is murdered 'again' by the dead man's wife (Kidder), who sees him as the reincarnation of her brutish husband. Directed with a total lack of finesse, the film is even more clumsily scripted (by Ehrlich from his own novel) and features a mass of flashbacks and some truly embarrassing interventions by Hecht as an excited parapsychologist.

d J. Lee Thompson *p* Frank P. Rosenberg *s* Max Ehrlich *c* Victor J. Kemper *lp* Michael Sarrazin, Jennifer O'Neill, Margot Kidder, Cornelia Sharpe, Paul Hecht

Seduzidas Pelo Demonio
(E. C. FILMES; BRAZIL) 108min
Like Rossi's previous horror movie, **O Homem Lobo** (1971), this picture warns against the moral corruption that befalls youngsters deprived of strong paternal authority. Roberto (Cesar) is rescued from devil worshippers as a boy and adopted by Mesquita and his wife. He appears normal until he causes the death of three youths at a party in his uncle's house. Judged to be possessed by the devil, he is incarcerated in an asylum from which he escapes. Finding his distraught father in a church, he attacks him but the righteous old man assumes his responsibilities at last and rams a crucifix into his son's gut with the desired results: as the writhing boy dies the wound disappears and the child begins to look his decent pre-demonic self again. As usual in overt exploitation films preaching overtly authoritarian messages, much of the film is devoted to depicting the sinful ways of the wicked.

d/co-p/s Raffaele Rossi *co-p* Cassiano Esteves *c* Pedro Luiz Nobile *lp* Roberto Cesar, Cassiano Ricardo, Shirley Stech, José Mesquita, Alfonso Arrichielo, Ivete Bonfá, Lorenia Machado, Elen Salvador, Marcio Camargo

Jacqueline Bisset in Peter Collinson's tepid reworking of The Spiral Staircase

The Spiral Staircase (RAVEN FILM; GB) scope 89min
Robert Siodmak's **Spiral Staircase** (1946) had transformed Ethel Lina White's routine mystery story *Some Must Watch* into a wonderfully shot psycho-thriller. Collinson's tepid version of the same plot exudes poverty of imagination as well as of production values: even the staircase is reduced to a few rickety steps leading down to a defective generator in the basement. The plot features a heroine (Bisset) suffering from hysterical dumbness, a mentally disturbed but apparently suave professor of psychology (Plummer) and sundry extra characters required for the sex interest (Law and Hunnicutt) or as victims for the maintenance of a semblance of suspense. Direction seems to have been limited to ordering the camera to dolly and pan along the rooms and corridors of the mansion, padding the film up to the necessary running-time. For extra atmosphere, the movie uses big closeups of the killer's eyes and organizes a thunderstorm to accompany the climactic scenes when Plummer attacks the mute Bisset before he is shot by his diabetic mother (Dunnock).

d Peter Collinson *p* Peter Shaw *s* Andrew Meredith (Alan Scott, Chris Bryant) *c* Ken Hodges *lp* Jacqueline Bisset, Christopher Plummer, Sam Wanamaker, Mildred Dunnock, Gayle Hunnicutt, Elaine Stritch, John Phillip Law, Sheila Brennan, Ronald Radd

1976

Anima Persa *aka* **Ames Perdues** *aka* **The Forbidden Room** *aka* **Lost Soul**
(DEAN FILM/FOX EUROPA; IT,FR) scope 102min
Italy's leading comedy director ventured into unfamiliar territory with this classic madman-in-the-attic story adapted from a novel by Giovanni Arping. The result is a delightful chiller shot in a cool, almost clinical, manner that enhances its overall impact and complexity. Picking up on the voyage of initiation motif he explored in his previous success, *Profumo di Donna* (1974), he introduces an adolescent boy (Mattei) into an oppressive, old Venetian house inhabited by the boy's aunt, Elisa (Deneuve) and her stuffy husband, Fabio Stolz (Gassman). She, like everybody else, calls him by his technocratic title, Engineer. The couple, surrounded by baroque furniture in the heavily draped rooms, arouse the boy's curiosity by forbidding him access to a room in which the Engineer's mad brother is supposed to be living. The narrative skilfully weaves its set of deceptive appearances: the Engineer's humiliations of his wife are simultaneously credible and excessively demonstrative; her resignation is both feeble and distant, almost playful; in a painting class, a classic Vermeer painting is transformed into an abstract painting by examining part of it in extreme closeup, and so on. The boy's maturation culminates in the discovery of the room's secret: straightlaced Gassman, whose world appears fixed according to the neatly labelled bits of knowledge contained in his collection of dictionaries, himself is its mad occupant.

The movie can be read on many levels – from a critique of filmic realism to an illustration of psychoanalytic processes – but is most convincing as a political argument, with Venice as the place where masks of respectability crumble to reveal, amid its shabby but fascinating props, the degeneration of a class that should have died long ago. Like **Psycho** (1960), the entire movie is constructed in terms of a process of splitting or 'doubling', making every identity suspect and undermining any sense of emotional and intellectual security. Only the boy's brief adventure with Lucia (Alvina), whose enchantingly sensuous naked presence disturbs him and measures the emotional distance he still must travel, breaks the eerily gloomy atmosphere that accompanies his journey towards 'knowledge' and maturity. Delli Colli's beautiful imagery of Venice and Francis Lai's excellent score match Gassman's commanding performance. Even Deneuve's acting conveys levels of complexity not manifested since **Repulsion** (1965) – a tribute to Risi's brilliant direction of actors.

Sissy Spacek defiled prepares for retribution in Carrie.

d/co-s Dino Risi *p* Pio Angeletti, Adriano de Micheli *co-s* Bernardino Zapponi *c* Tonino delli Colli *lp* Vittorio Gassman, Catherine Deneuve, Danilo Mattei, Anicee Alvina, Ester Carloni, Michele Capnist, Gino Cavalieri

Burnt Offerings
(PEA FILMS/DAN CURTIS PRODUCTIONS) 115min
This is an over-extended and only intermittently inventive treatment of the evil-house theme, handled much more dynamically in **The Amityville Horror** (1979). Meredith and Heckart play a sinister brother and sister whose isolated home in the country is rented out, complete with unseen 'mother', to a couple (Reed and Black) and their young son (Montgomery). They move in along with Reed's aunt (Davis), who becomes increasingly ill and eventually dies. Meanwhile Reed becomes violent and starts to suffer nightmarish visions, and after Montgomery almost dies when the swimming pool becomes inexplicably turbulent, the family opt to leave. However, they don't make it: Black goes to bid farewell to the unseen mother, and when Reed follows he finds his wife transformed into an old hag. The house 'claims' father and son, who die violently, and when Meredith and Heckart return, the house is its old self and they have a 'mother' upstairs once again.

Curtis, who directed a telefilm of **Dracula** (1973), brings off a few good sequences – notably the turbulent swimming pool – but is unable to do much about the meandering script. Davis, a long way from **What Ever Happened to Baby Jane?** (1962), has disappointingly little to do.

d/p/co-s Dan Curtis *co-s* William F. Nolan *c* Jacques Marquette *lp* Oliver Reed, Karen Black, Bette Davis, Lee Montgomery, Burgess Meredith, Eileen Heckart, Dub Taylor, Anthony James, Orin Cannon

Carrie (RED BANK FILMS) 98min
In *Carrie*, adapted from a Stephen King novel, the 'force' at the centre of the tale is not, as in **The Shining** (1980) or **Christine** (1982), an object, but a person; and the fact that this is an adolescent girl (Spacek) relates the film to the wider cycle of movies, beginning with **Rosemary's Baby** (1968) and continuing with **The Exorcist** (1973) and **The Omen** (1976), in which children become the destructive instruments of the ostensible order surrounding them. Compared with de Palma's other movies (**Phantom of the Paradise**, 1974, for example, or **The Fury**, 1978), *Carrie* is small scale and intimate, although he does make full use of elaborate camera movement and editing styles.

The heroine, the repressed daughter of a religious obsessive (Laurie) is unpopular at school and made by her classmates the butt of a hideous joke in which she is voted by a rigged ballot as queen of the senior prom, then gruesomely humiliated by being drenched by a bucket of pigs' blood. However, Carrie has discovered that she possesses telekinetic powers (as do two of the characters of *The Fury*) and wreaks an apocalyptic vengeance which reduces the school to rubble. There is an underlying logic here: Carrie's supernatural powers of destruction become a metaphor for her own repression, which in turn is complemented by the sexually predicted conformity of her peers. The trouble lies in the way that the couple who ultimately become the representatives of 'normality' and the audience's point of view (Irving and Katt) are themselves implicated in the ghastly prank against Carrie (apparently post-production cutting is partly responsible for this sense of confusion). Undeniably, however, the climactic effects' sequence is astonishing, especially the death of Laurie, who after denouncing her daughter as a witch is impaled by a veritable hail of flying implements. As in **Dressed to Kill** (1980), de Palma ends the film with a dream sequence in which, after Spacek has perished along with her mother, Irving is seen laying flowers on her grave. As she does so, a bloody hand suddenly emerges from the earth to seize hold of her. It is a moment as calculated to make an audience jump out of its seats as any in the cinema.

d Brian de Palma *p* Paul Monash *s* Lawrence D. Gordon *c* Mario Tosi *se* Gregory M. Auer *lp* Sissy Spacek, Piper Laurie, Amy Irving, Nancy Allen, William Katt, John Travolta, P. J. Soles, Betty Buckley, Sydney Lassick, Stefan Gierasch

La Casa dalle Finestre che Ridono
(AMA FILM; IT) scope 100min
The underrated Avati made a number of grotesque fantasy pictures, starting with *Balsamus* (1968), the story of a fake faith-healer who seems to acquire real powers but remains sexually impotent and commits suicide when faced with having to make love to his wife. His subsequent movies were uneven but always contained excellent uncannily atmospheric passages

ight: *Oliver Reed fails leave the haunted ouse in* Burnt fferings.

and genuinely bizarre scenes. With *La Casa*, his fifth feature, he produced one of the masterpieces of the genre, a film to rival the achievements of Mario Bava's best work (**Operazione Paura**, 1966).

The story, which is narrated with consummate skill, tells of a painter, Stefano (Capolicchio), who's invited to a small rural village to restore a giant fresco in the local church painted by a recently deceased local man. The painting is a horrific vision of St Sebastian being tortured and pierced by two figures. Gradually Stefano becomes aware that there is something hideously wrong in the village as well as with the painting – and the painter – and discovers that the morbidly obsessive artist, intent on capturing the last moments of a death agony on the canvas, worked from 'life': his two demented sisters sadistically tortured young male models to death, a practice they kept up after their artistic brother's death. As Stefano discovers the village's gruesome secret, he flees into the church, only to find that the priest is one of the sisters in drag.

As the film, shot with slow, deliberate camera movements and wonderfully surreal lighting, progresses, it is invaded by a creeping sense of putrefaction – the cancerous degeneration of the fresco itself, the rotting corpse of the dead painter lying in formaldehyde, the decrepit house of the painter with an old, dying woman in residence – up to the climactic scenes in which reason finally disintegrates into nightmare. The images of St Sebastian's martyrdom and similar pictures with viciously tortured bodies imprint themselves on the mind with a sickening clarity while the laughing mouths, playfully painted on to the windows of an old house, are transmuted into signs of the disturbingly sinister presence of the house's former occupants. Avati's reticent, cool but intensely obsessive direction achieves maximum effect with minimal gimmickry, as in an extraordinary scene where an attic is brought 'alive' by the simple device of having a sack of grain gently swinging throughout Stefano's exploration of the place.

The film's motifs refer back to **Peeping Tom** (1960), but also to popular Japanese terror stories (**Jigokuhen**, 1969), and the film itself achieves a hellishness in its examination of the neuroses that underpin the morbid fascination of depicting/filming 'death at work', 24 times a second. Avati immediately went on to make a horror-comedy, **Tutti Defunti Tranne i Morti** (1977), in which the traditional horror imagery is rendered grotesque, a more corrosively surreal achievement than the plethora of horror spoofs churned out by lesser talents.

d/co-s Pupi Avati *co-p* Gianni Minervini *co-p/co-s* Antonio Avati *co-s* Gianni Cavina, Maurizio Costanzo *c* Pasquale Rachini *lp* Lino Caplicchio, Francesca Marciano, Gianni Cavuna, Giulio Pizzirani, Vanna Busoni, Andrea Matteuzzi, Bob Tonelli, Pietro Brambilla, Ferdinando Orlandi, Ines Ciaschetti

Cauchemars *aka* **Cathy's Curse**
(MAKIFILMS/LES PRODUCTIONS AGORA; FR, CAN) 91(80)min
Unless the 11 missing minutes contain truly masterful material, this is a poverty-stricken child-possession story trying to cash in on the publicity surrounding **The Exorcist** (1973) and its many successors. Young Laura (Koot) dies with her father in a car-crash, leaving a doll with strangely covered eyes which, 30 years later, becomes the focus of evil when her grown-up brother George (Scarfe), his wife (Murray) and their daughter Cathy (Allen) return to the family home. The usual demonic paraphernalia – telekinesis, speaking in strange voices and causing unsightly messes – are fielded as Allen appears to be taken over by the malevolent spirit of Koot. Eventually Murray saves the day by tearing the covering from the doll's eyes. The uninspired direction and script devote a great deal of footage to showing cars driving up to the house and people getting in or out of them. The effects are basic, the acting nondescript and the script makes nothing of the interesting thematic possibilities of the alienation of a young girl from her female body.

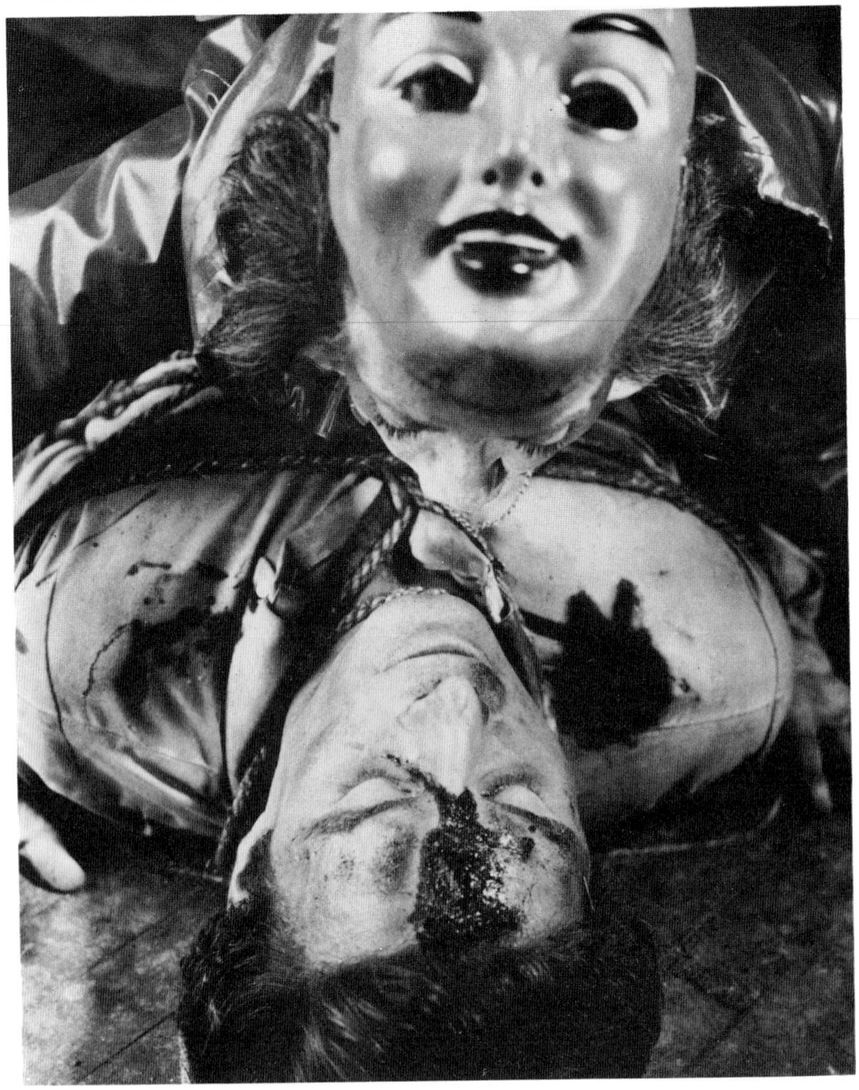

Above: *A typically bizarre image from Alfred Sole's inventive* Communion.

d/co-s Eddy Matalon *p* Nicole Mathieu Boisvert *co-s* Myra Clement, Alain Sens-Cazanave *c* Jean-Jacques Tarbès, Richard Cuipka *se* Eurocitel *lp* Alan Scarfe, Randi Allen, Beverly Murray, Roy Witham, Mary Morter, Dorothy Davis, Linda Koot, Peter McNeil

Communion *aka* **Alice, Sweet Alice** *aka* **Holy Terror**
(HARRISTOWN FUNDING) 108(96)min
Alongside the credits, while we hear the whispered mutter of prayer, we're shown the image of a veiled girl with a gold crucifix (in fact, as we see, a dagger) in her demurely gloved hands. Then Father Tom (Willrich) welcomes Catherine Spages (Miller) and her two daughters to the rectory. While eight-year-old Karen (Shields) is rewarded for her imminent first communion with cookies and a crucifix of her very own, her 12-year-old problem-child sister Alice (Sheppard) wanders the house in a monster mask and frightens the housekeeper. And when,with the congregation assembled on the day of the first communion, smoke curling from an oak chest leads to the discovery of Shields' charred and bloody body, all the evidence naturally points to Sheppard the culprit.

With superbly insolent skill, Sole plays the Hitchcock game to the hilt as the diminutive figure of the killer in a hooded yellow oilskin and flesh-pink mask pursues its path of vengeance, while red herrings multiply as semblances of culpability for the protestingly innocent Sheppard. The shock of the shower-bath murder from **Psycho** (1960) is recreated on a staircase as Sheppard's hostile aunt is repeatedly stabbed in the legs by an assailant from the basement. The hallucinating identity confusions of *Vertigo* (1958) reappear in a sequence where, answering a mysterious phone call, Sheppard's father (McMaster) pursues a figure purporting to be his possibly guilty niece, transformed in his mind into his daughter, but actually the murderer (Clinton), trapping him into a death as painfully prolonged as the one in *Torn Curtain* (1966). And *I Confess* (1953) looms in an ironic theological turnabout when the murderer, before being allowed to transfer the burden of guilt to the priest, receives for her long history of piety a vague absolution that leaves her free to continue the Lord's work by murdering with a clear conscience.

A pattern of purpose behind the display of horror-suspense pyrotechnics begins to emerge as the images hint at a web of frustrated or repressed sexuality, with the killer – the elderly housekeeper who has appointed herself mother superior to a succession of parish priests – 'protecting' Willrich as her surrogate lover/child. But Sole is concerned to take the matter further. Lurking behind the bland façade of the rectory, we discover a very old Monsignore, still nominally in charge of the parish though now rambling in his wits; and across the hallway from the Spages' apartment, the monstrously obese landlord, living in indescribably lewd squalor. Although arguably a trifle too grotesque to merge comfortably with the rest of the film, these two characters do act as powerful extensions to its theme. Menaced on the one hand by a Church in its dotage urging submission on pain of hellfire, and on the other by a corrupt society assuming eagerness to participate in its secret vices, the unhappy Sheppard – last seen furtively appropriating the killer's knife – almost inevitably takes over where her predecessor left off.

d/co-s Alfred Sole *p* Richard K. Rosenberg *co-s* Rosemary Ritvo *c* John Friberg, Chuck Hall *lp* Linda Miller, Mildred Clinton, Paula Sheppard, Niles McMaster, Rudolph Willrich, Brooke Shields, Jane Lowry

The Demon Lover (WOLF LORE CINEMA) 71min

This low-budget independent was made in Jackson, Michigan, by a group of horror fans. The plot has occultist Laval Blessing vow vengeance on his followers when they decide to break off their ritualistic meetings and call forth a hideous horned demon which sets about killing the members of the cult. The lack of budget shows in places although there is plenty of violence and bloodletting. The cast features Hansen (the alarming Leatherface in **The Texas Chainsaw Massacre**, 1974) and *Marvel* comic artist Mayerick, creator of Howard the Duck. The characters are all named after film and comic-book personalities – Professor Peckinpah, Detective Frazetta, Ormsby, Romero, Ackerman and so on.

d/p/s Donald G. Jackson, Jerry Younkins *lp* Christmas Robbins, Val Mayerick, Gunnar Hansen, Tom Hutton, Dave Howard, Susan Bullen, Phil Foreman, Linda Conrad, Ron Hiveley

Luan Peters about to be sacrificed in the silly The Devil's Men.

The Devil's Men *aka* **Land of the Minotaur** *aka* **The Devil's People**

(GETTY PICTURES CORP/POSEIDON FILMS; US,GB)
scope 94(83)min

An ancient religion wreaks havoc in the Balkans as Baron Corofax (Cushing) leads an entire village in nightly satanic rituals involving human sacrifices offered to a stone, fire-breathing minotaur in the ruins of a castle. The silliness is compounded by having the local children escape religiosity on the grounds that they are uncorruptibly innocent. The bulk of the picture is concerned with who dies how and when, with endlessly repeated shots of cowled figures mumbling incantations before their stone idol to pad out the proceedings. The director conforms to current standards by equipping the demon with genitals and having the young participants copulate extensively before falling victim to the hooded devil-worshippers. The climax is provided by an Irish priest (Pleasance) who brandishes a cross and sprinkles holy water on the villains and their idol, causing explosions which scatter bloody offal and rubble all over the set.

The only notable aspect of the film is rock musician Brian Eno's electronic score, a seventies equivalent to the psychedelics that used to signal 'with it' in the sixties. Appropriately, Eno's music also graced Derek Jarman's kitschy throwback to the sixties, *Sebastiane* (1976). Carayiannis, also known as Dacosta Carayan and Karayannis, studied in France before becoming one of Greece's most prolific directors of routinely commercial fare.

d Costas Carayiannis *p* Frixos Constantine *s* Arthur Rowe *c* Aris Stavrou *lp* Donald Pleasance, Peter Cushing, Luan Peters, Nikos Verlakis, Costas Skouras, Vanna Revilli, Anna Mentgosrani, Jane Lyle, Bob Behling, Fernando Bislani

Dr Black, Mr Hyde *aka* **The Watts Monster**

(CHARLES WALKER-MANFRED BERNHARD PRODUCTIONS)
87min

This is another blaxploitation variation on a staple horror myth from Crain, the director of **Blacula** (1972). Dr Henry Pride (Casey) is a black physician active in a free clinic and also involved in experimenting to regenerate dying cells. As a result of his experiments he discovers a formula which turns him into a raving murderer – and a white. With its seamy evocation of Watts street life and its careful delineation of Pride's poverty-stricken background (not to mention the connotations of his changes of colour), the film injects an interestingly critical social note into the tale. The film is beautifully shot by Fujimoto and climaxes in a spectacular and exciting chase around the Watts Towers.

d William Crain *p* Charles Walker *s* Larry LeBron *c* Tak Fujimoto *lp* Bernie Casey, Rosalind Cash, Marie O'Henry, Ji-Tu Cumbuka, Milt Kogan, Stu Gilliam

Eaten Alive *aka* **Death Trap** *aka* **Starlight Slaughter** *aka* **Horror Hotel Massacre**

(MARS PRODUCTION CORP) 89(86)min

Thanks to bad distribution, too many title changes and, one suspects, delayed, displaced critical resentment over the success of **The Texas Chainsaw Massacre** (1974), Hooper's follow-up has never really gained the reputation it deserves. Featuring Brand as the crazed proprietor of a hotel in the Louisiana swamplands who kills his guests with a scythe or by feeding them to a man-eating crocodile, the plot bears some relation to Jack Davis' *E.C.* comic story *Country Clubbing*, and

Left: *Eaten Alive*, *Tobe Hooper's Southern gothic follow-up to* The Texas Chainsaw Massacre *(1974)*.

is as much a blackly grotesque send-up of its predecessor as a continuation of it. In addition to the familiar swampland setting, there are references to Peter Pan and **Murders in the Zoo** (1933), various Tennessee Williams-type depictions of the decadence of rural life in the Deep South, and pokes at the macho cowboy tradition – 'you gotta do what you gotta do' mumbles Brand as he feeds yet another lady to the crocodile, while the radio cranks out a country and western song with the refrain 'oh the cowboy is a god-fearin' hard-working' man'.

Burns makes a reappearance from *The Texas Chainsaw Massacre*, and does Hooper and Wayne Bell's atmospheric and highly effective *musique concrète*. Although not as remorseless as its lurid predecessor, the film is far better than its neglect/dismissal would suggest. The scene in which a lovable little girl's pet dog is swallowed by the crocodile deserves a place in any pantheon of sick cinema.

d/co-s Tobe Hooper *p/co-s* Mardi Rustam, Alvin L. Fast *co-s* Kim Henkel *c* Robert Caramico *se* A & A Effects, Bob Mattey *lp* Neville Brand, Mel Ferrer, Carolyn Jones, Marilyn Burns, William Finley, Stuart Whitman, Roberta Collins, Kyle Richards, Robert Englund

Die Elixiere des Teufels *aka* The Devil's Elixir *aka* The Elixirs of the Devil

(ROXY/DIVINA FILM/BAYERISCHER RUNDFUNK; WG) 113min

This is a rather whimsical and wordy adaptation of E. T. A. Hoffmann's classic novel published in 1816, about a monk who drinks the fateful elixir and embarks on a series of uncanny adventures, involving doubles, murders, impersonations, flagellations, mad passions and insanity. Although not as perverse as M. G. Lewis's *The Monk*, Hoffmann's novel decisively inflected German gothic literature and eventually its silent movies when Offenbach's reworking of some Hoffmann tales was filmed repeatedly. This version of the author's most popular novel emphasizes the gothic trappings of the wayward monk's Faustian journey but appears unable to overcome the convoluted plot and extensive moralizing characteristic of the literature of the period. Although extra violence and eroticism were injected, those scenes have been removed, presumably to facilitate TV sales. What remains is a boringly flat, illustrator's approach to a story whose demonic dimensions appear not to have been grasped by the film-makers.

d/s Manfred Purzer *p* Luggi Waldleitner *c* Charly Steinberger *lp* Dieter Laser, Sylvia Manas, Christine Buchegger, Peter Brogle, Rudolf Fernau, Karl Maria Schley, Heinrich Schweiger, Horst Frank, Herbert Fuchs, Ellen Umlauf

Eraserhead (DAVID LYNCH) b/w 89min

This shoestring semi-underground feature by Lynch, who went on to the conspicuously overground features, *The Elephant Man* (1980) and *Dune* (1984), is difficult to describe and even harder to analyse.

Filmed in harsh black and white, it begins as a downbeat narrative in which a man (Nance) discovers that he and his girlfriend (Stewart) have created a premature and seemingly inhuman 'baby'. But subsequently, as the baby falls ill and Nance, who has been abandoned by Stewart, is attacked by peculiar wormlike creatures, fantasy of an increasingly macabre sort takes over. Nance's head is pushed off – the baby seems now to be growing inside of him – and ends up in a workshop being processed (hence the title) into pencil-top erasers. Even this is not the end: Nance first attempts to destroy the baby, but is eventually consumed by an alien planet. This cosmic illusion – echoed in more restrained fashion at the end of *The Elephant Man* – is certainly apocalyptic; but in the main the film sidesteps such overt symbolism in favour of an enveloping atmosphere of repulsiveness and unease.

d/p/s/se David Lynch *c* Frederick Elmes, Herbert Cardwell *lp* John Nance, Charlotte Stewart, Allen Joseph, Jeanne Bates, Judith Anna Roberts, Laurel Near, Jack Fisk, Jean Lange, V. Phipps-Wilson, John Monez

A Estranha Hospedaria dos Prazeres *aka* The Strange Inn of Pleasures

(PRODUÇOES CINEMATOGRAFICAS ZÉ DO CAIXAO; BRAZIL) 81min

With this picture and his next one, *Inferno Carnal* (1976), Marins' films entered the horror mainstream, containing, for the time being, the chillingly savage delirium of **Esta Noite Encarnarei no Teu Cadaver** (1966) and the other Zé do Caixao movies. Devised, produced and acted by Marins although directed by Motta, this film tries to combine the religious motif of sinners on their way to hell through purgatory with a more conventional iconography of death (the bowler-hatted skull) and a characteristically Brazilian carnivalesque exuberance. Indeed, the ritual of the carnival, when sacred time interrupts profane time to make way for the logic of wishes and fantasy, provides the model for the scenario. During a stormy night, a collection of characters, all of whom are involved in some sort of transgression of the social order, gather in an inn presided over by an enigmatic man dressed black and wearing a bowler hat (Marins). The travellers are intent on indulging their desires, whether it be simply making love as a couple or in an orgy, adultery or male prostitution, suicide or murder. In the morning, the nature of the place they have come to dawns upon them as the proprietor is revealed to be Death. Marins later returned to his earlier fantasies with **Delirios de um Amoral** (1978), a feature cobbling together bits from his previous films that had been censored, and *O Estupro* (1978), in which the savagery is even more directly sexual than in his earlier work. Having directed more than 30 features as well as about 130 films for TV, Marins can be regarded as the most prolific Brazilian film-maker to date.

d Marcelo Motta *p* José Mojica Marins *s* Rubens Luchelli *c* Giorgio Attili *lp* José Mojica Marins, Caçador Guerreiro, Maribeth Baumgarten, David Hyngaro, Vincenzo Colelia, Tomé Francisco, José Peres Ortega, José Nivaldo, Luiza Zaracausca

The Face of Darkness
(CROMDALE FILMS; GB) 58min
In this risibly contrived short-story feature, an MP (Pearce), whose wife has been murdered by terrorists, uses his knowledge of occult practices to raise one of the undead – a victim of the Spanish Inquisition – to commit a murder outrageous enough to create a climate which will favour enactment of his bill to reintroduce the death penalty. The plan comes off, which is more than can be said for the film which pretentiously seeks to draw parallels between medieval inquisitors and contemporary psychiatrists. Only Allister's performance as the undead lends any effectiveness to the proceedings.

d/p/s Ian F. H. Lloyd *c* Peter Harvey *lp* Lennard Pearce, John Bennett, David Allister, Roger Bizley, Gwyneth Powell, Jonathan Elsom, Susan Banaha

Full Circle *aka* **The Haunting of Julia**
(FETTER PRODUCTIONS/CLASSIC FILM INDUSTRIES; GB, CAN) 97min
The highly contrived narrative of this movie – which would seem to be attempting to emulate *Don't Look Now* (1972), though based in London – features a woman (Farrow) who, after being obliged to perform a fatal tracheotomy on her young daughter, suffers a nervous breakdown and goes to live in a large old house. After several mysterious happenings – her husband (Dullea) falls to his death in the cellar and a friend (Conti) is electrocuted in his bath – she discovers that the house is haunted by the evil presence of a little girl who had lived there, who was the leader of a gang of children who murdered one of their playmates, and had herself subsequently been killed by her mother (Nesbitt). At the conclusion, as bewildering as it is downbeat, Farrow has her own throat cut by a little girl who materializes in the house. Glossy camerawork and mannered direction are unable to lend much tension or credibility to the tale, which is derived from Peter Straub's story *Julia* and was adapted by Harry Bromley Davenport.

d Richard Loncraine *p* Peter Fetterman, Alfred Pariser *s* Dave Humphries *c* Peter Hannan *se* Thomas Clark *lp* Keir Dullea, Mia Farrow, Tom Conti, Jill Bennett, Cathleen Nesbitt, Robin Gammell, Edward Hardwicke, Mary Morris, Pauline Jameson, Peter Sallis, Nigel Havers

Eraserhead, *David Lynch's disturbing directorial debut.*

Grizzly *aka* **Killer Grizzly**
(FILM VENTURES INTERNATIONAL) 91(89)min
Having ripped off **The Exorcist** (1973) with **Abby** (1974, also directed by Girdler), and *Beyond the Door* (1975), the Atlanta-based Film Ventures International here turn to **Jaws** (1975) and replace Bruce the shark by what the advertising called '18 feet of gut-crunching man-eating terror'. The large bear terrorizes Montana state park, injuring and killing various hikers and hunters until forest ranger George tracks it down by helicopter and blows it apart with a bazooka. Most of his victims are young women (and, typically for the genre, scantily clad). Ecological messages and political machinations are hinted at but these themes are never properly developed and the special effects are routine at best (too many bear's-eye views, or low-angle shots of what might, with less stylistic manipulation, appear almost cuddly and cute).

d William Girdler *p/s* David Sheldon, Harvey Flaxman *c* William Asman *se* Phil Corey *lp* Christopher George, Andrew Prine, Richard Jaeckel, Joan McCall, Joe Dorsey, Vicki Johnson, Harvey Flaxman, Kermit Echols, Charles Kissinger, Tom Arcuragi

The Incredible Torture Show *aka* **Bloodsucking Freaks** (TROMA PRODUCTIONS) 88min
A deranged showbiz impresario (O'Brien) stages various sadistic entertainments in his off-Broadway Theater of the Macabre, which is also a front for a lucrative Gotham-based white slave trade in this cheerful piece of Grand Guignol butchery. When he captures a New York State Theater dancer his activities are investigated by the police.

Basically a series of grisly scenes from the 'show' linked by a shred of plot, the film is a totally gross exercise. Filmed in Ghoulovision and advertised as containing 'dental hi-jinks, human dartboards and home-style brainsurgery', the 'entertainments' include the Caged Sexoids (naked cannibal women tended by a dwarf), decapitation by guillotine and a woman having her brains sucked out through a straw. Something of a cult classic in the United States, and also the subject of a campaign by Women Against Pornography, the film is deliberately tacky and tongue-in-cheek (but distasteful enough nonetheless), in the spirit of Herschell Gordon Lewis.

d/s Joel M. Reed *p* Alan Margolin *c* Gerry Toll *se* Bob O'Bradovich *lp* Seamus O'Brien, Louie de Jesus, Niles McMaster, Viju Krim, Alan Dellay, Dan Fauci, Ernie Peysher, Lynette Sheldon

Inquisición (ANCLA ANUBIS; SP) 94min
Rather surprisingly for a Spanish movie, this story of 16th-century witch-hunting is set in France. For his directorial début, Molina, the leading horror scenarist and actor, chose a conventional witchfinding tale. Three legal gentlemen set out to rid the Peyriac region of undesirables, but Catherine (Randall) awakens lustful feelings in the timid judge de Fossey (Molina) who, after numerous sequences of torture and devilry, ends up being burnt as a warlock himself. Although not as sadistic as Adrian Hoven's **Hexen bis aufs Blut Gequaelt** (1969) and its sequel, Molina did avail himself of every opportunity to indulge in scenes of brutality and to undress his female protagonists. The settings, candlelit torture chambers and cavernous castles, are the work of the competent Gumersindo Andres, a specialist in this type of production.

Molina's next directorial contributions were **El Carnaval de las Bestias** and **El Retorno del Hombre Lobo** (both 1980) although his comedy about the devil's visit to earth, only to find humans more evil than he is (*El Caminante*, 1979), is his most entertaining movie for a long time.

d/s Jacinto Molina *c* Miguel Mila *lp* Paul Naschy (Jacinto Molina), Ricardo Merino, Toni Osbert, Monica Randall, La Pocha, Julia Saly, Tota Alba, Antonio Iranzo, Maria Salerno, Antonio Casas

J. D.'s Revenge (ARTHUR MARKS) 95min

This interesting variant on the Jekyll and Hyde theme features Turman as the New Orleans law student who gradually becomes possessed by the spirit of a dead gangster, J. D. Walker (McKnight), seeking to avenge a family feud. An efficient and effective piece of blaxploitation, the film is very much in the Southern gothic tradition and uses its New Orleans locations to great effect to create an atmosphere of incipient, imminent violence. Turman's slow transformation has its welcome moments of humour and the film is crisply photographed and tightly directed, with a fairly liberal helping of bloody scenes.

d/p Arthur Marks *s* Jaison Starkes *c* Harry May *lp* Glynn Turman, Joan Pringle, Lou Gossett, Carl Crudup, James Louis Watkins, Alice Jubert, Stephanie Faulkner, Fred Pinkard, Fuddle Bagley, David McKnight

Jack the Ripper *aka* Der Dirnenmoerderer von London

(CINEMAC/ASCOT/ELITE; WG, SWITZ) 108(95)min

After a series of sex and sadism pictures including *Juliette*, *La Fille au Sexe Brillant*, *Frauengefaengnis* and *Lèvres Rouges et Bottes Noires* (all 1975) starring Lina Romay and Monica Swinn, Franco only made three films in 1976: *Das Bildnis des Doriana Gray*, *Die Liebesbriefe einer Portuiesischen Nonne* and this rather better Ripper movie. Kinski's return to Franco is marked by a role that is tailormade for his screen persona. He is the philanthropic doctor obsessed by the fact that his mother was a prostitute, compulsively abducting, torturing and killing prostitutes in a London of foggy streets and dank basements. The killings are shown in colourful detail as are the sex scenes that set the tone of Kinski's panic fear of femininity transformed into sadistic aggression. Chaplin, the lover of the investigating policeman, agrees to function as bait to trap the maniac. With echoes of the surgical practices of Dr Orloff in **Gritos en la Noche** (1962), and overtones of the Jekyll and Hyde story, the film dwells on images of naked women, chained and mistreated, in its chronicle of the nightmares of someone simultaneously fascinated and repelled by sexual desire, having to maim and destroy in order to eradicate desire as such and whatever triggers it. As a film, Franco's version is well shot but doesn't come anywhere near **Murder By Decree** (1978), although it does highlight how plodding José Luis Madrid's **Jack el Destripador de Londres** (1971) and Fulci's **Lo Squartatore di New York** (1982) both are.

d/s Jesús Franco *p* Erwin Dietrich, Max Dara *c* Peter Baumgartner *lp* Klaus Kinski, Josephine Chaplin, Herbert Fuchs, Ursula von Wiese, Lina Romay, Andreas Mankopff, Hans Gaugler, Francine Custer, Olga Gebhard, Nicola Weisse

The Killer Behind the Mask *aka* Savage Weekend *aka* The Upstate Murders

(UPSTATE MURDER CO) 83(76)min

Made in 1976 (as *The Killer Behind the Mask*) but not released until 1981 (as *Savage Weekend*), this film actually pre-dates the body-count cycle initiated by **Friday the 13th** (1980) and, in its full-length American release version, is as much a sexploitation as a horror film. The plot has a group of friends visit a remote upstate New York country house for the weekend. While they are there, a masked killer starts to dispose of them one by one. The eruption of a crazed killer into this narrative of couplings seems almost like a tacked-on afterthought, although the murders (by a large range of domestic technology) are gruesome enough.

d/co-p/s David Paulsen *co-p* John Mason Kirby *c* Zoli Vidor *lp* Christopher Allport, James Doerr, Marilyn Hamlin, Kathleen Heaney, David Gale, Devin Goldenberg, Jeffrey David Pomerantz, William Sanderson, Yancy Victoria Butler, Adam Hirsch

Left: *Martin Sheen with Jodie Foster as* The Little Girl Who Lives Down the Lane.

King Kong (DEG/PARAMOUNT) scope 134min

An exercise in hubris on the part of De Laurentiis, this needless remake of the 1933 classic is not quite as bad as the comparison makes it seem. Semple's screenplay has a few witty lines, and the adequate performances of Lange and Bridges in the old Fay Wray and Bruce Cabot roles make up for Grodin's snarling villain.

That said, Rambaldi's much-trumpeted giant robot gorilla is a fake-looking contraption that fortunately only appears onscreen for a few frames, Baker's ape suit and his own miming are more effective, making the 'love' scenes, in which Kong toys with Lange, play surprisingly well. However, Guillermin's dreary direction is typical of the film's essential misreading of the Depression-era myth of the original movie. By exchanging the documentary film-making background of the original for a petro-chemical one, with an oil company set on ravaging the Third World coming up against Kong, the film tries to be modish, but merely ends up being silly as the indictments of corporate greed segue into ridiculous Toho-style monster-trampling-the-city sequences. Relocating the site of Kong's death from the Empire State Building to the World Trade Center is, as was said at the time, 'like Cecil B. De Mille having Christ crucified on a Star of David'.

Annik Borel as La Lupa Mannera.

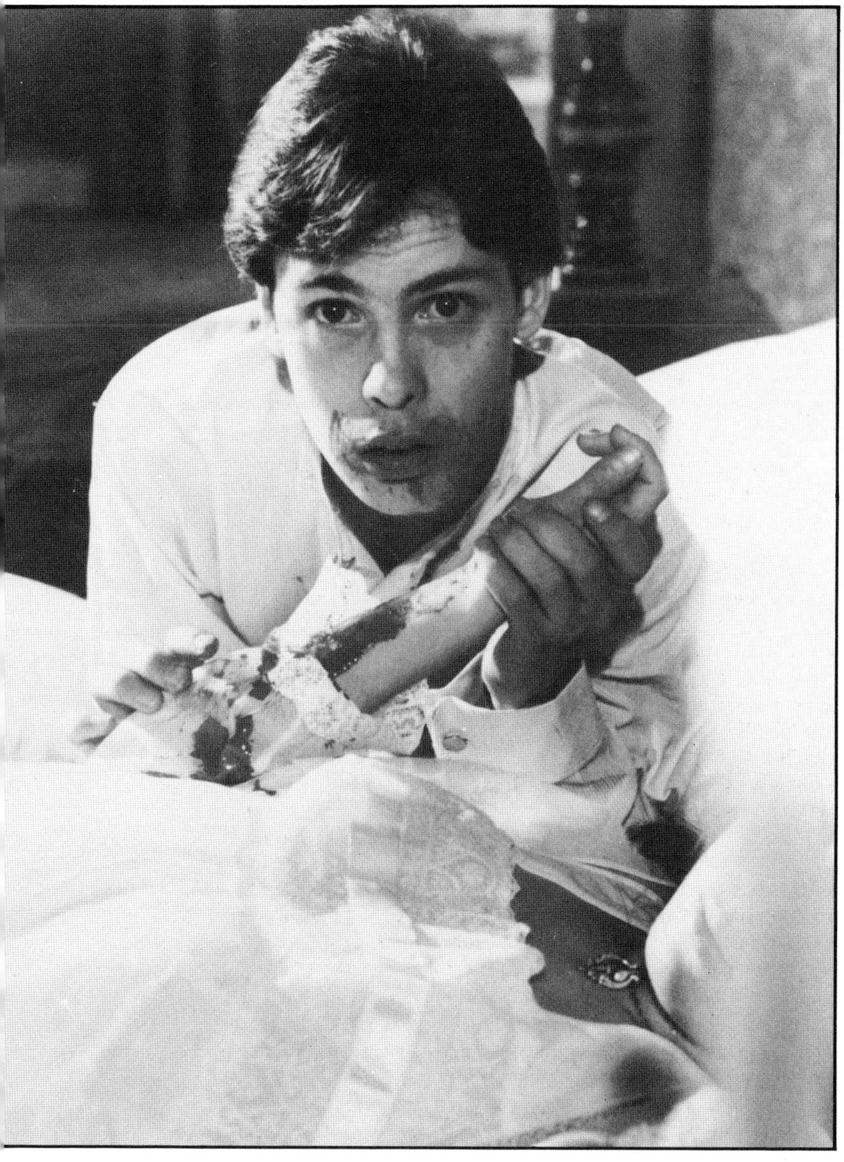

Above: *John Amplas as Martin, in George Romero's imaginative modern vampire movie.*

Mark Ferreri's *Bye Bye Monkey* (1978) is an unofficial, surreal sequel, while *King Kong Lives* (1986) is the official, disastrous one.

d John Guillermin *p* Dino De Laurentiis *s* Lorenzo Semple Jr *c* Richard H. Kline *se* Rick Baker, Carlo Rambaldi *lp* Jessica Lange, Jeff Bridges, Charles Grodin, John Randolph, Rene Auberjonois, Dennis Fimple, John Agar, Ed Lauter, Rick Baker

Lager SS5 – L'Inferno delle Donne

(SEFI CINEMATOGRAFICA; IT) scope 95(85)min

The box-office success of Liliana Cavani's picture about the pleasures of being tortured in a Nazi concentration camp, *Il Portiere de Notte* (1974) and, in America, the repulsively adolescent and racist torture-camp movies of Don Edmonds (*Ilsa, She Wolf of the SS*, 1974), triggered the nostalgic fantasies of explicit as well as crypto fascists, spawning a filmic equivalent of the established literary porn subgenre, 'il sadico-nazista'. Garrone contributed two filmic atrocities to this variation on the women's prison movies, *Lager SSadis Kastrat Kommandantur* (1976) and this movie which simply exploits 'entertaining' thrills such as Jewish women being undressed and divided into prostitutes and victims of medical atrocities. There is the obligatory Nazi lesbian, a crude abortion scene and a hefty smattering of assorted tortures. Titles in this series proliferated at a great speed: *La Svastica nel Ventre*, *L'Ultima Orgia del III Reich*, *Kaput Lager gli Ultimi Giorni delle SS*, *KZ 9 Lager di Sterminio*, *Le Deportate della Sezione Speciale SS*, *Le Lunghe Notti della Gestapo* and *Liebeslager* were all released in the 1976-77 season in Italy. Since nearly all the films flopped at the box office, the trend disappeared as quickly as it had emerged.

d/p/co-s Sergio Garrone *co-s* Vinicio Marinucci, Tacla Romanelli *c* Maurizio Centini *lp* Paola Corazzi, Paola d'Egidio, Giorgio Cerioni, Attilio Dottesio, Serafino Profumo, Patrizia Melega, Rita Manna, Vincenzo Amici

The Little Girl Who Lives Down the Lane

(ZEV BRAUN PRODUCTIONS/OCL INDUSTRIES/FILMEDIS-FILMEL; US, CAN, FR) 94min

Set in a small Canadian town, and designed as a vehicle for Foster, then aged 13, *The Little Girl Who Lives Down the Lane* inflects its French ancestry (and the nursery-rhyme allusion in its title) with elements of the whimsically macabre that bring the Gallic *comédie noire* tradition to mind. Foster plays a teenager, Rynn, living ostensibly with her father but actually on her own, with the corpses of both father (a suicide) and mother (whom she has murdered) in the cellar. An interfering estate agent (Smith), hysterical at finding the bodies, is killed in an accident on the premises, and eventually her disappearance leads to her child-molester son (Sheen) turning up, only to be given a cup of tea laced with the poison Foster used on her mother. Despite the potential for a comedy of manners, Koenig's script and (particularly) Gessner's direction have a literalness of approach and a lack of style that makes most of the humour unintentional. A subplot dealing with Foster's affair with the lame boy (Jacoby) who becomes her helpmate adds to the prevailing air of awkwardness.

d Nicolas Gessner *p* Zev Braun *s* Laird Koenig *c* René Verzier *se* Christoph Harbonville *lp* Jodie Foster, Martin Sheen, Alexis Smith, Scott Jacoby, Mort Shuman, Dorothy Davis, Hubert Noel

La Lupa Mannera *aka* Werewolf Woman *aka* Legend of the Wolfwoman *aka* The Wolf Man *aka* Daughter of a Werewolf

(DIALCHI FILM; IT) 100(84)min

Di Silvestro's stilted offering features a heroine, Daniela (Borel), whose sexual drives propel her into lycanthropy. The plot offers an opportunity to mix bloody and sexploitation scenes, and includes the obligatory lesbian and rape scenes. Stafford plays the police inspector in a manner that made his performance as OSS 117 in sixties secret-agent movies look convincing. The direction is virtually non-existent, the lighting worse and the imagery mercilessly ugly, the nadir being the tele-ad soft-focus rompings on the beach, which herald a 'cure' from lycanthropy. Di Silvestro is a minor practitioner of Z-grade pictures.

d/co-s Rino (Salvatore) di Silvestro *p* Diege Alchimded *co-s* Howard Ross (Renato Rossini) *c* Mario Capriotti *lp* Annik Borel, Frederick Stafford, Dagmar Lassander, Howard Ross (Renato Rossini), Tino Carraro, Osvaldo Ruggieri, Felicita Fanny, Andrea Scotti, Elio Zamuto

Martin (BRADDOCK ASSOCIATES) 95min

As electrically raw-edged as Romero's earlier **Night of the Living Dead** (1968), *Martin* opens with a ferociously 'naturalistic' account of its teenage hero's bloodlust in a railway compartment where he slashes a girl's wrist and drinks her blood in unambiguous sexual ecstasy. As the train pulls into the station, a snowy-bearded old man (Maazel), immaculately garbed in white, is waiting like an angel of retribution. 'Nosferatu!' the old man hisses, shepherding his young relative Martin (Amplas) off to the garlic-hung room he is to occupy in the family home. But, as Martin promptly demonstrates by ripping away the garlic and annexing his host's protective crucifix, the old talismans don't work any more. Wryly challenging genre assumptions, Amplas (and the film itself in a series of black-and-white inserts) pokes fun at the movie vampire lore, at one scarily absurd moment even swirling through the nocturnal streets in Lugosi outfit of bat-winged cloak and joke-shop incisors.

The notion of a blood-drinker living in the reassuringly familiar setting of a Pittsburg suburb where the old man owns a delicatessen and the clash of two worlds – the crumbling desolation of the immigrant ghetto and the refinements of the residential area invaded by Amplas for a bout of blood letting – make their own comments. In this context, Martin's problem is presented tellingly as derived from adolescent hesitance about sex, exacerbated by the social malaise surrounding him (reference to the Manson murders is very much in order). Although well on the way to self-exorcism after his discovery of normal sexual ecstasies with a sympathetically available woman (Nadeau), his 'vampirism' is meanwhile being subjected to traditional remedies by his elderly relative, who persuades (in neat mockery of **The Exorcist**, 1973) an amiably bleating old priest to mumble an exorcism ceremony. Naturally this fails, and the equally traditional answer is a stake through Martin's heart. Much of the charge here, questioning the validity of justice and capital punishment for 'monsters', is unfortunately undermined by the film's failure to confront (let alone resolve) the paradox presented by its rationalization of the vampire myths. Having his cake and eating it, Romero characterizes his hero simultaneously as a troubled teenager and as an age-old vampire kept youthful by infusions of blood. Message-wise, at least, the two characterizations tend to be mutually exclusive.

d/s George A. Romero *p* Richard Rubinstein *c* Michael Gornick *lp* John Amplas, Lincoln Maazel, Christine Forrest, Elyane Nadeau, Tom Savini, Fran Middleton, George A. Romero

Massacre at Central High *aka* Blackboard Massacre

(EVANS PRODUCTIONS) 88min

Pre-dating **Friday the 13th** (1980) by some four years, *Massacre at Central High* convincingly demonstrates that movies involving the violent deaths of numerous young people don't *necessarily* have to degenerate into mechanical body counts in which the victims are treated as so much cannon fodder for the special effects' men. Maury discovers on transferring to Central High that his friend Stevens belongs to a group of bullies who lord it over the other pupils. He refuses to join them, and in return they push a car over on him, permanently injuring his leg. This prompts him to engineer the deaths of the bullies, and life at Central High is much happier until other students attempt to form alliances with him and take over control of the place. Disillusioned, he initiates further deaths and eventually starts planning to blow the place up.

Starting out like a fifties AIP teen-rebel exercise and developing into a revenge tragedy à la Sam Peckinpah, the film ends up approaching the bleak nihilism of the superb *The Todd Killings* (1971), an impression only strengthened by the consistent abstraction of its realization and the laconic precision of the sequences in which Maury executes his grisly and imaginative murders. It would be a pity if the title's connotations caused the film to be passed over as simply another teenage-slash epic.

d/s Renee Daalder *p* Harold Sobel *c* Bert Van Munster *se* Roger George *lp* Derrel Maury, Andrew Stevens, Kimberly Beck, Robert Carradine, Ray Underwood, Steve Bond, Steve Sikes, Lani O'Grady, Damon Douglas, Rainbeaux Smith

Mosquito der Schander *aka* Bloodlust

(MONAREX; SWITZ) 88min

One of the rare Swiss contributions to the genre, this exercise ii psycho-horror anticipates Helma Sanders-Brahms' lurid **Di Beruehrte** (1981) in chronicling an anguished descent int madness and is based on an actual case history. A young ma (Pochath), overwhelmed by the memory of traumatic events in his childhood which left him with defective hearing and speech impediments, lives as a lonely outcast, surrounded by dolls and occasionally visiting prostitutes. When his insensitive office colleagues trigger a crisis, he takes to visiting mortuaries where he vampirizes the corpses with a pipette and steals bits of their bodies, such as eyes, which he keeps in glass jars in his room. When the only person he could relate to dies, he exhumes her body but leaves it unmolested and murders a young couple; this leads to his arrest.

Although the direction isn't nearly as flashy as Sanders-Brahms', Vajda's picture spends more time dwelling on the miserable lot of a hypersensitive youngster whose answer to a callously unfeeling world is to wallow in self-abasement, engage in zombieish practices and seek consolation among the downtrodden. That said, however, the perfunctory script simply connects up sensationalist and macabre scenes, interrupted now and then by solemn sentimentalism, as in the scenes with the girl (Zamula) who tries to dance on the rooftops and crashes to her death.

d Marijan Vajda *p* Manfred Dome *s* Nangoni Supasi *c* David Khan *lp* Werner Pochath, Ellen Umlauf, Birgit Zamula, Gerhard Ruhnke, Fred Berhoff, Peter Hamm, Marion Messner, Roswitha Guether, Charley Hiltl

The Omen (FOX) pv 111min

Following in the wake of **The Exorcist** (1973), this glossy and expensive production, with a cast of star names, confirmed the growing importance to the box office of the horror movie during the seventies. *The Omen* is, in fact, more functional and low-key than the *The Exorcist* and is propelled more by narrative invention than by elaborate effects. The story begins in Rome, where an American diplomat (Peck) whose wife (Remick) has just lost her baby, agrees to the suggestion of a priest (Benson) that another child (whose mother has died) be substituted. Five years later, the action continues in London, where the child, Damien (Stephens), becomes the focus of sundry grim happenings: his nanny (Palance) commits suicide, and Remick loses her expected new baby in an accident seemingly engineered by Damien and his sinister replacement nanny (Whitelaw). Meanwhile, a priest (Troughton) gives Peck scriptural warnings about the child, and is soon himself killed in a freak accident (a striking setpiece, in which he is transfixed by a lightning rod unlodged from a church during a storm). Peck follows Troughton's lead to Italy and through the repentant Benson unearths a plot to bring about the rebirth of the Antichrist. An exorcist (McKern) tells Peck that the child must be ritually killed in a church but as he prepares

Massacre at Central High, *one of the better 'teenage-slasher' movies of the seventies.*

The Omen, *one of the most commercially successful horror films of all times.*

to do this – having discovered that Remick has been killed by Whitelaw, whom he himself kills after an elaborate struggle – the police break into the church and shoot him dead. In a glib coda, Damien is seen being ushered into the White House, since the president is a friend of his 'parents'.

Though sometimes rather slowed down by its production values, *The Omen* is an atmospherically shot (by Taylor) accomplished entertainment, particularly in the climactic sequence in which Peck returns home to confront not only the evil Whitelaw but the ferocious hound of hell with which she is in league. The film's great popularity led to two sequels, **Damien – Omen II** (1978) and **The Final Conflict** (1981).

d Richard Donner *p* Harvey Bernhard *s* David Seltzer *c* Gilbert Taylor *se* John Richardson *lp* Gregory Peck, Lee Remick, Harvey Stephens, David Warner, Billie Whitelaw, Patrick Troughton, Leo McKern, Martin Benson, Robert Rietty, Holly Palance

The Redeemer ... Son of Satan! *aka* **The Redeemer**
(MLTD) 83min
Six students who graduated in 1967 from the Stuart Morse Academy are invited to the school for a class reunion. When they arrive they find the place deserted. It is revealed that each has committed various sins, and after a man grotesquely made up as a fairground barker puts on a show in the auditorium reviling sin and promising redemption, each is brutally murdered. Convoluted and confusing, *The Redeemer* displeases most on account of its dubious 'morality' – the only 'sins' which two of the class have committed (and they are the women, naturally) are being gay and leading an active sex life.

d Constantine S. Goochis *p* Sheldon Tromberg *c* John Michael Seymer *se* Jack Thompson *lp* Michael Hollingsworth, Damien Knight, Gyr Patterson, Nikki Barthen, Nick Carter, Jeannetta Arnette, Christopher Flint, T. G. Finkbinder, Eric Kjoenes, Larry Mooney

Satan's Slave
(MONUMENTAL PICTURES; GB) scope 86min
In this broad but rather effective foray into devil worship in the home counties, the heroine (Glendenning) gets caught up in strange goings-on at the country mansion of her uncle (Gough). He and his son (Potter) are necromancers intent on using her body to resurrect an ancestor burned as a witch two centuries before. A twist ending has her at first made to believe that the whole thing has been a dream, then delivered into the hands of the coven of satanists to which her father (Bree), who was supposedly killed early on, also belongs. Although the plot is highly artificial, it is tautly constructed by McGillivray, with some characteristically quirky reversals, such as the heroine's boyfriend (Craze) being casually killed off early in the action, an inversion of the situation in **Psycho** (1960). Young's camerawork uses garish colours and Gough's (literally) avuncular villain is enjoyably theatrical. Nevertheless, Warren's crude sensationalism (an eye gouging, Potter trailing a knife across women's nipples, and so on) causes the film to degenerate into a mere cocktail of sadistic and gory clichés culled from previous box-office hits and sexploitation-horror pictures, exemplified by the work of Jesús Franco, Renato Polselli and Claude Mulot, among others. Warren's subsequent work (**Prey**, 1977; **Terror**, 1978; *Inseminoid*, 1981) repeated the same formula.

d Norman J. Warren *co-p/c* Les Young *co-p* Richard Crafter *s* David McGillivray *lp* Candace Glendenning, Michael Gough, Martin Potter, Barbara Kellerman, Michael Craze, James Bree, Gloria Walker, Celia Hewitt

Schizo (PETE WALKER-HERITAGE-LTD; GB) 109min
Having, apparently, run out of institutional settings (used in *House of Whipcord* and **Frightmare**, both 1974 and *House of Mortal Sin*, 1975), Walker and McGillivray turn to the old standby for film-makers lacking inspiration: schizophrenia, explained to the audience with grotesque simple-mindedness by an American voice-over at the start of the picture. Since the title indicates that the beleaguered heroine and the bloodthirsty killer are one and the same, the movie exhausts itself scattering red herrings and studiously contriving nasty murders. Frederick is the victim-villain of the piece and Leyton the principal red herring, seeking to frighten Frederick into confessing to matricide. The rest is pointless mayhem and clichés as shadows lurk and doorknobs turn to the accompaniment of a ponderously predictable score, reducing the whole thing to risible absurdity. Walker's next effort, **The Comeback** (1977) tried to cash in on the success of **Phantom of the Paradise** (1974).

d/p Pete Walker *s* David McGillivray *c* Peter Jessop *lp* Lynne Frederick, John Leyton, Stephanie Beacham, John Fraser, Jack Watson, Queenie Watts, Trisha Mortimer, John McEnery, Victor Winding, David McGillivray

The Sentinel (U/JEFFREY KONVITZ PRODUCTIONS) 92min
When fashion model Alison Parker (Raines) rents an apartment in an old Brooklyn house, she is menaced by strange noises and weird apparitions. Eventually she discovers that the house is built over the entrance to hell and has been guarded through the years by a series of attempted suicide cases, the latest of which is the blind priest Father Halliran (Carradine).

In spite of a dazzling cast of character actors – including cameos by Ava Gardner and José Ferrer – and some reasonable special effects, *The Sentinel* is completely sunk by Winner's clumsy, sensationalism-at-all-costs direction. However, the film is not simply heavy-handed and mechanical it is also, like too much of Winner's *oeuvre*, extremely distasteful, particularly the sequence in which the 'legions of hell' erupt which uses *real* deformed and handicapped people in a sensationalist manner totally and utterly opposed to, say, **Freaks** (1932), in which Tod Browning treated his subjects with sympathy and dignity. A thoroughly execrable enterprise, it was parodied with *élan* by Ivan Reitman in the enormously successful **Ghostbusters** (1984).

d/co-p/co-s Michael Winner *co-p/co-s* Jeffrey Konvitz *c* Dick Kratina *se* Albert Whitlock *lp* Chris Sarandon, Cristina Raines, Martin Balsam, John Carradine, Arthur Kennedy, Burgess Meredith, Sylvia Miles, Deborah Raffin, Eli Wallach, Christopher Walken

Summer of Secrets

(SECRET PICTURE PRODUCTIONS; AUST) 100min

Better known as a director of theatre extravangazas, Sharman made the camp spectacle, *The Rocky Horror Picture Show* (1975), in Britain before returning to Australia for this silly fantasy picture. On an island, a mad doctor wearing a blonde wig (Dignam), abetted by his black assistant (Collins), busies himself in trying to remember, and then to revive, his dead wife (Fitzpatrick). This story is padded by that of another couple (Sharp and Campbell) indulging in nostalgia for an infantile existence. Most of the film is wasted on the doctor's inane musings and the screening of home movies. Sharman went on to ruin a Patrick White script, *The Night of the Prowler* (1978), and eventually went to the US. His first feature, *Shirley Thompson versus the Aliens* (1971), remains his best film, while *Rocky Horror* is enjoyable if experienced as a form of spectator sport in which the film plays but a minor part.

d Jim Sharman *p* Michael Thornhill *s* John Aitken *c* Russell Boyd *lp* Arthur Dignam, Rufus Collins, Nell Campbell, Kate Fitzpatrick, Andrew Sharp

Suspiria

(SEDA SPETTACOLI; IT) scope 97min

With **Profondo Rosso** (1975), Argento began to push his slasher movies – which had begun with **L'Uccello dalle Piume di Cristallo** (1970) – into gorier terrain, verging on the splatter genre. *Suspiria*, which established him as Italy's most efficient engineer of shock-horror pictures, is his best effort in the genre to date and looks both back to his earlier exercises in the mystery thriller, such as **Quattro Mosche di Velluto Grigio** (1971), for its highly wrought, decorative manner, and forward to his later work in the genre (**Inferno**, 1980; **Sotto gli Occhi dell'Assassino**, 1982) for its narrative design of an individual arriving in a strange locale and being plunged into a labyrinth of murders and sinister occurrences.

Here, the heroine (Harper) is a new student at a ballet school in Freiburg which was the home of a witch, the 'Black Widow'. Not too surprisingly, a coven still exists there, headed by the two principal teachers (Valli and Bennett). After a climactic confrontation with the materialized spirit of the Black Widow herself, Harper narrowly escapes as the building goes up in flames. Although the narrative is contrived and artificial, Argento's exceptionally skilful use of colour, jagged cutting and good sense of décor, as well as the recourse to a shower of maggots, traps of steel mesh to exsanguinate their victims, razors, and so on, combine to create a hallucinatory atmosphere of terror. The score, composed by the director and as usual performed by The Goblins rock group adds to the claustrophobia. Valli's performance is appropriately hieratic and the entire picture culminates in one of the most chillingly efficient sequences of the terror subgenre's brief history.

d/co-s Dario Argento *p* Claudio Argento *co-s* Daria Nicolodi *c* Luciano Tovoli *se* Germano Natali *lp* Jessica Harper, Stefania Casini, Udo Kier, Alida Valli, Joan Bennett, Flavio Bucci, Miguel Bosé, Rudolf Schuendler, Barbara Magnolfi

Un Sussurro nel Buio *aka* A Whisper in the Dark *aka* Sussurri nel Buio

(CINEMONDIAL; IT) scope 90min

This demonic-child movie, derived from Nicolas Roeg's *Don't Look Now* (1972), is set in an ancient Venetian villa where, to the consternation of his parents (Law and Delon), a little boy begins to see a sibling which turns out to be the ghost of the family's first child who died shortly after birth. The dead child insists on being recognized and accepted into the family and throws terrible tantrums when Law continues to disbelieve in his existence. The picture is both less pretentious and less extravagantly shot than its model, but as a supernatural thriller it works just as well, in spite of the routine acting.

d Marcello Aliprandi *p* Viero Spadoni *s* Nicolo Rienzi, Maria Teresa Rienzi *c* Claudio Cirillo *lp* Nathalie Delon, John Phillip Law, Olga Bisera, Joseph Cotton, Lucretia Love, Alessandro Poggi, Zora Welcova, Susanna Melandri, Simona Patilucci

To the Devil a Daughter *aka* Die Braut des Satans

(HAMMER/TERRA FILMKUNST; GB, WG) 93(92)min

With **Demons of the Mind** (1971), Sykes had shown he could imbue his horror pictures with a genuine sense of perverse eroticism, a skill that had previously seemed limited to Terence Fisher in Britain. Here he brings a satanic priest (Lee) who worships Astaroph and an American novelist (Widmark) specializing in the occult into conflict over the custody of a young girl (Kinski). The script effectively bends the original Wheatley story in the direction of Alastair Crowley's novel, *Moonchild*, and its emphasis on Sex Magick, justifying a brief full frontal shot of the beautiful Kinski during one of the occult rituals. The movie is skilfully constructed, allowing the manifestations of satanism and the explanations addressed to the viewer to increase in equal proportions, although the perfunctory ending somewhat spoils the mood. The staging of the murders, the occult manifestations and the climactic confrontation in which the novelist manages to divert the demonic forces on to the depraved cleric are considerably enhanced by excellent camerawork and Bowie's special effects, while Widmark and Lee – acting with more fervour than usual at this stage of his career – prove worthy opponents. Secondary roles are well handled by Denham as the distraught father, Valentine as the hysterical literary agent and Blackman as his sceptical wife, both helping Widmark at the cost of their lives.

Below: *Jessica Harper in action in Dario Argento's exercise in gore,* Suspiria.

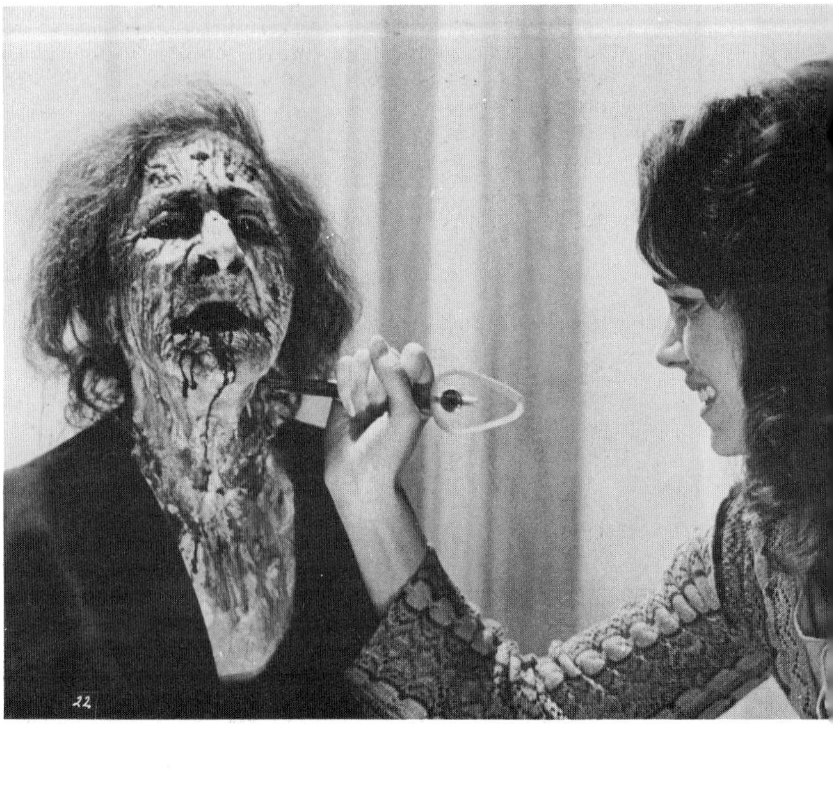

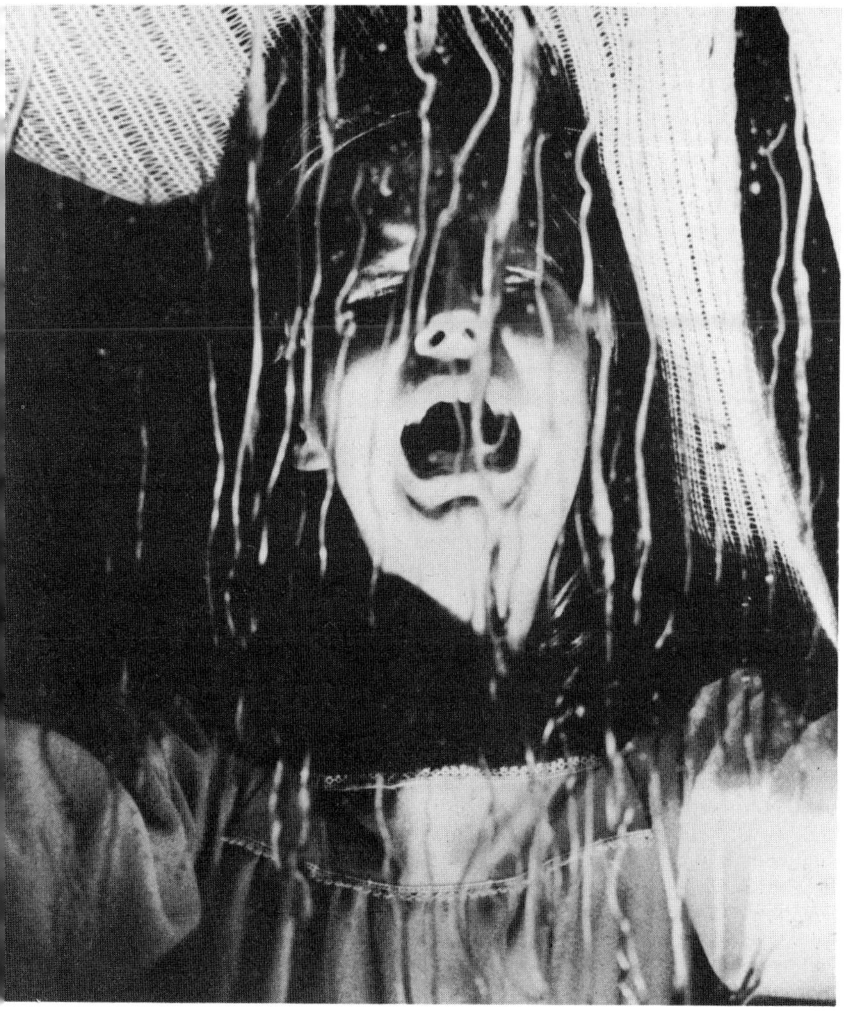

Susan Swift in a trance in Audrey Rose.

As a stylistic cross between **The Devil Rides Out** (1967) and **The Exorcist** (1973), Sykes' picture suggests new ways of exploring the gothic just when Hammer was about to collapse, leaving the terrain free for the demonic or psychological splatter movies that had evolved in America out of Dario Argento's Italian work. Unfortunately, the film also shows the limitations of exploitation movie budgets, with the superfluous Bavarian location scenes to satisfy co-production requirements and the glaringly obvious advertising spots for Lufthansa and British Airways.

d Peter Sykes *p* Roy Skeggs *s* Chris Wicking *c* David Watkin *se* Les Bowie *lp* Christopher Lee, Richard Widmark, Nastassia Kinski, Anthony Valentine, Honor Blackman, Denholm Elliott, Michael Goodliffe, Eva Maria Meineke

Ultimo Mondo Cannibale *aka* **The Last Survivor** *aka* **The Last Cannibal World**
(ERRE CINEMATOGRAFICA; IT) scope 92(88)min
An introductory title to this clumsy and unprepossessing exploitation movie claims that its story of an oil company expedition to discover the fate of two missing prospectors is based on fact and that the experiences of the sole survivor led to the discovery of a native tribe living in stone-age conditions on the island of Mindanao. This assertion does not, however, help to make the proceedings – which include an obligatory encounter with a jungle girl (Me Me Lay, a former TV presenter) – any more convincing or any less racist. The jungle setting occasionally has its moments but the film seems chiefly concerned with the gory simulation of cannibalistic rites and the realistic killing of animals, including the garrotting of a live crocodile. **La Montagna del Dio Cannibale** (1978) is a much more spirited Italian version of the same adventure-film conventions.

d Ruggero Deodato *p* Giorgio Carlo Rossi *s* Tito Carpi, Gianfranco Clerici, Renzo Genta, Giancarlo Rossi *c* Marcello Masciocchi *se* Paolo Ricci *lp* Massimo Foschi, Me Me Lay, Ivan Rassimov, Sheik Razak Shirkur, Judy Rosly, Suleiman Shamsi

Un Urlo dalle Tenebra *aka* **Naked Exorcism** *aka* **L'Esorcista n. 2** *aka* **Return of the Exorcist**
(COLOSSEUM INTERNATIONAL/MANILA CINEMATOGRAFICA; IT) 88min
This Italian spin-off from **The Exorcist** (1973) copies various details – flying furniture and so on – from its American model but fails to build them into a coherent whole. The possessed figure here is a teenage boy (Verne) and a pseudo-religious angle is stressed by making him the brother of a nun. Part of the story is told in flashback through the nun's confession to a priest, though it is characteristic of the feeble script that several episodes she recounts are ones at which she was not present. Conte, in one of his last roles, is wasted in a perfunctory appearance as the exorcist. Some isolated moments of atmospheric camerawork are about all that can be salvaged from the film. Pannaccio's previous effort in the genre was *Il Sesso della Strega* (1973).

d/co-s Elo Pannaccio *p* Luigi Fedeli *co-s* Aldo Crudo, Franco Brocani *c* Franco Villa, Mauricio Centini *lp* Richard Conte, Françoise Prévost, Jean-Claude Verne, Mimma Monticelli, Elena Svevo, Sonia Viviani, Patrizia Gori

1977

Audrey Rose (UA) pv 113min
Shades of **The Exorcist** (1973) and **The Omen** (1976) hang heavily over this occult thriller about a dead child reincarnated as another. Mason is alarmed by a sinisterly bearded man (Hopkins) who seems to be showing an undue interest in her 12-year-old daughter Ivy (Swift). When he explains that Ivy is, in fact, a reincarnation of his own daughter Audrey Rose, who was burned to death in a car-crash, Mason's husband (Beck) remains sceptical. But Ivy starts having screaming fits, mysteriously burning her hands (she is reliving the accident) and calmed only when Hopkins addresses her as Audrey Rose. Later, after a court case in which an Indian guru adds his authoritative testimony as to the reality of the transmigration of souls, an experiment is arranged in which a hypnotist takes Ivy back to relive Audrey Rose's death, and Hopkins completes the exorcism to set his daughter's soul at rest.

Solidly crafted by Wise and mercifully free of special effects trickery, *Audrey Rose* is a surprisingly watchable film if one can ignore the handicap of a script steeped in transcendental banality about the mystic East and indulging some spurious double-think to suggest that reincarnation is a legally acceptable reality.

d Robert Wise *co-p/s* Frank de Felitta *co-p* Joe Wizan *c* Victor J. Kemper *lp* Marsha Mason, Anthony Hopkins, John Beck, Susan Swift, Norman Lloyd, John Hillerman

The Axe *aka* **Lisa** *aka* **California Axe Massacre**
(FREDERICK PRODUCTIONS) 68(65)min
Three thugs (sadist, old lag, youth respectively played by Canon, Green and Friedel) torture and kill a man, terrorize the cashier of a small store, then hole up in a lonely house inhabited by a morose girl called Lisa (Lee) and her paralysed grandfather. When Green and Canon rape Lee in turn, one ends with his throat slit and is chopped up in the bath, the other is axed and shoved up the chimney. Friedel, having left shamefacedly, returns in time to be shot by the police. Largely motiveless and rudimentary in characterization, the film may be intended to suggest some sort of existential hopelessness (of her two murder weapons, Lee has earlier used the axe to cut chickens'

heads off, the razor to try to slash her wrists with), but ends up looking simply amateurish.

d/s Frederick R. Friedel *p* J. G. Patterson Jnr *c* Austin McKinney *lp* Leslie Lee, Jack Canon, Ray Green, Frederick R. Friedel, Douglas Powers

Bloedverwanten *aka* **Blood Relations** *aka* **Les Vampires en Ont Ras le Bol**

(JAAP VAN RIJ FILMPRODUCTIE/CTIS; FR,NETH) 97(90)min

The plot of this engaging horror comedy is derived from a story by the Dutch novelist Belcampo (Herman P. Schoenfeld Wichers) who often used medical settings for fantasy stories full of eccentric humour. A naïve young nurse (Deschamps) realizes that the hospital's blood plasma supplies are being stolen by the town's group of cheerfully down-at-heel vampires, led by a doctor (Hamel) and his policeman son (Arliss). Failing to get help from the village priest, played by, of all people, Constantine, she attempts to thwart them by injecting herself with some holy water, a trick she learned from an old vampire movie. The scheme fails and she ends up joining the genteel group of blood consumers. Even though the short story has been padded and stretched into feature length with lots of repetition, which considerably dissipates the situation's comic potential, the odd detail – the knitting spinster-vampire refusing to drink blood from the plasma bottle and insisting on a teacup, for example – raises a smile.

d Wim Lindner *p* Jaap Van Rij *s* John Brasom *c* Walter Bal *se* Kramsky *lp* Maxim Hamel, Gregoire Aslan, Sophie Deschamps, Robert Dalban, Eddie Constantine, Ralph Arliss, Elly Van Stekelenburg, Jacqueline Huet, Ronnie Bierman

The Car (U) pv 98(97)min

Offering an offbeat variation on the demonology theme much in evidence after **The Exorcist** (1973), though perhaps also influenced by *Duel* (1972), this film features a diabolic car, proceeding driverless through the south-west of America, mowing down anyone in its path. As directed by Silverstein, best known for the comedy western *Cat Ballou* (1965), the film is cleanly shot and enjoyably straight-faced, allowing the element of farce inherent in the basic idea to take care of itself. The small-town setting is effectively deployed, though some of the human interest is rather laborious. This centres on the deputy sheriff (Brolin), whose superior (Marley) has been killed by the car, and his girlfriend (Lloyd), the local schoolteacher, who succeeds in seeing off the car with appropriate imprecations after it corners a school party, but is later killed when the vengeful auto charges into her at home. The effects work is skilful throughout and culminates in a spectacular finale in which the car is blown up after being decoyed into a canyon stocked with explosives (a diabolical set of features are glimpsed as it blows up). Predictably, a coda shows another sinister car making its way through a different locale. However, the later **Christine** (1982) must be considered the cinema's definitive demon-car movie.

d/co-p Elliot Silverstein *co-p* Marvin Birdt *s* Dennis Shryack, Michael Butler, Lane Slate *c* Gerald Hirschfeld *se* Jack Faggard, Paul Hickerson, Ed Kennedy, Bill Aldridge *lp* James Brolin, Kathleen Lloyd, R. G. Armstrong, John Marley, John Rubinstein, Elizabeth Thompson, Roy Jenson, Kim Richards, Kyle Richards, Doris Dowling

The Child *aka* **Kill and Go Hide** *aka* **Zombie Child**

(PANORAMA FILMS) 83min

This film is quite a powerful combination of the evil-child subgenre and the zombie movie. During the thirties Barnett travels to a remote woodland area where she has been engaged by the widowed Janson to look after his daughter (Cole). Unbeknown to her father Cole has supernatural powers and uses them to summon up zombies from a nearby cemetery in order to avenge herself on those she considers responsible for her mother's death. Although obviously made on a limited budget, the subjective camera prowling through the woods, the odd angles and disjointed editing combine to provide a convincingly nightmarish atmosphere.

d Robert Voskanian *p* Robert Dadashian *s* Ralph Lucas *c* Mori Alavi *se* Jay Owens *lp* Laurel Barnett, Rosalie Cole, Frank Janson, Richard Hanners, Ruth Ballan, Blosson Bing Jong, Rod Medigovich, Wendell Hudiberg

Claws *aka* **Devil Bear** 90min

Like **Grizzly** (1976), this **Jaws** (1975)-inspired outing features a huge bear on the rampage, this time in the wilds of Alaska, although here the story is given supernatural overtones by the suggestion that perhaps the creature is the Kuh Tu Ka (a kind of Bigfoot) of Indian legend. But, as in the case of its predecessor, the bear evokes as much sympathy as terror, especially in the light of remarks like 'a few well-placed slugs will turn him into a rug'.

d Richard Banslach, Robert E. Pierson *p/co-s/c* Chuck D. Keen *co-s* Brian Russell *lp* Jason Evers, Leon Ames, Myron Healey, Anthony Caruso, Carla Layton, Glenn Sipes

The Comeback *aka* **The Day the Screaming Stopped**

(PETE WALKER-HERITAGE-LTD; GB) 100min

Not nearly as inventive as **Phantom of the Paradise** (1974), Walker's mixture of rock and horror stars Jones as an American singer recording an album in an isolated country house, where he comes across the putrefying corpse of his ex-wife (Palance) and later finds her head in a hat box in the cellar. His manager (Doyle) is revealed to be a transvestite and his new lover (Stephenson) is found dead, walled up in the attic with another cadaver. The villains are the house's caretakers (Keith and Owen) whose daughter committed suicide on hearing of her idol's marriage. Besides the miscasting of Jones, the inept picture simply shambles from one 'shock' to the next, substituting grotesque morsels of visceral horror, courtesy of George Partleton's makeup, for suspense. Not only is the identity of the culprits telegraphed long in advance of the ending, but by including a climactic scene in which Owen inadvertently axes his accomplice to death, the whole enterprise is rendered risible rather than simply meretricious. Stephenson later became a TV star and gossip columnists' delight as a comedienne in the Monty Python-derived *Not the Nine O'Clock News* teleseries.

Singer Jack Jones serenading what he thinks to be the corpse of his putrefying wife in The Comeback.

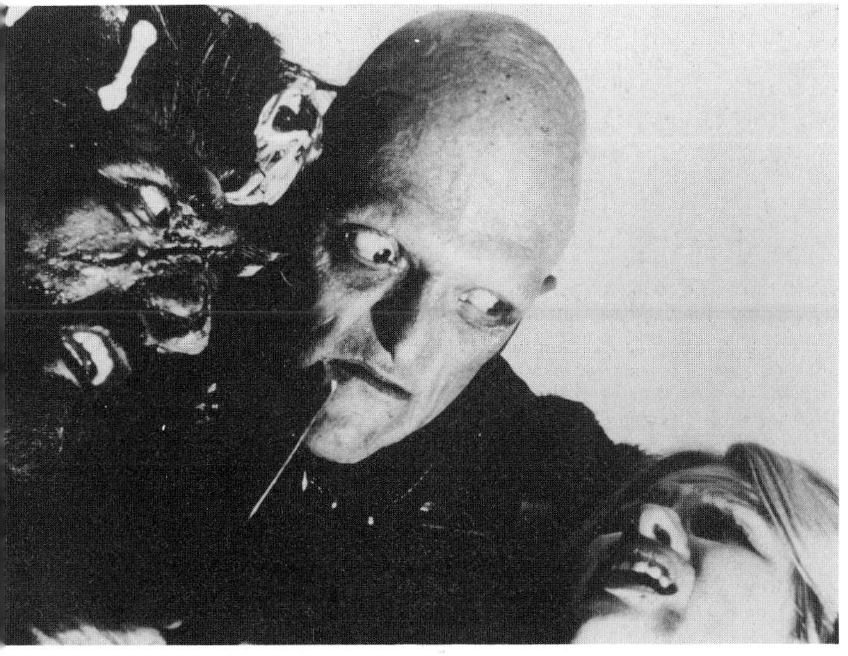

The monster family in Wes Craven's superior exploitation film, The Hills Have Eyes.

d/p Pete Walker *s* Murray Smith *c* Peter Jessop *lp* Jack Jones, Pamela Stephenson, David Doyle, Sheila Keith, Bill Owen, Holly Palance, Richard Johnson, Peter Turner

Dracula's Dog *aka* Zoltan ... Hound of Dracula

(VIC) 88min

When the Dracula family vault in Romania is disturbed by military manoeuvres, the coffins are hastily burnt by order of Inspector Branco (Ferrer), a noted vampire hunter. But two of the coffins are empty because the stakes have been withdrawn from the occupants by an unwary (and promptly dispatched) sentry. One contained Count Dracula's vampirized dog, Zoltan; the other a 'fractional lamia' (Nalder), a species not thirsting for blood itself and able to function in daylight and therefore of service in locating victims for its master. Unable to survive without a master, Nalder sails with Zoltan for Los Angeles, where the last of the Draculas (Pataki) – removed to safety as a child, unvampirized, before the Count and his entourage were staked – is living as Michael Drake, unaware of his heritage. Up to this point, the film is inventive and crudely but effectively staged, with Nalder's cadaverously ravaged features promising much menace. But the effort seems to have exhausted both writer and director, who can dream up nothing better than to have Nalder moon about endlessly intoning 'Soon!' to an impatient Zoltan while Pataki, his wife (Shutan) and two children embark on the inevitable camping holiday. Endless desultory attacks follow with Zoltan – lightbulb eyes shining and roaring like a lion – vampirizing other canine aides and Ferrer puffing heavily to the rescue.

d/co-p Albert Band *co-p/s* Frank Ray Perilli *c* Bruce Logan *lp* Michael Pataki, Reggie Nalder, José Ferrer, Jan Shutan, Libbie Chase

Emanuelle e gli Ultimi Cannibali *aka* Trap Them and Kill Them

(FULVIA CINEMATOGRAFICA/FLORA FILM/GICO CINEMATOGRAFICA; IT) 92(85)min

To a sexploitation director like Massaccesi (who was responsible for *Eva Nera*, 1976, and numerous *Emanuelle* pictures), the box-office success of the racist **Ultimo Mondo Cannibale** (1976) must have made a combination of sex and cannibalism seem like the next logical step. After a brief sequence in which a woman in an asylum eats part of a nurse's breast, the picture embarks on the routine expedition to the Amazon where most of the cast are eaten before Gemser is hailed as a goddess and escapes. The (badly done) gory sequences are interspersed with extended soft-core interludes featuring both black and white participants. The hero is played by Tinti, Gemser's husband, who had starred with her in Massaccesi's *Emanuelle in America* (1977).

d/co-s/c Joe d'Amato (Aristide Massaccesi) *p* Gianfranco Couyoumdjian *co-s* Romano Scandariato *se* Fabrizio de Angelis *lp* Laura Gemser, Gabriele Tinti, Susan Scott, Donald O'Brien, Percy Hogan, Monica Zanchi, Annemarie Clementi, Geoffrey Copplestone, Dirce Funari

The Exorcist II: The Heretic

(WB) 117(102)min

A critical and box-office disaster in America, cut and remodelled for European release, Boorman's sequel to **The Exorcist** (1973) treads much the same perilous tightrope of pretension as his earlier *Zardoz* (1973) and is just as fascinating. Trying to dispense with the crude shock tactics and religiosities of *The Exorcist* and fashion his sequel as a pure spiritual odyssey, Boorman fails because of a persistent thematic confusion and because his cast seems designed for another movie.

As the priest who fears a weakening in his faith, and who through his involvement with the possessed child of *The Exorcist* (Blair again, now a teenager) becomes aware of her demon's potential for good or evil, Burton reeks more of melodramatic than spiritual concern; while Blair's vacuous adolescent presence hardly substantiates the claim that she has the potential to become either a great destroyer or a great healer. What the film does have, on the other hand, is a considerably more complex view of the inter-relationship between good and evil than the earlier film's simple dichotomy. Moreover, in some sequences, Boorman's direction and Fraker's superb camerawork combine to produce a genuinely visionary quality: in particular the extraordinarily powerful evocation of a primitive landscape of incandescently fiery colours as the demon, a new Mephistopheles seducing his Faust with the aid of a stunning display of camera mobility and special effects, takes Burton on a hallucinatory tour of his domain.

d/co-p John Boorman *co-p* Richard Lederer *s* William Goodhart *c* William A. Fraker *lp* Linda Blair, Richard Burton, Louise Fletcher, Max von Sydow, Paul Henreid, James Earl Jones, Ned Beatty

The Hills Have Eyes

(BLOOD RELATIONS COMPANY) 90min

Craven's earlier **The Last House on the Left** (1972) has been seen as an updating of the folktale which provided the basis for Ingmar Bergman's *Jungfrukällen* (1960), and *The Hills Have Eyes* also seems to be inspired by an episode from folk history (in this case real): the activities of the cannibal Sawney Bean family who preyed on travellers in 17th-century Scotland. A family – ex-policeman (Grieve), his wife (Vincent), son (Houston), daughters (Lanier, Wallace), Wallace's husband (Speer) and their baby daughter – are on a camper holiday when their car breaks down in the desert. Grieve is warned – too late – by an old man (Steadman) about the activities of his 'monster' son, who after causing the deaths of his mother and sister had been cast out to die, but had survived and started a family with the woman he carried off into the hills.

From here on, the mayhem escalates. Steadman is killed by his son (Whitworth), Grieve is captured and burned alive by Whitworth and one of his sons (King), and his two other sons (Berryman, Gordon) attack the camper and seize the baby, which they propose to eat. However, though Vincent and Wallace die, the other three fight back, aided by their surviving dog, which eventually avenges its companion – killed and eaten by the crazies – by tearing out Berryman's throat. A booby trap is rigged up to dispose of Whitworth, while Gordon, about to kill Speer, is himself killed by a rattlesnake thrust at him by his 'sister' (Blythe), who proves to have secured the safety of the baby.

There are some potentially interesting elements in the film: the Grimm fairytale notion of the stolen baby; the fact that the dogs are named Beauty and Beast, with the latter at one stage taken by the cannibals to be the former's ghost; the role of family relationships – the booby trap, for instance, involves making use of Vincent's corpse – but the elements never fuse together. Over and above its rough technique and mediocre acting, the film is hobbled by its inability to confront the inference that the depraved 'family' of marauders are a dark mirror image of the 'typical' middle-American family they attack.

As it is, the attackers are just garishly repulsive, while their victims are neither likeable enough to serve as identification figures, nor placed in any critical perspective. Oddly, Wallace later played a comparable role, though as a survivor, in **Cujo** (1983), which dealt with partly related themes more cogently.

d/s Wes Craven *p* Peter Locke *c* Eric Saarinen *se* John Frazier, Greg Auer *lp* Russ Grieve, Virginia Vincent, Susan Lanier, Dee Wallace, Robert Houston, Martin Speer, John Steadman, Janus Blythe, Arthur King, James Whitworth, Michael Berryman, Lance Gordon

Holocaust 2000 *aka* The Chosen

(EMBASSY PRODUCTIONS/ASTON FILM; IT,GB) scope 102min

Just as de Martino's **L'Anticristo** (1974) sought to emulate **The Exorcist** (1973), so his *Holocaust 2000* follows in the footsteps of **The Omen** (1976). A Hollywood leading man, Douglas, and a supporting cast of British and Italian character actors try to cope, amid much supernatural mayhem, with the incarnation of the Antichrist, who happens to be an American tycoon's son, played rather appropriately by a British actor, Ward, previously seen spreading British colonialism in *Young Winston* (1972). Although box-office considerations must have dictated the wisdom of using an international cast, there is something felicitous about casting the young Churchill as a satanic executive whiz-kid trying to wrest control of a multinational company away from his American father by getting him declared insane. This then puts Ward in control of the construction of a thermonuclear plant in the Middle East. In the end the movie allows Douglas to escape but Ward remains in control in the boardroom, providing the unacceptable face of capitalism. Unfortunately, these overtones remain secondary and are not elaborated in any consistent nor even in any explicit manner, thus wasting an opportunity to make a wickedly subversive picture. Ennio Morricone's score is routine and obsessive, rehearsing some of the composer's familiar motifs.

d/co-s Alberto de Martino *p* Edmondo Amati *co-s* Sergio Donati, Michael Robson *c* Enrico Menczer *se* Giorgio de Rossi *lp* Kirk Douglas, Simon Ward, Anthony Quayle, Virginia McKenna, Agostina Belli, Romolo Valli, Adolfo Celi, Alexander Knox, Geoffrey Keen, Ivo Garrani

The Hound of the Baskervilles

(MICHAEL WHITE LTD; GB) scope 85min

Ex-Warhol acolyte Morrissey's third camp horror movie confirms that whatever was redeemable in his first two (**Il Mostro E in Tavola ...** and **Dracula Cerca Sangue**, both 1973) must have been due to Antonio Margheriti's presence as director. A self-confessed admirer of *Carry On* farces, he failed even to approximate these pictures' professionally competent displays of vulgarity. Britain's best comedy sketch performers, Cook and Moore, are wasted as a decadent Holmes and a bumbling Watson, stumbling from one tired, over-familiar routine to another. Other performers are wheeled on to do their star turns: Greenwood ejects some green vomit; Kinnear plays Ethel the axe-murderer; Wall and Handl are the eccentric housekeepers; Williams is a silly Sir Henry; Elliot breeds incontinent dogs; Terry-Thomas plays Dr Mortimer, Milligan a policeman, and so on. Cook and Moore are allowed to rely on funny voices and lavatorial humour while the rest is merely a collection of weak sketches loosely tied together by the period setting.

d/co-s Paul Morrissey *p* John Goldstone *co-s* Peter Cook, Dudley Moore *c* Dick Bush, John Wilcox *lp* Peter Cook, Dudley Moore, Denholm Elliot, Joan Greenwood, Terry-Thomas, Max Wall, Irene Handl, Kenneth Williams, Roy Kinnear, Spike Milligan

Ie *aka* House

(TOHO; JAP) scope 100(87)min

Elaborating the notion of a 'living room', invented by Jean Ray for his novel *Malpertuis* (filmed in 1972), this Japanese fairytale introduces a living house. The narrative – a rigorously consistent oedipal drama – has a teenage girl, whose 'good' pre-oedipal mother has died, unable to come to terms with a 'new' woman's sexual claims on her father. She takes refuge, with her siblings, in her aunt's house in the forest but her aunt cannot operate as a mother substitute since she's celibate and, by damming up her sexuality to the point where she refuses to die, has become a ghostly witch instead. Her overwhelming presence pervades the house which comes to function as a 'bad' maternal space: its furniture literally and often comically devours girls of marriageable age in marvellously orchestrated sequences. In order not to get eaten, the heroine must pass into adulthood, a transition she cannot achieve since she refuses to accept her own sexuality. Consequently, she becomes part of the house herself and awaits new victims – the first of whom is her father's lover – to nourish her world.

Ie is an uncanny mixture of comedy and horror, of gags and beautifully photographed spectral imagery and demonstrates how crude and pathologically 'male' Western fantasies – **Carrie** (1976), or the numerous Italian giallo films which deploy allegedly female fantasies, **Una Lucertola con la Pelle di Donna** (1971), **Macchie Solari** (1974) or **Setto Note in Nero** (1977), for example – about girls' sexual maturation can be.

d/p/co-s/se Nobuhiko Obayashi *co-s* Chiho Katsura *c* Y. Sakamoto *lp* Kimiko Ikegami, Kumiko Oda, Ai Matsubara, Miki Jinbo, Mieko Sato, Masayo Miyako, Enko Tanaka, Saho Sasazawa, Haruko Wanibuchi, Kiyoko Ozaki

The Island of Dr Moreau

(CINEMA 77/AIP) 104(98)min

H. G. Wells complained of **Island of Lost Souls** (1932) – the first authorized version of his novel, here filmed under its original title – that Charles Laughton's Moreau was a sadist

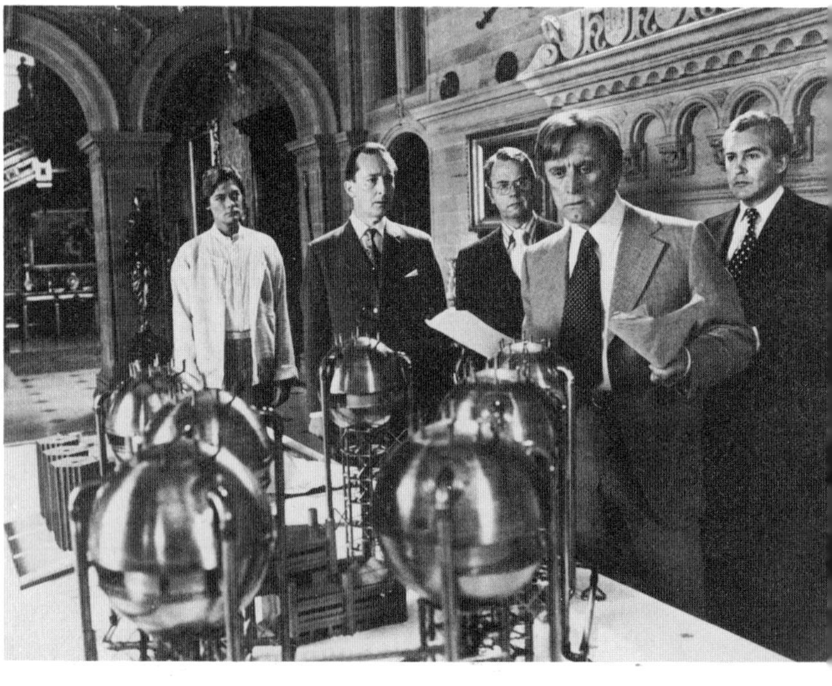

Kirk Douglas on the verge of realizing that hi planned thermonuclear plant is diabolically inspired in Holocaust 2000, *another film in the manner of* The Omen *(1973).*

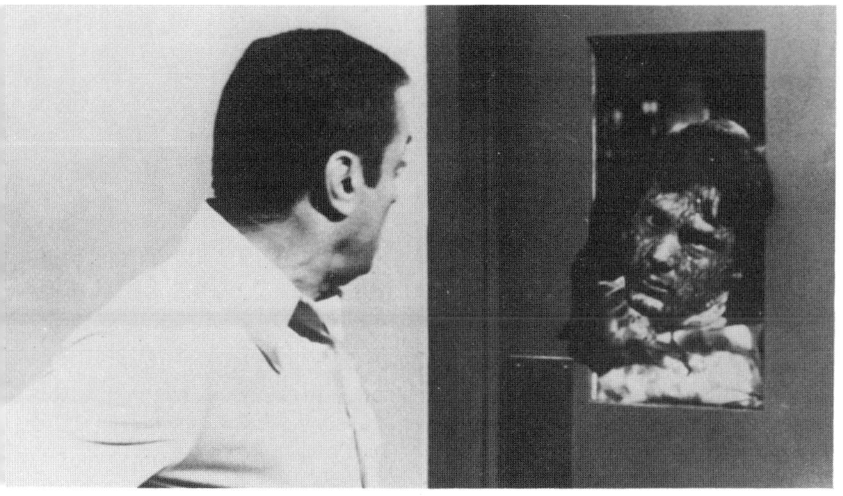

Tony Curtis surprised in the absurd but entertaining *The Manitou*.

rather than the basically kind man Wells had intended to conduct his genetic experiments. Lancaster rectifies this aspect of the character only to go arbitrarily and unconvincingly mad, whereupon he travesties not only Wells but his own life's work of turning beasts into men by vengefully turning the interfering humanitarian (York) into a beast. As silly as anything in a remarkably imbecilic film, which completely obviates the strange, brooding disquiet of the earlier version by giving it tropical paradise settings and an even lusher love interest, is the fairytale ending whereby York becomes a handsome prince again as soon as he and his beloved (Carrera) escape the island.

d Don Taylor *p* John Temple-Smith, Skip Steloff *s* John Herman Shaner, Al Ramrus *c* Gerry Fisher *lp* Burt Lancaster, Michael York, Nigel Davenport, Barbara Carrera, Richard Basehart, Nick Cravat

Lady Dracula

(TV 13/IFV PRODUKTION; WG) 86min

Although directed by Gottlieb, who was responsible for some of the most exploitative films to be made in Germany, this comedy is far less objectionable than Clive Donner's **Vampira** (1974). In 1876, Dracula, played with some relish by Boyd, bites a little girl whose coffin is dug up in 1976. After biting the dealer in antiques who purchased the coffin, she is transformed into an exceedingly attractive woman, Barbara (Kraft), who then has to drink five litres of fresh blood a day to survive. She works in a hospital, then in a morgue and anywhere else she can obtain the precious fluid, but is soon forced to start biting people.

The series of killings that follow draws the attention of the police and an inspector (Harris) falls in love with Kraft. The finale sees the two lovers, frustrated by the impossibility of meeting in the daytime, at last getting together in her coffin. The script is repetitive and the jokes often crude (the coffin bounces about when the hero and heroine mate, for instance), but some crazy-comedy situations involving a pair of undertakers and a recalcitrant cadaver work quite well. Kraft and Lingen, a veteran comic who appeared in Fritz Lang's *M* (1931) and *Das Testament des Dr Mabuse* (1933), acquit themselves honourably and the direction is routinely professional. The original story was provided by Harris.

d Franz-Joseph Gottlieb *p* Guenther Sturm, Kurt Kodal *s* Redis Read *c* Ernst W. Kalinke *se* Colin Chilvers *lp* Evelyne Kraft, Christine Buchegger, Brad Harris, Theo Lingen, Eddi Arent, Walter Giller, Klaus Hohner, Christine Schubert, Edith Leyrer, Zdenka Prohaskova, Ralph Boyd

The Manitou

(MANITOU PRODUCTIONS) pv 105min

An entertaining addition to the demonology cycle sparked off by **The Exorcist** (1973) and continued by numerous films, among them Girdler's earlier **Abby** (1974), *The Manitou* strikes a judicious balance between high production values and narrative vigour, and between 'serious' and tongue-in-cheek attitudes to its material. The setting is San Francisco and the heroine (Strasberg) has developed an unexplained tumour on her neck; an operation to remove it is disrupted when the surgeon (Cedar) is driven to cut his hand. Strasberg's boyfriend (Curtis), a professional mystic, intervenes on her behalf and this eventually leads him to seek the aid of a sympathetic Indian witch-doctor (Ansara) after it appears that the tumour is caused by the foetus of an evil witch-doctor, able to reincarnate himself at will. However, an operation to contain the manitou (spirit) of the evil one leads to the hideous-looking creature – the role is played by dwarfs Felix Silla and Joe Gieb – being re(born) and running amok in the hospital where he has been delivered. Finally, he is vanquished by the combined 'manitous' of the hospital's electronic devices being harnessed against him by Curtis, Ansara and Cedar, a trick which becomes effective when in time-honoured fashion it is realized that Curtis's love for Strasberg can be utilized to boost the positive energy needed to best the negative forces represented by the intruder. This conclusion may have it absurd side, but there is no denying the visceral impact of the sequence in which the witch-doctor makes his appearance. Elsewhere, the film is graced by expansive camerawork and the practised playing of its star-studded cast.

d/p/co-s William Girdler *co-s* Jon Cedar, Thomas Pope *c* Michael Hugo *se* Tom Burman *lp* Tony Curtis, Michael Ansara, Susan Strasberg, Stella Stevens, Jon Cedar, Ann Sothern, Burgess Meredith, Paul Mantee, Jeanette Nolan, Lurene Tuttle

Nurse Sherri *aka* Beyond the Living

(JER PICTURES) 88min

This particularly lame and clumsy exercise in demonic possession/hospital horrors has Jacobson as the eponymous nurse who becomes possessed by the spirit of a man who dies whilst being operated on, against his wishes, after a heart attack. Under the spirit's influence she sets out to kill all those involved in the operation. Adamson was one of the most productive exploitation directors of the seventies, interspersing biker films, like *Satan's Sadists* (1969) and *Hell's Bloody Angels* (1970), and, more unusually, westerns, such as *Jessie's Girls* (1975) with a string of horror and sex films.

d/co-s Al Adamson *p* Mark Sherwood *co-s* Michael Bockman, Greg Tittinger *c* Roger Michaels *se* Bob Lebar *lp* Geoffrey Land, Jill Jacobson, Marilyn Joi, Mary Kay Pass, Prentiss Moulden, Erwin Fuller, Clayton Foster, Caryl Briscoe, Bill Roy

Orca ... Killer Whale *aka* Killer Whale

(FAMOUS FILMS) pv 92min

An atrocious Dino de Laurentiis' **Jaws** (1975) spinoff. Here, a killer whale (having earlier kindly saved Carradine from the jaws of a giant white shark) seeks revenge on Harris for the murder of its pregnant mate. The film makes itself even more ridiculous by not only echoing the *Moby Dick* motif from *Jaws*, but making it the focal point of the film and allowing Harris to act it thoroughly badly. Rampling is the concerned marine biologist and Sampson the Red Indian mystic who understands all.

d Michael Anderson *p/co-s* Luciano Vincenzoni *co-s* Sergio Donati *c* Ted Moore *lp* Richard Harris, Charlotte Rampling, Will Sampson, Bo Derek, Keenan Wynn, Robert Carradine

Prey

(TYMAR FILM PRODUCTIONS; GB) 85(83)min

With a narrative that combines lesbianism and a cannibalistic alien, *Prey* is unmistakably a runner in the exploitation stakes.

Annen and Faulkner play the two women into whose home alien Stokes intrudes, in the human guise of a man he has murdered. By the end, both of them have been killed and eaten by the invader, who at the close radios a message to his 'control' recommending a larger-scale landing, as humans are not only rich in protein but easy prey. The film is well mounted and works up some suspense, but the gruesome eccentricity of the premise seems to call for a greater sense of humour than Warren's direction is able or willing to deliver. As in his later *Inseminoid* (1980) there is a gratuitous emphasis on violence and dismemberment. *Prey* bears some resemblance to the later low-budget British horror movie, **Xtro** (1982).

In Italy, Ferruccio Casacci used the film as a basis for his *Terrore ad Amityville Park* (1984), inserting new material and drastically re-editing Warren's silly story.

d Norman J. Warren *p* Terence Marcel, David Wimbury *s* Max Cuff *c* Derek V. Browne *lp* Glory Annen, Sally Faulkner, Barry Stokes, Sandy Chimney, Eddie Stacey

Ruby (STEVE KRANTZ PRODUCTIONS) 85min

This is an interesting, though idiosyncratic, film from Harrington, one of the most inventive American horror practitioners (**Games**, 1967; **What's the Matter with Helen?**, 1971). In a 1935 prologue, set to dreamlike effect in a mist-shrouded Florida swamp, singer and gangster's moll Ruby (Laurie) sees her lover (Vecchio) gunned down by fellow mobsters. The main action occurs 16 years on, with Ruby running a drive-in cinema in the same locality and providing employment for the now down-at-heel assassins (Whitman among them). They start to meet a variety of grisly fates, and it transpires that Ruby's teenage daughter (Baldwin), the child of her affair with Vecchio, has been telekinetically possessed by her father's avenging spirit. After the vendetta has been completed, the film elegiacally closes the circle by having Ruby go to meet her long-lost lover in a watery grave.

While clearly made on a modest budget, *Ruby* uses its B-picture format of a single setting and a limited number of characters to effectively stylized and claustrophobic ends. The plotting by Edwards and Schneider may be awkward at times, but the film is still a powerful example of Harrington's neo-gothic fascination with make-believe private worlds and with ringing the changes on showbusiness stereotypes, and Laurie – whose casting reflects the commercial influence of **Carrie** (1976), another movie about telekinetic powers, in which she had made a comeback – turns in an expert performance.

For movie buffs, perhaps the most supernatural – or at any rate, the oddest – aspect of *Ruby* is the fact that somehow, seven years before it was made, the drive-in manages to show *Attack of the 50-Foot Woman* (1958), interpolated excerpts from which amusingly comment on the movie's themes of revenge and thwarted desire.

d Curtis Harrington *p/co-s* George Edwards *co-s* Barry Schneider *c* William Mendenhall *lp* Piper Laurie, Stuart Whitman, Roger Davis, Janit Baldwin, Crystin Sinclaire, Paul Kent, Len Lesser, Jack Perkins, Sal Vecchio, Fred Kohler

Satan's Cheerleaders (WORLD AMUSEMENTS) 92min

Four Benedict High School cheerleaders on their way to the first game of the season are captured by backwoods' satanists led by the sheriff (Ireland) and his wife (de Carlo). After dispatching their captors, one of the girls, Sherman, turns out to have acquired black-magic powers and uses them to help the team win. Sadly, in spite of an inspired comic idea and a great title *Satan's Cheerleaders* is disappointingly lame, neither especially funny nor particularly horrific, and a general waste of the combined talents of Carradine, Ireland and de Carlo.

d/co-s Greydon Clark *p/co-s* Alvin L. Fast *lp* John Ireland, Yvonne de Carlo, Jack Kruschen, John Carradine, Kerry Sherman, Hillary Horan, Alisa Powell, Sherry Marks, Jacqulin Cole

Sette Note in Nero *aka* **Dolce Come Morire** *aka* **The Psychic**

(CINECOMPANY; IT) scope 95(86)min

Echoing some of the motifs treated earlier in his **Una Lucertola con la Pelle di Donna** (1971), this dull story about a woman (O'Neill) who has visions of various people's impending deaths, including her own, proves that in spite of the occasional effective scene, Fulci is a thoroughly average director simply filming what art directors and makeup people provide him with. Only one sequence at the beginning of *Sette Note* is worthy of note: the heroine as a little girl watches her mother's apparently suicidal leap off a cliff intercut with graphic closeups of the mother's head repeatedly cracking against the rocks. The rest consists of repetitious 'visions', each relentlessly preceded by a zoom into the heroine's eyes. In the last few minutes, the director tries to invent a few Poe-type twists playing on claustrophobia, but to no avail.

Two years after making this film, Fulci broke into the international market with his successful imitation of George Romero's *Dawn of the Dead* (1978), **Zombi 2** (1979). He returned to the claustrophobia theme with **Il Gatto Nero** (1981), using virtually the same ironic ending as the central character is walled in, echoing Poe's *The Casket of Amontillado*.

d/co-s Lucio Fulci *p* Franco Cuccu *co-s* Roberto Gianviti, Dardano Sacchetti *c* Sergio Salvati *lp* Jennifer O'Neill, Gabriele Ferzetti, Marc Porel, Gianni Garko, Evelyn Stewart (Ida Galli), Jenny Tamburi, Fabrizio Jovine, Luigi Diberti, Laura Vernier

Shock (Transfer Suspense Hypnos) *aka* **All 33 di Via Orologio Fa Sempre Freddo** *aka* **Beyond the Door II** *aka* **Suspense**

(LASER FILM; IT) scope 95(87)min

The great Bava's last feature confirms that he had lost none of his cinematic inventiveness since **La Maschera del Demonio** (1960). As in **The Omen** (1976), the movie centres on a young boy, Marco (Collin), with apparently supernatural powers, and his mother, Dora, played by Dario Argento's wife (Nicolodi). The story begins with the suggestion that Nicolodi's first husband, a drug addict and Collin's father, committed suicide, leaving her free to marry Bruno (Steiner). By the end, it has emerged that she in fact killed him and that Steiner walled up the corpse in the basement of their house. The movie chronicles Nicolodi's collapse into hysteria then utter dementia as her son, who is also playing at incest with her, appears to provoke hallucinations: she and Collin are in bed but Collin's hand caressing her changes into the putrid hand of a long-dead person and a similar hand grabs her ankle on the lawn and

Piper Laurie in Curtis Harrington's marvellously atmospheric Ruby.

assaults her with deadly weapons. At the end, she and her second husband perish in a bloodbath by the breached wall in their basement, leaving Collin sitting in the garden, drinking tea with an invisible guest who might be the ghost of his father.

The film was written and partly co-directed by Bava's son, Lamberto, who had been his directorial assistant since **Terrore nello Spazio** (1965). But the opening of the movie, with a restless camera, at floor level, prowling through a neglected garden, descending into a cobweb-ridden cellar full of odd objects and gliding along an ominous-looking wall before exploring an empty kitchen where a tap drips into fetid sinkwater, unmistakably betrays the guiding hand of the master. In addition, Bava's obsessive association of incestual sex with images of violent death and putrefaction, most strikingly realized in **Lisa e il Diavolo** (1972), is the structuring principle of the entire film. Bava's next (last) work, officially co-directed with his son, was a TV adaptation of a Prosper Mérimée story, *La Vénère d'Ille* (1978), about a bronze statue that comes alive in order to embrace a man to death. Lamberto Bava went on to direct films of his own, including **Macabro** (1980) and **La Casa con la Scala nel Buio** (1983). The American title of *Shock*, *Beyond the Door II*, indicates that the film was promoted as a follow-up to Ovidio Assonitis's **Chi Sei?** (1974), which was released in the US as *Beyond the Door*.

d Mario Bava *p* Turi Vasile *s* Lamberto Bava, Francesco Barbieri, Paolo Briganti, Dardano Sacchetti *c* Alberto Spagnoli *lp* Daria Nicolodi, John Steiner, David Collin Jnr, Ivan Rassimov, Nicola Salerno

Right: Shock, *the great Mario Bava's last feature film.*

Shock Waves *aka* Death Corps *aka* Almost Human

(LAURENCE FRIEDRICKS ENTERPRISES) 86min

The wildly eccentric notion of Nazi wartime experiments to create a 'zombie corps' of resuscitated troops is at the centre of this visibly cutprice movie. The setting is a Caribbean island to which a party of shipwrecked tourists make their way. They encounter first Cushing, who as a World War II officer had been given the task of assembling the 'zombie battalion', then the zombies themselves. Cushing had sought after the war to dispose of them by sending their ship to the bottom of the sea, but an underwater disturbance has brought them back to death-dealing life, and they proceed to kill not only Cushing but virtually all the rest of the cast. The sole survivor of the climactic escape attempt (Adams) proves to be insane – a cynically downbeat ending which in this respect foreshadows a number of rather later movies in the genre. Able performances and a few striking moments – especially the first appearance of the zombies, emerging from the sea with scarred faces and dark glasses – don't succeed in offsetting a rambling, repetitious script and a general air of impoverishment.

The Nazi and maritime motifs were combined again for **Death Ship** (1980).

d Ken Wiederhorn *p/c* Reuben Trane *s* John Harrison, Ken Pare *lp* Peter Cushing, John Carradine, Brooke Adams, Fred Buch, Jack Davidson, Luke Halpin

The Town That Dreaded Sundown (AIP) 90min

Ranging from the pseudo-documentary of the **The Legend of Boggy Creek** (1972) to the pseudo-history of the *Norsemen* (1978) by way of a couple of spuriously fulsome tributes to the noble savage (*Winterhawk*, 1975, and *Grayeagle*, 1977), Pierce's pursuit of the twin goals of 'truth' and 'Americana' has resulted in a growing number of poor films. Here, retelling the story of the Phantom Killer (a hooded sadist who bites, chews, tortures and slays) who terrorized Texarkana in 1946 with a minimum of talent but a maximum of graphic nastiness, he contributes one of the sleaziest and dullest entries in the teen-slaughter cycle.

d/p Charles B. Pierce *c* Earl E. Smith *c* Jim Roberson *lp* Ben Johnson, Andrew Prine, Dawn Wells, Jimmy Clem, Charles B. Pierce

Tutti Defunti Tranne i Morti (AMA FILM; IT) 105min

As if to exorcize the lugubrious intensity of his **La Casa dalle Finestre che Ridono** (1976), the talented Avati immediately produced this grotesque comedy with a *Ten Little Indians* plot set in his native Emilia Romagna. Dante (delle Piane) finds a manuscript which predicts the death of nine members of the Zanetti family, the decadent proprietors of an old castle. The prediction comes true as one after the other of the family comes to a sticky end. The culprit is Ignazio (Matteuzzi), the head of the family, presumed dead when the tale begins. However, since nine deaths are predicted, nine must occur, and in the end he dies at the hands of his nurse (and accomplice in the necrophiliac farce).

Avati's humour is blacker and more straight-faced than is usual for old-dark-house comedies, and he has a way of orchestrating 'variations on a theme', perhaps related to his experience as a jazz musician. After a few TV programmes (about jazz and cinema), he directed a weird fantasy, *Le Strelle nel Fosso* (1978), in which a sentimental and a misogynist view of women is condensed into a single story and character: an isolated farm with an all male family is accidentally visited by a woman who marries the four sons and the father all at the same time but leaves after an orgiastic wedding party that progressively degenerates into a funereal atmosphere. His later work, including a lovely musical fantasy (*Dancing Paradise*, 1982), evolved again towards the macabre with **Zeder** (1983).

d/co-s Pupi Avati *co-p* Gianni Minervini *co-p/co-s* Antonio Avati *co-s* Gianni Cavina, Maurizio Costanzo *c* Pasquale Rachini *lp* Carlo delle Piane, Gianni Cavina, Francesca Marcino, Greta Vaillant, Andrea Matteuzzi, Michele Mirabella, Flavia Giorgi, Bob Tonelli, Giulio Pizzirani

The Uncanny

(CINEVIDEO/TOR PRODUCTIONS; CAN, GB) 85min

An oddball addition to the ranks of the omnibus horror movie, *The Uncanny* is a stolid attempt to exploit the potential menace of cats, a theme better treated in **The Shadow of the Cat** (1961) and **Il Gatto Nero** (1981). In a framing sequence, writer Cushing visits publisher Milland in an attempt to interest him in a manuscript about a feline conspiracy to take over the world. Three episodes illustrate the notion. In the first, set in

London in 1912, a horde of cats belonging to a wealthy eccentric (Greenwood) take lethal revenge on the conspirators (Penhaligon, Williams) who murder their mistress, then seek to disinherit the cats who are her legatees. The second, set in present-day Quebec, involves a 'magic' cat who helps a little girl to dispose of her hated cousin. The third, which takes place in Hollywood in the thirties, has Pleasance and Eggar as actors involved in an off-screen love affair who do away with Pleasance's wife only to meet their fate at the claws of her pet pussy. A 'twist' ending has Cushing savaged to death by a tribe of cats while Milland is impelled by the gaze of his own pet cat to consign the manuscript to the fire. The flat-footed handling fails to achieve the tongue-in-cheek tone presumably being aimed for and treats the cats essentially as props, springing (or more accurately being thrown) toward their victims. The overall effect is of good actors wasted in laborious, under-written roles.

d Denis Héroux *p* Claude Héroux, René Dupont *s* Michael Parry *c* Harry Waxman, James Bawden *se* Michael Albrechtsen *lp* Peter Cushing, Ray Milland, Susan Penhaligon, Simon Williams, Joan Greenwood, Alexandra Steward, Samantha Eggar, John Vernon, Donald Pleasance

Victor Frankenstein *aka* Terror of Frankenstein

(ASPEKT FILM/NATIONAL FILM STUDIOS OF IRELAND; SW/EIRE) scope 92min

An American ex-patriot, writer/producer/director Floyd had previously made *In Search of Dracula* (1972), a silly TV travelogue through Transylvania beefed up with a few extracts from vampire movies and a guest appearance in costume by Christopher Lee. This picture, however, which was pretentiously promoted as yet another 'authentic' version of the 17-year-old Mary Shelley's novel and opts for a straightforwardly melodramatic rendering of the story. Partly shot in Ireland, where Wilcox orchestrated the photography, the film's pictorial style appears to derive from Stanley Kubrick's *Barry Lyndon* (1975), and features one of Kubrick's cast, Vitali, as the Baron and Oscarsson, a specialist in neurotic characters, as the creature. But whereas Terence Fisher managed to highlight the central dynamic of the myth by emphasizing the conflict between the Baron and the society in which he lived, with the creature merely as the concrete incarnation of that fraught relationship, Floyd's pretty pictures and psychological approach drain the myth of its power. Instead, the film chronicles the existential angst of the creation which, like a true adolescent, feels repulsive and is left to cope alone in the world, causing it to develop into a brutal delinquent. Floyd went on to make **The Inn of the Flying Dragon** (1981).

d/p/co-s Calvin Floyd *co-s* Yvonne Floyd *c* Tony Forsberg, John Wilcox *lp* Leon Vitali, Per Oscarsson, Nicholas Clay, Stacey Dorning, Jan Ohlsson, Olof Bergström, Mathias Henrickson, Archie O'Sullivan, Harry Brogan

A Virgem da Colina *aka* The Ring of Evil

(DRAGÃO FILMES; BRAZIL) 85min

This weird variation on Oscar Wilde's *The Picture of Dorian Gray* features a woman (Amaral) who receives an antique ring from her husband (Soares) on her wedding day. The ring causes her to develop a dual personality and while remaining the perfect lady in the evening, she becomes a prostitute by day. Gradually, her uninhibited side, manifested when her husband is at work, begins to leave its imprint on her face, forcing her to wear a mask to cover her luridly monstrous features. Soares eventually calls in an exorcist who reveals that the ring belonged to a prostitute witch. The evil thing is thrown into the water and peaceful domesticity is restored. The horror thus presented, in the form of physical corruption reflecting moral turpitude, is the woman's indulgence in all the desires which a marriage ring is supposed to stifle.

d/p/s Celso Falcão *c* Alfonso Vianna *lp* Jofre Soares, Christina Amaral, Edson Seretti, Marcos Lyra, Joel Barcellos, Wagner Tadeu, Wildemilson Arthur

1978

Bermuda: La Fossa Maledetta *aka* The Cave of Sharks *aka* Bermuda: La Cueva de los Tiburones

(KAOLA CINEMATOGRAFICA/AMANECER FILM/EMPRESA; IT,SP,VEN) 90(89)min

This is one of the many European attempts to cash in on the huge box-office success of **Jaws** (1975) and not even the best of a bad lot – **L'Ultimo Squalo** (1981) is at least more lively. The purported element of novelty in this clumsy picture involves setting most of the action in the Bermuda Triangle, where a crooked American (Kennedy) recruits the skindiver hero (Garcia), to help him filch treasure from a crashed plane on the seabed. They find a mysterious cave, which seems (though it never becomes clear) to be the entrance to some sinister magic kingdom. Sharks guard the cave mouth, and by the end they have chewed up quite a few of the supporting cast, though the double-dealing Kennedy is merely shot dead by the hero's brother. At the climax, Garcia fights off the sharks by feeding them the severed limbs of Kennedy's henchmen. But in one of the downbeat twist endings characteristic of exploitation movies of the period, the sharks catch up with him just as he is on the point of reaching his boat.

d Anthony Richmond (Teodoro Ricci) *p* Nino Segurini *s* Fernando Galiana, Manrico Melchiorre, Teodoro Ricci *c* Juan Jurado *se* Cineaudio FX *lp* Arthur Kennedy, Andrés Garcia, Janet Agren, Pino Collizi, Maximo Valverde, Sergio Doria

The Cat and the Canary

(GRENADIER FILMS; GB) scope 98(90)min

John Willard's 1922 stage play had previously been filmed by Paul Leni (1927), Rupert Julian (1930) and Elliott Nugent (1939) and was looking very tired by the time stylish sexploitation director Metzger got hold of it in the wake of the successful prewar nostalgia thrillers based on Agatha Christie's novels. Hyde-White is the deceased millionaire owner of Glencliffe Manor who leaves his testament in the form of a talking-head movie, gleefully insulting all his gathered relatives and bequeathing his fortune to Lynley. After this mildly entertaining opening, the various characters move mechanically through the stately home's corridors and rooms, waiting to be attacked by the madman who has escaped from a local asylum run by Fox. The masked killer, a dissolute ex-

The Uncanny, *a laborious addition to the omnibus cycle.*

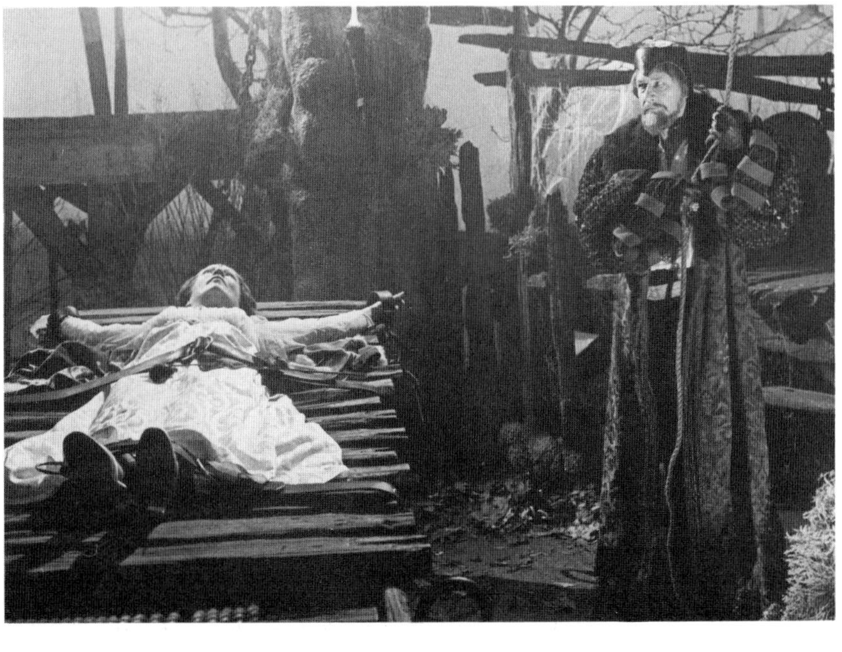

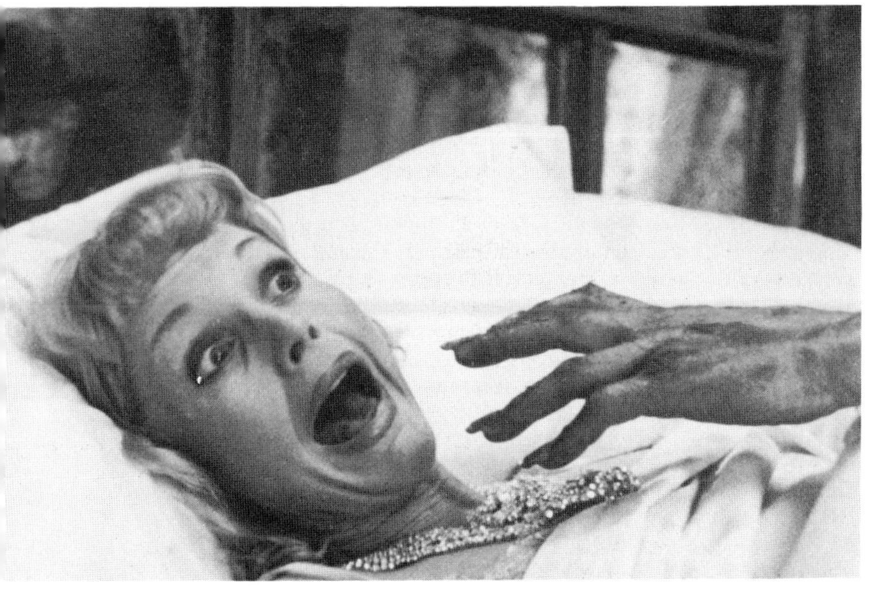

Carol Lynley menaced in yet another version of John Willard's 1922 stage play, The Cat and the Canary.

flying ace (McEnery), eventually drags Lynley to his basement torture chamber where he is shot by Lehmann and where the master villain, Fox, is disposed of by the wisecracking hero, Callan. Blackman and Hiller are the victims of the foot-dragging killer who emerges from behind sliding panels. The over-familiar plot looks both contrived and simplistic when compared with the labyrinthine plots that came into fashion with Hammer's psycho-thrillers in the sixties and the post-Argento giallo crime movies in the seventies. Metzger, who made his name with upmarket sexploitation (*Thérèse et Isabelle*, 1968; *L'Image*, 1976), often shooting both hard- and soft-core versions of his films, does a professional job but seems unable to decide whether he's aiming at suspense or parody and, as a result, achieves neither.

d/s Radley Metzger *p* Richard Gordon *c* Alex Thomson *lp* Honor Blackman, Carol Lynley, Michael Callan, Edward Fox, Peter McEnery, Wendy Hiller, Olivia Hussey, Beatrix Lehmann, Daniel Massey, Wilfrid Hyde-White

Damien – Omen II

(FOX) pv 109(107)min

This sequel to **The Omen** (1976) moves the story on seven years from the end of the previous film. Damien, the Antichrist (Scott-Taylor), is now 13, the ward of his uncle (Holden) and aunt (Grant) and a student at a military academy. During his time there, the boy – in one of the film's most eerily affecting sequences – agonizingly discovers the real nature of his identity. The plot of the film is broadly similar to that of its predecessor, with successive characters dying once they've learned Damien's secret, and includes a startling episode in which a journalist (Shepherd) is pursued and attacked by a large bird. Other victims include some of Holden's associates (Ayres, Arbus, Taylor) who discover elements of the truth in the course of a somewhat unsatisfactory subplot involving chicanery by an employee (Foxworth) who is 'in' with the forces of Satan. More surprisingly, Grant also proves to be on the side of darkness, and when Holden finally attempts to cast out the Antichrist by ritual slaying, she intervenes to murder her husband, although in the apocalyptic finale she is herself consumed by the flames which engulf Holden's skyscraper headquarters as Damien apparently sweeps all before him.

The storyline is handled in a desultory fashion and the actual machinations of the satanic forces seem somewhat irrelevant, but the film is composed with considerable skill, and the settings, especially the military academy, are cleverly used to heighten the implications of the otherwise banal material. In this respect, Butler's scope lensing is a considerable asset, giving the movie an expansive, four-square solidity which makes it far more memorable than *The Omen*. The third and last instalment in the saga is **The Final Conflict** (1981).

d Don Taylor *p* Harvey Bernhard *s* Stanley Mann, Michael Hodges *c* Bill Butler *se* Ira Anderson Jnr *lp* William Holden, Lee Grant, Jonathan Scott-Taylor, Lew Ayres, Sylvia Sidney, Robert Foxworth, Nicholas Pryor, Elizabeth Shepherd, Alan Arbus, Meshach Taylor

Darwasa

(KIRAN RAMSAY; IND) 133min

After their fairly successful zombie film **Do Gaz Jameen ke Neeche** (1972), the Ramsay family nearly bankrupted itself with the follow-up, *Andhera* (1975). *Darwasa* which marked their financial comeback, tells of a werewolf-like creature (Trilok Kapoor) engendered by the curse of the goddess Kali. The meandering plot also involves a mad scientist who invents a diabolical serum and various adventures involving Kali. The family went on to produce horror after horror for the next few years and the films, although crudely made and rather derivative, were always vigorously disliked by the censors. *Hotel* (1981) and *Maut Ka Saaya* (1982) are the highpoints of their achievement so far in the Hindu cinema.

d Tulsi Ramsay, Shyam Ramsay *p* Kiran Ramsay *s* Kumar Ramsay *c* Ganga Ramsay *lp* Sameer Khan, Imtiaz, Anil Dhawan, Shamlee, Trilok Kapoor, Shakti Kapoor, Anju Mahendru, Krishan Dhawan, Kumud Tripathi, Rakesh Pandey

Delirios de um Amoral

(PRODUÇOES CINEMATOGRAFICAS ZE DO CAIXAO; BRAZIL) 86min

A rather tired repetition of the gimmick Marins had used in **O Exorcismo Negro** (1974) in which he starred both as himself and as his creation, Zé do Caixao. Here, a psychiatrist, Dr Hamilton (Peres), becomes obsessed with the figure of Zé and as he studies the character his mind is taken over by Zé, plunging Peres into a delirium in which he hallucinates that Zé is about to take his wife, Tania (Miller). Peres's fellow doctors prove helpless and Miller is forced to call on Zé's creator, José Mojica Marins. Marins, fascinated by the effects of his creation on people's minds, resorts to hypnosis to cure Peres whose psyche now becomes the terrain of a duel between Zé, the malignant creature trying to possess him and Marins, the creature's inventor. After an exhausting struggle, Marins manages to persuade Peres that Zé doesn't really exist.

The movie presents the fairly transparent fantasy that Marins doesn't need psychiatric help since he can still re-assert control, however great the difficulties, over his psychopathic 'other', Zé do Caixao, the central figure of his sickest and most successful movies as well as of a popular comic strip he devised. By having the doctor hallucinate Zé's exploits, Marins also manages to reduce the picture's cost by inserting numerous scenes of his previous Zé do Caixao films, including *A Meia Noite Levarei a Sua Alma* (1965), **Esta Noite Encarnarei no Teu Cadaver** (1966) and **O Estranho Mundo de Zé do Caixao** (1968). Marins went on to direct and star in *Perversão* (1978) in which he mutilates a woman and is castrated by her vengeful sister, as well as a moral fable of sorts, *Mundo Mercade do Sexo* (1978), about a journalist who, having found his wife with his boss, kills them before committing suicide and thus, at last, provides a headline story. Subsequently, he returned to his Zé do Caixao world with *Encarnacão de Demonio* (1981).

d/p/co-s José Mojica Marins *co-s* Rubens F. Luchetti *c* Giorgio Attilli *lp* José Mojica Marins, Magna Miller, Jorge Peres, Lirio Bertelli, Anadir Goe, Valter Setembro, João da Cruz, Elza Perreira, Jaime Cortez, Andreia Bryan

A Deusa de Marmore – Escrava do Diabo

(PANORAMA DO BRAZIL; BRAZIL) 82min

This mixture of horror and pornochanchada – the Brazilian variety of sexploitation cinema – stars its director opposite

Marins, the leading Brazilian horror practitioner. Maldonado plays a 2000-year-old woman, Deusa de Marmore, who has a pact with the devil and preserves her youthful appearance by extracting a life-essence from people by means of a fatal kiss during sexual intercourse. A demon, Seu Sete Encruzilhada (Marins), acting for the devil, requires her to supply ever greater numbers of victims while he also maintains Deusa's lover (Ramayan) in a state of suspended animation (thereby providing an opportunity for necrophilia scenes as she briefly visits her man after lethal lovemaking bouts). In the end, while Maldonado is seducing Henrique (Paulo), his religious wife (Nunes) intervenes brandishing a cross, and Deusa reverts to her real age – in a scene reminiscent of Terence Fisher's **Dracula** (1958) – and dies.

Besides directing, scripting, producing and starring, Maldonado also took care of costumes and makeup, making her the female counterpart of José Mojica Marins, the one-man production house in São Paulo. The interesting credits were designed by Akira Murayama, who also makes a brief appearance in the movie, as do other members of the production team, including the composer Isnard Simone.

d/p/s Rosangela Maldonado *c* Giorgio Attilli *lp* Rosangela Maldonado, José Mojica Marins, João Paulo, Luandy Maldonado, Anadir Goe, Anita Nunes, Inaldo Ramayan, David Hungaro, Rubens de Souza, Adeluni Bonfim

Dominique

(GRAND PRIZE PRODUCTIONS; GB) 100(95)min

Dominique is a resolutely artificial 'twist' thriller, bringing to mind Hammer's psycho-horrors of the sixties (**Maniac** and **Paranoiac**, both 1962, for example), films whose narratives depend on pulling the wool over the audience's eyes and then delivering some outrageous final explanation. *Dominique* sets up a situation in which an ex-patriate American businessman in England (Robertson) is apparently trying to drive his wealthy wife (Simmons) to suicide. He evidently succeeds, but it then appears that she may not be really dead. He is in turn driven to taking his life – only for the whole thing to be revealed as a scheme engineered by his half-sister (Agutter), who is also his beneficiary. Such plots have by this time an unmistakably creaky air, which is hardly alleviated by the treatment this one receives. Moreover, the use of luckless British character actors in stock roles (Robson as the housekeeper, Ward as the ambiguous chauffeur) only serves to underline the lack of effective detail which might have served, as in *Les Diaboliques* (1955), to offset the essential contrivance of the storyline.

d Michael Anderson *p* Milton Subotsky, Andrew Donnally *s* Edward Abraham, Valerie Abraham *c* Ted Moore *lp* Jean Simmons, Cliff Robertson, Jenny Agutter, Simon Ward, Flora Robson, Jack Warner, Leslie Dwyer, Judy Geeson, David Tomlinson, Ron Moody

The Evil *aka* Cry Demon *aka* The Force Beyond

(RANGOON PRODUCTIONS) 89min

A psychologist (Crenna) and his wife (Pettet) buy an apparently haunted house which they intend to turn into a drug-rehabilitation centre. Although a friendly spirit tries to warn Pettet of the dangers ahead, the sceptical Crenna barges on regardless until he unwittingly removes a symbolic cross that locks the evil spirits in the basement. These go on the rampage, killing several of his patients and eventually he encounters the Devil himself (Buono). An extremely fast-paced, tightly constructed film in the tradition of, but far superior to, **The Legend of Hell House** (1973), the film milks the haunted-house subgenre for all it's worth. Effectively blending suspense and horror with credible psychologizing (Crenna's scepticism introduces a rational/supernatural opposition reminiscent of **Night of the Demon** (1957) and **Night of the Eagle**, 1961), *The Evil* is unusual for an American horror film in that it introduces the Devil himself, although his appearance was actually cut from some prints.

d Gus Trikonis *p* Ed Carlin *s* Donald G. Thompson *c* Mario di Leo *se* Hollywood Mobile Systems, Jack Young *lp* Richard Crenna, Joanna Pettet, Andrew Prine, Cassie Yates, Lynne Moddy, Victor Buono, George O'Hanlon Jnr, Mary Louise Weller, Robert Viharo, Milton Selzer

As Filhas do Fogo *aka* Daughters of Fire

(LYNXFILM/EDITORA TRES; BRAZIL) 98min

This is an interesting elaboration of the often used fantasy situation in which vegetation overwhelms a house, thereby returning it to 'nature'. The plot, set in Rio Grade do Sul, concerns two young women who come under the spell of a female necromancer and begin to experience strange events. Mysterious deaths occur and the women hear the voices of dead people. One of the women is found dead and the other kills their tormentor, but she finds herself imprisoned in the house which has been totally enveloped in forest foliage. In the morning, the house and the remnants of the haunting life and death spectacle which occurred there, have all been incorporated into the green Brazilian forest, as if Brazil itself had re-asserted its enduring construction of its history (the necromancer's relation to the voices of the dead). The São Paulo based Khouri, a former critic, became one of the new Brazilian cinema's best-known figures in the early sixties with such films as *Estranho Encontro* (1958) and *O Corpo Ardente* (1966).

d/s Walter Hugo Khouri *p* Cesar Memolo Jnr *c* Geraldo Gabriel *se* Geraldo Jose *lp* Paolo Morra, Maria Rosa, Rosina Malbouisson, Karin Rodrigues, Serafim Gonzalez, Selma Egrei, Maria Huseman, Helmut Hosse, Karin Haas, Rudolf Machalowsky

The Fury

(FOX/FRANK YABLANS PRESENTATIONS) 118min

The Fury, like de Palma's earlier **Carrie** (1976), is about people with telekinetic powers, but the film differs from its predecessor in adopting a far broader canvas. In part a conspiracy thriller, it begins in the Middle East where the widowed father (Douglas) of a teenage boy (Stevens) is apparently killed in a terrorist raid, which has been faked at the behest of his colleague (Cassavetes) so that the boy, possessor of 'superhuman' powers, can be enlisted into the services of the sinister intelligence agency Cassavetes works for. Douglas survives, though, and the main body of the action is concerned with his attempts to win back his son and exact revenge on his treacherous former friend. Ingenious plotting sets up a further series of parallels and oppositions as Douglas, outwitting the law and order agencies ranged against him, comes into contact with a teenage girl (Irving) who herself has telekinetic powers and is being studied at the research institute which is in part a

Andrew Stevens being tested for his telepathic powers in The Fury.

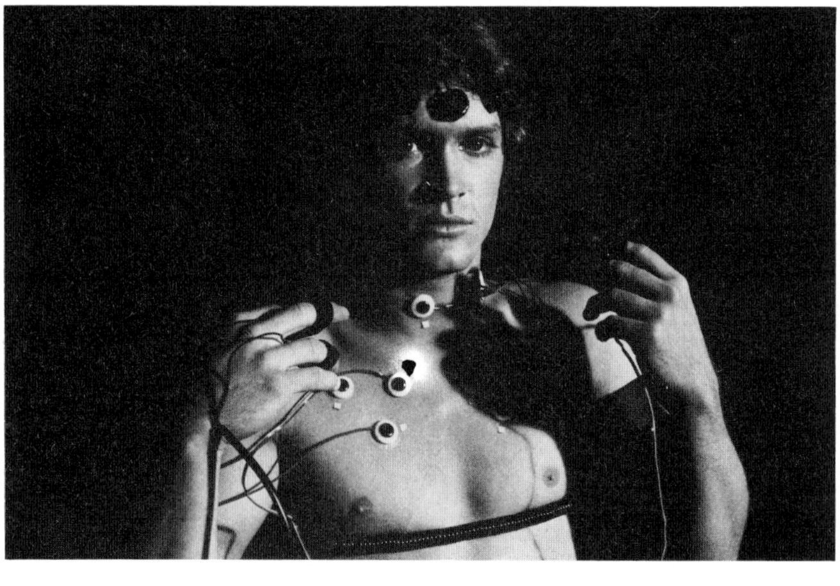

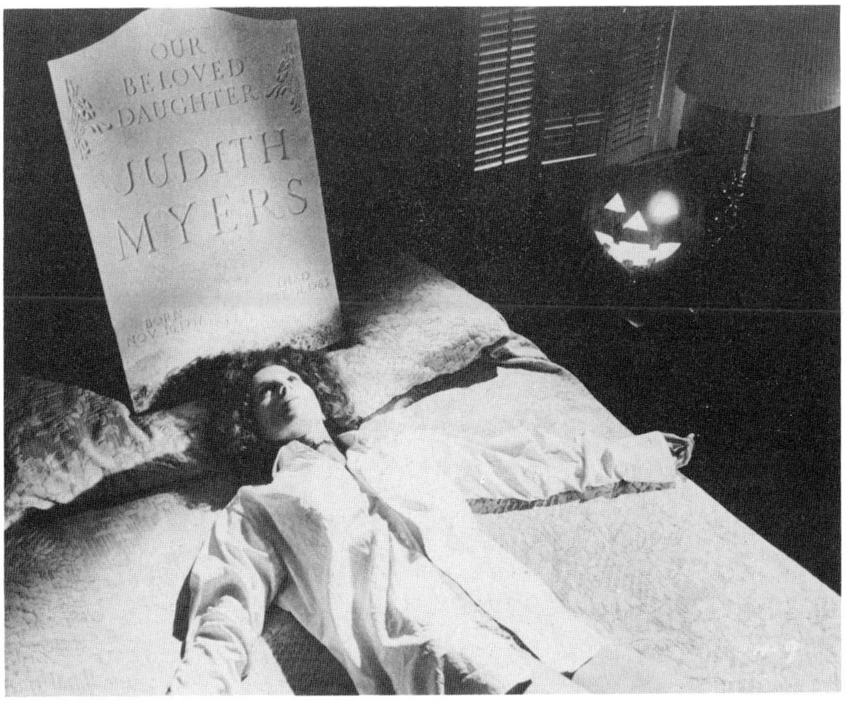

The baroque delights of Halloween, *John Carpenter's most accomplished film.*

front for Cassavetes' activities. The action sequences, including an extended nocturnal car-chase through the streets of Chicago, are handled with a brilliance de Palma has never matched, and the suspense sequence in which Douglas effects Irving's escape from the institute, though at the cost of the life of his girlfriend (Snodgrass), uses the potentially gimmicky device of slow motion to nailbiting effect.

The film builds to an apocalyptic conclusion in which, after seeing Douglas and his now deranged son perish, Irving turns her own 'fury' on Cassavetes' dissembling father-figure and literally blows him apart: the last sequence offers a pyrotechnic but judiciously brief display of special effects as Cassavetes' body appears to explode and his head goes sailing into the air. Far more than in **Phantom of the Paradise** (1974) or **Dressed to Kill** (1980), in *The Fury* de Palma strikes the ideal balance between narrative form and extravagant content.

d Brian de Palma *p* Frank Yablans *s* John Farris *c* Richard H. Kline *se* A. D. Flowers *lp* Kirk Douglas, John Cassavetes, Amy Irving, Carrie Snodgrass, Charles Durning, Carol Rossen, Rutanya Alda, William Finley, Joyce Easton, Jane Lambert, Andrew Stevens

Halloween (FALCON INTERNATIONAL) pv 91min
It is easy to see why *Halloween* became a favourite target for copyists: by sidestepping social or moral comment, it offers a foolproof blueprint for bloody violence. Unlike most of his imitators, however, Carpenter interprets that blueprint with a dazzling skill and mocking wit which invests it with a valid cinematic meaning. As in *Assault on Precinct 13* (1976), he begins with a subjective sequence: the camera prowling outside a house, peering in at the teenage couple necking behind its illuminated windows, watching in silent complicity as an unseen presence selects an enormous butcher's knife, dons a grotesque Halloween mask, and commits bloody murder. At this point, as the emerging killer is revealed to be a six-year-old boy, the camera cranes sharply up and away as if in shocked disbelief. Cut to 15 years later as the killer, now adult, escapes from an asylum and returns home to exorcize more demons (or necking couples).

Rarely have the remoter corners of the Panavision frame been used to such good effect as shifting volumes of darkness and light reveal the ineluctable presence of a sinister something. We know, and Carpenter knows we know, that it is all a game; and he delights in being just one step ahead of expectation, revealing nothing when there should be something, and something – as in the subtle reframing of Curtis sobbing in the doorway when she has finally managed to kill the killer, showing the corpse suddenly sitting bolt upright behind her – long after there should, by rights, be nothing. Fascinatingly, in a film devoted to the terrors of the night, Carpenter allows the mystery to be flooded by the light of reason. Despite all the talk of bogeymen by a frightened child, there is nothing of the supernatural in the film. His killer is a creature of flesh and blood who bleeds when stabbed, who can be stopped by bullets, yet who obstinately refuses to die. The analogy here is perhaps with Norman Bates' mother in **Psycho** (1960), a character given a terrible immortality by her son's mania. And in fact, playing the game with nice wit, Carpenter establishes quite a network of references (the victims are all voyeuristically observed in the sexual act; the heroine, Curtis, is the daughter of Janet Leigh; Pleasance's psychiatrist, a nominal hero unable to avert the disaster, is named after the John Gavin character), which allows him to refer to Mrs Bates' involuntary masquerade in two of the best scenes in the film. One is the chilling celebration of a love enduring beyond the grave when a murdered girl is found formally laid out on her bed with, at her head, the tombstone of the killer's first victim. The other, the hallucinating moment when the door opens, on her lover the victim thinks, but in fact on the killer demurely gowned from head to foot in a white shroud.

d/co-s John Carpenter *p/co-s* Debra Hill *c* Dean Cundey *lp* Jamie Lee Curtis, Donald Pleasance, Nancy Loomis, P. J. Soles, Charles Cyphers

I Spit on Your Grave *aka* **Day of the Woman**
(CINEMAGIC PICTURES) 101min
New Yorker Jenny (Keaton) goes to a secluded country retreat to finish her novel. There she is raped by four local louts (one of whom is mentally retarded) in the woods. Struggling to find her way home, she is assaulted by the same group again, and when she finally gets back to her cottage the ordeal begins yet again. They leave her for dead, but she survives and exacts a terrible revenge.

Taking its title from an American-set French film about racism, *J'Irai Cracher sur vos Tombes* (1959), which was based on a novel by Boris Vian, and its revenge-for-rape thematic from such films as *L'Amour Violé* (1977), *Rape Squad* (1974) and *Lipstick* (1976), *I Spit on Your Grave* is a film which sharply divides critical opinion and was one of the earliest targets of the 'video nasty' moral panic in Britain. Curiously enough one of the fiercest critics of the film was the *Chicago Sun-Times*'s film critic Roger Ebert, a former collaborator with Russ Meyer and normally a strong defender of the exploitation genres. The *argument*, of course, hinges on the question of whether the film encourages violence towards women whilst the *problem* is that many of those who pontificate for and against the film have clearly not actually seen it. Here, the men are so grossly unattractive and the rapes so harrowing, long-drawn-out and starkly presented that it is hard to imagine most male spectators identifying with the perpetrators, especially as the film's narrative structure and *mise-en-scène* force the spectator to view the action from Keaton's point-of-view. Further, there is no suggestion that she 'asked for it' or enjoyed it, except, of course, in the rapists' own perceptions, from which the film is careful to distance itself. Particularly relevant here are the scenes of revenge (grotesquely misread by some critics) in which Keaton *pretends* to have enjoyed the rape so as to lure the men to their destruction. In these scenes the familiar male arguments about women 'bringing it on themselves' and 'tempting' men by 'exposing' their bodies are exposed as simply sexist, self-excusing rhetoric and are quite clearly *presented as such*. More problematic, however, is Keaton's transformation into avenging fury: by allowing her to lapse into an almost catatonic, silent obsessive, the film distances the viewer from her, making her seem like a mere cipher and pushing her dangerously close to that negative female stereotype, the all-destructive *femme castratice* (quite literally, as it happens, in this case).

d/co-p/s Meir Zarchi *co-p* Joseph Zbeda *c* Yuri Haviv *lp* Camille Keaton, Eron Tabor, Richard Pace, Anthony Nichols

Jaws 2 (U) 116min
A lame sequel to **Jaws** (1975) in which the Long Island resort of Amity is menaced by another monster shark. Hamilton's mayor, apparently (and unbelievably) having learned nothing, once again suppresses police chief Scheider's shark alert, this time because lucrative property developments are in the offing. Since the teen-slaughter cycle was now under way, the menace is mostly directed at the town's tiresomely stupid teenagers, with an absurd finale in which the helicopter charging to the rescue is attacked and eaten by the shark. Lacking Spielberg's flair for building suspense, Szwarc's direction tends to undercut what tension there is by over-indulging in underwater shark's-view shots.

d Jeannot Szwarc *p* Richard D. Zanuck, David Brown *s* Carl Gottlieb, Howard Sackler, Dorothy Tristan *c* Michael Butler *lp* Roy Scheider, Lorraine Gary, Murray Hamilton, Joseph Mascolo, Jeffrey Kramer, Collin Wilcox

Killer's Moon (ROTHERNORTH; GB) 90min
This nastily exploitative quickie is an (incompetent) attempt to mine the vein opened by **The Texas Chainsaw Massacre** (1974) and gives four slobbering ghouls an entire busload of schoolgirls on a camping holiday with their boyfriends to slaughter in the Lake District. Gory murders and rape alternate with monotonous regularity in a script whose only function is to engineer the necessary encounters between maniacs and victims, and the token direction quickly loses track of which member of the cast is supposed to be involved in any given scene. The owner of a local hotel (Good) is simply forgotten halfway through the picture, only to reappear as a corpse behind the closing titles. Technical credits match the poverty of the acting and the only suspense is generated by challenging viewers to identify which scenes were shot day-for-night and which were not. Birkenshaw made another equally dismal effort in Italy, *Safari Senza Ritorno* (1983), a racist excursion into the Philippines jungle, featuring Stuart Whitman, Britt Ekland, Laura Gemser, Woody Strode and hordes of brutal 'savages'.

d/co-p/s Alan Birkinshaw *co-p* Gordon Keymer *c* Arthur Lavis *lp* Anthony Forrest, Tom Marshall, Georgina Kean, Nigel Gregory, David Jackson, Paul Rattee, Peter Spraggon, Jane Hayden, Alison Elliot, Jo-Anne Good, Jayne Lester

The Legacy *aka* **The Legacy of Maggie Walsh**
(PETHURST/A. TURMAN FOSTER; GB) scope 102(100)min
Ex-TV director Marquand enlivens this tired old-dark-house plot with stylish scenes of telekinesis, reincarnation, possession motifs and other assorted manifestations of the occult in an effort to out-sensationalize **The Omen** or **Suspiria** (both 1976). With at least one eye on the US gore market, the script has two Americans (Ross and Elliott) become reluctant guests at the stately house of Jason (Standing) – a shrivelled geriatric satanist breathing his last in an oxygen tent. Ross is supposed to be the reincarnation of Jason's mother, who was burned as a witch, and his successor as the head of the sinister cult. A group of fellow guests provide the victims: Broome is drowned; Daltry, looking moronically beatific, dies during a botched tracheotomy; Gray is burned alive; Neil impaled and Montague shot and telekinetically finished off by Ross. The direction and the equally insipid script make much of creaky doors opening, the knowing glances of servants and other antiquated clichés. Grantham's special makeup and Wingrove's effects work well, especially in the burning of Gray which leaves only a steaming heap of offal, but most of the picture is at best routine.

d Richard Marquand *p* David Foster *s* Jimmy Sangster, Patrick Tilley, Paul Wheeler *c* Dick Bush, Alan Hume *se* Ian Wingrove *lp* Katharine Ross, Sam Elliott, John Standing, Ian Hogg, Charles Gray, Margaret Tyzack, Roger Daltrey, Lee Montague, Hildegard Neil, Marianne Broome

Magic (JOSEPH E. LEVINE) 107min
This expansion by Goldman and Attenborough of Alberto Cavalcanti's contribution to **Dead of Night** (1945) is a sad piece of cinema that lacks both suspense and atmosphere. Goldman's original novel of a ventriloquist taken over by a dummy stimulated some interest by telling the tale through the dummy's eyes, recounting how the second-rate magician became a successful ventriloquist by using the gimmick of a foul-mouthed puppet. But the movie dwells on a sentimental account of the man's breakdown as he attempts to overcome the trauma of having been rejected by a girl (Ann-Margret) in his schooldays. As the character wanders through the various Catskills' resorts, the movie tries to squeeze some tension into the proceedings by resorting to the predictable Grand Guignol effects as Corky (Hopkins) allows the repressed side of his character (the dummy, Fats) to emerge, becoming increasingly schizophrenic and homicidal. The cast work hard, and Jerry Goldsmith's score valiantly tries to persuade viewers to feel affected, but the movie doesn't really come off.

d Richard Attenborough *p* Joseph E. Levine, Richard P. Levine *s* William Goldman *c* Victor J. Kemper *se* Robert MacDonald Jnr *lp* Anthony Hopkins, Ann-Margret, Burgess Meredith, Ed Lauter, Jerry Houser, Lillian Randolph, Joe Lowry

La Montagna del Dio Cannibale *aka* **Prisoner of the Cannibal God** *aka* **Slave of the Cannibal God**
(DANIA FILM; IT) scope 99(96)min
A special credit for Andress's leatherwear gives some indication of both the character and the slightly upmarket aspirations of this lurid jungle fantasy, in which Cassinelli and Andress play a brother and sister trekking through uncharted New Guinea ostensibly in search of Andress's missing husband but actually in hopes of locating some valuable uranium deposits. Keach has a rather thankless role as their guide, who

Katharine Ross in The Legacy, *a workmanlike offering at best.*

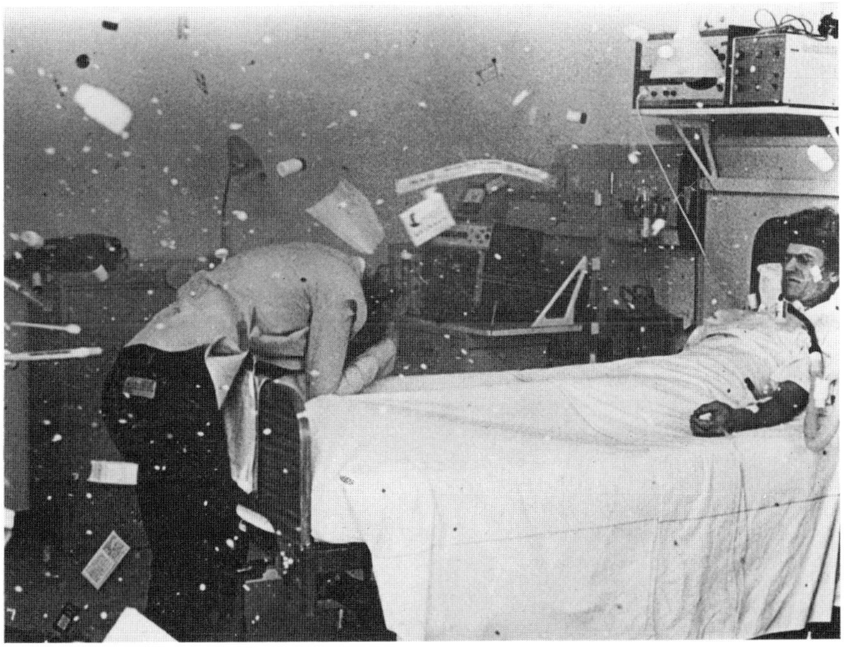

Robert Thompson lets loose his telekinetic powers in Patrick.

exits by being fatally swept over a waterfall. The Cannibal God proves to be the missing husband, or at least his remains, which the cannibals believe to have magic properties. Cassinelli is ultimately devoured for his pains, but the script effects an escape for Andress. The hokum is assembled with some assurance by Martino, formerly a director of sex and fantasy films, including **Tutti i Colori del Buio** (1972). As cannibal movies go, this one is undeniably superior to **Ultimo Mondo Cannibale** (1976).

d/co-s Sergio Martino *p* Luciano Martino *co-s* Cesare Frugoni *c* Giancarlo Ferrando *lp* Ursula Andress, Stacy Keach, Claudio Cassinelli, Antonio Marsina, Franco Fantasia, Lanfranco Spinola, Carlo Longhi, Dudley Wanagura

Murder by Decree *aka* **Sherlock Holmes and Saucy Jack** *aka* **Sherlock Holmes: Murder by Decree**
(SAUCY JACK INC/DECREE PRODUCTIONS; GB,CAN)
120(112)min
If the early one-reelers are included, this is Sherlock Holmes' 134th film and is enthralling and infuriating to equal degrees with a script that is both ingenuous and lacking in courage. An adaptation of John Lloyd and Elwyn Jones' *The Ripper File*, Clark's apocryphal adventure of Holmes (Plummer) and Watson (Mason) leads from Jack the Ripper (Jonfield) and his insane partner in crime, the royal physician (Lansford), to masonic worthies, including the Prime Minister Lord Salisbury (Gielgud), who are part of a plot to cover up the nauseating murders in order to prevent royal lechery from becoming public knowledge. The lengths they go to include kidnapping, baby-snatching and murder as well as the imprisonment of an innocent young woman (Bujold) in an insane asylum, and the delivery of her friend (Clark) into the hands of the sadistic physician. Holmes is impeded by Lestrade (Finlay) and the head of Scotland Yard (Quayle) as well as by a radical police officer (Hemmings) who wants to blow the establishment's cover of respectability.

Sadly, the script doesn't have the courage of its convictions and fudges the issue in a lengthy final scene in which Holmes directly confronts and accuses the leaders of government but then lets them off the hook, becoming part of the cover-up himself. Since this is totally out of character for the arrogantly logical detective, it suggests that it was the film-makers who suffered a sudden attack of cold feet. In a star-studded cast, Mason's Watson stands out as a particularly successful portrait but the credit for the stunningly filmed picture must go to the director and cameraman whose combined efforts create genuinely eerie surreal scenes and transform the city of London into a disturbing space, in which every dark recess and alleyway exudes a sense of corruption and menace that culminates in the hallucinatory dockside confrontation with the Ripper. If the film-makers had been able to muster more political courage their movie could have been a very powerful masterpiece.

d/co-p Bob Clark *co-p* René Dupont *s* John Hopkins *c* Reginald H. Morris *se* Michael Albrechtson *lp* Christopher Plummer, James Mason, David Hemmings, Suzan Clark, Genevieve Bujold, Anthony Quayle, John Gielgud, Frank Finlay, Peter Jonfield, Roy Lansford

Ninfas Diabolicas (PRESENCA; BRAZIL) 85min
While Rosangela Maldonado's **A Deusa de Marmore – Escrava do Diabo** (1978) presented a mixture of horror and pornochanchada, this picture combines the indigenously Brazilian sexploitation conventions with a ghost story. A man on a business trip (Hingst) offers a lift to two young women, apparently students (Mueller and Scalvi), and makes love to one of them. He turns to the other who appears to kill her friend before dragging the bewildered Hingst on to the ground with her in a wild embrace. As they drive back, the murdered woman appears on the back seat of the car and causes Hingst to crash. The two women, totally unscathed, are then seen walking away from the wreck and hitching a lift by the side of the road. The story has two morals: happily married men should stay away from loose women and female hitchhikers are sex-crazed predators, which makes it a fairly conventional story. Much of the film is devoted to the carnal encounters with the seductresses. The director, an immigrant from Shanghai, had co-directed a sexploitation film before, *O Puritano da Rua Augusta* (1966). This was his first solo effort.

d/p/co-s John Doo (Chien Lun Tu) *co-s* Ody Fraga *c* Ozualdo Candeias *lp* Sergio Hingst, Aldine Mueller, Patricia Scalvi, Dorothy Leiner, Misali Tanaka, Joseph Kang Doo, Andre Piacentini, Georgia Carolina

Patrick
(AUSTRALIAN INTERNATIONAL FILM CORP/ FILMWAYS AUSTRALASIA/AFC/VICTORIAN FILM COMMISSION; AUST) 110min
Ginnane, the prolific producer of fantasy potboilers, entrusted the direction of this **Carrie** (1976) derived story to Franklin, a sexploitation director who had studied at UCLA. Patrick (Thompson), having murdered his mother and her lover, has become a paralysed pre-oedipal, psychotic lump. From his bed, he manages to affect his surroundings, including the pretty nurse (Penhaligon) he fancies and his paternal – and therefore menacing – doctor (Helpmann), by telekinesis and causes havoc throughout the hospital. As usual with products from the Ginnane stable, the script is clumsy (here relying on repeated telephone calls to tell the audience what has happened) and the direction pedestrian, although Franklin does manage a sub-Argento shock scene. The non-Australian cast members are presumably to increase the picture's international bankability, and the film landed Franklin the job of directing **Psycho II** (1983) in the US. In Italy, Mario Landi made a sequel of sorts to this film called **Patrick Vive Ancora** (1980).

d/co-p Richard Franklin *co-p* Antony I. Ginnane *s* Everett de Roche *c* Don McAlpine *se* Conrad Rothmann *lp* Robert Thompson, Susan Penhaligon, Robert Helpmann, Rod Mullinar, Bruce Barry, Julia Blake, Helen Hemingway, Maria Mercedes, Everett de Roche, Walter Pym

Les Raisins de la Mort *aka* **Pesticide**
(LES FILMS ABC/RUSH PRODUCTIONS/ OFF PRODUCTION; FR) 90(85)min
Following on from **Phantasmes** (1975) and a series of particularly badly made hard-core porn movies, Rollin returned to the horror genre with this echo of George Romero's

Night of the Living Dead (1968) enhanced by aspects taken from **No Profanar el Sueño de los Muertos** (1974). Travelling to the South of France to join her lover, Elisabeth (Pascal) is assaulted in a deserted train carriage by what looks like a decomposing corpse. On her mad flight, she encounters hordes more of them. Eventually she teams up with two beer-drinking men who appear normal and shelters in an overgrown vineyard, only to find that the vines are infected by a pesticide and are the cause of the disease which turns the local population into walking zombies. She too will succumb as she sinks into insanity after being subjected to assaults and seeing her lover and her companions viciously killed.

Among the numerous gruesome scenes – heads cut off, bodies impaled upon pitchforks or crucified, faces disintegrating into a mouldering mess – are occasional visually stylish images as a reminder of what Rollin can achieve (**Le Frisson des Vampires**, 1970; **Requiem pour un Vampire**, 1971; **Lèvres de Sang**, 1975) but overall the movie remains a routinely gory potboiler, in spite of the felicitous idea of making France's national drink and major export asset into the source of putrefaction. For his next film, Rollin starred Agnes Coeur (he had used Joelle in *Jeunes Filles Impudiques* and **Les Démoniaques**, both 1973) and in the hard-core *Petites Pensionnaires Impudiques*, and a person called Orson Rosebud in *Pénetrations Vicieuses* (both 1979). With **Fascination** (1979) he again returned to the horror genre, this time with decidedly more success.

d/co-s Jean Rollin *p* Claude Guedj *co-s* Jean-Pierre Bouyxou, Christian Meunier *c* Claude Becognée *se* Alfredo Tiberi, Raphael Moronjiu, Yannick Josse *lp* Marie-Georges Pascal, Serge Marquand, Patricia Cartier, Felix Marten, Mirella Rancelot, Paul Biscaglia, Evelyne Thomas, Jean Rollin, Jean-Pierre Bouyxou

Suor Omicidi *aka* The Killer Nun

(CINESUD/IL GRUPPO DI LAVORO CALLIOPE; IT) 90(81)min

In spite of the cast of stars, Berruti offers a simple sexploitation variant on Domenico Paolella's intriguingly anti-clerical film, *Le Monache di Sant'Archangelo* (1973), the best of the many sex-and-violence-in-a-convent movies – themselves variants on the women's prison subgenre. A man-hating nun in an asylum slaughters male patients while diverting suspicion on to a fellow nun (Ekberg) who happens to be a drug addict. To avoid a scandal, the Mother Superior (Valli) has her quietly poisoned. Promoted with the sensational slogan: 'From the secret archives of the Vatican', the film was labelled 'unacceptable' by the Catholic censorship organizations in Italy.

d/co-s Giulio Berruti *p* Enzo Gallo *co-s* Alberto Tarallo *c* Tonino Maccoppi *lp* Anita Ekberg, Alida Valli, Massimo Serato, Lou Castel, Joe Dallesandro, Laura Nucci, Paola Morra, Lee de Barriault

Terror

(CRYSTAL FILM PRODUCTIONS; GB) 87min

Terror is an odd mixture, combining echoes of **The Exorcist** (1973) and **La Maschera del Demonio** (1960) into a plotline about a witch's curse bringing about the deaths of the last survivors (Nolan and Courage) of the family on whom it was visited 300 years before. Although the narrative is decidedly incoherent, with subsidiary characters meeting gory ends in random succession, the incidentals are often lively and distinctive. This is in great part due to McGillivray's script, with its amusing exploitation of the showbusiness milieu (Nolan plays a director of horror movies) as well as its capacity to reverse expectations (dripping 'blood' proves to be red paint; a 'monster' apparition turns out to be merely a harmless man walking stiffly in rain-soaked clothes). But the film also gains from Young's atmospheric camerawork and from well-contrived sequences such as the one in which a film studio comes supernaturally 'alive' with equipment and cans of film flying lethally through the air. It is unfortunate, though, that Warren's penchant for marking every climax with excited closeups of mangled and maimed throats – a tendency further aggravated in his *Inseminoid* (1980) – makes this a cheap and nasty movie.

d Norman J. Warren *co-p/c* Les Young *co-p* Richard Crafter *s* David McGillivray *lp* John Nolan, Carolyn Courage, James Aubrey, Sarah Keller, Milton Reid, Tricia Walsh, Glynis Barber, Patti Love, Peter Mayhew, David McGillivray

The Toolbox Murders

(CAL-AM PRODUCTIONS) 95(92)min

A number of women are brutally murdered in a Californian apartment block, where a 15-year-old girl has also disappeared. It transpires that the killer/kidnapper is the caretaker (Mitchell) who blames the death of his daughter on the 'evil' and 'corruption' of his victims and their like – almost inevitably, in this kind of film, attractive, sexually active women. Featuring death by power drill, nail gun, hammer, screwdriver, butcher's knife, scissors, car-crash and fire, *The Toolbox Murders* is, as the title might suggest, nothing if not gruesome. However, it's also remarkably suspenseless and surprisingly dull. The real problem, though, as with so many films of this type, is that no real distance is ever taken from the killer's scrambled perceptions and that the film ultimately condones a world view which it purports to condemn as lunatic.

d Dennis Donnelly *p* Tony Didio *s* Neva Friedenn, Robert Easter, Ann Kindberg *c* Gary Graver *lp* Cameron Mitchell, Pamelyn Ferdin, Wesley Eure, Nicolas Beauvy, Tim Donnelly, Aneta Corsaut, Faith McSwain, Marcie Drake

Tourist Trap (CHARLES BAND PRODUCTIONS) 90(85)min

A group of teenagers on a desert outing become marooned when their jeep breaks down at Slausen's Lost Oasis, a tourist-trap museum which houses a collection of remarkably lifelike mannequins. These have powers not only of animation but telekinesis and, aided by Slausen (Connors), rapidly turn on the young intruders. *Tourist Trap* exploits very effectively the peculiarly disturbing potentials of wax dummies, and does so with a comparatively restrained amount of gore and quite imaginatively suspenseful direction. Much more interesting, however, is the lack of any real explanation for the dummies' strange powers so that as the film progresses it becomes

A moment of terror in The Toolbox Murders.

Right: *Horror in outer space:* Alien.

increasingly nightmarish and delirious, reaching an impressive climax which leaves the only surviving character quite deranged.

d/co-s David Schmoeller *p/co-s* J. Larry Carroll *c* Nicholas von Sternberg *se* Richard O. Helmer, Karen Stern, David Ayres, Ken Horn, Robert A. Burns, Ve Neill *lp* Chuck Connors, Tanya Roberts, Keith McDermott, Dawn Jeffory, Jon Van Ness, Jocelyn Jones, Robin Sherwood

Die Woelfin von Teufelsmoor *aka* **Tod im November** *aka* **The Devil's Bed** *aka* **The She-Wolf of Devil's Moor**
(WOLFGANG ODELGA FILM/STAR FILM/WIEN FILM; AUSTRIA) 93min
Pfandler adapted his own story, *Walpurga*, to produce this thinly veiled, allegorical attack on the anti-nuclear movement. A young engineer (Law) arrives in an economically backward area to prepare for the building of a nuclear plant. The local opposition to the scheme is rooted in nature mysticism and manipulated by a menacing old man (Wischnewski), who relies on superstition and parapsychology to wield power over the region, and keeps the beautiful Walpurga (Bolkan) under his spell. But Bolkan and Law fall in love, which leads to the defeat of the 'green' forces of darkness exploited by the old wizard to keep the region under his control.

d/co-s Helmut Pfandler *p* Wolfgang Odelga *co-s* Karl Heinz Willschrei *c* Hanns Matula, Heinz Hoelscher *lp* John Phillip Law, Florinda Bolkan (José Soara Bulco), Siegfried Wischnewski, Claudia Rieschel, Dieter Jendreyko, Guido Wieland, Edd Stavjanik, Inge Toifl, Bruno Thost

1979

Alien
(FOX/BRANDYWINE-RONALD SHUSETT PRODUCTIONS; GB) pv 117min
Constructed as craftily as the commercials Scott first made his name with – the film opens with the crew of the *Nostromo* waking and ends with the sole survivor, Weaver, returning to sleep after her literal nightmare – *Alien* is nothing less than a gigantic 'Boo!' set in outer space where, as the film's advertising slogan went, 'No one can hear you scream'. At the heart of the movie lies H. R. Giger's alien (or, rather, aliens, as the prawn-like creature that bursts forth from Hurt's chest grows and grows) and its ferocious will to live and procreate at whatever cost to those around it.

Although the film can be seen as an inversion of the money-spinning science fiction films *Star Wars* and *Close Encounters of the Third Kind* (both 1977), in fact the movie is close to the tradition of H. P. Lovecraft. His tales about the 'Necronomicon' provided Giger, who illustrated the collected tales of Lovecraft, with his vision of the 'biomechanoid' being, a fusion of human and mechanical elements. Thus, it is entirely fitting that *Alien* was shot at Bray Studios, the long-time production base of Hammer, who had made some of the best (and worst) British horror films, and that the film's imagery should be sexual, rather than high tech.

d Ridley Scott *p* Gordon Carroll, David Giler, Walter Hill *s* Dan O'Bannon *c* Derek Vanlint, Denys Ayling *se* Filmfex Animation Services, Carlo Rambaldi, Clinton Cavers, Bernard Lodge, Brian Johnson, Nick Allder, Allan Bryce *lp* Tom Skerritt, Sigourney Weaver, Veronica Cartwright, Harry Dean Stanton, John Hurt, Ian Holm

Alison's Birthday
(DAVID HEMMINGS PRODUCTIONS/AFC/FONTANA FILMS; AUST) scope 95min
This, Coughlan's first movie plot starts from the idea that **Carrie** (1976) is **Rosemary's Baby** (1968), and throws in elements of **The Exorcist** (1973) for good measure. During a seance Alison (Samuel) is warned by her dead father to leave her uncle's house before her 19th birthday. She doesn't and the birthday celebration takes the form of black magic ceremony designed to transfer her personality into the wizened remains of a dead witch so that she can become a satanic cult's leader. The script is a cynical concoction of commercial elements from the previous money-makers, the direction is routine, the cinematography erratic and characters both stereotypical and misjudged.

d/s Ian Coughlan *p* David Hannay *c* Kevin Lind *se* Lu Kanturek *lp* Joanne Samuel, Bunny Brooke, Margie McCrae, Martin Vaughan, Rosalind Speirs, Ian Coughlan, Ralph Cotterill, Vincent Ball, John Bluthal, Eric Oldfield

The Amityville Horror
(CINEMA 77/AIP) 118min
Following the road to coffee-table horrors opened up by **The Exorcist** (1973), AIP came up with this, its biggest hit in years and a surprisingly effective film. The opening sequence is particularly striking in its attempt to characterize the demonic Long Island house, or rather to suggest an elemental quality to the murders taking place within it as the film begins: the booming thunder and flashes of lightning seem to co-exist with the gunshots that take out an entire family (except for the killer, the eldest son) while two lighted windows at the top of the house stare out like two baleful eyes. When the next family to move in (Brolin, Kidder and their two nice kids) are shown around by an eager estate agent, signs of anxious hype are apparent in the flash shots recapping the murders, not so much to suggest that the estate agent knows all about the house's history as to reassure the audience that something nasty lurks ready to spring again. Once the family have moved in, Rosenberg's direction settles down for some extremely effective tension-building as the priest arriving to bless the house (Steiger) finds himself blocked by an immovable malevolent force (eventually withdrawing into a broken, semi-catatonic silence); the little girl begins to enjoy a sinisterly secretive collusion with an invisible playmate; the family dog whines and scratches at the basement wall; the father grows increasingly morose; and his wife, troubled by his strange outbursts of violent irritability, discovers to her horror (from newspaper files) his uncanny resemblance to the original killer.

At this point, apparently intent on respecting the account of a real-life haunting which formed the basis for Jay Anson's novel, the script has nowhere to go. Having bolstered the first half with an over-emphasis on the family's Catholic background (the Church is always good for both satirical digs and a bit of spiritual mystification), the film ends rather lamely with the family fleeing the house – once the property of a notorious 18th-century satanist – after Brolin has thrown a murderous tantrum or two and glimpsed something nasty (but sensibly left very vague) in the basement. Having no such scruples as to credibility, the prequel **Amityville II: The Possession** (1982) and its sequel **Amityville 3-D** (1983), lose in effectiveness what they gain in exploitability.

d Stuart Rosenberg *p* Ronald Saland, Elliot Geisinger *s* Sandor Stern *c* Fred J. Koenekamp *lp* James Brolin, Margot Kidder, Rod Steiger, Don Stroud, Val Avery, Murray Hamilton

Bloodeaters (CM PRODUCTIONS) 84min
Shot on 16mm in Pittsburg – where **Night of the Living Dead** (1968) was also made – this low-low-budget picture has a partly amateur cast and a generally amateurish look to its technical aspects. The somewhat incoherent plot turns on a bunch of young hoodlums who are harvesting a marijuana crop in a remote forest which is the scene of a herbicide spraying experiment. The chemical has the effect of turning the crooks into zombies, who go on the rampage and attack anyone who comes in sight. A subplot about double-dealing federal agents doesn't go anywhere, and the attempts at comic relief, mainly involving Miller as a complaining wife, are less than engaging. Amplas, who played the title role in **Martin** (1976), is here confined to a stock role as one of the crooks.

d/p/s Chuck McCrann *c* David Sperling *lp* Charles Austin, Beverly Shapiro, Dennis Helfend, Harriet Miller, John Amplas, Paul Haskin

Buio Omega *aka* **Blue Holocaust** *aka* **Beyond the Darkness** (DR PRODUZIONI; IT) 94(85)min
Massaccesi, like the great Maria Bava, is a cameraman turned director but that is where the resemblance ends. Although here he makes isolated attempts at composing stylish images, the Grand Guignol fantasy smothers its potentially surreal love story in gore. The tale opens with the voodoo-induced death of a young woman. Her taxidermist lover, Francesco, exhumes her corpse, removes the intestines (in a scene which lingers on the messy details) and stuffs her. The girl who interrupts his activities is gratuitously tortured, killed and chopped to bits and his new girlfriend, Iris, helps him to dispose of the sludgy remains by pouring them on the rhubarb patch. The narrative then stumbles from shock to shock, including more chopping and eye-gouging, until a climactic orgy of gore brings it to a close.

Unfortunately, Massaccesi's approach is cheaply realist, trying to shock by unimaginatively filming butchery and cruelty. The potential poetry of a mad, necrophiliac passion that animates, for instance, Bava's **Lisa e il Diavolo** (1972) is kept at bay by the crudely exploitative approach, and nowhere does the director, a specialist in cheap sex movies, betray the fascination with the psychopathology of cinema and film-viewing itself which distinguishes Bava's work. Massaccesi's best movie is probably *Eva Nera* (1976), in which Jack Palance and Laura Gemser have fun with the Emanuelle motifs. Gemser also features in his **Emanuelle e gli Ultimi Cannibali** (1977) and **Le Notte Erotiche dei Morti Viventi** (1979).

d/c Joe d'Amato (Aristide Massaccesi) *p* Marco Rossetti *s* Ottavio Fabbri, Giacomo Guerrini *lp* Kieran Canter, Cinzia Monreale, Franca Stoppa, Sam Modesto, Anna Cardini, Lucia d'Elia, Simonetta Allodi, Klaus Rainer

Cannibal Holocaust (FD CINEMATOGRAFICA; IT) 95min
Attempting to cash in on the success of his **Ultimo Mondo Cannibale** (1976) as well as that of other lucrative depictions of unconsciously brutal visceral violence (**Zombi 2**, 1979; **La Regina dei Cannibali**, 1980), Deodato here tries to increase the sense of realism by resorting to an old literary trick. Whereas many porn novels pretended to be derived from 'found' manuscripts, Deodato's picture consists mainly of 'found' film – and, therefore, includes amateurish zooming, scratches, graininess and laboratory marks. The narrative excuse is that a group of sensationalist documentarists travelled to a remote Amazon tribe and incited the 'natives' to torture and cannibalism, which was eventually turned against the rich American film-makers. The film then presents the footage 'found' by a search party. Rarely screened in its complete version, the picture, which was shot on location, offers a catalogue of cruelty visited upon animals and people: a bound person is thrown into a river as bait for piranha fish, a naked woman in impaled, a tortoise skinned alive, a foetus is ripped out of a woman's womb and buried in mud, and so on.

As in so many movies of this nature, from **Horrors of the Black Museum** (1959) onwards, the film pretends to condemn what it exploits: the pseudo American film-makers are presented as the villains who shouldn't have filmed the very images which the Italian Deodato and others offer for sale. In view of the movie's pretend realism, it is worth noting that Deodato used to be Roberto Rossellini's assistant.

d Ruggero Deodato *p* Franco Palaggi *s* Gianfranco Clerici *c* Sergio d'Offizi *lp* Francesca Ciardi, Luca Barbareschi, Robert Kerman, Perry Pirkamen

The Changeling
(CHESSMAN PALK PRODUCTIONS; CAN) pv scope 107min
A rather oldfashioned tale of supernatural discovery – and, in theory, none the worse for that – *The Changeling* clearly aims to be a 'class' product, given the distinguished names in the cast, the recruitment as director of Medak (best known for prestige stage adaptations like *A Day in the Death of Joe Egg*, 1972), and the chosen milieu – a mansion near Seattle rented (if rather improbably) by a composer (Scott) and formerly owned by a distinguished politician (Douglas). It transpires, through Scott's realization that the house is haunted by the spirit of a dead child, that the politician is an impostor and that the real bearer of his name was murdered in infancy by his father to safeguard an inheritance. At the conclusion, the frustrated spirit sets the house alight and the politico dies simultaneously of a heart attack. Despite conscientiously active camerawork by Coquillon – notable in the genre for his contribution to **The Witchfinder General** (1968) – the film is desultory at best, and

The Amityville Horror, *the haunted house movie of the decade.*

certainly lacks the Jacobean overtones which its title hopefully suggests.

d Peter Medak *p* Joel B. Michaels, Garth H. Drabinsky *s* William Gray, Diana Maddox *c* John Coquillon *se* Gene Grigg *lp* George C. Scott, Trish Van Devere, Melvyn Douglas, John Colicos, Jean Marsh, Barry Morse, James Douglas, Roberta Maxwell

Dawn of the Dead *aka* **Zombies** (LAUREL GROUP PRODUCTIONS/DAWN ASSOCIATES) 127(125)min
This is not a conventional sequel to **Night of the Living Dead** (1968), but an enlargement of the premise of Romero's seminal movie, taking the crisis further by depicting an America where society has all but fallen apart. Television researcher Ross, helicopter pilot Emge and two National Guardsmen (Reininger, Foree) flee a collapsing city and take refuge in a vast shopping mall which they clear out and fortify against the flesh-eating zombies. The film first runs quickly through the rise and fall of a societal microcosm, with gung-ho Reininger getting himself needlessly killed and the pregnant Ross drifting away from her lover, before the survivors find themselves confronting a marauding band of survivalist bikers.

The Savini-designed atrocities (a helicopter rotor blade slicing off the top of a zombie's head like a breakfast egg) and the incongruities (a zombie nun or hare krishna) are humorous as well as horrible, but the central, slow movement of the film concentrates on the characters' disenchantment with a life of meaningless plenty and prepares us for a savage catharsis as the mall is invaded by the warring bands of bikers and zombies, who gleefully trash one another and the garish setting, throwing custard pies and wrenching off arms.

Co-produced with Dario Argento, *Dawn of the Living Dead* inaugurated a new phase in the 'splatter movie'. Certainly one of the bloodiest films ever made, it is also memorable for its unusual sensitivity and intelligence.

d/s George A. Romero *co-p* Richard P. Rubinstein, Dario Argento *c* Michael P. Gornick *se* Tom Savini *lp* David Emge, Ken Foree, Scott H. Reininger, Gaylen Ross, David Crawford, David Early

Dottor Jekyll e Gentile Signora *aka* **Dr and Mrs Jekyll** *aka* **Dr Jekyll Jr** *aka* **Il Dottore Jekill Jr** *aka* **Jekyll Jr** (MEDUSA; IT) 99(85)min
Veteran comedy director Steno conducts this crazy comedy with considerable gusto, obviously enjoying his games with gothic clichés. A multinational corporation run by merciless venal executives calls in Dr Jekyll, grandson of the famous father who appears to have survived the often depicted ending of Stevenson's story, to mount a super-villainous scheme to recruit the Queen of England for an advertising gimmick. Plagued by scruples, the young doctor (played by the podgy Villaggio), drinks a potion supplied by his grandfather in order to become really mean, but it turns out that the concoction had gone stale and makes him a benefactor of mankind instead. Fittingly for such an allegory about multinationals, the villains win and lock the Jekyll family into a cage while the masses demonstrate in favour of more exploitation and less leisure.

d/co-s Steno (Stefano Vanzina) *p* F. Poccioni *co-s* Leo Benvenuti, Piero de Bernardi, Giovanni Manganelli *c* Ennio Guarnieri, Sergio Salvati *lp* Paolo Villaggio, Edwige Fenech, Gianrico Tedeschi, Gordon Mitchell

Dracula (MIRISCH/U) pv 112min
Langella's striking matinée idol portrayal of Dracula apart, the special effects are the tail that wags the dog here. A lush, camp and stagy version of the Hamilton Deane and John L. Balderston adaptation of Bram Stoker's novel – which also provided the basis for the Bela Lugosi **Dracula** (1931) – the film is pointlessly given an Edwardian setting (and features a sports car improbably chasing the coach carrying Dracula's coffin). Although amusing, the movie does not bear comparison with the 1973 Dan Curtis-Richard Matheson-Jack Palance reworking for TV.

d John Badham *p* Walter Mirisch *s* W. D. Richter *c* Gilbert Taylor *lp* Frank Langella, Laurence Olivier, Donald Pleasance, Kate Nelligan, Trevor Eve, Tony Haygarth

The Driller Killer
(NAVARON FILMS) 85min
The object of some notoriety as the film most often cited, along with **I Spit on Your Grave** (1978), in the debate in the UK over 'video nasties', *The Driller Killer* is an undeniably unpleasant and disturbing film. The central figure, pseudonymously played by director Ferrara, is an unsuccessful painter struggling to make ends meet in a New York garret. His father is a derelict, and he becomes increasingly obsessed with avoiding the same fate, yet drawn to observing more closely the down-and-out community. Further unbalanced by a punk rock group who have moved into an adjacent apartment (adding an element of humour as well as cultural criticism), Ferrara makes nocturnal forays into the city streets to murder derelicts with an electric drill. Subsequently, this violence is turned back into his personal life, and he murders the art dealer (Schultz) who has rejected the painting over which he has been labouring, then tracks down his former girlfriend (Marz) who has left him for her ex-husband (Howorth). The movie ends enigmatically when, after killing Howorth, he takes his place in bed to await the arrival of Marz.

Though clearly cheaply made, the movie turns its impoverishment into an asset by adopting a hand-held shooting style for many of the exteriors, a technique which brings the squalid milieu fittingly to life: conversely, the sequences inside the apartment are quite precisely staged. Interestingly, too, in terms of the film's reputation, only one of the murders is shown in grisly detail. For the rest, the visual emphasis is placed squarely on the killer, with his victims frequently out of frame. In its lurid fashion, the film does succeed in presenting its protagonist as driven mad by being both trapped within his wretched environment and by his inability to transcend it in art.

d Abel Ferrara *p* Rochelle Weisberg *s* N. G. St John *c* Ken Kelsch *lp* Jimmy Laine (Abel Ferrara), Carolyn Marz, Harry Schultz, Baybi Day, Richard Howorth, Alan Wynroth, Maria Helhoski, James O'Hara, Rodney Montreal

Effects *aka* **The Manipulator**
(THE IMAGE WORKS) 87(79)min
This lacklustre play on the 'snuff'-movie mythology has the cast and crew of a low-budget horror movie called *Something's Wrong* discover that their voyeuristic megalomaniac director is setting up *Duped*, a film-about-a-film in which the killings are for real. However, though the Pittsburg-based production is of interest, utilizing several George Romero regulars on the technical side and also featuring special effects' wizard Savini in a small role (as Nicky), the film itself lacks any sense of the dramatic.

d/s Dusty Nelson *p* John Harrison, Pasquale Buba *c* Carl Augenstein *se* Tom Savini *lp* John Harrison, Susan Chapek, Joseph Pilato, Bernard KcKenna, Debra Gordon, Tom Savini, Chuck Hoyes, Blay Bahnsen

The Evictors
(CHARLES B. PIERCE FILM PRODUCTIONS) 92min
After a prologue to show their house's history of violence, with three people killed by the police while shooting it out after refusing to be evicted, a nice young couple (Parks and Harper) arrive in the small Louisiana town of Leadsville. It comes as no surprise at all when there are rumbles about subsequent deaths, sinister apparitions and an axe death; and very little

more surprise when it turns out that those three people didn't really die in the shootout, but escaped after substituting the bodies of people they had murdered, and are still lurking with mad intent. What takes the film watchably out of the rut is its determination (until it has to deliver the goods at the end) to try to show how people might really behave when faced with such circumstances by going for low-key, questioning performances that avoid the usual screaming hysteria, a calm and judicious directorial tempo and, above all, excellent locations that lend a genuine sense of place and community. The film doesn't quite come off, but at least it tries.

d/p/s Charles B. Pierce *c* Chuck Bryant *lp* Vic Morrow, Michael Parks, Jessica Harper, Sue Ann Langdon, Dennis Fimple

Fascination (LES FILMS ABC/COMEX; FR) 80min
Two mediocre hard-core porn movies provided Rollin with the necessary funds for his next fantasy picture which joined **Lèvres de Sang** (1975) as one of his best pictures to date. The decidedly misogynist story, set at the turn of the century, tells of a group of upper-middle-class women addicted to drinking blood. They meet in a castle and designate two of them to find a young man they can ritually slaughter and communally consume. A young hoodlum (Lemaire) falls into their hands and eventually discovers the fate awaiting him. While Lahaie expertly eliminates a gang of thieves by means of a scythe – no doubt inspired by Tobe Hooper's **Eaten Alive** (1976) – Mai tries to rescue their by now severely wounded victim because she has fallen in love with him. She kills Lahaie and lets her richly attired female companions feast upon her body. But Mai's own overpowering bloodlust eventually gets the upper hand and she slices up her lover, serving him to the congregation for the cannibalistic vampire feast.

The acting here is better than usual in a Rollin film, and Lahaie as the scythe-wielding avenger acquits herself honourably. But as usual, the picture's real delights are strictly visual: the camera sensuously caressing the bodies of a lesbian couple lying on a fur-covered bed, the thin mauve gowns floating around the women and a pale moon reflected in a lake illuminating the gently drifting naked body of an exsanguinated victim. While re-employing a number of his hard-core actresses (Lahaie was in *Vibrations Sensuelles*, 1976; Watteau in *Saute Moi Dessus* and *Lèvres Entrouvertes*, both 1977), Rollin also continued to collaborate with Bouyxou, a noted critic and historian of the genre.

Rollin's next picture used gamma rays as a plot device to generate zombielike creatures (*La Nuit des Traquées*, 1980; re-released with two extra sequences in 1981 as *Filles Traquées*). His next cannibal-zombie picture was an unmitigated disaster: **El Lago de los Muertos Vivientes** (1980).

The film was released in 1980.

d/s Jean Rollin *p* Joe de Lara *c* Georges Fromentin, D.Lacambe *lp* Franca Mai, Brigitte Lahaie, Jean-Marie Lemaire, Fanny Magier, Miriam Watteau, Alain Plumey, Muriel Montossè, Sophie Noel, Evelyne Thomas, Jacques Marboeuf

Il Fiume del Grande Caimano *aka* **The Great Alligator** *aka* **Great Alligator River** *aka* **Alligators**
(DANIA FILM/MEDUSA; IT) 91min
Martino (who was also responsible for **La Montagna del Dio Cannibale**, 1978) here transposes **Jaws** (1975) to an African setting, changes the monster to a giant crocodile adored as a god by the natives and manages to produce a mediocre, but therefore no less repulsively racist, fantasy. Ferrer is the entrepreneur who builds a holiday resort in the jungle and Bach and Cassinelli the tourists who finally escape from the crocodile by dynamiting it to bits, thereby reducing the previously restive natives back to their appropriate state – an apathetic but picturesque background for tourists – as the helicopters arrive to carry the survivors of the carnage back to civilization. Bach also serves to evoke horror at the thought of a white woman falling into the hands of 'tom tom banging, chanting and dancing savages'.

This inept film preceded *Alligator* (1980), which also trades on the body-in-pieces fantasy that has dominated the horror genre since the mid-seventies, and owes more to Tobe Hooper's **Eaten Alive** (1976), which also had Ferrer as a guest star in an isolated hotel setting. Some sources credit Antonio Vittori as cinematographer.

d/co-s Sergio Martino *p* Luciano Martino *co-s* Ernesto Gastaldi, Cesare Frugoni *c* Giancarlo Ferrando *lp* Barbara Bach, Mel Ferrer, Claudio Cassinelli, Romano Puppo, Richard Johnson, Fabrizio Castagnoli, Enzo Fizichella

The Fog
(DEBRA HILL PRODUCTIONS/AVCO EMBASSY) pv 90min
Once upon a time, on a dark and foggy night, a band of drowned mariners invaded a small Californian seaport seeking revenge on the wreckers who sent them to the bottom 100 years ago to the day.... Carpenter begins his film on precisely this delightfully time-honoured note with a pre-credit sequence in which an old salt (Houseman), holding up his watch to denote the witching hour, thrills a group of children round the campfire with the legend that tells how these dead men will return one day. But as the credit sequence begins with the clocks chiming midnight, the series of strange happenings that befall the sleeping town – glass suddenly shatters, cans jitter about on supermarket shelves, lights come on in a deserted garage, a car hoist sets itself in motion, an unattended pump gushes petrol – is recorded in a cold, clinical style that suggests some alien presence.

Whether intentionally or not, the film proper then seems to alternate the deceptively laconic precision that was so striking in *Assault on Precinct 13* (1976) with some curiously old-

A gnarled hand thrusts its way out of The Fog.

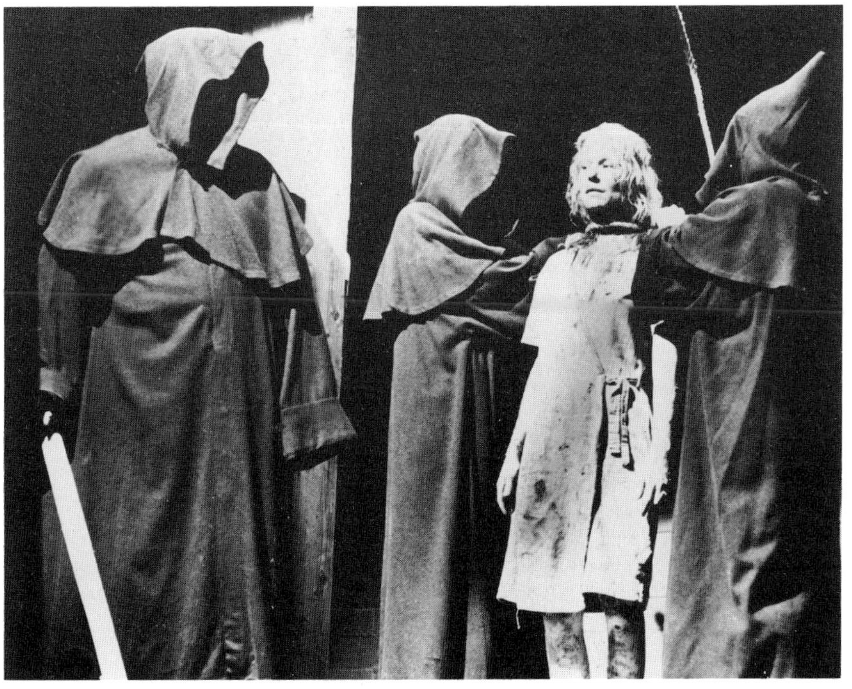

Above: *One of the attempts to terrify people into sanity in* Human Experiments.

fashioned hype (the bloodthirsty ghosts have the glowing red eyes of some Poverty Row monster, for example). The worst example of the hype, though, is the clumsy use of parallel montage. In **Halloween** (1978), Carpenter needed only a single set-up, plus a subtle reframing, to make a superb fright out of the moment when Jamie Lee Curtis thinks she has finally killed the killer, and suddenly he sits up behind her. A similar moment in *The Fog*, with Barbeau sitting beside a shrouded corpse unaware that it is slowly reviving, is made almost risible by repeated cutaways – will they or won't they enter in time? – to the doctor and her boyfriend talking outside. For all that, though, the film is wonderfully atmospheric, and Cundey's camerawork is stunning.

d/co-s John Carpenter *p/co-s* Debra Hill *c* Dean Cundey *lp* Adrienne Barbeau, Hal Holbrook, Janet Leigh, Jamie Lee Curtis, John Houseman, Tom Atkins

Graf Dracula Beisst Jetzt in Oberbayern *aka* Dracula Blows his Cool

(LISA FILM/BARTHONIA FILM; WG) 97(90)min

This is a soft-core imitation of **Love at First Bite** (1979) using plot elements derived from *Frankenstein 1970* (1958). The fashion photographer Stan (Garko) returns to his ancestral Bavarian castle where his vampiric great-grandfather (Garko again) still lives in the basement with the delectable Countess Olivia (Verges). After lots of shots of naked women, amorous encounters and disco dancing, the manor is transformed into Hotel Dracula, with staff playfully biting its tourist patrons. Marginally better than **Beiss Mich, Liebling** (1970), the picture was to be called *Dracula Sucks* in America, but this title was dropped when it emerged that Philip Marshak has used it for a harder sex film starring Jamie Gillis and Annette Haven.

d Carlo Ombra *p* Martin Friedman *s* Gruenbach and Rosenthal *c* Heinz Hoelscher *lp* Gianni Garko, Betty Verges, Giacomo Rizzo, Linda Grondier, Bea Fielder, Ralf Wolter, Herta Worell, Tobias Meister, Ellen Umlauf

Human Experiments

(PYRAMID ENTERTAINMENT) 86(78)min

Wrongly accused of mass murder, country singer (Haynes) is sent to Gates Prison. There psychiatrist Lewis engages in curious experiments, literally terrifying them out of their minds and then 'reprogramming' them, in order to break down his subjects' 'criminal personality'.

The result is a nasty and meretricious, albeit fast-moving and action-packed, decidedly voyeuristic 'back country' genre piece that clearly owes a debt to *Jackson County Jail* (1976). Coogan and Ray deliver particularly malevolent cameos as the backwoods' sheriff and his bar-owner brother, and the movie also features an appearance by Ellen Travolta, sister of John. The scenes in which Haynes is assailed by a number of fear-inducing occurrences, climaxing in an attack by a horde of insects, are, it has to be admitted, both imaginative and frightening. Nonetheless, it remains a film that puts action firmly before characterization.

d/co-p/co-s Gregory Goodell *co-p* Summer Brown *co-s* Richard Rothstein *c* João Fernandes *se* James Dannaldson, Knott Limited, Frank de Marco *lp* Linda Haynes, Geoffrey Lewis, Lurene Tuttle, Aldo Ray, Mercedes Shirley, Darlene Craviotto, Marie O'Henry, Wesley Marie Tackitt, Caroline Davies

Love at First Bite (SIMON PRODUCTIONS) 96min

This vampire parody begins delightfully with the traditional evocation of a cobwebby vault. A hand curls over the edge of a coffin and at a grand piano Dracula (Hamilton) sits in immaculate evening attire, mournfully playing to the accompaniment of howling wolves until, as they threaten to drown his music, he is moved to remonstrate: 'Children of the night – shut up!' Much of the film follows the path trodden by Mel Brooks' **Young Frankenstein** (1974), gleefully subjecting the genre to the same absurd incongruities but less often departing from it in a quest for laughs at any price. With Dracula fleeing to New York when a People's Commissar commandeers his Transylvanian castle as a gymnasium, the basic joke is that the film is designed as a thirties romantic comedy in which true love conquers all; and from that solid foundation it takes off in a witty proliferation of gags simultaneously poking fun at the Dracula myth and lamenting the pragmatic-neurotic modern society that no longer has any use for the wonder of romance.

Hamilton gives a fine high comedy performance as the magnificently suave, romantically tortured vampire who at last manages to find fulfilment in bed with a sexually liberated covergirl (Saint James): 'Oh, that's so kinky,' he croons to her, 'Are *you* biting *me*?'

d Stan Dragoti *p* Joel Freeman *s* Robert Kaufman *c* Edward Rosson *lp* George Hamilton, Susan Saint James, Richard Benjamin, Dick Shawn, Arte Johnson

Macabra *aka* Demonoid

(ZACH MOTION PICTURES/PANORAMA FILMS) 78min

Eggar and Jenson discover a severed hand in a miniature silver coffin whilst working their Mexican silvermine. This turns out to be a relic of an ancient devil-worshipping cult and proceeds to take over the left hands of various contemporary subjects, forcing them to commit grisly murders. Made in 1979 but not released until 1981 (presumably in an attempt to cash in on the success of **The Hand**, 1981), the film injects no new life into the well-tried theme: not only do acting and dialogue leave too much to be desired but some scenes don't fit together properly in sequence and stuntmen and technicians are visible in the corners of several shots. This wouldn't matter quite so much if the special effects were up to scratch, but once you've seen the devil's hand squash one skull you've seen them all.

d/p/co-s Alfred Zacharias *co-s* David Lee Fein, E. Amos Powell *c* Alex Phillips Jnr *se* Bob Burns *lp* Samantha Eggar, Stuart Whitman, Roy Cameron Jenson, Narcisco Busquets, Erika Carlsson, Lew Saunders

Mama Dracula

(VALISA FILMS/RADIO TELEVISION BELGE FRANÇAISE/SND; BEL) 90min

This eccentric picture, shot in English, tried to combine the sex comedy possibilities of the vampiric myth while stressing the maternal side of the vampire. The Countess (Fletcher), who runs a shop with her twin sons (the Wajnberg twins), preserves her beauty by bathing in virgins' blood. When abducting virgins becomes difficult, partly because of a policeman's (Hahn) suspicions, Dr Van Bloed (Shuman), a specialist in artificial blood, is recruited, but to no avail. A policewoman, Nancy (Schneider), is sent to the Countess's castle to investigate but comes under the vampire's spell and, after a chase during a fashion show, interrupted by the doctor who has finally found the correct formula for artificial blood, she ends up marrying both the twins. The photography and the settings are adequate but the farcical script never achieves the level of inventiveness required to get away with such a thin plot. Schneider, whose international fame rests on Bertolucci's *Last Tango in Paris* (1973) and Antonioni's *The Passenger* (1975), manages to convey a hint of comic talent although most of the time looks rather bored. Szulzinger is better known for the burlesque animation film he made with cartoonist Picha, *Tarzoon – Shame of the Jungle* (1975).

d/p/co-s Boris Szulzinger *co-s* Marc-Henri Wajnberg, Pierre Sterckx *c* Willy Kurant *lp* Maria Schneider, Louise Fletcher, Marc-Henri Wajnberg, Alexander Wajnberg, Jimmy Shuman, Jess Hahn, Michel Israel, Suzy Falk

Más Alla del Terror *aka* Beyond Terror *aka* Further Than Fear

(CINEVISION; SP) 89min

This obnoxious terror picture graphically depicts the revenge fantasies of bigoted Spanish conservatives who resent a younger generation's refusal to conform to their values. The movie opens with a tabloid-press account of 'contemporary youth': four cynical youngsters, drug addicts, indulge in an orgy of murder and theft. The second half of the movie chronicles the revenge of their victims: having sought refuge in an empty monastery, they become the prey of ghosts and mouldering corpses lurking in the attached church's subterranean vaults.

The story can best be seen as a companion piece to the wave of exorcism pictures which use a similar logic, except that this time the forces of decency and order, although half decayed, are shown to have enough life in them still to visit bloody retributions upon whoever they disapprove of. In this context it is interesting to note that some of the most sensationalist and gruesome violence which fuels the activities of conservative censorship lobbies, tends to occur mainly in pictures portraying extremely conservative fantasies.

d/co-s Tomas Aznar *p* Alfredo Casado *co-s* Miguel Lizondo, Alfredo Casado *c* Julio Bragado *se* Francisco Garcia, Pablo Perez *lp* Francisco Sanchez, Grajera Raquel Ramirez, Emilio Siegrist, Antonio Jabalera, Alexia Loreto, David Forrest, Andree van de Woestyne

Microwave Massacre

(A REEL LIFE PRODUCTION) 76min

This heavy-handed satire on gore movies bears some resemblance to **Please Don't Eat My Mother!** (1972) which in turn was based on **The Little Shop of Horrors** (1960). Donald (Vernon) is a construction worker who continually rows with his wife May (Ginsberg), not least over her penchant for elaborate meals prepared in their large microwave oven. One day in a rage he kills her, chops her body up and stores it in the freezer. Mistaking the pieces for meat, he discovers a taste for human flesh and is eventuallly forced into regularly replenishing his stocks. Overplayed for cheap laughs, even by the normally deadpan stand-up comedian Vernon, the film ends up by being neither horrific nor funny.

d Wayne Berwick *p/s* Thomas Singer, Craig Muckler *c* Karen Grossman *lp* Jackie Vernon, Loren Schein, Al Troupe, Claire Ginsberg, Lou Ann Webber, Anna Marlo, Sarah Alt, Cindy Gant, Karen Marshall, Marla Simon

Sigrid Thornton in peril in the lacklustre Snap-Shot.

Nightwing

(POLYC INTERNATIONAL; NETH) 105min

Derived from a novel by Martin Cruz Smith (better known as the author of *Gorky Park*), set largely on an Arizona Indian reservation and dealing with attacks by plague-carrying vampire bats, *Nightwing* – an American film in all but name – disregards the spare, documentary-like approach of its source, and opts instead (though without achieving any real *frisson*) for being a conventional shocker. Its forerunners are *The Birds* (1963) and more recent nature-on-the-offensive successors like *Frogs* (1972), but it is below the standard of even so minor an addition to the cycle as *Day of the Animals* (1976). Hiller is a long way from *Love Story* (1970) and the film has little atmosphere or momentum. Occasional plot details are quite inventive: scientist (Warner), lawman (Mancuso) and the Mancuso's girl (Harrold) use an electrified cage to protect themselves from the bats they are pursuing, and Warner fires a radio-transmitting dart into one of the creatures in order to discover its roosting place. But they are not assimilated interestingly into the narrative and the bat attacks themselves are repetitious in the extreme.

d Arthur Hiller *p* Martin Ransohoff *s* Steve Shagan, Bud Shrake, Martin Cruz Smith *c* Charles Rosher *se* Carlo Rambaldi *lp* Nick Mancuso, Kathryn Harrold, David Warner, Strother Martin, Steven Macht, Ben Piazza, George Clutesi

Nosferatu: Phantom der Nacht *aka* Nosferatu the Vampyre

(WERNER HERZOG/GAUMONT; WG,FR) 107min

This film is so nearly original in its approach to the Dracula story that one wonders why, instead of either going back to the Bram Stoker novel or letting his own imagination run free, Herzog chose to fetter himself to what is virtually a remake of one of the silent cinema's classics. Scene after scene simply re-creates images from Murnau's **Nosferatu** (1921), sometimes (as when Dracula steps ashore from the plague ship to dispose of his coffins) even reproducing whole sets and lighting effects, so that the only noticeable difference lies in the addition of colour and sound. Where the current trend has been to turn Dracula into a suave and socially acceptable seducer, Herzog reverts to the timeworn tradition of rattleboned monsters: cadaverously egg-headed, pointy-eared and mandarin-clawed, hideously suggestive of one of his own plague-bearing rats with his red-rimmed eyes and twin rodent fangs, his Dracula (Kinski) is an exact pastiche of Murnau's Count Orlock.

All too often, unfortunately, the result comes dangerously close to parody. Dracula's first appearance, a darker silhouette in the darkness as the door of his castle opens in silent answer to Jonathan Harker's knock, is magnificent; but as he steps into the light, graciously proffers a laden dinner-table with a wave of his six-inch talons, and moans in frustration at the wasted blood when Jonathan (Ganz) accidentally cuts his finger, he is so monstrously absurd that Ganz's studiously polite attempt not to notice anything out of the ordinary becomes merely risible. Imitating Murnau, the film gets tangled in the same weird mixture of acting styles, it reduces several of Stoker's characters (notably Renfield and Mina) to the same meaningless shadows of their proper selves, and it never quite sorts out its preoccupations from those of its model. One superbly minatory shot, however – a placid still-life of a canal lined with elegant homes, suddenly disrupted as the bowsprit of the plague ship noses menacingly into frame – indicates that what Herzog is after from his vampire is a salutary shock to bourgeois complacency. Devoted to the principle of material prosperity, erecting scientific procedure as a defence against the unknown, clinging to its fear of death as the ultimate terror, bourgeois society is delivered a double blow by the irruption of Dracula. Bringing the plague that means death, he also offers the secret of eternal life as a panacea against the old worry that you can't take it with you. But there is a snag: 'Can you imagine centuries enduring the same futilities?' murmurs Dracula, clearly pursued by a melancholy deathwish each time he greedily but wearily sinks his teeth into yet another victim's throat. If the film is something of a magnificent miscalculation, it's a haunting experience just the same.

d/p/s Werner Herzog *c* Joerg Schmidt-Reitwein *lp* Klaus Kinski, Isabelle Adjani, Bruno Ganz, Roland Topor, Walter Ladengast

Klaus Kinski as Dracula in Werner Herzog's homage to Murnau, Nosferatu: Phantom der Nacht.

El Sadico de Notre Dame *aka* **Exorcisme et Messes Noires** *aka* **Exorcisme** *aka* **La Sadique de Notre Dame** *aka* **The Ripper of Notre Dame** *aka* **L'Eventreur de Notre Dame** *aka* **The Black Masses of Exorcism**
(EUROCINE/CETELCI/TRITON; FR, SP, BEL) scope 92min
Five years after it was made, Franco's sadistic hard-core movie, *Exorcisme et Messes Noires* (1974) – a Franco-Belgian co-production which he directed under the pseudonym J. P. Johnson and which had already undergone one transformation with scenes featuring France Nicholas and Sam Marée cut and hard porn footage featuring Chireix and Atta added, released as *Sexorcisme* – was transformed into an outrageous sadean fantasy by the inclusion of extra footage featuring Pascal and Amiral. The plot concerns a deformed religious fanatic and sexual sadist who captures, tortures and kills young women, afterwards confessing his sins to a priest. Franco plays the lead himself, echoing José Mojica Marins' practice in his sick fantasy movies featuring Zé de Caixao (**O Estranho Mundo de Zé do Caixao**, 1968) and putting some of the most macabre and vicious scenes of eroticism available in mainstream cinema on the screen, with Lafférière, in particular, being given a hard time. The direction is mediocre but the picture's 'adult' comic-strip images are disturbingly impressive because of the intensity of the misogynist delirium they represent. Compared to Franco's many captive-women movies, many of which focus on sadism (*Frauengefaegnis*, 1975; *Die Teuflischen Schwestern* and *Frauen im Liebeslager*, both 1977; *Gefangene Frauen* and *Sadomania*, both 1980), *El Sadico* exudes a genuinely chilling sense of dementia instead of a routinely exploitative approach.

The 'hardest' version of the film was released in 1981. Belgian sources credit the cinematography to Raimond Heil while Italian sources credit Etienne Rosenfeld and Franco himself.

d James P. Johnson (Jesús Franco) *p* Marius Lesoeur, Daniel Lesoeur *s* David Kuhne (Jesús Franco), C. Gardner, Henri Bral, A. L. Miriaux *c* Jesús Franco, Etienne Rosenfeld *lp* Nadine Pascal, Jesús Franco, Rosa Amiral, Lina Romay, Olivier Mathot, Lynn Monteil, Monica Swinn, Catherine Lafférière, France Nicholas, Christine Chireix, David Atta

Screams of a Winter Night
(A FULL MOON PRODUCTION) 92min
This is one of the many horror films of the late seventies and eighties that were released as videos after the briefest of theatrical releases.

A compendium film made on 16mm (and then blown up) in Natichitoches, Louisiana, by local talent. A group of teenage campers tell each other tales while holed up in a cabin in the woods. The stories include a Big Foot-type creature which hangs its victims from trees, a group of guys who spend a night in a haunted house, a child-woman who kills anyone with interest in sex (an almost inevitable ingredient of contemporary American horror films, it sometimes seems), and more unusually, an Indian wind demon.

d/co-p James L. Wilson *co-p/s* Richard H. Wadsack *c* Robert E. Rogers *lp* Matt Borel, Gil Glascow, Patrick Byers, Marry Agen Cox, Robin Bradley, Ray Gaspard, Beverly Allen, Brandy Barrett, Charles Rucker, Jan Norton

Snap-Shot *aka* **Day After Halloween**
(FG FILMS/AUSTRALIA INTERNATIONAL FILM CORP; AUST) 92min
This horror-thriller set in the world of Melbourne fashion photography features Thornton as the model threatened by an unseen psychopath. The tale is reminiscent of *The Eyes of Laura Mars* (1978) but the pace is far too leisurely and time is wasted chronicling the rise to stardom of the one-time hairdresser's assistant and how this affects her relations with other people. As with nearly all Ginnane productions (**Thirst**, 1979; **Dead Kids** and *Turkey Shoot*, both 1981) the script is perfunctory. Wincer also directed **Harlequin** (1980) for Ginnane before embarking on a picture about Australia's favourite stuffed animal, the assassinated racehorse *Phar Lap* (1983).

d Simon Wincer *p* Anthony I. Ginnane *s* Chris de Roche, Everett de Roche *c* Vincent Monton *lp* Chantal Contouri, Robert Brunning, Sigrid Thornton, Hugh Keays-Byrne, Vincent Gil, Denise Drysdale, Jacqui Gordon, Peter Stratford, Lulu Pinkus

1979

Terror Train

(TRIPLE T PRODUCTIONS (ASTRAL) LTD; CAN) 97min

As the directorial début of distinguished editor Spottiswoode – who went on to direct the impressive *Under Fire* (1983) – and with cinematography by Alcott, cameraman of **The Shining** (1980), *Terror Train* might have been expected to be more than a routine addition to the teenage-massacre cycle started by **Halloween** (1978). The film certainly follows the *Halloween* model closely, even to the extent of casting Curtis as the beleaguered heroine. Once again, there is a pre-credits exposition – a student (MacKinnon) is unhinged by a macabre trick played on him by his confrères – and the main action is devoted to his subsequent lethal revenge on those responsible for his undoing. The setting is a privately chartered excursion train, aboard which a fraternity party is taking place. This provides some novelty, and the fact that the revellers are in carnival costume, allied to the introduction of a magician (Copperfield) who has been brought along to entertain them – the killer is finally revealed to have been disguised as the magician's female assistant – lends the proceedings an overtone of self-referential pastiche. But this and the concise technique are not enough to offset the thin and contrived plotting, which reaches a statutory climax as MacKinnon, now completely berserk, is dispatched with an axe by the conductor (Johnson) just before he can kill Curtis.

d Roger Spottiswoode *p* Harold Greenberg *s* T. Y. Drake *c* John Alcott *se* Josef Elsner *lp* Jamie Lee Curtis, Ben Johnson, Hart Bochner, Derek MacKinnon, David Copperfield, Sandee Currie, Timothy Webber, Anthony Sherwood, Howard Busgang, Steve Michaels

Thirst

(FG FILMS/NEW SOUTH WALES FILM CORP; AUST) scope 98min

A contemporary parable of industrially regulated vampirism, this film is set in a modern psychiatric hospital, located on an isolated Australian farm, where the 'patients' are kept in super-hygienic wards in order to be 'milked' of blood for their vampire hosts. The narrative follows the nightmarish progress of a young woman (Contouri) whom the sect believe to be a descendant of their founder, Countess Bathory. The film stresses the pedestrian qualities of the administrative detail – the blood is stored in milk bottles – without neglecting the conventional details of vampire lore – the fangs, the bite on the neck, and so on – but lacks the intelligence and punch of Alain Jessua's underestimated parable of colonialism, *Traitement de Choc* (1973) which uses a similar plot to far more subtle and ambiguous effect. Pickney's script is based on one of his *Instant Terror* plots, approached as a humourless thriller while Hardy fails to inject the necessary stylish eeriness required to make utterly unreal events cinematically effective. It remained the TV director's only feature. This was Ginnane's seventh feature in nine years, making him Australia's leading producer of straightforwardly commercial movies.

d Rod Hardy *p* Antony I. Ginnane *s* John Pinkney *c* Vincent Monton *se* Conrad Rothmann *lp* Chantal Contouri, David Hemmings, Henry Silva, Max Phipps, Shirley Cameron, Rod Mullinar, Robert Thompson, Walter Pym, Lulu Pinkus

When a Stranger Calls

(MELVIN SIMON PRODUCTIONS) 97min

While babysitting, Kane is terrorized by an anonymous phone-caller who threatens to kill her charges. Eventually it is discovered that the caller is on the upstairs phone and has indeed butchered the children. A deranged merchant seaman (Beckley), he is imprisoned in a mental institution but seven years later escapes and once more starts to terrorize Kane, who now has two children of her own. Durning, the policeman on the original case and now a private detective, vows to kill the madman. Part woman-in-peril film, part desperate manhunt,

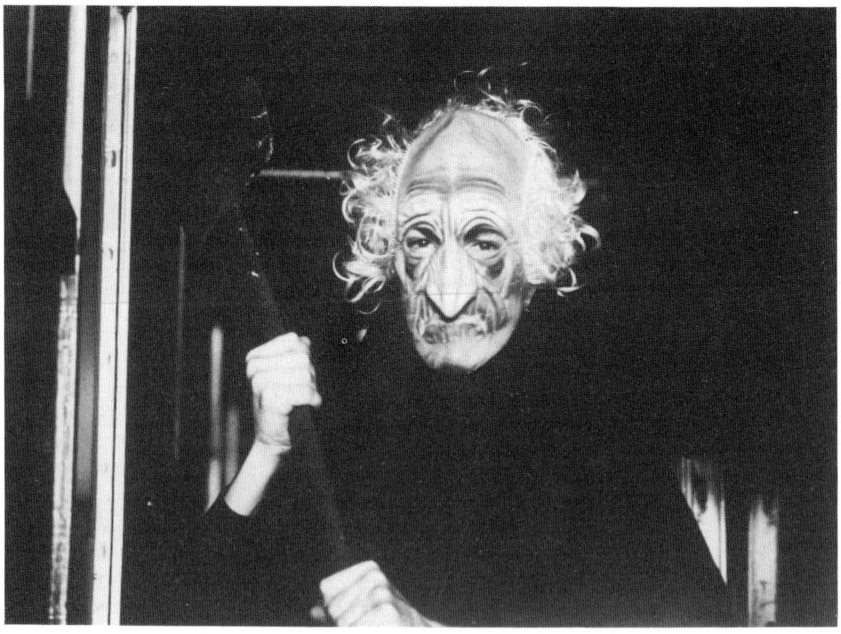

The crazed killer of Terror Train.

When a Stranger Calls is equally successful as both and manages to avoid the worst gory excesses of the former (in Britain it even achieved an AA as opposed to X certificate). It is also helped by an excellently atmospheric score by Dana Kaproff. The opening and closing sequences featuring Kane (who appears for only about 20 of the films 97 minutes) are genuinely frightening and have something of the threatening feel of *Cape Fear* (1962), whilst the middle sections in which Beckley is pursued by the obsessive Durning generate a certain amount of pity for Beckley which is not at all the usual stereotyped, psychopathic cipher but a slight, down-at-heel middle-aged bum. As a tight, economical thriller the film works very well and it would be a pity if its apparent proximity to the stalk-'n'-slash subgenre were to consign it to comparative oblivion.

d/co-s Fred Walton *co-p/co-s* Steve Feke *co-p* Doug Chapin *c* Don Peterman *se* B and D Special Effects *lp* Charles Durning, Carol Kane, Colleen Dewhurst, Tony Beckley, Rachel Roberts, Ron O'Neal, Steven Anderson, Rutanya Alda, Carmen Argenziano, Kirsten Larkin

Wolfman

(EO PRODUCTIONS) 101min

Wolfman is the first horror film produced by Owensby, sometimes referred to as the Cecil B. DeMille of North Carolina, where he owns a prolific studio in his home town of Shelby and turns out redneck action movies which seem to thoroughly clean up on the drive-in circuit without ever moving outside the Confederacy. In 1982 he entered the 3-D stakes with *Rottweiler*, planned as the first of ten 3-D movies to be made back-to-back. Though frequently directing and starring in his productions, Owensby here hands over direction to 22-year-old staffer Keeter and contents himself with playing the central character, Colin Glasgow, who, in 1910 in Georgia, becomes heir to 'the Devil's curse' when his father dies. Initially sceptical, before long Owensby has discovered that his father was a lycanthrope and that he too is beginning to turn into a werewolf. A series of grisly murders occurs, while he searches increasingly desperately for the source of the curse.

The result is a straightforward, efficiently directed werewolf tale, and although the special effects are not in **The Howling** (1980) league and Owensby is considerably more convincing as a werewolf than as Colin, the film does make good use of its backwoods' locations. Interestingly, it pre-dates Hollywood's early eighties rediscovery of the werewolf myths.

d/s Worth Keeter III *p* Earl Owensby *c* Darrell Cathcart *lp* Earl Owensby, Kristina Reynolds, Ed L. Grady, Maggie Lauterer, Richard Dedmon

Yashaga Ike *aka* **Demon Pond**
(SHOCHIKU; JAP) 124min
This bizarre fantasy which veers from arrestingly beautiful compositions to self-conscious artiness has all the hallmarks of Shinoda's cinema – his slow, ostentatiously stylized mode of narration, and adherence to classic Japanese theatrical forms – which became known in the West with *Shinju Tennu Amijima* (1969). Here, he adapts a story by Kuoka Izumi, set in 1913, about an explorer (Yamazaki) who meets up with an old friend (Kato) and his wife (Bando) in a remote village near a lake which is supposed to be haunted by demons. The demons can only be subdued by the ringing of a magic bell. When the superstitious rituals are infringed, supernatural forces which cause a tidal wave that drowns the entire village are unleased.

Presented as a mixture of Kaidan and disaster movies – but told in a manner derived from kabuki spectacles – the film illustrates that imaginative directors sometimes need the discipline of popular genres imposed by studios to counteract a tendency towards 'independent' self-indulgence and a straining towards a cosmic meaning where none exists. It is interesting, however, to see how the ancient convention of male actors playing female roles can still be made to work in the cinema. The celebrated kabuki actor Bando plays both the wife and a demon princess with consummate skill, in spite of the so-called 'ontological realism' of the cinematic image.

d Masahiro Shinoda *p* Kanji Nakagawa, Shigeru Sugisaki, Yukio Tomizawa *s* Haruhiko Minura, Takeshi Tamura *c* Masao Kosugi, Noritaka Sakamoto *lp* Tomasaburo Bando, Go Kato, Tsutomi Yamazaki, Koji Nanbara

Yuhuo Fen Qin *aka* **House of the Lute**
(HUNG WAY FILMS; HONG KONG) scope 97min
Released at the same time as Ann Hui's *The Secret* and Tsui Hark's *Butterfly Murders* (both 1979), this independently shot film – Lau's directorial début – was one of the first features to announce the 'new wave' of Hong Kong film-making. Lui, an elderly disabled landowner, lives in a large country house with his much younger wife. While he lives like a scholar and indulges his interest in the Chinese lute, she is drawn into an affair with a houseboy. They kill the old man and inherit his fortune but his ghost returns to haunt them.

Yuhuo Fen Qin is remarkable for its attempts to link the classical tradition of Chinese fantasy (Beauty's relationship with the scholar has a literary pedigree as long as that of her relationship with the Beast) to Western notions of surrealism. The film is constantly invested with visual and stylistic pleasures, including a relatively rare attempt to emphasize sensuality as opposed to lust in a lovemaking scene during the couple's brief venture into the modern city of Hong Kong. The classical strength of the pictorial composition – the scholar practising his lute on the roof of the old house, for example – throughout the movie creates an eerily subdued atmosphere, a feeling confirmed by the surrealist irruptions – the pair of bloody jaws suddenly appearing in the rice pot dinner, for example.

Lau, a respected writer on the Hong Kong and Chinese cinema, subsequently went into the straightforwardly commercial cinema with the thriller, *Headhunter* (1982) and an action film shot for the American market, *Horatio* (1983).

d/s Lau Shing-hon (Liu Chenghan) *p* Chan Hok-Yan *c* Koo Kwok-Wah *lp* Yum Tat-Wah, Kwan Koi-sham, Lok Bec-Kay, Chan Lap-Pun

Tony Beckley as the deranged maniac in the atmospheric When a Stranger Calls.

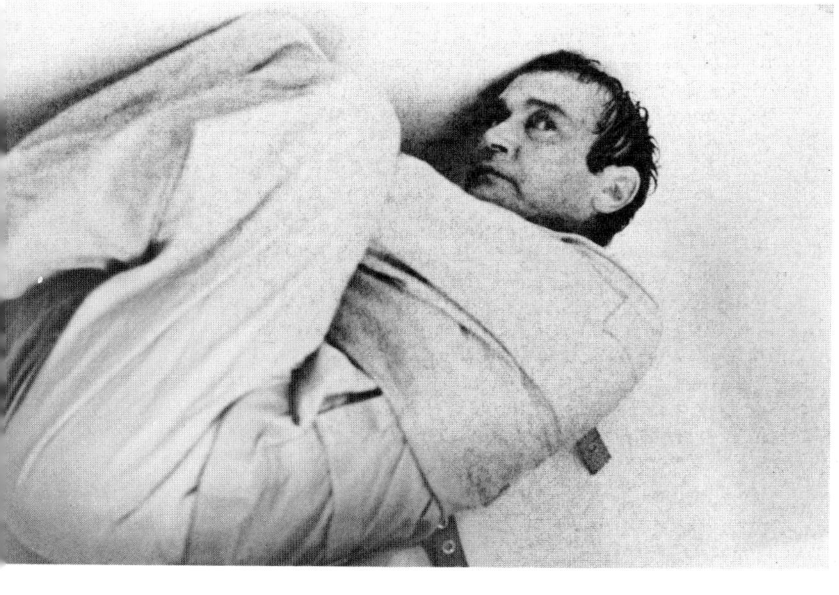

Zombi 2 *aka* **Island of the Living Dead** *aka* **Zombie Flesh Eaters**
(VARIETY FILM; IT) scope 95(98)min
Promoted as a sequel to George Romero's **Dawn of the Dead** (1978), Fulci's festival of gore bears little resemblance to Romero's model because it eliminates all vestiges of humour in favour of a relentless crescendo of visceral horror in which special effects and makeup easily steal the show. After a brief, atmospheric pre-credit sequence in New York's harbour when a decomposing corpse kills a policeman before disappearing into the water, the plot settles down to its mechanical business of sending two couples to a West Indian island called Matoul where Professor Menard (Johnson) conducts experiments on the dead but is overwhelmed by the powers of voodoo which cause a wholesale resurrection of corpses. Initially, the zombies are mainly blacks but then, in a well orchestrated sequence recalling Gilling's **The Plague of the Zombies** (1966), the earth of an entire forest begins to heave and split as decomposing corpses of the Spanish conquistadors rise from their graves and Johnson and the American couples are assailed by both the victims and the historical perpetrators of colonialism. In the end, the heroine (Farrow) and her infected boyfriend (McCullough) escape from the cinemascope image-filling conflagration and return to New York only to find hordes of zombies shuffling across Brooklyn Bridge.

De Rossi's special effects give the movie's physical violence an unprecedented intensity as, for example, a bamboo spike slices into an eye in full closeup, heads explode and bodies are torn to shreds in long, unconscionably gruesome sequences detailing activities of which cannibalism and disembowelling are the least repulsive, as in the death of Karlatos. Whereas Romero's film retained playful elements to soften the impact of the pre-oedipal body-in-pieces fantasy being enacted, this picture, after a pointed reference to **Jaws** (1975) in which a woman (Gay) sees a zombie devour an attacking shark underwater, lets rip the full force of a puritanical disgust at all things physical and channels this drive into a disturbing fantasy of the body politic, symbolized first by the white characters and then, more importantly, by New York, disintegrating as all the forces upon which 'civilization' has fed suddenly erupt and threaten to devour it in return. Like all coherently elaborated fantasies, the film works in many levels at once, with the psychic energies addressed by a regression to the pre-oedipal reinforcing the North/South, US/Third World axis of the conflicts. Although script and direction are rather peremptory, the film is given emotional punch by the sheer realism of its revolting imagery.

The picture spawned a flood of equally stomach-turning efforts, including **Le Notte del Terrore** (1980), Fulci's **Paura nella Citta dei Morti Viventi** (1980) and **... E Tu Vivrai nel Terrore! L'Aldila** (1981) and Lenzi's **Incubo sulla Citta Contaminata** (1980).

d Lucio Fulci *p* Ugo Tucci, Fabrizio de Angelis *s* Elisa Briganti *c* Sergio Salvati *se* Gianetto de Rossi *lp* Tisa Farrow, Ian McCullough, Richard Johnson, Auretta Gay, Olga Karlatos, Al Cliver (Pier Luigi Conti), Stefania d'Amario, Ugo Bologna, Monica Zanchi

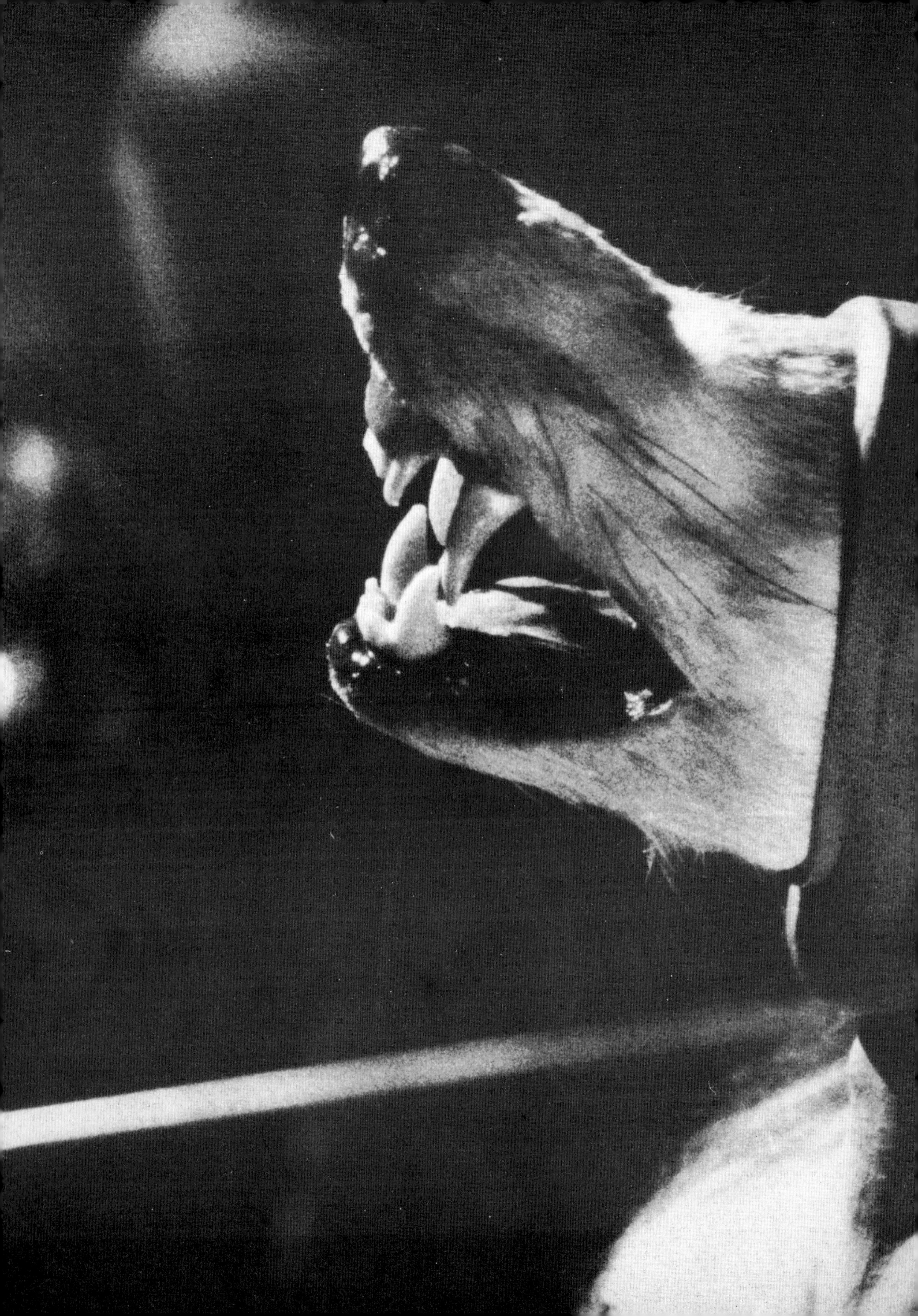

The 1980s

The Eighties

1980

Anthropophagus *aka* **The Grim Reaper** *aka* **Man Eater** *aka* **The Anthropophagous Beast**
(PCM INTERNATIONAL/FILMIRAGE; IT) 90(87)min
After numerous sexploitation movies, often starring Laura Gemser, Massaccesi ventured into cannibal and zombie films with **Emanuelle e gli Ultimi Cannibali** (1977) and **Le Notte Erotiche dei Morti Viventi** (1979). Here, however, he abandons sex for a straightforward visceral gore story. The monster is a shipwrecked man who ate his wife and son in order to survive on an abandoned Aegean island. Farrow, star of Lucio Fulci's **Zombi 2** (1979) and sister of the better known Mia, is the heroine who eventually fights off the degenerate cannibal with a pickaxe before her companion Vallone finishes the job. The film is ineptly directed and has some of the ugliest photography seen in cheap potboilers. The monster is played by Montefiori, who also helped concoct the script. Massaccesi returned to the theme of the deranged, seemingly indestructible monster-killer with **Anthropophagus II** (1981).

d/co-s Joe d'Amato (Aristide Massaccesi) *p* Oscar Santaniello *co-s* Luigi Montefiori *c* Enrico Biribicchi *lp* Tisa Farrow, Saverio Vallone, George Eastman (Luigi Montefiori), Vanessa Steiger, Mark Bodin, Margaret Donelly, Bob Larson, Rubina Rey, Zora Kerova

Previous pages: *The beast in the man, Neil Jordan's impressive* The Company of Wolves *(1984).*

Apocalisse Domani *aka* **Apocalypse Domani** *aka* **Virus** *aka* **Cannibal Apocalipsis** *aka* **Cannibal Apocalypse** *aka* **Apocalipse Cannibal** *aka* **Cannibals in the Streets** *aka* **The Cannibals Are in the Streets** *aka* **Savage Apocalypse** *aka* **The Slaughterers** *aka* **Cannibals in the City** *aka* **Invasion of the Flesh Hunters** *aka* **The Last Hunter**
(NEW FIDA ORGANISATION/JOSE FRADE PC; IT,SP) 95(90)min
The decline in Margheriti's uneven career, vividly illustrated by the two films usually credited to Paul Morrissey (**Il Monstro E in Tavola** and **Dracula Cerca Sangue**, both 1973), continued with this botched imitation of Lucio Fulci's imitation of George Romero's *Dawn of the Dead* (1978). The potentially interesting script starts in Vietnam where an American officer, Norman (Saxon), discovers two GIs in a bamboo-covered trap devouring a Vietnamese peasant. As he helps them out of the pit, one of the soldiers bites him in the arm. Later, back in Atlanta, Georgia, Saxon runs into the cannibalistic duo again and eventually joins them on a gory rampage as they slaughter, slash and chew their way through a

Director Mike Newell rehearsing a scene with Charlton Heston on the set of The Awakening.

Tales of Violence

The most marked feature of the horror film in the eighties was the intensity of the debate about it, which finally spilled over from the film journals into the mass media. The debate itself was often uninformed – in this echoing that of the fifties – linking together films that were purely exploitative and others that broached issues little treated outside the genre. Far more revealing was the venom with which it was conducted and the very title given the films in question, 'video nasties', which testified to the dramatic shift in the pattern of distribution and production – a significant number of the films were made for direct release as videos – of horror films.

Another element of eighties Horror was the number of sequels. The producers of key models, such as **Halloween** (1978), **Friday the 13th** (1980) and Wes Craven's groundbreaking **Nightmare on Elm Street** (1985) rushed to imitate Universal in the thirties by transforming the central concepts underlying the films into franchises. They had at least the legitimate rationale that the horror film had no final closure as part of its narrative structure, but was essentially open-ended. But, like the mainstream brothers and sisters they hoped to join, they quickly turned cautious. Accordingly, although in the eighties some films that spawned franchises (such as the innovative **Hellraiser**, 1987) were significant, it was generally the low-budget oddball exercises in genre and the oddities made from positions of power that were important in the second half of the decade. Ironically, the major horror films were almost mainstream, rather than genre, offerings: **The Keep** and **The Company of Wolves** (1984); **Blue Velvet** and **Manhunter** (1986); **Dead Ringers** and **Beetlejuice** (1988); and **Heathers** (1989).

The horrors of Blood Beach, *another* Jaws (1975) *imitation.*

gang of bikers, a nurse, a garage mechanic, and so on. The climax is set in the sewers, where the police finally exterminate the army of ghouls with flamethrowers.

The gore, courtesy of de Rossi, the man responsible for the visual impact of Lucio Fulci's **Zombi 2** (1979) is exceedingly graphic, but Margheriti wastes his opportunity to make telling points about the American involvement in Vietnam, the brutalization of its army personnel and the domestic results of a murderous foreign policy. Instead he directs the story as just another action picture, with the occasional flash of corrosive humour. Visually banal, the film reveals none of the stylish flair Margheriti had demonstrated so forcefully in the sixties, with his science fiction movies, *Il Pianeta degli Uomini Spenti* (1961) or *I Criminali della Galassia* (1966), for example. More striking than the film itself is the number of times it has been retitled.

d Anthony Dawson (Antonio Margheriti) *p/co-s* Marizio Amati, Sandro Amati *co-s* José Luis Martinez Molla, Dardano Sacchetti *c* Fernando Arribas *se* Gianetto de Rossi, Don Shelley *lp* John Saxon, Elisabeth Turner, Cindy Hamilton, May Heatherley, Cinzia Carolis, Tony King, Giovanni Lombardo Radice, Wallace Wilkinson, Ramiro Oliveiros, Venantino Venantini

Aquella Casa en las Afueras *aka* That House in the Outskirts *aka* That House on the Outskirts

(KALENDER FILMS INTERNATIONAL; SP) scope 101(98)min

Martin, whose best movie remains **Panico en el Transiberiano** (1972), made two atmospheric terror movies back-to-back for Kalender films, this and **Sobrenatural** (1980). Here, a pregnant woman, Nieves (Aguilar) is taken to a quiet, old house which turns out to be the site where, a few years earlier, she experienced a traumatic backstreet abortion, something she never told her husband (Escriva). The movie plays on the suspicion that her husband brought her there on purpose and heightens the terror by introducing one of the former abortion clinic nurses, Isabel (Valli), now a homicidal maniac living upstairs in a flat full of abortion memorabilia in glass jars. The ending has Valli going berserk but Aguilar emerges unscathed. If viewers accept the premiss that abortion is a vile crime perpetrated by perverted maniacs and of which 'the victims' should feel deeply ashamed, the script is convincing and tightly structured. Martin's direction is better than usual, handling the atmosphere of incipient lunacy and paranoid suspicion with considerable skill while avoiding most of the gore-orgies which characterize the genre in this period.

d/co-s Eugenio Martin *p/co-s* Antonio Cuevas *co-s* Manuel Summers, José G. Castillo, Eduardo Alvarez, Manuel Matji *c* Manuel Rojas *lp* Javier Escriva, Silvia Aguilar, Alida Valli, Maria Goyanes, Carmen Maura

The Awakening

(SOLOFILM/ORION PICTURES/EMI/BRITISH LION; GB) 105min

Heston's only foray into the horror genre, *The Awakening*, a relatively high-budget venture with location shooting in Egypt and camerawork by the distinguished veteran Cardiff, was adapted from Bram Stoker's novel *Jewel of the Seven Stars*, which also provided the basis for Seth Holt's **Blood from the Mummy's Tomb** (1971). As Egyptologist Corbeck (Heston) hammers his way into Queen Kara's tomb, intercut scenes show his wife (Townsend) giving birth to their little Margaret who emerges into the world as the tomb is finally opened. Years later, Townsend has been dispatched to the United States, Heston has married his assistant (York) and Margaret (Zimbalist) becomes her father's constant companion. He grows obsessed with the ritual that could bring the mummy back to life while the incestuous relation with his daughter is signified in terms of her becoming 'possessed' by the very figure which monopolizes his life. After some rather arbitrary deaths, including York's fall through layers of glass and Zimbalist's murder of her psychiatrist (McDiarmid), the film culminates with Heston in the British Museum, conducting the resurrection ritual which finally merges Kara and Margaret as he gets buried beneath collapsing masonry, in a scene which makes liberal use of red filters.

The film can perhaps best be seen as an awkward illustration of Freud's thesis that nightmares can function as a mask for even more terrifying fantasies: here the schizophrenia of the victim of paternal incest is reassuringly worked out in terms of classic possession motifs. Unfortunately, neither direction nor script seems prepared to explore this dream logic beyond its most superficial aspects while the claustrophobic dimension of Stoker's novel is dissipated by the picture's banal travelogue sequences. Claude Bolling's interesting score deserved a better film.

d Mike Newell *p* Robert Solo *s* Allan Scott, Chris Bryant, Clive Exton *c* Jack Cardiff *se* John Stears *lp* Charlton Heston, Susannah York, Jill Townsend, Stephanie Zimbalist, Patrick Drury, Bruce Myers, Ian McDiarmid, Roger Kemp, Nadim Sawalha

Blood Beach

(EMPRESS PRODUCTIONS) 89min

The premise of *Blood Beach* is somewhat akin to that of science fiction B-pictures of a generation earlier, such as *It Came from Beneath the Sea* (1955) or *The Giant Claw* (1957), although it is inevitably more expansive in style and also seeks to be more offbeat in tone. However, its story of an unexplained and largely unseen monster – when finally revealed toward the end, it rather resembles a giant artichoke – lurking beneath a southern Californian beach and preying on human victims is clearly derived from **Jaws** (1975). Indeed, that film is directly invoked at one point when the police chief (Saxon) sardonically observes, 'Just when you thought it was safe to go back in the water, you can't get across the goddam beach.'

The film makes atmospheric use of its setting, contrasting the sunny beach with the forbidding broken-down pier below which the monster is eventually found. There are, too, some adroit sequences, like that in which a would-be rapist (Bass) is seized and castrated by the monster as he advances upon his intended victim. But on the whole the effect is rather disjointed, with irrelevant emphasis on subsidiary characters like an uncouth police sergeant Burt (Young); there is also a curious plot construction which means that the ostensible hero (Huffman), a harbour patrolman who becomes involved after the mother (Medin) of his girlfriend (Hill) disappears, is barely involved in the climactic location and destruction of the monster. The film also leaves it unclear whether the monster has, in fact, finally been destroyed, since in a 'joke' ending the beach shows renewed signs of instability and a child suddenly disappears.

d/s Jeffrey Bloom *p* Steven Nalevansky *c* Steve Poster *se* Delwyn Rheume, Danny Cangemi, Bon Stokes Jnr, Bill Balles *lp* David Huffman, Marianna Hill, John Saxon, Burt Young, Stefan Gierasch, Otis Young, Darell Fetty, Harriet Medin, Pamela McMyler, Bobby Bass

Blood Tide

(CONNAUGHT INTERNATIONAL/ATHON; GB, GR) 82min

Filmed on location in Greece, and emphasizing scenic backgrounds at the expense of the plot, *Blood Tide* is a pedestrian attempt to dramatize the idea of an ancient monster resuscitated by latterday events: a somewhat similar premise to the later and better **The Winged Serpent** (1982). An American artist (Shelton) staying in Greece, becomes preoccupied by an ancient ritual in which virgin girls were sacrificed to a malign sea god. Her brother (Kove) and sister-in-law (Weller) are visiting when explosions caused by an American treasure hunter (Jones) free the monster from its undersea lair. Sundry killings ensue, but little tension or atmosphere is generated. Jones overplays alarmingly, while Ferrer and Kedrova have little to do as furrowed-browed locals, the latter a nun. The monster itself appears only briefly, which is perhaps just as well since it is all too obviously a rubber dummy.

d/co-s Richard Jefferies *co-p/co-s* Nico Mastorakis *co-p/co-s* Donald Langdon *c* Ari Stavrou *lp* James Earl Jones, Deborah Shelton, Jose Ferrer, Lila Kedrova, Mary Louise Weller, Martin Kove, Lydia Cornell

Bloody Birthday

(JUDICA PRODUCTIONS) 85min

An addition to the maniac-at-large cycle spawned by **Halloween** (1978), this feeble low-budget film attempts to ring the changes on the formula by having not one but three marauders and by making them young children. The unrelated trio (Hoy, Jacoby, Freeman) have been born during a total eclipse, which obscurely renders them homicidal, and as their mutual tenth birthday approaches they set about decimating the local community. Victims include Hoy's father, the sheriff (Kramer) and the schoolteacher (Strasberg), but the trio's attempts to kill the teenage sister (Lethin) of one of their classmates (Martel) prove unsuccessful. The far-fetched and under-nourished plot ends with Lethin and Martel agreeing to babysit to Hoy while her mother (Cordell) is away. Needless to say, the three malevolent children attempt to kill them, but in the nick of time they overpower Jacoby and Freeman and convince the police of what is happening. However, Hoy gets away and is seen at the close being escorted out of town by her mother.

d/co-s Ed Hunt *p* Gerald T. Olson *co-s* Barry Pearson *c* Stephen Posey *se* Roger George *lp* Susan Strasberg, José Ferrer, Lori Lethin, Melinda Cordell, Bert Kramer, Julie Brown, Joe Penny, K. C. Martel, Elizabeth Hoy, Billy Jacoby, Andy Freeman

The Boogeyman *aka* The Bogey Man

(INTERBEST AMERICAN ENTERPRISES) 83min

Though its story may be derivative and the special effects somewhat cheap, *The Boogeyman* rises way above the usual level of **Halloween** (1978) clones thanks to ex-Fassbinder collaborator Lommel's direction. From its darkly lurid opening in which a little boy dispatches his mother's lover (as powerful an evocation of the primal scene and its consequences as one could wish, later used in **Nightmare**, 1981), Lommel conjures a claustrophobic, fetid atmosphere well suited to this tale of unresolved sexual and familial conflicts. Love is the woman, haunted by the spirit of her mother's lover, killed years ago by her now mute brother. In an attempt to purge her mind of this scene of childhood trauma, she returns to the house where the murder took place and sees the lover in a mirror, which she smashes. However, one of the fragments now contains a malevolent force and causes a series of violent deaths. At times the supernatural element seems almost superfluous, but the scenes with the glowing mirror and those depicting the havoc wreaked by the telekinetic shard are imaginatively handled.

d/p/co-s Ulli Lommel *co-s* Suzanna Love, David Herschel *c* David Sperling, Jochen Breitenstein *se* Craig Harris *lp* Suzanna Love, Ron James, John Carradine, Nicholas Love, Raymond Boyden, Felicite Morgan, Bill Rayburn, Llewelyn Thomas, Jay Wright

The Burning (MIRAMAX) 91min

This slavish imitation of the already imitative **Friday the 13th** (1980) is the *reductio ad absurdum* of the body-count movie. After five years of unsuccessful skin grafts, a horribly disfigured camp counsellor – burned by a group of teenagers in a prank which misfired – returns to terrorize and murder as many teenage campers as possible. More than usually packed with the obligatry fare of teenage lust and all-American macho behaviour, the film is a particularly clear example of the *puritanism* of this particular subgenre, since virtually all the killings follow various scenes of sex play, and can thus all too easily be read as 'dire warnings' or 'punishments justly deserved'. Savini's special effects are as efficient as usual, but the direction – by Briton Maylam – and Rick Wakeman's score are both annoyingly insistent and nudging.

d/co-s Tony Maylam *p/co-s* Harvey Weinsten *co-s* Peter Lawrence, Bob Weinsten, Brad Grey *c* Harvey Harrison *se* Tom Savini *lp* Brian Matthews, Leah Ayres, Brian Backer, Larry Joshua, Jason Alexander, Ned Eisenberg, Garrick Glenn, Carolyn Houlihan, Fisher Stevens, Lou David

Il Cacciatore di Uomini *aka* The Man Hunter

(J/E FILMS/LISA FILMS; IT,SP,WG) 86min

Inevitably, the prolific Franco contributed to the cannibal subgenre with movies like *Mondo Cannibale* (1979) and this picture, which he took over from his colleague Armando de Ossorio. Conti (star of *Mondo Cannibale*) again takes the lead in a plot that involves kidnapped actresses and Vietnam veterans in a catalogue of repulsive events: a 'savage' priestess tears out young mens' hearts and eats them; shrieking women are sacrificed to a monster and a cannibalistic creature stalks

Bloody Birthday, *another of the cycle of teenage movies of the period.*

Lou David set alight in The Burning.

through the jungle and is eventually revealed to be a zombie. All this is further 'spiced' with images of chained women, 'native' dances in front of 'primitive' idols, scenes in which bodies are mangled and impaled and so on. As he had demonstrated many times before with films like **Fu Manchu y el Beso de la Muerte** (1968), Franco's sadistic delirium requires claustrophobic settings and does not adapt itself so well to exterior scenes. When he adopts the adventure-movie format, his pictures degenerate into repulsively racist misogynist tracts which in no way address the unpalatable aspects of cinephilia.

d/s Clifford Brown (Jesús Franco) *p* Franco Prosperi *c* Juan Soler *lp* Al Cliver (Pier Luigi Conti), Ursula Fellner, Gisela Han, Werner Pochat, Burt Altman, Robert Foster

El Carnaval de las Bestias *aka* **The Beasts' Carnival**
(DALMATA FILMS/HORI KIKAKU COMPANY; SP, JAP) 90min
Molina's first Japanese-Spanish co-production, this is an offbeat entry in the wave of cannibal movies. He plays a bandit who betrays his Japanese associates and absconds with a load of diamonds. His ex-lover, Mieko (Nagashima) pursues him from Japan to Thailand and eventually to Spain where she shoots him. On the point of dying, he seeks refuge in a house which turns out to be inhabited by cannibals. From then on, the film becomes a routine gore movie. Molina's next collaboration with a Japanese company yielded the tenth Waldemar Daninsky picture, **La Bestia y la Espada Magica** (1983).

d/p/s Jacinto Molina *c* Alejandro Ulloa *lp* Paul Naschy (Jacinto Molina), Eiko Nagashima, Lautaro Murua, Silvia Aguilar, Azucena Hernandez, Julia Saly, Kogi Maritugu, Mieko Gustanave

Death Ship
(ASTRAL BELLEVUE-PATHE-BLOODSTAR; CAN) 91min
Perhaps taking its cue from Steven Spielberg's *Duel* (1971), this picture also concentrates on a malevolent piece of transport machinery: it postulates a ship dedicated to the annihilation of its passengers. Ignoring the obvious means a ship has to terminate its life, the script has it rescue the nine survivors of a luxury liner after a collision with a mysterious vessel and then proceed to inflict grim ends on each one of the characters. Apart from the irritating appeal to idiot-logic (why didn't the ship allow the people to drown in the first place?), credibility and suspense are further undermined by the stooge-like stupidity of the victims who go out of their way to place themselves in jeopardy. Sandy Howard (executive producer of this picture) had been responsible for some entertaining low-budget efforts – including Roger Spottiswoode's **Terror Train** (1979) – but here the viewer has great difficulty in refraining from urging the ship to dispose of its cargo as soon as possible. It is pitiful to see Kennedy and Crenna, accomplished adventure film actors, stranded in such a picture.

d Alvin Rakoff *p* Derek Gibson, Harold Greenberg *s* John Robins *c* René Verzier *se* Mike Albrechtsen *lp* George Kennedy, Richard Crenna, Nick Mancuso, Sally Ann Howes, Kate Reid, Victoria Burgoyne, Jennifer McKinney, Danny Higham, Saul Rubinek

Diyu Wu Men *aka* **We Are Going to Eat You** *aka* **Hell Has no Gates** *aka* **No Door to Hell**
(SEASONAL FILMS; HONG KONG) scope
Presented initially as a black comedy, which is a debatable claim, this picture does point the way to Tsui's later commercial work (*Guima Zhiduo Xing*, 1981 and *Shushan*, 1983). But at the time of making this film, he had only completed the surreal *Diebian* (1979), and the sense of uncertainty resulting from that excellent movie's lack of success underlies much of this picture. Set in Republican China, the plot has an agent for the Central Surveillance Agency sent to capture a famous bandit, unaware that the village he goes to is inhabited by cannibals. The film falls squarely into the current trend of Hong Kong horror movies with some comic relief, except that here, even these moments are infused with poetic horror: hordes of skin-masked butchers à la **The Texas Chainsaw Massacre** (1974) chase the hapless agent through the village, in a manner evoking the Keystone Cops. Similarly, the agent's traumatic meeting with a fat and lascivious female impersonator pushes comedy into a kind of horrifying grotesquerie as repressions erupt and become writ large. In many ways, its delineation of sexuality as horror is superior to the better known *Diebian*, and the chillingly angry excess of the violence foreshadows his superb third feature, *Diyi Leixing Weixian* in its masterful presentation of a city imbued with both fear and smouldering hatred.

d/s Tsui Hark (Xu Ke) *p* Ng See Yuen (Wu Siyeun) *c* Liu Hongquan *lp* Xu Shaoqiang, Gao Xiong, Han Juocai, Zhang Nulian

Don't Answer the Phone *aka* **The Hollywood Strangler**
(SCORPION, FOR MANSON INTERNATIONAL) 95(93)min
Inspired by the Los Angeles Hillside Strangler case but with a late title-change to cash in on the success of the *Don't ...* series, *Don't Answer the Phone* is yet another woman-in-jeopardy movie. Here the killer is a disturbed photographer (Worth) who, having raped and killed five women, phones into psychologist Dr Lindsay Gale's (Gerrish) radio advice programmes complaining of headaches and feelings of aggression. Eventually he marks her down as his next victim. As in so many films of this type the covert suggestion that the female victims have 'asked for it' (on account of their sexual availability) is particularly objectionable whilst the psycho-killer's profile as a tormented Catholic with a father fixation, brain damage and a narcissistic obsession with body building, leather and chains who strangles his victims with coins wrapped in a stocking during bizarre pseudo-religious ceremonies can be guaranteed to offend most sensibilities. Worth's performance, however, is so outrageously over-the-top, and so bizarrely eccentric as to be horribly fascinating and the final line 'Adios, creep', delivered over a shot of Worth's corpse floating in Gerrish's swimming pool, is curiously resonant.

d/co-p/co-s Robert Hammer *co-p/co-s* Michael D. Castle *c* James Carter *se* Dick Albain *lp* James Westmoreland, Flo Gerrish, Ben Frank, Nicholas Worth, Pamela Bryant, Paula Warner, Gail Jensen, Denise Galik, Dale Kalberg, Susanne Severeid

Don't Go in the House (TURBINE FILMS) 83(81)min

One of the nastiest films in the women-in-jeopardy cycle, this addition to the *Don't ...* series has Grimaldi as the professional incinerator who, as a child, was punished by his mother holding his arms over a naked flame. Now, as an adult, he captures girls, incinerates them in a fireproof room which he has constructed, dresses the corpses in his mother's clothes and vents on them the hatred he feels for his long-dead mother. As if the grammatically inelegant title, the blatant thefts from Hitchcock (and especially **Psycho**, 1960) and the voyeuristic female nudity were not enough, *Don't Go in the House* makes matters even worse by its cynical pretence at an anti-child-abuse message. Until the title was snapped up by someone else, the film was going to be called *The Burning*.

d/co-s Joseph Ellison *p/co-s* Ellen Hammill *co-s* Joseph R. Masefield *c* Oliver Wood *se* Matt Vogel *lp* Dan Grimaldi, Charlie Bonet, Bill Ricci, Robert Osth, Dennis M. Hunter, John Hedburg, Ruth Dardick, Johanna Brushay, Darcy Shean, Mary Ann Chin

Dressed to Kill

(CINEMA 77/FILMWAYS/WARWICK ASSOCIATES) pv 104min

De Palma's copycat appropriation of Hitchcock tricks and mannerisms in films like *Obsession* (1976), **Carrie** (1976) and **The Fury** (1978) finally led to the logical conclusion of this shameless ripoff from **Psycho** (1960), which has not one but two shower-bath scenes, laconically kills Dickinson's heroine off at an early stage (not in the shower, just to tease, but an elevator), and has her young son (instead of sister) come looking for the killer. In the Norman Bates role as a trans-sexual psychiatrist who takes to blonde drag and a knife to exact revenge of women who rouse the hated masculine side of his nature, Caine is – to say the least – uncomfortably cast. As a series of suspense mechanisms the film works in a crude sort of way, but basically de Palma has nowhere to go.

d/s Brian de Palma *p* George Litto *c* Ralf Bode *lp* Michael Caine, Angie Dickinson, Nancy Allen, Keith Gordon, Dennis Franz

Fade to Black

(COMPASS INTERNATIONAL/LEISURE INVESTMENT CO/ MOVIE VENTURES LTD) 102min

Directed by Zimmerman (whose earlier *Unholy Rollers*, 1972, is a superior exploitation film) and co-produced by Irwin Yablans' Compass International (which was responsible for **Halloween**, 1978), *Fade to Black* is an intelligent, ingenious, imaginative and pleasingly self-reflexive horror movie. Eric Binford (Christopher of *Breaking Away*, 1979, fame) is an obsessive film fanatic who retreats from a world which treats him badly into a life of movie make-believe. After killing his aunt (Ashe), who is later revealed to be his mother, and after being stood up by Marilyn Monroe lookalike (Kerridge), Christopher embarks on a series of murders dressed up in various cinematic disguises and becomes known to the police as 'the Celluloid Killer'. Quite apart from the numerous movie references, which include Christopher's re-creation of Tommy Udo's murder-by-wheelchair in *Kiss of Death* (1947), his claims to live at 99 River Street, his dressing up as Dracula for a screening of **Night of the Living Dead** (1968) – at which, ironically, he looks no odder than the rest of the audience – and his end atop Grauman's Chinese Theatre à la *White Heat* (1949), the film is also distinguished by a carefully detailed, beautifully nuanced performance by Christopher, who in places achieves an almost Peter Lorre-like pathos. Helped enormously by Zimmerman's sense of irony and Christopher's sadly credible persona, the film succeeds in portraying the world of movie buffery as a seemingly seductive but in fact deadening, de-sensitizing cul-de-sac, in particular in its shots of the weird *Night of the Living Dead* audience blithely munching popcorn whilst watching scenes of appalling on-screen horror.

d/s Vernon Zimmerman *p* George G. Braunstein, Ron Hamady *c* Alex Phillips Jnr *se* James Wayne *lp* Dennis Christopher, Tim Thomerson, Gwynne Gilford, Normann Burton, Linda Kerridge, Morgan Paull, James Luisi, Eve Brent Ashe, John Steadman, Marcie Barkin

Friday the 13th

(GEORGETOWN PRODUCTIONS) 95min

This was one of the first of the teenage-jeopardy films which followed in the wake of the huge box-office success of **Halloween** (1978): among the many other subsequent examples are **My Bloody Valentine** (1981) and **Happy Birthday to Me** (1980).

Although *Friday the 13th* proved a huge commercial success (a fact which doubtless contributed to the continuation of the cycle), it is not only self-evidently made on the cheap but is almost completely lacking in style or invention. About the only interesting aspect of the film, really, is the slavishness with which it attempts to duplicate elements of *Halloween*: title, construction, even visual effects (notably in the climax, where, as in *Halloween*, the heroine attempts to hide in a closet). The film takes place at a summer camp which is reopening after being closed down many years previously in the wake of a succession of murders of the teenage occupants. The man behind the venture (Brouwer) hires a group of young people as counsellors. One (Morgan) is murdered even before she arrives; and during a long night of blood and (literal) thunder, Brouwer and five of his six helpers are murdered, two of them (Bacon and Taylor) just after they have made love (a juxtaposition that was to recur in sundry other movies of the subgenre). Finally, sole survivor King is confronted by 'friendly' neighbour (Palmer) who, in a remarkably arbitrary stroke of plotting, is revealed to be the killer, a woman whose teenage son was drowned in a swimming accident at the camp 20 years before and who has been taking revenge for the counsellors' supposed neglect. A lengthy struggle between the two women leaves King the survivor, but a downbeat coda suggests she may have been driven mad by the experience. The film's graphically gory makeup effects – by Savini who had

He Knows You're Alone, *an inept addition to the psycho-on-the-loose cycle.*

Angie Dickinson in Dressed to Kill.

previously worked on *Dawn of the Dead* (1978) – were perhaps responsible for its popularity. in any event, it spawned no fewer than three sequels: **Friday the 13th Part 2** (1981), **Friday the 13th Part III** (1982), and **Friday the 13th – The Final Chapter** (1984).

d/p Sean S. Cunningham *s* Victor Miller *c* Barry Abrams *se* Tom Savini, Taso Stavrakis *lp* Betsy Palmer, Adrienne King, Jeannine Taylor, Robbi Morgan, Kevin Bacon, Harry Crosby, Laurie Bartram, Mark Nelson, Peter Brouwer, Walt Gorney

The Godsend

(LONDON CANNON FILMS; GB) 90min
The Godsend has a moderately ingenious idea – the human 'cuckoo in the nest' – but is worked out in a thorough stilted and inconvincing way. A well-off couple (Stoddard and Hayman), parents of four children, take in a mysterious pregnant woman (Pleasance) who vanishes after giving birth to a baby girl, Bonnie. She causes their own children to meet violent ends, but though the husband latches on to what is happening, his wife steadfastly refuses to believe ill of Bonnie. The two young actresses who play Bonnie (Green and Boorman) look suitably menacing, but the atmosphere is too prosaic for the film to assume any imaginative life. The concluding twist, with the husband glimpsing the mysterious woman befriending another young wife, is too slight and predictable to have any effect.

d/p Gabrielle Beaumont *s* Olaf Pooley, Norman Warwick *lp* Malcolm Stoddard, Cyd Hayman, Angela Pleasance, Wilhelmina Green, Joanne Boorman

Happy Birthday to Me

(BIRTHDAY FILM CO/CFC/FAMOUS PLAYERS; CAN) 111min
Directed by veteran journeyman Thompson in a ponderously academic style, full of crane shots and shock cuts, and boasting expensive production values, *Happy Birthday to Me* is a lacklustre addition to the teenage horror cycle initiated by **Halloween** (1978). The action is set in a peculiar boarding school and the plot is complicated: Virginia (Anderson) has been unhinged by her mother's accidental death and is apparently responsible for the murders of a succession of her classmates although it eventually emerges that another girl, Ann (Bregman), has committed the killings disguised as Virginia as an elaborate revenge for the way the latter's mother (who had been Bregman's father's mistress) had brought shame upon her family. The climax, staged during a thunderstorm, has a gothic effectiveness: at a gruesome birthday party attended by the corpses of the assembled victims, the disguised Bregman murders Anderson's father (Dane), and then, in a black twist ending, Anderson struggles with and kills Bregman moments before the police arrive and find her apparently responsible for the mayhem. Unfortunately, the preceding events are artificially extended and the social background is at no point persuasively drawn.

Despite prominent billing Ford is consigned to a thankless minor role as a psychiatrist, while the film's star, Anderson is better known for her role in *The Little House on the Prairie* teleseries. Producers Link and Dunning were subsequently responsible for the more lively **My Bloody Valentine** (1981).

d J. Lee Thompson *p* John Dunning, André Link *s* Timothy Bond, Peter Jobin, John Saxton *c* Miklos Lente *se* King Hernandez, Bill Doane, Warren Keillor, Ron Otteson *lp* Glenn Ford, Melissa Sue Anderson, Lawrence Dane, Sharon Acker, Frances Hyland, Tracy Bregman, Jack Blum, Matt Craven, Lenore Zann, Earl Pennington

Harlequin *aka* The Minister's Magician

(ANTONY I. GINNANE PRODUCTIONS/AFC/ACE THEATRES/ WEST AUSTRALIAN FILM COUNCIL; AUST) scope 96min
Wincer followed his first feature, the derivative **Snap-Shot** (1979), with this updated version of the Rasputin story, located in Australian governmental circles and featuring Hemmings and Duncan as the central couple, Nick Rast and Sandra, and Powell as Gregory, the mad monk. The real villain of the piece is Crawford, Hemmings' ruthless political agent who tangles with the sinister faith-healer and provokes dramatically supernatural forms of retaliation. In the meantime, Powell has apparently cured the Hemmings' leukaemia-afflicted son, seduced Duncan as well as the maid (Best) and gained hypnotic power over the senator. The picture, erratically filmed with a predictable script, also features gratuitous examples of sex and cruelty, such as Best's commercially helpful nude bathing scene in which she finds her shampoo to have been replaced with caustic soda.

d Simon Wincer *p* Antony I. Ginnane *s* Everett de Roche *c* Gary Hansen *se* Conrad Rothman *lp* Robert Powell, David Hemmings, Carmen Duncan, Broderick Crawford, Gus Mercurio, Alison Best, Mark Spain, Sean Myers

He Knows You're Alone (MGM) 94min

A hamfisted addition to the psycho-on-the-loose cycle sparked off by **Halloween** (1978), this film attempts to adapt the formula to rather older characters and a more digressive, detective-story plot. A cop (Arlt) whose fiancée was murdered by a jilted lover realizes that the same unapprehended killer must be responsible for a more recent slaying. Meanwhile, another bride-to-be victim (O'Heaney) is being lined up; an attempt is made on her life which results in the murder of a dressmaker (Leon) in whose shop the murderer (Rolfing) has been hiding. Arlt obtains a clue to the next victim's identity, but inexplicably fails to warn her, and other incidental deaths ensue before a showdown, set in a morgue, in which Arlt is stabbed by Rolfing, but O'Heaney rescued by an ex-boyfriend (Scardino). In a fatuous conclusion, O'Heaney decides to marry Scardino rather than her fiancé (Carroll), and on the wedding day, the latter shows up in menacing mood. The laborious treatment entirely fails to mitigate the clumsy contrivance of the plot.

d Armand Mastroianni *p* George Manasse *s* Scott Parker *c* Gerald Feil *se* Taso N. Stavrakis *lp* Don Scardino, Caitlin O'Heaney, Elizabeth Kemp, Tom Rolfing, Lewis Arlt, Patsy Pease, James Rebhorn, Tom Hanks, Joseph Leon, James Carroll

The Howling

(AVCO EMBASSY PICTURES/INTERNATIONAL FILM INVESTORS/WESCOM PRODUCTIONS; CAN) 91(90)min

An alumnus from the unofficial Roger Corman film school, Dante named many of the cast members of this unusual werewolf tale after familiar horror movie directors: Terry Fisher (Balaski), Fred Francis (McCarthy), Erle Kenton (Carradine), Sam Newfield (Pickens), and so on, and threw in a few guest appearances of old stars for good measure, including Macnee of *The Avengers* teleseries and former Corman regular Miller as a quirky expert on lycanthropy. The story opens as a psycho-thriller with a TV anchorwoman, Karen (Wallace) using herself as bait for a maniac who gets shot by the police in a sex shop. The reporters then depart for a remote spa where they are joined by a few colleagues following up on the psychopath story which has yielded some evidence of lycanthropic activities. The rest of the picture, mainly set in and around the rest home, chronicles the expected encounters. The most effective sequence, largely courtesy of Rob Bottin's makeup artistry, comes in the middle of the picture and leaves no further shocks in reserve for the ending.

Although the blatant tongue-in-cheek approach does yield an occasional humorous line, it also signals that the film-makers really consider themselves above this sort of picture, implying a cynically manipulative or a contemptuous attitude towards the 'undiscriminating' audiences of horror movies. But considering the obvious zest with which Dante and Sayles espouse their mercenary work, the results are often better crafted and far less obnoxious than Sayles' 'personal' movies like *The Return of the Secaucus Seven* (1979) and *Lianna* (1982). Dante cut trailers for Corman before graduating to violent exploitation movies (*Piranha*, 1978; *Hollywood Boulevard*, 1976) and the Spielberg produced and promoted **Gremlins** (1984).

d Joe Dante *p* Michael Finnell, Jack Conrad *s* John Sayles, Terence H. Winkless *c* John Hora *se* Roger George *lp* Dee Wallace, Patrick Macnee, Dennis Dugan, Belinda Balaski, Christopher Stone, John Carradine, Dick Miller, Slim Pickens, Kevin McCarthy, Elisabeth Brooks

Humanoids from the Deep *aka* Monster

(NEW WORLD) 81min

This film starts like a throwback to the halcyon days of the fifties when monsters were always yearning after heroines but lumbered too slowly to catch them. But the difference is that here, the monsters, humanoid animals from the sea, *do* get to commit rape, not to mention a lot of mayhem, as they erupt into the middle of a carnival. As a *bonne bouche* at the end, courtesy of **Alien** (1979), a monster baby erupts through a pregnant woman's belly. Director Peeters claimed that Roger Corman had gingered the film up with some of the more exploitable bits, but, weighed down as it is with solemn musings about ecology and dispossessed Indians, it looks as if it was always a hopeless case.

d Barbara Peeters *p* Martin B. Cohen *s* Frederick James *c* Daniel Lacambre *lp* Doug McClure, Ann Turkel, Vic Morrow, Cindy Weintraub, Anthony Penya

Incubo sulla Città Contaminata *aka* Nightmare City *aka* City of the Walking Dead *aka* La Invasión de los Zombies Atomicos *aka* Invasion by the Atomic Zombies

(DIALCHI FILM/LOTUS FILM INTERNATIONAL; IT,SP) 92(81)min

The best part of this *Dawn of the Dead* (1978) meets the *The China Syndrome* (1979) is its beginning: Dean Miller (Stiglitz) goes to the airport to meet a professor but when the plane lands its doors disgorge a horde of mad ghouls who quickly take over the airport and swarm into the city – which according to the street signs is supposed to be American, although Spanish numberplates on the cars betray the real location. The motivation for the usual gore feast is that a radiation leak infected the professor which in turn infected the pasengers who now need human blood to replace their own rapidly mutating plasma. The military, represented by Ferrer and Rabal, send lots of hardware but to no avail as the zombies multiply faster than they can be killed and take over the world. Just as the hero's girlfriend, Sheyla (Trotter) drops from a helicoper's ladder back into the teeming zombie mass, Stiglitz wakes up from his nightmare. He goes to his appointment at the airport and arrives in time to witness a mysterious plane making an unscheduled landing .... The often-used circular ending here merely shows the film-makers didn't know how to end their story. The ecological overtones are hammered home in ponderously meaningful dialogues about nuclear accidents, while the story itself is handled with lighthearted carelessness (the central couple, on the run from the vampiric zombies, take time out for a coffee and some chat before resuming their mad flight, for instance). The images are routine, the effects cheap and the acting mediocre, but Lenzi at least made the effort to link the commercial images with a real issue, suggesting the film owes more to Romero's *The Crazies* (1973) than to his zombie pictures.

d Umberto Lenzi *p* Diego Alchimede, Luis Mendez *s* Antonio Corti, Piero Regnoli, Luis Maria Delgado *c* Hans Burman *se* Giuseppe Farranti, Franco di Girolami *lp* Hugo Stiglitz, Laura Trotter, Mel Ferrer, Francisco Rabal, Maria Rosaria Omaggio, Sonia Viviani, Eduardo Fajardo, Manolo Zarzo, Alejandro de Enciso

Inferno

(PRODUZIONI INTERSOUND; IT) scope 107(106)min

As the follow-up to Argento's **Suspiria** (1976), this must be considered a disappointment. The complicated, virtually incomprehensible plot – apparently derived from Alain Resnais' *L'Année Dernière à Marienbad* (1961) – concerns a New York apartment house which proves to house a coven of satanists, the 'Three Mothers'. A young woman who lives there (Miracle) discovers this and is murdered; her brother (McCloskey) investigates and narrowly escapes from the climactic conflagration in which the building is destroyed. The meandering narrative, strewn with murders of incidental characters like the brother's girlfriend (Giorgi), would hardly matter were the bravura sustained in a manner comparable with *Suspiria*. But only once or twice – the impressionistic use of pouring rain during the sequence in Rome which introduces McCloskey, for example, or the close-ups of fastening locks which punctuate the frantic attempts of one victim (Nicolodi) to flee from her unseen assailant – does Argento achieve that quality of technical display which is its own justification. The

The Howling, *Joe Dante's tongue-in-cheek essay in lycanthropy.*

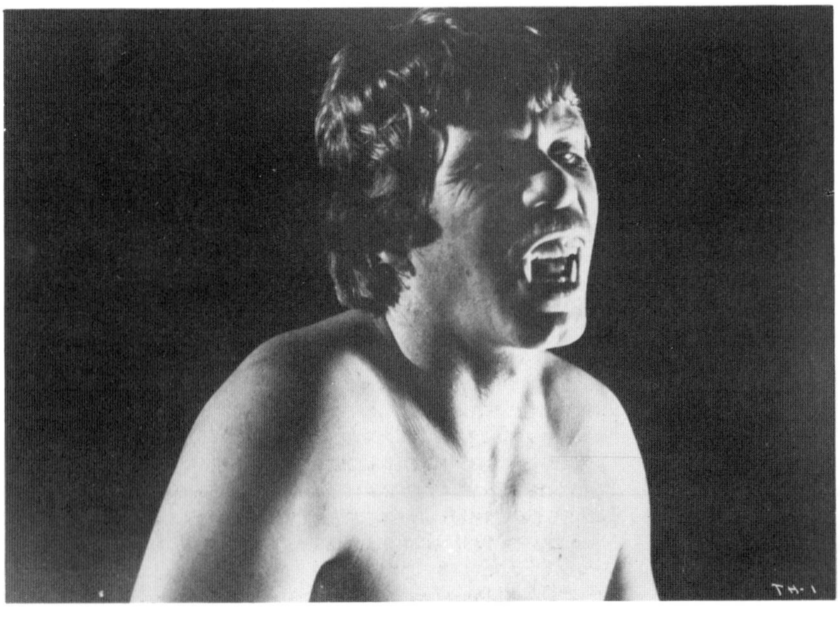

The disappointing Inferno.

fiery finale is characteristic of Argento in outline but realized in a distinctly perfunctory manner.

One of Argento's assistants on the film was Lamberto Bava, who subsequently made a noteworthy directorial début with **Macabro** (1980), and again assisted Argento on **Sotto gli Occhi dell'Assassino** (1982).

Inferno's score is by rock musician Keith Emerson.

d/s Dario Argento *p* Claudio Argento *c* Romano Albani *se* Germano Natali, Pino Leoni, (uncredited) Mario Bava *lp* Irene Miracle, Leigh McCloskey, Daria Nicolodi, Eleonora Giorgi, Alida Valli, Sacha Pitoeff, Feodor Chaliapin, Veronica Lazar, Gabriele Lavia

Just Before Dawn (OAKLAND PRODUCTIONS) 90min

Five young campers who obviously hadn't seen **The Hills Have Eyes** (1977) here head for the Oregon mountains. They too meet the mutant product of backwoods' inbreeding, notably a pair of giggling twins (both played by Hunsaker) armed with cleavers (which have saw-teeth just to make them nastier). Three of the campers die after the usual teasing preliminaries, but the characterization is so rudimentary that it is difficult to care when Benson and Henry are saved (forest-ranger Kennedy shoots one twin, the other chokes to death with Benson's arm rammed down his throat).

d Jeff Lieberman *p* David Sheldon, Doro Vlado Hreljanovic *s* Mark Arywitz, Gregg Irving *c* Joel King, Dean King *lp* George Kennedy, Deborah Benson, Gree Henry, Chris Lemmon, Ralph Seymour, John Hunsaker

El Lago de los Muertos Vivientes *aka* Le Lac des Morts Vivants *aka* The Lake of the Living Dead

(J.E. FILMS/EORINE; SP, FR) scope 91min

Although Jesús Franco was scheduled to direct this Nazi-zombie picture, the French producer assigned it to Rollin, Franco's less prolific but occasionally more stylish colleague in the sexy horror business. The plot concerns the return of a group of German soldiers who had been killed and dumped in a lake by villagers. Echoing the beginning of **Jaws** (1975), a young woman goes swimming and is caught by one of the zombies who rise from the bottom of the lake. The rest of the movie chronicles the ensuing battles between the undead Nazis and the locals until a youngster, the product of a Nazi's affair with a local woman, burns the mill where the zombies established their headquarters. The score is provided by one of Franco's regular collaborators, Daniel White, while actors Vernon and Foster are familiar from Franco's previous work. The film is not to be confused with Franco's own *El Lago de las Virgenes* (1981), nor with *L'Abîme des Morts Vivants* (1981), made by Lesoeur under the pseudonym A. M. Franck, and also featuring Nazi-zombies.

d Jean Rollin *p* Daniel Lesoeur *s* A. L. Mariaux *c* Max Monteillet *se* Christine Sauvage *lp* Howard Vernon, Robert Foster, Pierre Escourrou, Marcia Sharif, Anouchka, Nadine Pascal, Julian Atienza

Last Rites *aka* Dracula's Last Rites

(NEW EMPIRE FEATURES) 88min

The mortician's name – Lucard – indicates the level of imagination at work in this cheap and poorly made attempt to update vampire lore. In a small town in upstate New York the mortician, sheriff and local doctor are all vampires who manage to survive by drinking the blood of road-accident victims before burying them with stakes through their hearts so as to avoid unwelcome competition. For no apparent reason, the film features a family called the Fondas.

d/co-s/c Domonic Paris *p* Kelly van Horn *co-s* Ben Donnelly *lp* Patricia Lee Hammond, Gerald Fielding, Victor Jorge, Michael Lally, Mimi Weddell

Macabro *aka* Macabre

(AMA FILM/MEDUSA; IT) 91min

This aptly titled movie is the auspicious directorial début of Mario Bava's son and long-standing assistant and is co-scripted by Avati, the most stylish of the new Italian horror directors. The plot, which is more tightly constructed than those required by Mario Bava, concerns a woman, Jane (Stegers), who keeps the severed head of her lover (Molnar) in the fridge during the day, and in her bed at night. Her blind neighbour (Posse) becomes increasingly fixated on her and starts to spy. Every evening, he hears Stegers' preparations for the night: the sound of the fridge door opening and closing precedes noises suggesting intense experiences with an unseen lover. In the end, he's attacked by a demented Stegers and kills her, but when he reaches her bed and bends down to explore what's there, the hideous head sinks its teeth into his throat. Bava films the eerily obsessive story with unnerving coolness, allowing a genuinely venomous atmosphere, admirably sustained by the fine performance of Stegers (best known for her role in Fellini's *La Citta delle Donne*, 1980), to pervade the picture. Bava's next picture, **La Casa con la Scala nel Buio** (1983), confirmed that he is a worthy successor to his father.

d/co-s Lamberto Bava *co-p* Gianni Minervini *co-p/co-s* Antonio Avati *co-s* Pupi Avati, Roberto Gandus *c* Franco delli Colli *se* Piero Corridori, Angelo Mattei *lp* Bernice Stegers, Roberto Posse, Stanko Molnar, Veronika Zinny, Ferdinando Orlandi, Fernando Pannullo, Elisa Kadiga Bove

Mangiati Vivi *aka* Mangiati Vivi dai Cannibali *aka* Eaten Alive *aka* Eaten Alive by the Cannibals

(DANIA FILM/NAZIONALE CINEMATOGRAFICA/MEDUSA; IT) 90min

Lenzi's second gore movie of the year, after **Incubo sulla Citta Contaminata** (1980), rehearses the familiar savage-cruelty and cannibal motifs made popular by Ruggero Deodato's infamously racist fantasies (**Ultimo Mondo Cannibale**, 1976; **Cannibal Holocaust**, 1979). In New York, a mysterious assassin using a blow-pipe and arrows dipped in cobra venom, is crushed by a truck, leaving a can of film showing hideously sadistic scenes in a jungle setting. Sheila (Agren) and a mercenary (Kerman) set out to find the heroine's sister who featured in the footage, in New Guinea. They uncover a Jim Jones-type figure (Rassimov) lording it over the natives and hypnotically controlling Sheila's sister. He eventually orders his followers to commit mass suicide. The main point of the movie, usually severely curtailed by censorship cuts, is the depiction of gory brutality. The film is not to be confused with Tobe Hooper's **Eaten Alive** (1976), which also featured a guest appearance by Ferrer. Lenzi continued his obnoxious cannibal movies with **Cannibal Ferox** (1981).

d/s Humphrey Humbert (Umberto Lenzi) *p* Antonio Crescenzi *c* Federico Zanni *lp* Ivan Rassimov, Janet Agren, Paola Senatore, Robert Kerman, Mel Ferrer, Me Me Lai, Meg Fleming, Franco Fantasia, Michele Schniecenz

Mangryongui Kok *aka* **Bloody Smile**
(DEE YANG COMPANY; ROK) 88min
Though set in contemporary times, like the second story of Park's **Myonuriui Han** (1971), this tale is firmly rooted in feudal social relations. A wealthy patriarch picks up an orphan and weds her to his only son in order to ensure the family's continuation. When she becomes pregnant, a choice has to be made between the life of the mother and that of the child: the rich family chooses to sacrifice the young mother. She then returns as a ghost and takes possession of another woman who thus becomes the instrument of her revenge. Eventually, a Buddhist monk exorcizes the woman by persuading the ghost to forgive the selfish family for their lethal decision to put family status and property above the life of a person. The special effects associated with the haunting are limited to the use of filters and other image distortions easily achievable with the camera rather than with expensive process work. Within these limitations, the film works well although it doesn't match the stylishness of Park's **Two Women from the Nether World** (1982).

d Park Yoon Kyo *p* Han Sang Hoon *s* Yoo Il Soo *c* Ahn Chang Bok *lp* Chung Se Hyuk, Chi Mi Ok

Maniac (MAGNUM) 91min
A downbeat exploitation movie, *Maniac*, filmed in New York locations, focuses on a violently disturbed schizophrenic loner (Spinell) who was ill-treated in childhood by his mother and now devotes himself to the murder and mutilation of a succession of young women. There is some tension in the scenes which depict the life of the 'dark' side of his character alone in his drab room, in which he keeps a collection of mannequin dummies. But these are rather awkwardly offset by sequences showing him with the photographer (Munro), with whom in his 'normal' life he is having an affair. Savini, who was also responsible for the special effects for **Friday the 13th** (1980), contributes some graphically gory makeup effects in the murder scenes. A couple of hallucination scenes are quite imaginatively filmed, but Spinell's performance is unsubtle and the movie as a whole a fairly dubious undertaking.

d/co-p William Lustig *co-p* Andrew Garroni *s* C. A. Rosenberg, Joe Spinell *c* Robert Lindsay *se* Tom Savini *lp* Joe Spinell, Caroline Munro, Gail Lawrence, Kelly Piper, Rita Montone, Hyla Marrow, Tom Savini

Vincent Price at The Monster Club.

The Monster Club
(CHIPS PRODUCTIONS; GB) 97min
Subotsky was producer of some notable omnibus horror movies made under the Amicus banner (including **Torture Garden**, 1967, and **Tales from the Crypt**, 1972) but this attempt at resuscitating the formula in a semi-comic vein proved distinctly limp. Veterans Price and Carradine – hardly better served here than in **House of the Long Shadows** (1982) – appear in a laborious framing story in which the latter, playing a writer of horror stories, is initiated into the Monster Club; the subsequent stories elaborate on the club's various members. The first story deals with a 'shadmock', the possessor of a lethal whistle (Laurenson), and the manner in which it gets the better of the woman (Kellerman) who is trying to steal from him. The second story purports to be an autobiographical film by producer 'Lintom Busotsky' (Steel) involving his vampire father (Johnson) and the policeman (Pleasance) on whom he turns the tables and the third episode concerns a film director (Whitman) whose ideal horror movie location proves to be all too genuinely the province of ghouls. Any expectations of humour aroused by the presence of a producer and a director in the *dramatis personae* prove ill-founded. The individual narratives are slackly unfolded, while the scenes at the club are just embarrassingly silly. The stories are based on the work of R. Chetwynd-Hayes, who also provided the sources for the Amicus movie **From Beyond the Grave** (1973).

d Roy Ward Baker *p* Milton Subotsky *s* Edward Abraham, Valerie Abraham *c* Peter Jessop *lp* Vincent Price, John Carradine, Anthony Steel, Barbara Kellerman, Simon Ward, James Laurenson, Donald Pleasance, Richard Johnson, Britt Ekland, Stuart Whitman

Motel Hell (CAMP HILL PRODUCTIONS) 106(101)min
In Grainville California Ida and her brother Vincent (Parsons and Calhoun) are renowned for their home-cured meats – what no one knows is that these are spiced up with human flesh. The pair ambush people whom they consider weirdos and bury them alive in the garden, leaving only their heads protruding from the ground. Their vocal chords are slit and they are force fed on the best natural foods to fatten them up before being slaughterd.

Motel Hell marked the American début of British director Connor whose previous credits include *At the Earth's Core* (1976), **From Beyond the Grave** (1973) and *Arabian Adventure* (1979), all of whose elaborate and imaginative sense of style is

Left: *One of the hallucination sequences in* Maniac.

much in evidence here. Like **Eaten Alive** (1976), *Motel Hell* evokes much of *E. C.* comics' irreverent and perversely funny approach to horror and captures an American gothic feel not seen since such early *E. C.*s as *Tales from the Crypt* and *Vault of Horror*. The problem is, however, that the film can never quite make up its mind if it's an outrageously gross gore movie or a self-parodic and blackly ironic comedy, and much of the humour gets swallowed up in scenes involving blood and guts (especially those portraying the planting and harvesting of the victims) that are distinctly harrowing. Nonetheless the satire, when one can concentrate on it, is pretty juicy: the amiable Farmer Vincent feels his 'good work' is helping to solve the world's food problems – compounded of too many people and not enough food. Not only does he represent capitalism and the protestant work ethic at its most unrestrained, he also feels he is ridding America of 'undesirables': McCarthyism taken to its logical extreme. Thus the farm is the epitome of Reagan's America, where the grossest exploitation lurks just beneath the placid plastic surface, where murder is less blasphemous than sexual liberation, where idiotic families of tourists eat the most unutterable junk and the sheriff is 'the biggest cannibal around'. As one American critic put it, '*Motel Hell*'s eerie ambiance shows America and its simple-minded ideals through puke-colored lenses'. It should also be pointed out that the film's climax (from which most stills of the film are usually taken) which features a chainsaw duel inside the bloody slaughterhouse during which Calhoun wears a giant pig's head and a female victim slips inexorably towards a meat slicer is one of the truly great moments in the Grand Guignol pantheon.

d Kevin Connor *p/s* Robert Jaffe, Steven-Charles Jaffe *c* Thomas del Ruth *se* Adams R. Calvert *lp* Rory Calhoun, Paul Linke, Nancy Parsons, Nina Axelrod, Wolfman Jack, Elaine Joyce, Dick Curtis, Monique St Pierre, Rosanne Katon, E. Hampton Beagle

Mother's Day

(SAGA FILM/DUTY PRODUCTIONS) 98(93)min

McGuire and McQuade are psychopathic hillbilly brothers ruled by the iron hand of their mother in a shack deep in the woods. Mother is terrified of the prospect of an attack by her savage sister Queenie who she believes is lurking in the woods, and so trains her sons in all forms of combat, using kidnapped hikers and campers to practice on. When they capture three holidaying college girls – Hendrickson, Luce and Pierce – Luce dies but the others avenge her. As satire, *Mother's Day* works rather well, opening with a knock at encounter groups – the participants in one group planning murder in spite of their avowed intention to 'love' – and moving on to take a swipe at American motherhood. The film ends as a gross parody of consumerism, with McGuire and McQuade eating junk cereals by the bucketful, endlessly arguing whether punk is better than disco, collecting *Sesame Street* and *Star Trek* merchandising and raping and killing, 'just like I seen on TV ...'. The whole shack is a riot of consumer goods: John Travolta posters, Howdy Doody dolls and Batman ephemera, and model pink flamingoes adorn in the front lawn. As director Kaufman put it, 'this was Mother's perception of what society is about. As she says in the beginning of the film she wanted to take what was good from the city and the rest of it you can keep. This was her perception of what's good'. In this context it's entirely fitting that the brothers are done to death by radio aerial, electric meat carver, a can of Drano sink cleaner and a TV set. As a demented and anarchic version of *Deliverance* (1972), *Mother's Day* is hard to beat and it's good to see the perennial female victims getting their own back for a change.

Oddly enough, the film was banned in Britain.

d/co-p/co-s Charles Kaufman *co-p* Michael Kravits *co-s* Warren Leight *c* Joe Mangine *lp* Nancy Hendrickson, Deborah Luce, Tania Pierce, Holden McGuire, Billy Ray McQuade, Rose Ross

Rory Calhoun, wearing a pig mask, with Nina Axelrod in the Grand Guignol finale to Motel Hell.

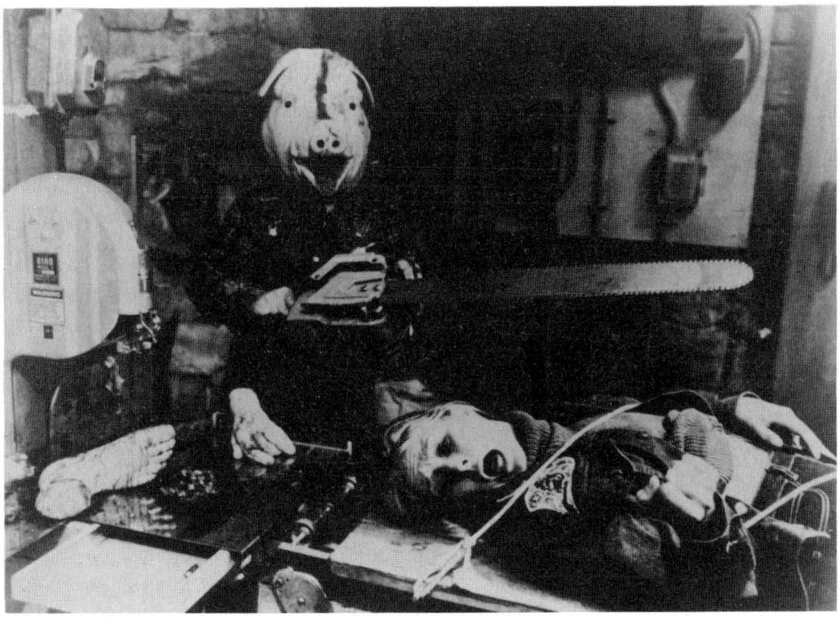

Ms 45 *aka* Angel of Vengeance

(NAVARON FILMS) 84(76)min

Thana (Tamerlis), a young garment worker in New York is raped on the way home only to find a burglar in her apartment who also tries to rape her. Killing him in self-defence, she carves up the body and puts the pieces in the fridge, gradually disposing of them around town. On her various forays she starts to dispose of lecherous males by shooting them and finally embarks on an all-out killing spree.

Like Ferrara's earlier **The Driller Killer** (1979), *Ms 45* is a stunning urban nightmare with distinct echoes of **Repulsion** (1965), and completely avoids the sadistic, voyeuristic sexism of so many recent American horror films. Whether the film could actually be termed 'feminist' is debatable, but what is undeniable is that the various assaults on Tamerlis are not filmed in such a way as to invite the audience to participate wallowingly in them, while the film's parade of unsympathetic male characters is quite relentless. Furthermore her transformation into an avenger is not achieved by her assuming the usual 'masculine' qualities, or even losing her positive 'feminine' ones.

Interestingly, when it was finally released in the UK in late 1984 in the midst of the 'video nasty' debate, it was reviewed very respectfully, in complete contrast to *The Driller Killer*.

d Abel Ferrara *p* Rochelle Weisberg *s* N. G. St John *c* James Momel *se* Matt Vogel, Sue Dalton *lp* Zoe Tamerlis, Steve Singer, Jack Thibeau, Peter Yellen, Darlene Stuto, Editta Sherman, Albert Sinkys, Jimmy Laine (Abel Ferrara)

The Nesting *aka* Phobia

(NESTING CO) 104min

This is an effective, spooky haunted-house story by one-time hard-core director Weston, who here demonstrates a strong visual sense and narrative skill. Lauren Cochran (Groves), an agoraphobic writer of gothic novels (the title of one of which gives the film its name), moves from New York to a remote, spooky Victorian mansion. Originally a brothel in which a massacre once took place, the house is now haunted by the ghosts of the victims and Groves becomes a pawn in their plans to revenge themselves upon their murderers. The movie also features the last film appearance of Grahame – as the ghost of the brothel madam.

d/p/co-s Armand Weston *co-s* Daria Price *c* João Fernandes *se* Matt Vogel *lp* Robin Groves, Christopher Loomis, Michael David Lally, John Carradine, Gloria Grahame, Bill Rowley, David Tabor, Patrick Farelley

Left: *Rachel Ward as the stalk-'n'-slasher of* Night School.

Le Notti del Terrore *aka* **Zombie Horror** *aka* **Zombie 3**
(ESTEBAN CINEMATOGRAFICA; IT) 92(83)min
The plot of this follow-up to Lucio Fulci's **Zombi 2** (1979) by Bianchi, a minor director of sexploitation and suspense movies, is devised with the intention of staging as many gruesomely visceral events as possible. The rotting undead emerge from an opened Etruscan tomb and invade a weekend party at a country mansion and, although some guests escape to a monastery, the carnage continues unabated there. De Rossi, who handled the special effects for *Zombi 2*, again orchestrates the gory events, which this time include the beheading with a scythe of a crucified young woman and the ripping away of one victim's breasts. The violence is more directly sexual, the victims more attractive and the overall effect more pathologically regressive than in Fulci's picture.

d Andrea Bianchi *p* Gabriele Crisanti *s* Piero Regnoli *c* Gianfranco Maioletti *se* Gianetto de Rossi *lp* Karin Weil, Maria Angela Giordan, Gian Luigi Chrizzi, Peter Bark, Simone Mattioli, Antonella Antinori, Roberto Caporali

L'Ossessione che Uccide *aka* **Murder Obsession** *aka* **Deliria** *aka* **Murderous Obsession** *aka* **Murder Syndrome** (DIONYSIO CINEMATOGRAFICA/NOUVELLE CINEVOG; IT,FR) 95min
After nearly a decade of silence, Freda, who started the horror revival with **I Vampiri** (1956), delivered this wonderfully stylish psycho-thriller, filmed with enchanting camera movements, half-tones and pastels, punctuated by bright splashes of colour and shock cuts. The tortuous plot is designed for suspense, but gives ample scope for a return to Freda's and Mario Bava's classic themes: the perversity of cinema as a maternal, all-encompassing space into which a network of looks traces, like incisions, a web that captivates the viewer and begins to tamper with the taboo undertones of the very desire for cinema as eerie images and the poisonous narrative both seduce and disturb us.

Mike (Patrizi) returns home to his mother, Glenda (Strindberg), together with his lover (Dionisio), a film director (Richardson) and two starlets (Gemser and Brochard). Assuming he killed his father, Patrizi gets drawn into a near-incestuous relationship with his mother while around him corpses begin to pile up (after a love session he wakes up next to a corpse, while the voyeur who photographed them and the woman who develops the pictures are both axed to death). In the end, Patrizi's oedipal guilt begins to unravel as he realizes

New Year's Evil (CANNON) 85min
This lacklustre, derivative stalk-'n'-slash movie has Kelly (of the *Happy Days* teleseries) as the host of a live New Year's Eve coast-to-coast TV rock show. A man identifying himself only as 'Evil' telephones to say that he has killed one of her friends and will kill again each time midnight strikes in the various time zones across America, finishing up by killing her. The routine affair seems interminable, drawn out as it is by the would-be punk numbers on the show.

The film's real point of interest and significance is as an example of how producers Globus and Golan, once they had hit on a successful formula – in this case the adolescent fantasies of the *Lemon Popsicle* series which began in 1978 – then mined it for all it was worth.

d/co-s Emmett Alston *p* Menahem Golan, Yoram Globus *co-s* Leonard Neubauer *c* Edward Thomas *lp* Roz Kelly, Kip Niven, Chris Wallace, Grant Cramer, Louisa Moritz, Jed Mills, Taaffe O'Connell, Jon Greene, Teri Copley, Anita Crane

Night School *aka* **Terror Eyes**
(LORIMAR) 88min
This dispiriting addition to the stalk-'n'-slash subgenre has a mysterious killer decapitating students at Wendell College, a night school for women. Suspicion falls on a professor, Snyder, who is known to have had affairs with several of the students, but the culprit turns out to be Ward, the research assistant with whom he lives, who has been attempting to remove some of the sources of temptation.

What makes the film so disappointing is the waste of the talents available – Ward (before she became better known through *The Thorn Birds* teleseries) and Hughes (of *Cromwell*, 1970, and *Chitty Chitty Bang Bang*, 1968, here making his horror début). Also depressing is the fact that this kind of mindless misogyny could be perpetrated by a woman scriptwiter (Avergon), who might at least have been expected to have Ward dispatch Snyder rather than the objects of his attentions! Alfred Sole, director of the excellent **Communion** (1976) and the underrated *Tanya's Island* (1980) was originally slated to direct.

d Ken Hughes *co-p* Larry Babb *co-p/s* Ruth Avergon *c* Mark Irwin *lp* Leonard Mann, Rachel Ward, Drew Snyder, Joseph R. Sicari, Nicholas Cairis, Karen MacDonald, Annette Miller, Bill McCann, Margo Skinner, Elizabeth Barnitz

Paura nella Citta dei Morti Viventi, *yet another Italian imitation of George Romero's zombie movies*.

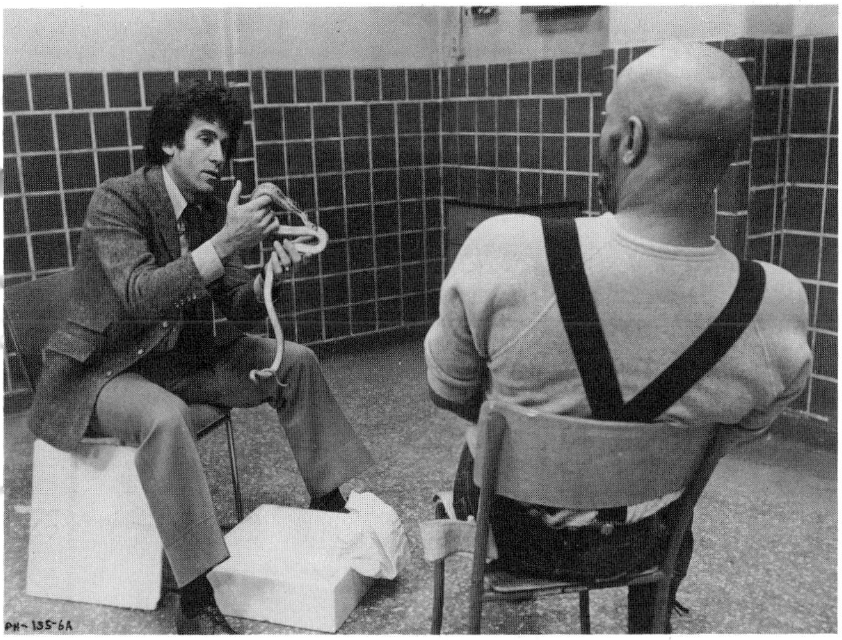

Paul Michael Glaser (left) as the doctor who treats phobias with death in Phobia.

he may not have committed patricide: his crazed mother is revealed to be the mad killer and she goes berserk in the grand finale. The picture's orchestration of eroticism in counterpoint to madness and horror imagery is expert. It was edited by Freda, who intensifies the morbid atmosphere with every twist of the plot, deploying motifs from Bach, Liszt and Vivaldi at opportune moments. In spite of a few awkward moments and, by comparison to the flood of entrails washing across the screens of the time, its somewhat oldfashioned look, Freda's movie clearly shows where the best Italian directors of the genre, from Bava to Avati, learned their trade.

d/co-s Riccardo Freda *p* Pino Collura, Enzo Boetani, Simon Mizrahi *co-s* Antonio Corti *c* Christiano Pogany *lp* Stefano Patrizi, Anita Strindberg, Laura Gemser, John Richardson, Martine Brochard, Silvia Dionisio, Henry Garcin, Fabrizio Moroni

Patrick Vive Ancora *aka* Patrick Still Lives *aka* Patrick Is Still Alive

(STEFANO FILM; IT) 94min

Landi's film is a drab imitation of Richard Franklin's mediocre **Patrick** (1978). The bedridden Patrick (Dei), disfigured and paralysed by an accident, lies in a house where several crimes have been committed, the vibrations of which begin to affect him. But his supernatural psychic powers eventually get the better of the evil forces that surround him. Landi's background as a TV director shows through in the numerous close shots of the hero's zombieish-looking face, mistakenly equating the size of the closeup with the dramatic intensity of the scene.

d Mario Landi *p/co-s* Gabriele Grisanti *co-s* Piero Regnoli *c* Franco Villa *lp* Sascha Pitoeff, Gianni Dei, Carmen Russo, Paola Giusti, Maria Angela Giordan, Franco Silva, Anna Veneziano, John Benedy

Paura nella Città dei Morti Viventi *aka* City of the Living Dead *aka* The Gates of Hell *aka* The Fear *aka* Fear in the City of the Living Dead *aka* Twilight of the Dead

(DANIA FILM/MEDUSA/INTERNATIONAL CINEMATOGRAFICA; IT) scope 93(92)min

Continuing the gory imitations of George Romero's zombie movies, Fulci followed his **Zombi 2** (1979) with this Grand Guignol piece ostensibly set in Lovecraft country but patently shot in Italy. When Dunwich's parish priest commits suicide in the cemetery, the gates of hell are opened and corpses rise up. Peter (George), a reporter, rescues Mary (MacColl) who apparently dies after hallucinating Dunwich's dead emerging from their tombs and taking over the world. The rest of the film consists of individual sketches, loosely connected, in which women (for the most part) vomit blood as their heads are torn open by the wormy fingers of the decaying dead. Other thrills include an outraged father forcing a retarded boy to undergo Fulci's trademark scene – an electric drill boring through his head from side to side – and plenty of intestines being pulled out of badly made dummies. The film's climax has George killed by a female zombie before a psychoanalyst friend (de Mejo) stabs the worm-eaten corpse of an undead priest in the crotch with a crucifix, inflicting acute discomfort on the devil and causing all the zombies to burn up.

The American version was supervised by Robert Warner.

d/co-s Lucio Fulci *p* Giovanni Masini *co-s* Dardano Sacchetti *c* Sergio Salvati *se* Gino de Rossi *lp* Christopher George, Janet Agren, Katriona MacColl, Carlo de Mejo, Antonella Interlenghi, Giovanni Lombardo Radice, Daniela Doria, Luca Paismer, Fabrizio Jovine

Phobia

(BOROUGH PARK PRODUCTIONS; CAN) 90min

Although he had been moving in that direction (with such films as *The List of Adrian Messenger*, 1963 and *Wise Blood*, 1979), this is Huston's only venture into the horror genre. The central character is an eminent psychotherapist (Glaser) who is conducting an experiment with a group of phobics who have been released from jail for the purpose. One by one, they are killed in mysterious ways, and it appears that the doctor is the victim of some peculiar conspiracy. Eventually, however, it turns out that he is himself the murderer, and has been seeking to punish his victims to compensate for his own phobic terror of water, which in childhood had prevented him saving his sister from drowning. This explanation may be pretty absurd – the artificiality of the plot echoes that found in much earlier Sangster scripts like **Maniac** and **Paranoiac** (both 1962) – and Glaser's performance is overly bland. But the film (essentially, perhaps, a detective story, though the central character represents a version of the mad-doctor stereotype) is cunningly well crafted in a self-effacing style. In keeping with the charade-like premise, Huston plays up the yarn-spinning conventions, capped by Glaser's casually abrupt suicide after he has obligingly explained his motives, and peoples the film with an amusing assortment of familiar types, all the way from the *femme fatale* (Stewart) who becomes the first victim to the foxy detective (Colicos) who investigates the case.

d John Huston *p* Zale Magder *s* Lew Lehman, Jimmy Sangster, Peter Bellwood *c* Reginald H. Morris *se* Martin Malivoire *lp* Paul Michael Glaser, John Colicos, Susan Hogan, Alexandra Stewart, David Bolt, Robert O'Ree, David Eisner, Lisa Langlois, Kenneth Welsh, Patricia Collins

Prom Night

(PROM NIGHT PRODUCTIONS) 95(93)min

This film clearly belongs to the contemporary cycle of teenage-jeopardy pictures initiated by **Halloween** (1978) (which also featured Curtis in a leading role), although the use of a high-school prom as the background for the action also recalls **Carrie** (1976), a film which perhaps influenced the subsequent jeopardy subgenre. As in *Halloween* and other films of the kind, the film begins with a prologue; in this case, a ten-year-old girl falls to her death after being taunted by four slightly older children. The action then moves on six years to the prom at which the girl's sister (Curtis) will be crowned queen by her father (Nielsen), the school head, whilst her brother (Tough) runs the disco. The four 'guilty' teenagers receive anonymous phone calls, and during the dance violence soon starts to erupt, and three of the four (Benton, Rubens and Thompson) and Mucci, mistaken for the fourth (Stevens), are killed. In a climactic ending, which takes place on the strobe-lit dance floor, the killer makes a renewed attempt on Stevens' life, before being wounded and unmasked by Curtis, and is revealed to be none other than Tough, who turns out to have witnessed his sister's death six years earlier. The plot here is rather more inventive and eventful than in some other similar movies, and whilst the film does not escape from the formula, Lynch's timing and response to the settings are sharp enough to lift it some way out of the rut.

d Paul Lynch *p* Peter Simpson *s* William Gray *c* Robert New *lp* Jamie Lee Curtis, Leslie Nielsen, Casey Stevens, Eddie Benton, Michael Tough, Antoinette Bower, David Mucci, Pita Oliver, Marybeth Rubens, Joy Thompson

La Regina dei Cannibali *aka* **Zombi Holocaust** *aka* **Dr Butcher MD** *aka* **Queen of the Cannibals** *aka* **The Island of the Last Zombies** (FLORA FILM/FULVIA CINEMATOGRAFICA/GICO CINEMATOGRAFICA; IT) 88(77)min

Borrowing heavily from Sergio Martino's gore movies, **La Montagna del Dio Cannibale** (1978) and **Il Fiume del Grand Caimano** (1979), *La Regina dei Cannibali* combines zombie and cannibal motifs. Also echoing Lucio Fulci's **Zombi 2** (1979), as well as Grau's **No Profanar el Sueño de los Muertos** (1974), the movie starts in New York morgue where orientals tear the hearts out of corpses. The heroine, a doctor (delli Colli), and her scientist friend (McCullough) set out to investigate the 'native' rites involving human sacrifices and cannibalism on Kito, an island in the Pacific, where they come into contact with Dr Abrera (O'Brien), who is practising transplants á la Dr Moreau, thereby creating misshapen zombies. Colli is captured, prepared for sacrifice, hailed as a goddess and rescued while the cannibals help the hero wipe out the zombies. The film's reason for being is to show bloody scalpings, bodies being eaten and ripped to bits, interspersed with shots of Colli's body.

d/co-s Frank Martin (Marino Girolami) *co-p* Gianfranco Couyoumdjian *co-p/co-s/co-se* Fabrizio de Angelis *c* Fausto Zuccoli *co-se* Maurizio Trani, Rosario Restopino *lp* Ian McCullough, Sherry Buchanan, Alexander Cole (Alexandra delli Colli), Peter O'Neal, Donald O'Brien, Walter Patriarca, Linda Fumis, Dakan, Roberto Resra

El Retorno del Hombre Lobo *aka* **The Return of the Wolfman** *aka* **La Noche del Hombrelobo**
(DALMATA FILMS; SP) 97min

Molina's ninth outing as Waldemar Daninsky, the werewolf, abandons the Tibetan extravagances of **La Maldición de la Bestia** (1975) and returns to the more familiar territory last used in **El Retorno de Walpurgis** (1973). Countess Bathory and Waldemar were executed in 16th-century Hungary but three German women, in search of the horrible duo's tombs in the Carpathians, resurrect the pair in a macabre ceremony while graverobbers remove the silver cross from the werewolf's heart. Waldemar and the Countess then try to settle old scores, with the werewolf eventually ripping out the vampire's throat. Since convention dictates that Waldemar shall be killed by someone who loves him, the final confrontation is between him and one of the German women armed with a silver cross. The movie rehearses well-known motifs and images while the soundtrack, provided by the group CAM, imitates Ennio Morricone's work.

Molina's next lycanthropic adventure, **La Bestia y la Espada Magica** (1983), was another Japanese-Spanish co-production – repeating his no doubt happy collaboration with Japan on **El Carnaval de las Bestias** (1980). *El Retorno*, however, was a major flop, threatening Molina's production company, Dulmata, with bankruptcy. The comedy director Mariano Ozores used the same sets for his spoof *El Liguero Magico* (1980) featuring Luis Lorenzo as a homosexual werewolf.

d/s Jacinto Molina *p* Modesto Perez Redondo *c* Alejandro Ulloa *lp* Paul Naschy (Jacinto Molina), Silvia Aguilar, Azucena Hernandez, Julia Saly, Beatriz Elorietta, Pilar Alcón, Pepe Ruiz, Tito Garcia, Riccardo Palacios, Mauro Rivera

Schizoid *aka* **Murder by Mail**
(CANNON) 91(88)min

Only the presence of Kinski – as a doctor who runs a therapy group – lifts this routine misogynist stalk-'n'-slash movie. When individual members of the group are murdered, agony columnist Hill (also one of Kinski's patients) starts to investigate. Kinski's scenes with his disturbed teenage daughter or those where he prowls restlessly through the house have a visual and dramatic resonance quite absent from the rest of the film, from most of its near relations and most certainly from Paulsen's earlier **The Killer Behind the Mask** (1976).

d/s David Paulsen *p* Menahem Golan, Yoram Globus *c* Norma Leigh *se* Joe Quinlivan *lp* Klaus Kinski, Mariana Hill, Craig Wasson, Donna Wilkes, Joe Regalbuto, Flo Gerrish, Richard Herd, Fredric Cook, Christopher Lloyd, Kiva Lawrence

The Shining (HAWK FILMS; GB) 146(119)min

In a typically Kubrickian conceit, the labyrinthine confines of a mountain hotel cut off from civilization by winter snowfall are the setting for a movie just as much about 'space' as the vast universes of *2001: A Space Odyssey* (1968). Struggling author Jack Torrance (Nicholson), paying his way as winter caretaker for the deserted Overlook hotel, remotely situated in the Colorado mountains, is haunted by his frustrated creative ambitions and fears of failure both as a husband and an artist. Nurtured by the claustrophobia and isolation of his surroundings, his underlying insanity gradually evolves into rampant madness as he attempts to murder with an axe the only other human occupants of the hotel, his wife (Duvall) and son (Lloyd).

Here, instead of evolving into a Nietzschean future, time has stopped: there is only space, and for Nicholson's tortured ego it proves both too great and too small. In adapting Stephen King's novel, Kubrick has ignored to a great extent its familiar theme that materialism provides the springboard for evil, eschewing exposition of the hotel's history (a fact accentuated by the truncated European version) to concentrate on the

Left: *The marvellous Klaus Kinski in the awful* Schizoid.

The Shining, *Stanley Kubrick's inner space movie.*

conflicts inside Nicholson's mind that lead to his destruction. Kubrick's central character is not haunted by ghosts of the past, but inspired by the grandiloquence of his opulent surroundings – the literal wealth of available space – until he comes to believe that his creative barrenness can be replaced by a kind of omnipotence as the immortal caretaker of the Overlook. This twinning of opposites, insignificance and omnipotence, is superbly visualized in Nicholson's conversations with two of the hotel's previous employees, bartender (Turkel) and caretaker (Stone), who actually did kill his family during winter isolation: a brilliant mixture of the blackest comedy and abstract reflections on power, responsibility, and duty to the hotel. This 'space trap' is also metaphorically suggested by the echo of the real maze in the hotel grounds – which becomes both Nicholson's downfall when he cannot find the way out and freezes to death, and his family's escape to freedom when they trap him there – in the hotel's carpet design. In the novel, Lloyd's gift for seeing things (the shining of the title) is used mainly as a means to reactivate horrific happenings in the hotel's history; in the film, this emphasis is somewhat lost, although Nicholson's jealousy of his son's gift is another factor in his feelings of inadequacy. Kubrick's mobile camera unerringly underlines the huge spaces of the building – roaming around enormous kitchens and ballrooms, tracking down unending corridors as the boy explores by bicycle – and encompasses one great moment of horror: a shot across a deserted lobby to the lift doors, and the doors open to disgorge a torrent of red, red blood. Nicholson's startling performance, beginning with the overdone charm at his job interview already showing signs of inherent insanity, through the later leering over-eagerness, to the final maniacal beast on the rampage, is perfectly realized.

d/p/co-s Stanley Kubrick *co-s* Diane Johnson *c* John Alcott *lp* Jack Nicholson, Shelley Duvall, Danny Lloyd, Scatman Crothers, Barry Nelson, Philip Stone, Joe Turkel

Silent Scream (AMERICAN CINEMA) 87min

Arriving too late to get college housing, Balding, Doubet, Widelock and Andelman are forced to rent rooms in a weird clifftop mansion owned by Mrs Engels (de Carlo) who lives there with her neurotic son Mason (Reardon). When Widelock is stabbed to death, investigating police lieutenant Mitchell finds de Carlo's daughter Victoria (Steele) who apparently left home years before but who is in fact mad and lives in a secret room in the house.

With its revelation of the identity of the murderer some time before the film's climax, its relatively low body count and avoidance of gory pyrotechnics, *Silent Scream* is by no means a typical teenagers-in-peril movie given the subject matter and date of release. Also untypical are the strengths of the performances, and the fact that one actually *cares* whether the intended victims survive or not. Among the kids Balding and Andelman are especially good, and any movie which unites two such horror veterans as de Carlo and Steele has to have something going for it. Director Harris shows himself capable of narrative economy and achieves a sense of style in a subgenre not noted for either: indeed, the scene in which Balding discovers the secret passage to Steele's room is impressively tense and atmospheric, and the climax is undeniably gripping.

d/co-p Denny Harris *co-p* Joan Harris *s* Ken Wheat, Jim Wheat, Wallace E. Bennett *c* Michael D. Murphy, David Shore *se* Steve Karkus *lp* Rebecca Balding, Cameron Mitchell, Avery Schreiber, Barbara Steele, Steve Doubet, Brad Rearden, John Widelock, Yvonne de Carlo, Juli Andelman, Jack Stryker

Sobrenatural *aka* **Supernatural**
(KALENDER FILMS/AQUARIUS FILMS/PARAGUAS FILMS; SP)
100min

Some seven years after his best Spanish horror movie, **Una Vela Para el Diablo** (1973), Martin made **Aquella Casa en las Afueras** (1980), immediately followed by *Sobrenatural*, which was released in 1982. Although full of quite eye-catching visual effects, it is essentially a mood piece about a woman (Galbo) who is haunted by the ghost of her pathologically authoritarian husband. His menacing presence pervades the house and all who enter it fall under his spell which even causes the decapitation of a maid by means of an electric knife. Galbo steadfastly refuses to go insane, a struggle that involves a medium (Losada), a boyfriend and a priest, until she frees herself, at a price: she must first acknowledge the reality of the supernatural before being able to turn it against her tormentor. Although the photography and Galbo's acting are very professional, Martin's talents lie more in the area of fast-moving stories like **Panico en el Transiberiano** (1973), and in the construction of individual scenes, than in mood pieces which, to succeed, require the sustained control of a complex rhythmical pattern.

d/co-s Eugenio Martin *p/co-s* Antonio Cuevas *co-s* Jose de Uña, Eduardo Alvarez *c* Antonio Cuevas Jnr *se* Antonio Molina, Estudio Moro *lp* Maximo Valverde, Cristina Galbo, Candida Losada, Gerardo Malla, Juan Jesús Valverde, Lola Lemos

The Survivor (TUESDAY FILMS/
FG FILM PRODUCTION/SOUTH AUSTRALIAN FILM CORP; AUST)
scope 100(84)min

The English actor-producer Hemmings continued his busy Australian career, which included **Thirst** (1979) and **Harlequin** (1980), with this muted supernatural story derived from a James Herbert novel about a pilot who virtually returns from the dead to revenge himself upon the person who put the bomb in his plane. The crash, filmed with a sense of journalistic urgency, is impressively staged, and the subsequent use of the charred wreck as the investigators get embroiled in increasingly chilling events, culminating in a revelatory flashback, provide the movie's highlights. When the pilot, played by a ghostly pale Powell, emerges unscathed from the wreck, echoes of the supernatural begin to reverberate through the picture, imbuing it with a disturbing sense of eeriness that could erupt into terror at any moment. The story could have been set anywhere and was originally to have been shot in Germany, but it was transferred to Australia for production reasons. Although the technical credits are adequate and Brian May's score effective, there are still too many *longueurs* and heavy-handed moments to justify the prizes the picture garnered at the Sitges (1981) and Trieste (1982) festivals. Cotten appears as a priest, mediating with the hereafter.

d David Hemmings *p* Antony I. Ginnane *s* David Ambrose *c* John Seale *se* Monty Fieguth, Victor Wilson *lp* Robert Powell, Jenny Agutter, Angela Punch-McGregor, Joseph Cotten, Ralph Cotterill, Peter Sumner, Denzin Howsen, Adrian Wright

Tattoo (JOSEPH E. LEVINE) 103min

In spite of Dern's convincing portrayal of one of his many psychopaths, *Tattoo* comes across as a rather contrived and 'arty' cross between *The Collector* (1965) and *Ai No Corrida* (1976). The plot features Dern as a tattooist hired by a New York magazine to decorate (though not actually tattoo) some of its models. He falls for one of the models, cover girl Maddy (Adams), kidnaps and drugs her, and begins to tattoo her in a most elaborate fashion.

Screenwriter Buñuel is Luis' daughter-in-law, whilst director Brooks made the excellent *The Knowledge* for British television.

d/co-s Bob Brooks *p* Joseph E. Levine, Richard P. Levine *co-s* Joyce Buñuel *c* Arthur Ornitz *lp* Bruce Dern, Maud Adams, Leonard Frey, Rikke Borge, John Getz, Peter Iacangelo, Alan Leach, Cynthia Nixon, Trish Doolan, Anthony Mannino

Viaje al Más Alla *aka* Trip to the Beyond

(D'ARBO PRODUCCIONES/JESÚS BALCAZAR; SP) 98min

This is a silly omnibus movie in the style of **Tales from the Crypt** (1972). Five guests at a mad professor's isolated Pyrenean mansion tell of their supernatural experiences, which include a haunted-house story, an exorcism, a case of reincarnation, a premonition of death come true and a wish-fulfilment tale of a driver who thinks he gave a lift to a man who has been run over by him. A second, slightly less loony professor of parapsychology leaves the mansion and is told that the place had burnt down years ago. The whole thing is recounted with ponderous solemnity by an ex-TV director who also ran the Ubesque 'Academy of Parapsychological Sciences'. D'Arbo went on to make more parapsychological inanities, including *El Ser* (1982).

d/co-p Sebastian d'Arbo *p* J. P. d'Arbo *c* Fernando Cobo *lp* Narcisco Ibañez Menta, Emilio Gutierrez Caba, Berta Singerman, Rosa Espinet, Dani Arbones, Rosa Morata, Montse Prous, Ramiro Oliveros

Wolnyoui Han *aka* Grudge of the Moon Lady

(HAN JIN ENTERPRISES; ROK) 100min

Like the same team's **Huphyokwi Yanyo** (1981) this bloody vampire movie is set in a medieval Korean village and has a standard melodramatic plot. A poor girl loves a man who is also coveted by the local landowner's daughter. The rich man buys the girl's father and sends the pair away. The young man, believing himself abandoned, then marries the scheming rich woman. When the faithful daughter returns home, she is attacked and takes refuge in a swamp where she is caught and possessed by an evil white cat spirit. Now a vengeful creature, she wreaks havoc in the village, murders her rival and is eventually killed by her 'true love'.

Although tragic figures and the focus of sympathy, the women in these fantasies are all invariably represented as creatures of desire, prepared to go to inordinate lengths to get their man or thwart a rival, while the male heroes tend to be somewhat passive and insipid 'innocents' overcome by circumstances. Nevertheless, the imagery of these Korean horror fantasies is eye-catching and the acting agreeably stereotyped, evoking characters in traditional folktales.

d Kim In Soo *p* Han Kap Chin *s* Lee Moon Woong *c* Lee Seung Un *lp* Chin Bong Chin, Huh Chin

Xie *aka* Hex

(SHAW BROTHERS; HONG KONG) scope 95min

Although not Gui Zhihong's first horror film, this movie confirms that he could practice the genre with considerable skill. The story is set in turn-of-the-century Republican China and uses the familiar beauty-and-the-scholar theme (as in *Gu Jing You Hun*, 1977) but with an unexpected twist: the scholar conspires with his mistress to kill his wife. He rapes his mistress, and pretends to allow himself to be drowned by her and his wife, then returns as a ghost to scare his wife to death. When he marries his mistress, they soon find themselves persecuted by the wife's ghost with hallucinatory visions which eventually drive him to his death and the mistress insane. The lighting is effective enough to make the scholar's ghost plausible even to his wife, the appearance of the wife after her death achieves a well-managed shock effect and the *mise-en-scène* effectively maintains the film's central ambiguity: does the wife return as a ghost or is she too merely pretending?

One of the steadiest contract directors at the Shaw studios, Gui studied film-making in Taiwan and joined Shaw in 1970. With the exception of brief forays into the Malaysian film industry in the mid-seventies and two films produced by a Hong Kong independent and directed under his pseudonym Xiao Gui (Gui Jnr), he has made all his films for Shaw. His varied career includes derivative work like *She Shashou* (1974), an imitation of **Willard** (1971); a German co-produced kung fu and sexploitation movie, *Yangji* (1974), directed with Ernst Hofbauer; and some very effective thrillers. *Xie* was followed by *Xie Douxie* (1980) and *Hex after Hex* (1982). However, these are too satirical and comic to be regarded as sequels to the original film. His **Shi Yao** (1981) is a horror film made as a thriller.

d/s Gui Zhihong (Kwei Chi-hung, Kuei Chih Hung) *p* Run Run Shaw *c* Li Hsin Yeh (Li Xinye, Li Sun Ip) *lp* Tanny, Wang Jung, Chen Szu-chia, Han Kuo-tsai

Yo *aka* Capriciousness

(WHA PUNG INDUSTRIAL COMPANY; ROK) 95min

Echoing the plot of Gui Zhihong's **Xie** (1980), this South Korean picture tells of a gambler who pretends to die in order to return as a ghost and scare his wife to death, after which he marries his accomplice, her best friend. The perfidious couple are then haunted by the wife's ghost. Exorcism is attempted to no avail, and the gambler is eventually burned to death while

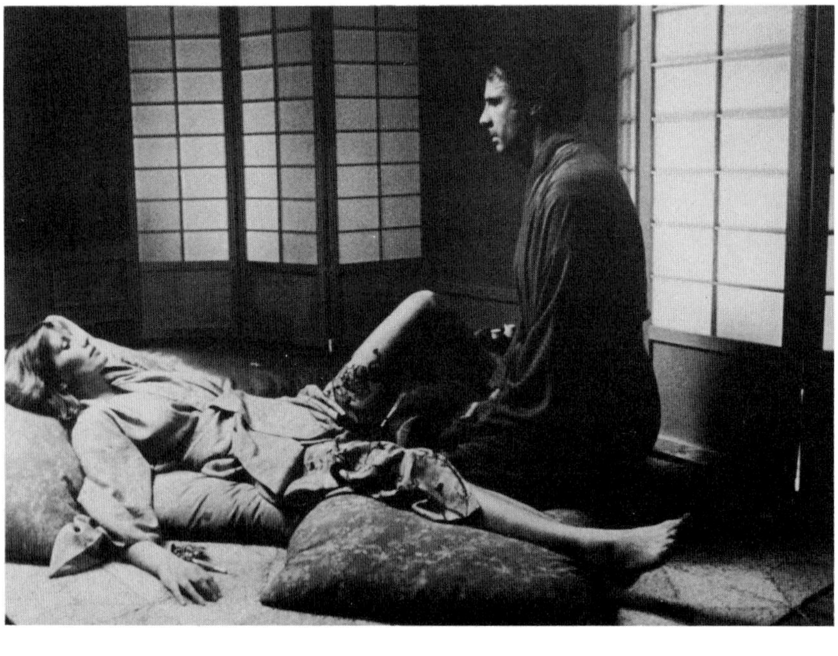

Maud Adams ritually submits herself to an obsessed Bruce Dern in Tattoo.

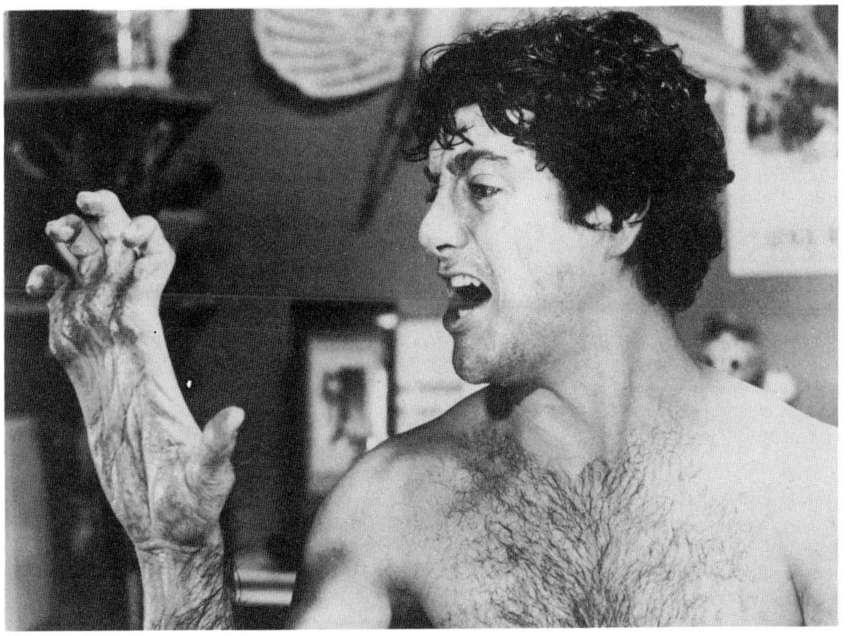

David Naughton watches himself metamorphoze in An American Werewolf in London.

his accomplice goes insane. The final twist is that the wife simply turned the tables on her tormentors since she too only pretended to die and be a ghost. In the end, her revenge completed, she becomes a Buddhist nun. The picture relies heavily on the credibility of the duplicitous ghost, but the spectral appearances lack conviction and the ritual exorcism is tediously expounded. Whereas Gui Zhihing's movie left it fairly ambiguous as to whether the ghost was 'real' or not, Kim's imitation leaves little room for doubt and takes the softest option by first blaming the women in the story and then redeeming the wife by making her take up the existence of a sexless nun.

d Kim Young Hyo *p* Chung Chang Wha *s* Sang Hak Chi *c* Sung Sub Lee *lp* Choo Ryun Kim, Soo Young Ran

1981

The Alchemist (IDEAL FILMS) 84min

The idea behind this film has possibilities but the turgid treatment it receives destroys any impact the film might have had. After accidentally killing his wife in an attempt to save her from the evil attentions of an alchemist (Glaudini), Ginty is cursed with eternal life as a ravening beast. Seventy-five years later, still young thanks to the blood he is forced to seek, he encounters his wife reincarnated as a waitress (Dooling). Ginty's now aged daughter (Stimpson) has become versed in alchemy in an attempt to save his soul by transferring the curse to herself, but Dooling's presence draws the evil. When a hellish doorway opens in the nearby graveyard, and three small demons emerge, the stage is set for the routine conflagration. The film isn't helped by its premises that demons can be clobbered and a satanic alchemist stabbed.

d Charles Band *p* Lawrence Appelbaum *s* Alan J. Adler *c* Andrew W. Friend *lp* Robert Ginty, Lucinda Dooling, John Sanderford, Viola Kate Stimpson, Robert Glaudini

An American Werewolf in London

(LYCANTHROPE FILMS; GB) 97min

Made by a director primarily associated with comedies – he was later responsible for the much praised *Trading Places* (1983) – *An American Werewolf in London* intriguingly proves to be only partly comic in tone. The opening, with a rock version of 'Blue Moon' heard over shots of sinister moorland vistas and two American hitch-hikers (Naughton and Dunne) straying into a village pub full of grotesquely uncommunicative locals, hints at broad parody. Later, however, after the youths are attacked by a werewolf and Dunne killed, the film adopts a two-way approach. On one hand, the scenes in which Naughton seeks to persuade other people, including the nurse (Agutter) who has fallen in love with him, of the real nature of the fate that has befallen him, are played for gentle humour. But the passages involving his transformation into a werewolf – the special effects are just as remarkable as in **The Howling** (1980) – and his attacks on sundry victims are handled unexpectedly straight. To some extent, this means that the film suffers from a split personality. But at times the two styles come fruitfully into conjunction, as when Naughton reverts to human form in a public place but minus clothes, or in the scenes where he is visited by the spectral Dunne, who begs him, as last of the werewolf bloodline, to kill himself and thus free the souls of the creature's previous victims. The remarkable sequence which precedes Naughton's being shot dead includes his transformation, surrounded by the ghosts of his victims, in a London sex cinema, and an elaborate mayhem of crashing cars as he escapes into Piccadilly Circus.

d/s John Landis *p* George Folsey Jnr *s* Robert Paynter *se* Rick Baker *lp* David Naughton, Jenny Agutter, Griffin Dunne, Brian Glover, John Woodvine, Lila Kaye, Frank Oz, Don McKillop, Colin Fernandes, Paul Kember

Anthropophagus II *aka* Absurd

(FILMIRAGE; IT) 96(91)min

Massaccesi, a diligent labourer in the undergrowth of Italian Z movies, made a large number of sexploitative films, including **Emanuelle e gli Ultimi Cannibali** (1977). In spite of the ineptness of his **Anthropophagus** (1980), there was sufficient response to the film for him to attempt this sequel, which features a similarly monstrous hero, again played by Montefiore, whose body keeps regenerating its tissue at the expense of his brain cells. This is supposed to turn him into an indestructible, mercilessly brutal killer. With risibly bad makeup and effects, the token script stumbles through six sequences signalled as 'shocks' by Carlo Maria Cordio's clichéd score. Most of the participants wisely hide behind pseudonyms.

d/co-p Peter Newton (Aristide Massaccesi) *co-p* Donatella Donati *s* John Cart *c* Richard Haller *lp* George Eastman (Luigi Montefiore), Annie Belle, Ian Danby, Charles Borromel, Katja Berger, Edmond Purdom, Ted Rusoff, Anja Kochansky

Basket Case

(BASKET CASE COMPANY) 90(89)min

Extremely low-budget, *Basket Case* seeks to make a deliberate appeal out of sleaziness and ineptitude, and is dedicated, significantly, to Herschell Gordon Lewis, father of the 'gore movie' with such films as **2000 Maniacs** (1964). The plot, which some have alleged is derivative of **Sisters** (1972), is rudimentary. The 'basket case' is Belial, a kind of dwarf, who was the Siamese twin of the young man (VanHentenryck) who now carries him about and is in telepathic communication with him. Belial, rescued by his brother after their father (Pierce) had them separated and sought to dispose of Belial, went on to kill the father, and is now – years later – conducting a vendetta against the doctors (Browne, Pace and Freeman), one of whom is, in fact, a vet, who conducted the illicit operation. After assorted gory mayhem, both twins die in a fall from a high window. Any intended pathos is scarcely achieved although there is a degree of slobbish humour in the scenes involving the skid row hotel where VanHentenryck is living. But on the whole, the grossness of tone and amateurishness of the production, especially where the animation of Belial is concerned, combine to make the film a repellent experience.

d/s Frank Henenlotter *p* Edgar Levins *c* Bruce Torbet *lp* Kevin VanHentenryck, Terri Susan Smith, Beverly Bonner, Robert Vogel, Diana Browne, Lloyd Pace, Bill Freeman, Joe Clarke, Ruth Neuman, Richard Pierce

1981

Die Beruehrte *aka* **No Mercy No Future**
(HELMA SANDERS-BRAHMS FILMPRODUKTION; WG) 108min
This is a highly romanticized presentation of psychotic delirium and is derived from a schizophrenic's journal. Whereas many horror films locate the threat to human existence in the rejects of a society – usually depicted as zombies or as gangs of brutalized psychopaths – this movie reverses the cliché and turns the devilish zombies into reincarnations of Christ with which the mad heroine obsessively seeks to merge. In artfully composed images, the agonies of a woman suffering a severe mental breakdown (Stepanek) are used to extol the moral virtues of a strictly visceral form of existence which even the heroine finds intolerable as she repeatedly and in glorious colour fantasizes gory deaths and bloodbaths. In refusing all forms of intelligence and wallowing in the exoticism of hallucinations and misery, the film is one of the few in the genre to invite us to side with the zombies. It forms part of a German fantasy genre – of which perhaps the best-known example is *Christiane F* (1981) – which presents as 'authentic experience' the mental or physical self-mutilations of those who have been mentally crippled.

d/p/co-s Helma Sanders-Brahms *co-s* Rita G *c* Thomas Mauch *lp* Elisabeth Stepanek, Hubertus von Weyraunch, Irmgard Mellinger, Carola Regnier, Nguyen Chi Danh, Erich Koitzch-Koltzack

The Boogens (TAFT INTERNATIONAL) 95min
In the manner of many other contemporary exercises in the genre, this low-budget undertaking, which proves to be almost as dreary as its title, centres on a past calamity haunting the present. The setting is a Colorado silvermine which is being reopened for the first time since a mysterious cave-in 70 years before. This eventually proves to have been caused by boogens, mysteriously scaly creatures of unexplained origin; needless to say, once their habitat is disturbed, they set about a renewed round of death-dealing. The monsters are tolerably well engineered, but aren't satisfactorily integrated by Conway into the largely incoherent plot. Much of the running-time is taken up with inane backchat between the two young engineers (McCarren and Harlan) involved in the project and their equally charmless girlfriends (Balding and Martin). There is, however, some consolation in Martin and Harlan falling prey to the boogens before the creatures are entombed once and for all by a handy charge of dynamite. By comparison with this film, the otherwise nondescript **My Bloody Valentine** (1981), which put a coalmine setting to atmospheric use, looks positively inspired.

d James L. Conway *p* Charles E. Sellier Jnr *s* David O'Malley, Bob Hunt *c* Paul Hipp *se* Jon Reeves, Doug Kramer, William Munns, Ken Horn *lp* Rebecca Balding, Fred McCarren, Anne-Marie Martin, Jeff Harlan, John Crawford, Jon Lormer

Campsite Massacre *aka* **The Final Terror**
(WATERSHED COMPANY) 84min
Set in California's Redwood national park, this standardized low-budget shocker is unmistakably derivative of **Friday the 13th** (1980). A group of young rangers and their girlfriends go on a canoeing trip accompanied by a sinister handyman (Pantoliano): it transpires that the latter was the offspring of a crazed rape victim (Maccario), who now lives wild in the woods, preying on campers. A lethal game of hide-and-seek ensues, though the body count is lower than in most examples of the genre, with only Metcalf and Harrell being murdered until the conclusion, in which the most aggressive of the rangers (Friedrich) – insistently characterized as a Vietnam veteran – dies along with the wild woman in a trap which the group have constructed. The film acquires a marginal retrospective interest for the early appearances by stars-to-be Rachel Ward and Daryl Hannah.

d Andrew Davis *p* Joe Roth *s* Jon George, Neill Hicks, Ronald Shusett *c* Andreas Davidescu *lp* John Friedrich, Adrian Zmed, Joe Pantoliano, Tony Maccario, Ernest Harden Jnr, Mark Metcalf, Akousa Busia, Lewis Smith, Cindy Harrell, Irene Sanders

Cannibal Ferox *aka* **Make Them Die Slowly**
(DANIA FILM/MEDUSA/NATIONAL CINEMATOGRAFICA; IT) 93(87)min
Following the pattern set by **Cannibal Holocaust** (1979) and his own **Mangiati Vivi** (1980), Lenzi here dispatches two attractive college girls and a boyfriend to Colombia in search of evidence to prove that cannibalism is a myth perpetrated by the whites.

In the jungle, they encounter a demented drug dealer who is revealed to have gruesomely tortured local indians. The 'natives' then return to wreak brutal and even more gruesome revenge upon the white party, castrating the drug dealer and hanging up one of the women with hooks through her breasts – as in *A Man Called Horse* (1969) – before finally eating them. Only the heroine (de Selle) escapes and, back in New York, receives her PhD with all references to cannibalism suitably passed over in silence. The direction is routine and concentrates on providing the target audience with the sickening thrills it expects. Like most of the other contributions to the series, the film tries to escape accusations of racism by stressing that the ferocity of the savages is 'merely' a response to savagery perpetrated by whites: except, of course, that the white savagery is assumed or quickly passed over, while that of the 'natives' forms the highlight and climax of the picture. The porn actor, Bolla, makes a brief appearance as a New York police lieutenant, which is only the trace of inspiration in the film.

d/s Umberto Lenzi *p* Antonio Crescenzi *c* Giovanni Bergamini *se* Gino de Rossi *lp* Lorraine de Selle, John Morghen, Bryan Redford, Zora Kerova, Venantino Venantin, Robert Kerman, John Bartha, Walter Lloyd, Meg Fleming, Richard Bolla

Dawn of the Mummy
(HARMONY GOLD; US,IT,EGYPT) 88min
The only gore mummy film to date, *Dawn of the Mummy* certainly lives up to expectations created by the Romero-esque title, even if only in the amount of blood and guts on display. The familiar storyline concerns an Egyptian royal personage who is entombed around 3000BC with his entire retinue of slaves, and the picture's tone is set right from the start with a

Deadly Blessing, *Wes Craven's rural gothic essay.*

Walerian Borowczyk's Docteur Jekyll et les Femmes.

detailed scene of organ-removal as part of the mummification process. When the tomb is desecrated by three present-day graverobbers, the mummy and his slaves run amok: their victims include a group of female American models working on an Egyptian photo-spread for a New York fashion magazine. The film was begun by Armand Weston until its producer also took over as director and is completely undistinguished.

d/p/co-s Frank Agrama *co-s* Daria Price, Ronald Dobrin *c* Sergio Rubini *se* Marizio Trani *lp* Brenda King, Barry Sattels, George Peck, John Salvo, Joan Levy, Diane Beatty

Dead Kids *aka* **Strange Behaviour**
(SOUTH STREET AUSTRALIA/HEMDALE/FAY RICHWHITE; NZ) scope 105min
Although shot on the north island of New Zealand, this film is set in the American mid-West where a series of bizarre stabbings is traced to the science department of the local college. Dignam – the Australian actor who had played the sinister doctor in Jim Sharman's **Summer of Secrets** (1976) – is the villain, while Murphy does the investigating. The prolific Ginnane worked with David Hemmings, who here is executive producer, on **Thirst** (1979) and *Turkey Shoot* (1981). His other exploitation picture credits include **The Survivor** and **Harlequin** (both 1980), but *Dead Kids*, courtesy of Laughlin's direction, must count as one of their most professional efforts.

d/co-s Michael Laughlin *p* Antony I. Ginnane, John Barnett *co-s* William Condon *c* Louis Horvath *se* Craig Reardon *lp* Michael Murphy, Louise Fletcher, Dan Shor, Fiona Lewis, Arthur Dignam, Scott Brady, Dey Young, Marc McClure, Beryl Te Wiata

Deadly Blessing
(INTER PLANETARY) 102(98) min
With this film Craven forsakes gore for suspense and essays – largely successfully – a relatively untapped subgenre, American rural gothic. Barr and Jensen are the married couple whose farm borders a fanatical Hittite community. One night Barr, an ex-Hittite now shunned by the rest for moving away, goes outside to find the word 'incubus' painted on his barn and is crushed to death by his own tractor. A bizarre series of murders begins, perpetrated, it seems, by Hartman, a hermaphrodite neighbour with a desperate desire to exclude anyone else from Jensen's life. At the last moment, however, an incubus suddenly erupts through the floorboards and whisks Jensen away to perdition.

The attempt at gothic is helped enormously by Borgnine's particularly threatening performance and a scene in which Jensen is unaware she is sharing her bath with a snake is milked for all the suspense it is worth, as is another girl's experience in a locked barn with an unseen but threatening intruder. Farmyard inhabitants also play a menacing role and a dream scene in which a spider falls into a girl's open mouth recalls the famous chisel nightmare in **The Last House on the Left** (1972). The fact that most of the scenes of terror take place in broad daylight and attractive surroundings also makes for a refreshing change from the old-dark-house format. The meeting of two irreconcilable ways of life is neatly developed and the series of oppositions and divisions on which the narrative is hinged find their apogee in the figure of Hartman. For a moment it really looks as if the film is going to lay bare the 'trouble' – the notion of bisexuality – which fuels, albeit in a covert and highly displaced, mediated fashion, the narrative of so many horror films. In the end, however, the supernatural is invoked instead.

Bizarrely, after the film was shown to the British critics, the distributors removed the arrival of the incubus, one of the very few instances, surely, in which commercial interference has increased rather than lessened a film's disturbing, subversive potential.

d/co-s Wes Craven *p* Micheline Keller, Max Keller, Pat Herskovic *co-s* Glenn M. Benest, Matthew Barr *c* Robert Jessup *se* Jack Bennett *lp* Maren Jensen, Susan Buckner, Sharon Stone, Jeff East, Lisa Hartman, Lois Nettleton, Ernest Borgnine, Coleen Riley, Doug Barr, Michael Berryman

Docteur Jekyll et les Femmes *aka* **The Blood of Doctor Jekyll** *aka* **Doctor Jekyll and Miss Osbourne**
(WHODUNIT PRODUCTIONS/ALLEGRO PRODUCTIONS/MULTIMEDIA; FR) 92(90)min
An expatriate Pole who made a stunning start in features (*Goto, l'Ile d'Amour*, 1969; *Blanche*, 1972) after a distinguished contribution to animation films, Borowczyk seems to have been driven ever deeper into the porn-exploitation ghetto since revealing his sympathies in *Une Collection Particulière* (1974), a superbly witty short about the more curious aspects of Victorian erotica. His characteristically idiosyncratic interpretation of Stevenson's novella – Mr Hyde (Kier) and Jekyll's fiancée depart together into the sunset after an orgy of killing, ecstatically lapping the blood that streams from each other's bodies – would undoubtedly have been a lot better had he not felt obliged to play the exploitation game by providing a tediously repetitive surfeit of rapes, murders, mutilations and perversions. Even so, Borowczyk's imagery, here fed by his fetishistic fascination with all things antiquarian, is often stunning and the film becomes a sort of still life in which familiar yet alien objects – an ancient dictaphone, a treadle sewing-machine, a book of remembrance – seem imbued with a secret significance all their own, and in which a glimpse of a whalebone corset or ruffled petticoat carries a heady whiff of eroticism.

d/s Walerian Borowczyk *p* Robert Kupferberg, Jean-Pierre Labrande *c* Noël Véry *lp* Udo Kier, Marina Pierro, Patrick Magee, Howard Vernon, Clément Harari

...E Tu Vivrai nel Terrore! L'Aldila *aka* **L'Aldila** *aka* **And You'll Live in Terror! The Beyond** *aka* **The Beyond**
(FULVIA FILM; IT) scope 90(86)min
Due particularly to the special makeup effects by de Rossi, who worked also on **No Profanar el Sueño de los Muertos** (1974), this is a film of considerable gruesomeness. Like Fulci's **Zombi 2** (1979) it belongs to a cycle of Italian movies sparked off by the success of George Romero's *Zombies* (1978), but also uses a two-part construction – the prologue is set in the 1920s, the main action in the present day – which echoes the different vein of American horror movies represented by **Halloween** (1978). As with several other Italian horror films of the same period, such as **Macabro** (1980) and Fulci's own **Quella Villa Accanto al Cimitero** (1981), the action is set in America, in this case Louisiana. The plot centres on a remote hotel which stands on one of the seven entrances to hell (the notion of a physical

doorway to hell echoes **The Sentinel**, 1976), through which, according to a sinister prophecy, the dead will on the appointed day issue forth to walk the earth. At the climax, the woman who has inherited the hotel (MacColl) and her helpmate (Warbeck) fight off a horde of the walking dead only to find themselves incarcerated in hell itself, the landscape of which has been foreshadowed in a painting on which the former manager of the hotel was working when he was seized and crucified as a satanist in the prologue. The intermediate plotting is even more random than in *Quella Villa Accanto al Cimitero*, but the setpieces, which include the supernatural manifestation of a mass of venomous spiders, are handled with undeniable gusto.

d/co-s Lucio Fulci *p* Fabrizio de Angelis *s* Giorgio Mariuzzo, Dardano Sacchetti *c* Sergio Salvati *se* Germano Natali, Gianetto de Rossi *lp* Katherine MacColl, David Warbeck, Sarah Keller, Antoine Saint John, Veronica Lazar, Anthony Flees, Giovanni de Nava, Michele Mirabella, Al Cliver (Pier Luigi Conti)

Estigma *aka* **Stigma**
(YANTRA CINEMATOGRAFICA/BALCAZAR; IT, SP) 94min
A male variation on **Carrie** (1976) with echoes of **The Fury** (1978) added for good measure, in which Sebastian (Borromeo) discovers at puberty that he has the ability to kill people by thought-power. Initially disturbed by the rumblings in his psyche, which terrify a medium (Liné) he accidentally encounters, he learns to use them and kills his brother out of jealousy for his girlfriend, Ana (Bastedo). Eventually he learns that he is the reincarnation of a boy who slaughtered his entire family and disheartened, no doubt at the loss of the sense of uniqueness, he kills Bastedo and commits suicide. Larraz's tame direction can't rescue a movie that appears too anxious to cram in scenes and motifs from recent box-office successes without worrying about the adolescent fantasy logic that underpins its models and gives them their coherence as fear-of-women movies. Larraz went on to make more explicit sex movies, including **Los Ritos Sexuales del Diablo** (1981).

d/s José Ramón Larraz *p* Jesús Balcazar *c* Giuseppe Bernardini *lp* Christian Borromeo, Alexandra Bastedo, Helga Liné, Emilio Gutierrez Caba, Irene Gutierrez Caba

Fear No Evil *aka* **Mark of the Beast**
(LA LOGGIA PRODUCTIONS) 99min
One of the most impressive demonic-possession films since **Rosemary's Baby** (1968) and certainly a great deal more interesting than the much-trumpeted **The Exorcist** (1973), *Fear No Evil* may borrow heavily from these and other precursors such as **Carrie** (1976), **The Omen** (1976) and **Night of the Living Dead** (1968) but does so in a manner wholly its own, one that is all the more remarkable since it was its writer/director/co-producer's first feature and cost a mere $1,500,000 – quite remarkable considering the complexity of some of the special effects.

The story has Andrew (Arngrim), a quiet, intense high-school student who gradually realizes not simply that he has supernatural powers but that he is the Devil incarnate. Whilst he is gradually coming to appreciate his newfound prowess, his classmate Julie (McAllen) and an old woman, (Hoffman) discover that they are, respectively, Gabrielle and Mikhail, the two angels sent to defeat Lucifer. A tremendous physical and spiritual struggle ensues in which Lucifer is finally defeated. At a time when the genre had become dominated by maniacs and psychopaths of one kind or another and Evil wins out with monotonous and cynical regularity, *Fear No Evil*, with its uncompromisingly metaphysical/supernatural concerns and its determination to see God ultimately triumphant, makes a refreshing, surprising and pleasant change. Strikingly directed and photographed, the film also benefits from excellent special effects courtesy of Visual Concepts Productions, whose work was seen in *The Empire Strikes Back* (1980), *Battlestar Galactica* (1979) and *The Dark* (1979). A fascinating début.

d/co-p/s Frank La Loggia *co-p* Charles M. La Loggia *c* Fred Goodich *se* Peter Kuran, Susan Turner, Robert Brown, John Eggett, Jon Seay, Jerome Seven *lp* Stefan Arngrim, Elizabeth Hoffman, Kathleen Rowe McAllen, Frank Birney, Daniel Eden, Jack Holland, Barry Cooper, Alice Sachs, Paul Haber, Richard Jay Silverthorn

The Final Conflict (FOX) pv 108min
The third and final film in the series started by **The Omen** (1976) and continued in **Damien – Omen II** (1978), *The Final Conflict* continues the story of the Antichrist, Damien (Neill) now aged 32. The head of a multinational corporation, as was his uncle in *Damien*, he is also US ambassador to Britain, as was his father in *The Omen*. He has assumed the latter post, having willed the 'suicide' of the former incumbent (Arden), because he has divined that the second coming of Christ will take place in England. This does indeed finally occur and, in a histrionic conclusion, full of lighting effects, the Evil One dies at the feet of his opposite number. In fact, he's been stabbed by a woman journalist (Harrow) whom he has seduced and whose son (Holm) has been killed as a result of her involvement with him. The weapon she uses is one of the seven daggers of Megiddo, the ritual instruments which have the power to destroy the Antichrist. Before this, the plot has concerned itself with the group of priests, headed by Brazzi, who are seeking to use the daggers to finish off Damien, an enterprise that causes the deaths of all but two of them, and with Damien's preparations for holding sway, which include an order to his disciples to kill every male baby born on the projected day of the return of Christ.

Like *Damien*, the film does not paint a very persuasive picture of how the forces of Satan might practically set about subverting world order, and this shortcoming is compounded by the script's gestures towards a serious consideration of the theological issues involved – something the melodramatic terms of reference can hardly accommodate.

d Graham Baker *p* Harvey Bernhard *s* Andrew Birkin *c* Robert Paynter, Phil Meheux *se* Ian Wingrove *lp* Sam Neill, Rosanno Brazzi, Lisa Harrow, Don Gordon, Barnaby Holm, Mason Adams, Robert Arden, Tommy Duggan, Marc Boyle, Richard Oldfield, Arwen Holm

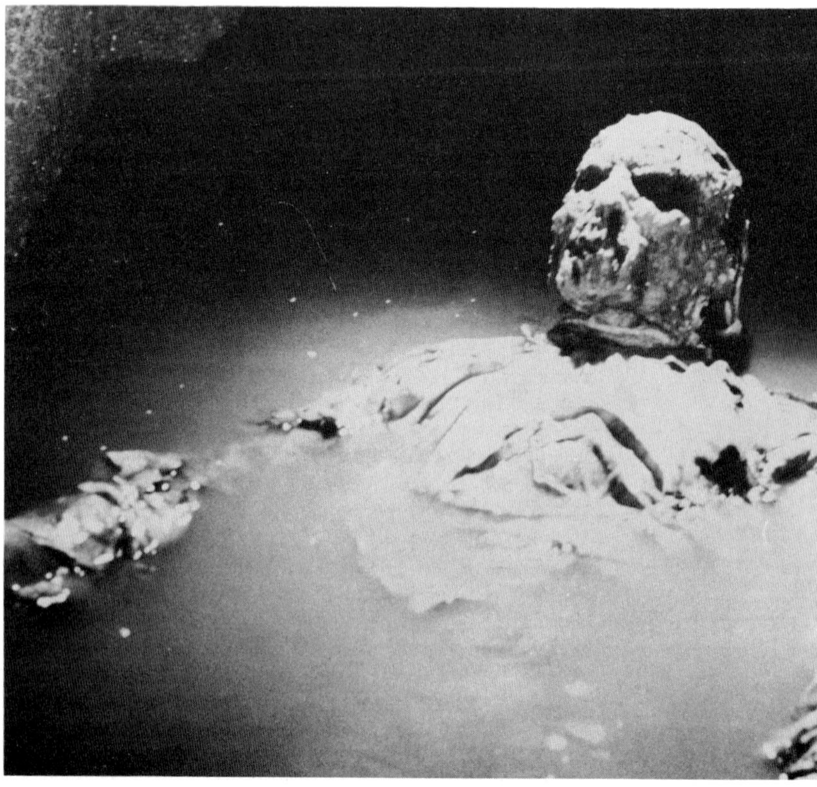

Gianetto de Rossi's gruesome make-up for ...E Tu Vivrai nel Terrore! L'Aldila.

Richard Jay Silverthorn as Leviathin in the impressive Fear No Evil.

Forfölgelsen *aka* The Witch Hunt

(NORSK FILM/SVENSKA FILM INSTITUTET; NOR,SW) 93min
This is the first costume picture by Breien, best known for her consciousness-raising bittersweet comedy *Hustruer* (1975). The story, set in 1625 when Denmark ruled Norway, tells of Eli (Terselius), a lively, independent-minded woman who returns to her native village after a long absence, and strikes up a relationship with a respected but weak farmworker, Aslak (Skagestad), which transgresses the restrictive conventions of the rural community. The villain, a bailiff (Mörk), selects Terselius as the scapegoat on whom all the local misfortunes can be blamed and, in spite of a courageous intervention by the mistress of a big farm (Bjork), once the bailiff sets the wheels of legalized religious superstition in motion, Terselius's fate is sealed from the moment she is labelled a witch. The film is shot as a rather academic TV drama and the surfeit of closeups framing anguished faces and meaningful looks help to reinforce the anachronistic account of witchcraft, superimposing late-20th-century psychological realism and notions of individualism on to the early-17th-century figures. Although strong on indignation, the movie sadly doesn't illuminate the socio-historical forces which governed people's lives and shaped their ways of thinking at the time. As a result, it lacks any explanatory force and blames witchcraft trials on the timeless evil inherent in men, with wonderfully warm and independent women as their uncomprehending victims.

d/s Anja Breien *c* Erling Thurman-Andersen *lp* Lil Terselius, Björn Skagestad, Anita Bjork, Erik Mörk

Friday the 13th Part 2

(GEORGETOWN PRODUCTIONS) 87min
A follow-up to the box-office success of **Friday the 13th** (1980), directed by the previous movie's executive producer, *Part 2* is more of a remake than a sequel. A somewhat arbitrary prologue shows the sole survivor (King) of the massacre in the previous film being killed by an unseen assailant. The action then moves on five years to a site near to Camp Crystal Lake, scene of the first film, where a group of students are assembling for a counsellor-training course. The organizer (Furey) assures them that they should pay no heed to tales of a 'wild' man loose in the woods. Naturally, the stories are only too well-founded: the marauder is Jason (Gillette), whose mother had perpetrated the earlier killings believing him to have been drowned. After butchering a policeman (Marks), who has found a cache of bodies at his secret hide-out, Gillette makes his way to the camp and proceeds to murder all six of the students remaining there while the rest are off at the town bar. When Furey and his girlfriend (Steel) return to camp, they are duly attacked: Furey, left for dead, recovers in time to save Steel, but later – in a muddled ending – Jason seems to return from the dead and launch a further onslaught.

The closing scene – Furey seemingly dead and a distraught Steel being escorted away by the police – leaves the way open for a further sequel, **Friday the 13th Part III** (1982), which was followed in turn by **Friday the 13th – The Final Chapter** (1984). Although *Part 2* is rather more skilfully assembled than its predecessor, the plotting is scarcely more original and the film as a whole has, to say the least, a statutory air about it.

d/p Steve Miner *s* Ron Kurz *c* Peter Stein *se* Carl Fullerton *lp* Amy Steel, John Furey, Adrienne King, Kirsten Baker, Stu Charno, Warrington Gillette, Walt Gorney, Marta Kober, Bill Randolph, Jack Marks

The Funhouse

(MACE NEUFELD PRODUCTIONS) pv 96min
Though marked by the same anarchic blend of black humour and horror comic violence, this is disappointingly ragged by comparison with **The Texas Chainsaw Massacre** (1974). Two teenage couples daringly elect to spend the night in a sleazy carnival funhouse, and are paid out for their 'permissive' sins – lovemaking, disobedience, petty theft – by finding a real murderous monster among the freakish exhibits. As in the earlier film, a normal family (parents watching **The Bride of Frankenstein**, 1935, on TV, kids paying them no heed) is contrasted with an abnormal one (father, mutant son, baby exhibited as a freak show foetus), but it all seems pretty arbitrary and makes only obvious capital out of the setting. The best thing about the film is the way the Dolby soundtrack is used to dislocatory ends.

d Tobe Hooper *p* Derek Power, Steven Bernhardt *s* Larry Block *c* Andrew Laszlo *lp* Elizabeth Berridge, Cooper Huckabee, Miles Chapin, Largo Woodruff, Shawn Carlson

Il Gatto Nero *aka* The Black Cat *aka* Il Gatto di Park Lane

(SELENIA CINEMATOGRAFICA; IT) scope 91(88)min
After filming the entrail-ridden zombie outings **Zombi 2** (1979) and **Paura nella Citta dei Morti Viventi** (1980), Fulci returned to the gothic with this Poe-inspired tale that repeats many aspects of his **Sette Note in Nero** (1977), including its ending as the heroine (Farmer) is immured alive. The plot is set in an English village where a mysterious Mr Miles (Magee in one of his last roles) wanders through the foggy cemetery trying to record messages from the dead. A detective (Warbeck) arrives to investigate a series of nasty murders, but it is Farmer, playing an American photographer, who realizes the link between Magee and his black cat, which commits the murders, leaving the odd paw-print on a wall or in the ground. Magee, in seemingly endless closeups intercut with similar shots of the cat, fights the feline for control but loses. Farmer, who assumed Miles was the real villain exercising hypnotic control over the poor cat, pays the price for her naïvety in an ironic ending.

The tale echoes themes from Poe, but with the exception of a few atmospheric cemetery scenes and the occasional judicious use of crane shots and high angles, Fulci's direction is uninspired, with an over-reliance on tight shots of eyes. He dismissed this low-budget effort, claiming he merely agreed to do it to keep his hand in, but the film shows that he is basically a realist director whose work derives its impact from what others put in front of Salvati's camera (gore and gruesomely made up figures). His next films, **... E Tu Vivrai nel Terrore! L'Aldila** and **Quella Villa Accanto del Cimitero** (both 1981), again rely on Grand Guignol setpieces arranged by Gianetto de Rossi and Germano Natali.

d/co-s Lucio Fulci *p* Giulio Sbarigia *co-s* Biagio Proietti *c* Sergio Salvati *se* Paolo Ricci *lp* Mimsy Farmer, Patrick Magee, David Warbeck, Dagmar Lassander, Daniela Doro, Al Cliver (Pier Luigi Conti), Bruno Corazzari, Geoffrey Copleston

Geburt der Hexe *aka* **The Birth of the Witch**
(JOCHEN RICHTER PRODUKTION/ZDF/SRG; WG,SWITZ) 95min
This highly schematic terror-morality play is set in a small medieval Castilian village and tells of a peasant woman (Berkewicz) who turns to Satan, transgressing the boundaries of life as prescribed by the State and the Church. Both the people and the aristocrats persecute her as a witch but when the local lords actually execute her, the peasants get very angry and take bloody revenge on the lords of the manor, posthumously revering the woman as a saint. Shot on location and using many non-professionals, the movie works with archetypes: the woman, the priest (Boehlke), the Lord (Pable), the peasants, and so on. Inspired by kitschy black and white paintings and drawings, Minks' picture presents a naïve account of the social causes of witchcraft which is both more pretentious and far less cinematic than Michael Reeves' impressive **The Witchfinder General** (1968). Minks is better known as a theatrical art director and has worked with Rainer Werner Fassbinder and other notable directors. Anja Breien's treatment of the subject, **Forfölgelsen** (1981), inspired by Dreyer's approach to superstitious cruelty, offers an equally indignant account of witchcraft trials but her feminist slant is more convincing.

d/s Wilfried Minks *p/c* Jochen Richter *lp* Ulla Berkewicz, Friedrich Karl Praetorius, Edgar M. Boehlke, Anja Silja, Lis Pitsos, Gonzalo Abril Vega, G. Pabel

Ghost Story (U) 110min
This is a lifeless adaptation of Peter Straub's novel about the legacy of social and sexual repression in a small New England town which has left four old men haunted by the memory of a youthful indiscretion that resulted in the death of a supposedly free-and-easy girl. Despite the atmospherics – the town locked in the icy grip of winter, the four old men exorcizing their fears by the telling of ghost stories – the film is without a real atmosphere, since all the subtlety of Straub's novel has gone. In its place, Irvin puts only the jumbled bones of a plot as the girl's spirit returns, alternating a face of beauty with one of rotting flesh, to exact revenge (even to a second generation) on the quartet. A conventional movie monster despite Krige's excellent performance, her ghostly presence never even begins to suggest the irresistible eruption of repressed forces that was the point of Straub's novel. Saddled with pedestrian direction in addition to a script littered with loose ends and extraneous characters, the film is remarkable chiefly in eliciting performances of embarrassing creakiness from its cast of seasoned veterans.

d John Irvin *p* Burt Weissbourd *s* Lawrence D. Cohen *c* Jack Cardiff *lp* Fred Astaire, Melvyn Douglas, Douglas Fairbanks Jnr, John Houseman, Craig Wasson, Patricia Neal, Alice Krige

Graduation Day
(BEDFORD PRODUCTIONS) scope 85min
The only point of originality in this film is that its orchestration of gory events was presided over by a woman, Rockow. Basically another **Halloween** (1978) derived body-count movie this one has an unidentified killer stalking members of a high-school track team. Fittingly, one member gets her throat cut while jogging, another is killed by a football with a spear attached, and yet another pole vaults into a bed of sharp spikes. Direction, script and acting are all routine.

d/co-p/co-s Herbert Freed *co-p* David Baughn *co-s* Anne Marisse *c* Daniel Yarussi *se* Jill Rockow *lp* Christopher George, Patch MacKenzie, E. Danny Murphy, E. J. Peaker

Gu *aka* **Bewitched**
(SHAW BROTHERS; HONG KONG) 98(93)min
Gui's highly successful, although erratically directed, gore thriller continues his attempts to mix magic, horror and thriller elements into a commercially viable formula (in the manner of **Shi Yao**, 1981); this time, however, the results are not as interesting as in his beauty-and-the-scholar picture **Xie** (1980). In Bangkok, a tourist (Ai Fei) from Hong Kong befriends a Thai girl (Chan) who casts a spell on him. Each full moon exercises a strange effect on him and he subsequently kills his daughter. Caught and sentenced to death, he tries to defend himself by claiming he was acting under the influence of an evil spell. Investigating this claim in Thailand, a police inspector (Wong) also comes under the fateful spell and, realizing what is happening to him, he calls in a high monk to perform an exorcism. The last scene, in which the monk fights and defeats the spell, allows Gui to draw on a battery of ritualistic effects which update the plethora of palm-power movies he made in the fifties and sixties. The sequel to this picture is **Mo** (1983).

d/co-s Gui Zhihong (Kwei Chih-hung, Kuei Chi-Hung) *p* Mona Fong (Fang Xihua) *co-s* Szu-Tu an (Situ an, Szeto An) *c* Li Hsin Yeh (Li Sun Ip, Li Xinye) *lp* Ai Fei, Melvin Wong (Kam Sun), Fen Ni (Fanny), Chen Lili (Lily Chan)

Gui da Gui *aka* **Encounter of the Spooky Kind** *aka* **Ghost against Ghost**
(BO HO FILM/GOLDEN HARVEST; HONG KONG) 119(98)min
Named after a well-known comic-strip character, Samo Hung, the plump but very agile martial arts actor/director was a child actor before becoming martial arts instructor and a supporting actor in a number of films by King Hu and others. He made his directorial début with *San De Hesheng Yu Chongmi Liu* (1977) and found box-office success with *Feilong Guojiang* (1978).

A chauffeur suspects that his wife is having an affair with his employer, so the boss engages a shaman to kill him by invoking various spirits. The film then culminates in a fierce fight in which the Monkey King and other gods as well as the shaman and his accomplices are defeated. The husband survives to beat his wife upon her return. While the film at times might be regarded as more comic than horrific, it is indicative of the essential shifts in tone which characterize much of the work in the genre in the contemporary Hong Kong cinema. Hung's sixth feature, it is considerably more sophisticated than his earlier efforts which tend towards martial arts slapstick. Its linking of the tragic with the supernatural and the use of genuine moments of terror – an overnight stay at a temple spent warding off corpses, for example – marks a maturity in Hung's work, confirmed by the wonderfully inventive comic-strip movie *Baijiazai* (1981) which he directed, and by his performance in Wu Ma's *The Dead and the Deadly* (1983).

d/co-s Samo Hung (Hung Kam-bo, Hong Jinbao) *p* Raymond Chow (Zou Wenhuai), Chan Pui-wah, Liu Chi-chung *co-s* Huang Ying *c* Ng Cho-wah, Lee Yau-tong *lp* Samo Hung, Cheung Fat, Chan Lung, Wong Har, Lam Cheng-Ying, Chang Ti-chiang

Douglas Fairbanks Jnr in Ghost Story.

Right: *Another corpse is discovered in* Hell Night.

Halloween II (DINO DE LAURENTIIS) pv 92min
The homicidal maniac of **Halloween** (1978) returns, this time to strew corpses around the hospital where Curtis is receiving treatment. She survives again, having at last learned that he is the little brother who killed their elder sister (in the prologue to *Halloween*). Thanks to Cundey's camerawork, the film *looks* much like its predecessor but is actually just another imitation (though better than most, no doubt because Carpenter supervised as well as co-scripting). The fact that there was nothing more to be had out of the story – unless by a cinematic intelligence the equivalent of Carpenter's – is amply demonstrated by the way the film can't wait to bring its murders to the forefront and regale the audience with gory helpings of stalk-and-slash.

d Rick Rosenthal *p/s* Debra Hill, John Carpenter *c* Dean Cundey *lp* Jamie Lee Curtis, Donald Pleasance, Charles Cyphers, Jeffrey Kramer, Lance Guest

The Hand (EDWARD R. PRESSMAN/IXTLAN) 104min
Caine is the strip cartoonist, already beset by marital problems, whose frustrations pile up when he loses his drawing hand in a car accident. Since the camera promptly starts lurking at floor level, it comes as no surprise when the severed hand (oddly accompanied by sounds of heavy breathing on the soundtrack) returns to do his subconscious bidding. Ineptly animated and given the full monster treatment, the murderous hand lacks the flesh-crawling horror of its more matter-of-fact ancestor in **The Beast with Five Fingers** (1946), and becomes simply absurd when (looking rather like a limp rubber glove) it topples full-grown adversaries to strangle them. As unsubtle as his scripts for *Midnight Express* (1978) and *Conan the Barbarian* (1981), Stone's adaptation of Marc Brandel's coolly reasoned novel (*The Lizard's Tail*) simply screws the hysteria to boiling point. An epilogue obviously modelled on **Psycho** (1960) – Caine giggling madly as a psychiatrist (Lindfors) is strangled by the hand even as she pronounces it to be imaginary – is perhaps the film's lowest point. Stone, now better known for *Platoon* (1986) and *Wall Street* (1987), made his horror début with **Seizure** (1973).

d/s Oliver Stone *p* Edward R. Pressman *c* King Baggot *lp* Michael Caine, Andrea Marcovicci, Annie McEnroe, Bruce McGill, Viveca Lindfors

Hannyo *aka* **Revenge of the Ghost**
(DONG HYOUP CORPORATION; ROK) 80min
Lee here combines the traditional vengeful-ghost story with European mad-plastic-surgeon motifs and sets the movie in a decidedly Europeanized Seoul of the thirties, throwing in Jack the Ripper overtones for good measure. The plot concerns an unsavoury medic who abducts women as raw material for operations to restore the beauty of a businessman's disfigured girlfriend. The ghostly elements are provided by the destructive flute-playing spectre of the surgeon's wife, poisoned by her husbnad. As in **Yo** (1981), it emerges that she hadn't died after all and is intent on a bloody revenge. The story is both awkward and full of undigested stereotypes which fit oddly into their inappropriate setting, although the rich woman married to and victimized by a neurotic, unworthy man is a familiar pair in transparently oedipal Korean narratives.

d Lee Yoo Sub *p* Kim Chi Han *s* Kim Young Han *c* Chung Kwang Suk *lp* Choi Suk, Lim Chung Ha

Hell Night (BLT PRODUCTIONS) 102min
Yablans produced **Halloween** (1978) and this is very much in the manner of the cycle spawned by that film. It is, however, a fairly creditable addition to the genre. A group of college freshers (Blair, Van Patten, Barton and Goodwin) have to undergo an initiation test by spending the night in a mansion still supposedly frequented by the sole survivor of a massacre in which a man killed his wife and three of his four deformed

children, then committed suicide. Older students (Brophy, Neumann and Sturtevant) attempt to scare their juniors with spook devices, but they are themselves polished off by one of what prove to be two marauders – the father is still alive – and by the end only Blair remains alive. In a spectacular finale, the mutant son is killed when, after jumping on to the roof of the car in which Blair is escaping, he is hurled off it and impaled on a spike-topped wall. Despite a number of holes in the plot (the bodies seem to have been left at the scene of the crime following the original massacre), the film is quite atmospherically handled by de Simone, with a strong performance from Blair, of **The Exorcist** (1973) fame, and elegant camerawork by Ahlberg.

d Tom de Simone *p* Irwin Yablans, Bruce Cohn Curtis *s* Randolph Feldman *c* Mac Ahlberg *lp* Linda Blair, Vincent Van Patten, Peter Barton, Kevin Brophy, Jenny Neumann, Suki Goodwin, Jimmy Sturtevant, Hal Ralston, Cary Fox, Ronald Gans

Humongous (HUMONGOUS PRODUCTIONS) 85min
Five teenagers on a weekend spree are shipwrecked on an island on which, 36 years before, a man was torn apart by the German shepherd dogs of the woman he had raped. One by one the teenagers are killed by a seven-foot-tall mutant.

Humongous is from the same writer-director team as **Prom Night** (1980) and displays neither logic, humanity, invention or imagination. The kids are treated as characterless cannon fodder and the director's flashy mannerisms (tilted camera angles and images obscured by dirty glass, bannisters and the like) are no subsititute for a genuine sense of style.

d Paul Lynch *p* Anthony Kramreither *s* William Gray *c* Brian R. R. Hebb *se* Martin Malivoire *lp* Janet Julian, David Wallace, John Wildman, Janet Baldwin, Joy Boushel, Layne Coleman, Shay Garner, Page Fletcher, John McFadyen, Garry Robbins

Huphyokwi Yanyo *aka* **The Vengeful Vampire Girl**
(HAN JIN ENTERPRISES; ROK) 96min
Set in the Korean middle ages, the story presents a traditional tale previously filmed by Korea's most important horror director, Park Yoon Kyo as **Myonuriui Han** (1971). Played for maximum shock effect, the film deploys a battery of standard

visual devices such as glowing blue lightning, dripping blood and a hissing soundtrack. A woman is raped by a wealthy governor but commits suicide during her ordeal by biting off her tongue and bleeding to death. She becomes a vampire ten years later when a couple of graverobbers dig her up, enabling her to achieve her revenge. However, she is finally killed by the governor's son, an expert martial artist who learns a secret method of killing vampires from a high priest. Uneven in tone, the movie oscillates between pure schlock and more seriously gruesome scenes, typifying the routine South Korean approach to the genre. Kim's previous horror fantasy, **Wolnyoui Han** (1980), also scripted by Lee, is an altogether more satisfactory effort.

d Kim In Soo *p* Han Kap Chin *s* Lee Moon Woong *c* Koo Choong Mo *lp* Choi Bong, Chong Hi Jung

Incubus

(GUARDIAN TRUST COMPANY; CAN) 92min

Incubus, a late entrant in the demonology cycle sparked off by **The Exorcist** (1973), is an adaptation of a novel by Ray Russell, about an incubus – a demon capable of assuming human form – who commits a series of murders in a small Californian town. In the novel, the incubus possesses an enormous phallus and sexually attacks its victims, a factor which, not surprisingly (even in the climate of 1981), is played down in the movie. Cassavetes and Ireland are the doctor and cop on the trail of the creature, and the plot quite intriguingly disentangles the dark history of the town's first family as their investigation proceeds. In the rather statutory twist ending, Cassavetes disposes of the apparently guilty party (McIntosh) only to discover that all is not what is seems and that his own lover (Keane) is really the incubus and has just killed his daughter (Flannery). Though Hough's direction is quite energetic in a mechanical fashion and Cassavetes provides a hard-working performance, the film is ultimately constricted by its formula-bound script.

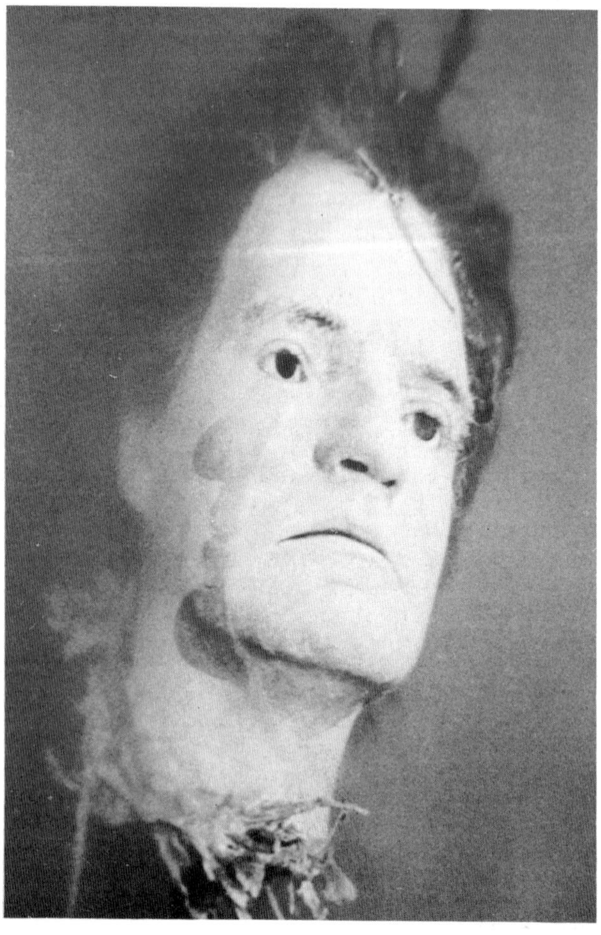

d John Hough *p* Marc Boyman, John M. Eckert *s* George Franklin *c* Albert J. Dunk *se* Colin Chilvers *lp* John Cassavetes, Kerrie Keane, John Ireland, Duncan McIntosh, Erin Flannery

Inferno dei Morti-Viventi *aka* Zombie Creeping Flesh *aka* Apocalipsis Canibal *aka* Cannibal Virus *aka* Virus – L'Inferno dei Morti Viventi *aka* Hell of the Living Death *aka* Virus Cannibale

(BEATRICE FILM/FILMS DARA; IT, SP) scope 99(90)min

A rock-bottom addition to the various European spin-offs from George Romero's *Zombies* (1978), such as **Zombi 2** (1979), this ridiculous movie takes place in Papua, where a medical research project goes wrong, turning the local workforce into flesh-eating zombies. A commando team (led by Giraldi) is sent in and manages to rescue some journalists (among them Newton) en route. When they eventually succeed, after numerous zombie attacks, in reaching the research centre, it transpires that the commandos' brief is to suppress the fact that the research was concerned with solving the problem of over-population by cannibalism. The group subsequently themselves fall victims to the zombies, and in a lamely apocalyptic ending, the zombie plague is said to be sweeping the world.

d Vincent Dawn (Bruno Mattei) *p* Sergio Cortona *s* Claudio Fragasso, J. M. Cunilles *c* John Cabrera *lp* Margit Evelyn Newton, Frank Garfield (Franco Giraldi), Selan Karay, Robert O'Neal, Gaby Renom, Luis Fonoll, Piero Fumelli, Patrizia Costa

The Inn of the Flying Dragon *aka* Ondskans Värdshus *aka* The Sleep of Death *aka* L'Auberge du Dragon Volant

(DRAGON CO/ASPEKT FILM/NATIONAL FILM STUDIOS OF IRELAND; SW, EIRE) scope 95(90)min

Rather unexpectedly, considering his weak **Victor Frankenstein** (1977), Floyd's free adaptation of Sheridan LeFanu's story *The Room in the Dragon Volant* is a well-made vampire tale which counts on suggestion and ambiguity to make its points. In 1815, a naïve young nobleman sets out to enjoy his adolescence travelling through Europe. He becomes fascinated by a mysterious beauty (Tolo) who is accompanied by a sinister, elderly man. Their encounter at a French inn leads to weird events: dead bodies are found in alcoves, an old hag dressed in the same black clothes as the beautiful countess appears during the daytime in places where the young beauty is supposed to be, while at night the countess appears as enchantingly youthful as ever, and so on.

The intensely romantic settings include glimpses of an ancient castle, a shadowy inn surrounded by the nocturnal howling of wolves and atmospheric sunsets shot in muted colours. Acting honours go to the brash hussar (Oscarsson) who acts as a catalyst: he is wiser than the hero and remembers that long ago, he too met a black clad woman – an encounter that marked his passage from adolescence to adulthood.

d/co-s Calvin Floyd *p* Rudolf Hertzog *co-s* Yvonne Floyd *c* Jiri Tirl, Tony Forsberg *lp* Per Oscarsson, Patrick Magee, Marilu Tolo, Curt Juergens, Brendan Price, Niall Toibin, Barry Cassins

Jigoku *aka* Inferno

(TOEI; JAP) scope 122min

A remake of Nakagawa's classic **Jigoku** (1960) – and like that film made for domestic consumption – this pushes the deliriously nightmarish images of suffering even further than the original. The strictly Buddhist conception of hell with its 'wheels' representing different levels of time as well as of spiritual life – or death – make for spectacular scope compositions. The basic story is a revenge plot. An adulterous couple have a baby just before being brutally slain by their respective families who want to eradicate the 'dishonour'. The baby grows into a young woman and takes bloody revenge on

Left: *The awful* Humongous.

John Ireland as the policeman of a small town beset by an Incubus.

the murderers of her parents. Starting with a crash during a car race, provoked by the apparition of a headless ghost, deadly events escalate with relentless inevitability until the picture culminates in an eerie depiction of hell with its imagery of torture and pain: severed and impaled limbs, putrefying corpses, bodies torn to shreds, cannibalism, sulphurous cauldrons and scarlet vortices.

d Tatsumi Kumashiro *s* Yozo Tanaka *c* Shigeru Akatsuka *se* Nobuo Yajima *lp* Mieko Harada, Kyoko Kishida, Ryuzo Hayashi, Kunie Tanaka, Renji Ishibashi

Koesi *aka* **Strange Dead Bodies**
(HAN LIM CINEMA CORP; ROK) 90min
This is quite an effective Korean version of **No Profanar el Sueño de los Muertos** (1974) in which scientists experimenting with a new insecticide inadvertently cause the dead to rise from their graves. Heavily laced with melodramic scenes, the picture wastes a lot of time with a single zombie-like figure's persecution of a young couple before settling down to the eerily filmed invasion of the undead as cadavers emerge from tombs and the dead in a hospital morgue come alive. When the heroic couple destroy the scientist's laboratory, they are able to see, in total silence, the cadavers shuffling back to their proper resting places. Unfortunately, the zombie makeup is limited to white greasepaint and red rings around the eyes, most of the horror being derived from the actual rising scenes and from the birth of three deformed children, a motif which suggests a possible analogy between the movie's insecticide and the use by the Americans of Agent Orange in Vietnam. Unfortunately, possibly because of the heavy censorship on South Korea, this motif is dropped as soon as it is introduced.

d Kang Bum Koo *p* Chung So Young *s* Choo Dong Woon *c* Yang Young Kil *lp* Kang Myung, Yoo Kwang Ok

Life After Life (CINEMA CITY; HONG KONG) 98min
After his routinely professional thriller *The System* (1981), cameraman turned director Yung made this supernatural thriller set in the fashion world. The ingenious script has a fashion-show designer, played by the comedy star Lam, discover a set of antique Chinese puppets owned by an old woman who looks after a temple. She agrees to lend them to Lam for a fashion show, but warns him not to keep them in his home. He ignores the warning and pays the price as weird things start happening in his study: he is assaulted by something that looks like a puppet and he becomes prey to unnerving hallucinations involving murder. An old newspaper clipping tells of the unexplained violent deaths of a puppeteer and his wife, but then the script begins to disintegrate as the story meanders through possession and reincarnation motifs. Lam seems uncomfortable in the dramatic part and Cheong, as the flighty model involved with both Lam and his producer, Tse, later gave a far better performance in Ho Fan's voyeuristic psycho-killer *Hua Jie* (1982). The potentially enchanting premise of Yung's movie is wasted as cod philosophy and glossy imagery take over halfway through.

d/s Peter Yung (Uong Weiquan) *p* Carl Mak (Mai Jia), Dean Shek *c* Arthur Young *lp* Ben Lam (Lin Quan), Flora Cheong, Tse Yin

Madhouse (O. G. ASSONITIS; US, IT) scope 90min
This exercise by Assonitis in the shock-machine type of cinema is very much in the style of Dario Argento. This effective concoction tells of a teacher in a school for deaf children, Julia (Everley) and her mad, hideously disfigured twin sister who escapes from the asylum with the aid of a ferocious killer dog. The mad twin vows to prepare a memorable birthday surprise for her sister, who was responsible for incarcerating her in the madhouse. She piles up corpses in the basement of Everley's deserted apartment block and after an extended, well-conducted chase sequence, the film ends with a surprise revelation of the identity of the 'real' psycho-killer. The violence involves the use of a power drill on someone's head and numerous other sickening bits of gory business. Replaying stock situations from the psycho-slasher genre, Assonitis also uses one of the more hallucinatory clichés which nevertheless retains its power to disturb: a festive table surrounded by cadavers in various stages of decomposition.

d/p/co-s Ovidio G. Assonitis *co-s* Stephen Blakely, Peter Shepherd, Robert Gandus *c* Piazzoli *lp* Trish Everley, Dennis Robertson, Michael Macrae, Morgan Hart, Richard Baker

Makai Tensho *aka* **Samurai Reincarnation**
(TOEI; JAP) 122min
Exploiting the success of Yoichi Takabayashi's *Honjin Satsujin Jiken* (1975) which was based on a thriller written by Sishi Yokomizo, the author's powerful publisher, Kadokawa, launched a production house devoted to making films of the novels published by his company. Many Yokomizo thrillers became box-office hits: the first of the series, *Inugamike no Ichizoku* (1976), directed by Kon Ichikawa, was so successful that Ichikawa spent the next few years imitating his own movie (*Gokumon-to*, 1977; *Joobachi*, 1978; *Byoin-zaka no Kubikukuri no Ie*, 1979). Kadokawa relentlessly mined the Yokomizo thrillers for his films, often gory affairs revolving around complicated family mysteries, adding other books in a similar vein to his production slate. This story by Futaro Yamada was one such addition.

The movie tells of Shiro Amakusa, a 17th-century christian rebel whose story had been filmed by Oshima as *Amakusa Shiro Tokisada* (1962). In Fukasaku's picture, the beheaded hero revives and summons other rebellious heroes from Japanese history to form a ghost army that seeks to subvert the rule of the Tokagawa shoguns. Although overlong, the film contains a few impressive scenes as the ghostly horde moves through a stylized landscape with swirling mists blanketing the earth. Fukasaku, an ex-critic, made his name with violent yakuza pictures before turning to science fiction with the end-of-the-world fantasy, *Fukkatsu no Hi* (1979).

d Kinji Fukasaku *p* Haruki Kadokawa *s* Tatsuo Nogami *c* Kiyoshi Hazegawa *lp* Shinichi Chiba, Kenji Sawada, Akiko Kana

Mangryongui Wechingturesu *aka* **Wedding Dress of the Ghost**
(HAP DONG FILMS; ROK) 92min
In this film, which is emblazoned with ritualistic imagery characteristic of fantasies with a rural grounding (decapitated pigs as part of a peasant girl's altar, for example), Park heightens the terror by locating much of the action in broad daylight around a businessman's home. Driving home, the wealthy entrepreneur accidently runs over a girl who resembles a hitchhiker whom he killed a month before. However, the girl is not a real person but a life-size effigy. Next, a shot begins to haunt him in this home every night and he exhumes the hitchhiker in order to practice an exorcism ritual, but the coffin is empty except for the doll-like effigy. In a blind panic, he falls into a well and drowns. The use of the hitchhiker/effigy/spirit triangle gives the film an elliptical appeal that is strengthened by its flashback structure, although it remains a very traditional vengeful-ghost story.

Park also made a fox-woman ghost story in a period setting, *Sex and Revenge* (1981) as well as a number of martial arts pictures. His best work in the fantasy genre is **Two Women from the Nether World** (1982), with its beautifully stylized sets, and **Mangryongui Kok** (1980).

d Park Yoon Kyo *p* Kwak Jung Hwan *s* Lee Jai Hun *c* Son Hyun Chae *lp* Chung Se Hyuk, Sunwoo Eun Sook

Midnight (CONGREGATION CO) 91min
After her policeman father has tried to rape her, Nancy (Verliin) leaves home to hitch to her sister in California. On the road she joins up with two young men before falling victim to a backwoods family of devil worshippers who plan to sacrifice her at midnight on Easter Sunday. Not unlike *Race with the Devil* (1971), *Midnight* is an effective mixture of road and horror movie and a refreshing break from the increasingly rigid formulae of many of its contemporaries. Scripted by the writer of **Night of the Living Dead** (1968), and with Savini's usual excellent special effects, the film continues its predecessor's stress on the racial issue by having the racially mixed trio encounter prejudice on the road and by making several of the family's victims black. Forties star Tierney is excellent as the heroine's stepfather, initially the villain of the piece, at the end, her stalwart protector.

d/s John A. Russo *p* Donald Redinger *c* Paul McCollough *se* Tom Savini *lp* Lawrence Tierney, Melanie Verliin, John Hall, Charles Jackson, Doris Hackney, John Amplas, Robin Walsh, David Marchick, Greg Besnak

Mil Gritos Tiene la Noche *aka* **1000 Cries Has the Night** *aka* **Pieces** (ALMENA FILMS/FORT FILMS; SP,PUERTO RICO) scope 87(85)min
This sleazy Puerto Rican exploitation movie was filmed in Boston and Madrid by an American producer based in Italy and a Spanish director. The nasty tendencies of a traditional psycho killer of women, manifested in his childhood, result in the decapitation of his mother when she berates him for playing with a nude jigsaw puzzle. In adult life, he (Purdom) then embarks on a series of gory murders of women, removing bits of their bodies in an effort to construct a new jigsaw puzzle. Taking its cue from **Macabro** (1980), the jigsaw woman is unkillable and returns from beyond the grave to torment her creator. The music track, provided by CAM, imitates Dario Argento's soundtracks.

Piquer had made his name with fairly respectable Jules Verne type stories, including *Misterio en la Isla de los Monstruos* (1981) and *Viaje al Centro de la Tierra* (1976), while producer Randall is best known for the infamous *Wild, Wild World of Jayne Mansfield* (1968), a pseudo-documentary which re-enacted the star's car-crash and decapitation.

d/s Juan Piquer Simon *p* Dick Randall, Steve Miniasian *c* Juan Marine *lp* Christopher George, Edmund Purdom, Lynda Day George, Paul L. Smith, Frank (Franco) Brana, Ian Sera, Jack Taylor, Gerard Tichy, Isabel Luque

La Momia Nacional *aka* **The National Mummy**
(JOSE FRADE; SP) scope 87min
A crazy terror-comedy with allegorical overtones set in 1900, this tells the story of a rich young archaeologist who is brought the recently discovered mummy of an ancient Egyptian princess by an old professor and his daughter. When divested of her wrappings, the mummy becomes a predatory female intent on raping all the men. Subsequent events include the usual doings of a vampire doctor, a weird dinner with a severed head in a dish and an incongruously happy ending. The main assets of the frenetically conducted mixture of farce, horror and sex are the odd surreal image and the beauty of its female lead, Hernandez, who also starred in Jacinto Molina's **El Retorno del Hombre Lobo** (1980) and Mariano Ozores's sexy witchcraft comedy, *Brujas Magicas* (1981). Larraz's best-known work remains **Vampyres** (1974) and the sadistic thriller, *Whirlpool* (1969), made under his English pseudonym Joseph Larraz. His next venture was a male version of **Carrie** (1976), **Estigma** (1981).

d/co-s José Ramón Larraz *p* José Frade *co-s* Juan Alonso Millan *c* Raúl Perez Cubero *lp* Paco Algora, Azucena Hernandez, Quique Camoiras, José Jaime Espinosa, Lili Murati, Paloma Hurtado, Carlos Lucena

My Bloody Valentine
(SECRET FILM CO/CANADIAN FILM DEVELOPMENT CORP/ FAMOUS PLAYERS; CAN) 91min
While *My Bloody Valentine* is clearly derived from **Halloween** (1978) and such spin-offs as **Terror Train** (1979) insofar as it's concerned with a collection of young people at the mercy of a maniac, it also displays certain divergences from its models. The setting is a mining town, where 20 years before, the crazed sole survivor of a cave-in had gruesomely murdered the two men deemed responsible for the accident. When the annual dance, during which the mayhem had occurred, is resumed, it becomes the cue for a succession of further murders, principally during a party which – improbably enough – a group of young miners and their girlfriends are holding illicitly at the pithead. The hero (Kelman) and heroine (Hallier) escape with their lives after a climactic chase in which the masked

Left: *The routine* My Bloody Valentine.

Isabelle Adjani as the schizoid woman in Possession.

assassin is revealed to be not the returned survivor (Cowper) but the son (Affleck) of one of his victims.

The film's strength lies in its atmospheric depiction of the bleak little town and, structurally, the movie differs from its models in recapitulating the past tragedy in a flashback rather than as a pre-credits prologue. Despite this degree of originality, though, and a lively climax, the film is weighed down by the contrivance of Beaird's script. However, as a foray into 'mining jeopardy', the movie is streets ahead of **The Boogens** (1981).

The special makeup effects are by Tom Burman, Ken Diaz and Tom Hoerber.

d George Mihalka *p* André Link, John Dunning, Stephen Miller *s* John Beaird *c* Rodney Gibbons *lp* Lori Hallier, Paul Kelman, Neil Affleck, Don Francks, Keith Knight, Cynthia Dale, Alf Humphreys, Terry Waterland, Jack Van Evera, Peter Cowper

Die Nacht des Schicksals

(HOCHSCHULE FUER FERNSEHEN UND FILM – MUENCHEN; WG) 80min

This is a straight-faced, highly stylized parody of both the horror and romance genres and was filmed on a shoestring, but the film achieves a glossy look by means of excellent photography and operatic stage designs. The narrative, reduced to a minimum, consists primarily of cliché scenes and motifs in the manner of Daniel Schmid's funnier and more accomplished *La Paloma* (1974). The plot, set in a gothic manor, involves an aristocratic baby – deposited in the woods by a homicidal maid (Zoeckler) – who returns 21 years later to her family castle as an opera singer (Wolke-Desinée). On the fateful night of her return, she and her companions are confronted by a series of doubles (each actor plays two roles), while the evil maid busies herself preparing a poisonous potato salad and sharpening her kitchen knife to the accompaniment of fifties German hit tunes. The climax consists of a murder, a suicide and a conflagration as the commonplaces of horror and sentimental romances are fused for the grand finale. Shot as a diploma film on 16mm for the Munich Film School in 1978, the 21-minute production was extended over the next few years, with virtually no extra funds, to feature length and was awarded the Max Ophuls prize in 1981.

d/co-s Helmer von Luetzelburg *co-s* Christoph Wagenknecht, Andreas Markus Klug *c* Alexander Witt *lp* Melitta Wolke-Desinée, Wolf Rettig, Billie Zoeckler, Ludwig Boettger, Traute Hoess, Marlene Moll, Christa Hiederer

Nightmare *aka* Nightmares in a Damaged Brain

(GOLDMINE PRODUCTIONS) 97(93)min

Just to show where his heart lies, Scavolini opens with an effectively nasty scene in which a man (Stafford) pulls back the bedclothes to find a severed head peering at him from a nest of blood, shredded tendons and goo. A schizophrenic under treatment for nightmares thought to be imaginary but in fact (flashback with more brutality here) deriving from a childhood trauma when he axed his parents for indulging in sexual bondage, he is supposedly cured by drug therapy, but a visit to a New York sex shop sets him off again. Murdering a girl for her car, he heads for Florida and starts playing cat and mouse with a single parent (Smith) and her three kids. Most of this part is a witless copy of **Halloween** (1978) with psychology that would make Robert Bloch at his worst look like Freud by comparison. And the ending, in which Stafford turns out to be Smith's missing son (with meaningful glances at Smith's other children) is even more stupid than the cops and psychologists who have to delay action to let the plot run its course.

With its cool Freud (primal scene, return of the repressed, etc), slavish borrowings from *Halloween et al*, and lashings of goo and extraneous nudity, *Nightmare* is nothing if not distasteful and opportunist. The film attempted to sell itself by crediting Tom Savini with its special effects but in fact he worked on it in only a minor consultative capacity. The opportunism did not stop there, however. When the film was released in Britain (with particularly unpleasant title change) the press shows were shrouded in secrecy, with the critics being provided with sick bags and not told what they were going to see until the film appeared on screen. Then, when the film was released on video, dealers were encouraged to enter a competition which consisted in guessing the weight of a model of a damaged brain in a jar of preserving fluid. Given these antics, and some particularly lurid advertising preceding the video's release it was hardly surprising that *Nightmares in a Damaged Brain* should feature as one of the main targets of the anti 'video nasty' campaigners. On the other hand, however, it seems grotesquely absurd that its distributor should have been imprisoned for six months for dealing in a print that was a mere 60 seconds longer than the BBFC certificated version. In the States the film was distributed with a self-imposed X rating and is indeed incredibly gory, especially in the oft-repeated trauma/nightmare sequence. However, apart from the effective opening sequence, and the atmospheric 42nd Street locations, the film is tediously routine and derivative.

d/s Romano Scavolini *co-p* John L. Watkins *co-p/co-se* William Milling *c* Gianni Fiore *co-se* Les Larrain, Edward French *lp* Baird Stafford, Sharon Smith, C. J. Cooke, Mik Cribben, Danny Ronen, John Watkins, William Milling, Scott Praetorius, William S. Kirksey, Christina Keefe

Possession

(OLIANE PRODUCTIONS/MARIANNE PRODUCTIONS/ SOMA FILM PRODUKTION; FR,WG) 127min

This misappropriation of the horror genre by an expatriate avant-garde Pole results in an indigestible wedge of psychology about a schizoid woman (Adjani) who, after much domestic recrimination, screaming and self-mutilation, deserts both husband (Neill) and lover (Bennent) for an empty apartment where her frustrated fury and desire apparently breed a monster. Starting as a fungus but developing into a slimy, tentacled pseudo-humanoid, this product (presumably) of her id is fertile enough to cause her to have a miscarriage on the underground in a welter of gore and pus. It eventually metamorphozes into an idealized double of her husband, but by that time most of the cast (all in some way abnormal) have either been fed to the creature or shot dead. The result is a very wearing film, with the English dialogue (although the setting is Berlin with the Wall much in evidence and presumably symbolic of schizo loyalties) gabbled by an hysterically over-the-top cast.

d/s Andrzej Zulawski *p* Marie-Laure Reyre *c* Bruno Nuytten *lp* Isabelle Adjani, Sam Neill, Margit Carstensen, Heinz Bennent, Johanna Hofer

The Prowler *aka* **Rosemary's Killer** *aka* **The Graduation** (CAROLCO) 88(87)min
At the end of the Second World War, a jilted soldier returns home and murders his unfaithful girlfriend and her new lover during a graduation dance. The dances are cancelled for the forseeable future but when the custom is revived 35 years later a series of similar brutal killings begins. Like **My Bloody Valentine** (1981), *The Prowler* moves away from the usual mid-Western setting but does little with its new location (New York) nor with its potentially interesting returning-GI motif. On the other hand, like *Valentine*, the film is, if hardly original, certainly polished, atmospheric and suspenseful. Savini's particularly graphic special effects resulted in most of the murders being trimmed in the British release print.

d/co-p Joseph Zito *co-p* David Streit *s* Glenn Leopold, Neal F. Barbera *c* Raúl Lomas *se* Tom Savini, Darryl Ferrucci *lp* Vicky Dawson, Christopher Goutman, Lawrence Tierney, Farley Granger, Cindy Weintraub, Lisa Dunsheath, David Sederholm, Bill Nunnery, Thom Bray, Diane Rode

Quella Villa Accanto al Cimitero *aka* **The House by the Cemetery** *aka* **The House outside the Cemetery**
(FULVIA FILM; IT) 86min
Fulci has acquired something of a cult following, but narrative cohesion is certainly not his strong point, and the fact that this film, like **...E Tu Vivrai nel Terrore! L'Aldila** (1981), is nominally set in America tends to underline this shortcoming. The arbitrary plot deals with an academic (Malco), his wife (MacColl) and young son who move into a New England house with a sinister history – a notion possibly derived from **The Amityville Horror** (1979). Once there, the little boy finds a mysterious playmate, and the cellar proves eventually to house an unsightly Dr Freudstein (de Nava), a 19th-century medical experimenter on Frankenstein lines who has managed to keep himself alive for 150 years by means of transplants from his victims' bodies (not surprisingly, he now looks pretty horrific). The parents are killed and the son ends in limbo with his playmate, who is Freudstein's daughter.

As is the case with so many Italian horror movies of this type, the film's qualities lie in its incidentals, with Freudstein's alarming appearance and the gruesome scenes in the cellar being offset by the chill vein of poetry attached to the episodes with the children, which is capped by the claustrophobic conclusion.

d/co-s Lucio Fulci *p* Fabrizio de Angelis *co-s* Dardano Sacchetti, Giorgio Mariuzzo *c* Sergio Salvati *se* Gino de Rossi, Maurizio Trani *lp* Katherine MacColl, Giovanni de Nava, Dagmar Lassander, Anja Pieroni, Giovanni Frezza, Silvia Collatina, Daniele Doria, Carlo de Mejo

Los Ritos Sexuales del Diablo
(HISPANIOLA; SP) 81min
Larraz had directed the derivative, though professional and at times fascinating, **Vampyres** (1974) and **Estigma** (1981), but in this sex film he simply uses satanism and possession as a narrative excuse to show sodomy, bestiality with goats, orgies and even less savoury happenings. The plot, set in England, has the sister of a murdered man fall into the hands of her devil-worshipping and lesbian sister-in-law. She is subjected to a catalogue of sexual 'horrors' and enforced drug usage. In the end all is revealed to have been a dream but then, the story appears to recommence as the first scenes are repeated in the manner of **Dead of Night** (1945). With the relaxation of censorship following General Franco's death, a number of almost hard-core porn movies such as this one – and a whole series of Jesús Franco movies – were manufactured and released in Spain with a special 'S' classification.

d/s José Ramón Larraz *c* Juan Marine *lp* Helga Liné, Vanesa Hidalgo, Mauro Rivera, Alfredo Lucheti

Die Saege des Todes *aka* **Bloody Moon**
(LISA FILM/RAPID FILM/METRO FILM; WG) 85(83)min
Routine fare from Franco, stringing together shock sequences and bare-breasted women by means of inept cutting and plentiful zooms. The plot uses the disfigured, lecherous Manuel (Warchter) as the red herring while his sister (Gerganoff) and her lover (Moosbrugger) terrorize young women and burn their aunt (Rubio) to a crisp in a wheelchair. Pascal is the woman in peril, around whom the corpses pile up. The result is a luridly meretricious picture which succeeds only in making the sight of attractive women and corpses extremely boring. Particularly tedious are the repeated scenes of Gerganoff alone in her room baring her breasts to the moon. Franco's movies continued to veer from the perversely sadistic to the routinely exploitative, with this picture firmly in the latter category, a far cry from his delirious **Les Avaleuses** (1973) or *Les Possedées du Diable* (1972).

d Jesús Franco *p* Wolf C. Hartwig *s* Rayo Casablanca *c* Juan Soler *lp* Olivia Pascal, Christoph Moosbrugger, Nadja Gerganoff, Alexander Waechter, Jasmin Losensky, Corinna Gillwald, Ann-Beate Engelke, Antonia Garcia, Maria Rubio

Samwonnyo *aka* **The Valley of Ghosts**
(YUN BANG FILMS; ROK) 80min
The traditional melodramatic plot is enlivened here by ghostly doings orchestrated by a rich landowner's foreman in order to obtain his master's fortune and position. Set in Manchuria, the last son of a wealthy landowner marries a Chinese woman and is falsely accused of murdering her. The real culprit, the foreman, then unleashes a horde of rather stylishly presented local ghosts upon the rich people although, eventually, he is suitably punished for his temerity. The picture is of interest partly as an illustration of the ubiquitousness of the association between women and cats as symbols of a malevolent 'other' sensuality. The association is also present in the Japanese bakeneko mono (**Yabu ni Naka Kuroneko**, 1968, for example) as well as in western legends such as **Cat People** (1942).

Kim, together with his star, Lee, and cinematographer made a second Manchurian picture, *The White Rose* (1981), a balletic martial arts film with excellently composed snowscapes and bright, enamelled colours. The prolific director and cinematographer team made two more martial arts pictures in 1981, revealing something about the rhythm of production in South Korea at this time.

d Kim Si Hyun *p* Choi Choon Joi *s* Lee Chung Keun *c* Shin Myung Ui *lp* Lee Ye Min, Choi Hyo Sun

Saturday the 14th (NEW WORLD) 77min
Despite its title, this is neither a satire nor an imitation of **Friday the 13th** (1980) and its successors, but a comic ragbag incorporating just about everything. Prentiss and Benjamin inherit an old dark house, and when their son opens a 'Book of Evil' that isn't supposed to be opened, a horde of monsters – and a couple of vampires who want to move in – are let loose. After a house-warming party at which sundry relatives are done to death in gouts of tomato ketchup, the boy (Brando) manages a successful exorcism and the family are at last able to settle

down in peace. There are a few pleasing notions (the creature from the black lagoon lurking in a bubble bath, for example, and the TV set which obstinately refuses to show anything except *The Twilight Zone*), but the humour is for the most part pitifully juvenile and the film itself crude. That said, it is far superior to *Friday the 13th: The Orphan* (1980), which is a faithful adaptation of Saki's *Sredni Vashtar*, but sadly to little effect.

d/s Howard R. Cohen *p* Julie Corman *c* Daniel Lacambre *lp* Richard Benjamin, Paula Prentiss, Jeffrey Tambor, Severn Darden, Kari Michaelsen, Kevin Brando

Sexo Sangriento *aka* **Bloodthirsty Sex**
(MANUEL ESTEBA PRODUCCIONES; SP) 105(84)min
This is a crude exploitation movie in the tradition of Jesús Franco's sex and sadism efforts. Three women, one of whom is a clairvoyant, become involved with a woman painter and her sinister, dumb servant. Although the clairvoyant anticipates the murderous events that follow, she is unable to forestall them and all get killed. The culprit is revealed to be the painter's father who went insane after his experiences in the Civil War and in a French concentration camp, a condition aggravated further upon his return to a Spain from which he felt alienated. Although the explanation for the psychotic's behaviour is more interesting than usual, the plot and imagery remain firmly within the conventions of traditional horror-sexploitation movies, confirming the status of Esteba, who signed titles such as *Horror Story* (1972) and *Viciosas al Desnudo* (1980), as a poor Catalonian cousin of Franco.

d/p/co-s Manuel Esteba Gallego *co-s* Xavier Flores *c* José Luís Valls *lp* Ovidi Montllor, Mirta Miller, Diana Conca, Viki Palma, Elisa Romero

The moment of death in The Prowler.

Shi Yao *aka* **Corpse Mania**
(SHAW BROTHERS; HONG KONG) scope 97min
After the successful **Xie** (1980), Gui made this horror thriller about an investigation of a recurrent case of necrophilia which leads to clues in a brothel and a suspect who has been recently released from an asylum. Although set in the Republican era, the movie clearly draws on Gui's *The Criminals* portmanteau films of the late seventies which were set in contemporary Hong Kong. There is the same sympathy for the innocent but obviously suspect culprit as in the *Lincum Da Xie An* episode of *The Criminals, part II* (1976). There is also a similar sense of violent horror in the discovery of the corpses as staged in this picture, and the murder of the brothel's madam. Both protagonists are mentally retarded and because of this are believed to be guilty. The film also draws on Gui's *Wanren Zhan* (1980), in which a web of intrigue is woven around the investigator who gradually realizes that he is in fact a possible victim himself: a motif that also informs Gui's **Gu** (1981). Of interest is the performance as a detective of Tso Tat-hua, a famous actor of detective parts in the Hong Kong cinema of the fifties and sixties.

d/co-s Gui Zhihong (Kwei Chi-hung, Kuei Chih-Hung) *p* Mona Fong (Fang Yihua) *co-s* Szu Tu-an (Situ An, Szeto An) *c* Li Hsin Yeh (Li Xinye) *lp* Tanny, Wang Jung, Yu Tsui-ling, Tso Tat-hua

Thrilled to Death *aka* **Momma's Boy** *aka* **Night Warning** *aka* **Butcher Baker Nightmare Maker**
(ROYAL AMERICAN PICTURES) 94min
A real oddity, this film – now banned in Britain as a 'video nasty' – features McNichol as a 17-year-old highschool basketball player brought up by his aunt (Tyrrell) after his parents died in a car-crash when he was three. Manically possessive, over-protective and fast going over the edge – she keeps a candlelit shrine to an old boyfriend in the basement – Tyrrell attempts to seduce a TV repairman and when that fails, kills him. The cop on the case, the homophobic (Svenson), ignores her incipient madness and tries to pin the killing on McNichol and his coach, whom he suspects of having an affair.

Notable primarily for Tyrrell's performance – which is almost in the **What Ever Happened to Baby Jane?** (1962) league – the film seems to be wrongly classed as horror for most of its length. The extremely bloody body count at the end makes the classification apparent, however. Apart from a horrifically convincing car-crash (great stunt footage), the film also contains a good deal of humour and a particularly ferocious example of small-town bigotry in Svenson's detective (very much in his bullying *Part II Walking Tall* (1975) role).

d William Asher *co-p/co-s* Stephen Breimer *co-p* Eugene Mazzola *co-s* Alan Jay Glueckman, Boon Collins *se* Al Apone *lp* Jimmy McNichol, Susan Tyrrell, Bo Svenson, Marcia Lewis, Julia Duffy, Britt Leach, Steve Eastin, Caskey Swaim, Cooper Neal, William Paxton

L'Ultimo Squalo *aka* **Shark** *aka* **The Great White** *aka* **The Last Jaws**
(UTI PRODUZIONI/HORIZON FILMS; IT) 87(80)min
'There's something fishy here', says one of the characters, apparently without punning intent – and there certainly is: *L'Ultimo Squalo* is about as bare-faced in its imitation of **Jaws** (1975) as a rip-off can possibly be. As in Spielberg's film, this one offers a resort celebrating its centennial, a local politician (Sinclair) who won't listen to reason about the danger of shark attacks because of the public relations risk, and a diffident shark expert (Franciscus) who together with a yo-ho-ho old man of the sea (Morrow in a fair variation on Robert Shaw's performance in *Jaws*) manages to put paid to the marauding shark, though at the cost of the latter's life. The only differences between the two movies boil down to the greater degree of on-screen mutilation and mayhem perpetrated by the shark in this one and the considerably greater degree of

directorial control and imagination evinced by its American predecessor.

d Enzo G. Castellari *p* Maurizio Amati, Ugo Tucci *s* Mark Princi *c* Alberto Spagnoli *se* Antonio Corridori *lp* James Franciscus, Joshua Sinclair, Vic Morrow, Micky Pignatelli, Timothy Brent, Stefania Girolami, Chuck Kaufman, Marko Lari

The Unseen (TRIUNE FILMS) 89min

Fairly restrained in terms of bloodletting but a women-in-jeopardy movie nonetheless, this features Bach as a telenews reporter on assignment in Solvang, California, covering a Danish festival with her camerawoman Lamm and helper Young. Lack of other accommodation forces them to stay at the remote mansion of museum keeper Lassick and his sister Goldoni, the monstrous offspring of whose incestuous relationship escapes from the basement during their stay. Quite imaginatively atmospheric, the film even allows itself a slight sense of compassion – a rare enough quality in this particular subgenre. The 'Danish' settings, if little more than local colour, make a pleasant change from the usual anonymous mid-Western locations.

d Peter Foleg *p* Anthony B. Unger *s* Michael L. Grace *c* Roberto Quezada *se* Harry Woolman *lp* Barbara Bach, Sydney Lassick, Stephen Furst, Lelia Goldoni, Karen Lamm, Doug Barr, Lois Young

Visiting Hours
(FILMPLAN INTERNATIONAL; CAN) 105(104)min

Returning home after a TV discussion on wife-battering, crusading journalist Grant is attacked by an intruder, Ironside, whose disturbed childhood has turned him into a psychopathic misogynist. Grant is taken to hospital only to be followed by the demented Ironside who continues to terrorize her there until – after the film has run through the whole gamut of women-in-jeopardy torments – she manages to dispatch him. That this kind of story is not hopelessly compromised from the start in terms of its representation of women, and may indeed be capable of quite progressive inflections is demonstrated by comparing *Visiting Hours* with *Coma* (1978), with which it shares a similarly independent heroine and a creepy hospital setting. The problem with this film is that the clichéd script, stock situations and overwrought, over-insistent direction simply exploit Grant and her plight as a means of generating shock and suspense in the most perfunctory, mechanical way imaginable.

d Jean-Claude Lord *p* Claude Héroux *s* Brian Taggert *c* René Verzier *lp* Michael Ironside, Lee Grant, Linda Purl, William Shatner, Lenore Zann, Harvey Atkin, Helen Hughes, Michael J. Reynolds

Wolfen (ORION) pv 115min

Wadleigh, director of the celebrated rock film *Woodstock* (1970), returned to the cinema with what he unwisely termed a 'thinking man's horror film.' The movie is elaborately made, with subjective camerawork and extensive optical effects, but low on thematic clarity and tension. The narrative concerns a series of murders in New York's South Bronx which are being investigated by an oddball detective (played by Finney in his first outing in the genre since **Night Must Fall**, 1964). Together with a female partner (Venora) and a coroner's officer (Hines), he gradually becomes convinced that the deaths are being perpetrated by marauding wolves. Ultimately, with the aid of an Indian acquaintance (Olmos), he discovers that the killers are 'wolfen', a species of sentient wolf that has always co-existed with humanity. This fanciful idea does not possess much evolutionary logic, and the portentous overtones – hinting at nothing less than the end of civilization – remain unassimilated, especially in a lame ending which leaves Finney and Venora surrounded by the wolfen pack, with whom they seem to have reached some kind of tacit understanding.

Albert Finney in Wolfen.

The film's major points of interest are the dialogue, which is humorous, and some arresting imagery. Joe Dante's **The Howling** (1980) is a much more striking combination of thriller plot and the supernatural.

d/co-s Michael Wadleigh *p* Rupert Hitzig *co-s* David Eyre *c* Gerry Fisher, Fred Abeles *lp* Albert Finney, Diane Venora, Edward James Olmos, Tom Norman, Gregory Hines, Dick O'Neill, Dehl Berti, Sam Gray, Ralph Ball, Peter Michael Goetz

Xiong Bang *aka* **The Imp**
(CENTURY MOTION PICTURE AND DISTRIBUTION CO; HONG KONG) scope 98min

Much influenced by **Rosemary's Baby** (1968) and **The Exorcist** (1973), Yu's first feature for his own (now defunct) production company plays on the purely exploitative aspects of its theme. With his wife about to have a baby, the long unemployed Ah Kan (Qin) finally gets a job as a night watchman in a commercial building. Strange events, including the death of colleagues (one of whom chokes on his dog stew), begin to happen. A newspaper reports on the building's troubled history and a Taoist priest is consulted. Realizing that Qin's baby could be the incarnation of evil, the priest takes steps to destroy the spirit of a corpse discovered buried in the basement of the block. The picture impressively delivers what it promises, creating terror through skilfully orchestrated audience identification with Qin's apparently innocent wife. Highlights include graphically portrayed surgery, zombie-like creatures and hallucinatory gruesome deaths.

Together with Ronny Yu (maker of **Pao Dan Fei Che**, 1983) and Yim Ho, Dennis Yu formed Film Force in the late seventies and studied film-making in the United States. Unlike other young directors of his generation, he has spent more time in production than directing. After his ill-fated management of the Century Motion Picture Company, where he directed the virulently racist anti-Filipino movie *Bun Mooi* (1982), he briefly resumed his career as an independent director before forming yet another production company.

d Dennis Yu (Yu Yunkang) *p* Jeff Lau *s* Kam Ping-Hing, Lee Ten, Cheung Kam-Moon *c* Bob Thompson *lp* Charlie Qin (Charlie Chin), Dorothy Yu, Yue Hua, Wong Ching, Kent Cheng, Chan Chen, Wong Chung, Yeung Chun-yiu

Right: *The marvellous opening sequence to* Alone in the Dark.

1982

Alone in the Dark

(NEW LINE PRODUCTIONS/MASADA PRODUCTIONS) 93min

This, the directorial début of Sholder (editor of **The Burning**, 1980), is an above average entry in the already crowded maniacs-on-the-loose subgenre, thanks to its tight, crisp look, imaginative use of sound, excellent playing by its veteran cast, and a nice line in humour. During a statewide power failure a group of homicidal maniacs escape from the maximum-security floor of a mental hospital and go on the rampage. If the film never quite lives up to its nightmarish opening in a diner where it rains indoors, the food consists of rotting raw fish and the crazed short-order cook brandishes a gleaming cleaver, it still has its moments in the performances of Landau's pyromaniac preacher and the massive Van Lidth (from *The Wanderers*, 1979) as a sex maniac, not to mention Pleasance's hippy-dippy psychiatrist for whom the inmates are not patients but voyagers and who calmly remarks of a murderous pyromaniac 'he's very deeply into his own space just now'.

The film's 'we're all crazy now' thesis is nicely summed up in the final scene in which Palance, the last remaining psycho, visits a punk gig in which the Sic F*cks perform numbers like 'Chop Up Your Mother' and 'Insects Rule My World' and where the punters misinterpret his psychotic violence as the height of radical chic.

d/s Jack Sholder *p* Robert Shaye *c* Joseph Mangine
se Tom Savini, Tom Brumberger, Don Lumpkin
lp Jack Palance, Donald Pleasance, Martin Landau, Dwight Schultz, Erland Van Lidth, Deborah Hedwall, Lee Taylor-Allan, Phillip Clark, Elizabeth Ward, Brent Jennings

Amityville II: The Possession

(ORION/DE LAURENTIIS/MEDIA TECHNOLOGY; US,MEX) 105min

This is a very different proposition from **The Amityville Horror** (1979). Not so much a sequel as a prequel, it gleefully catalogues the murders that happened more or less off-screen in the prologue to the earlier film, and makes blood and thunder its prime objectives. Within the first hour or so, to the accompaniment of a barrage of sleazy tricks and shock effects – exploding stomachs, rotating beds, oceans of blood, not to mention a wretchedly over-insistent use of the subjective camera – most of the principal characters have been summarily killed off. Having got its splatters out of the way, the film then proceeds to hedge its bets by offering a prolonged bout of exorcism which ends in comic-strip grotesquerie with the priest (Olson) becoming possessed. The dialogue is unspeakable, the acting little better, and the film itself a mess.

d Damiano Damiani *p* Ira N. Smith, Stephen R. Greenwald
s Tommy Lee Wallace *c* Franco di Giacomo
lp James Olson, Burt Young, Rutanya Alda, Jack Magner, Andrew Prine, Diane Franklin, Moses Gunn

Paul Clemens, en route to mutating into a flesh-eating insect, in the stylish The Beast Within.

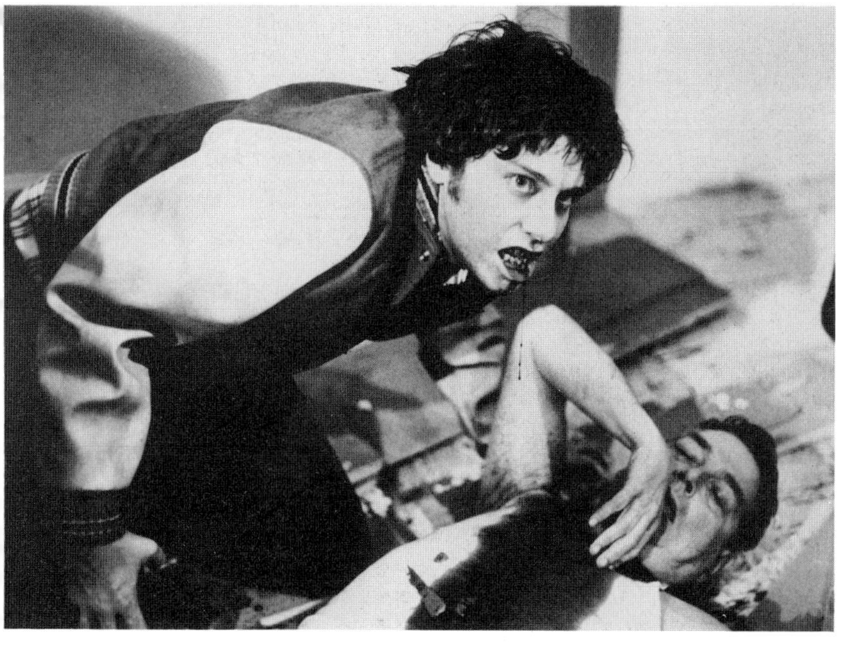

Assassino al Cimitero Etrusco *aka* Crime au Cimetière Etrusque *aka* Murder in the Etruscan Cemetery

(DANIA FILM/MEDUSA/IM. PEX. CI.; IT, FR) 90min

This rather oldfashioned, routinely directed, thriller with horror elements tries hard to infuse a sense of cruelty and uncanny menace into its prosaic drug-trafficking plot. Flashbacks masquerading as the heroine's dream sequences depict the ritual execution of a young couple in Etruscan times – recalling similar scenes in Terence Fisher's **The Mummy** (1959). The heroine (Audray), wife of a murdered Etruscanologist, is presented as the possible reincarnation of an ancient, immortal priestess. While the camera spends much time wandering around the murky graveyard and moving through dark, bluish catacombs, the villain turns out to be the heroine's best friend. As a mixture of horror and thriller genres, the movie is more successful that Armando Crispino's *L'Etrusco Uccide Ancora* (1972), but Crispino's picture is a better thriller.

d Christian Plummer *p* Luciano Martino *s* Ernesto Gastaldi, Dardano Sacchetti, Maria Chianetta, Jacques Leitienne *c* Giancarlo Ferrando *lp* Elvire Audray, Paolo Malco, Claudio Cassinelli, Marilu Tolo, Wandisa Guida, Ian Johnson

The Beast Within

(MGM/UA) 90min

In 1964 a newly married couple (Cox and Besch) have trouble with their car on a deserted Mississippi country road and while Cox goes off to look for help Besch is raped by a mysterious creature from a nearby swamp. Seventeen years later the couple's son (Clemens) contracts a mysterious illness and the family go back to Mississippi to look for a hereditary origin of the disease. Then Clemens starts to change.

For a comparatively late entry in the transformation stakes *The Beast Within* is unexpectedly effective, though given the excellence of Mora's earlier *Mad Dog* (1976) perhaps that isn't too surprising. Described by its director as 'an encyclopedia of horror films', the film nods towards **The Exorcist** (1973) and **The Howling** (1981), not to mention Dracula, Dr Jekyll and the werewolf, but does so in a style all its own; especially striking are the effective evocations of the swampland, the atmosphere of the tiny, incestuous Southern town, the uniformly excellent acting (including cameos from such stalwarts as R. G. Armstrong and L. Q. Jones), Les Baxter's score and the dazzling special effects: Clemens' climactic transformation into a giant, flesh-eating insect is really something to behold.

d Philippe Mora *p* Harvey Bernhard, Gabriel Katzka *s* Tom Holland *c* Jack L. Richards *se* Thomas R. Burman *lp* Ronny Cox, Bibi Besch, Paul Clemens, Don Gordon, Kitty Moffat, Ramsay King, John Dennis Johnston

Boogeyman II *aka* Revenge of the Boogeyman

(NEW WEST FILMS) 79min

More of remake than a sequel to **The Boogeyman** (1980), *Boogeyman II* uses almost half its length simply re-running its predecessor's highlights. Six months after the supernatural murders recounted in *The Boogeyman*, Love – the earlier film's heroine – moves from Maryland to Los Angeles to stay with film-maker Mickey Lombard (Lommel, director of *The Boogeyman*). When she tells her story to him and his friends, they all want to film it, whereupon the lethal mirror fragment from the first film turns up again and begins a fresh rampage. As interesting as this cannibalization of the earlier film is the even deeper level of self-reflection in the scenes with Lombard/Lommel and his friends, which become a hymn of hate to Hollywood that recalls Rainer Werner Fassbinder's jaundiced films-on-film. Attempting to make a serious movie, *Nathalie and the Age of Diminishing Expectations*, Lombard/Lommel is being forced to shoot some skin scenes by his producer who has already decided to retitle the film *Kiss and Tell*. Surrounded by self-seeking hangers-on only too eager to exploit Love for their own ends, the disillusioned director thumbs through his copy of *Hollywood Babylon* and muses about 'the good old days when Hollywood destroyed real people instead of toys' and sounds off against Brian de Palma (whose **Carrie**, 1976, provides the film's shock ending) and the like. Even more than in *The Boogeyman*, the telekinetic mirror is largely superfluous and is here played out with such cheap blood and gore effects as to appear merely parodic as the awful guests at the poolside party are dispatched with a garden hose, hedge clippers, corkscrew, barbecue tongs, an electric toothbrush and shaving foam.

A fascinating addition to the Hollywood-on-Hollywood subgenre, the film was bizarrely banned in Britain as a 'video nasty'.

d/co-p Bruce Starr *co-p/co-s* Ulli Lommel *co-s* Suzanna Love *c* Philippe Carr-Foster, David Sperling *se* CMI Ltd, Craig Foster *lp* Suzanna Love, Shannah Hall, Ulli Lommel, Shoto von Douglas, Bob Rosenfarb, Ahley DuBay, Rhonda Aldrich, Sarah Jean Watkins, Rock MacKenzie
Flashbacks: John Carradine, Ron James, Nicholas Love, Felicite Morgan, Bill Rayburn, Llewelyn Thomas

Cat People (RKO/U/FRIES) 118min

This is a curiously muffled remake of **Cat People** (1942) in which Schrader's Bressonian/Calvanist preoccupations clash rather horribly with horror movie conventions as he tries to bring the psychosexual hang-ups merely hinted at in the original out into the open. Crassly calculating in conception, the film emerges more than anything else as an undigested mess of half-baked ideas and wholesale borrowings. To begin with, there is the prologue set in a barbaric past on a stark plain where virgins are ritually mated to black leopards. Clearly derived from the similar evocation in **The Exorcist** (1973), impressively lowering but faintly absurd, this prologue not only attempts to present as a fact what was originally merely suggested as a legend, it also clashes disastrously with succeeding scenes shot on real locations in New Orleans. Then there is the fact that, whereas the Val Lewton-Jacques Tourneur version spent most of its running time subtly adducing psychological pros and cons to the heroine's belief that she is subject to feline metamorphosis, Schrader quickly stamps on all ambiguity by providing her with a brother (McDowell) who happily trots around from the outset as a black leopard chewing up girls of dubious virtue and trying to persuade his sister of the inevitability of incest. This leaves poor Irina (Kinski) nowhere much to go except into torments staged without much conviction, but given a seal of respectability by reference to Dante's *Inferno*, as she turns into a black leopard while making love with a zoo-keeper (Heard) whose hang-up is that he really prefers animals to people. Finally there is the problem of persuasive felinity. Simone Simon, the original Irina, set out with the sleek and sleepy advantage of looking astonishingly like a cat, but had obviously been drilled in movement and gesture. Kinski looks ravishing and McDowell suitably depraved, but with neither revealing much aptitude for echoing feline behaviour, Schrader resorts to the subterfuge of bouncing them off trampolines, with the unhappy result that they look less like cat people than refugees from a kung-fu movie.

The images are often striking, but the film itself is a pointless mess which makes fashionable nods towards explicit blood and sex. Symptomatically, the two best scenes – the jog through the park and attack in the swimming pool – are cribbed direct from the 1942 version and look as though they strayed in by mistake.

d Paul Schrader *p* Charles Fries *s* Alan Ormsby *c* John Barley, Paul Vom Brack *lp* Nastassia Kinski, Malcolm McDowell, John Heard, Annette O'Toole, Ruby Dee

Christine

(COL/DELPHI PRODUCTIONS) pv 110min

Adapted from a novel by Stephen King, as were **The Shining** (1980) and **Cujo** (1983) among several other horror movies, and directed by John Carpenter, maker of **Halloween** (1978) and **The Fog** (1979), *Christine* represents a fruitful conjunction. In common with other King stories, it posits a malign entity, in this case an automobile, a 1958 Plymouth Fury; and like other movies by Carpenter, it is concerned with a state of seige, individuals at the mercy of an unexplained phenomenon. Nonetheless *Christine* – the name is that of the car, and its classical allusion is that of an avenger – is not altogether satisfactory. This is not so much because the vehicle's demonic 'personality' is unexplained as because the malign empathy between the vehicle and the protagonist (Gordon), whom it transforms from schemiel to confident cad, is not dramatized to any real extent but has to be taken on trust. The high school butt's transformation and his capacity to wreak vengeance on his detractors – when they attack his beloved car with sledgehammers, the vehicle 'magically' reassembles itself, then

Nastassia Kinski ponders her fate in Paul Schrader's Cat People, *a curiously muffled remake of Jacques Tourneur's 1942 classic of the same title.*

Right: *The mechanical horrors attempt to destroy* Christine.

driverlessly tracks them down and kills them – recalls a variation on an earlier King adaptation, **Carrie** (1976).

But besides this thematic consistency, the appeal of *Christine* lies in the skill of its realization. The ambience of the California small-town setting is effortlessly caught by Morgan's mobile Panavision camerawork, and the incidental characters, especially the memorably uncouth garagiste (Prosky) on whose premises the car is repaired, are sketched in with just the right note of stylized realism. These qualities provide a beguiling framework for the film's *raison d'être*, the extraordinary sequences in which the car tracks down the four wreckers – in one case transforming itself into the motorized equivalent of a fiery steed – and the climactic episode where Gordon's girlfriend (Paul) and buddy (Stockwell) attempt to 'save' him by the perilous undertaking of destroying the car. In traditional fashion, the deranged Gordon himself dies in the melée, and in the tag scene, though Christine is seen reduced to a cube of squashed metal, one fragment of the package seems to be stirring in the breeze. Christine, it should be added, hailing from the heyday of rock'n'roll, will play nothing else on her radio, and signals her murderous intentions, as when she all but suffocates Paul after the girl has voiced 'jealousy' of her, with an impromptu 'blast from the past'. The result is a film of sly humour as well as (in all senses) spectacular efficiency.

d John Carpenter *p* Richard Kobrits *s* Bill Phillips *c* Donal M. Morgan *se* Roy Arbogast *lp* Keith Gordon, John Stockwell, Alexandra Paul, Robert Prosky, Harry Dean Stanton, Christine Belford, Roberts Blossom, William Ostrander, David Spielberg, Robert Darnell

Creepshow (UFD/LAUREL) 120min

Disappointingly, this tribute to *E. C.* horror comics turns out to be little more than a feeble echo of the Amicus anthology series that started with **Dr Terror's House of Horrors** (1964). One difference, though the effect is not particularly happy, is that in addition to beginning and ending each story with comic-strip versions of the opening or closing scenes, Romero indulges in a number of masking or split-screen devices. Far from enhancing the comic-strip ambience, these are at best coy, at worst unforgivably clumsy.

The film consists of five ghoulish stories. A murdered patriarch (Amplas) querulously returns from the grave to claim his birthday cake; a backwoods' farmer (King) turns into a fungus after breaking open a meteorite in the hope of finding riches; a jealous husband (Nielsen) buries his wife and her lover up to their necks as the tide comes in; a college professor (Holbrook) gets rid of his nagging wife (Barbeau) by feeding her to a thing crated by an Arctic expedition a century before but still very much alive and finally a ruthless tycoon (Marshall), who treats people as vermin, is overrun by cockroaches. With half the cast gleefully acting larger than life and the rest turning in more sophisticated performances, there seems to be some confusion as to whether the film's aim is psychological horror or comic-strip nastiness. Not that this matters too much, since King's stories are witless, overlong, and weakly derivative (notably from *The Thing* (1955), *The Quatermass Xperiment* (1955) and Poe's *The Cask of Amontillado*).

d George A. Romero *p* Richard P. Rubinstein *s* Stephen King *c* Michael Gornick *lp* Leslie Nielsen, E. G. Marshall, Adrienne Barbeau, Hal Holbrook, Carrie Nye, Viveca Lindfors, Stephen King, Fritz Weaver, John Amplas

Curtains

(CURTAIN PRODUCTIONS; CAN) 89min

After a conspicuously implausible red herring opening in which an actress (Eggar) pretends to be insane so as to be incarcerated in a mental hospital and afforded a chance to study insane behaviour at first hand for a film role, *Curtains* takes off into a drearily pedestrian variation on the masked-marauder theme. Eggar escapes to attend an ambiguous casting session being held by a director (Vernon) at an isolated country house. One by one, the rival aspirants are done to death by a masked attacker, as eventually is the director himself, until only Eggar and one other woman (Griffin) are left alive. In the upshot, needless to say it is the latter who proves to be the killer, but the script has not bothered to provide her with a semblance of motivation, any more than it has contrived any logic or suspense in the plotting of the attacks. The woebegone attempt to ring some changes on the format of **Halloween** (1978) by adopting a showbusiness milieu founders on a reef of affection, while the mental hospital scenes are gratuitously sensational. It seems only too appropriate that the director's pseudonym should be the name of the director within the film.

d Jonathan Striker (Richard Ciupka) *p* Peter R. Simpson *s* Robert Guza Jnr *c* Robert Paynter *lp* Samantha Eggar, John Vernon, Linda Thorson, Anne Ditchburn, Lynne Griffin, Lesleh Donaldson, Deborah Burgess, Michael Wincott, Maury Chaykin

Deadly Games *aka* Who Fell Asleep?

(GREAT PLAINS ENTERTAINMENT CORP) 95min

This fairly routine stalk-'n'-slash movie has a writer for a music magazine (Harris) return to her sleepy home town where a rash of murders has broken out. The perpetrator is a Vietnam war veteran, the best friend of the cop investigating the case. The only things that lift the film out of the rut are the relatively independent heroine and a number of generic in-jokes (the killer works as a projectionist in a horror-movie theatre and at one point shows **The Monster Walks**, 1932).

d/s Scott Mansfield *p* Raymond M. Dryden *c* R. Michael Stringer *se* John Eggett *lp* Sam Groom, Jo Ann Harris, Steve Railsback, Dick Butkus, Alexandra Morgan, Colleen Camp, Christine Tudor, June Lockhart, Denise Galik, Robin Hoff

Dracula Rises from the Coffin

(TAI CHANG INC; ROK) 92min

Based on the Shaw-Hammer co-production **The Legend of the Seven Golden Vampires** (1974), this film is a veritable oddity which can be read as a paranoid text on the fear of contamination from outside, political or spiritual. Dracula slips into Korea, obsessed with sucking the blood of a young Korean who has just returned from overseas study. Suitably garbed in Transylvanian black, Dracula appears at the girl's wedding, causing her to faint. Her husband and his friend, a Buddhist monk, devise a way to defeat Dracula but he has now sucked the blood of a foreign businesswoman and attempts to use her to attack the girl. In a forest which seems to be a cross between central Europe and Korea, Dracula meets his fate at the hands of spiritual kung fu.

The film is shot with a sensitive feel for the creation of horror in the daytime and the final climactic fight scene between the Buddhist monk and Dracula himself is replete with sudden entrances and exits (derived perhaps from King Hu's *Touch of Zen*) and the use of palm power and other such fantasies.

d Lee Hyoung Pyo *p* Lim Won Sik *s* Lee Hee Woo *c* Lee Sung Sub *lp* Kang Yong Suk, Park Yang Rae

Dr Jekyll's Dungeon of Death

(HYDE PRODUCTIONS) 91(88)min

Largely a one-man show featuring some particularly graphic on-camera injections and a decidedly low budget, this film, like *Son of Dr Jekyll* (1951), is one of the few spin-offs from Stevenson's original story not to feature a Hyde character (hence no transformations). Filmed in Nevada in 1978 and set in San Francisco in 1959 (though no exteriors are used and the choice of the fifties seems entirely arbitrary), the movie follows the experiments of the original Dr Jekyll's great-grandson (scriptwriter Mathers) with a mind-control serum, previously worked on by both his ancestor and Nazi scientists. The serum transforms his victims into martial arts' fighters with the result that the film becomes more and more of a bizarre generic mix.

d/p/c James Wood *s* James Mathers *lp* James Mathers, John Kearnery, Tom Nicholson, Dawn Carver Kelly, Nadine Kalmes

The Entity

(PELLEPORT INVESTORS/AMERICAN CINEMA) pv 125min

This late entry in the possession cycle offers a sex-starved demon. A Californian housewife (well played by Hershey) is raped by an invisible presence which returns repeatedly and insatiably for more. 'You are definitely not insane,' a friend assures her, 'but when men who are not actually there come in and have intercourse with you it's time to see a good psychiatrist.' Laughably described as a fictionalized account of a case history, the film rambles interminably through psychiatry's attempts to explain everything, and even more interminably through parapsychology's bleating efforts ('My God, I've never seen anything like it!!') to subdue the alien presence. Directed by Furie in his usual irritatingly mannered style, it features a barrage of uninteresting special effects. De Felitta's script for **Audrey Rose** (1977), which was also based on his own novel, is more persuasive.

d Sidney J. Furie *p* Harold Schneider *s* Frank de Felitta *c* Stepehn H. Burum *lp* Barbara Hershey, Ron Silver, David Labiosa, George Coe, Margaret Blye

Escrito en la Niebla *aka* It Is Written in the Fog

(FERNANDO BUTRAGUENO; SP) scope 90min

This belated imitation of **Psycho** (1960) by a newly formed production outfit has a small boy find his mother with her lover: he shoots the man and accuses his mother of murder, which causes her to become cataleptic. When he grows up, the son runs a restaurant and keeps his dumb wheelchair-ridden mother in his flat while he kills any woman he deems to be immoral. This tale can be seen as the portrait of a puritanically warped mind or as an indictment of female, particularly extramarital, sexuality. Whichever approach the viewer adopts, the film's thrills are provided by the traditional sex and women-in-peril sequences.

d Silvio F. Balbuena *p* Fernando Butragueno Benavente *s* Roberto Ibiricu Coto *c* Julio Bragado *lp* Terpy Ibir, Carmen Lujan, Carla Celia, Blanca de Burgos, Lili Danroe, Maribel Rivera, Rafael Conesa

The Evil Dead

(RENAISSANCE PICTURES) 86(85) min

Made on a shoestring by a tyro producer and director, both only just out of college at the time, *The Evil Dead* is an opportunist addition to the cycle of teenage-jeopardy horror films which followed in the wake of **Halloween** (1978). Clearly intended to be a 'calling card' to the industry for its youthful makers, though frankly absurd in any dramatic sense, it is a work of considerable energy and invention.

A group of five college students (the only players) arrive for a weekend at a spooky tumbledown house in the wilds of Tennessee. There they find an ancient book which has apparently been used to summon up a pack of demons. During the night, things start to happen. One girl (Sandweiss) ventures outside, to be assaulted by malevolent vines; later, with the bridge leading to the road collapsed, she goes berserk and the others confine her in the cellar; then another girl (York) falls under demonic influence and tries to kill the two men, though they dispatch her with an axe. By the time dawn arrives, the sole survivor is Campbell who has fought off the demonic attentions of the other three, decapitating Baker with a spade, and in the nick of time causing Sandweiss and Delrich to disintegrate by the ploy of consigning the crucial book to the fire. However, when Campbell ventures outside, an unseen demon launches itself upon him ...

Raimi makes no pretence at narrative integration. But what matters is the staging – virtuoso travelling shots, demon's-eye-view shots hurtling through the undergrowth, and above all the elaborate special effects: the sight of the grotesquely transmogrified Sandweiss straining to break through the trapdoor that confines her in the cellar is not easily forgotten. It is difficult to see how anyone could take the film seriously, though some arbiters of public morals appear to have done so.

d/s Samuel M. Raimi *p* Robert G. Tapert *c* Tim Philo *se* Bart Pierce, Tom Sullivan *lp* Bruce Campbell, Ellen Sandweiss, Betsy Baker, Hal Delrich, Sarah York

Evilspeak

(LEISURE INVESTMENT CO/CORONET FILM CORP) 89min

Weston's impressive horror début, *Evilspeak* is infinitely preferable to both the similarly set *An Officer and a Gentleman* and *Lords of Discipline*, and one of the best worm-turns horror movies since **Carrie** (1976). Howard plays a pudgy, lower-class

Barbara Hershey in danger in The Entity.

The inventive The Evil Dead.

orphan at a military academy. Plagued by his peers, he finds solace first in computers and later in a collection of black-magic books he finds in the crypt of the academy's chapel. With the help of his computer, he invokes a horde of razor-tusked wild pigs who eventually go on the rampage, kill his tormentors and destroy the academy. An extremely imaginative and energetic outing, the film's highlights include the scenes in which the pigs invade a luxurious bathroom and devour its occupant, and, later, run riot in the blazing chapel. After Howard's tormentors (including a particularly nasty Armstrong) have stabbed his puppy one really *wants* to see them get their porcine comeuppance.

d/co-p/co-s Eric Weston *co-p* Sylvio Tabet *co-s* Joseph Garofalo *c* Irv Goodnott *lp* Clint Howard, R. G. Armstrong, Joseph Cortese, Claude Earl Jones, Haywood Nelson, Don Stark, Charles Tyner, Lynn Hancock

Friday the 13th Part III

(JASON PRODUCTIONS/PAR) scope 95min

A sequel to both **Friday the 13th** (1980) and **Friday the 13th Part 2** (1981), *Part III* takes up the story in the immediate aftermath of *Part 2*, with a group of young people embarking – in improbable ignorance of the Camp Crystal massacre – on a country-based weekend in the area. But the death-dealing chain of events is much as before. About the only differences are that this film has a new actor (Brooker) as the maniacal killer Jason, and that it is made in 3-D. This device is perfectly in keeping with the sideshow aspects of the series as a whole, and no opportunity is lost for poking the audience in the eye with objects of every kind, notably the implements of Jason's death-dealing. In plot terms, the only slight divergence is that on this occasion the interlopers are menaced not only (as they eventually find out at the cost of seven of their eight lives) by Jason, but by a trio of aggressive bikers with whom two of their number (Parks, Zerner) have had a run-in. When the bikers come looking for trouble, however, they find it in the person of Jason, who disposes of them before getting around to his principal targets.

Little suspense is wrung out of this, though, or out of the subsequent events, and in what is by this time a ritual of expectation of the series, the movie ends with a pitched battle between Jason and the sole woman survivor (Kimmell); she is left paralysed with shock, and Jason is presumed dead, but yet another sequel, **Friday the 13th – The Final Chapter** appeared in 1984.

d Steve Miner *p* Frank Mancuso Jnr *s* Martin Kitrosser, Carol Watson *c* Gerald Feil *se* Martin Becker *lp* Dana Kimmell, Paul Kratka, Tracie Savage, Jeffrey Rogers, Catherine Parks, Larry Zerner, David Katims, Rachel Howard, Richard Brooker, Nick Savage, Gloria Charles, Kevin O'Brien

Full Moon High

(LARCO) 93min

Ironically, the first film to be completed during Hollywood's rediscovery of lycanthropy in the early eighties (**The Howling**, 1980; **An American Werewolf in London** and **Wolfen**, both 1981), *Full Moon High* was barely released commercially. Eschewing the complex special effects of its contemporaries, the film is really a comedy, a spoof on the werewolf subgenre in general and **I Was a Teenage Werewolf** (1957) in particular. Adam (son of Alan, who also appears in the film) Arkin plays the star of the Full Moon High School football team who in 1960 visits Romania with his father (McMahon), a CIA agent. There he is bitten by a werewolf. Doomed thereafter to wander the world, he finally returns to the States in 1980.

Cohen's first comedy, the film is kept deliberately low-key (in spite of makeup by Neill, a pupil of Rick Baker) to allow the satire to show through and to give full rein to Arkin's comic talents as the sympathetic, but incompetent, werewolf. Cohen himself said of the film, '... it's more than a comedy. It has some interesting ideas about how life in America has changed sexually and politically since the early sixties. All of Arkin's friends have changed but he hasn't. And whereas he changes into a werewolf all of the time, his friends change into middle aged people while he is gone, with different values and different ideas. They change as much as he does, actually.'

d/p/s Larry Cohen *se* Steve Neill *lp* Adam Arkin, Roz Kelly, Ed McMahon, Elizabeth Hartman, Alan Arkin, Bill Kirchenbauer, Joanne Nail

House of the Long Shadows

(LONDON-CANNON FILMS; GB) 101min

The assembly of veteran horror stars foregathered here deserved something better than a laborious revamping of *Seven Keys to Baldpate*, a play which was once a staple of provincial rep and has previously been filmed several times, most recently in 1947. The old dark house at the centre of the tale has been transplanted to Wales for this version. The principal figure now is an unlikely American writer (Arnaz) who accepts a bet from his publisher (Todd) that he will spend 24 hours in the mansion and write a gothic novel during his stay. Even more incredible than this is the succession of callers (Price, Lee and Cushing among them) who turn up and appear to be involved in some macabre family plot, leading to the 'deaths' of most of them. In a silly twist ending, lamely derivative of **Mark of the Vampire** (1935), the whole thing proves to have been a charade engineered by the publisher. In keeping with the prevailing sense of unreality of the whole enterprise, Arnaz not only finishes his book but tears up his winner's cheque.

d Peter Walker *p* Menahem Golan, Yoram Globus *s*Mitchell Armstrong *c* Norman Langley *lp* Vincent Price, Peter Cushing, John Carradine, Christopher Lee, Richard Todd, Desi Arnaz

The House on Sorority Row *aka* House of Evil

(VAE PRODUCTIONS) 92min

'Where's my baby?' screams Hunt after giving birth in the pre-credits sequence. The answer is that he's deformed and expected eventually to become insane because of an experimental fertility drug. The main action then starts 20 years later, with Hunt having turned her home into a sorority house. It comes as no surprise that a monster lurks in the attic and that, unhinged by a macabre joke the sorority girls play on his mother, he is soon running through victims like **Friday the 13th** (1980) and **Halloween II** (1981) rolled into one.

Something of a protégé of Brian de Palma and here making his first feature, Rosman has something of his mentor's gift for the showy, sub-Hitchcockian effect: a severed head in a toilet-bowl, for instance, whose eyes suddenly open. But despite the imaginative touches here and there, the film is still a copy of a copy of a copy, and the gore effects are depressingly crude.

d/co-p/s Mark Rosman *co-p* John G. Clark *c* Timothy Suhrstedt *lp* Kathryn McNeil, Eileen Davidson, Lois Kelso Hunt, Christopher Lawrence, Janis Zido, Charles Serio

The House Where Evil Dwells

(COHEN FEATURES) 88min

Set and shot in Japan at the Toei studios, Connor's adaptation of a James W. Hardiman novel is both routine and slightly comic. A love triangle in Kyoto of the 1840s revolving around Hattori, an unfaithful wife, ends in bloody slaughter and suicide, but the trio's ghosts remain to haunt the house now occupied by an American photographer (Albert), his wife (George) and, later, the family friend (McClure). The ghosts, shown in rather elementary superimpositions, take possession of the Anglo-Saxon visitors and their quarrels escalate into karate matches culminating in a replay of the gory events of 1840. Other ingredients in this familiar concoction which blames women for craving more sex than marriage affords (providing an opportunity to ask George to take her clothes off), involve a plague of insects and demonic rubber crabs as well as a phallic ivory carving that once belonged to the witch Okajima. The comic highlight comes when a Zen monk (Mitowa) tries to exorcize the house: Albert lets McClure into the house and the expelled ghosts, loitering in front of the place, rush back in through the open door. Connor was more at home with less demanding McClure dinosaur movies such as *The Land That Time Forgot* (1974).

d Kevin Connor *p* Martin B. Cohen *s* Robert A. Subotsky *c* Jacques Haitkin *se* Cruse and Co *lp* Edward Albert, Susan George, Doug McClure, Amy Barrett, Mako Hattori, Toshiyuki Sasaki, Toshiya Maruyama, Tsuyako Okajima, Henry Mitowa

Human Lanterns *aka* **The Human Skin Lantern**

(SHAW BROTHERS; HONG KONG) 95min

The Indonesian-born Lo Lieh shot to stardom as the naïve young hero of Cheng Chang-Ho's phenomenally successful *Tianxia Diyi Quan* (1972). Here, he reverts to his more familiar role as a villain, dominating the proceedings with his performance as a demented artisan who kills young women and skins them (a practice shown in graphic detail) in order to fashion uniquely covered lanterns in the shape of small dolls. The three main victims are Chu as a businessman's mistress, Liu as the man's sister and Tanny, his rival's wife. The narrative's sickeningly sadistic atmosphere is rendered even more unbearable by the beautifully controlled direction and stylish cinematography. Sun made his début in 1969 in Taiwan with comedies, and went on to direct action and martial arts' pictures. Most of his work is mediocre, a fact which leaves viewers unprepared for the poisonous intensity of the atmosphere created around Lieh's masterly performance.

d/co-s Sun Chung (Sun Zhong) *p* Mona Fong *co-s* I Kuang (Ni Kuang) *c* Tsao An-Shun *lp* Lo Lieh (Wang Lida, Luo Lie), Liu Yung, Chen Kuan-tai (Chen Guantai), Tanny, Linda Chu, Lin Hsiu-chun, Lo Mang, Sun chien

Husid *aka* **The House**

(SAGA FILM; ICELAND) 101(99)min

A cheaply made first feature by TV-trained film-makers, this psycho-horror movie proved extremely successful in the domestic Icelandic market, and was seen by one-third of the entire population within a ten-week run. The focus of the plot is an old house in Reykjavik. A young couple move in but when the man, a composer (Sigurdarson), leaves for a while, the memories (or ghosts) that seem to inhabit or be provoked by the gloomy place, invade the world of the young wife, Bjorg (Thorisdottir), who consults a medium (Skulason). She becomes prey to nightmarish visions of contorted faces and imitations of death and eventually succumbs to the increasingly demented atmosphere and meets a violent death.

Relying mostly on excellent cinematography and an artfully constructed soundtrack, Edvardsson manages to sustain a genuinely disturbing hesitation between a supernatural or a psychopathological explanation for the weird happenings. Although the notion of there being a special relationship between a woman's mind and her house is somewhat clichéd, Thorisdottir's performance is both sensitive and convincing. Compared to Harry Bromley Davenport's **Whispers of Fear** (1974), a picture with an almost identical situation, Edvardsson's film is a masterpiece.

d/co-s Egill Edvardsson *p* Jon Thor Hannesson *c/co-s* Snorri Thorisson *co-s* Björn G. Björnsson *lp* Lilja Thorisdottir, Johann Sigurdarson, Helgi Skulason, Baldvin Halldorsson, Margaret Olafsdottir, Thora Borg, Robert Arnfinnsson, Helga Oskarsdottir

Chard Hayward as the psychotic gardener in Lady, Stay Dead.

Lady, Stay Dead

(RYNTARE PRODUCTIONS; AUST) 95min

Eight years after his **Inn of the Damned** (1975), Bourke again mined the narrow seam of low-budget shock-horror. The film's suspense is provided by a psychopathic gardener (Hayward), who preys on the young women who employ him. He rapes and drowns his first victim in a fishtank. His second is the beach caretaker who sees him with the corpse (Coulls). His third victim (Howitt) escapes, in spite of the obligatory – at least since **Halloween** (1978) – return to life of the apparently dead villain. Some exploitative mileage is gained from dwelling on the gardener's sexual inadequacies – watching him with a female dummy and masturbating while spying on one of his victims on the beach – but no attempt is made to develop the voyeuristic or sexual themes latent in the situations. Instead, women are threatened simply as a way of titillating the audience's (assumed) misogynist impulses, for which an unimaginative script and banal dialogue suffice. Henman used the newly introduced lightweight Moviecam camera designed to save time and energy when shooting on location.

d/p/s Terry Bourke *c* Ray Henman *lp* Chard Hayward, Louise Howitt, Deborah Coulls, Roger Ward, Lex Foxcroft, James Elliott

Madman (THE LEGEND LIVES CO) 88min
An abandoned summer camp is reopened as a training centre for counsellors. Over the campfire the group leader recounts the episode that brought the closure of the camp in the first place – a rampage by the farmer 'Madman Marz' who killed his family, escaped the lynch mob and is said still to haunt the woods and to reappear if his name is called. It is and he does. Well photographed, reasonably suspenseful and boasting good special effects, the film is nonetheless an unoriginal, derivative carbon copy of **Friday the 13th** (1980).

d/s Joe Giannone *p* Gary Sales *c* James Momel *se* Jo Hansen *lp* Alexis Dubin, Tony Fish, Harriet Bass, Seth Jones, Jan Claire, Alex Murphy, Jimmy Steele, Paul Ehlers, Carl Fredericks, Michael Sullivan

Meurtres à Domicile *aka* **Home Murders**
(ODEC/BABY LONE FILMS; BEL,FR) 87min
This horror-thriller is based on the Belgian fantasy writer Thomas Owen's novel *Hôtel Meublé*, in which the author evokes an atmosphere of mysterious depravity punctuated with broad black humour as he sketches life in a gloomy apartment block in Brussels. The plot has a woman detective (Duperey) investigate a murder in the block, thereby presenting director and editor Lobet with an opportunity to review its eccentric inhabitants – a necrophiliac undertaker, a phoney clairvoyant who doubles as an exorcist (Dutheil), a sculptor and the young model he lives with, an aged theatrical ham (Giraudeau), and so on. The opportunity to rework the conventions of the genre by casting a woman as the detective is wasted as the unimaginative direction constantly allows suspense to degenerate into farce, largely through inept handling of the actors. The apartment house never becomes as malignant a dwelling as in **Malpertuis** (1972) nor does the film reveal the oppressive, slightly eerie mediocrity of Brussels, which is expertly conveyed in Chantal Akerman's *Jeanne Dielman* (1975).

d Marc Lobet *p* Violette Vercruyssen, Jacques Vercruyssen *s* Jean Van Hamme *c* Ken Legargeant *lp* Anny Duperey, Bernard Giraudeau, André Bernier, M. A. Dutheil, Daniel Emilfork, Alain Flick, Idwig Stephane

Morbus *aka* **Morbus, o Que Aproveche**
(PRODUCCIONES CINEMATOGRAFICAS TA. SOC. CO-OP; SP) 90min
Following the example of Jesús Franco and his *Macumba Sexual* (1981), Ferre's odd movie combines elements of zombieism with sex and satanism and ends up as nothing more than a macabre joke. The film starts with a mad scientist who discovers a serum to revive the dead; this results in the flesh-eating zombies. The sex is introduced as a pair of prostitutes take their clients into the forest, where the predictable zombie attack occurs. One of the women escapes and takes refuge in the house of a novelist who happens to be her ex-lover. The zombies' next victims are members of a satanic sect, who indulge in both bloody and sexual practices, and as a result of this attack, a second woman takes shelter in the novelist's house. The story's twist is that everything was a figment of the writer's drug-sodden imagination, whereupon the door opens and a horde of monstrous creatures invade the house. These are then revealed to be the writer's friends playing a practical joke. In the process, every opportunity to show sadism, cannibalism and, especially, lots of female nudity has been exploited to the commercially acceptable limit.

d/p Ignasi P. Ferre Serra *s* Isabel Coiset *c* Paco Riba *lp* Joan Borras, Carla Day, Mon Ferrer, Victor Israel, Montse Calvo, Irene Rives, Mireya Tejero, Sony Young

La Morte Vivante *aka* **The Living Dead Girl**
(LES FILMS ABC/FILMS ALERIAZ/FILMS DU YAKA; FR) 98min
In between the awful **El Lago de los Muertos Vivientes** (1980) and this rather well made zombie picture, Rollin had directed a sexy and violent thriller called *Les Echappées* (1981), his first attempt at a movie that was neither a fantasy nor a hard-core porn quickie. Returning to more familiar territory, he relied on aspects of **Les Yeux Sans Visage** (1959) to imbue this tale with a sense of the surreal: here too a woman goes out to procure victims for her friend, as did Alida Valli in Georges Franju's film. But that's where the resemblance ends. The plot has a lovely dead girl (Blanchard) revived by the gasses released by an earthquake. As she consumes more and more blood, haunting a castle in a volcanic area of the Auvergne where she once lived, she finds her memory and her consciousness returning to her, including an awareness of her death. A childhood friend (Pierro) proves to have remained devoted to her and agrees to provide victims to satisfy her bloodlust. But, as in **Fascination** (1979), lust is stronger than love and death triumphs as Blanchard eventually consumes her friend.

Although some sequences echo the surreal lyricism of his best pictures (**Lèvres de Sang**, 1975; **Requiem pour un Vampire**, 1971), bloody gore tends to swamp the proceedings. For his next picture, Rollin made his second thriller, *Les Meurtrières* (1983).

d/co-s Jean Rollin *p* Sam Selsky *co-s* Jean Ralf *c* Max Monteillet *se* Benoît Lestang *lp* Marina Pierro, Françoise Blanchard, Mike Marshall, Carina Barone, Fanny Magier, Jean-Pierre Bouyxou, Dominique Treillou, Jean Cherlian

Next of Kin
(FILM HOUSE/SIS PRODUCTIONS; AUST) 86min
This is an old-dark-house thriller with the added twist that the house is a home for the aged. A woman (Kerrin) returns to take charge of the house after her mother's death only to find strange goings-on, which echo those described in her dead mother's diary. Then, a long-lost and presumed dead relative (Gibson) is revealed. Neither the script nor the direction are able to sustain the intensity or the pace that would make such predictable material acceptable. Characterization is minimal, forcing the performers to emote within the impossibly narrow registers in a surfeit of reaction shots. The explosive climax is well orchestrated but echoes dozens of telefilms, and only Klaus Schulze's electronic score provides some interest.

d/co-s Tony Williams *p* Robert le Tet *co-s* Michael Heath *c* Gary Hansen *lp* Jackie Kerrin, John Jarratt, Gerda Nicolson, Alex Scott, Charles McCallum, Bernadette Gibson, Robert Ratti, Debra Lawrence, Tommy Dysart

Death stalks the old dark house in Next of Kin.

L'Occhio del Male *aka* **Manhattan Baby** *aka* **The Possessed** *aka* **The Eye of the Evil Dead**
(FULVIA FILM; IT) 91min
Having already pillaged George Romero for his **Zombi 2** (1979) and poorly imitated Jesús Franco in **Lo Squartatore di New York** (1982), for this film Fulci takes as his source Mike Newell's mediocre **The Awakening** (1980). An American Egyptologist is struck by blindness in a tomb he discovers (after, à la *Raiders of the Lost Ark*, 1981, overcoming numerous perils). Back in New York, his daughter, wearing an old medallion featuring the symbol of a malevolent Egyptian deity, appears to develop into a vehicle for the forces of evil. This leads into the usual scenes of mayhem until the picture culminates in its only genuine shock sequence. Among the undistinguished cast is Miss Italy 1979, de Ponti, whose subsequent career consisted of coming second in the Miss Universe 1982 contest and participating in eight sex films. Here she tries (in vain) to act fully clothed. For his next film, Fulci delivered a giallo version of the disco-movie genre, *Uccide a Passo di Danze* (1983).

d Lucio Fulci *p* Fabrizio de Angelis *s* Elisa Livia Brigante, Dardano Sacchetti *c* Guglielmo Mancori *lp* Christopher Connelly, Martha Taylor, Laura Lenzi, Giovanni Frezza, Brigitta Boccoli, Cinzia de Ponti

Pengabdi Setan *aka* **Satan's Slave**
(PT RAPI FILM; INDONESIA) 90min
Indonesia's prolific but severely censored film industry turned out a considerable number of horror and fantasy pictures in the early eighties, many of them merely translating Western box-office hits into local settings. This film takes its cue from Don Coscarelli's *Phantasm* (1978) and tells of a boy, Tommy, and his elder sister, Rita, who upon the death of their mother, become prey to a number of parapsychological phenomena apparently provoked by the boy. Rita begins to be haunted by ghostly apparitions, including the horrid spectre of her mother. The death of her boyfriend and that of a gardener then propel the film into gory zombie territory but, as in the zombie pictures of the forties, the undead are like mindless slaves of whoever recalls them to life. In the end, after much melodramatic and picturesque suffering, Rita discovers her governess to be the source of all evil and the witch is burnt. The direction is routine, mostly adopting an American narrative style and rhythm. Gautama made another such movie, *Nyi Blorong Putri Nyi Loro Kidul* (1982) also featuring Pelupessi.

d Sisworo Gautama Putra *p* Gope Samtani *c* F. E. S. Tarigan *lp* Ruth Pelupessi, W. D. Mochtar, Fachrul Rozy, Simon Cader, Diana Suarkom. J. M. Damsyik, Doddy Sukma

Poltergeist
(MGM/SIM ENTERTAINMENT) pv 114min
Produced and co-scripted by Spielberg, maker of the 'family' fantasy, *E.T.* (1982), but directed by Hooper, maker of the grimly gothic **The Texan Chainsaw Massacre** (1974) and **Eaten Alive** (1976), *Poltergeist* shows a split profile. (Indeed unsubstantianted rumours abound that Spielberg shot much of the film himself.) Thus, the story about a young girl (O'Rourke) who apparently becomes possessed by spirits who dwell inside the family TV set and then temporarily disappears into the set, has a whimsical Spielberg preoccupation with the rituals of suburban life. Uneasily integrated with this is the discovery that the housing tract on which the family live was built on the site of a cemetery, a subplot that reaches a climax as the remains of the dead come gruesomely hurtling to the surface in retaliation against those who have violated their domain. This sequence, expertly realized but somewhat conventional, reflects Hooper's sardonic view of the frailty of middle American values in the face of darker, primal forces. The film ends on a jokey note, though, after the family has managed to make its escape, with the father (Nelson) removing the TV set from the motel into which they have moved en route to a new future. Despite individually striking sequences, like the one in which the son (Robbins) is seized by the gaunt tree whose branches sprout through the window, the film leaves an impression of being fatally divided against itself.

d Tobe Hooper *p* Steven Spielberg, Michael Grais, Mark Victor *c* Matthew F. Leonetti *lp* Jobeth Williams, Craig T. Nelson, Beatrice Straight, Dominique Dunne, Oliver Robbins, Heather O'Rourke, Michael McManus, Virginia Kiser, Martin Casella, Richard Lawson, Dianne Freeling

Reversed Enemy (SAM YUNG FILMS; ROK) 82min
A martial arts' film in the fantastique tradition, this picture's plot is of less importance than its lugubrious special effects. In order to avenge the death of her father, a daughter helps another man fight his father but a martial arts' spirit refuses to take her side and defeats her instead. The ancient martial arts' spirit of Ho Ryong is particularly grotesque with his enormous red palpitating tongue and pale blue complexion. The special effects rely mainly on costume and lighting, avoiding both expense and process work.

d Lee Hyuk Soo *p* Kang Dai Jin *s* Ko Sung Ui *c* Chun Cho Myoung *lp* Kwon Il Soo, Choi Hyo Sun

O Secredo da Mumia *aka* **Lago Maldito**
(MAPA FILMES/SUPER 8 PRODUÇOES; BRAZIL) 85min
Not to be confused with *Il Secreto de la Momia* (1972), this Brazilian picture offers an entertaining although amateurish parody of the traditional mummy, as well as of the Dr Moreau, motifs. Cardozo also takes the opportunity to insert spoofs of other genres: the imaginings of a professor lead to a porn pastiche; the music of Curtiz's *The Egyptian* (1954) counterpoints the flashbacks to antiquity; a cellar full of captive creatures echoes mad-scientist movies; the ending, as the anything but frightening mummy (Stambovsky) enters a swamp, recalls Terence Fisher's **The Mummy** (1959) as well as *The Creature from the Black Lagoon* (1954), *The Robe* (1953) and many other films. The best gag of the picture comes when a piece of gauze covers the camera's lens to signify a subjective shot from the mummy's point-of-view. Cardozo learnt his trade under the wing of Marins, about whom he made a documentary in 1978 and who makes a guest appearance in the picture.

d/p Ivan Cardozo *s* Rubem Luchetti *c* Renato Laclete *se* Sergio Farjala *lp* Wilson Grey, Anselm Vasconcellos, Ana Maria Miranda, Clarice Piovesan, Felipe Falcao, Tania Boscoli, José Mojica Marins, Daniel Stambovsky, Regina Casé

Dominique Dunne and Oliver Robbins listen to the TV in Poltergeist.

Sean Hewitt's head is severed by the uncontrollable telepathic powers of Zeljko Ivanek (on screen) in The Sender.

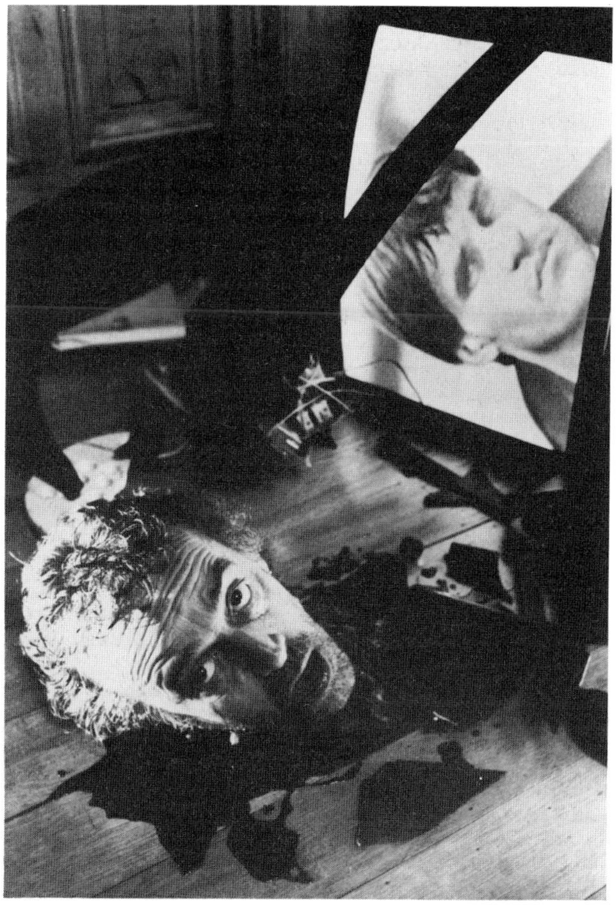

Secta Siniestra *aka* **The Bloody Sect**
(CONEXION FILMS; SP) scope 87min
An awkward mixture of psycho-killer movies, **Rosemary's Baby** (1968) and *Demon Seed* (1977), this film tells of a member of a satanist sect who infiltrates an artificial insemination establishment and puts three spermloads of the devil in circulation. The villain disposes of anyone who tries to interfere by providing an abortion or calling the police, and, although two of the recipients of the sperm are killed, a third victim, with a member of the bloody sect acting as a midwife, gives birth to a little devil who has a devastating effect on his environment. It may be of some interest to note that while a great many movies endow the devil with powerful sexual urges to be vented on women during black masses, this is the only picture to suggest that Beelzebub is an ardent onanist.

d/co-s Steve McCoy *co-s* John Wood (Ignacio F. Iquino), Jackie Kelly *c* Juan Gelpi *se* Anthony Basti, X. Lafita *lp* Mery Kerr, Carlos Martos, Josephine Varney, John Zanni, Henry Ragoud, Diana Conca, Sylvia Alain, Oscar Daniel

The Sender
(KINGSMERE PROPERTIES/PAR) 91min
A first feature by a British-born director who graduated from the National Film School, *The Sender* uses the premise of telepathic communication for the basis of a cleanly told narrative, as well as for some distinctive effects. The central character is a young amnesiac (Ivanek) who is taken to a psychiatric clinic after attempting to drown himself. He then establishes a telepathic link with a psychiatrist (Harrold), which causes her to experience his nightmares. Ivanek, the 'sender' of the title, cannot control his powers; when one of Harrold's colleagues (Freeman) subjects him to shock treatment, the result is that he begins to communicate telepathic images monstrous enough to disrupt the entire hospital. The clue to his condition ultimately proves to lie with his enigmatic mother (Knight). The notion of telepathic communication is made adroitly visual – it manifests itself in the hallucinations which the recipient undergoes – and which, uncommonly, were executed on the set rather than in post-production. To offset the impact of these sequences, Christian treats the main body of the action in functional, understated terms, drawing persuasively detailed performances from his actors, especially Knight. In keeping with this low-key approach, Baum's screenplay avoids predictable trimmings like an extra-mural relationship between Harrold and Freeman. The result is an ambitious and interesting addition to the genre.

d Roger Christian *p* Edward S. Feldman *s* Thomas Baum *c* Roger Pratt *se* Nick Allder *lp* Shirley Knight, Kathryn Harrold, Zeljko Ivanek, Paul Freeman, Sean Hewitt, Harry Ditson, Olivier Pierre, Tracy Harper, Al Matthews, Marsha Hunt, Angus McInnes

El Siniestro Dr Orloff *aka* **The Sinister Dr Orloff**
(GOLDEN FILMS INTERNATIONAL; SP) scope 88min
Still exploiting his first major horror success, **Gritos en la Noche** (1962), Franco here wheels out the demented son of Dr Orloff to perform sadistic surgery on kidnapped female victims, ostensibly to try and save his mother whose body got mangled in a car-crash. The aim is to supply her with new vital parts, but the young man's father intervenes and kills his crazed offspring. The scenes of sex and sadism are pushed as far as Spanish censorship, relaxed after the death of the director's namesake, allows although extra hard-core scenes were shot for more liberal markets. His next effort in the genre, **La Tumba de los Muertos Vivientes** (1982), resorted to the by-now familiar motif of Nazi zombies, while for his own production company, he remade Poe's *The Fall of the House of Usher*, as **El Hundimiento de la Casa Usher** (1983), starring Vernon and Lina Romay.

d/s Jesús Franco *c* Juan Soler *lp* Howard Vernon, Robert Foster, Rocio Freixas, Tony Skios, Tina Page, Mary Olsen, Juan Cozar, Teo Santander

The Slumber Party Massacre
(SANTA FE PRODUCTIONS) 84(76) min
A belated and conspicuously low-budget addition to the teenage massacre cycle begun by **Halloween** (1978), the virtually plotless *The Slumber Party Massacre* is chiefly notable for echoing **The Driller Killer** (1979) in featuring a maniac at large with an electric drill and for being a rare example of a horror movie directed by a woman: other instances are **The Velvet Vampire** (1971) and *Monster* (1980). The action occurs during a single night when an escaped homicidal maniac (Villela) gains access to the house where a teenage girl (Michaels) is giving a 'slumber party' for three of her girlfriends while her parents are away. The maniac puts paid to the three guests, two male classmates who have dropped in, and the girls' basketball coach (Roylance) who has also put in an appearance. But Michaels manages to evade the killer, and when a neighbourhood girl (Stille) and her younger sister (Meyers) arrive, the three girls manage, in what might possibly be seen as a crypto-feminist finale, to do the intruder to death. The film is nondescript but at least fast-paced and decorated by some slick repartee.

d/p Amy Jones *s* Rita Mae Brown *c* Steve (Stephen) Posey *lp* Michele Michaels, Robin Stille, Michael Villela, Debra DeLiso, Andree Honore, Gina Mari, Jennifer Meyers, Joe Johnson, David Millbern, Jean Vragas, Pamela Roylance

Something Wicked This Way Comes
(WALT DISNEY/BRYNA) 95min
A Walt Disney horror movie sounds somewhat implausible, and the texture of Bradbury's novel – about two small boys who realize that the mysterious carnival which stole into town by night has come to steal souls by granting the townsfolk their

secret desires – is here so thinned out that little is left but the bones. Shorn of the self-conscious poetics of Bradbury's prose style, all they add up to is a dismayingly schoolmarmish tale of fathers and sons, the vanity of illusions and homespun recipes for dealing with demons ('Happiness makes them run'). This might have worked well enough had the small-town setting been invested with any sort of reality. But Clayton sets off on the wrong foot by turning it into a Disney toytown, with landscape shots which colour bleaching turns into picture-book illustrations, and a set for the town centre which is attractive enough as a clean, cute idealization but hardly provides a basis for credibility. There is also the problem of the carnival itself, which Bradbury's novel invests with a marvellously shuddery Halloween quality as he describes how the two boys watch the big-top setting itself up in the moonlight without human help. Clayton's carnival, evocatively introduced by a low-angle shot of a locomotive roaring through the night like a black dragon, is a much more prosaic affair, content to settle for a few tacky illusions, some facile shocks (a horde of invading tarantulas), and indifferent special effects like the mist that pursues the boys (Peterson and Carson), or the lightning that threatens to rip their homes apart.

Aside from a few striking moments (significantly enough, they are the moments when the narrative comes closest to reality), the most impressive thing about the film is Pryce's performance as the gauntly top-hatted and alarmingly sinister carnival owner.

d Jack Clayton *p* Peter Vincent Douglas *s* Ray Bradbury *c* Stephen H. Burum *lp* Jason Robards, Jonathan Pryce, Diane Ladd, Pam Grier, Royal Dano, Vidal Peterson, Shawn Carson

Sotto gli Occhi dell'Assassino *aka* Tenebrae

(SIGMA CINEMATOGRAPHIA; IT) 110(101)min

Where the fanciful narratives of Argento's earlier **Suspiria** (1976) and **Inferno** (1980) were no more than pretexts for virtuosity, in *Sotto gli Occhi dell'Assassino*, the plot, while no less artificial, is considerably more important to the movie's function. This is, in fact, rather like an updated 'penny dreadful' in the Edgar Wallace manner. An American detective story writer (Franciosa) visits Rome on a promotional tour and finds himself embroiled in a series of murders of young women, seemingly imitative of his most recent novel. Coming under suspicion, he starts to play sleuth himself, aided by his agent (Saxon), who subsequently is himself murdered. In the end, it proves that though the murders were initiated by a deranged TV personality (Steiner), Franciosa has himself continued them out of psychopathic misogyny. Franciosa apparently commits suicide by cutting his throat, but his action seems to have been faked, and he subsequently murders the investigating policeman (Gemma) and is about to claim another victim (Nicolodi) when he is picturesquely killed by tripping over an elaborate steel sculpture.

Some elements of the material recall **Dressed to Kill** (1980) but Argento's film is in its own way considerably more effective. The killings are staged with a perhaps dubious relish, but visual detail – gloved hands, keys turning in locks – is brilliantly orchestrated to jangle the nerves, and in one extraordinary sequence the camera airily surmounts walls and glides through the windows as it undertakes a prowling inventory of an apartment house where a murder is about to be committed. The on-camera fake suicide might also be seen as a teasing objectification of the director's preferred technique of fooling his audience with sheer technical trickery.

Lamberto Bava, director of the excellent **Macabro** (1980), acted as assistant to Argento on the picture.

d/co-s Dario Argento *p* Claudio Argento *co-s* George Kemp *c* Luciano Tovoli *se* Giovanni Corridori *lp* Anthony Franciosa, John Saxon, Guiliano Gemma, Daria Nicolodi, Christian Borromeo, John Steiner, Veronica Laric, Lara Wendel, Ania Pieroni, Carola Stagnaro

Spasms (NATIONAL TRUST CO; CAN) 89min

A snake from Hell, rejoicing in the name of N'Gana Sunbu, is the supposed star attraction of *Spasms*. Captured in the Tropics by a white hunter, it becomes the property of a US millionaire (Reed), who professes to have been in telepathic contact with it since it killed his brother. Adherents of a sinister snake cult contrive to set it loose and it goes on the rampage – having by this time grown to enormous proportions as a result of the thermostat on its cage being altered. The creature eventually kills Reed before being machine-gunned to death by the parasychologist (Fonda) whom he has enlisted in his attempts to exorcise his obsession with the snake. Every bit as naïve as an old Monogram quickie, *Spasms* lacks the concomitant economy. Reed overacts, Fonda underacts, and Fruet, who previously made *Death Weekend* (1976), directs with noticeable lack of conviction.

The film was adapted from the novel *Death Bite* by Michael Maryk and Brent Monahan.

d William Fruet *p* John G. Pozhke, Maurice Smith *s* Don Enright *c* Mark Swain *se* Brian Warner *lp* Peter Fonda, Oliver Reed, Kerrie Keane, Al Waxman, Miguel Fernandes, Marilyn Lightstone, Laurie Brown, Gerard Parkes

Lo Squartatore di New York *aka* The New York Ripper *aka* The Ripper

(FULVIA FILM; IT) 92(87)min

After his Romero imitations and failed gothic efforts, from **Zombi 2** (1979) to **Il Gatto Nero** and **... E Tu Vivrai nel Terrore! L'Aldila** (both 1981), Fulci here ventures into Jesús Franco's favourite subgenre: the sadistic sex picture. But whereas Franco's **Jack the Ripper** (1976) benefited from the presence of Klaus Kinski and achieved an unpalatable but genuinely perverted delirium, Fulci's film merely records the slashing of eyes, breasts and other bits of anatomy with banal realism, desperately trying to make his picture look like an American product. With unnerving misogyny, every woman who dresses a little sexily, gets humiliated and slaughtered, while the only woman to escape from the Ripper is the one dressed according to provincial standards of Catholic decency. The script even spells out the moral of the story as the investigating detective informs a man whose wife (a nymphomaniac, of course, who dresses up in a raincoat to attend live sex shows) has just been murdered, that sexually 'free' women are fair game for any passing psychotic. The erratically strung together scenes of butchery, punctuated by routinely shot copulation sessions, emphasize the nauseatingly ultra-conservative point-of-view that underpins the film.

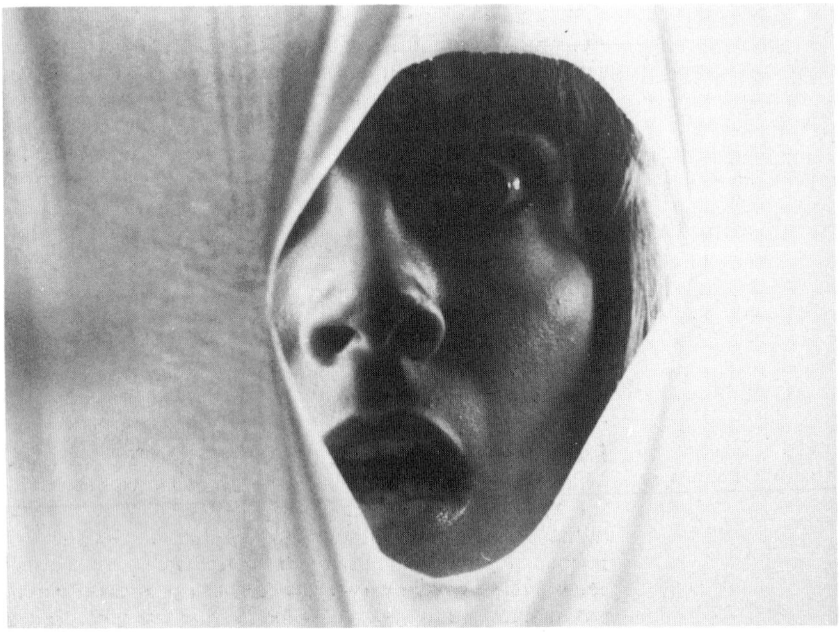

The shock-horror of Dario Argento: Sotto gli Occhi dell'Assassino.

soldiers, one English and one German, and their friends who return to the African desert in search of Rommel's treasure, which they find defended by an army of undead Nazis. The quickie, crammed with Franco's characteristic time-saving zooms and tourist-board footage offers nothing new to the by-now established Nazi zombie subgenre. Franco had been scheduled to make another such story, **El Lago de los Muertos Vivientes** (1980), but it seems that Jean Rollin directed it under the pseudonym J. A. Laser. Franco went on to make more, sexier zombie pictures, including *La Mansion de los Muertos Vivientes*, and the sadistic and racist *Macumba Sexual* (both 1982).

d/co-s Jesús Franco *p* Juan Couret, Miguel Tudela *co-s* Ramón Lido *c* Juan Soler *lp* Manuel Gelin, Eduardo Fajardo, Lina Romay, Antonio Mayans, Javier Maiza, Albino Graziani, Doris Regina, France Jordan

Bette Davis as the recluse in The Watcher in the Woods.

d/co-s Lucio Fulci *p* Fabrizio de Angelis *co-s* Gianfranco Clerici, Dardano Sacchetti, Vincenzo Mannino *c* Luigi Kuveiller *lp* Jack Hedley, Almanta Keller, Paolo Malco, Howard Ross (Renato Rossini), Alexandra delli Colli, Andrew Painter

El Tesoro de las Cuatro Coronas *aka* Treasure of the Four Crowns

(CANNON GROUP/MTG PRODUCTIONS/LOTUS FILMS; SP, US) scope 100(98)min

The veteran director Baldi made his name as a specialist in action-adventure movies, orchestrating the battle scenes in *Ben Hur* (1959), *El Cid* (1961) and *The Fall of the Roman Empire* (1964), among others. With those credits, he must have seemed the right choice to attempt an Italian imitation of *Raiders of the Lost Ark* (1981), combining adventure with horror motifs and designed for 3-D. The rather bovine hero, played by one of the producers (Petitto), goes in search of a legendary Visigoth treasure strictly for mercenary reasons. This requires him to wander through an old feudal castle where, after numerous attacks by snakes, wild dogs and other beasts, he stumbles upon a secret room. This offers an opportunity for special effects' man Unger and makeup wizard de Marchis, who received an Oscar for his work on *King Kong* (1976) and **Alien** (1979), to unleash their 3-D bag of tricks: suits of armour and skeletons come alive, as the forces of evil propel arrows, fireballs, spears and sundry objects towards the audience. The ending features a poltergeist and the villain's hideous head spinning like a top until it eventually disintegrates. Cheaply made, the film never overcomes the handicap of its rather thick hero, but the effects are entertaining.

d Ferdinando Baldi *p/co-s* Tony Anthony (Roger Petitto), Gene Quintano, Marshall Lupo *co-s* Lloyd Battista, Jim Bryce, Jerry Lazarus *c* Marcello Masciocchi, Giuseppe Ruzzolini *se* Fredy Unger, Germano Natali, Roberto Arcangeli, Carlo de Marchis *lp* Tony Anthony (Roger Petitto), Ana Obregon, Francisco Rabal, Gene Quintano, Jerry Lazarus, Emiliano Redondo, Francisco Villena, Kate Levan, Lewis Gordon

La Tumba de los Muertos Vivientes *aka* The Treasure of the Living Dead *aka* The Grave of the Living Dead *aka* Le Trésor des Morts Vivants

(EUROCINE/MARTE FILMS/DIASA; SP, FR) scope 94min

Predictably, the prolific Franco also contributed to the wave of zombie movies while maintaining his output of straight (and less straight) sex movies. Here he tells the story of two ex-

Two Women from the Netherworld

(HAN JIN ENTERPRISES; ROK) 98min

The betrothal of a young girl is broken off after she is raped by a rich warlord and abandoned. She commits suicide and becomes a ghost, condemned to wander the netherworld, where she meets another ghostly victim of the warlord. Together they conspire to return and avenge their deaths by persecuting and killing their tormentor.

With a considerable amount of studio work, Park weaves a credible netherworld parallel to the real world of ancient Korea and the special effects – including a scene in which a coffin rises to a vertical position in an eerily lit field – are an improvement on the results in his previous **Mangryongui Wechingturesu** (1981).

d Park Yoon Kyo *p* Han Kap Chin *s* Lee Jae Hun *c* Ahn Chang Bok *lp* Kim Ki Joo, Huh Jin

The Watcher in the Woods

(WALT DISNEY) 83min

A horror movie under the Disney aegis might seem like a contradiction in terms, and in the event the supernatural trimmings of *The Watcher in the Woods* prove to be of a very mild nature. This is basically an oldfashioned kind of juvenile fiction, in which an American couple (MaCallum and Baker) and their two daughters (Johnson and Richards) settle into an isolated corner of rural England – visualized in determinedly quaint terms – and the two girls become friendly with a strange elderly widow (Davis) whose own daughter disappeared 30 years before. The youthful heroines investigate and find that the missing daughter has been held captive by the alien force of the title. The alien, though, proves essentially well-intentioned, and everything ends up for the best. This is, in fact, family entertainment in the fullest sense, with family relationships seen as paramount – though the treatment is too sketchy, and the setting too unreal, for the film to work at all persuasively on any level. (The confused character of the project was reflected in a fraught production history, with the original version being subject to extensive cuts as well as to the additions of scenes shot under the uncredited supervision of Vincent McEveety.)

d John Hough *p* Ron Miller *s* Brian Clemens, Harry Spalding, Rosemary Anne Sisson *c* Alan Hume *lp* Bette Davis, Carroll Baker, David McCallum, Lynne-Holly Johnson, Kyle Richards, Ian Bannan

The Winged Serpent *aka* Q – The Winged Serpent

(LARCO PRODUCTIONS) 92min

On the strength of *It's Alive* (1973), *God Told Me To* (1976), and *It Lives Again* (1978), Cohen is undoubtedly an inventive film-maker, particularly in combining traditional horror elements with those of other genres. *The Winged Serpent* is also something of a hybrid: partly a traditional monster movie, partly a detective story. Two narratives are intertwined. One deals with the reincarnation of the 'flying serpent': (the Mexican god Quetzalcoatl), by a maniac who has himself been conducting a series of 'sacrificial' murders in the mode of Aztec rites. The other concerns a petty crook (Moriarty), who claims to have stashed his loot in the pinnacle of New York's Chrysler Building, where the serpent has made his home. The best things about the film are Moriarty's playing of the shifty, jazz-loving anti-hero, and the visual use of the Art Deco spire of the Chrysler Building, especially in the sequence in which Moriarty is saved from two suspicious colleagues by the appearance (as unexpected to him as to them) of the serpent. Some of the aerial camerawork is engaging, too, but the film is let down both the the somewhat rudimentary animation of the serpent and by the rambling nature of the storyline, which combines the two narrative strands through the investigations of a laconic cop (Carradine). The result is a movie distinctive in individual sequences, rather than as a whole.

d/p/s Larry Cohen *c* Fred Murphy *lp* David Carradine, Michael Moriarty, Candy Clark, Richard Roundtree, James Divon, Malachy McCourt, Fred J. Scollay, Peter Hock, Ron Cey, Mary Louise Weller

X-Ray *aka* **Hospital Massacre** *aka* **Ward 13**
(CANNON) 88(80)min
As children Susan and her brother David laugh at a Valentine card given her by young Harold. Shortly afterwards she finds David impaled on a coatrack. Nineteen years later Susan (Benton) goes into a hospital for a routine examination only to find herself relentlessly terrorized by Harold who wants to cut her heart out in revenge for his childhood humiliation. Though the film plays effectively enough on the audience's fear of hospitals (hardly very difficult), *X-Ray* is almost fatally undermined by the absurdity of its initial premise and the way in which mass murder is committed in the hospital without anybody seeming to notice. Ex-*Playboy* centrefold and country singer Benton displays her body in a lengthy examination scene which, one suspects, was a large part of the film's *raison d'être*.

Scriptwriter Behm was also responsible for the scripts of *Charade* (1963) and *Help!* (1965).

d/co-s Boaz Davidson *p* Menahem Golan, Yoram Globus *co-s* Marc Behm *c* Nicholas von Sternberg *se* Joe Quinlivan *lp* Barbi Benton, Chip Lucia, Jon Van Ness, Den Surles, Gay Austin, John Warner Williams, Lanny Duncan, Gloria Morrison, Karyn Smith, Michael Frost

Xiaosheng Papa *aka* **Till Death Us Do Scare** *aka* **Till Death Do We Scare**
(CINEMA CITY; HONG KONG) scope 100min
A particularly violent opening scene sets the tone for this horror comedy from one of Hong Kong's most successful family entertainment production companies. The ghosts of the three deceased husbands of an attractive widow try and arrange a match between her (Cheng) and a radio presenter (Tam) whose programme *Scary Ghost Stories* is a miserable flop. However they discover, just before the crucial moment, that the widow is a jinx to any man who tries to consummate a marriage to her. Tam eventually overcomes this problem and the movie has a happy ending. While the film does occasionally become comic, most damagingly in the climactic grand party during the Chinese halloween celebrations, its overall thrust is towards a kind of action horror characteristic of the director, who is the brother of martial arts' supremo film-maker Liu Jialiang (Lau Kar-leung), as well as being a martial artist and kung fu film director himself. The well-known makeup artist Savini was imported especially for this picture and the cast contains some stalwarts from the Cinema City stable, such as Tam, ex-beauty queen Cheng and Tsang, who also directed the company's very popular *Aces Go Places* (1981).

d Lau Kar-wing *p* Carl Mak (Mai Jia), Dean Shek *s* Raymond Wong, Ko Chi-sum *c* Brian Lai, Lam Ah-to *se* Tom Savini, Toho Film *lp* Alan Tam, Olivia Cheng, Eric Tsang, David Chiang (Jiang Dawei), Wong Ching, Raymond Wong, John Keung

Xtro (ASHLEY PRODUCTIONS; GB) 86min
'Not all aliens are friendly' ran the advertising line for this muddled movie – a claim which, along with the title, seems to suggest that the project was optimistically conceived as an adults-only variant of *E. T.* (1982). One of the film's principal characters is, in fact, a child (Nash), whose father (Sayer) has been abducted by UFO and subsequently returns to earth as an alien in human guise and 'converts' the boy to his own ways. This involves telekinesis, giving rise to a quite intriguing sequence in which the child uses his Action Man toy to exact a revenge on a disliked neighbour. The film is clumsily developed, however, with sundry murders of incidental characters and an excursion into triangle melodrama concerning the boy's mother (Stegers) and her lover (Brainin). The resolution, with father and son disappearing in a spaceship, is anti-climactic and Davenport's handling undynamic throughout. But some of the effects, especially the alarming sequence in which the father is 'reborn' fully grown from the woman his alien *alter ego* has just raped, contrive to be impressive in a gratuitous sort of way.

d Harry Bromley Davenport *p* Mark Forstater *s* Iain Cassie, Robert Smith *c* John Metcalfe *se* Tom Harris, Francis Coates *lp* Bernice Stegers, Philip Sayer, Danny Brainin, Simon Nash

Yin Ji *aka* **Kung Fu from Beyond the Grave**
(ETERNAL FILM-HONG KONG-CO; HONG KONG)
Nominally a martial arts' film centred around the themes of revenge and rivalry, this picture gives its plot a new twist by making ghosts its main protagonists. During the Feast of the Hungry Ghosts, spirits are allowed back on earth. In this case, two gangs of them return to earth and help individual humans compete for the *Wonderful Heaven Book* whose martial arts' instructions and invocations bestow upon its possessor the power to conjure up more ghosts and better magic tricks. But their game is brought to a close by a woman whose menstruation destroys all evil powers.

The mythological setting must have inspired the art direction which makes use of a wide variety of props and muticoloured costumes for the ghosts. Although their emergence out of the earth or from the sky recalls fifties and sixties martial arts movies, some of the gorier moments, like

Left: *Simon Nash (left) awaits with* Xtro *to be taken 'home'.*

Robert Joy meets a demon in Amityville 3-D.

the ceremony in front of an altar upon which a fresh human heart has been placed, emphatically characterize this as an eigthties product. The same feast was used as a setting for Li's **Mo Tai** (1983).

d Li Zhao *p* Bao Ming, Shao Weiying *s* Lu Feng *c* Zhang Dewei *lp* Zhuang Quanli, Luo Lie, Daxiyan, Xu Peirong

Das Zweite Gesicht *aka* The Second Face *aka* Second Sight

(BAYERISCHER RUNDFUNK/TURA FILM; WG) 101min

This first feature puts all its energies into creating a sophisticated, atmospheric *mise-en-scène*. The story concerns the attractive bookseller, Anna (Scacchi), who is hypnotically fascinated by a third-floor apartment which causes her to experience hallucinatory second-sight phenomena, suggesting 'she' might have committed suicide there 100 years before. Her boyfriend, meaningfully called Lichtsinn (Schuecke) to underline his immaturity, turns out to be a double for the man who broke her heart in the previous century, but who this time ends up slashing her to death with a piece of glass. The picture's effective scenes are primarily due to Weindler's excellent camerawork, circling around objects, gliding along old photographs and generally sustaining an intensity of vision which allows the props and the settings to take on a life of their own. But these efforts are largely ruined by inept dialogue, inappropriate Bartók music and distracting sound effects. Scacchi is pleasant to look at but that hardly justifies the Max Ophuls prize accorded to the picture in 1983.

d/s Dominik Graf *p* Michael Wiedemann *c* Helge Weindler *lp* Greta Scacchi, Thomas Schnecke, Irene Clarin, Brigitte Karber, Franz Buchrieser, Helene Gaubernack, Charles Brauer

1983

Las Amantes de Señor de la Noche *aka* The Lovers of the Lord of the Night

(CINEMATOGRAFICA FENIX; MEX) 97min

This is the début directorial feature of Vega, the villainess of the ill-fated Boris Karloff vehicle, **La Camara del Terror** (1968), who also appeared in *La Señora Muerte* (1968). The plot here has Vasquez, the lover of Venusita (de Haro), sent to the United States by his father in order to break up the romance. Encouraged by her governess (Vega), de Haro resorts to black magic in order to kill the unreasonable patriarch and to make her lover return to his native village. In its depiction of witchcraft as the embodiment of female strength in the face of an oppressively patriarchal social order, the movie can be seen as contributing to the current re-evaluation of witches in films like Anja Breien's **Forfölgelsen** and Wilfried Minks' **Geburt der Hexe** (both 1981).

d/p/s Isela Vega *c* Angel Bilbatua *lp* Isela Vega, Elena de Haro, Emilio Fernandez (El Indio), Arturo Vasquez, Irma Serrano, Lilia Prado

Amityville 3-D

(ORION/DE LAURENTIIS) 93min

Pretty much a re-run of **The Amityville Horror** (1979), this film has a sceptical journalist (Roberts) moving into the house and suffering much the same experiences as the earlier family except that he resorts to a parapsychologist (Joy) instead of a priest. A scene near the beginning – Roberts and a photographer colleague (Clark) attending a seance to expose it as fake, Roberts is ushered into what appears to be an empty room until, suddenly, a sinister figure looms out of the deep shadow in the *foreground* – suggests that Fleischer understands the potential of 3-D (which he had used before on *Arena*, 1953), but he isn't given much of a chance. Struggling to squeeze more mileage out of Amityville's already exhausted haunted house, the script simply cobbles together a random selection of standbys: deadly insects, self-willed lift, pop-up demon, menaced teenagers. Devoid of logic or excitement, things simply stagger along from manifestation to manifestation while the usual 3-D arsenal is hurled at the audience.

d Richard Fleischer *p* Stephen R. Kesten *s* William Wales *c* Fred Schuler *lp* Tony Roberts, Tess Harper, Robert Joy, Candy Clark, John Beal, Leora Dana

La Bestia y la Espada Magica *aka* The Beast and the Magic Sword *aka* La Bestia y los Samurais

(ACONITO FILMS/AMACHI; SP,JAP) 118(100)min

Although **El Retorno del Hombre Lobo** (1980) had flopped quite disastrously, Molina organized this, the tenth outing for his stock character, Waldemar Daninsky, made for his new Aconito company. The plot starts in 16th-century Japan with a wise man's vain efforts to remove the curse of lycanthropy from the unfortunate Daninsky. The action then moves to Europe where, after numerous sorties of the werewolf, he is put out of his misery by a Japanese woman who is in love with him and performs the final purification ritual by means of a silver sword. This was Molina's second Japanese co-production (after **El Carnaval de las Bestias**, 1980) and apparently benefited from a larger budget than usual for his films. There are some very atmospheric scenes and the overall impact of the picture is more impressive that that of his other self-produced effort that year, **Latidos de Pánico** (1983), a more conventional gothic story reminiscent of Antonio Margheriti's **La Danza Macabra** (1964).

d/p/s Jacinto Molina *c* Julio Burgos *lp* Paul Naschy (Jacinto Molina), Shigeru Amachi, Beatriz Escudero, Junko Asahina, Violeta Cela, Yoko Fuji, Gerard Tichy, Conrado San Martin

Bloodbath at the House of Death

(WILDWOOD PRODUCTIONS; GB) 92min

On his radio and TV shows, Everett created a sense of near hysteria through a frantic succession of gags. This film, scripted by his TV writers, adopts the same format, but what worked on radio and television fails in the cinema and the result is a poor imitation of *Carry On* movies, proving that without an even moderately funny script, even Stephenson, one of the stars to emerge from TV's *Not the Nine O'Clock News*, is boring. The situation invented to provide a setting for and unify the disparate sketches, is an old dark house called Headstone Manor where a great many people were said to have been slaughtered one night. Everett and Stephenson are the 'paranormal' researchers around whom the events – including a satanic ritual with exploding monks and the cloning of the heroes – unfold. The film ends with the house exploding. The references to generic conventions betray the writers' ignorance of the material they pretend to parody. The animation sequences are the work of Graham Garside.

d/p/co-s Ray Cameron *co-s* Barry Cryer *c* Brian West, Dusty Miller *se* Howell Opticals, Hugh Gordon *lp* Kenny Everett, Pamela Stephenson, Vincent Price, Gareth Hunt, Don Warrington, John Fortune, Sheila Staefel, Graham Stark, Pat Ashton, David Lodge

La Casa con la Scala nel Buio *aka* House of the Dark Stairway *aka* A Blade in the Dark

(NATIONAL CINEMATOGRAFICA/NUOVA DANIA CINEMATOGRAFICA; IT) 110min

Mario Bava's son pursued his career as a solo director (begun with **Macabro**, 1980) with this beautifully stylish tale of a composer commissioned to write the score for a giallo film who rents a large, empty house to get the feel of isolation, vulnerability and fear which his music requires. Soon, weird events, including apparently arbitrary murders and disappearing corpses, begin to haunt him as the plot intertwines the story of the composer with that of the film he is supposed to score, propelling the narrative into the realm of fantasy where fears are allowed to escalate according to a relentless dream logic. With the film, Bava explores the possibilities of combining the funereal lyricism of his father with the relentlessly manipulative shock-production techniques of his contemporary, Dario Argento.

d Lamberto Bava *s* Elisa Briganti, Dardano Sacchetti *c* Gianlorenzo Battaglia *lp* Andrea Occhipinti, Lara Naszinski, Anny Papa, Fabiola Toledo, Valeria Cavalli, Michele Soavi, Stanko Molnar

Cujo (TAFT ENTERTAINMENT CO) 91min

The prolific novelist Stephen King was a formative influence on the horror film of the seventies and eighties: adaptations of his work include **Carrie** (1976), **The Shining** (1980) and **Christine** (1982). In each of those films, the catalyst of the drama has been a particular entity – respectively, a person, a building, a car – and in *Cujo* the same applies. Here the catalyst is the eponymous dog, an appealing St Bernard which has the misfortune to be bitten by a rabid bat and turned into a marauder. In a tightly orchestrated narrative, the animal first attacks and kills the roughneck garagiste (Lauter), whose son is Cujo's owner, and one of his cronies (Watson), and subsequently menaces a middle-class mother (Wallace) and child (Pintauro), who have stopped at the garage for car repairs. There is a neat contrast between the two families – Lauter's wife (Lee) has gone away to visit relatives; Wallace's husband (Hugh-Kelly) is away on business – which points up the insecure status of the better-off couple: in fact, Hugh-Kelly is not only in a professional quandary over a key account at the advertising agency he works for but has been on the point of leaving his wife after discovering that she had had an affair with a neighbour (Stone). By extension of this scheme, Cujo becomes the external embodiment of the forces undermining the middle-class 'ideal'. (A similar premise, though articulated much more crudely, informs the low-budget **The Hills Have Eyes**, 1977.)

Interestingly, though, the film ends with the family reunited; Hugh-Kelly arrives just after Wallace has managed to kill Cujo before he can kill her and Pintauro, who have spent hours besieged in their car. This might be seen as a crypto-feminist twist; at any rate, 'traditional' family equilibrium has somewhat shifted. The flaw in the movie's conceptual scheme is perhaps that poor Cujo is a victim of misfortunes and not a product of social forces, as was the giant alligator in *Alligator* (1980), also directed by Teague, and rather more incisively handled.

d Lewis Teague *p* Daniel H. Blatt, Robert Singer *s* Don Carlos Dunaway, Lauren Currier *c* Jan de Bont *lp* Dee Wallace, Daniel Hugh-Kelly, Danny Pintauro, Christopher Stone, Ed Lauter, Kaiulani Lee, Billy Jacoby, Mills Watson, Sandy Ward, Jerry Hardin

Dracula Tan Exarchia (ALLAGI FILMS; GR) 84min

This rare Greek horror effort is an astonishingly bad variation on **Phantom of the Paradise** (1974). In Athens, Dracula and his servant spend their nights digging up famous musicians like Jimi Hendrix and Manos Hadjidakis in order to pillage parts of their anatomy. Their aim is to construct, Frankenstein-fashion, a hairy, invulnerable superstar rock singer. The last half of the film consists of the 'creature's ' performances. The most noteworthy aspect of the movie, besides its silly premise, is its unremitting ugliness.

d/co-s Nikos Zervos *co-s* Yannis Panousis, Vangelis Cotronis *lp* Kostas Soumas, Yannis Panousis, Vangelis Cotronis

Gui An Yan *aka* Obsessed

(CLIC LTD PRODUCTIONS; HONG KONG) 102min

Doubtless influenced by the local success of David Lai's **Possessed** (1983), a number of independent companies rushed to cash in on the horror film trend. This one, directed by King Hu's ex-cameraman, has a stylistic elegance lacking in a number of similar productions. A fireman faints when a charred corpse of a woman reaches out towards him during a fire. Regaining consciousness, he finds himself possessed by the dead woman's spirit and is driven to protecting her younger sister. This mission leads to his death when the sister becomes involved with a photographer who also practices black magic and sorcery. The film's strength derives largely from its intelligent elaboration of the link between sorcery and photography as a means of communication, both of these media also being concerned with the transference of 'a spirit' from one site to another. Chan, who plays a female impersonator killer in Leong Po-chih's *Ye Jinghum* (1982), here extends his range by becoming in effect a male pretence for a female spirit.

d/s/co-c Henry Chan *co-c* Paul Yip *lp* Eddie Chan, Anna Ho, Alexander Wong, Rainbow Ching

Cujo *attacks.*

Catherine Deneuve and David Bowie in the pedestrian The Hunger.

Halloween III: Season of the Witch

(DINO DE LAURENTIIS) pv 98min

Sensibly putting an end to the indestructible killer of **Halloween** (1978), after his poor performance in **Halloween II** (1981), Carpenter decided to start afresh with a script by Nigel Kneale (author of the *Quatermass* series). Described in advance as more in the tradition of *Invasion of the Body Snatchers* (1956), the film arrived looking rather like one might have expected a straight sequel to look, and with Kneale having removed his name from the credits.

The central idea is marvellous: at Halloween, children all over America are clamouring for the toy masks constantly advertised on TV with a habit-forming jingle, and which are in fact deadly destructive devices invented by a mad Irish toymaker (O'Herlihy) who intends to restore Halloween to its witch-cult origins. But instead of opening the way for Celtic mists of myth and magic, this purpose has been elbowed aside as a sort of joke. Kneale's further conception of O'Herlihy's plan as a diabolical revenge on the crass commercialization of Halloween – turning the consumer society's weaponry against itself in a grim and deadly joke – has also been garbled out of all recognition, leaving little more than another maniac running amok and repeatedly illustrating the deadliness of his device. Still, even if developed to formula, the plot *is* ingenious, and the film remains highly enjoyable thanks largely to Cundey's camerawork, which again perfectly captures the menace of small-town streets by night and of figures lurking at the edge of things.

d/s Tommy Lee Wallace *p* Debra Hill, John Carpenter *c* Dean Cundey *lp* Tom Atkins, Stacey Nelkin, Dan O'Herlihy, Ralph Strait, Michael Currie

The Hound of the Baskervilles

(MAPLETON FILMS; GB) 100min

This, the most recent adaptation of Conan Doyle's most famous and most filmed novel, initiated a series of telefilms derived from his stories. These were relatively straightforward, competently filmed dramatizations with one significant innovation: Holmes was presented as an irascible, rude snob whose insufferable arrogance gave the films a decidedly authentic period flavour. Here Holmes (Richardson) is mostly off-screen, leaving Churchill's Watson to take the limelight. Clay is the villain, Shaw the threatened Sir Henry and Lacey puts in an appearance as Lestrade. The acting is uniformly excellent in a theatrical sort of way befitting teledrama, while Taylor's camera manages to infuse the action-packed story with the required sense of eeriness, not an easy task in the small-screen format. The last of the series to date, Roy Ward Baker's *The Masks of Death* (1984) starred Peter Cushing again as the detective, reprising a role he had performed masterfully in Terence Fisher's **The Hound of the Baskervilles** (1958).

d Douglas Hickox *p* Otto Plaschkes *s* Charles Pogue *c* Ronnie Taylor *se* Pablo Perez *lp* Ian Richardson, Donald Churchill, Martin Shaw, Nicholas Clay, Denholm Elliott, Brian Blessed, Ronald Lacey, Glynis Barber, Eleonor Bron, Edward Judd

El Hundimiento de la Casa Usher *aka* The Fall of the House of Usher

(ELITE FILMS; SP) 90min

In between making racist cannibal movies (**El Tesoro de la Diosa Blanca**, 1983), zombie pictures (**La Tumba de los Muertos Vivientes**, 1982) and more or less straight porn films, Franco occasionally returned to gothic stories with films like **El Siniestro Dr Orloff** (1982) and this free adaptation of Poe's classic. Franco regulars Vernon – best remembered for his part in Jean Pierre Melville's *Le Silence de la Mer* (1947) – and Romay seem at home in this effectively shot tale of the neurotically jealous Usher (Vernon) who murders his young wife (Romay), believing her to be unfaithful, only for her to return as a ghost to drive him completely insane and encourage him to commit more and more crimes. When a visiting doctor (Foster) burns the young woman's corpse, Vernon collapses from a heart attack, underlining the fact that the evil female was none other than his *alter ego*. As he dies, the house begins to crumble.

The decidedly basic – though the settings are familiarly conventional – special effects betray both the speed and the budget of the production; besides producing and directing, Franco also scripted and photographed the movie while sharing the music credit with Pablo Villa.

d/p/s/c Jesús Franco *lp* Howard Vernon, Lina Romay, Robert Foster

The Hunger

(RICHARD SHEPARD COMPANY/MGM/UA) pv 99min

A determinedly upmarket vampire movie, full of modish trappings and haute couture, *The Hunger*, directed by former TV commercials' maker Scott – brother of Ridley Scott, maker of **Alien** (1979) – might be regarded as a transatlantic companion piece to the European *Daughters of Darkness* (1971). The high production values and insistent visual elaboration are not, however, organic to the film, but seem merely like glossy top-dressing to a fairly pedestrian narrative. This concerns a vampire couple (Bowie, Deneuve) who retain their youth via successive murders. But Bowie starts ageing and apparently dies; meanwhile, a policeman (Hedaya) is inquiring into Bowie's most recent victim (Ehlers), and a doctor (Sarandon), with whom Bowie has broken an appointment, becomes concerned about him. This leads rather arbitrarily into a secondary narrative concerning a lesbian relationship between Deneuve and Sarandon, with the latter's vampirization leading her first to murder a colleague (de Young), then to stab herself. In a somewhat confusing finale, Deneuve is destroyed by the remains of the sundry lovers she has stored in the attic, and Sarandon materializes elsewhere. Bowie, whose performance and costuming sometimes recall his role in *The Man Who Fell to Earth* (1976), is effective, but Deneuve is required to be little more than a clothes-horse.

d Tony Scott *p* Richard A. Shepherd *s* Ivan Davis, Michael Thomas *c* Stephen Goldblarr, Tom Mangravite *se* Graham Longhurst *lp* Catherine Deneuve, Susan Sarandon, David Bowie, Cliff de Young, Beth Ehlers, Dan Hedaya, Ann Magnusson, Rufus Collins, Suzanne Bertish, James Aubrey

Jaws 3-D

(MCA THEATRICALS/ARRIVISION) 99min

The police chief's kids from **Jaws 2** (1978) grow up. One (Quaid) works at Florida's 'Undersea Kingdom', a new multi-million dollar attraction offering closeup views of marine life. The other (Putch) nurses a pathological fear of water bred by his earlier experience, amply justified when a shark sneaks into the Undersea Kingdom's submarine tubes, killing three people. Helped out by performing dolphins (!), Quaid and Armstrong manage to anaesthetize the intruder, which dies. But in a twist borrowed from *Gorgo* (1961), the shark is followed by its vengeful mother, which wreaks considerable mayhem as the Undersea Kingdom is hurriedly cleared of its panic-stricken visitors. Excellent camerawork helps to prop up a comic-strip plot featuring the odd severed head or limb but remarkably free of gore.

d Joe Alves *p* Rupert Hitzig *s* Richard Matheson, Carl Gottleib *c* James A. Contner *se* Robert Blalack, Praxis Film Works Inc *lp* Dennis Quaid, Bess Armstrong, Simon MacCorkindale, Louis Gossett Jnr, John Putch

Latidos de Pánico *aka* Panic Beats

(ACONITO FILMS; SP) 92min

After the disastrous reception of **El Retorno del Hombre Lobo** (1980), Molina and Saly's production company, Dalmata, was nearly bankrupted; this picture was made in an attempt to re-float the business, and with the crew's agreement to defer payment. The story starts in the 16th century with a jealous knight killing his unfaithful wife. Centuries later, the satanic knight's ghost returns and commits a number of atrocities while his contemporary descendants are busy murdering each other. In the end, all the dead rise up again and gather for the climactic scenes in a church. Molina immediately followed this effort with a Japanese co-production, **La Bestia y la Espada Magica** (1983), his best (though not perfect) movie for years.

d/p/s Jacinto Molina *c* Julio Burgos *lp* Paul Naschy (Jacinto Molina), Julia Saly, Lola Goas, Manuel Zarzo, José Vivo, Paquita Ondiviela, Silvio Miro, Pedro Heras

Mo *aka* The Boxer's Omen

(SHAW BROTHERS; HONG KONG) 98min

Gui's sequel to his **Gu** (1981) begins with a Hong Kong boxer being rescued from a gang attack by a Thai monk who emerges out of nowhere bathed in a golden light. Subsequently, in a Bangkok temple, he is told by a monk that they were twin brothers in an earlier incarnation. The boxer takes on the monk's responsibilities, thereby allowing him to achieve nirvana. But the monk has been plagued by a spell which the boxer only discovers on his return to Hong Kong and which is only banished after a supernatural struggle somewhere in Nepal. Ostensibly a sequel, the film actually attempts to shift its ground more substantially. The visceral, external horror of *Gu* is here replaced by the classic principle of man carrying within himself the seeds of his own destruction. This is graphically illustrated in one of the film's most effectively terrifying moments as coils of worms begin to emerge from the protagonist's eyes during a boxing match. While the magic spells and the use of a Nepalese monk's bones and amulets yield impressive scenes, they cannot compete with the surreal image achieved by Dario Argento's worm shower in **Suspiria** (1976) and here are simply a crudely sensationalist device without any real metaphorical weight in the film's story.

d Gui Zhihong (Kwei Chi-hung, Kuei Chih Hung) *s* Szu-Tu An (Situ An, Szeta An) *c* Li Hsin Ye (Li Xinye, Li Sun Ip), Cao Huiqi, Li Yunkun *lp* Gao Fei, Lin Xiaoyin, Wei Jiawen

Mo Tai *aka* Devil Foetus

(LO WEI MOTION PICTURE CORP; HONG KONG) 95min

Like Dennis Yu's **Xiong Bang** (1981), this film takes its cue from **Rosemary's Baby** (1968) and **The Exorcist** (1973) while using the same festival setting as **Yin Ji** (1982). During the Feast of the Hungry Ghosts, a member of a rich landowning family buys an antique jade which is revealed to contain a monster. The thing materializes and makes love to the family's mother. The father destroys the jade but this causes him such physical agony that he commits suicide. The mother also dies in an accident soon afterwards, but an exorcist discovers that she was pregnant with a 'devil foetus' and drapes the coffin and the house with amulets which must stay in place for 12 years. Some 11 years later, the family's grandchildren interfere with the charms and trigger a new case of possession.

The redeeming feature of this contribution to the series of films derived from Western box-office hits, is its sense of the absurd, especially in the lovemaking scene with the mother. Sequences involving the exorcist are the most substantial aspect of the movie, largely because the incantations and the use of amulets appear to have been well researched and authentic. But the other elements of the story tend to veer between the usual conventions of melodrama and thrillers without any real commitment to explore or renovate either genre.

d/s/c Liu Honquan *p* Luo Wei, Xu Lihua *lp* Lu Xuiling, Eddie, Lu Beibei

Pao Dan Fei Che *aka* The Trail

(GOLDEN HARVEST; HONG KONG) 100min

The image of zombie-like creatures shepherded at night by shamans and monks is familiar from Chinese literature and folklore; the idea behind the imagery is that a man who dies away from home has to be brought back for burial. The motif is also part of Liu Jialiang's *Spiritual Boxer Part II* (1979) and Wu Ma's *The Dead and the Deadly* (1983). Here a band of smugglers disguise themselves as zombies to transport opium on the assumption that no one would be foolish enough to try and stop them. When one of the smugglers is killed, the survivors' investigation follows a trail of blood that leads to an ancient pagoda inhabited by a vampire.

Hui, best known as the director-star of some of Hong Kong's most successful comedies, was the moving force behind the movie. One of his brothers, Ricky – a regular star in Michael's comedies – is here played off against Zhang Zeshi, who assumes the same frustrated persona Michael incarnates in his own films. Yet, despite this, the film fits more comfortably into the horror – rather than comedy – genre, as Yu orchestrates the picture's horror around notions of power and manipulation so that the vampire is shown to be controlled by a heinously rich village leader just as, in their own way, the smugglers used and controlled the zombies. In addition, a considerable amount of

Disaster comes to Undersea Kingdom in Jaws 3-D, *one of the wave of 3-D films of the eighties.*

Tony Perkins returns home in Psycho II.

care has been taken to create the right atmospheres, as in the scene where the smugglers have to dispose of a corpse in a sulphurous pool. Dennis and Ronny Yu were the co-founders of the Film Force, a shortlived production company of young Hong Kong directors.

d/co-s Ronny Yu *p/co-s* Michael Hui (Xu Guanwen) *c* Chen Xiaoming (James Chan) *lp* Ricky Hui (Xu Guanying), Zhang Zeshi, Cheung Fat, Miao Tian, Tin Liang, Hsu Siu Ning

Possessed

(JOHNNY MAK PRODUCTION; HONG KONG) 100min

Drawing extensively on pop-folk superstition and a gamut of Hollywood films including **The Entity** (1982), **The Exorcist** (1973) and **Poltergeist** (1982), Lai presents a convincing tale of paranoia in the city. A pair of detectives (Lau and Xiao) follow a suspect to an old dark house where they catch a deranged murderer. The man turns on Lau, who shoots him. The two policemen then begin to experience strange events as a mysterious force kills Xiao's sister and rapes his girlfriend. A woman fortune-teller explains that all this is the handiwork of one of his dead father's victims seeking revenge (his father was also a cop). In a ritual of exorcism, the fortune-teller and her master invoke the power of the four-faced Buddha which breaks the curse but also kills everybody except for Xiao. As in *Poltergeist*, the picture's main preoccupation is the sins-of-the-fathers motif. The final struggle between good and bad, complete with umbilical cord imagery derived from the Hollywood film, is set in a 'home' which is destroyed. Both the subject and the quality of the special effects spawned a further series of derivations, including **Red Spells Red** (1983).

Following a successful career in local television, Mak specialized in producing a cinematic equivalent of the gutter press, taking sensational reports and turning them into exaggerated exploitation telefilms. On the basis of the production company's overall output, Lai, who previously directed *Lonely 15* (1982) for Mak, must be regarded as the producer's creature rather than as an individual film-maker.

d David Lai (Li Dawei) *p* Johnny Mak (Mai Dangxiong) *s* Ou Huahan (John Au) *c* Bob Thompson *lp* Liu Zhaoming (Lau Siu Ming), Xiao Yulong (Siu Yuk Lung), Wen Bixia, Chen Chisui (Sue Chan), Irene Wan

Psycho II (OAK INDUSTRIES/U) 113min

Released as cured after 22 years in an asylum, Norman Bates (Perkins) returns home – to a job in a diner pending new arrangements at the motel – for a sequel to **Psycho** (1960) which is a lot better than anyone could conceivably have anticipated. It opens with a truncated re-run of the original shower-bath murder. Although on the face of it an unwise move, this is amply justified by Franklin as he and cinematographer Cundey carefully resurrect Hitchcock's world through exact pastiche (shots of the looming house, the window with the mysteriously twitching curtain, Perkins silhouetted like a scarecrow in the night), through clever extension (the diner, crowded and utterly normal, yet somehow a twin to the Bates motel in its eerie isolation), and amused reference (a shot – when Perkins first goes upstairs and starts back in terror as his mother's voice calls from a slowly opening doorway – of his forgotten suitcase tumbling down the stairs in imitation of Arbogast's body).

The difficulty the film then faces is one of *déjà vu* concerning Perkins' propensities, and it falls back a little lamely on either comedy (blackish, but much too knowingly nudging), or on the convolutions of a plot which allows for as many stabbings as **Friday the 13th** (1980). With Miles still on the warpath and using her daughter (Tilly) to avenge Janet Leigh's death in *Psycho*, and with Perkins' *real* mother (Bryar) turning up and proving as possessive as the one now revealed as a foster parent, and with everybody seemingly taking their turn at being dead Mrs Bates, the film somehow threatens to turn into a mad mothers' convention.

Two sequences at least claw their way into authentic *Psycho* territory. One is a strange and tormented scene where Perkins entrusts Tilly to the room where he used to sleep as a child, and she wakes to find him standing guard with an enormous knife, a lover-executioner tenderly mumbling, 'You smell like the toasted cheese sandwiches my mother used to bring me'. The other is the wonderfully deadpan finale in which Perkins, his world on a recognizably even keel again, politely asks his mother if she's *sure* she doesn't want a sandwich before braining her with a shovel and going happily back to square one. Here, albeit briefly, the ghoulish chill of *Psycho* lives again.

Robert Bloch, author of the source novel for *Psycho* but left out in the cold on *Psycho II*, responded with a dispiriting novel – *Psycho II* – which uses dead psychology to suggest we are all Norman Bates under the skin.

d Richard Franklin *p* Hilton A. Green *s* Tom Holland *c* Dean Cundey *lp* Anthony Perkins, Vera Miles, Meg Tilly, Robert Loggia, Claudia Bryar, Dennis Franz

Pura Sangre *aka* Pure Blood

(LUIS OSPINA; COL) 98min

Ospina's début film is a macabre political allegory about a Howard Hughes-type tycoon who requires regular doses of fresh blood to survive. Three assistants, including nurse Florencia (Lemaitre), help the businessman/vampire's son and heir supply the patriarch with a steady stream of victims recruited from the nation's youngsters. The scenes showing the vampire recluse sitting in his room wired up to the blood machine, watching movies on TV, evoke both the Hughes and Getty business empires in terms of the behaviour of their founders but the various killings are treated exploitatively, undercutting both the political point of the movie and its nice line in bizarre black humour. Successful in Colombia, the picture spawned an imitation, **Carne de Tu Carne** (1984), co-edited by Ospina and directed by Mayolo, one of the scenarists of this picture.

d/p/co-s Luís Ospina *co-p* Rodrigo Castano *co-s* Alberto Quiroga *c* Ramón Suarez *lp* Florina Lemaitre, Carlos Mayolo, Humberto Arango, Luís Alberto Garcia, Gilberto 'Fly' Forero, Franky Linero

Red Spells Red

(NIKKO INTERNATIONAL FILMS; HONG KONG) 97min

This film draws on the special effects made popular by **Poltergeist** (1982) via its direct derivative, David Lai and Johnny Mak's **Possessed** (1983), but is the least successful of the three movies. While filming a cursed stone tablet on location in south-east Asia, Le Yiwei, an attractive TV presenter, unknowingly frees a 'little red devil' which proceeds to persecute the team. Shooting in Borneo, two members of the crew are killed in mysterious circumstances and the image of the 'red devil' appears on the rushes of their footage. A priest discovers the spell cast on Le and the subsequent exorcism leaves only the hero alive. There is an unevenness of tone in the film which results from the unresolved mixture of documentary footage of the south-east Asian locations and the totally studio-bound extended climactic sequence. The situation demanded some degree of plausibility but He Yong Lin's narrative moves along ploddingly, bogged down in artifice up to and including the explosion of effects during the final exorcism scenes.

d He Yong Lin *s* Chen Xueming *c* Chen Yongchang, Wang Yonglong *lp* Tang Zhenye, Pau Lixian, Jia Lun, Wan Tingfang

Die Schwarze Spinne *aka* The Black Spider

(PICA FILM; SWITZ) 98min

The early-19th-century preacher and novelist Jeremias Gotthelf wrote his edifying tales as a form of moral instruction for the Swiss peasantry. *Die Schwarze Spinne*, first published in 1842, encourages villagers to try and bear their lot, no matter how miserable their lives and tyrannical their rulers may be. It was made into an opera in 1936 and again in 1949, and Rissi here repeats the lesson for the benefit of today's generation. The story recounts how, in the Middle Ages, a tyrannical knight (Ehrlich) treated the peasants like slaves. A beautiful farmer's wife (Kessler), not a native of the area, makes a pact with the devil in order to lighten the burden weighing on their lives: she promises not to baptize her child. When she breaks her pledge, a black spider appears in the village and spreads the plague. Ehrlich, and many others, succumb to the illness before a virtuous woman catches and imprisons the spider. Although the spider – evil – is clearly closely connected with female sexuality, the story's main lesson is that a refusal to submit to injustice is against the 'rules' and will have dire consequences.

The story was written as an attack on the liberal ideas spreading from the corrupting and corrupted cities. Rissi incorporates that dimension into the picture by providing a modern-day framing narrative in which young drug addicts, cheated by their supplier, break into a chemical plant and unwittingly cause a major disaster which spreads lethal toxic substances through the region. *The Black Spider* story is then presented as the hallucination of a young woman on a drugs' trip. The parallel between a pact with the devil and drug usage as a means of alleviating intolerable pressures, which in fact end up doing untold harm, may be tenable to a degree but the film's lurid portrayal of the youngsters suggests Rissi isn't advocating a turn away from drugs into rationally revolutionary politics, but merely to try and be happy with the status quo.

d Mark M. Rissi *p* Edward Steiner *s* Walter Kauer *c* Edwin Horak *se* Giacomo Peier, Cornelius Defries, Bruno Reithaar *lp* Beatrice Kessler, Peter Ehrlich, Walo Lueoend, Walter Hess, Sigfrit Steiner, Henrik Rhyn, Peter Schneider, Christine Wipf, Michael Gempart

El Tesoro de la Diosa Blanca *aka* The Treasure of the White Goddess

(ELITE FILMS; SP) 91min

With this effective quickie patterned on the Tarzan story, Franco extended his series of racist sex-and-violence pictures begun in Italy with such films as **Ultimo Monde Cannibale** (1976), **La Montagna del Dio Cannibale** (1978) and **Il Fiume del Grande Carmano** (1979). An English expedition looking for treasure and for a white girl kidnapped by a black African tribe of cannibalistic headhunters, discover the latterday Jane to be the tribe's topless ruler. A black sorceress engineers some gory mischief but Wiener reasserts her authority over the 'nasty' blacks and saves the great white hunter (Foster) with whom she has fallen in love.

As in the Tarzan films, the heroine decides to stay in the jungle rather than 'return' to civilization, presumably (given the racial tone of the whole film) because women, children, blacks and animals are supposed to be closer to nature and 'the wild' than white men.

d/p/s Jesús Franco *c* Joan Almirall *lp* Katia Wiener, Robert Foster, Albino Grazianni, Javier Maiza

L'Ultima Casa Vicino al Lago *aka* The Last House Near the Lake

(CINEZETA; IT) 91min

With this movie, Girolami, a veteran of Italian westerns and action pictures, ventured into Jesús Franco's sexy-horror territory with some success, largely because of Fani's engaging personality which at times recalls Maria Schneider's brittle vulnerability. The narrative excuse to show her in morbidly sensual sex scenes is that a witch's curse makes her collapse into a faint when she has an orgasm, and she only revives when her partner dies. The 'modern' motorbike-riding heroine, living in an old, inherited castle, becomes hypnotically fascinated by another attractive woman, Lillith (Gardenia). One day, the pair begin a vicious fight with each other which gradually turns into a tenderly lesbian encounter, at which point both their bodies are suddenly engulfed by flames that appear to emerge out of the earth. This fantasy could have made an enchanting short and Girolami has to pad the movie with scenes involving an old painter in order to stretch it into feature length, but enough vividly erotic scenes – some set in a cemetery – remain to make this a very entertaining fairytale with deliciously subversive undertones, a rare event in cheap sex-and-horror films.

d Enzo G. Castellari (Girolami) *lp* Eleneora Fani, Wolfgang Soldati, V. Gardenia

La Villa delle Anime Maledette

(ANTONELLIANA CINEMATOGRAFICA; IT) 91min

After the well-received post-holocaust telefilm, *La Citta dell'Ultima Paura* (1975), and an alien body-snatcher picture called *Invasione* (1978), neither of which received a theatrical release, Ausino and Peyretti made this extremely stylish gothic tale set in Turin. Four young people inherit a house where once two men and a woman savagely destroyed each other. The house and its menacing caretaker begin to exercise their malevolent influence on the youngsters, which leads to more disturbingly orchestrated deaths. The villain is revealed to be the caretaker, a satanic sorcerer and instigator of a curse that has pursued the family for seven generations. Only the young Elisa (Grapputo) escapes the carnage.

Ausino makes ample and effective use of dolly-shots to create and sustain his parapsychological spells, and at times manages to evoke the flamboyantly funereal romanticism of the Italian master Mario Bava (shown in such classic films as his **Operazione Paura**, 1966, for example).

d/s Carlo Ausino *p* Michele Peyretti *se* Luciano Vittori, Lucia Laporta *lp* Annamaria Grapputo, Jean-Pierre Aumont, Beba Loncar, Giorgio Ardisson

Zeder *aka* **Zeder – Voices from the Beyond**
(AMA FILM/RAI; IT) 100(92)min
Avati is one of the most creative directors working in the horror genre today. This, his most recent horror movie, at times recaptures the uncannily chilling atmosphere he achieved in **La Casa dalle Finestre che Ridono** (1976). A writer (Lavia) is given an old typewriter by his wife (Canovas) and discovers strange sentences on its ribbon. He becomes intrigued by the theory he pieces together: a 19th-century writer, Paolo Zeder, maintained there were special areas in the world called K territories which were located out of time and where, since ageing and death don't exist, whoever is buried there can return from the dead. Lavia finds such a K territory in Italy where a group of Frenchmen are busy trying to resurrect a defrocked priest. The evil priest eventually materializes after many other bizarre events and gruesome crimes. As in *La Casa*, a sense of anguish filters into the story bit by bit, building up to an unnerving climax. But the main impact left by the picture, besides individual hallucinatory images, is the overwhelming morbidity written into the very texture of the movie: Avati even has Zeder's disciples put a camera inside a coffin in order to record what happens after burial, in one of the most macabrely voyeuristic scenes in the genre since **Peeping Tom** (1960). The script was inspired by the mysterious figure of Fulcanelli, the pseudonym of a 20th-century alchemist whose real identity still hasn't been settled. Although the best-known disciple of Mario Bava is undoubtedly Dario Argento, Avati is his talented successor. He also furnished the scenario for Lamberto Bava's extraordinary **Macabro** (1980).

d/co-s Pupi Avati *co-p* Gianni Minervini *co-p/co-s* Antonio Avati *co-s* Maurizio Costanzo *c* Franco delli Colli *lp* Gabriele Lavia, Anne Canovas, Bob Tonelli, Paola Tanziani, Cesare Barbetti, Aldo Sassi, Veronica Moriconi, Alessandro Partexano

1984

Body Double (COL/DELPHI PRODUCTIONS) 114min
De Palma's films have almost invariably aroused charges of voyeuristic sexism and unbridled cribbing from Hitchcock, but none more so than *Body Double*. In the last analysis, however, this may have more to do with external factors than with the film itself. Thanks to the recent revival of Hitchcock classics more people have actually *seen* the films de Palma so obsessively references in his own work, and in the wake of the recent spate of gore movies, debate about screen violence (and especially to women) has increased enormously.

Body Double shares the same movie-world setting as the under-rated *Blow Out* (1981). It concerns a struggling actor Jake who is fired from a vampire movie when his claustrophobia begins to interfere with his work. An actor friend lends him his home while he is away and Jake becomes fascinated by his neighbour Gloria, who nightly performs an erotic strip which he watches through a telescope. Fascinated, he begins to follow her, until she is gruesomely murdered ....

Stylistically and formally *Body Double* is one of de Palma's most virtuoso performances to date with the camera seductively and obsessively tracking, craning and zooming at every possible opportunity. Even though Jake's pursuit of Gloria does recall *Vertigo* (1958) and the museum scene in **Dressed to Kill** (1980) it is nonetheless intensely hypnotic and a real cinematic *tour de force*. Like **Blow Out**, *Body Double* is indeed ultimately *about* cinema itself, and thus, of course, *about* voyeurism too. The film is a labyrinth of mirrors in which, in the last analysis, there is only the play of looks, the interplay between truth and fakery, voyeurism and the real. *Body Double* is a truly modern work, concerned as it is with the confusion of perception, with uncertainty as to the limits of the tangible and the imaginary, of desire and fantasy.

d/p/co-s Brian de Palma *co-s* Robert J. Avrech, Brian de Palma *c* Stephen H. Burum *lp* Craig Wasson, Gregg Henry, Melanie Griffith, Deborah Shelton, Guy Boyd, Dennis Franz, David Haskell

Craig Wasson and Melanie Griffith in Body Double, *Brian de Palma's little-league version of Alfred Hitchcock's* Vertigo *(1958).*

Carne de Tu Carne *aka* **Flesh of Your Flesh**
(PRODUCCIONES VISUALES; COL) 85min
The domestic success of Luís Ospina's **Pura Sangre** (1983) spawned this imitation, co-edited by Ospina and directed by Mayolo, one of the scenarists on *Pura Sangre*. Set in 1956, shortly after Laureano Gomez had been ousted by General Pinilla, the story presents the country's political history in terms of the incestuous and gory goings-on, including vampirism, within a rich family. The film is dedicated to Roman Polanski and Roger Corman and told in the manner of an exploitative horror picture, but the rules of the genre, leavened with black comedy, take over and the film degenerates into an orgy of blood, totally losing control over the political dimensions of the tale.

d/co-s Carlos Mayolo *p* Berta del Carvajal, Fernando Baron *co-s* Elsa Vasquez, José Nieto *c* Luís Gabriel Beristain *lp* Adriana Herran, David Guerrero, José Angel

C.H.U.D. (COL/DELPHI PRODUCTIONS) 87(110)min
An interesting addition to the toxic-waste monster cycle (*Forbidden World*, 1982; *Impulse*, 1982; *The Toxic Avenger*, 1983) *C.H.U.D.* (an acronym for Cannibalistic Humanoid Underground Dwellers) concerns flesh-eating creatures living in the sewers of New York. As the film progresses the Malevolent Authority subtext common to almost all the films in this particular cycle comes to the fore with the revelation that hazardous radioactive waste has been dumped under the city, and that this has turned the derelicts who live in the sewers into ravening cannibals. Thus C.H.U.D. also stands for Contamination Hazard Urban Disposal.

Delayed by post-production tampering (which resulted in the removal of various above-ground scenes in the process of re-editing), rather too talky and with an awkward story structure, *C.H.U.D.* is nevertheless impressive. The acting and characterization are a good deal better than is customary in a low-budget exploitationer, making the above-ground scenes more than just a preamble to the subterranean ones, and the Malevolent Authority theme recalls the wonderful **Death Line** (1972). If the monsters look more like conventional demons than mutated derelicts they're nevertheless reasonably scary, and the underground scenes are pleasingly atmospheric.

d Douglas Cheek *p* Andrew Bonime *s* Parnell Hall, Shepard Abbott *c* Peter Stein *se* John Caglione Jnr *lp* John Heard, Kim Greist, Daniel Stern, Christopher Curry, George Martin, John Ramsey, Eddie Jones

Children of the Corn (NEW WORLD) 92 min
Based on a short story by Stephen King, this starts out well enough with a pre-credit sequence which establishes a small Nebraska town one tranquil Sunday morning just as church is coming out. Then, as people repair to the drugstore for refreshment, a guerrilla unit of children led by a youth in clerical garb suddenly dispose of their elders in an orgy of throat-cutting. The shock effect is neatly enhanced by a bland off-screen narration in which a small boy innocently recalls what happened that day. Three large flaws in the film soon become apparent, however. The first is that credibility is severely strained when the film proper begins with two strangers (Horton and Hamilton) driving into town – a cliché in itself – to find total dereliction, cut telephone wires and the children worshipping some dark god of the cornfields to whom they offer human sacrifices. Three years, we are told, have passed. Hasn't anybody noticed? The second flaw is the rather arty-crafty direction which seems more concerned to draw attention to itself than to develop a clean narrative-atmospheric line. But the definitive third flaw lies in the material itself. Instead of following up the intriguing implications of a middle American religious revival gone wrong, it opts for cheap supernatural thrills, with something or other tunnelling under cornfields like an angry mole. The result is a trite film.

d Fritz Kiersch *p* Donald P. Borchers, Terence Kirby *s* George Goldsmith *c* Raoul Lomas *lp* Peter Horton, Linda Hamilton, R. G. Armstrong, John Franklin, Courtney Gains

The Company of Wolves
(PALACE PICTURES; GB) 95min
Perhaps ironically, it took an Irish novelist to direct the most intelligent and visually stunning 'British' fantasy film since Hammer's heyday in the sixties. Jordan, whose previous feature (*Angel*, 1982) had revealed a lyrical sense bordering on the surreal, collaborated with fellow writer Carter on the script which is derived from a number of her tales, principally *Wolf Alice* and *The Company of Wolves*, to provide an imaginative rendition-cum-critique of Perrault's *Little Red Riding Hood*. The plot is constructed in Chinese-box fashion with one narrative generating another, each one elaborating or modifying the elements that went before. The main characters are the storytelling Granny (Lansbury) and the growing Rosaleen (Patterson) whose journey into sexual maturity provides the thread holding the fragmented narrative together. Refreshingly, the picture refuses any simple equation between wolves and male sexuality, preferring to dramatize the ambiguities inherent in the fantasy itself: Patterson's fear of wolves is matched by her erotic fascination with them, making 'the beasts' a metaphor of sexuality's awakening in both boys and girls.

Shot entirely in a studio, the visual intensity of Jordan's film has rarely been seen in British-produced pictures and the lovely, menacingly weird and wonderful forest and deliriously gothic village square are reminiscent of the best of German expressionism. The special effects, possibly inspired by the transformation scenes of **An American Werewolf in London** (1981), are uniformly excellent and integrate well into the story. The film's main achievement is its successful presentation of the very fabric of fantasy: whereas Mario Bava and others succeeded in this by neglecting the literary aspects of their often silly scripts, Jordan's audacious film goes for fantasy textures and dream logic from the start, making the picture uncontainable within any existing genre. It doesn't veer from fairytale to horror and black comedy but manages to be all at the same time throughout. The result is an unusual film, both beautiful and intelligent, a rare combination at the best of times, but especially so in British cinema.

The Company of Wolves, *the most intelligent British horror film since the heyday of Hammer.*

d/co-s Neil Jordan *p* Stephen Wolley, Nik Powell *co-s* Angela Carter *c* Bryan Loftus *se* Peter McDonald, Alan Whibley, Christopher Tucker *lp* Angela Lansbury, Sarah Patterson, David Warner, Graham Crowden, Brian Glover, Kathryn Pogson, Stephen Rea, Tusse Silberg, Micha Bergese, Georgia Slowe

Death Warmed Up
(TUCKER FILMS/NZFC; NZ) 90min
Blyth's second violent action film develops into what *Variety* called a 'surreal-art deco-punk' horror movie. A high-tech surgeon (Day), programmes the young hero (Hurst) to be mean to his parents, whereupon he slaughters them. On being released from the asylum, which proved a salutory experience for the deviant, the blonde hero runs across the intellectual villain again on a remote island where Dr Moreau-type experiments are in progress to produce an army of homicidal mutants. Hurst is then forced to become the brutal saviour of mankind – a mythical figure of impeccably Aryan descent entitled to rid the world of evil intellectuals and their accomplices, here led by the psychotic 'spider' (Letch). Like a great many of the films that invite audiences to root for a staunchly individualist superhero as he applies the 'final solution' to anyone who doesn't conform to the most conservative standards of lower-middle-class decency (and is therefore portrayed as inhumanly evil), this picture leaves a foul taste in the mouth, in spite of its technically competent manufacture and striking imagery.

d/co-s David Blyth *p* Murray Newey *co-s* Michael Heath *c* James Bartle *lp* Michael Hurt, Margaret Umbers, William Upjohn, Norelle Scott, David Letch, Gary Day, Jonathon Hardy

Don't Open Till Christmas
(SPECTACULAR TRADING INTERNATIONAL; GB) 86min
Producers Minasian (**Friday the 13th**, 1980) and Randall (**Il Castello della Paura**, 1973) bankrolled actor Purdom's inauspicious directing début, sadly notable only for Lake's performance as a psycho-killer shortly before he committed suicide after the death of his wife Diana Dors. The story concerns the slashing of a series of Father Christmas figures by Lake, a newspaper reporter with bad boyhood memories of Christmas. Suspects include the Yard's Chief Inspector Harris

(Purdom), who conspicuously fails to find the culprit, and the fiancé (Sundquist) of the daughter (Mayne) of one of the murdered Santas. While this is one of the very few psycho-horror pictures in which the victims are male, the tone of the tackily scripted shoestring effort can be gauged from its most exploitable scene: a Father Christmas being castrated while urinating in a public lavatory. The delightful Munro makes a brief appearance as herself in a cameo belatedly trying to cash in on the disco-dance movies. Al McGoohan received a credit for writing and directing 'additional scenes'.

d Edmund Purdom *p* Steve Minasian, Dick Randall *s* Derek Ford *c* Alan Pudney *se* Coast to Coast Ltd *lp* Edmund Purdom, Alan Lake, Belinda Mayne, Gerry Sundquist, Mark Jones, Caroline Munro, Kevin Lloyd, Kelly Baker, Pat Ashley, Des Dolan

Friday the 13th – The Final Chapter

(FRIDAY FOUR/PARAMOUNT) 91min
This, the fourth instalment in the saga of mass killer Jason Voorhees, has the same stultifying air as the other three – **Friday the 13th** (1980), **Friday the 13th Part 2** (1981) and **Friday the 13th Part III** (1982). Left for dead at the end of *Part III*, Jason (Brooker) escapes from cold storage at the morgue and goes on yet another drearily, cynically bloody spree in which sexual activity on behalf of any of the teenage holidaymakers inevitably leads to their death. A machete gets him in the end, but the final scene hints, depressingly, that his youthful conqueror (Feldman) may take over.

d Joseph Zito *p* Frank Mancuso Jnr *s* Barney Cohen *c* João Fernandes *lp* E. Erich Anderson, Kimberly Beck, Judie Aronson, Corey Feldman, Crispin Glover, Richard Brooker

Ghostbusters

(COL/DELPHI/BLACK RHINO/BERNIE BRILLSTEIN PRODUCTIONS) 105min
Originally conceived as a vehicle for John Belushi and Aykroyd, *Ghostbusters* is that most tricky of cross-generic hybrids, the horror-comedy. Directed by Reitman, of **Cannibal Girls** (1971) fame, it's the story of three parapsychologists (Murray, Aykroyd and Ranis) who turn freelance ghostbusters when they're made redundant from their academic jobs. As the number of ghost sightings increase, they discover that a building originally constructed by worshippers of a Sumerian demi-god is acting as the gateway from the spirit world.

Ghostbusters *to the rescue.*

The film takes the same basic plot as the execrable **The Sentinel** (1976) and treats it in a manner not dissimilar to the Bob Hope vehicles **The Cat and the Canary** (1939) and **The Ghost Breakers** (1940), with much of the movie's appeal lying in the bizarre collision of deadpan, throwaway humour and lavish high-tech visual effects.Indeed an important strand of the second half of the film is a celebration of its (assumed) success, with its extras – standing in for the audience, as it were – cheering on the Ghostbusters team. With an excellent cast and elaborate visuals (especially at the film's climax), *Ghostbusters* is as amusing as it is spectacular and treads the fine line between horror and comedy with notable success. Murray as the deadpan cynic transformed by love is particularly fine.

d/p Ivan Reitman *s* Dan Aykroyd, Harold Ramis *c* Laszlo Kovacs, Herb Wagreitch *se* Chuck Gaspar *lp* Bill Murray, Dan Aykroyd, Sigourney Weaver, Harold Ramis, Rick Moranis, Annie Potts, William Atherton, Ernie Hudson, David Margulies, Steven Tash

Ghoulies

(GHOULIES PRODUCTIONS/EMPIRE PRODUCTIONS) 84(81)min
Ghoulies emanates from the fruitful and productive stable of Empire Pictures which is run by Charles Band, the Roger Corman of the eighties. With a long apprenticeship as a producer of such low-budget fantasy fare as *Mansion of the Doomed* (1977), **Tourist Trap** (1978), *Laserblast* (1978), *Parasite* (1982), *Metalstorm* (1983), *Trancers* (1984) and *Swordkill* (1984), Band has established himself as a force to be reckoned with and his productions have now taken on their own distinctive look and feel, consisting of self-parodic humour, comic-strip vitality, narrative simplicity and a colourfully imaginative style.

Ghoulies is clearly inspired by **Gremlins** (1984) and concerns a horde of weird creatures who manage to penetrate this dimension thanks to the black magic rituals of an earnest youth who falls under the spell of his devil-worshipping father. It looks like a low-budget horror movie from the fifties, but its knowing, allusive, self-mocking tone is distinctly eighties. The real stars are, of course, the ghoulies themselves, who manifest an endearingly tacky quality and squeamishly cover their eyes in the gruesome scenes.

d/co-s Luca Bercovici *p/co-s* Jefery Levy *c* Mac Ahlberg *se* John Carl Buechler *lp* Peter Liapis, Lisa Pelikan, Michael des Barres, Jack Nance, Peter Risch, Tamara des Treaux, Scott Thomson

Gremlins (WB) 106min

A *Mad* parody of *E. T. and Mrs Hyde* might look something like this film. In the small town of Kingston Falls, one Christmas inventor Axton gives his son Galligan a mogwai, a strange creature which he has picked up in a Chinese curios shop. Mogwais aren't supposed to get wet, be fed after midnight or come into contact with sunlight, and after Galligan's mogwai, which he calls Gizmo, is accidentally dampened, it produces a number of less friendly creatures who proceed to go on the rampage. Like the *It's a Good Life* episode of *Twilight Zone* (1983), also directed by Dante, *Gremlins* is a wild, uproarious picture of unrestrained irresponsibility and childish malice triumphant. Gizmo may be particularly cute in the *E. T.* (1982) mould but Dante's essentially anarchic vision has – unlike Tobe Hooper's in **Poltergeist** (1982) – refused to be subdued by executive producer Spielberg's more sugary one. There is no doubt that it is the evil Stripe and his pals, and

A cool dude from Gremlins.

not the cuddly Gizmo, who are the narrative's driving force while the references to Capra's *It's a Wonderful Life* (1946) are as much in irony as homage. Dante's wholesale trashing of the Capra-esque small-town setting includes, as usual, a number of swipes at various media-saturated icons, including the YMCA, Walt Disney, *Phil Spector's Christmas Album*, Smokey the Bear and Santa Claus. The destruction of the town is paralleled by that of the narrative, as the film resolves itself in a disconnected series of anarchic, violent and blackly comic sketches.

d Joe Dante *p* Michael Finnell *s* Chris Columbus *c* John Hora *se* Bob McDonald Snr, Chris Walas *lp* Zach Galligan, Phoebe Cates, Hoyt Axton, Polly Holliday, Frances Lee McCain, Dick Miller, Glynn Turman, Keye Luke, Scott Brady, Corey Feldman

Hard Rock Zombies (PATEL/SHAH) 94min
A longhair discovers a guitar riff that re-animates the dead and, after experimenting on a squashed spider and a pickled hand, cuts a tape which is useful when his band is murdered with a lawn trimmer by a gardener. They return as strutting zombies to defy the conservative rulings of a rock-banning town council ('The only way we're gonna miss that concert is if you're dead') and face forces of evil: a senile Hitler (Bliesener) who sings 'The Führer's Face', a werewolf granny (Prevatte), a killer groupie, masked dwarves and a perverted photographer. Sadly death doesn't improve middle-of-the-road rocking.

d/p/s Krishna Shah *c* Tom Richmond *se* John Carl Buechler *lp* E.J. Curcio, Sam Mann, Jennifer Coe, Geno Andrews, Mick McMains, Jack Bliesener, Lisa Toothman, Susan Prevatte

I Married a Vampire (FULL MOON PRODUCTIONS) 88min
Neither very bad nor very good, though certainly cheap and strange, this straddles art and trash as small-town girl Golden has adventures in the big city (Boston). Preyed upon by a poetess (Aaron) who constantly steals from her friends, a huckstering religious cult, a lecher (Zalewski) who rapes her and then gives her a menial job, a landlord who overcharges for a vile apartment and a lawyer who promises to sort out her problems but takes the last of her cash, Golden finally reverses her streak of bad luck when (over halfway through the film) she meets Robespierre (Hickey), a romantic who helps her get revenge on all her persecutors. This displays a very matter-of-fact treatment of vampirism and a weird vein of buffery: Hickey has never seen a talking picture though he is enthusiastic about Eisenstein and his post-wedding treat is an apt trip to *Vampyr* (1932).

d/co-p/s Jay Raskin *co-p* Vicky Prodromidou *c* Oren Rudavsky *lp* Rachel Golden, Brendan Hickey, Ted Zalewski, Deborah Carroll, Temple Aaron, David Dunton

The Keep (PAR) scope 93min
The Keep was adapted from F. Paul Wilson's novel, which mixes themes from Bram Stoker and H.P. Lovecraft with a discussion of the nature of Evil as epitomized by the Third Reich. In this way the film fleshes out the key idea of *From Caligari to Hitler*, in which Siegfried Kracauer linked the German horror cinema of the twenties with the rise of fascism.

In 1941, a detachment of Nazi troops led by a humanitarian officer (Prochnow) occupies a mysterious Carpathian structure and unwittingly frees Molasar, an ancient evil force. The situation is complicated by SS officer Byrne, whose solution is to execute randomly-chosen 'partisans', Jewish professor McShane, who is lured into a Faustian pact when the monster promises to destroy the Nazi regime, and immortal warrior Glenn, whose mission is to keep Molasar imprisoned. Harking back to Kracauer, Prochnow upbraids Byrne with 'All that we are is coming out here in this Keep. You have scooped the many diseased psyches out of the German gutter ... you have infected millions with your twisted fantasies. What are you meeting in the granite corridors of this Keep? Yourself.' Maddeningly elliptical in its story-telling, this has a dreamlike, hypnotic fascination.

With images that echo **Nosferatu** (1921) and **Der Muede Tod** (1921), and McShane made up to look like Dr Caligari while Molasar more than resembles the 1919 Golem and the demon who breathes life into him, the mood of Expressionism is superbly evoked. Only the red of the monster's eyes and the swastika armbands break up the black, white and grey tones of slate walls, German uniforms, constant mists and charred corpses. In choosing to examine the unsettling kinship between Evil and Evil, Mann loses conventional heroism, neglecting in particular Glenn's enigmatic role and more or less throwing away the lightshow monster-vanquishing finale. Nevertheless, the mood of restless dread is like that of no other talking picture aside from **Isle of the Dead** (1945), and Mann stages astonishing moments of gloomy wonder, like the track away from the head of a soldier exploring a secret nook to reveal an unimaginably vast underground temple.

d/s Michael Mann *p* Gene Kirkwood, Howard W. Koch, Jr *c* Alex Thomson *se* Nick Allder *lp* Scott Glenn, Alberta Watson, Jurgen Prochnow, Ian McShane, Gabriel Byrne, Robert Prosky

Ninja III: The Domination (CANNON) 93min
Enter the Ninja (1982) and *Revenge of the Ninja* (1983) were simple action movies with little fantasy content. This sequel-in-name-only is a surprisingly brisk blend of swordplay and possession. After a golf-course massacre, a Black Ninja crawls away to die but passes on his haunted sword to telephone-line repairwoman Dickey. Under the influence of the sword, she becomes an agile avenger and kills the few survivors of the LAPD squad who killed the ninja, including her own boyfriend (Bennett). One-eyed White Ninja Kosugi appears from Japan to perform an exorcism during an earthquake and take on the dangerous ghost of his evil comrade. The film borrows from both the Western tradition of post-**Exorcist** (1973)

possession and the richly fantastical vein of Japanese and Chinese magical martial arts.

d Sam Firstenberg *p* Menahem Golan, Yoram Globus *s* James R. Silkie *c* Hanania Baer *se* Joe Quinlivan *lp* Lucinda Dickey, Sho Kosugi, Jordan Bennett, David Chung, Dale Ishimodo, James Hong

Nutriaman: The Copasaw Creature *aka* **Terror in the Swamp** (MARTIN FOLSE PRODUCTIONS) 83min
Though it boasts a modest, cynical first in the motivation for the creation of a monster – human hormones are injected into a nutria (swamp rat) to make it man-sized so that its pelts can be used by the fur trade – this Louisiana-shot community-theatre horror is a throwback to wandering-in-swamps quickies of earlier years (*Curse of the Swamp Creature*, 1966, *Sting of Death*, 1967, *Night Fright*, 1968, **Octaman**, 1971, **Blood Waters of Dr Z,** 1972, *The Creature From Black Lake*, 1976, *Bog*, 1978, *Rana: The Creature From Shadow Lake*, 1981). Due to a pathetic rat-man suit, the monster is represented by lengthy lurching subjective camera shots or glimpses as it darts between trees, which leaves too much running time for Sheriff's deputies, guilty scientists and swamp-rat poachers exchanging leaden dialogue.

d Joseph T. Catalanotto *p* Martin Folse *s* Billy Holliday *c* Wade Hanks *se* Ed Flynn *lp* Billy Holliday, Chuck Long, Chuck Bush, Mike Thomas, Ray Saadie, Gerald Daigal

Of Unknown Origin
(WB/DAVID-NESIS & CFDC/FAMOUS PLAYERS; CAN) 88min
In this adaption of G.C. Barker III's novel, *The Visitor*, a complacent character's middle-class home and illusory notions of stability are wrecked by the gnawing incursion of a barely-seen rat.

Weller, left alone for the summer by wife and children so he can work, is distracted by a growing obsession with an intelligent rat that attacks him where he is most vulnerable (in one sequence it hides in the toilet bowl). The initial lectures about the rat as a model of survival instinct recall **Jaws** (1975), and the film tries for a suggestive apocalypse as Weller determines to overcome and kill the verminous rodent. As he fights back, Weller becomes more and more primitive, wielding a spiked baseball bat and reducing his ideal home to a bloody shambles. The film suffers from Weller's overly shrill performance.

d George Pan Cosmatos *p* Claude Heroux *s* Brian Taggert *c* Rene Verzier *se* Jacques Godbout, Louis Craig *lp* Peter Weller, Jennifer Dale, Lawrence Dane, Kenneth Welsh, Shannon Tweed, Louis Del Grande

Razorback (WESTERN FILM PRODUCTIONS) 95min
A razorback is a particularly nasty and vicious kind of wild boar found in the Australian outback, and *Razorback* shows what happens when a rhino-sized example goes on the rampage and starts eating people. The film starts with a nod in the direction of the famous 'dingo baby' case, as the ravening porker storms an isolated homestead and seizes a child, whose grandfather is then charged with murder, but then rapidly becomes a strikingly bizarre amalgam of the man-against-Nature horrors of **Jaws** (1975) and its offshoots, the backwoods gothic of **The Texas Chainsaw Massacre** and **Deranged** (both 1974) and the peculiarly Australian horrors of *Outback* (1971), perhaps the most rancid picture of rural Australia ever committed to celluloid. These last two elements come to the fore in the scenes involving a couple of maniacal brothers who run a kangaroo meat factory and live in a disused mine decorated with Barry Manilow posters.

d Russell Mulcahy *p* Hal McElroy *s* Everett de Roche *c* Dean Semler *se* Mark Canny, Bob McCarron *lp* Gregory Harrison, Arkie Whiteley, Bill Kerr, Chris Haywood, David Argue, Judy Morris, John Howard

Schizophrenia (KARGL; WG) 95min
This downbeat true-life horror takes the subject of *Lady in a Cage* (1963) and the approach of **Henry, Portrait of a Serial Killer** (1987). After a documentary-style account of the history of just-released psychopath Leder, the calm madman invades the home of a young woman (Rabenreither) and her invalid parents. Thinking them his own abusive family, Leder humiliates, kills and violates them in lengthy, hard-to-sit-through sequences involving the torture of a wheelchair-bound cripple (Götz) who drags himself across the floor and the blood-boltered murder-rape of the woman. With a relentless interior monologue narration and remarkably convincing performances, this is a repellent and effective probing of the protagonist's fractured mind, often using exaggerated sound effects and slow pacing to convey Leder's dissociation from reality. Disoriented even by a gaggle of schoolgirls in sinister raincoats, Leder finally collapses completely and is apprehended by the authorities to return to an institution for the rest of his life.

d/p/co-s Gerald Kargl *co-s/c* Zbigniew Rybczynski *se* Mel Kutbay, Klaus Kovarik *lp* Erwin Leder, Silvia Rabenreither, Edith Rosset, Rudolf Götz, Renate Kastelik, Rosa Schandl

Silent Night, Deadly Night (TRI-STAR) 79min
A *cause célèbre* because American parent groups – who ignored **Tales From the Crypt** (1972), *To All a Goodnight* (1983), and the superior *You Better Watch Out* (1980) – protested its depiction of Santa Claus as a mad murderer, this is an entirely conventional slasher movie.

A child is traumatized in a pre-credits sequence, when he witnesses the murder of his parents by a mugger dressed as Santa Claus, and grows up in an oppressive orphanage to become a homicidal maniac (Wilson) who similarly disguises himself and commits Christmas-themed murders. Quigley is impaled on reindeer antlers, while others are killed while sleighing, hanged with Christmas tree lights or simply axed. With a few tough lines ('So it's not all phony sentiment, a lot of it's genuine greed') and undistinguished direction, this by-the-book holiday horror spawned several sequels. *Silent Night, Deadly Night, Part II* (1987) uses over half an hour of footage from the original film and a few comic sequences as the original madman's newly afflicted brother takes the axe to irritating characters. *Silent Night, Deadly Night, 3: Better Watch Out* (1989) was directed by down-on-his-luck Monte Hellman, while Brian Yuzna contributed *Silent Night, Deadly Night 4: Initiation* (1990) and *Silent Night, Deadly Night 5: The Toymaker* (1991), leaving behind the played-out psycho theme to concentrate on more occult and monster-laden plots.

d Charles E. Sellier *p* Ira Richard Barmak *s* Michael Hickey *c* Henning Schellerup *lp* Lilyan Chauvin, Robert Brian Wilson, Britt Leach, Toni Nero, Linnea Quigley

Terror in the Aisles (KALEIDOSCOPE/U) 83min
As an attempt to do a *That's Entertainment* (1974) of horror movies, *Terror in the Aisles* fails lamentably. Its definition of 'horror' is so broad as to be virtually meaningless – *Marathon Man* (1976), *Strangers on a Train* (1951), *Vice Squad* ((1982) and *Klute* (1971) rub shoulders with **Rosemary's Baby** (1968), **The Exorcist** (1973) and **The Shining** (1980) in a pointless collage of clips while the commentary intones banalities about why people go to scary movies. Moreover, the rapid juxtaposition techniques frequently rob the extracts of the very quality which is their reason for being there – suspense. The film also gives an extraordinarily partial account of horror film history that centres on the present and Hollywood.

d/co-p Andrew Kuehn *co-p* Stephen Netburn *s* Margery Doppelt *c* John A. Alonzo *lp* Donald Pleasence, Nancy Allen

Die Vierde Man *aka* **The Fourth Man** (DE VERENIGDE NEDERLANDSCHE FILMCOMPAGNIE; NETH) 102min
In this stylish outing drunken gay writer Krabbe is troubled by

prophetic dreams in which a gouged eyeball drips from a spy-hole in a hotel door. In Flushing on a speaking engagement, he becomes so consumed with lust for a young man (Hoffman) that he romances his girlfriend (Soutendijk), a minx who might be a witch who has already buried three husbands and set her sights on the fourth victim.

A breakthrough film for Verhoeven, who went Hollywood for *RoboCop* (1987), *Total Recall* (1990) and **Basic Instinct** (1992), this adaption of Gerard Reve's novel combines bizarre eroticism, weird religious imagery (a gay sex scene finds Hoffman on a cross and Krabbe's nurse guardian angel is the Virgin Mary), sly black humour, and Argento-style horror. It features perfectly balanced performances from Soutendijk, whose tightly marcelled hair and blood-red lips make her an unusual satanic seductress, and Krabbe, who persists in finding decency in the sleaziness of his character. Reminiscent of the films of Harry Kümel in its sado-erotic atmosphere, Low Countries setting and fusion of the supernatural with comedy of manners, *De Vierde Man* is an unusual picture that settles in a rarely travelled genre backwater, leavening audacious symbolism with wicked wit.

d Paul Verhoeven *p* Rob Houwer *s* Gerard Soetman *c* Jan De Bont *se* Chris Tucker *lp* Jeroen Krabbe, Rene Soutendijk, Thom Hoffman, Dolf De Vries, Geert De Jong, Hans Veerman, Hero Muller

1985

Appointment With Fear (GALAXY) 98min

Akkad's attempt to recreate the success of **Halloween** (1978), which he distributed, borrows the premise of *Psychic Killer* (1974) to dress up a standard slasher. A coma patient sends a psychic projection to slaughter his way through the usual complement of bubbleheaded teenagers to get to his son. Real strangeness is only demonstrated in the finale as Little stabs the killer's image only to have it dissolve in a flurry of leaves as his physical body explodes back in the asylum.

d Alan Smithee (Ramzi Thomas) *p* Moustapha Akkad *lp* Michelle Little, Michael Wyle, Kerry Remsen, Doug Rowe, Garrick Dowhen, Danny Dayton

Bloodsuckers From Outer Space (REEL MOVIES INTERNATIONAL) 78min

Like **Return of the Living Dead** (1985), this satirizes Romero's zombie films, even stumbling over several jokes used in O'Bannon's film: a zombie tied to a table for an autopsy, the inept use of nuclear weapons (the government bomb the wrong town) and innovative use of zombie dialogue.

An alien virus raises pasty-faced dead in Texas and the usual wandering-around ensues, climaxing in a town where the dead parody their former lives in a blunt manner that shows just how pointed **Dawn of the Dead** (1979) is.

d/s Glen Coburn *p* Garl Boyd Latham *c* Chad D. Smith *se* Tim McDowell, J.-P. Joyce *lp* Thom Meyers, Laura Ellis, Dennis Letts, Chris Heldman, Robert Bradeen, Pat Paulsen

The Blue Man *aka* Eternal Evil (FILMLINE INTERNATIONAL/NEW CENTURY PRODUCTIONS; CAN) 86min

This well-made, if leisurely, paranormal horror outing features discarnate spirits trying to possess suitable replacement bodies. Film-maker Rekert, who has interviewed the psychic vampires in aging incarnations (Sinelnikoff, Maxwell), is driven to despair in preparation for Sinelnikoff's migration into his skin from the sickly body of dancer Black. Concentrating on atmosphere, with blue backlighting and eerie music, this still litters the story with freak deaths as the spirits murder people who get in their way, and winds up with the expected series of twists as intervening cop Novak saves the day only to be possessed.

d George Mihalka *p* Pieter Kroonenburg *s* Robert Geoffrion *c* Paul Van Der Linden *lp* Winston Rekert, Karen Black, John Novak, Patty Talbot, Lois Maxwell, Michael Sinelnikoff

The Bride (COLGEMS; GB) 119min

This reworking of **The Bride of Frankenstein** (1935) opens with Frankenstein (Sting) toiling in an impressive laboratory, bringing to life a bandage-swathed perfect woman (Beals) as a mate for his cruder first effort, shambling giant Brown. Crisp is wittily cast as Ernest Thesiger and the sequence is impressive mock gothic.

Sumptuous production design conjures up the familiar Mittel Europa of the Universal and Hammer horrors, with Hungarian inns full of beer-swilling cockney louts and aristocratic balls staffed by impeccably costumed BBC classic serial leftovers, but Roddam takes a dreadfully obvious and lumbering approach to Mary Shelley (and James Whale). Brown's monster is a simple and loveable outcast, going through the plot of *Of Mice and Men* without ever suggesting menace or violence. Pompously uncommitted to genre, *The Bride* never approaches the effectiveness of Whale's (or Fisher's) approaches to Frankenstein.

d Franc Roddam *p* Victor Drai *s* Lloyd Fonvielle, Stephen H. Burum *se* Peter Hutchinson *lp* Sting, Jennifer Beals, Clancy Brown, David Rappaport, Geraldine Page, Quentin Crisp, Alexei Sayle, Phil Daniels, Anthony Higgins, Cary Elwes, Tim Spall, Ken Campbell, Guy Rolfe

Crimes of Passion (NEW WORLD) 107min

Bound here by Sandler's strong script, Russell's maniac energy and sexual stereotyping is, unusually, applied to good effect. By day, Joanna (Turner) is an uptight career woman with a line in grey suits and ballbreaking attitudes; by night, she is the blonde-wigged China Blue, a brassy hooker specializing in kinky role-playing games. Two men discover her dual life: surveillance expert Laughlin, an ordinary joe hired to discover whether Turner is an embezzler; and, more threatening, the sex-crazed skid-row evangelist Perkins, who kills prostitutes with his sharp-edged steel dildo and is driven to murder, possess or become China Blue.

The result is almost *Belle de Jour* (1967) meets **Psycho** (1960). With its sleazy ambience, limited sets, raucous music and wittily profane dialogue, the film has the feel of hardcore porn. The finale finds Turner and Perkins shuffling through their previous screen roles as bitch/goddess/whore and psycho/fanatic/transvestite in a sustained menace sequence which features an extraordinary moment when the mad preacher ties the heroine up so he can sing 'Get Happy' at her.

d Ken Russell *co-p/s* Barry Sandler *co-p* Donald P. Borchers *c* Dick Bush *se* John Hartigan *lp* Kathleen Turner, Anthony Perkins, John Laughlin, Annie Potts, Bruce Davison

Kathleen Turner and Anthony Perkins caught up in Crimes of Passion.

Jason rampant in Friday the 13th – A New Beginning.

Dark of the Night *aka* **Mr Wrong**
(CASTLE HILL; NEW ZEALAND) 88min
Bolton is the slightly dumpy girl dissatisfied with city life and the terrors of dealing with kiwi men called Wayne or Bruce. She feels compelled to buy a second-hand Jaguar car she can't really afford, and finds it haunted by a girl (Piercy) who was murdered in the front seat.

Literally driven to investigate the crime, she meets the psychopathic killer (Letch) and overcomes him with help from the car. More interested in being an antipodean *Georgy Girl* (1966) than in the supernatural, the film, like the similarly toned New Zealand psycho picture *Trial Run* (1984), works best as a character study.

d/co-p/co-s Gaylene Preston *co-p* Robin Laing *s* Geoff Murphy, Graham Tetley *c* Thom Burstyn *lp* Heather Bolton, David Letch, Margaret Umbers, Suzanne Lee, Gary Stalker, Danny Mulheron, Perry Piercy

Day of the Dead (LAUREL) 103min
This is a relentlessly horrific, ferociously intelligent follow-up to **Night of the Living Dead** (1968) and **Dawn of the Dead** (1979).

The Apocalypse is almost complete, and shuffling, flesh-eating dead outnumber the living 400,000 to one. In an underground research station in Florida, a handful of scientists still try to analyse the phenomenon, despite the unhelpful presence of a phalanx of soldiers under the command of Pilato, a gun-crazy psychotic. Cardille, a humanist scientist, is preoccupied with searching for other survivors and developing a cure, but the Frankensteinian Liberty hopes to domesticate the dead, keeping them well-fed and well-disciplined. The moral focus is an independent woman, the setting (a bleak, purpose-built bunker) is at once claustrophobic and microcosmic, and the hungry zombies are depicted in a less unpleasant light than the violent human characters who mistreat, but ultimately join, them.

The gruesome humour of **Re-Animator** (1985) is informed with the usual Romero intellectual rigour; in Savini's astonishing setpieces, Liberty tries to define the limits of zombie capability by such experiments as paring down a ghoul's head to a brain on a stalk or detaching all the digestive organs so they tumble out of the stomach cavity when a ravenous monster, who couldn't possibly slake his appetite, reaches out for human food. At the same time he lavishes care and attention on his prize pupil (Sherman), a zombie who has been taught to appreciate Beethoven. The finale is a black replay of the traditional E.C. comic finish as Sherman avenges the murder of his paternalist master by grimly leading the horde as they pull down and devour their oppressors. Here Savini and Romero fondly echo the E.C. spirit with ghastly visual puns (a head becomes a bowling ball with eye socket fingerholes) or moments of gruesome catharsis, as Pilato yells 'Choke on 'em!' to the zombies gobbling down his intestines.

d/s George A. Romero *p* Richard Rubinstein *c* Michael Gornick *se* Tom Seven *lp* Lori Cardille, Terry Alexander, Joe Pilato, Richard Liberty, Howard Sherman, Jarlath Conroy

Demoni *aka* **Demons** (DACFILM; IT) 93(86)min
Half-masked Soavi hands out tickets to a horror movie being previewed in a Berlin cinema. As a group of onscreen teens discover the tomb of Nostradamus, the evil in the movie gradually seeps into the audience. A girl who has scratched herself on a promotional prop in the foyer follows a film character in turning into a glowing-eyed, fanged monster, and the transformational plague spreads.

Demoni borrows the strategy of Giuliano Montaldo's *Circuito chiuso* (1978) and Woody Allen's *The Purple Rose of Cairo* (1985) in having a movie spill into reality, but Bava sadly populates the frame story with stereotypes as hackneyed and familiar as the film-within-a-film. Argento followed this commercial success by producing Bava's *Demoni 2* (1987) and, in an evolution of the series, actor-turned-director Soavi's *La Chiesa* (1989); several films, including Bava's TV movie *The Ogre* (1988) and a 1992 Umberto Lenzi feature, have been distributed in various territories as *Demoni 3*.

d/co-s Lamberto Bava *p/co-s* Dario Argento *co-s* Dardano Saccheti, Franco Ferini *c* Gianlorenzo Battaglia *se* Sergio Stivaletti *lp* Urbano Barberini, Natasha Hovey, Karl Zinny, Fiore Argento, Paolo Cozzo, Fabiola Toledo, Nicoletta Elmi, Michele Soavi

The Doctor and the Devils (BROOKSFILMS/FOX) 92min
In the forties, Dylan Thomas wrote a screenplay about Burke and Hare, but it wasn't filmed, perhaps because of the censorship problems run into by movies on the same subject: **The Body Snatcher** (1945) and the Tod Slaughter vehicle *The Greed of William Hart* (1948). Nicholas Ray revived the project in the sixties, announcing a production to star Laurence Harvey and Barbara Steele, but nothing came of it. This heavily reworked version retains the censor-imposed use of pseudonyms for well-known historical figures – Dr Rock (Dalton) for Dr Knox, and Fallon (Pryce) and Broome (Rea) for Burke and Hare – but is otherwise an inferior remake of **The Flesh and the Fiends** (1959), itself a reworking by John Gilling of his screenplay for *William Hart*.

19th-century Edinburgh becomes a non-specific, studio-bound city with stage-Irish and stage-cockney accents. The script is a conglomeration of aphorisms ('I don't need friends, I prefer enemies; they're better company and their feelings towards you are always genuine'), idiocies ('Society is a lot of people') and clichés ('We have to drag medicine into the 19th century'). Francis, returning after a spell as a cinematographer, recaptures the feel not of his best work but of shaky gothics like **Evil of Frankenstein** (1964).

d Freddie Francis *p* Jonathan Sanger *s* Ronald Harwood *c* Gerry Turpin, Norman Warwick *se* Alan Bryce *lp* Jonathan Pryce, Twiggy, Timothy Dalton, Julian Sands, Stephen Rea, Phyllis Logan, Lewis Fiander

Friday the 13th – A New Beginning
(TERROR INC/PAR) 92min
Giving the lie to the 1984 fourth instalment's subtitle, **The Final Chapter**, this restarts the series with Wieand imitating temporarily dead mass murderer Jason Voorhees by slaughtering mixed-up adolescents in a psychological rehabilitation centre where the sole survivor (Shepherd) of the previous film is gradually recovering from trauma.

With promiscuous teens, virginal nerds, backwoods retards and a Michael Jackson lookalike falling under the machete, the film covers the psycho bases, albeit with a reduction in the

Amanda Bearse as the girlfriend turned predator in Fright Night.

graphic gore: the splatter is reduced to a bland minimum as it would be for at least the next three sequels. Even by *Friday* standards, the story, direction and performances are terrible. Perhaps the worst of the run to date.

d/co-s Danny Steinmann *p* Timothy Silver *co-s* Martin Kitrosser, David Cohen *c* Stephen L. Posey *se* Martin Becker *lp* Melanie Kinnaman, John Shepherd, Shavar Ross, Mark St John, Richard Young, Juliette Cummins, Carol Locatell, Vernon Washington, Corey Feldman, Dick Wieand

Fright Night (COL) 105min

Fright Night has the feel of a well-mounted remake of **Count Yorga – Vampire** (1970).

High-schooler Ragsdale is distracted from the late-night horror film on TV by the arrival at the empty house next door of a coffin. While Jerry Dandridge (Sarandon), the new neighbour, impresses everyone with his suavity, swinging lifestyle and acidic wit, Ragsdale suspects, when blood-drained bodies turn up, that he is actually a vampire. The desperate teen calls in Peter Vincent (McDowell), a ham actor who specialized in fearless vampire killer roles and has been reduced to hosting the 'Fright Night' slot on local television, to confront the monster with crucifix, hammer and stakes. Doing for vampires what **The Howling** (1980) did for werewolves, this shows how much state-of-the-art make-up effects can improve traditionally ropey man-into-bat transformations, and otherwise revitalizes mythological clichés for the eighties. Hip, flip and cool in stylish sweaters, the vampire king is self-mocking enough to whistle 'Strangers in the Night' as he prowls for prey and smart enough to lock his coffin from the inside.

There is an interesting gay subtext in the hero's obsession with the handsome man next door, which makes him lose interest in his girlfriend (Bearse). The film was responsible for the commercial re-establishment of the vampire subgenre, and thus for the production of such imaginative items as **Vamp** (1986) and **Near Dark** (1987), as well as imitations like **The Lost Boys** (1987), the inevitable **Fright Night Part 2** (1988) and, ultimately, **Bram Stoker's Dracula** (1992).

d/s Tom Holland *p* Herb Jaffe *c* Jan Kiesser *se* Richard Edlund, John Bruno, Randy Cook, Steve Johnson *lp* Chris Sarandon, Roddy McDowell, William Ragsdale, Amanda Bearse, Stephen Geoffreys, Jonathan Stark, Dorothy Fielding, Art J. Evans

The Hills Have Eyes II (NEW REALM/VTC; US, GB) 88min

'I hadn't worked for three years,' Wes Craven claims in justification; 'I would have directed *Godzilla Goes to Paris*.' This perfunctory sequel drops the thematic drive of pitting two mirror-image families against each other and rehashes the uninteresting **Friday the 13th** (1980) strategy of isolating a group of teenagers in a rural locale and killing them one by one. Ruby (Blythe), the wild girl of the original film, returns, now civilized and guardian to a group of dirt bikers who unwisely choose to spend time racing around her old family property. An inordinate amount of footage from the first picture is used in flashback, before several of her relatives, including the once-dead Pluto (Berryman) and a new character called The Reaper (Bloom), turn up to dispose of the kids in familiar manners.

d/s Wes Craven *p* Barry Cahn, Peter Locke *c* David Lewis *lp* Michael Berryman, John Laughlin, Tamara Stafford, Kevin Blair, Janus Blythe, John Bloom, Peter Frechette

Jiangshi Xiansheng *aka* Mr Vampire

(BO HO FILMS; HONG KONG) 85min

One of the best Chinese horrors, this pits knockabout comedians against a vampire in a distinctive, flavourful mixture of Eastern and Western, comic and horrific, sophisticated effects and pleasant naïvety.

An undertaker cum exorcist (Ching-ying) struggles with his two over-enthusiastic apprentices (Hui, Sui-Ho) and searches for a prominent merchant's recently exhumed father. The dead man has returned as a bloodsucking corpse with long blue nails and hops in comically sinister fashion after victims, turning his son into a monster. He also infects the goofier of the apprentices, who, at one point, tries to resist the curse by painfully filing his fangs. To complicate matters, a lustful, lonely ghost has ensnared the other apprentice and keeps luring him to her haunted house for nights of exhausting passion. Further problems are caused by eight tame zombies left in the undertaker's care by his kung-fu master, the spiteful antics of a Clouseau-like police chief who resents the attention played to the vampire's beautiful daughter by the apprentices, and a duplicitous vendor who dilutes his supplies of sticky rice (an essential ingredient in Chinese vampire-killing rituals) with useless ordinary rice.

The big battle scenes combine slapstick comedy, mystic martial arts, James-Bernard-style music, distorted monster horror, arcane lore, comical grue and astonishing images. The lady ghost's head comes off and flies around the room, its hair spiked like porcupine quills, while the undertaker engages in an energetic fight with the headless body. The vampire bounces off a cat's cradle of inky strings which have the power to repulse evil beings, and unfamiliar bits of Chinese vampire mythology – the efficacy of a potential victim holding his breath (which makes him invisible to the monster), the powers of ideograph-covered yellow parchments to paralyse the walking dead when stuck to their foreheads – are brought ingeniously into play. Successful enough on its home turf to yield several sequels (Sung Kan Shing's *Jiangshi Jiazu/Mr Vampire, Part 2*, 1986, Wong Kee Hung's *Lianghuan Xiansheng/Mr Vampire, Part 3*, 1987, *Jiangshi Shushu/Mr Vampire Saga IV*, 1988) and imitations (Xen Lung Ting's *Jiangshi Fansheng/New Mr Vampire*, 1986, Yuen Woo-Ping's *Jiangshi Papa*, 1986), it still stands as the definitive entry in the 'Hopping Vampire' cycle.

d Lau Kun Wai *p* Samo Hung *s* Wong Ying, Szeto Cheuk Hon *lp* Ricky Hui, Moon Lee, Cin Sui-Ho, Lam Ching-Ying

Link (THORN EMI; GB) 116min

In lieu of the traditional mad wife in the attic, eccentric zoologist Stamp has three chimpanzees who help him in his studies but are unfortunately liable to turn ferocious at the least provocation. When he disappears, his assistant Shue is left in the house with the animals and finds herself conducting a battle of wits with Link, a circus-trained monkey who dresses as a butler and likes to play with matches.

An old-fashioned horror film, this uses *Animal Magic* lectures on the strength and intelligence of chimps much as fifties creature features contained educational slides to 'prove' A-bomb tests could cause giant ants. Stamp delivers an extravagantly loony performance before his offscreen demise but Shue screams, panics, and does all the wrong things to little effect.

d/p Richard Franklin *s* Everett De Roche *c* Mike Molloy *se* John Gant, Lyle Conway *lp* Elizabeth Shue, Terence Stamp, Steven Pinner, Richard Garnett

Medium *aka* **The Medium** (FILM POLSKI/POL) 100min
In a blue-lit Baltic seaport in 1933, a group of characters who resemble the principles in an 1897 murder triangle are drawn together to re-enact the tragedy.

The policeman investigating the peculiar events is worried because his ambitious junior has just joined the brownshirts and is noisily crusading for fascism, and he sees in himself a resemblance to one of the long-ago corpses. In the end, it turns out to be the work of a comatose psychic who plots, like the villains of **Patrick** (1978) and *The Medusa Touch* (1978), from his hospital bed to wreak havoc upon the world. With overtones of *Céline et Julie Vont en Bateau* (1974) in the obsessive repeating of a long-past murder mystery, and a few touches of **The Omen** (1976) in the presence of a malign but blank-faced child, this is an interesting attempt to use occult themes in a vaguely political manner, the ultimate suggestion being that fascism was rooted in supernatural evil.

d/s Jacek Koprowicz *c* Wit Dabal, Jerzy Zielinski *lp* Wladyslaw Kowalski, Michal Bajor, Grazyna Szapolowska, Jerzy Zelnik, Jerzy Stuhr, Jerzy Nowak, Ewa Dalkowska

Monster Dog *aka* **Leviatan**
(TRANS WORLD ENTERTAINMENT; US, SP) 87min
Cooper, whose seventies Grand Guignol rock was as much influenced by horror as David Bowie was by science fiction, fulfils expectations by taking the lead (and playing a monster) in his own horror film, on a slightly more serious if no less inept level than KISS in *Kiss Meets the Phantom of the Park* (1978). Without even the style of Aured's Paul Naschy vehicles, this is an old-fashioned werewolf B dressed up with hard rock leathers. Subsequently, Cooper has contributed songs and cameos to the **Friday the 13th** and **Nightmare on Elm Street** series and popped up in bits ranging from *Prince of Darkness* (1987) to *Wayne's World* (1992).

d/s Clyde Anderson (Claudio Fragasso) *p* Clark Tyrrel (Carlos Aured) *c* José García Galisteo *se* Carlo de Marchis *lp* Alice Cooper, Victoria Vera, Ricardo Palacios, Carlos Sanurio, Pepita James

Morirai a Mezzanotte *aka* **You Will Die at Midnight** *aka* **Carol Will Die at Midnight** *aka* **Midnight Killer** *aka* **Midnight Horror** (DANIA FILM/RETEITALIA; IT) 90min
A slavish imitation of Dario Argento's early giallo films, notably mendacious in virtually all its titles in that not only does Carol, doomed to die at midnight, survive after only the lightest of menacings, but the mad icepick killer stalking the cast, unusually, prefers daylight attacks.

Among the Argento-style sequences are a murder in an abandoned theatre very like the one in **Quattro Mosche di Velluto Grigio** (1971) and an encounter between Wendel and the killer in a deserted museum patterned on the art gallery in **L'Uccello dalle Piume di Cristallo** (1970). The final revelation of the murderer's identity, not to mention the most significant clue, is also derived from *L'Uccello*.

d John Old Jr (Lamberto Bava) *p* Mark Grillo Spina, Massimo Manasse *s* Dardano Sacchetti *c* Gianlorenzo Battaglia *se* Amedio Alessi *lp* Valeria D'Obici, Leonardo Treviglio, Lea Martino, Paolo Malco, Lara Wendel

Nail Gun Massacre (FUTURISTIC/REEL MOVIES) 84min
A Texas-shot implement movie which opens with good-ole-boy construction workers gang-raping a passer-by, then has a killer in black leathers and a motorcycle helmet prowl through the woods with the eponymous tool. As a great many Texans (guilty or innocent of the initial crime) are pinned to trees or nailed in the crotch, cackling wisecracks are dubbed onto the action. High on body-count but low on energy, this employs several stunt-persons (including a woman) as the murderer, who is finally unmasked as the most obvious supporting suspect.

co-d/p/s/se Terry Lofton *co-d/c* Bill Leslie *lp* Rocky Patterson, Michelle Meyer, Ron Queen, Beau Leland

A Nightmare on Elm Street (NEW LINE/MEDIA HOME ENTERTAINMENT/SMART EGG PICTURES) 91min
After a series of setbacks (*Swamp Thing*, 1982, *The Hills Have Eyes, Part 2*, 1984), Craven finally secured backing for this long-cherished project, and came up with a movie that revitalized the flagging teens-in-terror cycle, established independent production company New Line as an exploitation force, put his career back in gear, and introduced Freddy Krueger (Englund), *the* movie monster of the late eighties.

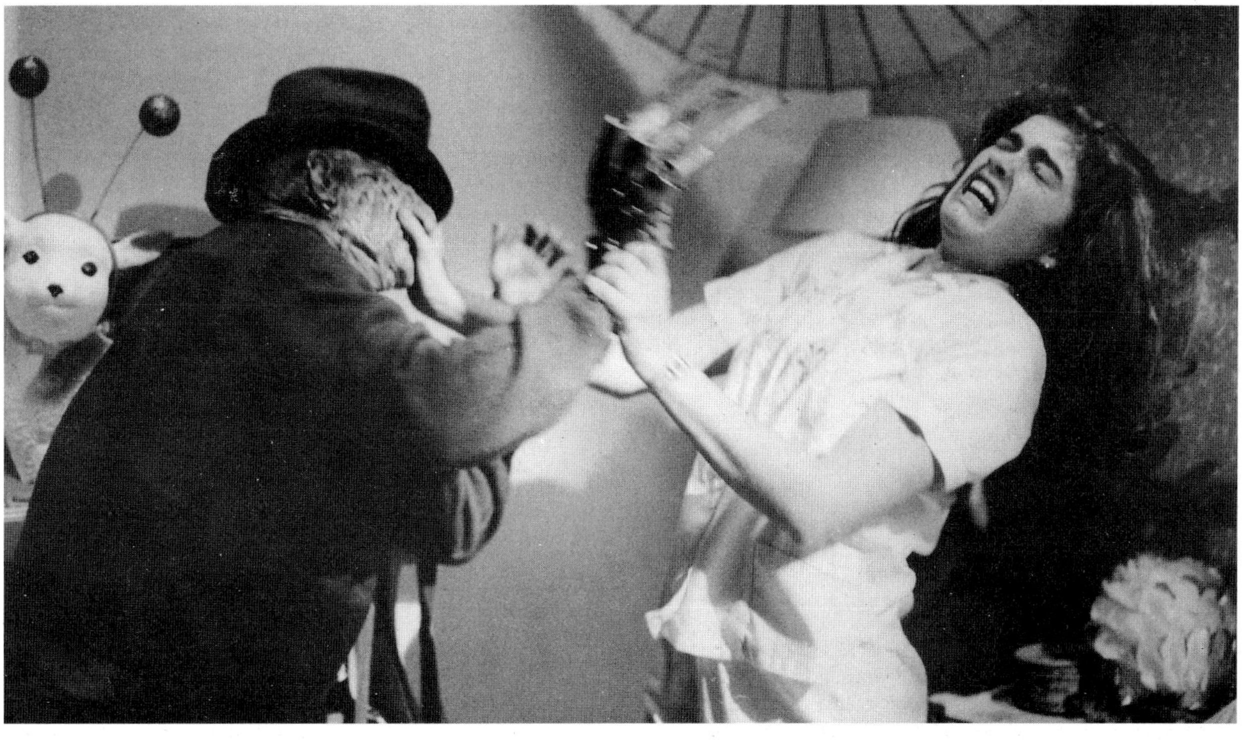

The monster of the eighties: Freddy Krueger makes his début in A Nightmare on Elm Street.

Set in Anytown, USA, which owes much to the milieu of Stephen King, the film deals with teenagers plagued by shared nightmares in which they are pursued by a disfigured murderer in a disgustingly striped jersey and porkpie hat who wears a razor-taloned glove. When Freddy kills a victim in a dream, he or she dies in reality. After her friends have been murdered, Langenkamp confronts her mother (Blakely), who explains the monster is the ghost of a child-killer set on fire by a lynch mob of Elm Street parents. In the finale, she lures Freddy out of dream into reality and fights back with a series of ingenious booby-traps.

Craven's **The Last House on the Left** (1972) and **Deadly Blessing** (1981) feature brief, surreally horrifying bad dreams. Here those moments become the whole film, allowing for impressively illogical images like the telephone that obscenely sprouts a tongue, the bathtub that turns into a bottomless well, the stairs which become swampy traps during a chase and Freddy's looming appearance behind the wallpaper of a victim's bedroom. Not the clown he becomes in the sequels, Freddy is kept in the shadows, adding nastily perverse touches like cackling as he slices off his own fingers, implying a deep perversity that makes him a more personal, sickening monster than rivals like Michael Myers and Jason Voorhees. Craven mixes smart throwaways ('God,' says the heroine after sleepless nights, 'I look twenty years old!') with comforting clichés, and contrives individual scare and suspense sequences with skill. The dangling plot-end allowed New Line to spin Freddy off into a series of follow-ups and a TV series, *Freddy's Nightmares*, which served, along with comics, books and other merchandise, to elevate the character to the monster movie pantheon.

d/co-s Wes Craven *p* Robert Shaye *co-s* Bruce Wagner *c* Jacques Haitkin *se* David Miller *lp* Heather Langenkamp, John Saxon, Ronee Blakely, Amanda Wyss, Nick Corri, Johnny Depp, Robert Englund, Charles Fleischer

Nomads (PSO) 95min

An ambitious, flawed début by McTiernan, who became a straightforward action man with *Predator* (1987), *Die Hard* (1988) and the mega-budgeted *Last Action Hero* (1993).

Los Angeles doctor Down is bitten by a dying derelict (Brosnan) and has psychic flashes to the last weeks of John Doe, who turns out to be a French anthropologist who fell to pieces while taking an obsessive interest in street gangs. It turns out the scientist has discovered a group of demon creatures he has previously encountered among Eskimos, and after death he is resurrected in leathers and chains to join their ranks. The disorientating plight of the doctor is well handled, especially when she visits the dead man's bewildered wife (Monticelli), but the monster villains are too-familiar faces (Woronov, Ant) dressed in biker outfits, and as such far less impressive than, say, the more-or-less alive gang members of *Assault on Precinct 13* (1976).

d/s John McTiernan *p* George Pappas *c* Stephen Ramsey *se* Paul Staples *lp* Lesley-Anne Down, Pierce Brosnan, Anna-Maria Monticelli, Hector Mercado, Mary Woronov, Adam Ant, Nina Foch

Once Bitten (SAMUEL GOLDWYN) 97min

An adequate-to-tiresome teen vampire comedy with a plot that was recycled seriously in **Near Dark** (1987) and **The Lost Boys** (1987) before **My Best Friend is a Vampire** (1988) and **Teen Vamp** (1989) played it for laughs again. Countess Hutton must dine on virgin blood, but supplies are short in Los Angeles, forcing her to prey on nerd Carrey, who gets cooler as he becomes vampirish but who ultimately throws off the condition before he becomes a full vampire. Hutton ('I'm so old I can't even remember my own sign') is better than the material.

d Howard Storm *p* Dimitri Villard, Robby Wald, Frank E. Hildebrand *s* David Hines, Jeffrey Hause, Jonathan Roberts *c* Adam Greenberg *se* Steve Laporte *lp* Lauren Hutton, Jim Carrey, Karen Kopins, Cleavon Little

The Oracle (REELTIME) 95min

In this piece of New York grunge from hardcore queen-turned-horrorist Findlay, a ghost uses a planchette to pester Powers, involving her in his revenge on the rival who had him killed and the wife who abetted the murder. The actual killer (Dryden) is a hulking female Joe Spinell who commits serial murders between professional hits. The convoluted story finds room for laughable but spirited gore effects, as when a supporting character hallucinates mouthed tentacles sprouting from his flesh, but often falls back on hackneyed mystic winds.

d/c Roberta Findlay *p* Walter E. Sear *s* R. Allem Leider *se* HorrorEFX, Jean Carballo *lp* Caroline Capers Powers, Roger Neil, Pam La Testa, Victoria Dryden

Phenomena *aka* Creepers (DACFILM; IT) 110(83)min

Argento's first film shot in English, this is his only unmitigated disaster.

Connelly, a pupil at an exclusive Zurich girls' school, is terrorized by a slasher. She has a psychic rapport with insects which enables her to expose the hideously deformed midget son of the tyrannical headmistress (Nicolodi) as the killer, precipitating a distastefully violent finale featuring Nicolodi's revenge-razoring by murdered entomologist Pleasence's pet chimpanzee.

A few bravura interludes are almost effective (Connelly dragging a telephone down a sewer tunnel only to have it disorientatingly start ringing) but the payoffs are unappetizingly horrid, mixing dodgy gore with unappealing misogyny.

d/p/co-s Dario Argento *co-s* Franco Ferrini *c* Romano Albani *se* Sergio Stivaletti *lp* Jennifer Connelly, Donald Pleasence, Daria Nicolodi, Dalila Di Lazzaro, Patrick Bauchau, Fiore Argento, Federica Mastroianni, Davide Marotta, Michele Soavi

Ping An Ye *aka* Night Caller (D&B/PYRAMID; HONG KONG) 96min

This opens, like **Sei Donne per L'Assasino** (1964) with a gloved murderer menacing a model and then knifing her to death while the victim's daughter cringes in a closet. A tightly-contrived Argento-style sequence, this also introduces a group of carol singers who intervene in the murder and a neat plot device whereby the killing is recorded on the cassette machine inside the little girl's talking doll.

The plot develops in the expected manner, with a blackmailer becoming the second victim as he is knifed during a televised fashion parade ('That show will do anything to get ratings,' a disgusted viewer snaps), but then takes a wild turn when the murderer is revealed at mid-point to be another model (Wong) with whom the first victim had a lesbian relationship, and the younger member of the buddy cop team is kidnapped by the killer and her demented assistant and tortured to reveal how he knows of her guilt. The finale is the cop-vs-killer confrontation.

d/s Philip Chan *p* Melvin Wong *c* Cai Huasheng *lp* Pauline Wong, Melvin Wong, Pat Ha, Philip Chan, Terry Hu, Lee Pu Wai, Deborah Sims

Psycho Girls (CAN) 92min

This outing echoes the home invasion and torture themes of **Last House on the Left** (1972), *Fight for Your Life* (1977) and *La Casa Sperduta nel Parco* (1982). A madwoman escapes to terrorize the sister who let her rot after the murder of their parents, and, with a couple of giggling torture-happy assistants, invades a chic party to find enough victims to stretch a thin story out to feature length with intense atrocities. Most of the film takes place in an abandoned madhouse where the chief crazy has a collection of Bowery Boys posters and a shrine to Sigmund Freud. Ciccoritti, who proceeded to the stylish and intriguing *Graveyard Shift* pictures, hits all the sleaze bases, turning in a competently made version of a H.G. Lewis gorefest.

d/s Cerard Ciccoritti *lp* John Haslett Cuff, Darlene Mignaccio, Agi Gallus, Rose Graham, Silvio Oliviero, Pier Giorgio Dicicco

Raiders of the Living Dead

(INDEPENDENT INTERNATIONAL) 83min

Independent International, the late-sixties and early-seventies grindhouse production company returns with producer Sherman replacing Al Adamson as director but no change in quality. A reporter, whose character trait is an obsession with the Three Stooges, investigates a terrorist incident at a nuclear power plant and comes across a plot by a crazed doctor to unleash skull-faced zombies on the world. As with previous I-I product, there is a superficial attempt to keep up with the modern genre scene, evoking Romero and Spielberg in the title, but its roots are in the thirties and forties, demonstrated by a one-scene cameo from Johann, unseen since her star turn in **The Mummy** (1932), and plot mechanics from **Revolt of the Zombies** (1936) or **King of the Zombies** (1941).

d/co-p Samuel S. Sherman *p* Dan Q. Kennis *co-s* Brett Piper *c* Douglas Meltzer *lp* Scott Schwartz, Robert Deveau, Doanna Asali, Bob Allen, Bob Sacchetti, Zita Johann

Re-Animator

(EMPIRE/RE-ANIMATOR) 86(84)min

Bespectacled fanatic Herbert West (Combs) perfects a glowing green reagent which re-animates dead tissue. Working at the Miskatonic Medical School of Arkham, Massachusetts, West uses his serum to graphically horrific effect. Dean Sampson becomes a drooling zombie and mad scientist Gale is turned into a megalomaniac head on a platter, collaborating with his headless body to wrest control of the reagent from its inventor.

Opening with Richard Band's disco remix of Bernard Herrmann's theme for **Psycho** (1960), this is a deliciously witty skit that perfectly catches the sick humour of H.P. Lovecraft's pulp pastiche, *Herbert West: The Reanimator*. The film extends the eighties trend for slapstick splatter of **The Evil Dead** (1982) and **Return of the Living Dead** (1985). Among the more astonishing sick jokes are the revivified dean head-butting the talking head, the disembodied Gale slobbering over the nude heroine (Crampton) and poking his bloody tongue in her ear, and West finally constricted to death by entrails. Gordon successfully uses the Corman trick of cutting back any footage that might be considered fat and lets the film leap from joke to joke with the minimum of interconnective tissue, logically advancing the plot with brief, pithy dialogue exchanges. Yuzna later directed the disastrous *Bride of Re-Animator* (1990).

d/co-s Stuart Gordon *p* Brian Yuzna *co-s* Dennis Paoli, William J. Norris *c* Mac Ahlberg *se* John Carl Buechler *lp* Jeffrey Combs, Bruce Abbott, David Hill, Barbara Crampton, Robert Sampson, Gerry Black, Carolyn Purdy-Gordon

Return of the Living Dead

(HEMDALE/FOX) 91min

After the success of **Night of the Living Dead** (1968) Romero's partner and co-writer John Russo penned *Return of the Living Dead*. In the early seventies, Romero agreed a 'quit claim' with regard to the property, which meant that Russo and the other two original partners on *Night* retained all the rights to *Return of the Living Dead* and to the use of the words 'Living Dead' in any future film titles, while Romero retained the word 'Dead'. Russo and the other partners then owned no part of Romero's properties, and vice versa.

In the late seventies, Fox, a Chicago stockbroker who dabbled in film finance, purchased the rights to *Return*. O'Bannon, writer of **Alien** (1979), *Dark Star* (1974), *Blue Thunder* (1983) and the under-rated **Dead and Buried** (1981) was brought in first as a writer and then, when Tobe Hooper dropped out, as director, thus making his directorial début.

The story tells what happens when metal cylinders that the army has put in storage after a disaster near Pittsburgh in the late sixties are accidentally broken open, and a spore that re-animates the dead seeps into a local cemetery where a gang of punks are having a party.

Eager to make it as different as possible from Romero's 'Dead' films, O'Bannon concentrates less on extreme gore and more on humour and characterization. The undead here are clearly individual characters who communicate with each other like normal human beings and the humour works particularly well in this context. Though less gruesome than Romero's creations, O'Bannon's zombies are pretty creepy, the inspiration behind them being an amalgam of the mummies of Guanajuato, the Bog People and E.C. comics. The film is graced with an excellent soundtrack.

d/s Dan O'Bannon *p* Tom Fox, Graham Henderson *c* Jules Brenner *se* Bill Munns, Tony Gardner *lp* Clu Gulager, James Karen, Don Calfa, Miguel Nuñez, Brian Peck, Linnea Quigley, Beverly Randolph

7, Hyde Park *aka* Formula for a Murder

(FULVIA; IT) 89min

This is a sustained variant on the cripple-in-jeopardy theme of **Taste of Fear** (1960). Nagy is a paraplegic heiress menaced by fortune-hunting husband Warbeck, who attempts to overstrain her weak heart with an excess of love-making. He also tries to fray her nerves by dressing up as a fake priest who raped her when she was a child, causing the fall that put her in a wheelchair, and lurking suggestively, dragging a sinister, bloodied doll that recites a threatening nursery rhyme.

The shocks come in the second half, which betrays the influence of American slasher movies as Warbeck dresses up in a practical oilcloth coat and takes a straight razor to Blumenberg for no rational plot reason.

d/co-s Martin Herbert (Alberto De Martino) *p* David Colby *co-s* Frank Walker *c* Lawrence Barkey *lp* Christina Nagy, David Warbeck, Carroll Blumenberg, Rossano Brazzi, Andrea Bosic, Loris Loddi, Adriana Giuffre, Daniela De Carolis, Arthur Webber Jr

Tom Mathews discovers a zombie's lot is not a happy one in Return of the Living Dead *while Beverly Randolph looks bravely on.*

Silver Bullet (DEG) 95(94)min
Scripted by King from his illustrated novella *Cycle of the Werewolf*, this, like such other Dino De Laurentiis-King collaborations as *Firestarter* (1984), *Cat's Eye* (1984) and *Maximum Overdrive* (1987), is half-hearted horror. 'This is a relationship movie,' claimed director Attias, 'filled with people who find themselves in situations that are both interesting and real.' Set in a rural community populated by hysterical, intolerant, booze-befuddled, trigger-happy rednecks, this displays King's cynicism about the common people. The plot winds down into a silly conflict between a lycanthrope, well-played in a script vacuum by McGill, and a pair of wholesome kids and their beery reprobate uncle (Busey). The monster is more ursine than lupine and Rambaldi's effects are weak in comparison with lycanthropic benchmarks like **The Howling** (1980) and **An American Werewolf in London** (1981).

d Daniel Attias *p* Martha Schumacher *s* Stephen King *c* Armando Nannuzzi *se* Carlo Rambaldi *lp* Gary Busey, Corey Haim, Everett McGill, Megan Fellows, Robin Groves, Leon Russom, Terry O'Quinn

Spookies *aka* **Twisted Souls**
(MIGGLES CORPORATION) 85min
Caricature teens are lured to an old dark house by an evil magician (Ward), who arranges for them to die one by one so he can revivify his sleeping-beauty wife. Conceived as a stringing together of effects showreels, this has a plot ploddingly in line with **The Evil Dead** (1982) or **Ghoulies** (1984) but is overrun by zombies roaming the estate, nasty little gremlins, toothy spider demons, melting possessees and a hook-handed teenage werewolf. After the collapse of the production, editor Joseph was required to piece together her co-directors' work.

co-d/co-p/co-s Thomas Doran, Brendan Faulkner *co-d/co-p* Eugenie Joseph *co-p/co-s* Frank M. Farel *c* Robert Chapell, Ken Kelsch *se* Arnold Gargiulo II, Vincent Guastini, Gabriel Bartalos, Jennifer Aspinall, John Dods *lp* Felix Ward, Dan Scott, Alec Nemser, Maria Pechukas, Peter Dain, Nick Gionta

Teen Wolf (ATLANTIC RELEASING CORP) 91min
Teen loser Fox sprouts fur and learns from his father (Hampton) that he's inherited the family curse. Rather than rip throats, Fox's wolf persona becomes a star basketball-player and the most popular kid in school. Despite nods to **I Was a Teenage Werewolf** (1957) and Larry Cohen's much snappier **Full Moon High** (1982), this is less a horror spoof than a geek-makes-good-but-learns-true-values high-school drama. The moral that it's better to be normally mediocre than weirdly outstanding is sneakily reactionary. Spun-off into an animated TV series and a dud Fox-free sequel, Christopher Leitch's *Teen Wolf Too* (1987), with Jason Bateman as a similarly afflicted cousin and Kim Darby as a tail-wagging werewolf teacher, this was the most prominent and influential of the rash of mild monster comedies of the mid-eighties.

d Rod Daniel *p* Mark Levinson, Scott Rosenfelt *s* Joseph Loeb III, Matthew Weisman *c* Tim Suhrstedt *se* The Burman Studios *lp* Michael J. Fox. James Hampton, Scott Paulin, Susan Ursitti, Jerry Levine, Jim MacKrell, Lorie Griffin, Mark Arnold, Matt Adler, Mark Holton

The Toxic Avenger (TROMA) 90(79)min
Set in Tromaville, New Jersey, 'the Toxic Waste Capital of America', this horror comedy was unaccountably popular.

Feeble weakling Melvin (Torgl) is abused by local louts and dumped into a vat of radioactive garbage to emerge as the Toxic Avenger, a tutu-clad mutant superhero (Cohen) who violently cleans up the streets while conducting a tender affair with a comely blind girl (Miranda). The team return to Tromaville for the similar **Class of Nuke 'Em High** (1986), and the Toxie comes back in *The Toxic Avenger, Part II* (1989) and *The Toxic Avenger Part III: The Last Temptation of Toxie* (1989), which are less distasteful but equally clod-hopping, also cameoing in *Class of Nuke 'Em High, Part 2: Subhumanoid Meltdown* (1991).

co-d/co-p Michael Herz *co-d* Samuel Weil *co-p/co-c* Lloyd Kaufman *s* Joe Ritter *co-c* James London *se* Jennifer Aspinall, Tom Lauten *lp* Andree Miranda, Mitchell Cohen, Jennifer Babtist, Cindy Manion, Robert Prichard, Gary Schneider, Pat Ryan Jr, Mark Torgl

Troll (EMPIRE/ALTAR) 82min
A normal family move into a new house and the daughter is replaced by a troll in disguise, prompting her brother (Hathaway) to appeal for help from the old lady upstairs (June Lockhart), who turns out to be a witch capable of becoming young (Anne Lockhart) and is dedicated to saving the world from a troll invasion. Originally conceived as a slasher movie, this was softened into a more fantasy-oriented picture, in which characters are magically transformed rather than horribly murdered: so Bono is impressively metamorphosed into a roomful of tropical greenery and dwarf Fondacaro is turned into an animated elf. Buechler re-uses a few creatures from **Ghoulies** (1984) and *RageWar* (1985), and seems more interested in the effects than in the jokey characterizations that had been the strength of such Empire successes as *Trancers* (1984) and *Zone Troopers* (1985). The cast mainly survive the neglect and there is an amusing fake fifties creature feature excerpt, *Invasion of the Pod People From Mars.*

d/se John Carl Buechler *p* Albert Band *s* Ed Naha *c* Romano Albani *lp* Noah Hathaway, Michael Moriarty, Shelley Hack, Jenny Beck, Sonny Bono, Phil Fondacaro, Brad Hall, Anne Lockhart, June Lockhart, Julia Louis-Dreyfus

Vampire Hunter D (EPIC-SONY/ASHI; JAP) 82(76)min
An animated horror-fantasy set in a distant future where society has decayed to the level of Hammer Films' Mittel Europa and vampire tyrants oppress the peasantry. Doris, the pure heroine, is bitten by Count Magnus Lee, an ancient monster who intends to bring her into his family against the wishes of his daughter Anneka. Doris and her young brother hire the eponymous hero, a dhampir (the son of a vampire and a human woman) who roams the land in Man With No Name fashion, advised by his talking hand and wielding a deadly sword against the vampires and their mutant or werewolf vassals. Though the plot outline is simplistic and characters are stick-thin even for a *manga* fairy-tale, the film has an outstandingly strange background and cleverly melds aspects of the traditional gothic horrors with the wandering samurai or spaghetti Western genres. An American-language edition was released in 1992 under the supervision of Carl Macek, with dialogue by Tom Wyner.

d Toyoo Ashida *p* Hiroshi Kato, Mitsuyshisa Koeda, Yukio Nagasaki *s* Yasushi Hirano

¡Vampiros en la Habana! *aka* **Vampires in Havana**
(ICAIC/TE/DURNIOK; CUBA, SP, WG) 78min
This colourful, inventive cartoon is similar in plot if not setting to **Sundown: The Vampire in Retreat** (1989).

In 1933, two rival vampire groups converge in Havana to squabble over Professor Von Dracula's invention 'vampisol', a cream which enables vampires to emerge in daylight. A group of European aristocrats want a monopoly on the formula, while a brasher bunch of Chicago gangsters wish it suppressed because they have a lucrative trade in underground 'beaches' where vampires can experience simulated sunlight. The hero is Dracula's nephew, Pepe, who has been raised on vampisol and doesn't even know he is a vampire, having passed his time joining the struggle to overthrow the Machado regime by singing subversive songs in public. The film is packed with amusing gags and ideas: a revolver which fires wooden stakes, a werewolf harassed by street mongrels, a pack of bloodsuckers seen cheering the villain of a vampire movie, and an amusingly prim heroine who refuses to enter a motel with a man even during a life-or-death chase. Finally, Pepe sings a song that reveals the vampisol formula over an international vampire radio hook-up, changing the undead way of life forever. With some good-natured politics (the villains are all national caricatures, the hero is a cheery revolutionary) and light-hearted spoofing of the melodramatic excesses of the hispanic vampire, this is very likeable.

d/s Juan Padrón *p* Paco Prats *c* Adalberto Hernández *lp* (voices) Frank González, Manuel Marín, Irela Bravo, Carlos González, Mirella Guillot, Carmen Solar, Juan Padrón

Witchboard (PARAGON ARTS PARTNERS) 98min
After a session with a ouija board, Californian bimbo Kitaen is possessed by the spirit of a mass murderer. Her boyfriend (Allen) collaborates with an obnoxious would-be suitor (Nicholas) to free her from the affliction. The film is mildly enlivened by Wilhoite's brief performance as a teenage Madame Arcati. Tenney's subsequent grindhouse items include **Night of the Demons** (1988), **The Cellar** (1990) and *Witchboard 2: The Devil's Game* (1993).

d/s Kevin S. Tenney *p* Gerald Geoffrey *c* Roy H. Wagner *se* Tassilo Baur *lp* Tawny Kitaen, Todd Allen, Stephen Nicholas, Kathleen Wilhoite, Burke Byrnes

1986

April Fool's Day (PAR) 88min
Heiress Foreman invites college friends to her island estate for an April Fool's party, and the plots of *The Last of Sheila* (1973) and **Friday the 13th** (1980) are combined as the guests' deepest secrets are exposed before they turn up horribly murdered. As in **Hell Night** (1981) and *Pranks* (1982), the film segues from gruesome practical jokes to actual murders but here the theme is taken to its logical conclusion by having all the horrors, even the regulation last-minute kicker, turn out to be stunts. There is even a subtly disturbing moment as Foreman explains it has all been faked in good fun and seems for a moment more seriously insane than she did when pretending to be her homicidal twin sister.

d Fred Walton *p* Frank Mancuso Jr *s* Danilo Bach *c* Charles Minsky *se* Martin Becker *lp* Jay Baker, Deborah Foreman, Deborah Goodrich, Ken Olandt, Griffin O'Neal, Leah King Pinsent, Clayton Rohner, Amy Steel, Thomas F. Wilson

Blue Velvet (DEG) 120min
In this, the most lyrical of his films, Lynch returns in gloriously saturated colour (rather than expressionist monochrome) to the fractured vision of small-town normality of **Eraserhead** (1976).

The opening sequence is lush, suggestive and unsettling: as Bobby Vinton's subtly fetishist title song plays, the camera tracks from a striking red, white and blue shot (blood-roses against a pristine white picket fence against an unnaturally clear sky) to a deliriously idyllic, slow-motion vision of a town that would suit Andy Hardy or Judy Garland. Lynch takes his camera in for a closer view and penetrates the thick grass of the garden to find a teeming, ravenous, carnivorous horde of insects chewing away at the underside of Norman Rockwell's America. The film follows this clue when college student MacLachlen returns home, gets involved in a local mystery and is exposed to the horrors that lurk underneath the Eisenhower-style perfection (it is impossible to tell whether the film is set in the fifties, the sixties or the eighties) of Lumberton, U.S.A. He first suspects something is amiss when he discovers a severed human ear in a vacant lot. The ear, naturally, is crawling with ants and Lynch, in an awe-inspiring effect, has the camera explore its interior as Alan Splet's unsettling sound effects suggest a universe inside the head as twisted and bizarre as that of *Eraserhead.*

The mystery revolves around a melancholy nightclub singer (Rossellini), and a frighteningly fiendlike and primal gangster (Hopper) who snorts gas through an insectlike mask, speaks only in the most basic terms ('Baby wants to fuck!') and forces Rossellini to have animalistic sex with him by threatening to further torture her kidnapped husband, the owner of the ear. Disturbingly, *Blue Velvet* refuses to let its Nancy Drew and Hardy Boys-style hero and heroine off the hook as MacLachlen becomes less an observer and more a participant in the sordid, insect nightlife of Lumberton. He overcomes his reluctance to hit Rossellini when she begs him to, and is dragged on a wild ride with Hopper where he finds himself watching Stockwell mime to Roy Orbison's 'In Dreams', the song Hopper later plays as he brutally beats up MacLachlen. The thriller-whodunnit plot eventually adds up, although not before the nightmare has thoroughly invaded MacLachlen's world with the appearance of a bruised and naked Rossellini on Dern's front lawn and a final confrontation with Hopper in an apartment that contains a still-standing, still-twitching corpse.

The coda replicates the opening sequence with all the proprieties restored – Frank is dead, a mechanical robin is eating the insects, the ear probed by the camera is MacLachlen's and still attached to his head, families are united – but the all-pervasive horrors have been so effectively summoned that we know they can never really be vanquished. Lynch further explored this eerie Americana in *Wild at Heart* (1990), the TV serial *Twin Peaks* and the spin-off **Twin Peaks: Fire Walk With Me** (1992).

d/s David Lynch *p* Richard Roth *c* Frederick Elmes *lp* Kyle MacLachlen, Isabella Rossellini, Dennis Hopper, Laura Dern, Dean Stockwell, Brad Dourif, Hope Lange

Camping del Terrore *aka* **Camping della Morte** *aka* **Body Count** (RACING PICTURES; IT) 90min
An entirely conventional summer-camp slaughter movie in the manner of **Friday the 13th** (1980), with tame gore and an interesting but sadly misused cast, this has a masked murderer prowling around a campsite in the woods where a massacre was once perpetrated. Hess, star of **Last House on the Left** (1972) and *La Casa Sperduta nel Parco*, runs the site with wife Farmer, and not the least of the improbabilities of the plot is that he could keep it open for business despite his habit of leaving vicious mantraps in the undergrowth.

d Ruggero Deodato *p* Alessandro Fracassi *s* Alex Capone, David Parker Jr *c* Emilio Loffredo *lp* Mimsy Farmer, Charles Napier, David Hess, Cynthia Thompson, Andrew Lederer, Ivan Rassimov, John Steiner

Class of Nuke 'Em High (TROMA) 85min
This is a lame follow-up to **The Toxic Avenger** (1985), with radioactive waste used as a growth agent in the cultivation of marijuana and an epidemic of mutation sweeping the high school of Tromaville.

The heroine (Brady) gives birth orally to a tadpole creature which festers into a monster in the school basement, and protects her from the local thug gang, only to be blasted with a handy laser weapon by its ungrateful 'father' (Brenton). Sadly the outing sprawls through too many plotlines as it pursues the usual teen-movie business of cramming as many loud songs onto the soundtrack and jiggling bikinis into the frame as is possible. The cast mug dreadfully in the usual Troma fashion and a few spots of genuine sadism merely add to the tasteless tedium. *Class of Nuke 'Em High, Part 2: Subhumanoid Meltdown* (1991) is, if anything, even worse, despite a guest appearance by Tromie the Giant Nuclear Squirrel.

co-d Richard W. Haines, Samuel Weil (Lloyd Kaufman) *co-p/co-s* Lloyd Kaufman *co-p* Michael Herz *co-s* Mark Rudnitsky *c* Michael Mayers *se* Tom Lauten *lp* Janelle Brady, Gilbert Brenton, Robert Prichard, R.L. Ryan, James Nugent Vernon, Brad Dunker, Gary Schneider

Crawlspace (EMPIRE) 77min
The doctor son (Kinski) of a Nazi war criminal flees South America after practising large-scale involuntary euthanasia in the hospital where he was working. Now he rents rooms to glamorous women upon whom he spies from ventilation ducts, occasionally killing tenants in experiments interrupted by periodic games of Russian roulette which he undertakes to give God a chance to stop him. This is a ridiculous melodrama. Set in America but shot in Italy, it wastes a competent cast on pretentious foolishness and contrived death traps.

d/s David Schmoeller *p* Roberto Bessi *c* Sergio Salvati *se* John Buechler, MMI Inc *lp* Klaus Kinski, Talia Balsam, Barbara Whinnery, Sally Brown, Carol Francis, Jack Heller, Kenneth Robert Shippy

Daemon (CHILDREN'S FILM UNIT; GB) 71min
In the UK the prolific Children's Film Unit makes films with the participation of an overwhelmingly junior cast and crew. Here, approaching the familiar 'evil child' theme from the child's point of view actually adds enough to the familiar subgenre to counterbalance the allowances one has to make for a degree of enthusiastic amateurism.

An eleven-year-old (Morell) having trouble settling into a new home and school develops symptoms (bruises and blisters, ghostly messages on his home computer) that convince his friends he has been possessed and prompt them to plot to drive a stake through his heart. A ghost story rather than a possession drama, the manifestations are actually of the hero's sympathy with a 19th-century sweep who was burned to death and bricked up in the chimney of his new house. While the use of children in all the lead roles, with only York intruding as a sympathetic psychiatrist, allows for some humorous touches (a fearless vampire hunter complains that he can't join his comrades on a nocturnal expedition because his mother won't let him out at night), it is also neatly worked into a script which explicitly links the problems of modern children with those of the abused urchins of the Victorian era. The achievement of *Daemon* can be gauged by comparison with *Suffer, Little Children* (1984), a similar project shot very badly on video by a far less talented group of British stage children.

d/p/s Colin Finbow *c* Titus Bicknell, Rory MacFarquhar, Orlando Wells, Leigh Melrose, Jason Wulfsohn *lp* Arnaud Morell, Susannah York, Bert Parnaby, Sadie Herlighy, Donna Glaser, Orlando Swayne

Deadly Friend (WB) 90min
The pendulum swing of Craven's career, between innovative genre movies and abortive fiascos, here rebounds from the height of **A Nightmare on Elm Street** (1985) to a depth to equal **The Hills Have Eyes II** (1985) or *Swamp Thing* (1982).

Teenage genius Laborteaux suffers two bereavements one Halloween: an intolerant old lady (Ramsey) takes a shotgun to his pet robot during a prank, and his girlfriend (Swanson) is battered to death by her drunken bum of a father. Naturally, he steals the girl from the morgue and re-animates her with vital circuits from the robot, whereupon she sets out on the familiar vengeance trail. The result is a film that lurches bewilderingly between the high-school genius genre of *Weird Science* (1985) and *Real Genius* (1985), with a cute robot in the *Short Circuit* (1986) mould, and a formulaic zombie picture rendered ridiculous by Swanson's literally stumbling, pasty-faced, arms-outstretched performance as Frankenstein's cheerleader.

d Wes Craven *p* Robert M. Sherman *s* Bruce Joel Rubin *c* Philip Lathrop *se* Robotics 21, Ray Raymond, Lance Anderson *lp* Matthew Laborteaux, Kristy Swanson, Michael Sharrett, Anne Twomey, Anne Ramsey

Deadtime Stories *aka* **Freaky Fairy Tales**
(BEDFORD ENTERTAINMENT) 81min
Plodding after **The Company of Wolves** (1984), this anthology has a baby-sitting uncle (Mesmer) tell his nephew (DePersia) splatter-laced fairy tales: *Peter and the Witches*, a new-minted medieval anecdote about an apprentice (Valentine) and three witches, and two dumbly comic updates of old tales. *Little Red Runninghood* features a horny werewolf pursuing a teenage bimbo (Picard) in a red jogging outfit, while *Goldie Lox and the Three Baers* has a telekinetic, homicidal blonde (De Prume) mixed up with a family of asylum escapees. The film was made over several years in Greenwich, Connecticut.

d/s Jeffrey S. Delman *p* Bill Paul *co-s* Charles F. Shelton *c* Daniel B. Canton *se* Bryant Tauser, Ed French *lp* Michael Mesmer, Brian DePersia, Scott Valentine, Nicole Picard, Catheryn de Prume, Melissa Leo

The Fantasist
(NEW IRISH FILM PRODUCTIONS/ITC; EIRE) 98min
Hardy's belated follow-up to **The Wicker Man** (1973) continues to suggest a link between sexual repression and getting murdered. An innocent girl (Harris) comes to Dublin and attracts the interest of a smooth-talking, phone-calling psychopath who, obsessed with a painting of a naked courtesan seen from the rear, has been back-stabbing women. The not-quite-virginal heroine is pursued by three creeps doubling as suitors and suspects: neurotic writer Bottoms, stomach fetishist Kavanagh and limping policeman Cazenove. From James McGinley's novel *Goosefoot*, this is more concerned with its heroine's odd character and exploring touristy bits of Dublin than with the psycho-on-the-loose plot, not taking any of its suspects seriously enough to make them menacing. Recognisably akin to Hardy's first film in its celtic themes and pitting of an innocent against a community of sinister decadents, this is notably less surprising and engrossing as mystery-horror.

d/s Robin Hardy *p* Mark Forstater *c* Frank Gell *se* Gerry Johnstone *lp* Moira Harris, Christopher Cazenove, Timothy Bottoms, John Kavanagh, Mick Lally, Bairbre Ní Chaoimh, James Bartley, Deirdre Donnelly, Liam O'Callaghan

The Deadly Friend.

Frenchman's Farm

(MAVIS BRAMSTON PRODUCTIONS; AUST) 96min

Driving through brushfire-blighted country, Tainsh timeslips to 1944 and witnesses an axe murder. In the present, she discovers the man found guilty was not the murderer she saw and police computers react to inquiries about the original crime by giving out a certificate of execution in Napoleonic French. The killer is a guillotine-happy French ghost compelled (always on February 29th) to decapitate anyone who comes near the treasure he guards. The detail is intriguing but the supernatural snippets are never satisfactorily bound together.

d Ron Way *p* James Fishburn, Matt White *s* William Russell, Keith Dewhurst *c* Malcolm McCulloch *lp* Tracey Tainsh, David Reyne, John Meillon, Norman Kaye, Tui Bow, Ray Barrett, Andrew Blackman

Friday the 13th, Part VI: Jason Lives *aka* Jason Lives: Friday the 13th, Part VI

(PAR/TERROR INC) 87min

This middle-of-the-road slasher opens with a resurrection along the lines of Universal monster sequels like **Ghost of Frankenstein** (1942) and **Frankenstein Meets the Wolf Man** (1943). The neurotic hero (Mathews), held over from the last two entries in the franchise, visits the grave of Jason Voorhees (Graham) and witnesses the mass murderer's resurrection as a lightning-powered killer zombie.

The final admission that the unkillable villain has supernatural powers theoretically breaks new ground, but this is as perfunctory and unsuspenseful an exercise as the other sequels. McLoughlin, who made the interesting *One Dark Night* (1982), shuffles the faceless central character through his pointless paces, finally sending him to the bottom of Crystal Lake. The zombie angle is an attempt to keep Jason up with his closest rival, Freddy Krueger, but he remains just an anonymous thug in a hockey mask with a machete.

d/s Tom McLoughlin *p* Don Behrns *c* Jon Kranhouse *se* Chris Swift, Bhan Wade *lp* Thom Mathews, Jennifer Cooke, David Kagen, Kerry Noonan, Renee Jones, Tom Fridley, C.J. Graham, Darcy Demoss

From Beyond (TARYN/EMPIRE) 85min

Reuniting the production team and cast of **Re-Animator** (1985), this is a messy, ambitious and perverse expansion of one of H.P. Lovecraft's briefer sketches.

Mad scientist Dr Pretorius (Sorel) invents a giant tuning-fork that brings creatures from another dimension into this reality and also stimulates the pineal glands of those who hear its unearthly tonalities. Pretorius disappears into the fifth dimension and returns as an increasingly mutated monstrosity, while his assistant (Combs) sprouts a brain-eating forehead tentacle, and a repressed scientific investigator (Crampton) trades her tight hairstyle and large glasses for chains and leather. Conceptually daring but sloppily executed, the film tries for the weird feel of a *Videodrome* (1982), but keeps trying to play safe by including the kinky sex, standard gore and horror-defusing humour expected of a run-of-the-splat exploitation movie.

d Stuart Gordon *p* Brian Yuzna *s* Dennis Paoli *c* Mac Ahlberg *se* John Carl Buechler, Mark Shostrom, John Naulin, Anthony Doublin *lp* Jeffrey Combs, Barbara Crampton, Ken Foree, Ted Sorel, Carolyn Purdy-Gordon

The Gate (THE GATE FILM PRODUCTIONS; CAN) 86min

With its young teenage heroes, plentiful effects, comparatively restrained horrors and an ending that takes back all the nastier aspects (the loveable dog killed by supernatural evil returns happily to life), this epitomizes mid-eighties Nancy Drew and the Hardy Boys-style 'safe' horror in the manner of **House**, (1986), *Critters*, (1986), **Neon Maniacs** (1986), **The Lost Boys** (1987) and **The Monster Squad** (1987).

Left to their own devices for the weekend, suburban brat Dorff and his snotty sister Denton throw a wild party and are menaced by phenomena stemming from the mysterious hole in their garden where an old tree has recently been struck by lightning. Everyone has bad dreams, kids levitate, geodes burst in the shape of an ancient curse, stop-motion imps scuttle, a bogeyman rumoured to be buried in the walls emerges, a demon is stabbed in the eye with a Barbie doll, a happy family photograph changes to show one smiling kid and three bloody corpses, a severed demon arm turns into scurrying maggots, and an ogre from the beyond turns up for the finale. Finally, from the sleeve notes of a Heavy Metal album, the kids deduce that the hole in the garden is a gateway to a nether world and that it must be closed before evil deities overrun the Earth. Takacs later made **I, Madman** (1989) and a limp *Gate II* (1990).

d Tibor Takacs *p* John Kemeny *s* Michael Nankin *c* Thomas Vamos *se* Randall William Cook *lp* Stephen Dorff, Christa Denton, Louis Tripp, Kelly Rowan, Jennifer Irwin

Girls' School Screamers *aka* The Portrait

(BANDIT/TROMA) 85min

Shot in Philadelphia, this community-theatre effort segues from ghost story to slasher. Convent girls spend a weekend in the mansion of a dead billionaire who has left his estate to the school. Supposedly cataloguing the bequest, they actually spend the time giggling, having seances, reading old diaries and being surprised by prank-playing boyfriends. The ghost of the billionaire's niece, murdered during an incestuous rape, returns to pester her reincarnation (O'Mara). The film is unusual in featuring the best-behaved victims in the stalker cycle: these girls don't have sex (or even talk about it), look after a sick supervisor, don't swear, do the washing up and are nice to the token fat girl.

d/co-p/s John P. Finegan *co-p* Pierce J. Keating, James W. Finegan *c* Albert R. Jordan *se* John Maffei *lp* Mollie O'Mara, Sharon Christopher, Vera Gallagher, Mari Butler

Gothic (VIRGIN) 87min

The first of several films – Gonzalo Suarez's *Rowing with the Wind* (1988), Ivan Passer's *Haunted Summer* (1988), Roger Corman's **Frankenstein Unbound** (1990) – set around the Villa Diodati on the shore of Lake Geneva in the summer of 1816, when Byron, Shelley, the future Mary Shelley, Claire Clairmont and Dr John Polidori passed time with ghost stories and Mary came up with the idea for Frankenstein while Polidori scribbled a tentative beginning for another subgenre with 'The Vampyre'.

This presents Byron (Byrne) as a limping mastermind who enjoys tormenting his friends, Shelley (Sands) as a posturing drug addict who walks nude on the roof during a thunderstorm, Claire (Cyr) as a neurotic seen in a vision with eyes for nipples, Polidori (Spall) as a comic loon who drips leeches, and Mary (Richardson) veering from long-suffering patience to wild abandon. Between shrieking and ranting, Russell recreates Fuseli's *Nightmare* and introduces a well-endowed spectral figure in armour who seems half *The Castle of Otranto* and half *Flesh Gordon* (1974).

d Ken Russell *p* Penny Corke *s* Stephen Volk *c* Mike Southon *se* Ace Effects *lp* Gabriel Byrne, Julian Sands, Natasha Richardson, Miriam Cyr, Timothy Spall

Haunted Honeymoon (ORION) 84min

Theoretically a tribute to forties programmers in which Bob Hope or Red Skelton wisecrack through haunted houses and solve mysteries, this oversteps the border between homage and plagiarism. Lifting its plot from **The Cat and the Canary** (1939) and *Whistling in the Dark* (1941) as radio personalities Wilder and Radner get mixed up in a complex game of murder and intrigue on a dilapidated estate, it winds up with a cop-out similar to those of *Shadow on the Stairs* (1942) or **The House of the Long Shadows** (1982). While on legitimate ground when recreating corridor sets from **The Old Dark House** (1932) or turning Pringle and Carter into lookalikes for Karloff and Lugosi, it gets shakier when it comes to stealing comic routines from *Murder, He Says* (1945).

d/co-s Gene Wilder *p* Susan Ruskin *co-s* Terence Marsh *c* Fred Schuler *se* John Stears *lp* Gene Wilder, Gilda Radner, Dom DeLuise, Jonathan Pryce, Peter Vaughan, Paul L. Smith, Eve Ferret, Jim Carter, Bryan Pringle

The Hitcher (HBO) pv 97min

'My mother told me never to do this,' says sleepy motorist Howell as he picks up thumbing John Ryder (Hauer) in a thunderstorm. Immediately, Hauer is waving a switchblade and making conversational gambits like 'Have you ever wondered just how much blood comes out of a punctured eyeball?' Howell manages to shove him out of the car but the hitcher dogs the boy's trail. He commits a series of murders, for which Howell is set up to take the blame, and contrives nasty jokes like dropping a severed finger into his portion of fries. Hauer's forceful, witty performance makes *The Hitcher* more personalized and deliberately malevolent than most eighties movie psychos. The sparse, harsh landscape and the simple storyline make the film a serious re-run of the eternal clash between the Road Runner and the Coyote, as the monstrous quarry turns all Howell's attempts to extricate himself back on him. Without overt gore (the nasty pulling-apart of Leigh is done entirely through suggestion), *The Hitcher* builds up a powerfully horrific drive.

d Robert Harmon *p* David Bombyk, Kip Ohman *s* Eric Red *c* John Seale *se* Art Brewer *lp* Rutger Hauer, C. Thomas Howell, Jennifer Jason Leigh, Jeffrey DeMunn, John Jackson, Billy Green Bush

Rutger Hauer is The Hitcher.

House (NEW WORLD) 93min

Novelist Katt, troubled by Vietnam memories, his recent divorce and the disappearance of his son, moves into the old house where his aunt has been mysteriously hanged. After comic business with the neighbours, the film gets down to the business of shouting 'boo!' every few minutes: monsters lunge from closets, gardening tools fly, a bloated toad-woman impersonates Katt's ex-wife (Lenz) and pesters him even after she has been dismembered to the tune of Betty Everett's *You're No Good*, the missing son cries from a limbo beyond the bathroom cabinet, and a zombie war buddy (Moll) turns up.

A non-serious, non-threatening horror, this juggles plot elements from *Poltergeist* (1982) with scary-cute monsters, contrived shocks, endearingly inappropriate pop music, a central performance that deserves a more substantial film to back it up, double-takes from Wendt and a reassuring but ultimately self-defeating lightness of tone. It was popular enough to yield the even more diffuse and ineffectual *House II: The Second Story* (1987), directed by Wiley; **The Horror Show** (1989), released in many territories as *House III*; and Lewis Abernathy's *House 4: The Repossession* (1991), with Katt returning in a token attempt at series continuity.

d Steve Miner *p* Sean S. Cunningham *s* Ethan Wiley *c* Mac Ahlberg *se* Backwood Film *lp* William Katt, Kay Lenz, George Wendt, Richard Moll, Mary Stavin

Howling II: Stirba – Werewolf Bitch *aka* Howling II: Your Sister is a Werewolf

(GRANTE FILM; US, FR, IT) 92min

An astonishing mish-mash sequel to **The Howling** (1980), with Brown as the brother of the Dee Wallace character, investigating a worldwide conspiracy of werewolves. In Transylvania, he tracks down Stirba (Danning), an imposing werewolf queen, and puts an end to a coven with the aid of her turncoat monster-killing brother (Lee), who has discovered that while lycanthropes are now immune to silver he can still destroy them with titanium bullets. One softcore scene manages to combine miscegenation, troilism, implied incest, bestiality, lesbianism, sadomasochism and lycanthropy to little effect.

Mora followed with the even more perverse *The Marsupials – Howling III* (1987), set in Australia and featuring pouched werewomen, a monster ballerina on the stage of the Sydney Opera House, a futuristic coda with Dame Edna Everage, and ecological sub-texts. John Hough's South-Africa-shot bore *Howling IV: The Original Nightmare* (1988), an adaptation of the Gary Brandner novel which Joe Dante mainly ignored, is more conventional but even more negligible. Neal Sundstrom's *Howling V: The Rebirth* (1989) returns to Eastern Europe and is an almost werewolf-free old dark castle story. Hope Perello's livelier *Howling VI: The Freaks* (1991), shot in America, enjoyably introduces vampires, freaks, a *Twin Peaks*-influenced small town, voodoo and a Bradburyish carnival to pep up the played-out theme. For all their sillinesses the *Howling* films have an unpredictability that puts them ahead of less adventurous series like the *Friday the 13th* or *House* films.

d Philippe Mora *p* Steven Lane *s* Robert Sarner, Gary Brandner *c* G. Stephenson *se* Jack Bricker, Scott Wheeler, Steve Johnson *lp* Christopher Lee, Annie McEnroe, Sybil Danning, Reb Brown, Marsha Hunt, Jimmy Nail, Judd Omen, Ferdinand Mayne

Hunter's Blood (CINEVENTURE) 102min

Based on Jere Cunningham's paperback, this returns to the country of *Deliverance* (1972), **The Texas Chainsaw Massacre** (1974) and **The Hills Have Eyes** (1977) with city slickers venturing into Arkansas backwoods and coming into conflict with inbred degenerates who poach game for a dog-food company and abduct women ('If you fed and watered your gals, they'd last longer'). An early sequence, in which city folks patronize a bar-room full of beer-guzzling rednecks, promises a more interesting social struggle than is eventually delivered by standard clashes between blowhard hunters and cretinous, perverted backwoodsmen. The few unsettling images of pastoral violence (a twitching corpse with most of its head shotgunned away, a skinned cop hanging from a tree, threads of blood in a fast-running river) are lost in the trite melodramatics of the capture-and-escape plot.

d Robert C. Hughes *p* Myrl A. Schreibman *s* Emmett Alston *c* Tom DeNove *se* Make-Up & Effects Laboratories *lp* Samuel Bottoms, Clu Gulager, Ken Swofford, Mayf Nutter, Joey Travolta, Ken Delaney, Lee DeBroux, Bruce Glover, Billy Drago, Charles Cyphers

Jiangshi Papa *aka* **Close Encounter of the Vampire** (FEITENG FILM CO; TAIWAN) 96min
An entry in the 'hopping vampire' genre established by Ronny Yu's **Pao Dan Fei Che** (1983) and Lau Kun Wai's **Jiangshi Xiansheng** (1985), this delivers mildly spectacular though essentially comic thrills, but not the UFO involvement promised by the English release title. Three bungling masters converge on a mission to end the nocturnal depredations of an apparently acromegalic vampire mandarin, using such bizarre equipment as a magic sword made of coins bound together, strings of fireworks and a lariat-shooting crossbow. The stiff-jointed monster survives so many foolproof vampire-killing devices that he has to be struck by lightning in the finale. Shrill in its comedy and skimpy in its production values, this was essentially a Hong Kong production with Taiwanese finance. Its commercial failure helped drive Yuen Woo-Ping back to his original field of action, choreography, distinguishing himself with the spectacular martial artistry of Tsui Hark's *Once Upon a Time in China* films.

d Yuen Woo-Ping *p/s* Yuen Family *c* Lam Chi-Wing, Kwok Muk-Sang *lp* Leung Ka-Yan, Yuen Cheung-Yan, Yuen Sun-Yi, Yeun Yat-Choch, Jan Chi-Jing, Lee Jok-Wai, Hui Fuk-Yin

Little Shop of Horrors (GEFFEN/WB) 88min
This adaptation of Ashman's off-Broadway musical version of Roger Corman's 1961 film is a vastly expensive and elaborate remake of a movie that was originally celebrated as one of the fastest and cheapest ever made.

In a Skid Row flower shop, nerdy florist's assistant Seymour (Moranis) adopts a small, cute plant from outer space and raises it from a cutting into a talking green behemoth by feeding it his own blood, and then the remains of various victims. A tacked-on happy ending loses the show's most ridiculously moving twist, as the heroine (Greene) willingly feeds herself to the plant to further Seymour's career, and falls back on a boring punchline as a sprout shoots from the ruins of the destroyed menace. There is also a major cop-out as the script exonerates Seymour of responsibility for the monster's crimes, thus losing the Faustian angle and fudging the shared guilt (equating social and financial success with mass murder) that is the whole point of the story.

Rick Moranis in one of his many nerd roles as the under assistant florist in Little Shop of Horrors.

The movie's one plus point is that it retains most of the lively, Phil Spectorish Alan Menken score, thus affording exhilarating show-stoppers for dumb blonde Greene as she dreams of an escape to a suburban kitsch paradise out of *Better Homes and Gardens*, Martin as a sadistic biker dentist who enjoys hurting his patients, and the disembodied voice of Levi Stubbs as the talking, singing, eating 'Mean Green Mother From Outer Space'.

d Frank Oz *p* David Geffen *s* Howard Ashman *c* Robert Paynter *se* Lyle Conway *lp* Rick Moranis, Ellen Greene, Steve Martin, Vincent Gardenia, Bill Murray, Jim Belushi, John Candy, Christopher Guest

Lucker *aka* **Necrophagous** (DESERT/VDS; BEL) 84min
This is a grim, effectively depressing portrait of John Lucker (Van Suyt), an alienated and flabby maniac who escapes from an institution and murders young women as a preparation for the slaking of his necrophile lusts but then waits for them to rot to the point when they are capable of arousing him.

A plotless film that captures the ghastly lifestyle of its listless protagonist, prefiguring the better-known but more superficial **Nekromantik** (1988), this features a setpiece sadistic murder filmed in unflinching detail as the protagonist ties up a prostitute and slits her throat, then watches her putrefy, before finally engaging in explicit acts of necrophilia guaranteed to offend the most hardened viewer.

With a grainy vision of Low Countries misery in the background, the film rarely attempts anything approaching a conventional thriller or horror approach, even throwing away the ambiguous ending as one of Lucker's victims manages to escape and he falls to his death in a lift-shaft only to appear in a clichéd evil-lives-on coda.

d/co-s/p Johan Vandewoestijne *co-s* John Kupferschmidt *c* Tony Castillo *lp* Nick Van Suyt, Helga Vandevelde, Let Jodts, Marie-Paule Claes, Martine Scherre, Carry Van Middel, John Edwards, Tony Castillo, Frank Van Laecke, Freek Neiryrick

Manhunter (DEG) pv 120min
A serial killer is plaguing the south-east, striking whenever the moon is full, slaughtering entire perfect families. Ex-FBI agent Will Graham (Peterson), who has taken early retirement after his special abilities – he can think like his psycho quarries – have led to a breakdown, reluctantly agrees to help, even if it plunges him back into the world of Dr Hannibal Lektor (Cox), the last killer he put away.

Poring over clues, looking at the dead families' home movies, consulting Lektor in his maximum security cell, and dealing with the sleazy media backwash of the killings, as Graham gets under the skin of the murderer, Francis Dolarhyde (Noonan), he wonders how close he is to the edge.

Adapted from Thomas Harris's *Red Dragon*, this chilly, haunting movie combines the sparse, striking imagery and inventive technique of Mann's *Miami Vice* TV production with the steady, hypnotic, disturbing atmospherics of his underrated films *Thief* (1981) and **The Keep** (1984). Mann makes exciting scenes in which the FBI experts do high-speed, high-tech analyses of clues, but also throws in out-of-the-blue eye-openers like the killer's bizarre date with a blind girl, whom he takes to a dental vet and introduces to a sleeping tiger. Steeped in both emotional and physical violence, *Manhunter* is surprisingly restrained in its action, which gives the final confrontation a real edge.

Noonan's creepy killer is stranded by the adaptation and his redeeming relationship with the blind girl (Allen) comes too late to have much impact, but the performances are spot on. Peterson is a coolly nervous hero, delicately trying to explain his hangups to his son in a somehow menacing supermarket, visibly falling under the killer's spell. Cox is monstrous as the sociopath psychiatrist who sits dangerously behind bars, sneering at Graham, defeating his doctors in their daily battles, and relishing his menace-edged dialogue ('You wouldn't care to give me your home address, would you, Will?') to scary/funny effect. The character recurs in **The Silence of the Lambs** (1991), also based on a novel by Harris and featuring Anthony Hopkins as a differently spelled Lector.

d/s Michael Mann *p* Richard Roth *c* Dante Spinotti *se* Joseph E. DiGaetano III *lp* William Peterson, Kim Griest, Dennis Farina, Tom Noonan, Brian Cox, Joan Allen, Stephen Lang

Matador (CIA IBEROAMERICANA DE TV; SP) 96min

Opening provocatively with a retired bullfighter masturbating in front of a video showing highlights of Bava's **Sei Donne per l'Assassino** (1964) and Franco's **Die Saege des Todes** (1981), Almodovar's labyrinthine tale of erotic horror follows several equally deranged characters.

Obsessed with bullfighting, lady lawyer Serna seduces young *torreros*, murdering them with a dagger hairpin on the point of orgasm. The matador himself (Martinez), forced into retirement by a goring, teaches most of Serna's victims and has necrophilic fantasies which he attempts to enact with his model girlfriend (Cobo) in between murdering disposable girls. While the two killers stalk each other, inevitably falling into a violently fetishist relationship, Martinez' repressed homosexual pupil (Banderas) tries to assert his masculinity, first in the comically fumbled attempted rape – using his penknife as a threat, he accidentally holds a bottle-opener to the victim's face – of Cobo, and then by confessing to both strings of murders. Police inspector Poncela and sympathetic psychiatrist Maura investigate Banderas' unlikely claims and Serna takes his case and tries to defend him. When the evidence implicating them gradually accumulates, Martinez and Serna, taking a cue from *Duel in the Sun* (1946), kill each other during sex.

A tribute to and a parody of the chic slasher films of Argento and Bava, with a few nods to such Spanish items as **La Semana del Asesino** (1972) and **La Campana del Infierno** (1973), this is the most extreme of Almodovar's internationally successful camp farces. Almodovar himself appears briefly as a fashion designer who makes up the models displaying his clothes as bloodied corpses (which Argento later did) and suggests he is as concerned with the striking objects (earrings, clothes, weapons) as the striking people in the film. Colourful and unreal enough to be less offensive than it sounds, this is nevertheless an intriguing meditation on sex and violence, linking the high style of the *corrida*, in which beautiful young men in tight and frilly clothes elegantly gore bulls to death, to that of the giallo film, with Bava's *Sei Donne* referred to throughout, even to the extent of having Serna recreate the famous image (see p.167) of Claudia Dantes drowned in the bathtub.

d/co-s Pedro Almodovar *p* Andres Vicente Gomez *co-s* Jesus Ferrero *c* Angel Luis Fernandez *lp* Assumpta Serna, Antonio Banderas, Nacho Martinez, Eva Como, Julieta Serrano, Chus Lampreave, Carmen Maura, Eusebio Poncela, Bibi Anderson

Necropolis (TYCIN) 77min

'I believe what I see,' snaps a New York cop, 'I can't book strange vibes.' In New Amsterdam in the 1680s, witch Baker performs a black mass and is thwarted as she tries to sacrifice a young bride. Three hundred years later, she stalks the modern city in heavy black eyeshadow, a peroxide punk haircut and black leather bondage gear, murdering the lookalike descendants of her original persecutors. In a plot lifted from **The Haunted Palace** (1963), *Superstition* (1982), *The Devonsville Terror* (1983) and *The Demons of Ludlow* (1983) she attempts to repeat her sacrifice.

d/s Brian Hickey *p* Tim Kincaid *c* Alfred D. Marks *se* Ed French *lp* LeeAnne Baker, Michael Conte, Jacquie Fitz, William K. Reed

Neon Maniacs (BEDFORD) 91min

This low-budget movie features a set of uninteresting monsters who wear Halloween costumes and live inside the Golden Gate Bridge, emerging at night to wreak havoc only to be destroyed by rainfall. It opens with a compressed slasher movie, introducing a group of teenagers who are killed within minutes, leaving the only virgin to return to school where she is viewed with suspicion because of her survival. This potentially interesting idea, focusing on survivor guilt, is dropped in favour of spotlighting a fourteen-year-old girl who directs her own video horror movies and comes from the *Famous Monsters* generation of cute but geeky kid monster-fighters, and a hero more concerned with the battle of the bands contest than rampaging killers even after he knows they've marked his girl for extermination.

d/c Joe Mangine *p* Steven D. Mackler *s* Mark Carducci *se* Al Apone, Doug White *lp* Allan Hayes, Donna Locke, Leilani Sarelle, Victor Elliott Brandt, Bo Sabato

A Nightmare on Elm Street, Part 2: Freddy's Revenge

(NEW LINE/HERON/SMART EGG) 85min

This is the least of the Nightmare movies.

There are clichés aplenty, including slow, low tracking shots past an ominously lit house that mark it as a 'bad place', and a ludicrous finale in which Myers defeats the monster by repeatedly and bathetically declaring her love. Freddy is much diminished, emerging from dreamshadows as a wisecracking goon surrounded by rubber effects. The sole interesting aspect is that, as in **Fright Night** (1985), the hero's problems are rooted less in the supernatural than repressed homosexual panic: Patton is more concerned with the body of the monster than the romantic advances of his girlfriend. This is extended in a distasteful but unconvincing scene in which a gay sports teacher is tied up naked in the showers, whipped with animated chains and slashed by Freddy, and in an odd moment when, needing to explain his plight to someone, Patton goes not to his girl but the macho jock (Rusler) who has previously humiliated him.

d Jack Sholder *p* Robert Shaye *s* David Chaskin *c* Jacques Haitkin *se* Kevin Yagher *lp* Mark Patton, Kim Myers, Clu Gulager, Hope Lange, Robert Rusler, Marshall Bell, Robert Englund, Sydney Walsh

Poltergeist II: The Other Side (MGM) pv 91min

After the destruction of their suburban home by an epidemic of evil spirits, the Freeling family – minus the elder daughter, written out due to the death of actress Dominique Dunne – move in with their slightly psychic grandmother (Fitzgerald) in Arizona. But the ghosts won't leave them alone and soon special effects are bursting out all over: Robins' braces expand and take over his whole body; Nelson swallows the worm in a bottle of mescal and it grows foetus-like inside him until it emerges in an orgy of monster-vomiting; slimy creatures (designed by H.R. Giger) emerge from the afterlife and threaten to cart them all into the void; and a dead preacher (Beck) stalks transparently through the walls in an attempt to spirit O'Rourke away.

Less a sequel than a footnote, this strings together set-pieces with turgid pretension. The effects are fine and the soundtrack boasts terrifically eerie whispers from beyond the grave, but the story is uninvolving.

d Brian Gibson *p/s* Mark Victor, Michael Grais *c* Andrew Laszlo *se* Richard Edlund, Boss Film *lp* Craig T. Nelson, JoBeth Williams, Heather O'Rourke, Zelda Rubinstein, Oliver Robins, Will Sampson, Julian Beck, Geraldine FitzGerald

Psycho III (U) 96(93)min

Following not only **Psycho** (1960) but the surprisingly tight and imaginative **Psycho II** (1983), Perkins' directorial début is accomplished and almost redeems the trite script.

Going for unexpected Hitchcockery, the film opens with a recreation of the finale of *Vertigo* (1958) as neurotic nun Scarwid semi-accidentally causes the death of a screeching mother superior. Fleeing from guilt, she winds up at that oasis of lost souls, the Bates Motel, and befriends nervous Norman (Perkins), who has recently reopened the place for business and is pathetically anxious its bad reputation be forgotten. Scarwid, subtly taking off Janet Leigh, reminds Norman of his original victim and soon the influence of Mrs Bates is reasserted. A recreation of the 1960 shower-bath murder pays off unexpectedly as Norman, dressed as his mother, looms over Scarwid with a knife only to find she has just cut her wrists; the would-be suicide looks up at the would-be killer and sees him as the Virgin Mary. Sadly, the film thereafter degenerates into a succession of knife killings.

Pogue's script contrives to drag Norman back into the bloodbath but Perkins' performance remains as delicate and hypnotic as ever: the masterstroke of the original, still shakily retained here, is the depiction of the murderer as the only humane, decent, morally untainted character in the vicinity of the Bates Motel, and Perkins plays off this with several chilly, moving little moments that depend on the other characters' and the audience's hope that the likeable young man can stay sane despite a world that forever contrives to drive him mad again. The next entry, Mick Garris's interesting *Psycho 4: The Beginning* (1991) was made, like the failed pilot *Bates Motel* (1987), for television: it features Henry Thomas and Olivia Hussey as the young Norman and his living mother, with Perkins in modern-set wraparound sequences.

d Anthony Perkins *p* Hilton A. Green *s* Charles Edward Pogue *c* Bruce Surtees *se* Michael Westmore *lp* Anthony Perkins, Diana Scarwid, Jeff Fahey, Roberta Maxwell, Hugh Gillin, Lee Garlington

Qi Yuan *aka* **Witch From Nepal** *aka* **Nepal Affair** *aka* **A Touch of Love** (GOLDEN HARVEST; HONG KONG) 90min
A modern fantasy combining the popular Chinese theme of a mortal who falls for an amorous supernatural female with large-scale fantasy action hijinx, demonstrating an early grasp of the possibilities of genre by Ching, later director of the *Chinese Ghost Story* films.

On holiday in Nepal, artist Chow falls off an elephant and breaks his leg, triggering his involvement in a magical underworld. Recovering in Hong Kong, he is approached by a winsome Nepalese acolyte who tells him he is destined to be her master and that a lion demon is coming to steal a pair of sacred marbles from him. In a long, comic central section, Chow discovers his psychic powers and finds himself in a triangular romance with his ballet-teacher girlfriend and the acolyte. When the impressive demon arrives, the film picks up considerably, commencing with a graveyard scene of George Romero-like intensity in which Chow and some children from the ballet school are attacked in their car by a platoon of rotting zombies and the demon turns an iron fence into a rack of spears. Chow, now confident in his magical abilities, confronts the demon in a knockdown fight that mixes martial arts, magical zapping effects and breaking glass, far more effectively catching the wild tone of the *Dr Strange* comics than the comparable *Highlander* (1986) as skyscrapers become canyons and the spell-casting antagonists resolve their ancient duel.

d Ching Siu-Tung *p* Raymond Chow, Leonard Ho *s* Tsui Jing-Hong *c* Lau Moon-Tong *lp* Chow Yun-Fat, Emily Chu, Nam Kit-Ying, Tik Wai, Ng Kong-Sang

Rawhead Rex (GREEN MAN) 89min
Agricultural workers dislodge a giant stone phallus from its place in an Irish field, unleashing a toothy eight-foot-tall monster (Von Schellendorf) in leather and chains.

This, the second filmed Clive Barker screenplay, is an adaptation of a story from his *Books of Blood* that reads like a treatment for a terrific monster movie, but the film shares the failings of the same team's *Underworld* (1985). The script treads a fine line between archetype and cliché but Pavlou plays up the latter, with especially hackneyed performances from Toibín and O'Brien as a mad verger and a raincoated policeman who fall under the monster's spell. The chief failure is the monster itself: the costume is rubbery and unconvincing.

d George Pavlou *p* Kevin Attew, Don Hawkins *s* Clive Barker *c* John Metcalfe *se* Peter Litten *lp* David Dukes, Kelly Piper, Ronan Wilmot, Niall Toibín, Niall O'Brien, Heinrich Von Schellendorf

Scared Stiff (MANSON INTERNATIONAL) 85min
A ghostly revenge tale, similar in concern to **The Oblong Box** (1969). In 1857, a cruel Southern plantation owner is cursed by voodoo-worshipping slaves and turned into a monster who locks his wife and children in a trunk. In modern times, psychiatrist Stevens and his ex-patient rock-star girlfriend (Keller) move into the mansion and find an old diary, a broken amulet and some dessicated corpses, whereupon the curse is passed on. There is tension between would-be subtle ghost story aspects and standard eighties effects (a zip-top cranium, bloated corpse people) yanked in to up the shock factor, but the film has a spirited climax in which the heroine is faced by the transformed Stevens, the ghost of the original villain, and phantoms from her own past. Friedman was evidently replaced by Bacaner for most of the shooting. The script was co-written by Frost, co-creator of *Twin Peaks*.

d/co-s Richard Friedman *p/co-s* Daniel F. Bacaner *co-s* Mark Frost *c* Yuri Denysenko *lp* Andrew Stevens, Mary Page Keller, David Ramsay, Josh Sega, Jackie Davis, Nicole Fourtier

Screamplay (TROMA) b/w 85min
This almost looks like a lost German Expressionist horror movie, with director-writer Seder playing the protagonist like a cross between Conrad Veidt's somnambulist and Dwight Frye's Renfield. In fact *Screamplay* is a black and white nightmare shot on the lowest of budgets, with sets painted to look like a fuzzy print of a silent film and action that often seems projected at the wrong speed.

A screenwriter (Seder) comes to Hollyweird, USA, to write his frustrations out in a script for a murder movie and winds up in a sleazy apartment building run by a thuggish super (Kuchar) and inhabited by an assortment of lost souls: a has-been actress, a has-been publicity agent, a nearly-was starlet, a would-be messiah. The murders in the script start taking place in real life and the hardboiled midget cop on the case wants to pin the crimes on the hero. With its hand-wringing performances, gloomy music, bizarrely perverse screenplay, neo-Underground attitudes and a modicum of sickly snide satire, *Screamplay* is genuinely unusual.

d/co-s/se Rufus Butler Seder *p/c* Dennis M. Piana *co-s* Ed Greenberg *lp* Rufus Butler Seder, George Kuchar, Katy Bolger, Nina Piana, Eugene Seder

As Sete Vampiros *aka* **The Seven Vampires** (EMBRAFILME/SUPEROITO PRODUCTIONS; BRAZIL) 100min
This is a Brazilian fantasy-comedy-horror-detective-nudie-musical-nostalgia movie. A carnivorous plant is imported to Brazil in the fifties and gobbles the face of a dedicated botanist before infecting his wife with a mysterious malady. Soon after, Rio is terrorized by a masked killer who drains his victims of blood. Meanwhile a Monroe-ish blonde poses in and out of dreamy fashions in sequences that could stand as a working definition of gratuitous nudity, and bumbling hard-boiled dick 'Raimundo Marlou' is distracted from comic books by a need to bring in the murderer. In a cabaret, vampirettes flounce in lingerie and serve as a warm-up for the hilarious 'Bob Rider and His Comets of Rhythm', an authentically pomaded Brazilian rocker (Jaime) with four out-of-step backing vocalists.

The horror is nostalgically reminiscent of continental mad-scientist shockers of the early sixties and the colours are pleasingly garish. The vampire turns out not to be the white-faced femme fatale but the mad scientist, hideously deformed behind his cloak, who has been haunting nightclubs in search of fresh blood for his experiments.

d/co-p Ivan Cardoso *co-p* Mauro Taubman, Claudio Klabin, Antonio Avilez, Flavio Holanda *s* R.F. Lucchetti *c* Carlos Egberto Silveira *se* Antonio Pacheco *lp* Alvamar Tadei, Andrea Beltraõ, Ariel Coelho, Bené Nunes, Colé Carlo Mossi, Danielle Daumerri, Dedina Bernardelli, Felipe Falcão, Ivon Curi, John Herbert, Leo Jaime

Sorority House Massacre (CONCORDE) 74 min

A blatant **Halloween** (1978) imitation, whose decent direction and acting don't outweigh the familiar premise. Sorority sister O'Neill, tormented by memories of the murders of her entire family, has **Don't Look Now** (1973) flashes of marbles rolling and knives poking through mirrors. The institutionalized killer (Russell) shares flashbacks inventively staged and edited to suggest a psychic link between heroine and murderer. After the careful build-up, Russell escapes and heads for the sorority house to slaughter supporting characters and menace O'Neill.

d/s Carol Frank *p* Ron Diamond *c* Mark Reshovsky *lp* Angela O'Neill, Wendy Martel, Pamela Ross, Nicole Rio, John C. Russell

Sotto il Vestito Niente *aka* Nothing Underneath (FASO FILM) 91min

An Italian giallo film in the old style, this reclaims the stalking-the-models subgenre of *The Eyes of Laura Mars* (1978) for the country which, with **Sei Donne per L'Assassino** (1964), originated it.

As a gloved killer menaces Milan, a Wyoming forest ranger (Schanley) psychically feels the death of his twin sister and goes to Italy with quizzical cop Pleasence to investigate the murders. Heavily influenced by Argento, the film presents its murders and confrontations as stylistic setpieces, distancing sadistic cruelty with beautiful camerawork and a lyrical Pino Donaggio score, and winds up with a genuinely revelatory revelation and some suspenseful slow-motion business with the embalmed corpse of the original victim, a plate-glass window and a touch of vertigo.

d/co-s Carlo Vanzina *p* Achille Manzotti *co-s* Enrico Vanzina, Franco Ferrini *c* Beppe Maccari *se* Corridorri *lp* Tom Schanley, Donald Pleasence, Renée Simonson, Nicola Perring

The Stepfather (ITC) 98(89)min

A commercial failure when set beside the similarly themed but reactionary **Fatal Attraction** (1987), this proved to be in the vanguard of a wave of interesting, questioning horror movies taking as their subject the eighties resurgence of fifties family values. It opens with a disturbing sequence of a quiet-seeming man (O'Quinn) in early middle age clearing up after a mass murderer, calmly making himself unrecognisable so he can establish a new identity. A chameleon-like psychopath who travels from community to community, he marries women with children and tries to establish a perfect family. When his loved ones fail to match his idealized vision of what a home should be, O'Quinn murders them and moves on to the next identity and the next family.

A skilfully made thriller, which works up suspense as O'Quinn's stepdaughter (Schoelen), in the manner of *Shadow of a Doubt* (1943) gradually realizes how well-founded her uneasy feelings about him are, the film is outstanding for its creation of a fully-rounded, sympathetic psychopath in the Norman Bates mould. The multiply-named madman is a creepily persuasive argument for the strength and validity of the American nuclear family as presented by *Leave It to Beaver* or *The Donna Reed Show*, and the most disturbing sequences show his frustration when the spiky, complicated, unreasonable people around him fail to slot into his mental stereotypes for them. O'Quinn returned from the dead in **Stepfather II** (1990).

d Joe Ruben *p* Jay Benson *s* Donald E. Westlake *c* John Lindley *lp* Terry O'Quinn, Jill Schoelen, Shelly Hack, Charles Lanyer, Stephen Shellen, Stephen E. Miller

Street Trash (CHAOS PRODUCTION) 91min

A case of 60-year-old wine is unearthed in a skid-row liquor store and sold cheap to winos, all of whom melt or explode in a graphic series of disgusting gags, the most elaborate of which involves a character literally flushing himself down the toilet.

These sequences are triumphs of cartoonish horror but hardly integrate into the rest of the film, which straggles all over the huge junkyard in which it is mostly set, pitting a hard-boiled killer cop against a Vietnam veteran psycho in a battle to the death which pays off with one of the most repulsive scenes in exploitation cinema: a group play piggy-in-the-middle with a ripped-off penis while the victim hops around trying to catch it so he can rush to hospital for emergency surgery. Muro also tries to find humour in unworkable necrophilia jokes, as when a slobbish passer-by who has taken the opportunity to have sex with the dead victim of a wino gangbang is told by the cop that one of his predecessors had syphilis. Originally a short, this expanded version remains intriguing but feels like an effects showreel padded out, however skilfully, with an anything-goes selection of subplots.

d Jim Muro *p/s* Roy Frumkes *c* Dennis Werner *se* Jennifer Aspinall, Mike Lackey *lp* Bill Chepil, Vic Noto, Mike Lackey, Jane Arkawa, Mark Sferrazza, Nicole Potter, R.L. Ryan

The Supernaturals (REPUBLIC) 80min

A promising but bland zombie movie influenced by *Southern Comfort* (1981).

During the Civil War, a cruel Northern officer forces Confederate POWS to walk through a minefield to clear the way; a century later, the dead rise from their graves to terrorize a group of modern soldiers. The dead turn out to have been revived via an optical effect by an immortal witch whose now very elderly son is the sole survivor of the massacre. Caulfield, the reincarnation of the witch's husband, is able to put an end to the curse. Sadly Mastroianni makes little of the Southern setting, the rising body-count or the 19th-century zombies.

d Armand Mastroianni *p* Sandy Howard *s* Michael S. Murphey, Joel Soisson *c* Peter Collister *se* Gregory Landerer *lp* Maxwell Caulfield, Talia Balsam, Bobby DiCicco, Nichelle Nichols, Bradford Bancroft, LeVar Burton

The Texas Chainsaw Massacre, Part 2 (CANNON) 95min

Less follow-up than parody, this was made after Hooper's disastrously extravagant science-fiction flops *Lifeforce* (1985) and *Invaders From Mars* (1986), and is a far more elaborate production than the cheapskate but intense original – hence the Sawyer family's move from an isolated farmhouse to extensive and impressive catacombs under a theme park. The elder Sawyer (Siedow, the only returning cast member) has expanded his cookery business and now wins state-wide chilli contests.

A Texas Ranger (Hopper) who wears mini-chainsaws in hip holsters is after the cannibal family to avenge his murdered relatives; and a disc jockey (Williams) gets involved when the monstrous Leatherface takes a shine to her. In the sequence where Leatherface confronts the girl and suffers an obviously sexual dysfunction when, after caressing the insides of her thighs with his chainsaw he is unable to pull-start the killer tool, and in Mosely's performance as a psychotic with a steel plate in his head who yells ''Nam flashback' when he is having a fit and loudly laments the sawing-in-half of his original Sonny Bono

Tony Fields returns from the dead to discover that he's not wanted in Trick or Treat.

wig, the film approximates the crazed tone of the first movie, but the plot fails to work up the relentless drive that makes **The Texas Chainsaw Massacre** (1974) a major classic.

The Savini effects that remain in the film (a character walking around with his face hanging off, a chainsaw buzzing right through Leatherface's stomach) are impressive in a *Fangoria* magazine sort of way, but seem to signal Hooper's admission that he is unable to do without splatter and rely on suspense and imagination as he was able to in his first film. The film fared badly at the box office, further handicapping Hooper's career.

d Tobe Hooper *p* Menahem Golan, Yoram Globus *s* L.M. 'Kit' Carson *c* Richard Kooris *se* Tom Savini *lp* Dennis Hopper, Caroline Williams, Bill Johnson, Jim Siedow, Bill Moseley, Lou Perry, Barry Kinyon, Chris Douridas

Trick or Treat (DEG) 97min

When Sammi Curr (Fields) dies in a hotel fire, teenager Price resurrects his idol by playing an acetate of the rocker's last album backwards. An electrified ghost Sammi zaps out of radios and cassette players when his songs are aired, punishing the preppies who terrorize his disciple. Naturally, it's Halloween and, naturally, the school has a Pumpkin Prom, and, even more naturally, Sammi decides to destroy it while Price has a change of heart and sets out to stop him.

The electrically generated satanic rock performer is a fresh monster and the business about appearing from appliances predates **The Horror Show** (1988) and **Shocker** (1989). But, as in Heavy Metal-themed horrors like **Hard Rock Zombies** (1984), *Rocktober Blood* (1985), **The Edge of Hell** (1987), **Slaughterhouse Rock** (1987) and **Black Roses** (1988), the undistinguished music never suggests, as Penelope Spheeris' documentary *The Decline of Western Civilisation, Part 2: The Metal Years* (1988) interestingly does, that Heavy Metal could be dangerous. There are a few clever stunts (TV preacher Osbourne is pulled through the screen and shrivels into a corpse), but most of the horrors are uninspired. First-time director Smith, typecast from *American Graffiti* (1973) as the wimp with glasses, ensures that the few good lines go to the hero's best friend, the wimp with glasses.

d Charlie Martin Smith *p/co-s* Michael S. Murphey, Joel Soisson *co-s* Rhet Topham *c* Robert Elswit *se* Kevin Yahger *lp* Marc Price, Tony Fields, Lisa Orgolini, Doug Savant, Elaine Joyce, Glen Morgan, Gene Simmons, Ozzy Osbourne

Turnaround (MAJOR ROSE; NORWAY) 87min

Set in wintery upstate New York but shot almost entirely in Norway, this is a bloodless **Last House on the Left** (1972) copy with a conjuring vigilante twist. Maier's rich bikers persecute McKeon, the grandson of stage magician Albert, by invading his Christmas party. To get even, McKeon has a New Year's Eve party in an old dark house and terrorizes the gate-crashers with hokey ghost train tricks (sawing a lady in quarters, floating masks, halls of mirrors, a guillotine stunt). Because the villains aren't threatening enough to do anything nasty beyond vandalizing McKeon's car, there is little tension, with the kindly magician never remotely suggesting that he might really decapitate Maier. Originally scripted as 'a British *Death Wish*' (1974) by David McGillivray for exploitation producer Ray Selfe, this was rewritten and toned down for Solum, of the Norwegian conspiracy thriller *Orions Belte* (1984).

d Ola Solum *p* Stuart Lyons *s* Sandra K. Bailey *c* Odd Geir Saether *lp* Doug McKeon, Tim Maier, Jonna Lee, Gayle Hunnicutt, Eddie Albert, Ed Bishop, Roman Sheen, David Healy

Vamp (NEW WORLD) 94min

Cheaper than **Fright Night** (1985), this is a more refreshing and intelligent turnaround of the vampire genre.

Three fraternity pledges have to secure the services of a stripper for their initiation and visit an out-of-the-way part of a down-at-heel city where, after being terrorized by psychotic albinos, they find the After Dark club, which turns out to be a nest of bloodsuckers. Undead entrepreneur Baron, a cockroach-muncher with dreams of relocating to Las Vegas, has hit on a sure-fire business, polishing off the unwanted low-lifes who frequent his club in order to feed his bevy of vampire ecdysiasts. When Katrina (Jones), the heart-ripping Queen of the Night, lunches on one of the college kids (Rusler), the smooth running of the establishment falls to pieces and the surviving hero (Makepeace) finds himself in an escalating nightmare that blends the plot structure of *After Hours* (1985) with the traditional fangs and stakes of the vampire movie.

Wenk confidently wields his effects sequences but also has an eye for creepy locales like a thirties hotel where the lifts have a nasty mind of their own, the almost deserted diner where the albinos hang out and the dark, disgusting club itself. The interesting vampires range from a tenacious waif who flies through the air and latches onto one victim, through the zombie-like strippers – two sit face to face applying their make-up while staring at each other as if looking in an absent mirror – to Jones' regal, silent, impressively costumed dancer, a character whose strange performances are truly perverse.

d/s Richard Wenk *p* Donald P. Borchers *c* Elliot Davis *se* Image Engineering *lp* Grace Jones, Chris Makepeace, Sandy Baron, Gedde Watanabe, Robert Rusler, Deedee Pfeiffer, Billy Drago, Lisa Lyon

Vec Videno *aka* **Reflections** *aka* **Déjà Vu** (ART FILM 80/ DFS AVALA/CROATIA FILM/SMART EGG; YUGOSLAVIA) 104min

A communist-bloc answer to **The Stepfather** (1986), focusing on a Yugoslav ex-concert pianist driven, by the pressures of his society and traumas relating to his wealthy family, to acts of psychotic violence. While at a re-education institute in 1971, the troubled Nadarevic becomes involved with a hard-bitten girl (Dobra) in a mini-skirt who teaches fashion modelling. Dobra stages a patriotic pageant in the hope that her career will take off, allowing her to move out of a cramped apartment where she has to move her sick brother out of bed whenever she brings home a lover. The shambolic pageant, with black-clad dancers as 'the forces of counter-revolution', reminds Nadarevic of his post-revolutionary nightmares, trapped behind a dresser as new co-tenants invaded the family flat while his mother noisily died. In a surpisingly gruesome and suspenseful finale, the madman goes wildly overboard and graphically murders Dobra and her new boyfriend with a sword. A stylish and strange anatomy-of-a-madman movie with a streak of satirical humour and some genuine shocks.

d/s Goran Marcovic *c* Zivko Slar *lp* Mustafa Nadarevic, Anica Dobra, Miroslav Mandic

White of the Eye (MRS WHITES PRODUCTION; GB) 111min

Arizona yuppies are terrorized by a serial murderer who specializes in waylaying wealthy women in their tastefully outfitted homes and disembowelling them on their stripped pine dinner tables in accordance with an ancient American Indian ritual. The police suspect Keith, an ex-hippie mechanics wizard who is now a comfortably-off stereo expert, but his wife (Moriarty) and daughter know he is innocent. Or is he? While Keith squirms under tactful persecution, Moriarty has interestingly washed-out flashbacks to the seventies and the circumstances whereby she ditched her cracked old boyfriend (Rosenberg), who has recently reappeared as a secondary suspect, in favour of the cool Westerner with perfect pitch and a roving eye.

Cammell's second and a halfth film in eighteen years – he co-directed *Performance* (1970) with Nicolas Roeg and did *Demon Seed* (1977) by himself – is a stylishly overblown thriller that shares with **The Stepfather** (1986) a penetrating insight into the corruption that lurks behind the Happy Families façade and a terrifically suspenseful finale in which a mother has to protect her offspring from a monstrous father figure. Although it opts for style rather than substance in its Argento-style execution, it reaches baroque heights of designer horror, skilfully deploying images like a flapping goldfish in an otherwise meticulously arranged gourmet dish.

d/co-s Donald Cammell *p* Sue Baden-Powell, Vicki Taft *co-s* China Cammell *c* Larry McConkey *se* Thomas Ford *lp* David Keith, Cathy Moriarty, Alan Rosenberg, Art Evans, Michael Greene, Danko Gurovich, David Chow

The Wraith

(NEW CENTURY/ALLIANCE ENTERTAINMENT) 92min

In effect this is Clint Eastwood's *High Plains Drifter* (1972) remade as a 'Brat Pack' movie, with a youthful cast who all seem to be related to someone more famous.

The new kid in town (Sheen) is the reincarnation of a high-school hero who was murdered on the road by a psychotic drag racer (Cassavetes) because he dared to go out with the girl (Fenn) the villain has a major crush on. Not only has Sheen come back from the dead to hang out at the local swimming hole or the hamburger bar; he can also transform himself into a high-tech spirit in black leathers who zooms about the desert murdering Cassavetes' gang-buddies in a sinister supercar whose prominent Ford logo suggests an intriguing link-up between big business and the afterlife.

The Wraith is a lot like the plentiful pop music on its soundtrack – well-produced, fast, eclectic, loud, flashy, insubstantial and unmemorable.

d/s Mike Marvin *p* John Kemeny *c* Reed Smoot *se* Alan Munro, VCE/Peter Kuran *lp* Charley Sheen, Nick Cassavetes, Sherilyn Fenn, Randy Quaid, Matthew Barry, David Sherrill, Jamie Bozian, Clint Howard, Griffin O'Neal

1987

Aenigma

(AM INTERNATIONAL/SUTJESKA; IT, YUGOSLAVIA) 85min

Wide-eyed Eirojvic is left in a coma after a cruel joke perpetrated by a group of schoolgirls and an insensitive gym teacher. She establishes a psychic link with new pupil Naszinski and drives her tormentors to bizarre fates.

Though girls are smothered by snails or crushed to death by an animated Greek statue, the horrors are mostly clumsy and familiar, involving shaky camerawork, unconvincing decapitations by window and hysterical overacting. The premise is stolen from **Patrick** (1978) and the overwhelmingly blue look borrowed from **Phenomena** (1986), which also inspired the school setting and a somewhat middle-aged idea of the behaviour patterns of teenage girls. The silly killer snails are in a tacky line of descent from the toy spider and bat sequences of **...E Tu Vivrai nel Terrore! L'Aldila** (1981) and **Quella Villa Accanto al Cimitero** (1981).

d/co-s Lucio Fulci *p* Ettore Spagnuolo *co-s* Giorgio Mariuzzo *c* Luigi Ciccarese *se* Giuseppe Ferranti *lp* Jared Martin, Lara Naszinski, Ulli Reinthaler, Sophie d'Aulan, Jennifer Naud, Riccardo Acerbi, Kathi Wise, Mijija Eirojvic

American Gothic *aka* **Hide and Go Shriek**

(VIDMARK; GB) 92min

In this minor outing a planeload of teens are stranded on a remote offshore island where they fall in with a godfearing psycho family who still live in the twenties.

Naturally, the teens get killed off, initially in amusing ways that are extensions of child's play (middle-aged kid Pollard hurtles one victim off a cliff with a swing) but mainly in the traditional **Friday the 13th** (1980) manner. Steiger manfully resists the temptation to chew scenery and underplays his stern patriarch role, leaving the campery to de Carlo as his wife. Initially promisingly unnerving as the off-centre lifestyle of the psycho family is gradually exposed, the film too quickly degenerates into an ordinary woodlands slasher movie.

d/co-s John Hough *p* John Quested *co-s* Terry Lens *c* Harvey Harrison *lp* Rod Steiger, Sarah Torgov, Yvonne De Carlo, Michael J. Pollard, Fiona Hutchinson, William Hootkins

Angel Heart (CAROLCO) 113min

In 1955, New York private eye Harry Angel (Rourke) is hired by mephistophelian Louis Cyphre (DeNiro) to find a missing singer. The case takes him to New Orleans and a circle of voodoo worshippers, all of whom turn up gruesomely murdered.

Like Dan Duryea in *Black Angel* (1946), Angel realizes he is the murderer for whom he has been searching, a lost soul attempting to avoid damnation. Parker opts to strain for significance by intercutting horrors with insistent shots of whirring fans, feet tap-dancing on rainy pavements and blood mingling with water. The grey look and frequent placing of Rourke in visual traps of bars and shadows (a noir commonplace) establishes the protagonist as doomed and damned but sadly the marvellously understated vision of a descent into Hell in a rattling skeleton lift is undercut by a banal, literal version of the Pit: screaming fat people.

d/s Alan Parker *p* Alan Marshall, Elliott Kastner *c* Michael Seresin *se* J.C. Brotherhood *lp* Mickey Rourke, Robert DeNiro, Charlotte Rampling, Lisa Bonet, Stocker Fontlieu

Anguista *aka* **Anguish** (SAMBA PC/LUNA FILMS; SP) 89min
This starts out as *The Mommy*, a slasher movie with smothering midget mother Rubinstein hypnotizing her blubbery psycho son (Lerner) into committing a series of eyeball-gouging murders. Then it shifts its layer of meta-fiction to a cinema where a psychopath has been hypnotized by the film, which features a subliminal gimmick along the lines of Hypno-Vision (*The Hypnotic Eye*, 1960) or Psychorama (**Terror in the Haunted House**, 1961), and feels driven to copycat killings. Then things get really complicated when the plot of *The Mommy* (the film-within-a-film) begins to mimic that of *Anguista* as the onscreen Lerner goes into a cinema to commit more atrocities while watching *The Lost World* (1925), while the real-life killer precipitates a siege situation in the downtown theatre (the characterless suburban cinema of the 'real' section contrasts neatly with the decaying art-deco movie palace of *The Mommy*) and the audiences panic. A pretentious cocktail of demented ideas, it is especially clever in its use of hackneyed William Castle devices, like an ominously meaningless warning placard, which turn out to be parts of *The Mommy*, not of *Anguista*.

d/s Bigas Luna *p* Pepon Coromina *c* Josep Maria Civit *se* Paco Teres *lp* Zelda Rubinstein, Michael Lerner, Talia Paul, Angel José, Clara Pastor, Isabel García Lorca

The Believers (ORION) 114min
Police psychiatrist Sheen, barely recovered from the accidental electrocution of his wife in a startling but irrelevant opening, is called in by cop Loggia to help with a case involving ritual child murder that leads him to discover a dark form of the voodoo-like faith Santeria.

Carl Crew as the cook in the inept gore comedy Blood Diner.

Based on Nicholas Conde's novel *The Religion*, this is all too clearly a retread of **Rosemary's Baby** (1968), as a coven of highly placed New York sorcerers try to get a parent to sacrifice a child for evil. Individual sequences work, particularly when horrible things happen: spiders erupt from a zit on Shaver's cheek, an autopsy reveals live snakes wriggling in a victim's guts, and Loggia is consumed more subtly by an unspeakable but unspecified spell. The suitably melodramatic finale involves a one-to-one confrontation between the hero and a scary witch doctor (Keyi) in the traditionally vast deserted warehouse where the sacrifices take place.

d/co-p John Schlesinger *co-p* Michael Childers, Beverly Camhe *s* Mark Frost *c* Robby Müller *se* Kevin Hayney *lp* Martin Sheen, Helen Shaver, Harley Cross, Robert Loggia, Elizabeth Wilson, Harris Yulin, Lee Richardson, Richard Masur, Carla Pinza, Jimmy Smits, Khali Keyi

Berserker: The Nordic Curse
(AMERICAN VIDEO/PARADISE FILMWORKS/SHAPIRO) 85min
A marginally competent death-in-the-woods movie with cabin-sitting teens pawed by a cannibal Viking who has possessed his descendant (Flower). Despite interesting Norse background, signalled mainly by Flower's 'yomping yiminy' John Qualen accent, this is underdeveloped. The script neglects to confirm or deny the survival of its wounded teen lead (Johnson) and sets up a legend whereby the berserker's spirit hops from descendant to descendant, then fails to have Flower's Sheriff cousin inherit the curse. The highlight is a tussle between the bear-masked berserker and a passing real bear.

d/s Jef Richard *p* Jules Rivera *c* Henning Schellerup *se* Perri Sorel, Carol Lynne Salonen *lp* Joseph Alan Johnson, Valerie Sheldon, Greg Dawson, Shannon Engemann, Beth Toussaint, George 'Buck' Flower

Blood Diner (LIGHTNING/VESTRON) 88min
'He has been spotted,' announces a radio, 'armed with a meat-cleaver in one hand and his genitals in the other. We return you to your usual program.'

Originally scripted as a sequel to H. G. Lewis's **Blood Feast** (1963), this gore comedy veers between knowing camp and ineptitude without ever really finding an identity of its own. A pair of Egyptian caterers (Burks, Crew) under the command of a disembodied brain in a jar (supposedly the villain of the Lewis film) kill a series of women in order to complete a ritual which will bring about the resurrection of the Ancient Egyptian goddess Sheetar.

d Jackie Kong *p* Jimmy Maslon *s* Michael Sonye *c* Jurg Walther *se* Bruce Zahlava *lp* Rick Burks, Carl Crew, Lisa Guggenheim, Roger Dauer, LaNette La France, Max Morris, Roxanne Cybelle

Blood Harvest (BUDDY'S INC/SHOOTING RANCH) 81min
This entire film is structured around the exploitable image of corpses hung upside-down in the villain's barn, as featured heavily in the promotional material and in irrelevant cutaways. The opening evokes the atmosphere of rural poverty and farm closures of the up-market *Country* (1985) with Salocheck returning home to find that her banker father, much hated for his part in evicting farmers, has disappeared. The social angle is swiftly dropped in favour of thin horror as Salocheck is pursued by a fresh-faced ex-boyfriend (West) who is transparently the psychopathic villain in a stocking mask who has been abducting and killing all those close to the girl. Wisconsin-based Rebane, a do-it-all-yourself film-maker, co-directed *Monster a-Go-Go* (1965) with H. G. Lewis and is best known for *The Giant Spider Invasion* (1975). Other genre works include *The Devil's Express* (1975), *The Alpha Incident* (1976), *Maggots* (1977), *The Capture of Bigfoot* (1979), *Rana: The Legend of Shadow Lake* (1980) and, probably his best work, *The Demons of Ludlow* (1983).

d Bill Rebane *p* Leszek Burzynski *s* Ben Bensen, Emil Joseph *c* Ito *se* Pat Cannon, Robert Johnson *lp* Tiny Tim, Itonia Salochek, Dean West, Lori Minneti, Peter Krause, Frank Benson

Blood Relations (SC ENTERTAINMENT; CAN) 90min
'Too much sex and violence, they say. Poppycock! Too much violence and not enough sex, that's their problem.'

An extravagantly mad neurosurgeon (Rubes) and his son (Hicks) play a game of multiple double-cross and attempted murder after the manner of *Les Diaboliques* (1955) or **Games** (1967) as Hicks dupes his girlfriend (Denier) into attempting to induce a heart attack in the older man. The intended victim is dying multi-millionaire Walston, who still hasn't decided who gets his fortune after he's gone. Glossily made and with some dry wit in the dialogue ('You know, you bring a girl home, you ask her to help you kill your father, and before you know it she's trying to run your life'), it's a generally enjoyable mystery with a wild finale as father and son try to resurrect Rubes' dead wife.

d Graeme Campbell *p* Nicolas Stilliadis *s* Stephen Saylor *c* Rhett Morita *lp* Jan Rubes, Lydie Denier, Kevin Hicks, Lynne Adams, Sam Malkin, Stephen Saylor, Carrie Leigh, Ray Walston

Blood Sisters (REELTIME) 86min
Sorority pledges spend the night in a former whorehouse that was the site of a shotgun massacre thirteen years ago and fall under the influence of the dead prostitutes, who appear in mirrors and trigger semi-erotic flashbacks, before being slashed by a male murderer in a frilly nightie. A combination of **The Nesting** (1980) and **Hell Night** (1981) – both, perhaps significantly, also by ex-porn film-makers – this begins as a somewhat clumsy ghost story and turns into a perfunctory body-count picture.

d/s/c Roberta Findlay *p* Walter Sear *lp* Amy Brentano, Shannon McMahon, Dan Erickson, Maria Machart, Elizabeth Rose, Cjerste Thor, John Fasano, Pam La Testa

Brain Damage (THE BRAIN DAMAGE COMPANY) 86min
Elmer, a hand-puppet parasite voiced by an uncredited Zacherle, latches onto Herbst, injecting his brain with a blue fluid that gives him amazing psychedelic experiences on the condition the kid helps him get plenty of his favourite food, human brains.

Like **Basket Case** (1981), to which there is a neat reference, this gives its monster a distinctive personality but doesn't come up with enough connective tissue to go around gory set-pieces. The scene that justifies *Brain Damage* is an intimate piece of torture in a shabby hotel room as Herbst suffers from withdrawal symptoms that make him hallucinate the pulling out of his brains through his ear in a long, bloody string while Elmer taunts him with a nasty rendition of Tommy Dorsey's *Elmer's Tune*. The monster – related to *The Brain Eaters* (1958), **The Tingler** (1959), the parasites from *Shivers* (1976) and the malicious frog in Chuck Jones' *One Froggy Evening* (1955) – provides ordinary drug visions out of *Liquid Sky* (1983) – lapping blue waters, negative images, droning music, lights in the sky – and sucks out victims' brains in overdone gross-out effects. The major 'gag' sequence has Elmer shoot out of Herbst's fly into a hooker's mouth for the screen's first fellatio/brain-eating sequence.

d/s Frank Henenlotter *p* Edgar Ievins *c* Bruce Torbet *se* Gabe Bartalos, David Kindlon *lp* Rick Herbst, Gordon MacDonald, Jennifer Lowry, Theo Barnes, Lucille Saint-Peter, John Zacherle, Kevin VanHentenryck

The Carrier (SWAN PRODUCTIONS) 99min
Outsider Fortescue, whose parents were murdered by greedy townsfolk, develops a condition whereby objects he has touched cause spontaneous combustion in those who touch them. The film takes an allegorical approach to its subject matter, condemning narrow-minded religion (the preacher is no help) and using Christ imagery (the carrier is crucified upside-down at the finale). Cut off from the world, the townsfolk dress in all-over plastic coverings and fortify two camps (one centred on church-going, the other on the local bar) who are spurred by Fortescue into a ridiculous but violent battle over possession of the cats used like mine-shaft canaries to detect the presence of the malady. By showing scientific method and fundamentalist religion as equally useless in the crisis, White takes an unusual, misanthropic line, suggesting that Fortescue's curse has come about as a reaction to evils done him by the locals. This stands out among the glut of regional horror films.

d/s Nathan J. White *p* Jeffrey Daugherty *c* Peter Deming *se* Roger White, Larry Larson, Brian Ochub *lp* Gregory Fortescue, Stevie Lee, Steve Dixon, Paul Urbanski, N. Paul Silverman, DeLaney Provencher, Marena Seeman, Patrick Butler, Julia Escher

La Casa no. 3 *aka* **Ghosthouse** (FILMIRAGE; IT) 94min
Though the title suggests a spurious sequel to **House** (1986) this was actually intended to cash in on **The Evil Dead** (1982) which was released in Italy as *La Casa*. That said, it is mainly an imitation of **Poltergeist** (1982).

The source of the horror is a little girl possessed by an evil doll which was stolen by her undertaker father from a dead child with whom it was supposed to be buried. Twenty years after killing the cat and her parents, she lurks around the house, luring dull teenagers to their doom with fake ham radio messages. The nastily leering puppet is patterned on the toy from *Poltergeist*, but the standard teen-kill sequences (involving quicklime, a guillotine or a psycho caretaker) are considerably less unnerving. In a dreary double-twist, the doll and the ghost girl's corpse are burned, banishing the evil, but the horror starts again when the doll turns up in a junk shop window while the hero is run over in the street. Further unrelated pseudo-sequels followed: *La Casa no. 4* (1989), with Linda Blair, was, almost coincidentally, released in the UK as *Ghosthouse II*, although its US title is *Witchery*.

d Humphrey Humbert (Umberto Lenzi) *p* Aristide Massacesi, Donatella Donati *s* Cinthia McGavin *c* Franco Delli Colli *lp* Lara Wendel, Gregg Scott, Mary Sellers, Kate Silver, Ron Houck, Martin Jay, Kristen Fougerousse, Willy H. Moon

La Casa al Fondo del Parco *aka* **Rat Man**
(FULVIA FILM; IT) 80min
This was apparently designed as a passenger on the very short coat-tails of Sondra Locke's unsuccessful fable *Ratboy* (1986). Exploiting the genuine deformities of a pygmy-like black child who, with the addition of some false fangs, appears as the film's genetically engineered human-rat cross-breed, the Florida-set film dispenses with scientific explanation before the opening credits and concentrates on puffily glamorous women wandering around in the dark, being leaped upon and gorily gnawed by the disturbing but fragile-seeming monster. Warbeck and Agren, veterans of Italian horrors, wearily walk through their paces, never quite catching on to the carnage around them, while the local police display no apparent interest in the mutilation murders of models taking place in the area.

d Anthony Ascot (Giuliano Carmineo) *p* Maurice Matthew *s* David Parker Jr *c* Robert Garder *se* Franco Giannini *lp* David Warbeck, Janet Agren, Eva Grimaldi, Luisa Menon, Werner Pochath, Nelson De La Rosa

Cellar Dweller (EMPIRE/DOVE) 77min
This is another Empire monster quickie along the lines of **Ghoulies** (1984), **Troll** (1985) and **Dolls** (1987).

Shot in Italy and pseudonymously written by the creator of the **Child's Play** series, the film deals with a monster brought to life in the fifties by a satanic horror comic artist (Combs), which menaces a houseful of neurotic would-be artists in the present day. As in **Screamplay** (1986), the central character (Mullowny) is an artist who works out personal frustrations by killing off annoying people in a gruesome storyline (here, a horror comic) only to have the deaths take place in real life.

d/se John Carl Buechler *p* Bob Wynn *s* Kit DuBois (Don Mancini) *c* Sergio Salvati *lp* Debrah Mullowney, Brian Robbins, Vince Edwards, Cheryl-Ann Wilson, Jeffrey Combs, Pamela Bellwood, Yvonne de Carlo

Combat Shock *aka* American Nightmare

(TROMA) 90min

This is an intense, grim psycho movie shot on a shoestring in New York, with traumatized Vietnam veteran Ricky Giovinazzo suffering nightmare flashbacks to a massacre in which he took part and being driven even crazier by his squalid surroundings.

His baby has been born as a squealing rubber-faced mutant thanks to his exposure to Agent Orange, his wife is a shrieking harridan who never lets up complaining, the only sustenance in his apartment is a bottle of milk that gets more and more rancid, and all his friends appear to be street people, junkies and deadbeats. Eventually, he becomes so crazed that he takes to the streets as a vigilante and blows away a few criminals before turning his gun on his family and himself. Giovinazzo is let down by his amateur cast and, even in this skid row context, the Vietnam trauma is hackneyed and conventional. It contains several hard-to-watch sequences (a drug addict shoving heroin into his arm with a bent coathanger, the protagonist's eventual killing of the baby) and certainly has a powerful sleaze atmosphere, but its one-note tone compares unfavourably with **The Driller Killer** (1979) or **Henry... Portrait of a Serial Killer** (1987).

d/p/s Buddy Giovinazzo *c* Stella Varveris *se* Ralph Cordero II, Ed Varuolo, Jeff Matthes *lp* Ricky Giovinazzo, Nick Nasta, Veronica Stork

Contagion

(PREMIERE FILM MARKETING/REEF FILMS; AUST) 86min

A makeshift but interesting Faust variant. Mid-level businessman Doyle comes across a mansion in the woods and is lured by suavely mephistophelean Roddy Bael (Barrett) into a life of unethical greed. Seduced by Bael's associates Cleo (Gaffney) and Helen (Hawksford), Doyle resorts to murder to further his success story, taunting a chubby competitor into a heart attack by agreeing to resign if he does another twenty weight-lifts. When others intervene in the evil idyll they see Bael's house as a dilapidated shack, and the film abandons unusual plotting for standard chase-and-chop as Bartlett eludes the demonic vagrants who inhabit this Australian corner of Hell.

d Karl Zwicky *co-p/s* Ken Methold *co-p* Leo Barretto *c* John Stokes *se* Springett Optical Services *lp* John Doyle, Nicola Bartlett, Ray Barrett, Kathy Gaffney, Pamela Hawksford

Creepshow 2 (LAUREL/NEW WORLD) 90min

Despite a screenplay by Romero working from stories by Stephen King, this second issue of Laurel's horror comic, directed by Romero's regular cinematographer, is an almost complete disaster.

A small boy leafs through a comic and a cartoon character called The Creep (Savini) introduces three pointless stories. In *Old Chief Wooden Head*, a wooden Indian outside a store avenges the murder of its kindly owners (Kennedy, Lamour) by a Native American hoodlum (Salsedo). In *The Raft*, four teenagers swimming on a lake are devoured by a slime monster that resembles an oil slick full of rubbish. In *The Hitch Hiker*, a hit-and-run driver (Chiles) is terrorized by her squashed victim, who reappears in increasingly bloody and decayed forms. As with **Creepshow** (1982), this suffers from King's inability to work in the rigid conventions of the E.C. comics he is supposed to be pastiching: these are less stories than situations and the all-important punchlines/twists never come along.

d Michael Gornick *p* David Ball *s* George A. Romero *c* Richard Hart, Tom Hurwitz *se* Howard Berger, Ed French *lp* Dorothy Lamour, George Kennedy, Frank S. Salsedo, Daniel Beer, Jeremy Green, Paul Satterfield, Page Hannah, Lois Chiles, Tom Wright, Tom Savini

The Curse *aka* The Farm

(TRANS WORLD; US, IT) scope 90min

Though closer in spirit and synopsis to H.P. Lovecraft's *The Color Out of Space* than the previous adaptation, **Monster of Terror** (1965), this is still a pedestrian effort.

The film begins with the cops drawing up at a homestead and carting away a screaming boil-faced man who rants about something in the water, then flashes back to 'six months earlier' and never bothers to return to its frame story. On the family farm, things are amiss: Pop (Akins) is a dour religious fanatic, Mom (Gregory) is a repressed neurotic, Junior Hero (Wil Wheaton) is a martyr to injustice, Brother (Danare) is a fat bully and Sis (Amy Wheaton) is a cute little girl with missing teeth. A fairly spectacular meteor comes out of the sky and glows in the dirt, prompting mass mutation. Anyone who drinks the water or eats the produce sprouts plasticine boils and an exaggerated attitude problem. A few effective licks turn up, as when Gregory quietly sews her embroidery to her hand, but it's mainly risible effects glop. Luckily, the Wheaton kids have been sneaking in bottled water and store-bought produce (underlining the film's message that healthy food is bad for you) and so are unboiled when the reservoir surveyor turns up out of nowhere to rescue them as the house implodes on itself.

d David Keith *p* Ovidio G. Assonitis *s* David Chaskin *c* Robert D. Forges *se* Franco Ruffini *lp* Claude Akins, Wil Wheaton, Malcolm Danare, Cooper Huckabee, John Schneider, Amy Wheaton, Kathleen Jordan Gregory

Dark Tower (SANDY HOWARD; US, SP) 96min

This troubled production was shot in Barcelona. Francis, who took it on as a follow-up to **The Doctor and the Devils** (1985), was replaced by Wiederhorn, of **Shock Waves** (1977) and **Return of the Living Dead, Part II** (1987). A pseudonym gets the final credit.

Sloppiness (Moriarty's main credit is misspelled) extends throughout the production, which uses the guest-stars-and-setpiece-death strategy of the *Omen* series while its plot attempts to cash in on the *Poltergeist* cycle. A modernist office block in Barcelona is plagued by accidents and investigator Moriarty comes to believe architect Agutter is the cause, her murdered husband returning for revenge by prompting normal people to turn into kill-crazy psychos in the lobby, throwing window-washers from a great height and staging freak accidents with the lifts. Finally, the ghost manifests itself as a tacky zombie from Wiederhorn's previous films and drags Agutter beyond the walls.

d Ken Barnett (Ken Wiederhorn, Freddie Francis) *p* John R. Bowey, David M. Witz *s* Robert J. Averech, Ken Blackwell, Ken Wiederhorn *c* Gordon Hayman *se* Enrique Jorba, Paco Teres *lp* Michael Moriarty, Jenny Agutter, Carol Lynley, Theodore Bikel, Anne Lockhart, Patch Mackenzie, Robin Sherman, Kevin McCarthy

Dead of Winter (MGM) 100min

Though it does not live up to the expectations raised by Penn's name, this is a perfectly acceptable lady-in-peril quickie, notionally inspired by Joseph H. Lewis' *My Name is Julia Ross* (1945) but also bearing striking plot similarities to Ken and Jim Wheat's *Lies* (1983).

Actress Steenbergen is lured to an old dark house by avuncular psychiatrist Rubes and his sinister valet McDowell, supposedly to audition for a movie role but actually as part of a triple-threat blackmail plot that involves a lookalike scheming murderess (also Steenbergen). With a blizzard raging outside, the heroine is pursued around the house by the crippled but apparently indestructible Rubes. As an entertaining minor horror along the lines of **Silent Scream** (1980) or **The House on Sorority Row** (1982), it's well above average, thanks to very subtly camp performances and decent production values; but it doesn't have a lot to do with the man who made *The Left-Handed Gun* (1958), *Bonnie and Clyde* (1967) or *Night Moves* (1975).

d Arthur Penn *p* John Bloomgarden, Marc Shmuger *s* Marc Shmuger, Mark Malone *c* Jan Weincke *lp* Mary Steenbergen, Jan Rubes, Roddy McDowell, William Russ, Ken Pogue, Wayne Robson, Mark Malone

Deliria *aka* **StageFright** *aka* **Aquarius** *aka* **Bloody Bird**
(FILMIRAGE; IT) 95min
An asylum escapee, called Irving Wallace after the author, is locked into a theatre where a dance company are rehearsing a pretentious ballet about an owl-masked Jack the Ripper.

In typical body-count fashion, the madman, once an actor himself, puts on the mask and employs a chainsaw, a power drill and an axe for a well-staged, fairly explicit deaths. *Deliria* has a highly conventional storyline, but Soavi, a former actor making his first feature, gives the familiar stalking added style in the Dario Argento manner. A key looms huge in the foreground as heroine Cupisti scrabbles for it, corpses are arranged artistically on the stage and covered with owl feathers, and various everyday objects are put to violent use by the killer and the surviving girl. Like many Argento movies, *Deliria* makes a connection between art and slaughter, with the killer seen as a demented artist whose victims become aesthetic objects for the camera. Unusually for an Italian director, Soavi also displays a sense of humour in his reworkings of the clichés of the Busby Berkeley putting-on-a-show movie even while he is setting up the next decapitation. The film was clearly an influence on Argento, Soavi's mentor, whose similarly-themed **Opera** (1988) also features a ruthless British director who doesn't mind using the murder of a colleague as an impetus to turn his latest show into a hit.

d/co-s Michele Soavi *p* Aristide Massacessi *co-s* Lew Cooper (Luigi Montefiore) *c* Renato Tafuri *se* Gianfranco Mecacci *lp* David Brandon, Barbara Cupisti, Roberto Gugorov, Martin Philip, Loredana Parella, Giovanni Lombardo Radice, Jo Ann Smith, Mary Sellers, John Morghen

Dentro al Cimitero *aka* **Graveyard Disturbance**
(DANIA FILM; IT) 90min
Five dull and obnoxious teens on a camping holiday – endearingly introduced shop-lifting from a store run by Bava – break down in a rural nowhere afflicted by dry-ice mists, howling wolves and ominous locals. In a riff on **La Danza Macabra** (1964), the kids bet they can survive the night in cobwebby catacombs where they are terrorized by monsters who specialize in lunging out of the shadows like ghost-train stunts rather than actually hurting anyone. The only trace of imagination is displayed in the odd but ridiculous design of the apparitions: a snaggle-toothed dwarf, a zombie with a rotting football head, a dowager with a flock of eyes.

d/co-s Lamberto Bava *p* Massimo Manasse *co-s* Dardano Sacchetti *c* Gianlorenza Battaglia *lp* Gregory Lech Thaddeus, Lea Martino, Beatrice Ring, Gianmarco Tognazzi

Dolls (EMPIRE) 75min
An American couple (Williams, Purdy-Gordon) travelling around rural England with the husband's daughter (Lorraine) get bogged down in a mudpatch during a storm and seek refuge in an old dark house which turns out to be home to master toymakers Rolfe and Mason.

During the night, more people turn up, and the toymakers' dolls come to life to administer rough justice to uncaring parents and larcenous punkettes. This apparently impersonal project proves a much more satisfactory follow-up to Gordon's impressive début film, **Re-Animator** (1985), than the more elaborate **From Beyond** (1986). As with **Troll** (1985) and **Cellar Dweller** (1987), also scripted by Naha, the film is structured like a body-count movie, with the creatures standing in for the more usual mad killer. The difference is that while the victims of teen stalk-and-slash films are usually marked for death only by youth and sexual activity, there is an E.C. comics morality at work here. The various characters attacked by (and turned into) dolls all invite their fates by exemplifying various evils.

d Stuart Gordon *p* Brian Yuzna *s* Ed Naha *c* Mac Ahlberg *se* Mechanical and Make-Up Imageries *lp* Stephen Lee, Guy Rolfe, Hilary Mason, Ian Patrick Williams, Carolyn Purdy-Gordon, Cassie Stuart, Carrie Lorraine

Don't Panic (DYNAMIC FILMS; US, MEX) 88min
One of a brief run of don't-mess-with-ouija-boards dramas (**Witchboard**, 1985, **The Oracle**, 1985), oddly set in Mexico City though all the teens appear very anglo. At a birthday party, a demonic spirit possesses teenager Aranda, whereupon he murders other kids and sprouts unimaginative blue, flaky make-up while ranting in the regulation gravelly voice. There are several messy murders but few plot surprises until the very last moment when, in place of the usual evil-lives-on punchline, there's a benevolent supernatural touch as heroine Hassel, at the grave of her boyfriend, senses his spirit ascending.

d/s Ruben Galindo Jr *p* Raul Galindo, Bruce Glenn *c* Muguel Arana, Daniel Lopez *se* Screaming Mad George *lp* Jon Michael Bischof, Gabriela Hassel, Helen Rojo, George Luke, Juan Ignacio Aranda

The Edge of Hell *aka* **Rock 'n' Roll Nightmare**
(THUNDER/SHAPIRO; CAN) 84min
Thor's Heavy Metal band retires to a haunted farmhouse to work on an album and some not-terribly-interesting supernatural monstrosities get them. After pointless softcore sex and even more pointless softcore Heavy Metal, ridiculous effects predominate: a pre-teen turns into a junior Morlock, a clawed hand explodes from a guitarist's chest to grope a groupie, a one-eyed hand-puppet with teeth lurks in the fridge. In an ambitious finale, Thor turns out to be an archangel who has created all the characters to lure demons with whom he engages in a supernatural duel, which consists of him posing in a studded jockstrap while the hellspawn throws starfish at him.

d John M. Fasano *p/s* Jon-Mikl Thor *c* Mark MacKay *lp* Jon-Mikl Thor, Frank Dietz, Jillian Peri, Teresa Simpson, Liane Abel, Jim Cirile, David Lane, Denise DiCandia, Clara Pater, Jesse D'Angelo

Epitaph (CITY LIGHTS) 90min
A twisted but uninteresting psycho movie. Middle-aged wife and mother Nascar resorts to bloody murder when threatened. Her tolerant husband (Williams) buries a still-living house-painter she has stabbed, but she eventually shoves a pickaxe into his back and further takes action against her mother-in-law, a concerned psychiatrist and her daughter's boyfriend (Keller). Pavlova, smothered by her mother, takes a shovel to her and inherits the insanity, driving off while holding a conversation with the corpse. A hectoring picture with overstated performances and padded dialogue between extensive if ordinary murder moments.

d/co-p/s Joseph Merhi *co-p/s* Richard Pepin *se* Constance J. Damron, Aaron Sims, Judy Yonemoto, Jim Crouch *lp* Natasha Pavlova, Delores Nascar, Jim Williams, Flint Keller, Linda Tucker Smith, Liz Kane

Evil Dead II

(ROSEBUD RELEASING/RENAISSANCE PICTURES) 84min

Less a sequel than an elaborate remake, this opens with a concentrated rerun of the story so far as Ash (Campbell) encounters Sumerian demons who possess his girlfriend and force him to decapitate her. A group of new characters, living and (evilly) dead, wander into the carnage and tip the film into a rollercoaster mode that never lets up. Ash suffers especial abuse as he resists the demons, taking Biblical measures when his possessed hand rebels and smashes plates over his head. Goblin monsters leer into reality, a popped eyeball flies into a girl's mouth, the undead girlfriend does a dance with her detachable head, gallons of blood gush from the walls, and the deadites run riot. After the humour-laced horror of **The Evil Dead** (1982), this adopts the crazy, cartoonish tone of Raimi's underrated *Crimewave* (1985) and goes for belly laughs. The film is especially well served by Campbell's gutsy performance as he goes from quivering wreck to functioning psychopath, strapping a chainsaw in place of his missing hand and taking a dive through a magical time-warp to confront the last of the demons in a medieval setting.

d/co-s Sam Raimi *p* Robert G. Tapert *co-s* Scott Spiegel *c* Peter Deming *se* Doug Beswick Productions *lp* Bruce Campbell, Sarah Berry, Dan Hicks, Kassie Wesley, Theodore Raimi, Denise Bixler

Fa Sempre, Fino alla Morte *aka* Until Death *aka* Changeling 2: The Revenge

(RETEITALIA/DANIA/DEVON; IT) 95min

In a conceptually gritty but botched opening, the pregnant Scola helps her lover bury her poisoned, still-living husband during a thunderstorm. The pay-off is a variation on *The Postman Always Rings Twice*, which is reprised by the bulk of the film, set six years later, in which the couple take in an itinerant handyman (Brandon) who is the reincarnation of the dead husband. Scola descends into madness, suffering – as does her young son (Vivio) – from bad dreams in which the maggot-ridden corpse rises from the ground to bear his family off. The sole eerie moment is a clever make-up stunt whereby Brandon turns from profile to reveal that half his face is that of the ghost.

d Lamberto Bava *p* Massimo Manasse, Marco Grillo Spina *s* Dardano Sacchetti *c* Gianlorenzo Battaglia *se* Fabrizio Sforza *lp* Gioia Scola, David Brandon, Giuseppe De Sando, Roberto Pedicini, Marco Vivio, Urbano Barberini

Fatal Attraction (PAR) 120min

Though, like **Jaws** (1975), this phenomenally successful talking-point movie owes almost everything to the horror genre, it too was not generally perceived as a horror movie. In its presentation of a spurned woman (Close) as a menace to the adulterous hero (Douglas) and his Ideal Family lifestyle, the film is a less rigorous, less interesting reworking of Clint Eastwood's *Play Misty for Me* (1971).

Close's crazed career woman, whose psychotic twitches include murdering a pet rabbit and returning from the dead like a *Halloween*-style unkillable psycho, is a glamorous monster who could never be accommodated within the confines of the innocent hero's life. Her insane drives mean Douglas can't be held responsible for his dalliance with her, whereas Eastwood and Jessica Walter played a more ambiguous game with the situation and used the woman's madness as a way of criticizing the hero's attitudes to her, rather than, as here, a way of exonerating him and of setting up a finale which almost echoes the ritual of the bullfight as it forces the audience to demand the bloody death of its monster. (In fact, Close's death was decreed by preview audiences who didn't approve of the original, inconclusive ending.) Lyne's taut, if obvious, direction can't cope with a flabby stretch in the middle, between the pruriently staged initial affair (sex in the kitchen sink and the lift) and the competently handled final stalk and slashing.

d Adrian Lyne *p* Stanley R. Jaffe, Sherry Lansing *s* James Dearden *c* Howard Atherton *lp* Glenn Close, Michael Douglas, Anne Archer, Ellen Hamilton Latzen, Stuart Pankin, Ellen Foley, Fred Gwynne, Meg Mundy, Tom Brennan, Lois Smith

Flowers in the Attic

(NEW WORLD/FRIES ENTERTAINMENT) 92min

In order to get into her dying millionaire father's good books (and will), the newly widowed Tennant moves back into the

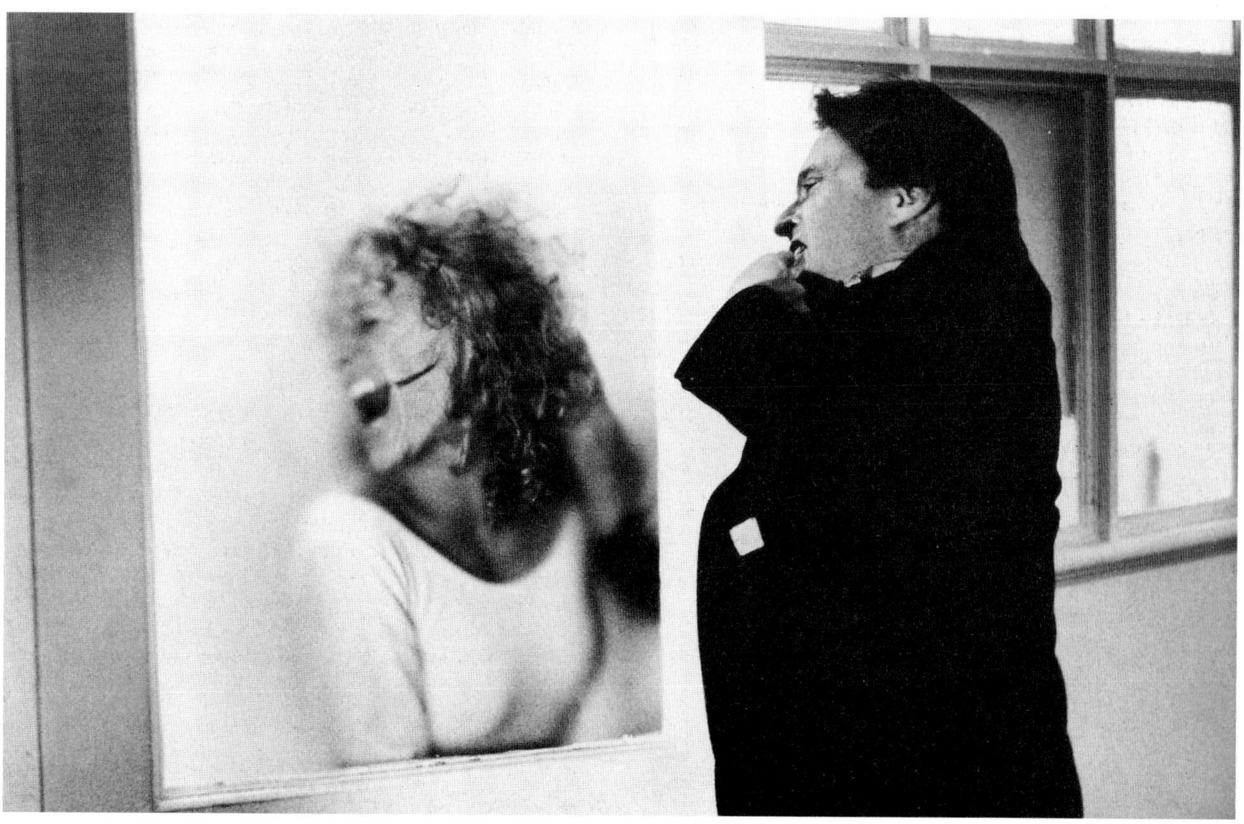

Glenn Close and Michael Douglas torment each other in Fatal Attraction.

family's old dark mansion and lets her mad mother (Fletcher) lock up her four children in a room that connects with the attic. If the old man finds out about the offspring, Tennant will lose her inheritance, so the children have to stay hidden, not to mention subject to their grandmother's ideas of punishment.

The kids grow pale and indulge in vampirism to keep alive when the food supply is suspended. All attempts at escape fail and gradually the elder children, Swanson and Adams, realize Mom has gone as crazy as the rest of her family and is conspiring to kill her offspring. Andrews, who makes a brief cameo appearance as a maid, is, after Stephen King, the world's most popular horror author, doubtless because she writes like Barbara Cartland in a shroud. In the one authetically camp moment, Swanson bursts into Tennant's wedding brandishing half a poisoned biscuit, shrieking 'Eat the cookie, momma!'

d/s Jeffrey Bloom *p* Sy Levin, Thomas Fries *c* Frank Byers, Gil Hubbs *lp* Victoria Tennant, Louise Fletcher, Kristy Swanson, Jeb Stuart Adams, Ben Ganger, Lindsay Parker, Marshall Colt, Nathan Davis

From a Whisper to a Scream *aka* The Offspring

(CONQUEST) 101(96)min

In this omnibus film Price recounts anecdotes to illustrate that the town of Oldfield is cursed. Gulager accidentally kills a girl he is molesting but continues to pay his attentions ('We can't let a little thing like this interrupt our romance,' he says of her death) and nine months later is attacked by a revolting zombie baby that crawls from her grave. In the fifties, an unscrupulous thug falls in with an immortal ex-slave and tries to get the secret himself only to wind up an undying basket case. In the thirties, a carnival is in town and the glass-eating star runs away from voodoo queen Cash only to become a bloody mess when the bits and pieces he's eaten explode from him. During the Civil War, Yankee raider Mitchell falls into the clutches of Oldfield's founders, cannibal children. Despite inept direction, this has more of the required mix of nastiness and morality than the **Creepshow** movies. Apart from the reliable Mitchell and the nerdy Gulager, none of the guest stars do much, with Price deadpanning in a hammy Southern accent through a role written for Forrest J. Ackerman. Not to be confused with *From a Whisper to a Scream* (1989), a Canadian thriller also known as *Love You to Death*.

d/co-s Jeff Burr *co-p* William Burr *co-p/co-s* Darin Scott *co-s* C. Courtney Joyner *c* Craig Green *se* Rob Burman *lp* Vincent Price, Susan Tyrrell, Clu Gulager, Cameron Mitchell, Martine Beswick, Terry Kiser, Harry Caesar, Rosalind Cash, Angelo Rossito, Terence Knox

Graveyard Shift

(LIGHTSHOW COMMUNICATIONS; CAN) 89min

This is a stylish, clever vampire movie.

Oliviero is an immortal bloodsucker who relaxes nude in a coffin as if it were a bath and has a fanged harem of former victims spread out across the city. He makes a living as a taxi driver, cruising the night for victims, and only gets into trouble when he decides that he wants to forsake the vampire girls for his true love, a suicidal film director (Papas) who specializes in mock-gothic rock videos. The film does well by its fetishist images (a trickle of blood running down a fishnet stocking and a stiletto heel) and its self-aware deployment of the classical trappings of the vampire movie in a modern context. Oliviero's not-quite-sympathetic vampire is an interesting figure who makes victims only of the terminally ill, the suicidal or vicious muggers, and seems convincingly detached from the neon-lit nightmare city that Ciccoritti naturally films in the style of Scorsese's *Taxi Driver* (1976). It spawned a lesser sequel, **The Understudy: Graveyard Shift II** (1988).

d/s Gerard Ciccoritti *p* Michael Bockner *c* Robert Bergman *se* Tim Mogg *lp* Silvio Oliviero, Helen Papas, Cliff Stoker, Dorin Ferber, Dan Rose, Don Jones

Top: Pinhead in Hellraiser.

Bottom: Government warning: Smoking kills. Oliver Smith in Hellraiser.

Hello Mary Lou: Prom Night 2 *aka* The Haunting of Hamilton High

(SIMCOM; CAN) 96min

A name-only sequel to the conventional psycho slasher **Prom Night** (1980), this is actually a cross between **Carrie** (1976) and **A Nightmare on Elm Street, Part 2: Freddy's Revenge** (1986) with the disfigured ghost of an evil 1957 prom queen (Schrage) returning to possess the heroine (Lyon) and destroy the school on prom night, with especial venom reserved for her old boyfriend (Ironside), who was partially responsible for her death and is now the principal.

Thoroughly ordinary in its competently marshalled horrors, this is given an edge by an interestingly conceived monster who combines the supernatural powers of Freddy Kruger with the temperament of a teenage bitch. While the film does briefly use the Ricky Nelson hit referred to in the title, the monster's signature song is actually Ronnie Hawkins' earthier 'Mary Lou'. Mary Lou (Courtney Taylor) returned in Ron Oliver's *Prom Night 3: The Last Kiss* (1990) but returned to Hell to sit out Clay Borris's *Prom Night IV: Deliver Us From Evil* (1991), whose villain is a pony-tailed devil monk.

d Bruce Pittman *p* Peter Simpson *s* Ron Oliver *c* John Herzog *se* Jim Doyle *lp* Michael Ironside, Justin Louis, Wendy Lyon, Lisa Schrage, Richard Monette

Hellraiser (NEW WORLD/FILM FUTURES; GB) 93min
Adapting his own novella *The Hellbound Heart*, Barker made a noteworthy début and introduced a genuinely unsettling set of extra-dimensional monsters.

Chapman solves a magical puzzle-box and summons the Cenobites, sado-masochistic demons who promise him experience beyond pleasure then tear him apart. His mistress (Higgins) learns she can gradually bring him back to life by spilling blood, wherupon she lures a succession of pick-ups to the attic and takes a hammer to them, causing the dead man to reappear in a wet and increasingly substantial shape (Smith). However, the ghost's niece (Lawrence), Higgins' stepdaughter, gets hold of the box and is visited by the Cenobites, who resent the undead's escape from his bargain, and the family incestuously destroys itself, with the useless father-figure (Robinson) killed to provide a skin for his brother, as the demons erupt into reality.

The overall approach, while not without wit, is unusually sober for a period characterized by such jokey items as **House** (1986), rooting its supernatural horror in human cruelty, and mainly treating its monsters not as jokes but as genuinely mind- (and flesh-) stretching menaces. The Cenobites (who boast unsettling features like sewn-shut eyelids behind dark glasses, a throat wound held open by a collar of surgical cramps, and traceries of pins hammered into a face) are well used and suggestive. For the most part, *Hellraiser* is a return to the cutting edge of horror, and in its inventively gruesome moments – Chapman turned inside-out by creaking millworks, his face put together on the floor like a jigsaw puzzle, the skinned monster lighting up a cigarette – is a reminder of the Grand Guignol intensity which was so unfashionable at the time of its release.

d/s Clive Barker *p* Christopher Figg *c* Robin Vidgeon *se* Bob Keen *lp* Andrew Robinson, Clare Higgins, Ashley Laurence, Sean Chapman, Oliver Smith, Doug Bradley, Robert Hines, Nicholas Vince

Henry... Portrait of a Serial Killer (MALJACK) 83min
Exceptionally well acted and shot for a zero-budget movie and resolutely unexploitative, this is loosely based on the confessions of mass murderer Henry Lee Lucas.

The product of a childhood trauma whose details change each time he recounts it, Henry (Rooker) drifts from job to job, murdering whenever the mood takes him. In the powerful opening sequence, the camera pans across the bodies of Henry's latest victims while their torture murders are heard on the soundtrack. Henry goes through the banal motions of everyday life, returning to the grim Chicago apartment he shares with his ex-cellmate Otis (Towles), and showing gentlemanly instincts by ceding his bedroom when Otis' sister Becky (Arnold) flees an abusive husband. The minimal plot follows Henry's developing relationship with the siblings, as he initiates Otis into the pleasure of killing, sharing practical tips on multiple murder, and moves towards a vaguely romantic liaison with Becky.

Michael Rooker as the serial killer in the disturbing Henry... Portrait of a Serial Killer.

Henry, a shell-shocked compulsive, is constantly compared with Otis, whose increasing delight in depravity shocks and disturbs Henry to the point where he kills his fellow-killer when he finds him raping Becky. Otis's verminous presence gives the lie to Henry's neutral sham of decency, forcing the killer to recognise his own monstrousness: the most explicit murder in the film is that of Otis, eye burst and head sawn off. Even the sub-title – which deliberately excludes Otis, unlike the co-murderers of *The Honeymoon Killers* (1967) or *The Case of the Hillside Stranglers* (1989) – suggests that Henry counts for more, by virtue of his status as a low-rent criminal mastermind in contrast to the genuine delight in appalling behaviour displayed by Otis. Clashes occur when Otis's primarily sexual degeneracy (expressed in rape, incest and necrophilia) cloud Henry's almost respectful, joyless recreations of the murder of his hooker mother.

The most deeply disturbing scenes are the quieter sequences that bracket the killings, as when Henry pulls Otis out of the shock that follows their first murders with coffee and fries, bringing him back to resolutely ordinary life. The strongest, hardest-to-sit-through sequence is a videotaped home invasion which, when the image becomes static because Henry has dropped the camera so he can kill the interloping son, strongly recalls *A Clockwork Orange* (1971) as it adopts the view of the torture, murder and rape that the Patrick Magee character had in Kubrick's film. The impact depends on an audience's instinct to turn away from the material Henry and Otis blankly watch on television. The most horrific moment is Otis's line 'I want to watch it again', which leads him to reshow on frame-advance the sequence of images an audience must be relieved to think over: McNaughton's camera homes threateningly on the television, holding it for a horrifying few seconds before a tactful fade to the film's single calming-down scene.

Like Norman Bates, Henry (who develops genuine if odd relationships) seems the most normal, well balanced person in the film, but he is even more chilling for his matter-of-fact explanations. The ambiguous but shattering finale refers to the finish of *Five Easy Pieces* (1970) as Henry literally dumps by the roadside the girl who might have been his only chance for normality. He disappears into the American vacuum from which he emerged in the beginning, to kill again without hindrance because – unlike the Thomas Harris-derived films and cycle entries like *While the City Sleeps* (1955), *The Boston Strangler* (1968) and *Dirty Harry* (1971) – *Henry* has no interest in the cocktail of issues surrounding serial murder, never cutting away to police, media or politicians. An unflinching portrait not only of its killer but of the world that at once turns him into what he is and allows him to get away with it.

d/co-p/co-s John McNaughton *co-p* Lisa Dedmond, Steven A. Jones *co-s* Richard Fire *c* Charlie Lieberman *se* Don Haberlorn *lp* Michael Rooker, Tom Towles, Tracy Arnold

Hide and Go Shriek *aka* **Close Your Eyes and Pray**
(NEW STAR ENTERTAINMENT) 94min
Borrowing the setting (a deserted department store) from *The Initiation* (1984) and a gimmick (the killer dresses as his last victim to fool the next) from **Terror Train** (1979), this is a late stalk-and-slash entry. Kids stage an all-night party in the store so they can get further aquainted with the mysteries of sex, and are murdered by a homicidal drag queen. The killer is the jilted jail boyfriend of the red herring ex-con caretaker.

d Skip Schoolnik *p* Dimitri Villard *s* Michael Kelly *c* Eugene Schlugleit *se* Screaming Mad George *lp* George Thomas, Donna Baltron, Brittain Frye, Annette Sinclair, Scott Fults, Ria Pavia, Sean Kanan, Bunky Jones, Jeff Levine, Scott Kubay

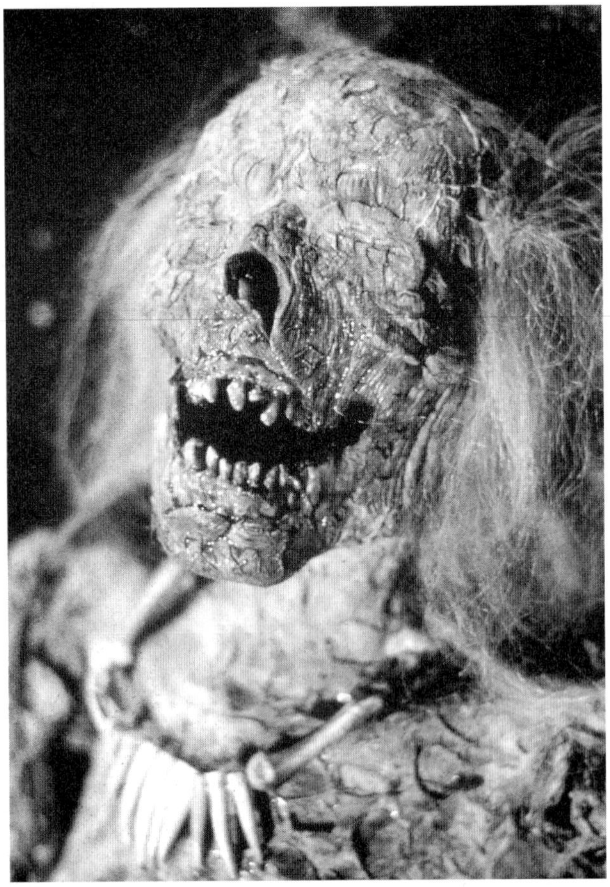

The uninspired The Lamp.

The Lamp *aka* **The Outing** (TMS) 85min
A group of kids spend the night in a creepy old museum and are killed one by one by a toothy creature who turns out to be the evil genie of a Middle Eastern lamp.

Even the terrible **Sorority Babes in the Slimeball Bowl-a-Rama** (1987), which has a similar wish-granting monster, makes more of the *Arabian Nights* overtone; this genie takes a familiar psycho approach to the murders, prowling like a subjective camera, lifting victims into propellor fans and chopping people in half. Though reasonably well made, with one effective scare as a mummified exhibit lurches suddenly to life, this is essentially just another programmer.

d Tom Daley *p/s* Warren Chaney *c* Herbert Raditschnig *se* Martin Becker *lp* Deborah Winters, James Huson, Andra St Ivanyi, Scott Bankston, Mark Mitchell, Andre Chimene, Damon Merrill, Barry Coffing

Livsfarlig Film *aka* **Lethal Film**
(SANDREW/SVT-1/FILM TEKNIK; SW) 108min
Set in the near future, this ambitious, incoherent comedy follows the bewilderment of Emil Frankenstein (Glaser), a director who usually turns out gore-drenched horror movies with titles like *Hack Me to Bits*. Traumatized because he no longer wants to 'show horror to people who are already afraid', Glaser searches Orpheus-like for his missing daughter in the Underworld-style depths of the studio, where he discovers refugees holed up in a sub-basement and decides to make a neo-realist film about them to show real horror.

Obviously influenced by *Sullivan's Travels* (1939) and *8½* (1964), it is full of jokes at the expense of film-making – a 'high concept' is a film about 'a sex fiend who drives a Ferrari who dies in a crash and returns as a ghost who rapes pregnant women' – and winds up with the decapitation of its hero.

d/co-s Suzanne Osten *p* Göran Lindström *co-s* Etienne Glaser, Niklas Radström *c* Göran Nilsson *lp* Etienne Glaser, Stina Ekblad, Henrik Holmborg, Lena T. Hansson, Agneta Ekmanner, Helge Skoog

The Lost Boys (WB) pv 97min
Originally conceived of as a vampiric reworking of *Peter Pan*, this has been stripped of its J.M. Barrie associations: all that remain are the title and the mixing of kindly father-figure and head villain into one role (Herrmann).

A family relocates in Santa Clara, California, 'murder capital of the world', and while divorced Weist tries to construct a new life, son Patric falls into the company of a gang of rock-video tearaways who turn out to be vampires, and his younger brother (Haim) joins a pair of junior mercenaries who run a comic-book store, assembling the stakes and garlic necessary to fight off the suckers. With the participation of producers Donner and Harvey Bernard and the casting of 13-year-olds (including Feldman) as heroes, the movie is a semi-sequel to *The Goonies* (1985). The selection of Schumacher, fresh from the 'Brat Pack' success of *St Elmo's Fire* (1985), edged the film towards an unrewarding commercial mode (MTV rock, pretty-boy teen vampires with trendy clothes and haircuts, doses of comedy whenever anything seems to get too horrific, special effects trickery, Spielbergian flying scenes) that eats away at more interesting ideas.

d Joel Schumacher *p* Richard Donner *s* Janice Fischer, James Jeremias, Jeffrey Boam *c* Michael Chapman *se* Greg Cannom *lp* Jason Patric, Corey Haim, Dianne Wiest, Barnard Hughes, Edward Herrmannn, Kiefer Sutherland, Jami Gertz, Corey Feldman, Jamison Newlander, Billy Wirth, Alexander Winter, Brooke McCarter

The Majorettes *aka* **One by One** (MAJOR FILMS) 92min
'We're looking for a man turned insane by guilt and his own repressed sexual urges.' Made by veterans of **Night of the Living Dead** (1968), this adaptation of Russo's competent novel starts as a slice-and-dice movie with a psycho dismembering a succession of jiggling majorettes, then turns into a combination of biker film and *Les Diaboliques* (1955).

A slobbering loon who surreptitiously photographs nude cheerleaders in the showers takes a picture of the fundamentalist sheriff killing a pneumatic bimbo, and his crazy mother blackmails the cop into murdering the nubile granddaughter of her crippled employer so she can make a profit on an inheritance. In a twist typical of Russo, the girl is caught in a shootout between a dope-dealing bike gang and a crazed football player and dies before her 18th birthday, which means the money goes to the state. The sheriff kills the mother and frames the voyeur, escaping in an amoral ending which finds him leering at the next generation of pom-pom tossers. Like Russo's **Midnight** (1981), this independent exploitation movie benefits from a twisted plot, marked by an especially disillusioned attitude to the police, but suffers from makeshift characterization, amateurish performances, and inept horror-action.

d Bill Hinzman *p/s* John Russo *c* Paul McCollough *se* Gerald Gergely *lp* Kevin Kindlin, Terrie Godfrey, Mark V. Jevicky, Sueanne Seamens, Denise Huot, Carl Hetrick, Russ Streiner, John Russo, Bill Hinzman

Mirror of Death *aka* **Dead of Night**
(VISTA STREET PRODUCTIONS) 85min
A programmer distinguished by Merrill's wide-eyed presence as an abused woman who practices voodoo in front of a mirror and is possessed by a malevolent goddess who helps her get revenge on a brutal boyfriend but becomes a danger to her decent sister (Browne). After a slow opening enlivened by a few shrieking transformations and heart-ripping deaths, the film perks up in an eventful and imaginative climax. The beleaguered sisters call in a psychic consultant (Kip) whose ad they find in the yellow pages and defeat the evil spirit with a neat if unlikely scam. The same team made *Bloodspell* (1988), a possession drama in which a sorcerer tries to displace his son's soul.

d Deryn Warren *p* Jessica Rains *s* Gerry Daly *c* Ronn Schmidt *se* Karen Westerfield *lp* Julie Merrill, Kuri Browne, John Reno, J.K. Dumont, Isaac Allan, Aarin Teich, Bob Kip

The Monster Squad (TAFT/BARISH/HBO) pv 82min
After a lush Hammer-style 1887 prologue, in which Van Helsing (Gwillim) fails to banish the forces of darkness to limbo, this cuts to a small town, where a gang of high-school kids pore over monster magazines in their clubhouse.

Dracula (Regehr) shows up with an entourage that includes the Frankenstein Monster (Noonan), a tormented Wolf Man (Gries), a mummy and a *Creature From the Black Lagoon* (1954) Gill Man. The Monsters are after an amulet which keeps the balance between the Forces of Good and Evil, and the kids, who happen upon Van Helsing's monster-defeating manual, set out to stop them. In a relishable finale, a ritual that has to be read by a virgin fails due to a teenage girl's reluctance to tell all to her younger brother ('Oh there was Steve, but he doesn't count') and the all-important bit of world-saving magic falls to Phoebe (Bank), a solemnly endearing four-year-old who has melted the heart of the Karloff-style Monster.

Far more effectively than **The Lost Boys** (1987), *The Monster Squad* pits monster-obsessed kids against real-life horrors. Intended by Dekker, of the hit-and-miss *Night of the Creeps* (1986), as a tribute to the Universal days of **House of Frankenstein** (1944) and **Abbott and Costello Meet Frankenstein** (1948), this one-ups its models with modern effects resources: the Wolf Man is blown apart and reforms, the mummy unravels like an old cardigan, and Regher's sardonically diabolical Dracula walks down Main Street bending members of the police force into interesting shapes. The post-Spielberg kids are funny in a genuinely childlike way rather than through smarmy wisecracks. Cimino is especially moving as Scary German Guy, a neighbourhood bogeyman called in to translate Van Helsing's diary who looks at his concentration-camp tattoo when one of the Squad compliments him on his extensive knowledge of monsters.

d/c-s Fred Dekker *p* Jonathan A. Zimbert *co-s* Shane Black *c* Bradford May *se* Stan Winston *lp* André Gower, Robby Kiger, Stephen Macht, Duncan Regehr, Tom Noonan, Brent Chalem, Ryan Lambert, Ashley Bank, Michael Faustino, Mary Ellen Trainor, Leonardo Cimino, Jonathan Gries, Stan Shaw, Lisa Fuller, Jack Gwillim, Tom Woodruff Jr, Michael MacKay, Carl Thibault

Hey, hey, we're the monsters: (from the left) Gill Man (Tom Woodruff Jr), Dracula (Duncan Regehr), Frankenstein (Tom Noonan), the Mummy (Michael Mackay) and the Wolf Man (Carl Thibault) came to town in the amiable The Monster Squad.

Munchies (NEW HORIZONS) 78min
Given that Roger Corman nurtured the talent of Joe Dante, it is fitting he should react to his protegé's successful **Gremlins** (1984) by mounting a cheapskate imitation, with bits of plot borrowed from Dante's earlier, Corman-produced *Piranha* (1978), itself imitative of **Jaws** (1975).

In Peru, an archaeologist (Korman) discovers a stone creature which, when brought back to America and hacked to pieces, becomes a horde of hungry little monsters. While earlier Corman quickies like *Piranha* are only half-comic, *Munchies* neglects to include any of the violence and nudity expected of grindhouse exploitation, though it does yank in a car chase, a motorcycle gang and a modish toxic waste subplot. The film is edited to the 78-minute bone in traditional Corman fashion. Accordingly, even dud jokes and stupid ideas get on and off screen quickly enough not to clutter up the movie. Reversing the process of **Alien** (1979) and *Aliens* (1986), the sequel is *Munchie* (1992).

d Bettina Hirsch *p* Roger Corman *s* Lance Smith *c* Jonathan West *se* Robert Short *lp* Harvey Korman, Charles Stratton, Nadine Van Der Velde, Alix Elias, Charlie Phillips, Robert Picardo, Wendy Schaal, Paul Bartel

My Demon Lover (NEW LINE) 87min
Originally written as a werewolf story, this was rethought on the assumption all the lycanthropic ground had been covered. Accordingly, Valentine, victim of a Romanian curse, turns into a variety of creations when aroused: a bloated pig-man, a Jerry Lewisian nerd, and the usual horned and fanged demon.

The story seems to have been substantially shaped by special-effects men, but the disparity between pre-release publicity (which shows imaginative monsters and freaks not actually in the film) and the final product suggests that yak-hair wielders and bladder inflaters were overruled to tone down the horrors in the hope of attracting fans of blander, minimally monstrous comedies like **Teen Wolf** (1986) and **My Best Friend is a Vampire** (1988). Apart from variably convincing monsters, the movie suffers from the enthusiastic but unappealing Valentine, its drippy middle-of-the-road score, a general assumption that people floundering and shouting constitutes comedy and the shallowness of its 'relationship' scenes.

d Charlie Loventhal *p* Robert Shaye *s* Leslie Ray *c* Jacques Haitkin *se* Carl Fullerton, John Caglione Jr, Doug Drexler, Neal Martz *lp* Scott Valentine, Michelle Little, Gina Gallego, Alan Fudge, Robert Trebor

Near Dark
(THE NEAR DARK JOINT VENTURE) 94min
Good ole boy Pasdar picks up winsome lass Wright at a gas station, and her love-bite gives him an intense aversion to sunlight and an unnatural craving for blood. Soon he is dragged back to meet her 'family', a group of po' white trash vampires who have travelled around the desert for over a century.

Led by Henriksen, a pony-tailed Civil War veteran ('we lost'), the vampires include Paxton as a grinning cowboy who disposes of victims with razor-edged spurs, Goldstein as a blowsy country and western gal, and Miller as a nasty old man in a twelve-year-old's body. Pasdar can't bring himself to kill and strikes out on his own in search of a cure, determined to save the girl and finish the rest. In a central horror scene, vampires take over a bar where The Cramps' *Fever* plays as they terrorize, kill, bleed and drink bikers, waitresses and beer-drinking thugs. Later Bigelow demonstrates all-action skills with a motel shootout where every bullet-hole lets in a deadly ray of sunlight and in a final confrontation between vampire and truck in a ghost town.

With on-the-road overtones in the manner of Red's work on **The Hitcher** (1986) and the lesser *Cohen and Tate* (1988), this is a more serious attempt to revive the vampire for the late eighties than **Fright Night** (1985) and **The Lost Boys** (1987). Its vampires are interesting and not completely unsympathetic characters, and their lifestyle is rigorously examined, demonstrating that (in contrast with the aristocrats of the Dracula movies) immortality hasn't gained them more than a tentative grasp on human society as they hurry from place to place, hiding by day under sun-blockers and nose-shields. Indebted both to the Western and the Walter Hill-style action movie, *Near Dark* is one of the key horror films of the eighties.

d/co-s Kathryn Bigelow *p* Steven-Charles Jaffe *co-s* Eric Red *c* Adam Greenberg *se* Steve Galich, Dale Martin *lp* Adrian Pasdar, Jenny Wright, Lance Henriksen, Bill Paxton, Jenette Goldstein, Joshua Miller, Marcie Leeds, Tim Thomerson

A Nightmare on Elm Street, Part 3: Dream Warriors

(NEW LINE/HERON/SMART EGG) 96min

Bringing back creator Craven as co-screenwriter, this wins back ground lost by **A Nightmare on Elm Street, Part 2: Freddy's Revenge** (1986), ignoring the events of the first sequel and bringing back surviving characters from **A Nightmare on Elm Street** (1985).

Langenkamp has become the world's only teenage psychiatrist but she still suffers from nightmares. She realizes that the mixed-up Elm Street kids she is counselling share her bad dreams, and that three deaths in two films hasn't been enough to keep Freddy (Englund) out of dreamland. Psychotherapist Wasson and cop Saxon disinter Freddy's bones and face him as a Harryhausen-style skeleton, while Langenkamp's wish-fulfilment warriors enter an old dark house of the psyche where Freddy lunges from mirrors with malicious wisecracks.

Not as suspenseful or scary as the initial instalment, this is nevertheless the first of the series really to get to grips with the potential of its subject matter. Russell, writer of the similarly themed *Dreamscape* (1984), gets exposition and characterization out of the way swiftly so he can concentrate on the kind of bizarre images usually found only on comic-book covers: a boy's veins are pulled from his limbs and used as strings to jerk him puppet-style towards death, an antique tap grabs a girl's hand and sprouts Freddy's razor fingernail extensions, a victim is literally tongue-tied, and, in a major coup, Freddy guests on the Dick Cavett Show and reaches out of the TV set, after slashing Zsa Zsa Gabor, to grab the next teenager.

d/co-s Chuck Russell *p* Robert Shaye *co-s* Wes Craven, Bruce Wagner, Frank Darabont *c* Roy H. Wagner *se* Kevin Yagher, Doug Beswick *lp* Heather Langenkamp, Patricia Arquette, Larry Fishburne, Craig Wasson, Priscilla Pointer, John Saxon, Robert Englund, Jennifer Rubin, Brooke Bundy, Rodney Eastman, Nan Martin

Open House *aka* Multiple Listings

(INTERCONTINENTAL) 97min

A run-of-the-mill slasher. A homeless hulk graphically murders LA realtors and calls shrink Bottoms' radio show to claim that 'them real-estate bitches deserved it'. Bottoms' girlfriend (Barbeau) is in the business and her circle of professional friends is cut down before she confronts the killer. After an interesting opening that sets up a potent contrast between have-alls who buy and sell Beverly Hills homes and the dog-food-eating vagrant killer, the film relies heavily on second-hand business like the phone-trace stunt from **Black Christmas** (1974) which reveals the killer's taunts are coming from the heroine's house. Barbeau, slumming somewhat, gives better than is really required.

d Jag Mudhra *p* Sandy Cobe *s* David Mickey Evans *c* Robert Hayes, Gary Louzon *se* John A. Naulin *lp* Joseph Bottoms, Adrienne Barbeau, Rudy Ramos, Mary Stavin, Scott Thompson Baker

Prince of Darkness (ALIVE) pv 101min

The Brotherhood of Sleep, an obscure Catholic sect, has guarded a terrible secret for centuries. When Father Pleasence is informed that a huge, green-slime-dripping cylinder that represents Ultimate Evil is in the basement of a Los Angeles church, he calls in physicist Wong and allows the scientist to import instruments and experts to deal with the mysterious menace.

Open the box, I dare you: Donald Pleasence about to unleash the ultimate evil in Prince Of Darkness.

As the investigators squabble about the phenomena they observe, sinister street people led by Cooper gather around with murderous intent, fuzzy messages from the future invade dreams, the insect population becomes highly agitated and animated, and several scientists dosed with the green slime return to life as satanic zombies. A long introductory scene scored with one of Carpenter's eerie synthesizer themes reveals that the director has not lost his ability to get a complicated plot in motion as he brings on all his characters and establishes an air of menace with a series of neatly edited snippets. Unlike *Assault on Precinct 13* (1976) and **Halloween** (1978) but like **The Fog** (1979), *Prince of Darkness* fails to take advantage of its claustrophobic setting and intercuts too many unconnected climaxes. Accordingly, although the film is consistently eerie and interesting, it is never really frightening or exciting. Carpenter's writing pseudonym is a tribute to Nigel Kneale, from whose TV scripts for *Quatermass and the Pit* and *The Stone Tape* he borrows extensively.

d John Carpenter *p* Larry Franco *s* Martin Quatermass (John Carpenter) *c* Gary B. Kibbe *se* Kevin Quibell *lp* Donald Pleasence, Jameson Parker, Victor Wong, Lisa Blount, Dennis Dun, Susan Blanchard, Anne Howard, Ann Yen, Ken Wright, Dirk Blocker, Alice Cooper

Prison (EMPIRE) 103min

'Just as **Halloween** (1978) took advantage of the very obvious, neglected fact that the most horrific night of the year had never been used for a horror movie,' claimed Yablans, 'it stands to reason that a prison, the most horrific place imaginable, ought to be used in that way, as well.' Yablans, who came up with the original ideas for *Halloween* and *Prison* was right: this is merely the best and most elaborate of a run of haunted prison films that include *Force of Darkness* (1986), **Slaughterhouse Rock** (1987), *Death Row Diner* (1988), **The Chair** (1988) and *Death House* (1989).

When warden Slate reopens a run-down penitentiary where he once allowed an innocent man to be electrocuted,he finds it possessed by the vengeful ghost. At heart another collection of bizarre deaths, *Prison* makes better use than its competitors of the oppressive setting, wittily re-using elements of the standard Hollywood prison movie, with an attempted break-out, a mess hall disturbance, sadistic guards, upstanding convicts and a climactic riot integrated into the ghostly goings-on. In an excellent cast, the Nixonian Slate plays just the right side of camp as the haunted monomaniac, while Buechler, away from his usual furry creatures, comes up with more grit and grue than usual for Empire.

d Renny Harlin *p* Irwin Yablans *s* C. Courtney Joyner *c* Mac Ahlberg *se* John Carl Buechler *lp* Viggo Mortensen, Chelsea Field, Lane Smith, Lincoln Kilpatrick, Tom Everett, Ivan Kane, Andre de Shields

Qian Nu Youhun *aka* A Chinese Ghost Story

(FILM WORKSHOP; HONG KONG) 95min

A humble tax-collector is forced to spend the night in the notoriously haunted Lan Ro Temple, where he incurs the wrath of a ghostbusting Taoist swordsman by getting in the way during a duel and falling in love with a mysterious and lovely ghost girl (Cheung). The winsome sprite is bound in fealty to a hermaphrodite vampire tree spirit with a mile-long tongue, and has been forced to entrap men so the monster can drain them of their yang elements, which reduces victims to withered zombie-mummy-vampires. Learning that Cheung has been promised in marriage to Lord Black, a particularly unpleasant demon who has a horde of long-haired living severed heads at his beck and call, the hero pursues her to the depths of one of many Chinese Hells.

Less concerned with realism than the average Western ghost story, this is a visual feast as spirits clash in mid-air in marvellously choreographed acrobatic brawls or the camera takes on the viewpoint of the deadly tongue as it rushes through the woods towards a character and then leaps down his throat into his stomach. The mood changes rapidly, with sensitive romantic scenes played under love songs and featuring much caressing of silk and the exposing of Cheung's belled anklet giving way to martial arts action/horror scenes, farcical knockabout comedy and special effects extravagances.

d Ching Siu-Tung *p* Tsui Hark *s* Ruan Jizhi *c* Pan Hengshen, Li Jiaogao, Liu Putang, Huang Yongheng *se* Xin Shi Technical Workshop *lp* Leslie Cheung, Wang Zuxian, Wu Ma, Liu Zhaoming, Lin Wei, Xue Zhilan, Wang Jang

Retribution (RENEGADE) 109min

Artist Lipscomb jumps off a building on Halloween night and wakes up partially possessed by a mobster who was tortured to death at exactly the moment of the suicide attempt. He tries to re-adjust by taking his hooker girlfriend (Snyder) to an art gallery but keeps having bad dreams.

This is an over-long movie that at least opts not to imitate the obvious models, deciding instead to collage bits and pieces from more obscure horrors: *High Plains Drifter* (1972), **The Possession of Joel Delaney** (1972), *The Tenant* (1976). Magar's functional style suddenly comes to life in scenes of gross violence, when Lipscomb's already hysterical performance cranks up until he appears as a green-eyed, cackling fiend. Victims are wrapped in a pig's carcass and buzz-sawed or have their heads burst by a fork-lift truck, to the accompaniment of telekinetic explosions, plenty of blue lights and a deafening score by John Carpenter's regular collaborator, Alan Howarth.

d/p/co-s Guy Magar *co-s* Lee Wasserman *c* Gary Thieltges *se* Court Wizard *lp* Dennis Lipscomb, Leslie Wing, Suzanne Snyder, Pamela Dunlap, Susan Preetz, Clare Peck, Chris Caputo, Hoyt Axton, Ralph Manza, Mario Roccuzzo

Return of the Living Dead, Part II

(LORIMAR) 89min

Less a sequel to **Return of the Living Dead** (1985) than an inferior comic remake, this finds Wiederhorn, of the pulpily enjoyable **Shock Waves** (1977), fruitlessly returning to the zombie genre.

Bratty kids discover a leftover zombie in an abandoned oil drum and let it out, wherupon bacterological warfare goo seeps into a graveyard and raises the dead. Karen and Mathews, stars of the first film, return in new roles as uninteresting body-snatchers forced to take refuge with even more uninteresting teenagers while cheap zombies in Halloween masks wander drearily about. A needless comedy working-over of material that was too broadly comic in the first place, this exemplifies every settle-for-less attitude of the late eighties horror cinema. *Return of the Living Dead, Part III* (1993) was inevitable.

d/s Ken Wiederhorn *p* Tom Fox *c* Robert Elswit *se* Kenny Myers *lp* James Karen, Thom Matthews, Dana Ashbrook, Marsha Dietlein, Suzanne Snyder, Philip Bruns, Michael Kenworthy, Thor Van Lingen

Return to Horror High (NEW WORLD/BALCOR) 95min

Not a sequel to *Horror High* (1974), this inventive little movie, like *Frankenstein 1970* (1958) and *House of the Seven Corpses* (1974), is structured around the blighted production of a horror film based on actual events. Accordingly, playing with the illusion-and-reality theme and offering a parodic subversion of the teenage splatter genre, it comes over as a low-budget blend of *The Stunt Man* (1980) and *Wacko!* (1981).

Detectives pore over the bloody site of the latest massacre and a demented screenwriter flashes back to the series of murders which has plagued the production of *Horror High*, an exploitative film about a real mass murder, and within the flashbacks cleverly misleading scenes are either further flashbacks to the original killings, extracts from the film in progress, or the confused nightmares of the leading lady (Lethin). Typical of the twisted approach is an intense teenage rape scene interrupted by a sleazy producer (Rocco) trying to make sure an actress's breasts are in shot, and then by Lethin, who protests the mistreatment of women in schlock like this.

d/co-s Bill Froehlich *p/co-s* Mark Lisson *co-s* Dana Escalante, Greg H. Sims *c* Roy Wagner *se* Make Up & Effects Labs Incorporated *lp* Brendan Hughes, Lori Lethin, Alex Rocco, Vince Edwards, Philip McKeon, Richard Brestoff, George Clooney, Al Fann, Scott Jacoby, Pepper Martin, Andy Romano

Mario Roccuzzo about to become dead meat in Retribution.

A Return to Salem's Lot (WB) 96min
This is not a sequel to Tobe Hooper's 1979 mini-series. Cohen plays the premise of a vampire-dominated town in Maine to different ends. Rather than import the ancient evil of a European Dracula figure, this has a vampire community cosily patterned after Thornton Wilder's *Our Town*.

Anthropologist Moriarty and his son (Reed) are lured to Jerusalem's Lot, where Judge Axel commissions the scientist to write a Bible for the undead. As usual, Cohen is more interested in filling in the background than telling the story. Cohen's Salem's Lot is a place of ceremonies by night (a secular wedding in which the bride and groom appear to be ten-year-olds, a recital of the Oath of Allegiance, even the orgies of bloodletting) and insidious banality by day, as abused and exploited human 'drones' look after the antique stores and guard the coffins. In the school, open from dusk till dawn, a class of ageless children recite a history of flight from persecution on the *Mayflower*'s supposedly lost sister ship, the *Speedwell*. The impeccably folksy patriarch prefers to drink from cattle because humans mainline heroin and transmit AIDS, but his wife (Keyes) persists in the old ways, confessing to 'a drinking problem'. Reed sums up the subtle evil with his initial comment on the sleepy place, 'This town sucks!' The depiction of a vampire lifestyle is effective and interesting, but Cohen has trouble with plot and pacing. Moriarty contributes another nervous, wisecracking hero and Fuller has his best-ever acting role as a half-Dutch, half-Romanian vigilante who is just as eager to stake a vampire as shoot a Nazi. Duggan, a Cohen fixture, gives an elegant, creepy performance as Axel, whose charm evaporates when he's angered enough to turn into a Nosferatu-faced goblin and who, in a film first, is impaled on the Stars and Stripes.

d/co-s Larry Cohen *p* Paul Kurta *co-s* James Dixon *c* Daniel Pearl *se* Steve Neill *lp* Michael Moriarty, Ricky Addison Reed, Andrew Duggan, Sam Fuller, Evelyn Keyes, Jill Gatsby, Ronee Blakely, June Havoc, James Dixon, Brad Rijn

The Serpent and the Rainbow (U) 98min
Based on a non-fiction book by Wade Davis, who discovered teterodotoxin (the drug used by voodoo priests to create a semblance of death) this entertaining, atmospheric, frequently creepy movie tries to make cinematic sense out of a book structured as scientific journalism cum travelogue rather than an action-horror story.

Anthropologist Pullman, who comes on like the pith-helmeted hero of a forties B-picture, visits Haiti in search of the secret of creating zombies. After doctor-priestess Tyson has explained the positive side of voodoo, Pullman confronts the forces of evil as represented by gold-toothed secret policeman/black magician Peytraud (Mokae), who warns him off the case by driving a nail through his scrotum. The film pulls marvellous coups in its trip around the real-life dream-world of Haiti, particularly an impressive pilgrimage to a huge waterfall that bests even **I Walked With a Zombie** (1943) as a depiction of the ceremony and magic of voodoo. Then at the mid-point, Craven switches from the mystic, erotic, primal melodrama of *The Emerald Forest* (1985) or *Walkabout* (1971) to a familiar effects-happy horror bonanza. By the finale, Craven's habitual nightmares have overwhelmed the plot while Peytraud has his face burned off and appears as a blaxploitation Freddy Krueger.

d Wes Craven *p* David Ladd, Doug Claybourne *s* Richard Maxwell, A.R. Simoun *c* John Lindley *se* Lance Anderson, David Anderson *lp* Bill Pullman, Cathy Tyson, Paul Winfield, Zakes Mokae, Brent Jennings, Conrad Roberts, Badja Djola, Theresa Merritt, Michael Gough

Slaughter High *aka* **April Fools' Day**
(VESTRON; GB) 88min
This imitation American splatter movie has an all-British cast assuming wonky transatlantic accents and a plot which fuses gimmicks from **Terror Train** (1979) and **The Burning** (1980) to come up with an apparently serious rerun of *National Lampoon's Class Reunion* (1982). Years after being humiliated and disfigured by the school's élite clique in an April Fool prank that misfires, nerd Scuddamore dresses in a clown outfit to kill his grown-up tormentors at a reunion in the now-deserted school. The murders (featuring poisoned beer, acid baths and electrified bedsteads) tend to reduce victims to semi-comic smoking messes, though there is a genuinely nasty moment when a guy under a car which has the jack pulled away holds up the vehicle with his arms only to have the killer slice his tendons until he is squashed. It winds up with a steal from **Maniac** (1980), or maybe *Dr Mabuse* (1923), as the killer is terrorized and eye-impaled by the ghosts of his victims.

co-d/co-s George Dugdale, Mark Ezra *co-d/co-s/se* Peter Litten *p* Steve Minasian, Dick Randall *c* Alan Pudney *lp* Caroline Munro, Simon Scuddamore, Carmine Iannaccone, Donna Yeager, Gary Hartman, Billy Martin, Michael Saffran, John Segal, Kelly Baker

Slaughterhouse Rock *aka* **Hell Island**
(FIRST AMERICAN/ARISTA) 82min
A minor but spirited haunting, with the ghost of cavalry commandant Fleming escaping from an urn hidden in the disused Alcatraz prison to possess the brother (Reilly) of a dream-plagued student (Celozzi). The teen-killing is enlivened by the ghost of necromantic rock star Basil, who apologizes for unleashing the evil in the first place and tries to help out, despite sarcastic comments from her murdered backing group. There is a deal too much murky wandering about the prison – considerably less eerie here than in *Point Blank* (1968) though a lot more interesting than in the comparable *Force of Darkness* (1986) – but snappy dialogue and off-kilter performances help. Logothetis even stages a few subtly eerie moments (Celozzi disoriented in a restaurant) among the usual fang attacks and fist-through-the-head gags. Unusually for rock-themed horror, a proper group (Devo) provide the music.

d Dimitri Logothetis *p* Louis George *s* Ted Landon *c* Nicholas von Sternberg *se* Ernest D. Farino, Wof N Bar Productions *lp* Nicholas Celozzi, Tom Reilly, Donna Denton, Toni Basil, Hope Marie Carlton, Tamara Hyler, Steven Brian Smith, Ty Miller, Al Fleming

Slumber Party Massacre II (CONCORDE) 86min
An eccentric follow-up to Amy Jones' 1982 film, making use of the original in a distinctly skewed manner.

Institutionalized Eilbacher, playing the surviving girl of *The Slumber Party Massacre*, is plagued with nightmares while her less traumatized younger sister (Bernard) is off at a slumber party herself, terrorized by the killer of Eilbacher's dreams. Illogical in a manner 'explained' by the tortuous revelation that the whole film is Eilbacher's fantasy of the dangers her sibling might be facing, this features the strangest psycho in the stalker cycle. Ilitch is an Eddie Cochran-style rock demon with a quiff and pointed leather boots who sports an outrageous drill at the end of his guitar and commits his murders while performing rockabilly numbers. Eye-openingly strange.

d/co-p/s Deborah Brock *co-p* Don Daniel *c* Thomas L. Callaway *se* James Cummins *lp* Crystal Bernard, Jennifer Rhodes, Kimberly McArthur, Patrick Lowe, Juliette Cummins, Heidi Kozak, Atanas Ilitch, Cindy Eilbacher

Sorority Babes in the Slimeball Bowl-a-Rama
aka **The Imp** (TITAN) 78min
'It's too bad we had to kill her,' a bimbo laments over the body of a possessed friend, 'I really liked the outfit she was wearing.' This is a no-budget horror comedy notable only for its assemblage of late eighties exploitation perennials Quigley, Bauer and Stevens in one movie.

The plot crosses *The Initiation* (1984) with **The Lamp** (1987). A punkette burglar (Quigley), two sorority pledges and three junior voyeurs break into a bowling alley to steal a trophy that contains a demon imp. The monster, who talks like a cross between Audrey II and Kermit the Frog, offers to fulfil its discoverers' wishes, but they all backfire. The sorority babes are turned into cackling she-demons like those of **The Evil Dead** (1982) – one imitates Margaret Hamilton – and fake-looking severed heads are used as bowling balls. Short on logic and long on gratuitous nude-ogling, this would-be camp item is scuppered by its thin wit and makeshift acting.

d/co-p David DeCouteau *co-p* John Schouwiler *s* Sergei Hasenecz *c* Stephen Ashley Blake *se* Craig Caton *lp* Linnea Quigley, Michelle Bauer, Andras Jones, Robin Rochelle, Brinke Stevens, Kathi Obrecht, Carla Baron

Spettri *aka* Specters (ITALY) 95min

A new section of catacombs comes to light in Rome and archaeologist Pleasence unwisely delves into it, freeing a barely-glimpsed demon that slaughters the supporting cast.

Vaguely inspired by the film-within-a-film section of **Demoni** (1985), this is atmospherically photographed (during one set-up scene in a laboratory, a monkey chatters unnervingly in the background) and loaded with ominous dialogue, but amounts to little more than an extended tease. An impressive cross between the minotaur and the fiend from **Night of the Demon** (1957), the monster, designed by *Demoni* veteran Stivaletti, barely gets a walk-on. Better is the subplot stolen from *Night Has a Thousand Eyes* (1948) in which an astrologer predicts that he will die in the jaws of a cat and has his throat cut on a stained-glass feline.

d/co-s Marcello Avallone *p/co-s* Maurizio Tedesco *co-s* Dardano Sachetti *c* Silvano Ippoliti *se* Sergio Stivaletti *lp* John Pepper, Katrine Michelsen, Donald Pleasence,

Strannyar Istoriyar Doktora Dzehila i Mistera Khaida *aka* The Strange Case of Dr Jekyll and Mr Hyde

(MOSFILM; USSR) 89min

This faithful filming of Stevenson's *The Strange Case of Dr Jekyll and Mr Hyde* unwisely preserves the novel's structure.

The first half has lawyer Utterson (Adoskin) trying to ascertain the precise link between distinguished and kindly Jekyll and degenerate murderer Hyde. The revelation that they are one and the same comes at mid-point, followed by a flashback in which Jekyll narrates his experiments. Stressing the addiction theme and borrowing from **I, Monster** (1970), this has the personality-altering drug administered via hypodermic needle rather than the familiar bubbling potion. In an approach not taken since *Dr Jekyll and Mr Hyde* (1912), with James Cruze and Harry Benham, two actors take the roles. Smoktunovski and Feklistov play the characters as they appeared in **The Two Faces of Dr Jekyll** (1960), an elderly, grey-haired, conscience-stricken Jekyll and a young, handsome, sadistic Hyde. Particularly effective are the transformation scenes – one has Hyde cover his face with his hands to emerge as Jekyll, while another cribs from **The Werewolf of London** (1935) as the metamorphosis occurs while Jekyll walks behind pillars.

d/co-s Alexander Orlov *co-s* Georgy Kapralov *c* Valery Shuvalov *lp* Innokenti Smoktunovsky, Alexander Feklistov, Anatoly Adoskin, Alexander Lazarev, Bruno Frienlich, Alla Budnitzskaya

The Taste of Hemlock

(SEAN S. CUNNINGHAM/TYNAN YOUNG) 90min

This strange little drama, based on Pauline Macaulay's play *The Astrakhan Coat*, strikes a bizarre note somewhere between *The Servant* (1964) and **Games** (1967), with the significant eighties reversal that here a trio of decadent rich folks invade the life of a humble dupe and destroy it completely.

Waiter Harrington answers an ad pinned up in a laundromat, hoping to get a leather jacket cheap, and finds himself involved with the coat's quixotic owner (Tynan Young) and a pair of sinister identical twins (Ramsay, Armstrong) who delight in setting him up to take several murder raps while initiating him into their circle of philosophical torturers. Pretentious but pointed, and filmed entirely in sombre shadows (with characters always dressed in black) this has a creepy style. Tynan Young wrote, produced and scored the film in addition to giving himself all the best lines.

d Geoffrey Darwin *p/s* Eric Tynan Young *c* Roger Tonry *lp* Randy Harrington, Eric Tynan Young, Anne Elizabeth Ramsay, Reed Armstrong, David McKnight, Barbara Pilavin, Shea Young

Terror at Tenkiller

(UNITED ENTERTAINMENT PICTURES) 90min

Logan holidays at an isolated lake to avoid her abusive fiancée, only to run into a charming handyman (Wiles) with the habit of slitting the throats of women who don't come up to his standards of purity. The result is a listless **Friday the 13th** (1980) clone (down to a final psycho-emerges-from-the-lake freeze-frame). A hint of the supernatural is the legend of an Indian maid who murdered ten braves of a rival tribe and reputedly lurks at the bottom of the lake. This Oklahoma-shot family affair is awkward regional film-making at its most minimal.

d/p Ken Meyer *s* Claudia Meyer *c* Steve Wacks *lp* Mike Wiles, Stacey Logan, Michele Merchant, Dale Buckmaster, Kevin Meyer, Dean Lewis, Debbie Killian, Jill Holmes

Through the Fire (TALON PRODUCTIONS) 85min

Made in Fort Worth, Texas, this low-budget Devil movie seems loosely inspired by **The Seventh Victim** (1943).

Heroine Hext is aided by tough cop Campitelli as she searches for her missing sister and gets caught up in a feud between occultist factions. The evil circle, who conjure a seldom-seen demon, are looking for a magic medallion Hext has come to own, while an ambiguously good group tries, fairly ineffectually, to help out. After sundry murky goings-on, the film winds up in a confrontation in a darkened building with slow-moving zombies. Sloppily constructed, this further suffers from indifferent acting, confused supernatural effects and suspenseless direction.

d/co-s G.D. Marcum *p* Charles C. Cunningham *co-s* Brad Potter *c* Roger Pistole *se* Jay A. Garris, Gregor Punchatz, K.C. Bryson *lp* Tamara Hext, Tom Campitelli, Randy Strickland, Billie Carroll, Dan Shackleford, John Davies, Wendy Wade

The Unholy

(LIMELITE STUDIOS/TEAM EFFORT) 102min

Having miraculously survived a five-storey fall, a priest (Cross) is assigned to an inner-city parish where two predecessors have been murdered in front of the altar on the night before Easter Sunday.

Since his only important parishioner is a crazy runaway virgin (Carroll) who works in the local satanic nightclub, he's soon glumly struggling with temptations of the flesh. Cross is also troubled by the mystery of who slaughtered the church dog and occasional flash-forwards to an effects-heavy climax in which a slime-dripping succubus tries to corrupt or kill him while the church floor gapes to reveal the fires of Hell. Written by Yordan as a companion piece to the cheap but interesting *Cataclysm* (1980), this emerges as a fudged attempt at an unfashionably theological horror film, albeit with a sneakily fundamentalist streak. The busy but unremarked Russ does well as the owner of the devil worshippers' hangout who winds up upside-down on a cross with his intestines spilling out. Demonic inserts were staged by Keen and spliced in after the departure of Vila to make the film more commercial. A dull stab at the thinking man's splatter movie.

d Camilo Vila *p* Matthew Hayden *s* Philip Yordan, Fernando Fonseca *c* Henry Vargas *se* Bob Keen *lp* Ben Cross, William Russ, Jill Carroll, Hal Holbrook, Trevor Howard, Ned Beatty, Peter Frechette

Uninvited

(AMAZING MOVIES/HERITAGE ENTERTAINMENT) 88min

Clark, an exploitation actor for Al Adamson and others, graduated to writing with the imaginative *Psychic Killer* (1975) then direction with the dire **Satan's Cheerleaders** (1977). His subsequent conventionally plotted, monster-filled horror and science-fiction efforts – *Without Warning* (1980), *The Return* (1980), the disarming spoof *Wacko!* (1980) – rely heavily on recognizable names, perhaps qualifying him as the genre equivalent of Western producer A.C. Lyles.

Crooked businessmen Kennedy, Cord and Gulager (who wears unbecoming false teeth) sail from Fort Lauderdale to the Cayman Islands in an unseaworthy luxury yacht to liberate funds from a tax shelter account. Refugees from a teenage beer 'n' bikinis comedy are aboard as a smokescreen for illegality and a girl brings a stray cat she has adopted. An escapee from a research centre, the cat contains a parasitic monster who emerges at intervals to infect people with a disease that prosthetically pops open their veins.

d/p/s Greydon Clark *c* Nicholas von Sternberg *se* Make Up Effects Lab, Jim & Debi Bouldon *lp* George Kennedy, Alex Cord, Clu Gulager, Toni Hudson, Eric Larson, Shari Shattuck

Vampire at Midnight (SKOURAS) 93min

Vintas, a bald hypnotist with a French accent, sleeps on a table and runs EST-style seminars while terrorizing the city as a vampire-killer. The cop on the case (Williams, who also produced and wrote the original story) talks to his goldfish and is handcuffed to the bed for sex by his partner. The victims are pretentious artist types who fill out the film with disco-dancing, piano-playing or nightclub acts.

This suspenseless, actionless vampire movie finally reveals its murderer to be an ordinary madman wearing a bulletproof vest and fake fangs. In the limp finale, Vintas gives up after a measly thump on the head and is taken to jail.

d Gregory McClatchy *p* Jason Williams, Tom Friedman *s* Dulhany Ross Clements *c* Daniel Yarussi *lp* Jason Williams, Gustav Vintas, Lesley Milne, Jeanie Moore, Esther Alise, Ted Hamaguchi

Vampire Knights (PETERSON-DODSON) 90min

This ultra-low-budget comedy clearly derives from **Fright Night** (1985).

A gaggle of vampirettes are alarmed when TV horror host Peterson forms a vampire-killing club called the Vampire Knights as a publicity stunt. They try to destroy the group only to discover that it consists of a lone horror nerd (Abraham) who'd rather watch a Linda Blair movie than have sex. Shot on very few cramped interiors, most of this consists of the vampire girls seducing and destroying macho studs, with attempted humour along the lines of **Beverly Hills Vamp** (1989).

d/s/co-p Daniel M. Peterson *co-p* James Dodson *c* Thomas Callaway *lp* Ken Abraham, Billy Frank, Daniel M. Peterson, Robin Rochelle, Thomas Kingsley, Ann Michaels, Mary Logan

The Video Dead (INTERSTATE 5/HIGHLIGHT) 90min

With its home-movie budget, this illogical comic splatter outing features an abandoned TV set which constantly rescreens *Zombie Blood Nightmare*, a cheapie starring badly made-up monsters who lurch into reality surrounded by tacky dry ice mist. For a while, the film almost scrapes by on dialogue turns (the hero is disgusted because his sister has chosen to go to college to 'major in aerobics, with a minor in music video'), suspense devices (in a possible film first, a nerve-wracking scene depends on trying to find the loose end of a roll of adhesive tape), or unfamiliar supernatural touches (copper bells sound whenever the walking dead are near) but monotony finally sets in as clay-faced zombies lumber slowly and one scene follows another with no rhyme or reason.

d/p/s Robert Scott *c* Greg Becker *se* Dale Hall, Jr *lp* Roxanna Augesen, Rocky Duvall, Vickie Bastel, Sam David McClelland, Michael St Michaels

The Wind *aka* The Edge of Terror

(OMEGA ENTERTAINMENT; GR) 93min

Best-selling novelist Foster leaves her lover (McCallum) floating in an LA pool with his cellphone while she rents the camp Morley's house in a Greek-island ghost town constantly racked by driving winds. As she writes a murder scene inspired by the tension between Morley and his handyman (Hauser), the madman really does take a sickle to his employer. Hauser, a great though usually ill-used villain, passes the rest of the film boringly chasing her about the house until the wind blows him off a cliff. Aside from the fact that Hauser is the first movie veteran killer to be unhinged by experiences in Nicaragua rather than Vietnam, this is a totally conventional stalker, without even the frills of Mastorakis' *Blind Date* (1984) or *The Zero Boys* (1986).

d/p/co-s Nico Mastorakis *co-s* Bred C. Perry *c* Andrew Bellis *lp* Meg Foster, Wings Hauser, David McCallum, Robert Morley, Steve Railsback

The Witches of Eastwick (WB) pv 118min

A big, impressive, floundering film, this is watchable and amusing. However, it is not as deep and clever as it would like to appear.

Darryl Van Horne (Nicholson), a millionaire with a topknot, lousy taste and a chauffeur who should work for The Addams Family, breezes into the New England town of Eastwick to

Heeeere's Jack!: Jack Nicholson surrounded by The Witches of Eastwick *(from the left), Michelle Pfeiffer, Susan Sarandon and Cher.*

answer the prayers of three repressed, depressed divorcées. He seduces each in turn and they set up an idyllic ménage in his mansion to concentrate on simple pleasures: massive sex, levitation, eating cherries and lounging *en deshabillé*. The pressure of giving equal weight to three independent-minded actresses, doubtless contractually enforced, requires the film monotonously to play scenes in threes, hiccoughing through three seductions, three repudiations, three break-ups, and so on. Nicholson, in outfits more horrible than the monster he briefly becomes, rants and raves, vomits in church, snores in stereo, makes vulgar remarks seem like epigrams and delivers a hilariously embittered keynote speech about why God invented women. Of the witches, only Sarandon – cast in Cher's role but shunted out of the spotlight by the complicated deal necessary to put the movie together – makes an impression, turning from a frigid cello teacher to a flamboyantly frizzy slut who munches pickles in public. It's a drama-comedy-horror-fantasy-satire-romance mainly because no one decided on a single, effective approach.

d George Miller *p* Neil Canton, Peter Guber, Jon Peters *s* Michael Cristofer *c* Vilmos Zsigmond *se* ILM *lp* Jack Nicholson, Cher, Susan Sarandon, Michelle Pfeiffer, Veronica Cartwright, Richard Jenkins, Keith Jochim, Carel Struycken

Zombie High (ELLIOTT KASTNER) 91min

Though the title suggests the camp of **Hard Rock Zombies** (1984) or **Class of Nuke 'Em High** (1986), this is an imitation of *The Stepford Wives* (1975) in which smiling normality turns out to conceal subtle horror.

An exclusive college whose alumni include presidents and billionaires is run by an ex-Cavalry colonel who learned the secret of immortality from Indians in the 1880s. It involves stolen brain-fluid and an operation which turns scruffy student layabouts into success-minded zombies with crystals in their brains. Freshwoman Madsen awakes the conscience of 102-year-old neurosurgeon Cox and the setup falls apart in an expected welter of bodies and instant-aging effects. In a straight-faced finale perhaps intended as comedy, a stately prom is destroyed when the soothing classical music which lulls the crystal-brain zombies is replaced by a Heavy Metal anthem, *Kiss My Butt*.

d Ron Link *p* Marc Toberman *s* Tim Doyle, Elizabeth Passarelli, Ghazai *c* David Lux, Brian Coyne *se* Chris Biggs, Mark Messenger *lp* Virginia Madsen, Richard Cox, Kay Kuter, James Wilder, Sherilyn Fenn, Paul Feig, T. Scott Coffey, Paul Williams

Zombie Nightmare
(GOLD GEMS LTD/NEW WORLD; CAN) 84min

A skid-row schlock movie, similar in plot to **The Toxic Avenger** (1985) but without even the attempted gore comedy. When a long-haired but law-abiding teenager (Thor) is killed by hit-and-run hoodlums, his mother has voodoo priestess Manuska raise him from the dead as an avenging zombie. Thor takes to the streets by night using a baseball bat to murder the delinquents who killed him, typically intervening as they are about to perpetrate more rape, brutality and lawlessness. The cop on the case (West) turns out to be an ex-hood who stabbed Thor's father in the prologue; in the finale, the zombie drags him to Hell after he has obligingly explained the transparent plot. Heavy Metal muscle-man Thor, also in *The Edge of Hell* (1987), struts in feeble white-face make-up, his presence cue for the use of Motorhead, Fist, Girlschool and Deathmask, although there is no thematic excuse for the music.

d Jack Bravman *p* Pierre Grisé *s* David Wellington *c* Robert Racine *se* Andy Clemens, Tony Bua, Jean Marc Cyr *lp* Adam West, Jon Mikl Thor, Tia Carrere, Manuska, Frank Dietz, Linda Singer, Linda Smith, Francesca Bonacorsa, John Fasano, Shawn Levy, Dean Hagopian

1988

Amsterdamned (FIRST FLOOR; NETH) 113min

While a hideously scarred skindiver slaughters at random in the canals of Amsterdam, Stapel's casual cop divides his time between autopsies, cynical dialogue and romancing a museum attendant. The action includes a high-speed powerboat chase that exceeds even the similar sequence in *Puppet on a Chain* (1970) in its combination of stunting and tourist locations. Maas plays the Hitchcock game of matching movie to setting, failing only to include tulips, but otherwise featuring all the trademarks of the city: a windmill, Flemish old masters in the museum, lots of canals, and discreet red-light district footage.

Like *De Lift*, *Amsterdamned* takes care to support thrills with well thought-out character drama: Stapel and Van De Ven, the stars of the earlier film, return as believably quirky protagonists, while Valcke is a diving expert who establishes a bantering rapport with the policeman and gets killed in an effective underwater fight. A semi-supernatural subplot, as the cop's daughter tries to to solve her father's case with psychic powers so he can spend more time with her, barely impinges on the *policier*, but serves to make the film even more reminiscent of the sixties and seventies run of Euro-thrillers – **Il Mostro di Venezia** (1965), *I Caldi Amori di una Minorenne* (1966), **Sette Scialli di Seta Gialla** (1972) – upon which it seems patterned.

d/s/co-p Dick Maas *co-p* Laurens Geels *c* Marc Felperlaan *se* Sjoerd Didden *lp* Huub Stapel, Monique Van de Ven, Serge-Henri Valcke, Tanneke Hartsuiker, Wim Zomer

Bad Dreams (FOX/NO FRILLS FILM/AMERICAN ENTERTAINMENT PARTNERS II) 84min

With a facially burned, dreamstalking bogeyman (Lynch) and heroine Rubin borrowed from **A Nightmare on Elm Street, Part 3: Dream Warriors** (1987), this is obviously an attempt to imitate the trappings of the successful *Elm Street* series.

Lynch is a Jim Jones cum Charles Manson cult leader who dies along with most of his followers in a suicidally set fire. Ruben, one of the survivors, wakes up after thirteen years in a coma to enter a group therapy session run by a pair of mad psychiatrists (Yulin, Abbott). Each patient dies in a manner appropriate to his or her neurosis, and finally it is revealed that all of the ghostly Lynch's appearances have been drug-induced hallucinations. Poorly constructed and directed, the film misuses the strikingly villainous Lynch in a cheat of a storyline.

d/co-s Andrew Fleming *p* Gale Anne Hurd *co-s* Steven E. de Souza *c* Alexander Gruszynski *se* Michele Burke, Fantasy II Film Effects *lp* Jennifer Rubin, Bruce Abbott, Richard Lynch, Dean Cameron, Harris Yulin, Susan Barnes, Elizabeth Daily, Sy Richardson

Beetlejuice (GEFFEN/WB) 96min

Returning to the parody-horror of his early shorts, *Vincent* (1982) and *Frankenweenie* (1984), this outing sees Burton develop further the gently bizarre sense of humour of his first feature, *Pee-Wee's Big Adventure* (1985).

Reversing the nice-young-couple-buy-a-haunted-house formula, newly dead innocents Davis and Baldwin find that they must spend eternity with an obnoxiously hip New York family, and call in Betelgeuse (Keaton), a crazed spirit who works as a bio-exorcist, ridding ghosts' houses of infestations of the living. With effects that turn characters into grotesques worthy of Don Martin or Basil Wolverton, a hilarous horror sequence in which rich guests are forced to lip-sync Harry Belafonte's *Banana Boat Song* while their dinner attacks them, and a twisted view of what normality actually is, the film mixes the satirical with the genuinely horrific. Keaton's Betelgeuse is a clever mix of the obnoxiously terrifying and the grossly funny, and both O'Hara and Ryder make the most of their roles as neurotic home-owner and gothic punkette daughter, Baldwin. A deliberate inversion of the gentle ghost subgenre of screwball comedy – which

Michael Keaton and friend in Beetlejuice.

includes the knockabout *Topper* (1937) and the bittersweet *The Ghost and Mrs Muir* (1947) – this is considerably more disturbing and intriguing than its exact contemporary, Neil Jordan's unsuccessfully whimsical *High Spirits* (1988).

d Tim Burton *p* Michael Bender, Larry Wilson, Richard Hashimoto *s* Michael McDowell, Warren Skaaren *c* Thomas Ackerman *se* Robert Short *lp* Alec Baldwin, Geena Davis, Michael Keaton, Jeffrey Jones, Catherine O'Hara, Winona Ryder, Sylvia Sidney, Glenn Shadix, Robert Goulet, Dick Cavett

Besøkarna *aka* **The Visitor** (SONET/MVM; SW) 104min
This is an unusually subtle and persuasive variation on the haunted mansion theme. An advertising executive (Bergqvist) moves with his family into a house deep in a forest, and is distracted from his overwrought attempt to solve a work problem by a succession of Amityville omens.

While Bergqvist is disturbed by mysterious noises and bloody footprints, his wife (Endre) and children are unimpressed, assuming him to be on the verge of a nervous collapse, which leads him to become argumentative and irrational. The traditional approach to this storyline would have the hero convincing his family of the truth of his suspicions, but *Besøkarna* renders the supernatural or extra-terrestrial status of the phenomena irrelevant by concentrating on the way Bergqvist's growing belief that something monstrous lurks in the sealed-off attic alienates him from his family. The result is successful primarily because brothers Joakim and Patrik Ersgard, the sons of the film's producer, concentrate on eerie visuals and sparse dialogue, opting for the weird rather than the obviously horrific.

d/co-s Joakim Ersgard *p* Hakan Ersgard *co-s* Patrik Ersgard *c* Hans-Ake Lerin *se* Olov Nylander *lp* Kjell Bergquist, Lena Endre, Joanna Berglund, Jonas Olsson, Johannes Brost, Patrik Ersgard, Bernt Lundquist

Black Roses (RAYVAN; CAN) 83min
A satanic rock group play in a small town, spreading evil among teenagers. Bigot Adams, the leader of an anti-rock crusade, is killed early but the film upholds her reactionary view of the Devil's music. Using a structure popular in paperback horror but comparatively rare in films, this intercuts between a dull but resolute hero (teacher Martin) who understands the crisis and tries to convince a disbelieving community, and gruesome vignettes in which ordinary people, under the spell of Black Roses, commit random acts of senseless violence or turn into silly effects.

d/co-p John Fasano *co-p* Ray Van Doorn *s* Cindy Sorrel *c* Paul Mitchnick *se* Richard Alonzo *lp* John Martin, Ken Swofford, Julie Adams, Carla Ferrigno, Carmine Appice, Sal Viviano, Frank Dietz, Robin Stewart

Blackout *aka* **The Attic**
(AMBIENT LIGHT ENTERTAINMENT) 90min
An overly leisurely psycho thriller. O'Grady receives a letter purporting to be from her long-disappeared father and visits her slightly mad mother (Lynley) and caring uncle (Hall), determined to discover how exactly her family broke up. Despite heavy attempts to make such details as a small hole in the ceiling seem significant and an occasional death among the supporting cast, this is resolutely unatmospheric, with the least ominous old dark house in the genre.

d/co-p Doug Adams *s/co-p* Joseph Stefano *c* Arledge Amenaki *se* Doug Smith *lp* Carol Lynley, Gail O'Grady, Michael Keys Hall, Joanna Miles, Joseph Gian, Deena Freeman

Blades (CINEMAX/TROMA) 98min
This is an over-long, straight-faced parody of **Jaws** (1975), set on a golf course terrorized by a giant runaway lawnmower.

After assorted golfers and interlopers have been shredded and dismembered, the alcoholic senior golf pro (North), the crazed mechanic son of the mower's first victim (Whelan) and a peppy young player (Scott) set out in a customized van to hunt down the killer. This is sadly limited by its major source, which demands the recreation of individual scenes from *Jaws* with mowers standing in for sharks, and Whelan doing a quite clever send-up of Robert Shaw. As monster-mower comedies go, *Blades* is not the equal of *Wacko!* (1983).

d/co-s Thomas R. Rondinella *p* John P. Finigan *co-s* William R. Pace *c* James Hayman *se* Wilfred Caban, Vincent Guastini *lp* Robert North, Jeremy Whelan, Victoria Scott, Holly Stevenson

The 'burbs (IMAGINE ENTERTAINMENT) 102min
In its twisted comic-horrific approach to suburbia, *The 'burbs* is one of several genre films (**Parents**, 1988, *Meet the Applegates*, 1989, **White of the Eye**, 1987, **The Stepfather**, 1986, *Life on the Edge*, 1989) to go against the nostalgic, family-centred vision of Reagan-Bush Americana by finding madness and monstrosity in the heart of the ideal home.

The film follows Dante's *Explorers* (1985) in its unusual (and unpopular) narrative strategy: presenting a situation filled with threat and mystery that turns out to be entirely innocent, forcing the audience to reassess the 'normal' point-of-view. Suburban hero Hanks's relaxing vacation at home is disturbed when neighbours (Dern, Ducommun) encourage his fantasies about the Klopeks, a seldom-seen family of newcomers whose bizarre habits include operating unidentifiable but noisy machinery after midnight during thunderstorms. The key speech has Hanks turning on his jovially paranoid neighbours as the Klopek house burns down, declaring 'Don't you see, we're the ones who are acting suspiciously!'.

The final revelation of genuine evil in the Addams-ish Klopek household is disappointing because it neither contradicts nor exceeds the neighbours' paranoia, merely confirms it.

d Joe Dante *p* Michael Finnell, Larry Brezner *s* Dana Olsen *c* Robert Stevens *se* Peter Kuran, ILM *lp* Tom Hanks, Carrie Fisher, Bruce Dern, Rick Ducommun, Corey Feldman, Wendy Schaal, Brother Theodore, Henry Gibson, Courtney Gains, Gale Gordon, Dick Miller, Robert Picardo

Cameron's Closet (SMART EGG) 86min

This outing teams Mastroianni (**He Knows You're Alone**, 1980, **The Supernaturals**, 1986) with Brandner, the author of the novel John Sayles and Joe Dante wisely ignored when scripting **The Howling** (1980).

Pudgy Cameron (Curtis) has been involved by his sweaty Dad (Hunter) in a psychic experiment that causes him to concentrate so hard on the figure of an Aztec demon that the malevolent creature is dragged into existence. Hunter falls on a machete, decapitating himself in a typically contrived shock sequence and Cameron's mother's moronic boyfriend gets blinded and thrown out of the window by the evil force. The cop on the case (Smith) has bad dreams about wandering through the corridors of Hell and the child's uncle (McCloskey) has an incestuous shower fantasy that ends in a bloody mess. While all this is happening a poorly articulated monster puppet occasionally looms out of the fog.

d Armand Mastroianni *p* Luigi Cingolani *s* Gary Brandner *c* Russell Carpenter *se* Carlo Rambaldi *lp* Cotter Smith, Mel Harris, Scott Curtis, Chuck McCann, Leigh McCloskey, Kim Lankford, Tab Hunter, Gary Hudson

Catacombs (EMPIRE/EDEN) 84min

Like **La Chiesa** (1989), this Italian-shot horror is heavily influenced by *The Name of the Rose* (1986), down to the casting of one of Jean-Jacques Annaud's actors, Chaliapin, as a dying monk.

A modern Catholic monastery is haunted by a possessed albino (Porter) who has been sealed in the catacombs for 400 years. Similar in plot to **Prison** (1987), it is a steadily paced, well produced tale, with an unusually detailed script and excellent performances from a mainly English supporting cast. The horrific aspects are comparatively mild – though the blasphemous image of a Christ statue coming to life and murdering the most sympathetic of the monks (Dobtcheff) with a nail pulled from his wooden hand is striking – and the finale depends rather too much on a conceptually daring miracle that unfortunately turns out to resemble an extra-strong spotlight.

d David Schmoeller *p* Hope Perello *s* Giovanni Di Marco, R. Barker Price *c* Sergio Salvati *se* Renato Agostini, Tom Floutz *lp* Timothy Van Patten, Laura Shaeffer, Jeremy West, Vernon Dobtcheff, Feodor Chaliapin, Brett Porter, Ian Abercrombie, Adriana Grampa Michel

The Chair

(ANGELIKA FILMS/URBAN ENTERTAINMENT) 90min

Like the superior **Prison** (1988), this features the ghost of an executed man haunting a jail's electrical systems.

Psychiatrist Coco, in charge of a group encounter rehabilitation program in a near-derelict correctional facility, tries to get through to a small group of mixed-up prisoners while clashing with the discipline-minded warden (Benedict). After a power-company repair man and a guard are killed by rampant machinery, Benedict confesses to Coco that he was a witness to the murder of a former warden (Bentley), fried in his own electric chair by rioters. Though the ghost eventually get his revenge on Benedict for leaving him to die, the film spends more time on Coco and his patients, cruelly and rather illogically having at least half of them turn out to be irredeemable psychopaths who casually murder their comic therapist in a genuinely unpleasant sequence. It has a gently eerie title sequence as the camera tracks through the deserted prison while Lonette McKee sings *The Folks Who Live on the Hill*, but the story straggles too much.

d Waldemar Korzeniowsky *p* Anthony Jones *s* Carolyn Swartz *c* Steven Ross *se* Tom Lauten, Irek Hartovich *lp* James Coco, Trini Alvarado, Paul Benedict, Gary McCleery, John Bentley, Stephen Geoffreys, Brad Greenquist

The Changer *aka* The Nostril Picker

(FRONT PORCH PRODUCTIONS) 76min

A Michigan-shot skid row dud. Unshaven slob Zschering learns a ritual which enables him to change his appearance. Unable to meet girls in his own disgusting person he assumes the likeness of a teenage girl and gains the confidence of local co-eds whom he proceeds to abuse and murder. The mildly unusual premise is barely used (the camera never sees Zschering's female persona, though it is illogically fooled by another disguise in the obvious twist finish).

d/co-p/c Patrick J. Mathews *co-p* Mark Nowicki *s/co-p* Steven Hodge *se* Gary Jones *lp* Carl Zschering, Edward Tanner, Laura Cummings, Gail Didia

Child's Play (UA) 87min

Owing rather more to *D.A.R.Y.L.* (1985) than *Devil Doll* (1936) or even *Pinocchio*, *Child's Play* constructs a world in which imaginative fear forever plays second fiddle to contrivance and special effects.

Dourif is the Lakeside strangler who dies in a toy shop and commits his soul to Chucky, a 'Good Guy Doll', and Hicks the mother who subsequently buys the doll for her six-year-old son, Vincent, only for it to transpire that to live Chucky needs Vincent's dead body. Holland's direction is efficient, and Sarandon is likeable enough as the cop who shot Dourif and is assigned to puzzle out the bizarre deaths associated with Vincent. However, though successful enough to spawn a couple of sequels (**Child's Play 2**, 1990 and **Child's Play 3**, 1991), the film remains mechanical.

d Tom Holland *p* David Kirschner *s* Don Mancini, John Lafia, Tom Holland *c* Bill Butler *se* Peter Donen *lp* Catherine Hicks, Chris Sarandon, Alex Vincent, Brad Dourif, Dinah Manoff, Tommy Swerdlow

Dangerous Games (QUANTUM; AUST) 97min

Though clearly derivative of both *The Initiation* (1984) and **Maniac Cop** (1988), this Australian-made psycho movie was a successful calling-card: it secured Hopkins the job of **A Nightmare on Elm Street: The Dream Child** (1989).

Murphy (Grives), an obsessive Irish cop, persecutes the teenage son of his old superior to such an extent that he is dismissed. However, the kid and his friends, as a prank, break into a department store and Grives follows them. One of the teens is accidentally killed, and Grives, actively demented, determines to make a suicidal clean sweep by slaughtering them and blowing up the store. Hopkins demonstrates skilled and assured handling of action, with the violence gradually getting out of hand and the department store eventually reduced to a shambles. Using slow motion, breaking glass, convincingly panicked performances and some shopping-mall survivalism left over from **Dawn of the Dead** (1979) and *Chopping Mall* (1986), the film stages a very effective mini-battle. The soundtrack makes use of *Fighting for Strangers* by Steeleye Span as a signature tune for the cop's psychosis.

d Stephen Hopkins *p* Judith West, Basil Appleby *s* Peter West *c* Peter Levy *se* David Young, Ray Fowler *lp* Miles Buchanan, Marcus Graham, Steven Grives, Sandy Lillingstone, Kathryn Walker, John Polson

The Dead Can't Lie *aka* **Gotham**
(SHOWTIME/THE MOVIE CHANNEL/KEITH ADDIS) 98min
The supernatural that is ever threatening to burst through in classic *films noir* like *Laura* (1944) or *Phantom Lady* (1944) here erupts.

Playboy Bruce hires hard-boiled private eye Jones to scare off his ex-wife Madsen, a femme fatale pestering him for the return of some jewels. The twist is that he claims the solid-seeming vixen has been dead for ten years. As he develops a relationship with the stylish spirit, Jones learns the jewels were actually stolen from the woman's grave and the ghost's characterization evolves from Kathleen Turner in *Body Heat* (1981) through Jennifer Jones in *A Portrait of Jennie* (1949) to Alice Krige in **Ghost Story** (1981). Appearing to the detective hero in anachronistic forties fashions, Madsen demonstrates increasingly alarming quirks, including the habit of lurking dead and nude in the bottom of his bath or inside a huge fridge that is the sole remaining item of furniture in her apartment.

Fonvielle, a writer on films as varied as *The Lords of Discipline* (1983), **The Bride** (1985) and *Good Morning, Babylon* (1987), plays with the visual conventions of the *film noir*, helped by a mainly monochrome colour-scheme from Carol Spier, David Cronenberg's usual production designer.

d/s Lloyd Fonvielle *p* David Latt *c* Michael Chapman *se* Michael Kavanagh *lp* Tommy Lee Jones, Virginia Madsen, Colin Bruce, Kevin Jarre, Dennis Stephenson, Frederic Forrest

Dead Heat (NEW WORLD) 86min
Combining the 1988 craze for bizarre cop team-ups (*Alien Nation, Red Heat, The Hidden*) with slapstick zombie gore after **Re-Animator** (1985) and **Return of the Living Dead** (1985), this also borrows from *DOA* (1949).

Los Angeles cops Williams and Piscopo are pursuing a gang of re-animated heistmen when Williams is killed; a handy machine returns him to life and his coroner girlfriend (Kirkconnell) gives him twelve hours to track down the culprits before he perishes. The most elaborately bizarre scene has Luke revive a roomful of meat, leading to disturbing images like a butchered cow carcass stumping after a victim or Williams wrestling with living liver. Price is the elitist behind the re-animation machine (his philosophy is 'God didn't mean for rich people to die and if he did we can buy him off') but has only one big scene, and McGavin's untrustworthily toupeéd stand-in doesn't adequately fill in as villain. The overwhelmingly light tone sits ill with a script involving the death of every sympathetic character.

d Mark Goldblatt *p* Michael Meltzer, David Helpern *s* Terry Black *c* Robert D. Yeoman *se* Steve Johnson *lp* Joe Piscopo, Treat Williams, Lindsay Frost, Darren McGavin, Vincent Price, Clare Kirkconnell, Keye Luke

Dead Ringers (MORGAN CREEK) 115min
Based on a *National Enquirer* headline (*Twin Docs Found Dead in Posh Pad*), this superior outing follows Beverly and Elliot Mantle, identical twins (both Irons), who develop a precocious and at the same time deeply repressed interest in the problems of sex and the female anatomy. They grow up to be a world-famous team of gynaecologists and divide their work strictly between themselves. Suave, outgoing Elliot accepts awards and research fellowships while the retiring, more overtly neurotic Beverly does the actual graft and takes care of the patients.

The twins live together in the one of Cronenberg's tasteful Hell-on-Earth luxury apartments and often replace each other at social functions. Accordingly, after Beverly takes a fancy to his latest patient, actress Claire Niveau (Bujold), Elliot seduces her, paving the way for Beverly to move in and establish a relationship that exposes him to a set of emotional dangers that lead to disaster. The set-up could almost work for a sophisticated farce: the sequence in which Claire discovers the deception and confronts the twins in a restaurant marvellously melds the ridiculous and the chilling. But far from taking a comic approach, *Dead Ringers* contains a horror and physicality more shattering than the goriest special-effects gimmick. What is deeply frightening about the movie is that it suggests we are willing to die – the twins operate on each other unto death – rather than change, so disturbing to a closed universe is change. Hence the bizarre subplot which pinpoints the fear of surgery as Beverly, increasingly infuriated that women's anatomies don't conform to textbooks, brings in a Giger-ish surrealist metalworker (Lack) to create a set of 'Gynaecological Instruments for Operating on Mutant Women'.

The end is profoundly depressing and yet deeply moving as the twins come to resemble each other more and more in their degradation, the calculating Elliot following Beverly into drug addiction on the theory that only if the Mantle brothers really become identical can the two inadequate personalities separate from each other and get back to functioning normality. Irons gives two of the subtlest, cleverest portrayals in the cinema of cruelty: the effects are invisible, with the acting doing more to create the illusion of duality than the optical splicing.

d/co-p/co-s David Cronenberg *co-p* Marc Boyman *co-s* Norman Snider *c* Peter Suschitzky *se* Lee Wilson *lp* Jeremy Irons, Genevieve Bujold, Heidi von Palleske, Barbara Gordon, Shirley Douglas, Stephen Lack, Nick Nichols

Reality intrudes on Dr Beverly Mantle in David Cronenberg's superior Dead Ringers.

Deadbeat at Dawn (ASMODEUS PRODUCTIONS) 82min
A semi-professional gore movie, unusual in that it eschews – aside from ominous touches with graveyards, amulets and ouija boards – the demonic trappings common in this area of film-making and hangs its splatter on a story straggling somewhere between *West Side Story* (1961) and *Reservoir Dogs* (1992).

As in H.G. Lewis's *She-Devils on Wheels* (1968), a gang-war plot is an excuse for a succession of low-budget atrocities: heads crushed, guts spilled, brains splattered, eyes gouged, throats cut. Achieving a species of downbeat intensity and on-the-streets grimness the comparatively inept and jokey Lewis never aspired to, this locates the Ohio-based VanBebber in the tradition of Buddy Giovinazzo (**Combat Shock**, 1987) and Jim Muro (**Street Trash**, 1986).

d/s/se Jim VanBebber *p/c* Michael King *lp* Paul Harper, Jim VanBebber, Megan Murphy, Ric Walker, Marc Pitman

Death Doll (WSM PRODUCTIONS) 82min
A no-budget psycho movie with supernatural frills. Pregnant Walters is imperilled after she and her husband (Boatwright) try Madame Zorba, a sinister fortune-telling machine. Boatwright dies mysteriously and Walters is terrorized by a bleeding china doll and a psychopath who, predictably, turns out to be her brother-in-law (Dance), cut out of the will if she gives birth and projecting his personality into the doll. With more talk than terror, this is deservedly obscure video fodder. Veteran Chauvin contributes the voice of Zorba, similar to but far less eerie than the machine in the fantasy *Big* (1988).

d/p William S. Mims *s* Sidney Mims *c* William Pope *se* Michael F. Jones *lp* Andrea Walters, William Dance, Jennifer Davis, Philip Boatwright, Lilyan Chauvin

Dream Demon (SPECTRAFILM/PALACE) 89min
Originally written by David Pirie and Richard Rayner for Christopher Petit, this then passed through several talented hands before emerging as an uneasy, compromised, tentative stab at a British **A Nightmare on Elm Street** (1985) with a few overtones from **Hellraiser** (1987).

Nervous bride-to-be Redgrave, tormented by bad dreams in which she decapitates her Falklands hero fiancé (Greenstreet) at the altar, is approached by American punkette Wilhoite who is trying to resolve a childhood trauma she experienced in the house the heroine has bought. The most interesting characters are sleazy tabloid journalists Spall and Nail who persecute the girl with intrusive questions and get sucked into dreams, where they become progresively more monstrous.

d/co-s Harley Cokliss *p* Paul Webster *co-s* Chris Wicking *c* Ian Wilson *se* Daniel Parker *lp* Jemma Redgrave, Kathleen Wilhoite, Timothy Spall, Jimmy Nail, Mark Greenstreet, Susan Fleetwood, Nickolas Grace

The Dreaming (GENESIS; AUST) 85min
Archaeologist Dignam delves into an aboriginal burial site on an island off the coast of Australia. Possessed by a 19th-century whaler, he is driven to re-enact the murder of an aborigine girl (Nehm). The scientist's doctor daughter (Cook) attends the mysterious death of the reincarnated victim, and is eventually pursued by her father, who wields a nasty blubber-carving implement, around a lighthouse.

In line with several other antipodean horrors – *The Lost Tribe* (1983), *Frog Dreaming* (1986), *Zombie Brigade* (1987) – this blends aboriginal mysticism with conventional melodramatics. There are effective sequences, as when the heroine hallucinates a band of barbarous whalers surrounding her car, and a few interesting ecological footnotes in the identification of the rapacious whale slaughterers with colonial oppressors and psychotic violence.

d/co-s Mario Andreacchio *p* Craig Lahiff, Wayne Groom *co-s* Rob George, Stephanie McCarthy *c* David Foreman *se* John Armstrong *lp* Arthur Dignam, Penny Cook, Gary Sweet, Laurence Clifford, Kristina Nehm

Jemma Redgrave and Timothy Spall, a journalist in extremis, in Dream Demon.

Edge of Sanity *aka* **Dr Jekyll and Mr Hyde**
(ALLIED VISION; GB) 90min
Another hack at the much-filmed novel, this adds a Jack the Ripper tie-in, a great deal of Freudian blather, plentiful Ken Russell-style degeneracy, a drug abuse angle lifted from *Jekyll and Hyde: Together Again* (1982) and a desperate dose of low camp.

Dr Jekyll (Perkins) is a limping pervert married to wax doll Barber, intent on liberating his repressed self. With the help of a lab chimp who tampers with an experiment – a device borrowed from Howard Hawks' *Monkey Business* (1952) – Jekyll comes up with a cocaine-like drug which turns him into a pasty-faced, lank-haired Olivier-voiced roué called Jack Hyde. With Hungary standing in for Victorian London, and a script heavily inclined towards irrelevant sex and violence, this is certainly not a serious attempt to do something radically new with the material. Victorian decadence is represented by a bully-boy pimp (Cole) who comes on like a cross between Bill Sikes and Julian Clary, and a succession of prostitutes in sub-Madonna underwear. The art direction is occasionally interesting – notably the catholic-themed brothel, or Jekyll's all-in-white laboratory.

d Gerard Kikoine *p* Edward Simmons, Harry Allan Towers *s* J.P. Felix, Ron Raley *c* Tony Spratling *se* Gordon Kaye *lp* Anthony Perkins, Glynis Barber, Sarah Maur-Thorp, David Lodge, Ben Cole, Ray Jewers, Jill Melford

Elvira, Mistress of the Dark (NEW WORLD) 96min
Actress-writer Peterson created the character of Elvira – a successor to Carolyn Jones' Morticia Addams, Yvonne de Carlo's Lily Munster and the pioneering 'horror hostess' Vampira, distinguished by her black beehive and prominent cleavage – for KHJ-TV's *Movie Macabre* in 1981.

This follows *Pee-Wee's Big Adventure* (1985), in which Peterson had a bit part, elaborating the heroine's limited character beyond a self-referential television environment (her previous appearances found her stretched out on a couch making jokes). Elvira travels to Fallwell, Massachusetts, to inherit an old dark house, feud with ultra-conservative locals and battle a rival warlock (Sheppard) for the title 'Master of the Dark'. Like Pee-Wee, Elvira is a childish creation: though heavily reliant on Mae West-ish sexual innuendoes, she never exchanges more than a chaste cuddle with her reticent leading man. Elvira's catty remarks about the low quality of the films she screens on her TV show rebound, since nothing here matches an opening clip from *It Conquered the World* (1956) either for humour or genuine weirdness.

d James Signorelli *p* Eric Gardner, Marc Pierson *s* Sam Egan, John Paragon, Cassandra Peterson *c* Hanania Baer *se* Doug Beswick *lp* Cassandra Peterson, W. Morgan Sheppard, Daniel Greene, Susan Kellermann, Jeff Conaway, Edie McClurg, Kurt Fuller

Evil Altar (OM) 87min
A bald and croaking warlock (Smith) orders an undead minion to sacrifice 103 children over a period of thirty years to help him become immortal ruler of the world. However, nearing the end of the run, the Collector goes against his master's wishes and tries to get local meat for the altar, precipitating the downfall of the diabolical scheme.

Despite its premise, this turns out not to be the expected teenkill clone but a relatively ambitious Faustian study, focusing on the bargains made with the warlock by the elders of a small town and the grief that comes when the younger generation revolts. With odd setpieces (an attack by a possessed baseball or a zombie killing a TV weatherlady) and surprisingly complex characters, this quickie rises momentarily above the rut, but only the French-accented Smith is up to the demands of the script and direction is hurried.

d Jim Winburn *p* Ryan Rao *s* Brend Friedman, Scott Rose, Jon Geilfuss *c* Peter Wolf *lp* William Smith, Pepper Martin, Robert Z'Dar, Theresa Cooney, Tal Armstrong

I Fantasmi di Sodoma *aka* **The Ghosts of Sodom**
(ALPHA CINEMATOGRAFICA; IT) 85min
Though bombed so severely in 1943 that all the extras unenthusiastically groping each other in the low-rent *Salon Kitty* (1975) opening are killed, a onetime Nazi brothel survives undamaged to the present day. Two young couples visit and are gradually seduced and menaced by phantoms of the dead Nazis. With plentiful nudity but little sex, the film meanders from scene to scene and winds up in a musak-scored vacuum.

d/co-s Lucio Fulci *p* Luigi Nannerini, Antonio Lucidi *co-s* Carlo Alberto Alfieri *se* Angelo Mattei *c* Silvano Tessicini *lp* Claus Aliot, Mary Salier, Robert Egon, Jessica Moore

Frankenstein General Hospital
(NEW STAR ENTERTAINMENT) 92min
This is a witless combination of **Young Frankenstein** (1974) and *Young Doctors in Love* (1982), with Dr Bob Frankenstein (Blankfield), descendant of the famous mad doctor, working on a monster in the basement laboratory of an ineptly run hospital.

Keyes apes Peter Boyle's monster while Jordan does a Dwight Frye impersonation as Iggy, the assistant who accidentally procures two left legs for the work-in-progress. Pickett, originator of the novelty record *The Monster Mash*, cameos as 'Man in Elevator'.

d Deborah Roberts *p* Dimitri Villard *s* Michael Kelly, Robert Deel *c* Tom Fraser *se* Doug White *lp* Mark Blankfield, Leslie Jordan, Jonathan Farwell, Kathy Shower, Hamilton Mitchell, Lou Cutell, Katie Couple, Dorothy Peterson, Irwin Keyes, Bobby 'Boris' Pickett

I Frati Rossi *aka* **The Red Monks**
(NATMAS PRODUCTIONS; IT) 84min
A confused 'old dark house' horror film, perhaps influenced in its dodgy thirties flavour by Mario Bava's **Lisa e il Diavolo** (1972), this concerns a heretical order of diabolists who ensnare innocents who venture into a haunted mansion, involving them in rituals which climax with the decapitation of the hero (Amato) by an apparently possessed heroine (Wendel).

Semi-erotic dream writhing, glowing-eyed skeletons, strikingly dressed apparitions, significant portraits, disposable servants, risibly fake spiders and slow-paced wandering combine in a mystifying but hardly intriguing horror movie, singularly lacking in narrative verve, involving characters or actual plot.

d/co-s Gianni Martucci *p/co-s* Pino Buricchi *c* Sergio Rubini *lp* Gerardo Amato, Lara Wendel, Malisa Longo, Richard Brown, Claudio Pacifico, Mary Maxwell, Ronald Russo

Friday the 13th, Part VII: The New Blood
(PAR) 90min
'I saw my father get killed when I was a kid and it's really messed up my head a lot.' Upping the supernatural content of this series, as part of a continuing war of one-upmanship with the rival **Nightmare on Elm Street** cycle, this pits zombie psycho Jason (Hodder) against a girl (Lincoln) with psychic powers borrowed from **Carrie** (1976). Lincoln is traumatized because she caused the death of her abusive father (Otrin), precipitating him into Crystal Lake where the temporarily dead Jason has been rotting since **Friday the 13th, Part VI: Jason Lives** (1986). During a lakeside party, she attempts to bring her father back but instead resurrects Jason, who emerges to slaughter another dozen or so undifferentiated teens. Stuntman Hodder was the first to play Jason more than once, returning in **Friday the 13th, Part VIII: Jason Takes Manhattan** (1989).

d John Carl Buechler *p* Iain Paterson *s* Daryl Haney, Manuel Fidello *c* Paul Elliott *se* Magical Media Industries *lp* Lar Park Lincoln, Terry Kiser, Kevin Blair, Susan Jennifer Sullivan, Heidi Kozak, Jennifer Banko, John Otrin, Susan Blu, Elizabeth Kaitan, Kane Hodder

Fright Night Part 2 (COL/VISTA) pv 104min
This is a bluntly unimaginative sequel to a film that was derivative in the first place.

College student Ragsdale has been persuaded by psychoanalysis that his brush with the undead was a psychotic episode, only to have Regine (Carmen), performance artist sister of the Chris Sarandon character, arrive to avenge the vampire's death. Though it returns to Bram Stoker for some wall-crawling antics and the deployment of communion wafers, the film experiments with new (and silly) vampire-killing methods: a bunch of roses in the face, or being wrapped in an altar cloth.

With McDowell hamming throughout, bland turns from Ragsdale and Lin as the young lovers and such promising monsters as Clark's black mute androgynous rollerskating vampire and Thompson's hulking Renfield-type reduced to one-joke bits, the acting weight falls on Carmen. Despite all the potentially intriguing frills given the character (her dancing, her sisterly devotion, her job as an Elvira-style horror hostess) she mainly shows off *Dynasty* reject fashions and keeps her unconvincing teeth in her mouth.

Julie Carmen, eyes aglow, out to avenge her vampire sister's death in Fright Night Part 2.

d/co-s Tommy Lee Wallace *p* Herb Jaffe, Mort Engelberg *co-s* Tim Metcalfe, Miguel Tejada-Flores *c* Mark Irwin *se* Make-Up FX Unlimited *lp* William Ragsdale, Roddy McDowell, Julie Carmen, Traci Lin, Jonathan Gries, Russell Clark, Brian Thompson

Ghost Town (EMPIRE) 85min
Like Empire's similarly well produced **Prison** (1987), this blends the horror genre with another classic form, in this case the Western.

Sheriff Luz pursues a missing girl in the desert and comes across a ghost town run by a 19th-century zombie outlaw. He is recruited by the ghost marshal – who was crucified on a watermill wheel – to defeat the gunslinger's band so the town can finally fade away. Death sits around in the form of a blind card-player dealing out aces and eights to doomed men and new uses are found for traditional Western props: a Sheriff's star is sharpened into a *shuriken*. Though a little slow-paced and just adequately acted, the film has a nice ghost-town atmosphere, thanks to Ahlberg's clever blending, as in his work on *Prison*, of genre conventions so that typical Western images work in a horror-movie context.

d Richard Governor *p* Timothy D. Tennant *s* Duke Sandefur *c* Mac Ahlberg *se* John Carl Buechler *lp* Franc Luz, Catherine Hickland, Jimmie F. Skaggs, Penelope Windust, Bruce Glover, Zitto Kazann

Ghostriders (GHOST RIDERS INC) 85min
This promising horror Western swiftly degenerates. An outlaw gang return after a hundred years to avenge themselves on descendants of the preacher who supervised their lynching. With incidents borrowed from *The Wild Bunch* (1967) (insects eating each other intercut with a shootout) and **Night of the Living Dead** (1968) (the apparent hero burned to death in a truck while escaping from a siege), this has interesting generic models but little to add. As in the similar but superior **Ghost Town** (1988), the ghost cowboys can only be sent back to Hell with a weapon from their period, a shotgun pistol which is fortunately a family heirloom.

d/co-p Alan Stewart *co-p/c* Thomas L. Callaway *co-p/co-s* James J. Desmarais *co-s* Clay McBride *lp* Bill Shaw, Mike Ammons, Arland Bishop, Ricky Long

Grandmother's House *aka* **Grandma's House** (OMEGA) 89min
This is an uninspired mad-relative-terrorizes-the-family movie in the tradition of **The Shuttered Room** (1966), **Crescendo** (1969) and **Silent Scream** (1980).

Despite the title, grandmother has little to do with the story, which concerns alleged orphans Foster and Valentine. They move in with their grandparents and are menaced by a crazed harridan (Stevens) who turns out to be their mother, unhinged because of childhood abuse by their grandfather-father (Lesser). The interminable climax features a lengthy chase during which plot revelations mechanically come tumbling out. The film bears the hallmarks of its producer, the Greek one-man horror industry responsible for *Island of Death* (1980), *Blood Tide* (1980), *Blind Date* (1984), **The Wind** (1987) and *The Zero Boys* (1988).

d Peter Rader *p* Nico Mastorakis *s/c* Peter Jensen *lp* Eric Foster, Kim Valentine, Brinke Stevens, Ida Lee, Len Lesser

Halloween 4: The Return of Michael Myers (TRANCAS INTERNATIONAL) 88min
Psychotic Michael (Wilbur) emerges from a ten-year coma and returns to Haddonfield, Illinois, to restart his killing spree and get to his niece (Harris), daughter of the written-out Jamie Lee Curtis. Sidestepping the interesting but unsuccessful **Halloween III: Season of the Witch** (1983), this picks up the plot of the original.

Typical of the sloppiness is the way the dialogue insists the windows have been barricaded, but minutes later director Little stages a death in front of a large, unboarded window to get a pretty backlighting effect. Only in a brief scene with still-pursuing Pleasence hitching a lift from a preacher who disturbingly proves even more fanatical than he is, and in the last scene, replicating the first moments of **Halloween** (1978) as a now-unhinged Harris takes over, does the film try to come up with new twists on the old themes. John Carpenter is credited only for the re-use of his synthesizer theme.

d Dwight H. Little *p* Paul Freeman *s* Alan B. McElroy *c* Peter Lyons Collister *se* John Buechler *lp* Donald Pleasence, Ellie Cornell, Danielle Harris, George P. Wilbur, Michael Pataki, Beau Starr, Gene Ross, Kathleen Kinmont, Sasha Jenson

Heart of Midnight (VESTRON) 105min
This is a wilfully perverse psychological study with overtones of high art and the slasher movie. Semi-crippled neurotic Leigh inherits the Midnight, a run-down inner-city nightclub, from her reputedly perverted uncle. She insists on restoring the club for re-opening and establishes an uneasy balance of tension with brutally unconcerned policeman Stallone and a mysteriously sympathetic stranger who claims to be a cop (Coyote). Leigh gradually realizes the Midnight was a sado-masochist brothel and that it is still inhabited by her transvestite cousin (Mayron). The villainess is a camp creation out of *Beyond the Valley of the Dolls* (1970) and her appearance as a last-reel menace seriously unbalances the decadent tone carefully established by the accumulation of odd details about the setting and the characters. Sharing the feel of such 'erotic thrillers' as **Crimes of Passion** (1985) and *Call Me* (1988), this is an unwieldy mix of the serious and the sleazy, but Leigh's powerful performance, vulnerable and yet stubborn, makes it a worthwhile picture.

d/s Matthew Chapman *p* Andrew Gaty *c* Ray Rivas *lp* Jennifer Jason Leigh, Peter Coyote, Frank Stallone, Brenda Vaccaro, Gale Mayron, Denise Dummont

Hellbound: Hellraiser II (NEW WORLD) 93min
A Caligari-ish asylum head (Cranham) takes charge of the traumatized Laurence, hoping to use the puzzle-solving ability of another inmate (Boorman) to open gateways to Hell.

Randel, working from a story by Clive Barker, re-establishes the visual and aural (Christopher Young's score is especially fine) feel of **Hellraiser** (1987) in a serviceable first half-hour, but once the characters enter Hell the plot flounders. Especially disappointing is Leviathan, the monster in the labyrinth, which turns out to look more like an image from an early seventies album cover than the promised fearsome Lord of Hell. Far better is Cranham as the icily perverse villain, whose reaction when turned into a grotesque with a fifteen-foot penile tentacle on his head is 'To think I hesitated!'. The best sequence has the raw and skinless Higgins flirt with the withdrawn and prissy Cranham, letting him mummify her in bandages before kissing him bloodily on the lips. In the end, however, this is undone by its echoing of **Dream Demon** (1988) and the **Nightmare on Elm Street** series as it spends too much time wandering around the gloomy passageways of the beyond.

d Tony Randel *p* Christopher Figg *s* Peter Atkins *c* Robin Vidgeon *se* Bob Keen *lp* Ashley Laurence, Clare Higgins, Kenneth Cranham, Imogen Boorman, Sean Chapman, William Hope, Doug Bradley

Hollywood Chainsaw Hookers *aka* **Hollywood Hookers** (CAMP MOTION PICTURES) 78min
Desperate, smarmy, would-be camp from Ray, whose low-rent output includes *Scalps* (1982), *The Tomb* (1985), **Beverly Hills Vamp** (1989) and **Evil Toons** (1990), this fails because it is

insufficiently inventive to duplicate the unintentional humour of Z-features like *Plan 9 From Outer Space* (1958). Private eye Richardson, who voice-overs third-rate Chandlerisms, traces runaway girls to an Ancient Egyptian prostitute cult who gain immortality by sacrificing clients with chainsaws. There is the odd joke (a hooker covering her velvet Elvis portrait before revving up her saw) but too much of the film consists of naked women waving chainsaws while thin stage blood is squirted at them from offscreen. Quigley, a poverty-row fixture of exploitation films of the period, performs 'the virgin dance of the two chainsaws' and is appealing in her nothing role, but the movie's bankruptcy is shown in a notably unexciting climax when she and villainess Bauer have a fight with buzzing but visibly switched-off chainsaws which the actresses are barely able to lift.

d/p/co-s Fred Olen Ray *co-s* T.L. Lankford *c* Scott Ressler *lp* Linnea Quigley, Gunnar Hansen, Jay Richardson, Michelle Bauer, Dawn Wildsmith

Intruder *aka* **Night Crew: The Final Checkout** (PHANTOM) 83(78)min

The directorial début of the co-writer of **Evil Dead II** (1987), this outing features that film's director as one of a group of supermarket staff murdered while working overnight in a soon-to-be-closed store.

The chief suspect for the person who makes unorthodox use of a billspike, a bandsaw, a meatcleaver, a meathook, a severed head and a machete is the ex-con ex-boyfriend (Byrnes) of cashier Cox. 'I'm just crazy about this store' giggles the hammy villain as Cox runs, whimpers, screams and fights back in approved Jamie Lee Curtis manner. To make up for his surprise-free, slasher script, Spiegel resorts to trick shots, filming through a bottle, from underneath a telephone dial or a wastepaper basket or from the point of view of a turning doorhandle.

d/s Scott Spiegel *p* Lawrence Bender *c* Fernando Arguelles *se* Greg Nicotero, Robert Kurtzman, Howard Berger *lp* Elizabeth Cox, Renée Estevez, Danny Hicks, David Byrnes, Sam Raimi, Eugene Glazer, Ted Raimi, Alvy Moore, Bruce Campbell

Jack's Back *aka* **Red Rain** (PALISADES) 96min

This slots into two 1988 cycles, cashing in on Jack the Ripper's centenary and a flurry of 'twin' movies (*Big Business*, **Dead Ringers**, *Twins*). A madman with some medical skill has been slaughtering prostitutes on the hundredth anniversaries of the Ripper murders. The first reel presents dedicated skid-row doctor Spader as either a suspect or a detective hero, but he is murdered, wherupon his estranged twin has a psychic nightmare in which he 'witnesses' the killing. Several promising themes (like the linking of present-day homeless and disenfranchised with the Victorian poor) are introduced only to be dropped. However, the script is suitably convoluted: the brother, a no-good drifter, is ignored by the police, who try to pin the killings on the dead man. Accordingly the brother takes over the detective role, sleuthing through an Argento-style whodunnit in which Spader's twinning is echoed when there turn out to be two psychos. The plot ties knots around the hero, so that when he definitively clears his brother, the eyewitness evidence that pointed to the dead man, plus his psychic inside knowledge, now casts him as the most likely suspect.

d/s Rowdy Herrington *p* Tim Moore, Cassian Elwes *c* Shelly Johnson *se* John Naulin *lp* James Spader, Cynthia Gibb, Rod Loomis, Rex Ryon, Robert Picardo, Jim Haynie, Wendell Wright, Chris Mulkey

The Jitters (SKOURAS/FASCINATION; US, CAN, JAP) 79min

A low-budget use of the impedimenta of the Hong Kong 'hopping vampire' genre, with prayers pasted to foreheads, heroes holding their breath to seem invisible to the undead and clumsy kung fu dressing up a slender story. Crooks murder a Chinese store-keeper who returns as a vengeful vampire, and ghostbuster Hong helps hero Viviano and the vampire's daughter (Tokuda) see off villains who are after a supposed treasure.

d/p John M. Fasano *s* Jeff McKay, Sonoko Kondo *c* Paul Mitchnick *se* Steven Wang, Richard Alonzo *lp* Sal Viviano, Marilyn Tokuda, James Hong, Frank Dietz

Kadaicha (PREMIERE FILM MARKETING; AUST) 88min

A lacklustre antipodean **Poltergeist** (1982). Teens receive curse stones from dream-stalking aboriginal ghosts and are subsequently killed by possessed fauna. It turns out that their suburb has unethically been built on the graves of massacred Native Australians, prompting a sole interesting character moment as Carides complains that it's not fair the ghosts should kill her teenage friends rather than their greedy parents.

d James Bogle *p* David Hannay, Charles Hannah *s* Ian Coughlan *c* Stephen F. Windon *se* Deryck de Niese *lp* Zoë Carides, Tom Jennings, Eric Oldfield, Kerry McKay, Fiona Gauntlett, Natalie McCurry, Bruce Hughes, Steve Dodd

The Kiss (COL) 98min

This Canadian-shot family-curse cum African-demon-parasite horror movie is multiply derivative, falling between the three stools of camp Hammer gothic, *Omen*-style mid-seventies gory blandness and early-eighties body horror.

Pacula, an international fashion model, visits her sister's family with a view to passing an ancient parasite on to her own niece (Salenger), wishing contrived freak accidents onto everyone who gets in the way. As in seventies movies, the family is the locus of horror, but rather than emerging from the poolside perfection of the heroine's suburban life, it is located in the exotic, otherly form of the aunt. With an array of leopard-print scarves and her feline looks, Pacula is a particularly reactionary idea of a monster, identified with various untenable 'others': a career-woman alternative to the happily married life of her sister, a follower of an African religion, an asexual who reproduces through a same-sex kiss. Like **Child's Play** (1988), this is mainstream, 'safe' horror.

d/co-p Pen Densham *co-p* John Watson *s* Stephen Volk, Tom Ropelewski *c* Francois Protat *se* Chris Walas *lp* Meredith Salenger, Joanna Pacula, Mimi Kuzyk, Nicholas Kilbertus, Peter Dvorsky, Pamela Collyer, Sabrina Boudot, Jan Rubes, Shawn Levy, Céline Lomez

Lady in White (NEW SKY/SAMUEL GOLDWYN) 113min

A personal project, this mix of *Stand By Me* (1986), *To Kill a Mockingbird* (1962), *Moonstruck* (1987) and **The Uninvited** (1944) confirms the promise of LaLoggia's Devil movie **Fear No Evil** (1981).

A horror writer returns to his home town and flashes back to 1962: on Halloween, young Haas is locked in a school cloakroom and sees a ghostly little girl who was the first victim of the child-killer who is terrorizing the community. The murderer himself turns up, looking for something he left behind, and tries to strangle Haas. The child survives apparent death and the black janitor is arrested for the crimes, but Haas knows the man is innocent, even if he can't identify his attacker, and continues to be visited by the ghost. While the low budget shows through in a few too many matte fringes, there are several magical sequences that provoke shivers and enchantment, as when the invisible ghost girl wanders through Haas's house, breathes on the window and draws a heart in the condensation. It's a simple trick, more convincingly supernatural than rotting zombies or broken mirrors. The Ray Bradbury-like small town, the understated period recreation, and the gently melancholy ghost story work well.

d/s/co-p Frank LaLoggia *co-p* Andrew G. LaMarca *c* Russell Carpenter *se* Fantasy II Film Effects *lp* Lukas Haas, Alex Rocco, Len Cariou, Katharine Helmond, Jason Presson, Renata Vanni, Angela Bertolini, Joelle Jacobi, Jared Rushton

The Lair of the White Worm (VESTRON) 93min
Dispensing with the tatters of literary respectability that cling to his other approaches to horror (*The Devils*, 1971, **Gothic**, 1986), Russell here adapts Bram Stoker's last and least novel.

Donohoe worthily combines the serpentine elegance of Jacqueline Pearce in **The Reptile** (1966) with the haughty vampire decadence of Ingrid Pitt in **The Vampire Lovers** (1970): her drowning of a venom-paralysed boy scout in a sunken bath by prodding him under soapy water with the toe of her thigh-length fetish boot is one of the few genuinely creepy-funny-sexy notes sounded in a pedestrian, smirking movie. However, the finale is a particular mess, with Donohoe – in body paint modelled on **Vampire Circus** (1970) and a huge false phallus like those of the rapist robots in *Flesh Gordon* (1974) – falling into the mouth of the muppet-like worm while Capaldi produces a hand grenade from his sporran (earlier, with even less explanation, he had found a mongoose there) to drop into the creature's lair. Russell leaves his signature in trippy dreams which involve nuns being raped by Roman soldiers while a huge snake strangles Jesus on the cross.

d/p/s Ken Russell *c* Dick Bush *se* Image Animation
lp Amanda Donohoe, Sammi Davis, Catherine Oxenburg, Hugh Grant, Peter Capaldi, Stratford Johns, Paul Brooke

Love at Stake (HEMDALE; CAN) 88min
Corrupt Puritan officials Pankin and Thomas stir up witch fever so they can seize the land they need for a colonial real-estate development. Genuine witch Carrera intervenes in the hope of winning pure-hearted cleric Cassidy from sweet orphan Preston, denouncing the girl as an acolyte of Satan. Despite a willing cast – in a variation of her role in **Wicked Stepmother** (1989), Carrera transforms into crone Ramsey – and an unfamiliar comedic subject, few laughs are wrung, with jokes too often depending on the low-comedy standbys of flatulence, bestiality and obscene bread-loaves.

d John Moffitt *p* Michael Gruskoff *s* Terry Sweeney, Lanier Laney *c* Mark Irwin *se* Cliff Wenger, Michael Kavanaugh
lp Patrick Cassidy, Kelly Preston, Bud Cort, David Graf, Stuart Pankin, Barbara Carrera, Dave Thomas, Anne Ramsey

Lurkers (REELTIME DISTRIBUTING CORPORATION) 90min
Co-creator of **Snuff** (1974) and **Shriek of the Mutilated** (1974), Findlay worked through the seventies and early eighties making porn movies. She returned to horror with a run of dreary New-York-shot occult quickies (**The Oracle**, 1985, **Blood Sisters**, 1986, *Prime Evil*, 1988). Combining themes from **Rosemary's Baby** (1968), **The Sentinel** (1977) and **Inferno** (1980) and also prefiguring **Jacob's Ladder** (1990), this is her most interesting film.

Haunted by memories of disfigured figures who loitered around the brownstone where her mad mother tried to kill her, Moore finds, during her engagement to a charming but untrustworthy photographer (Warner), the menacing apparitions have come back. Despite a slow-moving first hour and listless performances, the extended finale is decidely odd. Moore is dragged back to her childhood home for a nightmare party which proves that all the people in her life are part of a satanic plot, involving houses built as extensions of Hell, to lure her home to complete the once-thwarted murder attempt. With a more complicated satanic conspiracy than usual and even a few genuinely clever touches (interpolated scenes of Warner picking up a barmaid are not the character-underlining padding they at first seem to be, but actually set up a mildly neat twist), this stands out among Findlay's dull credits.

d/c Roberta Findlay *p* Walter E. Sear *s* Ed Kelleher, Harriette Vidal *se* Ed French *lp* Christine Moore, Gary Warner, Marina Taylor, Carissa Channing, Tom Billett

Maniac Cop (SHAPIRO-GLICKENHAUS) 85min
A killer dressed as a policeman plagues New York, but only burned-out lieutenant Atkins believes that the murderer might be a real cop. The case gets complicated when it turns out that the maniac (Z'Dar) is unkillable, a *Dirty Harry* (1971) crusader supposedly murdered in prison after he was indicted by the expedient-seeking police commissioner. During the St Patrick's Day parade, patrolman Campbell, on the run for the murders he didn't commit, finally confronts the hulking psychopath.

Directed by Lustig, whose earlier credits include such reactionary films as **Maniac** (1980) and *Vigilante* (1982), and financed by James Glickenhaus, author of the unredeemable *The Exterminator* (1980), this isn't free of formula, but Cohen, the most intriguing if variable creator in low-budget exploitation, imposes many of his trade-marks, including the weird police background of **The Winged Serpent** (1982) and *God Told Me To* (1978). The basic Halloween-style plot is complicated by the unusual setting (almost everyone in the film is a cop) and Cohen works in almost subliminal bits about the attitudes of (and to) the police. The opening is especially effective: a victim escapes from a gang of muggers and sighs with relief as the reassuring silhouette of a uniformed patrolman looms into view, only to have the authority-security figure throttle her. The killer is more impressive when glimpsed as a shadowy shape in police blues than when his not-too-scarred face is actually seen. Equally fine is the bizarre performance from former starlet North as the psycho's crippled girlfriend. Less succesful are the car chases and slugfests.

d William Lustig *p/s* Larry Cohen *c* Vincent J. Rabe
se Hollywood Special Effects *lp* Tom Atkins, Bruce Campbell, Robert Z'Dar, Laurene Landon, Richard Roundtree, Sheree North, William Smith

Monkey Shines *aka* **An Experiment in Fear** *aka* **Ella**
(ORION) 115min
Run down while road-training, athletic Allan Mann (Beghe) winds up an embittered paraplegic, tormented by an unsympathetic nurse (Forrest), smothered by his fussy mother (Van Patten) and a literally impotent witness as his girl goes off with the doctor who failed to save his limbs. His friend Pankow, a pasty-faced researcher with a drug habit, is raising the intelligence of capuchin monkeys through injections of pureed human brain; he donates Ella, his prize pupil, to a trainer (McNeil), who teaches the animal to be a nursemaid-companion to Beghe. Monkey and man develop an unnaturally close, perhaps even telepathic, relationship, and Ella picks up Beghe's unrepressed resentments and hatreds, eventually scuttling out to kill.

Like Cronenberg, Romero has fiercely cherished his independence; this, his first major-studio project, suffered from a little tampering (a regulation last-minute gratuitous shock was added to the otherwise subtly effective ending), but for the most part his style transfers seamlessly to the mainstream. Beghe is marvellous in an obviously restricted role, signalling his mind-link with the jungle creature by talking and spitting like Marlon Brando, and Ella the monkey is made to demonstrate an astonishing variety of response. The film is tighter than most of Romero's scattershot horrors, and his personality shows through in a gradual build-up of unbearable tension and profane, pithy dialogue. Particularly effective is the sustained suspense finale as Ella fumbles with hypodermic needles near the heroine's eyes, the drug-addled scientist is torn between saving his friend and his reputation, and the chairbound hero has to defend himself with only his head.

d/s George A. Romero *p* Charles Evans *c* James A. Contner
lp Jason Beghe, John Pankow, Melanie Parker, Joyce Van Patten, Christine Forrest, Stephen Root, Stanley Tucci, Janine Turner, William Newman

My Best Friend is a Vampire *aka* **I Was a Teenage Vampire** (KINGS ROAD ENTERTAINMENT) 90min
A high-school comedy monster movie in the tradition of **Teen Wolf** (1985) and **Once Bitten** (1985). Jerk Leonard is turned into a vampire by a seductress and is instructed in the ways of the undead by 200-year-old Auberjonois while intolerant

Warner seeks to destroy him. Better acted than usual for the sub-genre, with Pollak a strong teen queen, this still relies on too many second- or third-hand vampire jokes.

d Jimmy Huston *p* Dennis Murphy *s* Tab Murphy *c* James Bartle *se* Christy Belt *lp* Robert Sean Leonard, Cheryl Pollak, Rene Auberjonois, David Warner, Lee Anne Locken, Paul Willson

Necromancer
(BONNAIRE FILMS/SPECTRUM ENTERTAINMENT) 88min
Violated by a dope-dealing stud, prim drama student Kaitan consults a gypsy sorceress who has put a revenge-for-hire ad in the local paper. A demon manifests itself as her provocative doppelganger (also Kaitan), coming on to the rapist and his associates and turning into a cheapskate special effect to destroy them. Combining the revenge-for-rape drama of **I Spit On Your Grave** (1978) and *Sudden Impact* (1983) and the teenage-morality Faustian-pact subgenre of **Trick or Treat** (1986) and **976-EVIL** (1988), this is less interesting than Nelson's début feature **Effects** (1979). Kaitan (sometimes billed as Caytan) is poorly cast as a drama student – her wooden performance gets even worse when she does a scene from *The Taming of the Shrew* – leaving Tamblyn to steal the film as a boyishly lecherous professor who also falls victim to the succubus.

d Dusty Nelson *p* Roy McAree *s* Bill Naud *c* Richard Clabaugh, Eric Cayla *se* William J. Males & Associates *lp* Elizabeth Kaitan, Russ Tamblyn, Rhonda Durton, Stan Hurwitz, Edward Wright, Shawn Eisner, Lois Masten

Nekromantik (JELINSKI; WG) 73min
Described by its director as 'corpse-fucking Art', this minimally budgeted oddment deals with an eternal triangle between a mortuary driver (Lorenz), his twisted girlfriend (M) and a corpse. After an idyll in which the living couple experience 'the intense sensation of a necrophile sexual fulfilment', the situation inevitably begins to decay.

Horrific effects include the real killing and skinning of a rabbit (later reversed to symbolize 'that what has been destroyed is now restored'), a Romero-esque decapitation with the head severed above the lower lip rather than the more usual neck, clips from a sado-porn snuff movie, an eyeball licked out of its socket, much fondling of internal organs, the murder of a cat, the hero coming blood through a fake penis as he disembowels himself, and a droning synthesizer score. Unremittingly sleazy and downbeat, with an obsessional interest in bodily functions, fluids and decay, this is distinctive but ultimately not very interesting. As solemn and repetitive as the average German Schulmadchen-report sex film, it manages through its distance to be as an-horrific as they are an-erotic.

d/co-s/co-se Jorg Buttgereit *p* Manfred Jelinski *co-s/co-se* Franz Rodenkirchen *c* Uwe Bohrer *co-se* Daktari Lorenz *lp* Daktari Lorenz, Beatrice M, Harald Lundt, Susa Kohlstedt, Heike Surban

Night of the Demons *aka* **Halloween Party**
(MERIDIAN/PARAGON) 89min
Stereotypical movie teens attend a Halloween party thrown by gothic punkette Kinkade in a haunted house and mostly get turned into hideous demons.

Amid familiar fraternity slob comedy, softcore groping and teen-slaughtering, the script sometimes tries for character quirks the cast aren't up to. A nasty coda features the local Halloween-hater snacking on a pie made with his own razor-blade filled apples. Quigley, the most prolific starlet in eighties exploitation, is miscast as a giggling tease, introduced with a close-up of her pink-frilled bottom.

d Kevin S. Tenney *p/s* Joe Augustyn *c* David Lewis *se* Steve Johnson *lp* Lance Fenton, Cathy Podewell, Alvin Alexis, Hal Havins, Mimi Kinkade, Linnea Quigley, Philip Tanzini, Phillip Terashita, Allison Barron

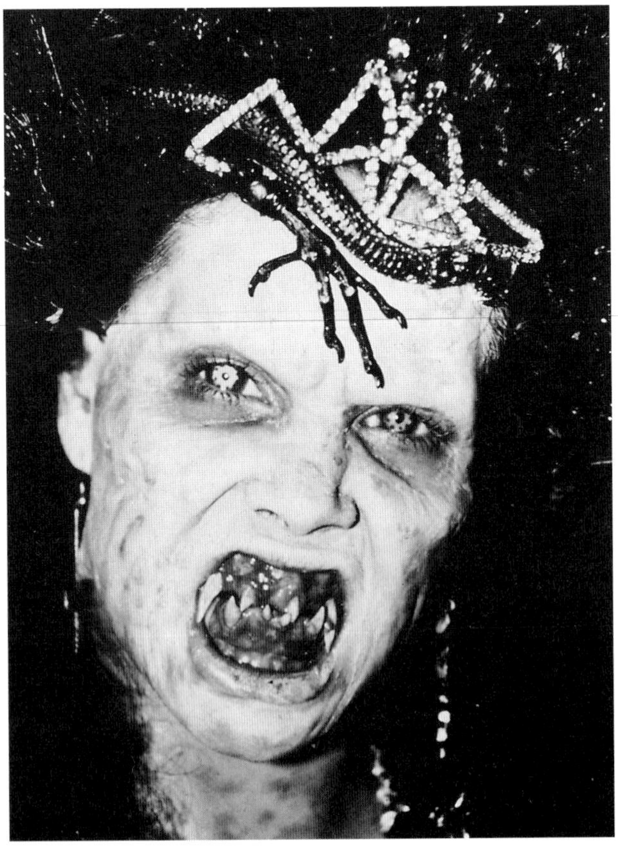

The punk as monster in Night of the Demons.

976-EVIL *aka* **HorrorScope** (NEW LINE) 93(100)min
Englund's directorial début is a lacklustre teenage *Faust*, similar to actor-turned-director Charlie Martin Smith's treatment of Topham's **Trick or Treat** (1986).

Put-upon Geoffreys stumbles on a telephone horoscope service that operates out of Hell, and falls under its influence as he gets back at the bullies who have made him miserable. Nothing much happens for the first half, outside a rain of fish that spooks Geoffreys' religious fanatic mother (Dennis), then a series of ordinary horror sequences trot out as the nerd turns into an oatmeal-faced demon, with Freddy-style wisecracks spicing gore murders and spider attacks. After butchering a couple of tormentors, Geoffreys crashes a poker party with 'Can I get into the game with a pair of hearts?' as he throws the organs on the table. It winds up in tolerably spectacular fashion with a gaping pit under the house revealing a frozen-over Hell.

Jim Wynorski's *976-EVIL II* (1991) purloins the plot of *Psychic Killer* (1974) and is undistinguished save for a scene in which a character is sucked into a TV set and channel-hops between *It's a Wonderful Life* (1947) and **Night of the Living Dead** (1968).

d Robert Englund *p* Lisa M. Hansen *s* Rhet Topham, Brian Helgeland *c* Paul Elliot *se* Kevin Yagher *lp* Stephen Geoffreys, Jim Metzler, Maria Rubell, Lezlie Deane, J.J. Cohen, Sandy Dennis, Pat O'Bryan, Robert Picardo

A Nightmare on Elm Street IV: The Dream Master (NEW LINE/HERON/SMART EGG) 93min
This was the film that saw Englund, billed sixth in **A Nightmare on Elm Street** (1984), win above-the-title billing. On the back of that Englund got himself the directorship of **976-Evil** (1988), the title role in the fifth remake of **The Phantom of the Opera** (1989) and the role, in the character of Freddy Kruger, of host of a particularly awful television horror show, *Freddy's Nightmares*. Concomitant with this entry into mainstream merchandising was the loss of the character's *Struwwelpeter* element. In its place came the wisecrackery of the Batman television series.

Finnish director Harlin handles the action sequences with the verve that later suited him well in such actioneers as *Die Hard II* (1990) and *Cliffhanger* (1993), but for the most part is constrained by a plot that is constructed to string together the setpiece special effects. Wilcox is the new girl on the block – all the children of the parents who killed Freddy now being dead – who functions as both the gateway through which Freddy enters reality and, as the film has it, 'the dream master' through which he can be repulsed. The net result is seemingly unending special effects in which characters we care little about meet a variety of would-be pertinent fates.

d Renny Harlin *p* Robert Shaye, Rachel Talalay *s* Brian Helgeland, Scott Pierce *c* Steven Fierberg *se* Dream Quest Images, Screaming Mad George *lp* Robert Englund, Lisa Wilcox, Rodney Eastman, Danny Hassel, Andras Jones, Tuesday Knight, Toy Newkirk, Ken Sagoes

Nosferatu a Venezia *aka* **Vampire in Venice**
(SCENA FILM/RETEITALIA; IT) 96min
This attractively photographed, impressively scored follow-up to **Nosferatu, Phantom der Nacht** (1979) is even statelier than the original.

Kinski's Nosferatu, fond of platitudes like 'There is no meaning in a life that never ends', has long white hair this time but keeps his rat teeth. Revived by a seance after 200 years in a Venetian tomb, he floats about the city, preying on aristocratic misses and flamenco dancers, and searching for the lookalike descendant (De Rossi) of a woman he once contaminated. In the Van Helsing role is Paris Catalano (Plummer), a student of vampirism. Slow and solemn as a Venetian funeral, this inevitably winds up with the neurotic Catalano losing and Nosferatu getting the girl.

d/p/s Augusto Caminito *c* Tonino Nardi *se* Franco Corridoni, Sergio Angeloni, Luigi Rocchetti *lp* Klaus Kinski, Barbara De Rossi, Yorgo Voyagis, Donald Pleasence, Christopher Plummer, Anne Knecht

Off-Balance *aka* **Un Delitto Poco Commune** *aka* **Phantom of Death** (GLOBE FILMS/TANDEM CINEMATOGRAFICA/ RETEITALIA/DMV DISTRIBUZIONE; IT) 95min
Youthful pianist York, struck by a disease which causes rapid aging, attempts a sincerely agonized performance under a rubbery Mr Hyde make-up job, but genre necessities require a series of bloody slasher murders. Pleasence, in a plodding copper role, is tormented by mocking phone calls after each woman has been cut up, but an illogical finale has the pathetic monster whimpering that he was only trying to force Pleasence to end his torment, moaning 'They say that death is God's cruelest joke, but not for me'.

d Ruggero Deodato *p* Pietro Innocenzi *s* Gianfranco Clerici, Vincenzo Mannino, Gigliola Battaglini *c* Giorgio Di Battista *se* Fabrizio Sforza *lp* Michael York, Donald Pleasence, Edwige Fenech, Mabi Galan, Caterina Boratto

Opera (CECCI GORI/GRUPPO TIGER CINEMATOGRAFICA; IT) scope 90min
A hooded maniac terrorizes an avant-garde production of Verdi's *Macbeth*, arranging for an accident to put the diva out of commission so the understudy (Marsillach) can play Lady Macbeth, then tying up Marsillach with needles taped to her eyelids to force her to watch as he slaughters various victims.

Flamboyant movie director Charleson, a self-portrait by Argento, stages the opera with plentiful trickery and fluttering ravens. In one sequence he tries to expose the killer by releasing into the audience a horde of vindictive birds who will recognise the murderer, whereupon a specially designed camera swoops around the huge auditorium in widescreen and the birds peck out the culprit's eye. Accordingly, though the film features one of the director's most infantile plots, it is nevertheless one of his most eye-opening, as well as eyeball-gouging, movies. The murders are astonishing set-pieces of designer violence (especially the slow-motion death of Nicolodi, shot through the head through a peephole in a door) and the camera continually prowls through the labyrinthine opera-house or luxury-apartment settings while Heavy Metal replaces opera on the soundtrack as the blood flows. Less colourful than Argento's supernatural masterpieces and afflicted with very silly dialogue, this nevertheless demonstrates the director's continuing mastery of sheer style.

d/co-s Dario Argento *p* Mario and Vittorio Cecci Gori *co-s* Franco Ferrini *c* Ronnie Taylor *se* Sergio Stivaletti *lp* Cristina Marsillach, Urbano Barberini, Ian Charleson, Antonella Vitale, Daria Nicolodi, William McNamara

Out of the Body (PREMIERE/MEDUSA; AUST) 89min
A competent psycho movie with a paranormal twist. A discarnate entity murders career women and puts out their eyes, and composer hero Hembrow has premonitions of the killings, putting him high on the suspect list. It unfolds predictably with the women in the cast getting slaughtered and dodgy telekinetic effects. The villain turns out anticlimactically to be an evil orange light which fuses symbiotically with Hembrow, yanking him out of his body as an astral projection whenever it kills. Humphries shoots the glow, wherupon Hembrow's stomach explodes. Unpretentious and unmemorable.

d Brian Trenchard-Smith *p* David Hannay, Charles Hannay *s* Kenneth G. Ross *c* Kevan Lind *se* Deryck de Niese *lp* Mark Hembrow, Tessa Humphries, Carrie Zivetz, Linda Newton, John Clayton, Shane Briant

Out of the Dark (ZEL FILMS) 89min
A clown-masked psychopath picks off girls who work for 'Suite Nothings', Black's skid-row phone porn business.

A throwback to the early eighties heyday of post-**Friday the 13th** (1980) splatter movies, this is an only slightly sent-up pastiche of the sleazy likes of **Don't Answer the Phone** (1980), **He Knows You're Alone** (1980) or *Eyes of a Stranger* (1981). Just as contrived as its predecessors, it features an especially over-the-top performance by the unmasked killer in the finale. Directed briskly by Schroeder, a protegee of Paul Bartel's also responsible for the dire necrophile farce *Mortuary Academy* (1988), and with likeable cameos from skid-row luminaries, this is funny enough to paper over the cracks in the would-be straight melodrama.

d Michael Schroeder *p/co-s* Zane W. Levitt *co-s* J. Gregory DeFelice *c* Julio Macat *se* Kevin McCarthy *lp* Cameron Dye, Karen Black, Lynne Danielson, Karen Witter, Starr Andreeff, Bud Cort, Geoffrey Lewis, Paul Bartel, Divine, Tracey Walter, Tab Hunter, Lainie Kazan, Karen Mayo-Chandler, Angela Robinson

Pandemonium
(KFM/SMART STREET/TRA LA LA; AUST) 88min
Loosely inspired by *The Rocky Horror Picture Show* (1975), this is wearisome, would-be cult offering.

In a Bondi Beach film studio, asylum escapee Argue and a buxom girl raised by dingoes (Dole) venture into a sub-culture of ranting lesbian Nazis, crippled movie stars, vampires, drag queens, mad scientists and maniacs, including a Hitler clone with a Pinocchio nose (Grenville) and a witch named Morticia (Deane-Jones). Dole, clad only in a loincloth, turns out to be a messiah-gone-wrong who has been fathered and abandoned by a Holy Ghost (Foley) who has been kicked out of the Trinity and turned into an aborigine. Everyone desires the innocent but finally she is seduced, in calculated blasphemy, by Foley, and the world is ambiguously redeemed.

d/co-p/co-s Haydn Keenan *co-p* Alex Cutler *co-s* Peter Gailey *c* David Sanderson *se* Monte Fieguth *lp* David Argue, Amanda Dole, Esben Storm, Rainee Skinner, Kery Mack, Ashley Grenville, Mercia Deane-Jones, Haydn Keenan

1988

Paperhouse (VESTRON; GB) 92min

A vaguely unhappy eleven-year-old (Burke) is confined against her will to bed; she passes the time by making a drawing of a house, and in her dreams finds herself in the weird landscape she has created. However, she's not a very talented artist and the things and people she draws don't come out right: when she draws her often-absent father (Cross), she makes him look angry and he becomes a threat.

Based on Catherine Starr's children's book *Marianna Dreams*, *Paperhouse*, ostensibly a children's film (though it was awarded a British '15' sequence for its intensity) is a more potent nightmare than such contemporaries as **Dream Demon** (1988) or **Hellbound: Hellraiser II** (1988). Burke is initially infuriating and feckless, but grows into a heroine of real maturity without suffering many blatant rites-of-passage. First-time director Rose does a startlingly good job of capping the psychologically astute twinning of father and monster in his presentation of Cross as a shadow-faced maniac, paying off with a shocking hammer attack. The film cannily peaks as horror half an hour from the end, switching into a suspenseful, melancholy mode that makes for a powerful, unashamedly emotional clifftop finale. It makes especially effective use of Gemma Jackson's dream designs, with objects like furniture or a bicycle built as the three-dimensional equivalent of Anna's fumbled drawings.

d Bernard Rose *p* Tim Bevan, Sarah Radcliffe *s* Matthew Jacobs *c* Mike Southon *se* Ace Effects *lp* Charlotte Burke, Ben Cross, Glenne Headly, Elliott Spiers, Gemma Jones

Parents (VESTRON) 82min

While mainstream horrors (**The Lost Boys**, 1987, **Fatal Attraction**, 1987, **Child's Play**, 1988) were affirming old values, this fits in with a more interesting strain (**The Stepfather**, 1986, **White of the Eye**, 1986, **The 'burbs**, 1988, **Society**, 1989) which exposes Reagan-Bush era virtues of middle-class family life as the root of all evil. In the manner of *Father Knows Best* and *Leave It to Beaver*, *Parents* recreates a fifties suburbia of tract homes, kidney-shaped coffee tables and canasta and then asks 'what's wrong with this picture of domestic bliss?'.

Young Madorsky begins to suspect there's something strange about his perfect parents: Dad (Quaid) develops defoliants for the Toxico company, while Mom (Hurt) slaves over the cooker. Madorsky is increasingly uncertain as to the ingredients of Mom's meat dishes: 'We've been having leftovers every day since we came here, I'd like to know what they were before they were leftovers.' Rarely has food looked so disgusting: burned hunks of dead flesh are pushed around on the barbeque, groaning platters of congealed nastiness are presented, livers are slit open in close-up, and one image (red-nailed female fingers pushing chunks of meat into the mincer) recalls nothing so much as the 'poundcake' inserts of hardcore porn.

Until the finale, which unnervingly turns into a bloodily straight stab session, the film plays ambiguously. A bizarre nostalgic fable with a darkly gruesome centre, decked out with period kitsch furniture and outfits, the film forsakes the foggy menace of straight horror for a hard, illuminated postcard look. The soundtrack brims with hits like Sheb Woolley's *The Flying Purple People Eater*, The Big Bopper's *Chantilly Lace* and Dean Martin's *Memories Are Made of This*, while Hurt and Quaid sport matched simpers that stand as the *Happy Days* equivalent of the American Gothic stare.

d Bob Balaban *p* Bonnie Palef-Woolf *s* Christopher Hawthorne *c* Robin Vidgeon *se* Gord Smith *lp* Randy Quaid, Mary Beth Hurt, Bryan Madorsky, Sandy Dennis, Juno Mills-Cockell, Kathryn Grody, Deborah Rush, Graham Jarvis

Phantom of the Ritz (HANCOCK PARK) 84min

Like *The Meateater* (1979), *Movie House Massacre* (1984) and **Popcorn** (1991), this sets the plot of *Phantom of the Opera* in an old cinema. Disfigured in a fifties drag race, the hulking and well-spoken phantom (Sussman) narrates and murders various people while amiable entrepreneur Bergman tries to make a success of the Ritz, which has re-opened as a fifties retro rock emporium. Surprisingly more concerned with likable eccentrics running a theatre than the monstrosity, this is notable as the only horror film appearance of The Coasters, who perform 'Yakity Yak' between killings.

The central image of the imaginative Paperhouse.

d Allen Plone *p* Carol Marcus Plone *s* Tom Dempsey *c* Ronald W. McLeish *se* Dean Gates *lp* Peter Bergman, Deborah Van Valkenburgh, Russel Curry, Joshua Sussman, B.J. McQueen, Cindy Vincino, Billy Gillespie, Steve Geng

Pin... (NEW WORLD/DAVID-MALO; CAN) 102min

This is a psychodrama in the Robert Bloch tradition. The disturbed son (Hewlett) of a wealthy doctor (O'Quinn) projects his voice and split personality into Pin (short for Pinocchio), his father's transparent teaching dummy. When their parents are killed in a car crash, Hewlett and his sister (Preston) are left to their own devices and his obsession intensifies, leading him to use Pin to murder the aunt who tries to take over their lives and attempt to kill Preston's sincere boyfriend when he feels they are conspiring to have him hospitalized. The final twist, when, after Preston has smashed the dummy, Hewlett takes on Pin's personality and sits immobile in a chair, is directly in the tradition of **The Psychopath** (1965) and **Dead of Night** (1945).

As in **The Stepfather** (1986), O'Quinn is effective as a subtly disturbed parent. Leisurely, with few contrived 'scare' sequences, this benefits from more complex than usual characterizations.

d/s Sandor Stern *p* René Malo *c* Guy Dufaux *lp* David Hewlett, Cyndy Preston, John Ferguson, Bronwen Mantel, Helene Udy, Patricia Collins, Terry O'Quinn

Poltergeist III (MGM) 98min

This represents further disappointment from Sherman, who has yet to live up to the promise of his first feature, **Death Line** (1972).

Following **Poltergeist II: The Other Side** (1986), O'Rourke is living in a Chicago high-rise with her Aunt (Allen) and Uncle (Skerritt). Kane (Davis), the evil dead preacher of the first sequel, is still after the little girl, and the irksome medium (Rubinstein) is on hand to drop ominous hints. Davis causes ice to spread throughout the building, and has a sideline in dropping child psychologists down elevator-shafts and sucking people into a limbo under a puddle in the carpark. Skerritt and Allen wrestle with a silly finale in which they have to reclaim O'Rourke from the beyond by re-affirming TV-movie style love for the girl. Monsters take a back seat, with most of the effects budget expended dully on sudden arctic freezes and repetitive, if ingenious, mirror conjuring tricks.

d/co-s Gary Sherman *p* Barry Bernardi *co-s* Brian Taggert *c* Alex Nepomniaschy *se* Cal Acord *lp* Heather O'Rourke, Zelda Rubinstein, Nancy Allen, Tom Skerritt, Lara Flynn Boyle, Kip Wentz, Richard Fire, Nathan Davis

Les Predateurs de la Nuit *aka* **Faceless**
(ATC 3000/FILMS DE LA ROCHELLE; FR) 98min
Like Franco's first major horror outing, **Gritos en la Noche** (1962), this is a blatant imitation of **Les Yeux Sans Visage** (1959).

Genius Berger supervises the kidnapping and surgical flaying of young girls to restore the beauty of his scarred sister (Jean). Franco wittily has Berger consult Dr Orloff (Vernon), the villain of *Gritos en la Noche* and subsequent movies, for advice on how to conduct evil experiments, then refers the case to a Nazi played by the iconic Diffring, whose icily crazed plastic surgeon is a reference to his role in **Circus of Horrors** (1959). The latest victim is cocaine-sniffing model Munro, whose father (Savalas) hires private eye and Vietnam veteran Mitchum to track the girl down. Mitchum's sleuthing consists of loitering in a Paris nightspot where Franco indulges a fondness for repetitive disco footage by having extras jive to an endlessly reprised song called *Frenchmen's Hearts Come Out at Night* and, in a distasteful would-be comic sequence, roughing up a fey homosexual, while Munro is raped by Berger's moronic handyman and makes feeble escape attempts.

In more oddly apt casting, porn star Lahaie takes the Alida Valli role of the mad scientist's perverse assistant, whose misdeeds include spearing Audran in the eye with a hypodermic needle.

d Jesus Franco *p* René Chateau *s* Fred Castle, Michel Lebrun, Jean Mazarin, Pierre Ripert *c* Maurice Fellous *se* Jacques Gastineau *lp* Helmut Berger, Brigitte Lahaie, Chris Mitchum, Telly Savalas, Anton Diffring, Caroline Munro, Christiane Jean, Howard Vernon, Stéphane Audran

Pulse (COL/ASPEN FILM SOCIETY) 87min
Similar in theme to Fritz Leiber's story *The Man Who Made Friends With Electricity*, this has a child (Lawrence) spending the summer against his wishes with his divorced father (De Young) and stepmother (Hart). Obsessed with a bizarre accident that killed everyone in the house next door, he becomes convinced that the electrical supply has come to malevolent life and murdered the family, and plans to do the same in his house.

With such a silly premise, which harks back to silent trick films like *Liquid Electricity* (1907), the film takes care to build slowly and not to be too sensationalist, establishing the tensions within the unsteady central family so that the boy's outrageous stories seem to be just another symptom of his maladjustment, before all the electrical devices in the house come to life. The finale, in which fanbelts spit deadly screws and wires spark near puddles of spilled water, is an effective mini-holocaust, finely orchestrated by Golding, without too many revolt-of-the-machine clichés. Unusually well acted and produced for a mid-rank horror film, this is an impressive minor entry in its subgenre, and makes very effectively subversive use of the imagery of humming wires and animated circuit boards familiar from cosily high-tech advertisements for the products and services here presented as monstrous menaces.

d/s Paul Golding *p* Patricia A. Stallone *c* Peter Lyons Collister *se* Richard O. Helmer *lp* Cliff De Young, Roxanne Hart, Matthew Lawrence, Charles Tyner, Dennis Redfield, Michael Rider

Pumpkinhead *aka* **Vengeance: The Demon**
(LION FILMS) 86min
Make-up effects supremo Winston's directorial début boasts an impressive monster along the lines of the creatures he created for *Aliens* (1986).

When careless city kids run down a child in the backwoods, the victim's father (Henriksen) consults a wizened witch woman who summons up a demon who sets out to kill off the road-hogs in standard body-count fashion until the grief-stricken Henriksen tries to stop it. The rural setting is hand-me-down from *The Waltons*, complete with harmonica score and dirty-faced children, and the victims are as undercharacterized a group of teens as assembled for any **Friday the 13th** (1980) sequel. Despite the startling demon, the horror sequences are boringly standardized, with claws reaching into the frame and bodies tossed about like sandbags. As demonstrated by **Who Fears the Devil?** (1972), adapted from the distinctive stories of Manly Wade Wellman, the folklore of the American backwoods is a rich source for horror; this disappointingly neglects that potential in favour of an ordinary monster-on-the-rampage story.

d Stan Winston *p* Richard C. Weinman, Howard Smith *s* Mark Patrick Carducci, Gary Gerani *c* Bojan Bazelli *se* Alec Gillis *lp* Lance Henriksen, Jeff East, John DiAquino, Kimberly Ross, Joel Hoffman, Cynthia Bain, Kerry Remsen

Quando Alice Ruppe lo Specchio *aka* **Touch of Death** (ALPHA CINEMATOGRAFICA; IT) 91min
Five years after his 1979-82 flurry of activity as a splatter auteur, Fulci returned to the genre with rapid, nasty gore movies (**I Fantasmi di Sodoma**, 1988, *Demonia*, 1988, **Voci dal Profondo**, 1990) lacking even the widescreen style and gothic fervour of his best-known films, albeit with an attempt to replace professional gloss with self-importance that climaxes in the mock autobiography of **Un Gatto nel Cervello** (1990). An almost plotless item – Halsey preys on rich widows, selecting women with mild deformities and slaughtering them in a frenzy of graphic but unconvincing effects – *Quando Alice Ruppe lo Specchio* is Fulci's reworking of *Monsieur Verdoux* (1947), playing chainsaw-dismemberments and microwave-melting for laughs with Mickey Mouse music and an absurdly precise performance from Halsey. In the film's single interesting scene, the killer spends five minutes propping up a corpse in the passenger seat of a car only to be stopped and given a speeding ticket by a cop who blithely ignores the body.

d/s Lucio Fulci *p* Luigi Nannerini, Antonino Lucidi *c* Silvano Tessicini *se* Angelo Mattei *lp* Brett Halsey, Ria De Simone, Pier Luigi Conti, Sasha Darwin, Zora Ulla Kesler, Marco Di Stefano

Ragno Gelido *aka* **Minaccia D'Amore** *aka* **Dial: Help**
(IMPACT FILM GROUP; IT) 95min
Continuing Deodato's drift towards the cosmopolitan mainstream, demonstrated by the ordinary **Camping nel Terrore** (1986) and **Off-Balance** (1988), this finds the uncompromising brutalist of **Cannibal Holocaust** (1979) and *La Casa Sperduta nel Parco* (1981) concocting a routine variant on **The Entity** (1982). Lewis is tormented by a lovestruck spirit who lurks in the Italian telephone system and uses it to get close to her. Deodato manages to get more from the menace of the phone than *Bells* (1980), with a mysterious whine killing Lewis' tankful of tropical fish or exploding occultist guest star Berger's heart pacemaker, spare change spurting out of the chute to kill a mugger, and tentacle-like cables striking, but the film does little but juxtapose silly horror with a selection of would-be stylish décors, *objets d'art*, clothes and people.

d/co-s Ruggero Deodato *p* Galiano Juso, Giovanni Bertolucci *co-s* Joseph and Mary Caravani *c* Renato Tafuri *se* Germano Natali *lp* Charlotte Lewis, Marcello Modugno, Mattia Sbragia, Victor Cavallo, Carola Stagnaro, Carlo Monni

1988

Rampage (DEG) 90min
An early 'serious' entry in the serial-killer cycle, concentrating on the legal and ethical issues raised by the trial of a handsome young man (McArthur) who has casually murdered several families, executing them with clean shots and drinking their blood.

Lawyer Biehn, who has always stood against the death penalty, is assigned the prosecution and gradually becomes convinced, especially after a bloody escape attempt, that the accused should not be kept alive. Having recently allowed his terminally ill daughter to die, Biehn feels McArthur's interests would similarly be served by mercy killing. After a grimly convincing outset, with understated but effective atrocities, the film gets hung up on talk, with an unnecessary soap-opera subplot about the break-up of Biehn's marriage intruding, and a shuffle of last-reel twists (the suggestion that McArthur's psychosis may be due to brain damage) never quite resolving the debate. Friedkin returned in 1991 to re-edit and reconstruct a new version which prunes much of Biehn's family life but also streamlines the argument into a less thought-provoking, more on-the-line indictment of the treatment of mass murderers, replacing McArthur's apparent suicide in prison with a caption, similar to the conclusion of *Helter Skelter* (1976), that declares the murderer still lives and will soon be eligible for parole.

d/s William Friedkin *p* David Salven *c* Robert D. Yeoman *lp* Michael Biehn, Alex McArthur, Nicholas Campbell, Deborah Van Valkenburgh, John Harkins, Art LaFleur, Grace Zabriskie, Roy London, Billy Green Bush

Raptors *aka* **Killing Birds**
(FILMIRAGE/FLORA FILM; IT) 90min
Shot in Louisiana, this is identikit Italian horror, with elements from Dario Argento, Lucio Fulci, Mario Bava and others stirred into the usual cocktail of second-hand American elements, from Hitchcock to Sam Raimi.

A group of youths venture out to an isolated house and, after half an hour of pointless but picturesque wandering, succumb to gory fates. Encounters with persistent Fulci-style zombies and Argento-ish necklace-in-the-lathe freak accidents account for most of the cast, but the sinister birds of the title flock ominously throughout and finally dispose, offscreen, of blind Vaughn, the film's name player.

d Claudio Lattanzi *s* Daniele Stroppa *c* Fred Slonisckо Jr *se* Harry Harris III, Robert Gould *lp* Lara Wendel, Timothy W. Watt, Leslie Cummins, James Villemaire, Sal Maggiore Jr, James Sutterfield, Lin Gathright, Robert Vaughn

Scarecrows (EFFIGY FILMS; AUST) 80min
Fleeing in a hijacked plane, a group of robbers fall out when one of their number grabs the stolen money and parachutes from the plane, leaving behind a grenade that just fails to destroy his comrades. They land and hunt him down, but find him a walking corpse, hollowed out and stuffed with high-denomination bills, who has to be dismembered to be killed. The group are attacked by three hideous scarecrows who seem to be all that's left of a backwoods family, and are gradually torn apart as pressures drive one mad, force another into uncharacteristic altruism, and so on. With no explanation of its fantasy content beyond a madman's musing that maybe they were all killed during the robbery and are being punished in Hell, the film is free to be suggestively bizarre in its gory horrors, as when a scarecrow replaces his missing hand with one sawn off a victim.

d/co-p/co-s William Wesley *p* Cami Winikoff *co-s* Richard Jefferies *c* Peter Deming *se* Norman Cabrera *lp* Ted Vernon, Victoria Christian, Richard Vidan, B.J. Turner, David Campbell, Michael Simms, Kristina Sanborn

The Seventh Sign (TRI-STAR) pv 97min
Opening with the suggestion that God and Ronald Reagan have the same foreign policy as the first signs of the Apocalypse involve smiting Haiti, the PLO and the Sandinistas, this fails to live up to the spectacular possibilities of the material. After a Palestinian hideout on the site of the Biblical Sodom is frozen into a striking ice palace, the film refuses to deliver further manifestations of equal weight. Impending doom is conveyed mainly by gloomy conversations in ill-lit rooms as Moore prepares to give birth to a soulless baby who will signal the End of All Things. Despite its immortal priestly villain and ambiguous Christ, the film embodies a return to the reactionary fundamentalism of the Devil Movie cycle inaugurated by **The Exorcist** (1973). Aside from God's apparent political sympathies, the film comes out against sex, incest, religious unorthodoxy and any kind of moral complexity. The heroine's baby, unlike Rosemary's, is a holy innocent who restores Jesus' faith in humanity.

d Carl Schultz *p* Ted Field, Robert W. Court *s* Roger Thornhill, W.W. Wicket (Clifford and Ellen Greene) *c* Juan Ruiz Anchia *se* Dream Quest Images *lp* Demi Moore, Michael Biehn, Jurgen Prochnow, Manny Jacobs, Frederic Forrest

Sister Sister (NEW WORLD/ODYSSEY) scope 91min
Directed by the co-writer of **Dead Kids** (1981) and *Strange Invaders* (1983), this effective Southern gothic tale has heroines named after the protagonists of **Strait-Jacket** (1964) and **Hush... Hush, Sweet Charlotte** (1965). In a swamplands hotel, disturbed and repressed Lucy (Leigh) suffers from hallucinations while her supposedly normal elder sister Charlotte (Ivey) looks after her. The arrival of handsome Stoltz during a thunderstorm triggers tensions and revives memories of the incident which warped the girls' psyches. Confident in its stormy melodramatics, with excellent and complementary lead female performances, this is an intriguing effort.

d/co-s Bill Condon *p* Walter Coblenz *co-s* Joel Cohen, Ginny Cerrella *c* Stephen M. Katz *se* Wayne Beauchamp, Paul Hickerson *lp* Eric Stoltz, Jennifer Jason Leigh, Judith Ivey, Dennis Lipscomb, Anne Pitoniak, Benjamin Mouton, Natalia Nogulich

Slaughterhouse
(AMERICAN ARTISTS/SLAUGHTERHOUSE/MANSON) 85min
'Jesus Christ Boy, you can't just slaughter people because they're messing with your hogs,' muses slaughterhouse proprietor Barrett when he finds his son (Barton) has killed and hung up a couple of teenagers, 'Still, you made a clean cut of it.' Another take on the familiar material of **The Texas Chainsaw Massacre** (1974), this has Barrett trying to discourage Barton's teen-killing and direct his murderousness towards the meat marketers who have been putting him out of business.

d/s Rick Roessler *p* Ron Matonak *c* Richard J. Benda *se* Robert Roscoe, Barney Burman, Mark Lane *lp* Sherry Bendorf, Don Barrett, William Houck, Joe Barton, Jane Higginson

Demi Moore pensive as the mother-to-be worried about what she's pregnant with in The Seventh Sign.

Spoorloos *aka* **The Vanishing**
(GOLDEN EGG FILM/INGRID PRODUCTIONS; FR, NETH) 106min
Though it has precedents in Robert Fuest's *And Soon the Darkness* (1970) and Richard Matheson's telefilm *Dying Room Only* (1973), this adaptation of Krabbé's novel *The Golden Egg* is consistently bewildering and surprising, chillingly unsensationalist and expertly constructed. Bervoets and Ter Steege, a young Dutch couple, enter France for a holiday; at a busy service station, Ter Steege goes off to get drinks and fails to return. Three years later, after Bervoets has become obsessive about the mystery, he is approached by Donnadieu, a Frenchman who claims to be the kidnapper.

The film gradually gets to the chilling heart of the matter, revealing not only Ter Steege's fate but the deceptively ordinary world of the monstrous sociopath. Donnadieu's extraordinarily subtle kidnapper emerges as one of the most memorable screen psychos, forever standing aside to admire his own handiwork but capable of almost endearing lapses like unthinkingly blowing his nose on a handkerchief he has just soaked with chloroform. He also displays a chilling callousness as he makes a move to grab his youngest daughter's nose when she sits next to him in the car, using fatherly horseplay to rehearse the doping of his victim. With a middle-class French lifestyle worthy of Simenon, Donnadieu is a genuinely frightening creation, and his final triumph over the rugged but obsessional Bervoets is an especially striking, understated moment of film horror. The film was pointlessly remade by Sluizer himself as **The Vanishing** (1992), one of the clutch of American remakes of European films in the nineties.

d/co-p George Sluizer *co-p* Anne Lordan *s* Tim Krabbé *c* Toni Kuhn *lp* Bernard-Pierre Donnadieu, Gene Bervoets, Johanna Ter Steege, Gwen Eckhaus, Bernadette Le Saché

The Stick
(DISTANT HORIZON/ARTISTIC FILM; SOUTH AFRICA) 90min
Like *Southern Comfort* (1981) and **The Supernaturals** (1986), this is a war movie overlaid with horror. A 'stick', a South African infantry unit, is sent into the bush to track white-painted guerillas who seem to represent the threat of the ghostly rather than of communism. After troops have semi-accidentally murdered a couple of native children, Taylor semi-deliberately shoots dead a strangely detached witch doctor and the rest of the stick, ignored by a cracked lieutenant, butcher an entire village. The witch doctor's influence lingers and the stick turn against each other, tormented by visions.

Banned in South Africa and easy to read as a political allegory of the story of a group of mutually hostile whites who tear at each other while tribespeople wait patiently to be slaughtered or get on with their lives, the movie resembles the North American 'Indian Curse' cycle of death-in-the-wilderness movies represented by **Death Curse of Tartu** (1966) and *Shadow of Chikara* (1978). Though the acting is irritatingly overstated and the voice-over could almost be a parody of *Platoon* (1987), *The Stick* benefits from the unfamiliar political and geographical landscape of its particular war and the well-evoked atmosphere of irrational horror.

d/co-s Darrell Root *p* Anant Singh *co-s* Carole Shore *c* Paul Witte *lp* Sean Taylor, Greg Latter, Nicky Rebelo, James Whyle, Frank Opperman, Winston Ntshona

Tainted *aka* **Body Passion** (CARDINAL PICTURES) 90min
A murky psycho movie following the incredible tribulations of bubblehead teacher Shattuck, who is surprised masturbating by a rapist (Fowler) and then, during her molestation, by her insanely jealous husband (Tootle). After stabbing Fowler and attacking his wife, Tootle has a fatal heart attack, leaving Shattuck (warned by the principal not to get involved in any scandal) to dispose of the corpses. After flirting with **Repulsion** (1965) as Shattuck feebly tries to simulate growing insanity, the film produces another psychopath (Schaus) for the regulation menace-and-murder finale.

d/s/co-p Orestes Matacena *co-p* Phyllis Redden *c* Ramon Suarez *se* Spectacular Effects International *lp* Shari Shattuck, Park Overall, Gene Tootle, Magilla Schaus, Blaque Fowler

Telesm *aka* **The Spell**
(FARABI CINEMA FOUNDATION/
INSTITUTE OF CINEMATIC AFFAIRS; IRAN) 94min
This is a lush period gothic melodrama, apparently influenced by Roger Corman and Hammer. A couple who have been joined in an arranged marriage to unite warring tribes are driven by a storm and vicious wolves to seek shelter in a decaying palace whose master, maddened by the disappearance of his bride on their wedding day, lives among the cobwebbed splendour of his interrupted wedding feast.

A sinister servant who has been gradually poisoning the prince for many years, a mirrored room that offers access to a labyrinth of secret passageways, the lingering presence of the missing bride, a white-faced inhabitant of the labyrinth and a last-reel holocaust in which the palace is spectacularly destroyed all suggest the Western horror movie tradition, while the subversive, in Iranian terms, triumph of put-upon women (the heroine, forbidden by tradition to speak to her husband for a year after the marriage, enters the underworld and allies herself with the ghostly disappeared woman to bring down the palace on the heads of the neurotic menfolk) suggests a thread of political allegory among the colourful haunted house trappings.

d/s Dariush Farhang *p* Mostazafan Foundation *c* Ali-Reza Zarrindast *lp* Jamshid Mashayekhi, Susan Taslimi, Parviz Poorhosseini, Attila Pessyani, S. Rahmani

To Die For *aka* **Dracula: The Love Story**
(ARROWHEAD) 90min
This is a romantic vampire movie, with a long-haired Vlad Tsepish (Hughes) wooing the real-estate agent (Walsh) who has sold him a Californian castle, and fighting off a fellow monster (Bond) whose true love he killed a century earlier and who is out for revenge. The film is more influenced by the late-eighties style-conscious movie vampirism of **Fright Night** (1985), **Vamp** (1986) and **Graveyard Shift** (1987) than Bram Stoker. Hughes' handsome but bland bloodsucker lurks at fashionable parties listening to middle-of-the-road rock and making smarmy advances, his seductive approach being contrasted with Bond's brutality (by comparison, Bond claims that his method of murder is 'as quick as ripping off a band-aid'). It was followed by David F. Price's *Son of Darkness: To Die For II* (1991), with Michael Praed as Vlad, renamed Max Schreck.

d Deran Sarafian *p* Brian Kumar *s* Leslie King *c* David Boyd *se* John Carl Buechler, Eddie Surkin *lp* Brendan Hughes, Sydney Walsh, Amanda Wyss, Scott Jacoby, Micah Grant, Duane Jones, Steve Bond

Twice Dead (CONCORDE PICTURES) 85min
A superior variation on **Turnaround** (1986), with a Hollywood ghost-story twist. A downwardly mobile family move into the decaying mansion where a thirties actor (Chapin) committed suicide; the neighbourhood has declined too, and a gang of violent punks loiter outside, threatening to rape Whitlow and kill her brother (Breznahan), while the ghost protects the family. In a three-act structure, the film sets up its conflicts, then has the gang lured to the house by Breznahan (a drama major who has become obsessed with Chapin's famous trickery) and terrorized by bogus horror stunts, with a second go-round as the gang return to exact bloody revenge only to have the ghost dispose of them through genuine supernatural intervention. The contrast between jokey mock horrors (an Alien-style rubber phallus exploding from a thug's crotch) and real deaths (a couple fried during sex by a faulty electric blanket) is effective, allowing the film to pull off a smooth mood switch between light and sombre.

d/co-s Bert Dragin *co-p/co-s* Robert McDonnell *co-p* Guy J. Louthan *c* Zoran Hochstatter *se* Michael Burnett *lp* Tom Breznahan, Jill Whitlow, Brooke Bundy, Jonathan Chapin, Christopher Burgard, Sam Melville, Charlie Spradling

The Understudy: Graveyard Shift II

(CINEMA VENTURES; CAN) 88min

Like its predecessor, this is a thoughtful vampire movie with an obsessive thread of sado-eroticism. Shadowy Baiser (Oliviero) invades the production of *The Blood Lover*, a film about a vampire pool hustler, taking over the lead role and possessing the actress (Gazelle) he must play opposite. The result is one of the better horror films about making a horror film (and unusually aware of the realities of film-making, with as much horror in the edit suite as on the set). Despite some confusion, *The Understudy* works in both its plots. Indeed, *The Blood Lover* is quite as strange an undertaking as the framing story. Both strands climax with Oliviero impaled on a pool cue by the screenwriter (Soper) and the regulation kicker in which Gazelle is reborn as the bloodsucking hustler she has been playing.

d/s Gerard Ciccoritti *p* Stephen R. Flacks, Arnold H. Bruck *c* Barry Stone *se* Adrianne Sicova *lp* Wendy Gazelle, Mark Soper, Silvio Oliviero, Ilse Von Glatz, Timothy Kelleher

The Unnameable (YANKEE CLASSIC PICTURES) 87min

Though H.P. Lovecraft became fashionable in the late eighties, most of the clutch of Lovecraft-derived films that followed Stuart Gordon's **Re-Animator** (1985) avoid using the Cthulhu mythos, his personalized horror mythology. *The Unnameable* resurrects some of the trappings, though they sit ill with formulaic teen-kill monster-movie conventions. An impressive copy of the *Necronomicon*, Lovecraft's oft-referred-to book of eldritch lore, is glimpsed, and the setting is the Miskatonic University in Arkham, but, owing little to the sketch it is supposed to be adapted from, the film takes its plot from the pared-down adaptation of August Derleth's Lovecraft elaboration **The Shuttered Room** (1966).

In 1670, a warlock is slaughtered by an unseen monstrosity he keeps locked up in his attic. Three hundred years later, his house is shunned and students staging a fraternity initiation rite decide to stay over, whereupon they are predictably killed by a monster seen mainly as a pair of hairy lower legs or a set of clawed hands. Incidentally, far from being unnameable, the creature is identified as Alyda Winthrop.

d/s/co-p Jean-Paul Ouelette *co-p* Dean Ramser *c* Tom Fraser *se* R. Christopher Biggs *lp* Charles King, Mark Kinsey Stephenson, Alexandra Durrell, Laura Albert, Eden Ham, Blane Wheatley, Mark Parra, Katrine Alexandre

Warlock (NEW WORLD) 102min

Devil-worshipper Sands, captured in 1691 by witchfinder Grant, prays to Satan and is whisked across time to Los Angeles, where he is supposed to assemble a grimoire and end the world. Grant follows and teams up with Singer, whom Sands has put under a curse which ages her twenty years every day.

The story dogs the tracks of chase-across-time tales like *Time After Time* (1979), *The Terminator* (1984) and *Trancers* (1984), but devotes time to unfamiliar superstitions: the warlock gains the power of flight by drinking boiled fat from an unbaptized child whom he finds in a playground while Christian children are in church. All three performers rise to the occasion, occasionally pulling nice reversals as when Singer tries to tell Grant about the 20th century with a patronizing 'Say, did you know the world was round?', or neat turns of phrase like a description of the warlock as 'the guy who finger-paints with body fluids'. Sands manages to be so verminously rotten that the film can get away with its blunt and (in the genre of **Witchfinder General**, 1968, and *Day of Wrath*, 1943) unfashionable endorsement of burning-at-the-stake as the only reasonable treatment for warlocks. Sands returns in Anthony Hickox's *Warlock: The Armageddon* (1993).

d/p Steve Miner *s* David T. Twohy *c* David Eggby *se* Make-Up Imagineering, Dream Quest Images *lp* Richard E. Grant, Julian Sands, Lori Singer, Mary Woronov

Waxwork (VESTRON) 97min

An imposing waxworks appears overnight in a small town, and sinister showman Warner invites a group of teens to a midnight party. However, the blundering kids find themselves transported via exhibits into the presence of 'the eighteen most evil men in history', which means gory vignettes featuring such famous names as Count Dracula (played inaptly with designer stubble and a Clint Eastwood croak by ex-Tarzan O'Keefe), a swashbuckling Marquis de Sade, an anonymous werewolf (Davies) with floppy bunny ears, the Phantom of the Opera and the Mummy. Galligan appeals to wheelchair-bound monster-fighter MacNee for help, and it winds up with a scrap between the forces of Good and a pack of monsters.

The tone veers between the comic – with Warner and MacNee turning in knowingly camp performances, and joke references to everything from **Crimes of Passion** (1985) to **The Little Shop of Horrors** (1960) – and the nasty – the De Sade scene, although inexplicit, features lurid dialogue, and the Dracula episode is especially blood-drenched.

d/s Anthony Hickox *p* Steffan Ahrenberg *c* Gerry Lively *se* Bob Keen *lp* Zach Gilligan, Deborah Foreman, Michelle Johnson, Miles O'Keefe, Dana Ashbrook, David Warner, John Rhys-Davies, Patrick Macnee

Der Werwolf von W. *aka* The Werewolf of W.

(REINERY/ZDF; WG) 82min

Pointless rather than mysterious, this follows a pretty girl (Schieber) as she investigates the death of a night watchman at a factory which has been built on a site associated with strange deaths as far back as the 16th century.

While the factory owner broods on his own secrets, the heroine, in concert with a mysteriously unmotivated detective and the watchman's successor, delves further into the unknown events and various supporting characters meet bloody fates. In an attempt to evoke an atmosphere of unexplained dread, the film omits its ending, never solving its mystery and never quite getting round to bringing the title character on screen, leaving the tantalizing possibility of a lycanthropic curse just one of any number of possible explanations.

d/co-s Manfred Müller *p* Peter Wohlgemuth-Reinery, Wolfgang Schulte *co-s* Werner Pilz *c* Wolfgang Pilgrim, Niki Stein *se* Brigitte Gruse *lp* Henry Hübchen, Michael Gwisdek, Martina Schieber, Werner Brehm, Horst Fechner

Witchcraft (VISTA STREET) 86min

Like *Sleepaway Camp* (1983), this unexceptional video item was successful enough to yield not just a sequel but a series. In a **Rosemary's Baby** (1968) riff, young wife Topol-Barzilai suspects satanic involvement when, shortly after giving birth, her husband (Sloan) requires they stay with his mother (Shelley) in the family mansion. A priest is cursed with boils and commits suicide, a magic mirror reflects a long-ago witch-burning, Sloan becomes doomily distant, Shelley occasionally dribbles blood and the heroine's best friend (Scott) is decapitated. It develops that Sloan and Shelley are man and wife, having returned after being burned at the stake, whereupon the sole surviving supporting character, a mute butler (Kissman), rescues Topol-Barzilai only to be killed before any motivation for his sudden spurt of decency can be advanced. With competent acting, a slow pace, cheapskate video effects and a standard story, this still led to Mark Woods' *Witchcraft, Part II: The Temptress* (1989), R.L. Tillmans' *Witchcraft III: The Kiss of Death* (1991) and James Mercadino's *Witchcraft IV: Virgin Heart* (1992).

d Robert Spera *p* Megan Barnett, Yoram Barzilai *s* Jody Savin *c* Jens Sturup *se* Angela Levin *lp* Anat Topol-Barzilai, Gary Sloan, Mary Shelley, Deborah Scott, Lee Kissman, Alexander Kirkwood, Edward Ross Newton

1989

Adrenaline (MANITOU/CLARA/CANAL +; FR) 80min
This collection of fourteen grotesque and bizarre shorts was made between 1987 and 1989 by mainly young French directors.

The overwhelming majority of the pieces have inanimate objects turn hostile: a spider-like surveillance robot (*Cyclope*), an underground train, a descending ceiling (*Revestriction*), an empty wine bottle. In *Cimetière des Eléphants*, the most effective of these black-outs, aged cars rumble towards an automobile graveyard with their hapless owners trapped inside to line up for the compressing machines. Other notable pieces are *T.V. Buster*, by Assal, and *Hudson*, in which a pair of couch potatoes assaulted by characters in their television call in an exorcist to deal with the problem. *Corridor*, by Robak (who made **Baby Blood**, 1990), is an enjoyable skit on the Indiana Jones booby-trapped passageway with a potential housebuyer negotiating the hazards of the home he is being shown around, while *Sculpture Physique*, by Piquer and Maddeddu, a 1988 Cannes prize-winner as a short, sees Maddeddu have his head punched into a shapeless mass so he can exhibit it in an abstract art show.

co-d/co-p Yann Piquer *co-d/s* Jean-Marie Maddeddu, Anita Assal, John Hudson, Barthelmy Bompard, Alain Robak, Philippe Dorison *se* Sylvain Nibart, Michel Soubeyrand *c* Bernard Cavalie *lp* Jean-Marie Maddeddu, Clementine Célarié, Bernadette Coqueret, Ged Marlon, Alain Aithnard, Jean-François Gallotte, Franck Baruk

Arabella, l'Angelo Nero *aka* **Arabella, the Black Angel** (LA ARPA; IT) 85min
This is a cross-breeding of the giallo film with the perennial 'serious' sexploitation, a tradition that runs from *Emmanuelle* (1976) to *9½ Weeks* (1986). The touchstones here are *Lady Chatterley's Lover* and **Crimes of Passion** (1985).

Cansino is the frustrated wife of a writer (Casale) crippled in a car accident on their honeymoon, who takes on the red light districts of Rome, indulging in bizarre and brutal sex acts with strangers. Dogging her career, and giving her a reputation as a jinxed 'black angel', is a regulation giallo slasher, who takes his scissors to anyone who involved with her. Also mixed up is a lesbian detective (Visconti) suffering from violent hallucinations that parallel the murders, including one surreally bizarre encounter far more sickening even than the atrocities of **Lo Squartatore di New York** (1982). A collection of vaguely perverse sex and violence scenes bluntly filmed and strung together at random, the film has a certain sleazy ambience.

d Max Steel (Arduino Sacco) *p* Francesco Vitulano *s* R. Filipucci, Vittorio Ferrero *c* Stefano Catalano *lp* Tini Cansino, Valentina Visconti, Francesco Casale, Carlo Mucari, Renato D'Amore, Evelyn Stewart

Beverly Hills Vamp
(AMERICAN INDEPENDENT/AUSTIN) 86min
Milder even than Ray's **Hollywood Chainsaw Hookers** (1988), this is another feeble entry in the post-**Vamp** (1986) comic vampire stakes, blending in perfectly with such mild cheapies as **Once Bitten** (1985), **My Best Friend is a Vampire** (1988), **Vampire Knights** (1987) and **Teen Vamp** (1989).

Aspiring film-makers Deezen and Conway come to Hollywood to tout their 'sincere love story' and fall in, first with Richardson, sleazeball producer of *Motorcycle Sluts in Heat* and then with vampire madame Ekland's bevy of seductive, bloodsucking bimbos. Conway is converted to pasty-faced monsterhood, but Deezen, who does his usual intolerable Jerry Lewis impersonation, takes advice from priest Quarry, who dutifully does an in-joke about his earlier incarnation as Count Yorga (in the 1970 outing **Count Yorga, Vampire**) and disposes of the creatures with stake, crucifix and 'Pope soda' (holy water).

d Fred Olen Ray *p* Grant Austin Waldman *s* Ernest D. Farino *c* Stephen Ashley Blake *se* Bret Mixon *lp* Britt Ekland, Eddie Deezen, Tim Conway Jr, Jay Richardsom. Michelle Bauer, Tom Shell, Debra Lamb, Jillian Kesner, Robert Quarry, Dawn Wildsmith

The Bite *aka* **Curse II: The Bite**
(VIVA/TOWA; IT, US, JAP) 98min
Blessed with one of the daftest premises of all time and distributed spuriously as a sequel to Assonitis' **The Curse** (1988), this is a surprisingly entertaining gore movie. The main reasons for this are the better-than-average performances and some interesting early tricks from George, the surrealistic make-up effects artist who worked on **A Nightmare on Elm Street IV: The Dream Master** (1988) and **Society** (1989).

Driving through an abandoned and tainted US Government military testing ground, young lovers Peck and Schoelen are menaced by aggressive snakes, one of which bites Peck on the hand, whereupon his arm slowly mutates into a snake hand-puppet and he takes to ripping out cops' insides and pulling doctors' chins off. In the finale, snakes erupt from Peck's body in a truly repulsive, completely absurd image. Sean Barton's South African *Curse III: Blood Sacrifice* (1991), top-lining Christopher Lee, is another unconnected follow-up, featuring witch doctors and an evil sea monster.

d/co-s Fred Goodwin (Federico Prosperi) *p* Ovidio G. Assonitis *co-s* Susan Zelouf *c* Roberto D'Ettore Piazzoli *se* Screaming Mad George *lp* Jill Schoelen, J. Eddie Peck, Jamie Farr, Savina Gersak, Marianne Muellerleile, Sidney Lassick, Terrence Evans, Bo Svenson

Blood Delirium (CINE DECIMA; IT) 85min
Castle-dwelling mad artist Law, who believes he is the reincarnation of Van Gogh, is obsessed with his dead wife, wiring her corpse to the piano to revive flagging artistic inspiration. Coming across a young musician (Christensen) who is the image of his wife, he tries to get her to recreate the dead woman in the manner of *Vertigo* (1958). Meanwhile, Law's butler (Mitchell), who was earlier caught molesting the wife's corpse, is abusing the local women, dismembering victims with a band-saw. Discovering his servant's crimes, Law realises that blood is the medium in which he can paint sunsets best, and is prepared to sanction the murders to continue his work. The heroine's helicopter-pilot boyfriend and the ghost of the wife, represented by three glowing balls, intervene and the castle falls down, though not before Law's Van Gogh obsession has been purged when the ghost cuts off his ear. Re-using bits of **L'Orribile Segreto del Dr Hichcock** (1962) and **Color Me Blood Red** (1964), this is a catalogue of sleazy subjects, with Law and Mitchell enthusiastically showing off their ranting insanity and clearly relishing the opportunity to slobber over starlets.

d Sergio Bergonzelli *p/co-s* Raffaella Mertes *co-s* Fratelli Cordi *c* Marce de Stefano *lp* John Phillip Law, Gordon Mitchell, Brigitte Christensen

Blood Games (BENTSVI/FORTUNE ENTERTAINMENT) 87min
An all-girl baseball team humiliates a team of backwoods rednecks by defeating them on their home ground in a sequence that effectively captures the growing frustration of the bested men as they try to disrupt the game the girls are taking seriously by groping scantily-dressed players and resorting to underhand violence. The victory triggers a set of escalating violent conflicts as local lout Cummings is egged on by his mercenary father (Shay) to take out his frustrations on the girls and is killed by the team captain (Albert) just after he has stabbed her father-coach (Hagen), whereupon Shay sets the community on the girls' trail, forcing their tour bus off the road and stalking them through the forests. With caricatured disgusting yokels and self-reliant athlete heroines who dress like bimbos and are duly ogled in the showers by the camera, the film can hardly be accused of subtle characterization,

except perhaps in the parallel father-child relationships in both camps, but Shay makes an effective villain, finally confronted by Albert in a ghost town.

d Tanya Rosenberg *p* Yakov Bentsvi *s* Craig L. Clyde, James L. Hennessy, George P. Saunders *c* Sam Gart *se* Greg Hendrickson *lp* Gregory Cummings, Laura Albert, Shelley Ablett, Luke Shay, Ross Hagen

Buried Alive (BRETON FILMS; SOUTH AFRICA) 89min

Allegedly derived from Poe's *The Premature Burial* (though a prowling cat and bricked-up victims suggest it could as easily be *The Black Cat*), this trite old-dark-house movie is notable as the last film Carradine completed before his death. At a school for disturbed girls, principal Vaughn, maddened because his psychologist father (Carradine) locked him in the dark as a child, walls up failed pupils in the basement. Pleasence is on hand in a disturbing toupee as a supporting loon and Carradine has two brief, ranting appearances as a perhaps-ghost.

d Gerard Kikoine *p* Harry Alan Towers *s* Jake Clesi, Stuart Lee *c* Gerard Loubeau *se* Scott Wheeler, Bill Butler *lp* Robert Vaughn, Donald Pleasence, Karen Witter, John Carradine, Ginger Allen, Nai Long

The Carpenter (GOLD GEMS; CAN) 87min

This quietly bizarre little drama crosses **The Hitcher** (1985) with *The Ghost and Mrs Muir* (1947). Neglected wife Adams, recovering from a breakdown while her philandering academic husband has an affair and lecherous workmen remodel her house, strikes up a relationship with the eponymous handyman (Hauser). He only works at night, and displays considerably more skill and pride in his work than the lazy regular builders, who assume he's scab labour brought in to make them look bad. When the workmen try to defraud, molest or rape Adams, he steps in with a nailgun or other convenient power tool and takes care of the problem. It develops that the charming, well-mannered Hauser is the ghost of the DIY enthusiast who built the house and went broke in the process, ultimately dying in the electric chair after taking his tools to a series of process servers and repossession men. *The Carpenter* is notable for Hauser's unusually subtle performance as the polite ghost, who tries to be reasonable throughout, reacting when the heroine hits him with a hammer by taking it away from her and patiently explaining, 'This is a tool, it's not a toy.'

d David Wellington *p* Pierre Grisé *s* Doug Taylor *c* David Franco *lp* Wings Hauser, Lynn Adams, Pierre Lenoir, Barbara-Ann Jones, Beverly Murray

La Chiesa *aka* The Church (CECCHI GORI/GRUPPO TIGER CINEMATOGRAFICA/RETEITALIA; IT) 96min

Opening in the spirit of de Ossorio's *Blind Dead* films with a medieval witch-hunt, this is set in a cathedral erected over the graves of a coven of devil-worshippers. The first half follows historian Arana as he investigates and falls under supernatural influences, but the ostensible hero all but vanishes from the second half, which resembles **Demoni** (1985) and *El Angel Exterminatador* (1962) as disparate characters are trapped by an ancient mechanism inside the church with the unleashed evil spirits.

Though it has some pleasing detail (the mechanical devices that bring the walls to life are especially well-realized) and the regulation horrific sequences (a girl dangled into a dark tunnel during an escape attempt through the cellars is splattered by a passing subway train) the film suffers from its scattered storyline and a typically Italian refusal to allow characters to be anything more than machine components. Indicative perhaps of the shrinking horizons of Italian horror is that, whereas Mario Bava (in **Lisa e il Diavolo**, 1972) followed Buñuel by staging a parodic version of Da Vinci's *Last Supper*, the equivalent scene here finds Soavi meticulously recreating in the flesh a well-known illustration of a demon embracing a naked woman by girlie/fantasy artist Boris Vallejo. The music is by Keith Emerson, but large sections are poached from the works of Philip Glass.

d/co-s Michele Soavi *p/co-s* Dario Argento *co-s* Franco Ferrini *c* Renato Tafuri *se* Sergio Stivaletti, Rosario Prestopino *lp* Tomas Arana, Barbara Cupisti, Feodor Chaliapin, Hugh Quarshie, Antonella Vitale, Asia Argento

Chopper Chicks in Zombie Town (CHELSEA PARTNERS/TROMA) 89min

In the spirit of *Piranha Women in the Avocado Jungle of Death* (1989), this Troma pick-up is a multi-pronged exploitation spoof with a mild feminist twist. The Cycle Sluts, a gang of leather-clad harpies, breeze into a town where evil undertaker Calfa is reprising the plots of **Plague of the Zombies** (1966) and **Dead and Buried** (1982), killing the locals and resurrecting them as zombies to toil in a radioactive mine. A conflict arises between Carlen, the aggressive lesbian leader of the pack (she performs a song *You Better Do What Your Big Mama Says*), and Rose, a former homecoming queen, as to whether the Sluts should help intolerant townsfolk against the shambling flesh-eaters, but in the end the gang come through in *Magnificent Seven* style. With a group of hard-bitten blind orphans, surprising character touches, neat gags ('If you don't eat anyone, maybe nobody'll notice', a young man tells his zombified Dad) and a refreshing generosity of spirit, this is far more likeable, exciting, well-made and worthwhile than anything actually produced by Troma.

d/s Dan Hoskins *p* Maria Snyder *c* Tom Fraser *se* Edward French *lp* Jamie Rose, Catherine Carlen, Lycia Naff, Vicki Frederick, Kristina Loggia, Don Calfa, Gretchen Palmer, Nina Petersen, Whitney Reis

Clownhouse (COMMERCIAL PICTURES) 84min

This is an amateurish psycho movie in which three homicidal maniacs 'denied circus privileges' escape from an asylum and dress up as clowns to terrorize three teenage brothers who have been left alone in their huge old house so the steadicam can rush around in pursuit.

Failing to make much use of the sinister side of clowning, the film's only perceptive point is in the characterizations of the boys: the elder brother bullying and intolerant, the middle one bespectacled and concerned, the youngest a nightmare-plagued bed-wetter with a convincingly irrational fear of clowns.

d/s/co-c Victor Salva *p* Michael Danty *co-c* Robin Mortarotti *lp* Nathan Forrest Winters, Brian McHugh, Sam Rockwell, Vileita Skillman, Timothy Enos

The Cook, the Thief, His Wife & Her Lover (ALLARTS COOK/ERATO; GB, FR, NETH) scope 126min

The nasty strain that runs through Greenaway's oeuvre – *The Draughtsman's Contract* (1982), *A Zed and Two Noughts* (1985), *The Belly of an Architect* (1987), *Drowning by Numbers* (1988) – comes to the surface in this horrific fable, which has the feel of **Cannibal Ferox** (1981) remade by Visconti.

In a car park, gangster Albert Spica (Gambon) has his thugs strip naked a restaurateur who has incurred his displeasure and, in a scene shot with all the exquisite perfection Greenaway can muster, forces the victim to eat several paperloads of dogshit. After this introduction, we move inside the restaurant, which Gambon has recently bought but which remains the domain of the Cook (Bohringer). Every night the Thief gorges himself on wonderfully cinematic meals while abusing his delicate wife (Mirren), driving her into the embrace of bookish diner Howard. When he discovers his wife and Howard are lovers he plots a terrible revenge on them. However, they are protected by the Cook which leads to Gambon's downfall. At the end he has to eat the perfectly prepared, glazed and garnished naked corpse of Howard, whom he has had tortured to death.

Beautifully art-directed, photographed, scored (by Michael Nyman) and acted, this is an intensely physical, repulsively fascinating meditation upon the nature of evil. Aside from De

The Cook, the Thief, His Wife and Her Lover; *well actually (front row) the Thief (Michael Gambon), the Wife (Helen Mirren), the Cook (Richard Bohringer) and the Lover (Alan Howard).*

Sade, who would have approved the indescribably ghastly finale, the film echoes Poe's *Masque of the Red Death,* to the extent of playing games with different-coloured rooms (the characters' Jean-Paul Gaultier clothes change to match the décor they walk through) derived from the 1964 Corman movie. At once disquietingly distanced and unremittingly confrontational, this is perhaps the ultimate drive-in/arthouse crossover film, wedding high-art production with video-nasty subject matter.

d/s Peter Greenaway *p* Kees Kasander *c* Sacha Vierny *se* Sjoerd Didden *lp* Richard Bohringer, Michael Gambon, Helen Mirren, Alan Howard, Tim Roth, Emer Gillespie, Ian Dury, Liz Smith

The Dead Pit (CORNERSTONE PRODUCTION CO) 101min
This is a a lively mix of the evil asylum theme with Romero-esque zombie rampages. After the gruesome opening sequence with Gochnauer killed by Slate and pushed into the eponymous pit of his victims, mental patients slaughtered in unethical experiments, the film cuts forward to twenty years later. Here Slate is the guilt-ridden head of the asylum and the amnesiac heroine (Lawson) is in his care. An earthquake unhinges some of the harmless patients and releases a red-eyed and decayed Gochnauer from the pit, whereupon he starts killing staff and patients with medical equipment, pre-empting **Dr Giggles** (1992). The doctor leads the shambling undead in an assault on the hospital which is only stopped when a patient with a compulsion to blow things up (Forster) demolishes a water-tower blessed by a hysterical nun, flooding the pit with holy water. This is a wilfully old-fashioned cheapjack B, evidently made as a calling card for Leonard and Everett. It clearly worked: they went on to make **The Lawnmower Man** (1992).

d/co-s Brett Leonard *p/co-s* Gimel Everett *c* Marty Collins *se* Ed Martinez *lp* Jeremy Slate, Danny Gochnauer, Steffen Gregory Forster, Cheryl Lawson, Joan Bechtel, Geha Getz, Mara Everett, Randy Fontana

Dr Caligari (STEINER) 80min
The new Dr Caligari (Reynal) is a fetish-garbed sexologist, granddaughter of the Werner Krauss character from the 1919 film. Operating out of the Caligari Insane Asylum (cue several limp CIA jokes), the doctor attempts to treat a sexually-obsessed woman (Albert) with hypothalamus liquid transplants that make her decide to murder her husband, while transforming her male colleague Dr Awol (Harris) into a Mamie Van Doren lookalike so they can engage in sex.

Albert, like the narrator of the original film, sees the world in surrealist terms, experiencing a low-budget sexual encounter with the television inspired by *Videodrome* (1983), having her arm turn briefly into a glove-puppet penis and surrendering to a doll-faced lesbian and a giant tongue. Like Sayadian's début feature *Café Flesh* (1982), made under the pseudonym 'Rinse Dream', this is a monotonous, if stylish, attempt to cross the borders between s-m porn, low-budget exploitation horror and high art. Like **The Cabinet of Caligari** (1962), to which it might also be considered a sequel, it's unusual enough to stand out among a rash of lookalike psycho movies.

d/co-s Stephen Sayadian *p* Joseph F. Robertson *co-s* Jerry Stahl *c* Ladi von Jansky *lp* Madeleine Reynal, Fox Harris, Laura Albert, Jennifer Balgobin, John Durbin, Gene Zerna

Dr Hackenstein (VISTA STREET) 86min
This has the sole distinction of being made before the 1990–1 craze for remake-parody-rip-offs of **Bride of Frankenstein** (1935): *Frankenhooker, Bride of Re-Animator,* **Frankenstein Unbound.**

In 1909, Dr Elliot Hackenstein (Muir) is striving to resurrect his fiancée (Baker), who has been decapitated by the propellors of the *Lusitania* during its maiden voyage. Three young women are forced by a motor accident to spend the night and he decides to take the legs from one, the arms of another and the eyes of the heroine (Travis) to attach to a torso body-snatched for him by local specialists (Ramsey and Ramsey). The film winds up with all the principals still alive, even if horribly altered, and a series of *American Graffiti* (1973) captions reveal their subsequent fates. The only amusing joke is the suggestion that the mute maid, who has torn her hair and wrung her hands throughout, went to Hollywood and became a silent film star.

d/s Richard Clark *p* Reza Mizbani, Megan Barnett *c* Jens Sturup *se* Kurtzman, Nicotero & Berger EFX Group *lp* David Muir, Stacey Travis, Catherine Davis Cox, Anne Ramsey, Logan Ramsey, Phyllis Diller, Sylvia Lee Baker

1989

Family Reunion (SPECTRUM/BULLSEYE) 85min
A minor demonic conspiracy movie, with young middle-aged Novak and his family drawn at Christmas to a ghost town he has dreamed of. Robed rednecks, led by Novak's still-young Satanist father (Andes), hope to induct him into the cult to further the Devil's ends. While the climactic confrontation is ordinary, featuring messy entrails and dry-ice-fogged caverns, there are a few unsettling touches in the build-up, involving a lost toy truck, the ghost town and the ageless villain's escape from the local jail. Starrett, director of the best of the robed redneck movies, **Race With the Devil** (1975), is the Sheriff.

d/p/s Michael Hawes *c* Jack Anderson *se* Jeff Varga
lp Mel Novak, Pam Phillips, John Andes, A.J. Woods, Jack Starrett, Kaylin Cool, Brad Kelly

Fatal Exposure (CIRCLE COMMUNICATIONS) 78min
Photographer Jack T. Rippington (Bahner), a descendant of Jack the Ripper (the script can't decide whether he is the famous killer's grandson or great-grandson), stages murders as works of art and searches for an ideal woman to bear his son and continue the line, maintaining sexual potency by drinking the blood of his victims. Encountering a dim but perkily morbid girl (Henderson), Bahner commences an affair with her, implicating her in the murders of several photographic models, and gets her pregnant, whereupon she discovers his bloody deeds and is imprisoned in the house. Henderson escapes and, in a confrontation, splashes acid in Bahner's face, posing him for one of his own photographs.

d/p/c Peter B. Good *s* Chris Painter *se* Scott Coulter
lp Blake Bahner, Ena Henderson, Dan Schmale, Julie Austin, Renee Cline, Gary Wise, Marc Griggs, Jah Riley, Joy Ovington

Friday the 13th, Part VIII: Jason Takes Manhattan
(PAR/HORROR INC) 100min
The eighth entry in the series, this rings changes on the tired formula by transporting hockey-masked maniac Hodder to two new locations, first a pleasure-boat full of the usual partying teens and then New York City (actually Toronto).

Daggett has the regulation role of the girl who survives after all her friends have been despatched, in the process coming to terms with the fear of water she developed as a child when her uncle tried to teach her to swim by throwing her in Crystal Lake for an encounter with the underwater Jason. Stabbed with a totemic object, the pen used in high school by Stephen King, Jason is finally dissolved in toxic waste in a sewer, his transformation back into a drowned child suggesting that not only has he been a zombie since *Part VI* but also a ghost since *Part II*.

d/s Rob Hedden *p* Randolph Cheveldave *c* Bryan England
se Jamie Brown *lp* Jensen Daggett, Scott Reeves, Peter Mark Richman, Barbara Bingham, V.C. Dupree, Kane Hodder, Sharlene Martin, Martin Cummins

Ghostbusters II (COL) 108min
This is less a sequel to than an inferior remake of **Ghostbusters** (1984).

This time, the Ancient Evil is a painting of a Carpathian tyrant who influences museum curator MacNicol to help him possess Weaver's baby son so he can rule the world, while a rising tide of psychoactive sewer slime feeds on the ill-will of the people of New York. Rather than confront a giant in the finale, the ghostbusters conjure one up, animating the Statue of Liberty to help them rescue Weaver and her child. Though the cast do the things that worked for them last time round, the film is a beat or two off the mark: Murray is snidely witty, while Aykroyd, Hudson and Ramis loon about behind him trying to steal back a few laughs.

d/p Ivan Reitman *s* Dan Aykroyd, Harold Ramis *c* Michael Chapman *se* Dennis Muren, Tim Lawrence *lp* Bill Murray, Sigourney Weaver, Dan Aykroyd, Rick Moranis, Harold Ramis, Annie Potts, Peter MacNicol, Ernie Hudson, Harris Yulin

Halloween 5 (MAGNUM PICTURES) 96min
This weak sequel, bearing the sub-title *The Revenge of Michael Myers* on advertising but not prints, opens by reversing the single interesting sequence in **Halloween 4: The Return of Michael Myers** (1988), revealing that Michael's 9-year-old niece (Harris) has not followed his footsteps by killing her stepmother.

The semi-supernatural psycho (Shanks) returns from his resting place at the bottom of a well to stalk yet another group of teens. Harris has psychic flashes whenever Michael is about to kill, Pleasence dies for the second time, and a mysterious gunslinger loiters in the background, intervening to help Michael escape from jail and presumably help out in future sequels. The central drama concentrates on Harris, as unkillable in this context because of her age as Michael is because of his importance to the series, so the mandatory make-out, practical joke and slaughter sequences seem intrusions. Late in the film, Othenin-Girard tries preposterously to work up sympathy for Michael, with Pleasence speechifying about the madman's need to slake the 'rage' inside him, and Harris coaxing the killer into removing his mask so a tear can be observed leaking from his eye before business as usual resumes with the murderer ineffectually trying to carve up his niece.

d/co-s Dominique Othenin-Girard *p* Ramsey Thomas
co-s Michael Jacobs, Shem Bitterman *c* Robert Draper
se KNB EFX Group *lp* Donald Pleasence, Danielle Harris, Wendy Kaplan, Ellie Cornell, Donald J. Shanks, Jeffrey Landman, Beau Starr, Betty Carvalho, Tamara Glynn

The Hand of Death *aka* **Unmasked: Hand of Death, Part 25** *aka* **Hand of Death, Part 25: Jackson's Back**
(STRANGE CINEMA; GB) 84min
Made in Britain, with teenagers sporting cockney accents and *The Face* cast-off fashions, this *Friday the 13th* parody finds Jackson (Cox), a hockey-masked serial killer who has purportedly starred in 24 previous *Hand of Death* movies, at large in London.

After slaughtering a partyload of the regulation promiscuous kids, Jackson corners a blind girl (Evans) who falls in love with him and brings him out of himself, forcing him to reveal a sensitive side as he recites Byron while wishing he could reject his murderous heritage. Fate and cliché dictate that his evil ways come back and, after more murders, he is compelled to stab his girlfriend. The scenes between Cox and Evans are quite well written and played, especially when the not-so-pure blind girl tries to get an unenthusiastic Jackson to be more aggressive in bed, but the rest too closely resembles any number of mindless slasher movies for satiric intent to be construed. However, it does feature a marvellously cod-existential horror ending, with Jackson crying in anguish as he collapses outside the Screen on Baker Street, the marquee above him announcing *Hand of Death 26: Jackson Returns*.

d Anders Palm *p/s* Mark Cutforth *c* John DeBorman
se Image Animation *lp* Gregory Cox, Fiona Evans, Edward Brayshaw

Headhunter
(GIBRALTAR RELEASING; SOUTH AFRICA) 88min
One of a wave of international-looking South African exploitation movies, this was at least partially shot in Florida. Nonetheless, the suggestion that Miami has a 'Nigerian ghetto' to excuse the presence in town of an African head-removing voodoo demon is somewhat suspect.

This does little with the theme of a Third World demon following emigrants to their new homes and, unsurprisingly, takes a racist attitude to African religions. Even a potentially amusing/intriguing scene, the murder of an evangelist's latest convert during a river baptism, falls flat due to indifferent staging and dud acting, though the enthusiastic head-chopping effects are almost ingratiating. The finale is lively, if perplexing, with Crawford and Lenz taking a chainsaw to a papier-mâché-swathed monster muscle-builder while the film keeps cutting away to a TV screening of *The Hideous Sun Demon* (1958).

d Francis Schaeffer *p* Jay Davidson *s* Len Spinelli *c* Hans Kuhle *se* Elaine Alexander, Kevin Brennan *lp* Kay Lenz, Wayne Crawford, June Chadwick, Steve Kanaly, John Fatooh, Sam Williams

Heathers

(NEW WORLD/CINEMARQUE ENTERTAINMENT) 102min

This is one of a run of movies (**The Stepfather**, 1986, **Parents**, 1988, **Society**, 1989) using standardized genre elements for comic and subversive ends.

Veronica (Ryder) is in the high school's élite clique, with three glamorous and variously obnoxious girls called Heather. Burdened with a conscience, she doesn't want to go along with the ruthless persecution, emotional torture and shallow vacuity that comes with the Miss Popularity crown. So when J.D. (Slater), her more-than-slightly psycho boyfriend, proposes they murder Bitch Queen Heather Number One (Falk) and pass it off as suicide, she encourages him until he actually commits the crime. The suicide turns the school upside-down, with the dead monster canonized, and J.D. decides to take his campaign of natural justice further. Despite a tangled plot that makes light of peer-group pressure, murder and suicide, *Heathers* is an astonishing variation on the 'youth problem' movie, mingling the approaches of John Hughes' comedies, *River's Edge* (1987), **Carrie** (1976) and **Massacre at Central High** (1976) to come up with an unsettling, painfully funny fable. The film bristles with nastily convincing teen slang ('Oh, fuck me gently with a chainsaw'), appalling but hilarious lapses of taste – a mourning teenager touching her hairstyle up with holy water from the font during her best friend's funeral – and spot-on performances from a young cast. Lehmann, working from Waters' supersmart script, choreographs stylized violence and sick humour with equal ease.

d Michael Lehmann *p* Denise Di Novi *s* Dan Waters *c* Francis Kenney *lp* Winona Ryder, Christian Slater, Shannen Doherty, Lisanne Falk, Kim Walker, Penelope Milford, Glenn Shadix, Lance Fenton

Winona Ryder at the funeral of bitch goddess Lisanne Falk in the edgy Heathers.

The Horror Show *aka* House III: The Horror Show

(MGM-UA) 95min

Planned as an entry in *The House* series, this was deemed by Cunningham too grim to be associated with those light-hearted charades and retitled, though the original tag was used for overseas release. A combination of *Cape Fear* (1962) and the *Elm Street* films, this pre-empted **Shocker** (1989) with an executed serial killer returning to life as an electric current.

Max Jenke (James), a jokey serial murderer whose last wish is 'to be buried with his meatcleaver', dies in the chair but survives because 'pure evil is a form of electrical energy' and attacks the family of the cop (Henriksen) who brought him to book. David Blyth, of **Death Warmed Up** (1984), was replaced after a week's shooting by effects specialist Isaac, whose work is competent but unexciting.

d James Isaac *p* Sean S. Cunningham *s* Allan Smithee (Allyn Warner), Leslie Bohem *c* Mac Ahlberg *se* VCE/Peter Kuran *lp* Lance Henriksen, Brion James, Rita Taggart, Deedee Pfeiffer, Aron Eisenberg, Thom Bray, Matt Clark

The House of Usher

(21ST CENTURY/BRETON; SOUTH AFRICA) 87min

A very camp melodrama. Windsor is brought to the House of Usher, within driving distance of London though the film was shot in Africa, by her fiancée (Swart), who is promptly buried alive by his oversensitive uncle Roderick (Reed). Finally the house self-destructs, featuring polystyrene bouncing masonry familiar from earlier Towers productions (**El Conde Dracula**, 1970, *King Solomon's Treasure*, 1976) falling upon the principals, and Windsor escapes to a perfunctory all-a-dream-or-was-it? ending.

d Alan Birkinshaw *p* Harry Alan Towers *s* Michael J. Murray *c* Jossi Wein *se* Scott Wheeler *lp* Oliver Reed, Donald Pleasence, Romy Windsor, Rufus Swart, Norman Coombes, Anne Stradi, Philip Godewa

I, Madman *aka* Hardcover

(TRANS WORLD ENTERTAINMENT; CAN) 89min

A stylish but insubstantial supernatural drama, harping on the levels-of-reality theme as it cuts between dramatizations of the fifties pulp-horror novels the heroine (Wright) is reading and a present-day, real-life re-enactment of their gruesome stories. The girl is haunted by Malcolm Brand (Cook), a ghost with a patchwork face, the author whose sleazily packaged books *I, Madman* and *Much of Madness, More of Sin* turn out to be autobiographical non-fiction. The screenplay laboriously telegraphs every turn of the plot, but Takacs brings off a few effectively creepy turns and Wright makes a wistfully vulnerable heroine, bringing a little more sensitivity to the role than the formulaic script demands. Cook also contributed effects, including a Jackal Boy that turns up as a *deus ex machina* in the finale.

d Tibor Takacs *p* Rafael Eisenman *s* David Chaskin *c* Brian England *se* Randy Cook *lp* Jenny Wright, Clayton Rohner, Randy Cook, Steven Memel

Ijintachi Tono Natsu *aka* The Discarnates

(SHOCHIKU EIZO COMPANY; JAP) 109min

Based on a novel by Taichi Yamada, this deceptive ghost story turns bloody in the climax. A television writer (Kazama) moves after divorce into an isolated flat, where his first action is to rebuff cruelly his attractive but neurotic neighbour (Natori). When he visits the neighbourhood where he was born, he meets a hospitable couple (Akiyoshi, Kataoka) who, he realizes, are the ghosts of his parents who died when he was a child. Disturbingly younger than he is, the parents project an idealized image of a sit-com couple, but Kazama adjusts and is soon playing catch with his father and having back-rubs from his mother. He reassesses his attitude to Natori and begins an affair with her, though she modestly conceals her chest as they make love, claiming to be scarred by a long-ago accident. However, as in all Japanese ghost stories, relationships between living and dead take a toll and Harada's mirror image ages rapidly. He is persuaded by Natori to bid reluctant farewell to his parents and embrace life, but, in a nastily ironic touch, Natori too turns out to be a ghost, having repeatedly stabbed herself in the chest after Kazama's initial rejection. A slow, careful and sincere movie about unfinished relationships, this is enlivened by a horror-movie strand which pays off with a gore-drenched ghost-laying. Unusually, the purpose of the supernatural intervention is to encourage the hero to grow psychologically rather than to visit a revenge upon him for his insensitivity. The result is a considerable picture.

d Nobuhiko Obayashi *p* Shigisemi Sugisaki *s* Shinichi Ichikawa *c* Yoshihisa Sakamoto *lp* Morio Kazama, Kumiko Akiyoshi, Tsurutaro Kataoka, Yuko Natori, Toshiyuki Nagashima

Kuutamosonaatti *aka* **Moonlight Sonata** (FIN) 86min

Similar to American rural horrors like **The Texas Chainsaw Massacre** (1974) or **Mother's Day** (1980), this Finnish suspense film is shot in the high style of European art cinema.

Model Bjorkman, fleeing from a breakdown to a remote cottage, is pestered by a family of degenerates. The lead heavy is a yokel out of *Straw Dogs* (1972), who constantly makes lewd advances, but the menace comes from his hulking brother (Sorvali), confined by day to a woodshed but allowed out at night to bay at the moon. Early on, the heroine's dog disappears, but rather than turn up as the expected corpse nailed to a door, the animal is adopted by the ox-like lunatic, who has been abused by his silent old mother until he can only relate to similarly whipped animals. The heroine's resourceful brother turns up and puts his skill with gadgets to good use as they defend their house against an attack by the maniacs. Soinio's broadly comic *Kuutamosonaatti 2: Kadunlakaisijat* (*Moonlight Sonata 2: The Street Sweepers*, 1991) has the family revived from frozen death in a sauna and moving to downtown Helsinki, where they are joined by a brigade of Red Guard zombies, killed in the civil war of 1918.

d/s Olli Soinio *p* Heikki Takkinen *c* Kari Sohlberg *lp* Tina Björkman, Kari Sorvali, Kim Gunell, Mikko Kivinen, Soli Labbart, Ville-Veikko Salminen

The Laughing Dead

(ARCHAEOPTERYX/TERCEL) 91min

This is a semi-vanity splatter from author Somtow Sucharitkul, made under the pseudonym used on his horror novels (*Vampire Junction*, *Moon Dance*). The busy auteur also provides music and plays the lead villain, the incarnation of an Aztec Death God who tries to dupe a neurotic priest (Sullivan) into sacrificing his illegitimate son to bring about 'the new age', while Sullivan is leading a party of holidaymakers around sites of archaeological interest in Mexico.

A mainly amateur cast – including many Californian science-fiction and horror writers – perform capably, and makeup effects account for a substantial proportion of the budget – featuring a gruesome exchange of hearts and some supremely tacky monsters – but it's essentially another wandering-around-in-corridors-waiting-to-be-decapitated movie.

d/s S.P. Somtow *p* Lex Nakashima *c* D.R. Boyd *se* MMI Inc *lp* Tim Sullivan, Wendy Webb, Premika Eaton, Ed Bryant, Larry Kagan, Krista Keim, S.P. Somtow

Living Doll (LIVING DOLL PRODUCTIONS; GB) 92min

Though made in Britain, this splatter movie – like the same producer's **Slaughter High** (1987) – is set unconvincingly in America, with a few exterior shots of New York traffic, a guest appearance by Kitt as a John Waters-esque landlady and very phony transatlantic accents attempting to give a more commercial flavour.

Similar in plot to **Nekromantik** (1988) but with failed humour replacing failed art, this follows the love-life of a lonely morgue attendant (Jax) who takes home a beautiful corpse (Orgill) and fantasizes a relationship with her. Orgill, who can no more hold her breath than Jax can his accent, slowly rots and the hero's life falls to pieces as he commits several murders to preserve his idyll. The finale, which makes creepy use of the title song, is almost clever in its cruelty – the dead girl deserts Jax for her newly murdered old boyfriend – but the build-up is interminable.

co-d Peter Litten *co-d/co-s* George Dugdale *p* Dick Randall *co-s* Mark Ezra *c* Colin Munn *se* Paul Catling *lp* Mark Jax, Katie Orgill, Eartha Kitt, Sean Aita

Malediction *aka* **Satan's Princess**

(SUN HEAT PICTURES) 88min

Though known for tacky science fiction (*The Amazing Colossal Man*, 1957), Gordon's occasional horror movies (**Tormented**, 1960, **Necromancy**, 1972, *The Coming*, 1980) tend to be more interesting, if not on a level with his best, the deliriously hard-boiled *The Mad Bomber* (1972).

Forster is the crippled ex-cop hired to track down a missing daughter. He comes across fashionable succubus Denier. 'I've existed for 500 years,' she claims, 'I've killed over a thousand men.' 'Two a year?' Forster sneers, 'My barber does better than that.' With interludes of unappetizing sadism, plot confusion about a magic flower and a silly final chase, this is hardly a sensible film, but there is a stress on off-beat characterizations and an unusually tactful use of the character of Forster's sometimes-possessed retarded son.

d/p Bert I. Gordon *s* Stephen Katz *c* Thomas F. Denove *se* David B. Miller *lp* Robert Forster, Lydie Denier, Caren Kaye, Phillip Glasser, M.K. Harris, Ellen Geer

Masque of the Red Death (CONCORDE) 85min

A remake of Roger Corman's 1964 production, in which a symbolic doom descends on a group of unpleasant medieval Italian aristocrats who take refuge from the plague in a cramped castle. Prince Prospero (Paul) is played as a sulky, neurasthenic adolescent and menace is handled by top-billed but briefly glimpsed MacNee, the Prince's Machiavellian tutor who finally incarnates the Red Death. Reiner, as the Prince's incest-minded sister, gives the most impressive performance while the rest of the cast, including Hoak as the innocent imported into the castle and Osterhage as an Abba-wigged captain of the guard, are hobbled by the pseudo-poetic wedges of philosophical chat inserted between extremely tame orgies, torture sequences and boil-bursting disease effects. The grandeur and elegance of Corman's earlier film are missing: in their place is plentiful dialogue about the cruelty of God and Death and the behaviour of princes.

d/co-s Larry Brand *p* Roger Corman *co-s* Darryl Haney *c* Edward Pei *se* Dean Jones, Starr Jones, Mark Buckmaster, Tom Poster, Jeannie Robinson, Kim Lampluh *lp* Patrick Macnee, Adrian Paul, Clare Hoak, Jeff Osterhage, Tracy Reiner

Mr Christmas Dinner *aka* **Lucky Stiff**

(NEW LINE) 79min

Following **Psycho III** (1986), Perkins relaxed with this shaggy dog story in the tradition of **The Folks at Red Wolf Inn** (1972) and **Motel Hell** (1980).

A chubby loser (Alaskey), ditched at the altar by the latest in a succession of fiancées, falls in with the glamorous elder daughter (Dixon) of a backwoods family that dates back to the Donner party and finds himself set up to feature on the menu at their Christmas hoedown. A sloppy farce, with Alaskey merely adequate in his handling of wisecracks and pratfalls that seem intended for John Candy, this nevertheless has amusing moments, especially the demented parody of *The Waltons*. While the cannibalism jokes are overfamiliar and fail to match the treatment of the theme in **Parents** (1988), the movie does come up with a few pleasingly deranged routines, as when the eldest son (Kober) tells a folk tale about a vixen who chews off her forefeet to feed her brood while Ma (Ryan) fusses with the lace cuffs around her own oversized replacement hands, or in the business with a suicidal son who has been encouraged to think he has succeeded and is now a ghost invisible to all.

d Anthony Perkins *p* Gerald T. Olson *s* Pat Proft *c* Jacques Haitkin *se* Mick Strawn *lp* Donna Dixon, Joe Alaskey, Jeff Kober, Elizabeth Arlen, Charles Frank, Morgan Sheppard, Barbara Gowards, Leigh McCloskey, Bill Quinn, Fran Ryan, Joe Unger

Never Cry Devil *aka* **Night Visitor**
(PREMIERE PICTURES) 88min
This is a bland thriller with a satanic theme. High school foulup Rydall, given to outlandish excuses, can't persuade friends that his glamorous neighbour (Tweed) is a hooker and takes to clambering over her roof with a camera to get evidence. He finds her being murdered by a Devil-masked satanist (Garfield) who turns out to be the prissy, intolerant history teacher. Unable to convince the police (Roundtree), Rydall is terrorized by Garfield and his idiot brother (Pollard), but calls in retired cop Gould, a drop-out friend of the family, to help him bring the cultists, who have murdered a succession of prostitutes in satanic rituals, to justice. This standard variation on the boy-who-cried-wolf theme introduced by *The Window* (1949) is distinguished only by the eccentric performances of has-been guest stars, with Gould so laid back that he barely registers, while Garfield, relishing uptight villainy and Latin mutterings, and Pollard, reprising his grey-haired child from **American Gothic** (1987), at least work up some interest as semi-comic villains. Silver is a former critic whose work includes *The Vampire Film*.

d Rupert Hitzig *p* Alain Silver *s* Randall Viscovich *c* Peter Jensen *lp* Elliott Gould, Allen Garfield, Michael J. Pollard, Shannon Tweed, Derek Rydall, Richard Roundtree, Henry Gibson

Night Life *aka* **Grave Misdemeanours**
(CREATIVE MOVIE MARKETING) 92min
Disadvantaged nerd Grimes is forced to spend his spare time working for his tyrannical undertaker uncle (Astin) and is frequently victimized by a group of preppies. Unusually the hazing is given an explicitly social aspect in the distinction between the put-upon heroes, who have to work at blue-collar jobs to get the money for college tuition if they are to escape the dead-end small town, and the snobbish villains, who breeze around destructively in sports cars, secure that their parents' money will buy them a comfortable future.

After the long build-up, the bullies are killed in an offscreen crash with a chemical truck and revived from the dead by that old melodrama standby, the streak of lightning. In the film's one effectively gruesome sequence, the re-animated teens avenge themselves on the undertaker by treating him as he has treated corpses, killing him with an airhose. The zombies pursue Grimes and his mechanic girlfriend (Pollak), surviving death by bullet, fire, furnace, axe, train and drowning before being put out of commission. Adequately acted, especially by Grimes and Pollak, this is a cut above such farces as *Beverly Hills Bodysnatchers* (1989). It should not be confused with the 1989 made-for-TV vampire movie of the same title, starring Ben Cross and Maryam D'Abo.

d David Acomba *p* Charles Lippincott *s* Keith Critchlow *c* Roger Tonry *se* Craig Reardon *lp* Scott Grimes, Cheryl Pollak, Anthony Geary, Alan Blumenfeld, John Astin, Phil Proctor, Severn Darden

A Nightmare on Elm Street: The Dream Child
(NEW LINE) 89min
Wilcox, heroine of the last film, is pregnant by her quickly-disposed-of boyfriend, and Freddy (Englund), existing this time in the dreams of the foetus, tries to return to real life by possessing the unborn child.

There are the usual excellent effects/dream scenes (Freddy as a motorbike engulfing a speeding teen, Freddy as a comic-book superhero cutting apart a paper man) but the story advances through disorienting lapses and leaps. The only new angle, apart from intermittent pro-life propaganda discussions about teenage pregnancy, is an underlining of Wes Craven's original thesis that it's all the parents' fault by outfitting the one-note teens with caricatured, feckless, and grotesque fathers and mothers, most nastily Minter's Mom. Like New Line's **Leatherface: Texas Chainsaw Massacre 3** (1990), this comes from and goes nowhere. It merely marks time between sequels.

d Stephen Hopkins *p* Robert Shaye, Rupert Harvey *s* Leslie Bohem *c* Peter Levy *se* David Miller, Peter Kuran, Chris Biggs, Todd Masters, Greg Nicotero *lp* Robert Englund, Lisa Wilcox, Danny Hassel, Kelly Jo Minter, Erika Anderson, Whitby Hertford, Nick Mele, Beatrice Boepple

El Niño de la Luna *aka* **The Moon Child**
(GANESH PRODUCCIONED CINEMATOGRAFICA; SP) 118min
An odd, fantastical melodrama set in the thirties, this features David (Saldana), an orphan in rural Spain who is told that he is 'the child of the moon', possessed of an occult ability to move objects by force of will.

Far from taking a **Carrie** (1976) approach to the material, Villaronga combines political paranoia – the child is abducted by a group of fascist scientists who wish to mate him with another prodigy to produce a psychic master race – with surreal effects as moon magic is worked. The second half of the film shifts locale to North Africa, where the boy's father might have come from, with parapsychologists now trying to track down and kill the escapee and Saldana trying to find a tribe who are awaiting his arrival as their God. Martin is excellent as the child's haunted mother.

d/s Augustin Villaronga *p* Julian Mateos *c* Jaime Peracaula *lp* Maribel Martin, Enrique Saldana, Lisa Gerrard, Lucis Bose, David Sust, Mary Carrollo

L'Ospite *aka* **The Guest** (ACO; IT) 90min
This is a standard Devil movie, set in Brazil with a few distinguishing touches of local colour, in which a glowing-eyed academic (Law) doing research in a convent library turns out to be the Devil himself. Law glooms through the library in search of rare books while Mother Superior Stevens stands around until it's time to be thrown off a balcony and a young nun, who has given birth to a demon child, puts an end to it all by stabbing the villain in the chest with an *Omen*-style dagger.

Little is made, apart from some tiresome travelogue sequences, of the unusual setting, but director Hansen pulls off a few horrific moments and Law's incarnation of Evil is persuasive.

d Carlos Pasini Hansen *p/co-s* Alberto Marras *co-s* Ronald Russo *c* Antonio Meliande *se* Zed Special Effects *lp* John Phillip Law, Eva Orlando, Stella Stevens, Thalis Panchancon

Pet Sematary (LAUREL) 102min
Like many King novels, *Pet Sematary*, an epic replay of *The Monkey's Paw*, overcomes hackneyed plotting through an accumulation of telling detail and in-depth characterization. However, King's screenplay prunes away the precise background and elaborate plot mechanisms to leave only a TV movie with added gore.

When his ideal family moves into an old dark house in Maine, Midkiff learns from eccentric neighbour Gwynne that things buried in the Micmac Indian graveyard beyond the pet cemetery come back to life as soulless monsters. A run-over cat returns as a neon-eyed fiend and Midkiff is warned that human beings come back as violent zombies, and a brain-splattered ghost pops up at odd intervals warning him never to tamper with the forces of life and death... and yet, when his son is killed on the road, he robs the grave and heads off to the cursed ground to bring the child back. From then on the film turns into another illogical spookshow, as a pint-sized zombie butchers the cast with a kitchen-knife.

d Mary Louise Lambert *p* Richard Rubinstein *s* Stephen King *c* Peter Stein *se* Lance Anderson *lp* Dale Midkiff, Fred Gwynne, Denise Crosby, Blaze Berdahl, Miko Hughes, Brad Greenquist

Phantom of the Mall: Eric's Revenge

(FRIES ENTERTAINMENT) 89min

Like **Phantom of the Paradise** (1974) and the telefilm *The Phantom of Hollywood* (1974), this reworks Gaston Leroux' *The Phantom of the Opera* by restaging its plot in a modern setting.

The teenage Phantom (Rydall) is disfigured during an arson attack on his parents' house, one of the many underhand tricks that clears the way for the erection by a group of corrupt businessmen of the mall of the title. Lurking under it, in NIKE sweatshirt and baseball cap, the Phantom plays guardian angel to his ex-girlfriend (Whitman) and brings vigilante-style justice to unsavoury characters upon whom he spies through closed-circuit television. Finally, rejected by the girl, he goes on a rampage and blows up the entire mall.

d Richard Friedman *p* Tom Fries *s* Scott J. Schneid, Tony Michaelman, Robert King *c* Harry Mathias *se* Matthew Mungle *lp* Derek Rydall, Morgan Fairchild, Kari Whitman, Rob Estes, Jonathan Goldsmith, Ken Foree

The Phantom of the Opera (21ST CENTURY) 90min

This is a mindless rehash, with bits of the original novel and moments copied from the 1925, 1943 and 1963 movies floating around in a scenario which opens, like the film-within-a-film from *Singin' in the Rain* (1952), with a modern day soprano (Schoelen) being hit on the head with a sandbag and sent back to Victorian London.

There she understudies an obnoxious diva (Lawrence) and is coached for her big break by a mysterious angel who turns out to be a composer (Englund) who has sold his soul to the Devil for musical genius. The Phantom skins victims and sews bits of their faces onto his own to cover not-terribly horrifying scars inflicted by a satanic dwarf in a silly flashback. After sundry murders and arias, the Phantom kidnaps the girl and takes her to his cramped lair, whereupon the hero (Hyde-White) and the police pursue him. 'There must be hundreds of miles of tunnel down here,' exclaims a bobby as they go through the same bit of sewer for the dozenth time. A further mark of its intelligence is that the films neglects the two scenes vital to any version of the story: it muffs its several unmaskings and omits entirely the falling chandelier.

d Dwight Little *p* Harry Alan Towers *s* Duke Sandefur, Gerry O'Hara *c* Elemer Ragalyi *se* Kevin Yagher *lp* Robert Englund, Jill Schoelen, Alex Hyde-White, Bill Bighy, Stephanie Lawrence, Terence Harvey

Posetitel Muzeia *aka* Visitor to a Museum

(LENFILM; USSR) 135min

From the director of the nuclear holocaust movie *Pisma Myortvoi Chelovyeka* (1986), this gloomy, arty Soviet horror film is pitched between **Day of the Dead** (1985) and Tarkovsky's *Offret* (1986).

After an ecological disaster has melted the polar ice-caps, Mikhailov travels at low tide to a ruined, near-inaccessible city to visit a famous, now-partially waterlogged museum where the treasures of the past remain. The journey is complicated by marauding bands of zombie mutants who have escaped from the concentration camps where surviving humans keep them penned. Distracted from his original purpose, Mikhailov becomes interested in mutants, two of whom are kept as servants by their parents in the house where he stays. Accepted by them as a saviour, Mikhailov finally allows himself to be transformed into a proselytizing zombie, chanting 'everything is foretold' over and over as he ventures out into the world. Unusually committed to embracing the monstrous, the film transforms mutants from menaces to pathetic former human beings, and isolates a bizarre strain of spirituality in their sub-human existence, depicting mutant masses where priests chant liturgical nonsense to hordes of pacified creatures. The climax features a perilous journey through tempest-tossed seas, but at 135 minutes the film is notably lengthy and hectoring.

d/s Konstantin Lopushanski *c* Nikolai Pokoptzev *lp* Viktor Mikhailov, Irina Rakshina, Vera Maiorova

Puppet Master (FULL MOON) 90min

In another of Charles Band's murdered-by-little-things supernatural slashers, a group of psychics gather at an old hotel where, in a 1939 prologue, alchemist-puppeteer Hickey has hidden his caseful of living, deadly puppets. The psychics have been summoned by evil magician Skaggs who is pretending to be dead so he can send the creatures to eliminate potential rivals. The monsters include a drill-headed bellhop, a pin-headed brute in a gray jersey, a knife-wielding slasher, a harlequin with changing faces and a ballerina who illogically but impressively vomits leeches onto victims. Schmoeller, returning to the territory of his unusual **Tourist Trap** (1978), makes effective use of the deco hotel and eerily designed monsters. In an above-average cast, Miracle is outstanding as a Southern-accented fortune teller ('I'm not a cynic, I prefer to think of myself as a nasty bitch') and Skaggs, the villain of **Ghost Town** (1988), enjoys himself as a death-faced bad guy illogically but predictably destroyed when the puppets turn on him. One of the first productions from Full Moon, the company Band set up to replace his troubled Empire, this was successful enough to warrant a sequel, David Allen's *Puppet Master II* (1990), and a World-War-Two-set prequel, David DeCoteau's *Puppet Master III: Toulon's Revenge* (1990).

d David Schmoeller *p* Hope Perello *s* Joseph G. Collodi *c* Sergio Salvati *se* David Allen *lp* Paul Le Mat, Irene Miracle, Matt Roe, Kathryn O'Reilly, William Hickey, Jimmie F. Skaggs, Robin Frates, Barbara Crampton

Rabid Grannies (STARDUST; BEL) 83min

As Belgian splatter movies dubbed inanely into British English go, *Rabid Grannies* is pretty awful. Grasping relatives who caricature various 'vices' (a cowardly priest, a fat condom manufacturer, an arms dealer, a lesbian fashion editor) arrive at the country estate of two dear old ladies (Aymerie, Broekman) to worm their way into the will. A disinherited Satanist sends a present which emits a smoke that turns the women into cackling monsters, in the style of **The Evil Dead** (1982), who proceed to slaughter everyone in sight. Though only released by

Catherine Aymerie and Caroline Broekman are Rabid Grannies.

Knife thrower Guy Stockwell and Thelma Tixou as the tattooed lady in the bizarre Santa Sangre.

Troma Films, it displays the company's usual style, mixing splatsick with genuinely offensive material: biddies turning into monsters is potentially funny, cutting off a little girl's legs is not.

The gore is unconvincing, but wall-to-wall when it starts: the fat manufacturer is debagged and has his buttocks shredded in close-up, limbs are lopped off wholesale, the priest's brains splash on the wall as he shoots himself, one of the monsters walks around with her insides hanging out. Incidentally, the old ladies are the victims' aunts, not grandmothers.

d/s Emmanuel Kervyn *p* James Desert *c* Hugh Labye *se* Steve Fernandez *lp* Catherine Aymerie, Caroline Broekman, Danielle Raven, Raymond Lescot

Regenerator *aka* **Metamorphosis**
(FILMIRAGE; IT) 96min
Though the title suggests an imitation of **Re-Animator** (1985), this Virginia-shot pseudo-American quickie was actually inspired by Cronenberg's remake of *The Fly* (1986).

An overly dedicated genetic scientist (Le Brock) working on a cure for old age and death is pressured by the university to produce concrete results. Unwisely, he injects himself in the eye with a serum which regresses him through the evolutionary process until he turns into a ridiculous man-sized vampire dinosaur and is gunned down by police in a throwaway finale. Montefiore, a familiar monster in cheapjack Italian films (notably as the cannibalistic killer of the **Anthropophagus** films but also Goliath in *King David*, 1983) signs himself with a variation on his 'George Eastman' pseudonym.

d/p G.L. Eastman (Luigi Montefiore) *c* Lorenzo Battaglia *se* Maurizio Trani *lp* Gene le Brock, Catherine Baranov, Harry Cason, David Wicker, Stephen Brown, Jason Arnold, Tom Story, Anna Colona, Wally Doyle, Laura Gemser

Return of the Family Man
(FOCUS FILMS; SOUTH AFRICA) 88min
There has always been a tradition of imitation English (*Dr Maniac*, 1972) and American (*The Demon*, 1980) horror movies in South Africa; this item comes from a late eighties run of direct-to-video exploitationers (*The Stay Awake*, *The Evil Below*, 1988, *Howling IV: The Original Nightmare*, 1989), all purporting not to be set in the country of production.

A 'Pacific Southwest', of variable American accents, is terrorized by an escaped maniac known as 'the Family Man' (Smerczak), who – in a promising but undeveloped throwaway – devised the Star Wars Strategic Defense Initiative. He returns to his abandoned mansion, where his own murdered family still sit around a table in a walled-up basement room, and menaces a group of teenagers who have been tricked into renting the dilapidated dump as a holiday villa.

d/co-s John Murlowski *p* Johan Van Rooyen, Karl Johnson *co-s* John Fox *c* René Smith *se* Tjaart Van Der Welt *lp* Ron Smerczak, Liam Cundill, Terence Reis, Debra Kaye, Michelle Constant, Victoria Bawcombe

Rush Week (NOBLE ENTERTAINMENT GROUP) 94 min
A hooded axe-murderer stalks a college rush week, casting a dampener over the butt-baring pranks by chopping girls who have posed for a crooked photographer. Despite a heavy-handed attempt to divert suspicion onto the hero's geeky best friend ('You can look after the axe'), the killer is transparently Thinnes, the spoilsport dean. Contemptuous enough to name one of the bisected bimbos 'Julie McGuffin', this is a plodding non-mystery scattered with naked co-eds and bloodless batterings, coming ten years after the heyday of the teenkill cycle.

d Bob Bralver *p/co-s* Michael W. Leighton *co-s* Russell V. Manzatt *c* Jeff Marc *lp* Dean Hamilton, Pamela Ludwig, Roy Thinnes, Courtney Gebhart, Gregg Allmann, Dan Grant, Kathleen Kinmont

Santa Sangre (INTERSOUND; IT) 118min
A come-back from the bizarre maker of *El Topo* (1970), substituting horror leftovers for the spaghetti Western furniture of the earlier film. In a garishly tatty Mexico, madman Axel Jodorowsky lives under the domination of his brutish, phoenix-tattooed, knife-throwing father (Stockwell) and aerialist mother (Guerra). Finding Stockwell in a lewd embrace with the tattooed lady, Guerra, acolyte of a heretical sect who revere as a saint a girl who had her arms cut off, castrates him with a phial of acid, whereupon he cuts off her arms. In later life, Jodorowsky emerges from an asylum and joins his mother in a mime act in which he functions as her arms, which leads him to commit Norman Bates-style murders at the behest of the mad woman, ultimately revealed to be only a life-sized puppet.

Among the horror highlights evoked are the twisted circus world of Browning's **The Unknown** (1927) and **Freaks** (1932), problems with recalcitrant arms and knife-throwing hands that rework the quandary of Stephen Orlac, a homage to James Whale as the hero tries to become the invisible image in bandages and a smoking jacket, gore-drenched knife murders and bird-of-prey imagery after the manner of the producer's brother Dario, a graveyard hallucination in the frenzied style of José Mojica Marins, an episode with a gargantuan female wrestler who recalls El Santo, and a twisted plot that echoes not only **Peeping Tom** (1960) but, even more disreputably, **Circus of Horrors** (19590) and **The Psychopath** (1965).

While dealing with degradation, violence and madness, Jodorowsky has mellowed enough to import a deal of humane feeling, allowing even the murderer's awful parents a strange dignity, struggling against the tide of gore to find a redemptive strain among the ruins of genre cinema.

d/co-s Alexandro Jodorowsky *p/co-s* Claudio Argento *co-s* Roberto Leoni *c* Daniele Nannuzzi *se* Marcelino Pacheco *lp* Axel Jodorowsky, Blanca Guerra, Guy Stockwell, Thelma Tixou, Sabrina Dennison

Shocker (ALIVE/U) 110min
Having lost control of of psycho superstar/moneymaking franchise Freddy Krueger, this was Craven's attempt to introduce a monster for the nineties. While it has interesting ideas – a few of which feature in the similar **The Horror Show** (1989) – the baneful spectre of Freddy loiters.

A serial killer slaughters families in a small town, and the hero – high school jock Berg – has bad dreams in which he sees the maniac at work. When he dreams of the murder of his adoptive mother and siblings, Berg helps his cop father (Murphy) identify limping TV repairman Horace Pinker (Pileggi) as the killer. Pinker is condemned to the electric chair and, in a melodramatic but well-staged execution sequence, dramatically reveals that the source of his psychic link with Berg is that he is the orphan's real father and vows to return from beyond the grave to continue his reign of terror. After death, Pinker moves into the same section of the afterlife as Freddy, and keeps popping up to make trouble. He can not only appear in dreams, but zip from place to place via TV signals, possess innocent people and make bad jokes.

d/co-p/s Wes Craven *co-p* Shep Gordon, Marianne Maddalena *c* Jacques Haitkin *se* Lance Anderson, Bruno George *lp* Peter Berg, Cami Cooper, Michael Murphy, Mitch Pileggi, Timothy Leary, Theodore Raimi, Alice Cooper, Heather Langenkamp

Society (SOCIETY PRODUCTIONS INC) 99min
An extraordinary genre début, this finds Yuzna, producer of **Re-Animator** (1985), taking up the megaphone for an unclassifiable fable that, like John Carpenter's *They Live* (1988), proposes that the rich are literally inhuman.

Warlock, son of a monied California family, confides to his psychiatrist that he suspects he is adopted, and can't stop feeling things are amiss with his family and their social circle. People die but turn up apparently unfazed, the Beverly Hills cops appear to be in on the conspiracy and people seem to perform anatomically impossible contortions. In an extended finale, Warlock crashes a social event and discovers the élite indulging in a bizarrely sexual ritual involving shape-shifting, plentiful slime, grotesque physical unions, po-faced pronouncements about the individual's responsibility to 'society', and tortuous duels. 'The rich have always sucked off low-class shit like you,' his sister's boyfriend tells him, while the cigar-smoking, slime-covered Judge explains 'You're a different race from us, a different species, a different class... You have to be born into society'. Flesh is twisted into surreal shapes and people are literally turned inside out, courtesy of grotesque effects by George, as the film segues from *The Graduate* (1967) into **From Beyond** (1986).

d Brian Yuzna *p* Keith Walley *s* Woody Keith, Rick Fry *c* Rick Fichter *se* Screaming Mad George *lp* Billy Warlock, Devin DeVasquez, Connie Danese, Ben Slack, Evan Richards, Patrice Jennings, Ben Myerson, Tim Bartell, Charles Lucia, Heidi Kozak

Sotto il Vestito Niente 2 *aka* **Too Beautiful to Die** (FILMIRAGE; IT) 97min
Another style-happy murder-the-models movie treading in the footsteps of **Sei Donne per l'Assassino** (1964). When Scola is raped in the jacuzzi by a VIP, abetted by her agent and a group of other models, she flees the house only to turn up mysteriously dead. Her sister (Guerin) arrives from America and takes her place in a Warriors of the Wasteland pop video being shot by director Gendron, wherupon the participants in the original rape are stalked by a masked figure whose favoured murder weapons are the sharp implements used in the video.

d/co-s Dario Di Piana *p* Achille Manzotti *co-s* Claudio Mancini *c* Alan Jones *lp* Francois Eric Gendron, Florence Guerin, Randi Ingermann, Giovanni Iamberi, Goia Maria Scola, Helena Jesus, Francois Marthouret

Spellbinder (MGM/INDIAN NECK ENTERTAINMENT) 99min
This is a Californian version of **The Wicker Man** (1973). Daly is the high-flying lawyer who rescues a battered witch (Preston) from a parking-lot assault, and tries to protect her from her ex-coven, who intend to sacrifice an innocent on the beach at the winter solstice. As is heavily signalled, Daly is himself the innocent who must 'come willingly' to the site of his death, and the kittenishly uninteresting Preston, along with his oafish best friend (Rossovich) and an assortment of local worthies, is in on the plot.

d Janet Greek *p* Joe Wizan, Brian Russell *s* Tracey Tormé *c* Adam Greenberg *se* Burt Dalton, Pat Lee, William Klinger *lp* Timothy Daly, Kelly Preston, Rick Rossovich, Audra Lindley, Diana Bellamy, Cary-Hiroyuki Tagawa, Stefan Gierasch

Streghe *aka* **Witch Story** (CLAUDIO BONIVENTO/UNITED ENTERTAINMENT CORPORATION; IT) 91min
This is an innovation-free mock-US horror movie in the tradition of **La Casa no. 3** (1987), incorporating snippets of plot and imagery from **La Maschera del Demonio** (1960), **...E Tu Vivrai nel Terrore! L'Aldila** (1981), **The Evil Dead** (1982) and **Night of the Demons** (1986).

The film opens with a sequence set in the Deep South in the thirties – in which a mob of angry villagers burn 'Satan's whore' Lund and the witch's influence causes a little girl (Law) to commit suicide. Then a busload of teenagers (integrated by sex, race and weight but uniformly lacking in acting ability) arrive in the locale in 1989 to holiday in the old house that was the site of the demonic doings. Any pretense of a story is jettisoned in favour of possessed girls cackling as they torture and murder perplexed boys with chainsaws, axes and shotguns. The single interesting teen (Sanderson) is too casually crushed under a falling crucifix after having unearthed clues that lead the survivors to dotty ex-priest Bannen, who explains at rambling length in a Scots-Florida accent why Lund, who has developed a Charlie's Angels perm in the afterlife, is influencing the ghost of Law to precipitate supernatural terrors.

d/co-s Alessandro Capone *p* Mauro Morigi, Giuseppe Pedersoli *co-s* Rosario Galli, Jeff Moldovan *c* Roberto Girometti *se* Rick Gonzales *lp* Ian Bannen, Christopher Peacock, Michelle Vannucchi, Deanna Lund, Gary Kerr, Amy Adams, Jeff Bankert, Charon Butler, Todd Conatser, Jason M. Lefkowitz, Nancie Sanderson, Suzanne Law

Sundown: The Vampire in Retreat (VESTRON) scope 104min
In this addition to the exclusive vampire western subgenre, fanged immortals shoot it out on Main Street at High Midnight, outlaw hordes ride into town popping off the civilized undead with sixgunloads of wooden bullets, whiskery old-timers in sombreros and shades stay out of the sun, and all the while the scenic splendours of Monument Valley are explored in glorious Panavision.

Haematologist Metzler is summoned to the vampire-run town of Purgatory to help the humanist Count Mardulak (Carradine) produce artificial blood so he can achieve integration with normal humanity. Meanwhile, vampire pilgrim father Ireland stirs up old-style predators and assembles an army of murderous saddle trash and drugged-out sleazeballs. The finale finds Mardulak revealing his true identity, thus giving Carradine the chance to take on the role his father essayed in the earlier vampire Western **Billy the Kid vs Dracula** (1965), and pulls a moving reversal as the good-hearted vampires, reconciled to the church, lose their fear of the cross.

d/co-s Anthony Hickox *p* Jef Richard *co-s* John Burgess *c* Levie Isaacs *se* Tony Gardner *lp* David Carradine, Jim Metzler, Morgan Brittany, Bruce Campbell, Deborah Foreman, John Ireland, Maxwell Caulfield, M. Emmet Walsh

Auditioning for ZZ Top: Sundown.

Teen Vamp
(NEW WORLD/JIM MCCULLOUCH PRODUCTIONS) 85min
A low budget, comedy-tinged vampire movie, similar to **Once Bitten** (1985) and **My Best Friend is a Vampire** (1988). In a thinly recreated fifties, high-school nerd Bishop is bitten by a prostitute and turns into a leather-jacketed cool juvenile delinquent with white-eye contact lenses and plastic fangs. Led by minister Gulager, a group of concerned citizens form a vigilante group and track Bishop to a local old dark house which is occasionally visited by apparitions, and a scrappy and protracted showdown sorts everything out. With minimal production values, amateurish performances and irritating music, this is a bottom-of-the-barrel quickie, slapped together to cash in on the success of **Teen Wolf** (1985).

d/s Samuel Bradford *p* Jim McCullough *c* Richard Mann *se* Jude Prest, Bill Davis *lp* Clu Gulager, Karen Carlson, Angie Brown, Beau Bishop

36:15 – Code Père Noel (LM/DEAL/GARANCE; FR) 90min
Though derivative of pictures like **Silent Night, Deadly Night** (1984), this fairy-tale action picture overcomes a familiar premise with post-Luc Besson/Beneix verve.

The child hero (Musy), who kits himself up Rambo-style to adventure with his dog in a castle-like home, hooks up through his computer with a psychotic (Florsheim) and attracts the Santa-suited madman on Christmas Eve. Florsheim arrives as Musy has staked out the fireplace to see whether Father Christmas really does come down the chimney, and the kid uses all his ingenuity to protect himself and to save his infirm grandfather (Ducreux). The film is mainly an extended game of cat and mouse, with explicit Tom and Jerry overtones, set in the rambling house, as Musy converts his toys into weapons. Manzor works up some sympathy for the put-upon madman, who is undone by fiendish tricks like a grenade wired to a toy train, and pulls clever bits of Hitchcockery, as when the nearly blind old man has to fire a gun at the struggling kid and villain. By concentrating on the bizarre child genius rather than a more usual screaming bimbo, and in using a deal of sly humour, Manzor's film emerges as a distinctive and offbeat entry in the Santa Psycho cycle. Made a year before *Home Alone* (1990), it has many striking plot similarities with John Hughes' box-office hit.

d/p/s René Manzor *c* Michel Gaffier *lp* Alain Musy, Brigitte Fossey, Louis Ducreux, Patrick Florsheim, François-Eric Gendron, Stephane Legros

Time of the Beast *aka* **Mutator**
(A CUT ABOVE; SOUTH AFRICA) 87min
Burned-out gene engineer James returns, disguised as a security guard, to the facility where he suspects his old employers, an unscrupulous corporation, are developing genetically engineered monsters. Trapped overnight in the premises are the corporation's untrustworthy owner (O'Shaughnessy), his eco-activist daughter (Davitz) who is intent on releasing experimental animals (an angle also exploited in *Primal Rage*, 1989), a couple of disposable guards and an unspecified number of monsters. The low-rent production has an impressive location, but the budget stretches to only one shaggy cat-monster suit.

d John R. Bowey *p* Russell D. Markowitz *s* Lynn Rose Higgins *c* Lynton Stephenson *se* Robert Burman Studios *lp* Brion James, Carolyn Ann Clark, Milton Raphael, Embeth Davitz, Neil McCarthy, Lindsay Orbach, Greg Latter, Brian O'Shaughnessy, Dennis Smith

Urotsukudoji *aka* **Legend of the Overfiend**
(TOSHIO MAEDA/JAPAN AUDIO VISUAL NETWORK/WEST CAPE CORPORATION; JAP) 108min
This feature-length compilation of the first four episodes of a serial, *The Wandering Kid*, finds the *manga* animation style usually expended on science fiction venturing into horror territory, albeit with messianic concerns and mass carnage similar in scope to such items as *Akira* (1989).

Along the lines of the wilder stretches of Clive Barker though also indebted to H.P. Lovecraft's Cthulhu mythos, the epic opens in a modern-day Osaka school where the beast-boy Amano, the Wandering Kid of the original title, is searching for the current incarnation of the Chojin, a long-forecast divinity and the Overfiend of the title who will remake the world into a peaceful utopia. Also on the case are demonic representatives out to stop the change, though the suitably apocalyptic finale presents the Chojin as hardly a benevolent God in that, to make way for its utopia, it is obliged entirely to destroy corrupt civilization. The human avatar of Chojin is Nagumo, a reject first seen masturbating while peeking into the girls' changing room, and the agent of his transformation into the giant monster god is his relationship with the innocent Akemi, who survives violation by a demon disguised as a lesbian teacher to become a mother-figure to the new world. Amano and his sister Megumi, who appear to have cat ancestors, finally turn against the creature's purpose in the city-destroying, open-ended, finale.

This is an all-out attempt to cover all shock bases, complete with a high body count as humans and demons are ripped to bloody shreds by magical forces, visionary depictions of hellish entities which combine the grosser elements of Marvel Comics characters with the bizarre excesses of Bosch, and nigh-hardcore sexual content that goes further than any live action film in the fusion of sado-erotic churning with special-effects demonology.

d Hideki Takayama *p* Yashuhito Yamaki *s* Noburu Aikawa *c* Shigeo Kamiyama, Susumu Yamakawa, Akihiko Takahashi

Vampire's Kiss (HEMDALE) 103min

Taking its title from the film-within-a-film found in **Body Double** (1984), this is a peculiar addition to the cinematic lore of the undead, poaching an idea or two from **Martin** (1976) and then playing like a big-city crack-up comedy – *Who Is Harry Kellerman and Why Is He Saying Those Terrible Things About Me?* (1971), *The Prisoner of Second Avenue* (1972) – with psychotic moments lifted from **The Driller Killer** (1979) or **Repulsion** (1965).

New York literary agent Cage picks up Beals, an exotic who bites him during sex and whom he fantasizes is a vampire. Cage takes to wearing dark glasses by day, sleeping under his couch, eating cockroaches, shunning crucifixes and buying plastic fangs to further his nocturnal rampaging, attempting a hilarious approximation of two of the hammiest vampire-related performances of the past, Max Schreck as the scuttling hunchbacked Dracula in **Nosferatu – Eine Symphonie des Grauens** (1921) and Dwight Frye as the wild-eyed, wild-haired, cockroach-eating Renfield in **Dracula** (1931). Given that at least as much time is spent on Cage's obsessional terrorizing of his assistant (Alonso) for her failure to locate a missing contract as it is on his excursions into vampirism, it barely qualifies as the horror movie which appears to be struggling towards birth in the sequences featuring Beals as the slinky vampirette, and settles into the nightmare comic course of Minion's earlier, far more sustained *After Hours* (1986).

d Robert Bierman *p* Barbara Zitwer, Barry Shills *s* Joseph Minion *c* Stefan Czapsky *se* Ed French *lp* Nicolas Cage, Maria Conchita Alonso, Jennifer Beals, Elizabeth Ashley, Kasi Lemmons, Bob Lujan

The Vineyard (NEW WORLD/NORTHSTAR) 90min

Hong, villain of John Carpenter's *Big Trouble in Little China* (1986), co-directs and co-writes in addition to taking the lead role of this low-budget attempt to follow Carpenter's crossbreeding of Chinese horror genre with its Western counterpart.

Po (Hong) is a centuries-old wine grower who retains his life thanks to a magic amulet and periodic infusions of a fluid made from the blood of young victims. He lures these to his island enclave by posing as a movie producer and holding 'auditions', the latest of which has brought him Witter, a blonde whom he intends, in an echo of the plot of *Big Trouble in Little China*, to marry and sacrifice in order to do without his amulet. In addition, the island is staffed by martial artists and Po's even more ancient and decrepit mother, and occasionally overrun by the lurching zombies buried in the vineyard.

co-d/co-s James Hong *co-d* Bill Rice *p* Harry Mok *co-s* Douglas Condo, James Marlowe *c* John Dirlam *se* Peter Konig *lp* James Hong, Karen Witter, Michael Wong, Cheryl Madsen, Lars Wanberg, Robert Ito, Rue Douglas

Voodoo Dawn *aka* Strange Turf

(STILLWELL PRODUCTIONS) 83min

A low-budget voodoo movie, with NYCU students Baily and Williams venturing onto a Southern plantation which is dominated by Haitian ex-secret-police chief and voodoo priest Todd who has turned one of their friends (Albrecht) into a zombie with his head sewn on. Consulting local Gershon, wise woman Merritt and fatherly refugee St Jacques, the city slickers learn enough voodoo to use against the villain. A last-reel revolution deposes the tyrant and disposes of the zombie. Sincere but drab, this benefits from mainly decent performances – the cadaverous Todd prefigures **Candyman** (1992) as a surprisingly underplayed and impressive chief baddie – and occasional effective moments, such as a zombie transfixed laterally by a spear stubbornly trying to walk through a doorway.

d Steven Fierberg *p* Steven Mackler *s* John Russo, Jeffrey Delman, Thomas Rendon, Evan Dunsky *c* James McCalmont *se* John Bisson *lp* Raymond St Jacques, Theresa Merritt, Gina Gershon, Kirk Baily, Billy 'Sly' Williams, Tony Todd, J. Grant Albrecht

Jennifer Beals as the slinky vampirette of Vampire's Kiss.

Bette Davis, in her last screen appearance, as the Wicked Stepmother.

Wicked Stepmother (MGM) 92min

This was a troubled production, even messier than most Cohen movies because Davis, in her last film, had to be replaced for much of the shooting with Carrera.

Rasche and Camp are disturbed when father (Stander) remarries late in life to Miranda (Davis), a witch who shrinks people. Miranda shares bodyspace with Priscilla (Carrera), another witch, with each spending time as a cat while the other is walking around, working spells, and disrupting the household. The witches' scheme is to make Stander wealthy by giving him the power to answer any question on a TV game show, and then take off with the money, leaving a literally diminished family behind. Cohen's fondness for players from the thirties and forties here appears to have rebounded with unfortunate effects (though there is a nice in-joke, with a picture of Joan Crawford standing in for Stander's first wife). Like **Full Moon High** (1982), this is essentially a sit-com, adopting some of the tone of TV's *Bewitched*, with magic used for joky ends, as when Carrera sprouts a cat's tail in the throes of orgasm or psychokinetically wrecks Camp's kitchen. Carrera enjoys herself in an unpromising role and there are funny turns from Moll as a clumsy private eye, Keyes as a witch who teaches an evening course and Landon as a dippy TV game-show hostess.

d/s Larry Cohen *p* Robert Littman *c* Bryan England
lp Bette Davis, Barbara Carrera, David Rasche, Colleen Camp, Lionel Stander, Tom Bosley, Shawn Donahue, Evelyn Keyes, Richard Moll, Laurene Landon

Zhuo Gui Dashi *aka* **Vampire Buster** *aka* **Ninja Vampire Busters**

(IN GEAR FILM PRODUCTION CO; HONG KONG) 90min

Despite its English-language titles (the appallingly ignorant use of the term Ninja is limited to UK video-box art and does not appear on any print), this is not an entry in the 'hopping vampire' cycle but a modern story of all-action exorcism and rampaging ghosts.

Opening during the Revolution with a chubby exorcist telling a Maoist mob not to break an ancient urn in which an ancestor of his once captured a demon, the film is mainly set in the present day. The urn is brought to Hong Kong by a politician who, after some complications, becomes possessed by the demon, who makes him reverse his position on nuclear power in an undeveloped subplot and turns into a glowing-eyed evil one. The now-venerable exorcist, who occasionally assumes the aspect of Buddha, is on the trail, with the help of a young conman who has been trying to defraud the politician and who gets brutally killed in a rare moment of non-comic violence. Predictable and hectic, but with intriguing political angles popping up amid the ghost-busting and family plotting.

d Siu Ka-Wing, Law Man *p* Alan Tang, Rover Tang
s Barry Wong, Wong Ching, Jeff Yuen *c* Lau Moon-Tong, Ngo Chi-Gwan, Lam Fai-Tai *lp* Simon Cheng, Fung Chui-Fen, Jacky Cheung, Chan Baak-Cheung, Chan Yi-Si

The 1990s

Arachnophobia (BUENA VISTA/AMBLIN) 109min
A near-perfect monster movie, *Arachnophobia* balances genre requirements with sly humour.

In a lengthy Venezuelan jungle prologue, a lethal new spider species stows away in the makeshift coffin of a bitten expedition member and is transported to a peaceful California township. Also new in town is Daniels, a doctor trying to escape big-city strain who immediately finds the country too stressful, with a house on the verge of falling down, an established town doctor (Jones) who decides not to retire and ruins Daniels' practice, and an arachnid invasion which exacerbates his arachnophobia. Things escalate and the professionals have to be called in: pony-tailed poseur Sands spouts hard-to-follow entomological theories while down-to-earth exterminator Goodman provides dry comedy relief and common-sense bugspray therapy. A high-quality version of *Kingdom of the Spiders* (1977) or *Frogs* (1972), this, like **Gremlins** (1984), evokes a traditional Spielberg-Frank Capra small town and proceeds to show the gnawing horrors lurking in the popcorn, the toilet bowl or the old barn. As in the best of Spielberg's early work, *Duel* (1972) and **Jaws** (1975), the climax finds an ordinary man standing alone, without any experts to help him, facing his own phobia and the monster that threatens his home. First-time director Marshall, previously one of Spielberg's trusty producers, comes into his own with a squirmy, cheeralong sequence that finds Daniels duelling with the Big Daddy spider in his own basement, protecting himself with only an ozone-unfriendly aerosol, a cigarette lighter, bottles of vintage wine and a nailgun.

d Frank Marshall *p* Kathleen Kennedy, Richard Vane *s* Don Jakoby, Wesley Strick *c* Mikael Salomon *se* Chris Walas *lp* Jeff Daniels, Harley Jane Kozak, John Goodman, Julian Sands, Stuart Pankin, Brian MacNamara, Henry Jones

Into the Mainstream

The arrival of the precisely titled **Bram Stoker's Dracula** in 1992, almost a full century after the novel was published, has been read as confirmation of the survival of the gothic tradition of horror. In truth, despite the fact that as I write (in the summer of 1993) another big-budget version of **Frankenstein** is about to go into production, horror in the nineties was generally less gothic than repetitive. The title of the decade was the marvellously grey **Henry... Portrait of a Serial Killer** (1991). That, far more than the Oscar-winning **Silence of the Lambs** (1991) broke new ground.

The amateur would-be gore-makers continued to exercise their fantasies on the direct-to-video sub-genre and the classics were revived (even by one-time directors of classics: Corman's **Frankenstein Unbound**, 1990). But most notable of all was the eruption of the horror narrative into mainstream Hollywood cinema. Consider **Basic Instinct** (1992). Its borrowings from *film noir* and *Bullitt* (1968)-type *policiers* have been noted, but of more fundamental interest is the movie's question, 'is she despite all the evidence nonetheless not the killer?...', with a visual to prove whatever you think to the contrary. This is a pure horror narrative strategy in which, since the story being told is not constrained by rationality, it is not reducible to a one-dimensional end, but the card is played in *Basic Instinct* with a commercial knowingness that is more evident than beguiling. The same is generally true of **Cape Fear** (1991). However, even this seems to be only a fad rather that a phase in the development of the genre. Indeed, the new caution that has made sequels the norm rather than the exception has been further supported by demographic evidence that in the nineties family films (as opposed to teen-oriented quickies) will be the most exploitable and spin-offable. As ever, horror stands at a crossroads. One the one hand the underlying narrative strategy of horror, in which anything can happen, is clearly easily utilizable by film-makers looking for visceral presence, a feature of contemporary film-making, yet as a genre horror doesn't fit the bill of family fare.

Baby Blood
(PARTNERS PRODUCTIONS/EXO 7 PRODUCTIONS; FR) 89min
A tentacle imported inside an African lion destined for a circus explodes forth and takes up residence in the womb of gap-toothed Escourrou. Pregnant and depressed, hearing the voice of her unnatural foetus, she flees the circus. Driven to kill obnoxious males, she drinks blood to help her child develop, finally giving birth to a normal baby who later is transformed into a

Previous pages: Something wicked this way comes: Tales from the Darkside: The Movie.

Left: John Goodman in Arachnophobia*: the common man as hero.*

monster. She loses the creature on a bus filled with drunken and abusive rugby players whose behaviour prompts her to induce a fatal crash from which only the monster emerges.

The result is a refreshingly vile alternative to the wholesome *Look Who's Talking* (1989). Enthusiastic in its application of grotesque gore effects, *Baby Blood* may be the only French film to feature a point-of-view shot of a knife repeatedly stabbing into the crotch of a lecher's Y-fronts. This is a relishably grotty trifle, flamboyantly mean-spirited with a sneaky gallic trace of wit.

d/s Alain Robak *p* Ariel Zietoun, Joelle Malberg, Irene Sohm *c* Bernard Dechet *se* Benoit Lestang, Jean-Marc Toussaint *lp* Emmanuelle Escourrou, Jean-François Gallotte, Christian Sinninger, Roselyn Geslot, Thierry LePortier

Bandh Darwaza

(RAMSAY FILMS COMBINE; INDIA) 145min

This is a Hindi vampire film, complete with elaborate musical numbers, martial arts, annoying comic relief, elementary gore, multi-faith religious overtones, chases, steamy romance and gothic horror.

After a lengthy period prologue in which a mob destroy Shaitan (a hugely fanged, grey-faced vampire who dresses like Dracula) the film skips to the present. Revived and dripping with slime, the monster emerges from his tomb to cast his influence over a voluptuous but intrepid young girl. While the heroine's sensuality marks her out as the wrong choice for the singing hero, who eventually settles for the demure and traditional second-string girl, she at least has the pluck to fight off attacking devil monks and dies, in a lift from *Salem's Lot* (1979) when, after failing to drive a knife through Shaitan's heart, she is tossed against a wall of spikes. The finale features a cross-country chase with the heroes' jeep in pursuit of the villains' hearse and a traditional confrontation between a torch-bearing mob and the vampire, which winds up with sympathetic magic as Shaitan spontaneously combusts when the bat-monkey idol in his temple is burned by a wise man. The credits reveal the timber was supplied by Jawahar Saw Mills.

d/p Tulsi Ramsay, Shyam Ramsay *s* Dev Kishan, Shyam Ramsay *c* Gangu Ramsay *se* Srinivas Roy *lp* Hashmat Khan, Manjeet Kular, Kunika, Satish Kaul, Anita Sareen

Basket Case 2

(SHAPIRO-GLICKENHAUS ENTERTAINMENT) 89min

Made back to back with *Frankenhooker* (1990), this demonstrates both Henenlotter's ingenuity at devising freakish monsters and his inability to create a coherent storyline peopled with believable characters.

Duane (VanHentenryck) and his monstrous separated Siamese twin Belial find themselves in the care of grandmotherly philanthropist Ross, who maintains a refuge for 'unique individuals': an array of rubber-faced freaks modelled on such sources as the pinhead geek from *The Brain That Wouldn't Die* (1962) and the grotesque cartoons of Basil Wolverton. Like **Basket Case** (1982), the film is stuck with a simplistic revenge plot as Belial and the other freaks terrorize exploitative showmen and tabloid journalists, while VanHentenryck has an awkwardly played romance with another of Henenlotter's unbelievably thin female characters (Rattray). Despite the haphazard and conventional gore-horror-suspense scenes, Henenlotter pulls off a few twisted, unclassifiably horrific moments, as in the magnificent punch line which finds the twins painfully and aptly sewn together again.

d/s Frank Henenlotter *p* Edgar Ievins *c* Robert M. Baldwin *se* Gabe Bartalos *lp* Kevin VanHentenryck, Annie Ross, Kathryn Meisle, Heather Rattray, Jason Evers, Ted Sorel

Blue Steel

(VESTRON) 106min

Like **Manhunter** (1986), **The Stepfather** (1986), and **Fatal Attraction** (1987), *Blue Steel* is a crossbreed of the slasher – with guns replacing knives as fetish objects of violence – with the psychological thriller and the relationship melodrama.

Rookie patrolwoman Curtis shoots dead an armed supermarket robber on her first night on the job, and is herself suspended because the dead man's gun has been stolen by one of the witnesses (Silver), a deranged stockbroker who becomes obsessed with the policewoman, murdering strangers with the gun after carving her name on bullet casings. Curtis and hulking homicide dick Brown try to catch the killer, while the charming Silver insinuates his way into her life, gradually revealing just how insane he is. Following **Near Dark** (1987) with this urban action movie, Bigelow concentrates unusually on characterizations, with Curtis's background filled in through scenes with her abused mother (Fletcher) and resentful father (Bosco), and Silver's psychopath given some intriguing psycho-babble to go along with traditional signifiers of instability like the home-exercise machine and the plausible lawyer.

d/co-s Kathryn Bigelow *p* Edward R. Pressman, Oliver Stone *co-s* Eric Red *c* Amir Mokri *se* Steve Kirshoff *lp* Jamie Lee Curtis, Ron Silver, Clancy Brown, Elizabeth Peña, Louise Fletcher, Philip Bosco

The Borrower

(ATLANTIC/VISION) 88min

McNaughton's follow-up to **Henry... Portrait of a Serial Killer** (1987) is more playful and more genre-oriented, a splattery monster movie in the line of descent from *Laserblast* (1977), *Critters* (1988), *Dark Angel* (1990) and *Peacemaker* (1990), in which alien criminals get loose on Earth and go on conventionally psychotic rampages. As in most of the films of this subgenre, the result is a crossbreed of invasion-from-space quickie and hard-boiled cop movie, with Chong as the driven LA cop tracking a recently-escaped rapist (Giuntoli) at the same time as she investigates a series of decapitations. The alien villain has been 'genetically devolved' from his insectoid original form into a human body, but the process hasn't quite worked and no sooner has he arrived on Earth and overpowered his guard than his head explodes, prompting him to borrow replacements from earthlings, allowing him, as in *The Hidden* (1985), to impersonate a succession of human beings and a dog. Not on a par with *Henry*, this is still well above average for its genre, and applies its gory jokes with relish, confirming McNaughton's promise if not really developing his potential.

d John McNaughton *p* R.P. Sekon, Steven A. Jones *s* Mason Nage, Richard Fire *c* Julio Macat, Robert New *se* Kevin Yagher *lp* Rae Dawn Chong, Don Gordon, Tom Towles, Antonio Fargas, Neil Giuntoli

Brain Dead

(CONCORDE) 85min

In 1963, Beaumont, who had scripted *The Intruder* (1962), **Premature Burial** (1962) and **The Haunted Palace** (1963) for Roger Corman, wrote a screenplay called *Paranoia*, expanding on the ideas he'd explored in his short fiction and *Twilight Zone* episodes. In 1990, Corman's company finally filmed it, and, surprisingly, much of Beaumont's distinctive plotting – a mix of panicky humour and deep-dyed paranoia – survived the updating rewrites.

Surgeon Pullman examines a genius (Cort) who has gone mad and killed his family, and finds his own identity alarmingly eaten away. His friends, colleagues and wife go along with the process, convincing him that he is the patient who needs brain surgery, so the boundaries between the sane neurosurgeon and the insane mathematician are gradually erased. In the wake of **A Nightmare on Elm Street** (1985), horror movies have domesticated the dream-or-reality theme as an excuse to pep up slow plot stretches with irrelevant but pointless shock scenes, but *Brain Dead* follows *Videodrome* (1982) in allowing the fantasies to fragment, multiply and take over the film.

d/co-s Adam Simon *p* Julie Corman *co-s* Charles Beaumont *c* Ronn Schmidt *se* Rob Burman, Barney Burman *lp* Bill Pullman, Bill Paxton, Bud Cort, Patricia Charbonneau, Nicholas Pryor, George Kennedy

The Cellar (INDIAN NECK ENTERTAINMENT) 85min

This formulaic Indian curse movie follows the expected pattern when a young couple (Kilpatrick, Savoy) move into a house. Kilpatrick's son (Miller) by a previous marriage visits and is disbelieved when he sees the creature, a combination of the most vicious parts of various animals, emerge from its cellar or a nearby sumphole to kill the supporting cast. It ends with a confrontation in the cellar as the family see off the monster, demonstrating the potency of a white-bread WASP nuclear family over Native American spiritualism. Despite attempts at the non-stereotyped characterization that marked Tenney's **Witchboard** (1985), this is a minor picture, with a plasticky monster and a seemingly interminable build-up.

d Kevin S. Tenney *p* Patrick Wells, Steven E. Berman *s* John Woodward *c* Thomas Jewett *se* Max, Kevin Brennan, Elaine Alexander *lp* Patrick Kilpatrick, Chris Miller, Suzanne Savoy, Ford Rainey, Michael Wren, Lou Perry, Danny Mora

Child's Play 2 (U) 85min

This sequel features a lavish major-studio budget, efficient special effects, up-front publicity articles in genre magazines and a snappy tag line, 'Sorry Jack ... Chucky's Back!'. Oddly, MGM-UA – producers of *Child's Play* (1988) – passed the property on, not wanting to make this on 'moral grounds', and left the doll-abusers at Universal to head for guaranteed box-office success.

A series of contrivances re-assemble the possessed killer doll and transfer the embattled child whose body he wants to usurp into the care of a foster family. Then the same old plot rolls, as pseudo-Mummy and Daddy Agutter and Graham refuse to believe ickle-wickle Vincent when he claims the doll in the basement contains the spirit of psycho Dourif. The adult cast are mechanically killed off one by one until a big showdown borrowed from *The Terminator* (1984). The movie winds up in a doll factory where the fight is on all over the automated production line, with attendants gored by doll-eyeball-inserting machinery, hot plastic slurping all over the place, and a succession of no-it's-not-dead-yet shocks.

d John Lafia *p* David Kirschner *s* Don Mancini *c* Stefan Czapsky *se* Kevin Yagher *lp* Alex Vincent, Jenny Agutter, Gerrit Graham, Christine Elise, Brad Dourif, Grace Zabriskie

Darkman (U) 95min

Obsessive scientist Neeson, working on artificial faces for the deformed, is mutilated when thugs in the pay of crooked tycoon Friels blow up his lab to destroy incriminating evidence. He escapes from unbilled Agutter's care after a revolutionary process has made him impervious to pain and dons perishable living disguises to get his revenge.

Working for the first time with a major studio, Raimi obviously feels himself the heir to a Universal tradition, fashioning a character designed to step into the footprints of **The Phantom of the Opera** or *The Invisible Man*, with both of whom the disfigured and masked Darkman, thwarted in love and prone to megalomania, has much in common. Raimi also draws on the thirties meld of science fiction and horror created by Warners and Michael Curtiz in **Doctor X** (1931), **Mystery of the Wax Museum** (1933) and *The Walking Dead* (1935), in which flesh-masked monsters mix with tough-talking gangsters. *Darkman* is an extraordinarily elaborate introduction, an 'origin story' in comics terms, that sadly hamstrings its central character with a multi-authored and diffuse plot. The action scenes, however, are effectively thrilling, as Darkman dangles from a speeding helicopter thwarting every attempt to dislodge him, or dodges hot rivets while playing cat and mouse with Friels in the girders of an unfinished skyscraper.

d/co-s Sam Raimi *p* Robert Tapert *co-s* Chuck Pfarrer, Ivan Raimi, Daniel Goldin, Joshua Goldin *c* Daryl Kass *se* Tony Gardner, Larry Hamlin *lp* Liam Neeson, Frances McDormand, Colin Friels, Larry Drake, Nicholas Worth, Jenny Agutter

Def By Temptation (TROMA) 95min

Animated by the guiding spirit of Spike Lee, the new black cinema here returns to the theme of **Blacula** (1972) and **Ganja and Hess** (1973).

The opening, with bartender Terrell spieling on the phone to a succession of girlfriends and then succumbing to a Temptress (Bond), appears to have strayed in out of *She's Gotta Have It* (1986), but the sharp, funny and borderline creepy social-sexual horror story continues with ambiguous sequences in the Temptress's red-sheeted four-poster as she disposes of sundry victims, either in the approved vampire fashion or in more bloody, bizarre manner, seducing a mainly gay muscle-man into a straight encounter only to penetrate him anally by (it is implied) growing outsized male genitalia, as she later grows fangs borrowed from Fredric March's Mr Hyde and serpent eyes like those of Jacqueline Pearce in **The Reptile** (1966). However, as the divinity student hero (Bond III) becomes the focus of the plot, the film unravels. The scenes between Bond and his best friend (Hardison) are marvellously written and played in Spike Lee's semi-improvised manner. The film's one major failing is that the complicated, amoral world of the bar and bedroom gives way too completely to a square morality that allows for an extreme re-use of the traditional vampire movie finish as faith literally conquers all, the Temptress being reduced to smoking bones by the sight of the cross and the hero's unshakeable faith.

d/p/s James Bond III *c* Ernest Dickerson *se* Rob Benevides *lp* James Bond III, Cynthia Bond, Kadeem Hardison, Bill Nunn, Samuel L. Jackson, John Canada Terrell

Demon Wind

(PRISM ENTERTAINMENT/UNITED FILMMAKERS) 97min

A lacklustre **Evil Dead** (1982) clone with a large-ish bunch of teenagers in a rural area whittled down as various of the group are possessed and turn bloodily upon the others. Relying heavily on the accepted signifiers of demonic malevolence (dribbled vomit, cackling taunts, rubbery make-up, horns, levitation, blasphemy) and without any real directorial verve, this fails to add anything to its crowded subgenre.

d/s Charles Philip Moore *p* Michael Bennett, Paul Hunt *c* Thomas Callaway *se* Lance Anderson *lp* Eric Larson, Francine LaPensée, Mark David Fritsche, Bobby Johnston, Jack Vogel, Stephen Quadros, Rufus Norris, Lynn Clark

Dracula's Widow (DEG) 86min

This is an old-fashioned vampire movie, more in tune with the late sixties and early seventies than the style-conscious mid-to-late eighties.

As in **Blacula** (1972), an antique coffin from Dracula's castle is imported to modern Los Angeles which contains his widow, Kristel. She bites Von Dohlen, impressionable proprietor of the Hollywood House of Wax, and makes him her slave while she predates singles-bar lounge lizards and devil-worshipping gangs, taking time out to avenge herself on Schnabel, dotty descendant of Dr Van Helsing. Kristel makes a stylish impression in severe suits but is a flavourless menace, alternating between whining fool and hissing monster in tacky Nosferatu make-up, coyly refraining from bringing to the role the sexual extremism of her Emmanuelle image.

d/co-s Christopher Coppola *p* Stephen Traxler *co-s* Kathryn Ann Thomas *c* Giuseppe Macari *se* Joe Quinlivan, Dean Gates *lp* Sylvia Kristel, Josef Sommer, Lenny Von Dohlen, Marc Coppola, Stefan Schnabel, Rachel Jones

Due Occhi Diabolici *aka* Two Evil Eyes

(ADC/GRUPPO BEMA; IT) 105min

A collaboration between two great genre auteurs, following their work on **Dawn of the Dead** (1979), this is essentially a remake of Roger Corman's **Tales of Terror** (1961) with a story dropped.

Johnny Depp is Edward Scissorhands.

Adapting Poe to a modern setting, the writer-directors take different approaches. Romero's *The Facts in the Case of M. Valdemar*, like Corman's, embroiders Poe's simple story, in which a man survives his death through hypnotism, with a typical lovers-plot-against-husband story as Barbeau, married to millionaire Valdemar (O'Malley) schemes with her hypnotist-doctor lover (Zada) to keep the old man going while his will can be processed. Barbeau's bitch performance keeps the story going, but Romero unwisely yanks in his trademark zombies and nebulous evil spirits, more at home in a *Poltergeist* sequel, for a series of false endings. The result is the slightest thing its creator has ever done. In *The Black Cat*, Argento – again, like Corman – brings in elements, incidents and characters from other stories (*The Tell-Tale Heart, The Pit and the Pendulum, The Fall of the House of Usher, Berenice*, even the poem *Annabel Lee*) to make less an adaptation of a specific story than an attempted evocation of the whole spectrum of Poe's work. Rod Usher (Keitel), a news photographer specializing in horrific images, is involved in a fraught relationship with Annabel (Potter), an ethereal cat-lover trying to escape from his brutality who, in an earlier incarnation seen in a dream, was a witch who led to Keitel's impaling. Keitel's half-comic, half-horrific performance is as much in the spirit of Poe as Vincent Price's Corman protagonists, and, along with Potter's fragile presence, provides a focus for Argento's camera tricks, elaborate effects and narrative confusion.

d/co-s George A. Romero *d/co-s/co-p* Dario Argento *co-p* Achille Manzotti *s* Franco Ferini *c* Peter Reniers, Giuseppe Macari *se* Tom Savini *lp* Harvey Keitel, Adrienne Barbeau, Madeleine Potter, Martin Balsam, E.G. Marshall, Ramy Zada, Bingo O'Malley, Kim Hunter, Sally Kirkland

Edward Scissorhands (FOX) 105min

This distinctive fable fuses images and themes from *Pinocchio, Frankenstein, Struwwelpeter* and **The 'burbs** (1988).

In an expressionist castle atop a Universal hill dwells Edward (Depp), a wild-haired artificial man left incomplete by the death of his fatherly inventor (Price), with sets of shears instead of hands. Avon lady Wiest brings him to the pastel suburbs and he becomes the rage of the neighbourhood because of his ability to work topiary and hairstyling miracles, and then an outcast freak when his good intentions are misunderstood. Not horror exactly, this is a more personal work than Burton's **Beetlejuice** (1988) and *Batman* (1989), blessed with a fascinating design scheme and a confident sense of fairytale absurdity. This is a curious big-studio project for the safety-conscious Hollywood of the nineties, but is nonetheless a welcome addition to whatever genre it is trying valiantly to create. Price contributes touching flashbacks as the Gepetto cum Frankenstein figure, choosing to educate his creation in the skills which will be of most use to him in an ideal world, etiquette and poetry. Depp's monster is at once a distorted image of his own creator, resembling Burton in hair and pallor, and a leather-swathed recreation of the silent-film school of Caligariesque monsters, his scissor-knife hands a unique image of the limited usefulness of formidable weapons.

d/co-p Tim Burton *co-p* Denise Di Novi *s* Caroline Thompson *c* Stefan Czapsky *se* Stan Winston *lp* Johnny Depp, Winona Ryder, Dianne Weist, Alan Arkin, Anthony Michael Hall, Kathy Baker, Vincent Price

Evil Toons

(AMERICAN INDEPENDENT PRODUCTIONS) 85min

The Evil Dead (1985) meets *Who Framed Roger Rabbit* (1988) to little effect. A cartoon character, vaguely resembling a lecherous Tasmanian Devil, emerges from an ancient grimoire to menace four bosomy babes who are usually seen naked or in skimpy underwear. The creature possesses one (Stone) and turns her into a demon-fanged monster, but is finally dispatched to Hell when the bespectacled but voluptuous heroine (Gabrielle) burns the book. At one level almost ironic, this nonetheless remains even less notable than **Sorority Babes in the Slimeball Bowl-a-Rama** (1987).

d/co-p Fred Olen Ray *co-p* Victoria Till *s* Sherman Scott *c* Gary Graver *se* Mark Heller *lp* Monique Gabrielle, David Carradine, Dick Miller, Suzanne Ager, Stacey Nix (Barbara Dare), Arte Johnson, Madison Stone

The Exorcist III (MORGAN CREEK/FOX) 110min

A belated second sequel, this comes over ten years after **The Exorcist II: The Heretic** (1977). Scott (in the role of the Lee J. Cobb character) puzzles out the fact that dead bodies carry the signs of mutilation by the Gemini Killer (Dourif), a serial killer who died in the electric chair just as Father Karras (Miller) took his fatal plunge. Then in hospital he discovers patient X who looks like Karras, except when he looks even more like the Gemini Killer, and has an unaccountable compulsion to explain the plot in ranting monologues. The actual exorcism was added by the producers, after Blatty completed the film, on the basis that given its title the film had to have one.

d/s William Peter Blatty *p* Carter DeHaven *c* Gerry Fisher *se* Bill Purcell *lp* George C. Scott, Ed Flanders, Brad Dourif, Jason Miller, Nicol Williamson, Scott Wilson

The First Power *aka* Pentagram

(INTERSCOPE COMMUNICATIONS INC) 98min

Homicide cop Phillips receives an anonymous phone call from cross-eyed clairvoyant Griffith tipping him off to the site of the next pentagram murder, and catches the killer (Kober). Despite warnings, Phillips sees to it that Kober goes to the gas chamber, whereupon, as in **Shocker** (1989), **Exorcist III** (1990) and **The Horror Show** (1989), he returns from the grave with the power to possess people. Phillips and Griffith, who get one 'character' scene apiece, team up to bring in the supernatural slasher, and a predictable mélange of body-hopping chase scenes and lunatic theological mumbling ensues.

d/s Robert Resnikoff *p* David Madden *c* Theo Van de Sande *se* Peter Chesney *lp* Lou Diamond Phillips, Tracy Griffith, Jeff Kober, Mykel T. Williamson, Dennis Lipscomb, Carmen Argenziano

Frankenstein Unbound (MOUNT COMPANY) 85min
Corman's first film as a director in 20 years, this adaptation of Brian Aldiss's novel is an interesting, if patchy, mix of slightly camp gothic and slightly pretentious science fiction.

Hurt, a 21st-century scientist whose wonder-weapon has created a time vortex, finds himself and his intelligent car transported back to Switzerland in 1817, in a world where Mary Shelley (Fonda) and her circle co-exist with the characters from her most famous novel. Hurt makes the aquaintance of Dr Frankenstein (Julia) and the scientists come to recognize their kinship, both having brought monsters into the world. Though stuck with an extremely reactionary return to the the venerable 'there are some things man is not meant to know' theme, especially belaboured during a hard-to-follow finale set in an other-time snowy waste where the characters have ended up, the film is often amusing in its recreation of the early Corman style, complete with shimmering dream sequences out of **House of Usher** (1960) and **The Masque of the Red Death** (1964).

d/co-p/co-s Roger Corman *co-p* Thom Mount, Kobi Jagger *co-s* F.X. Feeney *c* Armando Nannuzzi, Micahel Scott *se* Nick Dudman *lp* John Hurt, Raul Julia, Bridget Fonda, Nick Brimble, Catherine Rabbett, Michael Hutchence, Jason Patric

Il Gioco delle Ombre *aka* **The Shadow Game** (STALKER; IT) 108min
This is an arty ghost story halfway between Wim Wenders and Pupi Avati. Bussotti is the successful novelist who retreats to a remote village after the suicide of his lover (Carena). While writing a novel in his old dark house, he becomes obsessed with a disturbing fresco which reminds him of the dead woman and, though tempted back towards life by an appealing tightrope walker (Valentini), is drawn into an unhealthy relationship with the spirits of the dead and their world of shadows.

Though filmed on a meagre budget, the picture has a luxurious look, thanks to opulently gloomy interiors and Mertes's evocation of deserted and haunted beaches, with Popol Vuh contributing an eerie score. Too slow and slender to qualify as a shocker, with much repetition of admittedly impressive imagery, this nevertheless conjures up an air of dread more in line with M.R. or Henry James than the blood-and-monsters spectres that usually stalk Italian haunted-house pictures.

d/co-s Stefano Gabrini *p* Donatella Palermo *co-s* Roberto Marafante *c* Rafaele Mertes *lp* Fabio Bussotti, Mariella Valentini, Fiammetta Carena, Isa Gallinelli

Graveyard Shift (PAR) 86min
Adapted from a Stephen King short story, and not to be confused with the 1987 vampire movie of the same name, this is a fast and predictable monster movie. It deserves points for its teeth-clenched melodrama, demonstrated by villain Macht, the first character in a King movie to have an outrageous Maine accent, and Brad Dourif, given special billing as a Vietnam vet vermin exterminator ('I'm not one of those baby-burnin', flashbackin' fuck-ups you see Bruce Dern playin'').

A group of workers spend a holiday weekend cleaning out the Bachman Textile Mills, which are infested by hungry rats who have developed a taste for human meat from frequent snacking at the graveyard next door, and also harbour a cellar-dwelling monster resembling a giant rat-tailed fruitbat. Such B-movie favourites as the Fat Creep Who Gets What He Deserves, the Black Dude Who Ill-Advisedly Puts His Arm Into a Hole, the Stupid Woman Who Twists Her Ankle at the Worst Possible Moment and the Gutless Cretin Who Goes Hysterical become munchies, and the two main characters struggle with decidedly lame plotting and a laughable bit of neo-Marxist message-making, in which the factory is seen as an extension of the monster, grinding up working men for money.

d Ralph S. Singleton *p* William J. Dunn *s* John Esposito *c* Peter Stein *se* Peter Chesney, Albert J. Whitlock *lp* David Andrews, Kelly Wolf, Stephen Macht, Andrew Divoff

Gremlins 2: The New Batch (WB) 107min
Opening with promising buffoonery from Bugs Bunny and Daffy Duck directed by Chuck Jones, *Gremlins 2: The New Batch* is a run for commercial cover after the box-office failure of Dante's more interesting *Explorers* (1986) and **The 'burbs** (1988).

This mechanically relocates the story in a New York 'smart building', losing its cast amid Rick Baker's ingenious but unresonant effects. The influence of Jones is eclipsed here by that of Tex Avery, with gags – a step outside the body of the film as the image stalls and burns on the screen, cueing a cut to a cinema where gremlins are halting the projection of the movie – lifted from Avery's oeuvre. Even Dante's usual in-jokes are rather half-hearted, with Lee making a fine first impression as the mad geneticist but then being pointlessly killed off as a throwaway aside. Less like a sequel to *Gremlins* than a *MAD* magazine parody of it, complete with edge-of-the-panel details like the Batman-logo-shaped hole left in a wall by a flying gremlin, simple absurd dislocations of reference like the appearance of film critic Leonard Maltin who is repaid for his adverse review of the first film by a gremlin attack, and cynical skits like the replay of Cates' 'Christmas' speech as a knockabout lampoon.

d Joe Dante *p* Michael Finnell *s* Charlie Haas *c* John Hora *se* Rick Baker *lp* Zach Galligan, Phoebe Cates, John Glover, Robert Prosky, Robert Picardo, Christopher Lee, Dick Miller, John Astin, Paul Bartel, Belinda Balaski, Jackie Joseph, Tony Randall

Grim Prairie Tales (EAST/WEST) 94min
While making a long trip West, city slicker Dourif encounters bounty hunter Jones, and the pair spend the night, accompanied by a corpse, swapping horror stories.

Aware of the limitations of the omnibus movie, this curious hybrid subtly varies the stories, so that Jones' anecdotes of supernatural vengeance fail to prepare the audience for the creepier, character-based horror of Dourif's tale. The first couple of stories are simple sketches, with an old trapper falling foul of an Indian curse as he violates a burial ground, and a young man tempted to adultery by a pregnant woman he meets and protects on the trail and surprised by the fate that overtakes him.

Having irked Jones by his insistence on analysing the stories ('It's more about an old man's fear of death', he concludes of the first), Dourif surprises the old man with his own tale: in *Southerner* Atherton takes his family West, bringing an old evil along. The film finally has Jones pull a full-blooded story of hatred from beyond the grave, with a fastidious gunman (Paulin) facing down a bearlike murderer and then plagued by his uncouth ghost. Constantly throwing in odd effects – an outstanding animated dream sequence, a trick with flaring light that unnervingly catches the feel of being buried alive, a bit of precise historical detail, a nerve-shredding sequence with a straight razor, a liberal application of a gallon of gore – that flesh out the thin skeleton of its shaggy-dog structure, and with a posse of spot-on performances from under-used players, this is probably the best ever horror Western.

d/s Wayne Coe *p* Richard Hahn *c* Janusz Miniski *lp* James Earl Jones, Brad Dourif, William Atherton, Lisa Eichhorn, Scott Paulin, Mark McClure

The Guardian (U) 98min
A major-studio film with a competent cast, a name director and professional production values, this outing is betrayed by a screenplay that spins a hackneyed premise out with little imagination, zero suspense and a total lack of horrific verve. A pre-title caption and a brief introductory sequence destroys any possible mystery by establishing that the new nanny (Seagrove) in a California couple's ideal household is a druidical sprite who sacrifices babies to an evil tree. It then takes forever for Mom (Lowell) and Dad (Brown) to catch on that the servant is planning a nasty fate for their gurgling newborn brat.

d/co-d William Friedkin *p* Joe Wizan *s* Dan Greenburg, Stephen Volk *c* John A. Alonzo *se* Matthew Mungle *lp* Jenny Seagrove, Dwier Brown, Carey Lowell, Brad Hall, Miguel Ferrer

Hellgate (GHOST TOWN FILM MANAGEMENT/DISTANT HORIZON/ANANT SINGH; SOUTH AFRICA) 92min
This is the most watchable of the low-budget horror pictures (*The Evil Below*, 1989, *The Stay Awake*, 1989, **Headhunter**, 1989, **Return of the Family Man**, 1989) made in South Africa at the turn of the decade. That said, it is not up to even middle-ranking American quickies.

Set in a California where locals have to struggle to subsume Afrikaaner accents, it opens awkwardly with teens swapping ghost stories to fill in the flashback set-up, which concerns the ghost of a girl (Wolcott) killed by a bike gang in the fifties and also a magic crystal owned by the girl's father which can mutate dead or living beings into monstrous forms. Then the group encounter manifestations and monsters in an old Western ghost town and the film degenerates into an succession of (sometimes entertaining) tricks and jokes. Wolcott is a provocatively perverse presence as the victim cum vampire, and one or two of the stranger turns (the apparition of a troupe of can-can girls during one murder, the presence of a chatty severed head in the fridge, the mutation of a goldfish into a football-sized monster) pique the interest.

d William A. Levey *p* Anant Singh *s* Michael O'Rourke *c* Peter Palmer *se* Image Animation *lp* Ron Palillo, Abigail Wolcott, Petrea Curran, Evan J. Klisser, Joanne Ward, Carel Trichardt

I Bought a Vampire Motorcycle
(DIRK PRODUCTIONS) 104min
Despatch rider Morrissey buys a motorbike that is a vampire. The bike murders a mechanic (Peacock) who has stolen its petrol cap, leading to blackout nightmare sketches (the most bizarre and repulsive of which finds Peacock reincarnated as a giant turd that leaps out of the toilet bowl and crams itself down Morrissey's throat) and to more traditional action/splatter sequences as it goes after the cycle gang who murdered its former owner and then the hero's girlfriend (Noar). Priest Daniels performs an exorcism which fails, leaving the monster to be defeated by Elphick's garlic-breathing copper and a sun-lamp. It was filmed in Birmingham.

d Dirk Campbell *p/s* Mycal Miller, John Wolskel *c* Tom Ingle *se* Image Animation *lp* Neil Morrissey, Amanda Noar, Michael Elphick, Anthony Daniels, Daniel Peacock, Andrew Powell, George Rossi

Jacob's Ladder (CAROLCO) 113min
Suffering from flashbacks to Vietnam trauma, Jacob (Robbins) is persecuted by creatures in stocking masks, plagued by different versions of his everyday world (apparently, his son has died and he has left his wife for a co-worker at the post office, but occasionally this seems a nightmare alternative to his happy-families waking life) and the victim of a conspiracy to cover up a germ warfare experiment that went wrong. Because the film is a rip-off from *An Incident at Owl Creek Bridge* and, particularly, **Carnival of Souls** (1962), the footage-wasting conspiracy is a blind alley. Finally, Robbins, who has been imagining the whole film as he dies of a bayonet wound, is escorted to the afterlife by his dead son (Culkin) to the tune of Al Jolson's *Sonny Boy*. Despite Robbins's good performance and impressive visions of New York circa 1971 as Hell, this is ultimately more annoying than affecting, betraying the species of superficial grime-as-glamour razzamatazz that sunk Alan Parker's **Angel Heart** (1987) into an identical mire of pompous, post-generic sludge.

d Adrian Lyne *p* Alan Marshall *s* Bruce Joel Rubin *c* Jeffrey L. Kimball *se* Gordon J. Smith *lp* Tim Robbins, Elizabeth Peña, Danny Aiello, Matt Craven, Pruitt Taylor Vince, Jason Alexander, Macaulay Culkin

Leatherface: Texas Chainsaw Massacre III
(NEW LINE) 81min
An attempt by the distributors of **The Texas Chainsaw Massacre** (1974) to turn the property into a franchise to rival their Elm Street series, this is a listless sequel.

Heroine Hodge falls foul of a cannibal clan who include the *Hud*-ish Mortensen, a murderous matriarch and an evil little girl. Leatherface (Mihailoff) limps unmenacingly with a leg-brace (a sole attempt at continuity with the first film, which wound up with the killer being wounded in the thigh) and the attempt to characterize him (he is seen playing with a child's spelling game that buzzes an 'error' signal at him when he repeatedly types in FOOD under a picture of a boy) hardly makes him into a cult figure to equal Freddy Krueger. Shot in California with cowboy hats and armadilloes as set-dressing, this has none of the Texan atmosphere of the original. Novelist Schow's screenplay has a few memorably brutal lines – a shotgun-wielding rapist tells his victim 'I'm gonna fuck you in two' – but little else.

d Jeff Burr *p* Robert Engelman *s* David J. Schow *c* James L. Carter *se* Kurtzman, Nicotero & Berger Efx Group *lp* Kate Hodge, Viggo Mortensen, William Butler, Ken Foree, Joe Unger, Tom Everett, R.A. Mihailoff

El Leyenda del Cura de Bargota *aka* **The Legend of the Priest From Bargota**
(ORIGEN/TVE/RETEITALIA/TELECIP/RTP/TAURUS FILMS; SP) 88min
Told in flashback by a handsome priest (Cuervo) put to the torture by the Inquisition in 16th-century Spain, this is allegedly based on the historic case of Juan de Irusta, a priest of the Rioja Baja region. However, it seems to draw most of its inspiration from gothic novels like M.G. Lewis's *The Monk*.

On her death-bed, the hero's mother confides to him that he is the son of the Devil and tells him 'now go to your father', whereupon he falls from virtue, motivated mainly by lust for a woman (Fornar) who causes him to give up his vow of chastity and take part in demonic orgies. While a stone Satan talks to him, Cuervo suffers devilish torments (drenched by rainfall during a drought, pelted by snow in midsummer) which prompt his hypocritical parishioners to report him to the Holy Office.

d/co-s Pedro Olea *co-s* Juan Antonio Porto *c* Hans Surmann *lp* Fernando Guillín Cuervo, Lola Forner, Jaume Valls, Encarno Pasa, Raf Vallone

La Luna Negra *aka* **The Black Moon**
(ORIGEN; SP) 82min
Based on the legend of Lilith, the film opens with a pregnant modern Eve (Bosch) discovering that her husband is having an affair with a vaguely sinister architect with whom she has also been intimate. Bosch takes revenge by running the woman down with her car, putting the temptress into a permanent coma. Nine years later, Eve's daughter is the stereotypical Omen-style Devil Child (perhaps 'fathered' by the comatose woman) who demonstrates satanic powers by crucifying lizards, turning her eyes to grey marbles, arranging the slapstick murder of the gardener's boy (he steps on a scythe that jumps up and cuts his throat) and desecrating a church by urinating into a chalice. This is competently directed and photographed but uninterestingly acted, full of empty wandering about accompanied by crashing music to signify a climax that never arrives.

d Imanol Uribe *p* Antonio Cardenal *c* Javier Aguirresarobe *lp* Lydia Bosch, Fernando Guillín, José Coronado, Emma Suárez, Yolanda Rios, Mario Adorf, Amparo Munoz, Fernando Sancho

La Maschera del Demonio (RETEITALIA/ANFRI) 85min
In an example of ill-advised hubris, Bava *figlio* here remakes his father's best-known movie and miraculously transforms a Gogol-derived gothic fairy-tale into a teens-in-terror picture

which has more in common with his own minor offering **Dentro al Cimitero** (1987) than with the 1960 **La Maschera del Demonio**, a classic horror film.

A crowd of unappealing youths ski through the countryside and blunder into a crevice which contains the frozen corpse of Anibas (Kinski), a witch who was executed centuries earlier. The mask pounded onto her face is pulled off and she comes to life, sometimes possessing a lookalike girl (also Kinski), while the teens take refuge in an old church run by a blind cleric who remembers the original witch's reign of terror. The thick hero takes an unconscionable length of time to deduce that the name of his girlfriend, Sabina, is that of the witch spelled backwards. Stivaletti provides rubber monsters for several ridiculous scenes, in one of which Kinski turns into a chicken-foot hag while having sex with the hero, and another with a gorgon-haired witch with glowing teeth ranting over an arcane rite.

d Lamberto Bava *p* Andreas Pizzease *s* Giorgio Stegani, Massimo de Rita *c* Gianfranco Transunto *se* Sergio Stivaletti *lp* Debora Kinski, Eva Grimaldi, Giovanni Guidello, Michele Soavi, Piero Nomi

The Masque of the Red Death

(21ST CENTURY/BRETON; SOUTH AFRICA) 95min

This is one of several Poe adaptations – following **Buried Alive** (1989) and **The House of Usher** (1989) – made in the traditional Towers runaway fashion.

Birkinshaw had just directed Towers' third stab at *Ten Little Indians* (1989), and rather than compete with the Corman-produced **Masque of the Red Death** (1989) he reworked it, with the same actors, as yet another re-run of Agatha Christie's dwindling-party plot.

Millionaire Lom holds a Poe-themed masked ball in his castle, and a Red-Death-costumed psychopath murders several people. Lom seals all the suspects up with a time-lock security system and investigative reporter heroine McBride has to sleuth out the culprit before dawn, though in the end the usual bloody process of elimination unmasks the killer. It opens with a traditionally irrelevant dream sequence inspired by *The Tell-Tale Heart* and features a Poe-style death by razor-pendulum, but its nastiest moment is the sequence in which a fashion model is sewn into the warp of a loom and left to bleed to death.

d Alan Birkinshaw *p* Harry Allan Towers, Avi Lerner *s* Michael J. Murray *c* Jossi Wein *lp* Frank Stallone, Michelle McBride, Herbert Lom, Brenda Vaccaro

Meridian *aka* Kiss of the Beast *aka* Phantoms

(FULL MOON) 85min

This borrows some of its plot from heroine Fenn's *Two Moon Junction* (1988). Band also throws in a family curse and double-dealing prompted by the relationship between an evil magician and his afflicted werewolf twin brother (both Jamieson).

Fenn is the lady of an Italian castle, returning home after a spell in America and fascinated by the grotesques of a carnival magic show, all of whom turn out to be loitering immortals with parts to play in an eternally repeated tragedy that centres around her. A slow fantasy, with competent metamorphosis effects as Fenn becomes the monster's lover, this is less interesting than the best of Band's science-fiction films, but more ambitious than his run of killer-puppet horror movies, and is unusual in its emphasis on 'steamy' but romantic sex, scored by Pino Donaggio, with plentiful nudity and moaning. There is a surprisingly decent performance from Charlie as an art restorer who peels off one painting to discover another that explains the plot and is drawn hypnotically into a relationship with the evil twin.

d/co-p Charles Band *co-p* Debra Dion *s* Dennis Paoli *c* Mac Ahlberg *se* Greg Cannom *lp* Sherilyn Fenn, Malcolm Jamieson, Charlie (Spradling), Alex Daniels, Hilary Mason, Phil Fondacaro, Vernon Dobtcheff

Modeng Rulai Shenzhang *aka* Kung Fu Versus Acrobatic *aka* Thunderbolt '91

(WIN'S MOVIE & VE CO; HONG KONG) 97min

A light-hearted Hong Kong supernatural drama, with a pair of modern blunderers accidentally reviving the principals of a centuries-old conflict and taking home a princess and her handmaiden, whom they then have to protect from a moustachioed master of the magic arts.

Schooled in mystic kung fu by the heroine, the naïve hero (Lau) confronts villain Handicap Tin, whose powers are manifested by a spectral bare foot that gives a dangerous kick, using such trickery as the Laugh of Buddha, which emits pounding orange waves, and finally conjures up a unique ally in the shape of a buck-toothed cartoon turtle with an enormous hammer to see off the baddie, who has become addicted to television and incorporates break-dancing moves into his fighting style. Opening with clips from a vintage Cantonese kung fu movie of which this is an updated revamp, this is a knowing, affectionate salute to the simpler values of a traditional culture, which are seen in contrast to the hectic world of modern Hong Kong, where the heroes work in advertising and use their newly acquired magical skills to make burger commercials.

d Taylor Wong *p* Hueng Wah-Sing *s* Wong Ching *c* Chung Chi-Man *se* Cinefex Workshop *lp* Andy Lau, Joey Wang, Yuen Wah, Chan Pak-Cheung, Mui Siu-Wai, Cho Dat-Wah, Lau Chun, Lau Chi-Wing, Ngai Bing-Long

Mr Frost (AAA/HUGO FILMS; FR, GB) 103min

Having semi-accidentally captured polite mass murderer Frost (Goldblum), policeman Bates follows him from asylum to asylum, trying to convince the authorities that the killer, who has opted not to speak to anyone, is the Devil.

In a European madhouse where a dedicated team of crack and cracked psychologists are picking Frost apart, Baker makes a breakthrough when the madman decides she's the only person he will talk to, but becomes increasingly unnerved when her patient goes along with Bates's story, and claims to have allowed himself to be captured so he can restore age-old fear of the demonic by convincing an entirely rational person, her, that he is indeed the Prince of Darkness. Reminiscent in its weird, pretentious tone of oddities like *Hammersmith is Out* (1972) or *The Shout* (1978), *Mr Frost* is a promising drama of metaphysical horror that finally disappoints, thanks to lack of plot development.

d/co-s Philip Setbon *p* Xavier Gelin *co-s* Brad Lynch *c* Dominique Brencuier *lp* Jeff Goldblum, Alan Bates, Kathy Baker, Jean-Pierre Cassel, François Negret, Roland Giraud, Charley Boorman

Il Nido del Ragno *aka* The Spider Labyrinth

(RETEITALIA/SPLENDIDA; IT) 90min

This is an extension of the supernatural shockers of vintage Dario Argento and Pupi Avati. Academic arachnophobe Wybenga is sent to Budapest to track down a missing colleague and sucked into a labyrinth of the supernatural involving disappearances, giant spiders' webs, sinister local colour, the expected gore murders, unhelpful authorities, a world-wide cult marked by spider-marks on the arm, a black widow-like hotel manageress and enough spiders large and small to give **Arachnophobia** (1990) competition, though the film's human-spiders are more in line with the absurd creatures of *Mesa of Lost Women* (1963) and *Ein Toter Hing im Netz/Horrors of Spider Island* (1959). The early stretches are powerfully mysterious as Wybenga is bounced from one strange character and event to the next but the finale disappointingly devolves into excess. The hero is pinned down after he has shoved broken glass into the throat of a long-armed spider woman and initiated as a small spider crawls into a gash on his arm to make the cult's mark, while a rubbery special effects baby mutates into a horrible hybrid in an aside rather too obviously intended to be a showpiece highlight.

d Gianfranco Giagni *p/co-s* Tonino Cervi *co-s* Riccardo Arragno, Cesare Frugoni, Gianfranco Manfredini *c* Nini Celeste *se* Sergio Stivaletti *lp* Roland Wybenga, Paola Rinaldi, Marghareta Von Krauss, Claudia Muzli, William Berger, Stephane Audran, Valeriano Santinelli, Massimiliano Pavine, Arnaldo Dell'Aqua

Night of the Living Dead (21ST CENTURY) 89min
George Romero's 1968 classic, already expanded by sequels, imitations and parodies, was hardly in need of a colour remake; this was undertaken partly because a rights quirk meant that if the original production team did not undertake a remake, anyone else could. However, this is a surprisingly good job, compressing the plot of the original into its first four fifths, then coming up with potent new twists which cap the heroine's declaration of the zombies that 'we are them and they are us' with a startling, ambiguous and callous off-hand murder.

Romero shears away the 'scientific' explanation and sixties social satire, concentrating instead on divisions among the survivors cooped in a farmhouse by the rise of the dead. While the black hero (Todd) and his bigoted adversary (Towles) remain as they were, to the point of seeming men out of time, heroine Tallman is given a post-Sigourney Weaver attitude; her reaction to the flesh-eating ghouls is to become not an instant catatonic but a supercompetent guerilla whose anti-zombie violence is finally and devastatingly as insane a reaction as her predecessor's crawling into a psychological shell.

Make-up supremo Savini, in his directorial début, refrains from going as overboard into gore gags as in **Dawn of the Dead** (1979) and **Day of the Dead** (1985), and even plays the siege situation more for suspense than the blend of comedy and splatter that characterizes the series. With resources unavailable to the original (an original score rather than stock music, convincing make-up for the extras, consistent lighting, professional actors) he even brings up to standard the sometimes ropy qualities of the first film. Cannily, the shocks aren't reproduced exactly: the shambling graveyard wino in the first scene turns out to be exactly that and merely a precursor for the unexpected appearance from another part of the screen of the first attacking zombie. However, the film does have a few too many hand-through-the-window shock tricks and – like *Invasion of the Body Snatchers* (1954), *A Bout de Souffle* (1959) or **La Maschera del Demonio** (1960) – the original was so much a creation of its times while being at once important, influential and excellent, any remake, no matter how fine, is doomed to be a footnote.

d Tom Savini *p* John A. Russo, Russ Streiner *s* George A. Romero *c* Frank Prinzi *se* John Vulich, Everett Burrell *lp* Tony Todd, Pat Tallman, Tom Towles, William Butler, Katie Finneran, McKee Anderson, Bill Moseley

Nightbreed (MORGAN CREEK) 99min
Barker's second film lacks the claustrophobic tightness of **Hellraiser** (1987).

Sheffer is convinced by his psychoanalyst (the film director Cronenberg) that he is a masked serial murderer. Obsessed with the myth of Midian, a legendary city rumoured to be home to monsters, Sheffer encounters creatures who infect him with a bite so that when he is shot dead by the police he returns in a changed form. Cronenberg, who is himself the murderer, zealously attempts to destroy Midian, leading oppressive cops and priests and vigilantes there, and forcing Sheffer to defend his newfound people from the outside world. While the film features a startling array of briefly seen monsters, it doesn't find much for them to do except be unhelpful bystanders in the battle between the blandly unmonstrous hero and the mad doctor.

d/s Clive Barker *p* James G. Robinson *c* Robin Vidgeon *se* Image Animation *lp* Craig Sheffer, Anne Bobby, David Cronenberg, Charles Haid, Hugh Quarshie, Hugh Ross, Malcolm Smith, John Agar

Out for Blood (VIVID VIDEO) 105(60)min
In 1968, a hippie has an affair with a vampire, and in the present day their daughter (Welles) is a schizophrenic who transforms from repressed miss to vampire hoyden during dates with advertisers in a singles' magazine, draining the blood from their penises *à la* **The Case of the Full Moon Murders** (1973). The narrating cop-on-the-case (Spears), immaculately rumpled in trenchcoat and hat, appropriates the major plot device of *Sea of Love* (1989) and places a rhyming ad designed to attract the vampire's attention and meets up with Welles, who is redeemed by love. Similar in its use of video to **Dawn** (1991), this is nevertheless mainly concerned with extended sexual encounters between secondary characters. Good-humoured and cheesy, this suggests that, unlike most porn directors, Thomas at least puts some thought into scripts and camera angles.

d/p/s Paul Thomas *c* Jack Remy *se* Allan Bosshardt *lp* Tori Welles, Cheri Taylor, Kelly Royb

Pacific Heights (MORGAN CREEK) 100min
Like **The Amityville Horror** (1979), this is a horror story for home-owners, intended to elicit – as Stephen King pointed out – not the traditional feeling of fear and dread but the kind of nagging worry expressed in the phrase 'think of the bills'.

Griffith and Modine buy a dilapidated mansion and let out the first floor to the rich and persuasive Keaton, who sets about driving the couple crazy, doing noisy alteration work in the middle of the night, never paying rent, repeatedly using the law against his landlord, ignoring an eviction notice, and breeding cockroaches. Most effective with the simple, legal, nagging ways Keaton manages to irritate, this drags in melodramatic horror-movie plotting to keep it going until a reductive finale in which Keaton turns into yet another boring psycho, ranting incoherently as he wields a mean nailgun and finally perishing, like Francis Lederer in **The Return of Dracula** (1958), by falling backwards onto an awkwardly jutting pipe.

d John Schlesinger *p* Scott Rudin, William Sackheim *s* Daniel Pyne *c* Amir Mokri *lp* Melanie Griffith, Matthew Modine, Michael Keaton, Mako, Laurie Metcalf, Tippi Hedren

Paganini Horror (FULVIA; IT) 80min
Like **Il Gatto Nero** (1991), this finds Cozzi, a long-time collaborator with and booster of Dario Argento, clumping feebly in his master's footsteps, with script and performance input from Nicolodi, Argento's ex-partner and regular player, and a music background ludicrously less high-flown than that of **Opera** (1987).

Rock star Main rents the Venetian house in which Paganini is supposed to have sold his soul, planning to make a video based on a suppressed melody composed by the violinist. Following *Opera*, the clip is to be made by a world-renowned horror director, but this movie brat shows up with a shoulder-mounted cam-corder and no crew to stage a complex horror sequence that he makes up as he goes along. A masked Paganini slaughters model girls with a spiked violin, the laws of space and time break down, characters wander around tacky labyrinths, bloody fungus grows on faces and everyone breaks down in hysterical screaming. The only memorable touch is the devilish Pleasence's tossing-away of banknotes ('little demons') from a Venetian tower. The export version renders this even odder by using a deep voice very unlike the actor's distinctive whine.

d/co-s Lewis Coats (Luigi Cozzi) *p* Fabrizio De Angelis *co-s* Daria Nicolodi *c* Franco Lecca *se* Casagni-Prestopino *lp* Daria Nicolodi, Jasmine Main, Pascal Persiano, Donald Pleasence, Maria Cristina Mastrangeli, Michele Klippstein, Pietro Genuardi, Luana Ravagnini, Roberto Giannini, Giada Cozzi, Elena Pompei, Perla Agostini

Qumo Jingcha *aka* **Magic Cop**
(MOVIE IMPACT LTD/MILLIFAME; HONG KONG) 87min
An entertaining combination of two popular Hong Kong genres, horror-action and the tough-but-comic-cop story, which finds a veteran ghostbusting cop (Jing-Ying) partnered with younger, non-traditional team-mates as they take on an evil enchantress who uses voodoo to re-animate lumbering corpses.

With spirited use of unfamiliar ghost-fighting techniques and the usual excellent tumbling and tossing, this benefits from Jing-Ying's sternly Taoist Dirty Harry impersonation and features many wonderfully staged supernatural fights, with the interesting device that the cop and his nemesis slug it out through proxies until very late in the film, whereupon the ghost woman is turned from a winsome spirit into the requisite frightful hag for the final conflict. An especially well-staged sequence has the hero's initially disbelieving partner kung-fu-fighting a gangster who has been reanimated in the morgue through sympathetic magic.

d Dung Wai *p* Lam Jing-Ying *s* Wooi Gan-Cheung, Shum Ji-Leung *c* Lam Fai-Tai, Kwan Chi-Dung *se* Animation Shop *lp* Lam Jing-Ying, Lam Jun-Yin, Wong Mei-Wahj, Miu Kiu-Wai, Wu Ma, Chan Ji-Leung, Chow Bei-Lei, Nishiwaki Michiko

Repossessed (FIRST CLASS) 93min
In 1973, Nancy Aglet (Blair) was possessed by the Devil and exorcized by Father Jedidiah Mayii (Nielsen); now the Devil is back and she's been – wait for it – repossessed!

The title turns out to be the nearest thing to wit in this sophomoric skit of **The Exorcist** (1973), which relies on pea-soup vomit jokes, bare breast jokes, punch-in-the-crotch jokes, dog-killing jokes, faggot jokes, borrowed-badly-from-*Airplane!* (1979) jokes and overblown televangelist jokes. Narrated during a lecture by Nielsen, this touches all the bases of the original – a young priest struggling with his loss of faith (Starke), the heroine being tied to the bed and spewing up, the exorcists coming to grips with the Devil – but without any real comic approach. Blair does her own monster voice this time.

d/s Bob Logan *p* Steve Wizan *c* Michael D. Marguilies *se* Sam Nicholson *lp* Linda Blair, Leslie Nielsen, Ned Beatty, Anthony Starke, Lana Schwab

Rockula (CANNON) 91min
A vaguely amiable vampire musical. Cameron is an immortal virgin, dominated by his fanged sexpot mother (Basil) and doomed every 22 years to go through a cyclical relationship with a succession of reincarnations of his true love (Feré), always losing her to a hambone-wielding pirate.

Having done all the singing vampire jokes in his first routine, 'Rockula', Cameron proceeds to bash other styles in a 'Rapula' number and an Elvis parody. With a subplot about the hero's lost reflection, who obnoxiously gives him advice from behind an assortment of mirrors, and enlivened somewhat by Basil's presence as the Elvira-style mother, the film is mainly notable for the hero's band, which features a once-in-a-lifetime teaming-up of blues great Diddley and sleaze superstar Tyrrell.

d/co-s Luca Bercovici *p/co-s* Jefery Levy *co-s* Christopher Vierwel *c* John Schwartzman *se* Tony Gardner, Larry Hamlin *lp* Dean Cameron, Toni Basil, Tawny Feré, Thomas Dolby, Susan Tyrrell, Bo Diddley

Shakma (CURB ESQUIRE) 101min
This ridiculous Florida-filmed animal-on-the-rampage movie opens with tasteful open-heart surgery, then takes a long time to establish its premise, an ineffectual riff on the killer primate subgenre of **Link** (1985) and **Monkey Shines** (1988).

Students unwisely stage an all-night role-playing game in a locked and escape-proof campus building where Shakma, an experimental baboon, has just been dosed on a serum which has had the unfortunate side-effect of turning it homicidal. Naturally, the scuttling furball slaughters guest star McDowell first, then goes after the lesser lights, leaving them in bloody pools on the floor with portions of their faces missing. Though the film is unusually willing to dispose of both its female leads, the deaths are compromised by the directors' inability to get a sufficiently menacing trained baboon.

co-d/p Hugh Parks *co-d* Tom Logan *s* Roger Engle *c* Andy Bieber *se* Rick Gonzalez *lp* Christopher Atkins, Amanda Wyss, Ari Meyers, Roddy McDowell, Robb Morris, Gregg Flowers, Tre Loughlin

Shock 'Em Dead (ACADEMY) 94min
A formula rock 'n' roll Faust, with pizza functionary Quadros selling his soul to a voodoo bag-lady (Sodipe) to be 'the greatest rock star in the world' and finding the small print in his demonic contract means he can no longer eat anything and has to sustain himself by sucking out the souls of stabbed victims. This is low-budget and cramped, with scrappy green vomit and glowing eyes effects and a plodding, moralistic storyline. Porn queen Lords, not yet a competent actress, is a shrill heroine, while Quadros, borrowing the character name of 'Angel Martin' from Stuart Margolin on *The Rockford Files*, convinces neither as a nerd or a hair-freak rocker.

d/co-s Mark Freed *p* Eric Louzil *co-s* David Tedder *c* Ron Chapman *se* John 'J. Frog' Garcia *lp* Traci Lords, Stephen Quadros, Aldo Ray, Troy Donahue, Tim Moffet, Karen Russell, Gina Parks, Laurel Wiley, Tyger Sodipe

Simadia Tis Nichtes *aka* **Scars of the Night**
(GREEK FILM CENTER/ET 1; GR) 94min
A leisurely thriller with mythical overtones and apparently patterned on **The Wicker Man** (1973), down to the inclusion of a giant wooden symbol ritually burned in the climax. Ex-convict Tzortzoglou travels to an island to track down a former friend who owes him money. He arrives in time to attend the friend's funeral and notice claw-marks on his chest, then becomes involved with a mysterious baker (Katsaris) who may be an angel of death and Lehou, a local beauty who is the current incarnation of a sorceress entrusted with an amulet that protects the island. While searching for the missing amulet, Tzortzoglou witnesses primitive rituals and is pursued by an elemental whirlwind that barks like a rabid dog. Haunted by nightmares in which Lehou claws at his chest while making love to him, he becomes aware that he is trapped in a ritual of sacrifice, a confinement underlined when he falls down a well into a haunted cave. This was made as a theatrical feature and a four-part TV mini-series.

d/s Panos Kokkinopoulos *p* Bessie Voudouri *c* Dimitri Papacostandis *lp* Stratos Tzortzoglou, Katerina Lehou, Antonis Katsaris, Dimitri Katalifos

The Sleeping Car (VIDMARK ENTERTAINMENT) 86min
A wisecracking mature student (Naughton) rents a converted railway carriage and is persecuted by the ghost of an intolerant engineer (Buechler) who haunts the sofabed and uses springs to kill off anyone in the coach who so much as thinks of sex.

This is a standard ghost story, slow to build and predictable in the number of victims and the manner in which they are regularly killed off, but given a little snap by performances, especially winning heroine Aronson, who enjoys non-stop banter with Naughton, and crazy old guest star McCarthy, who plays a white witch and does his bit to exorcize the menace.

d/p Douglas Curtis *s* Greg O'Neill *c* David Lewis *se* Max W. Anderson, John Carl Buechler *lp* David Naughton, Judie Aronson, Jeff Conaway, Kevin McCarthy, Dani Minnick, John Carl Buechler

SoulTaker
(PACIFIC WEST ENTERTAINMENT/VICTORY PICTURES) 94min
'Led Zeppelin was wrong, man,' moans a new-made angel, 'There is no stairway to Heaven.' A low-key **Carnival of**

Souls (1962) or **Jacob's Ladder** (1990), with a young couple (Schilling, Thomsen) supposed to be killed in a car wreck evading a messenger from the beyond (Estevez) whose job is to ferry their souls to the afterlife.

Schilling's script gets hung up on the exact method of soul-taking, which involves a glowing teething ring, and glosses over such details as the process whereby angels are issued with stylish black coats and gloves. There are several unusual notions: that murderers have to pay their debt by becoming soul-taking angels, that discarnate spirits still use public transport, and that angels might be fallible.

d Michael Rissi *p* Eric Parkinson, Connie Kingrey *s* Vivian Schilling *c* James A. Rosenthal *se* Jerry Kitz *lp* Joe Estevez, Vivian Schilling, Gregg Thomsen, Robert Z'Dar, David Shark

Stepfather II (ITC) 86min

Given that **The Stepfather** (1986) hardly demanded a sequel, this is surprisingly adequate. Multi-identitied killer O'Quinn has survived being stabbed in the heart and escaped from an asylum to set up shop as a psychiatrist specializing in 'family problems', and now courts newly divorced realtor Foster, ingratiating himself with her alienated son and murdering anyone who stands in the way of his ideal union.

At the heart of the film lies O'Quinn's marvellously detailed and unsettling, by no means entirely unsympathetic, psycho performance. Whether listening to his breakfast cereal to make sure it provides the requisite TV commercial sound effects or casually conversing with the rival he has just murdered, O'Quinn's stepfather remains one of the strongest, strangest horror-movie villains of the age. In Guy Magar's cable TV *Stepfather III* (1992), O'Quinn is replaced, via plastic surgery, by Robert Wightman.

d Jeff Burr *p* Darin Scott, William Burr *s* John Auerback *c* Jacek Laskus *lp* Terry O'Quinn, Meg Foster, Caroline Williams, Jonathan Brandis, Henry Brown

Tales From the Darkside: The Movie

(LAUREL) 93min

Spun off from the TV series, this is above average by the standards of the *Creepshow* movies but doesn't rank with the best Amicus omnibuses.

In the frame story, witch Harry prepares to cook a little boy who, Scheherazade-like, puts her off by reading from a volume called *Tales From the Darkside. Lot 249*, from the story by Arthur Conan Doyle, is a standard tale of campus revenge, with an abused nerd getting back at preppie persecutors using a re-animated mummy. *Cat From Hell*, expanded from a sketch by Stephen King, is the slightest story but receives the most elaborate treatment, as an underworld hit man is hired to kill a cat that is persecuting a crippled pharmaceuticals millionaire (Hickey) whose fortune is based on animal experimentation. The most elaborate segment is *Lovers' Vow*, an original by Michael McDowell, unfortunately stuck with a guessable final revelation but trying for depth of character as a depressed and unsuccessful artist (Remar) encounters on the same night a murderous gargoyle who lets him live on the condition that he never tell anyone about its existence and a woman (Chong) who turns his life around but never talks about her background. Harrison takes standard tales with an especially feeble wrap-up 'happy ending' and shows considerable style in execution, drawing generally good performances and working a nice vein of black humour.

d John Harrison *p* Richard Rubinstein *s* Michael McDowell, George A. Romero *c* Robert Draper *lp* Deborah Harry, Christian Slater, William Hickey, James Remar, Rae Dawn Chong

Voci dal Profondo *aka* Voices From Beyond

(WIND FILMS/SCENA GROUP/EXECUTIVE CINE TV; IT) 85min

This listless mystery finds Fulci working for once with a tight, if trite, story. That said, few surprises are offered as a young woman (Huff) is influenced by her recently dead millionaire father (Del Prete) to discover which of his disinherited but grasping heirs put ground glass in his ice-cubes.

An almost original idea (Del Prete's spirit's ties to the world of the living diminish as his body decays) goes for little among the mix of tedious wandering around and soap-opera scheming as each of the dead man's various relatives and aquaintances is revealed, *Murder on the Orient Express*-style, to have reasons to want him dead. A typical Fulci touch is the use of an angelic child in a murder scheme, but more in key with his feeble attempts to recreate the tone of his most notorious pictures is a half-hearted nightmare in which an irrelevant character is attacked by zombies. In a dubious honour, Fulci dedicates the film 'to my few real friends, in particular to Clive Barker and Claudio Carabba.'

d/co-s Lucio Fulci *p* Luigi Nannerini, Antonio Lucidi *co-s* Pietro Ragnoli *c* Sandro Grossi *se* Pino Ferranti *lp* Karina Huff, Duilio Del Prete, Pascal Persiano, Lorenzo Flaherty, Damiano Azzos, Rosamaria Grauso, Bettina Giovannini, Frances Nacmen, Paolo Paoloni, Sacha Maria Darwin, Antonella Tinazzo

The Witches (LORIMAR) 90min

A misogynist horror film for children, adapted from Roald Dahl's highly regarded novel, this doesn't quite manage to make the transition from **Suspiria** (1976) to *Honey, I Shrunk the Kids* (1989).

Fisher, recently orphaned and in the care of his tale-telling Norwegian grandmother (Zetterling), is taken for a holiday break to a seaside hotel where a convention of the Royal Society for the Prevention of Cruelty to Children is a front for a gathering of all the witches in England. Bald and hideous under wigs and masks, with squared toes that prevent them wearing stylish shoes and a violet tint to their eyes, the witches, under the presidency of evil queen Huston – who appears as herself and as a ghastly Henson creation – plan to turn all the children in the country into mice. Fisher is so afflicted, but manages to adjust to rodenthood and, with the help of his superstitious granny, thwarts the evil scheme. Dahl's slyly nasty humour, and somewhat distasteful attitude to women, is retained by Roeg, which makes for a less amiable film than *Willy Wonka and the Chocolate Factory* (1971), but there are also all the effects expected of a muppet-style Hollywood movie, and several doses of 'British' comedy turns, courtesy of Atkinson and Paterson.

d Nicolas Roeg *p* Mark Shivas *s* Allan Scott *c* Harvey Harrison *se* Jim Henson *lp* Anjelica Huston, Mai Zetterling, Jasen Fisher, Jane Horrocks, Jenny Runacre, Bill Paterson, Rowan Atkinson, Brenda Blethyn

Anjelica Huston as Grand High Witch Miss Ernst in the disappointing The Witches.

Yangan Dou *aka* **A Chinese Ghost Story II**
(FILM WORKSHOP; HONG KONG) 104min
Taking characters from the first film – tax collector cum unwilling ghostbuster Leslie Cheung and Taoist Ma – this wisely avoids reprising the earlier plot, opting to have the heroine (Wang) reincarnated as the daughter of a disgraced imperial official. She enlists Cheung, mistaken for a wise and venerable magician, to help restore her father's honour and overthrow an evil magician – who appears as a yellow-hatted monk, a giant statue of Buddha or a 300-foot centipede – who has caused the family's downfall.

Siu Tung demonstrates his mastery of split-second comedy and suspense in a marvellous sequence involving a giant zombie, a magician (Jacky Cheung) who has had his own freeze spell cast on him, and the hero's attempts to save the magician while keeping the monster bound; or a scene in which the hero tries to conceal his innocent liaison with the heroine when her snappy sister (Li) intervenes with five loyal swordsmen while the girl is upstairs within reach of the still-living torso of the monster from the earlier sequence. The film misses the pure and melancholy love aspect of the earlier film (despite the English title, it does not even have a real ghost), but it makes up for the lack with spirited action adventure, plenty of enjoyable monstrosities and much sly humour.

d Ching Siu Tung *p* Tsui Hark *s* Lau Tai-Mok, Kan Kei-to, Leung Yu-ming *c* Arthur Wong *lp* Leslie Cheung, Joey Wang, Michelle Li, Wu Ma, Jacky Cheung, Waise Lee

Ye Mo Xiansheng *aka* **The Nocturnal Demon**
(LAU KOON-WAI/GOLDEN HARVEST; HONG KONG) 94min
A culture-shock crossbreed of violent slasher and kung-fu comedy, with a bizarre and unresolved doppelganger theme as the mad murderer, an impotent taxi driver who takes a Stanley knife to beautiful women, and the bumbling hero are presented as lookalikes, each resembling a Chinese Woody Allen to further the effect.

The moralizing plot involves a shrill-voiced innocent (Lee) from the mainland, who looks up a girl from her village who has gone to the bad by becoming a larcenous exotic dancer. When the dancer is murdered, Lee and her extended family hunt for the killer, which allows for strange asides like a *Clouseau*-ish comedy sequence as the heroine's blind grandfather dresses as a teenager to infiltrate a police station. A comedy thriller, with many disguises and slapstick tumbles, it turns surprisingly nasty in the sequences involving the murderer who is seen, in one unpleasant moment, pissing on his blade and his victim. The finale finds the killer displaying superhuman strength as Lee, dressed as a ridiculous hooker, kicks him into submission. There is one absolutely astonishing example of roller-skating martial-arts choreography as Lee disables a gang of muggers.

d/p Lau Koon-Wai *s* Lo Wing-Keung, Cheung Lei-Ling *c* Chan Chung-Chau, Lam Fai-Tai *sp* Cho Wing *lp* Alfred Cheung, Moon Lee, Lam Gau, Lau Naam-Kwong, Chow Keung, Yip Wing-Yin, Cho Wing

Zhuo Gui Hejia Huan II: Mayi Chuanqi *aka* **Ghost Legend** (WING FUNG FILM COMPANY/GOLDEN PRINCESS; HONG KONG) 92min
This fine Chinese ghost movie opens with an extraordinary exorcism-to-the-death between Ma, Hong Kong's Peter Cushing, and the King of Ghosts, a supernatural baddie who looks like a kung-fu Klingon.

200 years later, a doctor (Cheng) stumbles over the bones of a virgin victim of the King of Ghosts and accidentally bleeds onto her teeth, reviving her as a lovestruck spirit. In an original variation on the Dracula-reviving contrivances of the Hammer series, the King is brought back when Cheng plucks a herb bush that has grown from the fiend's heart and drops it in an alley while rushing to deliver a baby, later throwing a basinful of afterbirth onto the bush, whereupon the King regenerates, sucks the baby's soul and sets out to kill six more virgins which will bring his score up to 49 and mean he can never be killed again. Cheng's sister is involved with a novice monk in Ma's old monastery and the three, abetted by the ghost, join the tubby head priest, who has been developing a cannon which will be specially effective against spooks, in a campaign against the villain. It has the usual comedy and romance but is stronger than most Hong Kong films in its horror content, climaxing with a knock-down, drag-out fight between the goodies and the monster which winds up with the cannon, previously a slapstick dead loss, working properly and blowing the King of Ghosts to pieces.

d/p Ng Min-Kan *s* Lee Gwing-Kaai *c* Ng Man-Ding *lp* Ho Ka-Ging, Kent Cheng, Kwok Fu-Sing, Cheung Man, Wu Ma, Tong Lai-Kau, Chang Lung, Law Yim-Hung

Zombie '90: Extreme Pestilence
(BLOOD PICTURES/REEL GORE; WG) 75min
Typical of the sub-amateur efforts exposed through underground video distribution, this pastiche seems to come from morons who didn't notice the context of the atrocities in Romero's zombie movies. After an unseen plane crash leaks a toxin, zombies wander around Euro-nowhere killing walk-on characters. The ultimate product of the fanzine mentality, this is the equivalent of gorehound criticism: everything except carnage is ruled irrelevant to the quality of a movie. The wall-to-wall effects are notably ropey, without the low-budget irony of a **Braindead** (1992).

d/s/se Andreas Schnaas *p* The Violent Shitters *c* Steve Aquilina *lp* Matthias Kerl, Ralf Hess, Matthias Abbes, Marc Trinkhaus, Christian Biallas, Wolfgang Hinz

1991

The Addams Family (ORION) 99min
The film's opening, the family about to pour boiling oil on an unbearably merry group of carol singers, reproduces one of Charles Addams' most famous New Yorker cartoons. Over this is heard a snatch of Vic Mizzy's finger-snapping *Addams Family* TV theme, signalling a fusion of approaches to the material.

Stuck with a plot, about crooked lawyers passing off a ringer (Lloyd) as the long-lost Uncle Fester, as ephemeral as that of **Munster Go Home!** (1966) or (indeed) the TV special *Halloween With the Addams Family* (1977), the film still manages the basic joke that pure decadence can be touchingly like innocence, and the subversive notion that Morticia (Huston) and Gomez (Julia) have an intensely sexual marriage which, more than the sword-fighting, hungry tiger rug and active furniture, is their rebellion against the milk-and-water normality of sit-com couples. The best jokes are character-based: the oddly forlorn detail of Thing expelled from the Addams haven hauling a cart loaded with gloves, watches and rings; or Morticia's claim that her daughter's choice of an ancestor burned for witchcraft as a noteworthy hero is no stranger than that of a classmate who picks George Bush. There are casting coups all around, with Ricci achieving stellar magnitude with her blank-faced Wednesday, strapping her brother into an electric chair and informing him, as she throws switches, that this game is called 'Is there a God?'.

d Barry Sonnenfeld *p* Scott Rudin *s* Caroline Thompson, Larry Wilson *c* Owen Roizman *se* Chuck Comisky *lp* Anjelica Huston, Raul Julia, Christopher Lloyd, Christina Ricci, Christopher Hart, Jimmy Workman, Carel Struycken

Afraid of the Dark (SOVEREIGN/TELESCOPE/LES FILMS ARIANE/CINE CINQ; GB, FR) 91min
This restrained slasher starts with a young boy (Keyworth) peeping like a junior Hitchcock voyeur through windows and from behind railings at a curiously depopulated London caught somewhere between the nineties and an Edgar Wallace fifties of sinister stalkers and blind victims.

A mad razor-wielder attacks the patrons of a drop-in clinic and the hero's mother (Ardant) seems in line for victimization, while all the window-cleaners, locksmiths and photographers in the area are twitchily perverse suspects. Halfway through, after a tastelessly gory knitting-needle eye-gouging, this combination of *Emil and the Detectives* and **L'Uccello dalle Piume di Cristallo** (1970) pulls an arty about-face. The story breaks down to its constituent elements, recasting the actors and turning Keyworth from potential hero to psychotic menace, the preceding plot having been fantasized by him as a reaction to his own possibly impending blindness and his mother's new baby.

d/s Mark Peploe *p* Simon Bosanquet *c* Bruno De Keyzer *se* John Markwell *lp* Ben Keyworth, James Fox, Fanny Ardant, Paul McGann, Clare Holman, Robert Stephens

The Ambulance (EPIC-SARLUI/DIAMANT) 97min
Cohen's most coherent, controlled and effective film since **The Winged Serpent** (1982), this follows the strategy of *It's Alive* (1975) and *The Stuff* (1985) by taking an element (babies, ice cream) of ordinary life usually seen as reassuring, then revealing a paranoid, upsetting vision under the comforting surface.

Cartoonist Roberts approaches Turner on a street corner and tries to charm her into dating him, only for the girl to suffer a diabetic collapse and be swept away by a sinister ambulance. When he is unable to find a trace of her he gradually realizes that the ambulance is from a medical organization kidnapping diabetics for unethical research. Roberts, remarkably controlled, encounters a clutch of eccentric, unstereotyped characters during his investigation: harassed and more-neurotic-than-he-seems cop Jones and his supportive, slightly abrasive assistant Gallagher, and old-time newsman Buttons who snaps and wisecracks like Lee Tracy in a Warners newspaper drama as he brings in one last story. Having set up his ominous situation, Cohen plays the plot for suspense and humour, as, for example, when Roberts talks a gang of roughs who have just mugged him into tackling the ambulance attendants who are taking him away. Deeply suspicious of the medical profession, the film makes the trappings of the hospital into an infernal environment, with a sadistic fetishist villain (Braeden) who coos 'I love the feel of human flesh through surgical gloves'.

d/s Larry Cohen *p* Moctezuma Esparza, Robert Katz *c* Jacques Haitkin *se* Rob Benevides *lp* Eric Roberts, James Earl Jones, Megan Gallagher, Janine Turner, Jill Gatsby, Red Buttons, Eric Braeden, Richard Bright, Jim Dixon, Stan Lee, Laurene Landon

Basket Case 3
(SHAPIRO-GLICKENHAUS ENTERTAINMENT) 90min
This needless sequel lacks the edge of Henenlotter's earliest films.

Going back on the effective last image of **Basket Case 2** (1990), it has siamese twins Duane (VanHentenryck) and Belial re-separated then relocates to the Deep South. Elementary conflicts are settled by having Belial emerge from his basket to slaughter sundry Sheriff's deputies, twisting heads out of shape cartoon fashion, and hitting the vengeance trail in a contraption which combines the functions of tank and wheelchair. In a rare moment suggesting the skewed vision Henenlotter is capable of, jazz singer Ross leads assembled freaks in a singalong rendition of *Personality*.

d/co-s Frank Henenlotter *p* Edgar Ievins *co-s* Robert Martin *c* Bob Paone *se* Gabe Bartalos, David Kindlon *lp* Kevin VanHentenryck, Gil Roper, Annie Ross, Dan Biggers, Tina Louise Hilbert, Jim O'Doherty, Jackson Faw, Jim Grimshaw

Black Magic (POINT OF VIEW/MTE) 89min
This effective screwball horror features innocent insomniac Reinhold plagued by visions of a ghostly cousin (LaPaglia) who claims to have been cursed by his girlfriend (Ward). Visiting the eccentric community of Istanbul, North Carolina Reinhold finds town officials unperturbed by LaPaglia's disappearance and, despite warnings from demented local gangster James, falls for the winsome Ward. Alternating genuine creepiness with uneasy comedy, this plays like a more sinister *Bell, Book and Candle* (1958) as Reinhold is ensnared by the strange, sexy and sassy woman whom several ghosts urge him to destroy before the curse extends to him. Told that witches are unable to cry, Reinhold puts Ward to the test by taking her to 'the saddest movie ever made' only to find her alone in an audience chugging popcorn rather than clutching kleenex. Never falling back on obvious horror, this invents intriguing minor superstitions involving plagues of crows, obstreperous dogs and children, black tongues and constipation.

d/s Daniel Taplitz *p* Harvey Frand *c* Peter Fernberger *se* Dean Jones *lp* Rachel Ward, Judge Reinhold, Anthony LaPaglia, Brion James, Wendy Makkenna, Richard Whitting

Black Magic Woman (TRIMARK) 88min
A crossbreed of **Fatal Attraction** (1987) and **The Believers** (1987), with an LA art milieu and a genuinely surprising final twist.

Gallery owner Hamill, in an open relationship with girlfriend Wyss, has an affair with Apollonia which ends badly, whereupon he suffers from voodoo persecution as dead poultry is hung over his bed and blood-filled eggs are hidden under his pillow. When his sympathetic maid (Viera) recommends a hispanic exorcist, Hamill undergoes a ritual cleansing that lifts the curse, but supporting characters start to show up dead with their fingers severed. Because it follows so closely the structure of *Fatal Attraction*, the film cannily pulls its finish out of left field, at first appearing to set up a variant of the deleted 'Madame Butterfly' finale of Adrian Lyne's film only to redefine everything that has gone before, presenting an interesting opposition between old money witchcraft and ethnic voodoo.

d/co-p Deryn Warren *co-p* Marc Springer *s* Gerry Daly *c* Levie Isaacks *lp* Marc Hamill, Amanda Wyss, Apollonia, Victor Rivers, Abidah Viera, Carmen Moore, Bonnie Ebsen, Larry Hankin, Alan Toy

Bloodlust (WINDHOVER; AUST) 87min
This low-budget, disreputable punk vampire picture features three hip, violent, beautiful vampires who decide to relieve a drug dealer of $3 million to ensure their long-term financial security.

The introductory sequence contrasts the protagonists' methods of preying, with prostitute Chapman picking up a businessman in a hotel bar and draining him during sex, stylish lesbian Wallace murdering a foot fetishist (Flaus) and long-haired vigilante O'Neill gunning down a dope pusher. Escaping from a pair of comedy-relief cops and a group of survivalists led by a stake-wielding fanatic (Motherwell), the trio carry out their smash and grab, then retreat to a derelict country house for a bloody confrontation with the cops, gangsters and vigilantes. Painfully loud and hip, with a soundtrack from Revolting Cocks, Pailhead, Lead Into Gold and 1000 Homo DJs, and plentiful cocaine-snorting and explicit sex, this is rude, crude and invigorating, but a tad too self-conscious.

d/p/s Richard Wollstencroft, Jon Hewitt *c* Gary Ravencroft *lp* Jane Stuart Wallace, Kelly Chapman, Robert James O'Neill, Phil Motherwell, Paul Moder, James Young, Max Crawdaddy, Ian Rilen, John Flaus, Colin Savage, Big Bad Ralph

Bloodmoon
(VILLAGE ROADSHOW/MICHAEL FISHER; AUST) 90min
A late entry in the Australian sub-branch of the teenkill movie – following **Snap-Shot** (1979), *Nightmares* (1980), *An Early Frost* (1980) and **Lady, Stay Dead** (1982) – this hews fairly

close to its American model, **Prom Night** (1980). Lissek is the disturbed and cuckolded schoolmaster who garrottes courting couples with barbed wire in lovers' lane.

Though the prospect of seeing a collection of blonde and tanned perfect Australians bloodily disposed of after the manner of **Friday the 13th** (1980) has an undeniable appeal, this protracted thriller fails to capitalize on the possibilities. The only classy element is Brian May's orchestral score.

d Alec Mills *p* Stanley O'Toole *s* Robert Brennan *c* John Stokes *se* April Harvie *lp* Leon Lissek, Christine Amor, Ian Williams, Helen Thomson, Craige Cronnin, Hazel Howson, Suzie MacKenzie, Steve Bergin, Anya Molina

Body Parts (PAR) 88min

Officially based on Boileau-Narcejac's *Choice Cuts*, this is a patchwork of various screen versions of Maurice Renard's *The Hands of Orlac*. The result is a disorienting mixture of up-to-the-minute surgery and antiquated plot devices that is even less successful in its mix of old and new than **The Hand** (1981).

Psychiatrist Fahey loses his arm in a car crash, but experimental surgeon Duncan replaces it with one sawn off a living donor. Disturbed by his arm's tendency to violent acts, Fahey learns that it comes from an executed mass murderer and makes contact with other subjects of the Duncan treatment. Artist Dourif has received the killer's other arm and been transformed from journeyman to mad genius, while basketball player Murnik has new legs which tend to hit the accelerator pedal in heavy traffic. The film suddenly turns into an outrageous mad-science melodrama when the murderer (Walsh) shows up with his head sewn back on, an image borrowed from **Mad Love** (1935), to reclaim his missing pieces. Duncan keeps a straight face with leftover Lionel Atwill dialogue about the comparative unimportance of a few little atrocities when weighed against her great work.

d/co-s Eric Red *p* Frank Mancuso Jr *co-s* Norman Snider *c* Theo van de Sande *se* Neil N. Trifunovich *lp* Jeff Fahey, Lindsay Duncan, Brad Dourif, Kim Delaney, Zakes Mokae, Peter Murnik, John Walsh, Paul Benvictor

Bride of Re-Animator *aka* Re-Animator II

(WILDSTREET) 96min

This is doubly disappointing. Most of the cast and even incidentals like Richard Band's wittily Herrmannesque score are brought back from the 1985 original, but the script, which yokes in portions of **The Bride of Frankenstein** (1935), goes nowhere.

Returning from a sojourn in Peru, Dr Herbert West (Combs), the re-animator, and his assistant (Abbott) use a serum derived from the amniotic fluid of iguanas to bring to life a piecemeal creation (Kinmont) built around the heart of the heroine of the first film and the brain of a terminal patient. However, the severed head (Gale) of West's arch-enemy is still active, using bat's wings to get around, and West has also unwisely created a cellarful of monstrosities which finally, in an echo of *The Black Sleep* (1956), drag to him to his death in a collapsing crypt after his monster has rejected him and torn herself apart.

d/p Brian Yuzna *s* Woody Keith, Rick Fry *c* Rick Fichter *se* Screaming Mad George, John Carl Buechler, David Allen, KNB EFX Group, Doublin EFX *lp* Jeffrey Combs, Bruce Abbott, David Gale, Claude Earl Jones, Fabiana Udenio, Kathleen Kinmont

Cape Fear (AMBLIN/CAPPA/TRIBECA) 127min

This is another mainstream slasher in the manner of **Fatal Attraction** (1987) or **Sleeping With the Enemy** (1991), albeit with a more interesting dramatic core. Scorsese, a director of superior, personal, quirky films, here unashamedly applies himself to a large-scale quickie. The result is a triumph of technique over content.

Based on J. Lee-Thompson's 1962 thriller, De Niro is the just-released convict who persecutes the family of lawyer Nolte, who concealed evidence that might have got him off a rape charge. At first De Niro loiters around Nolte's wife (Lange) and daughter (Lewis), insinuating the disgusting things he plans to do but carefully not breaking laws, thereby forcing Nolte to realize that the law he lives by is a convenient fiction. Scorsese enters into the spirit of the gothic plotting, reusing Bernard Herrmann's original score, calling upon Saul Bass for a suitably ominous credit sequence, and respectfully casting the stars of the earlier film in telling cameos. The suspense rises in a crescendo in a swamp-set finale, as the truly demented De Niro invades a houseboat during a storm. Finally transforming into a Freddy-faced monster, De Niro is burned and battered but keeps crawling out of the waters to attack again. With *Taxi Driver* (1976), *The King of Comedy* (1983), *After Hours* (1985) and *GoodFellas* (1990), Scorsese demonstrated a flair for out-of-genre horror that proves his talent is ill served by the limitations of strict genre. *Cape Fear*, his most conventional film, is just a horror picture.

d Martin Scorsese *p* Barbara DeFina *s* Wesley Strick *c* Freddie Francis *se* Neal Martz, Derek Meddings *lp* Robert De Niro, Nick Nolte, Jessica Lange, Juliette Lewis, Joe Don Baker, Robert Mitchum, Gregory Peck, Martin Balsam, Illeana Douglas

Child's Play 3 (U) 89min

This is a few notches better than **Child's Play 2** (1990).

The hero isn't a squeaky brat but has grown up into Whalin, a maladjusted military school cadet, and Chucky, the freckle-faced doll possessed by serial killer Dourif, is given more interesting pranks to play, such as substituting live rounds for the paint cartridges issued during a war games exercise. Bender even has a few shots at atmosphere as the final showdown strays from the misty forests where the war game is played, allowing coward Jacobsen the chance stereotypically to redeem himself by falling on a live grenade, into a funfair where another ultimate destruction of Chucky is staged in an improbably elaborate ghost train.

d Jack Bender *p* Robert Lathan Brown *s* Don Mancini *c* John R. Leonetti *se* Kevin Yagher *lp* Justin Whalin, Perrey Reeves, Jeremy Sylvers, Travis Fine, Dean Jacobsen, Andy Robsinon, Brad Dourif, Peter Haskell

The Dark Backward (BACKWARD FILMS) 103min

This is an especially bizarre entry in the 'imaginary urban world' subgenre of **Eraserhead** (1976) and *Johnny Suede* (1991). Garbageman Nelson moonlights as a sweatily appalling comedian and achieves celebrity when a third arm grows between his shoulder-blades. A fable about the cruelty of comedy (Nelson's act is so terrible that when he appears on TV, his own mother turns over to watch the other side), the plot takes us on a lengthy detour through a garbage-strewn world dominated by disgusting-sounding products ('Pig Newtons', 'Beets and Raisins', 'Pork Juice', 'Weaselroni') issued by the ubiquitous Blump company. Paxton, as Nelson's hyperactive accordionist sidekick, enthusiastically performs not only a necrophile slobber over a nude corpse discovered in a garbage dump, but an orgy scene with three bizarre women. Completely consistent and undoubtedly a successful realization of Rifkin's off-centre vision, this is still a shuffling, miserable and repulsive, ultimately almost intolerable, viewing experience.

d/s Adam Rifkin *p* Brad Wyman, Cassian Elwes *c* Joey Forsyte *se* Tony Gardner *lp* Judd Nelson, Bil Paxton, Wayne Newton, Rob Lowe, Lara Flynn Boyle, James Caan, King Moody, Claudia Christian

Dawn (SHOOTING GALLERY; GB) 78min

Reputedly the cheapest horror feature ever made in Britain, this Bristol-based production uses video far more creatively than comparable items like *Suffer Little Children* (1983) and *Redneck Zombies* (1987).

Influenced by the novels of Anne Rice, *Dawn* has a disaffected young woman (Rees) picked up in a pub by Sloan, a suavely ordinary young man who turns out to be 200 years old and fleeing from a vengeful vigilante (Johnson). Rewriting the rules, *Dawn* has Sloan take his blood in a painful-looking transfusion and returns to mythology by emphasizing that the killing stake is just to secure the vampire to the earth while the sun does its work. Video limitations (static shots, unconvincing lighting, a tatty look) are largely avoided by Johnson's inventive corner-cutting. The cast perform remarkably well given the occasional solemn ludicrousness of the necessarily talky script.

d/p/s Niall Johnson *c* Nic Coleclough *se* Jon Rowlands, Harriet Braun *lp* Elizabeth Rees, Geoff Sloan, Craig Johnson, Kate Jones Davies, Meg Whelan, Graziella Jones

Dead Again (PAR) 101min

Alternating a lush black and white melodrama with a post-modern private-eye story, this mixes the supernatural with Hitchcockian romance, stirring *Spellbound* (1948) into **L'Uccello dalle Piume di Cristallo** (1970) with some verve.

Detective Branagh is given charge of amnesiac Thompson, and consults hypnotist Jacobi, who regresses her to a previous life in which she was mixed up in a famous forties murder case. Thompson comes to believe she is the reincarnation of the murdered wife of an exiled genius composer (Branagh) who was executed for the crime; eventually, Branagh realizes they have been cross-reincarnated and that he is actually the victim and the woman with whom he has become romantically involved is the returned composer. The defiantly ridiculous plot has to be unravelled by awkward speeches from heavily made-up Garcia and Schygulla, survivors of the flashbacks, but Branagh, following *Henry V* (1989) with another bit of amusing showing-off, knowingly skates over the silliness, laying on forties-style orchestral thunder and lightning even in the modern sequences, and ending with a trope worthy of Dario Argento as the surprise villain is impaled on a giant set of sculpted scissors.

d Kenneth Branagh *p* Lindsay Doran, Charles H. Maguire *s* Scott Frank *c* Matthew F. Leonetti *se* Tom & Bari Burman *lp* Kenneth Branagh, Emma Thompson, Andy Garcia, Derek Jacobi, Robin Williams, Hanna Schygulla, Campbell Scott

Emma Thompson distraught in Dead Again. *A mark of how carefully thought out was the design of the picture is the scissors motif behind her.*

Delicatessen (CONSTELLATION/UGC; FR) 97min

In a ravaged city, possibly a post-holocaust future but probably an alternate 1950s, very French apartment dwellers concentrate on very French concerns: adultery, suicide, music and, most of all, food.

The butcher (Dreyfus) who owns the block supports his tenants by hiring odd-job men, whom he fattens up and turns into meats that usefully supplement the lentils that have taken over as hard currency in the starving city. Into this tidily unhappy world comes Pinon, an ex-clown grieving over the death of his monkey. His good-natured decency moves the butcher's saintly daughter (Clapet) to betray the cannibals to subterranean vegetarian revolutionaries. The film features two priceless gag sequences built around creaking bedsprings, and has an unusal facility, akin to the films of Jean Renoir, to love all its characters, no matter how horrid.

d/co-s Jean-Pierre Jeunet, Marc Caro *p* Claudie Ossard *co-s* Gilles Adrien *c* Darius Khondji *se* Olivier Gleyze, Jean-Baptiste Bonetto, Yves Domenjoud *lp* Dominique Pinon, Julie Clapet, Jean Claude Dreyfus, Karin Viard, Ticky Holgado, Anne Marie Pisani, Jacques Mathou, Rufus, Howard Vernon

Demoni 3 *aka* **Black Demons** (FILMAKERS; IT) 86min

This is a spurious 'sequel' to Lamberto Bava's *Demoni* movies.

While holidaymaking in Rio de Janeiro, American siblings Van Hoven and Curtis and Curtis' British boyfriend (Balogh) get mixed up in Macumba voodoo. At a chicken-killing ritual dance, Van Hoven is given an amulet of Ogum and is transformed into a force of evil. Later the tourists' jeep breaks down near a cemetery where a tape of Macumba music conjures six worm-eaten negro zombies from their graves. Runaway slaves massacred a hundred years ago, they have returned to life to carry out a curse by slaughtering an equal number of white people. No less flip in its social content than the similarly race-motivated *Sugar Hill* (1972), this at least has an unusual marimba score to go with the familiar Italian horror business of zombies slowly chasing inane victims.

d Umberto Lenzi *p* Giuseppe Gargiulo *s* Olga Pehar *c* Maurizio Dell'Orco *se* Franco Casagni *lp* Keith Van Hoven, Joe Balogh, Sonia Curtis, Philip Murray, Juliana Texeira, Maria Alves

Demonic Toys (FULL MOON ENTERTAINMENT) 82min

Returning to the main feature (scurrying small creatures) of many other Charles Band quickies, this loose variant of **Child's Play** (1986) overleaps awkward initial exposition to deliver a neat, suspenseful, claustrophobic chiller.

Pregnant cop Scoggins pursues arms dealers who have just killed her partner into a warehouse full of discontinued toys, and a wounded crook bleeds onto the floor, re-activating the spirit of a demon who animates a selection of the toys as a warm-up for possessing the heroine's unborn child. Along with a security guard (Schrum), a runaway girl (Dunning) and a fast-food delivery boy (Mitchum), Scoggins and her handcuffed charge (Russo) are trapped overnight in the warehouse and attacked by the eponymous creatures, which include an especially malevolent baby doll, a reptilian clown jack-in-the-box, a feral teddy bear and a zap-gun-wielding plastic robot. By comparison with **Ghoulies** (1984) and **Dolls** (1987), the effects are unambitious but expert, with the monsters possessing a genuinely vicious/comic flair. The last-minute intervention by a heroic toy soldier provides a refreshingly resonant happy ending. Certainly more impressive than the vastly expensive *Toys* (1992).

d Peter Manoogian *p* Anne Kelly *s* David S. Goyer *c* Adolfo Bartoli *se* Magical Media Industries *lp* Tracy Scoggins, Bentley Mitchum, Michael Russo, Jeff Weston, Daniel Cerny, Ellen Dunning, Barry Lynch, William Thorne, Pete Schrum

Das Deutsche Kettensägenmassaker *aka* The German Chainsaw Massacre

(DME FILM/RHEWES FILPRODUKTION; G) 63min

As indebted to John Waters (especially *Desperate Living*, 1973) as to Tobe Hooper, this is a brief, satirical horror set in the first hours of a newly unified Germany.

Former East German Fallenstein reacts to the destruction of the Berlin Wall by leaving her husband and 'escaping' to the West in a Trabant. She finds capitalism represented by a demented cannibal family intent on turning former communists into frankfurters. An unsubtle critique of the rapacious new country, the film is marked by such touches as victim running from a chainsaw-wielding maniac screaming 'but we are one nation now'. The director's justification for the film is possibly the silliest ever: 'It's all irony, of course, you can easily see that the violence is not real. There are a few disgusting scenes, yes; but they are artistically made comments on what unification has done to this country.'

d/s/c Christoph Schlingensief *p* Christian Fürst *lp* Karina Fallenstein, Suzanne Bredehöft, Artur Albrecht, Volker Spengler, Alfred Edel, Brigitte Kausch, Dietrich Kuhlbrodt

Disturbed (WARNERS) 95min

An entry in the 'disappearing body' school of psycho-horror exemplified by *Les Diaboliques* (1955) and **Hush ... Hush, Sweet Charlotte** (1964), and influenced by the driven-to-extremes comedy of TV sit-com *Fawlty Towers*, this plays potentially offensive material for laughs.

McDowell, lecherous head of an insane asylum, habitually drugs and molests his female patients. When he mistakenly injects depressive Gidley with penicillin, to which she has an allergic reaction that puts her in a coma, patient Lewis steps in to help by suffocating her. The corpse is taken away and buried by a childlike retard and McDowell is driven crazy by apparitions (most disturbingly when he wakes from an erotic dream to find himself making love with a decapitated corpse) and a conspiracy of his patients, all intent on avenging Gidley's mother, an inmate he drove to suicide. McDowell delivers an over-the-top performance that builds to hysteria pitch and manages to be funny and almost sympathetic. The subject matter allows Winkler to excercise perhaps to excess a penchant for trick camera angles (a shot from the viewpoint of a thrown hypodermic syringe) but for the most part the playfully demented style complements the inventively twisted storyline.

d/co-s Charles Winkler *p* Brad Wyman *co-s* Emerson Bixby *c* Bernd Heinl *lp* Malcolm McDowell, Geoffrey Lewis, Priscilla Pointer, Pamela Gidley

Dolly Dearest

(PATRIOT PICTURES/CHANNELER ENTERPRISES) 89min

This is a cheap imitation of **Child's Play** (1988), with a competent cast failing to make an impression in thinly written parts.

A Mayan spirit possesses an entire line of prototype dolls (apparently numbering about three) in a Mexican factory recently taken over by a bewildered Bottoms. His daughter (Hutson) falls under the influence and becomes a staring brooder, shrieking in the presence of priests and getting her own doll to murder the servants. Crosby, Hutson's archaeology-buff brother (Demetral) and crusty archaeologist Torn chip in to help Bottoms blow up the factory and exorcize the little girl, mercifully ending the menace at a point when only Mexicans have been killed.

d/s Maria Lease *p* Daniel Cady *c* Eric D. Andersen *se* Alan G. Markowitz *lp* Denise Crosby, Sam Bottoms, Chris Demetral, Candy Hutson, Lupe Ontirveros, Will Gotay, Rip Torn

The Forgotten One

(WIND RIVER/SPIRITED PRODUCTIONS) 94min

A low-key ghost story with erotic and horrific elements, this is a refreshingly non-stereotypical offering.

Recently widowed writer O'Quinn discovers his new house has a ghost (Parker) in the basement, a murdered adulterous wife from the 19th century. She appears to him, seeing in him the reincarnation of her lover, and initiates an affair which she plans to culminate with his joining her in death. Segueing neatly from mystery to romance to horror, this benefits from a well-thought-out script and unusually detailed characterizations, especially of the burned-out but romantic hero and his concerned next-door neighbour (McNichol). In its later stretches, the film plays up the horror as Parker tries to gas or crash O'Quinn, finally luring him to a welcomed death in a lake.

d/s Phillip Badger *p* Peter Garrity *c* James Mathers *se* Tim Drnec *lp* Terry O'Quinn, Kristy McNichol, Elisabeth Brooks, Blair Parker

Freddy's Dead: The Final Nightmare

(NEW LINE) 90min

Coming on as if it's going to be different, this turns out to be exactly the same. It starts with a new title format (the film isn't called *A Nightmare on Elm Street, Part 6: The Dream Something*), a caption setting the action in 2001 (without any science-fiction content) and a declared intention to get Freddy out of his home town and into new locales ('after all, every town has an Elm Street'), but then a group of familiarly cut-out (and cut-up) characters are introduced and a few pathetic mysteries set in motion (who is the unseen father in psychiatrist Zane's childhood nightmares?), and the film delivers the usual succession of variably imaginative nightmares.

The stand-out is not the headachy 3-D finale, but a clever scene in which a deaf boy (Logan) is tormented by nightmare sounds, the inevitable *coup de grâce* coming when Freddy produces a blackboard and starts scraping. The gimmicks include unbilled cameos from Alice Cooper, Johnny Depp and Roseanne Barr, female characters who look like Madonna and Jodie Foster, and more Heavy Metal music. After this, Freddy may not be dead, but he certainly looks tired.

d Rachel Talalay *p* Robert Shaye, Aron Warner *s* Michael DeLuca *c* Declan Quinn *se* Mechanical Make-Up Images *lp* Robert Englund, Lisa Zane, Shon Greenblatt, Lezlie Deane, Ricky Dean Logan, Yaphet Kotto

Un Gatto nel Cervello: I Volti del Terrore *aka* A Cat in the Brain: The Face of Terror *aka* Nightmare Concert

(LA EXECUTIVE/CINE TV SRL; IT) 85min

In this vanity production, Fulci meditates on his life and work in the tradition of Bob Fosse's *All That Jazz* (1979), Woody Allen's *Stardust Memories* (1980) or Henry Jaglom's *Always* (1985), at the same time delivering a 'Greatest Hits' package by recycling gory sequences from movies like **Quando Alice Ruppe lo Specchio** (1988) and **I Fantasmi di Sodoma** (1988).

Fulci plays horror director 'Lucio Fulci', haunted by images of gruesome death which appear as he potters about glumly in an old pullover muttering about the cat in his brain. He consults psychiatrist Halsey, who suffers a bizarre transference and becomes a murderer. The finale finds Halsey dead, but Fulci, aboard a yacht named the *Perversion*, picks up the chainsaw in an identification of director with killer that goes beyond any of Argento's black-leather-glove tricks. Cheap, unpleasant, tasteless, repetitive and dull, this is the most pronounced example of Fulci's appalling misogyny since **Lo Squartatore di New York** (1982), with scene after scene of walk-on, mostly nude, women mutilated, decapitated, stabbed, abused, dismembered, turned to hamburger, garrotted, chainsawed and bludgeoned.

d/co-s Lucio Fulci *p* Luigi Nannerini, Antonio Lucidi *co-s* Giovanni Simonelli, Antonio Tentori *c* Alessandro Grossi *lp* Lucio Fulci, David L. Thompson, Jeoffrey Kennedy, Malisa Longo, Ria de Simone, Brett Halsey, Sasha Darwin

Il Gatto Nero *aka* Edgar Allan Poe's The Black Cat *aka* De Profundis *aka* Out of the Depths

(WORLD PICTURE/21ST CENTURY; IT) 85min

C.J. Graham as the cop from Hell in the silly but highly enjoyable Highway to Hell.

Like Fulci's **Un Gatto nel Cervello** (1991), this would-be self-reflective movie combines gory exploitation with meaningless in-jokes about the Italian schlock industry.

The plot revolves around the pre-production of the third instalment of the trilogy that Dario Argento abandoned after **Suspiria** (1976) and **Inferno** (1980). A crippled zombie movie producer, Munro as a scheming actress, a sinister boy who may not exist, a white witch whose stomach explodes in the style of Cozzi's *Contamination* (1980), a TV that vomits green innards and occasional cosmic trips are mixed in a cocktail that cashes in on the reputation of Argento's far more stylish movies.

d/s Lewis Coates (Luigi Cozzi) *p* Lucio Lucidi *c* Pasquale Rachini *se* Antonio Corridori, Armando Valcauda *lp* Florence Guerin, Urbano Barberini, Caroline Munro, Brett Halsey, Luisa Maneri, Karina Huff, Alessandra Accai, Jasmine Maimone, Antonio Marsina, Michele Soavi

Grave Secrets

(SHAPIRO-GLICKENHAUS ENTERTAINMENT) 85min

This is an unassuming, moderately effective ghost story which, despite the last-reel appearance of a toothy zombie, harks back to the conventions of **The Uninvited** (1944) for its understated horrors.

Parapsychologist LeMat is hired by Soutendijk, proprietor of a an old dark hotel, to tackle a haunting. With the help of medium Warner, LeMat discovers the culprit is Soutendijk's dead father, an abusive tyrant who raped her and then buried alive the baby born of their union, prompting her to decapitate him with a shovel. Though the subject matter is sensationalist, the steady pace and careful characterizations lift it out of the splatter rut.

d Donald P. Borchers *p* Michael Alan Shores *s* Jeffrey Polman, Lenore Wright *c* Jamie Thompson *se* Eric Dressor, Gregg Hendrickson, Kevin McCarthy *lp* Paul LeMat, Renee Soutendijk, David Warner, Lee Ving, Olivia Barashi, John Crawford, Bob Herron

The Hand That Rocks the Cradle

(HOLLYWOOD) 110min

This is a mainstream slasher movie modelled on **Fatal Attraction** (1987), pitting a female monster against the sanctity of an upper-middle-class nuclear family.

When her doctor husband (De Lancie) commits suicide in the face of sexual abuse charges, De Mornay loses her house to lawsuits and a baby to miscarriage, then sets out to avenge herself on the family who accused her husband. Moving into Sciorra's house as a nanny, De Mornay gradually alienates the housewife from friends and family, becoming a spade-wielding maniac for a regulation finale featuring sudden leaps out of dark spaces and unwise ventures into the cellar. Like the supernaturally themed **The Guardian** (1990), this fails to make much of the malevolent nanny theme. The true creepiness of the film comes of its complete espousal, down to the house-shaped bird table, of the values of the Terry O'Quinn character from **The Stepfather** (1986), demonizing the sweetly nasty De Mornay to such an extent it is hard not to feel she has a lot more going for her than her feeble-minded victims.

d Curtis Hansen *p* David Madden *s* Amanda Silver *c* Robert Elswit *lp* Annabella Sciorra, Rebecca De Mornay, Matt McCoy, Ernie Hudson, Julianne Moore, Madeline Zima, John de Lancie

Highway to Hell

(HIGH STREET) 94min

This reveals a horror comic sensibility blunted in *Drop Dead Fred* (1991), the more commercially streamlined star vehicle that De Jong made next.

Eloping, virginal young couple Lowe and Swanson are pulled over by Sgt Bedlam (Graham), a cop from Hell who carts Swanson off to the underworld. Opting for Fordian wide open spaces and dusty emptiness rather than the fiery pits of most Hell pictures, this manages both a suggestive vision of the inferno and an acceptable backdrop for an all-American road movie. Like *Bill and Ted's Bogus Journey* (1991), *Highway to Hell* deftly spoofs such cinematic precursors as *The Seventh Seal* (1956) and **Hellbound: Hellraiser II** (1988). Taking the myth of Orpheus as a rough guide, this is a joky travelogue of Hell, providing a modern American retread of a variety of underworld mythologies: an asphalt-laying device where the road to Hell is literally paved with souls damned for good intentions ('I only slept with the boss to advance my husband's career'), and a rowdy road-house run by Jimmy Hoffa where Hitler, Attila and Cleopatra sit around waiting to be joined by their still-living peers, Imelda Marcos, Colonel Qadaffi and Jerry Lewis.

d Ate de Jong *p* Mary Anne Page, John Byers *s* Brian Helgeland *c* Robin Vidgeon *se* Steve Johnson *lp* Chad Lowe, Kristy Swanson, Patrick Bergin, Adam Storke, Pamela Gidley, Richard Farnsworth, Anne Meara, C.J. Graham

Lisa

(UA) 93min

This bland women-in-jeopardy movie borrows the premise of William Castle's *I Saw What You Did* (1965).

Lisa (Keanan), 14-year-old daughter of overprotective single parent Ladd, is forbidden from dating and plays flirtatious phone games with randomly chosen handsome men. Bumping into restaurateur Moffett, Keanan begins a telephone romance, unaware that he is the Candlelight Killer, a serial slasher who has been leaving messages on his victims' answerphones informing them that he is in their apartments and about to kill them. *Lisa* turns in its last reel to a typical slasher movie as the heroines, who have acted throughout as if they didn't have a brain cell between them, co-operate to pitch the gravely wounded killer out the nearest window.

d/co-s Gary Sherman *p* Frank Yablans *co-s* Karen Clark *c* Alex Nepomniaschy *se* Guy Faria *lp* Cheryl Ladd, D.W. Moffett, Staci Keanan, Tanya Fenmore, Jeffrey Tambor, Edan Gross, Julie Cobb

Maniac Cop 2

(MOVIE HOUSE SALES/FADD ENTERPRISES) 87min

'You can shoot him with a gun, you can shoot him with an Uzi,' raps the theme song, 'but he'll turn up in your jacuzzi.' Poaching a trick, the early murders of the stars of the first film, from **The Mummy's Tomb** (1942), this is an old-style horror sequel, with the villain marking time between resurrections, plentiful flashback footage, and a redesign for the monster to make him more fearsome.

Matt Cordell (Z'Dar), the disfigured dead patrolman from **Maniac Cop** (1988), isn't dead after all (again) and this time he's partnered with a stripper-slaughtering serial killer (Rossi) who serves much the same plot function as Bela Lugosi's Ygor did in **Son of Frankenstein** (1939). There are flashes of Cohen's wit, but, despite the moose-jawed Z'Dar's impressive silhouette, the film suffers from Lustig's stodgy direction. Cohen, Lustig, Davi and Z'Dar returned with *Maniac Cop 3: Badge of Silence* (1992), a hospital-set slasher which feebly tries to be 'Bride of Maniac Cop'.

d William Lustig *p/s* Larry Cohen *c* James Lemmo *se* Dean Gates *lp* Robert Davi, Claudia Christian, Michael Lerner, Bruce Campbell, Laurene Landon, Robert Z'Dar, Leo Rossi

Midnight (SVS FILMS) 86min

An uncertain film – not, despite its campy central character, a comedy – about Midnight (Redgrave), an Elvira-style TV horror hostess in dispute with her crass producer (Curtis), and a series of throwaway murders that take place in her entourage.

Vane had done much better by Hollywood horror in his earlier *The Horror Star* (1981), with Ferdy Mayne as a zombie horror-movie performer avenging the desecration of his high-tech mausoleum, but his best work remains *The Black Room* (1981), a perverse and intriguing vampire film.

d/co-p/s Norman Thaddeus Vane *co-p* Gloria J. Morrison *c* David Golia *se* Elena M. Breckenridge *lp* Lynn Redgrave, Tony Curtis, Steven Parrish, Rita Gam, Gustav Vintas, Karen Witter, Frank Gorshin, Wolfman Jack

Mirror, Mirror

(ORPHAN EYES/LIMITED PARTNERSHIP) 100min

A entry in the limited 'haunted mirror' subgenre (*à la* **Dead of Night**, 1945) this is also a carefully written, acted and directed imitation of **Carrie** (1976).

Harvest is the victimized new girl in school, a California goth lost among squeaky clean cheerleaders. The only thing about their new house the girl likes is an antique mirror which proves home to a demonic entity that gives her the power to inflict horrible deaths upon her tormentors. Ordinary in its plot, *Mirror, Mirror* betrays a degree of thought uncommon in low-budget exploitation, and Harvest gives a fine, ambiguously sympathetic reading of the abused and gradually corrupted protagonist.

d/co-s Marina Sargenti *p* Jimmy Lifton *co-s* Annette Cascone, Gina Cascone, Yuri Zeltser *c* Robert Brinkmann *se* Chris Biggs, Kirk Karwacki *lp* Karen Black, Rainbow Harvest, Kristin Dattilo, Ricky Paull Goldin, Charlie (Spradling), Dorit Sauer, Stephen Tobolowsky, Anne Hearn, Yvonne DeCarlo, William Sanderson

Misery (CASTLE ROCK ENTERTAINMENT) 107min

Paul Sheldon (Caan), a successful novelist who has grown tired of his run of historical romances featuring the idealized heroine Misery, crashes his car in a Colorado blizzard just after he has completed a breakaway realistic novel. Annie Wilkes (Bates), who gushingly claims to be Sheldon's 'Number One Fan', abducts the wounded writer and cares for him in her isolated cottage, gradually revealing how unstable she is as she hints at her past as a baby-killing nurse. When Annie discovers Paul has killed Misery off, she terrorizes him into burning his just-completed manuscript and writing *Misery's Return*, in which her heroine is convincingly brought back from the dead.

The Oscar-winning Bates is a convincing and affecting monster, equipped with a bizarre and unsettling vocabulary of euphemisms and a scary run of folksy sayings that reveal precisely how her acceptance of romantic fictions has lead her to torture and murder. Regrettably, it somewhat smudges the power of its superbly staged climax with another re-use of the last-minute return from the dead, though, unlike **Fatal Attraction** (1987), it takes care not to turn its female monster into a misogynist's fantasy hate figure. Stephen King's novel is a deeper work, dealing with themes of fanatical devotion, the dilemma of the genre writer and the worthiness of commercial fiction.

d/co-p Rob Reiner *co-p* Andrew Scheinman *s* William Goldman *c* Barry Stonenfeld *se* KNB Effects *lp* James Caan, Kathy Bates, Richard Farnsworth, Frances Sternhagen, Lauren Bacall

Mo Chun Jie *aka* **The Holy Virgin Versus the Evil Dead**

(SAAM-WO FILMS; TAIWAN) 86min

Like **Mo** (1983) and **Qi Yuan** (1986), this has an ancient supernatural evil arrive in Hong Kong from a nearby country, then finds modern-day Chinese heroes, in this case a team of cops, joining up with a representative of the mystic culture that has produced the monster, in this case a virgin priestess, to defeat the evil on its own grounds.

While the other films have magical beings from Tibet, this chooses the politically and spiritually intriguing background of Cambodia, which produces a blue-faced hermaphrodite god and its evil disciple, an electric-eyed vampire-type who preys on young women and is at first treated as a sex murderer.

d Wong Jan-Yeung *p* Xu Shaohong *c* Wong Jit *lp* Jan Chi-Dan, Wu Wai-Chung, Yeung Bo-Ling, Chow Hoi-Mei

The Monk (CELTIC FILMS/MEDITERRANEO; GB, SP) 106min

Matthew Gregory Lewis's trendsetting gothic novel, loosely adapted for the screen by Luis Buñuel and Ado Kyrou in 1972, here receives an international co-production treatment that needlessly changes the protagonists' names. The film also prunes much of the supernatural and ghastly excesses, omits a subplot involving the Wandering Jew and, most bizarrely, alters the vividly repulsive finale, in which the novel's Ambrosio is dragged off to Hell by Lucifer and eaten by insects, to provide a pointlessly upbeat finish, in which Lorenzo (McGann) – condemned to burn at the stake for heresy, murder, rape and other crimes – is saved when he refuses to call upon the Devil, the punishment of the Inquisition actually achieving its stated purpose, to save his soul.

Without Lewis's delirious mix of melodrama, black humour and ironic morality, the film plods through one unlikely incident after another as the pure-hearted monk is seduced by a female libertine disguised as a male novice (Ward), then consumed with lust for a virginal girl (Linfield) whom he drugs, orphans, abducts and plans to ravish in a crypt. In a parallel story, fanatical lesbian nun Blair torments a pregnant sister (Sanchez-Gijon), whom she walls up in the basement of her convent, to the chagrin of the girl's lover (Elstob), who is forever turning up in a wig, waving letters from the Pope in attempts to rescue her. The film is curiously prosaic given its flamboyant source.

d/co-p/s Paco Lara *co-p* Muir Sutherland *c* Angel Luiz Fernandez *se* Alberto Nombela *lp* Paul McGann, Sophie Ward, Isla Blair, Freda Dowie, Marina Suara, Sophie Linfield, Aitana Sanchez-Gijon, Laura Davenport, Suzanne Bertish, Mark Elstob

Moonrise *aka* **Grampire** *aka* **My Grandad's a Vampire**

(TUCKER; NEW ZEALAND) 95min

This takes a more traditional approach to the vampire myth than Blyth's aggressively modernist **Red Blooded American Girl** (1991), even lifting a plot device (the power of the light of the full moon to give strength to the undead) from the first vampire story in English, Dr John Polidori's *The Vampyre*.

A gentle children's film, it eschews even the mock horror of the Munsters or the Addams Family, casting Lewis in a kinder variation of Granpa Munster, an 18th-century vampire who has chosen to live as a human in an out-of-the-way New Zealand town but returns from the dead to be with his grandson (Gocke). A kindly soul who adores Mozart and is squeamish about the idea of drinking blood, Lewis's vampire poses no threat and thus the film has problems finding enough plot to keep it going to feature length.

d David Blyth *p* Murray Newey *s* Michael Heath *c* Kevin Hayward *se* Bob McCarron *lp* Al Lewis, Justin Gocke, Milan Borich, Pat Evison, Noel Appleby

My Lovely Monster (XENON/WDR/SFB; G) 84min
This low-budget amiable comedy/horror spoof was clearly inspired by Woody Allen's *The Purple Rose of Cairo* (1985) and the real-life relocation from Hollywood, California (rather, Horrorwood, Karloffornia) of Forrest Ackerman's collection of horror-movie memorabilia.

A silent-movie monster (Francesco) patterned after Lon Chaney's top-hatted vampire in **London After Midnight** (1927) escapes from a burning piece of nitrate film and is stranded in a German cinema where he meets a young girl (Fischer) who assists him in finding his true home by getting him to the Ackermuseum, where he is able to slip into another print of his film. Made in English, with Ackerman providing pun-filled dialogue reminiscent of the worst of his *Famous Monsters of Filmland* and appearing in a cameo as himself, this has an oddball supporting cast of Ackerman's friends and hangers-on, including ersatz scream queen Bobbie Bresee, distinguished ham Mayne and Boris Karloff's daughter.

d/p/co-s Michel Bergmann *co-s* Forrest J. Ackerman *c* Fernando Arguelles *se* Rolf Baumann *lp* Silvio Francesco, Forrest J. Ackerman, Nicole Fischer, Matthias Fuchs, Marlen Diekhoff, Peter Voss, Olivia Davis, Ferdy Mayne, Bobbie Bresee, Sara Karloff

The Naked Lunch (FOX; GB, CAN) 115min
Having helped Bernardo Bertolucci embalm Paul Bowles' *The Sheltering Sky* (1990), producer Thomas here attacks another supposedly unfilmable underground classic.

William S. Burroughs is represented by William Lee (Weller), a skull-faced New York exterminator in 1953 who becomes addicted to his own poison and semi-accidentally shoots his wife (Davis) before fleeing to the North African city of Interzone. There, taking orders from giant insects with talking assholes disguised as typewriters, he tries to infiltrate an interlocking series of conspiracies that lead inexorably to the ever-changing drug guru Dr Benway (Scheider). Also involved are writer characters patterned on Paul and Jane Bowles, Brion Gysin, Jack Kerouac and Allen Ginsberg, and a race of scrotum-faced aliens called Mugwumps.

As in Cronenberg's *Videodrome* (1983), *The Fly* (1986) or **Dead Ringers** (1988), *The Naked Lunch* follows an apparently neutral but actually obsessive protagonist – ex-*RoboCop* Weller is a revelation in the part – into a world shaped by his own malformed psyche. But it is a retreat from the achievements of the earlier films. The drugs, images, homosexual themes, North African setting, period costumes and slang, and recurring characters are all well articulated by Cronenberg. But the vision they represent is Burroughs': the movie could almost be titled *William S. Burroughs' The Naked Lunch.* Distanced by the 'serious' literary tone from the lurid science-fiction horror of Cronenberg's earlier movies, this is a major film by a major film-maker, but also a studied grasp at respectability from someone whose absolute peak work needs no excuses.

d/s David Cronenberg *p* Jeremy Thomas *c* Peter Suschitzky *se* Chris Walas *lp* Peter Weller, Judy Davis, Ian Holm, Roy Scheider, Julian Sands, Nicholas Campbell, Michael Zelniker, Monique Mercure, Robert Silverman

Nekromantik 2 (MANFRED JELINSKI; G) 96min
This follow-up to Buttgereit's ridiculously well received original essentially reprises its taboo-breaking.

A nurse (Monika M) exhumes a corpse for sexual purposes, then enters into a relationship with an actor (Reeder) whom she finally decapitates, replacing his head with the corpse's but retaining his still-erect penis in the place of her true love's decayed and flaccid genitalia. The film tries rather badly to waver between porno-horror and the new wave, like some mutant offspring of **Living Doll** (1989) and *Jules et Jim* (1964), even throwing in a witless parody of *My Dinner With André*, though the exploitation bases are tackily covered with surprisingly elaborate H.G. Lewis-style gore and found footage ranging from seal-autopsies excerpted on video to the hardcore that Reeder is seen dubbing.

d/co-s Jörg Buttgereit *p/c* Manfred Jelinski *co-s* Franz Rodenkirchen *se* Alois Vollert, Sammy Bachaus *lp* Monika M, Mark Reeder, Wolfgang Müller, Beatrice M

Netherworld (FULL MOON) 81min
An occult film in the tradition of **The Mephisto Waltz** (1971).

Benedetti takes over the Louisiana manse left him by his recently deceased father (Sampson) and gets mixed up with voodoo in the basement of the nearby brothel, where witch queen Gentile performs rituals that will eventually resurrect the old man. While the bulk of the film strains after subtlety as Benedetti is seduced into following his father's plan – the obvious punchline being that Sampson intends to return to life by possessing his son – there are a few cut-aways of a stone hand that comes to life whenever Gentile is endangered and flies through corridors to latch gorily onto the heads of victims. Obviously influenced by Thing from **The Addams Family** (1991), the creation provides a few eye-opening (and gouging) moments with snake-fanged fingers, but its origin and relevance remain unexplained.

d David Schmoeller *p* Thomas Bradford *s* Billy Chicago *c* Adolfo Bartoli *se* Mark Shostrom *lp* Michael Benedetti, Denise Gentile, Anjanette Comer, Holly Floria, Robert Burr, Robert Sampson

Outcast (GOOD PRODUCTIONS) 92min
With a basic premise akin to the fantasy *Alias Nick Beal* (1949), this nerd revenge movie gradually turns into an **Omen** (1976)-style Antichrist exploitationer.

Rural geek Tench, abused by his foster father and the local louts, runs away to the big city and falls in with a gang of street-corner hoods who let him take the blame for an inept hold-up. Coming out of jail, he is accosted by a sidewalk preacher (Read) who turns out to be the Devil and offers him power over his enemies in exchange for his services in bringing the world to an end. The film takes on too much, and rushes through three or four mini-plots: Tench's humiliation, his revenge (involving chainsaws in the crotch and minor telekinesis), the investigation of a dogged private eye and a lady psychic who only turn up in the last half-hour, and a contrived bit whereby the Apocalypse can be forestalled if Tench's newborn child is baptized before he kills it.

d/s Roman Buchok *p* Philip M. Good *c* Gilles Corbeil *se* Nancy Howe *lp* John Tench, Peter Read, Tracey Hoyt, Paul Amato, Dean Richards, Krista Bulmer

The People Under the Stairs (ALIVE) 102min
13-year-old Adams is persuaded by his sister's boyfriend (Rhames) to help rob the landlords who have been running down the neighbourhood. Gaining entrance to the heavily fortified house, they find strange creatures lurking in the cellar. The man of the house (McGill) kills Rhames, and Adams discovers the landlords have been baby-snatching, rearing the fragile Langer as their perfect daughter, but mutilating failed sons and consigning them to the walls.

The house is a nightmare version of the Addams Family mansion, half booby-trapped funhouse and half corrupt-heart-of-America. The theme of Craven's early films – the opposition of 'monstrous' and 'normal' families, with the ultimate blurring of the boundaries between the two leading to a cynical vision of post-Vietnam/Watergate America – is resurrected

The People Under the Stairs, *a return to form from Wes Craven.*

here, with even the assumptions of **The Last House on the Left** (1972) and **The Hills Have Eyes** (1977) inverted. 'Normality' is represented by siblings McGill and Robie and their money-fuelled parody of the family values embodied and subverted by the heroes of the earlier films, whose inner violence only emerged under the pressure of attack from marginalized and poverty-stricken psychotics.

As in Craven's best work, the villains are intriguingly caricatured, though Robie and McGill never benefit from the kind of grudging sympathy accorded the mutants of *Last House* and *Hills*, even though Langer, more victim than monster, fulfils the plot function of the traitorous children of those films. Going beyond even the trashing of sit-com values in **The Stepfather** (1986) or **Parents** (1988), McGill and Robie, reunited after their double act on *Twin Peaks*, rank with Craven's best monsters, funny yet frightening. *The People Under the Stairs*, after several mis-steps, is a major return to form for the director.

d/s Wes Craven *p* Marianna Maddalena, Stuart M. Besser *c* Sandi Sissel *se* KNB *lp* Brandon Adams, Everett McGill, Wendy Robie, A.J. Langer, Ving Rhames, Kelly Jo Minter

The Pit and the Pendulum (FULL MOON) 96min

After a hiatus, marked by the troubled *Robot Jox* (1989) and the loss of *Honey, I Shrunk the Kids* (1989), Gordon returned to horror by reuniting with Charles Band to complete this long-cherished Poe project. Stirring in elements from *The Cask of Amontillado* and the witchfinding school of horror exploitation that stretches from *Vredens Dag* (1943) to **Witchfinder General** (1968), Gordon embeds his setpiece atrocity scenes – a long-dead heretic is exhumed and posthumously flogged, then ground into dust to fill an hourglass; a witch stuffs herself with gunpowder on her way to the stake, and explodes into spearlike bone fragments that scatter into the crowd at the *auto-da-fé* – in a conventional indictment of religious hypocrisy, with an irksomely innocent pair of young lovers similar to those of Corman's **The Masque of the Red Death** (1964) embroiled in the torture and plotting of Torquemada's castle because the Grand Inquisitor is consumed with lust for the baker's wife (De Ricci).

The finale, which trots out Poe's pendulum, is rather too well lit for maximum horror. However, Henriksen's performance as the tormented and tormenting Inquisitor, his expressive gestures and wild-eyed brooding conjuring memories of Conrad Veidt, elevates the film out of its jokiness ('One good turn deserves another,' snaps a torturer as he works the rack) and turns it into a portrait of a bizarrely twisted individual.

d Stuart Gordon *p* Albert Band *s* Dennis Paoli *c* Adolpho Bartoli *se* Greg Cannom *lp* Lance Henriksen, Rona De Ricci, Jonathan Fuller, Jeffrey Combs, Tom Towles, Stephen Lee, Oliver Reed, Carolyn Purdy-Gordon

Playroom *aka* **Schizo** (CINGOLINI) 87min

This is a well produced but ordinary horror movie of the haunted-castle and cursed-archaeological-expedition variety that gains some atmosphere value by its Yugoslav location.

Archaeologist McDonald returns to the castle where his family were murdered when he was a child, hoping to vindicate his father's name. Renewing a relationship with his demonic imaginary friend (Eisenberg), McDonald becomes obsessive, childish and irrational, then embarks on another killing spree, employing the implements he finds in a long-sealed torture chamber.

d Manny Coto *p* Luigi Cingolini *s* Keaton Jones *c* James L. Carter *se* Criswell, Johnson Effects *lp* Lisa Aliff, Aron Eisenberg, Maja, Christopher McDonald, James Purcell, Jamie Rose, Vincent Schiavelli

Popcorn (STUDIO THREE) 90min

A ramshackle horror comedy which manages to endear despite lapses, many doubtless due to its muddied production history.

A cash-starved university film department raises funds by holding an all-night horror festival in a soon-to-be-demolished theatre, screening new-minted fifties horror classics (*Attack of the Amazing Electrified Man, The Stench*) with the original William-Castle-style gimmicks (electrified seats, odorama) intact. Meanwhile, a scarred psychopath (Villard) in the Dr Phibes tradition, who has survived a sixties underground film massacre, stalks perky Winona Ryder lookalike Schoelen. There are pleasant running jokes, the spoof movies are funny, the script is peppered with in-jokes and the climax is a lively bit of on-stage carnage involving planned murder and a giant rubber mosquito. Particularly successful is the recreation of a Kenneth Anger-style demonic underground movie that turns out to be vital to the fudged backstory.

d Mark Herrier, Alan Ormsby *p* Torben Johnke, Gary Goch, Ashok Armitraj *s* Tod Hackett (Alan Ormsby) *c* Ronnie Taylor *se* Georgio Ferrari, Bob Clark *lp* Jill Schoelen, Tom Villard, Dee Wallace Stone, Derek Rydall, Ray Walston, Tony Roberts, Karen Witter

Pyushchye Krovy *aka* **Blood-Suckers**
(LENFILM; RUSSIA) 110min

This is a staid period literary adaptation rather than a full-blooded horror movie, faithfully using the intricate structure of Count Alexei Tolstoy's 1841 *The Vampire*, which has echoes of *The Queen of Spades*.

The film presents a young officer (Sokolov) involved with three generations of a matriarchal family. Falling for the winsome granddaughter of apparently ageless aristocrat Vlady, he is told by an aquaintance that Vlady and her line are vampires and that they have practised unspeakable rites in an Italian villa. With a series of dreams-within-flashbacks that get weirder the further from the frame story they are, the film reproduces Tolstoy's mix of folkloric vampirism, stuffy society comedy and wet romance. Among the gothic paraphernalia are ghosts who emerge from portraits, an Italian peasant girl who falls victim to the vampire, red-lit black masses, duels of honour, nights spent in the haunted chamber of an abandoned castle and multiple romantic misadventures. Tatarsky also made a version of Robert Louis Stevenson's *The Suicide Club* (1979–1980).

d Eugeny Tatarsky *s* Artur Makarov *c* Konstantin Ryzhov *lp* Milena Vlady, Andrey Sokolov, Marina Maiko

Qiann Youhun III: Zhi Dao Dao Dao *aka* **A Chinese Ghost Story III** (FILM WORKSHOP LTD/LONG SHONG/GOLDEN PRINCESS; HONG KONG) 115min

This, the third in the popular Chinese ghost series, retains Siu Tung and Hark and reincarnates the villainous Tree Princess of the first film while introducing a new cast who are remarkably similar to, though sadly less interesting than, the characters of earlier movies, shuffling them through a plot that consists entirely of off-cuts from the original.

A doddering but intrepid wise man and his naïve young monk sidekick try to use the force of a Golden Buddha against the Tree Princess, and the young hero falls in love with a female ghost in the thrall of the villainess. The ghost girl has been betrothed to a Mountain Demon and is willing to sacrifice herself for her living love, but the heroes, joined by a mercenary swordsman-magician, defeat the demons in time for the final song. There are some impressive moments – the heroes flying over a misty landsdcape trying to evade the suddenly-extruded stone fingers of the Mountain Demon – and the woodland settings are magical.

d Ching Siu Tung *p/co-s* Tsui Hark *co-s* Roy Szeto *c* Lau Moon-Tong *se* Cinefex Workshop *lp* Tony Leung (Leung Chiu Wai), Jacky Cheung, Joey Wang, Nina Li, Lau Siu-Meng, Lau Sheung, Lau Yuk-Ting, Wong Kwong-Leung

Qian Yunyu Qing *aka* **Ghostly Love** (HONG KONG) 98min

In the early nineties, the institution of a new censorship rating in Hong Kong, Category III, allowed sex and nudity in horror movies, resulting in a trickle of films similar in their mildly titillating aspects to early seventies Hammer or Paul Naschy vehicles.

One of many imitations of **Qian Nu Youhun** (1987), this takes advantage of the freedom by cutting away frequently from the formula story to protracted love-making scenes enthusiastically performed behind mosquito nets under pink lighting effects. Among the characters are a morally dubious monk who does an acrobatic and silly song and dance routine, and a naïve young hero in love with a ghost girl who finally helps him and the monk take on a vampiric villain, the Ghost King.

d/p Cheung Kit *lp* Wai Tin-Chi, Chu Bo-Yi, Ito Sayoko, Kishimoto Masami, Lam Wai, Lung Tin-Cheung

The Rapture (NEW LINE) 100min

This serious attempt to address born-again Christianity provides a pointed contrast to the Bible-thumping of **The Omen** (1976) or **The Seventh Sign** (1988).

The opening, in which a telephonist (Rogers) is drawn out of monotonous daytime work and night-time promiscuity by a growing involvement with millenarian religion, is profoundly expressive in its nightmarish modern despair. It also captures the conspiratorial creepiness of the sect to which she is drawn, with their blank-faced assertions that the world is about to end and that anyone not on their team will burn forever. The film leaps six years and presents Rogers with a husband (Duchovny) and child (Cullum), giving an audience little time to get used to the mood-switch before a passing psycho widows her and a vision tells her to go into the wilderness for transportation to Heaven. In the desert, fanaticism and despair lead her to a horrifying act of spiritual and physical violence. Then Tolkin stages a finale which can be taken as a dream or the literal truth as the trump of doom sounds, the Horsemen of the Apocalypse gallop and, in a wonderfully simple but effective image, prison bars fall apart. Having come through the unendurable, Rogers refuses to participate in the Judgement and the film poses very tough questions, not just for fundamentalists but for God himself. This is a complex, intellectual and important horror story.

d/s Michael Tolkin *p* Nick Wechsler, Nancy Tanenbaum, Karen Koch *c* Bojan Bozelli *se* Cinema Research Corporation *lp* Mimi Rogers, David Duchovny, Will Patton, Patrick Bauchau, Kimberly Cullum, Terri Hanauer, Dick Anthony Williams, James LeGros, Carole Davis

Red Blooded American Girl (SC ENTERTAINMENT/PRISM ENTERTAINMENT; CAN) 89min

Following the medical madness **Death Warmed Up** (1984), New Zealander Blyth – who had, in the interim, been fired from **The Horror Show** (1988) – returns to mysterious scientific institutions and unethical experiments for this offbeat vampire movie.

Drug designer Stevens is recruited by medical entrepreneur Plummer, who has become infected with an AIDS-like virus that makes its sufferers crave blood even as it gives them extra strength, to work on a method of stabilizing the condition. Fellow scientist Thomas, to whom Stevens is attracted, is bitten by an infectee and becomes a deranged, blood-addicted minx. The film has a confident grip on character – thanks to the input of screenwriter Moyle, director of *Pump Up the Volume* (1990) – and reworks the vampire mythology in terms of modern medicine more effectively than **The Hunger** (1983).

d David Blyth *p* Nicolas Stiliadis *s* Alan Moyle *c* Ludek Bogner *se* Brock Jolliffe *lp* Andrew Stevens, Heather Thomas, Christopher Plummer, Kim Coates, Lydie Denier

The Refrigerator (AVENUE D FILMS LTD) 90min

Despite a premise – a man-eating fridge – that might serve for a Troma item, this aligns itself not with the direct-to-video schlock its enthusiastic gore suggests but with the independent quirky art movies of Todd Haynes or Hal Hartley.

A young couple move into a run-down New York apartment dominated by an old-fashioned fridge, Simonds maniacally determined to get on in his office job, McNeal equally bent on a show-business career. The malign influence of the possessed appliance, which sometimes becomes a gateway to Hell, undoes their ambitions. Simonds learns that he comes at the bottom of the corporate food chain, while the fridge eats away at McNeal's ambitions, especially in an unnerving sequence that perfectly catches a sense of everyday horror as an escalation of minor incidents, climaxing with lost doorkeys, prevent her leaving the flat for an audition. With the help of a Bolivian repairman (Caban) and a local mystic (Sanz), McNeal confronts the fridge in a parody exorcism, which features Stephen King-style appliance fun as victims are shredded by rogue blenders and electric fans. Broad and cartoonish, with only McNeal and Caban underplaying, this is half-embarassed by its genre elements but nevertheless solidly in a resurgent tradition of domestic horror that echoes the trapped-in-a-house feel of **The Stepfather** (1986) but also ironically pulls apart the mortgage-strangled tone of **The Amityville Horror** (1979).

d/s Nicholas A.E. Jacobs *p* Christopher Oldcorn *c* Paul Gibson *se* Mike Deprez *lp* Julia McNeal, David Simonds, Angel Caban, Phyllis Sanz, Nena Segal, Jaime Rojo

The Revenge of Billy the Kid (MONTAGE; GB) 87min

A cheap British horror comedy in the tradition of **I Bought a Vampire Motorcycle** (1990), combining workable monster effects with bowel humour.

Set on an island off the coast of Cornwall, the film opens with drunken Farmer MacDonald (Balfour) forcing his sexual attentions on a goat. A hybrid is born and grows quickly to monstrous maturity, whereupon it slaughters some poachers and all of the MacDonald family except daughter Ronald (Perkins), who is rescued by her chainsaw-wielding mainland boyfriend (Williamson). There is one almost effective moment, derived from **I Was a Teenage Werewolf** (1957), when a victim hanging upside-down sees the monster advancing from the top of the screen.

d/co-s Jim Groom *p/co-s* Tim Dennison *co-s* Richard Mathews *c* David Read *se* Neill R. Gorton, Steven M. Painter *lp* Michael Balfour, Samantha Perkins, Jackie D. Broad, Bryan Healey, Trevor Peake, Norman Mitchell, Michael Ripper, Dean Williamson

Scissors (DDM FILM CORP) 105min

Best known as a writer – he was author of the source novel for **Audrey Rose** (1977) – DeFelitta here resurrects the sixties conventions of **Nightmare** (1963), **Strait-Jacket** (1964) and **Games** (1967).

The psychologically vulnerable Stone is the subject of a complex plot to drive her mad. Attacked in the lift of her apartment building, she becomes uncertain in her relationships with a variety of deceptively comforting or threatening men, most notably her suave psychiatrist (Cox) and twin neighbours (Railsback), a romantic soap-opera star and a sinister fake crippled artist. Lured to a luxurious show apartment in an unfinished building, she is locked in with a scissor-stabbed corpse and automated tricks that serve to unhinge her. With an overly complicated and melodramatic plot, this relies heavily on Stone's fragile performance and neat tricks involving scary *objets trouvés* like a collection of antique dolls and a squawking raven.

d/s Frank DeFelitta *p* Mel Pearl, Don Levin, Hal Polaire *c* Anthony B. Richmond *se* Andre Ellingson *lp* Sharon Stone, Steve Railsback, Ronny Cox, Michelle Phillips, Vicki Frederick

Servants of Twilight

(TRIMARK/GIBRALTAR ENTERTAINMENT) 92min

At the turn of the decade, Dean R. Koontz became the direct-to-video Stephen King, with adaptations of his supermarket best-sellers (*Watchers*, 1989, *The Face of Fear*, 1990, **Whispers**, 1991) almost entirely by-passing theatrical distribution.

In this, taken from Koontz's *Twilight*, private eye Greenwood is hired by single mother Bauer to protect her angelic son (Lennon) from a persistent group of homicidal religious fanatics, led by cast-offs from *Twin Peaks*, who believe him the Anti-Christ. Given that the only possible ending is the revelation that Lennon, conceived after Bauer had a fling with the Devil on a swinging singles cruise, is indeed diabolic, it's hard to sit through the predictable plot twists that precede this reversal.

d/co-p/co-s Jeffrey Obrow *co-p* Venetia Stevenson *co-s* Steven Carpenter *c* Antonio Soriano *se* Frank Ceglia *lp* Bruce Greenwood, Belinda Bauer, Grace Zabriskie, Richard Bradford, Jarrett Lennon, Jack Kehoe, Carel Struycken

La Setta *aka* The Sect *aka* The Devil's Daughter

(PENTA FILM/ADC; IT) 120min

This is a blend of Christian Devil movies like **Rosemary's Baby** (1968) with catch-all Lovecraft mythos.

A German schoolteacher (Curtis) is the victim of a conspiracy in which a shadowy group headed by a professorial Lom get her to give birth to a child who will be their 'revenge on God'. Lom impregnates Curtis by inserting a sacred scarab into her nose, and supervises the birth in an impressively symbolic underground well. The film then comes up with a happy ending as the normal-seeming baby sacrifices himself while destroying the sect and saving Curtis. Like Dario Argento's **Inferno** (1980), this resists interpretation by presenting less a story than a succession of setpieces which are either silly or gruesome, ranging from standard slashings to impressive face-ripping rituals, as sect members perpetrate atrocities. However, unlike *Inferno*, it has neither a lavish visual style nor a knowing sense of its own absurdity.

d/co-s Michele Soavi *co-p/co-s* Dario Argento *co-p* Mario & Vittorio Cecchi Gori *co-s* Gianni Romolo *c* Raffaele Mentes *se* Rosario Prestopino *lp* Kelly Curtis, Herbert Lom, Maria Angela Giordano, Michel Adatte, Carla Cassola, Angelika Maria Boeck, Tomas Arana

Shadows and Fog (ORION) 86min

In a non-specified monochrome 1920s city, pathetic clerk Allen is hauled out of bed by Kafkaesque vigilantes to pursue a monstrous murderer (Kirby). The film sees Allen paying homage to a number of expressionist German horror films, with swirling fog, shadowed streets and grotesque characters referring us to **Das Cabinet des Dr Caligari** (1919), **Nosferatu – Eine Symphonie des Grauens** (1921), *Die Buchse der Pandora* (1928) and *M* (1931) while Kurt Weill music jolts along.

Some circus characters led by the inevitable Farrow as a runaway sword-swallower stray in either from the likes of Igmar Bergman's *Gycklarnas Afton* (1953) or *Ansiktet* (1958) or the grotesque melodramas of Tod Browning, **Freaks** (1932) and **The Unknown** (1927). Allen is meticulous in his recreated visual style, but there is something arch about the way he uses images culled from coffee-table movie-still books to evoke an atmosphere of dread, especially in comparison with the genuinely demented and inventive reuse of the same material in Tim Burton's **Batman Returns** (1992) or Guy Maddin's *Tales From the Gimli Hospital* (1990) and *Archangel* (1991), which don't forget to be their own movies as well as being *hommages*.

d/s Woody Allen *p* Robert Greenhut *c* Carlo Di Palma *lp* Woody Allen, Mia Farrow, John Malkovich, Michael Kirby, John Cusack, Jodie Foster, Kathy Bates, Lily Tomlin, Kenneth Mars, Donald Pleasence, Madonna, Julie Kavner, Kate Nelligan

The Silence of the Lambs (ORION) 119min

Adapted from Thomas Harris's sequel to *Red Dragon*, which was filmed as **Manhunter** (1986), this takes a more gothic approach to Harris' psycho-procedural novel.

When FBI trainee Foster is sent by her superior (Glenn) to interview serial murderer Dr Hannibal Lecter (Hopkins), the mad genius, kept in a semi-medieval dungeon, offers to exchange insights relating to a murder spree for her own personal secrets. Buffalo Bill (Levine), the current killer, is a would-be transsexual who kidnaps and skins hefty young women; his current victim, whom he is starving in his basement to loosen her hide, is the daughter of a senator who exerts pressure on Glenn to crack the case, to the extent of offering Lecter a deal. The civilized psycho engineers an astonishing break from the cage he is being held in and Foster has to pursue leads which take her alone into the killer's lair, while knowing that the even more dangerous murderer is loose.

Hopkins is excellect as the imprisoned monster, if not quite up to the standard set by Brian Cox in *Manhunter*, but Foster carries the picture as Agent Clarice Starling, an unusually detailed protagonist who is presented as a complex individual without seeming to trail soap-opera traumas. With understated black humour – the punchline recalls **Cannibal Girls** (1971) – and almost operatic effects (cop Napier disembowelled and crucified on the bars of Lecter's cage) this edges out of the straight thriller into horror-movie territory, resolving its plot in a nightmare confrontation in Levine's vile workshop, where Foster flounders in the dark while he observes through night-sight goggles. Corman appears in a cameo as the head of the FBI, while George A. Romero is glimpsed as a background cop. The first horror movie to take a Best Picture Academy Award, it also won Oscars for Demme, Foster and Hopkins.

d Jonathan Demme *p* Edward Saxon, Kenneth Utt, Ron Bozman *s* Ted Tally *c* Tak Fujimoto *se* Carl Fullerton, Neal Martz *lp* Jodie Foster, Anthony Hopkins, Scott Glenn, Ted Levine, Anthony Heald, Charles Napier, Kasi Lemmons, Brooke Smith, Tracey Walter, Diane Baker, Roger Corman

Singapore Sling (GR) b/w 114min

In the line of black and white semi-art/semi-porn horrors, this is a direct descendant of **The Old Dark House** (1932), **The House on Haunted Hill** (1959), *Spider Baby* (1964) and *Thundercrack!* (1975), mixing film references, neo-noir visuals, insufferable pretension, considerable sadism and relentless sexual violence. In a storm-lashed mansion, a mad mother (Valley) and daughter (Herold) indulge in a series of games, which include re-enacting the abuse and murder of Laura, formerly a secretary in the house, and burying half-alive the chauffeur whose pulsating internal

Anthony Hopkins as Hanibal Lecter, the monster of the nineties, in The Silence of the Lambs.

organs they spread about a kitchen work surface. Into this English-speaking menage comes Singapore Sling (Thanassoulis), a wounded *noir* trenchcoat whose Greek voice-over explains his obsessive search for the lost Laura, which cues endless references to *Laura* (1944). Thanassoulis joins the games (notably a combination of S&M and ECT involving electrified handcuffs) and murders both women.

d/s Nicos Nicolaides *p* Maria-Louise Barthlomew *c* Aris Stavrou *lp* Meredyth Herold, Michele Valley, Panos Thanassoulis

Sleeping With the Enemy (FOX) 99min
This is a further continuation of the run of dressed-up-as-mainstream slashers (*Deceived*, **The Hand That Rocks the Cradle**, **Cape Fear**, **Misery** and even **The Silence of the Lambs**, all 1991, all fall into the genre) inaugurated by the success of **Fatal Attraction** (1987).

The beautifully bedraggled Roberts is married to Bergin, a fire-eyed swine who enjoys raping her to the tune of *Symphonie Fantastique* on CD and takes the time to beat her up if the cans aren't stacked properly in the cupboard. Faking her death, she makes a new life in an idyllic mid-west with the bearded care bear next door (Anderson) – whose lovability is signalled by his preference of Dion to Berlioz – but Bergin methodically tracks her down and the picture winds up with protracted stalking around a suitably old and dark house. With everything that made **The Stepfather** (1986) interesting trimmed away, this is an acceptable TV movie with a few moments of violence and Roberts in designer peril. It includes yet another irritating retread of the tired last-minute-return-from-the-dead stunt.

d Joseph Ruben *p* Leonard Goldberg *s* Ronald Bass *c* John W. Lindley *se* Calvin J. Acord *lp* Julie Roberts, Patrick Bergin, Kevin Anderson, Elizabeth Lawrence, Kyle Secor, Claudette Nevins

Tenkawa Densetsu Satsujin Jiken *aka* **Noh Mask Murders** (TOEI/KADOKAWA; JAP) 110min
Like *Ana/The Pit* (1957), *Inugami-ke no Ichizoku/The Inugamis* (1976) and *Gokumonto/Island of Horrors* (1977), this finds Ichikawa relaxing with one of the mysteries popular in the Far East which preserve the spirit of Edgar Wallace and Lafcadio Hearne.

Working from a novel by Yasuo Uchida, the film opens with three apparently unconnected events – the sudden death of a businessman in a Tokyo street, two lovers in a mountain region having a close call with a falling branch, and a young traveller's encounter with an attractive older woman – which turn out to be intimately interlinked. Intrigue and murders focus upon the intended retirement of the patriarch of a Noh theatre family, with factions backing either his granddaughter or his grandson as his successor. A 600-year-old Noh mask symbolizing Evil is a fetish for the murderer, actually used as a weapon when it is coated with poison and applied to the face of a victim.

d Kon Ichikawa *p* Haruki Kadokawa *s* Kuri-shitel *c* Yukio Isohata *lp* Takaaki Enoki, Takeshia Kusaka, Keiko Kishi, Ittoku Kishibe, Rei Okamoto, Shuji Otaki, Tomoko Naraoka, Takeshi Kato, Kyoko Kishida, Shiro Ito, Koji Ishizaka

Transylvania Twist (MIRACLE/CONCORDE) 82min
A jokey production from Roger Corman's Concorde, with widely accessible, if not very funny, gags about Jason, Leatherface, Freddy, Pinhead and **The Exorcist** (1973) jostling parodies of scenes from **Dracula** (1958), **House of Usher** (1960), **Premature Burial** (1961), **The Haunted Palace** (1963) and *Phantasm* (1979). The plot is borrowed from **The Cat and the Canary** (1939) as heirs search a castle for hidden treasure, while, in the most self-referential way imaginable, routines are stolen from the earlier spoof, **Young Frankenstein** (1974).

Dexter Ward (Altman) and Marisa Orlock (Copley) visit the castle of Lord Byron Orlock (Vaughn), aided by an intolerant Dr Van Helsing (Mask), searching for a book which will summon Lovecraftian demons, represented by the carrot from *It Conquered the World* (1957). Among the subtler gags is the constant re-use of the castle exterior shots created for **The Pit and the Pendulum** (1961) and worn ragged in Corman's pictures, including **The Terror** (1963), from which comes interpolated footage that enables Karloff to guest in a film made 20 years after his death. Wynorski's trademarks (movie references, large-breasted starlets, makeshift visuals) are in evidence. Miracle Pictures doesn't exist; the logo is borrowed from Joe Dante and Alan Arkush's wittier *Hollywood Boulevard* (1976).

d Jim Wynorski *p* Alida Camp *s* R.J. Robertson *c* Zoran Hockstatter *se* Jim Stewart *lp* Robert Vaughn, Teri Copley, Steve Altman, Ace Mask, Angus Scrimm, Steve Franken, Howard Morris, Jay Robinson, Brinke Stevens, Kelli Maroney, Forrest J. Ackerman, Boris Karloff

Whispers (LIVE HOME VIDEO/ITC/CINEPIX; CAN) 93min
A characterless Canadian production, this Dean R. Koontz adaptation features Tennant as the independent heroine irrationally victimized by a wealthy man (Leclerc) whom she shoots dead.

While she is forming a relationship with the cop on the case (Sarandon), evidence gradually suggests that Leclerc, who apparently kills women he believes to be the incarnations of his hated mother, is still alive. A final flurry of exposition reveals that the murderer is a set of identical twins conceived in father-daughter incest and raised as one personality. The finale, which is too clumsily staged to be anything more than a conceit, features Leclerc being overwhelmed by cockroaches – whose 'whispers' traumatized him as a child – in the cellar where his mother once punished him for not acting enough like himself.

d Douglas Jackson *p* Don Carmody, John Dunning *s* Anita Doohan *c* Peter Benison *se* Joe Blasco, Ed French *lp* Victoria Tennant, Jean Leclerc, Chris Sarandon, Peter MacNeill, Linda Sorensen, Eric Christmas

1992

Amityville 1992: It's About Time

(STEVE WHITE PRODUCTIONS) 95min

Though officially it ended with **Amityville 3-D** (1983), there have been several attempts to revive the Amityville franchise. These include *Amityville 4: The Evil Escapes* (1989), a cable TV movie with Patty Duke, and *The Amityville Curse* (1989), a low-budget splatter movie based on a book by Hans Holzer.

This is virtually a a remake of *Amityville 4.* Architect Macht brings a haunted clock (in the TV movie, it's a free-standing lamp) from the Amityville mansion to his house on the other side of the country, whereupon its evil influence wrecks his home and family. Savaged by a supernatural dog, Macht becomes bedridden and tetchy, while his ex-girlfriend (Weatherley), who moves in to look after him, is menaced by slime. Macht's daughter (Ward) becomes a hoyden who tempts her boyfriend to death by mutation in a pit of ooze and makes incestuous advances to her metalhead brother (Martin). An imaginative touch has the clock, which came originally from the house of Gilles de Rais, slow down or speed up so that simple actions seem to take hours or time stops entirely.

d Tony Randel *p/co-s* Christopher Defaria *s* Antonio Toro *c* Christopher Taylor *se* KNB EXF Group *lp* Stephen Macht, Shawn Weatherley, Megan Ward, Damon Martin, Jonathan Penner, Nita Talbot, Dick Miller

Army of Darkness *aka* Evil Dead III: Army of Darkness *aka* Army of Darkness: The Medievil Dead *aka* Bruce Campbell vs Army of Darkness

(RENAISSANCE/DE LAURENTIIS) 89min

The third entry in the *Evil Dead* series opens with the much-abused Ash (Campbell) in 12th-century England. Thrown into a pit by a nobleman (Gilbert), he uses 20th-century savvy and a chainsaw to rise to command of the armies of good against the the Deadites. While questing for the *Necronomicon* and a way back to the present, Campbell enters a haunted mill where his mirror image is split into many fragments, creating mischievous Lilliputians who torment him; then an eye in his neck grows into a separate body, as in *The Split* (1960), which becomes the rotted leader of the armies of the dead.

Less a splattercoaster than an attempted fantasy adventure in the Ray Harryhausen tradition, this is awkwardly neither a straight sequel – like **Evil Dead II** (1987), it rewrites the ending of the last film – nor a free-standing story. The spectacular shocks are strung on an attenuated plot, which re-runs *A Connecticut Yankee at the Court of King Arthur* with fondly remembered riffs from earlier *Evil Dead* movies. There is a slyly unsettling theme in Campbell's obsessive attempts to escape from a time in which he is a hero with princesses at his feet to an era where he is a supermarket functionary. Early versions have a *Planet of the Apes* (1968) unhappy ending in which Campbell overshoots centuries and arrives in a devastated post-nuclear landscape, but release prints feature a last-minute shootout in the supermarket.

d/co-s Sam Raimi *p* Robert Tapert *co-s* Ivan Raimi *c* Bill Pope *se* KNB Effects Group, Tony Gardner, Introvision International *lp* Bruce Campbell, Embeth Davitz, Marcus Gilbert, Ian Abercrombie, Michael Earl Reid, Richard Grove, Bridget Fonda

Bad Lieutenant

(PRESSMAN) 96min

'Vampires are lucky,' an ethereal drug addict (Lund) tells Keitel as he mainlines heroin, 'they can feed on others. We get to eat ourselves.'

Having established mainstream credentials with TV work for *Miami Vice* and *Crime Story* and the films *China Girl* (1987) and *Cat Chaser* (1989), Ferrara returned to his early concerns (**The Driller Killer**, 1979, **Ms 45**, 1980) with the Grand Guignol of *King of New York* (1990). This follow-up, co-written by the actress who (as Zoe Tamerlis) played the title role in *Ms 45*, returns to the rough, semi-improvisational tone of the early films, abandoning tight plotting for an impressionistic series of individually downbeat, cumulatively shattering scenes.

The bad lieutenant, played by Keitel with a rawness no other name actor would dare, shakes down drug dealers for crack he himself uses and runs an illegal book in his department to finance his mountaining gambling debts. He is affected by the unbearable world he inhabits to such a degree that he takes advantage of a minor traffic offence to sexually harass a pair of underage girls. The catalyst for ambiguous redemption is a Viridiana-like nun (Thorn) raped in a church by teenage louts. Catholic gangsters post an unofficial reward that could help Keitel out of a growing debt hole, but the most shocking aspect of the crime, to audiences used to the vigilante spirit of American movies, is that the nun is able to forgive her attackers, prompting Keitel to brutally ecstatic visions of Jesus (Hipp) which finally drive him, in a frenzy of torment, to help the bewildered rapists save themselves before he is himself shot by a random murderer. As in *The Driller Killer* and *Ms 45*, Ferrara's tormented protagonist is unable to deal with the New York City chaos, but here the conclusion of the psychosis is a turning-away from violence which leads to a moment of transcendence and almost merciful death.

d/co-s Abel Ferrara *p* Edward R. Pressman, Mary Kane *co-s* Zoe Lund *c* Ken Kelsch *lp* Harvey Keitel, Victor Argo, Paul Calderone, Leonard Thomas, Robin Burrows, Frankie Thorn, Victoria Bastel, Paul Hipp, Zoe Lund

Basic Instinct

(CAROLCO/STUDIO CANAL +) scope 127min

Another mainstream slasher, this intricate but clumsy tease features Douglas as the burned-out detective who gets involved with an ice-cool author (Stone) who may well be a murderess. The opening, which sees the murderess take an icepick to a retired rock star during a bout of energetic love-making, segues from explicit sex to explicit violence in a manner that makes De Palma seem restrained.

A potentially neat little mystery is inflated to overkill proportions as Verhoeven turns a piece which might have worked in the intimate, ironic style of his **Die Vierde Man** (1984) into a worthy successor to such super-genre items as *RoboCop* (1986) and *Total Recall* (1990), with swoopingly filmed car chases, too much loving San Francisco travelogue footage, more costume and location changes than are necessary and bursts of violence and sexual activity far in excess of anything in big-budget cinema. Stripped of its lush trimmings, the film fits most comfortably into that direct-to-video genre loosely inaugurated by **Fatal Attraction** (1987), the 'erotic thriller' in which ice-cold *femmes fatales* lure menopausal men into the murky mysteries of sex.

The film is riven by a tension between the strict narrative requirements of the Hollywood thriller and the lavish but random tendencies of the European horror tradition represented by Eszterhas's contrived script, with sudden shocks, self-justifying excesses and periodic explosions of stylish self-indulgence.

d Paul Verhoeven *p* Alan Marshall *s* Joe Eszterhas *c* Jan DeBont *se* Rob Bottin *lp* Michael Douglas, Sharon Stone, Jeanne Tripplehorn, George Dzundza, Denis Arndt, Leilani Sarelle, Dorothy Malone

Batman Returns

(WB) 127min

As signalled by the use of the character name Max Shreck and incidentals like a cameo (in a Red Death outfit) from the 1925 **Phantom of the Opera**, Burton is even more committed here to Expressionism than in *Batman* (1989). Taking his superhero further into the realms of gothic horror with malformed characters, he creates a despairing tone that undercuts any cape-swinging action. Accordingly, Gotham City is a dark Metropolis where the worlds of Robert Wiene, Fritz Lang and Orson Welles meet, with a fairy-tale scattering of snow over rusted girders and granite blocks adding much-needed visual relief from the almost unrelieved darkness of the plot.

Keaton's Batman is a top-billed supporting player, his familiar trauma given far less weight than the appalling pressures which create a pair of further grotesques, DeVito's spherical Penguin, modelled after Werner Krauss's Dr Caligari, and Pfeiffer's schizophrenic Catwoman, a ditzy loser reincarnated as a PVC pervert. Hints of a romance are carried through in fetishist clashes of leather and rubbers, as the strangest sadomasochistic relationship in mainstream cinema, epitomized by the potent image of Catwoman licking Batman's face from chin to cowl, threatens to reconcile their fractured personalities but remains hauntingly unfulfilled. First seen as an unknown thing in a Frank Henenlotter basket delicately floating into the sewers as he is abandoned by his snobbish parents, the Penguin generates a sympathy which evaporates as DeVito's intensely sewer-level performance ('You're just jealous because I'm a real freak and you have to wear a mask') becomes ever more demented ('I'm not a human being,' he shouts, 'I'm an animal.'). But the pathos reappears for a finale even more bizarrely affecting than that of **Edward Scissorhands** (1990), as a troupe of loyal pall-bearers ease the bloated corpse into the water for a Viking funeral.

d/co-p Tim Burton *co-p* Denise DiNovi *s* Daniel Waters *c* Stefan Czapsky *se* Stan Winston *lp* Michael Keaton, Danny DeVito, Michelle Pfeiffer, Christopher Walken, Michael Gough, Michael Murphy, Pat Hingle

Braindead (WINGNUT FILMS; NEW ZEALAND) 102min
A sick comedy set in genteel 1957 New Zealand, where a strain of rabies-like zombiehood is imported by a Sumatran rat-monkey.

While spying on her intimidated son (Balme) and his 'unsuitable' ethnic girlfriend (Peñalver) on a trip to the zoo, interfering and snobbish Moody is bitten by the animated beast and becomes a ravenous cannibal. Balme tries to conceal his mother's infirmity, but the plague spreads and soon he has to deal with a zombified nurse, priest and juvenile delinquent. The early stretches feature grotesque comedy (Moody eats her own ear with custard, the nurse has a china bird embedded in her forehead, a splattery conflict is played out against an episode of *The Archers*) but Jackson loses control when the nurse and the priest mate to produce a hideous zombie baby who needs barbed wire over his pram to keep him down.

d/co-s Peter Jackson *p* Jim Booth *co-s* Stephen Sinclair, Frances Walsh *c* Murray Milne *se* Bob McCarron, Richard Taylor *lp* Timothy Balme, Diana Peñalver, Elizabeth Moody, Ian Watkin, Brenda Kendall, Stuart Devenie, Jed Brophy

'It was terrible, he nearly bled on my prom dress,' exclaims Buffy the Vampire Slayer *(Kristy Swanson) to would-be rebel Luke Perry, who tries to comfort her when they find another dead body.*

Bram Stoker's Dracula *aka* **Dracula**
(COL/AMERICAN ZOETROPE/OSIRIS FILMS) 123min
Visually magnificent, this attempt to provide a 'definitive' film of Stoker's novel – note the author's possessive credit in the title – suffers from a fatal misreading of its original. Stoker's novel is about lust, not love. The film's other major failing is the unfocused lead performance. In impressive make-ups and (especially) remarkable costumes by Eiko Ishioka, Oldman's Dracula veers between medieval knight, Edith Evans with a Bela Lugosi accent, a lovelorn swain with blue-tinted glasses and a *Fright Night*-ish creature. At its best, Coppola's artificial vision shows what Georges Méliès might do with the resources of a modern studio, but at its worst it looks like a horror film by Christine Edzard, as costume, set design and sentiment overwhelm a compressed and fragile story.

Like Richard Matheson (**Dracula**, 1973), screenwriter Hart links Stoker's vampire and the historical Vlad the Impaler and revives the most tiresome monster motivation (compare **The Mummy**, 1932, **Blacula**, 1972), the search for the reincarnation of lost love, with Dracula coming from Transylvania to London less as conquering invader than mail-order husband. Heroine Ryder is introduced in the prologue as the bride of Vlad, mistakenly committing suicide and prompting the Prince to renounce God and become a vampire, then re-appears as a New Woman, dissatisfied with her priggish fiancé (Reeves) and secretly admiring the mercilessly flirtatious friend (Frost), who becomes an undead hoyden when the Count seduces her.

While closer to Stoker's text than other attempts to be definitive (**El Conde Dracula**, 1970), it still gabbles through the convoluted plot without giving any of the heroes except Hopkins' battle-scarred and intense Van Helsing a chance to register. Typical of the attempt to have Stoker's cake and eat Hart's love story is the finale, a dramatization of Stoker's breathless trains-boats-horses chase across Europe which has Dracula wounded in a desperate knife-fight, but finally plumps for bathetic *liebestod* as Ryder mercifully decapitates her life-weary lover in a bloody and flat consummation.

Coppola treats the film as an exercise in gothic style, borrowing images from **Nosferatu** (1922) and **Dracula** (1930) and going beyond the heavy breathing of Hammer with explicit sex sequences, including Reeves' extraordinary draining by the concubines and Ryder's discovery of Frost rutting in the garden with a hirsute wolf-man. While the prospect of a vampire movie by the man who directed *Apocalypse Now* (1979) seems enticing, this unfortunately seems to come from the anonymous hand that was turned to *Gardens of Stone* (1986).

d/co-p Francis Ford Coppola *co-p* Fred Fuchs, Charles Mulvehill *s* James V. Hart *c* Michael Balhaus *se* Roman Coppola, Michele Burke, Greg Cannom, Fantasy II Film Effects *lp* Gary Oldman, Winona Ryder, Anthony Hopkins, Keanu Reeves, Richard E. Grant, Cary Elwes, Bill Campbell

Buffy the Vampire Slayer (FOX) 86min
Buffy (Swanson), a Californian teenager interested only in clothes and cheerleading, is told by Sutherland that she is the latest incarnation of a long line of vampire-slaying heroines. A 'high concept' teen movie, this is a higher-budgeted, but still relatively cheapskate, version of direct-to-video bloodsucking nerd comedies: **Once Bitten** (1985), **My Best Friend is a Vampire** (1988), **Beverly Hills Vamp** (1989), **Teen Vamp** (1989).

Oddly, the most effective strand is the parody of California lifestyles, as a socially conscious student committee hold a 'Hug the World' dance, and a New Age basketball coach gives a pep talk that concludes 'Remember, you have to make a statement, "I have a right to the ball".' Sutherland tries hard to seem serious as the plot-explaining slayer-trainer and Reubens makes a remarkable amount of the nothingy role of the chief disciple, his sarcastic death scene funny enough to warrant a reprise under the end titles. Hauer's lisping, English-accented King Vampire is a fey and self-mocking performance ill-served by an especially feeble demise.

d Fran Rubel Kuzui *p* Kaz Kuzui, Howard Rosenman *s* Joss Whedon *c* James Hayman *se* William Forsche, Mark Maitre *lp* Kristy Swanson, Donald Sutherland, Paul Reubens, Rutger Hauer, Luke Perry, Candy Clark, David Arquette, Michele Abrams

C'Est Arrivé Près de Chez Vous *aka* Man Bites Dog *aka* It Happened in Your Neighborhood

(LES ARTISTES ANONYMES; BEL) 96min

If **Henry... Portrait of a Serial Killer** (1987) resembles a fly-on-the-wall documentary on a mass murderer, this sprightly, sick Belgian comedy adopts the mock approach of *This is Spinal Tap* (1985) and *Bob Roberts* (1992) to present itself as an actual documentary.

A director (Belvaux) and his team traipse around with Benoit (Poelvoorde), a compulsive but professional criminal who always begins the month by murdering a postman and sorting through the mail to track down lonely pensioners. As the film progresses, the crew, at first disturbed enough to avoid eating with their subject, become implicated in his misdeeds, eventually joining him in a Christmas rape massacre and suffering during the crossfire as a feud develops between Benoit and some other crooks, including one who has also had a film crew following him.

Poelvoorde creates a remarkably complex and repulsive portrait of a killer desperate for attention and respect, who intersperses helpful lectures on the correct way to weight a body for disposal with pompous thoughts on architecture, art, music and family values, somehow contriving in his jolly way to be even more obnoxious when not slaughtering people. Filmed on the cheap, with the lack of funds even worked into the script as Benoit offers to chip in the proceeds of robberies to finance the documentary, this surrenders occasionally to artiness, but manages to pull off the difficult trick of making potentially offensive subject matter at once funny and pointed.

co-d/co-p/co-s Rémy Belvaux, Benoit Poelvoorde *co-d/co-p/co-s/c* André Bonzel *co-s* Vincent Tavier *lp* Benoit Poelvoorde, Rémy Belvaux, Jacqueline Poelvoorde Pappaert, Jenny Drye, Malou Madou, Rachel Deman, André Bonzel, Willy Vanderbroeck

Candyman

(PROPAGANDA) 98min

In adapting *The Forbidden*, Rose, the director of **Paperhouse** (1988), does an even more skilful job of translating Clive Barker's approach to the screen than the author himself in **Hellraiser** (1987). Chicago academic Madsen investigates a series of folk tales about Candyman (Todd), a hook-handed murderer, that emerge from the run-down Cabrini Green estates, tapping the vein of urban legendry that underscores the *Halloween* and *Elm Street* sagas by addressing the process of mythification itself rather than simply using a nursery rhyme to 'explain' a monster's origins.

After establishing the grimness of the urban environment, culminating in a brutal encounter with a street gang in a malodorous public toilet, the film turns into a gruesome variation on the 'wrong man' theme as Candyman's misdeeds (beheading a dog, kidnapping a baby, gutting a woman) are attributed to the heroine. Candyman, a striking black figure who is at once a grimmer literal spook than Freddy Krueger and a menacing incarnation of the metaphorical 'spook' seen as a threat by white America, draws his strength from the stories told about him and, in passages of dialogue lifted from the original, almost seductively asks Madsen to join him in an anecdote: 'Your death would be a parable to frighten children with, lovers would use it as an excuse to cling closer together'.

d/s Bernard Rose *p* Steve Golin, Sigurjohn Sighvatsson, Alan Poul *c* Anthony B. Richmond *se* Bob Keen *lp* Virginia Madsen, Tony Todd, Xander Berkeley, Vanessa Williams, Kasi Lemmons, Dejuan Guy

Children of the Corn II: The Final Sacrifice

(FIFTH AVENUE ENTERTAINMENT/STONE STANLEY) 103min

A belated follow-up to the 1984 film, this, along with **A Return to Salem's Lot** (1987), **Pet Sematary II** (1992) and **The Lawnmower Man** (1992), demonstrates that the power of the King name in video marketing is enough to green-light any unpromising project.

It opens in the aftermath of the first film, with the surviving children of Gatlin, Nebraska, taken in by a neighbouring community and the evil of He Who Walks Behind the Rows still in evidence as *Omen*-ous freak deaths befall newsmen who seek to exploit the tragedy and unsympathetic adults who abuse the children (in a skit on *The Wizard of Oz*, a harridan is squashed by a house). Burned-out journo Knox tries to get the full story while his rebellious son Scherrer, in a development lifted from *A Return to Salem's Lot*, is inducted into the adult-hating agrarian cult. Several 'explanations' are raised as an American Indian anthropology professor (Romero) discovers ancient evidence that a spirit turns children against the adults when the grown-ups desecrate the land and also learns of a scheme to palm off blighted corn with the healthy crop, yielding a toxic waste which can cause hallucinogenic homicidal mania.

d David F. Price *p* Scott A. Stone, David G. Stanley *s* A.L. Katz, Gilbert Adler *c* Levie Isaacks *se* Bob Keen *lp* Terence Knox, Paul Scherrer, Ryan Bollman, Christie Clark, Rosalind Allen, Ned Romero

Children of the Night

(FANGORIA) 92min

One of three 1992 films (with the science-fiction outing *Mindwarp* and the mad-science quickie *Severed Ties*) produced by *Fangoria*, which was to the eighties what *Famous Monsters of Filmland* was to the sixties, the prime interface between the horror-movie industry and a loyal fan following.

Set in a typical small town, the film deals with the *Salem's Lot*-style transformation of almost all the population into vampires by Vlado Czakyr (Sawyer), a Dracula-style Romanian vampire. At its centre are the attempts of teacher DeLuise, virginal teen Dolenz and town drunk Morris to eliminate the monsters. An effective early sequence, cribbed from **Inferno** (1980), has Dolenz and McLaughlin encounter underwater vampires in a flooded crypt but the tone veers wildly between relatively serious and well-played horror and a lazy, witless comedy-of-gore approach (a folksy vampire with a golf-club embedded in her forehead) typical of the worst of *Fangoria*.

d Tony Randel *p* Christopher Webster *s* Nicolas Falacci *c* Richard Michalak *se* KNB Effects Group *lp* Karen Black, Peter DeLuise, Ami Dolenz, Maya McLaughlin, Evan MacKenzie, Garrett Moorris, David Sawyer, Josette DiCarlo

Cronos *aka* Chronos *aka* The Cronos Device

(PRODS. IGUANA/VENTANA/IMCINE/FFCC/U OF GUADALAJARA/GRUPO DEL TORO; MEX) 92min

This rethink of the vampire myth makes more of the Central American experience than imitation Universal-Hammer Mexican horrors like **El Vampiro** (1957), extending its theme on a nationalist level by depicting Mexico as vampirized by first Europe and then the United States.

In 1536, an alchemist flees the Spanish Inquisition to the colonies and invents the 'chronos device', a clockwork contraption which enables its creator to live forever but gives him a thirst for human blood. When the alchemist is killed in an explosion in the 1930s, the machine is incorporated into a statue – a development paralleling **Hellraiser III: Hell on Earth** (1992) – which falls into the hands of antique dealer Luppi. Dying American millionaire Brook, having learned of the device in the alchemist's lost diaries, sends his ruthless nephew Perlman to obtain the life-ensuring machine, and a struggle ensues for its possession, with rival vampires of several literal and metaphorical types striving for immortality.

d/s Guillermo del Toro *p* Bertha Navarro, Arthur Gorson *c* Guillermo Navarro *se* Necropia *lp* Federico Luppi, Ron Perlman, Claudio Brook, Margarita Isabel, Tamara Shanath

Larry Drake is Dr Giggles.

Death Becomes Her (U) 113min

Marketed under the relatively tame tag of 'your basic black comedy', this revolves around a fraught triangular relationship between fading movie-star Streep, first seen in a horribly tasteless seventies Broadway musical of *Sweet Bird of Youth*, talented plastic surgeon Willis, who sinks to becoming a morgue beautician during a nightmare marriage to Streep, and jilted-at-the-altar authoress Hawn, who grows into a grossly fat and insane slob before metamorphosing into a svelte super-success.

Envious of Hawn, Streep consults a perhaps diabolic beauty specialist (Rossellini) who claims to be 71 and swans around in Theda Bara costumes. Given a potion, which Hawn has also taken, that brings eternal youth and beauty, Streep is fated to remain gorgeous, but also cursed to survive death. After violent confrontations, Streep is left with a broken neck and Hawn with a shotgun-hole through her stomach, whereupon Willis is bullied into providing cosmetic and embalming services.

The first two-thirds is wonderfully played and caustically written, with Rossellini inhabiting a Universal horror estate amid a caricatured Beverly Hills, and a platoon of effects people providing seamless illusions: Streep's neck elongates and twists so she literally faces backwards, Hawn walks around with a see-through hole in her midriff. The pace falters in the climax, set at a party attended by a host of dead celebrities (Elvis, James Dean, Andy Warhol, etc), but picks up for a very tart coda set 37 years in the future. A major-league answer to low-budget zombie comedies like **Re-Animator** (1985) and **Braindead** (1992), this benefits from setting astonishing (and expensive) imagery amid a plot worth talking about and generously risk-taking unsympathetic performances from well cast and intriguingly horrible stars.

d/co-p Robert Zemeckis *co-p* Steve Starkey *s* Martin Donovan, David Koepp *c* Dean Cundey *se* Ken Ralston, Dick Smith, Kevin Haney, Tom Woodruff Jr, Alec Gillis *lp* Meryl Streep, Bruce Willis, Goldie Hawn, Isabella Rossellini, Ian Ogilvy, Adam Storke, Sydney Pollack

Doppelganger (ITC) 98min

A cunningly contrived psychological thriller about multiple personality, with a mystery villain convincing disturbed Barrymore that she is haunted by a double who murders people she finds inconvenient, this transforms into supernatural horror with last-reel effects in which the schizoid girl fissures in two, emerging from a wormy cocoon as a demonic creature who destroys her tormentor.

Despite incoherence, the movie works on a moment-by-moment basis, with surprisingly well-written dialogue and an amusing Hollywood background as Barrymore rooms with a struggling screenwriter (Newbern) who attempts to puzzle out her complicated backstory as a distraction from his stalled screenplay. Israeli Nesher, best known for *She* (1982) and *Time Bomb* (1991), pays especial care to the minor characters, with Kellerman in a cameo as an ex-nun running a phone sex service, and Hope doing wonders in the thankless second-string girlfriend role as Newbern's cynical writing partner.

d/s Avi Nesher *p* Donald P. Borchers *c* Sven Kirsten *se* KNB Effects *lp* Drew Barrymore, George Newbern, Dennis Christopher, Sally Kellerman, Leslie Hope

Dr Giggles (LARGO/U) 95min

A throwback to the psycho boom of 1978–1982, this is a capable but unimpressive job. With a theme (doctors and surgery) rather than a national holiday as a central thread, it follows exactly the outline of **Halloween** (1978), **The Prowler** (1980) or **My Bloody Valentine** (1981).

Drake is the asylum escapee, a killer with delusions that he is a doctor, who returns to the town where his similarly murderous surgeon father was killed by a mob. Traumatized because his father sewed him into his mother's corpse, Drake, who has an unsettling nervous laugh, stalks teenagers, cops and bystanders, killing with a variety of medical implements (hardly original, as demonstrated by **X-Ray**, 1982, **Halloween II**, 1981, and **Visiting Hours**, 1981). Heroine Combs has a heart murmur and a deep-seated fear of operations. With clichéd old dark house, fairground, asylum, hospital and high-school settings, this has all the distasteful callousness of the worst of the slice 'n' dice cycle, as Drake spouts sub-Krueger witticisms on a medical theme every time he smothers someone with a blood-pressure sleeve or takes a set of **Dead Ringers** (1988) surgical tools to an abdomen.

d/co-s Manny Coto *p* Stuart M. Besser *co-s* Graeme Whifler *c* Robert Draper *se* KNB Effects Group *lp* Larry Drake, Holly Marie Combs, Cliff DeYoung, Glenn Quinn, Keith Diamond, Richard Bradford

Dr Mordrid (FULL MOON ENTERTAINMENT) 89min

This fantasy-horror quickie introduces a possible continuing character, Dr Mordrid (Combs), a Manhattan-based sorcerer who seems to be a blatant steal – lock, stock and amulet – from Marvel Comics' Dr Strange.

Working on Earth under the orders of an extra-dimensional pair of blue eyes known as 'The Monitor', the immortal Mordrid is confronted by an evil sorcerer (Thompson) who has escaped from an extra-dimensional prison and is intent on summoning a horde of demons (of whom only a feeble two are glimpsed) to destroy the Earth. With his impressive lair, pet raven and serious tone, Mordrid is potentially interesting, but a tight budget minimizes the supposedly titanic conflict between hero and villain while the film gets sidetracked by a relationship with a police researcher (Nipar) whose jealous superior (Acavone) tries to pin Thompson's crimes on the doctor.

co-d Albert Band *co-d/p* Charles Band *s* C. Courtney Joyner *c* Adolfo Bartoli *se* David Allen Productions *lp* Jeffrey Combs, Yvette Nipar, Jay Acavone, Brian Thompson, Keith Couloris, Ritch Brinkley, Pearl Shaw, Murray Rubin

Dust Devil (PALACE; GB) 107(87)min

More personal than Stanley's début, the efficient science-fiction outing *Hardware* (1990), this mystical slasher follows Hitch (Burke), a shape-shifting serial killer who is at once the incarnation of an African spirit and a style-conscious retread of Clint Eastwood's Man With No Name.

Burke stalks the roads of the Namib desert preying on lost souls who secretly desire his murderous intervention, hooking up with a nearly-but-not-quite-suicidal runaway South African wife (Field). Westernized black policeman Mokae, another lonely outcast, pursues them, unsure whether he seeks to kill or be killed, dragging Field's obnoxious husband (Swart) into the wasteland. This is mainly a hallucinatory picture, more interested in eerie desert images and oddly unsettling touches like an abandoned cinema half-buried under drifting sands or the melancholy monster's almost-delicate dance with Field to Hank Williams' *Rambling Man*. Based on an actual case – also the subject of the conspiracy movie *Windprints* (1990) – this tackles incipient political themes in its precise evocation of the South Africa-Namibian border, with white cops beating up black witnesses, but is more concerned with thanatophilic romance and an evocation of ancient magic. In any of its several editions (Stanley's preferred cut has slightly more detours), this is a considerable and remarkable picture.

d/s Richard Stanley *p* JoAnne Sellar *c* Steve Chivers *se* Dream Machine *lp* Robert Burke, Chelsea Field, Zakes Mokae, Marianne Sägebrecht, William Hootkins, Rufus Swart

The Fear Inside (VIACOM) 96min
This above-average entry in the 'home invasion' cycle echoes both *Lady in a Cage* (1964) and *The Servant* (1963), though its *raison d'être* is the string of more stereotyped, higher-profile 1992 suspensers **The Hand That Rocks the Cradle**, **Single White Female** and *Unlawful Entry*.

Agoraphobic divorcee Lahti takes in student Rubin as a boarder and is none too upset when her tenant's sympathetic 'brother' (McDermott) shows up. Rubin and McDermott are actually lovers, fleeing from the robbery-and-killing of a rich old lady with souvenirs like a valuable antique ring and a severed finger. The criminals, who have a complicated relationship of betrayal and dependency, become erratic, with Rubin deteriorating from perky girl-next-door into fright-wigged horror harridan, and McDermott, a trigger-happy panicker, torn between the two psychologically damaged women. The ring disappears, causing everybody to suspect and persecute everybody else, only to turn up in a thieving parrot's cage after fatal injuries have been inflicted, prompting Rubin to blow the bird away in a feathery close-up.

d Leon Ichaso *p* John Broderick *s* David Birke *c* Bojan Bazelli *lp* Christine Lahti, Dylan McDermott, Jennifer Rubin, David Ackroyd, Thomas Ian Nicholas, Paul Linke

Hellraiser III: Hell on Earth
(FIFTH AVENUE/MORTORFF) 92min
An improvement on **Hellbound: Hellraiser II** (1988), this further transforms Clive Barker's distinctive 1986 début into a mall-cinema horror franchise. Barker's terminology is dropped (his Cenobites become plain demons) and arbitrary, plot-driven 'rules' are invented for Hell, but the most obvious Elm Street influence is the turning of Bradley's Pinhead (billed 17th as 'Lead Cenobite' in *Hellraiser*) into a cult creature worthy of *Fangoria* covers.

Pinhead is released from a pillar of souls that has been acquired by a decadent nightclub owner (Bernhardt), and TV journalist Farrell sets out, armed with the familiar puzzle box, to send the demon back to Hell. An unusual concentration on characterization – the relationship between Farrell and the lost clubgirl (Marshall) who liberates the monster is especially well developed – sits alongside the expected deployment of horror apparatus as sundry characters are skinned instantly, sliced with CDs, have drills or cameras rammed through their heads, smoke cigarettes from open wounds, explode in bloody chunks or distort like toffee. In the tradition of sequel-as-spectacle, this is almost as effective and crowd-pleasing a recap of basic principles as **A Nightmare on Elm Street, Part 3: Dream Warriors** (1987) or **Evil Dead II** (1987).

d Anthony Hickox *p* Lawrence Mortorff *s* Peter Atkins *c* Gerry Lively *se* Bob Keen *lp* Terry Farrell, Doug Bradley, Paula Marshall, Kevin Bernhardt, Ken Carpenter

Innocent Blood (WB) 112min
This promising but messy hybrid pits vampirette Parillaud against a Pittsburgh mafia don (Loggia) she has accidentally turned into an undead monster. Undercover cop LaPaglia falls for the ethical bloodsucker, who preys only on victims who deserve to die, while Loggia transforms his entourage into a platoon of new-made vampire hoods.

Of all the entries in the 1992 vampire cycle, this is at once the most hung-up on horror history (shown by Landis's in-joke cameo casting of splatter celebs like Forrest J. Ackerman, Dario Argento and Tom Savini, and use of television excerpts from **Dracula**, 1931, *The Beast From 20,000 Fathoms*, 1953, **Phantom of the Rue Morgue**, 1954, and **Dracula**, 1958) and the most revisionary in its rewriting of the basic mythology. Archly refraining from using the word 'vampire' to the extent that its characters seem unbelievably ignorant, this substitutes a pump-shotgun to the head for a stake in the heart, fractal-glowing eyes for fangs, and rawly gushing open wounds for tiny neck-punctures.

d John Landis *p* Lee Rich, Leslie Belzberg *s* Michael Wolk *c* Mac Ahlberg *se* Steve Johnson *lp* Anne Parillaud, Robert Loggia, Anthony LaPaglia, David Proval, Don Rickles

Knight Moves (KNIGHT MOVES/CINEVOX; US, G) 116min
This is a rare non-Italian entry in the giallo genre, intercutting pointlessly bizarre crimes with a plodding police investigation.

Chess master Lambert is targeted by a psycho who drains the blood of young women as 'moves' in an obscure game. Among typical giallo touches are a black and white opening sequence establishing how the murderer was driven crazy, the periodic introduction and disposal of pretty women who are stalked and exsanguinated by the gas-masked slayer, and the killer's voice-disguised phone calls which, through a plot contrivance, have to be received in the flooded and eerie cellar of Lambert's hotel, setting up a watery locale for the the final confrontation.

d Carl Schenkel *p* Ziad El Khoury, Jean-Luc Defait *s* Brad Mirman *c* Dietrich Lohmann *se* Gary Paller *lp* Christopher Lambert, Diane Lane, Tom Skerritt, Daniel Baldwin, Ferdinand Mayne, Charles Bailey-Gates, Arthur Strauss

The Lawnmower Man *aka* **Stephen King's The Lawnmower Man** (ALLIED VISION/LANE PRINGLE; GB, US) 108min
Though up-to-the-minute in its use of new-fangled technology, this is an update of George Zucco mad-scientist movies like **The Monster and the Girl** (1941) or **The Mad Ghoul** (1943). Brosnan, upset because the government is using his Virtual Reality experiments to turn chimpanzees into homicidal maniacs, turns his work to noble ends by raising the mentally handicapped gardener (Fahey) to genius level in imitation of *Charly* (1968).

The film takes its reputed source seriously enough to use elements from King's world (The Shop, the covert agency from *Firestarter* and *Golden Years*) and his favoured plot devices (the *Carrie-Christine* story of a put-upon victim elevated to demigod status who takes spectacular vengeance upon his small-minded persecutors). However, King reasoned that the title of his unconnected story had been grafted onto an extant script called *Cybergod*, and took legal action to remove his name.

d/co-s Brett Leonard *p/co-s* Gimel Everett *c* Russell Carpenter *se* Jonathan Keeton *lp* Pierce Brosnan, Jeff Fahey, Jenny Wright, Mark Bringleson, Geoffrey Lewis, Jeremy Slate, Dean Norris, Caroline Coffey, Troy Evans, John Laughlin

Leprechaun (TRIMARK) 88min
Malevolent leprechaun Davis, complete with buckled shoes and oversized hat, murders people who have discovered his pot of gold, wisecracking in a slippery Oirish accent as he massacres.

Less distinctive than innumerable Charles Band quickies, this puts the star of *Willow* (1988) under rubbery make-up and has him pursue *Friday the 13th*-style characterless victims around a rural nowhere. Uncertain of its intent, it veers between campy would-be comedy, with the leprechaun speeding around in a kiddie kar, and unpleasant sadism, as a lovable retard (Holton) is slashed about the face. Jones touches folktale bases (inventing the ludicrous notion that leprechauns are affected by four-leaf clover as vampires are by crucifixes) but makes absolutely nothing of them, having obviously learned mythology from *Darby O'Gill and the Little People* (1958) and *Finian's Rainbow* (1968) rather than, say, Arthur Machen.

d/s Mark Jones *p* Jeffrey B. Mallian *c* Levie Isaacks *se* Gabe Bartalos *lp* Warwick Davis, Jennifer Aniston, Ken Olandt, Mark Holton, Robert Gorman, Shay Duffin, John Volstad, John Sanderford

Matinee (U) 99min

Like *Explorers* (1985), this is as much a meditation on the cultural legacy of the monster movie as a coming-of-age drama. In 1962, during the Cuba Missile Crisis, huckstering horror movie producer Lawrence Woolsey (Goodman), who is modelled on William Castle, hosts a pre-release screening of his latest quickie, *Mant!*, at a Florida theatre he has rigged up with gimmicks from Rumble-rama to Atomo-Vision. In the audience are a navy brat (Fenton), worried because his father is on the ships blockading Cuba, a juvenile delinquent (Villemaire) dressed as a monster, a theatre manager (Picardo) obsessed with his fall-out shelter and a precocious girl (Jakub) who has dared sneer at 'duck and cover' air raid precautions. Affectionate if broad in its parody of *The Fly* (1958) and *Them!* (1954), *Mant!* features uncredited genre veterans Robert Cornthwaite, William Schallert and Kevin McCarthy. The film at first seems happy to be a clever pastiche of fifties paranoia, but Dante steps beyond that when Goodman explains a philosophy of horror, linking his attempts to be safely scary with the real-life horror of potential atomic war. With wonderful and rare performances from its junior cast and amusingly caricatured adults (including Miller and Sayles as anti-horror protestors hired by Goodman to stir up publicity) this is a warm and unfashionable movie.

d Joe Dante *p* Michael Finnell *s* Charlie Haas *c* John Hora *se* James McPherson *lp* John Goodman, Cathy Moriarty, Simon Fenton, Omri Katz, Kellie Martin, Lisa Jakub, Dick Miller, John Sayles, James Villemaire, Robert Picardo

Pet Sematary II (PAR) 101min

Stephen King was persuaded to accept a sequel clause in the rights contract for **Pet Sematary** (1989) by an assurance that this follow-up was impossible. Nothing is impossible in Hollywood.

When his actress mother (Fluegel) is electrocuted in an on-set accident while making a horror film, the alienated Furlong moves to Ludlow, Maine, to live with his veterinarian father Edwards. Bullied at school and suspicious of Edwards's relationship with a younger woman, Furlong becomes involved with a put-upon kid (McGuire) who is abused by his brutal Sheriff stepfather (Brown). When Brown kills his dog, Furlong resorts to the cursed Indian burial ground of the first film.

The dog returns as a glowing-eyed hellhound whose physiological deadness confounds scientific tests. It protects its master by ripping out Brown's throat, whereupon the kids (in a decidedly odd development) bring Brown back as a stumbling, grinning, sadistic zombie, and Furlong revives his screen queen mother for a gory finish.

d Mary Lambert *p* Ralph S. Singleton *s* Richard Outten *c* Russell Carpenter *se* Steve Johnson, Peter M. Chesney *lp* Edward Furlong, Anthony Edwards, Clancy Brown, Jared Rushton, Sarah Trigger, Darlanne Fluegel, Jason McGuire

Psychic (TRIMARK/ALLEGRO/WESTWIND; CAN) 88min

Galligan has trick-photography dreams in which he witnesses strangulation murders and is made to look especially guilty to the cops when he gets the feeling that the mad killer terrorizing the city is a respected psychology professor (Nouri) who happens to be dating the teacher (Stewart) he himself has a crush on.

The psychic-vs-psycho plot is one of the most overworked themes in low-budget cinema and TV (*Visions*, 1972, *Man on a Swing*, 1974, *Mind Over Murder*, 1979, *The Killing Hour*, 1984, *Fear*, 1990), but this is at least snappily scripted, properly acted and directed with some style by Mihalka, who has improved considerably since **My Bloody Valentine** (1981).

d George Mihalka *p* Tom Berry *s* Miguel Tejada-Flores, Paul Koval *c* Ludek Bogner *se* Brock Jolliffe *lp* Zach Galligan, Catherine Mary Stewart, Michael Nouri, Albert Schultz, Ken James, Clark Johnson

Raising Cain (U) 92min

After variously successful (*The Untouchables*, 1987), disappointing (*Casualties of War*, 1989), disastrous (*The Bonfire of the Vanities*, 1990) and invisible (*Wise Guys*, 1986) ventures away from the psycho field, De Palma returned with this wittily outrageous item, derived in great part from **Peeping Tom** (1960).

Lithgow, in audaciously insane performances, is a child psychologist with a multiple personality who is kidnapping children to recreate the psychological experiment which his evil Norwegian father carried out on him in infancy. Urged to murderous extremes by his imaginary twin Cain and cautioned by the spectre-like appearance of his father, Lithgow's experiments with his own child are complicated by his wife (Davidovich) who has resumed an affair with an old aquaintance (Bauer), whom Lithgow elegantly frames for murder even as he is trying to dispose of Davidovich with the **Psycho** (1960) car-shoved-in-a-lake stunt.

De Palma's script lacks the dangerous edge of his superior **Sisters** (1972) but is similarly very cleverly constructed. Its conjuring tricks include a marvellously extended tracking shot while psychologist Sternhagen provides reams of plot exposition during a trip through a busy building, a last-minute surprise involving the discrete existence of one of Lithgow's personalities, and an even-more-baroque reprise of the baby-in-slow-motion-danger gambit from *The Untouchables*.

d/s Brian De Palma *p* Gale Anne Hurd *c* Stephen H. Burum *se* Robbie Knott *lp* John Lithgow, Lolita Davidovich, Steven Bauer, Frances Sternhagen, Gregg Henry, Tom Bower

The Runestone (HYPERION/SIGNATURE) 101min

Though spun off from an indecently ancient premise, this is a well thought-out horror picture.

When a pre-Columbian artefact covered in runic carvings is unearthed in Pennsylvania, the ailing survivors of a circle of Scandinavian immigrants pass on a sacred duty to a disbelieving younger man (Jacob), and archaeologist Laurance metamorphoses into Fenrir, a Norse wolf monster who can only be defeated by the God Tyr, who happens to be incarnated at present as a one-handed clock-mender (Godunov). The long-fingered monster is strictly stock, but Carroll takes odd story paths and the cast invest even minor characters with individuality. Riegert's foulmouth cop is an unusual hero – even stranger is the film's refusal to give him a conventional relationship with the artist heroine (Severance). There is a priceless gag as the creature invades an art gallery and slaughters a living sculpture in front of supercilious patrons ('It's art, but do I like it?').

d/s Willard Carroll *p* Harry E. Gould Jr, Thomas Wilhite *c* Misha Suslov *se* Lance Anderson *lp* Peter Riegert, Joan Severance, William Hickey, Tim Ryan, Mitchell Laurance, Lawrence Tierney, Chris Young, Alexander Godunov

Shadow Hunter (ROPE OF SAND) 90min

A sincere low-budget cross between *Thunderheart* (1992) and **Dust Devil** (1992). Glenn is the burned-out LA cop sent to the reservation to pick up a Navajo serial killer (Bratt) who escapes after stabbing him with a bone-bead which enables the magically powered murderer to enter his dreams. With a tribal policeman (Beltran) and an expert tracker (Alvarado), Glenn takes to the trail on horseback and pursues the 'skinwalker' into the wilderness.

Though well written, this suffers from its simple chase structure and lack of incident. There are Western touches, as when the sniping villain guns down horses to force his pursuers on foot, but the climax depends too much on serial-style dangling, with Alvarado suspended over a pit of rattlesnakes and Glenn literally cliff-hanging as Bratt, an initially intriguing character who turns out to be another cackling psycho, indulges in hammy gloating. Cardone made similarly ambitious if ultimately formula genre items in the monster-slasher-dream movie *The Slayer* (1980) and the *Outer Limits*-styled *Shadowzone* (1990).

d/s J.S. Cardone *p* Carol Kottenbrook, Scott Einbinder *c* Michael Cardone *se* Mark Shostrom *lp* Scott Glenn, Angela Alvarado, Robert Beltran, Benjamin Bratt

Sherlock Holmes in Caracas

(FONCINE/BIG BEN/TIUNA; VENEZUELA) 95min

Made in English, this comedy is very loosely derived from Arthur Conan Doyle's *The Adventure of the Sussex Vampire*.

A wild comedy with plentiful anachronisms and attempts to deconstruct the familiar characters, this opens with Holmes (Montesinos), who complains about his feeble characterization, and Watson (Dacournan), who records the case with a video camcorder, arriving in South America, actually pausing only briefly in Caracas en route to Maracaibo, where an old friend has vague suspicions about the beauty queen (Cruz) he has married. After exposing the governess (Luzardo) as a pagan worshipper, Holmes deduces that Cruz, as opposed to the character in the story, really is a vampire. Crammed with off-the-wall Pythonesque gags, this lively footnote to the screen career of Sherlock Holmes is more concerned with laughs than chills.

d/co-p/s Juan E. Frísan *co-p* Franklin Whaite *c* Ricardo Younis *lp* Jean Manuel Montesinos, Gilbert Dacournan, Carolina Luzardo, Maria Eugenia Cruz, Giles Bickford

Single White Female (COLUMBIA) 107min

This is one of the early nineties cuckoo-in-the-nest cycle (**The Hand That Rocks the Cradle**, 1991, *Poison Ivy*, 1992, *Unlawful Entry*, 1992) in which apparently trustworthy characters are invited into homes only to take over and turn homicidally dangerous.

In New York, Fonda splits up with her boyfriend (Weber) and takes mousy Leigh as a roommate. Gradually, Leigh makes herself over into a copy of Fonda, spinning out of control when Fonda and Weber reconcile. Like most mainstream slashers, it falls down by co-opting the ridiculous conventions of its low-budget cousins, complete with dead characters returning to life and simplistic abnormal psychology.

d/p Barbet Schroeder *s* Don Roos *c* Luciano Tovoli *se* Matthew W. Mungle *lp* Bridget Fonda, Jennifer Jason Leigh, Steven Weber, Peter Friedman, Stephan Tobolowsky

Sleepwalkers (COL) 91min

Posing as the new kid in town, shape-shifter Krause asks out high-schooler Amick, while his mother (Krige), with whom he has an incestuous relationship, sits in a house besieged by cats, begging him to suck out the girl's soul so they can get on with living forever. A conflict develops between the monsters, with his growing attachment to Amick triggering a transfer of loyalties, but this plot is ditched when Krause turns into a cat-faced date rapist, tossing off Freddy-isms.

Having served an apprenticeship with *Critters 2: The Main Course* (1988) and the surprisingly effective made-for-cable *Psycho IV: The Beginning* (1990), Garris here does as good a job as possible but King's terrible script trips him up. It is hard to credit that any creatures could live forever if to destroy them takes not the spiritual and moral strength of a Dr Van Helsing, but merely the panicky reactions of a popcorn girl and a horde of housecats. Matey cameos from King, Clive Barker, Tobe Hooper, Joe Dante and John Landis hardly help.

d Mick Garris *p* Mark Victor, Michael Grais, Nabeel Zahid *s* Stephen King *c* Rodney Charters *se* Tony Gardner *lp* Alice Krige, Brian Krause, Madchen Amick, Ron Perlman, Jim Haynie, Cindy Pickett, Lyman Ward, Dan Martin, Glenn Shadix, Mark Hamill

Tale of a Vampire *aka* A Tale of Vampire

(STATE SCREEN; GB) 100min

A cross-cultural oddity with the feel of a seventies British horror retranslated from Japanese, as Sato elaborates on the tone of **Vampyres** (1974), pruning away the exploitative aspects to focus on haunted melancholia.

Inspired by the poem *Annabel Lee*, the film evokes the morbid and twisted romanticism of Edgar Allan Poe, who appears personally as a slouch-hatted avenger (Cranham) tracking down the vampire (Sands) who has stolen his wife from him and who is now intent on seducing Hamilton, the long-gone Virginia's exact double. Set in a dusty dead-end library and a minimally populated fringe London, the film is a tight, intimate drama that suffers from a curtailed ending. The slow-paced film creates a unique and disturbing atmosphere, with effective images of a blood-boltered Sands outweighed by weirder moments like Cranham's presentation of Hamilton, tied to a bed with red ribbons, as an offering to his nemesis.

d/co-s Shimako Sato *p* Simon Johnson *co-s* Jane Corbett *c* Zubin Mistry *se* Dave Watkins *lp* Julian Sands, Suzanna Hamilton, Kenneth Cranham, Marian Diamond

To Sleep With a Vampire (CONCORDE) 92min

Described by Friedman as 'a cross between *The Vampire Lestat* and *My Dinner With André*', this follows two characters – stripper Spradling and vampire Valentine – through a night of debate as Valentine, who preys only on those who want to die, determines whether Spradling is suicidal or not. The film is let down by its shallow depiction of the heroine's G-string angst over the son from whom she is separated and suffers from Valentine's wooden performance. Nonetheless, Spradling's speech about what a disappointment Valentine is ('you can't turn into a bat and you're not rich') is pointed and there is a surprisingly moving moment when the girl takes the vampire, who has never seen the sun, down to the beach at night and shines a floodlight on him to explain what the day is like. An oddly arty exploitationer, this shows that executive producer Corman has lost none of his peculiar ambitions nor any of his inherent delight in recycling and penny-pinching. It is an exact remake of Katt Shea Ruben's *Dance of the Damned* (1988).

d Adam Friedman *p* Mike Elliott *s* Patricia Harrington *c* Michael Craine *lp* Scott Valentine, Charlie Spradling

Turn of the Screw

(ELECTRIC PICTURES; US, GB, FR) 95min

A plodding adaptation of Henry James's novella, set for no discernible reason in the 1960s.

In a black and white framing sequence, mental patient Faithfull, who may or may not be the heroine grown old, recounts in group therapy the story of a repressed young girl (Kensit) who takes a job at Bly House as governess to two angelic but creepy kids (Szekeres, England) and gradually comes to believe they have fallen under the influence of the ghosts of a dead estate manager and his mistress. The vagaries of multi-national co-production mean Audran is oddly cast as the housekeeper, while Sands puts in a minimal cameo as the Master of Bly, puffing on a hookah during a job interview.

Kensit hardly eclipses Deborah Kerr in **The Innocents** (1961) while Lemorande takes far too simplistic an approach to James's carefully complicated story, presenting the governess as being so repressed at the outset that her descent into madness hardly needs supernatural intervention.

d/s Rusty Lemorande *p* Steffan Ahrenberg *c* Witold Stok *se* Effects Associates *lp* Patsy Kensit, Stephane Audran, Marianne Faithfull, Clare Szekeres, Joseph England, Julian Sands, Olivier Debray

Twin Peaks: Fire Walk With Me

(NEW LINE/BOUYGES) 135min

This spin-off from the TV series may well be the director's cruelest film since **Eraserhead** (1977).

In pruning the catch-phrases, comic subplots, big-business soap, playful eroticism and detective-story elements, not to mention choosing to tell the backstory of Laura Palmer rather than resolve the cliffhanger ending by showing what happens next, the film deliberately alienates a large segment of the show's fan following to concentrate on a genuinely disturbing descent into Hell. After a flurry of re-establishing touches (micro-cameos from series regulars, Angelo Badalamenti's theme music) to suggest familiar territory, the film plunges into a degradation which is spiritually as devastating as the physical tortures of **I Spit on Your Grave** (1978) or **The Last House on the Left** (1972). In the monster father-figure of Leland/Bob, Lynch has a bogeyman who puts Freddy Krueger to shame by bringing into the open the incest, abuse and brutality that the *Elm Street* movies conceal behind MTV surrealism and flip wisecracks. When a character hallucinates, the images (and, as usual with Lynch, the multi-layered and terrifying soundtrack) cannot get any more disturbing, while the film's many moments of horror (a peer into a drab picture of an open door, Laura's hysterical and numbed laughter, the alternations of the glowering Leland with the insanely evil Bob) show how tidy, conventional and domesticated the generic horror movie of the nineties has become. *Fire Walk With Me* succeeds in showing the sourness that has always been at the heart of the television series.

d/co-s David Lynch *p* Gregg Fienberg *co-s* Robert Engels *c* Ron Garcia *lp* Sheryl Lee, Ray Wise, Moira Kelly, Kyle MacLachlen, Chris Isaak, David Lynch, David Bowie, Harry Dean Stanton, Grace Zabriskie, Dana Ashbrook, James Marshall, Pamela Gidley, Miguel Ferrer, Eric DaRe, Mädchen Amick, Kiefer Sutherland, Frank Silva

The Unnameable Returns *aka* H.P. Lovecraft's The Unnameable Returns

(YANKEE CLASSIC/AM EAST/PRISM/NEW AGE) 89min

This superior sequel takes a more interesting approach than the student-slaughtering of **The Unnameable** (1988).

Loosely inspired by H. P. Lovecraft's *The Statement of Randolph Carter*, Stephenson, an authentically neurotic and irritating Lovecraft protagonist, ventures into a labyrinth under a graveyard to find the unnameable, a demon (Strain) whose physical form is combined with that of a 300-year-old girl. A ritual from the *Necronomicon* frees Ford, a naked innocent who develops a crush on the embarassed scholar, but the demon pursues them to the Miskatonic University.

d/p/s Jean-Paul Ouellette *c* Gregg Gardner, Roger Olkowski *se* R. Christopher Biggs *lp* Mark Kinsey Stephenson, Maria Ford, Charles Klausmeyer, John Rhys-Davies, David Warner, Julie Strain, Peter Breck

Urotsukudoji II *aka* Legend of Demon Womb

(TOSHIO MAEDA/JAPANAUDIO VISUAL NETWORK/WEST CAPE CORPORATION; JAP) 87min

This is the second cutting-together of episodes from Takayama's animated serial. Less apocalyptic and cluttered than **Urotsukudoji** (1989), this has teenager Nagumo, avatar of the godlike Chojin, giving blood to a cousin injured in a plane crash. Takeaki, recipient along with the blood of Nagumo's incipient monstrousness, periodically becomes a demon serial killer and is manipulated by the green-haired, floating son of a mad Nazi necromancer, who pits Takeaki against his cousin, hoping to kill the Chojin and take over the world.

d Hideki Takayama *p* Yasuhito Yamaki *s* Noburu Aikawa *c* Hideo Okazaki

The Vanishing (FOX) 110min

In remaking his own **Spoorloos** (1988), Sluizer coarsens the psychology and delivers a slam-bang shocker without subtlety.

Disturbed family man Bridges sets out to do evil and is somehow involved in the disappearance from a busy roadside area of the girlfriend (Bullock) of a young man (Sutherland) who becomes obsessed with solving the puzzle. In lieu of the chilling collision of two separate obsessives, the film provides an escalating series of physical conflicts which leave the cast bruised and bloody for a woodland finale which verges on *Evil Dead* comedy as Travis scrabbles in a freshly dug grave and Bridges consistently revives from fatal wounds. Flailing in the wake of Bernard-Pierre Donnadieu's performance, Bridges adopts a goofy walk, a whiny accent and a bad haircut to suggest evil. Graff muddies a near-perfect construction by heavy-handedly foreshadowing the horrific stretches while the finale consistently cuts away from the point of the story to Sutherland's Number Two Girl (Travis) sleuthing her way to the rescue. Like mainstream slashers **Cape Fear** (1991) and **Basic Instinct** (1992), the film goes overboard with thunderstorms, crashing music (Jerry Goldsmith), flashy effects and general directorial business, at the expense of characterization, plot or sincere chills.

d George Sluizer *p* Larry Brezner, Paul Schiff *s* Todd Graff *c* Peter Suschitzky *se* James Hart *lp* Jeff Bridges, Kiefer Sutherland, Nancy Travis, Sandra Bullock, Park Overall

Waxwork II: Lost in Time *aka* Lost in Time

(ELECTRIC PICTURES) 104min

Like its predecessor, this is more appealing for its ingredients than its execution.

Galligan and his girlfriend (Schnarre) enter 'God's Nintendo Game', where Good and Evil eternally battle in zones of time and space that resemble sundry horror movies, allowing Hickox to do an especially expert pastiche of the black and white style of **The Haunting** (1963), though his low-budget attempt at duplicating the epileptic camerawork of **Alien** (1979) is more reminiscent of the numberless B-picture imitations than the original model. Zipping between a Poe/Corman-inspired medieval England, where magician Godunov attempts to usurp the throne of King Arthur (Ireland), and various brief sketches that allow glimpses of a George Romero-style zombie shopping mall, the besieged mansion of Baron Frankenstein (Kemp), and a silent and jerky print of **Nosferatu** (1921), *Dr Jekyll and Mr Hyde*, *Jack the Ripper* and *Godzilla*, the characters pick up enough plot coupons to be rewarded with an ending in which Schnarre produces a living severed hand in court to demonstrate that she is innocent of a murder charge.

d/s Anthony Hickox *p* Nancy Paloian *c* Gerry Lively *se* Bob Keen *lp* Zach Galligan, Monica Schnarre, Sophie Ward, Alexander Godunov, Bruce Campbell, Patrick Macnee, Martin Kemp, David Carradine, John Ireland, Michael Des Barres, Marina Sirtis, Maxwell Caulfield, Juliet Mills, Drew Barrymore

Appendix 1

All-Time Horror Rental Champs

This chart is derived from *Variety*'s 1993 list of All-Time Rental Champs, which is compiled and estimated by Lawrence Cohn, and includes films which have secured rentals (i.e. distributors' receipts, not ticket sales) in America and Canada of $3 million and over for films released before 1981, and $10 million for films released after 1981. *Variety* suggests as a rough guide that foreign rentals 'sometimes equal or slightly surpass American and Canadian rentals'. Thus doubling the figures listed here would give an indication of world-wide rentals. The figures relate, in the main, to the first release of a title. In the case of some older titles a successful release could well have significantly increased rental revenue. Because the revenues of some films have been recalculated, they will be different from those listed in the First Edition of this book. It is also worth pointing out that these figures do not include non-theatrical revenue, for example from television sales, which could be substantial. Needless to say, the list is biased in favour of recent titles and their higher seat prices.

in thousands of dollars

Batman 1989	150,500
Ghostbusters 1984	132,720
Jaws 1975	129,549
Batman Returns 1992	100,100
The Exorcist 1973	89,000
Gremlins 1984	79,500
Fatal Attraction 1987	70,000
Ghostbusters II 1989	60,490
The Silence of the Lambs 1991	59,883
The Addams Family 1991	56,200
Basic Instinct 1992	53,000
Jaws II 1978	50,432
Bram Stoker's Dracula 1992	47,200
Sleeping With the Enemy 1991	46,629
Alien 1979	40,300
Cape Fear 1991	39,490
The Hand That Rocks the Cradle 1991	39,334
Young Frankenstein 1974	38,823
Poltergeist 1982	38,249
King Kong 1976	36,915
The Amityville Horror 1979	35,000
Beetlejuice 1988	33,200
The Witches of Eastwick 1987	31,800
Arachnophobia 1990	31,366
The Shining 1980	30,900
Death Becomes Her 1992	30,433
The Goonies 1985	29,900
Flatliners 1990	28,800
The Omen 1976	28,544
Edward Scissorhands 1990	27,500
Jaws 3-D 1983	27,035
Misery 1991	26,880
Pet Sematary 1989	26,400
A Nightmare on Elm Street, IV: The Dream Master 1988	22,000
A Nightmare on Elm Street, Part 3: Dream Warriors 1987	21,345
Single White Female 1992	21,100
Gremlins 2: The New Batch 1990	20,800
Love at First Bite 1979	20,600
Poltergeist II: The Other Side 1986	20,483
Little Shop of Horrors 1986	19,300
Halloween 1978	18,500
Freddy's Dead: The Final Nightmare 1991	17,700
Dead Again 1991	17,500
Friday the 13th 1980	17,113
Friday the 13th Part III 1982	16,500
Darkman 1990	16,158
Friday the 13th – The Final Chapter 1984	16,000
Psycho II 1983	15,908
Carrie 1976	15,208
Dressed to Kill 1980	15,000
Rosemary's Baby 1968	15,000
The Texas Chainsaw Massacre 1974	14,421
Child's Play 2 1990	14,077
The Exorcist II: The Heretic 1977	13,900
An American Werewolf in London 1981	13,764
The Lawnmower Man	13,600
A Nightmare on Elm Street, Part 2: Freddy's Revenge 1986	13,500
Magic 1978	13,268
Sleepwalkers 1992	13,200
Damien – Omen II 1978	12,100
Halloween II 1981	11,920
Jacob's Ladder 1990	11,600
Psycho 1960	11,200
Ghost Story 1981	11,136
Fury, The 1978	11,100
Jaws – the Revenge 1987	10,850
When a Stranger Calls 1979	10,828
Dracula 1979	10,738
Fright Night 1985	10,710
Final Conflict, The 1981	10,000
A Nightmare on Elm Street: The Dream Child 1989	10,000
Candyman 1992	10,000
Friday the 13th – A New Beginning 1985	10,000
Creepshow 1982	10,000
Fog, The 1979	9,905
House of Wax 1953	9,500
Orca... Killer Whale 1977	9,430
Willard 1971	9,300
The Silent Scream 1980	7,900
Grizzly 1976	7,563
Prom Night 1980	6,126
The Changeling 1979	5,300
The Reincarnation of Peter Proud 1975	5,000
The Sentinel 1976	4,383
The Awakening 1980	4,250
What Ever Happened to Baby Jane? 1962	4,050
The Nutty Professor 1963	4,000
The Island of Dr Moreau 1977	4,000
King Kong 1933	4,000
Scared Stiff 1952	3,500
The Town That Dreaded Sundown 1977	3,500
The Legend of Boggy Creek 1972	3,000

Appendix 2

Most-Filmed Horror Writers

The following is a list of writers who have had three or more horror films based on their work. The date of first publication of a work is given after the title in brackets, followed by the dates of any films based on the work. Where the film uses a different title, this is given; where it is the same, the abbreviation '*ot*' for 'original title' is used. For ease of reference, a writer's works are given in alphabetical order (except where several stories are used in a single film); film versions are given in chronological order. For the record, the most-filmed horror author is Edgar Allan Poe, and the most-filmed horror book is Robert Louis Stevenson's *The Strange Case of Dr Jekyll and Mr Hyde*.

Clive Barker
Cabal (novel, 1988): Nightbreed 1990
The Hellbound Heart (novella, 1988): Hellraiser 1987
'Rawhead Rex' (story, 1984): *ot* 1986

Robert Bloch
'Enoch' (1946), 'Terror Over Hollywood' (1957), 'Mrs Steinway' (1954), 'The Man Who Collected Poe' (1951) (all stories): Torture Garden 1967
'Frozen Fear' (1946), 'The Weird Tailor' (1950), 'Lucy Comes to Stay' (1952), 'Mannikins of Horror' (1939) (all stories): Asylum 1972
'Method for Murder' (1962), 'Waxworks' (1938), 'Sweets to the Sweet' (1947), 'The Cloak' (1939) (all stories): The House That Dripped Blood 1970
Psycho (novel, 1959): *ot* 1960
'The Skull of the Marquis de Sade' (story, 1965): The Skull 1964

Paul Dickey and Charles W Goddard
The Ghost Breaker (play, 1909): *ot* 1922, The Ghost Breakers 1940, Scared Stiff 1952

Sir Arthur Conan Doyle
'The Hound of the Baskervilles' (story, 1902): Den Graa Dame 1909, Der Hund von Baskerville 1914, Der Hund von Baskerville 1915, Der Hund von Baskerville 1920, Der Hund von Baskerville 1929, *ot* 1931, *ot* 1939, *ot* 1958, *ot* 1977, *ot* 1983
'Lot No. 249' (story, 1892): Tales from the Darkside 1990

Hanns Heinz Ewers
Alraune (novel, 1913): *ot* 1918, *ot* 1918, *ot* 1928, *ot* 1930

Victor Hugo
L'Homme Qui Rit (novel, 1869): The Man Who Laughs 1928
Notre Dame de Paris (novel, 1831): The Hunchback of Notre Dame 1923, *ot* 1956, The Hunchback of Notre Dame 1939

Stephen King
Carrie (novel, 1974): *ot* 1976
'Cat From Hell' (story, 1977): Tales from the Darkside 1990
'Children of the Corn' (story, 1977): *ot* 1984
Christine (novel, 1983): *ot* 1982
'The Crate' (story, 1979): Creepshow 1982
Cujo (novel, 1981): *ot* 1983
Cycle of the Werewolf (novella, 1984): Silver Bullet 1985
'Graveyard Shift' (story, 1970): *ot* 1990
Misery (novel, 1987): *ot* 1991
Pet Sematary (novel, 1983): *ot* 1989
'The Raft' (story, 1982): Creepshow 2 1987
The Shining (novel, 1977): *ot* 1980

Sheridan Le Fanu
'Carmilla' (story, 1872): Vampyr 1931, Et Mourir de Plaisir 1960, La Cripta e l'Incubo 1964, The Vampire Lovers 1970, La Novia Ensangrientada 1972
'The Room at the Dragon Volant' (story, 1872): Inn of the Flying Dragon 1981

Gaston Leroux
Balaoo (novel, 1913): *ot* 1913
The Phantom of the Opera (novel, 1910): *ot* 1925, *ot* 1943, *ot* 1962, *ot* 1989

H.P. Lovecraft
'The Case of Charles Dexter Ward' (story, 1941): The Haunted Palace 1963
'The Color Out of Space' (story, 1927): The Curse 1989
'The Dreams in the Witch House' (story, 1933, with August Derleth): The Curse of the Crimson Altar 1968
'The Shuttered Room' (story, 1945, with August Derleth): *ot* 1966
'The Statement of Randolph Carter' (story, 1920): The Unnameable Returns 1992
'The Unnameable' (story, 1923): *ot* 1988

Edgar Allen Poe
'Annabel Lee' (poem, 1849): A Tale of Vampire 1992
'The Black Cat' (story, 1843): Unheimliche Geschichten 1919, Unheimliche Geschichten 1932, *ot* 1934, Maniac 1934, *ot* 1941, Tales of Terror 1961, *ot* 1966, The Sabbat of the Black Cat 1971, Il Gatto Nero 1981, Due Occhi Diabolichi 1990
'The Cask of Amontillado' (story, 1846): Tales of Terror 1961, Obras Maestras del Terror, 1960
'The Facts in the Case of M. Valdemar' (story, 1845): Obras Maestras del Terror, 1960, Tales of Terror, 1961, Due Occhi Diabolichi, 1990

'The Fall of the House of Usher' (story, 1839): La Chute de la Maison Usher 1928, House of Usher 1960, El Hundimiento de la Casa Usher 1983
'Ligeia': The Tomb of Ligeia 1964
'The Masque of the Red Death' (story, 1842): Die Pest in Florenz 1919, *ot* 1964, *ot* 1989, *ot* 1990
'Morella' (story, 1835): Tales of Terror 1961
'The Murders in the Rue Morgue' (story, 1841): Murders in the Rue Morgue 1932, Phantom of the Rue Morgue 1954, *ot* 1971
'The Oblong Box' (story, 1844): *ot* 1969
'The Pit and the Pendulum' (story, 1842): The Pit and the Pendulum 1961, Die Schlangengrabe und das Pendel 1967, 1991
'The Premature Burial' (story, 1844): The Crime of Dr Crespi 1935, Premature Burial 1961, Buried Alive 1989
'The Raven' (poem, 1845): *ot* 1935, *ot* 1964
'The System of Dr Tarr and Professor Fether' (story, 1845): Le Système de Dr Goudron et du Professeur Plume 1912, Unheimliche Geschichten 1919, Unheimliche Geschichten 1932, La Mansión de la Locura 1971
'The Tell-Tale Heart' (story, 1843): *ot* 1960, Obras Maestras del Terror 1960, El Demonio en la Sangre 1964

Maurice Renard
Les Mains d'Orlac (novel, 1920): Orlacs Haende 1924, Mad Love 1935, The Hands of Orlac 1960, Hands of a Stranger 1962

Mary Shelley
Frankenstein, or the Modern Prometheus (novel, 1818): Frankenstein 1910, Life Without Soul 1915, Il Mostro di Frankenstein 1920, Frankenstein 1921, The Curse of Frankenstein 1957, Frankenstein: The True Story 1973, Victor Frankenstein 1973, Frankenstein Unbound 1990

Robert Louis Stevenson
'The Body Snatcher' (story, 1884): *ot* 1945
'The Sire de Malétroit's Door' (story, 1882): The Strange Door 1951
The Strange Case of Dr Jekyll and Mr Hyde (novel, 1886): Dr Jekyll and Mr Hyde 1920, Dr Jekyll and Mr Hyde 1920, Dr Jekyll and Mr Hyde 1931, Dr Jekyll and Mr Hyde 1941, Le Testament du Dr Cordelier 1959, The Two Faces of Dr Jekyll 1960, I, Monster 1970, Dr Jekyll and Sister Hyde 1971, The Man with Two Heads 1972, Dr Jekyll et les Femmes 1983, Strannayar Istoriyar Doktora Dzhekila i Mister Khaida 1987, Edge of Sanity 1988
'The Suicide Club' (story, 1882): Unheimliche Geschichten 1919, Unheimliche Geschichten 1932
The Wrong Box (novel, 1889; with Lloyd Osbourne): *ot* 1966

Bram Stoker
Dracula (novel, 1897): Nosferatu – Eine Symphonie des Grauens 1922, *ot* 1931, *ot* 1958, El Conde Dracula 1970, *ot* 1973, *ot* 1979, Nosferatu, Phantom der Nacht 1979
'Dracula's Guest' (story, published posthumously 1914): Dracula's Daughter 1936
Jewel of the Seven Stars (novel, 1903): Blood from the Mummy's Tomb 1971, The Awakening 1980
The Lair of the White Worm (novel, 1911): *ot* 1988

Namboko Tsuruya
Tokaido Yotsuya Kaidan (play, 1825): Shinsaku Yotsuya Kaidan 1949, *ot* 1959, Yotsuya Kaidan 1965, Yotsuya Kaidan – Oiwa no Borei 1969

Edgar Wallace
The Squeaker (novel, 1927): Der Hexer 1964
The Terror (play, 1927): *ot* 1928
The Testament of Gordon Stuart (novel, 1924): Dark Eyes of London 1939, Die Toten Augen von London 1961

H.G. Wells
'The Inexperienced Ghost' (story, 1903): Dead of Night, 1945
The Island of Dr Moreau (novel, 1896): Island of Lost Souls 1932, *ot* 1977

Oscar Wilde
The Picture of Dorian Gray (novel, 1890): Das Bildnis des Dorian Grey 1917, Il Dio Chiamato Dorian 1917, *ot* 1945

John Willard
The Cat and the Canary (play, 1922): *ot* 1927, The Cat Creeps 1930, *ot* 1939, *ot* 1978

Index

Thing in the Attic, The *see* The Ghoul 1974
Thing That Couldn't Die, The 1958
Thirst 1979
Thirst of Baron Blood, The *see* Gli Orrori del Castello di Norimberga 1972
36:15 – Code Père Noel 1989
Three Cases of Murder 1954
Three Faces of Fear, The *see* I Tre Volti della Paura 1963
Three Faces of Terror, The *see* I Tre Volti della Paura 1963
Three Lights, The *see* Der Muede Tod 1921
Three Wax Men *see* Das Wachsfigurenkabinett 1924
Three's Company 1953
Thrilled to Death 1981
Throne of the Blood Monster *see* El Processo de las Brujas 1969
Through the Fire 1987
Thunderbolt '91 *see* Modeng Rulai Shenzhang 1990
Thy Soul Shall Bear Witness *see* Körkarlen 1920
'Til Death Us Do Part *see* La Nova Ensangretada 1972
Till Death Do We Scare *see* Ziaosheng Papa 1982
Time of the Beast 1989
Tina, La Naufrageuse Perverse *see* Les Démoniaques 1973
Tingler, The 1959
To Die For 1988
To Love a Vampire *see* Lust for a Vampire 1970
To Sleep With a Vampire 1992
To the Devil a Daughter 1976
Tod in November *see* Die Woelfin von Teufelsmoor 1978
Todeskuss Des Dr Fu Manchu, Der *see* Fu Manchu y el Beso de la Muerte 1968
Todos los Colores de la Oscuridad *see* Tutti i Colori del Buio 1972
Tokaido Yotsuya Kaidan 1959
Tokugawa Onna Keibatsushi 1968
Tomb of Ligeia, The 1964
Tombs of Horror *see* La Danza Macabra 1964
Tombs of Horror, The *see* Cinque Tombe per un Medium 1966
Tombs of the Blind Dead *see* La Noche del Terror Ciego 1971
Tonight I Will Make Your Corpse Turn Red *see* Esta Noite Encarnarei no Teu Cadaver 1966
Tonight I Will Paint in Flesh Colour *see* Esta Noite Encarnarei no Teu Cadaver 1966
Too Beautiful to Die *see* Sotto il Vestito Niente 2 1989
Toolbox Murders, The 1978
Tormented 1960
Torre de los Siete Jorobados, La 1944
Torso *see* I Corpi Presentano Tracce di Violenza Carnale 1973
Torture Chamber of Baron Blood, The *see* Gli Orrori del Castello di Norimberga 1972
Torture Chamber of Dr Sadism, The *see* Die Schlangengrube und das Pendel 1967
Torture Dungeon 1970
Torture Garden 1967
Torture Room, The *see* Die Schlangengrube und das Pendel 1967
Toten Augen von London, Die 1961
Totentanz 1919
Toter Sucht Seiner Moerder, Ein *see* Vengeance 1962
Toto all'Inferno 1954
Toto in Hell *see* Toto all'Inferno 1954
Touch of Death *see* Quando Alice Ruppe lo Specchio 1988
Touch of Love, A *see* Qi Yuan 1986
Tourist Trap 1978
Tower of Evil 1972
Tower of London 1939
Tower of London 1962
Tower of the Seven Hunchbacks, The *see* La Torre de los Siete Jorobados 1944
Town That Dreaded Sundown, The 1977
Toxic Avenger, The 1985
Track of the Vampire *see* Blood Bath 1966
Trail, The *see* Pao Dan Fei Che 1983
Transylvania Twist 1991
Trap Them and Kill Them *see* Emanuelle e gli Ultimi Cannibali 1977
Trauma *see* Exposé 1975
Tre Volti della Paura, I 1963
Treasure of the Four Crowns *see* El Tesoro de las Cuatro Coronas 1982
Treasure of the White Goddess, The *see* El Tesoro de la Diosa Blanca 1983
Trésor des Morts Vivants, Le *see* La Tumba de los Muertos Vivientos 1982
Trial of the Witches, The *see* El Processo de las Brujas 1969
Trick or Treat 1986
Trilogia de Terror 1968
Trilogy of Terror *see* Trilogia del Terror 1968
Trip to the Beyond *see* Viaje al Más Alla 1980
Trog 1970
Troll 1985
Trono di Fuco, Il *see* El Processo de las Brujas 1969
Tumba de la Isla Maldita, La 1973
Tuo Vizio E una Stanza Chiusa e Solo Io ne Ho la Chiave 1972
Turn of the Screw 1992
Turnaround 1986
Tutti Defunti Tranne i Morti 1977
Tutti i Colori del Buio 1972
Twelfth Hour, The *see* Nosferatu – Eine Symphonie des Grauens 1921
Twice Dead 1988
Twice Told Tales 1963
Twilight of the Dead *see* Paura nella Città dei Morti Viventi 1980
Twin Peaks: Fire Walk With Me 1992
Twins of Dracula *see* Twins of Evil 1971
Twins of Evil 1971
Twisted Nerve 1968
Twisted Souls *see* Spookies 1985
Twitch of the Death Nerve *see* Ecologia del Delitto 1971
Two Evil Eyes *see* Due Occhi Diabolici 1990
Two Faces of Dr Jekyll, The 1960
Two Monks *see* Dos Monjes 1934
Two on a Guillotine 1964
2000 Maniacs 1964
Two Women from the Netherworld 1982
Uccello dalle Piume di Cristallo, L' 1970
Ultima Casa Vicino al Lago, L' 1983
Ultima Preda del Vampiro, L' 1960
Ultimo Mondo Cannibale 1976
Ultimo Squalo, L' 1981
Ultratumba *see* Al Otro Lado del Espejo 1973
Uncanny, The 1977
Uncle Was a Vampire *see* Tempi Duri per i Vampiri 1959
Undead, The 1956
Undead, The 1973 *see* From Beyond the Grave 1973
Understudy, The: Graveyard Shift II 1988
Undertaker and His Pals, The 1967
Undying Monster, The 1942
Ungeheuer von London City, Das 1964
Unheimliche Geschichten 1919
Unheimliche Geschichten 1932
Unholy, The 1987
Unholy Love *see* Alraune 1928
Unholy Three, The 1925
Unholy Three, The 1930
Uninvited, The 1944
Uninvited 1987
Unknown, The 1927
Unknown, The 1946
Unknown Treasures 1926
Unmasked: Hand of Death, Part 25 *see* The Hand of Death 1989
Unnameable, The 1988
Unnameable Returns, The 1992
Unnaturals, The *see* Contronatura 1969
Unseen, The 1981
Until Death *see* Fa Sempre, Fino alla Morte 1987
Up Frankenstein *see* Il Mostro E in Tavola . . . Barone Frankenstein 1973
Upstate Murders, The *see* The Killer Behind the Mask 1976
Urlo dalle Tenebra, Un 1976
Urotsukudoji 1989
Urotsukudoji II 1992
Valkoinen Peura 1952
Valley of Ghosts, The *see* Samwonnyo 1981
Valley of the Zombies 1946
Vamp 1986
Vampir *see* Vampira 1974
Vampira 1974
Vampiras, Las *see* Vampyros Lesbos 1970
Vampire *see* Vampyr 1931
Vampire, The 1957
Vampire, The 1957 *see* El Vampiro 1957
Vampire and the Ballerina, The *see* L'Amanate del Vampiro 1960
Vampire at Midnight 1987
Vampire Bat, The 1933
Vampire Beast Craves Blood, The *see* The Blood Beast Terror 1967
Vampire Buster *see* Zhuo Gui Dashi 1989
Vampire Castle *see* Captain Kronos – Vampire Hunter 1972
Vampire Circus 1971
Vampire for Two, A *see* Un Vampiro para Dos 1965
Vampire Happening, The *see* Gebissen Wird nur Nachts 1970
Vampire Hunter D 1985
Vampire in Venice *see* Nosferatu a Venezia 1988
Vampire Killers, The *see* Dance of the Vampires 1967
Vampire Knights 1987
Vampire Lovers, The 1970
Vampire Man *see* Onna Kyuketsuki 1959
Vampire Nue, La 1969
Vampire of Dr Dracula, The *see* La Marca del Hombre Lobo 1967
Vampire of the Highway, The *see* El Vampiro de la Autopista 1970
Vampire of the Opera, The *see* Il Mostro dell'Opera 1964
Vampire over London *see* Old Mother Riley Meets the Vampire 1952
Vampire People *see* The Blood Drinkers 1966
Vampire Thrills *see* Le Frisson des Vampires 1970
Vampire Woman 1962 *see* Xi Xuefu 1962
Vampire Woman 1973 *see* La Tumba de la Isla Maldita 1973
Vampire Women 1967 *see* Le Viol du Vampire 1967
Vampire Women 1973 *see* La Tumba de la Isla Maldita 1973
Vampire's Coffin, The *see* El Ataud del Vampiro 1957
Vampire's Crypt, The *see* La Cripta e l'Incubo 1964
Vampire's Dream, A *see* Um Sonho de Vampiros 1969
Vampire's Ghost, The 1945
Vampire's Kiss 1989
Vampire's Last Victim, The *see* L'Ultima Preda del Vampiro 1960
Vampire's Lover, The *see* L'Amante del Vampiro 1960
Vampire's Niece, The *see* Malenka – La Nipote del Vampiro 1968
Vampirella *see* Vampira 1974
Vampires, The 1956 *see* I Vampiri 1956
Vampires, The 1961 *see* Maciste contro il Vampiro 1961
Vampires en Ont Ras le Bol, Les *see* Bloedverwanten 1977
Vampires in Havana *see* ¡Vampiros en la Habana! 1985
Vampires vs Hercules, The *see* Ercole al Centro della Terra 1961
Vampiri, I 1956
Vampiro de la Autopista, El 1970
Vampiro dell'Opera, Il *see* Il Mostro dell'Opera 1964
Vampiro, El 1957
Vampiro para Dos, Un 1965
Vampiro y el Sexo, El *see* Santo y el Tesoro de Dracula 1968
¡Vampiros en la Habana! 1985
Vampiros Tambien Duermen, Los *see* El Extraño Amor de los Vampiros 1975
Vampyr 1931
Vampyre Orgy, The *see* Vampyres 1974
Vampyres – Daughters of Darkness *see* Vampyres 1974
Vampyros Lesbos 1970
Vanishing, The 1988 *see* Spoorloos 1988
Vanishing, The 1992
Vanishing Body, The *see* The Black Cat 1934
Vargtimmen 1968
Vault of Horror 1973
Vec Videno 1986
Vela Para el Diablo, Una 1973
Velvet House, The *see* The Corpse 1969
Velvet Vampire, The 1971
Vendetta dei Morti Viventi, La *see* La Rebellion de las Muertas 1972
Venganza de la Momia, La 1973
Venganza de las Mujeres Vampiro, La 1969
Vengeance 1962
Vengeance of the Monster, The *see* Daimajin 1966
Vengeance of the Mummy, The *see* La Venganza de la Momia 1973
Vengeance of the Vampire Women, The *see* La Venganza de las Mujeres Vampiro 1969
Vengeance of the Zombies *see* La Rebellión de las Muertas 1972
Vengeance: The Demon *see* Pumpkinhead 1988
Venin de la Peur, Le *see* Una Lucertola con la Pelle di Donna 1971
Venus im Pelz *see* Venus in Furs 1969
Venus in Furs 1969
Vera, un Cuento Cruel 1973
Vergine di Norimberga, La 1963
Vergini Cavalcano la Morte, Le *see* Ceremonia Sangrienta 1972
Veronique's Long Night *see* La Lunga Notte di Veronique 1966
Viaje al Más Alla 1980
Victor Frankenstein 1977
Video Dead, The 1987
Vienna Strangler, The *see* Il Strangolatore di Vienna 1971
Vierde Man, Die 1984
Vierges et Vampires *see* Requiem pour un Vampire 1971
Villa delle Anime Maledette, La 1983
Vineyard, The 1989
Viol du Vampire, Le 1967
Violated Angels *see* Okasaretu Byuakui 1967
Violated Women *see* Okasaretu Byuakui 1967
Virgem da Colina, A 1977
Virgin of Nuremberg, The *see* La Vergine di Norimberga 1963
Virgin Vampires *see* Twins of Evil 1971
Virgin Witch 1970
Virgins and the Vampires, The *see* Requiem pour un Vampire 1971
Virgins and Vampires *see* Requiem pour un Vampire 1971
Virus *see* Apocalisse Domani 1980
Virus Cannibale *see* Inferno dei Morti-Viventi 1981
Virus – L'Inferno dei Morti Viventi *see* Inferno dei Morti-Viventi 1981
Visiting Hours 1981
Visitor, The *see* Besøkarna 1988
Visitor to a Museum *see* Posetitel Muzeia 1989
Voci dal Profondo 1990
Voices 1973
Voices From Beyond *see* Voci dal Profondo 1990
Voodoo Blood Death *see* Curse of Simba 1964
Voodoo Dawn 1989
Voodoo Girl *see* Sugar Hill 1974
Voodoo Man, The 1944
Vulture, The 1966
Wachsfigurenkabinett, Das 1924
Wahnsinn 1919
Waking Hour, The *see* The Velvet Vampire 1971
War of the Zombies *see* Roma contra Roma 1963
Ward 13 *see* X-Ray 1982
Warhol's Frankenstein *see* Il Mostro E in Tavola . . . Barone Frankenstein 1973
Warlock 1988
Warning Shadows *see* Schatten 1923
Watcher in the Woods, The 1982
Watts Monster, The *see* Dr Black, Mr Hyde 1976
Waxwork 1988
Waxwork II: Lost in Time 1992
Waxworks *see* Das Wachsfigurenkabinett 1924
Way and the Body, The *see* La Frusta e il Corpo 1963
We Are Going to Eat You *see* Diyu Wu Men 1980
Weary Death, The *see* Der Muede Tod 1921
Web of the Spider *see* Nella Stretta Morsa del Ragno 1970
Wedding Dress of the Ghost *see* Mangryongui Wechingturesu 1981
Weird Tales *see* Kwaidan 1964
Weird Woman 1944
Welcome to Arrow Beach 1973
Werewolf, The 1913
Werewolf, The 1956
Werewolf, The 1971 *see* O Homem Lobo 1971
Werewolf and the Yeti, The *see* La Maldición de la Bestia 1975
Werewolf in a Girl's Dormitory *see* Lycanthropus 1962
Werewolf of London, The 1935
Werewolf of W., The *see* Der Werwolf von W. 1988
Werewolf of Washington, The 1973
Werewolf versus the Vampire Women, The *see* La Noche de Walpurgis 1970
Werewolf Woman *see* La Lupa Mannera 1976
Werewolf's Shadow, The *see* La Noche de Walpurgis 1970
Werewolves on Wheels 1971
Werwolf von W., Der 1988
West of Zanzibar 1928
What *see* La Frusta e il Corpo 1963
What a Carve-up ! 1961
What Ever Happened to Aunt Alice? 1969
What Ever Happened to Baby Jane? 1962
What's the Matter with Helen? 1971
When a Stranger Calls 1979
When the Screaming Stops *see* Las Garras de Lorelei 1972
Where East Is East 1929
Where Has Poor Mickey Gone? 1964
While London Sleeps 1926
While Paris Sleeps 1923
Whip and the Body, The *see* La Frusta e il Corpo 1963
Whip and the Flesh, The *see* La Frusta e il Corpo 1963
Whisper in the Dark, A *see* Un Sussurro nel Buio 1976
Whispers 1991
Whispers of Fear 1974
White of the Eye 1986
White Reindeer, The *see* Valkoinen Peura 1952
White Zombie 1932
Who? *see* Chi Sei? 1974
Who Can Kill a Child? *see* Quien Puedo Matar a un Niño? 1975
Who Fears the Devil? 1972
Who Fell Asleep? *see* Deadly Games 1982
Who Slew Auntie Roo? *see* Whoever Slew Auntie Roo? 1971
Whoever Slew Auntie Roo? 1971
Wicked Stepmother 1989
Wicker Man, The 1973
Wild Jungle Captive *see* Jungle Captive 1945
Willard 1971
Wind, The 1987
Winged Serpent, The 1982
Witch, The 1952 *see* Noita Palaa Elämään 1952
Witch, The 1954 *see* La Bruja 1954
Witch, The 1966 *see* La Strega in Amore 1966
Witch and Warlock *see* Witchcraft 1964
Witch From Nepal *see* Qi Yuan 1986
Witch Hunt, The *see* Forfolgelsen 1981
Witch in Love, The *see* La Strega in Amore 1966
Witch Killer of Blackmoor, The *see* El Processo de las Brujas 1969
Witch Returns to Life, The *see* Noita Palaa Elämään 1952
Witch's Curse, The *see* Maciste all'Inferno 1962
Witch's Mirror, The *see* El Espejo de la Bruja 1960
Witchboard 1985
Witchcraft 1959 *see* The Devil's Hand 1959
Witchcraft 1964
Witchcraft 1988
Witchcraft Through the Ages *see* Häxan 1922
Witches Mountain *see* El Monte de las Brujas 1972
Witches of Eastwick, The 1987
Witches, The 1966
Witches, The 1990
Witches Trial, The *see* El Processo de las Brujas 1969
Witchfinder General 1968
With Hercules to the Centre of the Earth *see* Ercole al Centro della Terra 1961
Wizard, The *see* Der Hexer 1964
Wizard of Gore, The 1968
Woelfin von Teufelsmoor, Die 1978
Wolf Forest, The *see* El Bosque del Lobo 1968
Wolf Man, The 1941
Wolf Man, The 1976 *see* La Lupa Mannera 1976
Wolf's Forest, The *see* El Bosque del Lobo 1968
Wolfen 1981
Wolfman, The *see* The Curse of the Werewolf 1960
Wolfman 1979
Wolfman of Count Dracula, The *see* La Marca del Hombre Lobo 1967
Wolfman of Galicia, The *see* El Bosque del Lobo 1968
Wolnyoui Han 1980
Woman of the Snow *see* Kaidan Yukigoro 1968
Woman Who Came Back, The 1945
Woman Who Wouldn't Die, The *see* Catacombs 1964
Womaneater 1957
Women of Doom *see* Las Melancolicas 1971
Women Vampire, The *see* Onna Kyuketsuki 1959
Women's Prison *see* Hiroku Onna-ro 1967
World of the Vampires *see* El Mundo de las Vampiros 1960
Would You Kill a Child? *see* Quien Puedo Matar a un Niño? 1975
Wraith, The 1986
Wrestling Women vs the Aztec Mummy *see* Las Luchadoras contra la Momia 1964
Wrestling Women vs the Murdering Robot *see* Las Luchsdoras contra el Robot Asesino 1969
Wrong Box, The 1966
Wuerger Kommit auf Leisen Socken, Der *see* Il Strangolatore di Vienna 1971
X-Ray 1982
Xi Xuefu 1962
Xiaosheng Papa 1982
Xie 1980
Xiong Bang 1981
Xtro 1982
Yabu no Naka Kuroneko 1968
Yacula *see* Les Avaleuses 1973
Yangan Dou 1990
Yashaga Ike 1979
Ye Bang Ge Sheng 1961
Ye Mo Xiansheng 1990
Yeux Sans Visage, Les 1959
Yin Ji 1982
Yin-Yang Chieh 1974
Yo 1980
Yokai Daisenso 1968
Yokai Hyaku Monogatari 1968
Yotsuya Kaidan 1965
Yotsuya Kaidan – Oiwa no Borei 1969
You Will Die at Midnight *see* Morirai a Mezzanotte 1985
You'll Find Out 1940
Young Frankenstein 1974
Young Hannah, Queen of the Vampires *see* La Tumba de la Isla Maldita 1973
Young Man, I Think You're Dying *see* The Beast in the Cellar 1970
Your Vice Is a Closed Room and Only I Have the Key *see* Il Tuo Vizio E una Stanza Chiusa e Solo Io ne Ho la Chiave 1972
Yuhuo Fen Qin 1979
Yukionna *see* Kaidan Yukigoro 1968
Yureiyashiki no Kyofu-Chi Wo Suu Ningyo *see* Chi o Suu Ningyo 1970
ZaAT *see* Blood Waters of Dr Z 1972
Zaertlichkeit der Voelfe 1973
Zeder 1983
Zeder – Voices from the Beyond *see* Zeder 1983
Zhi Mo Nu 1968
Zhuo Gui Dashi 1989
Zhuo Gui Hejia Huan II: Mayi Chuanqi 1990
Zoltan . . . Hound of Dracula *see* Dracula's Dog 1977
Zombie, The *see* The Plague of the Zombies 1966
Zombie 2 1979
Zombie 3 *see* Le Notti del Terrore 1980
Zombie '90: Extreme Pestilence 1990
Zombie Child *see* The Child 1977
Zombie Creeping Flesh *see* Inferno dei Morti-Viventi 1981
Zombie Flesh Eaters *see* Zombie 2 1979
Zombie High 1987
Zombie Holocaust *see* La Regina dei Cannibali 1980
Zombie Horror *see* Le Notti del Terrore 1980
Zombie Nightmare 1987
Zombies 1964 *see* I Eat Your Skin 1964
Zombies, The *see* The Plague of the Zombies 1966
Zombies 1979 *see* Dawn of the Dead 1979
Zombies of Mora Tau 1957
Zombies on Broadway 1945
Zweite Gesicht, Das 1982
Zwoelfte Stunde, Die *see* Nosferatu-Eine Symphonie des Grauens 1921